# STATISTICAL TECHNIQUES IN BUSINESS AND ECONOMICS

**Eighth Edition**

# STATISTICAL TECHNIQUES IN BUSINESS AND ECONOMICS

ROBERT D. MASON

•

DOUGLAS A. LIND

*Both of The University of Toledo*

## IRWIN

Homewood, IL 60430
Boston, MA 02116

© Richard D. Irwin, Inc. 1967, 1970, 1974, 1978, 1982, 1986, 1990, and 1993

Senior sponsoring editor:   Richard T. Hercher, Jr.
Developmental editor:   Jim Minatel
Marketing manager:   Kurt Messersmith
Project editor:   Waivah Clement
Production manager:   Bob Lange
Designer:   Heidi J. Baughman
Art manager:   Kim Meriwether
Compositor:   The Clarinda Company
Typeface:   9.5/12 Helvetica
Printer:   Von Hoffmann Press

**Library of Congress Cataloging-in-Publication Data**

Mason, Robert Deward,
    Statistical techniques in business and economics / Robert D. Mason, Douglas A. Lind.—8th ed.
        p.      cm.
    ISBN 0-256-10338-0   0-256-10811-0 (International ed.)
    ISBN 0-256-12828-6 (Instructor's Edition)
    1. Social sciences—Statistical methods.   2. Economics—Statistical methods.   3. Commercial statistics.   I. Lind, Douglas A.   II. Title.
    HA29.M268   1993
    519.5—dc20                                           92−9933

*Printed in the United States of America*
2 3 4 5 6 7 8 9 0 VH 9 8 7 6 5 4 3

To Anita and Jane

## Preface to the Student

**A**s the name implies, the purpose of the eighth edition of *Statistical Techniques in Business and Economics* is to provide students in marketing, accounting, finance, international trade, management, and other fields of business administration and economics with a sound introduction to the many applications of descriptive and inferential statistics. The book, however, is also very appropriate for use in other subject areas, such as the various social sciences. You will find that the text provides excellent preparation for decision-making problems in various facets of business and economics and a good background for advanced courses involving statistical techniques.

## LEARNING AIDS

We have designed the text to assist you in approaching this course without the anxiety often associated with statistics. This teaching-learning orientation has resulted in a large number of very effective learning aids. The following aids have been retained and improved from previous editions of *Statistical Techniques in Business and Economics*.

**Goals.** Each chapter opens with a set of goals. They indicate what you should be able to do after completing the chapter.

**Examples and solutions.** After the discussion of a concept in a chapter, there is at least one example and its solution. Any numbers involved are kept manageable so that you can concentrate on the technique and solution.

**Self-review problems.** A large number of self-review problems are interspersed throughout each chapter. They are designed to give you an opportunity to work problems similar to the preceding examples. They serve to reinforce understanding of the material just covered.

**Exercises.** The number of exercises within chapters and at the end of chapters has been increased significantly. Usually, the first few chapter exercises stress computations, and the remaining incorporate interesting real-world data. The answer and method of solution to every odd-numbered exercise can be found at the end of the text.

**Definitions.** The definitions of new terms, such as the coefficient of correlation, are boxed and highlighted in color for emphasis.

**Marginal notes.** There are nearly 700 concise notes in the margin. Each is aimed at reemphasizing an important concept or facet immediately adjacent to it.

**Chapter outline.** At the end of the chapter discussion is an outline, including formulas, that brings together in brief form the material covered in the chapter.

**Chapter examination.** There is an examination at the end of each chapter covering all the material in the chapter. It allows you to quickly evaluate your overall comprehension of the subject matter. The answers and methods of solution for the examination questions are also at the end of the chapter.

**Review section.** After each major *group* of chapters is a section aimed at providing an overall understanding of the preceding chapters.

**Symbols.** At the end of the book is a listing of the major statistical symbols, their meaning, and the page on which a particular symbol first appears.

## NEW LEARNING AIDS

**Formulas.** Formulas in a chapter are numbered starting with 1. Reference is made in the chapter to these formula numbers, giving you quick access to the appropriate formula.

**Color format.** This edition is the first to be published using a five-color design. The intent of this pedagogical device is to underscore important features for you, to provide clarity, and to reinforce learning. In addition, the use of color will add to the visual stimulation and interest for motivation. The use of five colors allows anyone using the book to easily locate and recognize key learning aids by color. For instance, MINITAB input and output are always denoted by a light blue border, and the self-reviews and their answers are printed over a cream-colored background.

**Photographs.** We have also added color photographs throughout the text. The photographs at the beginning of the chapters depict activities in such industries as retailing, transportation, advertising, manufacturing, and entertainment. The 21 industries shown were selected from industry classification lists published by the U.S. government and *Fortune* magazine, with modifications. They represent a broad cross section of the areas involving problems that require the collection of data and the application of statistical techniques for their solution. In addition, within each chapter we have added occasional color photos that match an example or problem. We worked hard, in cooperation with Irwin, to make this edition more interesting and stimulating through the use of color in photographs and graphic art. We hope you will find the color to be helpful and interesting and that, at least partially as a result of these enhancements, you will enjoy your study of statistics.

## CHANGES IN THE CONTENT OF THE EIGHTH EDITION

We very much appreciate the positive support and encouragement of the many instructors who adopted previous editions of this book and the students who have studied from it. Many of their suggestions for improvement, as well as those of the reviewers, were incorporated in the eighth edition. An overview of the major changes in this edition is provided below.

The introductory chapter and the following three chapters on descriptive statistics have been revised and expanded by the inclusion of many interesting illustrations from *Business Week, The Wall Street Journal,* NCR's 1990 *Annual Report,* and other publications. They include examples of descriptive and inferential statistics, qualitative and quantitative data, and levels of measurement. We start in these early chapters to emphasize the important role of computers in data analysis. We use mainly MINITAB as the statistical software package. The commands needed to solve problems involving stem-and-leaf charts, histograms, and measures of central tendency appear at the top of the outputs. At the request of our users, the number of exercises in each of these early chapters is more than double the number in the seventh edition.

In Chapters 5, 6, and 7, dealing with probability, discrete distributions, and continuous distributions, we maintained the same writing style and general format found in the previous edition. In Chapter 5, the section on Bayes' theorem has been revised and expanded significantly. Also, there is more stress on tree diagrams, and the number of exercises has been increased. Chapter 6, on discrete probability distributions, and Chapter 7, on the normal probability distribution, still include the binomial, the cumulative binomial, the hypergeometric, the Poisson, and the normal probability distributions. We revised and increased the number of exercises both within the chapters and at the end of the chapters.

Chapter 8, on sampling methods and sampling distributions, stresses the reasons why sampling is necessary in certain situations, the methods of selecting a sample from a population, the sampling distribution of the means, and the central limit theorem. Several computer simulations are used to reinforce the idea of the central limit theorem and to emphasize the changing shapes of sampling distributions. As in previous chapters, the number of exercises has been increased significantly.

Chapters 9, 10, and 11 examine the concept of hypothesis testing and the steps needed to arrive at a decision. The discussion of the $p$-value and its use has been greatly expanded from earlier editions and is used again in the following chapter, Chapter 12, on the analysis of variance.

In Chapters 13, 14, and 15 we stress standard correlation and regression measures and a test of significance. MINITAB is used as an aid in computing the coefficient of correlation, the regression equation, and related statistical measures. The two chapters on nonparametric methods (Chapters 16 and 17) still include such topics as chi-square, the sign test, the Mann-Whitney test, the Kruskal-Wallis one-way analysis of variance, the median test, and the Wilcoxon matched-pair signed rank test. New to this edition is an extensive discussion of the goodness-of-fit test, which can be applied to test for normality.

Chapter 18, on index numbers, has been updated, and the discussion of the number of uses of indexes worldwide has been expanded. Also added are a number of new exercises based on current data. Again, the total number of exercises in this chapter is double those in the seventh edition. The material in Chapter 19, on time series and forecasting, has also been updated, and a new section regarding the use of deseasonalized data to forecast has been added. In Chapter 20, on decision making, we use a program by Hall and Adelman, *Computerized Business Statistics,* to demonstrate how a problem requiring a decision-making approach can be solved by a computer. In the chapter on quality control (Chapter 21) we show how a computer can be used to design various types of quality-control charts. The exercises have been revised and updated and include more problems dealing with quality in services, retailing, and other current issues.

## COMPUTER DATA EXERCISES

The last few exercises in most chapters are based on three large data sets found at the end of the book. The first set contains data on 75 homes sold in Sarasota, Florida, during the year. Included for each home is the selling price, the size of the home, the number of bedrooms, and other data. The second set has data on the 200 largest corporations in the United States. For each corporation there are figures on annual sales, profits, share turnover, dividends paid, and so on. The third set gives the number of games won, team batting average, and other statistics for each of the 26 major league baseball teams for the 1991 season. Since the data sets are large, a computer and software, such as MINITAB, are needed to answer such questions as: What are the mean and median annual attendance? What is the relationship between sales and profits for the 200 largest firms? Can we conclude that the mean selling price for homes with a pool is different from the mean selling price for homes without a pool?

## SUPPLEMENTS

The **Study Guide** that accompanies the eighth edition is written by the authors. Each chapter includes the chapter goals, an introduction, a discussion of the important concepts and terms, a glossary, chapter problems with solutions, student exercises with answers in the back of the guide, and chapter assignments that may be assigned at the option of the instructor. The exercises and assignments have been updated and revised. The Study Guide can be purchased from your campus bookstore, or they can order it for you.

A **Data Disk** is also available. This diskette contains the three large data sets and data for many of the examples and exercises. The data are included in both ASCII and MINITAB formats. Ask your instructor for details.

**Bob Mason**
**Doug Lind**

# Acknowledgments

The eighth edition of *Statistical Techniques in Business and Economics* is the product of many people—students, colleagues, reviewers, and the staff at Richard D. Irwin, Inc. We thank them all. We also wish to express our gratitude to:

| | |
|---|---|
| Diane L. Stehman | Northeastern Illinois University |
| Jonas Falik | Queensborough Community College |
| Louis A. Patille | University of Phoenix |
| Wendy J. McGuire | Santa Fe Community College |
| J. B. Orris | Butler University |
| David R. Hoffman | University of Phoenix |
| Joseph F. Kearney | Davenport College |
| Robert J. Miller | Missouri Southern State College |
| Bob McManus | Algonquin College |
| Leonard Gaston | Central State University |
| Linda Stroh | Sacramento City College |
| John Shannon | Suffolk University |
| Blake L. Friesen | Saskatchewan Institute of Applied Science and Technology—Palliser Campus |

Their suggestions and thorough reviews of the seventh edition and the manuscript for this edition made this a better text. Many of these reviewers also contributed their expertise by reviewing the supplements.

Special thanks go to Louis A. Patille and Wendy McGuire, who each solved all of the exercises and checked our answers for accuracy. Thanks are also due to Joseph F. Kearney and Patricia Buchanan, Pennsylvania State University, who each checked the accuracy of all of the examples and self-reviews. Stephen D. Lind, Vijay Venbakkam, and Anita R. Ford are deserving of thanks for their tremendous help with the solutions manual and computer problems.

Lloyd Landau of Mercy College prepared the Test Bank and Denise McGinnis prepared the Transparency Masters. These supplements are a great deal of work to write and we appreciate the work in them which makes teaching the course easier for everyone who uses the text.

Many of the tables in the appendix were computer-generated for greater accuracy. We are indebted to Goldstein Software, Inc. for the program *GoldSpread Statistical,* which was used to generate these tables.

**R.D.M.**
**D.A.L.**

# Contents in Brief

# Contents

## CHAPTER FOUR

**Measures of Dispersion and Skewness**  111

## CHAPTER FIVE

**A Survey of Probability Concepts**  161

## CHAPTER SIX

**Discrete Probability Distributions**  211

## CHAPTER SEVEN

**The Normal Probability Distribution**  249

CHAPTER EIGHT

## Sampling Methods and Sampling Distributions  285

CHAPTER NINE

## Tests of Hypotheses: Large Samples  333

## CHAPTER TEN

**Tests of Hypotheses: Proportions**  *369*

## CHAPTER ELEVEN

**Student's *t* Test: Small Samples**  *393*

CHAPTER TWELVE

## Analysis of Variance  *423*

CHAPTER THIRTEEN

## Simple Correlation Analysis  *465*

CHAPTER FOURTEEN

## Simple Regression Analysis  *497*

CHAPTER FIFTEEN

**Multiple Regression and Correlation**  *531*

CHAPTER SIXTEEN

**Analysis of Nominal-Level Data: The Chi-Square Distribution**  *575*

## CHAPTER SEVENTEEN

**Nonparametric Methods: Analysis of Ranked Data**  *605*

**Index Numbers**  *649*

**Time Series and Forecasting**  *683*

## CHAPTER TWENTY

## An Introduction to Decision Making under Uncertainty   721

## CHAPTER TWENTY-ONE

## Statistical Quality Control   743

## APPENDIXES

## Tables and Data Sets   781

## ANSWERS

### Odd-Numbered Chapter Exercises   *817*

## ANSWERS

### Odd-Numbered Review Exercises   *862*

### Index   *867*

Electronics—Courtesy Zenith Electronics Corporation

# WHAT IS STATISTICS?

GOALS

When you have completed this chapter, you will be able to:

1. Define what is meant by statistics.

2. Cite some uses of statistics in business and other areas.

3. Explain what is meant by descriptive statistics and inferential statistics.

4. Distinguish between nominal, ordinal, interval, and ratio levels of measurement.

**A**bout 100 years ago H. G. Wells noted that "statistical thinking will one day be as necessary for efficient citizenship as the ability to read and write." He made no mention of business simply because the Industrial Revolution was still in its infancy. Were he to comment on statistical thinking today he would probably say that "statistical thinking is necessary not only for efficient citizenship, but also for effective decision making in various facets of business."

A recent article in the *Washington Post* by Michael Schrage emphasizes the importance of statistics.[1] He states that America is not going to have a quality revolution until its managers and workers get some grasp of probability and statistics. Unfortunately, corporate statistical literacy is abysmally low, Schrage points out. Brian Joyner, a Wisconsin-based consultant, agrees. To his dismay, he finds that much of his consulting time is spent on remedial statistical education. Author Andrea Gabor points out in the same article that "Japanese students are inundated with statistics in high school. You realize that statistics is now part of their culture. Just as our bookstores have sections on science and technology, their bookstores have sections on quality control and statistics." No doubt the emphasis on quality control, statistics, and probability has played a major part in the huge success of their Toyotas, Hondas, Sonys, Minoltas, and other manufactured product brands.

W. Edwards Deming, noted statistician and quality control expert, insists that we should start statistics education before high school. He likes to tell the story of an 11-year-old who devised a quality control chart to track the on-time performance of his school bus. Deming commented, "He's got a good start in life." It is hoped that this book will give you a solid foundation in statistics for your future life in marketing, accounting, management, or some other facet of business.

## WHAT IS MEANT BY STATISTICS?

Whether you are listening to your favorite local radio station, watching the Cubs play the Dodgers on television, or reading *USA Today, The Wall Street Journal,* or *Sports Illustrated,* you are the target of a barrage of assorted figures commonly referred to as statistics. Statistics might pertain to sports, the stock market, employment, agricultural production, and so forth. You may hear that Kroger has lettuce on sale for 69 cents a head, 216 died in a plane crash in Iran, IBM common stock is up $\frac{1}{8}$ to $106\frac{1}{4}$, and the Lakers defeated the Pistons 109 to 108. Some other examples:

- *Financial statistics:* The *Chicago Tribune* reported that the top three Chicago-based firms, ranked according to their 1990 revenues, were Sears, Roebuck and Co. ($55,972,000,000); Amoco Corp. ($31,581,000,000): and Sara Lee Corp. ($11,606,000,000).

- *Sales statistics:* Browsing through some recent issues of *Business Week,* we find that a pair of Rhead's bass flies tied by Louis Rhead in the 19th century sells for $250 and a near-mint fly rod built by Pinky Gillum in 1963 lists for $10,000. Pfizer's Procardia XL, a cardiovascular drug, had worldwide sales of $700,000,000 in 1991, and sales of Diflucan, an antifungal for AIDS patients, totaled $400,000,000.

- *Sports-related statistics:* Roger Clemens (Boston Red Sox) will earn $4,656,250 in 1993, Dwight Gooden (New York Mets) $5,916,667, and Jose Canseco

---

[1]Michael Schrage, "If Statistics Are the Key to Quality, Our Students Need Some Chance Encounters," *Washington Post* (March 15, 1991).

(Oakland Athletics) $4,800,000. Sales of tennis rackets increased from 2.2 million in 1985 to 4.0 million in 1990.

• *Statistics from* The Wall Street Journal: Florists' Transworld Delivery Association handled 55,200 orders for flowers last Father's Day, up from 49,600 the previous year. The number of people who consider flowers appropriate for men has risen to 63 percent from just 44 percent in 1982.

• *Other assorted statistics:* The U.S. Department of Justice reported that 12.5 percent of the personnel in sheriffs' departments are women, 7.6 percent of local police are women, and 4.2 percent of state police are women. Barbara Franklin is paid $315,600 as the director of seven major corporations. About 5.5 million children in the United States are hungry, and another 6 million are not getting enough to eat.

Statistic

One figure is called a **statistic** (singular). The closing price of Boeing common stock (44½) is a statistic. Your cumulative grade point average (4.0) is a statistic. The total retail sales for May, $131.88 billion, is a statistic. A collection of figures or facts is

Statistics

referred to as **statistics** (plural). For example, a collection of data such as 55,200 flower orders for Father's Day, 30,000 travel agencies in the United States, 2.2 percent of the labor force employed in farming, and $10,000 for a fly rod is commonly referred to as statistics.

However, the subject of statistics as we will explore it in this text has a much broader meaning than just collecting and publishing numerical facts and figures. Statistics is defined as:

Statistics defined

| Statistics   The science of collecting, organizing, presenting, analyzing, and interpreting numerical data for the purpose of assisting in making a more effective decision. |
| --- |

Just as attorneys have "rules of evidence" and accountants have "commonly accepted practices," persons dealing with numerical data follow some standard guidelines. Some of the basic statistical techniques they use in decision problems are presented in the following chapters.

Many first approach the application of numerical data to solve a problem with some trepidation. They have heard such often-quoted phrases as "statistics lie," and they might have seen a book in the bookstore entitled *How to Lie with Statistics*. Statistics "lie" only if they are not applied correctly. For illustration, suppose the sales of Carter Marine for the past 20 years were depicted as in Chart 1–1 on the following page. Initially, you might conclude that sales increased at a very rapid rate since 1972 (the lie).

However, a closer look reveals that sales increased only about 1 percent—from $100 million to $101 million (the truth). The designer of the chart—intentionally or unintentionally—scaled the vertical (sales) axis incorrectly, leaving us with the wrong impression regarding the trend of sales since 1972. Graphic representation is covered in Chapter 2.

Our objectives in this book are many. One, of course, is to alert you of possible misuses of charts, averages, correlation and regression techniques, and other statistical tools. Another is to introduce you to the usefulness of statistical techniques in marketing, accounting, finance, international trade, economics, law enforcement, and other fields. Specifically, who uses statistics?

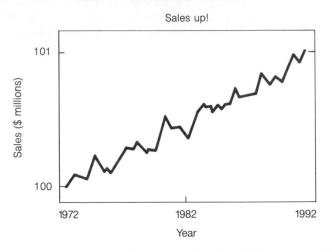

### CHART 1—1

**Sales of Carter Marine since 1972**

Sales up!

# WHO USES STATISTICS?

*Use in business and other fields*

As noted, statistical techniques are used extensively by marketing, accounting, quality control, and other departments; consumers; professional sports people; hospital administrators; educators; political parties; physicians; and others involved in making decisions. The following examples suggest the wide use of statistics in decision problems.

*Some specific uses of statistics in problem solving*

1. The research analysts for such firms as Merrill Lynch evaluate many facets of a stock before making a "buy" or "sell" recommendation. They collect the past sales data of the company and estimate future earnings. Other factors, such as projected worldwide demand for the company's products, the strength of the competition, and the effect of the new management-union contract, are also considered before a recommendation is made.

2. The Republican party wants to determine its chances of winning at least five of the seven contested seats in the Senate. How can the chances of challenger A. J. Farley in Oklahoma be assessed? A sample survey of potential voters in the state could be conducted. The party could hire pollsters, such as Gallup or Harris; or the party could undertake the survey. Scientifically selecting, say, 2,000 registered voters in Oklahoma and evaluating the results require a knowledge of the techniques of probability and sampling (covered in Chapters 5–8).

*Statistics imperative in quality assurance*

3. Management must make decisions on the quality of current production. For example, automatic drill presses do not produce a perfect hole 1.3000 inches in diameter each time a hole is drilled (because of drill wear, vibration of the machine, and other factors). Slight tolerances are permitted, but when the hole is too small or too large, production is considered defective (not usable). The quality assurance department is charged with continually monitoring production using sampling and other standard statistical techniques (covered in Chapter 21).

4. Consumers shopping for a grocery item, such as canned pork and beans, often use unit pricing to decide which size to purchase. Is the 21-ounce size of Van Camp pork and beans at 69 cents, the 31-ounce size at 98 cents, or the 53-ounce size at $1.55 the best buy? If price is the only consideration, converting each price to cost per ounce will lead to the answer.

Statistics use in professional sports

5. Professional football teams computerize data on college prospects in order to decide which prospect to draft. The record for Clint Sawyer of Texas Tech might include: 4.3 seconds in the 40-yard dash, weight 230 pounds, and bench press 420 pounds. Should the Dallas Cowboys draft him or Keith Dresser of Idaho State in the first round?

6. The hospital administrator must act on a proposal that a new wing be added to alleviate crowded conditions. To determine whether or not a new wing is actually needed, the administrator must gather and evaluate data such as bed occupancy rates. Then data must be collected on the cost of the wing, sources of financing, and projected income, in order to justify the construction to the board of directors.

7. Internally, the controller and the accounting department of a firm are charged with the accuracy of various financial documents. Since it is physically impossible to check every document for accuracy, a sampling of the invoices is made, and decisions are based on the sample results (sampling techniques are covered in Chapter 8).

Statistics use in marketing

8. The marketing department of a soap manufacturer has the responsibility of making recommendations regarding the potential profitability of a newly developed group of face soaps having fruit smells, such as pineapple, orange, and lime. Likewise, the marketing department of a nationally known soft drink bottler must make a similar decision regarding a newly developed group of drinks having such unique tastes as avocado and plum. Both departments will conduct consumer tests and make profit projections based on sample results. The *Chicago Tribune* reported in February 1991 that market research has developed into a $2.5 billion business. It was noted that surveys conducted for major industries help to determine what type of car we will drive, the kinds of food we will eat, the pain killers we take, and the deodorants, toothpaste, soap, and perfume we use.

Use of statistical techniques by government

9. The federal government is particularly concerned with the present condition of our economy and with predicting future economic trends. The government conducts a large number of surveys to determine consumer confidence and the outlook of management regarding sales and production for the next 12 months. Indexes, such as the Consumer Price Index (covered in Chapter 18), are constructed each month to assess the trend of inflation. Department store sales, housing starts, money turnover, and industrial production statistics are just a few of the hundreds of economic indicators evaluated monthly. These evaluations are used to make decisions regarding the prime rate charged by banks and are used by the Federal Reserve Board to decide the level of control to place on the money supply.

Statistics use by TV networks, in medicine, in education

10. The following situations require the use of statistical techniques: Management must decide whether or not to build a new plant in South Carolina, Arkansas, or Wyoming; taxes, transportation costs, building costs, and the willingness of key personnel to move must be considered. NBC must decide whether or not to add another soap, "Mama Knows Best" to its

prime-time offerings. A college must decide whether or not to admit an applicant from Skipton, England, who had a D+ average in a private school. A doctor must decide what tests to conduct for a patient exhibiting certain symptoms. Based on blood tests, electrocardiograms, and other test results, a course of action is taken. Finally, you are considering opening a pizza restaurant. Before making a decision, you will collect and evaluate data on such items as the initial cost, competition, and potential profit.

## TYPES OF STATISTICS

### DESCRIPTIVE STATISTICS

*Descriptive statistics*

The definition of statistics in the introduction referred to "organizing, presenting, and analyzing numerical data." This facet of statistics is commonly referred to as **descriptive statistics.** What is a **descriptive statistic?**

- According to NCR's 1990 annual report, the company's total number of employees is 55,000. The figure 55,000 merely describes the company's total employment. Thus, it is considered a descriptive statistic.

- The Electronic Industries Association in their *Electronic Market Data Book* reported that factory sales of color TVs last year were $6.6 billion. The figure $6.6 billion is a descriptive statistic; it merely describes the total annual sales.

> **Descriptive statistics** The procedures used to organize and summarize masses of numerical data.

Masses of unorganized numerical data—such as the census of population, the hourly earnings of thousands of computer programmers, and the individual responses of 2,340 registered voters regarding their choice for President of the United States—are of little value. However, statistical techniques are available to organize this type of data into a meaningful form. Some data can be organized into a **frequency distribution.** (The procedure for doing this is covered in Chapter 2.) Various **charts** may be used to describe data; several basic chart forms are also presented in Chapter 2.

*Median—another descriptive tool*

Specialized averages, such as the *median,* may be computed to describe the central value of a group of numerical data. These averages are presented in Chapter 3. A number of statistical measures may be used to describe how closely the data are clustered about an average. These measures are examined in Chapter 4.

### INFERENTIAL STATISTICS

*A population of individuals, objects, or measurements*

Another facet of statistics is **inferential statistics**—also called **statistical inference** and **inductive statistics.** Our main concern regarding inferential statistics is finding out something about a population based on a sample taken from that population. For example, based on a survey by the federal government reported in *USA Today,* only 46 percent of high school seniors can solve problems involving fractions, decimals, and percentages. And, only 77 percent of these seniors correctly totaled the cost of soup, a burger, fries, and a cola on a restaurant menu. Since these are inferences about the population (all high school seniors) based on sample data, we refer to them as inferential statistics.

> **Inferential statistics**   The methods used to find out something about a population, based on a sample.

Note the words "population" and "sample" in the definition of inferential statistics. We often make reference to the population living in the United States or the 1 billion population of China. However, in statistics the word *population* has a broader meaning. A **population** may consist of *individuals*—such as all the students enrolled at State University, all the students in Accounting 201, or all the inmates at Attica prison. A population may also consist of *objects,* such as all the XB-70 tires produced during the week at the Cooper Tire and Rubber Company in Findlay, Ohio, or all the trout in a stock pond. A population may also consist of a group of *measurements,* such as all the weights of the defensive linemen on the Penn State University football team or all the heights of the basketball players in the Southeastern Conference. Note that a population in the statistical sense of the word does not necessarily refer to people.

> **Population**   A collection of all possible individuals, objects, or measurements of interest.

To infer something about a population, we usually take a **sample** from the population.

> **Sample**   A portion, or part, of the population of interest.

Why take a sample instead of studying every member of the population? A sample of registered voters is necessary because of the prohibitive cost of contacting millions of voters before an election. Testing wheat for moisture content destroys the wheat, thus making a sample imperative. If the wine tasters tested all the wine, none would be available for sale. It would be physically impossible for a few marine biologists to capture and tag all the seals in the ocean. (These and other reasons for sampling are discussed in Chapter 8.)

As noted, taking a sample to find out something about a population is done extensively in business, agriculture, politics, and government, as shown in the following examples:

1. Before an election, such professional polling organizations as Gallup and Harris sample only about 2,000 registered voters out of the millions eligible to vote. Based on sample results, certain inferences are made regarding how all voters will cast their ballots on election day. Historically, the actual election results have been remarkably close to the sample results. The following figures are based on Gallup's predictions: for Roosevelt (1944), 51.5 percent estimated versus 53.3 percent actual; for Reagan (1984), 59.0 percent of the total vote prior to the election versus 59.2 percent actual; for Bush (1988), 52.9 percent estimated versus 53.4 percent actual.

2. One automobile manufacturer takes a sample of five pinion gears (used in the transmission) every hour. On the basis of the sample results, a decision is made as to the quality of all pinion gears produced during the hour.

3. A small scoop of wheat is taken from a truck as it waits to be unloaded at Anderson's grain elevator in Maumee, Ohio. Based on the results of this sample, a price is established for the whole truckload.

4. The U.S. Department of Labor constantly monitors employment, unemployment, wages, and labor turnover based on sample surveys. Their release for March 1991 included these statistics: 6.8 percent of those 16 years and over searching for work were unemployed, and 947,000 had been unemployed 27 weeks or longer. For the same month the average weekly earnings in mining were $621.28, in manufacturing $444.31, and in retail trade $195.01.

5. Television networks constantly monitor the popularity of their programs by hiring Neilsen and other organizations to sample the preferences of TV viewers. These program ratings are used to set advertising rates and to cancel programs.

6. Marine biologists tag a few seals to chart their migratory patterns.

7. Wine tasters sip a few drops of wine to make a decision with respect to all the wine waiting to be released for sale.

8. The accounting department checks only a few invoices to find out something about the accuracy of all the invoices.

9. Consumers sample pizza and other products at the grocery store. If you like the sample, you may purchase a whole pizza.

**Risks of sampling**

There are certain risks involved in using sample results to infer something about an unknown population. Five pinion gears selected at random by the quality assurance department from all the pinion gears manufactured during the past hour might be acceptable. Thus, it might be inferred from the sample of five that all the gears produced were satisfactory. However, since this inference was based on only a portion of the population, there is a chance that not all gears are satisfactory. In fact, it might be that the five gears chosen at random were the only acceptable ones produced during the hour! Pollsters such as Gallup and Harris might predict that John Corrigan will win the vacant House seat by a landslide. However, there is a chance that Sue Bronner might win.

Extensive consumer research involving sophisticated sampling techniques is conducted on a continuing basis by a large number of research firms. Despite their advanced sampling methods, their recommendations regarding particular new TV programs, for example, are often rejected by the general public. According to Ralph Looney, writing for the *Chicago Tribune,* "It probably comes as a surprise to the TV big shots that so many of their programs end up as duds." He mused that "when you wonder why some TV shows are so bad, blame it on the surveyors who tell the network bosses what you want to watch."[2] The discussion of sampling techniques (starting with Chapter 5) will assess the risks of making an incorrect decision.

*Following is a self-review problem. There are a number of them interspersed throughout each chapter. They test your comprehension of the preceding material. The answer and method of solution are given at the end of the chapter. We recommend that you solve each one and then check your answer.*

---

[2]Ralph Looney, "Pollsters Fret as Americans Learn to Say No." *Chicago Tribune* (February 5, 1991).

### Self-Review 1–1

*The answers are at the end of the chapter.*

Chicago-based Market Facts asked a sample of 1,960 consumers to try a newly developed frozen fish dinner by Morton called Fish Delight. Out of the 1,960 sampled, 1,176 said they would purchase the dinner if it is marketed.

1. What would Market Facts report to Morton Foods regarding acceptance of Fish Delight?
2. Is this an example of descriptive statistics or inferential statistics? Explain.

## TYPES OF VARIABLES

Qualitative variable

There are two basic types of data: (1) those obtained from a qualitative population and (2) those obtained from a quantitative population. When the characteristic or variable being studied is nonnumeric, it is called a **qualitative variable.** Examples of qualitative variables are gender, religious affiliation, type of automobile owned, state of birth, and eye color. In quality control work (see Chapter 21), qualitative variables are also referred to as *attribute variables.* When the data being studied are qualitative, we are usually interested in how many or what proportion fall in each category. For example, what percent of the population have blue eyes? How many Catholics and how many Protestants are there in the United States? What percent of the total number of cars sold last month were Buicks? Qualitative data are often summarized in charts and bar graphs (Chapters 2 and 21).

Quantitative variable

When the variable studied can be reported numerically, the variable is called a **quantitative variable,** and the population is called a quantitative population. Examples of quantitative variables are: the balance in your checking account, the ages of company presidents, the life of a battery (such as 42 months), the speeds of automobiles traveling along Interstate 5 near Seattle, and the number of children in a family.

Discrete variable

Quantitative variables are either discrete or continuous. **Discrete variables** can assume only certain values, and there are usually "gaps" between the values. Examples of discrete variables are the number of bedrooms in a house (1, 2, 3, 4, etc.), the number of cars arriving at a tollbooth on I-75 at Berea, Kentucky, over an hour (16, 19, 30, etc.), and the number of students in each section of a statistics course (25 in section A, 42 in section B, and 18 in section C). Notice that a home can have 3 or 4 bedrooms, but it cannot have 3.56 bedrooms. Thus, there is a "gap" between possible values. Typically, discrete variables result from counting. We count, for example, the number of cars arriving at the Berea exit on I-75, and we count the number of statistic students in each section.

Continuous variable

Observations of a **continuous variable** can assume any value within a specific range. Examples of continuous variables include the air pressure in a tire and the weight of a shipment of grain (which, depending on the accuracy of the scales, could be 15.0 tons, 15.01 tons, 15.03 tons, etc.). The amount of raisin bran in a box and the time it took to fly from Orlando to San Diego are other variables of a continuous nature. The Orlando–San Diego flight could take 7 hours and 30 minutes; or 7 hours, 30 minutes and 45 seconds; or 7 hours, 30 minutes, and 45.1 seconds, depending on the accuracy of the timing device. Typically, continuous variables result from measuring something. When the population is quantitative, we are usually interested in determining how the observations are distributed among all the possible outcomes, what a typical value is (Chapter 3), and the amount of variability in the data (Chapter 4).

The types of variables are shown in the following diagram.

```
                          ┌──────────────┐
                          │     Data     │
                          └──────┬───────┘
                  ┌──────────────┴───────────────┐
         ┌────────────────┐              ┌─────────────────┐
         │  Qualitative or │              │  Quantitative   │
         │    attribute    │              │  or numerical   │
         └────────────────┘              └────────┬────────┘
                                    ┌──────────────┴──────────────┐
                            ┌───────────────┐         ┌───────────────┐
                            │   Discrete    │         │  Continuous   │
                            └───────────────┘         └───────────────┘
```

Examples:

| Qualitative | Discrete | Continuous |
|---|---|---|
| Type of car owned | Number of children | Weight of a shipment |
| Color of pens | Number of employees | Miles driven between oil changes |
| Gender | Number of TV sets sold last year | Distance between New York and Bangkok |

## LEVELS OF MEASUREMENT

"Level of measurement" will be mentioned frequently in the following chapters. The four general types, or levels, of measurement are nominal, ordinal, interval, and ratio.

### NOMINAL LEVEL

The information presented in Table 1–1 and Table 1–2 represents nominal measurement. This level is considered the most "primitive," the "lowest," or the most limited type of measurement.

---

**TABLE  1–1**

**Religion Reported by the Population of the United States 14 Years Old and Older**

| Religion | Total |
|---|---|
| Protestant | 78,952,000 |
| Roman Catholic | 30,669,000 |
| Jewish | 3,868,000 |
| Other religion | 1,545,000 |
| No religion | 3,195,000 |
| Religion not reported | 1,104,000 |
| Total | 119,333,000 |

Source: U.S. Department of Commerce, Bureau of the Census, *Current Population Reports,* series P-20, no. 79.

---

**TABLE  1–2**

**Top Seven New Passenger Car Sales in Canada, by Company**

| Company | Annual sales (number of units) |
|---|---|
| General Motors | 379,159 |
| Ford | 193,000 |
| Chrysler | 156,078 |
| Honda | 72,976 |
| Toyota | 68,753 |
| Hyundai | 50,648 |
| Volkswagen | 41,470 |
| All others | 187,648 |

Source: Member companies of the Motor Vehicle Manufacturers Association and the Automobile Importers of Canada.

Nominal level: Data can only be classified into categories

The terms **nominal level of measurement** and **nominal-scaled** are commonly used to refer to data that can *only be classified into categories*. In the strict sense of the words, however, there are no measurements and no scales involved. Instead, there are just counts.

The arrangement of the religions in Table 1−1 could have been changed. Roman Catholic could have been listed first, Jewish second, and so on. This essentially indicates that for the nominal level of measurement, *there is no particular order for the groupings.* Further, the categories are considered to be **mutually exclusive,** meaning, for example, that a person could not be a Protestant and have no religion at the same time. In the case of Table 1−2, a car could not be a Ford and a Hyundai at the same time.

Mutually exclusive

| Mutually exclusive   An individual, object, or measurement is included in only one category. |
| --- |

It should be noted that the categories in Table 1−1 and Table 1−2 are **exhaustive,** meaning that every member of the population, or sample, must appear in one of the categories. If a person refused to give her religion, she would be included in the category "religion not reported." If she embraced Buddhism, her religion would be included in the category "other religion." In Table 1−2, a Mercedes Benz would fall in the category "all others."

Exhaustive

| Exhaustive   Each individual, object, or measurement must appear in one category. |
| --- |

In order to process data on religious preference, sex, employment by industry, and so forth, the categories are often coded 1, 2, 3, . . . with, say, 1 representing Protestant, 2 representing Roman Catholic, and so on. This facilitates counting when a computer or other counting device is used. It is not permissible, however, to manipulate these numbers algebraically. For example, $1 + 2$ does not equal 3; that is, a Protestant plus a Roman Catholic does not equal a person of the Jewish religion. Likewise, if a General Motors car was coded 1, a Ford 2, and so on, a GM plus a Ford does not equal a Chrysler.

Don't try to add 1 + 2

Tests applied to nominal-scaled data do not make any assumptions regarding the underlying distribution of the population from which the sample was selected. Thus, these tests are called *distribution-free* or *nonparametric* tests. Some of these tests will be discussed starting with Chapter 16.

## ORDINAL LEVEL

Ordinal level means ranking

Table 1−3 on the following page, which lists ratings of the company commander by the nurses under her command, is an illustration of the **ordinal level of measurement.** One category is higher than the next one; that is, "superior" is a higher rating than "good," "good" is higher than "average," and so on.

If 1 is substituted for "superior," 2 substituted for "good," and so on, a 1 ranking is obviously higher than a 2 ranking, and a 2 ranking is higher than a 3 ranking. However, it cannot be said that (as an example) a company commander rated good is twice as competent as one rated average, or that a company commander rated superior is twice as competent as one rated good. It can only be said that a rating of superior is greater than a rating of good, and a good rating is greater than an average rating.

---

### Table 1—3

**Ratings of the Company Commander**

| Rating | Number of nurses |
|---|---|
| Superior | 6 |
| Good | 28 |
| Average | 25 |
| Poor | 17 |
| Inferior | 0 |

---

In review, the major difference between a nominal level and an ordinal level of measurement is the "greater than" relationship between the ordinal-level categories. Otherwise, the ordinal scale of measurement has the same characteristics as the nominal scale, namely, the categories are mutually exclusive and exhaustive.

## Interval Level

The **interval scale of measurement** is the next higher level. It includes all the characteristics of the ordinal scale, but in addition, the distance between values is a constant size. Temperature on the Fahrenheit scale is an example. Suppose the high temperatures for three consecutive days in January in North Platte, Nebraska, are 28, 31, and 20. These temperatures can easily be ranked, but we can also determine the differences between the temperatures. This is possible because 1 degree Fahrenheit represents a constant unit of measurement. It is important to note that the zero point is arbitrary—just another point on the Fahrenheit scale. Zero degrees Fahrenheit does not represent the absence of heat, just that it is cold! Suppose that the August temperature of 96 degrees is to be compared with the three North Platte January temperatures of about 30 degrees. We can say that it is more than 60 degrees warmer on an August day than on a day in January, but we cannot say that it is three times as hot. Scores on an SAT examination and scores on a history or a math examination are also examples of the interval scale of measurement.

The interval scale of measurement has mutually exclusive and exhaustive properties. An August high temperature, for example, cannot be both 88 and 76. Hence, the mutually exclusive feature is met. We can list the high temperatures for all days in August. Thus, the exhaustive feature is met.

## Ratio Level

**Ratio level** is the "highest" level of measurement. This level has all the characteristics of interval level: the distances between numbers are of a known, constant size; the categories are mutually exclusive; and so on. The major differences between interval and ratio levels of measurement are these: (1) Ratio-level data has a *meaningful* zero point, and (2) the ratio between two numbers is meaningful. Money is a good illustration. Having zero dollars has meaning—you have none! Weight is another ratio-level measurement. If the dial on a scale is zero, there is a complete absence of weight. Also, if you earn $40,000 a year and Keith earns $10,000, you earn four times what he does. Likewise if you weigh 240 pounds and Pat weighs 80 pounds, you weigh three times what she does. We can say that you earn $30,000 a year more than Keith does and weigh 160 pounds more than Pat does. Other examples of the ratio level of measurement are the number of years doctors spend in medical practice and the number of Hondas sold last month by the salespeople at Westgate Honda.

## Self-Review 1–2

*The answers are at the end of the chapter.*

1. *Canadian Statistics* reported these populations:

| Province or territory | Number of people |
|---|---|
| Newfoundland | 567,681 |
| Nova Scotia | 847,442 |
| New Brunswick | 691,403 |
| Northwest Territories | 45,741 |
| Yukon | 23,153 |

What level of measurement is reflected by these data? Why?

2. Test scores on a special examination given to Army enlisted personnel interested in attending Officer Candidate School are:

| Scores | Number of applicants |
|---|---|
| 90–99 | 42 |
| 80–89 | 19 |
| 70–79 | 7 |
| 60–69 | 4 |
| Below 60 | 3 |

What level of measurement do these data represent? Explain.

## SOME LEARNING AIDS

Valuable learning aids

As you progress through each chapter, you will notice a number of learning aids designed to help you determine immediately whether or not you have grasped the preceding subject matter. Among these are:

- **Self-review problems** scattered throughout every chapter. We suggest that you solve each of these review problems and check your answers against those provided at the end of the chapter.

- **Exercises** interspersed throughout each chapter. The answers and methods of solution to the odd-numbered exercises are at the end of the book.

- A section entitled **Computer Data Exercises** at the end of most chapters. It contains more challenging problems and larger data sets. A computer is essential to solve them.

- An **examination** at the end of each chapter. Included are objective-type questions and problems covering the entire chapter. This test allows you to pull together the main ideas presented in the chapter. The answers are at the end of the chapter.

- A **review section** after a group of chapters consisting of the highlights of the preceding chapters, a glossary, and a comprehensive group of exercises.

A word of encouragement          Such symbols as $\chi^2$, $\Sigma$, $\sigma$, and $\rho$ are used in this text. So are formulas such as:

$$s = \sqrt{\frac{\Sigma fX^2 - \frac{(\Sigma fX)^2}{n}}{n-1}} \qquad z = \frac{\overline{X}_1 - \overline{X}_2}{\sqrt{\left(\frac{s_1}{\sqrt{n_1}}\right)^2 + \left(\frac{s_2}{\sqrt{n_2}}\right)^2}}$$

They should not intimidate or discourage you! These symbols and formulas are merely a way of condensing the subject matter. However, since many of the symbols, formulas, and terms (e.g., *standard deviation, coefficient of correlation, chi-square,* and *decision rule*) might be unfamiliar to you, the material may be slow reading, and you may have to read some material several times. Should you need to know the meaning of a certain symbol, there is a listing of symbols at the end of the text.

## COMPUTER APPLICATIONS

The use of personal computers and computer applications in business are increasing at a rapid rate. As evidence, the revenue of IBM, the world's largest computer manufacturer, went from $52 billion in 1986 to over $69 billion in 1990, an increase of 32 percent in just four years (see Chart 1–2).

Courtesy International Business
Machines Corporation

---

### CHART   1–2

**Revenue of IBM, 1986–1990**

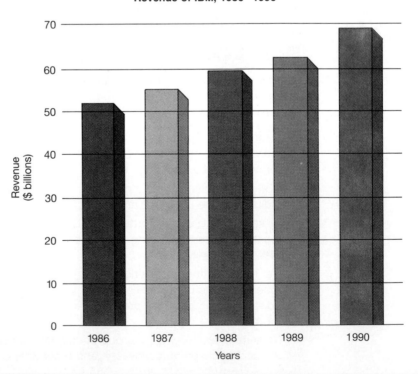

Minitab's new version 8
features easy-to-use
pull-down menus.
Courtesy Minitab, Inc.

Computers are now available for student use at most colleges and universities, as are such software systems as MINITAB, SAS, and the Statistical Package for the Social Sciences (SPSS). We chose MINITAB for most of the statistical applications in this text. It is user-friendly, meaning that it is easy to operate and does not require learning a special programming language. To help you, we've given the MINITAB commands at the top of each computer output.

To illustrate the use of a computer and the application of MINITAB, we discuss the monthly rental rates of condominiums in the Sarasota and Bradenton, Florida, area in Chapters 2, 3, and 4. The following MINITAB output reveals, among other things, that 120 condominiums were studied, the mean rental amount was $1,457.90, and the rental prices ranged from a low of $640 to a high of $2,187. The headings used, such as STDEV and Q3 will be explained when we get to Chapter 4.

```
MTB > describe c1

                 N      MEAN    MEDIAN    TRMEAN    STDEV    SEMEAN
Rentals        120    1457.9    1464.5    1462.3    307.6      28.1
               MIN       MAX        Q1        Q3
Rentals      640.0    2187.0    1288.3    1639.3
```

Had we used a calculator to arrive at these measures and others needed to fully analyze the rental amounts, many hours of calculations would be required. The likelihood of an error in arithmetic is very high when a large number of values are considered. MINITAB can provide us with the needed information in just seconds.

At the end of most chapters are exercises involving large data sets designed for computer analysis. One data set provides information on the sales of 75 homes in Florida. The information for each of the homes includes the selling price, size in square feet, the distance from the center of the city, whether or not it has a pool, and so on. A second data set provides summary statistics for the major league baseball season. Information on each team, such as the number of home runs hit, total attendance, and the number of games won, is provided. Another data *set* includes business and economic statistics on several hundred top firms in the United States. The purpose of these exercises is to illustrate computer usage involving real data.

At the option of your instructor, and depending on the operating system and equipment available, we urge you to apply a statistical computer package to the exercises having large data sets. It will relieve you of tedious manipulations and allow you to concentrate on data analysis.

## CHAPTER OUTLINE

I. Definition of statistics.
   A. *Statistics* may be thought of as a collection of numerical data.
   B. As used in a broader sense, statistics refers to the statistical tools used to collect, present, analyze, and interpret data for the purpose of making more effective decisions.
II. Subdivisions of statistics.
   A. *Descriptive statistics* deals with presenting data in a graph or a frequency distribution and with applying various averages and measures of dispersion.
   B. *Inferential statistics* deals with taking a sample from a population and making estimates about a characteristic of that population based on the sample results.

III. Types of variables.
   A. *Qualitative variables* presumes that the variable is nonnumeric, such as make of motorcycle (Harley-Davidson, Yamaha).
   B. *Quantitative variable* deals with variables that can be measured, such as weight (110 pounds, 304 pounds) or annual sales ($10.1 million, $7.6 million).
IV. Levels of measurement.
   A. *Nominal level of measurement* refers to data that can only be counted and put into categories. There is no particular order to the categories.
   B. *Ordinal level of measurement* presumes that one category is higher than another. Freshman, sophomore, junior, and senior illustrates this kind of ranking.
   C. *Interval level of measurement* includes the ranking characteristics of the ordinal measurement and specifies that the distance between numbers is the same.
   D. *Ratio level of measurement* has all the characteristics of the interval level of measurement. In addition, the zero point is meaningful, and the ratio between two numbers is meaningful.

# EXERCISES

*The answers to the odd-numbered exercises are at the end of the book.*

1. One definition of statistics is that they are a collection of facts and figures. In business and other fields, statistics is thought of as a science. Discuss the difference between the two concepts.

2. Distinguish between *descriptive statistics* and *inferential statistics*.

3. A sample of 200 executives revealed that 60 of them had some degree of hypertension due in part to their job. What could be inferred about all executives? Why?

4. Numerous complaints have been received by the management of the food-processing plant where you work part-time. It is claimed that there is an excessive amount of liquid in some cans of cherries. The plant has no systematic quality assurance program. If you were named the quality assurance manager, what steps would you take to check production?

5. You have just been appointed the chief marketing executive for Fun Enterprise, a company that specializes in designing and erecting amusement parks near large cities. F.E. is primarily interested in a location in the Southeast. Once the site has been selected, you must recommend whether the park should be oriented toward persons of all ages, just children, or just retired persons. How would you proceed with making recommendations regarding (1) the location of the park and (2) the group orientation (all ages, young, old)?

6. The average annual salary for full professors at selected universities and colleges in California are (in $ thousands):

| University | Average Salary |
|---|---|
| Azusa Pacific University | $37.1 |
| California Institute of Technology | 86.0 |
| California Maritime Academy | 50.5 |
| California Lutheran University | 45.6 |
| Cal. St. Univ-Long Beach | 59.7 |

Source: The Annual Report on the Economic Status of the Profession 1990–1991, *Academie,* page 36.

    a.   Is this listing a sample or a population? Explain.

    b.   Are the categories considered to be mutually exclusive? Explain.

    c.   What approximate salary would you choose to be a typical salary for these five universities? Explain.

7.   You are studying the price movements of a selected group of stocks listed on the New York Stock Exchange. Referring to the Sarasota *Herald–Tribune* for January 26, 1992, p. 3C you found:

| Movement of Stock | Number |
|---|---|
| Increased | 69 |
| Decreased | 32 |
| Stayed the same | 11 |

    a.   Are the 112 stocks considered a sample or a population? Explain.

    b.   What is the level of measurement? Explain.

    c.   Are the categories mutually exclusive? Explain.

    d.   In your study IBM increased 2¼. What is that one figure called?

8.   Prior to the Democratic National Convention Gordon S. Black Corp. made a telephone poll of 906 adults nationwide regarding these Democrats as presidential candidates.

---

### A LOOK AT POLITICIANS AND THE PRESIDENCY

**Opinions of These Democrats as Presidential Candidates**

| | Favorable | Not favorable | Undecided | Not enough information |
|---|---|---|---|---|
| Mario Cuomo | 26% | 23% | 16% | 33% |
| Jerry Brown | 17% | 28% | 13% | 40% |
| Tom Harkin | 9% | 8% | 8% | 73% |
| Bob Kerrey | 10% | 7% | 10% | 71% |
| Paul Tsongas | 9% | 8% | 9% | 71% |
| Douglas Wilder | 11% | 10% | 11% | 66% |
| Bill Clinton | 9% | 6% | 9% | 74% |

---

Data collected by Gordon S. Black Corp. Telephone poll of 806 adults nationwide on December 9–10. Margin of error: 3.5%.
Source: *USA Today,* December 12, 1991, p. 4A.

    a.   Is this a sample or a population?

    b.   What level of measurement are the candidates opinions? Explain.

    c.   Write an analysis of the results of the poll.

9.   A survey of U.S. households regarding their confidence in the American economy revealed the following data portrayed graphically. Note that 1985 = 100. The 100 represents the "average" confidence of Americans during a given year. A figure such as 75.0 would indicate that consumer confidence in the economy is 25 percent below normal.

       Write an analysis of consumer confidence in the economy for the years 1980 to 1991.

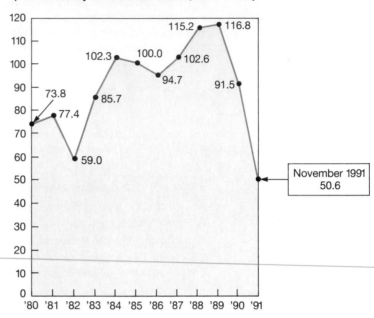

**CONSUMER CONFIDENCE**

**(from a survey of U.S. households, *1985 = 100*)**

Source: The Conference Board.

# CHAPTER 1 EXAMINATION

*The answers are at the end of the chapter.*

Indicate whether the statement is true or false. If false, give the correct answer.

1. Another name for inferential statistics is descriptive statistics.
2. A sample of consumers tasted a new cheese chip and rated it either excellent, very good, fair, or poor. The level of measurement for this market research problem is ordinal.
3. The Pipe Fitters and Plumbers Union consists of 5,020 members. A representative group of 248 members were selected and asked questions. The 248 is considered the population.
4. A total of 9,386 unmarried mothers under 15 had a baby last year, there were 6,950 accidental deaths in January, and the record Atlantic halibut weighed 250 pounds. This collection of facts and figures is called statistics.
5. The method used to find out something about the cutthroat trout population in Yellowstone National Park based on a sample of 40 trout is called inferential statistics.
6. Gallup and other pollsters seldom employ sampling methods because the populations they work with are so large.
7. The chamber of commerce asked a sample of persons sunbathing on Siesta Beach, Sarasota, Florida, if they lived in Sarasota or within 30 miles of the beach, lived out-of-state, or lived in a foreign country. This research project involved nominal-level data.
8. The Bureau of the Census reported that there are 12,955,000 production workers in manufacturing. This one figure is called a statistic.
9. The nominal level is considered the "lowest" level of data, and the data must be mutually exclusive.
10. A sample of 3,014 steelworkers was selected to find out if they will go on strike on Monday. Over 50 percent of those in the sample said they would go out on strike. Since the number sampled is large and those advocating a strike constitute over 50 percent, we can assume that the majority of all the steelworkers favor a strike.

## Self-Review

# ANSWERS

1–1 1. Based on the sample of 1,960 consumers, we estimate that, if it is marketed, 60 percent of all consumers will purchase Fish Delight (1,176/1,960) × 100 = 60 percent.)

2. Inferential statistics, because a sample was used to make an inference about how all consumers in the population would react if Fish Delight were marketed.

1–2 1. Nominal level. There is no particular order to the provinces and territories. Yukon, for example, could have been listed first. And the categories are mutually exclusive, meaning that a person could not be a resident of the Yukon and Nova Scotia at the same time.

2. The scores can be ranked, but in addition, we can determine the differences between the scores. These differences are of a known, constant size. The score of 95 is 10 points higher than a score of 85, a score of 85 is 10 points higher than a score of 75, and so on. Hence, the level of measurement is interval.

## Answers

# CHAPTER 1 EXAMINATION

1. False. Inductive statistics.
2. True.
3. False. A sample.
4. True.
5. True.
6. False. Most of their polls and surveys involve a sample selected from the population of interest.
7. True.
8. True.
9. True.
10. False. There is always a chance that the sample results will not accurately reflect the characteristics of the population.

Office Equipment and Services—Courtesy of International Business Machines Corporation

# SUMMARIZING DATA: FREQUENCY DISTRIBUTIONS AND GRAPHIC PRESENTATION

When you have completed this chapter, you will be able to:

1. Organize raw data into a frequency distribution.
2. Portray the frequency distribution in a histogram, a frequency polygon, and cumulative frequency polygons.
3. Develop a stem-and-leaf display.
4. Present data using such common graphic techniques as line charts, bar charts, and pie charts.

I n Chapter 1 we noted that the area of statistics called descriptive statistics involves techniques used to organize and summarize a mass of raw data into some meaningful form. This chapter begins our study of two of these valuable techniques. We will first discuss how to organize a set of raw numbers into a *frequency distribution* and portray the distribution graphically in a *histogram,* a *frequency polygon,* and a *cumulative frequency polygon.* Then other types of numerical information will be summarized and presented in the form of a *line chart,* a *bar chart,* or some other type of chart.

## CONSTRUCTION OF A FREQUENCY DISTRIBUTION

A **frequency distribution** is a very useful statistical tool for organizing a mass of observations into some meaningful form.

> Frequency distribution    A grouping of data into categories showing the number of observations in each mutually exclusive category.

Frequency distribution— a valuable tool for organizing data

A frequency distribution gives the number of times each value (such as incomes) occurs in each class. The steps in the construction of a frequency distribution are best shown using an example.

### ■ EXAMPLE

First step: Collecting raw data

The sales manager of Arvidus, a large construction and rental firm specializing in vacation condominiums in the area of Sarasota and Bradenton, Florida, wants guidelines regarding monthly rentals to send to potential vacationers. As a first step, she selected a sample of 120 rentals, which are shown in Table 2–1. These figures are generally referred to as the **raw data.** We can find the lowest and highest monthly rentals, but that is about all we can glean from this unorganized mass of raw data. How can the monthly rentals be reorganized to better describe the data?

### TABLE 2–1

**Monthly Rentals of Condominiums**

| | | | | | | | | | |
|---|---|---|---|---|---|---|---|---|---|
| $1,170 | $1,207 | $1,581 | $1,277 | $1,305 | $1,472 | $1,077 | $1,319 | $1,537 | $ 1,849 |
| 1,332 | 1,418 | 1,949 | 1,403 | 1,744 | 1,532 | 1,219 | 896 | 1,500 | 1,671 |
| 1,471 | 1,399 | 1,041 | 1,379 | 821 | 1,558 | 1,118 | 1,533 | 1,510 | 1,760 |
| 1,826 | 1,309 | 1,426 | 1,288 | 1,394 | 1,545 | 1,032 | 1,289 | 695 | 803 |
| 1,440 | 1,421 | 1,329 | 1,407 | 718 | 1,457 | 1,449 | 1,455 | 2,051 | 1,677 |
| 1,119 | 1,020 | 1,400 | 1,442 | 1,593 | 1,962 | 1,263 | 1,788 | 1,501 | 1,668 |
| 1,352 | 1,340 | 1,459 | 1,823 | 1,451 | 1,138 | 1,592 | 982 | 1,981 | 1,091 |
| 1,428 | 1,603 | 1,699 | 1,237 | 1,325 | 1,590 | 1,142 | 1,425 | 1,550 | 913 |
| 1,470 | 1,783 | 1,618 | 1,431 | 1,557 | 896 | 1,662 | 1,591 | 1,551 | 1,612 |
| 1,249 | 1,419 | 2,162 | 1,373 | 1,542 | 1,631 | 1,567 | 1,221 | 1,972 | 1,714 |
| 949 | 1,539 | 1,634 | 1,637 | 1,649 | 1,607 | 1,640 | 1,739 | 1,540 | 2,187 |
| 1,752 | 1,648 | 1,978 | 640 | 1,736 | 1,222 | 1,790 | 1,188 | 2,091 | 1,829 |

↑

Low

High

Before we reorganize the monthly rentals, it should be mentioned that the raw data are often referred to as *ungrouped data.* That is, the condominium data in Table 2–1 are not grouped in any way into a frequency distribution. Data organized into a frequency distribution are referred to as *grouped* data.

## ☑ SOLUTION

There are two methods of organizing the raw data into a frequency distribution. The first requires setting up an **array.**

| | |
|---|---|
| Array | An ordering of the observations from smallest to largest, or vice versa. |

Compiling an array

Referring to Table 2–1, the monthly rentals are scanned for the lowest rental ($640) and the highest ($2,187). Then the values are arranged from the lowest to the highest. (See Table 2–2).

### TABLE 2–2

#### An Ordered Array for 120 Monthly Rentals

| $ 640 | $1,041 | $1,222 | $1,332 | $1,421 | $1,470 | $1,545 | $1,607 | $1,677 | $1,826 |
|---|---|---|---|---|---|---|---|---|---|
| 695 | 1,077 | 1,237 | 1,340 | 1,425 | 1,471 | 1,550 | 1,612 | 1,699 | 1,829 |
| 718 | 1,091 | 1,249 | 1,352 | 1,426 | 1,472 | 1,551 | 1,618 | 1,714 | 1,849 |
| 803 | 1,118 | 1,263 | 1,373 | 1,428 | 1,500 | 1,557 | 1,631 | 1,736 | 1,949 |
| 821 | 1,119 | 1,277 | 1,379 | 1,431 | 1,501 | 1,558 | 1,634 | 1,739 | 1,962 |
| 896 | 1,138 | 1,288 | 1,394 | 1,440 | 1,510 | 1,567 | 1,637 | 1,744 | 1,972 |
| 896 | 1,142 | 1,289 | 1,399 | 1,442 | 1,532 | 1,581 | 1,640 | 1,752 | 1,978 |
| 913 | 1,170 | 1,305 | 1,400 | 1,449 | 1,533 | 1,590 | 1,648 | 1,760 | 1,981 |
| 949 | 1,188 | 1,309 | 1,403 | 1,451 | 1,537 | 1,591 | 1,649 | 1,783 | 2,051 |
| 982 | 1,207 | 1,319 | 1,407 | 1,455 | 1,539 | 1,592 | 1,662 | 1,788 | 2,091 |
| 1,020 | 1,219 | 1,325 | 1,418 | 1,457 | 1,540 | 1,593 | 1,668 | 1,790 | 2,162 |
| 1,032 | 1,221 | 1,329 | 1,419 | 1,459 | 1,542 | 1,603 | 1,671 | 1,823 | 2,187 |

The ordered array does have some advantages. The low ($640) and high ($2,187) values can be readily perceived, and there seems to be a large number of rentals between $1,400 and $1,700. However, the construction of an array is a tedious process—even though there are only 120 values. A second and better way to summarize the rentals is to organize them directly into a frequency distribution.

Constructing an array is time-consuming

Steps in constructing a frequency distribution

The usual steps in organizing data into a frequency distribution are:

1. Decide on a set of groupings called **classes.** A class might contain all the rentals from $600 through $799, inclusive. The next class would be $800 through $999 inclusive, and so on.

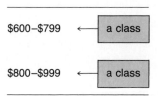

$600–$799  ←—  a class

$800–$999  ←—  a class

Each category (class) has two limits—a *lower stated class limit* and an *upper stated class limit.* A common practice is to let the lower limit of the first class be a number slightly below the first or lowest observation and to make all the classes have the same width. In this example it was decided to make the lower class limit of the first class $600 (slightly below $640) and the upper limit of that class $799. The next class is written $800–$999 and includes the rentals $800, $801, $802, . . . , $999. In other words, both the upper and lower limits of each class are included in that class.

Recall from the definition of a frequency distribution that the classes must be *mutually exclusive.* This means that the classes are formulated so that a particular value can occur *in only one class.* Thus, there is no overlapping of classes. For example, if the classes are $600–$799, $800–$999, and so forth, the value $799 lies in the first class ($600–$799) and the value $800 in the second class.

2. *Tally* the rental payments into the classes. The usual practice is to use a tally mark (/) to represent a rental. The rental of $1,170 in the upper left-hand corner of the table containing the raw data (Table 2–1) is tallied in the $1,000–$1,199 class. The next number in that column ($1,332) is tallied in the $1,200–$1,399 class, and so on. When completed, the tallies would appear as:

| | |
|---|---|
| $ 600–$ 799 | /// |
| 800–   999 | 卌 // |
| 1,000– 1,199 | 卌 卌 / |
| 1,200– 1,399 | 卌 卌 卌 卌 // |
| 1,400– 1,599 | 卌 卌 卌 卌 卌 卌 卌 卌 |
| 1,600– 1,799 | 卌 卌 卌 卌 //// |
| 1,800– 1,999 | 卌 //// |
| 2,000– 2,199 | //// |

3. Count the number of tallies in each class. Note there are three tallies, or **class frequencies,** in the $600–$799 class, seven class frequencies in the $800–$999 class, and so forth. The classes and the class frequencies are shown in Table 2–3 in the form of a frequency distribution.

### TABLE   2–3

**Distribution of the Monthly Rentals of 120 Condominium Units**

| Monthly rentals | Number of units |
|---|---|
| $ 600–$ 799 | 3 |
| 800–   999 | 7 |
| 1,000– 1,199 | 11 |
| 1,200– 1,399 | 22 |
| 1,400– 1,599 | 40 |
| 1,600– 1,799 | 24 |
| 1,800– 1,999 | 9 |
| 2,000– 2,199 | 4 |
| Total | 120 |

What observations can the sales manager now make about the monthly rentals? (1) The lowest rental is about $600, the highest about $2,200. (2) Most of the rentals are between $1,000 and $1,800 a month. (3) The largest concentration is between $1,400 and $1,600.

It should be noted that forcing the monthly rentals into a frequency distribution has caused some loss of information. That is, by organizing the raw data into classes, we can no longer pinpoint exact rentals such as $692 or $1,218. However, the advantages of condensing the data into an understandable form have more than offset this disadvantage.

In summary, organizing raw data into a frequency distribution allows us to quickly determine the approximate low and high values, a typical value near the center of the distribution, and the variation (how the data are concentrated and spread) around that value.

*Again we want to call your attention to the self-review problems. They appear in each chapter following the discussion of a major topic. By solving each one of them, you can immediately test your comprehension of the preceding text material. The answers are given at the end of the chapter.*

### Self-Review 2–1

Suggestion: Do each self-review

*The answers are at the end of the chapter.*

The monthly incomes of a small sample of new computer operators in the Cleveland metropolitan area are: $1,650, $1,475, $1,760, $1,540, $1,495, $1,590, $1,625, and $1,510.

1. What are the ungrouped numbers ($1,650, $1,475, and so on) called?

2. Using $1,400–$1,499 as the first class, $1,500–$1,599 as the second class, and so forth, organize the monthly incomes into a frequency distribution.

3. What are the numbers in the right column of your frequency distribution called?

4. Describe the distribution of monthly incomes.

## STATED AND REAL CLASS LIMITS

Stated class limits and true class limits

The classes in the frequency distribution of 120 monthly condo rentals from Table 2–3 are $600–$799, $800–$999, and so on. These classes are called the *stated classes,* and the lower and upper limits are called the *stated class limits.*

The monthly rentals were rounded to the nearest dollar. For example, a rental of $799.50 was rounded *up* to $800 and tallied in the second class. Any amount over $799 but under $799.50 was rounded *down* to $799 and included in the first class. Thus, the $600–$799 class actually encompasses all rentals from $599.50 inclusive up to but not including $799.50. Likewise, the next stated class, $800–$999, includes rentals between $799.50 and $999.50. These class limits are called the *true class limits.* True limits are such that the upper true limit of a class is the same as the lower true limit of the next class.

For comparison, the stated class limits and the true class limits are given in Table 2–4.

### TABLE  2−4

**Stated Class Limits and True Class Limits**

| Stated limits | True limits | Number of rental units |
|---|---|---|
| $ 600–$ 799 | $  599.50 up to but not including $  799.50 | 3 |
| 800–   999 | 799.50 up to but not including    999.50 | 7 |
| 1,000–  1,199 | 999.50 up to but not including  1,199.50 | 11 |
| 1,200–  1,399 | 1,199.50 up to but not including  1,399.50 | 22 |
| 1,400–  1,599 | 1,399.50 up to but not including  1,599.50 | 40 |
| 1,600–  1,799 | 1,599.50 up to but not including  1,799.50 | 24 |
| 1,800–  1,999 | 1,799.50 up to but not including  1,999.50 | 9 |
| 2,000–  2,199 | 1,999.50 up to but not including  2,199.50 | 4 |

## MIDPOINTS

*Midpoint—halfway between lower and upper class limits*

The **midpoint** of a class, often called a **class mark,** is determined by *going halfway between either the stated class limits or the true class limits.* It is obtained by adding the lower and upper limits and dividing the total by two. For example, halfway between the stated limits of $600 and $799 is $699.50, found by ($600 + $799)/2. The midpoint best represents, or is typical of, the values in that class. Class midpoints will be used to construct a frequency polygon in the following section.

## CLASS INTERVAL

*Class interval*

A **class interval** may be determined by subtracting the lower stated limit of a class from the lower stated limit of the next higher class. For our monthly rental example, the first two classes are:

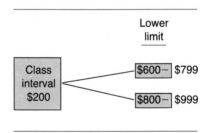

If all the classes in a distribution are the same size, the class interval may be found by determining the distance between any two successive midpoints. In the monthly rental example, the first two midpoints are $699.50 and $899.50 (computed from the true limits in Table 2−4). Subtracting $699.50 from $899.50 gives us $200.00, the class interval of the distribution.

## HINTS ON CONSTRUCTING A FREQUENCY DISTRIBUTION

*Try to have equal class intervals*

1.   Whenever possible, the class intervals used in a frequency distribution should be equal. Unequal class intervals present problems when the distribution is portrayed graphically. Unequal class intervals, however, may be necessary in certain situations in order to avoid a large number of empty, or almost empty, classes. Such is the case in the following example. The Internal Revenue Service used unequal-size class

intervals to give the distribution of adjusted gross incomes of individuals (see Table 2−5). Had the IRS used an equal-size class interval of $1,000, more than 1,000 classes would have been required to encompass all the incomes! It would, of course, be almost impossible to analyze this large a frequency distribution.

---

## TABLE 2−5

### Adjusted Gross Income for Individuals Filing Income Tax Returns

| Adjusted gross income class | Number of returns (in thousands) |
|---|---|
| Under $  2,000 | 135 |
| $    2,000–$  2,999 | 3,399 |
| 3,000–    4,999 | 8,175 |
| 5,000–    9,999 | 19,740 |
| 10,000–  14,999 | 15,539 |
| 15,000–  24,999 | 14,944 |
| 25,000–  49,999 | 4,451 |
| 50,000–  99,999 | 699 |
| 100,000– 499,999 | 162 |
| 500,000– 999,999 | 3 |
| $1,000,000 and over | 1 |

---

2.   Suppose you have a mass of raw data to organize into a frequency distribution and want to use the same interval for each class. What class interval should you use? The following formula gives a suggested common class interval. Note that the number (2−1) is to the right of the formula. We will refer to these formula numbers in future discussions.

Determining class interval

$$\text{Suggested class interval} = \frac{\text{Highest value} - \text{Lowest value}}{\text{Number of classes}} \qquad (2-1)$$

Suppose you want to condense the raw data for the rentals in Table 2−1 into eight classes. The lowest charged is $640, and the highest is $2,187. What is the suggested class interval?

$$\text{Suggested class interval} = \frac{\$2,187 - \$640}{8} = \frac{\$1,547}{8} = \$193.375$$

Use of rounded values for class interval

A class interval of $193.375 would be very awkward to work with. It would be much easier to tally the rentals into a frequency distribution if the interval were rounded to say, $200.[1]

---

[1]If you are uncertain about the number of classes to use, the following formula will give a suggested class interval.

$$\text{Suggested class interval} = \frac{\text{Highest observed value} - \text{Lowest observed value}}{1 + 3.322(\text{logarithm of the total frequencies})} \qquad (2-2)$$

For the monthly rentals:

$$\frac{\$2,187 - \$640}{1 + 3.322(\text{log of } 120)} = \frac{\$1,547}{1 + 3.322(2.0792)} = \frac{\$1,547}{7.9071024} = \$195.65$$

To find the logarithm of 120 using a scientific hand calculator, depress 120 then log . The display will show 2.079181246.

3. Normally, your personal judgment can influence the number of classes. Too many or too few classes, however, might not reveal the basic shape of the distribution. In the condo rental problem, for example, a class interval of $900 would not give much insight into the pattern of rentals. (See Table 2−6.) About all we could say is that approximately half of the monthly rentals are below $1,499.50 and half are above $1,499.50. As a general rule, no fewer than 5 or more than 15 classes should be used in the construction of a frequency distribution.

*Have from 5 to 15 classes*

*Unwise to have too few or too many classes*

---

**TABLE   2−6**

**An Example of Too Few Classes**

| Monthly rentals | Number of units |
|---|---|
| $  600–$1,499 | 63 |
| 1,500–  2,399 | 57 |
| Total | 120 |

---

One guideline that can be used to determine the suggested number of classes, $k$, follows. It is the smallest integer $k$, such that $2^k \geq n$, where $n$ is the total number of observations. Using the 120 monthly condominium rentals to illustrate, let us try the integer 6. Thus, $2^6 = 64$ which is not equal to or greater than 120. Trying 7 classes, $2^7 = 128$ which is equal to or greater than an $n$ of 120. So the recommended number of classes is at least 7. (We used 8 in Table 2−3.) Based on this guideline, the following table shows the number of classes recommended for a specified number of observations.

| Total number of observations | Recommended number of classes |
|---|---|
| 9–16 | 4 |
| 17–32 | 5 |
| 33–64 | 6 |
| 65–128 | 7 |
| 129–256 | 8 |
| 257–512 | 9 |
| 513–1,024 | 10 |

4. Usually, the lower limit of the first class is an even multiple of the class interval. In the monthly rental problem, the class interval was selected to be $200. Multiplying this by 3.0 (an even multiple) gives $600, the lower limit of the first class. As another example, suppose that some price data range from $23 (low) to $69 (high), and we want the class interval to be $10. The lower limit of the first class would be $20, found by multiplying 2.0 (the even multiple) by $10, the class interval.

5. Avoid overlapping stated class limits, such as $1,300–$1,400, $1,400–$1,500, and $1,500–$1,600. Classes established in this way are not mutually exclusive, thus violating the definition of a frequency distribution. With overlapping classes it would not be clear where to tally $1,400, for example. Does it belong in the $1,300–$1,400 class or the $1,400–$1,500 class? Stating the classes as $1,300–$1,399, $1,400–$1,499, and $1,500–$1,599 avoids this problem; or we could state a class as "$1,300 up to but not including $1,400."

6. Try not to have *open-ended classes.* The classes "Under $2,000" and "$1,000,000 and over" used by the IRS in Table 2−5 are examples of open-ended classes. They cause problems in graphing, described in the next section, and in using certain measures of central tendency and dispersion, described in Chapters 3 and 4.

## Self-Review 2−2

*The answers are at the end of the chapter.*

1. The monthly salaries of a sample of the 87 employees of Acklin Stamping were rounded to the nearest dollar. They ranged from a low of $1,041 to a high of $2,548.
   a. Suppose we want to condense the data into seven classes. Using the same interval for each class, determine a suggested class interval.
   b. What class interval would be easier to work with?
   c. What are the stated class limits for the first class? The next class?

2. Suppose classes are written as:

   40−60
   60−90
   90−150
   150 and greater

   These classes illustrate three practices that should be avoided. What are they?

# RELATIVE FREQUENCY DISTRIBUTION

*A relative frequency is a percent*

It may be desirable to convert class frequencies to **relative class frequencies** to show the percent of the total number of observations in each class. In our monthly rental example, we may want to know what percent of the rentals are in the $600–$799 class. In another study we may want to know what percent of the employees are absent between one and three days a year due to illness.

To convert a frequency distribution to a **relative frequency distribution,** each of the class frequencies is divided by the total number of frequencies. Using the distribution of the monthly rentals again, the relative frequency for the $600–$799 class is computed as: 3 ÷ 120 = 0.025. That is, 2.5 percent of the rental units are between $600 and $799. Likewise, 3.3 percent of the units rent for $2,000 or more, found by 4 ÷ 120. The relative frequencies must total 1.000. (See Table 2−7.)

*Total of relative frequencies = 1.000*

## TABLE 2−7

### Monthly Rentals, Class Frequencies, and Relative Frequencies

| Monthly rentals | Class frequency | Relative frequency | Found by |
|---|---|---|---|
| $ 600–$ 799 | 3 | 0.025 | 3 ÷ 120 |
| 800– 999 | 7 | 0.058 ⟵ | 7 ÷ 120 |
| 1,000– 1,199 | 11 | 0.092 ⟵ | 11 ÷ 120 |
| 1,200– 1,399 | 22 | 0.183 | 22 ÷ 120 |
| 1,400– 1,599 | 40 | 0.333 | 40 ÷ 120 |
| 1,600– 1,799 | 24 | 0.200 | 24 ÷ 120 |
| 1,800– 1,999 | 9 | 0.075 | 9 ÷ 120 |
| 2,000– 2,199 | 4 | 0.033 | 4 ÷ 120 |
| | 120 | 0.999* | |

*Slight discrepancy due to rounding. Should be 1.000.

## EXERCISES

*The answers to the odd-numbered exercises are at the end of the book.*

1. What is an array?

2. What is meant by a frequency distribution?

3. In a frequency distribution the classes must be mutually exclusive. Explain.

4. A set of raw data contains 53 observations. The lowest value is $42, the highest $142. The data has to be organized into a frequency distribution. Starting with 40, how many classes would you suggest?

5. The director of the honors program at Eastern University has 16 applications for admission next fall. The composite ACT scores of the applicants are:

| | | | | | | | |
|---|---|---|---|---|---|---|---|
| 27 | 27 | 27 | 28 | 27 | 25 | 25 | 28 |
| 26 | 28 | 26 | 28 | 31 | 30 | 26 | 26 |

The ACT scores are to be organized into a frequency distribution.
   a. How many classes would you recommend?
   b. What class interval would you suggest?
   c. What lower limit would you recommend for the first class?
   d. Organize the scores into a frequency distribution.
   e. Comment on the shape of the distribution.

6. The Quick Change Oil Company has a number of outlets in the metropolitan area. No appointment is required. The number of oil changes at the Oak Street outlet in the past 20 days are:

| | | | | | | | | | |
|---|---|---|---|---|---|---|---|---|---|
| 65 | 98 | 55 | 62 | 79 | 59 | 51 | 90 | 72 | 56 |
| 70 | 62 | 66 | 80 | 94 | 79 | 63 | 73 | 71 | 85 |

The data are to be organized into a frequency distribution.
   a. How many classes would you recommend?
   b. What class interval would you suggest?
   c. What lower limit would you recommend for the first class?
   d. Organize the number of oil changes into a frequency distribution.
   e. Comment on the shape of the frequency distribution.

7. The local manager of Food Queen is interested in the number of times a customer shops at her store during a two-week period. The responses of 51 customers were:

| | | | | | | | | | | | | | |
|---|---|---|---|---|---|---|---|---|---|---|---|---|---|
| 5 | 3 | 3 | 1 | 4 | 4 | 5 | 6 | 4 | 2 | 6 | 6 | 6 | 7 | 1 |
| 1 | 14 | 1 | 2 | 4 | 4 | 4 | 5 | 6 | 3 | 5 | 3 | 4 | 5 | 6 |
| 8 | 4 | 7 | 6 | 5 | 9 | 11 | 3 | 12 | 4 | 7 | 6 | 5 | 15 | 1 |
| 1 | 10 | 8 | 9 | 2 | 12 | | | | | | | | |

   a. Starting with 0 as the lower limit of the first class and using a class interval of 3, organize the data into a frequency distribution.

b. Describe the distribution. Where does the data tend to cluster?

c. Convert the distribution to a relative frequency distribution.

8. Moore Travel Agency, a nationwide travel agency, offers special rates on certain Caribbean cruises to senior citizens. The president of Moore Travel wants additional information on the ages of those people taking cruises. A random sample of 40 customers taking a cruise last year revealed these ages.

| 77 | 18 | 63 | 84 | 38 | 54 | 50 | 59 | 54 | 56 | 36 | 26 | 50 | 34 | 44 |
|----|----|----|----|----|----|----|----|----|----|----|----|----|----|----|
| 41 | 58 | 58 | 53 | 51 | 62 | 43 | 52 | 53 | 63 | 62 | 62 | 65 | 61 | 52 |
| 60 | 60 | 45 | 66 | 83 | 71 | 63 | 58 | 61 | 71 |    |    |    |    |    |

a. Organize the data into a frequency distribution, using seven classes and 15 as the lower limit of the first class. What class interval did you select?

b. Where do the data tend to cluster?

c. Describe the distribution.

d. Convert the distribution to a relative frequency distribution.

## STEM-AND-LEAF DISPLAYS

In the previous sections, we showed how to organize data into a frequency distribution in order to summarize the raw data into some meaningful form. A disadvantage of that approach is the loss of some information when tallying. For example, it is not clear from the following distribution of the ages of new employees at the Young Foundry how the ages in the 20–29 age group are distributed. Are they clustered close to 20 years or somewhat evenly distributed throughout the class?

| Ages of new employees | Tally | Frequency |
|-----------------------|-------|-----------|
| 20–29 | 𝓣𝓗𝓛 // | 7 |
| 30–39 | 𝓣𝓗𝓛 𝓣𝓗𝓛 𝓣𝓗𝓛 𝓣𝓗𝓛 / | 21 |
| 40–49 | //// | 4 |
| 50–59 | // | 2 |
| 60–69 | / | 1 |

A technique that has gained popularity in recent years offsets the loss of information that occurs from summarizing raw data. It is called a **stem-and-leaf display.** To construct such a display using the ages of the new employees at Young Foundry, a tally is replaced by the last digit of an employee's age. Thus, the ages of the seven employees in the 20–29 class might appear as:

Stem-and-leaf display

$$2 \mid 3 \quad 4 \quad 5 \quad 5 \quad 7 \quad 8 \quad 9$$

We can see that the ages are spread somewhat evenly through the 20–29 age class. Note that the values within a class are ordered from smallest to largest. The first value is 23, the second is 24, and so on.

The following example shows the steps needed to construct a stem-and-leaf display.

### ■ EXAMPLE

The selling prices of 45 single-family two-bedroom homes in Cartersville, Georgia, are given in Table 2–8. How are the price data organized into a stem-and-leaf display?

Chapter 2

Courtesy USX Corporation

### TABLE 2–8

**Selling Prices of Single-Family Two-Bedroom Homes, Cartersville, Georgia ($000)**

| $ 96 | $ 93 | $ 88 | $117 | $127 |
|------|------|------|------|------|
| 95   | 113  | 96   | 108  | 94   |
| 148  | 156  | 139  | 142  | 94   |
| 107  | 125  | 155  | 155  | 103  |
| 112  | 127  | 117  | 120  | 112  |
| 135  | 132  | 111  | 125  | 104  |
| 106  | 139  | 134  | 119  | 97   |
| 89   | 118  | 136  | 125  | 143  |
| 120  | 103  | 113  | 124  | 138  |

Stem is leading digit. Leaf is trailing digit.

## ✅ SOLUTION

The *stem* is the *leading digit or digits.* The *leaf* is the *trailing digit.* The stem is placed to the left of a vertical line and the leaf (trailing digit) to the right of the line. For example, note in Table 2–8 that the sale price in the upper left is $96,000. The stem is 9 and the leaf 6. The vertical line merely separates the two parts of each number.

| Stem, or leading digit | Leaf, or trailing digit |
|:----------------------:|:-----------------------:|
| 9                      | 6                       |

The leading digits for the raw data in Table 2–8 are 9, 10, 11, . . . , 15. The trailing digit for each sale price is recorded on the same line as its leading digit (stem). Thus, the first three prices in the left column of Table 2–8 would appear as:

| Stem | Leaf |
|:----:|:-----|
| 9    | 6 5  |
| •    |      |
| •    |      |
| •    |      |
| 15   | 8    |

Organizing all the sale prices:

| Stem | Leaf |
|:----:|:-----|
| 8  | 9 8 |
| 9  | 6 5 3 6 4 4 7 |
| 10 | 7 6 3 8 3 4 |
| 11 | 2 3 8 7 1 3 7 9 2 |
| 12 | 0 5 7 0 5 5 4 7 |
| 13 | 5 2 9 9 4 6 8 |
| 14 | 8 2 3 |
| 15 | 6 5 5 |

The trailing digits in each row are then rank-ordered to form a stem-and-leaf display. The first row would appear as:

| Stem | Leaf |
|------|------|
| 8    | 8  9 |

The leaves for each row when ranked from low to high are:

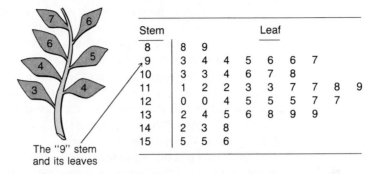

| Stem | Leaf |
|------|------|
| 8  | 8  9 |
| 9  | 3  4  4  5  6  6  7 |
| 10 | 3  3  4  6  7  8 |
| 11 | 1  2  2  3  3  7  7  8  9 |
| 12 | 0  0  4  5  5  5  7  7 |
| 13 | 2  4  5  6  8  9  9 |
| 14 | 2  3  8 |
| 15 | 5  5  6 |

The "9" stem and its leaves

Each row in this display has a stem and a leaf. The "9" stem has seven leaves and could be pictured as shown above.

The stem-and-leaf approach is very flexible. For example, following are the number of Kentucky Fried Chicken Drummer Boys (dinners containing drumstick, mashed potatoes, and slaw) sold during a four-week period: 2,463, 2,412, 2,543, and 2,488. The stem-and-leaf display would be

| Stem | Leaf |
|------|------|
| 24 | 1   6   8 |
| 25 | 4 |

The stem includes the hundreds and thousands digits. The units digit is dropped. The leaf therefore becomes the tens digit.

The output from the MINITAB system for the procedure called "stem" is shown below. The data are from Table 2–8. In this book the material entered by the computer user is shaded in color, and the output by the computer is in black. The MINITAB system will offer the prompt MTB>. When you see this prompt, MINITAB is asking what procedure you would like to run. In this case, the desired procedure is called "stem," and the subcommand is called "increment." Here the desired increment is 10. The data are located in a column, which is called C1. The variable is called "Price." The output follows.

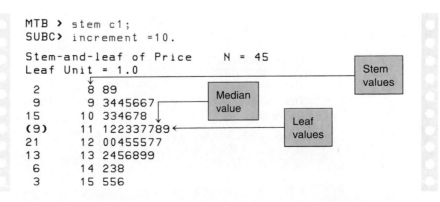

```
MTB > stem c1;
SUBC> increment =10.
Stem-and-leaf of Price      N = 45
Leaf Unit = 1.0
    2      8  89
    9      9  3445667
   15     10  334678
  (9)     11  122337789
   21     12  00455577
   13     13  2456899
    6     14  238
    3     15  556
```

Stem values

Median value

Leaf values

Note that some additional information is provided by the MINITAB solution in the column to the left of the stem values. The values 2, 9, 15, and so on are the cumulative totals. The number 15, for example, indicates that a total of 15 observations have occurred *before* the value of 110. About halfway down that column, the number 9 appears in parentheses. The parentheses indicate the location of the middle observation. That is, the value below which half the observations occur is in this row. There are a total of 45 observations, so the middle value, if the data were arranged in an array, would be the 23rd value. In this example, 15 observations fall below 110. The value 9 in parentheses indicates that there are nine observations in the row with a stem of 110. The middle value would be the 23rd observation, or the 8th value in this row. Hence, the middle value, or the *median,* as it is called, is 118, found by counting over 8 values in the 110 row. *After the median row, the values decline.* These values represent the "more than" cumulative totals. That is, there are 21 observations of 120 or more, 13 of 130 or more, and so on.

The following MINITAB output also employs the data in Table 2–8 with respect to the selling prices of two-bedroom homes in Cartersville, Georgia. Note, however, that the increments are 5 instead of 10 as used before. The median, or middle value, is still 118, found by noting that 20 observations are 114 or less and that there are 4 observations between 115 and 119. We are looking for the third observation, which is 118.

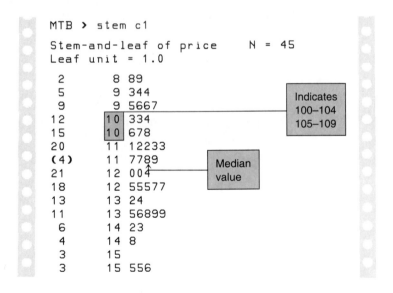

## Self-Review 2–4

*The answers are at the end of the chapter.*

The price-earnings ratios for 20 selected stocks are:

8.3, 9.6, 9.5, 9.1, 8.8, 11.2, 7.7, 10.1, 9.9, 10.8, 10.2, 8.0, 8.4, 8.1, 11.6, 9.6, 8.8, 8.0, 10.4, 9.8

1. Design a stem-and-leaf display.
2. Interpret the display.

## EXERCISES

*The answers to the odd-numbered exercises are at the end of the book.*

9. The first row of a stem-and-leaf chart appears as 62|1 3 3 7 9. Explain.

10. The following stem-and-leaf chart represents the daily production of VCRs.

```
      Stem-and-leaf of production     N = 80
      Leaf unit = 1

               Stem     Leaf
         5        8      12334
        15        8      5566667899
        30        9      011111233333344
       (10)       9      555666777778888888899999
        25       10      00111223334444
        11       10      5566678
         4       11      2334
```

    a.    What is the smallest number of VCRs produced during a day?

    b.    How many observations are in the first class?

    c.    What is the middle value of the production data?

    d.    During how many days was production less than 95 VCRs?

    e.    During how many days were 105 or more VCRs produced?

11. A survey of the number of calls received by a sample of Southern Phone Company subscribers last week revealed the following. Develop a stem-and-leaf chart.

| 52 | 43 | 30 | 38 | 30 | 42 | 12 | 46 | 39 | 37 |
|----|----|----|----|----|----|----|----|----|----|
| 34 | 46 | 32 | 18 | 41 | 5  |    |    |    |    |

12. Citizens Banking is studying the number of times their automatic teller, located in a Loblaws Supermarket, is used daily. Following is a list of the number of times the teller was used during the last 30 days. Develop a stem-and-leaf chart.

| 3  | 64 | 84 | 76 | 84 | 54 | 75 | 59 | 70 | 61 |
|----|----|----|----|----|----|----|----|----|----|
| 63 | 80 | 84 | 73 | 68 | 52 | 65 | 90 | 52 | 77 |
| 95 | 36 | 78 | 61 | 59 | 84 | 95 | 47 | 87 | 60 |

## PORTRAYING A FREQUENCY DISTRIBUTION GRAPHICALLY

*Chart commands attention*

Sales managers, stock analysts, hospital administrators, and other busy executives often need a quick picture of the trends in sales, stock prices, or hospital costs. These trends can be shown by use of *charts* or *graphs.* Three charts that will help portray a frequency distribution graphically are the *histogram,* the *frequency polygon,* and the *cumulative frequency polygon.*

### HISTOGRAM

*Histogram defined*

The histogram is one of the most widely used charts and one of the easiest to understand. A **histogram** describes a frequency distribution using a series of adjacent rectangles, where the height of each rectangle is proportional to the frequency of the class it represents. The construction of a histogram is illustrated by reintroducing the example of monthly rentals of vacation condominiums in the Sarasota-Bradenton area (Tables 2–1 and 2–3).

## ■ EXAMPLE

| Monthly rentals | Number of units |
|---|---|
| $ 600–$ 799 | 3 |
| 800– 999 | 7 |
| 1,000– 1,199 | 11 |
| 1,200– 1,399 | 22 |
| 1,400– 1,599 | 40 |
| 1,600– 1,799 | 24 |
| 1,800– 1,999 | 9 |
| 2,000– 2,199 | 4 |

How is a histogram constructed for this frequency distribution?

## ☑ SOLUTION

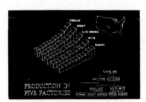

Some computer programs such as StatSofts CSS: STATISTICA feature stunning graphical displays.
Courtesy StatSoft, Inc.

To construct a histogram, the class frequencies are scaled on the vertical axis (the Y-axis), and either the stated limits, the true limits, or the midpoints are on the horizontal axis (the X-axis). We will use the stated limits and show only the lower limit of each class on the X-axis.

Note from the frequency distribution that there are three rental units in the $600–$799 class. Therefore, the height of the column for that class is 3. There are seven units in the next class ($800–$999), and logically the height of the column is 7. (See Chart 2–1). The height of each bar thus represents the number of observations in that class.

---

### CHART 2–1

**Construction of a Histogram**

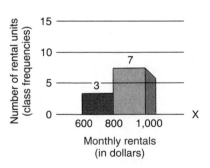

---

This procedure is continued for all the classes until the histogram is completed, as shown in Chart 2–2.

A histogram

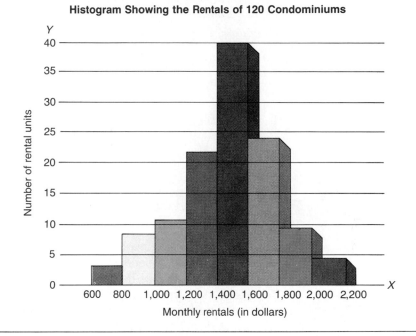

CHART 2-2

**Histogram Showing the Rentals of 120 Condominiums**

The following features are apparent from the histogram: (1) The lowest monthly rental is about $600. (2) The highest is about $2,200. (3) Most of the rentals are between $1,200 and $1,800. (4) The largest concentration is between $1,400 and $1,600. Thus, this histogram provides an easily interpreted visual picture of the monthly rentals. Had we plotted relative frequencies (instead of class frequencies), the general shape of the distribution would be the same.

MINITAB has several procedures that will produce graphs. Shown below are the **dotplot** and the **histogram.** Both of these graphs are closely related to a frequency distribution. The raw data from Table 2-1 and the frequency distribution of Table 2-3 regarding the monthly rentals of 120 condominium units in the Sarasota-Bradenton, Florida, area are used to illustrate a dotplot and a histogram.

MINITAB dotplot

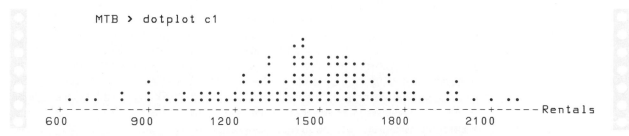

MINITAB histogram

```
MTB > hist c1;
SUBC> increment = 200;
SUBC> start = 700.

Histogram of rentals     N = 120

Midpoint  Count
     700      3  ***
     900      7  *******
    1100     11  ***********
    1300     22  **********************
    1500     40  ****************************************
    1700     24  ************************
    1900      9  *********
    2100      4  ****
```

## FREQUENCY POLYGON

Frequency polygon
defined

A frequency polygon is closely related to a histogram. The **frequency polygon** consists of line segments connecting the points formed by the intersection of the class midpoint and the class frequency. Empty classes are usually included at each end so the curve will anchor with the horizontal axis ($X$-axis).

The frequency polygon is again illustrated using the monthly rentals of condominiums. We need the class midpoints, which are scaled along the $X$-axis, and the class frequencies, which are scaled on the $Y$-axis. Recall that the class midpoint is the value that represents the class and is determined by going halfway between the two stated class limits.

| Stated limits | Midpoints | Class frequencies |
|---|---|---|
| $ 600–$ 799 | $ 699.50 | 3 |
| 800– 999 | 899.50 | 7 |
| 1,000– 1,199 | 1,099.50 | 11 |
| 1,200– 1,399 | 1,299.50 | 22 |
| 1,400– 1,599 | 1,499.50 | 40 |
| 1,600– 1,799 | 1,699.50 | 24 |
| 1,800– 1,999 | 1,899.50 | 9 |
| 2,000– 2,199 | 2,099.50 | 4 |

As noted, the $600–$799 class is represented by its midpoint, $699.50. To make the first plot, move horizontally to $699.50, the midpoint, and then vertically to 3, the class frequency, and place a dot. The $X$ and $Y$ values that form this dot are known as its *coordinates*. The coordinates of the next plot are $X = \$899.50$, $Y = 7$. This process is continued until all the classes are accounted for. Then the dots are connected *in order*. The point representing the first class is joined to the one representing the second class, and so forth.

Note in Chart 2–3 that, to complete the frequency polygon, midpoints of $499.50 and $2,299.50 were added to the two extremes, and the polygon was "anchored" to the horizontal axis at zero frequencies. Those two values—$499.50 and $2,299.50— were derived by subtracting the class interval of $200 from the lowest midpoint in the distribution ($699.50) and by adding $200 to the highest midpoint ($2,099.50). By anchoring the two extremes of the frequency polygon to the $X$-axis, the total area under the polygon is now equal to the total of the frequencies (120).

Both the histogram and frequency polygon allow us to get a quick picture of the main characteristics of the data (highs, lows, point of concentration, etc.). Although the

Frequency polygon

## Chart 2–3

**Frequency Polygon Showing the Monthly Rentals of 120 Condominium Units**

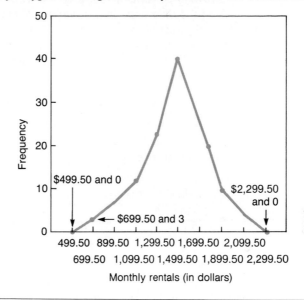

Frequency polygon preferred when comparing distributions

two representations are similar in purpose, the histogram has the advantage of depicting each class as a rectangle, with the area of each rectangular bar representing the total number of frequencies in the class. The frequency polygon, in turn, has an advantage over the histogram. It allows us to compare directly two or more frequency distributions. Suppose, for example, that the monthly condominium rentals in the Sarasota-Bradenton area are to be compared with those in the Jackson, Mississippi, area. Both frequency distributions are plotted in Chart 2–4. It is obvious from the chart

## Chart 2–4

**Distribution of Monthly Rentals in the Sarasota-Bradenton and Jackson Areas**

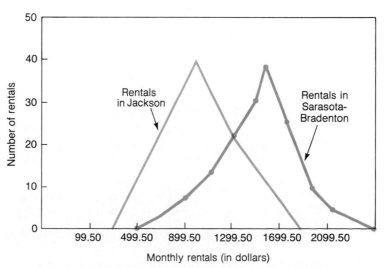

that the rentals in the Sarasota-Bradenton area are generally higher than those in the Jackson area.

The number of class frequencies in Chart 2–4 is about equal between the two areas. If the difference in the number of class frequencies were quite large, say, 40 units in Sarasota-Bradenton and 500 in Jackson, changing the class frequencies to relative frequencies and then plotting the data would allow for a better comparison. This situation occurs in Exercises 15 and 16.

### Self-Review 2–5

*The answers are at the end of the chapter.*

The annual exports of a group of small pharmaceutical firms are:

| Exports ($ millions) | Number of firms |
|---|---|
| $ 2–$ 4 | 6 |
| 5– 7 | 13 |
| 8– 10 | 20 |
| 11– 13 | 10 |
| 14– 16 | 3 |

1. Portray the exports in the form of a histogram.
2. What are the midpoints?
3. Portray the exports in the form of a frequency polygon.
4. Interpret the charts.

## EXERCISES

*The answers to the odd-numbered exercises are at the end of the book.*

13. The following frequency distribution represents the number of days during a year that employees at the E. J. Wilcox Manufacturing company were absent from work due to illness.

| Number of days absent | Number of employees |
|---|---|
| 0–2 | 5 |
| 3–5 | 12 |
| 6–8 | 23 |
| 9–11 | 8 |
| 12–14 | 2 |
| Total | 50 |

a. Assuming that this is a sample, what is the sample size?
b. What is the midpoint of the first class?
c. Construct a histogram.
d. A frequency polygon is to be drawn. What are the coordinates of the plot for the first class?
e. Construct a frequency polygon.
f. Interpret the rate of employee absenteeism using the two charts.

14. A large retailer is studying the lead time (elapsed time between when an order is placed and when it is filled) for a sample of recent orders. The lead times are reported in days.

| Lead time (days) | Frequency |
|---|---|
| 0–4 | 6 |
| 5–9 | 7 |
| 10–14 | 12 |
| 15–19 | 8 |
| 20–24 | 7 |
| Total | 40 |

a. How many orders were studied?

b. What is the midpoint of the first class?

c. What are the coordinates of the first class?

d. Draw a histogram.

e. Draw a frequency polygon.

f. Interpret the lead times using the two charts.

15. A study is being conducted with respect to the time it takes to assemble a plug-in unit using the Wilcox Method versus the Lambert Method. The times using the Wilcox Method were stored in the computer, and it was a simple job to organize them into a frequency distribution. However, considerable effort had to be expended to determine the assembly times using the Lambert Method, so only 50 were selected. The two distributions are:

| Time, in minutes | Number studied | |
| | Wilcox Method | Lambert Method |
| --- | --- | --- |
| 5– 7 | 120 | 4 |
| 8–10 | 426 | 11 |
| 11–13 | 1,060 | 25 |
| 14–16 | 286 | 7 |
| 17–19 | 108 | 3 |

In order to compare the two methods using frequency polygons, it is first necessary to convert the class frequencies to relative frequencies (because the number studied for the Wilcox Method is so much greater than for the Lambert Method).

a. Convert the class frequencies for both distributions to relative frequencies.

b. On one chart portray the two polygons representing the assembly times.

c. Draw conclusions regarding the assembly times.

16. Western Insurance Company is studying automobile damage claims for cars five years old and older and those less than five years old. The raw data were tabulated into the following frequency distributions.

| Amount of claim | Number of claims | |
| | Autos five years old and older | Autos less than five years old |
| --- | --- | --- |
| $  200–$  499 | 30 | 86 |
| 500–   799 | 129 | 212 |
| 800– 1,099 | 20 | 368 |
| 1,100– 1,399 | 10 | 480 |
| 1,400– 1,699 | 6 | 1,806 |
| 1,700– 1,999 | 2 | 898 |
| 2,000– 2,299 | 3 | 150 |

The distributions are to be portrayed on one chart to facilitate comparison.

a. Convert the class frequencies for each distribution to relative frequencies.

b. Depict the relative frequencies for both distributions on one chart.

c. Interpret the chart.

## CUMULATIVE FREQUENCY POLYGONS

We return to the previous example using the monthly rentals of condominiums. (See Table 2–3.) How many rent for over $950 a month? What percent rent for less than $1,900 a month? The answers to these questions can be approximated by developing a **cumulative frequency distribution** and drawing a **cumulative frequency polygon,** often called an *ogive.* A cumulative frequency polygon is used *when we want to determine how many observations lie above or below certain values.*

A *less-than cumulative frequency polygon* can be used to answer such questions as, "What percent of the rentals are less than $1,700?" and "How many rentals are less than $900 a month?" A less-than cumulative frequency distribution tells how many items in the distribution have a value equal to or less than the upper class limit of the first class, of the second class, of the third class, and so forth.

Likewise, a *more-than cumulative frequency polygon* can give the answers to these questions: "What percent of the rentals are equal to or more than $1,000 a month?" "How many rentals in the study are equal to or more than $2,000 a month?" A more-than cumulative frequency distribution tells how many items in the distribution have a value equal to or greater than the value of the lower limit of the first class, of the second class, of the third class, and so on. We will now construct a less-than cumulative frequency polygon.

## LESS-THAN CUMULATIVE FREQUENCY POLYGON

### ■ EXAMPLE

The frequency distribution for the monthly rentals in the Sarasota-Bradenton area is repeated below.

| Monthly rentals | Number of rentals (class frequencies) |
|---|---|
| $ 600–$ 799 | 3 |
| 800– 999 | 7 |
| 1,000– 1,199 | 11 |
| 1,200– 1,399 | 22 |
| 1,400– 1,599 | 40 |
| 1,600– 1,799 | 24 |
| 1,800– 1,999 | 9 |
| 2,000– 2,199 | 4 |
| Total | 120 |

Construct a **less-than cumulative frequency polygon.** Then answer these questions: Fifty percent of the condo rentals are equal to or less than what amount? Seventy-five percent of the rentals are equal to or less than what amount?

### ☑ SOLUTION

Referring to the preceding table, note that three rentals are in the $600–$799 class. However, we know that the upper true limit of that class is really $799.50, since it includes all rentals up to $799.50. Those 3 rentals plus the 7 in the next lowest class, a total of 10 rentals, are less than $999.50. The cumulative number of frequencies for the next class is 21, found by 3 + 7 + 11. This process for determining the cumulative frequencies is continued for all the classes.

| Monthly rentals | Class frequencies | | Cumulative frequencies | Found by |
|---|---|---|---|---|
| Less than $ 599.50 | 0 | Add | 0 | |
| Less than     799.50 | 3 | down | 3 | |
| Less than     999.50 | 7 | ↓ | 10 | ←—3 + 7 |
| Less than  1,199.50 | 11 | | 21 | ←—3 + 7 + 11 |
| Less than  1,399.50 | 22 | | 43 | ←—3 + 7 + 11 + 22 |
| Less than  1,599.50 | 40 | | 83 | |
| Less than  1,799.50 | 24 | | 107 | |
| Less than  1,999.50 | 9 | | 116 | |
| Less than  2,199.50 | 4 | | 120 | |

Less-than cumulative frequency polygon

The upper true limits and the cumulative frequencies are plotted to construct a less-than cumulative frequency polygon. (See Chart 2–5.) The first plot is $X =$ $599.50, $Y = 0$. The coordinates of the next plot are $799.50 and 3; the next are $999.50 and 10; and so on. (A technical note: If we did not know how the data were rounded, or if the values were whole numbers—such as the number of children, i.e., 0, 1, 2, 3, . . .—we could use in this problem $600, $800, $1,000, and so on for the $X$-axis.) Note that "percent of the total" is scaled on the $Y$-axis.

## CHART   2–5

### Less-than Cumulative Frequency Polygon for the Monthly Rentals

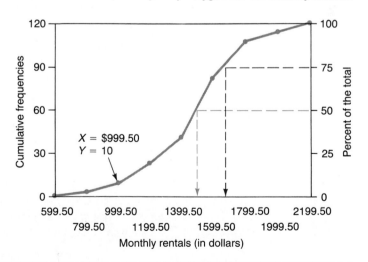

A few approximate figures from the above chart follow. Fifty percent of the rentals are equal to or less than $1,500 monthly. This is arrived at by drawing a dashed line from 50 percent to the distribution curve and dropping vertically to the $X$-axis. Three out of every four rentals (75 percent) are equal to or less than about $1,675 monthly.

## MORE-THAN CUMULATIVE FREQUENCY POLYGON

A more-than cumulative frequency distribution is constructed by starting with the highest class and working backward, adding the frequencies *up* to the lowest class. To draw a more-than cumulative frequency polygon, the *lower* true limits and their corresponding cumulative frequencies are used. Again we use the true limit. We know that the lower limit of the $800–$999 class is not really $800 because it includes all the rentals from $799.50. Therefore, $799.50 and 117 are the coordinates of the point for that class (see Chart 2–6).

| Rentals | Class frequencies | | Cumulative frequencies | Found by |
|---|---|---|---|---|
| More than $   599.50 | 3 | | 120 | |
| More than      799.50 | 7 | | 117 | |
| More than      999.50 | 11 | | 110 | |
| More than   1,199.50 | 22 | | 99 | |
| More than   1,399.50 | 40 | ↑ | 77 | |
| More than   1,599.50 | 24 | | 37 | ⟵  4 + 9 + 24 |
| More than   1,799.50 | 9 | Add | 13 | ⟵  4 + 9 |
| More than   1,999.50 | 4 | up | 4 | |
| More than   2,199.50 | 0 | | 0 | |

### CHART   2–6

More-than cumulative
frequency polygon

**More-than Cumulative Frequency Polygon for the Monthly Rentals**

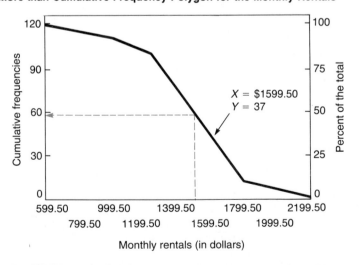

If we wanted to determine how many monthly rentals are equal to or more than $1,500, a line would be drawn vertically from $1,500, as shown, to the polygon and then left to the *Y*-axis. The corresponding number on the *Y*-axis is about 57, meaning that the prices of 57 rentals are equal to or more than $1,500 a month.

## Self-Review 2–6

*The answers are at the end of the chapter.*

A sample of the hourly wages of 80 part-time and full-time employees at Food City Supermarkets was organized into the following table. An hourly wage of, say, $4.49 was included in the $2–$4 class, but a wage of $4.50 was included in the next higher class ($5–$7).

| Hourly wages | Number of wages |
|---|---|
| $ 2–$ 4 | 18 |
| 5– 7 | 36 |
| 8– 10 | 20 |
| 11– 13 | 6 |

1. What is the table called?
2. Develop a less-than cumulative frequency distribution, and portray the distribution in a less-than cumulative frequency polygon.
3. Develop a more-than cumulative distribution, and draw the appropriate cumulative polygon.
4. Based on the two cumulative polygons, how many employees earn $6 an hour or less? Half of the employees earn an hourly wage of how much or more? How many employees earn $10 or more? Twenty employees earn how much or more?

## EXERCISES

*The answers to the odd-numbered exercises are at the end of the book.*

17. The frequency distribution representing the number of days annually the employees at the E. J. Wilcox Manufacturing Company were absent from work due to illness is repeated from Exercise 13.

| Number of days absent | Frequency |
|---|---|
| 0–2 | 5 |
| 3–5 | 12 |
| 6–8 | 23 |
| 9–11 | 8 |
| 12–14 | 2 |
| Total | 50 |

a. How many employees were absent less than three days annually? How many were absent less than six days due to illness?
b. Convert the frequency distribution to a less-than cumulative frequency distribution.
c. Portray the cumulative distribution in the form of a less-than cumulative frequency polygon. Since these are whole numbers, we can use stated or true limits.
d. About three out of four employees were absent for how many days or less due to illness?

18. The frequency distribution with respect to the lead time it takes to fill an order from Exercise 14 is repeated below.

| Lead time (days) | Frequency |
|---|---|
| 0–4 | 6 |
| 5–9 | 7 |
| 10–14 | 12 |
| 15–19 | 8 |
| 20–24 | 7 |
| Total | 40 |

   a.  How many orders were filled in less than 10 days? In less than 15 days?
   b.  Convert the frequency distribution to a less-than cumulative frequency distribution.
   c.  Develop a less-than cumulative frequency polygon. Use stated or true limits.
   d.  About 60% of the orders were filled in less than how many days?
19. Refer to Exercise 17. Convert the frequency distribution to a more-than cumulative frequency distribution.
   a.  How many employees were absent from work more than five days?
   b.  Draw a more-than cumulative frequency polygon. Use stated or true limits.
   c.  Interpret the chart.
20. Refer to Exercise 18. Convert the frequency distribution to a more-than cumulative frequency distribution.
   a.  How many orders had a lead time of 15 days or more?
   b.  Draw a more-than cumulative frequency polygon. Use stated or true limits.
   c.  Interpret the chart.

## GRAPHIC REPRESENTATION OF DATA

The frequency polygon, the histogram, the less-than cumulative frequency polygon, and the more-than cumulative frequency polygon have strong visual appeal. There are other graphs. Chart 2–7 is an example. They are used extensively in government

---

### CHART   2–7

**Life Expectancy at Birth, by Race and Sex, 1900 to 1990**

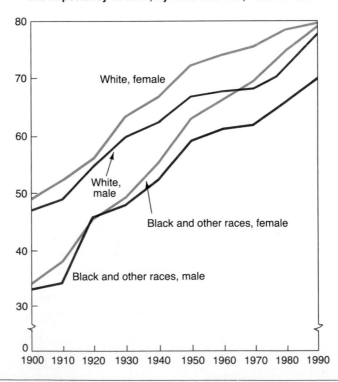

Source: National Center for Health Statistics, U.S. Department of Health and Human Services.

reports, research reports, newspapers, and journals. Several of these are presented in this section. Others, such as the scatter diagram, are introduced later.

Chart 2–7 on the previous page is an example of the use of graphs. The purpose of that graph is to show the steady increase in the life expectancy of non-whites and whites since 1900. We interpret the line labeled "non-white, male" by stating that only half of a large group of these children born in 1900 lived to the age of 33. Now half of those born in 1990 can expect to live to age 70. Note too that since 1900 the life expectancy of non-white females has increased more rapidly than for whites.

Likewise, data such as the sales of NCR since 1970 and the imports of Honda Civics since 1984 can be depicted graphically in a chart. A well-drawn chart has the advantage of attracting reader attention and clearly showing trends and other important features of the data.

We will now show how to portray data in the form of line charts, bar charts, and pie charts. (Charts are commonly referred to as graphs.)

**The four quadrants**    Recall from algebra that there are four quadrants to a grid. Note in the following illustration that both the *X* values and the *Y* values are positive in quadrant I. Since most business data are positive, it is the quadrant most frequently used. Also note that the divisions on the *Y*-axis (vertical axis) are equidistant. So are the divisions on the *X*-axis (horizontal axis). Paper showing axes with these characteristics is called *arithmetic*
**Arithmetic paper**    *paper.*

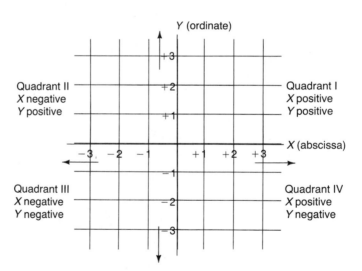

# Simple Line Charts and Simple Bar Charts

*Simple line charts* are ideal for portraying the trends of sales, imports, and other business series over a period of time. Chart 2–8 shows the earnings per share of common stock for Abbey-Green, Inc. Note that in 1989 Abbey-Green suffered a loss, and hence the earnings per share are negative. In this case both quadrants I and IV are required.

Two other examples of line charts follow. Chart 2–9 shows the dramatic increase in the sales of cellular phones since 1986. The sales, in thousands of units, increased from 280.0 in 1986 to 1,190.0 in 1990. This is about a fourfold increase in only four years!

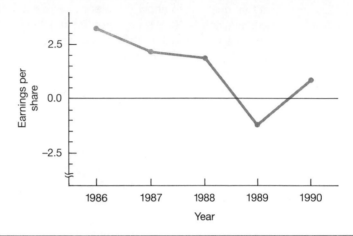

### CHART 2–8

**Abbey-Green, Inc. Earnings per Share, 1986 to 1990**

Source: Abbey-Green, Inc., *Annual Report,* 1990, p. 6.

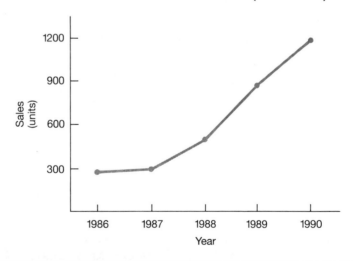

### CHART 2–9

**Sales of Cellular Phones from 1986 to 1990 (000s of units)**

Source: *The Universal Almanac,* 1991, p. 242.

Chart 2–10 illustrates an excellent way of depicting the change in two or more series of data over a period of time. This chart allows us to quickly compare the median price of existing homes in the United States and in California. Note that in 1970 the selling price of a home in California and in the United States overall was about the same—slightly below $40,000. However, since 1970 the median selling price of an existing home in California has increased to about $200,000. In the nation as a whole the price rose to only about $100,000.

## CHART 2—10

**Median Sales Price of Existing Homes, California and the United States ($000)**

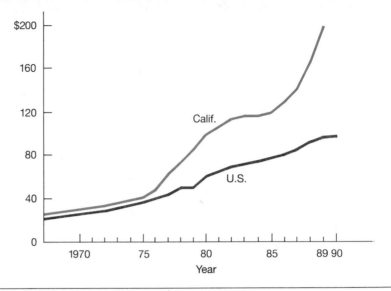

Source: *U.S. News & World Report,* April 8, 1991, p. 56.

Chart 2—11 is a simple *vertical bar chart.* This type of chart is appropriate for showing a single series over a period of time. It is very similar to a line chart, except that bars are used instead of points connected with a straight line. This chart shows the amounts spent, in billions of dollars, at vending machines in the United States from 1985 to 1989.

## CHART 2—11

**Amounts Spent at Vending Machines, 1985 to 1989 ($ billions)**

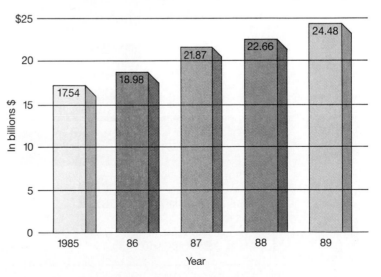

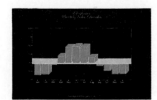

A bar graph generated by computer using SPSS.
Courtesy SPSS, Inc.

Source: *Toledo Blade,* March 10, 1991, p. 15.

A simple line chart and a bar chart may be combined to gain reader attention. The following figure combines Chart 2–9 and an unusual bar chart to illustrate.

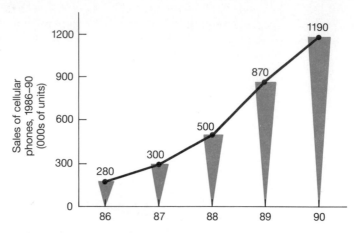

The U.S. Bureau of Labor Statistics recently estimated percentage increases in selected occupations from 1988 to 2000. These projected increases are shown in Chart 2–12 in the form of a *horizontal bar chart.* Note that the bureau estimates that the number of computer analysts will increase 53 percent from 1988 to 2000.

Horizontal bar chart

### Chart 2–12

**Percentage Increases in Civilian Jobs for Selected Occupations, 1988 to 2000**

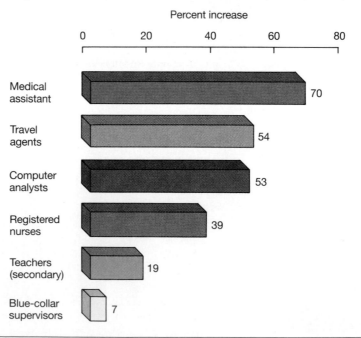

Source: *The Universal Almanac,* 1991, p. 223.

## COMPONENT-PART BAR CHARTS

Component-part bar chart

Sidens, a chain of discount stores, is organized into three groups for sales and purchasing. Each is headed by a general manager. The change in total sales for the three years 1989, 1990, and 1991 and the change for each group relative to the total is to be portrayed in a *component-part bar chart.* (In many of the new graphic computer packages, such as CHARTMASTER, it is called a *stacked bar chart.*) The sales of each group are:

| | Sales ($ millions) | | |
|---|---|---|---|
| Group | 1989 | 1990 | 1991 |
| Clothing | $ 2 | $ 3 | $ 2 |
| Drug/Hardware | 10 | 8 | 3 |
| Auto/Sports | 4 | 8 | 18 |
| Total | $16 | $19 | $23 |

To construct a component-part bar chart, the clothing sales of $2 million for 1989 are plotted first (step 1).

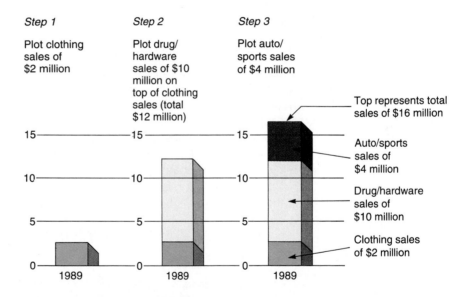

*Step 1*

Plot clothing sales of $2 million

*Step 2*

Plot drug/hardware sales of $10 million on top of clothing sales (total $12 million)

*Step 3*

Plot auto/sports sales of $4 million

Top represents total sales of $16 million

Auto/sports sales of $4 million

Drug/hardware sales of $10 million

Clothing sales of $2 million

The sales for all three years are shown in Chart 2–13 on the following page. Note that for each year, clothing sales were plotted first, at the bottom of the bar, drug/hardware sales were plotted on top of clothing sales, and auto/sports sales were the last component plotted. The top of each bar represents total sales for the year.. The interpretation of the component-part bar chart is:

1. Total sales increased during the three years.
2. Clothing sales remained relatively constant over the three-year period.
3. Drug/hardware sales decreased as a component of the total.
4. Auto/sports sales increased rapidly as a component of the total.

---

## CHART 2—13

**A Component-Part Bar Chart**

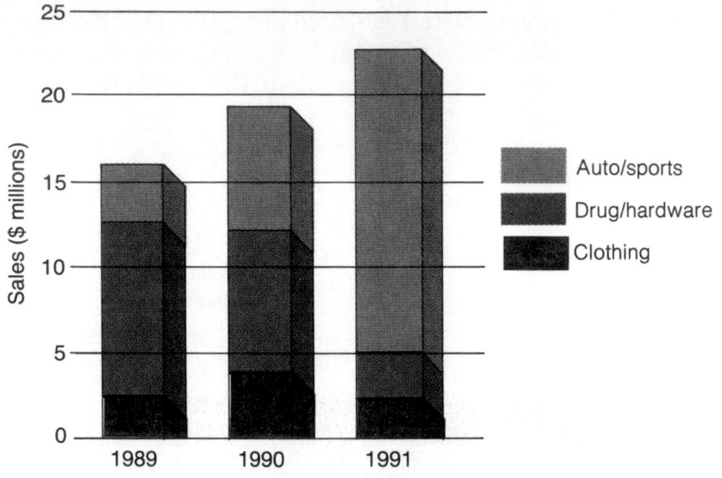

---

## TWO-DIRECTIONAL BAR CHARTS

Two-directional chart

A **two-directional chart** is alternately called a *duo-directional, two-way, or bilateral chart.* A two-directional chart can be used to show profit and loss, above-normal and below-normal activity, and percentage changes from one period of time to another. To illustrate, suppose that the sales of cassette decks, compact disc players, etc. at Kidans Music Store for the first six months of 1992 are to be compared with those for the first six months of 1991. The objective in this problem is to show the *percent change* in sales, not the change in the dollar amounts. The sales data are:

| | Sales the first six months | | Percent change from 1991 to 1992 |
|---|---|---|---|
| | 1991 | 1992 | |
| Cassette decks | $ 4,000 | $ 3,000 | −25 |
| Compact disc players | 1,000 | 1,500 | 50 |
| Radios | 10,000 | 5,000 | −50 |
| TVs | 100,000 | 110,000 | 10 |
| Camcorders | 25,000 | 50,000 | 100 |

Note that cassette deck sales decreased 25 percent from 1991 to 1992: [($3,000 − $4,000)/$4,000](100). Compact disc player sales increased 50 percent during the same period: [($1,500 − $1,000)/$1,000](100).

The percentage changes are divided into two groups. The percentage increases are usually arranged in descending order. The percentage decreases are usually arranged in ascending order.

| Percentage increases | Percentage decreases |
|---|---|
| 100 Camcorders | −25 Cassette decks |
| 50 Compact disc players | −50 Radios |
| 10 TVs | |

To construct a two-directional bar chart, the percentage changes are usually plotted in the same ascending/descending order (Chart 2–14). The center line is the origin for each bar. The most common method is to plot the percentage increases to the right of the origin and the percentage decreases to the left of the origin, as illustrated.

---

## CHART 2–14

### A Two-Directional Bar Chart

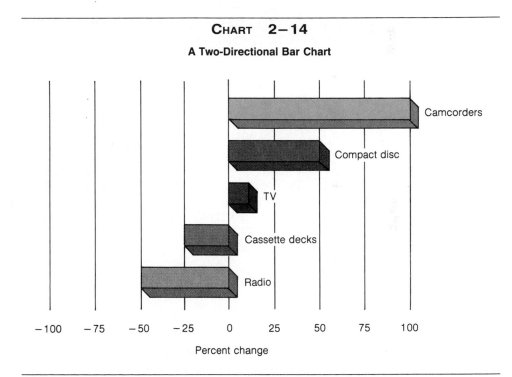

Percent change

---

## PIE CHARTS

A **pie chart,** also referred to as a *circle chart,* is especially useful for depicting a relative frequency distribution. The procedure followed in constructing a pie chart will be described using the data in Table 2–9, provided by the FBI.

To construct a pie chart, the obvious first step is to draw a circle. There are 360 degrees in a circle. To plot the 26.3 percent for the "19 and under" age group in the relative frequency distribution, we convert that percentage to degrees. The answer is 94.68 degrees, found by 26.3 percent × 360. Then, using a protractor, locate 94.68 degrees on the circumference of the circle. Lines drawn from 0 and 94.68 degrees to

### TABLE 2—9

**Arrests, by Age**

| Age | Number of arrests | Relative frequency |
|---|---|---|
| 19 and under | 2,734,756 | 26.3% |
| 20–29 | 4,201,950 | 40.4 |
| 30–39 | 2,122,973 | 20.4 |
| 40–49 | 790,535 | 7.6 |
| 50 and over | 541,963 | 5.3 |
| Total | 10,392,177 | 100.0 |

Source: Federal Bureau of Investigation, *Uniform Crime Reports for the United States.*

the center of the circle encompass the percentage of total arrests (26.3 percent) attributed to the "19 and under" age group, as shown below.

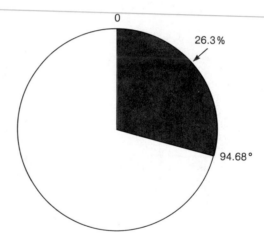

An easier and more understandable way of portraying the relative frequencies in a pie chart is to consider only the percents. As shown in Chart 2–15, the percents 0, 5, 10, 15, and so on are scaled evenly around the circumference of the circle. To plot the 26.3 percent for the "19 and under" age group, a line is drawn from 0 to the center of the circle and another line from the center to 26.3 percent on the circle. Then, adding 26.3 percent to 40.4 percent for the 20–29 age group, we get 66.7 percent. A line is drawn from the center of the circle to 66.7 percent. Thus, the area of the circle between 26.3 percent and 66.7 percent represents the percent of the total number of arrests attributed to the 20–29 age group. Continuing, we add 20.4 percent to 66.7 percent, which gives 87.1 percent. A line is drawn from the center to 87.1 percent. The area between 66.7 and 87.1, or 20.4 percent, shows the percent of the total number of arrests attributed to the 30–39 age group. This procedure is continued until all the age groups are accounted for. (See Chart 2–15).

## CHART   2-15

**Arrests by Age Group**

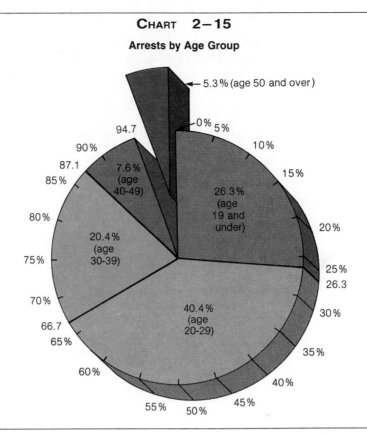

Chart 2-15 illustrates a distinct advantage of the pie chart. Since the areas in the circle correspond directly to the relative frequencies, we can quickly grasp which area is the largest—in this case, 40.4 percent, representing the 20-29 age group—and which sector is the smallest (5.3 percent for the "50 and over" age group).

### Self-Review 2-7

*The answers are at the end of the chapter.*

The Clayton County Commissioners want to design a chart to show the taxpayers attending the forthcoming meeting what happens to their tax dollars. The total amount of taxes collected is $2 million. Expenditures were: $440,000 for schools, $1,160,000 for roads, $320,000 for administration, and $80,000 for supplies. A pie chart seems ideal to show the portion of each tax dollar going for schools, roads, administration, and supplies. Convert the dollar amounts to percents of the total, and portray the percents in the form of a pie chart.

## EXERCISES

*The answers to the odd-numbered exercises are at the end of the book.*

21. The net incomes of the NCR Corporation for the years 1980–1990, in millions of dollars, are:

| Year | Net income ($ millions) | Year | Net income ($ millions) |
|------|------|------|------|
| 1990 | $369 | 1985 | $315 |
| 1989 | 412 | 1984 | 343 |
| 1988 | 439 | 1983 | 288 |
| 1987 | 419 | 1982 | 234 |
| 1986 | 337 | 1981 | 208 |
|      |      | 1980 | 255 |

Source: NCR Corporation, *Annual Report,* 1990, p. 26–27.

Portray the net incomes in the form of a line graph.

22. During 1991 the federal government spent 25 percent of its revenue on defense, 43 percent on payments to individuals, 14 percent on interest, 12 percent on grants to state and local governments, and the remaining 6 percent on other federal operations. Develop a pie chart to graphically portray these percents. (Source: Office of Management and Budget, *Budget of the Federal Government, Fiscal Year 1991.*)

23. The federal government reported these average weekly earnings for production workers by major industry for 1966 and 1990:

|      | Mining | Construction | Manufacturing | Transportation and public utilities | Wholesale trade |
|------|------|------|------|------|------|
| 1966 | $130.34 | $146.26 | $112.19 | $128.13 | $111.11 |
| 1990 | 580.32 | 528.61 | 442.56 | 501.43 | 409.85 |

Source: Bureau of Labor Statistics.

Rearrange the data and show, in the form of a bar chart, either the percent change in weekly earnings by industry from 1966 to 1990, or the dollar change in earnings by industry between these two periods.

24. A report is to be made to the management of Boise Cascade regarding the sales volume of selected building products from 1980 to 1990. The annual report of the company gives these figures (in millions):

|      | 1980 | 1990 |
|------|------|------|
| Plywood (square feet) | 1,256 | 1,682 |
| Lumber (board feet) | 670 | 782 |
| Particleboard (square feet) | 108 | 179 |
| Building materials distribution (sales dollars) | $552 | $289 |

Source: Boise Cascade Corporation, *Annual Report,* 1990, p. 43.

Depict the percent changes from 1980 to 1990 in the form of a two-directional bar chart.

## CHAPTER OUTLINE

I. Frequency distributions.
   A. A frequency distribution is a grouping of data into mutually exclusive categories showing the number of observations in each category. Its purpose is to show the data in some meaningful form.

B. Steps in developing a frequency distribution.
1. Construct an array—a listing of the raw data from smallest to largest, or vice versa.
2. Decide on the size of the class interval. If the number of classes has been established, a suggested class interval can be determined by

$$\frac{\text{Highest value} - \text{Lowest value}}{\text{Number of classes}} \qquad (2-1)$$

If the number of classes is uncertain, a suggested class interval can be found by

$$\frac{\text{Highest value} - \text{Lowest value}}{1 + 3.322(\text{logarithm of the total frequencies})} \qquad (2-2)$$

3. Set up the classes.
4. Tally the raw data into the classes to arrive at the frequency distribution.
5. Constructing an array is rather tedious and can be omitted. Instead, the data can be tallied directly into the appropriate classes.
C. Criteria in constructing a frequency distribution.
1. Avoid having fewer than 5 or more than 15 classes.
2. Avoid open-ended class.
3. Keep the class intervals the same size.
4. Do not have overlapping classes.
II. Relative frequency distribution: Similar to the frequency distribution, but instead of giving the number of observations in each class, it gives the percent of the total number of observations.
III. Stem-and-leaf displays.
A. The purpose of a stem-and-leaf display is to organize ungrouped (raw) data into some meaningful form.
B. Data are partitioned into a stem and a leaf. The first digit (digits) of a number is the stem. The trailing digit (digits) is the leaf.
IV. Graphic presentation of a frequency distribution.
A. A histogram depicts the number of frequencies in each class in the form of bars.
B. A frequency polygon and a relative frequency polygon have the classes scaled on the X-axis and the class frequencies on the Y-axis. The midpoint of a class and its corresponding class frequency are plotted using a dot. The dots are connected to form the polygon. The area under the polygon, as for the histogram, is equal to the total number of frequencies.
V. Cumulative frequency polygons.
A. A less-than cumulative frequency polygon allows us to determine how many, or what percent, of the observations are equal to or less than a certain value.
B. A more-than cumulative frequency polygon is constructed by accumulating the class frequencies starting with the highest class. The lower true limits and the cumulative frequencies are plotted. From the polygon we can determine how many, or what percent, of the values are equal to or more than a selected amount.
VI. Other graphs.
A. Line charts are ideal for portraying the trend of data over a period of time.
B. Bar charts are also used to show the long-term trend of sales, production, and other business and economic series.
C. Two-directional charts are ideally suited for depicting the profit or loss of a group of firms, the increase or decrease in the price of a select number of common stocks, and so forth.
D. Pie charts can be effectively used to portray the components of the total.

# EXERCISES

*The answers to the odd-numbered exercises are at the end of the book.*

25. Adventure Shops, a chain of sport shops catering to beginning skiers, located in Sylvania, Ohio, plans to conduct a study of how much a beginning skier spends on his or her initial purchase of equipment and supplies. Based on these figures, they want to explore the possibility of offering combinations, such as a pair of boots and a pair of skis, in order to induce customers to buy more. A sample of their cash register receipts revealed these initial purchases:

| $140 | $ 82 | $265 | $168 | $ 90 | $114 | $172 | $230 | $142 |
|------|------|------|------|------|------|------|------|------|
| 86 | 125 | 235 | 212 | 171 | 149 | 156 | 162 | 118 |
| 139 | 149 | 132 | 105 | 162 | 126 | 216 | 195 | 127 |
| 161 | 135 | 172 | 220 | 229 | 129 | 87 | 128 | 126 |
| 175 | 127 | 149 | 126 | 121 | 118 | 172 | 126 | |

    a. Arrive at a suggested class interval. Use five classes, and let the lower limit of the first class be $80.

    b. What would be a better class interval?

    c. Organize the data into a frequency distribution.

    d. Interpret your findings.

26. A 100-bed hospital at Rome, Georgia, had 1,820 patients during the year for an annual turnover rate of 18.2 patients per bed (1,820/100 = 18.2). The hospital administrator believes turnover is too low—that is, patients are remaining in the hospital beds too long. Other staff members think that the turnover rate is about average compared with those of other hospitals in the South and Southwest. In order to compare the turnover rate of 18.2 patients per bed with experience in other states, data from the American Hospital Association were secured.

| State | Turnover rate | State | Turnover rate |
|-------|-------|-------|-------|
| Alabama | 29 | Missouri | 29 |
| Arizona | 33 | Nebraska | 26 |
| Arkansas | 31 | New Mexico | 28 |
| District of Columbia | 22 | North Carolina | 26 |
| Florida | 29 | Oklahoma | 29 |
| Georgia | 30 | South Carolina | 28 |
| Kentucky | 34 | Tennessee | 29 |
| Louisiana | 30 | Texas | 31 |
| Maryland | 22 | Virginia | 24 |
| Mississippi | 27 | West Virginia | 27 |

Assume that the patient turnover rates per hospital bed have been rounded using conventional rounding rules (31.5 is rounded up to 32, but 31.49 is rounded down to 31).

    a. Using formula 2–2, determine the size of the class interval.

    b. Tally the turnover rates into a frequency distribution.

    c. Draw a histogram.

    d. Construct a less-than cumulative frequency polygon.

    e. Summarize your findings.

27. The numbers of shareholders for a selected group of large companies (in thousands) are:

| Company | Number of shareholders (000s) | Company | Number of shareholders (000s) |
|---|---|---|---|
| Pan American World Airways | 144 | Northeast Utilities | 200 |
| General Public Utilities | 177 | Standard Oil (Indiana) | 173 |
| Occidental Petroleum | 266 | Atlantic Richfield | 195 |
| Middle South Utilities | 133 | Detroit Edison | 220 |
| Chrysler Corporation | 209 | Eastman Kodak | 251 |
| Standard Oil of California | 264 | Dow Chemical | 137 |
| Bethlehem Steel | 160 | Pennsylvania Power | 150 |
| Long Island Lighting | 143 | American Electric Power | 282 |
| RCA | 246 | Ohio Edison | 158 |
| Greyhound Corporation | 151 | Transamerica Corporation | 162 |
| Pacific Gas & Electric | 239 | Columbia Gas System | 165 |
| Niagara Mohawk Power | 204 | International Telephone & | |
| E. I. du Pont de Nemours | 204 | Telegraph | 223 |
| Westinghouse Electric | 195 | Union Electric | 158 |
| Union Carbide | 176 | Virginia Electric and Power | 162 |
| BankAmerica | 175 | Public Service Electric & Gas | 225 |
| | | Consumers Power | 161 |

The numbers of shareholders are to be organized into a frequency distribution and several graphs drawn to portray the distribution.

a. Using seven classes and a lower limit of 130, construct a frequency distribution.

b. Portray the distribution in the form of a frequency polygon.

c. Portray the distribution in a less-than cumulative frequency polygon.

d. Based on the cumulative polygon, three out of every four (75 percent) of the companies have how many shareholders or less?

e. Write a brief analysis of the number of shareholders based on the frequency distribution and graphs.

28. The scores on a mechanical aptitude test were organized into the following distribution.

| Test scores | Number of scores |
|---|---|
| 100–119 | 6 |
| 120–139 | 17 |
| 140–159 | 38 |
| 160–179 | 15 |
| 180–199 | 4 |

a. Portray the distribution in the form of a histogram.

b. Portray the distribution in the form of a frequency polygon.

c. Using the two charts, interpret the distribution of test scores.

29. The weights of 75 ears of Growfast, an eating corn, were recorded and condensed into the following distribution.

| Weights in ounces | Numbers of ears |
|---|---|
| 16–17 | 12 |
| 18–19 | 36 |
| 20–21 | 14 |
| 22–23 | 8 |
| 24–25 | 4 |
| 26–27 | 1 |

a. Portray the weights in a histogram.

b. Portray the weights in a frequency polygon.

c. Based on the charts, interpret the distribution of weights.

30. According to the United States Bureau of Justice, the numbers of prisoners under sentence of death, by age group, are:

| Age | Number |
|---|---|
| Under 20 years | 13 |
| 20–24 years | 212 |
| 25–34 years | 804 |
| 35–54 years | 531 |
| 55 years and over | 31 |

a. Select an appropriate chart to portray the data graphically.

b. Using the age distribution and your chart, interpret the data.

31. A recent survey showed that the typical American car owner spends $2,950 per year on operating expenses. Below is a breakdown of the various expenditure items. Draw an appropriate chart to portray the data.

| Expenditure item | Amount |
|---|---|
| Fuel | $ 603 |
| Interest on car loan | 279 |
| Repairs | 930 |
| Insurance and license | 646 |
| Depreciation | 492 |
| Total | $2,950 |

32. The Midland National Bank selected a sample of 40 student checking accounts. Below are their end-of-the-month balances.

| $404 | $ 74 | $234 | $149 | $279 | $215 | $123 | $ 55 | $ 43 | $321 |
|---|---|---|---|---|---|---|---|---|---|
| 87 | 234 | 68 | 489 | 57 | 185 | 141 | 758 | 72 | 863 |
| 703 | 125 | 350 | 440 | 37 | 252 | 27 | 521 | 302 | 127 |
| 968 | 712 | 503 | 498 | 327 | 608 | 358 | 425 | 303 | 203 |

a. Tally the data into a frequency distribution using $100 as a class interval and $0 as the starting point.

b. Draw a less-than cumulative frequency polygon.

c. The bank considers any student with an ending balance of $400 or more a "preferred customer." Estimate the percent of preferred customers.

d. The bank is also considering a service charge to the lowest 10% of the ending balances. What would you recommend as the cutoff point between those who have to pay a service charge and those who do not?

33. Following are the numbers of games won by each of the 26 major league baseball teams during the 1990 season.

| 95 | 91 | 85 | 77 | 77 | 70 | 91 | 86 | 85 |
|---|---|---|---|---|---|---|---|---|
| 75 | 75 | 65 | 88 | 86 | 79 | 77 | 76 | 74 |
| 67 | 103 | 94 | 83 | 80 | 77 | 75 | 74 | |

Develop a stem-and-leaf chart.

34. Refer to the numbers of wins in the previous problem.

a. Organize the data into a frequency distribution. Use a class interval of 5, and let 65 be the lower limit of the first class.

b. How many games did a typical team win?

c. Develop a less-than cumulative frequency distribution. How many games did half or more of the teams win?

    d.   Estimate the number of teams that won 80 games or less.

    e.   Twenty-five percent of the teams won how many games or less?

35. We wish to portray the current gold reserves of central banks and governments for selected countries.

| | Reserves (in millions of troy ounces) |
|---|---|
| United States | 261.93 |
| Canada | 16.10 |
| Japan | 24.23 |
| France | 81.85 |
| Italy | 66.67 |
| Switzerland | 83.26 |

Source: *International Financial Statistics.*

Rearrange the reserves, and portray them in a horizontal bar chart.

36. According to a sales survey, for the first half of the model year 1991 the best-selling vehicle in the United States was the Honda Accord, followed by two light-duty trucks. The five largest sellers are shown below. Draw a chart to show the survey results.

| Model | Units sold |
|---|---|
| Honda Accord | 192,268 |
| Ford F Series truck | 187,270 |
| Chevrolet CK truck | 181,176 |
| Chevrolet Cavalier | 148,022 |
| Ford Taurus | 147,468 |

Source: *USA Today,* April 5, 1991, p. B2.

37. The salaries (in $000) of the baseball players on the 1991 opening-day roster and the disabled list of the Cleveland Indians are:

| | | | | | | | | |
|---|---|---|---|---|---|---|---|---|
| $2,500 | $100 | $410 | $2,050 | $1,450 | $115 | $ 125 | $175 | $ 900 |
| 2,025 | 345 | 550 | 100 | 165 | 800 | 100 | 575 | 1,750 |
| 1,150 | 110 | 102 | 100 | 155 | 100 | 1,368 | 100 | 750 |

Source: *USA Today,* April 5, 1991, p. C5.

Courtesy the Cleveland Indians.

a.   Organize the salary data into a frequency distribution.

b.   Comment on the shape of the distribution.

c.   About 10 percent of the players earn what amount or more?

38. An economist wants to show graphically the percent changes in U.S. direct investments abroad from 1988 to the present time for selected countries.

|  | Direct investment ($ millions) | |
|---|---|---|
|  | 1988 | Present year |
| South Africa | $ 1,269 | $    714 |
| India | 436 | 549 |
| Taiwan | 1,622 | 1,949 |
| Canada | 62,610 | 66,856 |
| Greece | 195 | 265 |
| Ecuador | 431 | 395 |
| Bermuda | 19,040 | 17,849 |
| All countries | 333,501 | 373,436 |

Source: Bureau of Economic Analysis,
U.S. Department of Commerce.

Rearrange the data, and show the percent changes from 1988 to the present in the form of a two-directional chart.

39. Annual tax revenues, by type of tax, for the state of Georgia are as follows:

| Type of tax | Amount ($000) |
|---|---|
| Sales | $2,812,473 |
| License | 185,198 |
| Income (individual) | 2,732,045 |
| Corporate | 525,015 |
| Property | 22,647 |
| Death and gift | 37,326 |
| Total | $6,314,704 |

a.   Develop a chart showing the relationship of each type of tax to the total.

b.   What percent of the total tax revenue is attributed to Georgia's sales tax?

40. A major manufacturer of light-duty trucks has four assembly plants. Careful records are kept with respect to the number of trucks assembled during an eight-hour shift. (*Note:* in several of the plants there are two or three shifts.) A sample of the shift productions at the four plants revealed the following:

| | | | | | | | | |
|---|---|---|---|---|---|---|---|---|
| 348 | 371 | 360 | 369 | 376 | 397 | 368 | 361 | 374 |
| 410 | 374 | 377 | 335 | 356 | 322 | 344 | 399 | 362 |
| 384 | 365 | 380 | 349 | 358 | 343 | 432 | 376 | 347 |
| 385 | 399 | 400 | 359 | 329 | 370 | 398 | 352 | 396 |
| 366 | 392 | 375 | 379 | 389 | 390 | 386 | 341 | 351 |
| 354 | 395 | 338 | 390 | 333 | | | | |

a.   Construct a frequency distribution. Use a class interval of 20 units.

b.   Construct a stem-and-leaf display.

c.   Comment on the shape of the distribution.

41. Population figures for Canada, by decade over the period 1901–1991, are:

|      | Population  |      | Population   |
|------|-------------|------|--------------|
| 1901 | 5,371,000   | 1951 | 14,009,000   |
| 1911 | 7,207,000   | 1961 | 18,238,000   |
| 1921 | 8,788,000   | 1971 | 21,568,000   |
| 1931 | 10,377,000  | 1981 | 24,343,000   |
| 1941 | 11,507,000  | 1991 | 27,000,000*  |

*Estimated.
Source: Canadian Almanac & Directory, 1991, pp. 6–77, and previous issues.

Depict the population of Canada from 1901 to the present time in the form of either a line chart or a vertical bar chart.

42. Infant mortality figures (rates per 1,000 live births) for Canada and other selected countries are:

|        | Infant mortality |               | Infant mortality |
|--------|------------------|---------------|------------------|
| Canada | 8                | Pakistan      | 111              |
| Brazil | 65               | Uganda        | 105              |
| China  | 35               | United States | 10               |
| Greece | 12               | USSR          | 29               |
| India  | 86               | Vietnam       | 47               |

Source: World Bank, World Development Report, 1990.

Rearrange the infant mortality rates, and portray the data in a horizontal bar chart.

43. Annual imports from selected Canadian trading partners are:

| Partner        | Annual imports ($ millions) |
|----------------|-----------------------------|
| Japan          | $9,550                      |
| United Kingdom | 4,556                       |
| South Korea    | 2,441                       |
| China          | 1,182                       |
| Australia      | 618                         |

Source: Canadian Almanac & Directory, 1991, pp. 6–80.

Portray the Canadian import data in a pie chart.

44. Most of the exports from Canada to commonwealth, preferential, and other foreign countries total less than $70 million per country annually. We are interested in organizing those exports into a frequency distribution and portraying them in a frequency polygon and a histogram. Countries purchasing Canadian exports under $70 million and the amounts of the merchandise (in $ millions) are:

|            | Export amount |                | Export amount |                     | Export amount |
|------------|---------------|----------------|---------------|---------------------|---------------|
| Bahamas    | $29           | Benin          | $ 1           | Lebanon             | $ 6           |
| Bahrain    | 6             | Bolivia        | 1             | Liberia             | 4             |
| Bangladesh | 65            | Bulgaria       | 12            | Libya               | 62            |
| Barbados   | 47            | Cameroon       | 38            | Luxembourg          | 4             |
| Belize     | 5             | Costa Rica     | 23            | Madagascar          | 1             |
| Bermuda    | 39            | Czechoslovakia | 13            | Mozambique          | 10            |
| Cyprus     | 5             | Dominican      |               | Nepal               | 1             |
| Fiji       | 2             | Republic       | 62            | Netherlands Antilles| 12            |

(continued)

| | Export amount | | Export amount | | Export amount |
|---|---|---|---|---|---|
| Gibraltar | $ 1 | Ecuador | $34 | Nicaragua | $23 |
| Ghana | 33 | Egypt | 61 | Oman | 4 |
| Kenya | 6 | El Salvador | 11 | Panama | 19 |
| Malawi | 5 | Ethiopia | 25 | Paraguay | 1 |
| Malta | 3 | French Africa | 43 | Peru | 58 |
| Mauritius | 1 | French Oceania | 2 | Poland | 37 |
| Nigeria | 33 | Gabon | 6 | Romania | 41 |
| Pakistan | 69 | Greece | 60 | Senegal | 18 |
| Papua, N.G. | 31 | Greenland | 10 | Somalia | 3 |
| Qatar | 5 | Guatemala | 21 | St. Pierre | 29 |
| Sri Lanka | 11 | Guinea | 4 | Sudan | 9 |
| Tanzania | 21 | Haiti | 19 | Suriname | 1 |
| Trinidad | 58 | Honduras | 14 | Synan | 5 |
| Uganda | 5 | Hungary | 6 | Togo | 4 |
| Zambia | 19 | Iceland | 11 | Tunisia | 40 |
| Zimbabwe | 17 | Ivory Coast | 11 | Arab Emirates | 33 |
| Albania | 1 | Korea, DPR | 1 | Virgin Islands | 4 |
| Angola | 11 | Kuwait | 26 | Uruguay | 26 |
| Argentina | 39 | Khmer | 1 | Vietnam | 2 |

Source: *Canadian Almanac & Directory*, 1991, pp. 6–80.

a. Organize the Canadian exports into a frequency distribution. (It is suggested that you use classes 0–9, 10–19, etc.).

b. Portray the frequency distribution in the form of a frequency polygon.

c. Draw a histogram.

d. Depict the distribution in a less-than frequency polygon.

e. Based on the graphs, about half of the countries who bought merchandise valued at less than $70 million paid about what amount?

f. Analyze the exports going to these 80 countries.

45. There has been a substantial increase in enrollment at the University of Toledo over the last 12 years. The president has asked Dr. Patsy Scott, Director of Institutional Research, to provide student enrollment figures. Full-time and part-time enrollment is shown in the following table. What long-term trends, if any, are indicated? Which group accounts for the increase? Draw appropriate charts and graphs to depict the enrollment data.

| Year | Full-time | Part-time | Total |
|---|---|---|---|
| 1979 | 10,127 | 8,112 | 18,239 |
| 1980 | 11,684 | 8,586 | 20,270 |
| 1981 | 12,173 | 8,944 | 21,117 |
| 1982 | 12,540 | 8,846 | 21,386 |
| 1983 | 12,748 | 8,841 | 21,589 |
| 1984 | 12,612 | 8,427 | 21,039 |
| 1985 | 12,725 | 8,513 | 21,238 |
| 1986 | 12,826 | 8,350 | 21,176 |
| 1987 | 13,341 | 8,399 | 21,740 |
| 1988 | 14,433 | 8,373 | 22,806 |
| 1989 | 15,430 | 8,498 | 23,928 |
| 1990 | 16,227 | 8,554 | 24,781 |

Source: University of Toledo, Department of
Institutional Research, *Resource and
Consumption Report*, January 1990. p. 9

46. Continuing Exercise 45, Dr. Scott has also been asked by the president to study the ethnicity of the students. The following information is obtained.

| Ethnic group | 1986 enrollment | 1990 enrollment |
|---|---|---|
| Unknown | 441 | 392 |
| American Indian/Alaskan native | 109 | 172 |
| Asian or Pacific Islander | 195 | 251 |
| Black/non-Hispanic | 1,253 | 1,684 |
| Hispanic | 260 | 365 |
| White/non-Hispanic | 8,313 | 9,843 |
| Nonresident alien | 1,297 | 1,070 |

Source: The University of Toledo, Department of Institutional Research, *Resource and Consumption Report,* January 1990, p. 24.

  a. Draw an appropriate chart showing the percent changes in the various categories. Which groups changed the most?

  b. Has there been a change in the makeup of the student body from 1986 to 1990? Compare the percent of each ethnic group for the two years.

47. The numbers of persons with AIDs per 100,000 population for selected metropolitan areas as of July 1990 were:

| | Number with AIDS (per 100,000 population) |
|---|---|
| Atlanta, Ga. | 922 |
| Austin, Tex. | 245 |
| Dallas, Tex. | 711 |
| Houston, Tex. | 1,245 |
| New York, N.Y. | 6,565 |
| San Francisco, Calif. | 1,935 |
| Washington, D.C. | 1,059 |
| West Palm Beach, Fla. | 353 |

Source: Department of Health and Human Services, *HIV/AIDS Survellance Report.*

Rearrange the AIDs data, and portray them in either a vertical or a horizontal bar chart.

## COMPUTER DATA EXERCISES

48. Refer to data set 1, which reports information on homes sold in Florida during 1990.

  a. Select an appropriate class interval, and organize the selling prices into a frequency distribution.

  b. What is the typical selling price of a home?

  c. Draw a less-than cumulative frequency distribution. Twenty percent of the homes sold for less than what amount? About what percent of the homes sold for more than $100,000?

  d. Comment on the shape of the distribution of selling prices.

  e. Draw a graph that depicts the number of homes sold in each of the townships.

49. Refer to data set 2, which reports information on 200 corporations in the United States.

  a. Organize the information on market value into a frequency distribution. Select an appropriate class interval.

  b. What is the typical market value for these 200 corporations?

  c. Draw a less-than cumulative frequency distribution. Eighty percent of the market values are less than what amount? About what percent of the market values are more than $20,000 (million)?

  d. Comment on the shape of the distribution.

50. Refer to data set 3, which reports information on the 26 major league baseball teams for the 1991 season.

    a.  Organize the information on total salaries for the 26 teams into a frequency distribution. Select an appropriate class interval.

    b.  What is the "typical" team paying in total salary?

    c.  Draw a less-than cumulative frequency distribution. Forty percent of the teams are paying less than what amount in total salary? About what percent of teams are paying less than $25,000,000 in salary?

    d.  Comment on the shape of the distribution. Does it appear that some teams are "out of line" on the high and low sides?

    e.  Develop a graph that reports the fraction of games won on the X- axis and the salary on the Y- axis. Comment on the graph.

# CHAPTER 2  EXAMINATION

*The answers are at the end of the chapter.*

For Questions 1–10, indicate whether the statement is true or false.

1.  An array is a listing of all the values from the smallest to the largest or the largest to the smallest.

2.  The number of observations in each class is called a frequency distribution.

3.  A sample of 85 observations is to be organized into a frequency distribution. The suggested number of classes is 7.

4.  Generally speaking, we should construct a frequency distribution with at least 20 classes.

5.  A histogram is a graph representing the corresponding frequency distribution.

6.  The class midpoint is obtained by adding the lower and upper class limits and dividing by 2.

7.  To construct a frequency polygon, we need the class midpoints and the class frequencies.

8.  A frequency polygon and a relative frequency distribution are similar in that they are both based on a frequency distribution.

9.  The class interval is obtained by subtracting the lower stated limit of a class from the lower stated limit of the next higher class.

10. Relative frequency distributions are developed by dividing each class frequency by the total number of observations.

For questions 11–25, give the letter that represents the correct answer.

11. We constructed the following by tallying the ages of our employees into classes.

| Ages | Number of ages |
|------|------|
| 20–29 | 16 |
| 30–39 | 25 |
| 40–49 | 51 |
| 50–59 | 80 |
| 60–69 | 20 |
| 70–79 | 8 |

This arrangement is called:

a.  A histogram.        b.  A frequency polygon.

c.  An ogive.           d.  A frequency distribution.

e.  None of the above.

12. Refer to Question 11. What is the class interval?
    a.  50, found by 70 − 20.      b.  59, found by 79 − 20.
    c.  10, found by 30 − 20.      d.  9, found by 29 − 20.
    e.  None of the above.
13. Refer to Question 11. What are the stated lower limits?
    a.  20, 30, 40, etc.      b.  19.5, 29.5, 39.5, etc.
    c.  29, 39, 49, etc.      d.  24.5, 34.5, 44.5, etc.
    e.  None of the above.
14. Refer to Question 11. What is the relative class frequency for the lowest class (20−29)?
    a.  16.                    b.  0.08, or 8 percent.
    c.  100 percent.      d.  200
    e.  None of the above.
15. Refer to Question 11. What are (is) the true class limits for the first class?
    a.  19.5 and 29.5      b.  16.
    c.  20 and 29.            d.  Less than 20 and more than 30.
    e.  None of the above.
16. Using the data in Question 11, the following picture was drawn. The picture is called:
    a.  A histogram.
    b.  A frequency polygon.
    c.  A less-than cumulative frequency polygon.
    d.  A more-than cumulative frequency polygon.
    e.  None of the above.

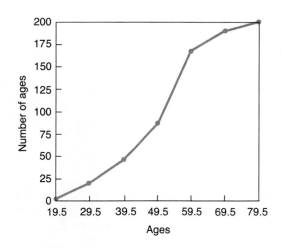

17. Refer to the picture in Question 16. About half of the employees are:
    a.  79 or older.          b.  20 or younger.
    c.  51 or younger.      d.  40 or younger.
    e.  None of the above.
18. Refer to the picture in Question 16. About 25 percent of the employees are what age or less?
    a.  20.      b.  80.
    c.  41.      d.  52.
    e.  None of the above.

19. Two distributions are plotted in the following chart. What are the two pictures called?

    a.   Frequency polygons.    b.   Relative frequency polygons.

    c.   Ogives.    d.   Histograms.

    e.   None of the above.

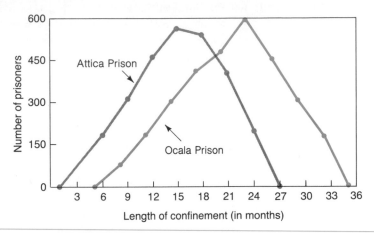

20. Refer to Question 19. In general, is the length of confinement longer in Attica Prison or in Ocala Prison?

    a.   Attica Prison.    b.   Ocala Prison.

    c.   Cannot tell based on the picture.    d.   None of the above.

21. The following type of chart is called:

    a.   A simple bar chart.    b.   A pie chart.

    c.   A two-directional bar chart.    d.   A component-part bar chart.

    e.   None of the above.

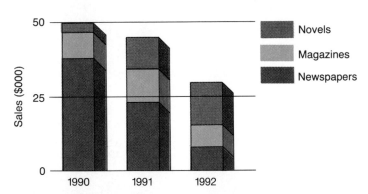

22. Refer to Question 21. With respect to total sales from 1990 to 1992:

    a.   Total sales increased.    b.   Total sales decreased.

    c.   Total sales stayed about the same.    d.   None of the above.

23. Refer to Question 21. With respect to sales of newspapers from 1990 to 1992:

    a.   Newspaper sales declined but in 1992 were a larger proportion of the total compared with 1990.

    b.   Newspaper sales declined and in 1992 were a smaller proportion of the total compared with 1990.

    c.   Newspaper sales increased from 1990 to 1992.

    d.   None of the above.

24. Refer to Question 21. With respect to the sale of novels:
   a.   Sales of novels increased as a proportion of total sales from 1990 to 1992.
   b.   Sales of novels decreased as a proportion of total sales from 1990 to 1992.
   c.   Sales of novels stayed about the same from 1990 to 1992.
   d.   None of the above.

25. The percentages of the total annual sales of Manchini shirts, ties, socks, and robes for 1992 are shown in the following pie chart. Annual sales of which clothing item is the largest?
   a.   Shirts.      b.   Ties.
   c.   Socks.      d.   Robes.
   e.   None of the above.

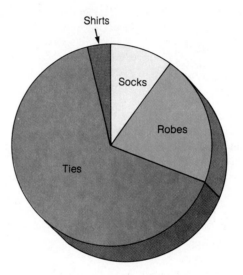

# ANSWERS

2–1  1.  The raw data.

2.

| Monthly incomes | Tallies | Number |
|---|---|---|
| $1,400–$1,499 | // | 2 |
| 1,500– 1,599 | /// | 3 |
| 1,600– 1,699 | // | 2 |
| 1,700– 1,799 | / | 1 |
| Total | | 8 |

3.  Class frequencies.
4.  The lowest monthly income is about $1,400 and the highest $1,799. The largest concentration of incomes is in the $1,500–$1,599 class.

2–2  1.  a. $215.29, found by ($2,548 − $1,041)/7.
b. $200.
c. $1,000–$1,199.
  $1,200–$1,399.
2.  Unequal size class intervals.
Open-ended class.
Overlapping classes.

2–3  1.  24.
2.  20 percent.
3.  10.8 percent.

2–4  1.

| Stem | Leaf |
|---|---|
| 7 | 7 |
| 8 | 0 0 1 3 4 8 8 |
| 9 | 1 5 6 6 8 9 |
| 10 | 1 2 4 8 |
| 11 | 2 6 |

2.  The price-earnings ratios are concentrated in the 8 and 9 percent classes. For each class, the price-earnings ratios are distributed somewhat evenly throughout the class.

2–5  1.

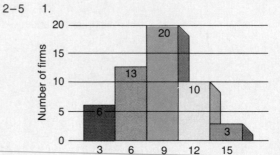

2.  $3, $6, $9, $12, $15 million.

3.

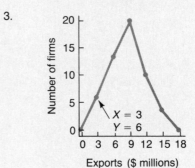

4.  None of the firms had exports less than $2 million or more than $17 million. The largest concentration (20) is between $8 million and $11 million.

2–6  1.  A frequency distribution.

2.

| Hourly wages | Cumulative number |
|---|---|
| Less than  $1.50 | 0 |
| Less than  $4.50 | 18 |
| Less than  $7.50 | 54 |
| Less than $10.50 | 74 |
| Less than $13.50 | 80 |

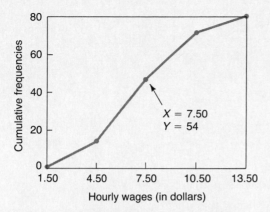

the curve and then moving horizontally to the *Y*-axis.

About \$6.30, found by going horizontally from 40 on the *Y*-axis to the curve and then vertically down to the *X*-axis.

About 9, found by going to \$10 on the *X*-axis of the more-than polygon, moving vertically to the curve, and then moving horizontally to the *Y*-axis.

About \$8, found by going to 20 on the more-than polygon, moving horizontally to the curve, and then moving vertically to the *X*-axis.

2–7

3.

| Hourly wages | Cumulative number |
|---|---|
| More than $1.50 | 80 |
| More than $4.50 | 62 |
| More than $7.50 | 26 |
| More than $10.50 | 6 |
| More than $13.50 | 0 |

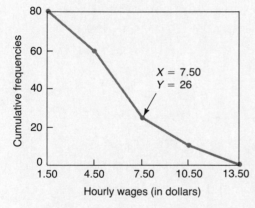

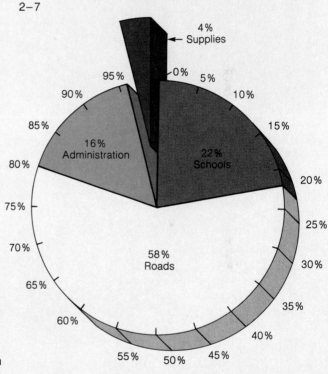

4. About 36, found by going to the less-than polygon and drawing a line vertically from \$6 to

## Answers

# CHAPTER 2 EXAMINATION

| | | | | | |
|---|---|---|---|---|---|
| 1. | True. | 9. | True. | 18. | *c.* |
| 2. | False. | 10. | True. | 19. | *a.* |
| 3. | True. | 11. | *d.* | 20. | *b.* |
| 4. | False. | 12. | *c.* | 21. | *d.* |
| 5. | True. | 13. | *a.* | 22. | *b.* |
| 6. | True. | 14. | *b.* | 23. | *b.* |
| 7. | True. | 15. | *a.* | 24. | *a.* |
| 8. | True. | 16. | *c.* | 25. | *b.* |
| | | 17. | *c.* | | |

# DESCRIBING DATA—MEASURES OF CENTRAL TENDENCY

When you have completed this chapter, you will be able to:

1. Calculate the arithmetic mean, median, mode, and geometric mean.

2. Explain the characteristics, use, advantages, and disadvantages of each average.

3. Identify the position of the arithmetic mean, median, and mode for both a symmetrical distribution and a skewed distribution.

**C**hapter 2 began our study of descriptive statistics. In order to transform a mass of raw data into some meaningful form, we organized it into a frequency distribution and portrayed it graphically in a histogram and a frequency polygon. We also examined other tools used to describe data, including line, bar, and pie charts.

This chapter is concerned with yet another way of describing numerical data, namely, a *measure of central tendency* commonly referred to as an **average.** The purpose of an average is to pinpoint the center of a set of observations. You are familiar with averages. If you follow the sports scene, you are bombarded with them (for example, "Larry Bird of the Boston Celtics is averaging 28.1 points a game"). Other examples: The average life expectancy of white females in 1900 was 49.2 years; in 1990 it was 78.5 years. The 10 highest paid executives averaged $3,580,945 last year.

Four measures of central tendency commonly used in business and economics are examined in the following sections. They are the *arithmetic mean, median, mode,* and the *geometric mean.*

## WHAT IS AN AVERAGE?

Average: A representative value for a group of data

We often need a single number to represent a set of data. This one number can be thought of as being "typical" of all the data. A typical college football tackle weighs about 230 pounds. Thus, a 415-pound tackle would be well above average. Likewise, if the average annual salary of 966 top executives is $505,687, a salary of $506,000 would be "about average." What is an average?

> Average   A single value that represents a set of data. It pinpoints a center of the values.

As noted above, the word *average* occurs frequently in our everyday language. It usually refers to the arithmetic mean, discussed in the next section, but it could refer to any of the averages (the mean, median, or mode). A more precise term than *average* is a *measure of central tendency.*

## THE SAMPLE MEAN

As explained in Chapter 1, a statistician must frequently take a sample from the population in order to find out something about a specific characteristic of the population. The quality assurance department, for example, needs to be assured that the ball bearings being produced have an acceptable outside diameter. It would be very expensive and time-consuming to check the outside diameter of all the bearings being mass-produced. Therefore, a sample of five bearings might be selected and the mean outside diameter of the five bearings calculated in order to estimate the mean diameter of all the bearings produced.

The measure of central tendency (average) most widely used is the **arithmetic mean,** usually shortened to the **mean.** For raw data, that is, ungrouped data, *the mean is the sum of all the values divided by the total number of values.* To find the mean for a sample, use the following formula.

Mean of ungrouped sample data

$$\text{Sample mean} = \frac{\text{Sum of all the values in the sample}}{\text{Number of values in the sample}}$$

Instead of writing out in words the full directions for computing the mean (or any other measure), it is more convenient to use the shorthand notation of algebra. At times, we will be concerned with a *sample,* which is part of a population, and at other times, with the entire *population.* The mean of a sample and the mean of a population are computed in the same way, but the shorthand notation used is different. The formula for the mean of a *sample* is:

$$\overline{X} = \frac{\Sigma X}{n}$$ (3–1)

To determine $\overline{X}$: Sum the sample values and divide by the number of values

where:

$\overline{X}$   stands for the sample mean—it is read "$X$ bar."

$X$   stands for a particular value.

$\Sigma$   is the Greek capital sigma and indicates the operation of adding.

So

$\Sigma X$   stands for the sum of all the $X$s,

  $n$   is the total number of values in the sample.

A statistic is a sample value

The mean of a sample, or any other measure based on sample data, is called a **statistic.** If the mean outside diameter of a sample of ball bearings is computed to be 0.625 inches, that sample value is a statistic.

---

Statistic   A measurable characteristic of a sample.

---

## ■ EXAMPLE

The net weights of the contents of five Giorgio perfume bottles selected at random from the production line are (in grams): 85.4, 85.3, 84.9, 85.4, and 85.0. What is the arithmetic mean weight of the sample observations?

## ☑ SOLUTION

Using formula (3–1), the sample mean is computed as follows:

$$\text{Sample mean} = \frac{\text{Sum of all the values in the sample}}{\text{Number of values in the sample}}$$

$$\overline{X} = \frac{\Sigma X}{n}$$

$$= \frac{85.4 + 85.3 + 84.9 + 85.4 + 85.0}{5}$$

$$= \frac{426.0}{5}$$

$$= 85.2$$

Mean of ungrouped sample data is 85.2.

The arithmetic mean weight is 85.2 grams.

Highland Salesman
Courtesy Highland Superstores, Inc.

## THE POPULATION MEAN

Many studies involve all the population values. To illustrate, if a study were concerned with all the weekly commissions earned by the full-time salespersons employed by Highland Superstores in Plymouth, Michigan, the entire set of weekly commissions would be considered the population. The mean of the population, in terms of symbols, is:

$$\mu = \frac{\Sigma X}{N}$$

(3–2)

To determine $\mu$: Total the population values and divide by the number of values

where:

$\mu$   stands for the population mean. It is mu, the Greek letter for lowercase *m*.

$N$   is the total number of observations in the population.

As before, $\Sigma X$ stands for the sum of all the *X*s.

A parameter is a population value

As noted, any measurable characteristics of a sample is called a statistic. Any measurable characteristic of a population, such as the mean, is called a **parameter.** A sample statistic is used to estimate a population parameter.

| Parameter | A measurable characteristic of a population. |
|---|---|

### Self-Review 3–1

*The answers are at the end of the chapter.*

Again, we recommend you solve these self-review problems.

1. The annual incomes of a sample of several middle-management employees at Westinghouse are (to the nearest $100): $42,900, $49,100, $38,300, and $56,800.
   a. Give the formula for the sample mean.
   b. Find the sample mean rounded to the nearest $100.
   c. Is the mean you computed in b a statistic or a parameter? Why?
   d. What is your best estimate of the population mean?

2. All the students in advanced computer science S411 are considered the population. Their course grades are 92, 96, 61, 86, 79, and 84.
   a. Give the formula for the population mean.
   b. Compute the mean course grade.
   c. Is the mean you computed in b a statistic or a parameter? Why?

## THE PROPERTIES OF THE ARITHMETIC MEAN

Properties of the mean

As noted, the arithmetic mean is a widely used measure of central tendency. It has several properties:

1. Every set of interval-level and ratio-level data has a mean. (Recall from Chapter 1 that interval- and ratio-level data include such measurable data as ages, incomes, and weights, with the distance between numbers being constant.)

2. All the values are included in computing the mean.

3. A set of data has only one mean. This is unique. (Later in the chapter we will discover an average that might appear twice, or more than twice, in a set of data.)

4. The mean is a very useful measure for comparing two or more populations. It can, for example, be used to compare the performance of the production employees on the first shift at the Chrysler transmission plant with the performance of those on the second shift.

5. The arithmetic mean is the only measure of central tendency where *the sum of the deviations of each value from the mean will always be zero.* Expressed symbolically:

$$\Sigma(X - \overline{X}) = 0 \qquad\qquad (3\text{--}3)$$

**Sum of deviations from mean = 0**

As an example, the mean of 3, 8, and 4 is 5. Then:

$$\Sigma(X - \overline{X}) = (3 - 5) + (8 - 5) + (4 - 5)$$
$$= -2 + 3 - 1$$
$$= 0$$

**Mean as a balance point**

Thus, we can consider the mean as a balance point for a set of data. To illustrate, suppose we had a long board with the numbers 1, 2, 3, . . . , *n* evenly spaced on it. Suppose three gold bars of equal weight were placed on the board at numbers 3, 4, and 8, and the balance point was set at 5, the mean of the three numbers. We would find that the board balanced perfectly! The deviations below the mean (−3) are equal to the deviations above the mean (+3). Shown schematically:

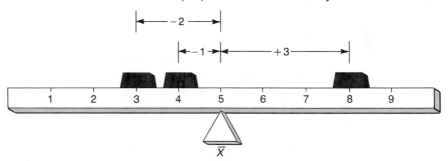

**Mean unduly affected by unusually large or small values**

The mean does have several disadvantages, however. Recall that the mean uses the value of every item in a sample, or population, in its computation. If one or two of these items is either extremely large or extremely small, the mean might not be an appropriate average to represent the data. For example, suppose the annual incomes of a small group of stockbrokers at Merrill Lynch are $62,900, $61,600, $62,500, $60,800, and $1.2 million. The mean income is $289,560. Obviously, it is not representative of this group because all but one broker has an income in the $60,000 to $63,000 range. One income ($1.2 million) is unduly affecting the mean.

**Cannot determine mean for open-ended data**

The mean is also inappropriate if there is an *open-ended class* for data tallied into a frequency distribution. If a frequency distribution has the open-ended class "$100,000 and more," and there are 10 persons in that class, we really do not know whether their incomes are close to $100,000, $500,000, or $16 million. Since we lack information about their incomes, the arithmetic mean income for this open-ended distribution cannot be determined.

# EXERCISES

*The answers to the odd-numbered exercises are at the end of the book.*

1. What are the differences between a sample mean and a population mean?
2. List the characteristics of the mean.
3. a. Compute the mean of the following sample values: 5, 9, 4, 10.
   b. Show that $\Sigma(X - \bar{X}) = 0$.
4. a. Compute the mean of the following sample values: 1.3, 7.0, 3.6, 4.1, 5.0.
   b. Show that $\Sigma(X - \bar{X}) = 0$.
5. Compute the mean of the following sample values: 16.25, 12.91, 14.58.
6. Compute the mean hourly wage paid carpenters who earned the following wages: $15.40, $20.10, $18.75, $22.76, $30.67, $18.00 respectively.
7. There are 10 salespeople employed by Midtown Ford. The numbers of new cars sold last month by each salesperson were: 15, 23, 4, 19, 18, 10, 10, 8, 28, 19.
   a. Compute the mean number of cars sold.
   b. Is this a sample statistic or a population parameter?
8. The accounting department at a mail order company counted the following numbers of incoming calls per day to the company's toll-free number during a seven-day period: 14, 24, 19, 31, 36, 26, 17.
   a. Compute the mean number of calls per day.
   b. Is this a sample statistic or a population parameter?
9. The Cambridge Power and Light Company selected 20 residential customers. Following are the amounts, to the nearest dollar, the customers were charged for electrical service last month:

| 54 | 48 | 58 | 50 | 25 | 47 | 75 | 46 | 60 | 70 |
|----|----|----|----|----|----|----|----|----|----|
| 67 | 68 | 39 | 35 | 56 | 66 | 33 | 62 | 65 | 67 |

   a. Compute the mean monthly charge.
   b. Is this a sample statistic or a population parameter?
10. The personnel director at Mercy Hospital began a study of the overtime hours of the registered nurses. Fifteen RNs were selected at random, and these overtime hours during June were noted:

| 13 | 13 | 12 | 15 | 7 | 15 | 5 | 12 |
|----|----|----|----|----|----|----|----|
| 6 | 7 | 12 | 10 | 9 | 13 | 12 | |

   a. Compute the mean number of overtime hours.
   b. Is this a sample statistic or a population parameter?

# WEIGHTED MEAN

Hillman's Cards and Gifts pay their salespeople either $6.50, $7.50, or $8.50 an hour. It might be concluded that the arithmetic mean hourly wage is $7.50, found by ($6.50 + $7.50 + $8.50)/3. However, this is true only if there are the *same* number of salespeople earning $6.50, $7.50, and $8.50 an hour. However, suppose 14 salespeople earn $6.50 an hour, 10 are paid $7.50, and 2 get $8.50. To find the mean, $6.50 is *weighted,* or multiplied, by 14; $7.50 is weighted by 10; and $8.50 is weighted by 2. The resulting average is aptly called the *weighted mean.*

Weighted mean: Each value weighted according to its importance

In general, the weighted mean of a set of numbers designated $X_1, X_2, X_3, \ldots, X_n$ with corresponding weights $w_1, w_2, w_3, \ldots, w_n$ is computed by:

$$\overline{X}_w = \frac{w_1 X_1 + w_2 X_2 + w_3 X_3 + \cdots + w_n X_n}{w_1 + w_2 + w_3 + \cdots + w_n}$$   (3−4)

This may be shortened to:

$$\overline{X}_w = \frac{\Sigma(w \cdot X)}{\Sigma w}$$

For the card and gift store problem:

$$\overline{X}_w = \frac{14(\$6.50) + 10(\$7.50) + 2(\$8.50)}{14 + 10 + 2}$$

$$= \frac{\$183}{26}$$

$$= \$7.038$$

The weighted mean hourly wage is $7.04.

### Self-Review 3−2

*The answers are at the end of the chapter.*

Springers sold 95 Antonelli men's suits for the regular price of $400. For the spring sale the suits were reduced to $200, and 126 were sold. At the final clearance, the price was reduced to $100, and the remaining 79 suits were sold.

a. What was the weighted mean price of an Antonelli suit?

b. Springers paid $200 a suit for the 300 suits. Comment on the store's profit on the suits if a salesperson receives a $25 commission for each one sold.

## EXERCISES

*The answers to the odd-numbered exercises are at the end of the book.*

11. Calico Pizza sells colas in three sizes: small, medium, and large. The small size costs $0.50, the medium $0.75, and the large $1.00. Yesterday 20 small, 50 medium, and 30 large colas were sold. What was the weighted mean price per cola?

12. A specialty bookstore concentrates mainly on used books. Paperbacks are $1.00 each, and hardcover books are $3.50. Of the 50 books sold Tuesday morning, 40 were paperback and the rest were hardcover. What was the weighted mean price of a book?

13. Metropolitan Hospital employs 200 persons on the nursing staff. Fifty are nurse's aides, 50 are practical nurses, and 100 are registered nurses. Nurse's aides receive $8 an hour, practical nurses $10 an hour, and registered nurses $14 an hour. What is the weighted mean hourly wage?

14. Andrews and Associates specialize in corporate law. They charge $100 an hour for researching a case, $75 an hour for consultations, and $200 an hour for writing a brief. Last week one of the associates spent 10 hours consulting with her client, 10 hours researching the case, and 20 hours writing the brief. What was the weighted mean hourly charge for her legal services?

# THE MEDIAN

Median of ungrouped data

It has been pointed out that for data containing one or two very large or very small values, the arithmetic mean may not be representative. The center point for such problems can be better described using a measure of central tendency called the **median.**

To illustrate the need for a measure of central tendency other than the arithmetic mean, suppose you are seeking to buy a condominium in Palm Aire. Your agent said that the average price of the units currently available is $110,000. Would you still want to look? If you had budgeted your maximum purchase price between $60,000 and $75,000, you might think they were out of your price range. However, checking the individual prices of the units might change your mind. They are $60,000, $65,000, $70,000, $80,000, and a superdeluxe penthouse costs $275,000. The arithmetic mean price is $110,000, as the real estate agent reported, but one price ($275,000) is pulling the arithmetic mean upward, causing it to be an unrepresentative average. It does seem that a price between $65,000 and $75,000 is a more typical or representative average, and it is. In cases such as this, the median provides a more accurate measure of central tendency.

Median: Value of middle item

| **Median** The midpoint of the values after they have been ordered from the smallest to the largest, or the largest to the smallest. There are as many values above the median as below it in the data array. |
| --- |

The median price of the units available is $70,000. To determine this, the prices were ordered from low ($60,000) to high ($275,000) and the middle value ($70,000) selected.

| Prices ordered from low to high | | Prices ordered from high to low |
| --- | --- | --- |
| $ 60,000 | | $275,000 |
| 65,000 | | 80,000 |
| 70,000 | ←Median→ | 70,000 |
| 80,000 | | 65,000 |
| 275,000 | | 60,000 |

Median unaffected by extreme values

Note that there are the same number of prices below the median of $70,000 as above it. The median is, therefore, unaffected by extremely low or high observations. Had the highest price been $90,000, or $300,000, or even $1 million, the median price would still be $70,000. Likewise, had the lowest price been $20,000 or $50,000, the median price would still be $70,000.

In the previous illustration there is an *odd* number of observations (five). How is the median determined for an *even* number of observations? As before, the observations are ordered. Then the usual practice is to find the arithmetic mean of the two middle observations. Note that for an even number of observations, the median may not be one of the given values.

## ■ EXAMPLES

1. A sample of the paramedical fees charged by Baltimore clinics revealed these amounts: $35, $29, $30, $25, $32, $35. What is the median charge?
2. The lengths of time several underwriters took to review applications for similar insurance coverage are (in minutes): 50, 230, 52, 57. What is the median length of time required to review an application?

## ☑ SOLUTIONS

1. Arranging the paramedical fees from low to high:

$25
29
30
   ← Median
32
35
35

The median fee is $31, found by determining the arithmetic mean of the two center observations: ($30 + $32)/2 = $31.

2. Arranging the lengths of time from low to high:

50
52
   ← Median
57
230

The median length of time is 54.5 minutes, found by (52 + 57)/2 = 54.5. Notice that 54.5 is not one of the values.

Again, we see that there are the same number of observations below the median as above it. An easy way to locate the position of the middle item for raw (ungrouped) data is by the formula:

$$\text{Location of median value} = \frac{n+1}{2}$$

(3–5)

where $n$ is the total number of items.

For Example 1 there are six items, so $(n + 1)/2 = (6 + 1)/2 = 3.5$. After arranging the data from low to high, we locate the middle item by counting down to the 3.5th item and then determining its value, the median. It is $31.

| Item number | 1 | 2 | 3 | 4 | 5 | 6 |
|---|---|---|---|---|---|---|
| Value of item | $25 | $29 | $30 | $32 | $35 | $35 |

$31
Median

If there are five items, for example, $7, $2, $4, $8, and $15, $(n + 1)/2 = (5 + 1)/2 = 3$. Arranging these values from low to high, we find the value of the third item. It is $7, the median.

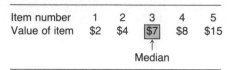

## PROPERTIES OF THE MEDIAN

1. The median is unique; that is, like the mean, there is only one median for a set of data.
2. To determine the median, arrange the data from low to high, and find the value of the middle observation.
3. It is not affected by extremely large or small values and is therefore a valuable measure of central tendency when such values do occur.
4. It can be computed for an open-ended frequency distribution if the median does not lie in an open-ended class. (We will show the computations for the median of data grouped in a frequency distribution shortly.)

*Median can be determined for all levels of data except nominal*

5. It can be computed for ratio-level, interval-level, and ordinal-level data. (Recall from Chapter 1 that ordinal-level data can be ranked from low to high—such as the responses "excellent," "very good," "good," "fair," and "poor" to a question on a marketing survey.) To use a simple illustration, suppose five people rated a new fudge bar. One person thought it was excellent, one rated it very good, one called it good, one rated it fair, and one considered it poor. The median response is "good." Half of the responses are above "good"; the other half are below it.

---

### Self-Review 3–3

*The answers are at the end of the chapter.*

1. A sample of single persons in Towson, Texas, receiving social security payments revealed these monthly benefits: $426, $299, $290, $687, $480, $439, and $565.
   a. What is the median monthly benefit?
   b. How many observations are below the median? Above it?

2. The numbers of work stoppages in the automobile industry for selected months are 6, 0, 10, 14, 8, and 0.
   a. What is the median number of stoppages?
   b. How many observations are below the median? Above it?

## THE MODE

The **mode** is another measure of central tendency.

> Mode   The value of the observation that appears most frequently.

Mode of ungrouped data

## ▌ EXAMPLE

The annual salaries of quality-control managers in selected states are:

| | | | | | |
|---|---|---|---|---|---|
| Arizona | $35,000 | Illinois | $58,000 | Ohio | $50,000 |
| California | 49,100 | Louisiana | 50,C00 | Tennessee | 50,000 |
| Colorado | 50,000 | Maryland | 60,000 | Texas | 71,400 |
| Florida | 50,000 | Massachusetts | 40,000 | West Virginia | 50,000 |
| Idaho | 40,000 | New Jersey | 65,000 | Wyoming | 55,000 |

What is the model (mode) annual salary?

## ☑ SOLUTION

A perusal of the salaries reveals that the annual salary of $50,000 appears more often (six times) than any other salary. The mode is, therefore, $50,000.

The mode is especially useful in describing nominal and ordinal levels of measurement. As an example of its use for nominal-level data, a company has developed five bath oils. Chart 3–1 shows the results of a marketing survey designed to find out which bath oil consumers prefer. The largest number of respondents favored Lamoure, as evidenced by the highest bar. Thus, Lamoure is the mode.

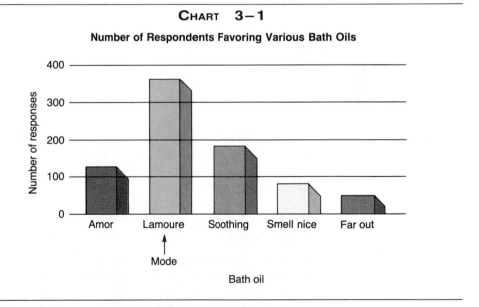

### CHART   3–1

**Number of Respondents Favoring Various Bath Oils**

In summary, we can determine the mode for all levels of data—nominal, ordinal, interval, and ratio. The mode also has the advantage of not being affected by extremely high or low values. Like the median, it can be used as a measure of central tendency for open-ended distributions.

Disadvantages of the mode

The mode does have a number of disadvantages, however, that cause it to be used less frequently than the mean or median. For many sets of data, there is no mode because no value appears more than once. For example, there is no mode for this set of price data: $19, $21, $23, $20, and $18. Since every value is different, however, it could be argued that every value is the mode. Conversely, for some data sets there is more than one mode. Suppose the ages of a group are 22, 26, 27, 27, 31, 35, and 35. Both the ages 27 and 35 are modes. One would question the use of two modes to represent the central tendency of this set of age data.

## A COMPUTER EXAMPLE

A computer can be used to organize a mass of raw data and determine various measures of central tendency.

### ■ EXAMPLE

Table 2−1 in the preceding chapter gave the raw monthly data on condominium rentals in the Sarasota-Bradenton area. What are the mean and median monthly rental amounts?

### ☑ SOLUTION

The data consisted of 120 observations, so to perform the calculations by hand would be very tedious. The following output is from the MINITAB system.

```
MTB > MEAN C1
    MEAN     =    1457.9
MTB > MEDIAN C1
    MEDIAN   =    1464.5
```

You may want to check these two measures of central tendency by referring to the raw data in either Table 2−1 or Table 2−2. The computer formula (3−5), uses $(n + 1)/2$, to determine the median ($1,464.50). Incidentally, the MINITAB system does not provide the mode.

## EXERCISES

*The answers to the odd-numbered exercises are at the end of the book.*

15. Employees at Houghton Steel took several short refresher courses. During the course several different teaching methods were used. At the completion of the courses, each employee indicated his or her first preference regarding the teaching methods. The results are:

| Teaching method | Number of first preferences |
|---|---|
| Television | 86 |
| Lecture | 142 |
| Group discussion | 17 |
| Programmed learning | 49 |

a.   What level of measurement is this?

b.   What is the modal teaching preference? Why?

c.   Can the median be determined? Explain.

d.   Can the mean be determined? Explain.

16.  The results of a survey regarding the political affiliations of a sample of registered voters in Lucas County are:

| Political affiliation | Number of registered voters |
|---|---|
| Republican | 1,027 |
| Democrat | 842 |
| Socialist | 21 |
| Independent | 1,146 |
| All others | 17 |

a.   What level of measurement is this—ratio, interval, ordinal, or nominal?

b.   What is the modal affiliation? Why?

c.   Can the median be determined? Explain.

d.   Can the mean affiliation be determined? Explain.

17.  The daily take-home pay amounts of a sample of steel fabricators in Quebec is $96.70, $67.10, $89.70, $96.70, $91.40, $96.70, and $82.60 respectively.

a.   What is the modal daily take-home pay amount?

b.   Does the mode seem to be a representative average? Explain.

c.   What is the median take-home pay amount?

d.   What is the mean daily take-home pay amount?

e.   Which measure of central tendency seems to best describe the typical take-home pay amount of the steel fabricators in Quebec?

18.  The numbers of dry wells completed worldwide by the Chevron Corporation during each of the past 11 years are:

|  | Number of dry wells |  | Number of dry wells |
|---|---|---|---|
| 1990 | 79 | 1984 | 202 |
| 1989 | 71 | 1983 | 90 |
| 1988 | 77 | 1982 | 108 |
| 1987 | 44 | 1981 | 102 |
| 1986 | 79 | 1980 | 65 |
| 1985 | 160 |  |  |

Source: Chevron Corporation, *Annual Report,* 1990, pp. 70–71.

a.   What is the modal number of dry wells completed during this period?

b.   Does the mode seem to be a representative value? Explain.

c.   What is the arithmetic mean number of dry wells?

d.   What is the median number of dry wells?

e.   Which one(s) of the measures of central tendency seem to best describe the data?

19.  The numbers of new cars sold by the 10 salespeople at Midtown Ford last month are: 15, 23, 4, 19, 18, 10, 10, 8, 28, 19. Which one(s) of the three measures of central tendency best describes the typical number of new cars sold last month by a salesperson?

# THE GEOMETRIC MEAN

Two uses of the geometric mean

There are two main uses of the geometric mean: (1) to average percents, indexes, and relatives; and (2) to determine the average percent increase in sales, production, or other business or economic series from one time period to another.

The **geometric mean** of a set of $n$ positive numbers is defined as the $n$th root of the product of the $n$ numbers. Thus, the formula for the geometric mean is written:

$$\text{G.M.} = \sqrt[n]{(X_1)(X_2)(X_3) \cdots (X_n)} \qquad (3-6)$$

Note: If one of the numbers is zero or negative, the geometric mean cannot be computed.

## ■ EXAMPLE

To illustrate the use of the geometric mean in averaging percents, suppose the profits earned by the Atkins Construction Company on four projects were 3, 2, 4, and 6 percent, respectively. What is the geometric mean profit? (Note: $n = 4$, the number of observations.)

## ✓ SOLUTION

$$\begin{aligned}
\text{G.M.} &= \sqrt[n]{(X_1)(X_2)(X_3) \cdots (X_n)} \\
&= \sqrt[4]{(3)(2)(4)(6)} \\
&= \sqrt[4]{144}
\end{aligned}$$

A calculator is very useful

The geometric mean percent is therefore the fourth root of 144. If a calculator with either a $\sqrt[x]{y}$ or $y^x$ key is available, the geometric mean can be quickly determined:

|  | | Display |
|---|---|---|
| | Multiply $3 \times 2 \times 4 \times 6$ | 144 |
| | Depress $\sqrt[x]{y}$ or $y^x$ key* | |
| number of observations | Depress $4^\dagger$ = | 3.464101615 |

*On some calculators you must depress the 2nd function mode before depressing $y^x$.

†If the key is $y^x$, the reciprocal of $n$ must be used. The reciprocal of 4 is $\frac{1}{4} = .25$.

The geometric mean profit is 3.46 percent.

Geometric mean—a more conservative average

The arithmetic mean profit is 3.75 percent, found by $(3 + 2 + 4 + 6)/4$. Although the profit of 6 percent is not extremely large, it is weighting the arithmetic mean upward. The geometric mean of 3.46 gives a more conservative profit figure because it is not so heavily weighted by extreme values. It will be, in fact, either equal to or less than the arithmetic mean.

## ▮ EXAMPLE

Suppose the prices of five high-tech stocks increased by 37.1, 1,140.0, 0.927, 2.7, and 842.0 percent, respectively, since 1988. What is the geometric mean percent increase in the price of the five stocks?

## ☑ SOLUTION

Using a calculator:

|  | Display |
|---|---|
| Multiply 37.1 × 1,140 × .927 × 2.7 × 842 | 89132143 |
| Depress $\sqrt[x]{y}$ or $y^x$ key* |  |
| Depress 5† = | 38.9051299 |

*On some calculators you must depress the ⃞2nd function mode before depressing $y^x$.

†Use reciprocal of 5, or $\frac{1}{5} = .20$, if $y^x$ key is used.

The geometric mean percent increase is 38.9 percent. Contrast the geometric mean of 38.9 percent with the arithmetic mean of 404.5 percent, found by 2,022.727/5. Again, it is evident that the geometric mean is not so highly influenced by extreme values as is the arithmetic mean.

Geometric mean gives the correct average percent increase

Now to explore the second application of the geometric mean: determining the average percent increase in sales, exports, or other business series from one time period to another. The formula for the geometric mean as applied to this type of problem is:

$$\text{G.M.} = \sqrt[n-1]{\frac{\text{Value at end of period}}{\text{Value at beginning of period}}} - 1 \qquad (3-7)$$

## ▮ EXAMPLE

The population of Haarlan in 1980 was 2 persons, and in 1990 it was 22. What was the average annual percentage increase during this period?

## ☑ SOLUTION

Note that there is an 11-year span. Thus, $n = 11$. The 11 years are 1980, 1981, 1982, 1983, 1984, 1985, 1986, 1987, 1988, 1989, and 1990. Even though there are 11 years involved, there are only 10 annual rates of change, namely, from 1980 to 1981, from 1981 to 1982, and so forth up to the change from 1989 to 1990.

Formula (3–7) for the geometric mean as applied to this type of problem is:

$$\text{G.M.} = \sqrt[n-1]{\frac{\text{Population at end of period}}{\text{Population at beginning of period}}} - 1$$

$$= \sqrt[11-1]{\frac{22}{2}} - 1$$

$$= \sqrt[10]{\frac{22}{2}} - 1$$

Problem solved quickly
using a calculator

Using a calculator:

|                                        | Display     |
| -------------------------------------- | ----------- |
| $22 \div 2$                            |             |
| Depress $\sqrt[x]{y}$ or $y^x$ key*    | 11          |
| Depress $10^\dagger$ =                 | 1.270981615 |
| Depress $-1$ =                         | .270981615  |

*On some calculators you must depress the
2nd function mode before depressing $y^x$.

†If $y^x$ key is on calculator, use the reciprocal
of 10, or $\frac{1}{10} = .1$.

The final value of .270981615 is multiplied by 100 to express it as a percent. The geometric mean annual percent increase in Haarlan's population is approximately 27 percent.

### Self-Review 3–4

*The answers are at the end of the chapter.*

1. The annual yield, in percent, of four computer stocks are: 4.91, 5.75, 8.12, and 21.60.
   a. Find the geometric mean yield.
   b. Find the arithmetic mean yield.
   c. Is the arithmetic mean equal to or greater than the geometric mean? It should be.

2. Production increased from 23,000 units in 1971 to 120,520 units in 1991. Find the geometric mean annual percent increase.

### Exercises

*The answers to the odd-numbered exercises are at the end of the book.*

20. a. Under what conditions is the geometric mean more representative of a set of data than the arithmetic mean?

    b. Under what conditions, if any, will the geometric mean be *larger* than the arithmetic mean?

21. Compute the geometric mean of the following values: 8, 12, 14, 26, 5.

22. Compute the geometric mean of the following values: 2, 8, 6, 4, 10, 6, 8, 4.

23. In 1983 there were 30,948 minivans sold in the United States. By 1990 sales had increased to 926,429. Determine the geometric mean yearly rate of increase. (Source: *USA Today,* April 5, 1991, p. B1.)

24. In 1975 there were 9.19 million cable TV subscribers. In 1990 the number had increased to 54.87 million. Determine the geometric mean yearly rate of increase. (Source: *USA Today,* March 22, 1991, p. A1.)

## The Mean, Median, and Mode of Grouped Data

Quite often data on incomes, ages, and so on are grouped and presented in the form of a frequency distribution. It is usually impossible to secure the original raw data. Thus, if we are interested in a typical value to represent the data, we must *estimate* it based on the frequency distribution.

## THE ARITHMETIC MEAN

Arithmetic mean of grouped data

To approximate the arithmetic mean of data organized into a frequency distribution, the observations in each class are represented by the *midpoint* of the class. The mean of a sample of data organized in a frequency distribution is computed by:

$$\bar{X} = \frac{\Sigma fX}{n}$$
(3–8)

where:

$\bar{X}$    is the designation for the arithmetic mean.

$X$    is the mid-value, or midpoint, of each class.

$f$    is the frequency in each class.

$fX$    is the frequency in each class times the midpoint of the class.

$\Sigma fX$    is the sum of these products.

$n$    is the total number of frequencies.

## ▩ EXAMPLE

The computations for the arithmetic mean of data grouped into a frequency distribution will be shown using the distribution repeated below from Table 2–4 in Chapter 2.

| Monthly rentals of new condominium units | Number of units |
|---|---|
| $ 600–$ 799 | 3 |
| 800– 999 | 7 |
| 1,000– 1,199 | 11 |
| 1,200– 1,399 | 22 |
| 1,400– 1,599 | 40 |
| 1,600– 1,799 | 24 |
| 1,800– 1,999 | 9 |
| 2,000– 2,199 | 4 |
| Total | 120 |

What is the mean monthly rental?

## ☑ SOLUTION

Midpoint represents values in the class

It is assumed that the midpoint of the first class ($699.50) represents the three rental units in that class. That midpoint was determined by ($600 + $799)/2. Thus, the three rentals in that class cost an approximate total 3 × $699.50, or $2,098.50. Next, the class midpoint of $899.50 represents the rentals in the $800–$999 class. The total in that class is $6,296.50, found by 7 × $899.50. This process is continued for all the classes. The total amount of the monthly rentals is $175,340. (See Table 3–1.)

---

## TABLE   3–1

### Monthly Rentals of 120 New Condominium Units

| Monthly rentals | Number (f) | Midpoint (X) | Frequency × midpoint (fX) |
|---|---|---|---|
| $  600–$  799 | 3 | $   699.50 | $    2,098.50 |
| 800–    999 | 7 | 899.50 | 6,296.50 |
| 1,000–  1,199 | 11 | 1,099.50 | 12,094.50 |
| 1,200–  1,399 | 22 | 1,299.50 | 28,589.00 |
| 1,400–  1,599 | 40 | 1,499.50 | 59,980.00 |
| 1,600–  1,799 | 24 | 1,699.50 | 40,788.00 |
| 1,800–  1,999 | 9 | 1,899.50 | 17,095.50 |
| 2,000–  2,199 | 4 | 2,099.50 | 8,398.00 |
| Total | 120 | | $175,340.00 |
| | ↑ | | ↑ |
| | $\boxed{n}$ | | $\boxed{\Sigma fX}$ |

---

Solving for the arithmetic mean of the sample using formula (3–8):

$$\overline{X} = \frac{\Sigma fX}{n}$$

$$= \frac{\$175,340}{120}$$

$$= \$1,461.17$$

**Mean of grouped data only an estimate**

It was emphasized that the mean of data grouped into a frequency distribution may be different from the mean using raw data. The grouping results in some loss of information. In the monthly rental problem, the mean using the raw data in Chapter 2 was computed to be $1,457.90 (reported on page 84 using MINITAB), which is fairly close to the mean just computed ($1,461.17) using the frequency distribution. The difference of $3.27 is less than 0.25 percent. The mean of grouped data is considered an *estimate* of the ungrouped (raw) data.

## Self-Review 3–5

*The answers are at the end of the chapter.*

The net incomes of a sample of large importers of antiques were organized into the following table:

| Net income ($ millions) | Number of importers |
|---|---|
| 2– 4 | 1 |
| 5– 7 | 4 |
| 8–10 | 10 |
| 11–13 | 3 |
| 14–16 | 2 |

a. What is the table called?

b. Estimate the arithmetic mean net income.

# EXERCISES

*The answers to the odd-numbered exercises are at the end of the book.*

25. When we compute the mean of a frequency distribution, why do we refer to this as an *estimated* mean?

26. Determine the estimated mean of the following frequency distribution.

| Class | Frequency |
|-------|-----------|
| 0– 4  | 2         |
| 5– 9  | 7         |
| 10–14 | 12        |
| 15–19 | 6         |
| 20–24 | 3         |

27. Determine the estimated mean of the following frequency distribution.

| Class | Frequency |
|-------|-----------|
| 20–29 | 7         |
| 30–39 | 12        |
| 40–49 | 21        |
| 50–59 | 18        |
| 60–69 | 12        |

28. Last month a total of 60 antique cars were sold in the metropolitan Erie, Pennsylvania, area. The selling prices were organized into the following frequency distribution.

| Selling price ($000) | Frequency |
|----------------------|-----------|
| 30.0–39.0            | 3         |
| 40.0–49.0            | 7         |
| 50.0–59.0            | 18        |
| 60.0–69.0            | 20        |
| 70.0–79.0            | 12        |

Estimate the mean selling price.

29. FM radio station WLQR recently changed its format from easy listening to contemporary. A recent sample of 50 listeners revealed the following age distribution. Estimate the mean age of the listeners.

| Age   | Frequency |
|-------|-----------|
| 20–29 | 1         |
| 30–39 | 15        |
| 40–49 | 22        |
| 50–59 | 8         |
| 60–69 | 4         |

# THE MEDIAN

**Median: Half the values are above it, half below**

Recall that the median is defined as the value below which half of the values lie and above which the other half of the values lie. Since the raw data have been organized into a frequency distribution, some of the information is not identifiable. As a result we cannot determine the exact median. It can be estimated, however, by (1) locating the class in which the median lies and then (2) interpolating within that class to arrive at the median. The rationale for this approach is that the members of the median class are assumed to be evenly spaced throughout the class. The formula is:

Median of grouped data

$$\text{Median} = L + \frac{\frac{n}{2} - CF}{f} \ (i) \qquad (3-9)$$

where:

    $L$  is the lower *true* limit of the class containing the median.

    $n$  is the total number of frequencies.

    $f$  is the frequency in the median class.

  $CF$  is the cumulative number of frequencies in all the classes immediately preceding the class containing the median.

    $i$  is the width of the class in which the median lies.

First, we shall estimate the median by locating the class in which it falls and interpolating. Then the formula for the median will be applied to check our answer.

## ■ EXAMPLE

The problem of monthly rentals of 120 condominiums is used again to show the procedure for estimating the median (see Table 3–2). The cumulative frequencies in the right column will be used shortly. What is the median monthly rental?

### TABLE  3–2

**Monthly Rentals**

| Monthly rentals | Frequencies (f) | Cumulative frequencies (CF) |
|---|---|---|
| $ 600–$ 799 | 3 | 3 |
| 800– 999 | 7 | 10 |
| 1,000– 1,199 | 11 | 21 |
| 1,200– 1,399 | 22 | 43 |
| 1,400– 1,599 | 40 | 83 |
| 1,600– 1,799 | 24 | 107 |
| 1,800– 1,999 | 9 | 116 |
| 2,000– 2,199 | 4 | 120 |

## ☑ SOLUTION

Locate class containing median

The monthly rentals have already been arranged in ascending order from $600 to $2,199. It is common practice to locate the middle observation by dividing the total number of observations by 2. In this case, $n/2 = 120/2 = 60$.[1] The class containing the 60th condominium unit is located by referring to the cumulative frequency column in Table 3–2. Note that 43 units cost $1,399 or less, and 83 cost $1,599 or less. Hence,

---

[1]Technically, it should be $(n + 1)/2$, but the difference is usually negligible.

the 60th rental is in the $1,400 to $1,599 class. Recall that the lower limit of that class is really $1,399.50 and the upper limit $1,599.50. We have, therefore, located the median monthly cost somewhere between the true class limits of $1,399.50 and $1,599.50.

Interpolate to find median

To interpolate in the $1,399.50–$1,599.50 class, recall that the monthly rentals are assumed to be evenly distributed between the lower and upper true limits. There are 17 rentals between the 43rd and 60th condominium, and there are 40 units in the class containing the median. (See Chart 3–2.) The median is therefore 17/40 of the distance between $1,399.50 and $1,599.50. That distance is $200. Thus, 17/40 of $200, or $85, is added to the lower true limit of $1,399.50 to give $1,484.50, the estimated median rental. To summarize:

$$\text{Median} = \$1,399.50 + \frac{60 - 43}{40}\,(\$200)$$

$$= \$1,399.50 + \frac{17}{40}\,(\$200)$$

$$= \$1,399.50 + \$85$$

$$= \$1,484.50$$

The median, using the formula

If we use formula (3–9) for the median of grouped data given previously, $L$ is $1,399.50, the lower true limit of the class containing the median; $n$ is 120 units; $CF$ is 43, the cumulative number of rentals preceding the median class; $f$ is 40, the frequency in the median class; and $i$ is $200, the width of the class containing the median.

$$\text{Median} = L + \frac{\frac{n}{2} - CF}{f}\,(i)$$

$$= \$1,399.50 + \frac{\frac{120}{2} - 43}{40}\,(\$200)$$

$$= \$1,399.50 + \frac{17}{40}\,(\$200)$$

$$= \$1,399.50 + \$85$$

$$= \$1,484.50 \text{ (same as determined previously)}$$

The assumption underlying the approximation of the median—that the frequencies in the median class are distributed evenly between $1,399.50 and $1,599.50—may not be correct. Therefore, it is safer to say that *about* half of the monthly rentals are less than $1,484.50 and the other half more than $1,484.50. Again, the median estimated from data grouped in a frequency distribution ($1,484.50 in this case) and the median of ungrouped data ($1,464.50 from Table 2–2 and the MINITAB output on page 142) will probably be somewhat different, but the differences are usually small.

Median can be determined for distributions having open ends

A final note: The median is based only on the frequencies and the true class limits of the median class. The open-ended classes that occur at the extremes are rarely needed. Therefore, the median of a frequency distribution having open ends can be determined. The arithmetic mean of a frequency distribution with an open-ended class cannot be accurately computed—unless, of course, the midpoints of the open-ended classes are estimated. Further, the median can be determined if *percentage*

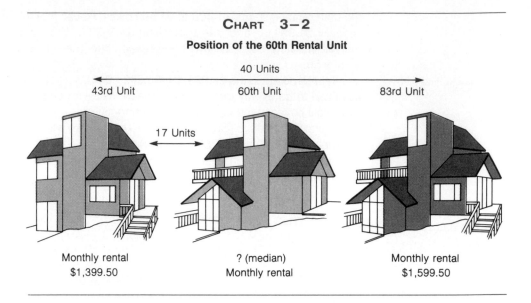

**CHART    3−2**

**Position of the 60th Rental Unit**

40 Units

43rd Unit                    60th Unit                    83rd Unit

17 Units

Monthly rental              ? (median)                   Monthly rental
$1,399.50                   Monthly rental               $1,599.50

*frequencies* are given instead of the actual frequencies. This is because the median is the value with 50 percent of the distribution above it and 50 percent below it and does not depend on actual counts. The percents are considered substitutes for the actual frequencies. In a sense, they are actual frequencies whose total is 100.0. Problem 2 in Self-Review 3−6 has both an open end and percentage frequencies.

## THE MODE

Class midpoint— estimated mode

Recall that the mode is defined as the value that occurs most often. For data grouped into a frequency distribution, the mode can be approximated by the *midpoint of the class containing the largest number of class frequencies*. For Problem 2 in Self-Review 3−6, the modal net sales is found by first locating the class containing the greatest number of percents. It is the $7–$9 class because it has the largest number of percents (40). The midpoint of that class ($8 million) is the estimated mode. This indicates that more stamping plants had net sales of $8 million than any other amount. If the raw data were available, the value appearing most often would probably be slightly different from $8 million.

Bimodal—having two modes

Two values may occur a large number of times. The distribution is then called *bimodal.* Suppose the ages of a sample of workers are 22, 27, 30, 30, 30, 30, 34, 58, 60, 60, 60, 60, and 65. The two modes are 30 years and 60 years. Often two points of concentration develop because the population being sampled is probably not homogeneous. In this illustration, the population might be composed of two distinct groups—one a group of relatively young employees who have been recently hired to meet the increased demand for a product, and the other a group of older employees who have been with the company a long time.

If a large number of workers were sampled, the distribution of their ages when plotted might appear as shown in Chart 3−3. Note that the two peaks need not be exactly equal in height in order for us to consider the distribution bimodal.

## Self-Review 3–6

*The answers are at the end of the chapter.*

1. A sample of the daily production of transceivers at Scott Electronics was organized into the following distribution.

| Daily production | Frequencies |
|---|---|
| 80– 89 | 5 |
| 90– 99 | 9 |
| 100–109 | 20 |
| 110–119 | 8 |
| 120–129 | 6 |
| 130–139 | 2 |

Assuming that the true class limits are 79.5–89.5 and so on, estimate the median daily production.

2. The net sales of a sample of small stamping plants were organized into the following percentage frequency distribution.

| Net sales ($ millions) | Percent of total |
|---|---|
| 1– 3 | 13 |
| 4– 6 | 14 |
| 7– 9 | 40 |
| 10–12 | 23 |
| 13 and greater | 10 |

What is the median net sales?

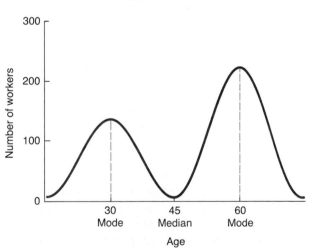

CHART  3–3

**A Bimodal Distribution**

As shown in the chart, the median age is approximately 45 years. This would not be a representative age for those recently hired. Neither would the older group of employees consider it a typical age. Thus, a logical decision would be to divide the employees into two distinct groups before continuing the analysis of the data.

If the set of data has more than two modes, the distribution is referred to as being *multimodal.* In such cases we would probably not consider any of the modes as being representative of the central value of the data.

## EXERCISES

*The answers to the odd-numbered exercises are at the end of the book.*

30. Refer to Exercise 26. Compute the median. What is the mode?
31. Refer to Exercise 27. Compute the median. What is the mode?
32. The ages of newly hired, unskilled employees were grouped into the following distribution:

| Ages | Number |
|------|--------|
| 18–20 | 4 |
| 21–23 | 8 |
| 24–26 | 11 |
| 27–29 | 20 |
| 30–32 | 7 |

    a. Compute the median age.

    b. What is the modal age?

33. A sample of light trucks using diesel fuel revealed these mileages per gallon of fuel used:

| Mileage | Number of trucks |
|---------|------------------|
| 10–12 | 2 |
| 13–15 | 5 |
| 16–18 | 10 |
| 19–21 | 8 |
| 22–24 | 3 |
| 25–27 | 2 |

    a. What is the median mileage per gallon of fuel used?

    b. What is the modal mileage?

## SELECTING AN AVERAGE FOR DATA IN A FREQUENCY DISTRIBUTION

*For a symmetrical distribution mean, median, and mode are equal.*

Refer to the frequency polygon in Chart 3–4. It is symmetrical and bell-shaped, meaning that *the distribution has the same shape on either side of the center axis.* If the polygon were folded in half, the two halves would be identical. For a symmetric distribution, the mode, median, and mean are located at the center and are always equal. They are all 20 years in Chart 3–4.

The length of service at the highest point of the curve is the *mode* (20 years). Because the frequency curve is symmetrical, the *median* corresponds to the point where the distribution is cut in half (20 years). The total of the lengths of service for employees with long service with the company is offset by the total service of newer employees, resulting in an *arithmetic mean* of 20 years. Logically, any of the three averages would be appropriate to represent the lengths of service.

*A skewed distribution is not symmetrical*

As the distribution becomes asymmetrical, or **skewed,** the relationship among the three averages changes. In a *positively skewed distribution,* the arithmetic mean is the largest of the three averages. Why? Because the mean is influenced more than the median or mode by a few extremely high values. The median is generally the next largest average in a positively skewed frequency distribution. The mode is the smallest of the three averages.

If the distribution is highly skewed, such as the monthly incomes in Chart 3–5, the mean would not be a good average to use. The median and mode would be more representative.

---

### CHART 3—4

**A Symmetrical Distribution**

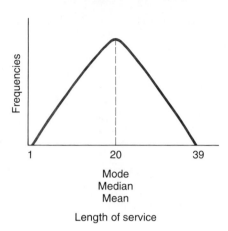

Mode
Median
Mean

Length of service

---

Extremely large values
"pulling" mean upward

### CHART 3—5

**A Positively Skewed Distribution**

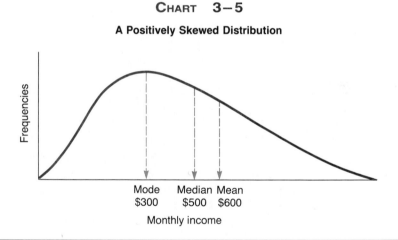

| Mode | Median | Mean |
| $300 | $500 | $600 |

Monthly income

---

Conversely, in a distribution that is *negatively skewed,* the mean is the lowest of the three averages. The mean is, of course, influenced by a few extremely low observations. The median is greater than the arithmetic mean, and the modal value is the largest of the three averages. Again, if the distribution is highly skewed, such as the distribution of tensile strengths shown in Chart 3—6, the mean should not be used to represent the data.

An approximate relationship among the three averages is: If there is a sufficiently large number of observations to suggest a smoothed distribution and if the shape of the curve is only moderately skewed, *the median is approximately one third of the distance from the arithmetic mean to the mode.*

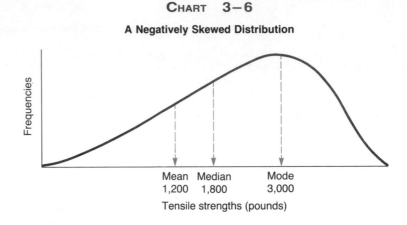

**CHART   3–6**

**A Negatively Skewed Distribution**

If two averages of a moderately skewed frequency distribution are known, the third can be approximated. The formulas are:

$$
\begin{aligned}
\text{Mode} &= \text{Mean} - 3(\text{Mean} - \text{Median}) \\
\text{Mean} &= \frac{3(\text{Median}) - \text{Mode}}{2} \\
\text{Median} &= \frac{2(\text{Mean}) + \text{Mode}}{3}
\end{aligned}
\qquad (3-10)
$$

We noted before that if the distribution is open-ended, the mean cannot be computed—unless the midpoint of the open-ended class, or classes, can be approximated. Consider, for example, the following distribution. Unless the midpoint of the "less than $50,000" class and the midpoint of the "$250,000 and more" class can be estimated, the mean cannot be determined.

| Annual income | Number of executives |
|---|---|
| Less than $50,000 | 17 |
| $50,000 to $100,000 | 62 |
| $100,000 to $150,000 | 103 |
| $150,000 to $200,000 | 73 |
| $200,000 to $250,000 | 41 |
| $250,000 and more | 20 |

However, the median and mode could be used to represent the typical annual income of the executives.

### Self-Review 3–7

*The answers are at the end of the chapter.*

The weekly sales from a sample of Hi-Tec electronic supply stores were organized into a frequency distribution. The mean of weekly sales was computed to be $105,900, the median $105,000, and the mode $104,500.

a. Sketch the sales in the form of a smoothed frequency polygon. Note the location of the mean, median, and mode on the *X*-axis.

b. Is the distribution symmetrical, positively skewed, or negatively skewed? Explain.

## EXERCISES

*The answers to the odd-numbered exercises are at the end of the book.*

34. A machine weighs coal that is being loaded on barges and automatically records the total every hour. After 132 hours of operation, the total weights were organized into a frequency distribution, and based on that distribution a curve was drawn. It was approximately symmetrical in shape. The mean weight loaded per hour was computed to be 1,200 tons.

    a. What is the median? Explain.

    b. What is the mode? Explain.

35. The price-earnings ratios for a selected group of common stocks were organized into a frequency distribution, and the following frequency polygon was drawn. Three averages (mean, median, and mode) were computed. One of the three was 10.2, another 10.8, and the other 11.1.

    a. Which price-earnings ratio is the median? What does this indicate?

    b. Which price-earnings ratio is the mode? Interpret.

    c. Which price-earnings ratio is the mean?

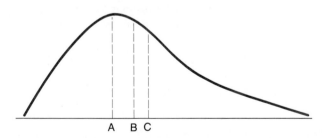

36. Idaho Trout Farm, Inc. raises trout commercially. Management is concerned about the length and weight of the trout and continually samples the ponds. A sample from pond 42 revealed that the modal length is 12.0 inches and the mean 12.9 inches.

    a. What is the approximate median length?

    b. Draw a picture of the distribution, and identify each of the averages.

37. The Special Education department at Coldstream University administered a test to disadvantaged children. The modal score was 72.0 and the median 78.0.

    a. What is the approximate mean score?

    b. Sketch the distribution, and identify each of the averages.

# CHAPTER OUTLINE

I. An average is a single value used to represent a set of data.
   A.   There are many types of averages, such as the mean, median, mode, and geometric mean.
   B.   The mean is the average reported most often.
II. To compute the arithmetic mean the values are summed, and the sum is divided by the total number of observations. For a sample, the sample mean is found by

$$\bar{X} = \frac{\Sigma X}{n} \tag{3-1}$$

For a population, the population mean is found by

$$\mu = \frac{\Sigma X}{N} \tag{3-2}$$

For the arithmetic mean:
   A.   The interval scale of measurement is required.
   B.   All the values are used in the calculation.
   C.   A set of data has only one mean.
   D.   The sum of the deviations from the mean is zero.

$$\Sigma(X - \bar{X}) = 0 \tag{3-3}$$

For data grouped into a frequency distribution, the formula is

$$\bar{X} = \frac{\Sigma fX}{n} \tag{3-8}$$

III. The weighted mean is found by multiplying each observation by its corresponding weight and dividing by the sum of the weights.

$$\bar{X}_w = \frac{w_1 X_1 + w_2 X_2 + w_3 X_3 + \cdots + w_n X_n}{w_1 + w_2 + w_3 + \cdots + w_n} \tag{3-4}$$

IV. The geometric mean is the $n$th root of the product of $n$ values.
   A.   To measure the average of a set of percentages,

$$\text{Geometric mean} = \sqrt[n]{(X_1)(X_2)(X_3) \cdots (X_n)} \tag{3-6}$$

   B.   To measure the average annual percent increase in business or economic data from one time period to another,

$$\text{Geometric mean} = \sqrt[n-1]{\frac{\text{Value at end of period}}{\text{Value at beginning of period}}} - 1 \tag{3-7}$$

V. The median is the middle value in a set of values ordered from smallest to largest. It can be located by

$$\frac{n + 1}{2} \tag{3-5}$$

   A.   To determine the median, the ordinal scale of measurement is required.
   B.   It is not influenced by extreme values.
   C.   Fifty percent of the observations are greater than the median.
   D.   It does not need to be one of the values in the data set.
   E.   It is unique for a set of data.

$$\text{Median} = L + \frac{\frac{n}{2} - CF}{f} \ (i)$$

(3–9)

VI. The mode is the value that occurs most often in a set of data.
  A.  The mode can be determined for nominal data.
  B.  A set of data can have more than one mode.
VII. Skewness is the lack of symmetry in a set of data.
  A.  If there is no skewness in the data, the mean, median, and mode are equal. Half of the values are above these values and half below them. Shown graphically:

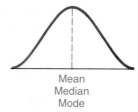

Mean
Median
Mode

  B.  If the long tail of the distribution is to the right, the set of values is positively skewed.
    1.  The mode is the value at the highest point of the distribution.
    2.  The mean is the largest of the three averages.

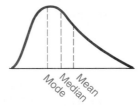

Mode Median Mean

  C.  If the long tail of the distribution is to the left, the set of values is negatively skewed.
    1.  The mode is the value at the highest point of the distribution.
    2.  The mean is the smallest of the three averages.

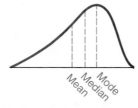

Mean Median Mode

# EXERCISES

*The answers to the odd-numbered exercises are at the end of the book.*

38.  The accounting firm of Crawford and Associates has five senior partners. Yesterday the senior partners saw six, four, three, seven, and five clients, respectively.
  a.  Compute the mean number and median number of clients seen by a partner.
  b.  Is the mean a sample mean or a population mean?
  c.  Verify that $\Sigma(X - \bar{X}) = 0$.
39.  Owens Orchards sells apples in a large bag by weight. A sample of seven bags contained the following numbers of apples: 23, 19, 26, 17, 21, 24, 22.
  a.  Compute the mean number and median number of apples in a bag.
  b.  Verify that $\Sigma(X - \bar{X}) = 0$.

40. A sample of households that subscribe to the United Bell Phone Company revealed the following numbers of calls received last week. Determine the mean and the median numbers of calls received.

| 52 | 43 | 30 | 38 | 30 | 42 | 12 | 46 | 39 | 37 |
|----|----|----|----|----|----|----|----|----|----|
| 34 | 46 | 32 | 18 | 41 | 5  |    |    |    |    |

41. The Citizens Banking Company is studying the number of times the automatic teller, located in a Loblaws Supermarket, is used per day. Following are the numbers of times the machine was used over each of the last 30 days. Determine the mean number of times the machine was used per day.

| 83 | 64 | 84 | 76 | 84 | 54 | 75 | 59 | 70 | 61 |
|----|----|----|----|----|----|----|----|----|----|
| 63 | 80 | 84 | 73 | 68 | 52 | 65 | 90 | 52 | 77 |
| 95 | 36 | 78 | 61 | 59 | 84 | 95 | 47 | 87 | 60 |

42. Following are the numbers of games won by the 26 major league baseball teams during the 1990 season.

| 95 | 91  | 85 | 77 | 77 | 70 | 91 | 86 | 85 |
|----|-----|----|----|----|----|----|----|----|
| 75 | 75  | 65 | 88 | 86 | 79 | 77 | 76 | 74 |
| 67 | 103 | 94 | 83 | 80 | 77 | 75 | 74 |    |

Determine the mean and median numbers of games won.

43. Repeated below are the salaries (in $000) of the players on the 1991 opening-day roster and the disabled list of the Cleveland Indians.

| 2,500 | 100 | 410 | 2,050 | 1,450 | 115 | 125   | 175 | 900   |
|-------|-----|-----|-------|-------|-----|-------|-----|-------|
| 2,025 | 345 | 550 | 100   | 165   | 800 | 100   | 575 | 1,750 |
| 1,150 | 110 | 102 | 100   | 155   | 100 | 1,368 | 100 | 750   |

Determine the mean salary and the median salary. Which average is more representative? Why? (Source: USA Today, April 5, 1991, p. C5.)

44. The numbers of Temban camcorders produced during eight-hour shifts for 50 shifts selected at random are:

| 348 | 371 | 360 | 369 | 376 | 397 | 368 | 361 | 374 |
|-----|-----|-----|-----|-----|-----|-----|-----|-----|
| 410 | 374 | 377 | 335 | 356 | 322 | 344 | 399 | 362 |
| 384 | 365 | 380 | 349 | 358 | 343 | 432 | 376 | 347 |
| 385 | 399 | 400 | 359 | 329 | 370 | 398 | 352 | 396 |
| 366 | 392 | 375 | 379 | 389 | 390 | 386 | 341 | 351 |
| 354 | 395 | 338 | 390 | 333 |     |     |     |     |

Determine the mean number of camcorders produced during an eight-hour shift.

45. In 1980 the average daily number of stocks traded on the New York Stock Exchange was 44,871. In 1989 the daily average increased to 165,470. Determine the geometric mean yearly rate of increase. (Source: New York Stock Exchange, Fact Book, 1990.)

46. The metropolitan area of Los Angeles–Long Beach, California, is the area expected to show the largest increase in the number of jobs between 1989 and 2010. The number of jobs is expected to increase from 5,164,900 to 6,286,800. What is the geometric mean expected yearly rate of increase?

47. Wells Fargo Mortgage and Equity Trust gave these occupancy rates in their annual report for various office income properties the company owns.

| Pleasant Hills, California | 100% |
|----------------------------|------|
| Lakewood, Colorado         | 90   |
| Riverside, California       | 80   |
| Scottsdale, Arizona         | 20   |
| San Antonio, Texas          | 62   |

What is the geometric mean occupancy rate?

48. Wells Fargo Mortgage and Equity Trust also reported these occupancy rates for some of its industrial income properties:

| | |
|---|---|
| Tucson, Arizona | 81% |
| Irvine, California | 100 |
| Carlsbad, California | 74 |
| Dallas, Texas | 80 |

What is the geometric mean occupancy rate?

49. The 12-month returns on five aggressive-growth mutual funds were 32.2 percent, 35.5 percent, 80.0 percent, 60.9 percent, and 92.1 percent. Determine the arithmetic mean and the geometric mean rates of return. (Source: *U.S. News & World Report,* April 22, 1991, p. 68.)

50. In 1970 the mean salary for a major league baseball player was $29,303. In 1991 the salary increased to $597,537. Determine the geometric mean yearly rate of increase. (Source: *USA Today,* April 5, 1991, p. C1.)

51. Mid South University has seven defensive linemen who weigh 240 pounds each, four who weigh 212 each, three who weigh 190 each, and one who tips the scales at 314. What is the weighted mean weight of the defensive linemen?

52. A Nashville, Tennessee, bottling company offers three kinds of delivery service—instant, same day, and within five days. The profit per delivery varies according to the kind of delivery. The profit for an instant delivery is less than that for the other kinds because the driver has to go directly to a grocery store with a small load and return to the bottling plant. To find out what effect, if any, each type of delivery has on the profit picture, the company has made the following tabulation based on deliveries for the previous quarter.

| Type of delivery | Number of deliveries during the quarter | Profit per delivery |
|---|---|---|
| Instant | 100 | $ 70 |
| Same day | 60 | 100 |
| Within five days | 40 | 160 |

a. What is the weighted mean profit per delivery?

b. Suppose the bottling company were able to eliminate instant orders through special promotions and careful planning. What would their profit per delivery be if all 100 grocery stores previously requesting instant delivery changed to same day delivery?

53. The Oriental Star, a steamship line, is studying various facets of the business, including the length of time required to load and unload a ship and the weight of containers. The number of containers and their weights loaded on a ship bound for Hong Kong are:

| Number of containers | Weight per container (pounds) |
|---|---|
| 60 | 1,000 |
| 40 | 3,000 |
| 20 | 6,000 |

a. Adding 1,000, 3,000, and 6,000 gives 10,000 pounds. Dividing 10,000 pounds by 3 is 3,333 pounds, the mean weight of a container. Is that the average weight of a container on the ship bound for Hong Kong? Explain.

b. Compute the weighted mean of the 120 containers. Explain why this weight is different from the 3,333 pounds computed in a.

54. An automatic machine that fills containers appears to be performing erratically. A check of the weights of the contents of a number of cans revealed:

| Weight (grams) | Number of cans |
|----------------|----------------|
| 130–139 | 2 |
| 140–149 | 8 |
| 150–159 | 20 |
| 160–169 | 15 |
| 170–179 | 9 |
| 180–189 | 7 |
| 190–199 | 3 |
| 200–209 | 2 |

a.    To the nearest tenth of a gram (such as 161.3), estimate the arithmetic mean weight of the contents of a can.

b.    To the nearest tenth of a gram, estimate the median weight of the contents of a can.

55.   The Department of Commerce, Bureau of the Census, reported that 515,600 unmarried women gave birth last year. The ages and numbers of unmarried mothers are presented in a frequency distribution:

| Age of mother | Number (in thousands) |
|---------------|-----------------------|
| Under 15 years | 10.1 |
| 15–19 years | 239.7 |
| 20–24 years | 168.6 |
| 25–29 years | 62.4 |
| 30–34 years | 23.7 |
| 35–39 years | 8.8 |
| 40 years and older | 2.3 |

Estimate the median age of the unmarried mothers. Interpret.

56.   The U.S. Department of Commerce in the *County and City Data Book* gave these household incomes for Alaska and Connecticut:

| Incomes | Percent of households | |
|---------|--------|-------------|
|         | Alaska | Connecticut |
| Less than $20,000 | 18.3 | 22.2 |
| $20,000–$29,999 | 21.2 | 27.6 |
| 30,000– 39,999 | 18.4 | 24.1 |
| 40,000– 49,999 | 15.1 | 13.1 |
| 50,000– 59,999 | 11.3 | 6.0 |
| 60,000 and greater | 15.7 | 7.0 |

For the distribution of incomes for Alaska:

a.    What is the median income? Interpret.

b.    What is the modal income? Interpret.

57.   Refer to Exercise 56. For the distribution of incomes for Connecticut:

a.    What is the median income? Interpret.

b.    What is the modal income? Interpret.

58.   The Department of Commerce, Bureau of the Census, reported on the number of income earners in American families:

| Number of earners | Number (in thousands) |
|-------------------|-----------------------|
| 0 | 7,083 |
| 1 | 18,621 |
| 2 | 22,414 |
| 3 | 5,533 |
| 4 or more | 2,797 |

a. What is the modal number of income earners in a typical American family? Explain what this indicates.

b. Would the mean or median number of earners be a representative average? Explain.

59. The Bureau of the Census, in *Current Population Reports,* series P-20, gave the ages of divorced males and females (in thousands of persons 18 years old and older):

| Age | Males | Females |
|-----|-------|---------|
| 18–19 | 5 | 9 |
| 20–24 | 80 | 210 |
| 25–29 | 174 | 303 |
| 30–34 | 210 | 315 |
| 35–44 | 385 | 656 |
| 45–54 | 450 | 656 |
| 55–64 | 295 | 409 |
| 65–74 | 174 | 200 |
| 75 and older | 56 | 69 |

a. Estimate the median age of divorced males. Interpret.

b. Estimate the median age of divorced females. Interpret.

c. Estimate the modal age for the males. Do the same for the females.

60. Questions a through h refer to the following measures of central tendency and the shapes of a distribution.

| Measure of central tendency | Shape of distribution |
|-----------------------------|-----------------------|
| Arithmetic mean | Symmetrical |
| Median | Positively skewed |
| Mode | Negatively skewed |
| Geometric mean | |

a. Which measure of central tendency is defined as the value of the item that appears most frequently?

b. Which measure of central tendency is affected the most by extremely small or extremely large values?

c. Which measure must be used to determine the average annual percent increase in sales, for example, from 1962 to 1992?

d. How is the shape of a frequency distribution described if the three measures of central tendency are equal?

e. How is the shape of a frequency distribution described if the mean is the largest of the three measures of central tendency?

f. Which measure of central tendency is determined by summing all of the values and dividing the sum by the number of values?

g. Which measure of central tendency is defined as the point above which half of the values lie and below which the other half lie?

h. In a negatively skewed frequency distribution, which measure of central tendency is the largest?

61. An auctioneer specializes in used cars that are about 10 years old. The selling prices of a large number of automobiles were grouped into a frequency distribution, and a smoothed frequency polygon was drawn.

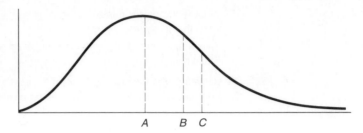

The average represented by the letter *A* was computed to be $3,000 and the average represented by *B* $3,220.

a. Approximate the average represented by the letter *C*.

b. What is the average in part a called, and why is it larger than the other two averages?

c. What is the modal price?

d. Is the distribution of the prices symmetrical, positively skewed, or negatively skewed? Cite evidence.

62. Each employee is given a production rating that represents her/his efficiency on the job. The ratings were organized into a frequency distribution and then portrayed in the form of a less-than cumulative frequency polygon. Based on the chart, what is the approximate median rating?

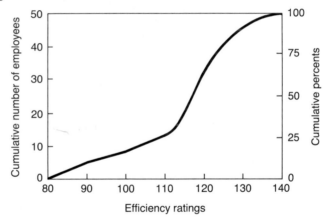

63. Motor vehicle registration in Canada increased from 22,000 in 1911 to an estimated 17,000,000 in 1991. What was the geometric mean annual percent increase in vehicle registration from 1911 to 1991? (Source: *Canadian Almanac & Directory,* 1991, p. 6–82.)

64. Canadian fisheries production figures for 1941 and 1989 were:

| Year | Production |
|------|------------|
| 1941 | $   62,259,000 |
| 1989 | 3,013,090,000 |

Source: *Canadian Almanac & Directory,* 1991, p. 6–81.

What was the geometric mean annual percent increase in fisheries production from 1941 to 1989?

65. Cunard's Queen Elizabeth 2 takes a world cruise every year. The 1992 cruise is a 100-day cruise starting on January 6, 1992, from Ft. Lauderdale, Florida. It goes to South America, Australia, Hong Kong, Tokyo, Mombasa, Haifa, and other places.

Courtesy Cunard

a.  The price for an outside luxury double room with a veranda on the signal deck is $126,900 per person. This price is up from $88,300 per person in 1986. What is the geometric mean annual rate of increase in the cruise price from 1986 to 1992?

b.  You could join the QE 2 in Sidney and take a 22-day partial cruise disembarking in Hong Kong. The ship stops at such places as Perth, Bali, Kota Kinabalu, Tokyo, and Taipei. The price per person for an outside room on the Mauretania deck is $8,910. This is up from $6,240 in 1986. What is the geometric mean annual rate of increase in price from 1986 to 1992? (Source: Cunard, *World Cruises and Winter Vacations,* 1992, pp. 53–54.)

66. The Sagafjord, a Cunard cruise-line ship, offers a full world cruise of 107 days starting January 6, 1992, from Ft. Lauderdale, Florida. It stops at such places as Lima, Punta Arenas, Rio, Zanzibar, Madras, Kuala Lumpur, and Bangkok.

a.  A luxury suite on the officers deck costs $119,900. In 1984 such a suite cost only $78,200. What is the geometric mean annual rate of increase from 1984 to 1992?

b.  If you want to take only a 46-day segment from Ft. Lauderdale to Mombasa in Africa, an outside cabin on the main deck is $16,660 per person. The corresponding 1984 price was $11,160. What is the geometric mean annual rate of increase from 1984 to 1992? What is the arithmetic mean daily cost per person in 1992 for this 46-day trip? (Source: *World Cruises and Winter Vacations,* 1992, pp. 65–66.)

## COMPUTER DATA EXERCISES

67. Refer to data set 1, which reports information on homes sold in Florida during 1990.

a.  Determine the mean and the median selling prices of the 75 homes. Is one a better measure of central tendency than the other?

b.  How many bedrooms does the typical home have?

c.  How many bathrooms does a typical home have? What is the modal number of bathrooms?

d.  How many miles is the typical home from the center of the city?

68. Refer to data set 2, which reports information on 200 corporations in the United States.

a.  Determine the mean and the median sales for the selected companies.

b.  Determine the mean and median profits for the selected companies.

69. Refer to data set 3, which reports information on the 26 major league baseball teams for the 1991 season.
    a.   Determine the mean and the median salaries for the 26 teams.
    b.   What is the "typical" team paying in total salary?
    c.   Determine the mean and the median attendance figures for the 26 teams.
    d.   What is the typical attendance?

# CHAPTER 3   EXAMINATION

*The answers are at the end of the chapter.*

For Questions 1 through 10, fill in the blank with the correct answer.

1. The _____ is found by arranging the data from low to high and selecting the middle value.
2. The _____ cannot be computed if the frequency distribution has an open-ended class.
3. The _____ cannot be computed if one of the values is 0.
4. If the mean is larger than the median, the distribution is _____ skewed.
5. If the mean, median, and mode are all equal, the distribution is _____.
6. If the mean is smaller than the median, the distribution is _____ skewed.
7. The _____ is not recommended if one extremely large value is found in the data set.
8. The _____ is found by adding all the values and dividing by the number of observations.
9. If the deviations from the mean are totaled, the result is always _____.
10. The value that occurs most often in a set of data is called the _____.
11. A sample of five employees from Pelton Tool and Die, Inc. revealed the following lengths of service, in years: 13, 22, 27, 24, 19.
    a.   Compute the mean length of service.
    b.   Determine the median length of service.
12. A sample of 50 antique dealers in the southeast United States revealed the following sales last year:

| Sales ($000) | Number of firms |
|---|---|
| 100.0–119.0 | 5 |
| 120.0–139.0 | 7 |
| 140.0–159.0 | 9 |
| 160.0–179.0 | 16 |
| 180.0–199.0 | 10 |
| 200.0–219.0 | 3 |

    a.   Estimate the mean sales.
    b.   Estimate the median sales.
    c.   What is the modal sales amount?
13. The mean of a frequency distribution is 230, and the mode is 200. Estimate the median.

3-1  1.  a.  $\bar{X} = \dfrac{\Sigma X}{n}$

b.  $= \dfrac{\$187,100}{4}$

$= \$46,775$

$= \$46,800$ rounded

c.  Statistic, because it is a sample value.
d.  $46,800. The sample mean is our best estimate of the population mean.

2.  a.  $\mu = \dfrac{\Sigma X}{N}$

b.  $\mu = \dfrac{498}{6} = 83$

c.  Parameter, because it was computed using all the population values.

3-2  a.  $237, found by:

$$\frac{(95 \times \$400) + (126 \times \$200) + (79 \times \$100)}{95 + 126 + 79}$$

$$= \frac{\$71,100}{300} = \$237$$

b.  The profit per suit is $12, found by $237 − $200 cost − $25 commission. The total profit for the 300 suits is $3,600, found by $300 × $12.

3-3  1.  a.  $439.
         b.  3, 3.
     2.  a.  7, found by $(6 + 8)/2 = 7$.
         b.  3, 3.

3-4  1.  a.  About 8.39 percent.
         b.  About 10.1 percent.
         c.  Yes, $10.1 > 8.39$.
     2.  About 8.63 percent.

3-5  a.  Frequency distribution.
     b.  $9.15 million, found by:

| f | X | fX |
|---|---|---|
| 1 | $ 3 | $ 3 |
| 4 | 6 | 24 |
| 10 | 9 | 90 |
| 3 | 12 | 36 |
| 2 | 15 | 30 |
| 20 | | $183 |

$\bar{X} = \dfrac{\Sigma fX}{n} = \dfrac{\$183}{20} = \$9.15$

3-6  1.  105.0 transceivers.

| True class limits | f | CF |
|---|---|---|
| 79.5– 89.5 | 5 | 5 |
| 89.5– 99.5 | 9 | 14 |
| 99.5–109.5 | 20 | 34 |
| 109.5–119.5 | 8 | 42 |
| 119.5–129.5 | 6 | 48 |
| 129.5–139.5 | 2 | 50 |

$n/2 = 50/2 = 25$. The 25th transceiver is in the 99.5–109.5 class.

$$99.5 + 11/20\,(10) = 105.0$$

or

$$99.5 + \frac{\dfrac{50}{2} - 14}{20}(10) = 105.0$$

2.  $8.225 million.

| True class limits ($ millions) | Cumulative percent |
|---|---|
| 0.5– 3.5 | 13 |
| 3.5– 6.5 | 27 |
| 6.5– 9.5 | 67 |
| 9.5–12.5 | 90 |
| 12.5 and greater | 100 |

$$n/2 = 100/2 = 50$$

Median is in the 6.5 to 9.5 class.

$$\$6.5 + \frac{50\% - 27\%}{40\%}\,(\$3)$$

$$= \$6.5 + \frac{23\%}{40\%} \times \$3$$

$$= \$8.225 \text{ or } \$8,225,000$$

3–7   a.

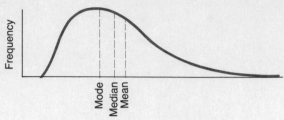

Weekly sales ($000)

b.   Positively skewed, because the mean is the largest average and the mode is the smallest.

## Answers

# CHAPTER 3 EXAMINATION

1.   Median.
2.   Mean.
3.   Geometric mean.
4.   Positively.
5.   Symmetric.
6.   Negatively.
7.   Mean.
8.   Mean.
9.   Zero.
10.  Mode.

11.  a.   21 years, found by 105/5.
     b.   22 years, found by arranging the lengths of service from low to high and selecting the middle observation.
12.  a.   $160,700, found by $8,035,000/50.
     b.   $164,500, found by $159.5 + 4/16($20) (in $000).
     c.   $169,500, which is the midpoint of the class with the largest number of frequencies.
13.  About 220, found by [2(mean) + mode]/3.

Automotive—Courtesy The Goodyear Tire and Rubber Company

CHAPTER

4

# MEASURES OF DISPERSION AND SKEWNESS

When you have completed this chapter, you will be able to:

GOALS

1. Compute various measures of dispersion for raw data.
2. Compute various measures of dispersion for data organized in a frequency distribution.
3. Explain the characteristics, uses, advantages, and disadvantages of each measure of dispersion presented.
4. Explain Chebyshev's theorem and the Empirical, or Normal, Rule.
5. Compute and explain the uses of the coefficient of variation and the coefficient of skewness.

C hapter 2 began our study of descriptive statistics. We organized a mass of raw data into a table called a frequency distribution and then portrayed the distribution graphically in a histogram, a frequency polygon, and a cumulative frequency polygon to further describe the shape and other important characteristics of the data. In Chapter 3 several averages were computed to describe a typical value near the center of the observations.

We will now examine several measures that describe the *dispersion, variability,* or *spread* of the data. Discussed in this chapter are the *range, average deviation, variance, standard deviation, interquartile range, quartile deviation,* and *percentile range.*

## WHY STUDY DISPERSION?

**Measure of central tendency is representative if data clustered close to it**

There are several reasons for analyzing the dispersion in a set of data. First, by applying a measure of dispersion, we can evaluate the measure of central tendency being used. A small value for a measure of dispersion indicates that the data are clustered closely, say, around the arithmetic mean. The mean is therefore considered quite representative of the data. That is, the mean is a reliable average. Conversely, a large measure of dispersion indicates that the mean is not very reliable— that is, it is not very representative of the data. Such is the case in Chart 4–1. Note that the ages of the employees range from 18 to 85. This large spread results in an average (50) that is not very meaningful.

---

**CHART 4–1**

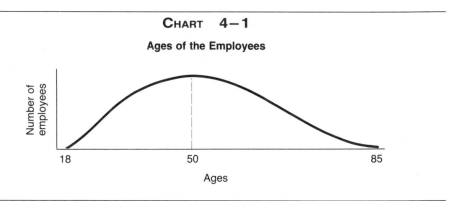

**Ages of the Employees**

**Average unrepresentative because of large spread**

---

Photo courtesy of Hewlett-Packard Company

A second reason for studying the dispersion in a set of data is to compare the spread in two or more distributions. Suppose, for example, that the new PDM/3 computer is assembled in Baton Rouge and also in Tucson. The arithmetic mean daily output in the Baton Rouge plant is 50, and in the Tucson plant the mean output is also 50. Based on the two means, one might conclude that the distributions of the daily outputs are identical. Production records for nine days at the two plants, however, reveal that this conclusion is not correct. (See Chart 4–2.) Baton Rouge production varies from 48 to 52 assemblies a day. Production at the Tucson plant is more erratic, ranging from 40 to 60 assemblies a day.

A measure of dispersion can be used to evaluate the reliability of two or more averages

## CHART 4–2

**Daily Production of Computers at the Baton Rouge and Tucson Plants**

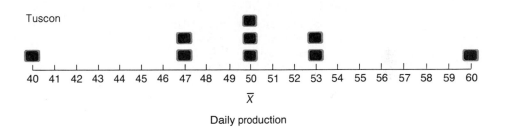

Daily production

# MEASURES OF DISPERSION—UNGROUPED DATA

## RANGE

The simplest measure of dispersion is the **range.** It is the difference between the highest and lowest values in a set of data. In the form of an equation:

Definition of range

$$\boxed{\text{Range} = \text{Highest value} - \text{Lowest value}} \qquad (4-1)$$

The range is widely used in statistical process control (SPC) applications. It is easy to calculate and to understand. For these applications see Chapter 21.

### ■ EXAMPLE

The capacities of several metal containers are 38, 20, 37, 64, and 27 liters, respectively. What is the range?

### ☑ SOLUTION

Range of ungrouped data

The range is 44 liters, found by 64 − 20.

Returning to the example of daily production of computers in Chart 4−2, note that the range of the production in the Baton Rouge plant is 4, found by 52 − 48. The range of the daily production in the Tucson plant is 20 computers (60 − 40). It can be concluded, therefore, that (1) there is less dispersion in the daily production in the Baton Rouge plant than in the Tucson plant because the range of 4 computers is less than the range of 20 computers, and (2) the production in the Baton Rouge plant is clustered more closely about the mean of 50 than is the production in the Tucson plant (because the range of 4 is less than the range of 20). Thus, the mean production in the Baton Rouge plant (50 computers) is a more representative average than the mean of 50 computers for the Tucson plant.

## Self-Review 4–1

*The answers are at the end of the chapter.*

The annual travel costs for executives and middle management at Trion Chemicals were organized into frequency distributions and portrayed in frequency polygons.

1. What is the approximate arithmetic mean travel cost for executives? For middle management?

2. What is the range for the executives? For middle management?

3. Compare the dispersion for the two distributions, and explain what it indicates.

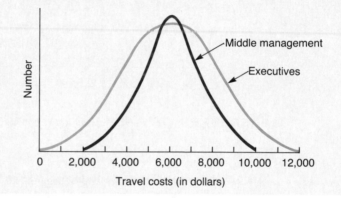

## AVERAGE DEVIATION

Average deviation: Mean of the deviations from the mean

A serious defect of the range is that it is based only on two values, the highest and the lowest; it does not take into consideration all of the values. The **average deviation** does. Often referred to as the *mean deviation,* it measures the average amount by which the values in a population, or sample, vary from their mean. In terms of a definition:

Average deviation or mean deviation

> Average deviation   The arithmetic mean of the absolute values of the deviations from the arithmetic mean.

In terms of a formula, the average deviation, designated A.D., is computed for a sample by:

$$\text{A.D.} = \frac{\Sigma|X - \bar{X}|}{n}$$

(4–2)

where:

$X$   is the value of each observation.

$\overline{X}$   is the arithmetic mean of the values.

$n$   is the number of observations in the sample.

‖   indicates the absolute value. In other words, the signs of the deviations from the mean are disregarded.

Why do we ignore the signs of the deviations from the mean? If we didn't, the positive and negative deviations from the mean would exactly offset each other, and the average deviation would always be zero. Such a measure (zero) would be a useless statistic. Because we use absolute deviations, the mean deviation is often called the *mean absolute deviation (MAD).*

**Mean absolute deviation (MAD)**

### ▮ EXAMPLE

The weights of a sample of crates ready for shipment to France are (in kilograms): 103, 97, 101, 106, and 103.

1. What is the mean deviation?
2. How is it interpreted?

### ☑ SOLUTION

The arithmetic mean weight is 102 kg, found by $(103 + 97 + 101 + 106 + 103)/5$.

1. To find the average deviation:
   a. The mean is subtracted from each value.
   b. The absolute deviations are summed.
   c. The sum of the absolute deviations is divided by the number of values.

| Weights (in kg.) $X$ | $X - \overline{X}$ | | Absolute deviation | $\text{A.D.} = \dfrac{\Sigma\lvert X - \overline{X}\rvert}{n}$ |
|---|---|---|---|---|
| 103 | $\lvert +1 \rvert$ | = | 1 | |
| 97 | $\lvert -5 \rvert$ | = | 5 | $= \dfrac{12}{5}$ |
| 101 | $\lvert -1 \rvert$ | = | 1 | |
| 106 | $\lvert +4 \rvert$ | = | 4 | |
| 103 | $\lvert +1 \rvert$ | = | 1 | $= 2.4$ kg |
| | | | 12 | |

The average deviation of the sample is 2.4 kilograms.

2. Interpretation: The weights of the crates deviate, on the average, 2.4 kilograms from the arithmetic mean weight of 102 kilograms.

**Advantages of average deviation**

**Disadvantage of average deviation**

   The average deviation does have two advantages. It uses the value of every item in a set of data in its computation, and it is easy to understand—it is the average amount by which the values deviate from the mean. However, absolute values are difficult to work with, so the average deviation is not frequently used.

### Self-Review 4–2

*The answers are at the end of the chapter.*

The weights of a group of crates being shipped to Ireland are (in kilograms): 95, 103, 105, 110, 104, 105, 112, and 90.

1. Compute the average deviation.
2. Interpret your findings.

3. Compare the dispersion in the weights of the shipments going to France with the dispersion in the weights of shipments to Ireland.

## A Computer Application

If there are a large number of observations, the MINITAB system can be applied to reduce computational time and ensure better accuracy. The weights from the preceding example are used to show the procedure.

```
MTB > set c1
DATA > 103, 97, 101, 106, 103
DATA > end
MTB > mean c1
   MEAN      =        102.00
MTB > let c2=c1 - 102
MTB > absolute c2 c3
MTB > mean c3
   MEAN      =        2.4000
```

## Exercises

*The answers to the odd-numbered exercises are at the end of the book.*

1.  There were five customer service representatives on duty at the Electronic Super Store during last Friday's sale. The respective numbers of VCRs these representatives sold during the first four hours of the sale are: 5, 8, 4, 10, and 3.
    a.  What is the range?
    b.  What is the arithmetic mean?
    c.  What is the average deviation?
    d.  Interpret the range.
2.  The Department of Statistics at Western State University offers eight sections of basic statistics. Following are the numbers of students enrolled in these sections: 34, 46, 52, 29, 41, 38, 36, and 28.
    a.  What is the range?
    b.  What is the arithmetic mean number of students enrolled in a section?
    c.  What is the average deviation?
    d.  Interpret the range.
3.  Dave's Automatic Door installs automatic garage door openers. The following list indicates the number of minutes needed to install a sample of 10 doors: 28, 32, 24, 46, 44, 40, 54, 38, 32, and 42.
    a.  What is the range?
    b.  What is the arithmetic mean?
    c.  What is the average deviation?
    d.  Interpret the average deviation.

4.  A sample of eight companies in the aerospace industry were surveyed as to their return on investment last year. The results are (in percent): 10.6, 12.6, 14.8, 18.2, 12.0, 14.8, 12.2, and 15.6.

    a.  What is the range?
    b.  What is the arithmetic mean return on investment?
    c.  What is the average deviation?
    d.  Interpret the average deviation.

5.  Ten experts rated a newly developed pizza on a scale of 1 to 50. The ratings were: 34, 35, 41, 28, 26, 29, 32, 36, 38, and 40.

    a.  What is the range?
    b.  What is the arithmetic mean rating?
    c.  What is the average deviation? Interpret.
    d.  A second group of experts rated the same pizza. The range was 8, the mean 33.9, and the average deviation 1.9. Compare the dispersion in these ratings with that of the first group of experts.

6.  A sample of the personnel files of eight male employees employed by Acme Carpet revealed that, during a six-month period, they lost the following numbers of days due to illness: 2, 0, 6, 3, 10, 4, 1, and 2.

    a.  What is the range?
    b.  What is the arithmetic mean number of days lost?
    c.  What is the average deviation? Interpret.
    d.  A sample of the personnel files of female employees revealed that they lost 3.48 days on the average during the same six-month period due to illness. The range was computed to be 10 and the average deviation 2.381. Compare the two groups.

## VARIANCE AND STANDARD DEVIATION

*Variance and standard deviation based on squared deviations*

The **variance** and the **standard deviation** are also based on the deviations from the mean.

| |
|---|
| Variance   The arithmetic mean of the squared deviations from the mean. |

| |
|---|
| Standard deviation   The square root of the variance. |

Note in the definition of variance that the deviations from the mean are squared. The signs of the deviations ($+$ or $-$) are not ignored as they were for the average deviation. Squaring the deviations from the mean eliminates the chance of having negative numbers because multiplying two negative numbers gives a positive number.

### POPULATION VARIANCE

The formulas for the *population variance* and the *sample variance* are slightly different. The population variance is considered first. (Recall that a population is the totality of all observations being studied.) The **population variance** is found by:

$$\sigma^2 = \frac{\Sigma(X - \mu)^2}{N} \qquad (4-3)$$

where:

$\sigma^2$   is the symbol for the population variance ($\sigma$ is the lower-case Greek letter sigma).

$X$   is the value of the observation in the population.

$\mu$   is the mean of the population.

$N$   is the total number of observations in the population.

## ◼ EXAMPLE

The ages of all the patients in the isolation ward of Yellowstone Hospital are 38, 26, 13, 41, and 22 years. What is the population variance?

## ☑ SOLUTION

| Ages (X) | $X - \mu$ | $(X - \mu)^2$ |
|---|---|---|
| 38 | +10 | 100 |
| 26 | − 2 | 4 |
| 13 | −15 | 225 |
| 41 | +13 | 169 |
| 22 | − 6 | 36 |
| 140 | 0* | 534 |

$$\mu = \frac{\Sigma X}{N} = \frac{140}{5} = 28$$

$$\sigma^2 = \frac{\Sigma (X - \mu)^2}{N}$$

$$= \frac{534}{5}$$

$$= 106.8$$

*Sum of the deviations from mean must equal zero.

The preceding approach for determining the population variance was used mainly to show that the variance is based on the *squared deviations from the population mean.* The mean is a whole number, and the computations for this small population of ages were relatively easy. Usually, however, the population is large, and the mean is not a whole number. For these problems a more efficient formula can be used. Note that the following formula is not based on deviations from the mean, but rather on the actual values, thus eliminating a large number of subtractions.

$$\sigma^2 = \frac{\Sigma X^2}{N} - \left(\frac{\Sigma X}{N}\right)^2 \qquad (4-4)$$

Applying the formula to the previous problem:

$$\sigma^2 = \frac{(38)^2 + (26)^2 + (13)^2 + (41)^2 + (22)^2}{5} - \left(\frac{38 + 26 + 13 + 41 + 22}{5}\right)^2$$

$$= \frac{4,454}{5} - \left(\frac{140}{5}\right)^2$$

$$= 106.8 \text{ (which is the same answer as before)}$$

Like the range and the average deviation, the variance can be used to compare the dispersion in two or more sets of observations. For example, the variance for the ages of the patients in isolation was just computed to be 106.8. If the variance in the ages of all the cancer patients in the hospital is 342.9, it can be said: (1) There is less dispersion in the distribution of the ages of patients in isolation than in the age distribution of all cancer patients (because 106.8 is less than 342.9). (2) The ages of the patients in isolation are clustered more closely about the mean of 28 years than are the ages of those in the cancer ward. Thus, the mean age for the patients in isolation is a more representative average compared to the mean for all cancer patients.

### POPULATION STANDARD DEVIATION

*Variance: Difficult to interpret*

Both the range and the average deviation are easy to interpret. The range is the difference between the high and low values of a set of data, and the average deviation is the mean of the deviations from the mean. However, the variance is difficult to interpret for a single set of observations. The variance of 106.8 for the ages of the patients in isolation is not in terms of years, but rather "years squared."

*Standard deviation in same units as data*

There is a way out of this dilemma. By taking the square root of the population variance, we can transform it to the same unit of measurement used for the original data. The square root of 106.8 is 10.3 years. The square root of the population variance is called the **population standard deviation.** In terms of a formula:

$$\sigma = \sqrt{\frac{\Sigma(X - \mu)^2}{N}} \quad \text{or} \quad \sigma = \sqrt{\frac{\Sigma X^2}{N} - \left(\frac{\Sigma X}{N}\right)^2} \tag{4-5}$$

### Self-Review 4-3

*The answers are at the end of the chapter.*

A population consists of the weights of all defensive tackles on St. Norbet's football team. They are: Johnson, 204 pounds; Patrick, 215 pounds; Juniors, 207 pounds; Kendron, 212 pounds, Nicko, 214 pounds; and Cochran, 208 pounds.

1. What is the population variance?
2. What is the population standard deviation?

## EXERCISES

*The answers to the odd-numbered exercises are at the end of the book.*

7. Consider these five values a population: 8, 3, 7, 3, and 4.
   a. Compute the variance by squaring the individual deviations from the mean. (See formula 4-3.)
   b. Determine the variance by squaring the individual values as in formula 4-4.
8. These values are a population: 12, 6, 10, 4, 8, and 16.
   a. Determine the variance by squaring the individual deviations from the mean.
   b. Determine the variance by squaring each individual value as in formula 4-4.
9. The annual report of Dennis Industries cited these primary earnings per common share for the past five years: $2.68, $1.03, $2.26, $4.30, and $3.58. Considering these as population values, what is:
   a. The arithmetic mean primary earnings per comon share?
   b. The variance?

10. Referring to Exercise 9, the annual report of Dennis Industries also gave these returns on stockholder equity for the same five-year period (in percent): 13.2, 5.0, 10.2, 17.5, and 12.9.

   a. What is the arithmetic mean return?

   b. What is the variance?

11. Plywood, Inc. reported these returns on stockholder equity for the past five years: 4.3, 4.9, 7.2, 6.7, and 11.6. Consider these as population values.

   a. Compute the range, the arithmetic mean, the variance, and the standard deviation.

   b. Compare the return on stockholder equity for Plywood, Inc. with that for Dennis Industries cited in Exercise 10.

12. The annual incomes of the five vice presidents of TMV industries are: $75,000, $78,000, $72,000, $83,000, and $90,000. (Consider this a population.)

   a. What is the range?

   b. What is the arithmetic mean income?

   c. What is the population variance? The standard deviation?

   d. The annual incomes of another firm similar to TMV Industries were also studied. $\mu = \$79,900$, and $\sigma = \$8,612$. Compare the means and dispersions in the two firms.

## SAMPLE VARIANCE

Sample variance used as an estimator of population variance

The formula for the population mean given in Chapter 3 is $\mu = \Sigma X/N$. We just changed symbols for the sample mean, that is, $\bar{X} = \Sigma X/n$. Unfortunately, the conversion from the population variance to the sample variance is not quite that direct. It requires a slight change in the denominator. Instead of substituting $n$ (number in the sample) for $N$ (number in the population), the denominator is $n - 1$. Thus, the formula for the **sample variance** used as an estimator of the population variance is:

Sample variance— ungrouped data

$$s^2 = \frac{\Sigma(X - \bar{X})^2}{n - 1} \qquad (4-6)$$

where:

   $s^2$  is the symbol used to represent the sample variance.

   $X$   is the value of the observations in the sample.

   $\bar{X}$   is the mean of the sample.

   $n$   is the total number of observations in the sample.

Converting the more direct formula for the population variance $\sigma^2$ to the sample variance $s^2$, we have

$$s^2 = \frac{\Sigma X^2 - \dfrac{(\Sigma X)^2}{n}}{n - 1} \qquad (4-7)$$

Why is this seemingly insignificant change made in the denominator? It can be proven that, had the sample variance been computed using just $n$ in the denominator, the result would *underestimate* the population variance.[1] That is, the sample variance would be a *biased* estimator of the population variance. This is especially true when the sample size is small. Using $n - 1$ compensates for this underestimation. Thus, the sample variance $s^2$ is considered an *unbiased estimator of the population variance.*[2]

Sample variance—an unbiased estimator

## ■ EXAMPLE

The hourly wages for a sample of part-time employees at Fruit Packers, Inc. are: $2, $10, $6, $8, and $9. What is the sample variance?

## ☑ SOLUTION

Using squared deviations from the mean:     Using the more direct formula:

$$\bar{X} = \frac{\Sigma X}{n} = \frac{\$35}{5} = \$7$$

| Hourly wage (X) | $X - \bar{X}$ | $(X - \bar{X})^2$ |
|---|---|---|
| $ 2 | −$5 | 25 |
| 10 | 3 | 9 |
| 6 | − 1 | 1 |
| 8 | 1 | 1 |
| 9 | 2 | 4 |
| $35 | 0 | 40 |

$$s^2 = \frac{\Sigma(X - \bar{X})^2}{n - 1}$$

$$= \frac{40}{5 - 1}$$

$$= 10$$

Variance of ungrouped data

| Hourly wage (X) | $X^2$ |
|---|---|
| $ 2 | 4 |
| 10 | 100 |
| 6 | 36 |
| 8 | 64 |
| 9 | 81 |
| $35 | 285 |

$$s^2 = \frac{\Sigma X^2 - \frac{(\Sigma X)^2}{n}}{n - 1}$$

$$= \frac{285 - \frac{(35)^2}{5}}{5 - 1}$$

$$= \frac{40}{5 - 1}$$

$$= 10$$

### Self-Review 4–4

*The answers are at the end of the chapter.*

The weights of the contents of several small aspirin bottles are (in grams): 4, 2, 5, 4, 5, 2, and 6. What is the sample variance?

---

[1]To state it another way, the formula for the sample variance should be

$$\frac{\Sigma(X - \mu)^2}{n}$$

However, $\bar{X}$ is used to estimate $\mu$. Thus, the sum in the numerator is too small. Dividing by $n - 1$ instead of $n$ compensates for the underestimation in the numerator.

[2]If the sample variance has been computed using just $n$ in the denominator, it can be converted to the unbiased estimator $s^2$ by:

$$s^2 = \frac{n}{n - 1}(\hat{s}^2)$$

where $\hat{s}^2$ is the sample variance computed using just $n$.

### SAMPLE STANDARD DEVIATION

The sample standard deviation is used as an estimator of the population standard deviation. As noted previously, the population standard deviation is the square root of the population variance. Likewise, the *sample standard deviation is the square root of the sample variance.* The sample standard deviation is found by:

**Formulas for the sample standard deviation**

$$s = \sqrt{\frac{\Sigma(X - \overline{X})^2}{n - 1}} \qquad\qquad (4\text{--}8)$$

or, using the more direct formula given in formula (4–9):

$$s = \sqrt{\frac{\Sigma X^2 - \dfrac{(\Sigma X)^2}{n}}{n - 1}} \qquad\qquad (4\text{--}9)$$

### ■ EXAMPLE

The sample variance in the previous example involving hourly wages was computed to be 10. What is the sample standard deviation?

### ☑ SOLUTION

The sample standard deviation is $3.16, found by $\sqrt{10}$. Note again that the sample variance is in terms of dollars squared, but taking the square root of 10 gives us $3.16, which is in the same units (dollars) as the original data.

---

### Self-Review 4–5

*The answers are at the end of the chapter.*

Refer to Self-Review 4–4.

1. What is the sample standard deviation?

2. Is the standard deviation in the same unit of measurement as the original problem?

---

## EXERCISES

*The answers to the odd-numbered exercises are at the end of the book.*

13. Consider these values a sample: 7, 2, 6, 2, and 3.
    a. Compute the sample standard deviation by squaring the individual deviations from the mean. [See formula (4–8).]
    b. Compute the variance by squaring the original values. [See formula (4–7).]
14. The following five values are a sample: 11, 6, 10, 6, and 7.
    a. Compute the sample standard deviation by squaring the deviations from the mean.
    b. Compute the sample standard deviation by the more direct formula [formula (4–9)].
15. Dave's Automatic Door, referred to in Exercise 3, installs automatic garage door openers. Based on a sample, following are the times, in minutes, required to install 10 doors: 28, 32, 24, 46, 44, 40, 54, 38, 32, and 42.
    a. Compute the sample variance by squaring the deviations from the mean.

b. Compute the sample variance by using the more direct computational formula.

c. Determine the standard deviation.

16. The sample of eight companies in the aerospace industry, referred to in Exercise 4, were surveyed as to their return on investment last year. The results are: 10.6, 12.6, 14.8, 18.2, 12.0, 14.8, 12.2, and 15.6.

a. Compute the sample variance by squaring the deviations from the mean.

b. Compute the variance by using the more direct computational formula.

c. Determine the standard deviation.

17. Trout, Inc. feeds fingerling trout in special ponds and markets them when they attain a certain weight. A sample of 10 trout were isolated in a pond and fed a special food mixture designated RT-10. At the end of the experimental period, the weights of the trout were (in grams): 124, 125, 125, 123, 120, 124, 127, 125, 126, and 121.

a. What is the range?

b. What is the arithmetic mean of the sample?

c. Compute the sample variance.

d. Compute the standard deviation of the sample.

18. Refer to Exercise 17. Another special mixture, AB-4, was used in another pond. The mean of a sample was computed to be 126.9 grams and the standard deviation 1.2 grams. Which food results in a more uniform weight?

# MEASURES OF DISPERSION FOR DATA GROUPED INTO A FREQUENCY DISTRIBUTION

## RANGE

Range from grouped data

Recall that the range is defined as the difference between the highest and lowest values. To estimate the range from data already grouped into a frequency distribution, subtract the lowest stated limit of the smallest class from the highest stated limit of the largest class. For example, suppose a sample of 40 hourly wages were grouped into this frequency distribution:

| Hourly earnings | Number |
|---|---|
| $ 6–$ 9 | 10 |
| 10– 13 | 21 |
| 14– 17 | 9 |

The range is $11, found by $17 − $6.

Some prefer to use the true class limits. In this case, the range would be $12, found by $17.50 − $5.50.

## Self-Review 4–6

*The answers are at the end of the chapter.*

Consumers reported on the number of miles the Bridgeport XCB tire traveled before it became bald. The mileages were tallied into the following distribution. What is the range in mileage?

| Mileage | Number of tires |
|---|---|
| 25,000–29,000 | 16 |
| 30,000–34,000 | 45 |
| 35,000–39,000 | 78 |
| 40,000–44,000 | 56 |
| 45,000–49,000 | 21 |
| 50,000–54,000 | 9 |

## STANDARD DEVIATION

Recall that for *ungrouped* data, one formula for the sample standard deviation is:

$$s = \sqrt{\dfrac{\Sigma X^2 - \dfrac{(\Sigma X)^2}{n}}{n-1}}$$

Formula for sample standard deviation— grouped data

If the data of interest are in *grouped* form (in a frequency distribution), the sample standard deviation can be approximated by substituting $\Sigma fX^2$ for $\Sigma X^2$ and $\Sigma fX$ for $\Sigma X$. The formula for the *sample standard deviation* then converts to:

$$s = \sqrt{\dfrac{\Sigma fX^2 - \dfrac{(\Sigma fX)^2}{n}}{n-1}} \qquad (4-10)$$

where:

$X$   is the midpoint of a class.

$f$   is the class frequency.

$n$   is the total number of sample observations.

### ◼ EXAMPLE

A sample of the semimonthly amounts invested in the Dupree Paint Company's profit-sharing plan by employees was organized into a frequency distribution for further study. (See Table 4–1.) What is the standard deviation of the grouped data? What is the sample variance?

---

### TABLE    4–1

**A Sample of Semimonthly Amounts Invested by Employees in the Profit-Sharing Plan**

| Amount invested | Number of employees |
|---|---|
| $30–$34 | 3 |
| 35– 39 | 7 |
| 40– 44 | 11 |
| 45– 49 | 22 |
| 50– 54 | 40 |
| 55– 59 | 24 |
| 60– 64 | 9 |
| 65– 69 | 4 |

---

### ☑ SOLUTION

Following the same practice used in Chapter 3 for computing the arithmetic mean of grouped data, $X$ represents the midpoint of each class. For example, the midpoint of the \$30–\$34 class is \$32. (See Table 4–2.) It is assumed that the amounts invested in the \$30–\$34 class are evenly distributed throughout that class. Therefore, the three amounts average \$32. All seven amounts in the \$35–\$39 class average \$37, and so on.

---

### TABLE 4–2

#### Calculations Needed for the Sample Standard Deviation

| Amount invested | Number ($f$) | Midpoint ($X$) | $fX$ | $fX \cdot X$, or $fX^2$ | |
|---|---|---|---|---|---|
| \$30–\$34 | 3 | \$32 | \$ 96 | 3,072 | ← $\$32 \times \$96$ |
| 35– 39 | 7 | 37 | 259 | 9,583 | |
| 40– 44 | 11 | 42 | 462 | 19,404 | |
| 45– 49 | 22 | 47 | 1,034 | 48,598 | ← $\$47 \times \$1,034$ |
| 50– 54 | 40 | 52 | 2,080 | 108,160 | |
| 55– 59 | 24 | 57 | 1,368 | 77,976 | |
| 60– 64 | 9 | 62 | 558 | 34,596 | |
| 65– 69 | 4 | 67 | 268 | 17,956 | |
| | 120 | | \$6,125 | 319,345 | |

---

To find the standard deviation of these data grouped into a frequency distribution:

*Step 1.* Each class frequency is multiplied by its class midpoint. That is, for the first class multiply $f$ times $X$, written $fX$. Thus, $3 \times \$32 = \$96$. For the second class, $fX = 7 \times \$37 = \$259$, and so on.

*Step 2.* Calculate $fX^2$. This could be written $fX \cdot X$. For the first class it would be $\$96 \times \$32 = 3,072$; for the second class, $\$259 \times \$37 = 9,583$; and so on.

*Step 3.* Sum the $fX$ and $fX^2$ columns. They are \$6,125 and 319,345, respectively.

Inserting these sums in formula (4–10) and solving for the sample standard deviation:

$$s = \sqrt{\frac{\Sigma fX^2 - \dfrac{(\Sigma fX)^2}{n}}{n - 1}}$$

$$= \sqrt{\frac{319,345 - \dfrac{(\$6,125)^2}{120}}{120 - 1}}$$

$$= \sqrt{\frac{319,345 - 312,630.2}{119}}$$

$$= \$7.51$$

The sample standard deviation is \$7.51. The sample variance is $(\$7.51)^2$, or about 56.4.

## Self-Review 4–7

*The answers are at the end of the chapter.*

The ages of a sample of the quarter-inch drills available for rental by Tool Rental, Inc. were organized into the following table:

| Ages (in years) | Number |
|---|---|
| 2– 4 | 2 |
| 5– 7 | 5 |
| 8–10 | 10 |
| 11–13 | 4 |
| 14–16 | 2 |

1. What is the grouping called?
2. Estimate the sample standard deviation.
3. Estimate the mean age of the drills (to the nearest tenth of a year).
4. What is the sample variance?

# EXERCISES

*The answers to the odd-numbered exercises are at the end of the book.*

19. Refer to the following frequency distribution.

| Class | Frequency |
|---|---|
| 0– 4 | 2 |
| 5– 9 | 7 |
| 10–14 | 12 |
| 15–19 | 6 |
| 20–24 | 3 |

   a. Determine the range.
   b. Compute the standard deviation.

20. Refer to the following frequency distribution.

| Class | Frequency |
|---|---|
| 20–29 | 7 |
| 30–39 | 12 |
| 40–49 | 21 |
| 50–59 | 18 |
| 60–69 | 12 |

   a. Determine the range.
   b. Compute the standard deviation.

21. Each person who applies for an assembly job at North Carolina Furniture is given a mechanical aptitude test. One part of the test involves assembling a dresser based on numbered instructions. A sample of the lengths of time it took 42 persons to assemble the dresser was organized into the following frequency distribution.

| Length of time (in minutes) | Number |
|---|---|
| 1– 3 | 4 |
| 4– 6 | 8 |
| 7– 9 | 14 |
| 10–12 | 9 |
| 13–15 | 5 |
| 16–18 | 2 |

   a. What is the range?

b.   What is the standard deviation?

c.   What is the variance?

22.   A sample of the amounts paid for parking on Saturday at the Downtown Parking Garage in Toronto was organized into the following frequency distribution.

| Amount paid | Number |
|---|---|
| $0.50–$0.74 | 2 |
| 0.75– 0.99 | 7 |
| 1.00– 1.24 | 15 |
| 1.25– 1.49 | 28 |
| 1.50– 1.74 | 14 |
| 1.75– 1.99 | 9 |
| 2.00– 2.24 | 3 |
| 2.25– 2.49 | 2 |

a.   Compute the range.

b.   Compute the sample standard deviation.

c.   What is the sample variance?

## INTERPRETATION AND USES OF THE STANDARD DEVIATION

Standard deviation used to compare dispersions

The standard deviation is commonly used as a measure to compare the spread in two or more sets of observations. For example, the standard deviation of the semimonthly amounts invested in the Dupree Paint Company profit-sharing plan was just computed to be $7.51. Suppose these employees are located in the South. If the standard deviation for a group of employees in the West is $10.47, and the means are about the same, it indicates that the amounts invested by the southern employees are not dispersed as much as those in the West (because $7.51 < $10.47). Since the amounts invested by the southern employees are clustered more closely about the mean, the mean for the southern employees is a more reliable measure than the mean for the western group.

## CHEBYSHEV'S THEOREM

Chebyshev's theorem: Applies regardless of shape of distribution

We have stressed that a small standard deviation for a set of values indicates that these values are located close to the mean. Conversely, a large standard deviation reveals that the observations are widely scattered about the mean. The Russian mathematician P. L. Chebyshev (1821–1894) developed a theorem that allows us to determine the minimum proportion of the values that lie within a specified number of standard deviations of the mean. For example, based on *Chebyshev's theorem,* at least three of every four values, or 75 percent, must lie between the mean plus two standard deviations and the mean minus two standard deviations. This relationship applies regardless of the shape of the distribution. Further, at least eight of every nine values, or 89.9 percent, will lie between plus three standard deviations and minus three standard deviations of the mean. At least 24 of 25 values, or 96 percent, will lie between plus and minus five standard deviations of the mean.

Chebyshev's theorem

In general terms, Chebyshev's theorem states:

---

Chebyshev's theorem   For any set of observations (sample or population), the minimum proportion of the values that lie within $k$ standard deviations of the mean is at least $1 - 1/k^2$, where $k$ is any constant greater than 1.

---

## ■ EXAMPLE

In the previous example and solution, the mean semimonthly amount contributed by the Dupree Paint employees to the company's profit-sharing plan was $51.04, and the standard deviation was computed to be $7.51. At least what percent of the contributions lie within plus two standard deviations and minus two standard deviations of the mean?

## ☑ SOLUTION

About 75 percent, found by

$$1 - \frac{1}{k^2} = 1 - \frac{1}{2^2} = 1 - \frac{1}{4} = \frac{3}{4} = 0.75$$

### Self-Review 4–8

*The answers are at the end of the chapter.*

Referring to the previous example regarding the contributions to the company's profit-sharing plan, these figures were arrived at. $\overline{X} = \$51.04$, $s = \$7.51$.

1. At least what percent of the contributions

to the plan lie within three standard deviations of the mean?

2. At least what percent of the contributions lie between $34.14 and $67.94?

## THE EMPIRICAL RULE

*Empirical Rule: Applies only to symmetrical distributions*

*Chebyshev's theorem is concerned with any set of values;* that is, the distribution of values can have any shape. However, for a symmetrical, bell-shaped distribution curve, such as the one in Chart 4–3, we can be more precise in explaining the dispersion about the mean. These relationships involving the standard deviation and the mean are included in the *Empirical Rule,* sometimes called the *Normal Rule.*

---

### CHART   4–3

**A Symmetrical, Bell-Shaped Curve Showing the Relationships between the Standard Deviation and the Mean**

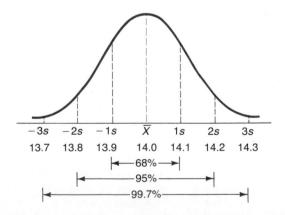

---

> **Empirical Rule** For a symmetrical, bell-shaped frequency distribution, approximately 68 percent of the observations will lie within plus and minus one standard deviation of the mean; about 95 percent of the observations will lie within plus and minus two standard deviations of the mean; and practically all (99.7 percent) will lie within plus and minus three standard deviations of the mean.

68 percent within
$\overline{X} \pm 1s$;
95 percent within
$\overline{X} \pm 2s$;
99.7 percent within
$\overline{X} \pm 3s$

These relationships are portrayed graphically in Chart 4–3.

It has been noted that if a distribution is symmetrical and bell-shaped, practically all of the observations lie between the mean plus and minus three standard deviations. Thus, if $\overline{X} = 100$ and $s = 10$, practically all the observations lie between $100 + 3(10)$ and $100 - 3(10)$, or 70 and 130. The range is therefore 60, found by $130 - 70$.

Conversely, if we know that the range is 60, we can approximate the standard deviation by dividing the range by 6. For this illustration: range $\div 6 = 60 \div 6 = 10$, the standard deviation.

## ■ EXAMPLE

A sample of the monthly amounts spent for food by families of four receiving food stamps approximates a symmetrical, bell-shaped frequency distribution. The sample mean is $150; the standard deviation is $20. Using the empirical rule:

1. About 68 percent of the monthly food expenditures are between what two amounts?
2. About 95 percent of the monthly food expenditures are between what two amounts?
3. Almost all of the monthly expenditures are between what two amounts?

## ☑ SOLUTION

1. About 68 percent are between $130 and $170, found by $\overline{X} \pm 1s = \$150 \pm 1(\$20)$.
2. About 95 percent are between $110 and $190, found by $\overline{X} \pm 2s = \$150 \pm 2(\$20)$.
3. Almost all (99.7 percent) are between $90 and $210, found by $\overline{X} \pm 3s = \$150 \pm 3(\$20)$.

---

### Self-Review 4–9

*The answers are at the end of the chapter.*

The distribution of a sample of the outside diameters of PVC gas pipes approximates a symmetrical, bell-shaped distribution. The arithmetic mean outside diameter of the sample is 14.0 inches, and the standard deviation is 0.1 inches.

1. About 68 percent of the outside diameters lie between what two amounts?

2. About 95 percent lie between what two amounts?

3. Almost all (99.7 percent) lie between what two amounts?

4. Portray the preceding percentages and amounts graphically.

## EXERCISES

*The answers to the odd-numbered exercises are at the end of the book.*

23. According to Chebyshev's theorem, at least what percent of any set of observations will be within 1.8 standard deviations of the mean?

24. The mean income of a group of sample observations is $500; the standard deviation is $40. According to Chebyshev's theorem, at least what percent of the incomes will lie between $400 and $600?

25. The distribution of the weights of a sample of 1,400 cargo containers is somewhat normally distributed. Based on the Empirical Rule, what percent of the weights will lie:
    a.   Between $\bar{X} - 2s$ and $\bar{X} + 2s$?
    b.   Between $\bar{X}$ and $\bar{X} + 2s$? Below $\bar{X} - 2s$?

26. The following figure portrays the symmetrical appearance of a sample distribution of efficiency ratings.

a.   Estimate the mean efficiency rating.
b.   Estimate the standard deviation to the nearest whole number. (Hint: Since the mean plus and minus three standard deviations encompasses practically all of the values, the range divided by 6 should give a good approximation of the standard deviation.)
c.   About 68 percent of the efficiency ratings fall between what two values?
d.   About 95 percent of the efficiency ratings fall between what two values?

## SOME OTHER MEASURES OF DISPERSION

Three other measures of dispersion will be considered briefly. They are: the *interquartile range,* the *quartile deviation,* and the *percentile range.*

### INTERQUARTILE RANGE

Interquartile range: Distance between $Q_1$ and $Q_3$

The **interquartile range** is the distance between the third quartile and the first quartile.

> Interquartile range = Third quartile − First quartile = $Q_3 - Q_1$    (4−11)

Recall that the median value, $Q_2$, separates the top 50 percent of a set of observations from the bottom 50 percent. In a similar fashion, the *first quartile, $Q_1$,* is the value corresponding to the point below which 25 percent of the observations lie. The *third quartile, $Q_3$,* is the value corresponding to the point above which 25 percent of the observations lie. Therefore, the middle 50 percent of the observations are located between $Q_3$ and $Q_1$.

Formulas for $Q_1$ and $Q_3$      The formulas for $Q_1$ and $Q_3$ are:

$$Q_1 = L + \frac{\frac{n}{4} - CF}{f} \; (i)$$        (4–12)

where:

    *L*   is the lower true limit of the class containing the first quartile.

    *n*   is the total number of frequencies (not classes).

   *CF*   is the cumulative number of frequencies in all of the classes preceding the class containing the first quartile.

    *f*   is the frequency in the class containing the first quartile.

    *i*   is the size of the class in which the first quartile lies.

$$Q_3 = L + \frac{\frac{3n}{4} - CF}{f} \; (i)$$        (4–13)

where:

    *L*   is the lower true limit of the class containing the third quartile.

    *n*   is the total number of class frequencies (not classes).

   *CF*   is the cumulative number of frequencies in all of the classes preceding the class containing the third quartile.

    *f*   is the frequency in the class containing the third quartile.

    *i*   is the size of the class in which the third quartile lies.

### ■ EXAMPLE

What is the first quartile for the distribution of the semimonthly contributions to the Dupree Paint profit-sharing plan in Table 4–3? The cumulative frequencies in the right column are needed for the computation of $Q_1$.

---

## TABLE 4–3

**Calculations Needed for the First and Third Quartiles**

| Stated limits | True limits | Class frequency | Cumulative frequency |
|---|---|---|---|
| $30–$34 | $29.50–$34.50 | 3 | 3 |
| 35– 39 | 34.50– 39.50 | 7 | 10 |
| 40– 44 | 39.50– 44.50 | 11 | 21 |
| 45– 49 | 44.50– 49.50 | 22 | 43 |
| 50– 54 | 49.50– 54.50 | 40 | 83 |
| 55– 59 | 54.50– 59.50 | 24 | 107 |
| 60– 64 | 59.50– 64.50 | 9 | 116 |
| 65– 69 | 64.50– 69.50 | 4 | 120 |

---

## ☑ SOLUTION

You will no doubt notice that the procedure for determining the first and third quartiles is quite similar to that presented in Chapter 3 for the median (which is the second quartile, $Q_2$). Interpolating for the first quartile:

*Step 1.* Determine the class in which $Q_1$ lies. Note that there are 120 employees. One fourth of 120 is 30. Observe in the *CF* column that there are 21 contributions below the *true* upper class limit of $44.50 and 43 contributions below the true upper limit of $49.50. Logically, the 30th contribution falls in the $44.50–$49.50 class. So *L,* the lower true limit of the class containing $Q_1$, is $44.50.

*Step 2.* Determine the cumulative number of frequencies, *CF,* in all of the classes immediately preceding the class containing the first quartile. Referring to Table 4–3, *CF* is 21.

*Step 3.* Determine *f,* the frequency of the class containing the first quartile. There are 22 frequencies in the $44.50–$49.50 class.

*Step 4.* Determine *i,* the class interval of the class containing $Q_1$. The class interval is $49.50 − $44.50 = $5.

Substituting all these values in the formula for $Q_1$:

$$Q_1 = L + \frac{\frac{n}{4} - CF}{f} \quad (i)$$

$$= \$44.50 + \frac{\frac{120}{4} - 21}{22} \; (\$5)$$

$$= \$44.50 + \frac{9}{22} \; (\$5)$$

$$= \$46.55$$

The interpretation is that one fourth of the employee contributions are below $46.55.

### Self-Review 4–10

*The answers are at the end of the chapter.*

Refer to the distribution of the contributions of the employees to the Dupree Paint Company's profit-sharing plan in Table 4–3. What is the third quartile? Interpret.

*Interquartile range can also be used to compare spreads*

Recall that the interquartile range is the distance between the third quartile and the first quartile. The interquartile range for the distribution of semimonthly amounts contributed to the company's profit-sharing plan is $9.41, found by $Q_3 - Q_1 = \$55.96 - \$46.55$. This indicates that the middle half of the contributions by the employees is between $46.55 and $55.96, with the distance between these two quartiles being $9.41. The interquartile range can also be used to compare the dispersion between two or more distributions. For example, suppose that the interquartile range for another distribution of employee contributions is $14.96. Two things may be said: (1) The contributions with the interquartile range of $9.41 are clustered more closely around their mean than are the contributions with an interquartile range of $14.96 (because

$9.41 < $14.96). (2) The mean of the contributions with the interquartile range of $9.41 is a more representative average than is the mean of the distribution of contributions with an interquartile range of $14.96.

## QUARTILE DEVIATION

Quartile deviation

The **quartile deviation** is half the distance between the third quartile, $Q_3$, and the first quartile, $Q_1$.

$$Q.D. = \frac{Q_3 - Q_1}{2}$$

(4–14)

For the semimonthly contributions to the Dupree Paint profit-sharing plan:

$$
\begin{aligned}
Q.D. &= \frac{Q_3 - Q_1}{2} \\
&= \frac{\$55.96 - \$46.55}{2} \\
&= \$4.71
\end{aligned}
$$

## APPROXIMATING THE QUARTILES

The first and third quartiles may be approximated from a cumulative frequency polygon.

### ■ EXAMPLE

The annual incomes of a sample of a group of self-employed salespeople were organized into a frequency distribution. The distribution was portrayed in a less-than cumulative frequency polygon. What are the approximate first and third quartiles?

### ☑ SOLUTION

Note that the number of salespersons is shown on the left side of the cumulative polygon, and the percent of the total is on the right side.

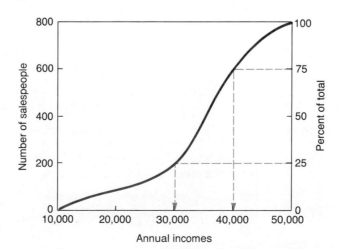

*First quartile:* Recall that the first quartile is the point below which 25 percent of the incomes lie. What is that point? Go to either one fourth of 800, or 200, on left side, or 25 percent on the right vertical axis. Then move horizontally to the curve and down to the X-axis, and read the income. It is about $30,000.

*Third quartile:* Three fourths of 800 is 600. Go either to 600 or to 75 percent on the Y-axis. Then move horizontally to the curve and down to the X-axis, and read the income. It is about $40,000.

## PERCENTILE RANGE

Percentile range

As noted, there are three quartiles ($Q_1$, $Q_2$, and $Q_3$). They divide a distribution into four parts. Likewise, the 99 *percentiles* divide a distribution into 100 parts. The 10-to-90 *percentile range* is the distance between the 10th and 90th percentiles. The percentiles are computed and interpreted in a manner similar to the quartiles. The symbol $P_{10}$ is used to represent the 10th percentile and $P_{90}$ the 90th percentile.

The formulas for these two percentiles are:

$$P_{10} = L + \frac{\frac{10n}{100} - CF}{f} \ (I) \qquad (4\text{–}15)$$

$$P_{90} = L + \frac{\frac{90n}{100} - CF}{f} \ (i) \qquad (4\text{–}16)$$

### ■ EXAMPLE

What is the 10th percentile for the distribution of Dupree Paint Company's semimonthly profit-sharing contributions in Table 4–3?

### ☑ SOLUTION

$$P_{10} = L + \frac{\frac{10n}{100} - CF}{f} \ (i)$$

$$= \$39.50 + \frac{\frac{10(120)}{100} - 10}{11} \ (\$5)$$

$$= \$39.50 + \frac{2}{11} \ (\$5)$$

$40.41, the 10th percentile

$$= \$40.41$$

### Self-Review 4–11

*The answers are at the end of the chapter.*

Refer to Table 4–3. What is the 90th percentile?

The 90th percentile (from Self-Review 4–11) is $60.06. The 10th percentile, computed in the preceding example solution, is $40.41. The percentile range is the distance between the 90th and 10th percentiles. It is $19.65, found by $60.06 − $40.41. Interpreting, the middle 80 percent of the employee contributions lie between $40.41 and $60.06 (approximately). A total of 20 percent lie either below $40.41 or above $60.06.

## EXERCISES

*The answers to the odd-numbered exercises are at the end of the book.*

27. The data from Exercise 19 are repeated below.

| Class | Frequency |
|-------|-----------|
| 0– 4 | 2 |
| 5– 9 | 7 |
| 10–14 | 12 |
| 15–19 | 6 |
| 20–24 | 3 |

   a. Compute the value of the first quartile.
   b. Compute the value of the third quartile.
   c. Compute the interquartile range.
   d. Compute the value of the 10th percentile.
   e. Compute the value of the 90th percentile.

28. The data from Exercise 20 are repeated below.

| Class | Frequency |
|-------|-----------|
| 20–29 | 7 |
| 30–39 | 12 |
| 40–49 | 21 |
| 50–59 | 18 |
| 60–69 | 12 |

   a. Compute the value of the first quartile.
   b. Compute the value of the third quartile.
   c. Compute the interquartile range.
   d. Compute the value of the 10th percentile.
   e. Compute the value of the 90th percentile.

29. The example of monthly rentals of condominiums from Chapter 2 is repeated below.

| Monthly rentals | Number of units |
|-----------------|-----------------|
| $ 600–$ 799 | 3 |
| 800– 999 | 7 |
| 1,000– 1,199 | 11 |
| 1,200– 1,399 | 22 |
| 1,400– 1,599 | 40 |
| 1,600– 1,799 | 24 |
| 1,800– 1,999 | 9 |
| 2,000– 2,199 | 4 |
| Total | 120 |

   a. What is the first quartile?
   b. What is the third quartile?

    c.    What is the interquartile range? Interpret.

    d.    What is the quartile deviation? Interpret.

30. The weekly incomes of part-time employees were tallied into the following distribution:

| Weekly incomes | Number |
|---|---|
| $ 40–$ 49 | 8 |
| 50–  59 | 16 |
| 60–  69 | 24 |
| 70–  79 | 48 |
| 80–  89 | 22 |
| 90–  99 | 14 |
| 100– 109 | 11 |
| 110– 119 | 7 |

    a.    What is the first quartile?

    b.    What is the third quartile?

    c.    What is the interquartile range? Interpret.

    d.    What is the quartile deviation? Interpret.

    e.    Determine the 10-to-90 percentile range. Interpret.

31. The number of air miles logged by a sample of executives during the year were grouped into the following distribution:

| Number of miles | Class frequency |
|---|---|
| 10,000–19,000 | 16 |
| 20,000–29,000 | 31 |
| 30,000–39,000 | 86 |
| 40,000–49,000 | 103 |
| 50,000–59,000 | 120 |
| 60,000–69,000 | 99 |
| 70,000–79,000 | 71 |
| 80,000–89,000 | 30 |
| 90,000–99,000 | 10 |
| 100,000 and over | 4 |

    a.    Estimate the interquartile range. Interpret.

    b.    Estimate the quartile deviation. Interpret.

    c.    What is the 20-to-80 percentile range? Interpret.

## RELATIVE DISPERSION

Coefficient of variation

A direct comparison of two or more measures of dispersion—say, the standard deviation for a distribution of annual incomes and the standard deviation of a distribution of absenteeism for this same group of employees—is impossible. Can we say that the standard deviation of $1,200 for the income distribution is greater than the standard deviation of 4.5 days for the distribution of absenteeism? Obviously not, because we cannot directly compare dollars and days absent from work. In order to make a meaningful comparison of the dispersion in incomes and absenteeism, we need to convert each of these measures to a *relative* value—that is, a percent. Karl Pearson (1857–1936), who contributed significantly to the science of statistics, developed a relative measure called the **coefficient of variation** (C.V.). It is a very useful measure when:

When to use C.V.

1. The data are in different units (such as dollars and days absent).
2. The data are in the same units, but the means are far apart (such as the incomes of the top executives and the incomes of the unskilled employees).

---

**Coefficient of variation**    The ratio of the standard deviation to the arithmetic mean, expressed as a percent.

---

Formula for coefficient of variation

In terms of a formula for a sample:

$$\text{C.V.} = \frac{s}{\overline{X}} (100)$$    $\leftarrow$    Multiplying by 100 converts the decimal to a percent    (4–17)

## ■ EXAMPLE

A study of the test scores for an in-plant course in management principles and the years of service of the employees enrolled in the course resulted in these statistics: The mean score was 200; the standard deviation was 40. The mean number of years of service was 20 years; the standard deviation was 2 years. Compare the relative dispersion in the two distributions using the coefficient of variation.

## ☑ SOLUTION

The distributions are in different units (test scores and years of service). Therefore, they are converted to coefficients of variation.

For the test scores:

$$\text{C.V.} = \frac{s}{\overline{X}} (100)$$

$$= \frac{40}{200} (100)$$

$$= 20 \text{ percent}$$

The standard deviation is 20 percent of the mean.

For years of service:

$$\text{C.V.} = \frac{s}{\overline{X}} (100)$$

$$= \frac{2}{20} (100)$$

$$= 10 \text{ percent}$$

The standard deviation is 10 percent of the mean.

Interpreting, there is more dispersion relative to the mean in the distribution of test scores compared to the distribution of years of service (because 20 percent > 10 percent).

The same procedure is used when the data are in the same units but the means are far apart. (See the following example.)

## ■ EXAMPLE

The variation in the annual incomes of executives is to be compared with the variation in incomes of unskilled employees. For a sample of executives, $\overline{X}$ = $500,000 and $s$ = $50,000. For a sample of unskilled employees, $\overline{X}$ = $12,000 and $s$ = $1,200. We are tempted to say that there is more dispersion in the annual incomes of the executives because $50,000 > $1,200. The means are so far apart, however, that we need to convert the statistics to coefficients in order to make a meaningful comparison of the variation in annual incomes.

## ☑ SOLUTION

For the executives:

$$C.V. = \frac{s}{\overline{X}}(100)$$

$$= \frac{\$50,000}{\$500,000}(100)$$

$$= 10 \text{ percent}$$

For the unskilled employees:

$$C.V. = \frac{s}{\overline{X}}(100)$$

$$= \frac{\$1,200}{\$12,000}(100)$$

$$= 10 \text{ percent}$$

There is no difference in the relative dispersion of the two groups.

---

### Self-Review 4–12

*The answers are at the end of the chapter.*

A large group of air force inductees were given two experimental tests—a mechanical aptitude test and a finger dexterity test. The arithmetic mean score on the mechanical aptitude test was 200, with a standard devi- ation of 10. The mean and standard deviation for the finger dexterity test were: $\overline{X}$ = 30, $s$ = 6. Compare the relative dispersion in the two groups.

## EXERCISES

*The answers to the odd-numbered exercises are at the end of the book.*

32. For a sample of students in the College of Business Administration at Eastern University, the mean grade point average is 3.10 with a standard deviation of 0.25. Compute the coefficient of variation. [See formula (4–17).]

33. Mountain Airlines is studying the weight of luggage for each pasenger. For a large group of domestic passengers the mean is 47 pounds with a standard deviation of 10 pounds. For a large group of overseas passengers the mean is 78 pounds and the standard deviation is 15 pounds. Compute the relative dispersion of each group. Comment on the difference in relative dispersion.

34. The research analyst for the Sidde Financial stock brokerage firm wants to compare the dispersion in the price-earnings ratios for a group of common stocks with the dispersion

Courtesy United Airlines

of their return on investment. For the price-earnings ratios, the mean is 10.9 and the standard deviation 1.8. The mean return on investment is 25 percent and the standard deviation 5.2 percent.

    a. Why should the coefficient of variation be used to compare the dispersion?

    b. Compare the relative dispersion for the price-earnings ratios and return on investment.

35. The spread in the annual prices of stocks selling under $10 and the spread in prices of those selling over $60 are to be compared. The mean price of the stocks selling under $10 is $5.25 and the standard deviation $1.52. The mean price of those stocks selling over $60 is $92.50 and the standard deviation $5.28.

    a. Why should the coefficient of variation be used to compare the dispersion in the prices?

    b. Compute the coefficients of variation, and explain any difference.

## SKEWNESS

Some distributions symmetrical

Some distributions positively skewed

Some distributions negatively skewed

Chapter 3 described the central tendency of a set of observations using the mean, median, and mode. This chapter has showed several measures that describe the spread in the data. Another characteristic that can be measured is the degree of *skewness* of a distribution. Recall that if a frequency distribution is *symmetrical,* it has no skewness—that is, the skewness is zero. If one or more observations are extremely large, the mean of the distribution becomes greater than the median or mode. In such cases the distribution is said to be *positively skewed.* Conversely, if one or more extremely small observations are present, the mean is the smallest of the three averages, and the distribution is said to be *negatively skewed.* (See Chart 4–4).

---

### CHART 4–4

**Shapes of Frequency Polygons Depicting Skewness**

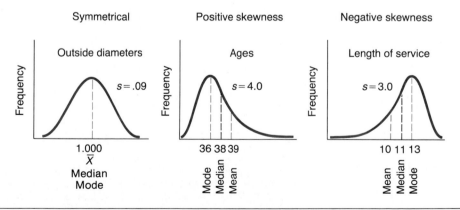

---

Coefficient of skewness

Karl Pearson also developed a measure to describe the degree of skewness, called the **coefficient of skewness:**

$$Sk = \frac{3(\text{mean} - \text{median})}{\text{Standard deviation}} \qquad (4-18)$$

## ■ EXAMPLE

The lengths of stay on the cancer floor of Sunnyside Hospital were organized into a frequency distribution. The mean length of stay was 28 days, the median 25 days, and the modal length 23 days. The standard deviation was computed to be 4.2 days.

1. Is the distribution symmetrical, positively skewed, or negatively skewed?
2. What is the coefficient of skewness? Interpret.

## ☑ SOLUTION

1. The distribution is positively skewed because the mean is the largest of the three averages.
2. The coefficient of skewness is 2.14, found by

$$Sk = \frac{3(\text{mean} - \text{median})}{\text{Standard deviation}} = \frac{3(28 - 25)}{4.2} = \frac{9}{4.2} = 2.14$$

Interpreting, the coefficient of skewness generally lies between $-3$ and $+3$. In this case the coefficient of $+2.14$ indicates a substantial amount of positive skewness. Apparently, a few cancer patients are staying in the hospital for a long time, causing the mean to be larger than the median or mode.

### Self-Review 4−13

*The answers are at the end of the chapter.*

A sample of experienced data entry clerks revealed that their mean typing speed is 87 words per minute and the median is 73. The standard deviation is 16.9 words per minute. What is the coefficient of skewness? Interpret.

## A COMPUTER APPLICATION

A MINITAB statistical package was applied in Chapter 3 to arrive at such measures of central tendency as the arithmetic mean and the median. Other packages are available, including the Statistical Package for the Social Sciences, or SPSS$^x$, as it is usually called. The following is the output from the SPSS$^x$ system for the condominium rental data introduced in Table 2−1 and repeated in Exercise 29 in this chapter.

```
NUMBER OF VALID OBSERVATIONS (LISTWISE) =    120.00
VARIABLE RENTAL        MONTHLY RENTALS


             MEAN          1457.933
             STD DEV        307.595
             KURTOSIS          .272
             SKEWNESS         -.263
             RANGE         1547.000
             MINIMUM            640
             MAXIMUM           2187
```

# KURTOSIS

Kurtosis: a measure of peakedness

One summarizing measure not included in the foregoing discussion but given in the SPSS[x] computer printout is **kurtosis**, which measures the peakedness of a distribution. Note in Figure A that although both curves are symmetrical and have the same mean, one curve is more peaked. The curve in Figure B is called a *mesokurtic* curve (*meso* means "intermediate"). The curve in Figure C is called a *leptokurtic* curve (*lepto* means "slender"). The curve in Figure D is called a *platykurtic* curve (*platy* means "flat"). As shown, symmetrical distributions can have varying degrees of peakedness, but so can skewed distributions. We will not show the computations for the degree of kurtosis. Note, however, that the coefficient of kurtosis for the condominium rental problems, as shown on the SPSS[x] output, is .272.

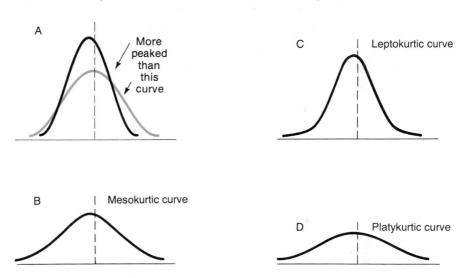

# EXERCISES

*The answers to the odd-numbered exercises are at the end of the book.*

36. For a particular distribution of wages, the arithmetic mean was computed to be $25,000, the median $25,000, and the mode also $25,000. The standard deviation was $1,000. Determine the coefficient of skewness. Comment on your findings.

37. Referring to the data in Chapter 2 regarding the salaries of the 1991 Cleveland Indians, the mean salary is $673,000, and the median is $345,000. The standard deviation is $729,000. Determine the coefficient of skewness. Comment on the shape of the distribution.

38. A sample of the homes currently offered for sale in Walla Walla, Washington, revealed that the mean asking price is $75,900, the median $70,100, and the modal price $67,200. The standard deviation of the distribution is $5,900.
    a.   Is the distribution of prices symmetrical, negatively skewed, or positively skewed?
    b.   What is the coefficient of skewness? Interpret.

39. A study of the net sales of a sample of small corporations revealed that the mean net sales is $2.1 million, the median $2.4 million, and the modal sales $2.6 million. The standard deviation of the distribution is $500,000.
    a.   Is the distribution of net sales symmetrical, negatively skewed, or positively skewed?
    b.   What is the coefficient of skewness? Interpret.

## A COMPUTER APPLICATION

The analysis of monthly rentals of new condominium units in the Sarasota-Bradenton area began in Chapter 2. The rentals were organized into a frequency distribution. In Chapter 3 the measures of central tendency, such as the arithmetic mean and the median, were computed for both grouped and ungrouped data. In this chapter, the standard deviation was just one of the measures of dispersion we discussed. These descriptive measurers give a visual picture of the data and describe the central tendency and spread. In many cases the calculations are quite lengthy. The MINITAB software system can be used to improve the accuracy and reduce the computational burden.

The results from the MINITAB procedure *describe* for the condominium rental data originally presented in Table 2–1 and used again in Exercise 29 of this chapter is:

```
MTB > describe c1
                N       MEAN    MEDIAN   TRMEAN    STDEV    SEMEAN
Rentals       120      1457.9   1464.5   1462.3    307.6    28.1

                MIN      MAX      Q1        Q3
Rentals       640.0    2187.0   1288.3    1639.3
```

You are familiar with most of the terms in the output, but some may be new. *N* refers to the number of rentals, which is 120; the mean rental is $1,457.90; and the median rental is $1,464.5. STDEV is the standard deviation, $307.6; MIN the smallest rental, $640; and, MAX the largest rental, $2,187. Q1 is the first quartile, and Q3 is the third quartile. Thus, 25 percent of the rentals are less than $1,288.30, and 75 percent are less than $1,639.30. Because the actual data are used instead of the grouped data, some of the values are slightly different from those computed from the grouped data in the frequency distribution.

Also included in the output are two values not yet discussed. SEMEAN refers to the *standard error of the mean,* which will be discussed in Chapter 8. TRMEAN refers to the trimmed mean. MINITAB deletes the smallest 5 percent and the largest 5 percent of the values and computes the mean of the remaining values; this is called the *trimmed mean.*

## CHAPTER OUTLINE

   I. A measure of dispersion, such as the standard deviation, is used to evaluate a measure of central tendency. A larger amount of dispersion indicates that the data are more widely spread out from the mean.
   II. The range is the difference between the largest and the smallest values.

$$\text{Range} = \text{Highest value} - \text{Lowest value} \qquad (4-1)$$

   A.   It is easy to compute and easy to understand.
   B.   Only two observations are used in its calculation.
   C.   It is influenced by large or small values.
   III. The average deviation is the mean of the absolute differences between each observation and the mean.

$$\text{A.D.} = \frac{\Sigma|X - \bar{X}|}{n} \qquad (4-2)$$

A. All the values are used in its calculation.
B. It is not influenced by an extreme value in the way that the range is.
C. To compute the average deviation:
  1. Determine the mean of the values.
  2. Compute the difference between the mean and each value.
  3. Sum these differences without regard to their signs.
  4. Divide the sum of the differences by the number of observations.

IV. The variance is the mean of the squared deviations between the mean and each value. The formulas for a population as applied to ungrouped data are:

$$\sigma^2 = \frac{\Sigma(X - \mu)^2}{N} \quad \text{or} \quad \frac{\Sigma X^2}{N} - \left(\frac{\Sigma X}{N}\right)^2 \qquad (4-3), (4-4)$$

for grouped data the formula is:

$$\sigma^2 = \frac{\Sigma fX^2}{N} - \left(\frac{\Sigma fX}{N}\right)^2$$

A. All the values are used in its calculation.
B. It is not influenced by large or small values.
C. The units are cumbersome to work with. (It is in the original units squared.)
D. To calculate the variance:
  1. Compute the mean.
  2. Determine the difference between each value and the mean.
  3. Square each of these differences.
  4. Sum the squared differences.
  5. If the data are a sample, divide by $n - 1$; divide by $N$ if they represent a population.

V. The standard deviation is the square root of the variance. The formulas for a sample as applied to ungrouped data are:

$$s = \sqrt{\frac{\Sigma(X - \bar{X})^2}{n - 1}} \quad \text{or} \quad \sqrt{\frac{\Sigma X^2 - \frac{(\Sigma X)^2}{n}}{n - 1}} \qquad (4-8), (4-9)$$

for grouped data the formula is:

$$s = \sqrt{\frac{\Sigma fX^2 - \frac{(\Sigma fX)^2}{n}}{n - 1}} \qquad (4-10)$$

A. Its value is in the same units as the original data.
B. The standard deviation is the most widely reported measure of dispersion.

VI. Chebyshev's theorem states that, regardless of the shape of the distribution, at least $1 - 1/k^2$ of the observations will be within $k$ units of the mean.

VII. The quartile deviation is the difference between the first quartile and the third quartile divided by 2.

$$\text{Q.D.} = \frac{Q_3 - Q_1}{2} \qquad (4-14)$$

where the third quartile ($Q_3$) and the first quartile ($Q_1$) are found by:

$$Q_3 = L + \frac{\frac{3n}{4} - CF}{f}(i) \qquad Q_1 = L + \frac{\frac{n}{4} - CF}{f}(i) \qquad (4-13), (4-12)$$

The distance between the first quartile and the third quartile is called the interquartile range.

$$\text{Interquartile range} = Q_3 - Q_1 \qquad\qquad (4-11)$$

    A.   Both of these measures are concerned with the middle 50 percent of the data.

    B.   They are not influenced by extreme values.

VIII. The Empirical, or Normal, Rule states that:

$\mu \pm \sigma$ encompasses about 68 percent of the values.

$\mu \pm 2\sigma$ encompasses about 95 percent of the values.

$\mu \pm 3\sigma$ encompasses about 99.7 percent of the values.

  IX. The coefficient of variation is a measure of relative dispersion.

    A.   It is computed by dividing the standard deviation by the mean.

$$\text{C.V.} = \frac{s}{\overline{X}}(100) \qquad\qquad (4-17)$$

    B.   The coefficient of variation reflects the variation in a distribution, relative to the mean. Use this measure:

       1.  When there is a wide difference in the magniude of the means being compared.

       2.  When the distributions being compared are in different units.

   X. The coefficient of skewness is a measure of the lack of symmetry in a distribution.

$$Sk = \frac{3(\text{mean} - \text{median})}{\text{Standard deviation}} \qquad\qquad (4-18)$$

    A.   It may range from $-3.00$ up to 3.00.

    B.   A value of 0 indicates a symmetric distribution.

    C.   If the long tail of the distribution is to the right, the distribution is positively skewed.

    D.   If the long tail of the distribution is to the left, the distribution is negatively skewed.

## EXERCISES

*The answers to the odd-numbered exercises are at the end of the book.*

40.  Discuss the advantages and disadvantages of the range as a measure of dispersion.

41.  What are the differences in computation between the standard deviation of a population and the standard deviation of a sample?

42.  If the coefficient of skewness is computed to be $-2.25$, describe the shape of the distribution. Include comments on the direction of the tail and whether the mean or the median is larger.

43.  Two distributions are being compared; one has a coefficient of variation of 20 percent and the other 30 percent. Comment on the relative dispersion of the two distributions.

44.  The hourly outputs of a group of employees assembling plug-in units at Zenith were selected at random. The sample outputs were: 8, 9, 8, 10, 9, 10, 12, and 10.

    a.   Compute the range.

    b.   Compute the average deviation.

    c.   Compute the standard deviation.

45.  The ages of a sample of Canadian tourists flying from Toronto to Hong Kong were: 32, 21, 60, 47, 54, 17, 72, 55, 33, and 41.

    a.   Compute the range.

    b.   Compute the average deviation.

    c.   Compute the standard deviation.

Courtesy Zenith Electronics Corporation

46. The weights (in pounds) of a sample of five boxes being sent by UPS are: 12, 6, 7, 3, and 10.
    a. Compute the range.
    b. Compute the average deviation.
    c. Compute the standard deviation.

47. A southern state has seven state universities in its system. The numbers of volumes (in thousands) held in their libraries are 83, 510, 33, 256, 401, 47, and 23.
    a. Is this a sample or a population?
    b. Compute the standard deviation.
    c. Compute the coefficient of variation.

48. The heights, in inches, of the starting five for the basketball team of the University of the West are: 74, 79, 81, 80, and 78.
    a. Is this a sample or a population?
    b. Compute the standard deviation.
    c. Compute the coefficient of variation.

49. A recent report in *Woman's World* magazine suggested that the typical family of four with an intermediate budget spends about $96 per week on food. The following frequency distribution was included in the report.

| Amount spent | Frequency |
|---|---|
| $ 80–$ 84 | 6 |
| 85– 89 | 12 |
| 90– 94 | 23 |
| 95– 99 | 35 |
| 100– 104 | 24 |
| 105– 109 | 10 |

    a. Compute the range.
    b. Compute the standard deviation.
    c. Compute the interquartile range.
    d. Compute the 10-to-90 percentile range.

50. Bidwell Electronics, Inc. recently surveyed a sample of their employees to determine how far they lived from corporate headquarters. The results are:

| Distance (miles) | Frequency |
|---|---|
| 0–4 | 4 |
| 5–9 | 15 |
| 10–14 | 27 |
| 15–19 | 18 |
| 20–24 | 6 |

    a. Compute the range.
    b. Compute the standard deviation
    c. Compute the interquartile range.
    d. Compute the 20-to-80 percentile range.

51. Houston Memorial Hospital wants to compare its annual patient turnover rate per bed with those published by the American Hospital Association. The turnover rates for a sample of 80 beds were organized into the following frequency distribution. (An annual turnover rate of 21.0 per bed indicates that, during a year, 21 different patients occupied the same hospital bed.)

| Annual turnover rate per bed | Number |
|---|---|
| 17–19 | 4 |
| 20–22 | 9 |
| 23–25 | 13 |
| 26–28 | 20 |
| 29–31 | 15 |
| 32–34 | 7 |
| 35–37 | 5 |
| 38–40 | 5 |
| 41–43 | 2 |

a.  Compute the arithmetic mean and median turnover rate per bed.

b.  Determine the standard deviation.

c.  What is the coefficient of variation?

d.  Is the distribution negatively or positively skewed? Cite evidence.

Exercises 52 through 55 are based on the following problem. The quality control department at GE constantly monitors three assembly lines producing built-in ovens for home use. The oven is designed to preheat to a temperature of 240 degrees Fahrenheit in four minutes and then shut off. However, the oven may not reach 240 degrees in the allotted time because of improper installation of the insulation and other reasons. Likewise, the temperature might go over 240 degrees during the four-minute preheat cycle.

A large number of ovens were sampled, and the following measures were computed on each line:

| | Temperature | | |
|---|---|---|---|
| Statistical measure | Line 1 | Line 2 | Line 3 |
| Arithmetic mean | 238.1 | 240.0 | 242.9 |
| Median | 240.0 | 240.0 | 240.0 |
| Mode | 241.5 | 240.0 | 239.1 |
| Standard deviation | 3.0 | 0.4 | 3.9 |
| Mean deviation | 1.9 | 0.2 | 2.2 |
| Quartile deviation | 1.0 | 0.1 | 1.7 |

52. The distribution of the oven readings from which line is a symmetrical, bell-shaped distribution?

a.  Line 1.

b.  Line 2.

c.  Line 3.

d.  Cannot determine based on the information given.

53. The coefficient of variation for the temperatures from line 3 is:

a.  1.6 percent.

b.  60.6 percent.

c.  3.9 degrees.

d.  242.9 degrees.

e.  Cannot be computed based on the information given.

54. According to the Empirical Rule, about 95 percent of the temperatures from line 2 were between:

a.  238.8 and 241.2.

b.  239.9 and 240.1.

c.  239.2 and 240.8.

d.  239.6 and 240.4.

e.  None of these is correct.

55. The distribution of the oven temperatures at the end of the four-minute preheat period for line 1 is:
    a. Not skewed.
    b. Negatively skewed.

56. The U.S. Bureau of the Census, in a study of households with an income of more than $75,000, reported the following percentage distribution of the ages of the heads of the households.

| Age | Percent |
|-----|---------|
| 15–24 | 0.8 |
| 25–34 | 16.9 |
| 35–44 | 28.2 |
| 45–54 | 29.3 |
| 55–64 | 17.5 |
| 65 or more | 7.3 |
| | 100.0 |

   a. Compute the first and third quartiles.
   b. Determine the quartile deviation.
   c. Compute the 10th and 90th percentiles.
   d. Determine the 10-to-90 percentile range.
      (Source: *The Universal Almanac*, 1991, p. 210.)

57. The Britten Turkey Farm delivers turkeys to a distributor in the metropolitan Detroit area. The percentage distribution below shows the weights of the turkeys delivered.

| Weight (pounds) | Percent |
|-----------------|---------|
| 10–14 | 4.7 |
| 15–19 | 27.8 |
| 20–24 | 51.6 |
| 25 or more | 15.9 |

   a. Compute the first and third quartiles.
   b. Determine the quartile deviation.

58. Health issues are a concern of managers, especially as they evaluate the cost of medical insurance. In a recent survey of 150 executives at Elvers Industries, a large insurance and financial firm located in the Southwest, the numbers of pounds by which the executives were overweight were reported.

| Pounds overweight | Frequency |
|-------------------|-----------|
| 0–5 | 14 |
| 6–9 | 42 |
| 10–19 | 58 |
| 20–29 | 28 |
| 30 or more | 8 |

   a. Compute the first and third quartiles.
   b. Determine the quartile deviation.
   c. Compute the 30th and 70th percentiles.
   d. Determine the 30-to-70 percentile range.
   e. Interpret part c and part d.

59. The following percentage distribution reports the incomes of U.S. households for the year 1987. (This is the latest year for which complete data are available.)

| Income | Percent |
|---|---|
| Under $5,000 | 6.9 |
| $ 5,000 to $10,000 | 11.5 |
| 10,000 to  15,000 | 10.6 |
| 15,000 to  25,000 | 19.2 |
| 25,000 to  35,000 | 16.1 |
| 35,000 to  50,000 | 17.2 |
| 50,000 to  75,000 | 12.2 |
| 75,000 or more | 6.3 |

Use stated lower limits in your calculations to:

a.    Compute the first and third quartiles.

b.    Determine the quartile deviation.

c.    Compute the 20th and 80th percentiles.

d.    Determine the 20-to-80 percentile range.

e.    Interpret part c and part d. (Source: *The Universal Almanac,* 1991, p. 210.)

60.  A large brokerage firm computed an arithmetic mean of 58.5 opening transactions per day. The standard deviation is 15.8 and the median 63.5 opening transactions.

a.    Using Chebyshev's theorem, what percent of the days will there be between 19.0 and 98.0 transactions.

b.    Determine the coefficient of variation.

c.    Determine the coefficient of skewness.

61.  The arithmetic mean discount based on the list price of toothpaste and other such items at Merrill's Discount Drug stores is 24 percent, with a standard deviation of 2 percent. The median discount is 25.5 percent.

a.    Using Chebyshev's theorem, what percent of the discounts will be between 21 and 27 percent?

b.    What is the coefficient of variation? Explain what it indicates.

c.    What is the coefficient of skewness? Explain its meaning.

62.  The National Video Rental Association reported the following data regarding the number of videotapes rented per family unit last month.

| Number rented | 0 | 1–4 | 5–9 | 10–19 | 20–39 | 40 or more |
|---|---|---|---|---|---|---|
| Number of households | 54 | 10 | 16 | 34 | 18 | 6 |

a.    How many videos does a typical family rent per month?

b.    Seventy-five percent of the households rent how many videos or less per month?

c.    Determine the interquartile range.

## COMPUTER DATA EXERCISES

63.  Refer to data set 1, which reports information on homes sold in Florida during 1990.

a.    Determine the standard deviation of the selling prices of the 75 homes. Using the mean and median computed earlier, determine the coefficient of variation and the coefficient of skewness. Comment on these values.

b.    Determine the standard deviation of the distance from the center of the city to the 75 homes. Using the mean and median computed earlier, determine the coefficient of variation and the coefficient of skewness. Comment on these values.

64.  Refer to data set 2, which reports information on 200 corporations in the United States.

a.    Determine the standard deviation of the sales for the 200 selected companies. Using the mean and median computed earlier, determine the coefficient of variation and the coefficient of skewness. Comment on these values.

b.    Determine the standard deviation of the profits for the selected companies. Using

Courtesy Blockbuster Video

the mean and median computed earlier, determine the coefficient of variation and the coefficient of skewness. Comment on these values.

65. Refer to data set 3, which reports information on the 26 major league baseball teams for the 1991 season.

    a. Determine the standard deviation of the total salary for the 26 teams. Using the mean and median computed earlier, determine the coefficient of variation and the coefficient of skewness. Comment on these values.

    b. Determine the standard deviation of the attendance for the 26 teams. Using the mean and median computed earlier, determine the coefficient of variation and the coefficient of skewness. Comment on these values.

# CHAPTER 4 EXAMINATION

*The answers are at the end of the chapter.*

Questions 1–5 are based on the following statistics. Samples of copper wire were submitted for testing by two companies. The sample pieces for each company were tested for tensile strength and the results organized into a frequency distribution. Then the mean, median, and other measures were computed. (Tensile strengths are in pounds per square inch.)

| | Company | |
| Statistic | Tanyo | Artin |
| --- | --- | --- |
| Arithmetic mean | 500 | 600 |
| Median | 500 | 500 |
| Mode | 500 | 300 |
| Standard deviation | 40 | 20 |
| Mean deviation | 32 | 16 |
| Quartile deviation | 25 | 14 |
| Range | 240 | 120 |
| Number in sample | 100 | 80 |

1. According to the Empirical Rule, the middle 95 percent of the wires from the Tanyo Company tested between approximately what two values?

2. The middle 50 percent of the wires of the Tanyo Company tested between what two values?

3. What is the coefficient of variation for the Tanyo distribution?

4. Which distribution has the larger dispersion? Explain.

5. What is the variance for the Tanyo distribution?

Questions 6 and 7 are based on the following sample weights: 7, 9, 11, 9, and 4 grams.

6. Compute the average deviation.

7. Compute the variance and the standard deviation.

Questions 8–10 are based on the following frequency distribution.

| Days absent during year | Number (f) |
| --- | --- |
| 2– 5 | 7 |
| 6– 9 | 11 |
| 10–13 | 20 |
| 14–17 | 30 |
| 18–21 | 14 |
| 22–25 | 10 |
| 26–29 | 8 |

8. Determine the range. Explain what it indicates.

9. Determine the 10-to-90 percentile range.

10. Is the distribution symmetrical, positively skewed, or negatively skewed? (It is not necessary to compute any measures, such as the coefficient of skewness.)

# ANSWERS

4–1   1.   $6,000; $6,000.

2.   $12,000 for executives, found by $12,000 − $0; $8,000 for middle management, found by $10,000 − $2,000.

3.   There is more spread in the annual travel costs for the executives because the range for their distribution ($12,000) is greater than the range of $8,000 for middle management. Thus, the $6,000 arithmetic mean for middle management is more representative of the typical travel cost.

| X | $X - \mu$ | $(X - \mu)^2$ |
|---|---|---|
| 204 | −6 | 36 |
| 215 | +5 | 25 |
| 207 | −3 | 9 |
| 212 | +2 | 4 |
| 214 | +4 | 16 |
| 208 | −2 | 4 |
| | 0 | 94 |

$$\mu = \frac{\Sigma X}{N} = \frac{1260}{6} = 210 \text{ pounds}$$

4–2       $\overline{X} = \dfrac{824}{8} = 103$

$$\sigma^2 = \frac{\Sigma(X - \mu)^2}{N} = \frac{94}{6} = 15.67$$

2.   3.96 pounds, found by $\sqrt{15.67}$.

1.   5.25 kg, found by:

4–4   2.33, found by:

$$\overline{X} = \frac{\Sigma X}{n} = \frac{28}{7} = 4$$

| X | $X - \overline{X}$ | Absolute deviation |
|---|---|---|
| 95 | \|− 8\| | 8 |
| 103 | \| 0\| | 0 |
| 105 | \|+ 2\| | 2 |
| 110 | \|+ 7\| | 7 |
| 104 | \|+ 1\| | 1 |
| 105 | \|+ 2\| | 2 |
| 112 | \|+ 9\| | 9 |
| 90 | \|−13\| | 13 |
| Total | | 42 |

$$\text{A.D.} = \frac{42}{8} = 5.25 \text{ kg}$$

| X | $X - \overline{X}$ | $(X - \overline{X})^2$ | $X^2$ |
|---|---|---|---|
| 4 | 0 | 0 | 16 |
| 2 | −2 | 4 | 4 |
| 5 | 1 | 1 | 25 |
| 4 | 0 | 0 | 16 |
| 5 | 1 | 1 | 25 |
| 2 | −2 | 4 | 4 |
| 6 | 2 | 4 | 36 |
| 28 | 0 | 14 | 126 |

2.   The weights of the crates going to Ireland deviate 5.25 kilograms on the average from the mean of 103 kilograms.

3.   There is more dispersion in the crates going to Ireland compared with those going to France (because 5.25 kilograms is greater than 2.4 kilograms).

$$s^2 = \frac{\Sigma(X - \overline{X})^2}{n - 1} \quad \text{or} \quad s^2 = \frac{\Sigma X^2 - \dfrac{(\Sigma X)^2}{n}}{n - 1}$$

$$= \frac{14}{7 - 1}$$

$$= 2.33$$

$$= \frac{126 - \dfrac{(28)^2}{7}}{7 - 1}$$

$$= \frac{126 - 112}{6}$$

$$= 2.33$$

4–3   1.   15.67, found by:

4–5  1.  1.53 grams, found by $\sqrt{2.33}$.
    2.  Yes, the original data were in grams. The standard deviation is 1.53 grams.
4–6  29,000 miles, found by $54{,}000 - 25{,}000$. Using true limits it would be 30,000 miles.
4–7  1.  A frequency distribution.
    2.  3.2 years, found by:

| Ages | $f$ | $X$ | $fX$ | $fX^2$ |
|------|----|----|-----|-------|
| 2– 4 | 2 | 3 | 6 | 18 |
| 5– 7 | 5 | 6 | 30 | 180 |
| 8–10 | 10 | 9 | 90 | 810 |
| 11–13 | 4 | 12 | 48 | 576 |
| 14–16 | 2 | 15 | 30 | 450 |
|  | 23 |  | 204 | 2,034 |

$$s = \sqrt{\frac{2{,}034 - \dfrac{(204)^2}{23}}{23 - 1}}$$

$$= \sqrt{\frac{2{,}034 - 1{,}809.3913}{22}}$$

$$= \sqrt{10.209486}$$

$$= 3.195 \text{ years}$$

    3.  8.9 years, found by 204/23.
    4.  10.208, found by $(3.195)^2$.
4–8  1.  At least 88.9 percent, found by:

$$1 - \frac{1}{3^2} = 1 - \frac{1}{9} = \frac{8}{9} = 0.889$$

    2.  About 80.2 percent found by:

$$1 - \frac{1}{(2.25)^2} = 1 - \frac{1}{5.0625} = 1 - 0.198$$

    Both \$34.14 and \$67.94 are 2.25 standard deviations from the mean.
    $(\$34.14 - \$51.04)/\$7.51 = -2.25$,
    and $(\$67.94 - \$51.04)/\$7.51 = +2.25$.
4–9  1.  13.9 and 14.1 inches, found by $14.0 \pm 1(0.1)$.
    2.  13.8 and 14.2 inches, found by $14.0 \pm 2(0.1)$.

    3.  13.7 and 14.3 inches, found by $14.0 \pm 3(0.1)$.
    4.

| | $-3s$ | $-2s$ | $-1s$ | $\overline{X}$ | $+1s$ | $+2s$ | $+3s$ |
|---|---|---|---|---|---|---|---|
| | 13.7 | 13.8 | 13.9 | 14.0 | 14.1 | 14.2 | 14.3 |

68%
95%
99.7%

4–10  $Q_3 = \$55.96$, found by $3/4 \times 120 = 90$. $Q_3$ lies in the \$54.50–\$59.50 class. $L = \$54.50$, $CF = 83$, $f = 24$. Solving:

$$\$54.50 + \frac{\dfrac{3(120)}{4} - 83}{24}(\$5) = \$55.96$$

One fourth of the commissions are above \$55.96.
4–11  \$60.06, found by:

$$\$59.50 + \frac{\dfrac{90(120)}{100} - 107}{9}(\$5)$$

4–12  C.V. for mechanical is 5 percent, found by $(10/200)(100)$. For finger dexterity C.V. is 20 percent, found by $(6/30)(100)$. Thus, relative dispersion in finger dexterity scores is greater than relative dispersion in mechanical, because 20 percent > 5 percent.
4–13  2.49, found by:

$$Sk = \frac{3(87 - 73)}{16.9} = 2.49$$

There is considerable positive skewness in the distribution of the typing speeds. A few extremely fast typists are causing the mean to be greater than the median or mode.

# Answers

## CHAPTER 4 EXAMINATION

1. About 420 and 580, found by $\bar{X} \pm 2s = 500 \pm 2(40)$.
2. About 475 and 525, found by median $\pm$ Q.D. $= 500 \pm 25$.
3. 8 percent, found by $(s/\bar{X})100 = (40/500)100$.
4. Tanyo. The range of 240 is greater than the range of 120. Also, standard deviation of 40 is greater than 20, and C.V. of 8 percent for Tanyo is greater than 3.3 percent for Artin.
5. 1,600, found by $(40)^2$.
6. A.D. $= 10/5 = 2$.
7. Variance $= 28/(5 - 1) = 7$. Standard deviation $= \sqrt{7} = 2.65$.

| $X$ | $X - \bar{X}$ | $(X - \bar{X})^2$ |
|---|---|---|
| 7 | $|-1|$ | 1 |
| 9 | $|+1|$ | 1 |
| 11 | $|+3|$ | 9 |
| 9 | $|+1|$ | 1 |
| 4 | $|-4|$ | 16 |
| 40 | 10 | 28 |

8. Either 27 (found by $29 - 2$) or 28 (found by $29.5 - 1.50$).
9. 18.1, found by $24.7 - 6.6$

$$P_{10} = 5.5 + \frac{\frac{10(100)}{100} - 7}{11}(4) = 6.6$$

$$P_{90} = 21.5 + \frac{\frac{90(100)}{100} - 82}{10}(4) = 24.7$$

10. It appears to be about symmetrical.

# A Review of Chapters 1—4

This section is a review of the major concepts and terms introduced in Chapters 1 through 4. These chapters were concerned with describing a set of data by organizing it into a *frequency distribution* and then portraying the distribution in the form of a *histogram,* a *frequency polygon,* and a *cumulative frequency polygon.* The purpose of these graphs is to visually reveal the important characteristics of the data.

Computing a central value to represent the data is another way of summarizing a mass of observations. Chapter 3 looked at several measures of central tendency, including the *mean, weighted mean, median,* and *mode.* Chapter 4 described the *dispersion,* or spread, in the data by computing the *range, standard deviation,* and other measures. Further, *skewness* or lack of symmetry in the data was described by determining the *coefficient of skewness.*

We stressed the importance of computer software packages, including MINITAB. Several computer outputs in these chapters demonstrated how quickly and accurately a mass of raw data can be organized into a frequency distribution and a histogram. Also, we noticed that the computer outputs present a large number of descriptive measures, including the mean, the variance, and the standard deviation.

## Glossary

### Chapter 1

**Descriptive statistics**   The techniques used to describe the important characteristics of a set of data. These may include organizing the values into a frequency distribution and computing measures of central tendency and measures of spread and skewness.

**Exhaustive**   Each observation must fall into one of the categories.

**Inferential statistics,** also called **statistical inference** or **inductive statistics**   This facet of statistics deals with estimating a population parameter based on a sample statistic. For example, if 2 out of the 10 hand calculators sampled are defective, we might infer than 20 percent of the production is defective.

**Interval measurement**   If one observation is greater than another by a certain amount, and the zero point is arbitrary, the measurement is on at least an interval scale. For example, the difference between temperatures of 70 degrees and 80 degrees is 10 degrees. Likewise, a temperature of 90 degrees is 10 degrees more than a temperature of 80 degrees, and so on.

**Mutually exclusive**   An observation cannot fall into more than one category.

**Nominal measurement**   The "lowest" level of measurement. If data are classified into categories and the order of those categories is not important, it is nominal level of measurement. Examples are sex (male, female) and political affiliation (Republican, Democrat, Independent, all others). If it makes no difference whether male or female is listed first, the data are nominal-level.

**Ordinal measurement**   Data that can be logically ranked are referred to as ordinal measures. For example, consumer response to the sound of a new speaker might be excellent, very good, fair, or poor.

**Population**   The collection, or set, of all individuals, objects, or measurements whose properties are being studied.

**Ratio measurement**   If the distances between numbers are of a known constant size *and there is a true zero point,* the measurement is on a ratio scale. For example, the distance between $200 and $300 is $100, and in the case of money there is a true zero point. If you have zero dollars, there is an absence of money (you have none).

**Sample**   A portion, or subset, of the population being studied.

**Statistics**   The science of collecting, organizing, analyzing, and interpreting numerical data for the purpose of making more effective decisions.

## CHAPTER 2

**Array**   An ordering of the observations from the smallest to the largest or vice versa.

**Charts**   Special graphical formats used to portray a frequency distribution, including histograms, frequency polygons, and cumulative frequency polygons. Other graphical devices used to portray data are line charts, bar charts, and pie charts. They are very useful, for example, for depicting the trend in long-term debt or percent changes in profit from last year to this year.

**Class**   The interval in which the data are tallied. For example, $4–$7 is a class; $8–$11 is another class.

**Class frequency**   The number of observations in each class. If there are 16 observations in the $4–$7 class, 16 is the class frequency.

**Frequency distribution**   It is often difficult to analyze a large mass of raw data. To summarize the data, they can be organized into classes such as $1,000–$1,999 and $2,000–$2,999. The resulting grouping is called a frequency distribution.

**Midpoint**   The value that divides the class into two equal parts. For the classes $4–$7 and $8–$11, the midpoints are $5.50 and $9.50, respectively.

## CHAPTER 3

**Arithmetic mean**   The sum of the values divided by the number of values. The symbol for the mean of a sample is $\bar{X}$, and the symbol for a population is $\mu$.

**Average**   A number that describes the central tendency of the data. There are a number of specialized averages, including the arithmetic mean, weighted mean, median, mode, and geometric mean.

**Geometric mean**   The $n$th root of the product of all the values. It is especially useful for averaging rates of change and index numbers. It minimizes the importance of extreme values. A second use of the geometric mean is determining the mean percent change over a period of time. For example, if gross sales were $245 million in 1981 and $692 million in 1992, what is the average annual percent increase?

**Median**   The value of the middle observation after all the observations have been arranged from low to high. For example, if observations 6, 9, 4 are rearranged to read 4, ⑥, 9, the middle value is 6, the median.

**Mode**   The value of an item that appears most frequently in a set of data. For grouped data, it is the *midpoint* of the class containing the largest number of values.

**Weighted mean**   Each value is weighted according to its relative importance. For example, if 5 shirts cost $10 each and 20 shirts cost $8 each, the weighted mean price is $8.40: [(5 × $10) + (20 × $8)]/25 = $210/25 = $8.40.

## CHAPTER 4

**Average deviation,** also referred to as the **mean deviation** or **mean absolute deviation (MAD).** The mean of the deviations from the mean, disregarding signs.

**Coefficient of skewness**   A measure that describes the lack of symmetry in a distribution. For a symmetrical distribution there is no skewness so the coefficient of skewness is zero. Otherwise, it is either positive or negative, with the limits of its value being about +3 and −3.

**Coefficient of variation**   The standard deviation divided by the mean, expressed as a percent. It is especially useful for comparing the relative dispersion in two or more sets of data where (1) they are in different units, or (2) one mean is larger than the other mean.

**Dispersion** or **spread**   A measure of central tendency pinpoints a single value that is typical of the data. A measure of dispersion indicates how close or far apart the values are from the mean or other measure of central tendency. Such a measure of dispersion indicates how reliable the average is.

**Interquartile range**   The distance between the third quartile and the first quartile.

**Kurtosis**   A measurement of the peakedness of a distribution.

**Percentile range**   The distance between any two selected percentiles.

**Quartile deviation**   Half the distance between the third quartile and the first quartile.

**Range**   Distance between the highest and lowest values: Range = Highest value − Lowest value.

**Standard deviation**   Square root of the variance.

**Variance**   Mean of the squared deviations from the mean.

## EXERCISES

*The answers to the odd-numbered exercises are at the end of the book.*

1. A small number of employees were selected from all the employees at NED Electronics and their hourly rates recorded. The rates were: $9.50, $9.00, $11.70, $14.80, and $13.00.
   a.   Are the hourly rates a sample or a population?
   b.   What is the level of measurement?
   c.   What is the arithmetic mean hourly rate?
   d.   What is the median hourly rate? Interpret.
   e.   What is the variance?
   f.   What is the coefficient of skewness? Interpret.

2. The weekly overtime hours worked by all the employees at the Publix Market are: 1, 4, 6, 12, 5, and 2.
   a.   Is this a sample or a population?
   b.   What is the mean number of overtime hours worked?
   c.   What is the median? Interpret.
   d.   What is the mode?
   e.   What is the average deviation?
   f.   What is the standard deviation?
   g.   What is the coefficient of variation?

3. The tourist bureaus of St. Thomas and other Caribbean islands surveyed a sample of tourists as they left to return to the United States. One of the questions was: How many rolls of film did you expose when visiting our island? The sample responses were:

   | 8 | 6 | 3 | 11 | 14 | 8 | 9 | 16 | 9 | 10 |
   |---|---|---|----|----|---|---|----|---|----|
   | 5 | 11 | 7 | 8 | 8 | 10 | 9 | 12 | 13 | 9 |

   a.   Using five classes, organize the sample data into a frequency distribution.
   b.   Portray the distribution in the form of a frequency polygon.
   c.   What is the mean number of rolls exposed?

   d.    What is the median?

   e.    What is the mode?

   f.    What is the range?

   g.    What is the sample variance?

   h.    What is the sample standard deviation?

   i.    Assuming that the distribution is symmetrical and bell-shaped, about 95 percent of the tourists exposed between _____ and _____ rolls.

4. The annual amounts spent on research and development for a sample of electronic component manufacturers are (in $ millions):

| | | | | | | | | | |
|---|---|---|---|---|---|---|---|---|---|
| 8 | 34 | 15 | 24 | 15 | 28 | 12 | 20 | 22 | 23 |
| 14 | 26 | 18 | 23 | 10 | 21 | 16 | 17 | 22 | 31 |
| 13 | 25 | 20 | 28 | 6 | 20 | 19 | 27 | 16 | 22 |

   a.    What is the level of measurement?

   b.    Using six classes, organize the expenditures into a frequency distribution.

   c.    Portray the distribution in the form of a histogram.

   d.    Portray the distribution in the form of a less-than cumulative frequency polygon.

   e.    Based on the less-than cumulative frequency polygon, what is the *estimated* median amount spent on research and development? Interpret.

   f.    What is the mean amount spent on research and development?

   g.    Based on the less-than cumulative frequency polygon, what is the interquartile range? The quartile deviation?

5. The rates of growth of Bardeen Chemicals for the past five years are 5.2 percent, 8.7 percent, 3.9 percent, 6.8 percent, and 19.5 percent, respectively.

   a.    What is the arithmetic mean annual growth rate?

   b.    What is the geometric mean annual growth rate?

   c.    Should the arithmetic mean or geometric mean be used to represent the average annual growth rate? Why?

6. Kaiser Aluminum & Chemical Corporation noted in its 1989 second-quarter report that as of June 30, 1989, notes payable amounted to $284.0 million. For the same date in 1984, they were $113.0 million. What is the geometric mean yearly percent increase (June to June) from June 1984 to June 1989?

7. BFI in its annual report revealed that working capital was (in billions) $4.4, $3.4, $3.0, $4.8, $7.8, and $8.3 consecutively for the years 1986–1991. Present these figures in either a simple line chart or a simple bar chart.

8. Suppose an executive of OCM wants to show graphically at the board meeting the change in selected items from the statements of income and other financial reports. From the August *Quarterly,* these items are of interest:

| | Six months ended June 30 (in $ millions) | |
|---|---|---|
| | 1990 | 1991 |
| Income from operations | $ 74.4 | $123.1 |
| Interest income | 2.7 | 3.3 |
| Investments in joint ventures | 118.5 | 105.0 |
| Inventory of logs | 21.9 | 6.6 |
| Net income per common share | 0.54 | 1.16 |

Present the percent changes from 1990 to 1991 in the form of a two-directional bar chart.

For exercises 9—18, fill in the blanks.

9. Employees in a company training course were asked to rate it as either outstanding, very good, good, fair, or poor. The level of measurement is _____.

10. A sample of senior citizens revealed that their mean annual retirement income is $16,900. Since the mean is based on a sample, the $16,900 is called a _____.

11. Refer to the following picture. It is called a _____. The third quartile is about _____, the first quartile _____, the interquartile range _____, the quartile deviation _____, and the range _____.

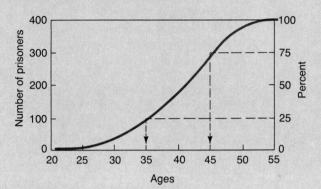

12. Refer to the following picture, which is based on a frequency distribution. It is called a _____. Describe the skewness in the distribution. Explain.

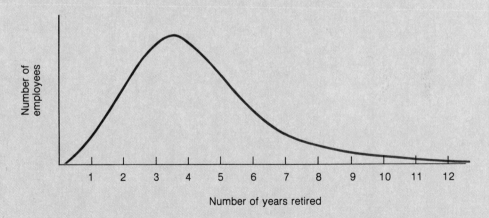

13. Mean = $64, median = $61, mode = $60, standard deviation = $6, and range = $40. The coefficient of variation is _____.

14. Refer to Exercise 13. The coefficient of skewness is _____.

15. A useful measure to compare the relative dispersion in two or more distributions, if they are in different units, is the _____.

16. Mean = 100, median = 100, mode = 100, and $s$ = 4. The range is about _____.

17. Refer to Exercise 16. About 95 percent of the values lie between _____ and _____.

18. Fine Furniture, Inc. produced 2,460 desks in 1980 and 6,520 in 1990. To find the average annual percent increase in production, the _____ should be used.

A sample of the amounts of funds customers first deposited in First Federal's MCA (miniature checking account) revealed the following.

| $124 | $ 14 | $150 | $289 | $ 52 | $156 | $203 | $ 82 | $ 27 | $248 |
|------|------|------|------|------|------|------|------|------|------|
| 39   | 52   | 103  | 58   | 136  | 249  | 110  | 298  | 251  | 157  |
| 186  | 107  | 142  | 185  | 75   | 202  | 119  | 219  | 156  | 78   |
| 116  | 152  | 206  | 117  | 52   | 299  | 58   | 153  | 219  | 148  |
| 145  | 187  | 165  | 147  | 158  | 146  | 185  | 186  | 149  | 140  |

19. Using the preceding raw data and a statistical package (such as MINITAB),
    a. Organize the data into a frequency distribution.
    b. Calculate the mean, median, and other descriptive measures. Include charts, if available. You decide on the class interval.
    c. Interpret the computer output; that is, describe the central tendency, spread, skewness, and other measures.

20. If a computer is not available, organize the miniature checking accounts into a frequency distribution. You decide on the class interval. Portray the distribution in chart form, and compute measures of central tendency, spread, and skewness. Then interpret the important characteristics of the miniature checking accounts

21. Since the year 1789, 85 judges have served as associate justices of the Supreme Court of the United States. Their lengths of service are given below. (Those serving presently are not included.) Analyze the data.
    a. What is a typical length of service.
    b. What is the variation in the lengths of service?
    c. Is the distribution skewed?
    d. Develop a stem-and-leaf chart.

| 8  | 1  | 20 | 5  | 9  | 0  | 13 | 15 | 30 | 3  |
|----|----|----|----|----|----|----|----|----|----|
| 30 | 16 | 18 | 23 | 33 | 20 | 2  | 31 | 14 | 32 |
| 4  | 28 | 14 | 18 | 27 | 5  | 23 | 5  | 8  | 23 |
| 18 | 28 | 14 | 34 | 10 | 21 | 9  | 33 | 6  | 7  |
| 20 | 11 | 5  | 20 | 15 | 10 | 2  | 16 | 13 | 26 |
| 29 | 19 | 3  | 4  | 5  | 26 | 4  | 10 | 26 | 22 |
| 5  | 15 | 16 | 7  | 16 | 15 | 6  | 34 | 19 | 23 |
| 36 | 9  | 1  | 13 | 6  | 13 | 17 | 7  | 16 | 5  |
| 23 | 2  | 3  | 15 | 14 |    |    |    |    |    |

22. The per-capita personal income by state (including the District of Columbia), in thousands of dollars, for 1986 follows.
    a. Organize these data into a frequency distribution.
    b. What is a "typical" per-capita income for a state?
    c. How much variation in the income data is there?
    d. Is the distribution symmetrical?
    e. Summarize your findings.

| 11.1 | 17.7 | 13.2 | 10.7 | 16.8 | 15.1 | 19.2 | 15.1 |
|------|------|------|------|------|------|------|------|
| 18.9 | 14.3 | 13.2 | 14.7 | 11.4 | 15.4 | 12.9 | 13.2 |
| 14.4 | 11.1 | 11.2 | 12.7 | 16.6 | 17.5 | 14.1 | 14.7 |
| 9.5  | 13.6 | 11.9 | 13.8 | 15.1 | 15.9 | 18.3 | 11.1 |
| 17.1 | 12.2 | 12.3 | 13.7 | 12.4 | 12.2 | 13.9 | 14.7 |
| 11.1 | 11.9 | 11.8 | 13.5 | 10.7 | 12.8 | 15.4 | 14.5 |
| 10.5 | 13.8 | 13.2 |      |      |      |      |      |

23. The following frequency distributions show the earnings of year-round full-time workers by sex. Compare the two distributions, and comment on the differences. You may want to draw some charts. Interesting comparisons might be the earnings of the highest 25

percent and the lowest 25 percent; the median, mean, and modal incomes; and the disperson in the two distributions.

| Earnings group | Women | Men |
|---|---|---|
| $ 2,999 or less | 533 | 924 |
| $ 3,000–$ 4,999 | 401 | 422 |
| 5,000– 6,999 | 1,108 | 814 |
| 7,000– 9,999 | 3,218 | 2,233 |
| 10,000– 14,999 | 7,527 | 5,872 |
| 15,000– 19,999 | 5,926 | 6,621 |
| 20,000– 24,999 | 4,085 | 6,425 |
| 25,000– 49,999 | 4,297 | 17,489 |
| $50,000 or over | 287 | 4,141 |
| Total | 27,382 | 44,941 |

24. Following are the ages at which the 41 U.S. presidents began their terms in office. Organize the data into a stem-and-leaf chart. Determine a typical age at the time of inauguration. Comment on the variation in age.

| 57 | 61 | 57 | 57 | 58 | 57 | 61 | 54 | 68 | 51 | 65 |
|---|---|---|---|---|---|---|---|---|---|---|
| 49 | 64 | 50 | 48 | 65 | 52 | 56 | 46 | 54 | 49 | |
| 50 | 47 | 55 | 55 | 54 | 42 | 51 | 56 | 55 | 51 | |
| 54 | 51 | 60 | 62 | 43 | 55 | 56 | 61 | 52 | 69 | |

Leisure and entertainment—Courtesy Busch Gardens

# A SURVEY OF PROBABILITY CONCEPTS

When you have completed this chapter, you will be able to:

1. Define the term *probability*.
2. Describe the classical, the relative frequency, and the subjective approaches to probability.
3. Understand the terms *experiment, event,* and *outcome.*
4. Define the terms *conditional probability* and *joint probability.*

5. Calculate probabilities, applying the rules of addition and multiplication.
6. Determine the number of possible permutations and combinations.
7. Calculate a probability using Bayes' theorem.

T he emphasis in Chapters 2 through 4 was on descriptive statistics. In Chapter 2 monthly condominium rentals were organized into a frequency distribution to show the lowest and highest rentals and where the largest concentration of data lay. We also portrayed the distribution graphically in a histogram and several polygons. In Chapters 3 and 4 a number of measures of central tendency and dispersion were used to pinpoint a typical monthly rental (about $1,475) and to examine the spread in the data. The spread was described using such measures of dispersion as the range and the standard deviation. Descriptive statistics, therefore, is concerned with *describing something that has already occurred.*

We now turn to the second facet of statistics, namely, *computing the chance that something will occur.* This facet of statistics is referred to as **inferential statistics** or **statistical inference.**

Seldom does a decision maker have complete information from which to make a decision. For example:

- Toys and Things, a toy and puzzle manufacturer, has developed a new game based on sports trivia and wants to know whether or not sports buffs will purchase the game. "Slam Dunk" and "Home Run" are two of the names under consideration. One way to minimize the risk of making a wrong decision is to hire pollsters to take a sample of, say, 2,000 from the population and ask each respondent for a reaction to the new game and its proposed titles.

- The quality assurance department of Bethlehem Steel mill must assure management that the quarter-inch wire being produced has an acceptable tensile strength. Obviously, not all the wire produced can be tested for tensile strength because testing requires the wire to be stretched until it breaks—thus destroying it. So a sample is selected at random, say, 10 pieces. Based on the test results, all the wire produced is deemed to be either satisfactory or unsatisfactory.

- Other questions involving uncertainty are: Should the daytime drama "Mama Knows Best" be discontinued immediately? Should the New York Giants select Sammy Uwea or Clint Murray in the first round of the college draft? Will a newly developed mint-flavored cereal be profitable if marketed? Should I marry Jean? Should I buy a new Rolls Royce? Should I vote for Charles Linden for town commissioner?

Statistical inference deals with inferences about a population based on a sample taken from that population. (The populations for the preceding illustrations are: all consumers who like sports trivia games, all the quarter-inch steel wire produced, all television viewers who watch soaps, all the college football players to be drafted by the professional teams, and so on.)

Since there is considerable uncertainty in decision making, it is important that all the known risks involved be scientifically evaluated. Helpful in this evaluation is *probability theory,* which has often been referred to as the science of uncertainty. The use of probability theory allows the decision maker with only limited information to analyze the risks and minimize the gamble inherent, for example, in marketing a new product or accepting an incoming shipment containing defective parts.

Because probability concepts are so important in the field of statistical inference (to be discussed starting with Chapter 8), this chapter introduces the basic language of probability, including such terms as *experiment, event, subjective probability,* and *addition and multiplication rules.*

# What Is a Probability?

No doubt you are familiar with terms such as *probability, chance,* and *likelihood.* They are often used interchangeably. The weather forecaster announces that there is a 70 percent chance of rain for Super Bowl Sunday. Based on a survey of consumers who tested a newly developed pickle with a banana taste, the probability is .03 that, if marketed, it will be a financial success. (This means that the chance of the banana-tasting pickle being accepted by the public is rather remote.) What is a probability? In general, it is the chance that something will happen.

Probability defined

> **Probability**   A measure of the likelihood that an event in the future will happen; it can only assume a value between 0 and 1, inclusive.

Three key words are used in the study of probability: *experiment, outcome,* and *event.* These terms are used in our everyday language, but in statistics they have specific meanings.

Experiment:
An observed activity

> **Experiment**   The observation of some activity or the act of taking some measurement.

This definition is more general than the one used in the physical sciences, where we picture someone manipulating test tubes or microscopes. In reference to probability, an experiment has two or more possible results, and it is uncertain which will occur.

Outcome:
A particular result

> **Outcome**   A particular result of an experiment.

For example, the tossing of a coin is an experiment. You may observe the coin toss, but you are unsure whether it will come up "heads" or "tails." Similarly, asking 500 college students whether or not they would purchase a new IBM PS/2 at a particular price is an experiment. If the coin is tossed, one particular outcome is a "head." The alternative outcome is a "tail." In the computer purchasing experiment, one possible outcome is that 273 students indicate they would purchase a PS/2 computer. Another outcome is that 317 students would purchase the computer. Still another outcome is that 423 students indicate that they would purchase the PS/2 computer. When one or more of the experiment's outcomes is observed, we call this an **event.**

Event: Several outcomes

> **Event**   A collection of one or more outcomes of an experiment.

Following are some examples to clarify the definitions of the terms *experiment, outcome,* and *event.*

| Experiment | Observe whether or not your car starts when the ignition is turned to the "on" position |
|---|---|
| Possible outcomes | Yes, it starts |
| | No, it does not start |
| Possible events | It starts |

| Experiment | Roll a die |
|---|---|
| Possible outcomes | Observe a 1 |
| | Observe a 2 |
| | Observe a 3 |
| | Observe a 4 |
| | Observe a 5 |
| | Observe a 6 |
| Possible events | Observe an even number |
| | Observe a number greater than 4 |
| | Observe a number 3 or less |
| Experiment | Count the number of inmates at the Nebraska State Prison that are over 60 years of age |
| Possible outcomes | Counted 0 that are over 60 |
| | • |
| | • |
| | • |
| | Counted 29 that are over 60 |
| | • |
| | • |
| | • |
| | Counted 48 that are over 60 |
| | • |
| | • |
| | • |
| Possible events | More than 13 are over 60 |
| | Fewer than 20 are over 60 |
| | • |
| | • |
| | • |

Notice in the first example that there are only two possible outcomes: the car starts or it doesn't. In the die-rolling experiment there are six possible outcomes, but there are many possible events. As for counting the number of inmates in the Nebraska State Prison over 60 years of age, the number of possible outcomes can be anywhere from zero to the total number of inmates. There are a large number of possible events in this experiment.

How is a probability expressed?

A probability is expressed as a decimal, such as .70, .27, or .50. However, it may be given as a fraction such as $7/10$, $27/100$ or $1/2$. It can assume a number from 0 to 1 inclusive. If a company has only five sales regions, and each region's name or number is written on a slip of paper and the slips put in a hat, the probability of selecting one of the five regions is 1. The probability of selecting from the hat a slip of paper that reads "Pittsburgh Steelers" is 0. Thus, the probability of 1 represents something that is certain to happen, and the probability of 0 represents something that cannot happen.

The closer a probability is to 0, the more improbable it is that something will happen. The closer the probability is to 1, the more sure we are it will happen. The relationship is shown in the following diagram along with a few of our personal beliefs.

0 means no chance;
1 means certainty

You might, however, assign a different probability to Slo Poke's chances or to an increase in federal taxes.

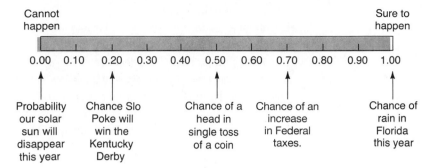

Cannot happen                    Sure to happen

0.00  0.10  0.20  0.30  0.40  0.50  0.60  0.70  0.80  0.90  1.00

Probability our solar sun will disappear this year

Chance Slo Poke will win the Kentucky Derby

Chance of a head in single toss of a coin

Chance of an increase in Federal taxes.

Chance of rain in Florida this year

## Self-Review 5–1

*The answers are at the end of the chapter.*

1. A new hand-held video game has been developed. Its market potential is to be tested by 80 veteran game players.
   a. What is the experiment?
   b. What is one possible outcome?

2. a. Suppose 65 players tried the new game and said they liked it. Is 65 a probability?
   b. The probability that the new hand-held video game will be a success is computed to be −1. Comment.
   c. Specify one possible event.

Courtesy Nintendo

## EXERCISES

*The answers to the odd-numbered exercises are at the end of the book.*

1. What is the difference between an experiment and an event?
2. What is the difference between an event and an outcome?

3. Answer the following questions:
    a.   What is the lowest and highest value a probability can assume?
    b.   When is a probability greater than 1?
    c.   When is a probability less than 0?
    d.   What conclusion can be drawn if a probability is between .8 and 1.0?
4. Is it possible for probability to assume a value of 0?
5. The Streets Department in Whitehouse, Illinois, is considering widening Indiana Avenue to three lanes. Before a final decision is made, 500 citizens are asked if they support the widening.
    a.   What is the experiment?
    b.   What are some of the possible events?
    c.   List two possible outcomes.
6. The chairman of the board of Rudd Industries is delivering a speech to the company stockholders tomorrow explaining his position that the company should merge with Zimmerman Plastics. He has received six pieces of mail on the issue and is interested in the number of writers who agree with him.
    a.   What is the experiment?
    b.   What are some of the possible events?
    c.   List two possible outcomes.

# WHY STUDY PROBABILITY?

What role does probability have in decision making? This question can be answered by citing two cases that will be discussed in forthcoming chapters.

## CASE 1

Could the difference between 20 percent and 19 percent be due to sampling?

Based on past experience, a publishing company has determined that at least 20 percent of a certain group, such as musicians, must subscribe to a monthly magazine to make it a financial success. The company is considering a monthly magazine for bird-watchers. A special copy was designed and mailed to a sample of 1,000 bird-watchers. In response, 190 out of 1,000, or 19 percent, said they would subscribe to the magazine if it were published. Should we state that this proportion is less than 20 percent and make an immediate decision not to publish the magazine? Or could the difference between the required percent (20) and the sample percent (19) be attributed to sampling, that is, chance? Probability will help us arrive at a decision for this type of problem, which will be discussed in Chapter 10.

## CASE 2

Could the difference between 1,070 psi and 1,062 psi be due to chance?

A very large construction project requires thousands of concrete blocks. Specifications state that the blocks must stand up to pressures of 1,050 pounds per square inch (psi) on the average. Two firms manufacturing these blocks submitted samples for testing. The arithmetic mean strength of the Strong Block Company blocks was 1,070 psi; those from the Taylor Company tested at 1,062 psi. Strong Block thinks it should be awarded the contract because its blocks have a higher psi. Taylor disagrees, saying that the difference of only 8 psi could be due to sampling (chance). If Strong Block's claim is correct, it will be awarded the contract. If Taylor's statement is correct, the contract will be divided between the two companies. Probability will help us reach a decision for a problem such as this in Chapter 9.

## APPROACHES TO PROBABILITY

Two approaches to probability will be discussed, namely, the *objective* and the *subjective* viewpoints. **Objective probability** can be subdivided into (1) *classical* or *a priori* probability and (2) the *relative frequency* or *a posteriori concept.*

## CLASSICAL PROBABILITY

Classical probability

The **classical** or a priori approach to probability is predicated on the assumption that the outcomes of an experiment are *equally likely.* Using the classical viewpoint, the probability of an event's happening is computed by dividing the number of favorable outcomes by the total number of possible outcomes:

$$\text{Probability of an event} = \frac{\text{Number of favorable outcomes}}{\text{Total number of possible outcomes}} \qquad (5-1)$$

### ▩ EXAMPLE

The experiment is to observe the "up" face on a six-sided die. What is the probability that a two-spot ⚁ will appear face up? There is only one "favorable" outcome, a two-spot.

### ☑ SOLUTION

The possible events are:

a one-spot ⚀

a two-spot ⚁

a three spot ⚂

a four-spot ⚃

a five-spot ⚄ and

a six-spot ⚅

All six results for the toss of the die are equally likely. Therefore:

$$\text{Probability of a two-spot} = \frac{1}{6} \quad \begin{array}{l} \leftarrow \\ \leftarrow \end{array} \quad \frac{\text{Number of favorable outcomes}}{\text{Total number of possible outcomes}}$$

$$= .167$$

Mutually exclusive events

If *only one* of several events can occur at one time, we refer to the events as being **mutually exclusive.**

Mutually exclusive  The occurrence of any one event means that none of the others can occur at the same time.

In the die-tossing experiment, the six possible outcomes are mutually exclusive events. If a two-spot comes face up on the toss of the die, a five-spot cannot occur at the same time.

**Collectively exhaustive**

If an experiment has a set of events that includes every possible outcome, such as the die-tossing experiment, the set of events is called **collectively exhaustive.**

> **Collectively exhaustive**   At least one of the events must occur when an experiment is conducted.

For the die-tossing experiment, the set of events consists of 1, 2, 3, 4, 5, and 6. The set is collectively exhaustive because it includes all possible outcomes.

**Sum of probabilities = 1**

If the set of events is collectively exhaustive and the events are mutually exclusive, the sum of the probabilities equals 1. For the coin-tossing example:

|  | Probability |
|---|---|
| Event: Head | .50 |
| Event: Tail | .50 |
| Total | 1.00 |

For the classical approach to be applied, the events must have the same chance of occurring (called *equally likely events*). Also, the set of events must be mutually exclusive and collectively exhaustive.

Historically, the classical approach to probability was developed and applied in the 17th and 18th centuries to games of chance, such as cards and dice. Note that it is unnecessary to do any experiment to determine the probability of an event occurring using the classical approach; we can logically arrive, for example, at the probability of getting a tail on the toss of one coin or three heads on the toss of three coins. Nor do we have to conduct an experiment to determine the probability that your income tax return will be audited if there are 2 million returns mailed to your district office and 2,400 are to be audited. Assuming that each return has an equal chance of being audited, your probability is .0012—found by 2,400 divided by 2 million. Obviously, the chance of your return being audited is rather remote.

## Self-Review 5–2

*The answers are at the end of the chapter.*

1. Featherstone has warehouses in four regions: southern, midwestern, Rocky Mountain, and far western. One of the regions is to be selected at random to store a seldom-used item. What is the probability that the warehouse selected would be the one in the Rocky Mountain region?

2. One card from a standard 52-card deck is to be selected at random. Express as a fraction and as a decimal:

   a. The probability the card will be a spade.
   b. The probability the card will be the jack of hearts.
   c. The probability the card will be a queen.

3. The above two examples illustrate what approach to probability?

## RELATIVE FREQUENCY CONCEPT

Relative frequency concept

Another probability concept is based on **relative frequencies.** The probability of an event happening in the long run is determined by observing what fraction of the time like events happened in the past. In terms of a formula:

$$\text{Probability of event happening} = \frac{\text{Number of times event occurred in past}}{\text{Total number of observations}}$$

### ▨ EXAMPLE

A study of 751 business administration graduates at the University of Toledo was conducted. This is the experiment. It revealed that 383 out of the 751 were *not* employed in their major area of study in college. For illustration, a person who majored in accounting is now the marketing manager of a tomato processing firm. What is the probability that a particular business graduate will be employed in an area other than his or her college major?

### ☑ SOLUTION

$$\text{Probability of event happening} = \frac{\text{Number of times event occurred in past}}{\text{Total number of observations}}$$

$$P(A) = \frac{383}{751}$$

$$= .51$$

> To simplify, letters or numbers may be used. *P* stands for probability, and in this case *P(A)* stands for the probability that a graduate is not employed in his or her major area of college study.

Since 383 out of 751, or .51 in terms of a probability, are in a different field of employment from their major in college, we can use this as an estimate of the probability. In other words, based on past experience, the probability is .51 that a business graduate is employed in a field other than his or her college major.

### Self-Review 5–3

*The answers are at the end of the chapter.*

The National Center for Health Statistics reported that of every 883 deaths in recent years, 24 resulted from an automobile accident, 182 from cancer, and 333 from heart disease.

1. Using the relative frequency approach, approximate the probability that a particu-

lar death is due to an automobile accident. Express it as a fraction and as a decimal.

2. Using the relative frequency approach, estimate the probability that a particular death is caused by cancer. Express it as a fraction and as a decimal.

# SUBJECTIVE PROBABILITY

If there is little or no past experience on which to base a probability, a probability may be arrived at subjectively. Essentially, this means evaluating the available opinions and other subjective information and then arriving at the probability. This probability is aptly called a **subjective probability.**

---

Subjective concept of probability    The likelihood (probability) of a particular event happening that is assigned by an individual based on whatever information is available.

---

Illustrations of subjective probability are:

1. Estimating the likelihood that the New England Patriots will play in the Super Bowl next year.
2. Estimating the probability that General Motors Corp. will lose its number 1 ranking in total units sold to Ford Motor Co. or Chrysler Corp. within two years.
3. Estimating the likelihood that you will earn an *A* in this course.

## Self-Review 5–4

*The answers are at the end of the chapter.*

1. What probability would you assign to the likelihood that the Dow Jones Industrial Average will climb to 3,500 this year?

2. What probability would you assign to the likelihood that you will buy a new automobile this year?

In summary, there are two viewpoints regarding probability—the objective and the subjective viewpoints. We noted that a probability statement always constitutes an estimate of an unknown value that will govern an event that has not yet occurred. There is, of course, a considerable latitude in the degree of uncertainty that surrounds this estimate, based primarily on the knowledge possessed by the individual concerning the underlying process. The individual possesses a great deal of knowledge about the toss of a die and can state that the probability that a one-spot will appear face up on the toss of a true die is one sixth. But we know very little concerning the acceptance in the marketplace of a new and untested product. For example, even though a market research director tests a newly developed product in, say, 40 retail stores and states that there is a 70 percent chance that the product will have sales of more than 1 million units, she still has very little knowledge of how consumers will react when it is marketed nationally. In both cases (the case of the person rolling a die and the testing of a new product) the individual is assigning a value to an event of interest, and a difference exists only in the predictor's confidence in the precision of the estimate. However, regardless of the viewpoint, the same laws of probability (presented in the following sections) will be applied.

# EXERCISES

*The answers to the odd-numbered exercises are at the end of the book.*

7. In each of the following cases indicate whether classical, relative frequency, or subjective probability is used.

   a. A basketball player makes 30 out of 50 foul shots. The probability is .6 that she makes the next foul shot attempted.

   b. A seven-member committee of students is formed to study environmental issues. What is the likelihood that any one of the seven is chosen as the spokesperson?

   c. You purchase one of 5 million tickets sold for Lotto Canada. What is the likelihood you win?

   d. The probability of an earthquake in northern California in the next 10 years is .80.

8. Define the term *mutually exclusive* in your own words.

9. There are 52 cards in a standard deck.

   a. What is the probability that the first card selected is a spade?

   b. What is the probability that the first card selected is the jack of spades?

   c. What concept of probability do a and b illustrate?

10. A single die is rolled.

    a. What is the probability that a two-spot will show face up?

    b. What concept of probability does this illustrate?

    c. Are the events equally likely and mutually exclusive? Explain.

11. Before a nationwide survey was conducted, 40 people were selected to test the questionnaire. One question about whether or not abortions should be legal required a yes or no answer.

    a. What is the experiment?

    b. List one possible event.

    c. Ten of the 40 favored legalized abortions. Based on these sample responses, what is the probability that a particular person will be in favor of legalized abortions?

    d. What concept of probability does this illustrate?

    e. Are the events equally likely and mutually exclusive?

12. A large number of automobile drivers were selected at random, and the number of traffic violations they had, if any, were recorded.

    | Number of violations | Number of drivers |
    |:---:|:---:|
    | 0 | 1,910 |
    | 1 | 46 |
    | 2 | 18 |
    | 3 | 12 |
    | 4 | 9 |
    | 5 or more | 5 |

    a. What is the experiment?

    b. List one possible event.

    c. What is the probability that a particular driver had exactly two violations?

    d. What concept of probability does this illustrate?

# SOME BASIC RULES OF PROBABILITY

Now that we have defined probability and described the different approaches to probability, we turn our attention to combining events by applying rules of addition and multiplication.

# Rules of Addition

## Special Rule of Addition

Two mutually exclusive events cannot both happen at one time

To apply the **special rule of addition,** the events must be mutually exclusive. Recall that *mutually exclusive* means that when one event occurs, none of the other events can occur *at the same time.* As illustrations, if a two-spot comes face up on the roll of a die, none of the other faces (1, 3, 4, 5, or 6) can be face up at the same time. And a product coming off the assembly line cannot be defective and satisfactory at the same time.

Add probability of A and B to get P(A or B)

If two events A and B are mutually exclusive, the special rule of addition states that the probability of one *or* the other event's occurring equals the sum of their probabilities. This rule is expressed in the following formula.

$$P(A \text{ or } B) = P(A) + P(B) \qquad\qquad (5-2)$$

For three mutually exclusive events designated A, B, and C, the rule is written:

$$P(A \text{ or } B \text{ or } C) = P(A) + P(B) + P(C)$$

## ■ Example

An automatic CIncinnati machine fills plastic bags with a mixture of beans, broccoli, and other vegetables. Most of the bags contain the correct weight, but because of the slight variation in the size of the beans and other vegetables, a package might be slightly underweight or overweight. A check of many packages in the past revealed:

| Weight | Event | Number of packages | Probability of occurrence | |
|---|---|---|---|---|
| Underweight | A | 100 | .025 | ← $\dfrac{100}{4{,}000}$ |
| Satisfactory | B | 3,600 | .900 | |
| Overweight | C | 300 | .075 | |
| | | 4,000 | 1.000 | |

What is the probability that a particular package will be either underweight or over-weight?

## ☑ Solution

The outcome "underweight" is the event A. The outcome "overweight" is the event C. Applying the special rule of addition:

$$P(A \text{ or } C) = P(A) + P(C)$$
$$= .025 + 0.75$$
$$= .10$$

Note that the events are mutually exclusive, meaning that a package of mixed vegetables cannot be underweight, satisfactory, and overweight at the same time. (Note that *P*(*A* or *B* or *C*) = 1.000.)

**Venn diagram: A useful tool to depict addition or multiplication rules**

English logician J. Venn (1834–1888) developed a diagram to portray graphically the outcome of an experiment. The *mutually exclusive* concept and various other rules for combining probabilities can be illustrated using this device. To construct a Venn diagram, a space is first enclosed representing the total of all possible outcomes. This space is called the *sample space,* and it is usually in the form of a rectangle. A particular outcome (for example, that the bag of mixed vegetables was overweight) is called a *sample point.* The total of all sample points equals the sample space. The following Venn diagram represents the *mutually exclusive* concept. There is no overlapping of events, meaning that the events are mutually exclusive.

**Sample point, sample space**

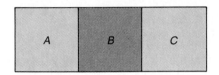

### Self-Review 5–5

*The answers are at the end of the chapter.*

A selected group of employees of Worldwide Enterprises is to be surveyed with respect to a new pension plan. In-depth interviews are to be conducted with each employee selected in the sample. The employees are classified as follows:

| Classification | Event | Number of employees |
|---|---|---|
| Supervisors | A | 120 |
| Maintenance | B | 50 |
| Production | C | 1,460 |
| Management | D | 302 |
| Secretarial | E | 68 |

1. What is the probability that the first person selected is a maintenance employee?

2. What is the probability that the first person selected is a secretary?

3. What is the probability that the first person selected is either in maintenance or a secretary?

4. What rule of probability did you use to determine the answer to 3?

5. What is the probability that the first person chosen to be interviewed is either a supervisor or in maintenance or a production worker or a manager or a secretary?

6. Draw a Venn diagram to depict these events.

7. Are these events mutually exclusive?

The probability that a bag of mixed vegetables selected is underweight *P*(*A*), plus the probability that it is not an underweight bag, written *P*(~*A*) and read "not *A*," must logically equal 1. This is written:

$$P(A) + P(\sim A) = 1$$

**The complement rule**

This can be revised to read:

$$P(A) = 1 - P(\sim A) \tag{5–3}$$

This is called the **complement rule.**

What is the complement rule? It is a way to determine the probability of an event occurring by subtracting the probability of the event *not* occurring from 1. A Venn diagram illustrating the complement rule might appear as:

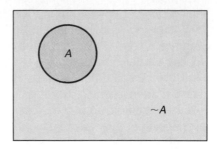

### ■ EXAMPLE

Recall that the probability that a bag of mixed vegetables is underweight is .025 and that the probability of an overweight bag is .075. Use the complement rule to show that the probability of a satisfactory bag is .900. Show the solution using a Venn diagram.

### ☑ SOLUTION

The probability that the bag is unsatisfactory equals the probability that the bag is overweight plus the probability that it is underweight. That is, $P(A \text{ or } C) = P(A) + P(C) = .025 + .075 = .100$. The bag is satisfactory if it is not underweight or overweight, so $P(B) = 1 - [P(A) + P(C)] = 1 - [.025 + .075] = 0.900$. The Venn diagram portraying this situation is:

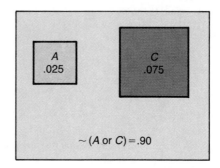

The complement rule is very important in the study of probability. In many situations it is more efficient to calculate the probability of an event happening by determining the probability of it not happening and subtracting the result from 1.

### Self-Review 5–6

*The answers are at the end of the chapter.*

Refer to Self-Review 5–5. Portray the following in the form of one Venn diagram. On the first selection, what is the probability of:

1. Selecting a maintenance employee (designated event *B*)?

2. Selecting a secretary (designated event *E*)?

3. Selecting a person in management (designated event *D*)?

4. Not selecting event *B*, or *D*, or *E*?

# EXERCISES

*The answers to the odd-numbered exercises are at the end of the book.*

13. The events *A* and *B* are mutually exclusive. Suppose $P(A) = .30$ and $P(B) = .20$. What is the probability of either *A* or *B* occurring? What is the probability that neither *A* nor *B* will happen?

14. The events *X* and *Y* are mutually exclusive. Suppose $P(X) = .05$ and $P(Y) = .02$. What is the probability of either *X* or *Y* occurring? What is the probability that neither *X* nor *Y* will happen?

15. A study of 200 grocery chains revealed these incomes after taxes:

| Income after taxes | Number of firms |
|---|---|
| Under $1 million | 102 |
| $1 million to $20 million | 61 |
| $20 million or more | 37 |

   a. What is the probability that a particular chain has under $1 million in income after taxes?

   b. What is the probability that a grocery chain selected at random has either an income between $1 million and $20 million, or an income of $20 million or more? What rule of probability was applied?

16. A study of the opinions of designers with respect to the primary color most desirable for use in executive offices showed:

| Primary color | Number of opinions |
|---|---|
| Red | 92 |
| Orange | 86 |
| Yellow | 46 |
| Green | 91 |
| Blue | 37 |
| Indigo | 46 |
| Violet | 2 |

   a. What is the experiment?

   b. What is one possible event?

   c. What is the probability of selecting a particular response and discovering that the designer prefers red or green?

   d. What is the probability that a designer does not prefer yellow?

   e. Are the events mutually exclusive? Explain.

## THE GENERAL RULE OF ADDITION

The outcomes of an experiment may not be mutually exclusive. Suppose, for illustration, that the Florida Tourist Commission selected a sample of 200 tourists who visited the state during the year. The survey revealed that 120 tourists went to Disney World and 100 went to Busch Gardens near Tampa. What is the probability that a person selected visited either Disney World or Busch Gardens? If the special rule of addition is used, the probability of selecting a tourist who went to Disney World is .60, found by 120/200. Similarly, the probability of a tourist going to Busch Gardens is .50. The sum of these probabilities is 1.10. We know, however, that this probability cannot be greater than 1. The explanation is that many tourists visited both attractions and are being counted twice! A check of the survey responses revealed that 60 out of the 200 sampled did, in fact, visit both attractions.

To answer our question, "What is the probability that a person selected visited either Disney World or Busch Gardens?" (1) add the probability that a tourist visited Disney World and the probability he/she visited Busch Gardens, and (2) subtract the probability of visiting both. Thus:

$$P(\text{Disney or Busch}) = P(\text{Disney}) + P(\text{Busch}) - P(\text{both Disney and Busch})$$

$$= \frac{120}{200} + \frac{100}{200} - \frac{60}{200}$$

$$= \frac{160}{200} = .80, \text{ or}$$

$$= .60 + .50 - .30 = .80$$

When two events overlap, the probability is called a **joint probability.** The probability that a tourist visits both attractions (.30) is an example of a joint probability.

Joint probability:
Occurrence of two or
more events at the same
time

> **Joint probability**   A probability that measures the likelihood that two or more events will happen concurrently.

In summary, the general rule of addition is used to combine events that are not mutually exclusive. This rule for two events designated $A$ and $B$ is written:

$$P(A \text{ or } B) = P(A) + P(B) - P(A \text{ and } B) \tag{5-4}$$

For the expression $P(A \text{ or } B)$, the word *or* suggests that $A$ may occur or $B$ may occur. This also includes the possibility that $A$ and $B$ may occur. This use of *or* is sometimes called an "inclusive."

### ■ EXAMPLE

An example involving joint
probability

What is the probability that a card chosen at random from a standard deck of cards will either be a king or a heart?

### ◪ SOLUTION

We may be inclined to add the probability of a king and the probability of a heart. But this creates a problem. If we do that, the king of hearts is counted with the kings and also with the hearts. So, if we simply add the probability of a king (there are 4 in a deck of 52 cards) to the probability of a heart (there are 13 in a deck of 52 cards) and report that 17 out of 52 cards meet the requirement, we have counted the king of hearts twice. We need to subtract 1 card from the 17 so that the king of hearts is counted only once. Thus, there are 16 cards that are either hearts or kings. So the probability is 16/52 = .3077.

| Card | Probability | | Explanation |
|------|------|------|------|
| King | $P(A)$ | = 4/52 | 4 kings in a deck of 52 cards |
| Heart | $P(B)$ | = 13/52 | 13 hearts in a deck of 52 cards |
| King of hearts | $P(A \text{ and } B)$ | = 1/52 | 1 king of hearts in a deck of 52 cards |

Solving:

$$P(A \text{ or } B) = P(A) + P(B) - P(A \text{ and } B)$$
$$= 4/52 + 13/52 - 1/52$$
$$= 16/52, \text{ or } .3077$$

A Venn diagram portrays these outcomes, which are not mutually exclusive.

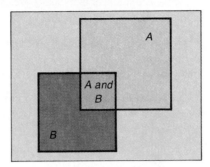

### Self-Review 5–7

*The answers are at the end of the chapter.*

Routine physical examinations are conducted annually as part of a health service program for the General Cement employees. It was discovered that 8 percent of the employees needed corrective shoes, 15 percent needed major dental work, and 3 percent needed both corrective shoes and major dental work.

1. What is the probability that an employee selected at random will need either corrective shoes or major dental work?
2. Show this situation in the form of a Venn diagram.

## Exercises

*The answers to the odd-numbered exercises are at the end of the book.*

17. The probabilities of the events A and B are .20 and .30, respectively. The events are not mutually exclusive. The probability that both A and B occur is .15. What is the probability of either A or B occurring?

18. Let $P(X) = .55$ and $P(Y) = .35$. Assume that these events are not mutually exclusive and that the probability that they both occur is .20. What is the probability of either X or Y occurring?

19. Suppose the two events A and B are mutually exclusive. What is the probability of their joint occurrence?

20. A student is taking two courses, history and math. The probability that the student will pass the history course is .60, and the probability of passing the math course is .70. The probability of passing both is .50. What is the probability of passing at least one?

21. A survey of top executives revealed that 35 percent of them regularly read *Time* magazine, 20 percent read *Newsweek,* and 40 percent read *U.S. News & World Report.* Ten percent read both *Time* and *U.S. News & World Report.*

    a. What is the probability that a particular top executive reads either *Time* or *U.S. News & World Report* regularly?

    b. What is the probability .10 called?

    c. Are the events mutually exclusive? Explain.

22. A study by the National Park Service revealed that 50 percent of the vacationers going to the Rocky Mountain region visit Yellowstone Park, 40 percent visit the Tetons, and 35 percent visit both.

    a.    What is the probability that a vacationer will visit at least one of these magnificent attractions?

    b.    What is the probability .35 called?

    c.    Are the events mutually exclusive? Explain.

## RULES OF MULTIPLICATION

### SPECIAL RULE OF MULTIPLICATION

The special rule of addition requires that two events $A$ and $B$ be **independent.** Two events are independent if the occurrence of one does not alter the probability of the other. So if the events $A$ and $B$ are independent, the occurrence of $A$ does not alter the probability of $B$.

> Independent    The occurrence of one event has no effect on the probability of the occurrence of any other event.

For two independent events $A$ and $B$, the probability that $A$ and $B$ will both occur is found by multiplying the two probabilities. This is called the **special rule of multiplication** and is written symbolically as:

$$P(A \text{ and } B) = P(A) \times P(B) \text{ or}$$
$$= P(A) \cdot P(B)$$

(5–5)

Raised dot means to *multiply.*

This rule for combining probabilities presumes that a second outcome does *not* depend on the first outcome. To illustrate what is meant by independence of outcomes, suppose two coins are tossed. The outcome of one coin (head or tail) is unaffected by the outcome of the other coin (head or tail). To put it another way, two events are independent if the outcome of the second event does not depend on the outcome of the first event.

For three independent events $A$, $B$, and $C$, the special rule of multiplication used to determine the probability that all three events will occur is:

$$P(A \text{ and } B \text{ and } C) = P(A) \cdot P(B) \cdot P(C)$$

### ■ EXAMPLE

Two coins are tossed. What is the probability that both will land tail up?

## ✓ SOLUTION

The probability of a tail showing face up on one of the coins, written $P(A)$, is one half, or .50. The probability that the other coin will land tail up, written $P(B)$, is one half, or .50. Using formula (5–5), the probability that both will happen is one fourth, or .25, found by:

$$P(A \text{ and } B) = P(A) \cdot P(B)$$

$$= \frac{1}{2} \times \frac{1}{2}$$

$$= \frac{1}{4}, \text{ or } .25$$

This can be shown by listing all of the possible outcomes. Two tails is only one of the four possible outcomes:

$$\text{T} \quad \text{T}$$

$$\text{or} \quad \text{T} \quad \text{H}$$

$$\text{or} \quad \text{H} \quad \text{T}$$

$$\text{or} \quad \text{H} \quad \text{H}$$

### Self-Review 5–8

*The answers are at the end of the chapter.*

1. From long experience, Teton Tire knows that the probability is .80 that their XB-70 will last 40,000 miles before it becomes bald or fails. An adjustment is made on any tire that does not last 40,000 miles. You purchase four XB-70s. What is the probability that all four tires will last at least 40,000 miles?

2. As cited in an earlier example, an automatic Cincinnati machine inserts mixed vegetables into a plastic bag. Past experience revealed that some packages were underweight

and some overweight, but most of them had satisfactory weight.

| Weight | Probability |
|---|---|
| Underweight | .025 |
| Satisfactory | .900 |
| Overweight | .075 |

a. What is the probability of selecting three packages from the food processing line today and finding that all three of them are underweight?
b. What does this probability mean?

If two events are not independent, they are referred to as being *dependent*. To illustrate dependency, suppose there are 10 rolls of film in a box, and it is known that 3 are defective. A roll of film is selected from the box. Obviously, the probability of selecting a defective roll is ³/₁₀, and the probability of selecting a good roll is ⁷/₁₀. Then a second roll is selected from the box without the first one being returned to the box. The probability that it is defective *depends on* whether the first roll selected was defective or good. The probability that the second roll is defective is:

²/₉, if the first roll selected was defective. (Only two defective rolls remain in the box containing nine rolls.)

³/₉, if the first roll selected was good. (All three defective rolls are still in the box containing nine rolls.)

Conditional probability

The fraction ⅔ (or ²⁄₉) is aptly called a **conditional probability** because its value is conditional on (dependent on) whether a defective or a good roll of film is chosen in the first selection from the box.

> Conditional probability   The probability of a particular event occurring, given that another event has occurred.

If we want to determine the probability that two defective rolls of film are selected one after the other, the general rule of multiplication is applied.

### GENERAL RULE OF MULTIPLICATION

General rule of multiplication

The **general rule of multiplication** is used to find the *joint probability* that two events will occur, such as selecting 2 defective rolls from the box of 10 rolls, one after the other. In general, the rule states that for two events *A* and *B,* the joint probability that both events will happen is found by multiplying the probability that event *A* will happen by the conditional probability of event *B*'s occurring. Symbolically, the joint probability *P(A and B)* is found by:

$$P(A \text{ and } B) = P(A) \cdot P(B|A) \qquad (5-6)$$

where $P(B|A)$ stands for the probability that *B* will occur *given that* A *has already occurred.* The vertical line means "given that."

### ■ EXAMPLE

To illustrate the formula, let's use the problem with 10 rolls of film in a box, 3 of which are defective. Two rolls are to be selected, one after the other. What is the probability of selecting a defective roll followed by another defective roll?

### ✓ SOLUTION

The first roll of film selected from the box being found defective is event *A.* $P(A) = \frac{3}{10}$ because 3 out of the 10 are defective. The second roll selected being found defective is event *B.* Therefore, $P(B|A) = \frac{2}{9}$, because after the first selection was found to be defective, only 2 defective rolls of film remained in the box containing 9 rolls. Determining the probability of two defectives [see formula (5−6)]:

$$P(A \text{ and } B) = P(A) \cdot P(B|A)$$
$$= \frac{3}{10} \times \frac{2}{9}$$
$$= \frac{6}{90}, \text{ or about .07}$$

This means that if this experiment were repeated 100 times, in the long run seven experiments would result in defective rolls of film on both the first and second selections.

Incidentally, it is assumed that this experiment was conducted *without replacement*—that is, the defective roll of film was not thrown back in the box before the next roll was selected. It should also be noted that the general rule of multiplication can be extended to more than two events. For three events, *A, B,* and *C,* the formula would be:

$$P(A \text{ and } B \text{ and } C) = P(A) \cdot P(B|A) \cdot P(C|A \text{ and } B)$$

For illustration, the probability that the first three rolls chosen from the box will all be defective is .00833, found by:

$$P(A \text{ and } B \text{ and } C) = P(A) \cdot P(B|A) \cdot P(C|A \text{ and } B)$$
$$= \frac{3}{10} \times \frac{2}{9} \times \frac{1}{8}$$
$$= \frac{6}{720} = .00833$$

### Self-Review 5–9

*The answers are at the end of the chapter.*

The board of directors of Tarbell Industries consists of eight men and four women. A four-member search committee is to be chosen at random to recommend a new company president.

1. What is the probability that all four mem-

bers of the search committee will be women?

2. What is the probability that all four members will be men?

3. Does the sum of the probabilities for 1 and 2 equal 1? Explain

Another application of the general rule of multiplication follows. A survey of executives dealt with their loyalty to the company. One of the questions asked was, "If you were given an offer by another company equal to or slightly better than your present position, would you remain with the company or take the other position?" The responses of the 200 executives in the survey were cross-classified with their length of service with the company. (See Table 5–1.) The type of table that resulted is usually referred to as a *contingency table.*

Contingency table

#### TABLE 5–1

**Loyalty of Executives and Length of Service with Company**

| Loyalty | Less than 1 year | 1–5 years | 6–10 years | More than 10 years | Total |
|---|---|---|---|---|---|
| Would remain | 10 | 30 | 5 | 75 | 120 |
| Would not remain | 25 | 15 | 10 | 30 | 80 |
| | | | | | 200 |

### ■ EXAMPLE

What is the probability of randomly selecting an executive who is loyal to the company (would remain) and who has more than 10 years of service?

## ☑ SOLUTION

Note that two events occur at the same time—the executive would remain with the company, and he or she has more than 10 years of service.

1. Event *A* is an executive who would remain with the company despite an equal or slightly better offer from another company. To find the probability that event *A* will happen, refer to Table 5–1. Note that there are 120 executives out of the 200 in the survey who would remain with the company, so $P(A) = 120/200$, or .60.

2. Event *B* is an executive who has more than 10 years of service with the company. Thus, $P(B|A)$ is the conditional probability that an executive with more than 10 years of service would remain with the company despite an equal or slightly better offer from another company. Referring to the contingency table, Table 5–1, 75 of the 120 executives who would remain have more than 10 years of service, so $P(B|A) = 75/120$.

Solving for the probability that an executive randomly selected will be one who would remain with the company and who has more than 10 years of service with the company, using the general rule of multiplication in formula (5–6):

$$P(A \text{ and } B) = P(A) \cdot P(B|A)$$
$$= \frac{120}{200} \times \frac{75}{120}$$
$$= \frac{9,000}{24,000}$$
$$= .375$$

### Self-Review 5–10

*The answers are at the end of the chapter.*

Refer to Table 5–1. Using the general rule of multiplication, what is the probability of selecting at random an executive who would not remain with the company and has less than one year of service?

## TREE DIAGRAMS

A *tree diagram* is very useful for portraying conditional and joint probabilities. A tree diagram is particularly useful for analyzing business decisions where there are several stages to the problem. The contingency table (Table 5–1) is used to show the construction of a tree diagram.

Steps in constructing a tree diagram

1. The construction diagram is begun by drawing a heavy dot on the left to represent the trunk of the tree (see Chart 5–1).

2. For this problem, two main branches go out from the trunk, the upper one representing "would remain" and the lower one "would not remain." Their probabilities are written on the branches, namely, 120/200 and 80/200. These are $P(A)$ and $P(\sim A)$.

3. Four branches "grow" out of each of the two main branches. These branches represent the length of service—less than 1 year, 1–5 years,

## CHART 5–1

**Tree Diagram Showing Loyalty and Length of Service**

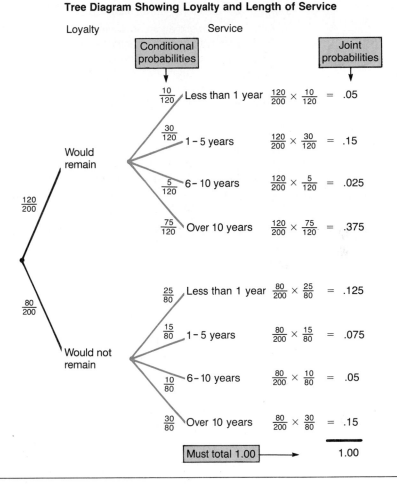

6–10 years, and more than 10 years. The conditional probabilities 10/120, 30/120, 5/120, and so on are written on the appropriate branches. These are $P(B_1|A)$, $P(B_2|A)$, $P(B_3|A)$, and $P(B_4|A)$, where $B_1$ refers to less than 1 year of service, $B_2$ 1 to 5 years, $B_3$ 6 to 10 years, and $B_4$ more than 10 years.

4. Finally, joint probabilities, that $A$ and $B$ will occur together, are shown on the right side. For example, the joint probability of randomly selecting an executive who would remain with the company and who has less than one year of service, using formula (5–6), is:

$$P(A \text{ and } B_1) = P(A) \cdot P(B_1|A)$$

$$= \left(\frac{120}{200}\right)\left(\frac{10}{120}\right) = .05$$

Because the joint probabilities represent all possible selections (would remain, 6–10 years service; would not remain, more than 10 years of service; etc.), they must sum to 1.00. (See Chart 5–1.)

### Self-Review 5–11

*The answers are at the end of the chapter.*

1. Refer to the tree diagram in Chart 5–1. Explain the path you would follow to find the joint probability of selecting an executive at random who has 6–10 years' service and who would not remain with the company upon receipt of an equal or slightly better offer from another company.

2. A random sample of the employees of the Hardware Manufacturing Company was chosen in order to determine their retirement plans after age 65. Those selected in the sample were divided into management and production. The results were:

| Employee | Plans after age 65 | | |
|---|---|---|---|
| | Retire | Not retire | Total |
| Management | 5 | 15 | 20 |
| Production | 30 | 50 | 80 |
| | | | 100 |

a. What is the table called?
b. Draw a tree diagram, and determine the joint probabilities.
c. Do the joint probabilities total 1.00? Why?

## EXERCISES

*The answers to the odd-numbered exercises are at the end of the book.*

23. a.  What is a joint probability?
    b.  What is a conditional probability?
24. What is a contingency table? What does it show?
25. a.  What is the following picture called?
    b.  What is the name of the total area encompassed by the large rectangle?
    c.  Are the events $D$ and $H$ mutually exclusive? Explain.
    d.  What is the formula for arriving at the probability of $D$ or $H$ happening?

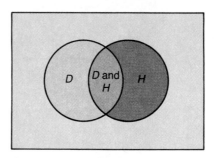

26. Suppose $P(A) = .40$ and $P(B|A) = .30$. What is the joint probability of $A$ and $B$?
27. Suppose $P(X_1) = .75$ and $P(Y_2|X_1) = .40$. What is the joint probability of $X_1$ and $Y_2$?
28. Refer to the following table.

| Second event | First event | | | |
|---|---|---|---|---|
| | $A_1$ | $A_2$ | $A_3$ | Total |
| $B_1$ | 2 | 1 | 3 | 6 |
| $B_2$ | 1 | 2 | 1 | 4 |
| Total | 3 | 3 | 4 | 10 |

a.  Determine $P(A_1)$.
b.  Determine $P(B_1|A_2)$.
c.  Determine $P(B_2 \text{ and } A_3)$.

29. Three defective electric toothbrushes were accidentally shipped to a drugstore by Cleanbrush Products along with 17 nondefective ones.
   a. What is the probability that the first two electric toothbrushes sold will be returned to the drugstore because they are defective?
   b. What is the probability that the first two electric toothbrushes sold will not be defective?

30. Each salesperson at Stiles-Comptom is rated either below average, average, or above average with respect to sales ability. Each salesperson is also rated with respect to his or her potential for advancement—either fair, good, or excellent. These traits for the 500 salespeople were cross-classified into the following table.

| Sales ability | Potential for advancement | | |
|---|---|---|---|
| | Fair | Good | Excellent |
| Below average | 16 | 12 | 22 |
| Average | 45 | 60 | 45 |
| Above average | 93 | 72 | 135 |

   a. What is this table called?
   b. What is the probability that a salesperson selected at random will have above-average sales ability and excellent potential for advancement?
   c. Construct a tree diagram showing all the probabilities, conditional probabilities, and joint probabilities.

## BAYES' THEOREM

In the 18th century Reverend Thomas Bayes, an English Presbyterian minister, pondered this question: Does God really exist? Being interested in mathematics, he attempted to develop a formula to arrive at the probability that God does exist based on evidence that was available to him on earth. Later Laplace refined Bayes' work and gave it the name "Bayes' theorem." In a workable form, **Bayes' theorem** is:

What is the probability of A, given B has occurred?

$$P(A_1|B) = \frac{P(A_1) \cdot P(B|A_1)}{P(A_1) \cdot P(B|A_1) + P(A_2) \cdot P(B|A_2)} \qquad (5-7)$$

(The meaning of each of these letters will be explained in the following example, but note that they refer to conditional probabilities.)

Consider the following problem. Suppose 5 percent of the population of Umen, a fictional Third World country, have a disease that is peculiar to that country. We will let $A_1$ refer to the event "has the disease" and $A_2$ refer to the event "does not have the disease." Thus, we know that if we select a person from Umen at random, the probability that the individual chosen has the disease is .05, or $P(A_1) = .05$. This probability, $P(A_1) = P(\text{has the disease}) = .05$, is called the *prior probability*. It is given this name because the probability is assigned before any empirical data are obtained. The prior probability that a person is not afflicted with the disease is therefore .95, or $P(A_2) = .95$, found by $1 - .05$.

Prior probability

There is a diagnostic technique to detect the disease, but it is not very accurate. Let B denote the event "test shows the disease is present." Assume that historical evidence shows that if a person actually has the disease, the probability that the test will indicate the presence of the disease is .90. Using the conditional probability definitions developed earlier in this chapter, this statement is written as:

$$P(B|A_1) = .90$$

Assume the probability is .15 that a person actually does not have the disease but the test indicates the disease is present.

$$P(B|A_2) = .15$$

Let's randomly select a person from Umen and perform the test. The test results indicate the disease is present. What is the probability that the person actually has the disease? In symbolic form, we want to know $P(A_1|B)$, which is interpreted as: $P$(has the disease|the test results are positive). The probability $P(A_1|B)$ is called a *posterior* or *revised probability*. With the help of Bayes' theorem, we can determine the revised probability.

Bayes' theorem

$$P(A_1|B) = \frac{P(A_1) \cdot P(B|A_1)}{P(A_1) \cdot P(B|A_1) + P(A_2) \cdot P(B|A_2)}$$

$$= \frac{(.05)(.90)}{(.05)(.90) + (.95)(.15)}$$

$$= \frac{.0450}{.1875}$$

$$= .24$$

The revised or posterior probability that a person has the disease, given that he or she tested positive, is .24. How is the result interpreted? If a person is selected at random from the population, the probability that he or she has the disease is .05. If the person is tested and the test result is positive, the probability that the person actually has the disease is increased about five-fold, from .05 to .24.

The preceding problem included only two events, $A_1$ and $A_2$, as prior probabilities. If there are more than two prior probabilities, the denominator of Bayes' theorem requires additional terms. If the prior probability distribution consists of $n$ mutually exclusive events, Bayes' theorem reads as follows.

$$P(A_i|B) = \frac{P(A_i) \cdot P(B|A_i)}{P(A_1) \cdot P(B|A_1) + P(A_2) \cdot P(B|A_2) + \cdots + P(A_n) \cdot P(B|A_n)}$$

where $A_i$ refers to any of the $n$ possible outcomes.

Using the preceding notation, the calculations for the Umen problem are summarized in the following table.

| Events, $A_i$ | Prior probability, $P(A_i)$ | Conditional probability, $P(B|A_i)$ | Joint probability, $P(A_i \text{ and } B)$ | Posterior probability, $P(A_i|B)$ |
|---|---|---|---|---|
| Disease, $A_1$ | .05 | .90 | .0450 | .0450/.1875 = .24 |
| No disease, $A_2$ | .95 | .15 | .1425 | .1425/.1875 = .76 |
| | | | $P(B) = .1875$ | 1.00 |

Another illustration of Bayes' theorem follows.

## ■ EXAMPLE

A manufacturer of VCRs purchases a particular microchip, called the LS-24, from three suppliers: Hall Electronic, Schuller Sales, and Crawford Components. Thirty percent of the LS-24 chips are purchased from Hall Electronics, 20 percent from Schuller Sales,

Photo courtesy of Hewlett-Packard Company

and the remaining 50 percent from Crawford Components. The manufacturer has extensive histories on the three suppliers and knows that 3 percent of the LS-24 chips from Hall Electronics are defective, 5 percent of chips from Schuller Sales are defective, and 4 percent of the chips purchased from Crawford Components are defective.

When the LS-24 chips arrive at the manufacturer, they are placed directly in a bin and not inspected or otherwise identified by supplier. A worker selects a chip for installation in a VCR and finds it defective. What is the probability that it was manufactured by Schuller Sales?

## ☑ SOLUTION

As a first step, let's summarize some of the information given in the problem statement.

- There are three events, that is, three suppliers.

  $A_1$    The LS-24 was purchased from Hall Electronics
  $A_2$    The LS-24 was purchased from Schuller Sales
  $A_3$    The LS-24 was purchased from Crawford Components

- The prior probabilities are:

  $P(A_1) = .30$    The probability the LS-24 was manufactured by Hall Electronics
  $P(A_2) = .20$    The probability the LS-24 was manufactured by Schuller Sales
  $P(A_3) = .50$    The probability the LS-24 was manufactured by Crawford Components

- The additional information is that the LS-24 to be assembled is defective.

  $B_1$    The LS-24 is defective
  $B_2$    The LS-24 is not defective

- The following conditional probabilities are given.

  $P(B_1|A_1) = .03$    The probability that an LS-24 chip produced by Hall Electronics is defective
  $P(B_1|A_2) = .05$    The probability that an LS-24 chip produced by Schuller Sales is defective
  $P(B_1|A_3) = .04$    The probability that an LS-24 chip produced by Crawford Components is defective

- A chip is selected from the bin. Because the chips are not inspected or otherwise identified by supplier, we are not certain which supplier manufactured the chip. We want to determine the probability that the defective chip was purchased from Schuller Sales. This probability is written $P(A_2|B_1)$.

Look at Schuller's quality record. It is the worst of the three suppliers. Now that we have found a defective LS-24 chip, we suspect that $P(A_2|B_1)$ is greater than $P(A_2)$. That is, we expect the revised probability to be greater than .20. But how much greater? Bayes' theorem can give us the answer. As a first step, consider the tree diagram in Chart 5–2.

The events are dependent, so the prior probability in the first branch is multiplied by the conditional probability in the second branch to obtain the joint probability. The joint probability is reported in the last column of Chart 5–2. To construct the tree diagram of Chart 5–2, we used a time sequence that moved from the supplier to the determination of whether the chip was acceptable or unacceptable.

What we need to do is reverse the time process. That is, instead of moving from left to right on Chart 5–2, we need to move from right to left. We have a defective chip, and we want to determine the likelihood that it was purchased from Schuller Sales. How is that accomplished? We first look at the joint probabilities as relative frequencies

## Chart 5-2

### Tree Diagram of VCR Manufacturing Problem

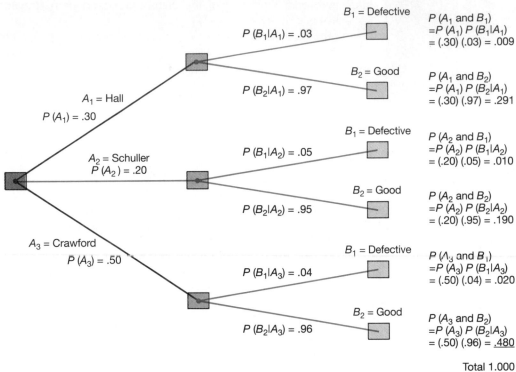

out of 1,000 cases. For example, the likelihood of a defective LS-24 chip that was produced by Hall Electronics is .009. So out of 1,000 cases we would expect to find 9 defective chips produced by Hall Electronics. We observe that in 39 of 1,000 cases the LS-24 chip selected for assembly will be defective, found by 9 + 10 + 20. Of these 39 defective chips, 10 were produced by Schuller Sales. Thus, the probability that the defective LS-24 chip was purchased from Schuller Sales is 10/39 = .2564. We have now determined the revised probability of $P(A_2|B_1)$. Before we found the defective chip, the likelihood that it was purchased from Schuller Sales was .20. This likelihood has been increased to .2564.

This information is summarized in the following table.

| Events, $A_i$ | Prior, probability, $P(A_i)$ | Conditional probability, $P(B_1|A_i)$ | Joint probability, $P(A_i \text{ and } B_1)$ | Posterior probability, $P(A_i|B_1)$ |
|---|---|---|---|---|
| Hall | .30 | .03 | .009 | .009/.039 = .2308 |
| Schuller | .20 | .05 | .010 | .010/.039 = .2564 |
| Crawford | .50 | .04 | .020 | .020/.039 = .5128 |
| | | | $P(B_1)$ = .039 | 1.0000 |

The probability that the defective LS-24 chip came from Schuller Sales can be found by using Bayes' theorem. We want to compute $P(A_2|B_1)$, where $A_2$ refers to Schuller Sales and $B_1$ to the fact that the selected LS-24 chip was defective.

$$P(A_2|B_1) = \frac{P(A_2)P(B_1|A_2)}{P(A_1)P(B_1|A_1) + P(A_2)P(B_1|A_2) + P(A_3)P(B_1|A_3)}$$

$$= \frac{(.20)(.05)}{(.30)(.03) + (.20)(.05) + (.50)(.04)}$$

$$= \frac{.010}{.039} = .2564$$

This is the same result obtained from the Chart 5–2 and from the conditional probability table.

### Self-Review 5–12

*The answers are at the end of the chapter.*

Refer to the preceding example and solution.

1. Design a formula using words to find the probability that the part selected came from Crawford Components, given that it was a good chip.

2. Compute the probability using Bayes' theorem.

## EXERCISES

*The answers to the odd-numbered exercises are at the end of the book.*

31. $P(A_1) = .60$, $P(A_2) = .40$, $P(B_1|A_1) = .05$, and $P(B_1|A_2) = .10$. Use Bayes' theorem to determine $P(A_1|B_1)$.

32. $P(A_1) = .20$, $P(A_2) = .40$, and $P(A_3) = .40$. $P(B_1|A_1) = .25$, $P(B_1|A_2) = .05$, and $P(B_1|A_3) = .10$. Use Bayes' theorem to determine $P(A_3|B_1)$.

33. The Ludlow Wildcats baseball team, a minor league team in the Cleveland Indians organization, plays 70 percent of their games at night and 30 percent during the day. The team wins 50 percent of their night games and 90 percent of their day games. According to today's newspaper, they won yesterday. What is the probability the game was played at night?

34. Dr. Stallter has been teaching basic statistics for many years. She knows that 80 percent of the students will complete the assigned problems. She has also determined that among those who do their assignments, 90 percent will pass the course. Among those students who do not do their homework, 60 percent will pass. Mike Fishbaugh took statistics last semester from Dr. Stallter and received a passing grade. What is the probability he completed the assignments?

35. The credit department of Lion's Department Store in Anaheim, California, reported that 30 percent of their sales are cash, 30 percent are paid for by check at the time of the purchase, and 40 percent are charged. Twenty percent of the cash purchases, 90 percent of the checks, and 60 percent of the charges are for more than $50. Ms. Tina Stevens just purchased a new dress that cost $120. What is the probability that she paid cash?

36. The Lorrange Plastics Company has four raw-material suppliers. The following table shows the proportion purchased from each supplier and the percent of material that is defective from that supplier.

| Supplier | Percent purchased | Percent defective |
|---|---|---|
| Roberts, Inc. | 30.0 | 2.50 |
| Asmus Mfg. | 20.0 | 1.75 |
| Lewis, Ltd. | 25.0 | 3.00 |
| Melvin, Inc. | 25.0 | 1.00 |

The material used this morning was defective. What is the probability it was purchased from Asmus Mfg.?

## SOME PRINCIPLES OF COUNTING

*Three formulas for determining the total number of events*

If the number of possible outcomes in an experiment is small, it is relatively easy to list and count all of the possible events. There are six possible events, for example, resulting from the roll of a die, namely:

If, however, there are a large number of possible outcomes, such as the number of boys and girls for families with 10 children, it would be tedious to list and count all the possibilities. They could have all boys, one boy and nine girls, two boys and eight girls, and so on. To facilitate counting, three counting formulas will be examined: the *multiplication formula,* the *permutation formula,* and the *combination formula.*

### THE MULTIPLICATION FORMULA

> Multiplication formula   If there are $m$ ways of doing one thing and $n$ ways of doing another thing, there are $m \times n$ ways of doing both.

In terms of a formula:

$$\text{Total number of arrangements} = m \times n \qquad (5-8)$$

This can be extended to more than two events. For three events $m, n,$ and $o$:

*Multiplication formula for three events*

$$\text{Total number of arrangements} = m \times n \times o$$

### ■ EXAMPLE

An automobile dealer wants to advertise that for $19,999 you can buy either a convertible, a two-door, or a four-door model with your choice of either wire wheel covers or solid wheel covers. How many different arrangements of models and wheel covers can the dealer offer?

## ☑ SOLUTION

Of course, the dealer could determine the total number of arrangements by picturing and counting them. There are six.

*For $19,999 you have a choice of six. Hurry, buy now.*

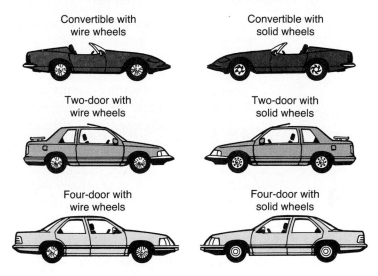

Convertible with wire wheels · Convertible with solid wheels

Two-door with wire wheels · Two-door with solid wheels

Four-door with wire wheels · Four-door with solid wheels

We can employ the multiplication formula as a check (where *m* is the number of models and *n* the wheel cover type). Using formula (5–8):

$$\text{Total possible arrangements} = m \times n$$
$$= 3 \times 2$$
$$= 6$$

It was not difficult to list and count all the possible models and wheel cover arrangements in this example. Suppose, however, that the dealer decided to offer eight models and six types of wheel covers. It would be tedious to picture and count all the possible alternatives. Instead, the multiplication formula can be used. In this case, $m \times n = 8 \times 6 = 48$ possible arrangements.

Note in the preceding applications of the multiplication formula that there were *two or more groupings*. The automobile dealer, for example, offered a choice of models and a choice of wheel covers. If a home builder offered you four different exterior styles of a home to choose from and three interior floor plans, the multiplication formula would be used to find how many different arrangements were possible.

*Two groups—exterior style and interior floor plan*

### Self-Review 5–13

*The answers are at the end of the chapter.*

1. Stiffin Lamps has developed five lamp bases and four lamp shades that can be used together. How many different arrangements of base and shade can be offered?

2. Pioneer manufactures three models of stereo receivers, two cassette decks, four speakers, and three turntables. When the four types of compatible components are sold together, they form a "system." How many different systems can the electronics firm offer?

## THE PERMUTATION FORMULA

Permutation applicable for one group of objects

As noted, the multiplication formula is applied to find the number of possible arrangements for two or more groups. The **permutation formula** is applied to find the possible number of arrangements where there is only *one* group of objects. As illustrations of this type of problem:

- A group of three electronic parts is to be assembled into a plug-in unit for a television set. The parts can be assembled in any order. The question involving counting is: In how many different ways can the three parts be assembled?

- A machine operator must make four safety checks before starting his machine. It does not matter in which order the checks are made. In how many different ways can the operator make the checks?

One order for the first illustration might be: transistor first, the LEDs second, and the synthesizer third. This arrangement is called a **permutation.**

---

Permutation    Any arrangement of *r* objects selected from *n* possible objects.

---

Permutation formula

Note that the arrangements *a, b, c,* and *b, a, c* are *different* permutations. The formula employed to count the total number of different permutations is:

$$_nP_r = \frac{n!}{(n-r)!}$$ (5–9)

where:

- *P* is the number of permutations, or ways the objects can be arranged.
- *n* is the total number of objects. In the first illustration, there are three electronic parts, so $n = 3$.
- *r* is the number of objects to be used at one time. In the electronics problem, all the objects (electronic parts) are to be assembled, so $r = 3$. If only two out of the three electronic parts were to be inserted in the plug-in unit, *r* would be 2.

4! means $4 \times 3 \times 2 \times 1$

Before we solve the two problems illustrated, note that permutations and combinations (to be discussed shortly) use a notation called *n factorial.* It is written *n!* and means the product of $n(n-1)(n-2)(n-3) \cdots [n-(n-1)]$. For instance, 5! would be found by $5(5-1)(5-2)(5-3)[5-(5-1)]$. Thus, $5 \cdot 4 \cdot 3 \cdot 2 \cdot 1 = 120$.

As shown below, numbers can be canceled when the same numbers are included in the numerator and denominator.

$$\frac{6!3!}{4!} = \frac{6 \cdot 5 \cdot \not{4} \cdot \not{3} \cdot \not{2} \cdot \not{1}(3 \cdot 2 \cdot 1)}{\not{4} \cdot \not{3} \cdot \not{2} \cdot \not{1}} = 180$$

0! = 1

By definition, zero factorial, written 0!, is set equal to 1. That is, $0! = 1$.

## ▪ EXAMPLE

Referring to the group of three electronic parts that are to be assembled in any order, in how many different ways can they be assembled?

## ☑ SOLUTION

$n = 3$ because there are three electronic parts to be assembled. $r = 3$ because all three are to be inserted in the plug-in unit. Solving using formula (5–9):

$$_nP_r = \frac{n!}{(n-r)!} = \frac{3!}{(3-3)!} = \frac{3!}{0!} = \frac{3!}{1} = 6$$

### Self-Review 5–14

*The answers are at the end of the chapter.*

1. What does 6! equal?
2. What does 6!2!/4!3! equal?
3. Recall that a machine operator must make four safety checks before starting to machine a part. It does not matter in which order the checks are made. In how many different ways can the operator make the checks?
4. The 10 numbers 0 through 9 are to be used in code groups of four to identify an item of clothing. Code 1083 might identify a blue blouse, size medium. The code group 2031 might identify a pair of pants, size 18, and so on. Repetitions of numbers are not permitted. That is, the same number cannot be used twice (or more) in a total sequence. For example, 2256, 2562, or 5559 would not be permitted. How many different code groups can be designed?

Another approach to the number of permutations

A check can be made of the number of permutations arrived at using the permutations formula. To check we merely determine how many spaces have to be filled and the possibilities for each space. In the problem involving three electronic parts, there are three locations in the plug-in unit for the three parts. There are three possibilities for the first space, two for the second (one has been used up), and one for the third, as follows:

$$(3)(2)(1) = 6 \text{ permutations}$$

The six ways in which the three electronic parts, lettered *A, B, C,* can be arranged are:

$$\begin{array}{ccc} ABC & BAC & CAB \\ ACB & BCA & CBA \end{array}$$

To cite another example:

## ■ EXAMPLE

Suppose that there are eight machines but only three spaces on the floor of the machine shop for the machines. In how many different ways can eight machines be arranged in the three available spaces?

## ☑ SOLUTION

There are eight possibilities for the first space, seven for the second space (one has been used up), and six for the third space. Then:

$$(8)(7)(6) = 336 \text{ permutations}$$

As before, this may also be expressed mathematically by saying that the number of permutations, *P,* of *n* items is dependent on the number of spaces, *r,* available:

$$_nP_r = \frac{n!}{(n-r)!} = \frac{8!}{(8-3)!} = \frac{8!}{5!} = \frac{(8)(7)(6)5!}{5!} = 336 \text{ permutations}$$

### Self-Review 5–15

*The answers are at the end of the chapter.*

A musician wants to write a score based on only five chords: B-flat, C, D, E and G. However, only three chords out of the five will be used in succession, such as C, B-flat, and E. Repetitions, such as B-flat, B-flat, and E, will not be permitted.

1. How many permutations of the five chords, taken three at a time, are possible?

2. Using formula (5–9), how many permutations are possible?

### PERMUTATIONS ALLOWING FOR REPETITIONS

Formula for number of permutations when repetitions allowed

The previous discussion of permutations did not allow for any repetition. If repetitions are permitted, the permutation formula is:

$$\boxed{_nP_r = n^r} \qquad\qquad (5-10)$$

To illustrate the point, assume that two letters, *A* and *B,* are to be taken two at a time. With repetitions, such as *AA,* there are four permutations possible, found by $P = n^r = 2^2$. The four permutations are *AA, AB, BA,* and *BB.*

### Self-Review 5–16

*The answers are at the end of the chapter.*

In Self-Review 5–15, the musician decided to use five chords taken three at a time. Repetitions—such as B-flat, B-flat, and E—were not permitted. There are 60 possi-ble arrangements (permutations) of three chords. If repetitions are permitted, how many permutations are possible?

No repetitions allowed

In brief review of permutations, if a set of objects designated by *a, b, c, d,* and *e* can also be arranged as *a, c, d, e,* and *b;* and if they can be arranged as *c, a, e, b,* and *d;* and so on, then there are 120 permutations of these five objects taken five at a time, found by

$$_nP_r = \frac{n!}{(n-r)!} = \frac{5!}{(5-5)!} = 120$$

where:

*n*   is the total number of objects.

*r*   is the number of objects considered for each permutation.

If only two of the five objects were considered—such as *a, b; d, a;* or *c, e*—then there are a total of 20 permutations possible, found by:

$$_nP_r = \frac{n!}{(n-r)!} = \frac{5!}{(5-2)!} = 20$$

Note that in permutations *the order in which the objects are listed differs from one arrangement to the next* (that is, *a, b* differs from *b, a; e, a* differs from *a, e;* and so on). Each arrangement is counted.

Repetitions allowed

If repetitions are permitted, such as *a, a, a, b, b,* or *a, a, b, b, d,* the number of permutations can be determined by $_nP_r = n^r$. For the five objects ($n = 5$) taken five at a time ($r = 5$), there are 3,125 possible arrangements, found by $_nP_r = n^r = 5^5$, using formula (5–10).

## THE COMBINATION FORMULA

In determining the number of permutations of *n* different things taken *r* at a time, the order of things is of concern. For example, in painting three color dots on a resistor, the order could be red, orange, and blue (meaning, say, a 500-ohm resistor); or the order could be orange, blue, and red (meaning a 1,000-ohm resistor); and so on. There are six permutations of the three colors, found by:

$$_nP_r = \frac{n!}{(n-r)!} = \frac{3 \cdot 2 \cdot 1}{(3-3)!} = 6$$

Combination formula

Suppose, however, it has been decided that *any combination* of red, orange, and blue will be used on a resistor to identify it as a 750-ohm resistor; *the order is not important.* In effect, the many different ways of ordering the three colors are disregarded. That is, the combination of red, blue, and orange on a resistor is considered the same as orange, blue, and red; both would identify a 750-ohm resistor. This means that the combination of red, orange, and blue can be used only once for identification purposes.

> Combination   The number of ways to choose *r* objects from a group of *n* objects without regard to order.

The **combination formula** is:

$$\boxed{_nC_r = \frac{n!}{r!(n-r)!}}$$                                                (5–11)

## ■ EXAMPLE

The paint department has been given the assignment of designing color codes for 42 different parts. Three colors are to be used on each part, but a combination of three colors used for one part cannot be rearranged and used to identify a different part. This means that if green, yellow, and violet were used to identify a camshaft, yellow, violet, and green (or any other combination of these three colors) could not be used to identify, say, a pinion gear. Would seven colors taken three at a time be adequate to color-code the 42 parts?

## ☑ SOLUTION

Using formula (5–11) there are 35 combinations, found by

$$_7C_3 = \frac{n!}{r!(n-r)!} = \frac{7!}{3!(7-3)!} = \frac{7!}{3!4!} = 35$$

The seven colors taken three at a time (i.e., three colors to a part) would not be adequate to color-code the 42 different parts because they would provide only 35 combinations. Eight colors taken three at a time would give 56 different combinations. This would be more than adequate to color-code the 42 different parts.

### Self-Review 5–17

*The answers are at the end of the chapter.*

1. In the preceding solution we said that eight colors taken three at a time would give 56 different combinations. Using formula (5–11), is that true?

2. As an alternative plan for color-coding the 42 different parts, it has been suggested that only two colors be placed on a part. Would 10 colors be adequate to color-code the 42 different parts? (Again, a combination of two colors could only be used once—that is, if pink and blue were coded for one part, blue and pink could not be used to identify a different part.)

## SUMMARIZING THE DIFFERENCE BETWEEN A PERMUTATION AND A COMBINATION

For a permutation, each different order of objects is counted

To qualify as a *permutation*, the *order of the objects for each possible outcome is different*. For three objects, *a, b,* and *c,* the order *a, b, c* is one order (permutation); *b, a, c* is another permutation; *c, a, b* is another permutation; and so on. There are six possible arrangements of these three objects taken three at a time. Using the permutation formula:

$$_nP_r = \frac{n!}{(n-r)!} = \frac{3!}{(3-3)!} = \frac{3 \cdot 2 \cdot 1}{1} = 6$$

For a combination, order *ab* considered same as order *ba*

If the order of the objects is not important, the total number of orders is called a *combination*. For example, if executives Able, Baker, and Chauncy are to be chosen as a committee to negotiate a merger, there is only one possible combination of these three; the committee of Able, Baker, and Chauncy is the same as the committee of Baker, Chauncy, and Able. Using the combination formula:

$$_nC_r = \frac{n!}{r!(n-r)!} = \frac{3 \cdot 2 \cdot 1}{3 \cdot 2 \cdot 1(1)} = 1$$

## EXERCISES

*The answers to the odd-numbered exercises are at the end of the book.*

37. a. Describe what is meant by a permutation.
    b. Describe what is meant by a combination.
38. Solve the following:
    a. 40!/35!.

b.    $_7P_4$.

c.    $_5C_2$.

39. Solve the following:

a.    20!/17!

b.    $_9P_3$.

c.    $_7C_2$.

40. A pollster randomly selects 4 of 10 available people. How many different groups of 4 are possible?

41. A telephone number consists of seven digits, the first three representing the exchange. How many different numbers are possible within the 537 exchange?

42. An overnight express company must include five cities on its route. How many different routes are possible assuming that it does not matter which order the cities are included in the routing?

43. A representative of the Environmental Protection Agency (EPA) wants to select samples from 10 different landfills. He has 15 landfills from which he can collect samples. How many different samples are possible?

44. A national pollster has developed 15 questions designed to rate the performance of the president of the United States. The pollster will select 10 of these questions. How many different arrangements are there for the order of the 10 selected questions?

*Courtesy Airborne Express*

# CHAPTER OUTLINE

I.   A probability is a value between 0 and 1 that represents the likelihood that a particular event will happen.

   A.   An experiment is the observation of some activity or the act of taking some measurement.

   B.   An outcome is a particular result of an experiment.

   C.   An event is the collection of one or more outcomes of an experiment.

II.  There are three definitions of probability.

   A.   The classical definition applies when there are $n$ equally likely outcomes to an experiment.

   B.   The relative frequency definition occurs when the number of times an event happens is divided by the total number of observations.

   C.   A subjective probability is based on whatever information is available. It is applied only when there is not enough information for another method to be used.

III. Two events are mutually exclusive if by virtue of one event happening the other cannot happen.

IV.  Events are independent if the occurrence of one event does not affect the occurrence of another event.

V.   The rules of addition are used to combine events.

   A.   The special rule of addition is used to combine events that are mutually exclusive.

$$P(A \text{ or } B) = P(A) + P(B) \qquad (5-2)$$

   B.   The general rule of addition is used to combine events that are not mutually exclusive.

$$P(A \text{ or } B) = P(A) + P(B) - P(A \text{ and } B) \qquad (5-4)$$

   C.   The complement rule is used to determine the probability of an event happening by subtracting the probability of the event not happening from 1.

$$P(A) = 1 - P(\sim A) \qquad (5-3)$$

VI.   The rules of multiplication are also used to combine events.
   A.   Events are independent if the occurrence of one event has no effect on the occurrence of any other event.
   B.   The special rule of multiplication is used to combine events that are independent.

$$P(A \text{ and } B) = P(A)P(B) \qquad (5-5)$$

   C.   The general rule of multiplication is used to combine events that are not independent.

$$P(A \text{ and } B) = P(A)P(B|A) \qquad (5-6)$$

   D.   A joint probability is the likelihood that two or more events will happen at the same time.
   E.   A conditional probability is the likelihood that an event will happen, given that another event has already happened.
   F.   Bayes' Theorem is a method of revising a probability, given that additional information is obtained. For two events:

$$P(A_1|B) = \frac{P(A_1) \cdot P(B|A_1)}{P(A_1) \cdot P(B|A_1) + P(A_2) \cdot P(B|A_2)} \qquad (5-7)$$

VII.  There are three counting rules that are useful in determining the total number of ways in which events can occur.
   A.   The multiplication rule states that if there are $m$ ways one event can happen and $n$ ways another event can happen, then there are $mn$ ways the two events can happen.

$$\text{Number of arrangements} = m \times n \qquad (5-8)$$

   B.   A permutation is an arrangement in which the order of the objects is important.

$$_nP_r = \frac{n!}{(n-r)!} \qquad (5-9)$$

   C.   A combination is an arrangement where the order of the objects is not important.

$$_nC_r = \frac{n!}{r!(n-r)!} \qquad (5-10)$$

# EXERCISES

*The answers to the odd-numbered exercises are at the end of the book.*

45.  The marketing research department at Vernors plans to survey teenagers regarding their reactions to a newly developed soft drink. They will be asked to compare it with their favorite soft drink.
   a.   What is the experiment?
   b.   What is one possible event?

46.  The number of times an event occurred in the past is divided by the total number of occurrences. What is this approach to probability called?

47.  The probability that the cause and the cure of cancer will be discovered before the year 2000 is .02. What viewpoint of probability does this statement illustrate?

48.  Is it true that, if there is absolutely no chance a person will recover from 50 bullet wounds, the probability assigned to this event is $-1.00$?

49.  On the throw of one die, what is the probability that a one-spot or a two-spot or a six-spot will appear face up? What definition of probability is being used?

50.  A study of the weekly offering in the envelopes at the First Baptist Church in Warren, Pennsylvania, revealed the following:

| Offering in envelope | Number |
|---|---|
| $ 0 up to $ 5 | 200 |
| 5 up to 10 | 100 |
| 10 up to 20 | 75 |
| 20 up to 50 | 75 |
| 50 or more | 50 |
| Total | 500 |

a. What is the probability of selecting an envelope at random and finding $50 or more in it?

b. Are the classes "$0 up to $5," "$5 up to $10," and so on considered mutually exclusive?

c. If the probabilities associated with each class were totaled, what would the total be?

d. What is the probability of selecting an envelope at random and finding it to contain up to $10?

e. What is the probability of finding less than $50 in an envelope selected at random?

51. Define each of these terms:
a. Conditional probability.
b. Event.
c. Joint probability.

52. The first card selected from a standard 52-card deck was a king.
a. If it is returned to the deck, what is the probability that a king will be drawn on the second selection?
b. If the king is not replaced, what is the probability that a king will be drawn on the second selection?
c. What is the probability that a king will be selected on the first draw from the deck and another king on the second draw (assuming that the first king was not replaced)?

53. Armco, a manufacturer of traffic light systems, found that under accelerated life tests, 95 percent of the newly developed systems lasted three years before failing to change the signals properly.
a. If a city purchased four of these systems, what is the probability that all four systems would operate properly for at least three years?
b. Which rule of probability does this illustrate?
c. Using letters to represent the four systems, design an equation to show how you arrived at the answer to part a.

54. Refer to the following picture.

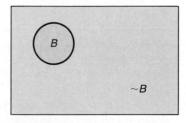

a. What is the picture called?
b. What is the total area called?
c. What rule of probability is illustrated?
d. B represents the event of choosing a family that receives welfare payments. What does $P(B) + P(\sim B)$ equal?

55. In a management trainee program at Claremont Enterprises, 80 percent of the trainees are female and 20 percent male. Ninety percent of the females attended college, and 78 percent of the males attended college.

    a.   A management trainee is selected at random. What is the probability that the person selected is a female who did not attend college?

    b.   Construct a tree diagram showing all the probabilities, conditional probabilities, and joint probabilities.

    c.   Do the joint probabilities total 1.00? Why?

56. A coin is tossed four times.

    a.   What is the probability that each of the four tosses will result in a head face up?

    b.   Using the letters A, B, C, and D, write the formula for the probability of this outcome.

    c.   Suppose four heads did appear face up on the tosses of the coin. What is the probability that a head will appear face up on the next toss of the coin?

57. Three young children approach a gumball machine, each with a nickel to spend. The machine has just been filled with 50 black, 150 white, 100 red, and 100 yellow balls, which have been thoroughly mixed.

    a.   Sue and Jim approach the machine first. They both say they want red gumballs. What is the likelihood they will get their wish?

    b.   Sue and Jim did get red gumballs. Sammie approaches the machine next and says he does not want a red gumball. What is the chance he will get his wish?

    c.   What is the probability that Sammie will not get his wish?

58. Of every 100 employees at Kiddie Carts, 57 are production workers (designated as A), 40 are supervisors (designated as B), 2 are secretaries (designated as C), and 1 is with either middle or top management (designated as D). If an employee is selected at random, what does P(A or B or C) equal?

59. A punchboard has 50 squares numbered 1, 2, 3, . . . , 50. It was announced that there are three winning numbers on the board.

    a.   Using letters, design a formula to calculate the probability that a winning number will be chosen on both the first and second selections from the punchboard.

    b.   Compute the probability.

60. Harvey Kuenn played major league baseball from 1954 until 1966. During that time his career batting average was .308. Assume that the probability of getting a hit is .308 for each time at bat. (To put it another way, for every 1,000 times at bat, he had 308 hits.) In a particular game he batted three times.

    a.   What is the probability that he had three hits?

    b.   What is the probability that he did not get any hits in the game?

61. The probability that a bomber hits its target on any particular run is .80. If four bombers are sent after the same target, what is the probability that they all hit the target? What is the probability that none of the bombers hits the target?

62. Ninety students will graduate from Lima Shawnee High School this year. Out of the 90 graduates fifty are planning to attend college. Two students are selected at random to carry the flag at graduation. What is the probability that both of them are planning to attend college?

63. The board of directors of Saner Automatic Door Company consists of 12 members, 3 of whom are women. A new policy and procedures manual is to be written for the company. A committee of 3 is randomly selected from the board to do the writing.

    a.   What is the probability that all members of the committee are men?

    b.   What is the probability that at least 1 member of the committee is a woman?

64. A survey of undergraduate students in the School of Business at Northern University revealed the following regarding the sex and majors of the students:

|  | Major | | | |
| Sex | Accounting | Management | Finance | Total |
| --- | --- | --- | --- | --- |
| Male | 100 | 150 | 50 | 300 |
| Female | 100 | 50 | 50 | 200 |
| Total | 200 | 200 | 100 | 500 |

    a.    What is the probability of selecting a female student?

    b.    What is the probability of selecting a finance or accounting major?

    c.    What is the probability of selecting a female or an accounting major? Which rule of addition did you apply?

    d.    What is the probability of selecting an accounting major, given that the person selected is a male?

    e.    Suppose two students are selected randomly to attend a lunch with the president of the university. What is the probability that both of those selected are accounting majors?

65. The Wood County sheriff classifies crimes by age (in years) of the criminal and whether the crime is violent or nonviolent. As shown below, a total of 150 crimes were reported by the sheriff last year.

|  | Age (in years) | | | |
| Type of crime | Under 20 | 20 to 40 | 40 or older | Total |
| --- | --- | --- | --- | --- |
| Violent | 27 | 41 | 14 | 82 |
| Nonviolent | 12 | 34 | 22 | 68 |
| Total | 39 | 75 | 36 | 150 |

    a.    What is the probability of selecting a case to analyze and finding it involved a violent crime?

    b.    What is the probability of selecting a case to analyze and finding the crime was committed by someone less than 40 years old?

    c.    What is the probability of selecting a case that involved a violent crime or an offender less than 20 years old? Which rule of addition did you apply?

    d.    Given that a violent crime is selected for analysis, what is the probability the crime was committed by a person under 20 years old?

    e.    Two crimes are selected for review by Judge Tybo. What is the probability both are violent crimes?

66. Mr. and Mrs. Wilhelms are both retired and living in a retirement community in Arizona. Suppose the probability that a retired man will live another 10 years is .60. The probability that a retired woman will live another 10 years is .70.

    a.    What is the probability that both Mr. and Mrs. Wilhelms will be alive 10 years from now?

    b.    What is the probability that in 10 years Mr. Wilhelms is not living and Mrs. Wilhelms is living?

    c.    What is the probability that in 10 years at least one is living?

67. Flashner Marketing Research, Inc. specializes in providing assessments of the prospects for women's apparel shops in shopping malls. Al Flashner, president, reports that he assesses the prospects as good, fair, or poor. Records from previous assessments show that 60 percent of the time the prospects were rated as good, 30 percent of the time fair, and 10 percent of the time poor. Of those rated good, 80 percent made a profit the first year; of those rated fair, 60 percent made a profit the first year; and of those rated poor, 20 percent made a profit the first year. Connie's Apparel was one of Flashner's clients. Connie's Apparel made a profit last year. What is the probabiity that it was given an original rating of poor?

68. A test contains five multiple-choice questions. Each question has four answers, labeled *a, b, c,* and *d.* Only one answer is correct. What is the probability of answering all five questions correctly, assuming that the person taking the test knows nothing about the subject and just guessed the answers?

69. A round-robin chess tournament involving the 10 members of the chess club must be scheduled. (In a round-robin tournament, each member plays every other member.) How many matches must be scheduled? (Of course, if Smith plays Jones, it is the same as Jones playing Smith.)

70. A new job consists of assembling four different parts. All four have different color codes, and they can be assembled in any order. The production department wants to determine the most efficient way to assemble the four parts. The supervisors are going to conduct some experiments to solve the problem. First, they plan to assemble the parts in this order—green, black, yellow, and blue—and record the time. Then the assembly will be accomplished in a different order. In how many different ways can the four parts be assembled?

71. It was found that 60 percent of the tourists to China visited the Forbidden City, the Temple of Heaven, the Great Wall, and other historical sites in or near Beijing. Forty percent visited Xi'an with its magnificent terracotta soldiers, horses, and chariots which lay buried for over 2,000 years. Thirty percent of the tourists went to both Beijing and Xi'an. What is the probability that a tourist visited at least one of these places?

72. Two boxes of men's Arrow shirts were received from the factory. Box 1 contained 25 sport shirts and 15 dress shirts. Box 2 contained 30 sport shirts and 10 dress shirts. One of the boxes was selected at random, and a shirt was chosen at random from that box to be inspected. The shirt was a sport shirt. Given this information, what is the probability that the box the sport shirt came from is box 1?

73. Refer to Exercise 72. What is the probability that the sport shirt came from box 2?

74. Refer to Exercise 72. Suppose the shirt selected from the box was a dress shirt (instead of a sport shirt). What is the probability that the dress shirt came from box 1?

75. Refer to Exercise 72. Suppose the shirt selected at random from the box was a dress shirt (instead of a sport shirt). What is the probability the dress shirt came from box 2?

76. The operators of Riccardo's Restaurant want to advertise that they have a large number of different meals. They offer 4 soups, 3 salads, 12 entrees, 6 vegetables, and 5 desserts. How many different meals do they offer? In addition, Riccardo's has an "early bird" special: You may omit any part of the meal except the entrees for a reduced price. How many different meals do they have for the "early birds"?

77. Wendy's Hamburgers advertised that there are 256 different ways to order your hamburger. You may choose to have, or omit, any combination of the following on your hamburger: mustard, catchup, onion, pickle, tomato, relish, mayonnaise, and lettuce. Is the advertisement correct?

78. Reynolds Construction Company has agreed not to erect all "look-alike" homes in a new subdivision. Five exterior designs are offered to potential home buyers. The builder has standardized three interior plans that can be incorporated in any of the five exteriors. How many different ways can the exterior and interior plans be offered to potential home buyers?

79. A small rug weaver has decided to use seven compatible colors in her new line of rugs. However, in weaving a rug, only five spindles can be used. In her advertising she wants to indicate the number of different color groupings for sale. How many color groupings using the seven colors taken five at a time are there? (This assumes that five different colors will go into each rug—i.e., there are no repetitions of color.)

80. Consideration is being given to forming a Super Ten football conference. The top 10 football teams in the country, based on past records, would be members of the Super Ten conference. Each team would play every other team in the conference during the season. The team winning the most games would be declared the national champion.

How many games would the conference commissioner have to schedule each year? (Remember, Oklahoma versus Michigan is the same as Michigan versus Oklahoma.)

81. In a recent study of court cases it was found that 85 percent of the divorced women did not receive alimony. If five divorced women are selected, what is the probability none receive alimony?

82. A new chewing gum has been developed that is helpful to those who want to stop smoking. If 60 percent of those people chewing the gum are successful in stopping smoking, what is the probability that in a group of four smokers at least one quits smoking?

83. The state of Ohio has license plates with three numbers followed by three letters. How many different license plates are possible?

84. A new sports car model has defective brakes 15 percent of the time and a defective steering mechanism 5 percent of the time. Let's assume (and hope) that these problems occur independently. If one or the other of these problems is present, the car is called a "lemon." If both of these conditions are present, the car is a "hazard." Your instructor purchased one of these cars yesterday. What is the probability it is:

   a. A lemon?
   b. A hazard?

85. Tim Bleckie is the owner of Bleckie Investment and Real Estate Company. The company recently purchased four tracts of land in Holly Farms Estates and six tracts in Newburg Woods. The tracts are all equally desirable and sell for about the same amount.

   a. What is the probability that the next two tracts sold will be in Newburg Woods?
   b. What is the probability that of the next four sold at least one will be in Holly Farms?
   c. Are these events independent or dependent?

86. There are four people being considered for the position of chief executive officer of Dalton Enterprises. Three of the applicants are over 60 years of age. Two are female, of which only one is over 60. All four applicants are either over 60 years of age or female.

   a. What is the probability that a candidate is over 60 and female?
   b. Given that the candidate is male, what is the probability he is less than 60?
   c. Given that the person is over 60, what is the probability the person is female?

87. A case of 24 cans contains 1 can that is contaminated. Three cans are to be chosen randomly for testing.

   a. How many different combinations of 3 cans could be selected?
   b. What is the probability that the contaminated can is selected for testing?

88. A high school basketball player is a 60 percent foul shooter. If she attempts three foul shots in a game, and the shots are assumed to be independent, what is the probability that she makes:

   a. All three?
   b. At least one?
   c. At least two?

89. A recent study of how 670 Americans get to work revealed the following data.

|  | Type of worker | | |
|---|---|---|---|
|  | Urban | Rural | Total |
| Automobile | 400 | 200 | 600 |
| Public transportation | 50 | 20 | 70 |
| Total | 450 | 220 | 670 |

If a worker is selected at random, what is the probability that the worker:

a. Is a rural worker?
b. Uses public transportation?

    c.   Is a rural worker or uses public transportation?

    d.   Is a rural worker, given that he or she uses public transportation?

    e.   Uses public transportation, given that he or she is an urban worker?

90. A recent report indicated the ages of drunk drivers in Ohio for the year 1991 and whether the drunk drivers were first-time or repeat offenders.

| Age | First-time | Repeat | Total |
|---|---|---|---|
| 16–20 | 5,311 | 519 | 5,830 |
| 21–25 | 10,713 | 4,104 | 14,817 |
| 26–30 | 10,301 | 5,719 | 16,020 |
| 31–35 | 8,246 | 4,344 | 12,590 |
| 36–40 | 5,442 | 2,596 | 8,038 |
| 41–45 | 3,474 | 1,719 | 5,193 |
| Total | 43,487 | 19,001 | 62,488 |

Source: *Toledo Blade,* May 15, 1991, p. 21.

A drunk driver is selected at random.

    a.   What is the probability that the driver is a repeat offender?

    b.   What is the probability that the driver is under 21 or a first-time offender?

    c.   What is the probability that the driver is a repeat offender, given that the driver is over 30?

    d.   Is a first-time offender or a repeat offender more likely to be over 30?

    e.   What is the probability of selecting two drunk drivers and finding they are both first-time offenders?

91. Betts Electronic, Inc. purchases TV picture tubes from four different suppliers. Tyson Wholesale supplies 20 percent of the tubes, Fuji Importers 30 percent, Kirkpatricks 25 percent, and Parts, Inc. 25 percent. Tyson Wholesale tends to have the best quality, as only 3 percent of their tubes arrive defective. Fuji Importers tubes are 4 percent defective, Kirkpatricks 7 percent, and Parts, Inc. 6.5 percent defective.

    a.   What is the overall (average) percent defective?

    b.   A defective picture tube was discovered in the latest shipment. What is the probability that is came from Tyson Wholesale?

    c.   What is the probability that the defective tube came from Fuji Importers? From Kirkpatricks? From Parts, Inc.?

92. The following diagram represents a system of two components, *A* and *B,* which are in series. (Being in series means that for the system to operate, both components *A* and *B* must work.) Suppose that the probability that *A* functions is .90, and the probability that *B* functions is also .90. Assume that these two components are independent. What is the probability that the system operates?

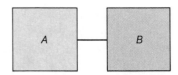

93. Refer to the system diagram above, but suppose the system works if *either A* or *B* works. What is the probability the system works under these conditions?

94. A puzzle in a newspaper presents a matching problem. The names of 10 U.S. presidents are listed in one column, and their vice presidents are listed in random order in the second column. The puzzle asks the reader to match each president with his vice president. If you make the matches randomly, how many matches are possible? What is the probability all 10 of your matches are correct?

95. To reduce theft, the Meredeth Company screens all its employees with a lie detector test that is known to be correct 90 percent of the time (for both guilty and innocent subjects). George Meredeth decides to fire all employees who fail the test. Suppose 5 percent of the employees are guilty of theft.
    a. What proportion of the workers are fired?
    b. Of the workers fired, what proportion are actually guilty?
    c. Of the workers not fired, what proportion are guilty?
    d. What do you think of George's policy?

## COMPUTER DATA EXERCISES

96. Refer to data set 1, which reports information on homes sold in Florida during 1990.
    a. Sort the data into a table that shows the number of homes that have a pool versus the number that don't have a pool in each of the five townships.
       (1) What percent of the homes sold are in township 1 or have a pool?
       (2) Given homes sold in township 3, what percent of the homes have a pool?
       (3) What percent of the homes sold both have a pool and are in township 3?
    b. Sort the data into a table that shows the number of homes that have a garage versus those that don't have a garage in each of the five townships.
       (1) What percent of the homes sold have a garage?
       (2) Given homes sold in township 5, what percent of the homes do not have a garage?
       (3) What percent of the homes sold both have a garage and are in township 3?
       (4) What percent of the homes do not have a garage or are in township 2?

97. Refer to data set 3, which reports information on the 26 major league baseball teams for the 1991 season. Set up a variable that divides the teams into two groups, those that had a winning season and those that did not. That is, create a variable to count the cases where the variable "fraction" is less than .500 and those where it is .500 or more. We'll call this variable "winning." Next create a new variable for attendance using three categories: attendance less than 1,500,000 (shown in the data as 1.5), attendance of 1.5 million up to 2.5 million, and attendance of more than 2.5 million.
    a. Create a table that shows the number of teams with a winning season versus those with a losing season by the three categories of attendance.
       (1) What percent of the teams had a winning season?
       (2) What percent of the teams had a winning season or attendance of more than 2.5 million?
       (3) Given teams with attendance of more than 2.5 million, what percent had a winning season?
       (4) What percent of the teams had a losing season and drew less than 1.5 million?
    b. Create a table that shows the number of teams that play on artificial turf fields by winning and losing records.
       (1) What percent of the teams play on turf fields?
       (2) Is the percent of teams with winning records larger on grass or on turf fields?
       (3) What percent of the teams have winning records or play on turf fields?

## CHAPTER 5 EXAMINATION

*The answers are at the end of the chapter.*

For Questions 1–7 indicate whether the statement is true or false. If false, correct the statement.

1. Two coins are tossed. The tossing of the coins is called an experiment, and one possible event is a head.

2. The outcomes must be equally likely for the relative frequency probability approach to be used.

3. The complement rule states that the probability of an event not occurring is equal to 1 minus the probability of its occurrence.

4. The classical approach to probability is based on a person's degree of belief and hunches that a particular event will happen.

5. If two events are mutually exclusive, then $P(A \text{ or } B) = P(A) + P(B)$.

6. There are five vacant parking places. Five automobiles arrive at the same time. There are 25 different ways they can park.

7. This Venn diagram shows that the events are mutually exclusive.

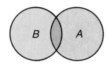

Questions 8–11 are based on the following tabulation of the status of the employees at BMD. Indicate whether the statement is true or false. If false, correct the statement.

| Status | Male | Female | Total |
|---|---|---|---|
| Executive | 80 | 20 | 100 |
| Supervisors | 100 | 300 | 400 |
| Production | 150 | 250 | 400 |
| Clerical | 40 | 60 | 100 |
| Total | 370 | 630 | 1,000 |

8. The probability of selecting at random a female executive is 20.0.

9. The probability of selecting a supervisor or a female is about .716.

10. The probability of selecting a supervisor given that a female employee is selected is .476.

11. The probability of selecting a clerical employee is .10.

Questions 12 and 13 are based on the following problem. A machine operator grinds a very thin disk the size of a dime. One side of the disk is plain, but the operator mills a slot on the other side. The disks are immediately wrapped for shipment. The operator suddenly realized that he did not machine in the slot in one of the last four disks he made but cannot recall which one was neglected.

12. What is the probability that one of the four pieces selected at random (say, the one on the extreme right) is defective? What is this probability called?

13. As an experiment, the machine operator unwrapped the disk on the extreme right and tossed it in the air. If it lands with the slot face up, the machine operator would know it is not the defective disk. However, if the disk landed with a plain face up, the machine operator would be uncertain whether that particular disk is defective or not defective. The disk landed with a plain face up. What is the probability that it is the defective disk? What is the probability called?

14. The First National Bank has two computers. The probability that the newer one will be inoperative in any particular month is .05. The probability that the older one will be inoperative in any particular month is .10. Assuming that these events are independent, what is the probability that they both become inoperative during a month?

15. The shipping department has just received 20 orders. A shipping clerk will be given 8 orders to fill. How many different groups of 8 orders could shipping clerk Catlin be given to fill?

16. The Swatzi motorbike dealer is promoting two top-of-the line motorbikes by offering the buyer one of three free options. In how many different ways can the two bikes and three options be arranged?

## ANSWERS

5–1  1.  a.  Testing of the new computer game.
    b.  Seventy-three players liked the game.
2.  a.  No. Probability cannot be greater than 1. The probability that the game, if put on the market, will be sucessful is $\frac{65}{80}$, or .8125.
    b.  Cannot be less than 0. Perhaps a mistake in arithmetic.
    c.  More than half of the persons testing the game liked it. (Of course, other answers are possible.)

5–2  1.  $\frac{1}{4}$ = .25
2.  a.  $\dfrac{13 \text{ spades in deck}}{52 \text{ cards total}}$
        $= \frac{13}{52} = \frac{1}{4} = .25.$
    b.  $\dfrac{1 \text{ jack of hearts in deck}}{52 \text{ cards total}}$
        $= \frac{1}{52} = .0192.$
    c.  $\dfrac{4 \text{ queens in deck}}{52 \text{ cards total}}$
        $= \frac{4}{52} = .0769.$
3.  Classical.

5–3  1.  $\dfrac{24}{883} = .027.$
2.  $\dfrac{182}{883} = .206.$

5–4  1.  The author's view of the chance that the DJIA will climb to 3,500 is .25. You may be more optimistic or less optimistic.
2.  .90 if you have been looking for a new car, or, say, .01 if you have no intention of buying or trading.

5–5  1.  .025, found by 50/2,000.
2.  .034, found by 68/2,000.
3.  .059, found by $P(B \text{ or } E) = .025 + .034.$
4.  Special rule of addition.
5.  1.
6.

| A | B | C | D | E |
|---|---|---|---|---|

7.  Yes.

5–6  For 1, 2, 3, and 4, the Venn diagram might appear as:

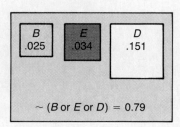

$\sim (B \text{ or } E \text{ or } D) = 0.79$

We found .79 by $1 - (.025 + .034 + .151)$.

5–7  1.  Need for corrective shoes is event $A$. Need for major dental work is event $B$.

$$P(A \text{ or } B) = P(A) + P(B)$$
$$- P(A \text{ and } B)$$
$$= .08 + .15 - .03$$
$$= .20$$

2.  One possibility is:

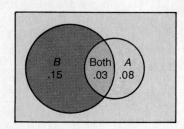

5–8  1.  $(.80)(.80)(.80)(.80) = .4096.$
2.  a.  .0000156, found by: $.025 \times .025 \times .025.$
    b.  The chance of selecting three bags and finding them all underweight is rather remote.

5–9  1.  .002, found by:

$$\frac{4}{12} \times \frac{3}{11} \times \frac{2}{10} \times \frac{1}{9} = \frac{24}{11,880} = .002$$

2.  .14, bound by:

$$\frac{8}{12} \times \frac{7}{11} \times \frac{6}{10} \times \frac{5}{9} = \frac{1,680}{11,880} = .1414$$

3. No, because there are other possibilities, such as three women and one man.

5–10
$$P(A \text{ and } B) = P(A) \cdot P(B|A)$$
$$= \frac{80}{200} \times \frac{25}{80}$$
$$= .125$$

5–11 1. Go out from the tree trunk on the lower branch, "would not remain." The probability of that event is 80/200. Continuing on the same path, find the branch labeled "6–10 years." The conditional probability is 10/80. To get the joint probability:

$$P(A \text{ and } B) = \frac{80}{200} \times \frac{10}{80}$$
$$= \frac{800}{16,000}$$
$$= .05$$

2. a. Contingency table.
   b.

   c. Yes, all possibilities are included.

5–12 1. $P(A_3|B_2) = \dfrac{P(A_3)P(B_2|A_3)}{P(A_1)P(B_2|A_1) + P(A_2)P(B_2|A_2) + P(A_3)P(B_2|A_3)}$
$$= \frac{.50(.96)}{(.30)(.97) + (.20)(.95) + (.50)(.96)}$$
$$= \frac{.480}{.961} = .499$$

5–13 1. There are 20, found by $5 \times 4$.
      2. There are 72, found by $3 \times 2 \times 4 \times 3$.
5–14 1. 720, found by $6 \times 5 \times 4 \times 3 \times 2 \times 1$.
      2. 10, found by:

$$\frac{6 \cdot 5 \cdot 4 \cdot 3 \cdot 2 \cdot 1(2 \cdot 1)}{4 \cdot 3 \cdot 2 \cdot 1(3 \cdot 2 \cdot 1)}$$

3. 24, found by:

$$\frac{4!}{(4-4)!} = \frac{4!}{0!}$$
$$= \frac{4!}{1}$$
$$= \frac{4 \cdot 3 \cdot 2 \cdot 1}{1}$$

4. 5,040, found by:

$$\frac{10!}{(10-4)!} = \frac{10!}{6!}$$
$$= \frac{10 \cdot 9 \cdot 8 \cdot 7 \cdot 6 \cdot 5 \cdot 4 \cdot 3 \cdot 2 \cdot 1}{6 \cdot 5 \cdot 4 \cdot 3 \cdot 2 \cdot 1}$$

5–15 1. 60, found by $(5)(4)(3)$.
      2. 60, found by:

$$\frac{5!}{(5-3)!} = \frac{5 \cdot 4 \cdot 3 \cdot 2 \cdot 1}{2 \cdot 1}$$

5–16   125, found by $_nP_r = n^r = 5^3$.
5–17 1. 56 is correct, found by:

$$_8C_3 = \frac{n!}{r!(n-r)!}$$
$$= \frac{8!}{3!(8-3)!}$$
$$= \frac{8!}{3!5!}$$
$$= \frac{8 \cdot 7 \cdot 6 \cdot 5!}{3 \cdot 2 \cdot 1 \cdot 5!}$$
$$= 56$$

2. Yes. There are 45 combinations, found by:

$$_{10}C_2 = \frac{n!}{r!(n-r)!}$$
$$= \frac{10!}{2!(10-2)!}$$
$$= \frac{10!}{2!8!}$$
$$= \frac{10 \cdot 9 \cdot 8!}{2 \cdot 1 \cdot 8!}$$
$$= 45$$

## CHAPTER 5 EXAMINATION

1. True.
2. False. The outcomes are equally likely in the classical approach.
3. True.
4. False. This is the definition of the subjective approach.
5. True.
6. False. There are 120, found by 5!/0!.
7. False. The events are not mutually exclusive. That is, there is an overlapping of events.
8. False. It is .020, found by 20/1,000.
9. False. It is about .730, found by:

$$P(S \text{ or } F) = P(S) + P(F) - P(S \text{ and } F)$$
$$= \frac{400}{1,000} + \frac{630}{1,000} - \frac{300}{1,000} = .730$$

10. True.
11. True.
12. .25. Prior probability.
13. .40, found by using Bayes' theorem:

$$\frac{(.25)(1.00)}{.25(1.00) + .75(.50)}$$

The value .40 is called a posterior probability.
14. .005, found by $P(A \text{ and } B) = P(A) \cdot P(B) = (.05)(.10)$.
15. 125,970, found by 20!/8!(20 − 8)!.
16. 6, found by 2 × 3.

*Food—Photo courtesy of Kellogg Company © 1991 Kellogg Company*

# DISCRETE PROBABILITY DISTRIBUTIONS

When you have completed this chapter, you will be able to:

GOALS

1. Define a probability distribution.
2. Distinguish between a discrete probability distribution and a continuous probability distribution.
3. Calculate the mean, variance, and standard deviation of a discrete probability distribution.
4. Describe the characteristics of the binomial, the hypergeometric, and the Poisson distributions.
5. Determine which probability distribution to use in a given situation.

**C**hapters 2 through 4 were devoted to descriptive statistics. We described raw data by organizing them into a frequency distribution and portraying the distribution in charts. Also, we computed an average—such as the arithmetic mean, median, or mode—to represent a typical value near the center of the distribution. The range and the standard deviation were used to describe the spread in the data. These chapters, therefore, focused on describing *something that has already happened.*

Starting with Chapter 5, the emphasis changed—we began examining *something that would probably happen.* We noted that this facet of statistics is called *statistical inference.* The objective is to make inferences (statements) about a population based on a small number of observations, called a sample, selected from the population. In Chapter 5, we stated that a probability is a value between 0 and 1 inclusive, and we examined how probabilities can be combined using rules of addition and multiplication.

This chapter will begin the study of **probability distributions.** A probability distribution gives the entire range of values that can occur based on an experiment. In this chapter we consider *discrete distributions,* where the outcome of an experiment can assume only certain values. For the toss of a die, as an example, only a one-, two-, three-, four-, five-, or six-spot can appear face up. Three discrete distributions are examined, namely, the *binomial, hypergeometric,* and *Poisson.*

## What Is a Probability Distribution?

A probability distribution shows the expected outcomes of an experiment and the probability of each of these outcomes.

Probability distribution defined

> Probability distribution   A listing of all the outcomes of an experiment and the probability associated with each outcome.

How can we generate a probability distribution?

### ■ Example

Suppose we are interested in the number of heads showing face up on three tosses of a coin. This is the experiment. The possible results are: zero heads, one head, two heads, and three heads. What is the probability distribution for the number of heads?

### ✓ Solution

There are eight possible results. A tail might appear face up on the first toss, another tail on the second toss, and another tail on the third toss of the coin. Or we might get a tail, tail, and head, in that order. The following table shows the eight possibilities (H represents a head and T a tail).

| Possible result | Coin toss | | | Number of heads |
|:---:|:---:|:---:|:---:|:---:|
| | First | Second | Third | |
| 1 | T | T | T | 0 |
| 2 | T | T | H | 1 |
| 3 | T | H | T | 1 |
| 4 | T | H | H | 2 |
| 5 | H | T | T | 1 |
| 6 | H | T | H | 2 |
| 7 | H | H | T | 2 |
| 8 | H | H | H | 3 |

Note that the outcome "zero heads" occurred only once, "1 head" occurred three times, "two heads" occurred three times, and the outcome "three heads" occurred only once. That is, "zero heads" happened one out of eight times. Thus, the probability of zero heads is one eighth, the probability of one head is three eighths, and so on. The distribution of probabilities is shown in Table 6–1. Note that the total of the probabilities of all possible events is 1.000. This is always true.

The same information can be portrayed graphically using a chart, such as Chart 6–1.

---

## TABLE    6–1

**Probability Distribution for the Outcomes of Zero, One, Two, and Three Heads Showing Face up on Three Tosses of a Coin**

| Number of heads, $r$ | Probability of outcome, $P(r)$ |
|:---:|:---:|
| 0 | $\dfrac{1}{8} = .125$ |
| 1 | $\dfrac{3}{8} = .375$ |
| 2 | $\dfrac{3}{8} = .375$ |
| 3 | $\dfrac{1}{8} = .125$ |
| Total | $\dfrac{8}{8} = 1.000$ |

---

## CHART    6–1

**Graphical Presentation of the Number of Heads and the Associated Probability Resulting from Three Tosses of a Coin**

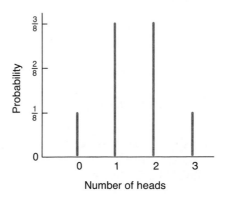

---

Characteristics of a
probability distribution

Before continuing, we should note two important characteristics of a probability distribution.

1. The probability of a particular outcome must always be between 0 and 1 inclusive. (The probabilities of $r$, written $P(r)$ in the coin tossing example, were .125, .375, etc.)

2. The sum of the probabilities of all mutually exclusive outcomes is 1.000. (Referring to Table 6–1, .125 + .375 + .375 + .125 = 1.000.)

### Self-Review 6–1

*The answers are at the end of the chapter.*

The possible outcomes of an experiment involving the roll of a six-sided die are: a one-spot, a two-spot, a three-spot, a four-spot, a five-spot, and a six-spot.

1. Develop a probability distribution for these outcomes.
2. Portray the probability distribution graphically.
3. What is the total of the probabilities?

## RANDOM VARIABLES

A few examples will best illustrate what is meant by a **random variable.**

- If we count the number of employees absent on Monday, there might be 0, 1, 2, 3, . . . . The number absent is the random variable.
- If we weigh a steel ingot, it might be 2,500 pounds, 2,500.1 pounds, 2,500.13 pounds, and so on depending on the accuracy of the scale.
- If we toss two coins and count the number of heads, there could be zero, one, or two heads. Since the exact number of heads resulting from this experiment is due to chance, the number of heads appearing is the random variable.
- Other random variables might be: the number of defective light bulbs produced during the week, the heights of the members of the girls' basketball team, the number of runners in the Boston Marathon, and the daily number of drivers charged with driving under the influence. In the last case there may be 0, 1, 2, 3, 4, . . . drivers.

Definition of a random variable

> Random variable　A quantity resulting from a random experiment that, by chance, can assume different values.

A random variable may be either *discrete* or *continuous.*

## DISCRETE RANDOM VARIABLE

Discrete random variable can assume only certain separated values in an interval

A discrete random variable can assume only a certain number of separated values. If there are 100 employees, then the count of the number absent on Monday can only be 0, 1, 2, 3, . . . , 100. A discrete random variable is usually the result of counting something. By way of a definition:

> Discrete random variable　A variable that can assume only certain clearly separated values resulting from a count of some item of interest.

It should be noted that a discrete variable can, in some cases, assume fractional or decimal values. These values must be separated, that is, have distance between them. As an example, the scores awarded by judges for technical competence and artistic form in figure skating are decimal values, such as 7.2, 8.9, and 9.7. Such values are discrete because there is a distance between scores of, say, 8.3 and 8.4. (A score cannot be 8.34 or 8.347.)

Continuous random variable can assume any value in an interval

If we measure something such as the width of a room, the height of a person, or the outside diameter of a bushing, the variable is called a *continuous random variable.* It can assume one of an infinitely large number of values, within certain limitations. As examples:

- The distance between Atlanta and Los Angeles could be 2,254 miles, 2,254.1 miles, 2,254.162 miles, and so on, depending on the accuracy of our measuring device.

- Tire pressure could be 28 pounds per square inch (psi), 28.6 psi, 28.62 psi, 28.624 psi, and so on, depending on the accuracy of the gauge.

Logically, if we organize a set of discrete random variables in a probability distribution, the distribution is called a **discrete probability distribution.** Several discrete probability distributions will be presented in this chapter. Chapter 7 will examine a very important continuous probability distribution—the normal probability distribution.

## THE MEAN, VARIANCE, AND STANDARD DEVIATION OF A PROBABILITY DISTRIBUTION

In Chapters 3 and 4, measures of location and variation were discussed for a frequency distribution. The mean reports the central location of the data, and the variance describes the spread in the data. In a similar fashion, a probability distribution is summarized by its mean and variance. The mean of a probability distribution is denoted by the lower-case Greek letter mu ($\mu$) and the variance by the lower-case Greek letter sigma (squared) ($\sigma^2$).

### MEAN

The mean is a typical value used to represent a probability distribution. It also is the long-run average value of the random variable. The mean of a probability distribution is also referred to as its expected value, $E(X)$. It is a weighted average where the possible values are weighted by their corresponding probability of occurrence.

The mean of a discrete probability distribution is computed by the formula:

$$\mu = E(X) = \Sigma[XP(X)] \qquad (6-1)$$

where $P(X)$ is the probability of the various outcomes $X$. In words, multiply each $X$ value by its probability of occurrence, and then add these products.

### VARIANCE AND STANDARD DEVIATION

As noted, the mean is a typical value used to represent a discrete probability distribution. However, it does not describe the amount of spread (variation) of a distribution. The variance does this. As explained in Chapter 4, a comparison of two variances allows you to compare the variation in two distributions having the same mean but different spreads. The formula for the variance of a probability distribution is:

$$\sigma^2 = \Sigma[(X - \mu)^2 P(X)] \qquad\qquad (6-2)$$

The computational steps are:

1. Subtract the mean from each value, and square this difference.
2. Multiply each squared difference by its probability.
3. Sum the resulting products to arrive at the variance.

The standard deviation $\sigma$ of a discrete probability distribution is found by taking the square root of $\sigma^2$, that is, $\sigma = \sqrt{\sigma^2}$.

## ▉ EXAMPLE

John Ragsdale sells new cars for Pelican Ford. John usually sells the largest number of cars on Saturday. He has established the following probability distribution for the number of cars he expects to sell on a particular Saturday.

| Number of cars sold, $X$ | Probability, $P(X)$ |
|:---:|:---:|
| 0 | .10 |
| 1 | .20 |
| 2 | .30 |
| 3 | .30 |
| 4 | .10 |
| Total | 1.00 |

1. What type of a distribution is this?
2. On a typical Saturday, how many cars should John expect to sell?
3. What is the variance of the distribution?

## ☑ SOLUTION

1. This is an example of a discrete probability distribution. Note that John expects to sell only within a certain range of cars; he does not expect to sell 5 cars or 50 cars. Further, he cannot sell half a car. He can only sell 0, 1, 2, 3, or 4 cars. Note that the outcomes are mutually exclusive—he cannot sell a total of both 3 and 4 cars on the same Saturday.
2. The mean number of cars sold is computed but weighting the number of cars sold by the probability of selling that number and totaling the products using formula (6−1):

$$\mu = E(X) = \Sigma[XP(X)]$$
$$= 0(.10) + 1(.20) + 2(.30) + 3(.30) + 4(.10)$$
$$= 2.1$$

These calculations are summarized in the following table.

| Number of cars sold, X | Probability, P(X) | X · P(X) |
|---|---|---|
| 0 | .10 | 0.00 |
| 1 | .20 | 0.20 |
| 2 | .30 | 0.60 |
| 3 | .30 | 0.90 |
| 4 | .10 | 0.40 |
| | 1.00 | $E(X) = 2.10$ |

How do we interpret a mean of 2.1? This value indicates that, over a large number of Saturdays, John Ragsdale expects to sell an average of 2.1 cars a day. (Of course, it is not possible for him to sell *exactly* 2.1 cars on any particular Saturday.)

3. Again, a table is useful for systemizing the computations for the variance. It is 1.290.

| Number of cars sold, X | Probability, P(X) | $(X - \mu)$ | $(X - \mu)^2$ | $(X - \mu)^2 P(X)$ |
|---|---|---|---|---|
| 0 | .10 | 0 − 2.1 | 4.41 | 0.441 |
| 1 | .20 | 1 − 2.1 | 1.21 | 0.242 |
| 2 | .30 | 2 − 2.1 | 0.01 | 0.003 |
| 3 | .30 | 3 − 2.1 | 0.81 | 0.243 |
| 4 | .10 | 4 − 2.1 | 3.61 | 0.361 |
| | | | | $\sigma^2 = 1.290$ |

Recall that the standard deviation, $\sigma$, is the square root of the variance. In this problem, $\sqrt{\sigma^2} = \sqrt{1.290} = 1.136$ cars. How do we interpret a standard deviation of 1.136 cars? If salesperson Rita Kirsch also sold a mean of 2.1 cars on Saturdays, and the standard deviation in her sales was 1.91 cars, we would conclude that there is more variability in the Saturday sales of Ms. Kirsch (because 1.91 > 1.136).

## Self-Review 6–2

*The answers are at the end of the chapter.*

The Pizza Palace offers three sizes of cola—small, medium, and large—to go with its pizza. The colas are sold for 50 cents, 75 cents, and 90 cents, respectively. Thirty percent of the orders are for small, 50 percent are for medium, and 20 percent are for the large size. Organize the size of the colas and the probability of a sale into a probability distribution.

1. Is this a discrete probability distribution? Indicate why or why not.

2. Compute the mean amount charged for a cola.

3. What is the variance of the amount charged for a cola? The standard deviation?

# EXERCISES

*The answers to the odd-numbered exercises are at the end of the book.*

1. Describe the difference between a discrete distribution and a continuous distribution.
2. Describe the characteristics of a discrete probability distribution.
3. Compute the mean and variance of the following discrete probability distribution.

| $X$ | $P(X)$ |
|---|---|
| 0 | .20 |
| 1 | .40 |
| 2 | .30 |
| 3 | .10 |

4. Compute the mean and variance of the following discrete probability distribution.

| $X$ | $P(X)$ |
|---|---|
| 2 | .50 |
| 8 | .30 |
| 10 | .20 |

5. Dan Woodward is the owner and manager of Dan's Truck Stop. Dan offers free refills on all coffee orders. He gathered the following information on the number of coffee refills.

| Refills | Percent |
|---|---|
| 0 | 30.0 |
| 1 | 40.0 |
| 2 | 20.0 |
| 3 | 10.0 |

Compute the mean, variance, and standard deviation for the number of refills.

6. The director of admissions at Kinzua University in Nova Scotia estimated the student admission for the fall semester based on past experience.

| Admission | Probability |
|---|---|
| 1,000 | .60 |
| 1,200 | .30 |
| 1,500 | .10 |

What is the expected number of admissions for the fall semester? Compute the variance and the standard deviation.

# BINOMIAL PROBABILITY DISTRIBUTION

The binomial distribution is a discrete distribution

The **binomial probability distribution** is a discrete probability distribution. One of the characteristics of a binomial distribution is that it is concerned with experiments where each outcome can take only one of two forms. For example, the statement in a true/false question is either true or false. Each outcome is *mutually exclusive*—meaning, in this case, that the answer to a true/false question cannot be correct and wrong *at the same time*. A common way to designate the two outcomes is "success" and "failure." If, for example, you guessed the correct answer to a true/false question, the outcome would be classified as a success. If not, it is a failure. Other illustrations of experiments that have this characteristic (only two outcomes) are:

Experiment: Selecting a mechanical toy from the production line.

Outcomes: Toy works correctly (a success).

Toy does not work correctly (a failure).

Experiment: Asking a five-year-old child whether he likes a newly developed cereal.

Outcomes: He likes it (a success).

He does not like it (a failure).

*A binomial distribution is a result of counts*

A second characteristic of a binomial distribution is that the data collected are the *result of counts*. This is one reason that the binomial distribution is classified as a discrete distribution.

A third characteristic of a binomial distribution is that the probability of a success remains the same from one trial to another. Examples:

- The probability that you will guess the first question of a true/false test correctly (a success) is one half. This is the first "trial." The probability that you will guess right on the second question (the second trial) is also one half, the probability of success on the third trial is one half, and so on.

- If past experience revealed that the drawbridge over the Gulf Intracoastal Waterway was raised one out of every five times you approached it, then the probability is one fifth that it will be raised (a success) the next time you approach it, one fifth the following time, and so on.

A fourth characteristic of a binomial probability distribution is that one trial is *independent* of any other trial. In effect, this is the same as saying that there is no rhythmic pattern with respect to the outcomes. As an example, the answers to a true-false test are not arranged T, T, T, F, F, F, T, T, T, and so forth.

*A binomial distribution has these characteristics*

In summary, a binomial distribution has these characteristics:

1. An outcome of an experiment is classified into one of two mutually exclusive categories—namely, a success or a failure.

2. The data collected are the result of counts.

3. The probability of a success stays the same for each trial. So does the probability of a failure.

4. The trials are independent, meaning that the outcome of one trial does not affect the outcome of any other trial.

## Self-Review 6–3

*The answers are at the end of the chapter.*

The professor teaching Horticulture 101 made an assignment involving the memorization of the Latin names of flowers. Unfortunately, none of the students studied the chapter. A pop quiz the next day consisted of 20 multiple-choice questions, each having five choices. All the students guessed the answer to each question.

1. Why would the binomial probability distribution be used to determine the probabilities of guessing 0, 1, 2, . . . , 20 questions correctly?

2. What is the probability that a student will guess all 20 questions correctly? (It is not necessary to calculate this probability. Instead, show in fractional form how it would be determined.)

# How Is a Binomial Probability Distribution Constructed?

Formula for binomial

To construct a binomial probability distribution, we must know (1) the number of trials and (2) the probability of success on each trial. For example, if an examination at the conclusion of a management seminar consists of 20 multiple-choice questions, the number of trials is 20. If each question has five choices and only one choice is correct, the probability of success on each trial is one fifth, or .20. Thus, the probability is .20 that a person with no knowledge of the subject matter will guess the answer to a question correctly. So the conditions of the binomial distribution just noted are met.

The binomial probability distribution can be described using the formula:

$$P(r) = \frac{n!}{r!(n-r)!} p^r q^{n-r} \qquad (6-3)$$

where:

   $n$   is the number of trials.

   $r$   is the number of observed successes.

   $p$   is the probability of success on each trial.

   $q$   is the probability of a failure, found by $1 - p$.

## ■ Example

As we all know, the answer to a true/false question is either correct or incorrect. Assume that (1) an examination consists of four true/false questions, and (2) a student has no knowledge of the subject matter. The chance (probability) that the student will guess the correct answer to the first question is one half, or .50. Likewise, the probability of guessing each of the remaining questions correctly is .50. What is the probability of:

   1. Getting exactly none out of four correct?
   2. Getting exactly one out of four correct?

## ☑ Solution

   1. The probability of guessing exactly none out of the four correctly is .0625, found by applying formula (6–3). (Recall from Chapter 5 that 0! is equal to 1.)

$$P(r) = \frac{n!}{r!(n-r)!} p^r q^{n-r}$$

Substituting:

$$P(0) = \frac{4!}{0!(4-0)!} (.50)^0 (1 - .50)^{4-0}$$

$$= \frac{4 \cdot 3 \cdot 2 \cdot 1}{(1)(4 \cdot 3 \cdot 2 \cdot 1)} (1)(.50)^4$$

$$= (1)(1)(.50)^4$$

$$= .0625$$

2. The probability of getting exactly one out of four correct is .2500, found by:

$$P(1) = \frac{4!}{1!(4-1)!} (.50)^1 (1 - .50)^{4-1}$$

$$= \frac{4 \cdot \cancel{3} \cdot \cancel{2} \cdot \cancel{1}}{1(\cancel{3} \cdot \cancel{2} \cdot \cancel{1})} (.50)^1 (.50)^3$$

$$= (4)(.50)(.125)$$

$$= .2500$$

### Self-Review 6−4

*The answers are at the end of the chapter.*

Refer to the preceding example and solution. Note that there are four true/false questions. Using formula (6−3), what is the probability of getting exactly two of the four questions correct?

The probabilities of getting exactly zero, one, two, three, and four questions correct out of a total of four questions are shown in Table 6−2.

---

TABLE  6−2

**Binomial Probability Distribution for $n = 4$, $p = .50$**

| Number of correct guesses | Probability Fraction | Decimal |
|:---:|:---:|:---:|
| 0 | $\frac{1}{16}$ | .0625 |
| 1 | $\frac{4}{16}$ | .2500 |
| 2 | $\frac{6}{16}$ | .3750 |
| 3 | $\frac{4}{16}$ | .2500 |
| 4 | $\frac{1}{16}$ | .0625 |
| Total | $\frac{16}{16}$ | 1.000 |

---

The data in Table 6−2 have been plotted in Chart 6−2, which falls on page 222, mainly to show the symmetrical nature of the binomial probability distribution when $p = .50$.

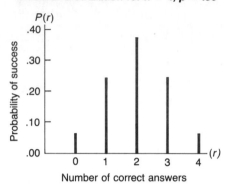

CHART    6–2

**Binomial Distribution for $n = 4$, $p = .50$**

*Number of correct answers*

## EXERCISES

*The answers to the odd-numbered exercises are at the end of the book.*

7.  List the characteristics of the binomial distribution.

8.  In a binomial situation $n = 5$ and $p = .20$. Determine the following probabilities using formula (6–3).

    a.  $r = 1$     b.  $r = 3$

9.  In a binomial situation $n = 4$ and $p = .25$. Determine the following probabilities using the binomial formula.

    a.  $r = 2$     b.  $r = 3$

10. In a binomial situation $n = 5$ and $p = .40$. Determine the following probabilities using the binomial formula.

    a.  $r = 1$     b.  $r = 2$

## USING BINOMIAL PROBABILITY TABLES

Binomial table: Quick way of determining a probability

A binomial probability distribution is a theoretical distribution that, as has been shown, can be generated mathematically. However, except for problems involving small $n$ (say, $n = 3$ or 4), the calculations for the probabilities of 0, 1, 2, . . . successes can be rather tedious. As an aid in finding the needed probabilities, an extensive table has been developed that gives the probabilities of 0, 1, 2, 3, . . . successes for various values of $n$ and $p$. This table is in Appendix A, and a small portion of the table needed for the following example is shown in Table 6–3.

### ■ EXAMPLE

Based on recent experience, 5 percent of the worm gears produced by an automatic, high-speed Carter-Bell milling machine are defective. What is the probability that out of six gears selected at random, exactly zero gears will be defective? Exactly one? Exactly two? Exactly three? Exactly four? Exactly five? Exactly six out of the six? (Note: $n = 6$, $p = .05$.)

## TABLE 6–3

### Binomial Probabilities for $n = 6$

| $r$ | .05 | .1 | .2 | .3 | .4 | .5 | .6 | .7 | .8 | .9 | .95 |
|---|---|---|---|---|---|---|---|---|---|---|---|
| 0 | .735 | .531 | .262 | .118 | .047 | .016 | .004 | .001 | .000 | .000 | .000 |
| 1 | .232 | .354 | .393 | .303 | .187 | .094 | .037 | .010 | .002 | .000 | .000 |
| 2 | .031 | .098 | .246 | .324 | .311 | .234 | .138 | .060 | .015 | .001 | .000 |
| 3 | .002 | .015 | .082 | .185 | .276 | .313 | .276 | .185 | .082 | .015 | .002 |
| 4 | .000 | .001 | .015 | .060 | .138 | .234 | .311 | .324 | .246 | .098 | .031 |
| 5 | .000 | .000 | .002 | .010 | .037 | .094 | .187 | .303 | .393 | .354 | .232 |
| 6 | .000 | .000 | .000 | .001 | .004 | .016 | .047 | .118 | .262 | .531 | .735 |

## ☑ SOLUTION

Note that the binomial conditions are met: (1) There is a constant probability of success (.05), (2) there is a fixed number of trials (6), (3) the trials are independent, and (4) there are only two possible outcomes (a particular gear is either defective or acceptable).

Binomial probability distribution

Refer to Table 6–3 for the probability of exactly zero defective gears. Go down the left margin to an $r$ of 0. Now move horizontally to the column headed by a $p$ of .05 to find the probability. It is .735.

The probability of exactly one defective in a sample of six worm gears is .232. The complete binomial probability distribution for $n = 6$ and $p = .05$ is:

| Number of defective gears, $r$ | Probability of occurrence, $P(r)$ |
|---|---|
| 0 | .735 |
| 1 | .232 |
| 2 | .031 |
| 3 | .002 |
| 4 | .000 |
| 5 | .000 |
| 6 | .000 |

Of course, there is a slight chance of getting exactly five defective gears out of six random selections. It is .00000178, found by inserting the appropriate values in the binomial formula:

$$P(5) = \frac{6!}{5!(6-5)!}(.05)^5(.95)^1$$
$$= (6)(.05)^5(.95)$$
$$= .00000178$$

For six out of the six, the probability is .000000015. Thus, the probability is very small that five or six defective gears will be selected in a sample of six.

This problem can also be solved on the MINITAB system. The command PDF is used to access the probability density function. The subcommand BINOMIAL is used with $n$, the number of trials (or sample size), and $p$, the probability of a success. The output follows.

```
MTB > pdf;
SUBC> binomial n=6 p=.05.
    BINOMIAL WITH N = 6   P = 0.050000
    K              P(X = K)
    0              0.7351
    1              0.2321
    2              0.0305
    3              0.0021
    4              0.0001
    5              0.0000
```

Probability of one defective

The output is the same as in Table 6–3 except for the difference in the number of digits after the decimal.

### Self-Review 6–5

*The answers are at the end of the chapter.*

One of every five times you approached the drawbridge over the Gulf Intracoastal Waterway, it was raised, and you had to wait. Using the binomial probability table in Appendix A:

1. What is the probability that on your next seven approaches to the drawbridge it will not be raised?

2. What is the probability that it will be raised exactly one out of the seven approaches?

3. What is the probability that it will be raised exactly twice? Exactly three times? Exactly four times? Exactly five times? Exactly six times? All seven times?

4. What should the probabilities in 1, 2, and 3 total?

Appendix A is somewhat limited in that it gives probabilities only for $n$ values of 1 to 25 and $p$ values of .05, .10, .20, . . . , .95. There are two methods for arriving at a binomial distribution for an $n$ over 25 and/or a $p$ not found in the table (say, .07): (1) The normal approximation to the binomial may be used. This will be presented in Chapter 7. (2) A computer can generate the probabilities for a specified number of successes, given an $n$ and a $p$. To illustrate, following are two MINITAB outputs—one for an $n$ of 40 and a $p$ of .09, and the other for an $n$ of 27 and a $p$ of .376.

```
MTB > pdf;
SUBC> binomial n=40 p=.09.
    BINOMIAL WITH N = 40 P = 0.090000
       K         P(X = K)
       0         0.0230
       1         0.0910
       2         0.1754
       3         0.2198
       4         0.2011
       5         0.1432
       6         0.0826
       7         0.0397
       8         0.0162
       9         0.0057
      10         0.0017
      11         0.0005
      12         0.0001
      13         0.0000
```

```
MTB > pdf;
SUBC> binomial n=27 p=.376.
      BINOMIAL WITH N = 27 P = 0.376000
           K        P(X = K)
           1        0.0000
           2        0.0004
           3        0.0019
           4        0.0068
           5        0.0189
           6        0.0418
           7        0.0756
           8        0.1139
           9        0.1448
          10        0.1571
          11        0.1463
          12        0.1175
          13        0.0817
          14        0.0492
          15        0.0257
          16        0.0116
          17        0.0045
          18        0.0015
          19        0.0004
          20        0.0001
          21        0.0000
```

As *p* becomes larger, binomial distribution becomes more symmetrical

Several additional points should be made about binomial distributions:

1. If *n* remains the same but *p* increases from .05 to .95, the shape of the distribution changes. Note in Table 6–4 that the probabilities for a *p* of .05 are positively skewed. As *p* approaches .50, the distribution approaches a symmetrical distribution. As *p* goes beyond .50 and moves toward .95, the probability distribution becomes negatively skewed. Table 6–4 gives probabilities for *n* = 10 and probabilities of success of .05, .10, .20, .50, and .70. The plots of these values are shown in Chart 6–3.

## TABLE 6–4

**Probability of 0, 1, 2, . . . Successes for a *p* of .05, .10, .20, .50, and .70 and an *n* of 10**

| r | .05 | .1 | .2 | .3 | .4 | .5 | .6 | .7 | .8 | .9 | .95 |
|---|------|------|------|------|------|------|------|------|------|------|------|
| 0 | .599 | .349 | .107 | .028 | .006 | .001 | .000 | .000 | .000 | .000 | .000 |
| 1 | .315 | .387 | .268 | .121 | .040 | .010 | .002 | .000 | .000 | .000 | .000 |
| 2 | .075 | .194 | .302 | .233 | .121 | .044 | .011 | .001 | .000 | .000 | .000 |
| 3 | .010 | .057 | .201 | .267 | .215 | .117 | .042 | .009 | .001 | .000 | .000 |
| 4 | .001 | .011 | .088 | .200 | .251 | .205 | .111 | .037 | .006 | .000 | .000 |
| 5 | .000 | .001 | .026 | .103 | .201 | .246 | .201 | .103 | .026 | .001 | .000 |
| 6 | .000 | .000 | .006 | .037 | .111 | .205 | .251 | .200 | .088 | .011 | .001 |
| 7 | .000 | .000 | .001 | .009 | .042 | .117 | .215 | .267 | .201 | .057 | .010 |
| 8 | .000 | .000 | .000 | .001 | .011 | .044 | .121 | .233 | .302 | .194 | .075 |
| 9 | .000 | .000 | .000 | .000 | .002 | .010 | .040 | .121 | .268 | .387 | .315 |
| 10 | .000 | .000 | .000 | .000 | .000 | .001 | .006 | .028 | .107 | .349 | .599 |

## CHART   6−3

### Chart Representing the Binomial Probability Distribution for a
### p of .05, .10, .20, .50, and .70 and an n of 10

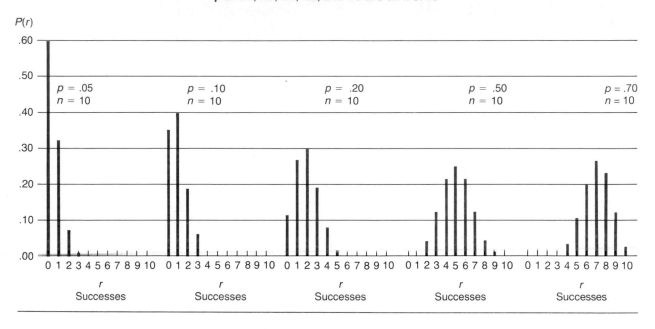

2. If *p,* the probability of success, remains the same but *n* becomes larger and larger, the shape of the binomial distribution becomes more symmetrical. Chart 6−4 shows a situation where *p* remains constant at .10 but *n* increases from 7 to 40.

## CHART   6−4

### Chart Representing the Binomial Probability Distribution
### for a p of .10 and an n of 7, 12, 20, and 40

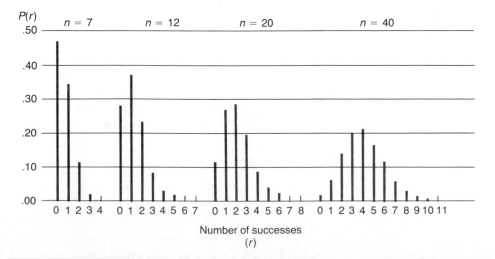

3. The mean ($\mu$) and the variance ($\sigma^2$) of a binomial distribution can be computed by:

$$\mu = np \qquad (6-4)$$
$$\sigma^2 = np(1 - p) \qquad (6-5)$$

For the previous example regarding defective worm gears, recall that $p = .05$ and $n = 6$. Hence:

$$\mu = np = 6(.05) = .30$$
$$\sigma^2 = np(1 - p) = 6(.05)(1 - .05) = .285$$

The mean of .30 and the variance of .285 can be verified using formula (6–1) and (6–2). The probability distribution from Table 6–3 is repeated below.

| Number of defects, $r$ | $P(r)$ | $rP(r)$ | $r - \mu$ | $(r - \mu)^2$ | $(r - \mu)^2 P(r)$ |
|---|---|---|---|---|---|
| 0 | .735 | 0 | −0.30 | 0.09 | 0.06615 |
| 1 | .232 | 0.232 | 0.70 | 0.49 | 0.11368 |
| 2 | .031 | 0.062 | 1.70 | 2.89 | 0.08959 |
| 3 | .002 | 0.006 | 2.70 | 7.29 | 0.01458 |
| 4 | .000 | 0 | 3.70 | 13.69 | 0 |
| 5 | .000 | 0 | 4.70 | 22.09 | 0 |
| 6 | .000 | 0 | 5.70 | 32.49 | 0 |
| | | 0.30 | | | 0.284* |

*The slight discrepancy between .285 and .284 is due to rounding.

# EXERCISES

*The answers to the odd-numbered exercises are at the end of the book.*

11. Assume a binomial distribution where $n = 3$ and $p = .60$.
    a.  Refer to Appendix A, and list the probabilities of a success for values of $r$ from 0 to 3.
    b.  Determine the mean and standard deviation of the distribution.

12. Assume a binomial distribution where $n = 5$ and $p = .30$.
    a.  Refer to Appendix A, and list the probabilities of a success for values of $r$ from 0 to 5.
    b.  Determine the mean and standard deviation of the distribution.

13. On a very hot summer day, 10 percent of the production employees at Nome Steel are absent from work. Ten production employees are to be selected at random for a special in-depth study on absenteeism.
    a.  What is the random variable in this problem?
    b.  Is the random variable discrete or continuous? Why?
    c.  What is the probability of selecting 10 production employees at random on a hot summer day and finding that none of them is absent?
    d.  Develop a binomial probability distribution for this experiment.
    e.  Compute the mean, variance, and standard deviation of the distribution.
    f.  Portray the binomial probability distribution in the form of a chart.
    g.  Why is the binomial probability distribution appropriate for this type of problem?

14. The marketing department of the Kellogg Company plans to conduct a national survey to find out whether or not consumers of flake cereals can distinguish one of their favorite flake cereals from other flake cereals. To test the questionnaire and procedure to be used, eight persons were asked to cooperate in an experiment. Five very small bowls of flake cereals were placed in front of a person. The bowls were labeled A, B, C, D, and E. The person was informed that only one bowl contained his or her favorite flake cereal.

   a.  Suppose a person could not identify his or her favorite cereal and just guessed it was in bowl C. What is the probability that the person guessed correctly?

   b.  What is the random variable in this problem?

   c.  Is the random variable discrete or continuous? Why?

   d.  Suppose that all of the eight persons in the experiment were unable to identify their favorite cereal and just guessed which bowl it was in. What is the probability that none of the eight guessed correctly?

   e.  Develop a binomial probability distribution for this experiment.

   f.  Compute the mean, variance, and standard deviation of the distribution.

   g.  Portray the binomial probability distribution in the form of a chart.

   h.  Suppose seven of the eight persons identified the cereal they liked best. Is it reasonable to assume that they were just guessing? Explain. What would you conclude?

   i.  Why is the binomial probability distribution appropriate for this problem?

## USES AND IMPORTANCE OF THE BINOMIAL PROBABILITY DISTRIBUTION

Some uses of the binomial distribution

We have cited several examples of the use and importance of a probability distribution in this chapter. In brief, we noted that any probability distribution is a theoretical distribution showing how the outcomes of an experiment are expected to be distributed. Specifically, a binomial probability distribution shows how an experiment involving only two outcomes (a success or a failure) is expected to be distributed. In the examples, the chapter exercises, and the self-reviews, we also illustrated some uses of the binomial probability distribution. Here are two other cases:

### CASE 1

Suppose that past experience revealed that 5 percent of the automobile doors coming off the production line are defective. A defective door is defined by quality control as a door with one or more defects, such as an exposed sharp burr, faulty paint, or a dent. Ten doors are to be selected at random by quality control. The binomial distribution for the number of defects in 10 doors with $p = .05$ is shown in Table 6–5.

Note that the probable number of defective doors in the sample of 10 is either 0 or 1. Three or more defective doors is quite improbable. If 6 doors were defective out of the 10, quality control would no doubt investigate the causes of the defects and take corrective action. Thus, knowledge of the distribution tells us, in advance of the experiment, what we can expect to occur and what are unusual results.

### CASE 2

Surveys are conducted continuously by various research groups regarding voting preference, consumer protection policies, product preference, and so on. A set of

## TABLE  6−5

**Binomial Probability Distribution for an *n* of 10 and a *p* of .05**

| Number of defects | Probability of occurrence | |
|---|---|---|
| 0 | .599 ⎫ | Most |
| 1 | .315 ⎬ | probable |
| 2 | .075 | |
| 3 | .010 ⎫ | |
| 4 | .001 | |
| 5 | .000 | |
| 6 | .000 | Quite |
| 7 | .000 | improbable |
| 8 | .000 | |
| 9 | .000 | |
| 10 | .000 ⎭ | |

multiple-choice questions is often used, and the respondent checks what he or she considers the correct answer. The researcher is always concerned that uninformed respondents may merely guess the answers to avoid embarrassment. The researcher, therefore, generates a binomial probability distribution and matches it with the *actual responses* in order to help identify the guesses. For example, a questionnaire consists of six questions, and each question has five choices. Only one answer is correct. The binomial probability distribution for the number of correct answers arrived at *by chance* is shown in Table 6−6. If the respondents were just guessing the answers to avoid embarrassment, the probable number they would guess correctly is zero, one, or two. However, if most of the respondents had five or six correct out of six, we would assume that they knew the answers to most of the questions because the chance of guessing five or six out of six correctly is only .002, or about 2 out of 1,000.

In summary, we generate an appropriate theoretical probability distribution to identify the expected outcomes of an experiment. We then match the actual outcomes with the expected outcomes in order to evaluate the results of the experiment.

## TABLE  6−6

**Binomial Probability Distribution for an *n* of 6 and a *p* of .20**

| Number of correct answers | Probability of occurrence | |
|---|---|---|
| 0 | .262 ⎫ | Most |
| 1 | .393 ⎬ | probable |
| 2 | .246 ⎭ | |
| 3 | .082 | |
| 4 | .015 ⎫ | Least |
| 5 | .002 ⎬ | probable |
| 6 | .000 ⎭ | |

## CUMULATIVE PROBABILITY DISTRIBUTIONS

We may want to know the probability of correctly guessing the answers to 6 *or more* true/false questions out of 10. Or we may be interested in the probability of selecting *less than* two defectives at random from the production during the previous hour. This sounds like we need cumulative frequency distributions similar to the ones developed in Chapter 2. We do.

First let us convert the binomial probability distribution in Table 6–6 to both a less-than and a more-than binomial probability distribution. Recall from Chapter 2 that for a less-than distribution we add the probabilities successively down, and for the more-than distribution the probabilities are added up. (See Table 6–7.)

---

### TABLE   6–7

**Less-Than and More-Than Cumulative Binomial Distributions**
**($n = 6$, $p = .20$)**

| Number of correct answers, $r$ | Probability of occurrence, $P(r)$ | | Less-than probability | | More-than probability |
|:---:|:---:|:---:|:---:|:---:|:---:|
| 0 | .262 | Add | .262 | | 1.000 |
| 1 | .393 | down | .655 | | .738 |
| 2 | .246 | | .901 | | .345 |
| 3 | .082 | ↓ | .983 | ↑ | .099 |
| 4 | .015 | | .998 | | .017 |
| 5 | .002 | | 1.000 | Add | .002 |
| 6 | .000 | | 1.000 | up | .000 |

---

Refer to the cumulative probability distributions to answer the following questions. What is the probability of selecting the responses of six respondents and finding *by chance* two or fewer correct responses? The probability is .901. What is the probability of three or more correct responses? It is .099. What is the probability of more than three correct responses? It is .017. (The probability of "more than three" means four or more.)

Charting the less-than cumulative probabilities

Chart 6–5 portrays the less-than cumulative probability distribution. To plot, start at 0 on the *X*-axis, and draw a line vertical to .262. Then go horizontally to 1 on the *X*-axis, and draw a vertical line to .655, and so on. Note that the probability of one or fewer correct responses is read using the *top* of the vertical line. Also note that the chart representing the less-than cumulative probability distribution goes upward and to the right stepwise. The plots cannot be connected successively using straight lines because the data are discrete—that is, there are no values between 0 and 1, 1 and 2, and so on.

More-than cumulative binomial

A more-than cumulative binomial distribution is portrayed in a chart the same way. The cumulative probabilities, however, are read from the *lowest* point of the vertical lines. (You will have the opportunity to draw both a less-than chart and a more-than chart in the following self-review and in the chapter exercises.) A cumulative binomial probability table for selected values of *n* is provided in Appendix B.

A cumulative frequency distribution is useful for computing the probability that the number of successes is *r* or less. This is discussed in the following example.

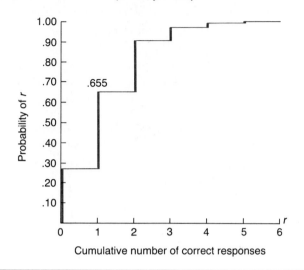

CHART 6–5

**Chart Representing a Less-Than Cumulative Binomial Distribution**
**(*n* = 6, *p* = .20)**

### EXAMPLE

A recent study by the American Highway Patrolman's Association revealed that 60 percent of American drivers use their seat belts. A sample of 10 drivers on the Florida Turnpike is selected.

1. What is the probability that exactly 7 were wearing seat belts?
2. What is the probability that 7 or fewer of the drivers were wearing seat belts?
3. What is the probability that more than 7 of the drivers were wearing seat belts?

### SOLUTION

This situation meets the binomial requirements, namely:

- A particular driver either is wearing his or her seat belt or is not. There are only two possible outcomes.
- The probability of a "success" (wearing a seat belt) is the same from driver to driver: 60 percent.
- The trials are independent. If the fourth driver selected in the sample is wearing a seat belt, for example, it has no effect whatsoever on whether the fifth driver selected is or is not wearing a seat belt.
- There is a fixed number of trials—10 in this case, because 10 drivers were checked.

    1. To find the likelihood of *exactly* 7 drivers, we use Appendix A. Locate the page for *n* = 10. Next find the column for *p* = .60 and the row for *r* = 7. The

value is .215. Thus, the probability of finding 7 out of the 10 drivers in the sample wearing their seat belts is .215. This is often written as follows:

$$P(r = 7 \mid n = 10 \text{ and } p = .60) = .215$$

where $r$ refers to the number of successes, $n$ the number of trials, and $p$ the probability of a success. The bar "|" means "given that."

2. There are several methods for determining the probability of 7 or fewer of the drivers wearing seat belts. One method is to use Appendix B, where the probability of $r$ or fewer successes is reported. We first locate the page in the appendix for $n = 10$, and then we find the column for $p = .60$ and the row for $r = 7$. The intersection where $r = 7$ and $p = .60$ is .833. So the probability that 7 or fewer of the drivers were wearing seat belts is .833. This could be written as follows:

$$P(r \le 7 \mid n = 10 \text{ and } p = .60) = .833$$

This probability could also be determined from Appendix A and applying the special rule of addition. Because these events are mutually exclusive, we could determine the probability that of the 10 drivers, none was wearing a seat belt, 1 was wearing a seat belt, 2 were wearing seat belts, and so on up to 7 drivers. These eight possible outcomes are then totaled. From Appendix A for $n = 10$ and $p = .60$, the result is the same:

$$\begin{aligned} P(r \le 7 \mid n = 10 \text{ and } p = .40) &= P(r = 0) + P(r = 1) + P(r = 2) + P(r = 3) \\ &\quad + P(r = 4) + P(r = 5) + P(r = 6) + P(r = 7) \\ &= .000 + .002 + .011 + .042 + .111 + .201 + .251 + .215 \\ &= .833 \end{aligned}$$

This is the probability of 7 or less.

3. Suppose the question was, "What is the probability that *more than 7* drivers are found wearing their seat belts when checked?" Is the possibility of 7 of the 10 drivers included in this probability or excluded from the question? It is excluded. The question is equivalent to asking, "What is the probability that *8 or more* drivers are wearing seat belts?" To answer this question we use Appendix B and the complement rule. First we determine the probability of 7 or fewer wearing seat belts, and we subtract this probability from 1.

$$P(r > 7) = 1 - P(r \le 7) = 1 - .833 = .167$$

## Self-Review 6–6

*The answers are at the end of the chapter.*

1. For a case where $n = 4$ and $p = .60$, determine the probability that:
   a. $r = 2$.
   b. $r \le 2$.
   c. $r > 2$.

2. Develop a less-than cumulative binomial probability distribution for an $n$ of 5 and $p$ of .50. Portray this distribution in a chart.

## EXERCISES

*The answers to the odd-numbered exercises are at the end of the book.*

15. In a binomial distribution $n = 8$ and $p = .30$. Find the following probabilities.
    a.   $r = 2$.
    b.   $r \leq 2$ (the probability that $r$ is equal to or less than 2).
    c.   $r \geq 3$ (the probability that $r$ is equal to or greater than 3).

16. In a binomial distribution $n = 12$ and $p = .60$. Find the following probabilities.
    a.   $r = 5$
    b.   $r \leq 5$
    c.   $r \geq 6$

17. In a recent study 90 percent of the homes in the United States were found to have color TVs. In a sample of nine homes what is the probability that:
    a.   All nine have color TVs?
    b.   Less than five have color TVs?
    c.   More than five have color TVs?
    d.   At least seven homes have color TVs?

18. A manufacturer of window frames knows from long experience that 5 percent of the production will have some type of minor defect that will require a slight adjustment. What is the probability that in a sample of 20 window frames:
    a.   None will need adjustments?
    b.   At least 1 will need adjustment?
    c.   More than 2 will need adjustment?

19. Your instructor gave a pop quiz consisting of 10 true/false questions during the second week of class. Unfortunately, you neither attended any previous classes nor read the textbook (a common occurrence). You decide, however, to take the quiz and just guess the answer to each question. The instructor announces that six or more correct answers are needed to pass the test.
    a.   For each question, what is the probability you will guess the correct answer?
    b.   The following chart shows the more-than cumulative binomial probabilities for an $n$ of 10 and a $p$ of .50. Based on the chart, approximately what is your chance of passing the test?

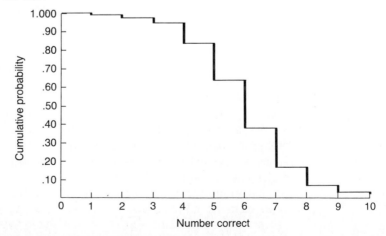

    c.   What is the exact probability of passing with six or more correct answers? (Refer to Appendix A or B for the probabilities of 6, 7, 8, 9, and 10 out of 10 correct.)

20. The sponsors of Cancer Research came up with a unique idea to attract wealthy patrons to a $500-a-plate dinner. It was announced that, after the dinner, each patron attending could buy a set of 20 tickets for the gaming tables (such as roulette). The chance of winning a prize for each of the 20 plays is 50-50. You bought a set of 20 tickets.

    a. What is the chance that you will win 15 or more prizes?
    b. What is the probability that you will win exactly four prizes?
    c. What is the probability you will have no successes—that is, you will not win a prize?
    d. What is the probability you will win 5 or fewer prizes?
    e. What is the probability you will win fewer than 5 prizes?

## HYPERGEOMETRIC DISTRIBUTION

We pointed out that for the binomial distribution to be applied, the probability of a success must stay the same for each successive trial. For example, the probability of guessing the correct answer to a true/false question is .50. This probability remains the same for each question on an examination. Likewise, suppose that 40 percent of the registered voters in a precinct are Republicans. If 27 registered voters are to be selected at random, the probability of choosing a Republican on the first selection is .40. The chance of choosing a Republican on the next selection is also .40, assuming that the sampling is done *with replacement,* meaning that the person selected is put back in the population before the next person is selected.

Most sampling is done *without replacement.* Thus, the outcomes are not independent—meaning that the probability for each successive observation will change. For example, if the population consists of 20 items, the probability of selecting a particular item from that population is ¹⁄₂₀. If the sampling is done without replacement, there are only 19 items remaining; the probability of selecting a particular item on the second selection is only ¹⁄₁₉. For the third selection, the probability is ¹⁄₁₈, and so on. This assumes that the population is *finite*—that is, the number in the population is known.

*Finite population*

---

Finite population   A population consisting of a fixed number of known individuals, objects, or measurements.

---

Examples of a finite population are 2,842 Republicans in the precinct, 9,241 applications for medical school, and the 18 Pontiac Sunbirds currently in stock at North Pontiac.

Recall that one of the criteria for using the binomial distribution is that the probability of success remain the same from trial to trial. Since the probability of success does not remain the same from trial to trial when sampling is done without replacement, the binomial distribution should not be used. Instead, the **hypergeometric distribution** should be applied. Therefore, (1) if a sample is selected from a finite population without replacement and (2) if the size of the sample $n$ is greater than 5 percent of the size of the population $N$, then the hypergeometric distribution is used to determine the probability of a specified number of successes and/or failures. It is especially appropriate when the size of the population is small.

The formula for the hypergeometric distribution is:

*Hypergeometric distribution*

$$P(r) = \frac{(_sC_r)(_{N-S}C_{n-r})}{_NC_n} \qquad (6-6)$$

where:

   $N$   is the size of the population.
   $S$   is the number of successes in the population.
   $r$   is the number of successes of interest. It may be 0, 1, 2, 3, . . . .
   $n$   is the size of the sample or the number of trials.
   $C$   is the symbol for a combination.

### ▮ EXAMPLE

Suppose 50 transceivers were manufactured during the week ($N = 50$). Forty operated perfectly ($S = 40$), and 10 had at least one defect. A sample of 5 is selected at random ($n = 5$). Using the hypergeometric formula, what is the probability that 4 ($r = 4$) of the 5 will operate perfectly? (Note that sampling is done without replacement, and the sample size of 5 is $\frac{5}{50}$, or 10 percent of the population. This is greater than the 5 percent requirement.)

### ▨ SOLUTION

In this problem,

   $N = 50$, the number of transceivers manufactured.
   $n = 5$, the size of the sample.
   $S = 40$, the number of transceivers in the population operating perfectly.
   $r = 4$, the number in the sample operating perfectly.

We want to find the probability that 4 transceivers of the 5 selected will operate perfectly.

Inserting these values in formula (6−6) and solving for the probability that 4 out of 5 transceivers in the sample operate perfectly:

$$P(r) = \frac{(_sC_r)(_{N-S}C_{n-r})}{_NC_n}$$

$$P(4) = \frac{(_{40}C_4)(_{50-40}C_{5-4})}{_{50}C_5}$$

$$= \frac{\left(\dfrac{40!}{4!36!}\right)\left(\dfrac{10!}{1!9!}\right)}{\dfrac{50!}{5!45!}}$$

$$= \frac{(91,390)(10)}{2,118,760} = .431$$

Thus, the probability of selecting 5 transceivers at random out of 50 and finding that 4 of the 5 operate perfectly is .431.

The hypergeometric probabilities of finding 0, 1, 2, 3, 4, and 5 working transceivers of the 5 transceivers selected at random are given in Table 6−8.

## TABLE 6–8

**Hypergeometric Probabilities ($n = 5$, $N = 50$, $S = 40$) that Transceivers Operate Correctly**

| Number operating correctly | Probability |
|:---:|:---:|
| 0 | .000* |
| 1 | .004 |
| 2 | .044 |
| 3 | .210 |
| 4 | .431 |
| 5 | .311 |

*Actually .0001.

Hypergeometric probabilities closely approximate binomial probabilities. For comparison, Table 6–9 gives the hypergeometric and binomial probabilities for the transceiver problem. (Since 40 of the 50 transceivers operated correctly, the binomial probability of selecting a perfect transceiver is $^{40}\!/_{50} = .80$. The binomial probabilities for Table 6–9 come from the binomial table in Appendix A, $n = 5$, $p = .80$.)

## TABLE 6–9

**Hypergeometric and Binomial Probabilities for the Transceiver Problem**

| Number of transceivers in sample operating correctly, $r$ | Hypergeometric probability, $P(r)$ | Binomial probability* ($n = 5$, $p = 40/50 = .80$) |
|:---:|:---:|:---:|
| 0 | .000 | .000 |
| 1 | .004 | .006 |
| 2 | .044 | .051 |
| 3 | .210 | .205 |
| 4 | .431 | .410 |
| 5 | .311 | .328 |

*From Appendix A for an $n$ of 5 and a $p$ of .80, found by 40/50.

We pointed out that when the binomial requirement of a constant probability of success cannot be met, the hypergeometric distribution should be used in its place. However, as Table 6–9 shows, under many conditions the results of the binomial closely approximate those of the hypergeometric. As a rule of thumb, if the selected items are not returned to the population and the sample size is less than 5 percent of the population, the binomial distribution can be used to approximate the hypergeometric distribution. That is, when $n < .05N$, the binomial appoximation should suffice.

### Self-Review 6–7

*The answers are at the end of the chapter.*

Refer to the transceiver example and Table 6–8. Verify the hypergeometric probability of .210 that three of the five randomly selected transceivers will operate correctly.

# EXERCISES

*The answers to the odd-numbered exercises are at the end of the book.*

21. Suppose a population consists of 10 items, 6 of which are defective. A sample of 3 items is selected. What is the probability that exactly 2 are defective?

22. Suppose a population consists of 15 items, 10 of which are acceptable. A sample of 4 items is selected. What is the probability that exactly 3 are acceptable?

23. Kolzak Appliance Outlet just received a shipment of 10 TV sets. Shortly after they were received, the manufacturer called to report that he had inadvertently shipped 3 defective sets. Ms. Kolzak, the owner of the outlet, decided to test 2 of the 10 sets she received. What is the probability that neither of the 2 sets tested was defective?

24. The Computer Systems Department consists of eight faculty, six of whom are tenured. Dr. Vonder, the chairman, wants to establish a committee of three department faculty members to review the curriculum. If she selects the committee at random:

    a.   What is the probability all members of the committee are tenured?

    b.   What is the probability that at least one member is not tenured?

    (Hint: For this question use the complement rule.)

25. Keith's Florists has 15 delivery trucks, used mainly to deliver flowers and flower arrangements in the Tulsa area. Suppose 6 of the 15 trucks have brake problems. Five trucks were selected at random to be tested. What is the probability that 2 of those tested have defective brakes?

26. Professor Jon Hammer has a pool of 15 multiple-choice questions regarding probability distributions. Four of these questions involve the hypergeometric distribution. What is the probability at least 1 of these hypergeometric questions will appear on the 5-question quiz on Monday?

# POISSON PROBABILITY DISTRIBUTION

Poisson probability distribution—a discrete distribution

The binomial probability distributions for probabilities of success (*p*) less than .05 could be computed, but the calculations would be quite time-consuming (especially for a large *n* of, say, 100 or more). The distribution of probabilities would become more and more skewed as the probability of success became smaller. The limiting form of the binomial distribution where the probability of success is very small and *n* is large is called the **Poisson probability distribution.** The distribution is named after Simeon Poisson, who described it in 1837. It is often referred to as the *law of improbable events,* meaning that the probability *p* of a particular event's happening is quite small. The Poisson distribution is a discrete probability distribution because *it is formed by counting something.*

This distribution has many applications. It is used as a model to describe such phenomena as the distribution of errors in data entry, the number of scratches and other imperfections in newly painted panels, the number of defective parts in outgoing shipments, the number of customers waiting to be served at a restaurant or waiting to get into an attraction at Disney World, and the number of accidents on Interstate I-75 during a three-month period.

The Poisson distribution can be described mathematically using the formula:

$$P(x) = \frac{\mu^x e^{-\mu}}{x!} \qquad \text{or} \qquad P(x) = \frac{\mu^x}{x! e^{\mu}} \qquad (6-7)$$

where:

$\mu$ (mu)   is the arithmetic mean number of occurrences (successes) in a particular interval of time.

$e$   is the constant 2.71828 (base of the Naperian logarithmic system).

$x$   is the number of occurrences (successes).

$P(x)$   is the probability to be computed for a specified value of $x$.

**Mean of a Poisson distribution**

The mean number of successes $\mu$ can be determined in binomial situations by $np$, where $n$ is the total number of trials and $p$ the probability of success.

$$\mu = np \qquad (6-8)$$

The variance of the Poisson is also equal to $np$. If, for example, the probability that a check cashed by a bank will bounce is .0003, and 10,000 checks are cashed, the mean number of bad checks is 3.0, found by $\mu = np = 10{,}000\ (.0003) = 3.0$.

Recall that for a binomial distribution there is a determinate number of successes. For example, for a four-question multiple-choice test there can only be zero, one, two, three, or four successes (correct answers). The random variable $x$ for a Poisson distribution, however, can assume an *infinite number of values*—that is, 0, 1, 2, 3, 4, 5, . . . . However, *the probabilities become very small after the first few occurrences* (successes).

To illustrate the computation of a Poisson probability, assume that billing clerks rarely make errors in data entry on the billing statements. Many statements, of course, have no mistakes; some have one; a very few have two mistakes; rarely will a statement have three mistakes; and so on. A random sample of 1,000 statements revealed 300 errors. Thus, the arithmetic mean number of mistakes per billing statement is 0.3, found by 300/1,000. This is a sample mean, $\overline{X}$, which is used to estimate the population mean, $\mu$, for a model (Poisson) of the process.

The probability of no (0) mistakes appearing in a statement is computed by:

$$P(x) = \frac{\mu^x}{x!e^{\mu}}$$

Substituting:

$$P(0) = \frac{0.3^0}{0!(2.71828)^{0.3}} = .7408$$

**Use a table to determine Poisson probabilities**

However, the computations of the probabilities for a Poisson distribution using the formula are time-consuming. As an aid, a table of Poisson probabilities is given in Appendix C for various values of $\mu$.

## ■ EXAMPLE

Recall from the previous illustration that the mean number of errors per billing statement was estimated to be 0.3. That is, $\mu = 0.3$. What is the probability that no mistakes will be found on a randomly selected billing statement? What is the probability that exactly one mistake will be found?

### ✓ SOLUTION

Refer to Appendix C. Locate the column headed by $\mu = 0.3$. Read down that column to the row labeled 0, and read the value. It is .7408. The probability of exactly one error is .2222. The Poisson distribution for zero, one, two, three, and four successes (errors) is given below using the MINITAB system. The output is graphed in Chart 6−6.

```
MTB > pdf;
SUBC> poisson mu = .3.
       POISSON WITH MEAN = 0.300
          K              P(X = K)
          0              0.7408
          1              0.2222
          2              0.0333
          3              0.0033
          4              0.0003
          5              0.0000
```

### CHART 6−6

**Poisson Probability Distribution for $\mu = 0.3$**

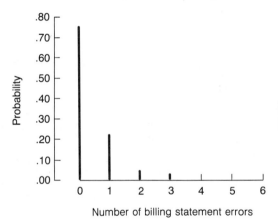

Number of billing statement errors

### Self-Review 6−8

*The answers are at the end of the chapter.*

A hybrid seed grower is experiencing trouble with corn borers. A random check of 5,000 ears revealed the following: Many of the ears contained no borers; some ears had one borer; a few had two borers; and so on. The distribution of the number of borers per ear approximates the Poisson distribution. The grower counted 3,500 borers in the 5,000 ears.

1. What is the probability that an ear of corn selected at random will contain no borers?
2. Develop a Poisson probability distribution for this experiment.

The Poisson probability distribution is always positively skewed. Also, the Poisson random variable has no specific upper limit. The Poisson distributions for the data entry illustration, where $\mu = 0.3$, and for the corn borer experiment in Self-Review 6–8, where $\mu = 0.7$, are highly skewed. As $\mu$ becomes larger, the Poisson distribution becomes almost symmetrical. For illustration, the distributions for means of 0.7, 2.0, and 6.0 are shown in Chart 6–7.

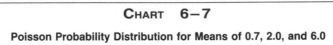

CHART    6–7

**Poisson Probability Distribution for Means of 0.7, 2.0, and 6.0**

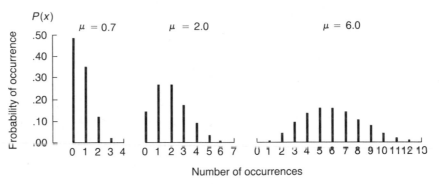

Only $\mu$ needed to construct Poisson

In brief summary, the Poisson distribution is actually a group of discrete distributions. To apply it, $n$ must be large, such as 1,000 sheared pieces. Conversely, the probability $p$ of a defect, error, and the like must be small. All that is needed to construct a Poisson probability distribution is the average number of defects, errors, and so on—designated as $\mu$. Mu is computed by $np$.

# EXERCISES

*The answers to the odd-numbered exercises are at the end of the book.*

27. In a Poisson distribution $\mu = 0.4$.
    a.  What is the probability that $x = 0$?
    b.  What is the probability that $x \geq 0$?
28. In a Poisson distribution $\mu = 4$.
    a.  What is the probability that $x = 2$?
    b.  What is the probability that $x \leq 2$?
    c.  What is the probability that $x > 2$?
29. Ms. Bergen is a loan officer at Coast Bank and Trust. Based on her years of experience she estimates that the probability is .025 that an applicant will not be able to repay his or her installment loan. Last month she made 40 loans.
    a.  What is the probability that 3 loans will be defaulted?
    b.  What is the probability that at least 3 loans will be defaulted?
30. Automobiles arrive at the Elkhart exit of the Indiana Turnpike at the rate of two per minute. The distribution of arrivals approximates a Poisson distribution.
    a.  What is the probability that no automobiles arrive in a particular minute?
    b.  What is the probability at least one automobile arrives during a particular minute?

31. It is estimated that 0.5 percent of the callers to the billing department of the U.S. West Telephone Company will receive a busy signal. What is the probability that of today's 1,200 callers at least 5 received a busy signal?

32. Textbook authors and publishers work very hard to minimize the number of errors in a text. However, some errors are unavoidable. Mr. J. A. Carmen, statistics editor, reports that the mean number of errors per chapter is 0.8. What is the probability that there are less than 2 errors in a particular chapter?

## CHAPTER OUTLINE

I.   A random variable is a numerical value determined by the outcome of an experiment.
II.  A probability distribution is a listing of all the outcomes of an experiment and the probability associated with each outcome.
    A. A discrete probability distribution can assume only certain values. The main features are:
        1. The sum of the possible outcomes is 1.00.
        2. The probability of a particular outcome is between 0.00 and 1.00.
        3. The outcomes are mutually exclusive.
    B. A continuous distribution can assume an infinite number of values within a specific range.
III. The mean and variance of a probability distribution are computed as follows.
    A. The mean is equal to:

$$\mu = \Sigma[XP(X)] \tag{6-1}$$

    B. The variance is equal to:

$$\sigma^2 = \Sigma[(X - \mu)^2 P(X)] \tag{6-2}$$

IV. The binomial distribution has the following characteristics.
    A. Each outcome is classified into one of two mutually exclusive categories.
    B. The probability of a success remains the same from trial to trial.
    C. Each trial is independent.
    D. The distribution results from a count of the number of successes in a fixed number of trials.
    E. A binomial probability is determined as follows.

$$P(r) = {}_nC_r\, p^r q^{n-r} \tag{6-3}$$

    F. The mean is computed as:

$$\mu = np \tag{6-4}$$

    G. The variance is

$$\sigma^2 = np(1 - p) \tag{6-5}$$

V.  The hypergeometric distribution has the following characteristics.
    A. There are only two possible outcomes.
    B. The trials are not independent, so the probability of a success is not the same on each trial.
    C. The distribution results from a count of the number of successes in a fixed number of trials.
    D. A hypergeometric probability is computed from the following equation.

$$P(r) = \frac{({}_SC_r)({}_{N-S}C_{n-r})}{{}_NC_n} \tag{6-6}$$

VI.  The Poisson distribution has the following characteristics.
   A.  Each outcome is classified into one of two mutually exclusive categories.
   B.  The probability of a success remains the same from trial to trial.
   C.  Each trial is independent.
   D.  The distribution results from a count of the number of successes in a fixed number of trials.
   E.  A Poisson probability is determined from the following equation.

$$P(x) = \frac{\mu^x}{x!e^\mu} \hspace{3cm} (6-7)$$

   F.  The probability of a success is usually small, and the number of trials is usually large.
   G.  The mean and variance of a Poisson distribution are the same and are equal to $np$.

## EXERCISES

*The answers to the odd-numbered exercises are at the end of the book.*

33.  List the characteristics of the hypergeometric distribution.

34.  What is a binomial distribution?

35.  Under what conditions will the Poisson and the binomial distributions give roughly the same results?

36.  What is a discrete probability distribution?

37.  Samson Apartments has a large number of units available to rent each month. A concern of management is the number of vacant apartments each month. A recent study revealed the percent of the time that a given number of apartments are vacant.

| Number of vacant units | Probability |
| --- | --- |
| 0 | .10 |
| 1 | .20 |
| 2 | .30 |
| 3 | .40 |

Compute the mean and standard deviation of the number of vacant apartments.

38.  An investment will be worth $1,000, $2,000, or $5,000 at the end of the year. The probabilities of these values are .25, .60, and .15, respectively. Determine the mean and variance of the worth of the investment.

39.  The personnel manager of the Cumberland Pig Iron Company is studying the number of on-the-job accidents over a period of one month. He developed the following probability distribution.

| Number of accidents | Probability |
| --- | --- |
| 0 | .40 |
| 1 | .20 |
| 2 | .20 |
| 3 | .10 |
| 4 | .10 |

Compute the mean, variance, and standard deviation of the number of accidents in a month.

40.  Corso Bakery offers special decorated cakes for birthdays, weddings, and other occasions. They also have regular cakes available in their bakery. The following table gives the total number of cakes sold per day and the corresponding probability.

| Number of cakes sold in a day | Probability |
|---|---|
| 12 | .25 |
| 13 | .40 |
| 14 | .25 |
| 15 | .10 |

Compute the mean, variance, and standard deviation for the number of cakes sold per day.

41. A stock analyst watched Corbin common stock very closely for 50 trading days and recorded the following data.

| Amount of change | Number of days |
|---|---|
| $-\dfrac{1}{4}$ | 6 |
| $-\dfrac{1}{8}$ | 12 |
| 0 | 17 |
| $\dfrac{1}{8}$ | 9 |
| $\dfrac{1}{4}$ | 4 |
| $\dfrac{1}{2}$ | 2 |

Does this information qualify as a discrete probability distribution? If yes, convert the information to a probability distribution. Compute the mean and the variance.

42. A Tamiami shearing machine is producing 10 percent defective pieces, which is abnormally high. The quality-control engineer has been checking the output by almost continuous sampling since the abnormal condition began. What is the probability that in a sample of 10 pieces:

a. Exactly 5 will be defective?

b. 5 or more will be defective?

43. A mechanical aptitude test includes five problems to determine whether or not the person taking the test can distinguish the sizes of objects. For example, a person is given four blocks of slightly different sizes and must quickly indicate which one is the largest.

The person can choose only one block. Thus, the choice is either right or wrong. This is repeated with round blocks, diamond-shaped blocks, and so on. Assuming that the person cannot distinguish sizes:

a. What is the probability that he/she will guess all five identifications correctly?

b. What is the probability that he/she will get none out of the five correct?

c. What is the probability of getting one or more identifications correct?

44. The first-grade classes in the Maumee school district are filled, and several new classes must be added. Assume that half of the seven-year-olds who will enroll are boys and the other half are girls. The class size is limited to 18 children.

    a. What is the probability that exactly 9 boys and 9 girls will be in the class?

    b. What is the probability that there will be 11 or more boys in the newly created class? Is this the same as the probability of having 7 or fewer girls in the class of 18?

    c. What is the probability that exactly 7 girls and 11 boys will enroll in the new class?

    d. When the doors open the first day of class, what is the probability that the first seven-year-old child who walks into the room will be a girl?

45. Thirty percent of the population in a southwestern community are Spanish-speaking Americans. A Spanish-speaking person is accused of killing a non-Spanish-speaking American. Of the first 12 potential jurors, only 2 are Spanish-speaking Americans, and 10 are not. The defendant's lawyer challenges the jury selection, claiming bias against her client. The government lawyer disagrees, saying that the probability of this particular jury composition is common. What do you think?

46. A new chassis was put into production by Fisher. Production involved soldering, inserting transistors, and so on. Each chassis was inspected at the end of the assembly line, and the number of defects per unit were recorded. For the first 100 chassis produced, there were 40 defects. Some of the chassis had no defects; a few had one defect; and so on. The distribution of defects followed a Poisson distribution. Based on the first 100 produced, about how many out of every 1,000 chassis assembled should have one or more defects?

47. The Ford production department has installed a new spray machine to paint automobile doors. As is common with most spray guns, unsightly blemishes sometimes appear because of improper mixture or other problems. A worker counted the number of blemishes on each door. Most doors had no blemishes, a few had one, a very few had two, and so on. The average number was 0.5 per door. The distribution of blemishes followed the Poisson distribution.

    a. Out of 10,000 doors painted, about how many would have no blemishes?

    b. Out of 10,000 doors painted, how many would have two or more blemishes?

48. L. L. Bean advertised same-day service. Unfortunately, the movement of orders did not go as planned, and there were a large number of complaints. A complete change in the handling of incoming and outgoing orders was then made. An internal goal was set to have fewer than five unfilled orders on hand (per picker) at the end of 95 out of every 100 working days. Frequent checks of the unfilled orders at the end of the day revealed that the distribution of the unfilled orders approximated a Poisson distribution; that is, most of the days there were no unfilled orders, some of the days there was one order, and so on. The average number of unfilled orders per picker was 2.0.

    a. Has L. L. Bean lived up to its internal goal? Cite evidence.

    b. Draw a histogram representing the Poisson probability distribution of unfilled orders at the end of the day.

49. West Virginia Tool and Die has 100 drill presses and other machines in constant use. The probability that a machine will become inoperative during a given day is .002. During some days no machines are inoperative; during other days one, two, three, or more are broken down.

    a. What is the probability that for a particular day no machines will be inoperative?

    b. What is the probability that fewer than two machines will be inoperative during a particular day?

    c. A machine operator claims that she noticed on many occasions three or more machines broken down during the day. Does her claim seem logical? Why or why not?

Courtesy Ford Motor Company

50. Suppose 1.5 percent of the plastic spacers produced by a Corson high-speed mold injection machine are defective. The distribution of defectives follows a Poisson distribution. For a random sample of 200 spacers, find the probability that:

    a.    None of the spacers is defective.

    b.    Three or more of the spacers are defective.

51. A study of the lines at the checkout registers of Safeway Supermarket revealed that, during a certain period at the rush hour, the number of customers waiting averaged four. What is the probability that during that period:

    a.    No customers were waiting?

    b.    Four customers were waiting?

    c.    Four or fewer were waiting?

    d.    Four or more were waiting?

52. A box of electric hedge trimmers contains six Cummings trimmers. Two are defective; four operate correctly. Three trimmers are selected from the box.

    a.    What is the probability that exactly one of the Cummings trimmers is defective?

    b.    What is the probability that two trimmers of the three selected are defective?

53. The sales of Lexus automobiles in the Detroit area follow a Poisson distribution with a mean of 3.00 per day.

    a.    What is the probability that no Lexus is sold on a particular day?

    b.    What is the probability that for five consecutive days at least one Lexus is sold?

54. A new flavor of Ipana toothpaste has been developed. It was tested by a group of 10 people. Six of the group said they liked the new flavor, and the remaining four indicated they did not. Four of the 10 are selected to participate in an in-depth interview. What is the probability that of those selected for the in-depth interview two liked the new flavor and two did not?

55. Suppose it is known that 5 out of 25 Chrysler subcompact automobiles off the assembly line require adjustment of some kind. Four subcompacts are selected at random. We are interested in the probability that exactly one will require adjustment.

    a.    Solve the problem assuming that out of the 25 subcompacts, the samples are drawn without replacement.

    b.    Solve the problem assuming the sampling is done with replacement.

    c.    Assuming replacement, work the problem using the Poisson distribution.

56. The South Bend Football Booster Club conducts a raffle at each home football game. For this week's game 1,000 tickets are sold for $5 each. A single winner will be randomly drawn and awarded a prize of $500. What is the mean amount won, or lost, by each person who bought a ticket? Interpret.

57. In an effort to avoid detection at customs at the Miami airport, a traveler placed five narcotic tablets in a bottle containing seven vitamin pills similar in appearance. If the customs official selects three of the tablets at random for analysis, what is the probability that the traveler will be arrested for illegal possession of narcotics?

58. A bowl contains 10 nickels, 10 dimes, 15 quarters, and 15 half-dollars. A coin is randomly selected from the bowl.

    a.    What is the probability a dime is selected?

    b.    What is the mean payoff for each selection?

    c.    What is the variance of the payoff?

59. On January 29, 1986, the space shuttle *Challenger* exploded at an altitude of 46,000 feet, resulting in the death of all seven astronauts. A 1985 study published by the National Aeronautics and Space Administration (NASA) suggested that the probability of a catastrophic occurrence such as this was about 1 in 60,000. A similar report by the air

force set the likelihood of a catastrophe at 1 in 35. The *Challenger* flight was the 25th mission in the shuttle program. Use the Poisson distribution to compare the probabilities of at least one disaster in 25 missions using both estimates of the probability of occurrence.

60. According to the "January theory," if the stock market is up for the month of January, it will be up for the year. If it is down in January, it will be down for the year. According to an article in *The Wall Street Journal,* this theory held for 29 out of the last 34 years. Suppose there is no truth to this theory. What is the probability this could happen by chance? (You will probably need a computer. Use the binomial distribution.)

## COMPUTER DATA EXERCISES

61. Refer to data set 1, which reports information on homes sold in Florida during 1990.
    a. Create a probability distribution for the number of bedrooms. Compute the mean and standard deviation of this distribution.
    b. Create a probability distribution for the number of bathrooms. Compute the mean and standard deviation of this distribution.

## CHAPTER 6 EXAMINATION

*The answers are at the end of the chapter.*

For Questions 1–10 fill in the correct answer.

1. A _____ is a listing of the possible outcomes from an experiment and the probability associated with each of these outcomes.
2. In a _____ distribution the probability of a success is *not* the same for each trial.
3. In a _____ distribution the probability of a success is usually small.
4. In a _____ distribution the mean and the variance are equal.
5. In a binomial experiment there are _____ possible outcomes.
6. The Poisson distribution is an example of a (discrete, continuous) _____ probability distribution.
7. The Poisson distribution is _____ skewed.
8. A _____ population consists of a fixed number of individuals, objects, or measurements.
9. For a discrete probability distribution, the sum of the probabilities is _____.
10. For a discrete probability distribution, the outcomes must be_____.
11. Current medical studies indicate that 30 percent of the population will suffer from the flu each winter. A group of 12 people is randomly selected.
    a. What is the probability that exactly 5 in the group will have the flu this winter?
    b. What is the probability that a least 5 in the group will have the flu this winter?
    c. Compute the mean and variance of the number in the group that will suffer with the flu this winter.
12. A college basketball coach has 12 players on his roster. Eight of the players are receiving basketball scholarships, and 4 are not. Recently the team has been losing most of their games. The coach decided to draw the names of 5 players out of a hat and designate them as the starting lineup. What is the probability that 4 of the 5 players selected are on a scholarship?
13. Suppose there were 200 students in your high school graduating class. Current statistics indicate that 0.5 percent, or .005, of the population will become millionaires. What is the probability that at least one student from your class becomes a millionaire?

# ANSWERS

6–1 1.

| Number of spots | Probability |
|---|---|
| 1 | $\frac{1}{6}$ |
| 2 | $\frac{1}{6}$ |
| 3 | $\frac{1}{6}$ |
| 4 | $\frac{1}{6}$ |
| 5 | $\frac{1}{6}$ |
| 6 | $\frac{1}{6}$ |
| Total | $\frac{6}{6} = 1.00$ |

2.

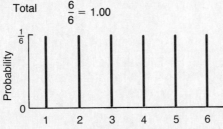

3. $\frac{6}{6}$, or 1.

6–2 1. Yes. The sum of the probabilities is 1.00, and the outcomes are mutually exclusive.

2.

| x | P(X) | xP(X) |
|---|---|---|
| 50 | .30 | 15.0 |
| 75 | .50 | 37.5 |
| 90 | .20 | 18.0 |
| | | 70.5 |

The mean is 70.5 cents.

3.

| X | P(X) | $(X - \mu)$ | $(X - \mu^2 P(X)$ |
|---|---|---|---|
| 50 | .30 | − 20.5 | 126.075 |
| 75 | .50 | 4.5 | 10.125 |
| 90 | .20 | 19.5 | 76.050 |
| | | | 212.25 |

The variance is 212.25, and the standard deviation is 14.57 cents.

6–3 1. a. For each multiple-choice question, a student either guesses the answer correctly (a success) or does not (a failure).
b. The distribution of successes is discrete, resulting from a count of the number of successes.
c. The probability that a student will guess each question correctly is one fifth, or .20.
d. The trials are independent, meaning that a success, or failure, for any question does not affect the outcome of any other question.

2. $\left(\dfrac{1}{5}\right)^{20}$

6–4 .3750, found by:

$$P(2) = \frac{4!}{2!(4 - 2)!}(.50)^2(.50)^{4-2}$$
$$= (6)(.50)^2(.50)^2$$
$$= (6)(.25)(.25)$$

6–5 $n = 7, p = .20$.

| | r | Probability |
|---|---|---|
| 1. | 0 | .210 |
| 2. | 1 | .367 |
| 3. | 2 | .275 |
| | 3 | .115 |
| | 4 | .029 |
| | 5 | .004 |
| | 6 | .000 |
| | 7 | .000 |
| 4. | 1.000 | |

6–6 $n = 4, p = .60$
a. $P(r = 2) = .346$
b. $P(r \le 2) = .526$
c. $P(r > 2) = 1 - .526$
$= .474$

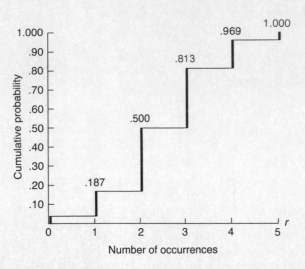

Number of occurrences

6–7 .210, found by:

$$P(3) = \frac{(_{40}C_3)(_{10}C_2)}{_{50}C_5}$$

$$= \frac{\left(\dfrac{40 \cdot 39 \cdot 38}{3 \cdot 2 \cdot 1}\right)\left(\dfrac{10 \cdot 9}{2}\right)}{\left(\dfrac{50 \cdot 49 \cdot 48 \cdot 47 \cdot 46}{5 \cdot 4 \cdot 3 \cdot 2 \cdot 1}\right)}$$

$$= \frac{(9{,}880)(45)}{(2{,}118{,}760)} = .210$$

6–8 1. .4966. $\mu = 0.7$, found by 3,500/5,000. Refer to Appendix C, for a $\mu$ of 0.7 and an $x$ of 0.

2.

| Number of occurrences, $x$ | Probability of occurrence, $P(x)$ |
|---|---|
| 0 | .4966 |
| 1 | .3476 |
| 2 | .1217 |
| 3 | .0284 |
| 4 | .0050 |
| 5 | .0007 |
| 6 | .0001 |

## Answers

# CHAPTER 6 EXAMINATION

1. Probability distribution.
2. Hypergeometric.
3. Poisson.
4. Poisson.
5. Two
6. Discrete.
7. Positively.
8. Finite.
9. 1.00.
10. Mutually exclusive.
11. $n = 12, p = .30$
   a. $P(r = 5 \mid n = 12 \text{ and } p = .30) = .158$
   b. $P(r \geq 5 \mid n = 12 \text{ and } p = .30) = 1 - .724 = .276$
   c. $\mu = np = 12(.30) = 3.6$
      $\sigma^2 = np(1 - p) = 12(.30)(.70) = 2.52$

12. .354, found by:

$$P(4) = \frac{(_8C_4)(_4C_1)}{_{12}C_5} = \frac{\left(\dfrac{8!}{4!4!}\right)\left(\dfrac{4!}{3!1!}\right)}{\left(\dfrac{12!}{7!5!}\right)}$$

$$= \frac{\left(\dfrac{8 \cdot 7 \cdot 6 \cdot 5}{4 \cdot 3 \cdot 2 \cdot 1}\right)4}{\left(\dfrac{12 \cdot 11 \cdot 10 \cdot 9 \cdot 8}{5 \cdot 4 \cdot 3 \cdot 2 \cdot 1}\right)} = \frac{280}{792} = .354$$

13. $\mu = np = 200(.005) = 1.00$. $P(X \geq 1) = 1 - P(X = 0)$
    $= 1 - .3679 = .6321.$

# THE NORMAL PROBABILITY DISTRIBUTION

When you have completed this chapter, you will be able to:

## GOALS

1. List the characteristics of a normal probability distribution.

2. Define and calculate z values.

3. Determine the probability that an observation will lie between two points, using the standard normal distribution.

4. Determine the probability that an observation will be above, or below, a value, using the standard normal distribution.

5. Compare two or more observations that are in different probability distributions.

6. Use the normal probability distribution to approximate the binomial probability distribution.

Courtesy Alcoa

**C**hapter 6 dealt with three *discrete* probability distributions: the binomial distribution, the hypergeometric distribution, and the Poisson distribution. Recall that these distributions are based on discrete random variables, which can assume only specified values. For example, the number of correct answers on a 10-question examination can only be 0, 1, 2, 3, . . ., 10. There cannot be a negative number of responses, such as $-7$, nor can there be $7\frac{1}{4}$ or 15 correct answers.

We will continue our study of probability distributions in this chapter by examining a very important *continuous* probability distribution, namely, the **normal probability distribution.** As noted in the preceding chapter, a continuous random variable is one that can assume an *infinite* number of possible values within a specified range. It usually results from measuring something, such as the weight of an individual. The weight might be 112.0 kilograms, 112.1 kilograms, 112.12 kilograms, and so on, depending on the accuracy of the scale. Other continuous random variables are the life expectancy of alkaline batteries, the volume of a shipping container, and the weight of impurities in a steel ingot.

The probability distributions of the life expectancies of some products, such as batteries, tires, and light bulbs, tend to follow a "normal" pattern. So do the weights of boxes of Kellogg's Special K cereal, the lengths of rolls of aluminum, and other variables measured on a continuous scale.

In this chapter the main characteristics of a normal probability distribution and the normal curve are examined first. Then the *standard normal distribution* and its uses are presented. Finally, we will look at how the normal distribution can be used to estimate binomial probabilities.

## CHARACTERISTICS OF A NORMAL PROBABILITY DISTRIBUTION

The normal probability distribution and its accompanying normal curve have the following characteristics:

**Bell-shaped**

1. The normal curve is *bell-shaped* and has a single peak at the exact center of the distribution. The arithmetic mean, median, and mode of the distribution are equal and located at the peak. Thus, half the area under the curve is above this center point, and the other half is below it.

**Symmetrical**

2. The normal probability distribution is *symmetrical* about its mean. If we cut the normal curve vertically at this central value, the two halves will be mirror images.

**Asymptotic**

3. The normal curve falls off smoothly in either direction from the central value. It is *asymptotic,* meaning that the curve gets closer and closer to the X-axis but never actually touches it. That is, the "tails" of the curve extend indefinitely in both directions. In real-world problems, however, this is somewhat unrealistic. The life of an alkaline battery, for example, could not be 300 years.

These characteristics are summarized in Chart 7–1.

## THE FAMILY OF NORMAL PROBABILITY DISTRIBUTIONS

**Family of normal distributions**

Generally speaking, there is not just one normal probability distribution. Instead, there is a "family" of them. There is one normal probability distribution for the lengths of

---

**CHART 7–1**

**Characteristics of a Normal Distribution**

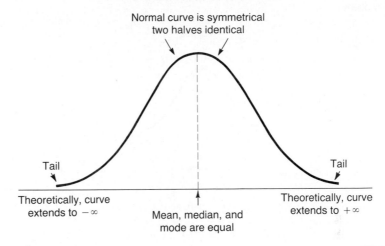

Normal curve is symmetrical
two halves identical

Tail                                                                 Tail

Theoretically, curve          Mean, median, and          Theoretically, curve
extends to $-\infty$              mode are equal              extends to $+\infty$

---

service of the employees in our Camden plant, where the mean is 20 years and the standard deviation is 3.1 years. There is another normal probability distribution for the lengths of service in our Dunkirk plant, where $\mu = 20$ years and $\sigma = 3.9$ years. Chart 7–2 portrays three such normal distributions, where the means are the same but the standard deviations are different.

---

**CHART 7–2**

Equal means, unequal
standard deviations

**Normal Probability Distributions with Equal Means but Different Standard Deviations**

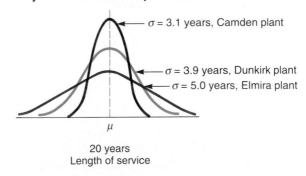

$\sigma = 3.1$ years, Camden plant

$\sigma = 3.9$ years, Dunkirk plant
$\sigma = 5.0$ years, Elmira plant

$\mu$

20 years
Length of service

---

Chart 7–3 shows the weights of three different cereals. The distributions are normally distributed with different means but identical standard deviations.

Finally, Chart 7–4 shows the curves for three normal distributions having different means and standard deviations. They show the distribution of tensile strengths, measured in pounds per square inch (psi), for three types of cables.

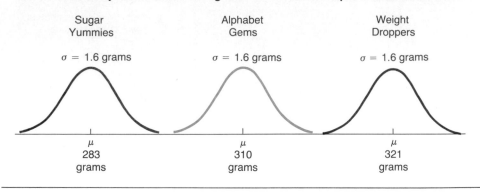

## Chart 7—3

**Unequal means, equal standard deviations**

**Normal Probability Distributions Having Different Means but Equal Standard Deviations**

## Chart 7—4

**Unequal means, unequal standard deviations**

**Normal Probability Distributions with Different Means and Standard Deviations**

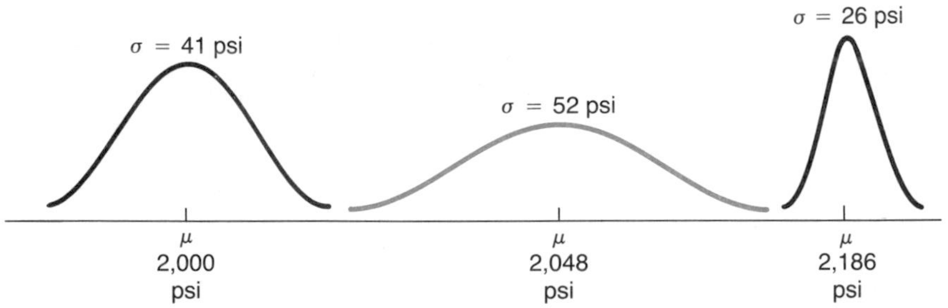

# THE STANDARD NORMAL PROBABILITY DISTRIBUTION

**Standard normal probability distribution**

We noted that there is a family of normal distributions. Each distribution has a different mean ($\mu$) or standard deviation ($\sigma$). The number of normal distributions is therefore unlimited. It would be physically impossible to provide a table of probabilities (such as for the binomial and Poisson) for each combination of $\mu$ and $\sigma$. Fortunately, one member of the family of normal distributions can be used for all problems where the normal distribution is applicable. It has a mean of 0 and a standard deviation of 1 and is called the **standard normal distribution.**

First it is necessary to convert, or *standardize,* the actual distribution to a standard normal distribution using a *z value,* also called a *z score,* a *z statistic,* the *standard normal deviate,* or just the *normal deviate.*

---

*z* value    The distance between a selected value, designated *X,* and the population mean, $\mu$, divided by the population standard deviation, $\sigma$.

---

In terms of a formula:

$$z = \frac{X - \mu}{\sigma}$$

(7–1)

where:

$X$   is the value of any particular observation or measurement.

$\mu$   is the mean of the distribution.

$\sigma$   is the standard deviation of the distribution.

As noted in the above definition, a $z$ value measures the distance between a particular value of $X$ and the arithmetic mean in units of the standard deviation. Knowing the $z$ value determined using formula (7–1), we can find the area or probability under the normal curve by referring to Appendix D.

Suppose, for illustration, we computed $z$ to be 1.91. What is the area under the normal curve between the mean and $X$? Go down the left margin of the table in Appendix D headed by the letter $z$, to 1.9. Then move horizontally to the right and read the area (probability) under the column headed 0.01. It is .4719. This is the area under the normal curve between the mean and $X$.

What is the area under the curve between the mean and $X$ for the following $z$ values? Check your answers against those given.

| Computed $z$ value | Area under curve |
|:---:|:---:|
| 2.84 | .4977 |
| 1.00 | .3413 |
| 0.49 | .1879 |

Now we will compute the $z$ value given the population mean $\mu$, the population standard deviation $\sigma$, and a selected $X$.

### EXAMPLE

The weekly incomes of a large group of middle managers are normally distributed with a mean of $1,000 and a standard deviation of $100. What is the $z$ value for an income $X$ of $1,100? For $900?

### SOLUTION

Using formula (7–1), the $z$ values for the two $X$ values ($1,100 and $900) are computed as follows:

For $X = \$1,100$:

$$z = \frac{X - \mu}{\sigma}$$

$$= \frac{\$1,100 - \$1,000}{\$100}$$

$$= 1.00$$

For $X = \$900$:

$$z = \frac{X - \mu}{\sigma}$$

$$= \frac{\$900 - \$1,000}{\$100}$$

$$= -1.00$$

The z of 1.00 indicates that a weekly income of $1,100 for a middle manager is one standard deviation above the mean, and a z of −1.00 shows that a $900 income is one standard deviation below the mean. Note that both incomes ($1,100 and $900) are the same distance ($100) from the mean.

## AREAS UNDER THE NORMAL CURVE

Before examining various applications of the standard normal probability distribution, we will consider three areas under the normal curve that will be used extensively in the following chapters.

*Areas under the normal curve*

1. About 68 percent of the area under the normal curve is within plus one and minus one standard deviation of the mean. This can be written as $\mu \pm 1\sigma$.
2. About 95 percent of the area under the normal curve is within plus and minus two standard deviations of the mean, written $\mu \pm 2\sigma$.
3. Practically all (99.74 percent) of the area under the normal curve is within three standard deviations of the mean, written $\mu \pm 3\sigma$.

Shown diagramatically, using more precise percentages:

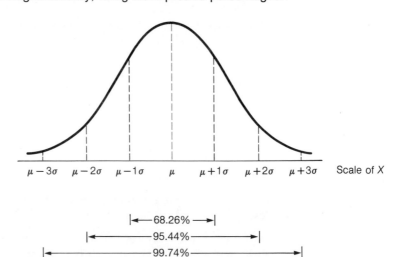

Transforming measurements to standard normal deviates changes the scale. The conversions are shown in the following graph. For example, $\mu + 1\sigma$ is converted to a z value of +1.00. Likewise, $\mu - 2\sigma$ is transformed to a z value of −2.00. Note that the center of the z distribution is zero, indicating no deviation from the mean, $\mu$.

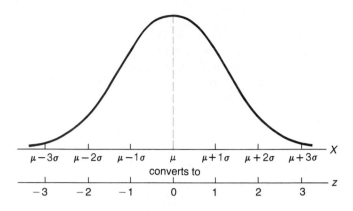

These concepts can be stated somewhat differently: The area under the normal curve within plus and minus one standard deviation of the mean is about .6826. The area within plus and minus two standard deviations of the mean is about .9544. The area within three standard deviations of the mean is about .9974. The total area under the normal curve is 1.0000.

*Total area under normal curve is 1*

### █ EXAMPLE

An accelerated life test on a large number of type D alkaline batteries revealed that the mean life for a particular use before failure is 19.0 hours. The distribution of the lives approximated a normal distribution. The standard deviation of the distribution was 1.2 hours.

1. About 68.26 percent of the batteries failed between what two values?
2. About 95.44 percent of the batteries failed between what two values?
3. About 99.74 percent of the batteries failed between what two values?

### ☑ SOLUTION

1. About 68.26 percent failed between 17.8 hours and 20.2 hours, found by 19.0 ± 1(1.2).
2. About 95.44 percent failed between 16.6 hours and 21.4 hours, found by 19.0 ± 2(1.2).
3. About 99.74 percent failed between 15.4 hours and 22.6 hours, found by 19.0 ± 3(1.2).

Shown in a diagram:

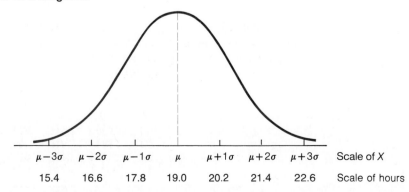

## Self-Review 7–2

*The answers are at the end of the chapter.*

The distribution of the annual incomes of a group of middle-management employees at Compton Plastics approximates a normal distribution with a mean of $37,200 and a standard deviation of $800.

1. About 68.26 percent of the incomes lie between what two amounts?

2. About 95.44 percent of the incomes lie between what two amounts?

3. About 99.74 percent of the incomes lie between what two amounts?

4. What are the median and the modal incomes?

5. Is the distribution of incomes symmetrical?

## EXERCISES

*The answers to the odd-numbered exercises are at the end of the book.*

1. Explain what is meant by this statement: "There is not just one normal probability distribution but a 'family' of them."

2. List the major characteristics of a normal probability distribution.

3. The mean of a normal probability distribution is 500; the standard deviation is 10.
   a. About 68 percent of the observations lie between what two values?
   b. About 95 percent of the observations lie between what two values?
   c. Practically all of the observations lie between what two values?

4. The mean of a normal probability distribution is 60; the standard deviation is 5.
   a. About what percent of the observations lie between 55 and 65?
   b. About what percent of the observations lie between 50 and 70?
   c. About what percent of the observations lie between 45 and 75?

## APPLICATIONS OF THE STANDARD NORMAL DISTRIBUTION

First application of the standard normal distribution

The first application of the standard normal distribution involves the determination of the area under the normal curve between the mean and a selected value, designated X. Using the same problem as in the previous weekly income example ($\mu$ = $1,000, $\sigma$ = $100), what is the area under the normal curve between $1,000 and $1,100?

What is area between $1,000 and $1,100?

We have already converted $1,100 to a z value of 1.00 using formula (7–1). To repeat:

$$z = \frac{X - \mu}{\sigma} = \frac{\$1,100 - \$1,000}{\$100} = 1.00$$

The probability associated with a z of 1.00 has been computed and is found in Appendix D. A small portion of that appendix table follows. To locate the area, go down the left column to 1.0. Then move horizontally to the right, and read the area under the curve in the column marked .00. It is .3413.

| z | .00 | .01 | .02 |
|-----|-------|-------|-------|
| 0.7 | .2580 | .2611 | .2642 |
| 0.8 | .2881 | .2910 | .2939 |
| 0.9 | .3159 | .3186 | .3212 |
| 1.0 | .3413 | .3438 | .3461 |
| 1.1 | .3643 | .3665 | .3686 |

Shown in a diagram:

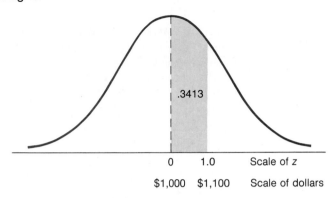

0        1.0         Scale of z

$1,000   $1,100    Scale of dollars

The area under the normal curve between $1,000 and $1,100 is .3413, and the total area under the curve is 1.0000. One can also say that 34.13 percent of the weekly incomes are between $1,000 and $1,100 and that the probability of a particular income being between $1,000 and $1,100 is .3413.

### ■ EXAMPLE

Refer to the previous problem ($\mu$ = $1,000, $\sigma$ = $100).

1. What is the probability that a particular weekly income selected at random is between $790 and $1,000?
2. What is the probability that the income is less than $790?

### ✓ SOLUTION

Computing the z value for $790 using formula (7−1):

$$z = \frac{X - \mu}{\sigma} = \frac{\$790 - \$1,000}{\$100} = \frac{-\$210}{\$100} = -2.10$$

1. The area under the normal curve between $\mu$ and $X$ for a z value of −2.10 is .4821 (from Appendix D). Since the normal curve is symmetrical, the minus sign in front of 2.10 indicates that the area is to the left of the mean.
2. The mean divides the normal curve into two identical halves. The area under the half to the left of the mean is .5000, and the area to the right of the mean is also .5000. Since the area under the curve between $790 and $1,000 is .4821, the area below $790 can be found by subtracting .4821 from .5000. Thus, .5000 − .4821 = .0179. Shown in a diagram:

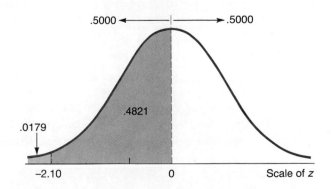

.5000 ◄————————|————————► .5000

.4821

.0179

−2.10                    0            Scale of z

### Self-Review 7–3

*The answers are at the end of the chapter.*

The employees of Cartwright Manufacturing are awarded efficiency ratings. The distribution of the ratings approximates a normal distribution. The mean is 400, the standard deviation 50.

1. What is the area under the normal curve between 400 and 482?

2. What is the area under the normal curve which is greater than 482?

3. Show the facets of this problem in a chart.

## EXERCISES

*The answers to the odd-numbered exercises are at the end of the book.*

5. A normal population has a mean of 20.0 and a standard deviation of 4.0.
   a. Compute the $z$ value associated with 25.0.
   b. What percent of the population is between 20.0 and 25.0?
   c. What percent of the population is less than 18.0?

6. A normal population has a mean of 12.2 and a standard deviation of 2.5
   a. Compute the $z$ value associated with 14.3.
   b. What percent of the population is between 12.2 and 14.3?
   c. What percent of the population is less than 10.0?

Courtesy Delta Air Lines, Inc.

7. A recent study of the hourly wages of maintenance crews for major airlines showed the mean hourly salary was $16.50, with a standard deviation of $3.50. If we select a crew member at random, what is the probability:
   a. The crew member earns between $16.50 and $20.00 per hour?
   b. The crew member earns more than $20.00 per hour?
   c. The crew member earns less than $15.00 per hour?

8.  The mean of a normal distribution is 400 pounds. The standard deviation is 10 pounds.
    a.  What is the area between 415 pounds and the mean of 400 pounds?
    b.  What is the area between the mean and 395 pounds?
    c.  What is the probability of selecting a value at random and discovering it has a value of less than 395 pounds?

A similar application of the standard normal distribution involves combining areas to the right and to the left of the mean.

### ■ EXAMPLE

Another application of standard normal distribution

Returning to the distribution of weekly incomes ($\mu$ = $1,000, $\sigma$ = $100), what is the area under the normal curve between $840 and $1,200?

### ☑ SOLUTION

The problem is divided into two parts. For the area between $840 and the mean of $1,000:

$$z = \frac{\$840 - \$1,000}{\$100} = \frac{-\$160}{\$100} = -1.60$$

For the area between the mean of $1,000 and $1,200:

$$z = \frac{\$1,200 - \$1,000}{\$100} = \frac{\$200}{\$100} = 2.00$$

The area under the curve for a $z$ of $-1.60$ is .4452 (from Appendix D). The area under the curve for a $z$ of 2.00 is .4772. Adding the two areas: .4452 + .4772 = .9224.

Thus, the probability of selecting an income between $840 and $1,200 is .9224. In other words, 92.24 percent of the managers have a weekly income between $840 and $1,200. Shown in a diagram:

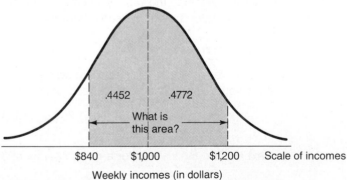

Weekly incomes (in dollars)

Another application of standard normal distribution

Another application of the standard normal distribution is finding the area above, or below, a specified value.

### ■ EXAMPLE

Returning again to the weekly incomes illustration ($\mu$ = $1,000, $\sigma$ = $100), what percent of the executives earn weekly incomes of $1,245 or more?

## ✓ SOLUTION

Find the area above
$1,245

We first need to find the area between the mean of $1,000 and an $X$ of $1,245. We will first use formula (7–1) to find $z$.

$$z = \frac{X - \mu}{\sigma} = \frac{\$1,245 - \$1,000}{\$100} = \frac{\$245}{\$100} = 2.45$$

Then, referring to Appendix D, the area associated with a $z$ of 2.45 is .4929. This is the area between $1,000 and $1,245. Logically, the area for $1,245 and beyond is found by subtracting .4929 from .5000. This area is .0071, indicating that only 0.71 percent of the executives earn weekly incomes of $1,245 or more.

The following diagram shows the various facets of this problem.

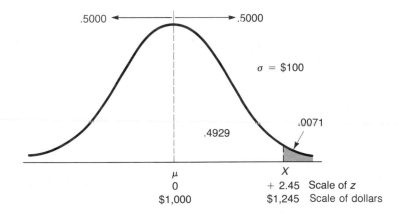

Still another application of the standard normal distribution involves determining the area between values on the *same* side of the mean.

## ▮ EXAMPLE

Returning again to the weekly incomes example ($\mu$ = $1,000 and $\sigma$ = $100), what is the area under the normal curve between $1,150 and $1,250?

## ✓ SOLUTION

The problem is again separated into two parts, and formula (7–1) is used. First we find the $z$ value associated with a weekly salary of $1,250:

$$z = \frac{\$1,250 - \$1,000}{\$100} = 2.50$$

Next we find the $z$ value for a weekly salary of $1,150:

$$z = \frac{\$1,150 - \$1,000}{\$100} = 1.50$$

From Appendix D the area associated with a $z$ value of 2.50 is .4938. So the probability of a weekly salary between $1,000 and $1,250 is .4938. Similarly, the area associated with a $z$ value of 1.50 is .4332, so the probability of a weekly salary between $1,000 and $1,150 is .4332. The probability of a weekly salary between $1,150 and $1,250 is found by subtracting the area associated with a $z$ value of 1.50 (.4332) from that associated with a $z$ of 2.50 (.4938). Thus, the probability of a weekly salary between $1,150 and $1,250 is .0606. Shown in a diagram:

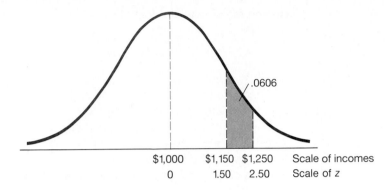

$1,000          $1,150  $1,250     Scale of incomes
   0             1.50    2.50      Scale of z

### Self-Review 7–4

*The answers are at the end of the chapter.*

Refer to the previous example ($\mu = \$1,000$, $\sigma = \$100$).

1. What percent of the executives earn a weekly income of $925 or less?

2. Portray the facets of this problem in a diagram.

Previous examples required finding the percent of the observations located between two observations or the percent of the observations above, or below, a particular observation X. A further application of the standard normal distribution involves finding the value of the observation X when the percent above or below the observation is given.

Another application

### ◼ EXAMPLE

Given a percent, find X

Suppose a tire manufacturer wants to set a mileage guarantee on its new MX100 tire. Life tests revealed that the mean mileage is 47,900, and the standard deviation of the normal distribution of mileages is 2,050 miles. The manufacturer wants to set the guaranteed mileage so that no more than 5 percent of the tires will have to be replaced. What guaranteed mileage should the manufacturer announce?

### ☑ SOLUTION

The facets of this problem are shown in the following diagram. X represents the guaranteed mileage.

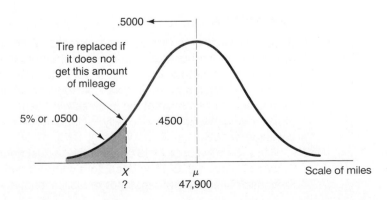

Inserting these values in formula (7–1) for z:

$$z = \frac{X - \mu}{\sigma} = \frac{X - 47,900}{2,050}$$

There are two unknowns, z and X. To find z, note that the area under the normal curve to the left of X is .0500. Logically, the area between $\mu$ and X is .4500, found by .5000 − .0500. Now refer to Appendix D. Search the body of the table for the area closest to .4500. There are two values equidistant from .4500, namely, .4505 and .4495. Move left from these values, and read the z values in the margin: 1.65 and 1.64. "Split the difference," and say the z score is 1.645. (It is really −1.645 because it is to the left of the mean.)

Knowing that the distance between $\mu$ and X is −1.645$\sigma$, we can now solve for X (the guaranteed mileage):

$$z = \frac{X - 47,900}{2,050}$$

$$-1.645 = \frac{X - 47,900}{2,050}$$

$$-1.645(2,050) = X - 47,900$$

$$X = 44,528 \text{ miles}$$

How is the value 44,528 interpreted? If the manufacturer advertises that its tires will last 44,528 miles, only 5 percent of the tires will fail to last that long.

---

### Self-Review 7–5

*The answers are at the end of the chapter.*

An analysis of the final test scores for a computer programming seminar revealed that they approximate a normal curve with a mean of 75 and a standard deviation of 8. The instructor wants to award the grade of A to the upper 10 percent of the test grades. What is the dividing point between an A and a B grade?

---

**Final application of standard normal distribution**

A final use of the standard normal distribution is to compare two or more observations that are on different scales or in different units. That is, the observations are in different distributions.

### ■ EXAMPLE

**Comparing observations on different scales**

Suppose a study of the inmates at a correctional institution is concerned with the social adjustment of the inmates in prison and their prospects for rehabilitation upon being released. Each inmate was given a test regarding social adjustment. The scores are normally distributed, with a mean of 100 and a standard deviation of 20. Prison psychologists rated each of the inmates with respect to the prospect for rehabilitation. These ratings were also normally distributed, with a mean of 500 and a standard deviation of 100.

Tora Carney scored 146 on the social adjustment test, and her rating with respect to rehabilitation is 335. How does Tora compare with the group with respect to social responsibility and the prospect for rehabilitation?

## ☑ SOLUTION

Converting her social responsibility test score of 146 to a $z$ value using (7–1):

$$z = \frac{X - \mu}{\sigma} = \frac{146 - 100}{20}$$

$$= \frac{46}{20} = 2.30$$

Converting her rehabilitation rating of 335 to a $z$ value:

$$z = \frac{X - \mu}{\sigma} = \frac{335 - 500}{100}$$

$$= \frac{-165}{100} = -1.65$$

The standardized test score and the standardized rating are shown below.

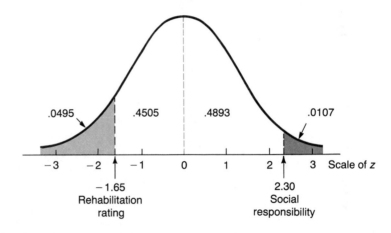

### INTERPRETATION

With respect to social responsibility. Tora Carney is in the highest 1 percent of the group. However, compared with the other inmates, she is among the lowest 5 percent with regard to the prospect for rehabilitation.

Self-Review 7–6 illustrates the use of the standard normal distribution for comparing data in different units—ratios and percent changes, in this case. The ratios are in one distribution and the percent changes in another.

### Self-Review 7–6

*The answers are at the end of the chapter.*

The price-earnings (PE) ratios and the changes in price over a three-year period for selected stocks were studied. For the PE ratios, $\mu = 10.0$ and $\sigma = 2.0$. For the price changes, $\mu = 50$ percent and $\sigma = 10$ percent. Both distributions are normally distributed. Radnor Industries had a PE of 11.2 and a 75 percent increase in price in the three-year period.

1. Convert Radnor's PE and percent change to $z$ values.

2. Show the two $z$ values on a standardized normal curve.

3. Compare Radnor's PE ratio and percent change with those of the other selected stocks.

# EXERCISES

*The answers to the odd-numbered exercises are at the end of the book.*

9. A normal population has a mean of 50.0 and a standard deviation of 4.0.
   a.   Compute the probability of a value between 44.0 and 55.0.
   b.   Compute the probability of a value greater than 55.0.
   c.   Compute the probability of a value between 52.0 and 55.0.
   d.   Determine the value of X below which 95 percent of the values will occur.

10. A normal population has a mean of 80.0 and a standard deviation of 14.0.
   a.   Compute the probability of a value between 75.0 and 90.0.
   b.   Compute the probability of a value of 75.0 or less.
   c.   Compute the probability of a value between 55.0 and 70.0.
   d.   Determine the value of X above which 80 percent of the values will occur.

11. A cola-dispensing machine is set to dispense 7.00 ounces of cola per cup. The standard deviation is 0.10 ounces. What is the probability that a machine will dispense:
   a.   Between 7.10 and 7.25 ounces of cola?
   b.   7.25 ounces of cola or more?
   c.   Between 6.8 and 7.25 ounces of cola?
   d.   How much cola is dispensed in the largest 1 percent of the drinks?

12. The amounts of money requested in home loan applications at Dawn River Federal Savings is approximately normally distributed with a mean of $70,000 and a standard deviation of $20,000. A loan application is received this morning. What is the probability that:
   a.   The amount requested is $80,000 or more?
   b.   The amount requested is between $65,000 and $80,000?
   c.   The amount requested is $65,000 or more?
   d.   Twenty percent of the loans are larger than what amount?

13. WNAE, an FM stereo station with a rock and roll format, finds that the mean length of time a person is tuned to the station is 15.0 minutes with a standard deviation of 3.5 minutes. What is the probability that a particular listener will tune in:
   a.   For 20 minutes or more?
   b.   For 20 minutes or less?
   c.   Between 10 and 12 minutes?
   d.   Seventy percent of the listeners are tuned in for how many minutes or less?

14. Landrum Airlines flies the route between Chicago and Pittsburgh. The mean number of passengers per flight is 160 with a standard deviation of 20. The aircraft used for the route has 200 seats.
   a.   What percent of the flights are sold out?
   b.   The airline must sell 150 seats to break even on this particular flight. On what percent of the flights does the airline make money?
   c.   The airline would like to reduce the number of flight attendants on 20% of the flights. This will be done on the flights with the fewest passengers. Below what number of passengers on a flight will the airline reduce the number of flight attendants?

# THE NORMAL APPROXIMATION TO THE BINOMIAL

Normal approximation to the binomial

Chapter 6 discussed the binomial probability distribution, which is a discrete distribution. The table of binomial probabilities in Appendix A goes successively from an *n* of 1 to an *n* of 25. Suppose a problem involved taking a sample of 60. Generating a binomial distribution for that large a number would be very time-consuming—even using a computer. A more efficient approach is to apply the *normal approximation to the binomial.*

Using the normal distribution (a continuous distribution) as a substitute for a binomial distribution (a discrete distribution) for large values of $n$ seems reasonable because as $n$ increases, a binomial distribution gets closer and closer to a normal distribution. The change in the shape of the binomial distribution from an $n$ of 1 to an $n$ of 20 is depicted in Chart 7–5.

---

### CHART 7–5

**Binomial Distributions for an $n$ of 1, 3, and 20, where $p = .50$**

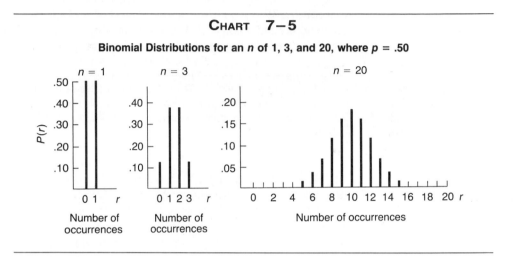

---

When to use the normal approximation

When can we use the normal approximation to the binomial? The *normal probability distribution is generally deemed a good approximation to the binomial probability distribution when np and n(1 − p) are both greater than 5.* However, before we apply the normal approximation, we must make sure that our distribution of interest is in fact a binomial distribution. Recall from Chapter 6 that to qualify, four criteria must be met:

1. There are only two mutually exclusive outcomes to an experiment: a "success" and a "failure."
2. A binomial distribution results from counting the number of successes.
3. Each trial is independent.
4. The probability $p$ must remain the same from trial to trial, and there must be a fixed number of trials, $n$.

## CONTINUITY CORRECTION FACTOR

To show the application of the normal approximation to the binomial and the need for a correction factor, suppose that the management of the Santoni Pizza Restaurant found that 70 percent of their new customers return for another meal. For a week in which 80 new (first-time) customers dined at Santoni's, what is the probability that 60 or more will return for another meal?

We could use the binomial formula (6–3)

$$P(r) = \frac{n!}{r!(n-r)!}(p)^r(q)^{n-r}$$

to calculate this probability. It would mean, however, computing the probabilities of 60, 61, 62, . . ., 80 and adding them to arrive at the probability of 60 or more. No doubt you will agree that using the normal approximation to the binomial is a much more efficient method of estimating the probability of 60 or more.

Since we are going to determine the binomial probability of 60 or more successes using the normal curve, we must subtract, in this case, .5 from 60. The value .5 is called the **continuity correction factor.** This small adjustment must be made because a continuous distribution (the normal distribution) is being used to approximate a discrete distribution (the binomial distribution). Subtracting, $60 - .5 = 59.5$.

Continuity correction factor

| **Continuity correction factor**   The value .5 subtracted or added, depending on the problem, to a selected value when a binomial probability distribution, which is a discrete probability distribution, is being approximated by a continuous probability distribution—the normal distribution. |
|---|

Notice that the binomial conditions are met: (1) There are only two possible outcomes—a customer either returns for another meal or does not return. (2) We can count the number of successes, meaning, for example, that 57 of the 80 customers return. (3) The trials are independent, meaning that if the 34th person returns for a second meal, that does not affect whether the 58th person returns. (4) The probability of a customer returning remains at .70 for all 80 customers.

The steps in determining the probability that 60 or more first-time Santoni customers out of 80 will return are:

**STEP 1**   Find the z value corresponding to an X of 59.5 using formula (7–1), and formulas (6–4) and (6–5) for the mean and variance of a binomial distribution:

$\mu = np = 80(.70) = 56.$
$\sigma^2 = np(1 - p) = 80(.70)(1 - .70) = 16.8.$
$\sigma = 4.0988$, found by $\sqrt{16.8}$.
$z = 0.85$, found by:

$$z = \frac{X - \mu}{\sigma} = \frac{59.5 - 56}{4.0988} = 0.85$$

**STEP 2**   Determine the area under the normal curve between $\mu$ (56) and X (59.5). From step 1 we know that the z value corresponding to 59.5 is 0.85. So we go to Appendix D and read down the left margin to 0.8, and then we go horizontally to the area under the column headed by .05. That area is .3023.

**STEP 3**   Calculate the area beyond 59.5 by subtracting .3023 from .5000 (.5000 − .3023 = .1977). Thus, .1977 is the probability that 60 or more first-time Santoni customers out of 80 will return for another meal.

The facets of this problem are shown graphically:

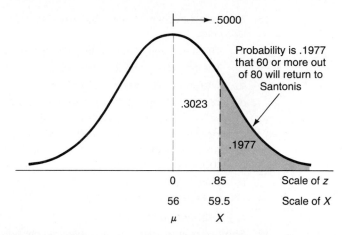

The MINITAB system can be used to check this binomial probability (.1977) by using the normal distribution. The MINITAB probability of .8034 in the following output is a cumulative probability and must be subtracted from 1.00.

```
MTB > cdf 59.5
SUBC> normal 56 4.0988.
     59.5000      0.8034
```

Using the computed MINITAB probability of .8034, we can determine the probability that 60 or more customers will return for another meal. It is .1966. (The slight discrepancy between .1977 and .1966 is due to rounding.)

$$P(z > 0.85) = 1 - P(z < 0.85)$$
$$= 1 - .8034$$
$$= .1966$$

### Self-Review 7–7

*The answers are at the end of the chapter.*

A study by Great Southern Home Insurance revealed that none of the stolen goods were recovered by the homeowners in 80 percent of the reported thefts.

1. During a period in which 200 thefts occurred, what is the probability that no

stolen goods were recovered in 170 or more of the robberies?

2. During a period in which 200 thefts occurred, what is the probability that no stolen goods were recovered in 150 or more robberies?

## Exercises

*The answers to the odd-numbered exercises are at the end of the book.*

15. Suppose $X$ has a binomial probability distribution with $n = 50$ and $p = .25$. Compute the following:
    a.   The mean and standard deviation of the random variable.
    b.   The probability that $X$ is 15 or more.
    c.   The probability that $X$ is 10 or less.

16. Suppose $X$ has a binomial probability distribution with $n = 40$ and $p = .55$. Compute the following:
    a.  The mean and standard deviation of the random variable.
    b.  The probability that $X$ is 25 or greater.
    c.  The probability that $X$ is 15 or less.
    d.  The probability that $X$ is between 15 and 25 inclusive.

17. Theresa's Tax Service specializes in federal tax returns. A recent audit of her returns indicated that an error was made on 10 percent of the returns she prepared last year. Assuming this rate continues into this year and she prepares 60 returns, what is the probability that she makes:
    a.  More than nine errors?
    b.  At least nine errors?
    c.  Exactly nine errors?

18. Shorty's Muffler advertises that they can change a muffler in 30 minutes or less. However, the work standards department at corporate headquarters recently conducted a study and found that 20 percent of the mufflers were not installed in 30 minutes or less. The Maumee branch installed 50 mufflers last month. If the corporate report is correct:
    a.  How many of the installations at the Maumee branch would you expect to take more than 30 minutes?
    b.  What is the likelihood that fewer than eight installations took more than 30 minutes?
    c.  What is the likelihood that eight or fewer installations took more than 30 minutes?
    d.  What is the likelihood that exactly eight of the 50 installations took more than 30 minutes?

19. A study conducted by the nationally known Taurus Health Club revealed that 30 percent of its new members are significantly overweight. A membership drive in a metropolitan area resulted in 500 new members.
    a.  It has been suggested that the normal approximation to the binomial be used to determine the probability that of the 500 new members, 175 or more are significantly overweight. Does this problem qualify as a binomial problem? Explain.
    b.  What is the probability that 175 or more of the new members are overweight?
    c.  What is the probability that 140 or more new members are significantly overweight?

20. Research on new juvenile delinquents who were put on probation by Judge Conners revealed that 38 percent of them committed another crime.
    a.  What is the probability that of the last 100 new juvenile delinquents put on probation, 30 or more will commit another crime?
    b.  What is the probability that 40 or fewer of the delinquents will commit another crime?
    c.  What is the probability that between 30 and 40 of the delinquents will commit another crime?

## CHAPTER OUTLINE

I.  The normal distribution is a continuous probability distribution with the following major characteristics.
    A.  It is bell-shaped and the mean, median, and mode are equal.
    B.  It is symmetrical.
    C.  It is asymptotic, meaning the curve approaches but never touches the $X$-axis.
    D.  It is completely described by the mean and the standard deviation.
    E.  There is a family of normal distributions. Each time the mean or the standard deviation change, a new distribution is created.

II. The standard normal distribution is a particular normal distribution.
    A. It has a mean of 0.00 and a standard deviation of 1.00.
    B. Any normal distribution can be converted to the standard normal distribution by the following formula.

$$z = \frac{X - \mu}{\sigma}$$

(7–1)

    C. By standardizing a normal distribution we can report the distance from the mean in units of the standard deviation.
III. The normal distribution can be used to approximate a binomial distribution under certain conditions.
    A. $np$ and $n(1 - p)$ must both be greater than 5.
        1. $n$ is the number of observations.
        2. $p$ is the probability of a success.
    B. The four conditions for a binomial distribution are:
        1. There are only two possible outcomes.
        2. $p$ remains the same from trial to trial.
        3. The trials are independent.
        4. The distribution results from a count of the number of successes in a fixed number of trials.
    C. The mean and the variance of a binomial distribution are computed as follows:

$$\mu = np$$
$$\sigma^2 = np(1 - p)$$

    D. The continuity correction factor of .5 is used to extend the continuous value of $X$ one-half unit in either direction. This correction compensates for estimating a discrete distribution by a continuous distribution.

## EXERCISES

*The answers to the odd-numbered exercises are at the end of the book.*

21. Ball-Bearings, Inc. produces ball bearings automatically on a Kronar BBX machine. For one of the ball bearings, the arithmetic mean diameter is set at 20.00 mm (millimeters). The standard deviation of the production over a long period of time was computed to be 0.150 mm.
    a. What percent of the ball bearings will have diameters between 20.00 mm and 20.27 mm?
    b. What percent of the ball bearings will have diameters of 20.27 mm or more?
    c. What percent of the ball bearings will have diameters between 19.85 mm and 20.30 mm?
    d. What percent of the ball bearings will have diameters 19.91 mm or less?

22. Weston, a national manufacturer of unattached garages, discovered that the lengths of time it takes two construction workers to erect the Red Barn model are approximately normally distributed with a mean of 32 hours and a standard deviation of 2 hours.
    a. What percent of the garages take between 32 hours and 34 hours to erect?
    b. What percent of the garages take 28.7 hours or less to erect?
    c. What percent of the garages take between 29 hours and 34 hours to erect?
    d. Of the garages, 5 percent take how many hours or more to erect?

23. The net sales and the number of employees for aluminum fabricators with similar characteristics were organized into frequency distributions. Both were normally distributed. For the net sales, $\mu = \$180$ million and $\sigma = \$25$ million. For the number of

employees, $\mu = 1,500$ and $\sigma = 120$. Clarion Fabricators had sales of $170 million and 1,850 employees.

   a. Convert Clarion's sales and number of employees to z values.

   b. Locate the two z values on a standard normal distribution.

   c. Compare Clarion's sales and number of employees with those of the other fabricators. What percent of the fabricators have more sales than Clarion? More employees?

24. A mechanical aptitude test designed for entering college students has a mean of 1,000 and a standard deviation of 150. An IQ test designed for college students has a mean of 110 and a standard deviation of 10. Shawn Bucci scored 1,310 on the mechanical aptitude test and 122 on the IQ test. Evaluate his test scores relative to those of others who took the tests.

25. A study of Furniture Wholesales, Inc. regarding the payment of invoices revealed that, on the average, an invoice was paid 20 days after it was received. The standard deviation equaled 5 days.

   a. What percent of the invoices are paid within 15 days of receipt?

   b. What is the probability of selecting any invoice and finding it was paid between 18 and 26 days after it was received?

   c. The management of Furniture Wholesales wants to encourage their customers to pay their monthly invoices as soon as possible. Therefore, it was announced that a 2 percent reduction in price would be in effect for customers who pay within 7 working days of the receipt of the invoice. Assuming the payments are normally distributed, out of 200 customers during July, how many would normally be eligible for the reduction?

26. The mean score of a college entrance test is 500; the standard deviation is 75. The scores are normally distributed.

   a. What percent of the students scored 320 or below?

   b. Twenty percent of the students had a test score equal to or above what score?

   c. Ten percent of the students had a test score equal to or below what score?

27. The annual commissions per salesperson employed by Machine Products, which is a manufacturer of light machinery, averaged $40,000, with a standard deviation of $5,000. What percent of the salespeople earn between $32,000 and $42,000?

28. The weights of cans of Monarch pears are normally distributed with a mean of 1,000 grams and a standard deviation of 50 grams. Calculate the percentage of the cans that weigh:

   a. 860 grams or less.

   b. Between 1,055 and 1,100 grams.

29. Past experience with respect to the number of passengers on the *Queen Elizabeth II*, offering one-week cruises to the Caribbean, revealed that the mean number of passengers is 1,820 and the standard deviation of the normal distribution of the number of passengers is 120.

   a. What percent of the cruises will have between 1,820 and 1,970 passengers?

   b. What percent of the cruises will have 1,970 passengers or more?

   c. What percent of the Caribbean cruises will have 1,600 or fewer passengers?

30. Management at Gordon Electronics is considering adopting a bonus system to increase production. One suggestion is to pay a bonus on the highest 5 percent of production based on past experience. Past records indicate that, on the average, 4,000 units of a small assembly are produced during a week. The distribution of the weekly production is approximately normal with a standard deviation of 60 units. If the bonus is paid on the upper 5 percent of production, the bonus will be paid on how many units or more?

31. Past experience of Eltron Chemicals with administering a test to recent college graduates who had applied for a job revealed that the mean test score was 500 and the standard deviation was 50. The distribution of the test scores was normal.

   a. Based on this experience, management is considering placing a person whose score is in the upper 6 percent of the distribution directly into a responsible position. What is the lowest score a college graduate must earn to qualify for a responsible position?

   b. Also based on past performance, the personnel director plans to give no consideration to anyone who scores 400 or less on the test. About what percent of the applicants will receive no consideration?

   c. Because of the limited number of vacancies this year, applicants with scores between 400 and 485 will be put on a "hold" status. What *percent* of the applicants will be put on "hold" status? If a total of 1,000 applied for a job with the company, *how many* would be put in the "hold" classification?

32. The tensile strengths of a large number of wires were determined and then organized into a frequency distribution. The distribution approximated a normal distribution with a mean of 300 pounds and a standard deviation of 20 pounds.

   a. What percent of the wires tested between 296 pounds and 310 pounds?

   b. What percent tested 332 pounds or over?

   c. Eighty percent of the wires tested over what amount?

33. Fast Service Truck Lines uses the Ford Super 1310 exclusively. Management made a study of the maintenance costs using a sample. It revealed that the arithmetic mean number of kilometers traveled per truck during the year was 60,000. The distances traveled during the year were normally distributed. The standard deviation of the normally distributed distances in the sample of Ford 1310s was 2,000 kilometers.

   a. What percent of the Ford Super 1310s logged 65,200 kilometers or more?

   b. The truck line owns 3,500 Ford Super 1310s. Based on the sample findings, how many of them traveled 55,000 kilometers or less?

   c. How many of the Fords traveled 62,000 kilometers or less during the year?

34. The annual incomes of a large group of supervisors at Belco are normally distributed with a mean of $28,000 and a standard deviation of $1,200. The length of service of the same supervisors is also normally distributed with a mean of 20 years and a standard deviation of 5 years. John McMaster earns $30,400 annually and has 10 years of service.

   a. Compare his income with those of the other supervisors.

   b. Compare this length of service with those of the other supervisors.

35. An executive at Westinghouse drives from his home in the suburbs near Pittsburgh to his office in the center of the city. The driving times are normally distributed with a mean of 35 minutes and a standard deviation of 8 minutes.

   a. In what percent of the days will it take him 30 minutes or less to drive to work?

   b. In what percent of the days will it take 40 minutes or more to drive to work?

   c. Explain to the executive why the probability is nearly 0 that it will take him exactly 40 minutes to get to work.

   d. Since the executive didn't understand your answer to part c, how would you estimate the percent of days in which it takes 40 minutes to drive to work? (Hint: Within what range of values would the times be rounded to 40?)

   e. Some days there will be accidents or other delays, so the trip will take longer than usual. How long will the longest 10 percent of the trips take?

36. Wal-Mart, a large discount retailer, offers a "no hassle" returns policy. The mean number of customers returning items is 10.3 with a standard deviation of 2.25 customers per day.

   a. In what percent of the days are there 8 or fewer customers returning items?

b.  In what percent of the days are there between 12 and 14 customers returning items?

c.  Is there any chance of a day with no returns?

(Source: *USA Today,* June 2, 1988, p. B1.)

37. Steve Lindowski is the punter for the Perrysburg Yellow Jackets high school football team. Coach Pohlman reports that Steve averages 39.5 yards per punt. Steve's father maintains additional data on his son's punting. The distribution of yards per punt is approximately normal, and 20 percent of his punts are longer than 45 yards.

a.  What is the standard deviation of the distribution of the lengths of Steve's punts?

b.  The mighty Yellow Jackets are pinned back deep in their own territory. Steve must punt the ball from his 8-yard line. What is the probability he kicks it beyond the 50-yard line?

c.  How far did the longest 5 percent of his punts go?

d.  Several of Lindowski's punts were blocked and traveled less than 10 yards. What effect did these blocked punts have on the arithmetic mean, the standard deviation, and the shape of the distribution of yardage?

38. A recent study showed that 20 percent of all employees steal from their company each year. If a company employs 50 people, what is the probability that:

a.  Fewer than 5 employees steal?

b.  More than 5 employees steal?

c.  Exactly 5 employees steal?

d.  More than 5 but fewer than 15 employees steal?

(Source: "Truth Cops," *Toledo Blade,* June 2, 1991, p. F1.)

39. The American Dietetic Association reported that 64 percent of American men over the age of 18 consider nutrition a top priority in their lives. A sample of 60 men is selected. What is the likelihood that:

a.  32 or more consider diet important?

b.  44 or more consider diet important?

c.  More than 32 but fewer than 43 consider diet important?

d.  Exactly 44 consider diet important?

(Source: "Men Are Weighing in with Improved Diets", *USA Today,* June 5, 1991, p. D8.)

40. Two-liter plastic bottles used for bottling cola are shipped in lots of 100. Suppose the lots are 5 percent defective. Some bottles leak, some are too small, and so forth.

a.  What is the probability that a shipment of plastic bottles contains 8 or more defectives?

b.  What is the probability that between 8 and 10 bottles are defective?

c.  What is the probability that there are exactly 8 defectives?

d.  What is the probability of no defectives?

41. At Casper State College 20 percent of the students drop basic statistics the first time they enroll. There are 50 students enrolled in Dr. Corbell's statistics class this semester. Compute the following probabilities.

a.  What is the probability that at least 8 drop?

b.  What is the probability that exactly 8 drop?

c.  What is the probability that 8 or less drop?

42. Assume that 10 percent of those taking the statistics part of the examination to qualify as a certified public accountant fail. Sixty students are taking the exam this Saturday.

a.  What is the probability that exactly two students will fail?

b.  What is the probability at least two students will fail?

43. The Tri-State county traffic division reported that 40 percent of the high-speed chases

Courtesy George J. Meyer Manufacturing,
a Figgie International Company

involving automobiles result in a minor or major accident. During a month in which 50 high-speed chases occur, what is the probability that 25 or more will result in a minor or major accident?

44. Cruise ships of the Royal Viking line report that 80 percent of their rooms are occupied during September. For a cruise ship having 800 rooms, what is the probability that 665 or more are occupied in September?

45. The Immigration and Naturalization Service (INS) has set as a goal that the Federal Inspection Service clear each international flight within 45 minutes after its arrival in the United States. Let's interpret this to mean that 95 percent of the flights are cleared in 45 minutes, so 5 percent of the flights take longer to clear. Let's also assume that the distribution of times is normal.

    a.  If the standard deviation of the time to clear an international flight is 5 minutes, what is the mean time to clear a flight?

    b.  Suppose the standard deviation is 10 minutes, not the 5 minutes suggested in part a. What is the new mean?

    c.  If an executive has 30 minutes from the time her flight landed to catch her limousine, assuming the information in part b, what is the likelihood that she will be cleared by INS in time?

    (Source: "Inspection Process to Slow Travelers Entering the USA," *USA Today,* June 5, 1991, p. 9A.)

46. Refer to Exercise 59 in Chapter 6. In this problem an air force study indicated that the probability of a disaster such as the January 28, 1986, explosion of the space shuttle *Challenger* was 1 in 35. Use the normal approximation to the binomial to compute the probability of at least one disaster in 25 missions. How does this compare with your result in Chapter 6?

47. The registrar at Elmwood University studied the grade point averages (GPAs) of students over many years. He has discovered that the distribution is approximately normal with a mean of 2.80 and a standard deviation of 0.40.

    a.  What is the probability that a randomly selected student has a GPA of from 2.00 up to 3.00?

    b.  What percent of the students are on probation, that is, have a GPA less than 2.00?

    c.  The student population at EU is 10,000. How many students are on the dean's list, that is, have GPAs of 3.70 or higher?

    d.  To qualify for a Bell scholarship, a student must be in the top 10 percent of the student body. What GPA must a student have to qualify for a Bell scholarship?

48. Mr. Jon Molnar will graduate from Eastwood High School this year. He took the American College Test (ACT) for college admission and received a score of 30. The high school principal informed him that only 2 percent of the students taking the exam receive a higher score. The mean score for all students taking the exam is 18.3. Jon's friends Karrie and George also took the test but were not given any information by the principal other than their scores. Karrie scored 25 and George 18. Based on this information, what were Karrie's and George's percentile ranks? What assumption is necessary?

49. Canned hams processed at the Henline Ham Company are normally distributed with a mean of 9.20 pounds and a standard deviation of 0.25 pounds. The label weight is given as 9.00 pounds.

    a.  What proportion of the hams actually weigh less than the amount claimed on the label?

    b.  The owner, Glen Henline, is considering two proposals to reduce the proportion of hams below label weight. He can increase the mean weight to 9.25 and leave the standard deviation the same, or he can leave the mean weight at 9.20 and reduce the standard deviation from 0.25 pounds to 0.15. Which change would you recommend?

## COMPUTER DATA EXERCISES

50. Refer to data set 1, which reports information on homes sold in Florida during 1990.

   a.  The mean selling price (in $000) of the homes was computed earlier to be $166.67, with a standard deviation of $35.68. Use the normal distribution to estimate the percent of homes selling for more than $210. Compare this to the actual percent. Does the normal distribution yield a good approximation of the actual results?

   b.  The mean distance from a home to the center of the city is 14.893 miles with a standard deviation of 4.892 miles. Use the normal distribution to estimate the percentages of homes within 19, 20, and 21 miles from the center of the city. Compare each result to the actual percent. Does the normal distribution yield a good approximation of the actual results?

51. Refer to data set 2, which reports information on 200 corporations in the United States.

   a.  The mean market value, in millions, is $10,304 with a standard deviation of $11,018. Use the normal distribution to estimate the percent of companies with a market value less than $5,000. Compare this to the actual percent.

   b.  The mean profit for the year 1991 is 620.0 ($ millions) with a standard deviation of 802.4 ($ millions). Use the normal distribution to estimate the percent of companies that lost money. Compare that percent to the actual percent. Comment on the accuracy of the estimate.

52. Refer to data set 3, which reports information on the 20 major league baseball teams for the 1991 season.

   a.  The mean number of home runs hit by a major league team is 130.12 with a standard deviation of 32.01. Use the normal distribution to estimate the percent of teams that hit fewer than 110. Compare this to the actual number. Comment on the accuracy of the estimate.

   b.  The mean team salary is $24.24 million with a standard deviation of $6.51 million. Use the normal distribution to estimate the number of teams with a salary of over $30 million. Compare this estimate to the actual number. Comment on the accuracy of the estimate.

# CHAPTER 7  EXAMINATION

*The answers are at the end of the chapter.*

For Questions 1 to 10 indicate whether the statement is true or false. If it false, correct it.

 1.  The normal probability distribution is a continuous probability distribution.

 2.  There is only one normal distribution.

 3.  The normal distribution is positively skewed.

 4.  The curve representing a normal distribution has its tallest point at the mean.

 5.  The binomial distribution may be approximated by the normal distribution when $np$ and $n(1 - p)$ are both greater than 3.

 6.  The $z$ value for the area under the normal curve between 0 and 1.34 is .4099. Likewise, the $z$ value for the area between 0 and $-1.34$ is also .4099.

 7.  For a normal distribution where $\mu = 10$, $\sigma = 2$, and $X = 13$, the corresponding $z$ value for $X$ is 3.00.

 8.  Refer to Question 7. The probability of a value of 13 or greater is .0668.

 9.  For a binomial random variable $p = .70$ and $n = 50$. The mean and variance are 35 and 10.5, respectively.

10.  Refer to the data in Question 9. If $X = 38$, the likelihood of a value of 38 or less is .8599.

11. The seasonal output of a new experimental strain of pepper plants was carefully weighed. The mean weight per plant is 15.0 pounds, and the standard deviation is 1.75 pounds. The weights are approximately normally distributed.

    a. What proportion of the plants will weigh between 13 and 16 pounds?

    b. What proportion of the plants will weigh 13 or more pounds?

    c. The largest 5 percent of the plants are to be studied further to evaluate why they were so large. What is the cutoff point between those plants that will be studied and those that will not be studied?

12. A new dental study reported that 40 percent of children under 10 years of age now wear braces. In a group of 30 children what is the likelihood that:

    a. More than 15 wear braces?

    b. Fewer than 8 wear braces?

    c. Between 8 and 15 inclusive wear braces?

# ANSWERS

7–1   1.   2.25, found by:

$$z = \frac{\$1,225 - \$1,000}{\$100} = \frac{\$225}{\$100} = 2.25$$

2.   −2.25, found by:

$$z = \frac{\$775 - \$1,000}{\$100} = \frac{-\$225}{\$100} = -2.25$$

7–2   1.   $36,400 and $38,000, found by $37,200 ± 1($800).
2.   $35,600 and $38,800, found by $37,200 ± 2($800).
3.   $34,800 and $39,600, found by $37,200 ± 3($800).
4.   $37,200. Mean, median, and mode are equal for a normal distribution.
5.   Yes, a normal distribution is symmetrical.

7–3   1.   Computing z:

$$z = \frac{482 - 400}{50} = +1.64$$

Referring to Appendix D, the area is .4495
2.   .0505, found by .5000 − .4495.
3.

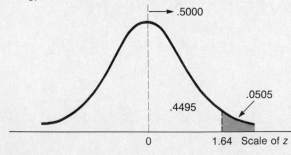

7–4   1.   About 22.66 percent, found by:

$$z = \frac{\$925 - \$1,000}{\$100} = -0.75$$

Area = .2734 from Appendix D. Then .5000 − .2734 = .2266.

2.

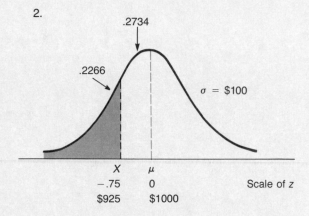

7–5   85.24 (instructor would no doubt make it 85). The closest area to .4000 is .3997; z is 1.28. Then:

$$1.28 = \frac{X - 75}{8}$$

$$10.24 = X - 75$$

$$X = 85.24$$

7–6   1.   $z = 0.60$ for PE ratio, found by:

$$z = \frac{11.2 - 10.0}{2.0} = 0.60$$

$z = 2.50$ for percent change, found by:

$$z = \frac{75 - 50}{10} = 2.50$$

2.

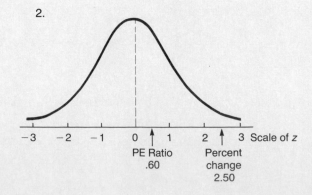

3. Compared with the other selected stocks, Radnor's PE Ratio is slightly above average; the percent increase is well above average.

7-7  1.  0.465, found by $\mu = np = 200(.80) = 160$, and $\sigma^2 = np(1 - p) = 200(.80)(1 - .80) = 32$. Then,

$$\sigma = \sqrt{32} = 5.66$$

$$z = \frac{169.5 - 160}{5.66} = 1.68$$

Area from Appendix D is .4535. Subtracting from .5000 gives .0465.

2. .9686, found by $.4686 + .5000$. First calculate $z$:

$$z = \frac{149.5 - 160}{5.66} = -1.86$$

Area from Appendix D is .4686.

## Answers

# CHAPTER 7 EXAMINATION

1. True.
2. False. There is a family of normal distributions. A new distribution is created each time the mean or standard deviation changes.
3. False. The normal distribution is symmetrical.
4. True.
5. False. $np$ and $n(1 - p)$ should be greater than 5.
6. True.
7. False. $z = (13 - 10)/2 = 1.50$.
8. True.
9. True.
10. True.
11. a. .5886, found by

$$z = \frac{13.0 - 15.0}{1.75} = -1.14$$

Area under the curve is .3729.

$$z = \frac{16.0 - 15.0}{1.75} = 0.57$$

Area under the curve is .2157.
Adding, $.3729 + .2157 = .5886$.

b. .8729, found by $.5000 + .3729$.

c. 17.88 pounds, found by

$$1.645 = \frac{X - 15.0}{1.75}$$

$$X = 15.0 + 1.645(1.75)$$

$$= 15.0 + 2.88 = 17.88$$

12.
$$\mu = np = 30(.40) = 12$$
$$\sigma^2 = np(1 - p) = 30(.40)(.60) = 7.2$$
$$\sigma = \sqrt{7.2} = 2.6833$$

a. .0968, found by

$$z = \frac{15.5 - 12.0}{2.6833} = 1.30$$

Area beyond 1.30 is $.5000 - .4032 = .0968$.

b. .0465, found by

$$z = \frac{7.5 - 12.0}{2.6833} = -1.68$$

Area less than $-1.68$ is $.5000 - .4535 = .0465$.

c. .8567, found by $.4032 + .4535$.

## Section Two

# A Review of Chapters 5−7

Thissection is a review of the major concepts, terms, symbols, and equations introduced in Chapters 5, 6, and 7. These three chapters are concerned with methods of dealing with uncertainty. As an example of the uncertainty in business, consider the role of the quality assurance department in most mass-production firms. Usually, the department has neither the personnel nor the time to check, say, all 200 plug-in modules produced during a two-hour period. Standard procedure may call for taking a sample of 5 modules and shipping all 200 modules out if those 5 operate correctly. However, if 1 or more in the sample are defective, all 200 are checked. Assuming that all 5 function correctly, quality assurance personnel cannot be absolutely certain that their action (allowing shipment of the modules) will prove to be correct. It could be that the 5 selected at random are the only ones out of the 200 that function properly! Probability theory lets us measure the uncertainty involved, in this case, of shipping out defective modules. Also, probability as a measurement of uncertainty comes into play when Gallup, Harris, and other pollsters predict that Jim Barstow will win the vacant senatorial seat in Georgia.

Chapter 5 noted that a *probability* is a number between 0 and 1 inclusive that measures one's belief that a particular event will occur. A weather forecaster might state that the probability of rain tomorrow is .20. The project director of a firm bidding on a subway system in Bangkok might assess the firm's chance of being awarded the contract at .50. We looked at the ways probabilities can be combined using rules of addition and multiplication, some principles of counting, and the importance of Bayes' theorem.

Chapter 6 presented three *discrete* probability distributions—the *binomial distribution,* the *hypergeometric distribution,* and the *Poisson distribution.* Other probability distributions will be discussed in forthcoming chapters (*t* distribution, chi-square distribution, etc.). Probability distributions are simply listings of all the possible outcomes of an experiment and the probability associated with each outcome. A probability distribution allows us to evaluate sample results.

As an example, suppose a consumer research firm, such as National Family Opinion, conducted a survey to find out whether or not grocery shoppers can identify the brand name of a product if the name does not appear on the can, box, or package. For question 1, NFO deleted the name of a soup and gave the shopper five choices: (1) Campbell's, (2) Knorr, (3) Progresso, (4) Chalet Suzanne, and (5) Heinz.

There were six similar questions, and 1,000 shoppers participated in the experiment. There is a possibility that shoppers unfamiliar with various labels and brand names would select a name at random—that is, guess the brand name. So a binomial probability distribution is generated to see what a random distribution of choices would look like. These probabilities are in column 2 of the following table; the numbers expected are in column 3. Note that we expect only 2 of the 1,000 shoppers to *guess* five of the six questions correctly. We expect practically no shoppers to guess six out of six. The actual responses are in column 4. A comparison of columns 3 and 4 indicate that a large percentage of the shoppers can identify the brand name of the product by looking at the label. NFO would conclude that it is highly unlikely for such a large number of shoppers to select so many correct brand names by chance.

| 1<br>Number of<br>correct<br>identifications | 2<br><br><br>Probability* | 3<br><br>Expected number<br>by chance | 4<br><br>Actual number<br>in survey |
|---|---|---|---|
| 0 | .262 | 262 | 5 |
| 1 | .393 | 393 | 16 |
| 2 | .246 | 246 | 10 |
| 3 | .082 | 82 | 27 |
| 4 | .015 | 15 | 81 |
| 5 | .002 | 2 | 346 |
| 6 | .000 | 0 | 515 |
|  | 1.000 | 1,000 | 1,000 |

*Probabilities from Appendix A.

MINITAB and other computer programs can generate a binomial distribution given *n* and *p*. Following is the MINITAB output for the preceding illustration.

```
MTB > pdf;
SUBC> binomial n=6, p=20.
    BINOMIAL WITH N = 6   P = 0 .200000
    K       P(X = K)
    0       0.2621
    1       0.3932
    2       0.2458
    3       0.0819
    4       0.0154
    5       0.0015
    6       0.0001
```

In Chapter 7 the very important continuous *normal probability distribution* was introduced. Some phenomena, such as the tensile strength of wires and the weights of the contents of cans and bottles, approximate a normal, bell-shaped distribution. Actually, there is a family of normal distributions—each with its own mean and standard deviation. There is a normal distribution, for example, for a mean of $100 and a standard deviation of $5, another for a mean of $149 and a standard deviation of $5.26, and so on. It was noted that a normal probability distribution is bell-shaped and symmetrical about its mean and that the tails of the normal curve extend in either direction infinitely. Since there are an unlimited number of normal distributions, it is difficult to compare two or more distributions directly. Instead, the distributions of interest can be *standardized*. The distribution of these standardized values is aptly called the *standard normal distribution*. The standard normal distribution has a mean of 0 and a standard deviation of 1. It is very useful, for example, for comparing distributions in different units. The distribution of the incomes of middle managers and the distribution of their efficiency ratings is an example of distributions in different units.

# GLOSSARY

## CHAPTER 5

**Bayes' theorem**   Developed by Reverend Bayes in the 1700s, a rule designed to find the probability of one event, *A*, occurring, given that another event, *B*, has occurred.

**Classical probability**   Probability based on the assumption that each of the outcomes is equally likely. On the toss of a coin, for example, a head or tail is equally likely. Using this concept of probability, if there are *n* possible outcomes, the probability of a particular outcome is $1/n$. Thus, on the toss of a coin, the probability of a head is $1/n = \frac{1}{2}$.

**Combination formula**   If the order *a, b, c* is considered the same as *b, a, c,* or *c, b, a,* and so on, the number of arrangements is found by:

$$_nC_r = \frac{n!}{r!(n - r)!}$$

**Conditional Probability**   The likelihood that an event will occur given that another event has already occurred.

**Event**   A collection of one or more outcomes of an experiment. For example, an event may be three defective valves in an incoming shipment of valves for a 351 cu. in. Ford V8 engine.

**Experiment**   An activity that is either observed or measured. An experiment may be counting the number of correct responses to a question, for example.

**General rule of addition**   Used to combine probabilities when the events are *not* mutually exclusive.

$$P(A \text{ or } B) = P(A) + P(B) - P(A \text{ and } B)$$

**General rule of multiplication**   Used when the events are not independent. Example: It is known that there are 3 defective radios in a box containing 10 radios. What is the probability of selecting 2 defective radios on the first two selections from the box?

$$P(A \text{ and } B) = P(A) \cdot P(B \mid A) = \frac{3}{10} \times \frac{2}{9} = \frac{6}{90} = .067$$

where $P(B \mid A)$ means the "probability of *B* occurring given that *A* has already occurred."

**Independent**   The occurrence of one event has no effect on the probability of the occurrence of any other event.

**Multiplication formula**   One of the formulas that can be used to count the number of possible outcomes of an experiment. It states that if there are *m* ways of doing one thing and *n* ways of doing another, there are $m \times n$ ways of doing both. Example: A sports shop offers two sports coats and three contrasting pants for $400. How many different outfits can there be? Answer: $m \times n = 2 \times 3 = 6$.

**Outcome**   A particular result of an experiment.

**Permutation formula**   A formula used to count the number of possible outcomes. If *a, b, c* is one arrangement, *b, a, c* another, *c, a, b* another, etc., the total number of arrangements is determined by

$$_nP_r = \frac{n!}{(n - r)!}$$

**Probability**   A number between 0 and 1 inclusive that gives the likelihood that a specific event will occur.

**Relative frequency**   A concept of probability based on past experience. For example, the Metropolitan Life Insurance Company reported that during the year, 100.2 of every 100,000 persons in Wyoming died of accidental death (motor vehicle accidents, falls, drowning, firearms, etc.). Based on this experience, Metropolitan can estimate the probability of accidental death for a particular person in Wyoming: $100.2/100,000 = .001002$.

**Special rule of addition**   For this rule to apply, the events must be mutually exclusive. For two events, the probability of $A$ or $B$ occurring is found by:

$$P(A \text{ or } B) = P(A) + P(B)$$

Example: The probability of a one-spot or a two-spot occurring on the toss of one die is

$$P(A \text{ or } B) = \frac{1}{6} + \frac{1}{6} = \frac{2}{6} = \frac{1}{3}$$

**Special rule of multiplication**   If two events are not related—that is, they are independent—this rule is applied to determine the probability of their joint occurrence.

$$P(A \text{ and } B) = P(A) \cdot P(B)$$

Example: The probability of two heads on two tosses of a coin is:

$$P(A \text{ and } B) = P(A) \cdot P(B) = \frac{1}{2} \times \frac{1}{2} = \frac{1}{4}$$

**Subjective probability**   The chance of an event happening based on whatever information is available—hunches, personal opinion, opinion of others, rumors, and so on.

## CHAPTER 6

**Binomial probability distribution**   A discrete random variable with the following characteristics:

1. Each outcome is mutually exclusive, meaning that it cannot be a "success" and a "failure" at the same time. Example: The answer to a multiple-choice question is either correct or wrong.
2. The distribution is the result of counting the number of successes. The counts may be, for example, the number of correct answers to a 10-question multiple-choice test. The counts listed would be 0, 1, 2, . . . , 10.
3. Each trial is independent, meaning that the answer to trial 1 (correct or wrong) in no way affects the answer to trial 2, for example.
4. The probability of a success stays the same from trial to trial. Example: For a multiple-choice quiz having four choices per question, the probability of guessing the answer to question 1 is .25, that of guessing the answer to question 2 is also .25, and so on.

**Continuous random variable**   A random variable that may assume an infinitely large number of values with certain limitations. Example: The height of the power forward on Indiana's basketball team may be 78.0 inches, 78.01 inches, 78.014 inches, and so on, depending on the accuracy of the measuring device being used.

**Discrete random variable**   A random variable that can assume only certain specific values. Example: A family can consist of 1, 2, 3, . . . persons, not $-14$ or $2\frac{1}{4}$ persons.

**Hypergeometric probability distribution**   A probability distribution based on a discrete random variable. Its major characteristics are:

1. There is a fixed number of trials.
2. The probability of success is not the same from trial to trial.

**Poisson distribution**   A distribution often used to approximate binomial probabilities when $n$ is large and $p$ is small. What is considered "large" or "small" is not precisely defined, but a general rule is that $n$ should be equal to or greater than 20 and $p$ equal to or less than .05.

**Probability distribution**   A distribution in the form of a table listing all the possible outcomes of an experiment and the probability associated with each outcome.

**Random variable**   A quantity obtained from an experiment that may, by chance, result in different values. For example, a count of the number of accidents (the experiment) on I-75 during a week might be 10, or 11, or 12, or some other number.

### Chapter 7

**Continuity correction factor**   Used to improve the accurcy of the approximation of a discrete distribution (binomial) by a continuous distribution (normal).

**Normal probability distribution**   A continuous distribution that is bell-shaped and symmetrical, with the mean dividing the distribution into two equal parts. Further, the normal curve extends infinitely in either direction; that is, it never touches the X-axis. By converting a normal distribution to a *standard normal distribution,* we can, for example, compare two or more distributions having significantly different means or that are in different units (such as incomes and years of service).

**z value**   The distance between a selected value and the population mean divided by the standard deviation.

## Exercises

*The answers to the odd-numbered exercises are at the end of the book.*

## Part 1 — Fill in the Blanks

1. Based on your assessment of the stock market, you state that chances are 50–50 that stock prices will start to go down within two months. This concept of probability based on your belief is called _____.

2. A study of absenteeism from the classroom is being conducted. In our study of probability, this particular activity is called _____.

3. Refer to Exercise 2. It was found that 126 students were absent from Monday morning classes. This number (126) is called _____.

4. To apply this rule of addition:

$$P(A \text{ or } B \text{ or } C) = P(A) + P(B) + P(C)$$

   the events must be _____.

5. Management claims that the probability of a defective relay is only .001. The rule to use for finding the probability of the relay *not* being defective is _____. The formula for that rule is _____. The probability of a particular relay not being defective is

   _____.

6. For a probability distribution, the sum of all possible outcomes must equal _____.

7. Is the binomial distribution discrete or continuous? _____

8. The characteristics of a binomial probability distribution are:  _____, _____,

   _____, _____.

9. The Poisson probability distribution is (discrete or continuous?) _____.

10. To construct a Poisson distribution, you need _____.

11. The characteristics of a normal probability distribution and its accompanying normal curve are: _____, _____, _____.

12. If we convert values of a normal distribution to a distribution that has a mean of 0 and a standard deviation of 1, this probability distribution is called _____.

# PART II—PROBLEMS

13. A self-study course on management principles was offered to all employees of TMC Electronics. At the end of the time period, the employees were tested, with the following results:

| Course grade | Number of employees |
|---|---|
| A | 20 |
| B | 35 |
| C | 90 |
| D | 40 |
| F | 10 |
| Withdrew | 5 |

What is the probability that an employee selected at random:

a. Earned an A?

b. Earned a C or better?

c. Did not fail or withdraw?

14. It is claimed that Aldradine, a new medicine for acne, is 80 percent effective—that is, of every 100 persons who apply it, 80 show significant improvement. It is applied to the affected areas of a group of 15 people.

a. What is the probability that all 15 will show significant improvement?

b. What is the probability that fewer than 9 of the 15 will show significant improvement?

c. What is the probability that 12 or more people will show significant improvement?

15. First National Bank thoroughly investigates its applicants for small home-improvement loans. Their default record is very impressive: the probability that a homeowner will default is only .005. The bank has approved 400 small home-improvement loans. Assuming the Poisson probability distribution applies to this problem:

a. What is the probability that no homeowners out of the 400 will default?

b. How many of the 400 will not default?

c. What is the probability that 3 or more homeowners will default on their small home-improvement loans?

16. A study of the attendance at the University of Toledo's basketball games revealed that the distribution of attendance is normally distributed with a mean of 10,000 and a standard deviation of 2,000.

a. What is the probability of a particular game having an attendance of 13,500 or more?

b. What percent of the games had an attendance between 8,000 and 11,500?

c. Ten percent of the games had an attendance of how many or less?

17. The following table shows a breakdown of the U.S. Congress by party affiliation and branch.

| | Party | |
|---|---|---|
| | Democrats | Republicans |
| House | 258 | 177 |
| Senate | 54 | 46 |

a. A member of Congress is selected at random. What is the probability of selecting a Republican member of Congress?

b. Given that the person selected is a member of the House of Representatives, what is the probability of selecting a Republican?

c. What is the probability of selecting a member of the House of Representatives or a Democrat?

18. The Internal Revenue Service has set aside 200 tax returns where the amount of charitable contributions seemed excessive. A sample of six returns is selected from the group. If two or more of this sampled group have "excessive" amounts deducted for charitable contributions, the entire group will be audited. What is the probability that the entire group will be audited, if the true proportion of "excessive' deductions is 20 percent? What if the true proportion is 30 percent?

19. The Daniel-James Insurance Company will insure an offshore Mobil Oil production platform for one year. The president of Daniel-James estimates the following losses for that platform (in $ millions) with the accompanying probabilities:

| Amount of loss ($ millions) | Probability of loss |
|---|---|
| 0 | .98 |
| 40 | .016 |
| 300 | .004 |

a. What is the expected amount Daniel-James will have to pay to Mobil in claims?

b. What is the likelihood that Daniel-James will actually lose less than the expected amount?

c. Given that Daniel-James suffers a loss, what is the likelihood that it is for $300 million?

d. Daniel-James has set the annual premium at $2.0 million. Does that seem like a fair premium? Will it cover their risk?

20. The distribution of the number of school-age children per family in the Whitehall Estates area of Boise, Idaho, is:

| Number of children | 0 | 1 | 2 | 3 | 4 |
|---|---|---|---|---|---|
| Percent of families | 40 | 30 | 15 | 10 | 5 |

a. Determine the mean and standard deviation of the number of school-age children per family in Whitehall Estates.

b. A new school is to be built in Whitehall Estates. An estimate of the number of school-age children is needed. There are 500 family units. How many children would you estimate?

c. Some additional information is needed about only the families having children. Convert the preceding distribution to one for families with children. What is the mean number of children among families that have children?

Law enforcement, Chicago police—photo by the Illinois Department of Commerce and Community Affairs

# SAMPLING METHODS AND SAMPLING DISTRIBUTIONS

When you have completed this chapter, you will be able to:

## GOALS

1. Explain why in many situations a sample is the only feasible way to learn something about a population.

2. Explain the various methods of selecting a sample.

3. Distinguish between probability sampling and nonprobability sampling.

4. Define and construct a sampling distribution of sample means.

5. Explain the central limit theorem and its importance in statistical inference.

6. Calculate confidence intervals for means and proportions.

7. Determine how large a sample should be for both means and proportions.

**C**hapters 1 through 4 emphasized the techniques used to describe data. To illustrate these techniques, we organized the monthly rentals of condominiums into a frequency distribution and computed various averages and measures of dispersion. Such measures as the mean and the standard deviation were computed to describe the central tendency of the data and the extent of its spread. These chapters were concerned with *describing something that has already occurred.*

We started to lay the foundation for the inference facet of statistics in Chapter 5 with the study of the basic concepts of probability. Three discrete distributions—hypergeometric, binomial, and Poisson—were discussed at length in Chapter 6. The normal probability distribution, which is a continuous distribution, was presented in Chapter 7. Probability distributions encompass all possible outcomes of an experiment and the probability associated with each outcome. Distributions are generated mainly to evaluate *something that might occur.*

We are going to look at another probability distribution in this chapter, called the *sampling distribution of the means.* Before we do, however, can you discover what these four cases have in common?

Courtesy USX Corporation

*Case 1:*   The quality-control department at USX has the job of assuring the quality of production. To check the tensile strength of drawn steel wire, five small pieces are selected every three hours, and the tensile strength of each piece is determined by stretching it until it breaks.

*Case 2:*   The marketing department of Lever Bros. has the responsibility of determining consumer opinion with respect to new products. To determine the sales potential of a new soap named Ahhh, 452 consumers were asked to try it for one week. At the end of one week, each consumer completed a questionnaire regarding Ahhh.

*Case 3:*   Harris Polls was hired to gather the opinion of registered voters regarding policies of the federal government. Two thousand registered voters were selected at random. Their opinions regarding our immigration policy, measures being taken to curb inflation, and other strategies were recorded.

*Case 4:*   In a study of the migratory pattern of seals, 50 seals were tagged by marine biologists in California, and their movements were charted for a period of three years.

The cases have these common characteristics: (1) It would be very expensive, if not impossible, to contact all the registered voters in the United States, all the seals, and all the consumers. Further, checking all the drawn wire produced at USX in a three-hour period for tensile strength would destroy it, and none would be available for sale! (2) Only a relatively small group was involved in each study. Only five pieces of wire were tested, only 50 seals tagged, and so on.

The cases illustrate one way to evaluate the quality of steel wire and the opinions of consumers about a product—namely, to take a *sample* from the *population* of interest. In Chapter 1 we noted that *a sample is a part of the population.* The populations in these cases are all the seals in the ocean, all the registered voters in the United States, all the adult consumers, and all the wire drawn in a three-hour period. Note that the population might be persons, objects, or other phenomena of interest. Making general conclusions about the entire group (the *population*) based on statistical information obtained from a small group (the *sample*) is called *statistical inference.* For example, finding that all five pieces of wire tested for tensile strength did not meet specifications, the quality-control inspector would conclude that production during the three-hour period was not satisfactory. If 403 of the 452 consumers in the sample *disliked* Ahhh, no doubt Lever Bros. would not manufacture and market Ahhh.

Making decisions based on incomplete information is not new. For centuries wine tasters, for example, have made predictions about the vintage based on a few sips. Many shoppers purchase a pizza at the grocery store after sampling a small wedge. (The inference is that if the small sample tastes good, the whole pizza will taste equally good.) In industry, a random sample of 50 ball bearings might result in an inference (generalization) that 5 percent of all ball bearings produced are defective. Similarly, an inventory of a few items in a department store might result in a prediction that if the present security measures remain unchanged, 8 percent of the stock will be stolen during the month. In medicine, a sample of blood might result in an inference that the patient is anemic.

This chapter will first explain why, in many cases, sampling may be the only logical way to find out something about a population. Then some of the basic methods of selecting a probability sample will be discussed. Then we will explain why sample statistics may differ from the corresponding population parameters. The central limit theorem, confidence intervals, and required sample size are also covered in this chapter.

## WHY SAMPLE THE POPULATION?

Why taking a sample from a population is often necessary

As noted previously, it is often not feasible to study the entire population. Some of the major reasons why sampling is necessary are:

1. **The destructive nature of certain tests.** If the wine tasters at the Sutter Home Winery in California drank all the wine to evaluate the vintage, they would consume the entire crop, and none would be available for sale. In the area of industrial production, steel plates, wires, and similar products must often have a certain minimum tensile strength. To ensure that the product meets the minimum standard, a relatively small sample is selected. Each piece is stretched until it breaks, and the breaking point (usually measured in pounds per square inch) is recorded. Obviously, if all the wire or all the plates were tested for tensile strength, none would be available for sale or use. For this same reason, only a sample of photographic film is selected to determine the quality of all the film produced. Only a few seeds are tested for germination by Burpee prior to the planting season.

2. **The physical impossibility of checking all items in the population.** The populations of fish, birds, snakes, mosquitoes, and the like are large and are constantly moving, being born, and dying. Instead of even attempting to count all the ducks in Canada or all the fish in Lake Erie, we make estimates using various techniques—such as counting all the ducks on a pond picked at random, making creel checks, or setting nets at predetermined places in the lake.

3. **The cost of studying all the items in a population is often prohibitive.** Public opinion polls and consumer testing organizations, such as Gallup Polls and Marketing Facts, located in Chicago, usually contact fewer than 2,000 families out of approximately 50 million families in the United States. One consumer panel-type organization charges about $40,000 to mail out samples and tabulate the responses in order to test a product (such as cereal, cat food, or perfume). The same product test using all 50 million families would cost about $1 billion.

4. **The adequacy of sample results.** Even if funds were available, it is doubtful whether the additional accuracy of a 100 percent sample—that is, studying the entire

population—is essential in most problems. For example, the federal government uses a sample of grocery stores scattered throughout the United States to determine the monthly index of food prices. The prices of bread, beans, milk, and other major food items are included in the index. It is unlikely that the inclusion of all grocery stores in the United States would significantly affect the index, since the prices of milk, bread, and other major foods usually do not vary by more than a few cents from one chain store to another.

5. **To contact the whole population would often be time-consuming.** A candidate for a national office may wish to determine her chances for election. A sample poll using the regular staff and field interviews of a professional polling firm would take only one or two days. By using the same staff and interviewers and working seven days a week, it would take nearly 200 years to contact all the voting population!

Even if a large staff of interviewers could be assembled, the cost of contacting all of the voters would probably not be worth the expense. If the candidate were extremely popular, the sample poll might indicate that she would most certainly receive between 79 percent and 81 percent of the popular vote. The additional expense and time needed to find out that she might receive exactly 80 percent of the popular vote does not seem justified.

## WHAT IS A PROBABILITY SAMPLE?

In general, there are two types of samples: a probability sample and a nonprobability sample. What is a probability sample?

> Probability sample   A sample selected in such a way that each item or person in the population being studied has a known (nonzero) likelihood of being included in the sample.

Nonprobability sample: Results may be biased

If probability sampling is done, each item in the population has a chance of being chosen. If **nonprobability methods** are used, not all items or people have a chance of being included in the sample. In such instances the results may be **biased,** meaning that the sample results may not be representative of the population. Panel sampling and convenience sampling are two nonprobability methods. For example, a panel may consist of 2,000 cat owners or mothers of new babies. The panel is formed to solicit opinions on a newly developed cat food or a disposable baby diaper. Selection of panel members is based on the judgment of the person conducting the research, and the sample results may therefore not be representative of the entire population of cat owners or new mothers (since not all cat owners or all new mothers have a chance of being chosen). The statistical procedures used in this text to evaluate sample results are based on probability sampling. Therefore, only the methods of probability sampling will be discussed in the following section.

## METHODS OF PROBABILITY SAMPLING

There is no one "best" method of selecting a probability sample from a population of interest. A method used to select a sample of invoices in a file drawer might not be the most appropriate method for choosing a national sample of voters. However, all probability sampling methods have a similar goal, namely, *to allow chance to determine the items or persons to be included in the sample.* The first method presented is **simple random sampling.**

# SIMPLE RANDOM SAMPLING

Simple random sample

> **Simple random sample**   A sample formulated in such a manner that each item or person in the population has the same chance of being included.

To illustrate simple random sampling and selection, suppose a population consists of 845 employees of Nitra Industries. A sample of 52 employees is to be selected from that population. One way of ensuring that every employee in the population has a chance of being chosen is to first write the name of each one on a small slip of paper and deposit all of the slips in a box. After they have been thoroughly mixed, the first selection is made. This process is repeated until the sample of size 52 is chosen.

Table of random numbers: Efficient way to select members of the sample

A more convenient method of selecting a random sample is to use the identification number of each employee and a *table of random numbers.* As the name implies these numbers have been generated by a random process (in this case, by a computer). For each digit of a number, the probability of 0, 1, 2, . . . , 9 is the same. Thus, the probability that employee number 011 will be selected is the same as for employee 722 or employee 382. Bias is therefore completely eliminated from the selection process.

A portion of a table of random numbers is shown in the following illustration. To use such a table to select a sample of employees, you must first choose a starting point in the table. Suppose the time is 3:04. You might look at the third column and then move down to the fourth set of numbers. The number is 03759. Since there are only 845 employees, 037 is the number of the first employee to be a member of the sample. To continue selecting employees, you could move in any direction. Suppose you decide to move right. The first three digits of the number to the right of 03759 are 447—the number of the employee selected to be the second member of the sample. The next three-digit number to the right is 961. You cannot use 961 because there are only 845 employees. You continue to the right and select employee 784, then 189, and so on. Another way of selecting the starting point is to close your eyes and point at a number in the table. A table of random numbers is included in Appendix E.

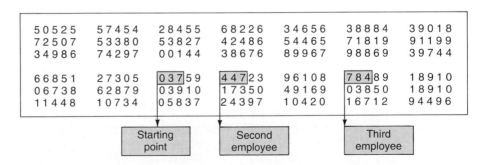

A study conducted by Marion Bryson and Robert Mason[1] further illustrates the use of a table of random numbers and simple random sampling.

Located in 18 warehouses on a U.S. Army ordnance depot were 186,810 different ordnance items such as tires, nuts, bolts, tank treads, and tire irons. In each warehouse

---

[1]Office of Ordnance Research, *Physical Inventory Accounting Program,* Technical Report Number 1.

there were bays, and in each bay there were bins. For example, in warehouse 17 motor vehicle parts were stored. Bay 260, bin 2, contained Jeep cranks. Bay 260, bin 3, had Jeep radiator caps.

The problem involved selecting a bin at random from a warehouse and counting all the items found in the bin. This physical count was compared with the count that computer inventory records indicated should be on hand. Thus, the problem was essentially a physical inventory problem involving sampling methods. The objective of the research project was to determine how accurate the computer records were.

To ensure that each bin had an equal chance of being selected, a table of random numbers was used to choose the warehouse, bay, and bin.

If warehouse 5, bay 455, and bin 6 were selected, a checker went to that location and counted the number of items in that bin.

**Using a table of random numbers to prevent bias**

Why was such a time-consuming method used to select the bins to sample? The alternative would have been to allow the checkers to count the items in any bins they wished. No doubt the checkers would have avoided counting the items in bins containing heavy or greasy parts. And they probably would have shunned the top bins, 20 feet from the floor of a warehouse. The omission of the items in these bins from this physical inventory research project might have biased the results—that is, their omission might have given a false picture of the accuracy of the computer records.

---

### Self-Review 8–1

*The answers are at the end of the chapter.*

Following is the class roster for an introductory course in business statistics. Three students are to be randomly selected and asked various questions regarding course content and method of instruction.

1. The numbers 00 through 45 are handwritten on slips of paper and placed in a bowl.

The three numbers selected were 31, 7, and 25. Which students would be included in the sample?

2. Now use the table of random digits, Appendix E, to select your own sample.

3. What would you do if you encountered the number 59 in the table of random digits?

---

```
          CSPM 264 01 BUSINESS & ECONOMIC STAT

          8:00 AM  9:40 AM MW      ST 118    LIND D
RANDOM
NUMBER       NAME                          CLASS RANK
  00         SPILLSON JOHN                     SO
  01         ANGER CHERYL RENEE               SO
  02         BALL CLAIRE JEANETTE             FR
  03         BERRY CHRISTOPHER G              FR
  04         BOBAK JAMES PATRICK              SO
  05         BRIGHT M STARR                   JR
  06         CHONTOS PAUL JOSEPH              SO
  07         DETLEV BRIAN HANS                JR
  08         DUDAS VIOLA                      SO
  09         DULBS RICHARD ZALFA              JR
  10         EDINGER SUSAN KEE                SR
  11         FINK FRANK JAMES                 SR
  12         FRANCIS JAMES P                  JR
  13         GAGHEN PAMELA LYNN               JR
  14         GOULD ROBYN KAY                  SO
```

```
RANDOM
NUMBER      NAME                              CLASS RANK
   15       GROSENBACHER SCOTT ALAN               SO
   16       HEETFIELD DIANE MARIE                 SO
   17       KABAT JAMES DAVID                     JR
   18       KEMP LISA ADRIANE                     FR
   19       KILLION MICHELLE A                    SO
   20       KOPERSKI MARY ELLEN                   SO
   21       KOPP BRIDGETTE ANN                    SO
   22       LEHMANN KRISTINA MARIE                JR
   23       MEDLEY CHERYL ANN                     SO
   24       MITCHELL GREG R                       FR
   25       MOLTER KRISTI MARIE                   SO
   26       MULCAHY STEPHEN ROBERT                SO
   27       NICHOLAS ROBERT CHARLES               JR
   28       NICKENS VIRGINIA                      SO
   29       PENNYWITT SEAN PATRICK                SO
   30       POTEAU KRIS E                         JR
   31       PRICE MARY LYNETTE                    SO
   32       RISTAS JAMES                          SR
   33       SAGER ANNE MARIE                      SO
   34       SMILLIE HEATHER MICHELLE              SO
   35       SNYDER LEISHA KAY                     SR
   36       STAHL MARIA TASHERY                   SO
   37       STJOHN AMY J                          SO
   38       STURDEVANT RICHARD R                  SO
   39       SWETYE LYNN MICHELE                   SO
   40       WALASINSKI MICHAEL                    SO
   41       WALKER DIANE ELAINE                   SO
   42       WARNOCK JENNIFER MARY                 SO
   43       WILLIAMS WENDY A                      SO
   44       YAP HOCK BAN                          SO
   45       YODER ARLAN JAY                       JR
```

## SYSTEMATIC RANDOM SAMPLING

**Systematic random sample: First sample member chosen at random**

The simple random sampling procedure may be awkward to use in certain research situations. For example, suppose that the population of interest consists of 2,000 invoices located in file drawers. Drawing a simple random sample would first require numbering the invoices from 0000 to 1999. Using a table of random numbers, a sample of, say, 100 numbers would then have to be selected. An invoice to match each of these 100 numbers would have to be located in the file drawers. This would be a very time-consuming task. Instead, a **systematic random sample** could be selected by simply going through the file drawers and selecting every 20th invoice for study. The first invoice would be chosen using a random process—a table of random numbers, for example. If the 10th invoice were chosen, the sample would consist of the 10th, 30th, 50th, 70th, . . . invoices.

**Members of sample chosen systematically**

---

Systematic random sample   The items or individuals of the population are arranged in some way—alphabetically, in a file drawer by date received, or some other method. A random starting point is selected, and then every *k*th member of the population is selected for the sample.

---

A systematic sample should not be used, however, if there is a predetermined pattern to the population. For example, in the physical inventory study mentioned previously, some of the warehouses in the ordnance depot have bays six bins high. In the bottom row of bins are fast-moving ordnance items, such as grease, touch-up spray paint, and hardware. These items are stored on the floor-level bins to speed the work of the pickers who must fill the requisitions. In the top row of bins are slow-moving items, such as tire rims, half-track treads, and firing pins. The middle four rows are stocked with moderately fast-moving items, such as tires, headlights, and cotter pins. If a systematic sample is used to check the inventory, then it is quite possible that a biased sample will be selected. Suppose the sampling procedure called for a selection of every third bin, and bin 1 is selected first. Then bins 1, 4, 7, 10, 13, 16, 19, and 22 would be selected systematically.

| 6 | 7 | 18 | 19 | }  ← Slow-moving items |
|---|---|----|----|---|
| 5 | 8 | 17 | 20 | |
| 4 | 9 | 16 | 21 | ← Moderately fast-moving items |
| 3 | 10 | 15 | 22 | |
| 2 | 11 | 14 | 23 | |
| 1 | 12 | 13 | 24 | }  ← Fast-moving items |

*A systematic sample may produce biased results*

The systematic procedure automatically selected 4 bins filled with moderately fast-moving items and a total of 4 bins filled with either fast-moving or slow-moving items. This 50-50 division of the sample does not coincide with the actual population characteristics. The population consists of 16 bins of moderately fast-moving items, 4 bins of fast-moving items, and 4 bins of slow-moving items. The sample results would undoubtedly be biased toward the slow- and fast-moving items.

## Self-Review 8–2

*The answers are at the end of the chapter.*

Refer to Self-Review 8–1. Suppose the sample is to consist of every ninth student enrolled in the class. Initially, the fourth student down on the list was selected at random. That student is numbered 03. Remembering that the random numbers start with 00, which students will be chosen to be members of the sample?

## Exercises

*The answers to the odd-numbered exercises are at the end of the book.*

1. The following is a list of Marco's Pizza stores in Lucas County. Also noted is whether the store is corporate-owned (C) or manager-owned (M). A sample of four locations is to be selected and inspected for customer convenience, safety, cleanliness, and other features.

    a. The random numbers selected are 08, 18, 11, 54, 02, 41, and 54. Which stores are selected?

    b. Use a table of random numbers to select your own sample of four locations.

| Random number | Marco's Pizza store | Ownership type | Random number | Marco's Pizza Store | Ownership type |
|---|---|---|---|---|---|
| 00 | 2607 Starr Av | C | 12 | 2040 Ottawa River Rd | C |
| 01 | 309 W Alexis Rd | C | 13 | 2116 N Reynolds Rd | C |
| 02 | 2652 W Central Av | C | 14 | 3678 Rugby Dr | C |
| 03 | 630 Dixie Hwy | M | 15 | 1419 South Av | C |
| 04 | 3510 Dorr St | C | 16 | 1234 W Sylvania Av | C |
| 05 | 5055 Glendale Av | C | 17 | 4624 Woodville Rd | M |
| 06 | 3382 Lagrange St | M | 18 | 5155 S Main | M |
| 07 | 2525 W Laskey Rd | C | 19 | 106 E Airport Hwy | C |
| 08 | 303 Louisiana Av | C | 20 | 6725 W Central & McCord | M |
| 09 | 149 Main St | C | 21 | 4252 Monroe | C |
| 10 | 835 S McCord Rd | M | 22 | 2036 Woodville Rd | C |
| 11 | 3501 Monroe St | M | 23 | 1316 Michigan Av | M |

2. The following is a list of the Wendy's Old Fashioned Hamburgers store locations in the Cordon metropolitan area. Also noted is whether the location has a salad bar.

   a. A sample of five locations is to be randomly selected and inspected by the corporate quality-assurance department. The random numbers obtained were 09, 16, 00, 49, 54, 12, and 04. What locations are included in the sample?

   b. Use a table of random numbers to develop your own sample of five locations.

| Random number | Wendy's Old Fashioned Hamburgers store | Salad bar | Random number | Wendy's Old Fashioned Hamburgers store | Salad bar |
|---|---|---|---|---|---|
| 00 | 5555 Airport Hwy | S | 09 | 3124 Monroe St | S |
| 01 | 6525 Airport Hwy | S | 10 | 27393 Helen Dr | NS |
| 02 | 5166 Airport Hwy At Reynolds Rd | NS | 11 | 4277 Monroe St | S |
| 03 | E Alexis Rd & Telegraph Rd | S | 12 | 5804 Monroe | S |
| 04 | 2124 W Alexis Rd | S | 13 | 2866 Navarre Av | S |
| 05 | 5560 W. Central Av | S | 14 | 3435 Secor Rd | NS |
| 06 | 914 Conant St | NS | 15 | 1109 South Av | NS |
| 07 | 3454 Dorr St | S | 16 | 3465 Stickney Av | S |
| 08 | Front St & Main St | S | 17 | 1945 Woodville Rd | S |

3. Refer to Exercise 1, regarding the Marco's Pizza locations. A sample is to consist of every seventh location. The number 03 is selected as the starting point. Which locations will be contacted?

4. Refer to Exercise 2, regarding the Wendy's locations. A sample is to consist of every fifth location. A random starting point of 02 is selected. Which stores are included in the sample?

## STRATIFIED RANDOM SAMPLING

Another type of probability sampling is referred to as **stratified random sampling.**

> Stratified random sample   A population is first divided into subgroups, called strata, and a sample is selected from each stratum.

Stratified sample guarantees representation of each subgroup

After the population has been divided into strata, either a *proportional* or a *nonproportional* sample can be selected. As the name implies, a proportional sampling procedure requires that the number of items in each stratum be in the same proportion as found in the population. For instance, the problem might be to study the advertising expenditures of the 352 largest companies in the United States. Suppose that the objective of the study is to determine whether firms with high returns on equity (a measure of profitability) spent more or less of each sales dollar on advertising than firms with a low return or a deficit. Assume that the 352 firms were divided into five strata. (See Table 8–1.) If, say, 50 firms are to be selected for intensive study, then 1 firm with a level of profitability of 30 percent and more would be studied, 5 firms in the 20–30 percent stratum would be selected at random, and so on.

### TABLE  8–1

**Number Sampled for a Proportional Stratified Random Sample**

| Stratum | Profitability (return on equity) | Number of firms | Percent of total | Number sampled |
|---|---|---|---|---|
| 1 | 30 percent and over | 8 | 2 | 1* |
| 2 | 20 up to 30 percent | 35 | 10 | 5* |
| 3 | 10 up to 20 percent | 189 | 54 | 27 |
| 4 | 0 up to 10 percent | 115 | 33 | 16 |
| 5 | Deficit | 5 | 1 | 1 |
| Total | | 352 | 100 | 50 |

*2 percent of 50 = 1; 10 percent of 50 = 5; etc.

In a *nonproportional* stratified sample, the number of items studied in each stratum is disproportionate to the respective numbers in the population. We then weight the sample results according to the stratum's proportion of the total population. For example, if nonproportional sampling were used in the preceding case, we would weight the results of stratum 1 by 2/100, stratum 2 by 10/100, stratum 3 by 54/100, and so on. Regardless of whether a proportional or a nonproportional sampling procedure is used, every item or person in the population has a chance of being selected for the sample.

Stratified sampling has the advantage, in some cases, of more accurately reflecting the characteristics of the population than does simple random or systematic random sampling. Note in Table 8–1 that 2 percent of the firms have a return on equity of 30 percent or more (stratum 1), and 1 percent have a deficit (stratum 5). If a simple random sample of 50 were taken, we might not *by chance* select any firms in stratum 1 or 5. A stratified random sample, however, would ensure that at least one firm in stratum 1 and one firm in stratum 5 are represented in the sample.

## EXERCISES

*The answers to the odd-numbered exercises are at the end of the book.*

5. Refer to Exercise 1, regarding Marco's Pizza. Suppose a sample is to consist of three locations, of which two are corporate-owned and one is manager-owned. Select a sample accordingly.

6. Refer to Exercise 2, regarding Wendy's. A sample of four restaurants is to consist of three locations with salad bars (S) and one without a salad bar (NS). Select the sample accordingly.

## CLUSTER SAMPLING

Cluster sampling reduces
sampling cost

Another common type of sampling is **cluster sampling.** It is often employed to reduce the cost of sampling a population scattered over a large geographic area. Suppose you want to conduct a survey to determine the views of industrialists in the state with respect to state and federal environmental protection policies. Selecting a random sample of industrialists in the state and personally contacting each one would be time-consuming and very expensive. Instead, you could employ cluster sampling by subdividing the state into small units—either counties or regions. These are often called *primary units.* Suppose you divided the state into 12 primary units. Suppose you then selected at random four regions—2, 7, 4, and 12—and concentrated your efforts in these primary units. You could take a random sample of the industrialists in each of these regions and interview them. (Note that this is a combination of cluster sampling and simple random sampling.)

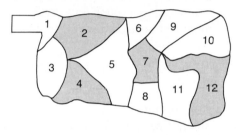

Many other sampling
methods

The discussion of sampling methods in the preceding sections did not include all the sampling methods available to a researcher, and the presentation was greatly oversimplified. Should you become involved in a major research project in marketing, finance, accounting, or other areas, you would need to consult books devoted solely to sample theory and sample design.

## SAMPLING ERROR

The previous discussion stressed the importance of selecting a sample so that every item or individual in the population has a known chance of being selected. To accomplish this, we could choose a simple random sample, a systematic sample, a stratified sample, a cluster sample, or a combination of these methods. Logically, it is unlikely that a sample mean would be *identical* to the population mean. Likewise, the sample standard deviation or other measure computed from a sample would probably not be *exactly* equal to the corresponding population value. We can therefore expect some difference between a *sample statistic,* such as the sample mean or sample standard deviation, and the corresponding *population parameter.* The difference between a sample statistic and a population parameter is called the **sampling error.** This error is simply due to chance.

Sampling error defined

> Sampling error   The difference between a sample statistic and its corresponding population parameter.

Suppose a population of five production employees had efficiency ratings of 97, 103, 96, 99, and 105. Further suppose that a sample of two ratings—97 and 105—was selected from that population to estimate the population mean rating. The mean of that sample would be 101, found by (97 + 105)/2. Another sample of two is selected: 103 and 96, with a sample mean of 99.5. The mean of all the ratings (the population mean) is 100, found by: (97 + 103 + 96 + 99 + 105)/5 = 500/5 = 100.0. The sampling error for the first sample is 1.0 determined by $\overline{X} - \mu = 101 - 100$. The second sample has a sampling error of $-0.5$. Each of these differences, 1.0 and $-0.5$, is the error that would be made in estimating the population mean based on a sample mean, and these sampling errors are due to chance.

Now that we have discovered the possibility of a sampling error when sample results are used to estimate a population parameter, how can the marketing research department make an accurate prediction about the possible success of a newly developed toothpaste or other product, based only on sample results? How can the quality-assurance department in a mass-production firm release a shipment of microchips based only on a sample of 10 chips? How can Gallup or Harris polls make an accurate prediction about a presidential race based on a sample of 2,000 registered voters out of a voting population of nearly 90 million? To answer these questions, we must first develop a *sampling distribution of the means.*

## SAMPLING DISTRIBUTION OF THE MEANS

*Sample means vary from sample to sample*

The efficiency rating example showed how the means for samples of a specified size vary from sample to sample. The mean efficiency rating of the first sample of two employees was 101, and the second sample mean was 99.5. A third sample would probably result in a different mean. The population mean was 100. If we organized the means of all possible samples of size 2 into a probability distribution, we would obtain the **sampling distribution of the means.**

*Sampling distribution defined*

> Sampling distribution of the means    A probability distribution consisting of a list of all possible sample means of a given sample size selected from a population, and the probability of occurrence associated with each sample mean.

The following example illustrates the construction of a sampling distribution of the means.

### ■ EXAMPLE

Tartus Industries has seven production employees (considered the population). The hourly earnings of each employee are given in Table 8–2.

---

#### TABLE  8–2

**Hourly Earnings of the Production Employees of Tartus Industries**

| Employee | Hourly earnings |
|----------|-----------------|
| Joe | $7 |
| Sam | 7 |
| Sue | 8 |
| Bob | 8 |
| Jan | 7 |
| Art | 8 |
| Ted | 9 |

---

Suppose that all possible samples of size 2 were selected from the population

1. What is the population mean?
2. What is the sampling distribution of the means for a sample of size 2?
3. What is the mean of the sampling distribution?
4. What observations can be made with respect to the population and the sampling distribution?

## ☑ SOLUTION

1. The population mean is $7.7143, found by:

$$\mu = \frac{\$7 + \$7 + \$8 + \$8 + \$7 + \$8 + \$9}{7}$$

2. In order to arrive at the sampling distribution of the means, all possible samples of size 2 were selected without replacement from the population, and their means were computed. (See Table 8–3.)[2] The 21 distinct sample means from all possible samples of size 2 that can be drawn from the population are shown in Table 8–4. This probability distribution is the sampling distribution of the means.

---

### TABLE 8–3

**Sample Means for All Possible Samples of Size 2**

| Sample | Employees | Hourly earnings | Sum | Mean |
|--------|-----------|-----------------|------|------|
| 1 | Joe, Sam | $7, $7 | $14 | $7.00 |
| 2 | Joe, Sue | 7, 8 | 15 | 7.50 |
| 3 | Joe, Bob | 7, 8 | 15 | 7.50 |
| 4 | Joe, Jan | 7, 7 | 14 | 7.00 |
| 5 | Joe, Art | 7, 8 | 15 | 7.50 |
| 6 | Joe, Ted | 7, 9 | 16 | 8.00 |
| 7 | Sam, Sue | 7, 8 | 15 | 7.50 |
| 8 | Sam, Bob | 7, 8 | 15 | 7.50 |
| 9 | Sam, Jan | 7, 7 | 14 | 7.00 |
| 10 | Sam, Art | 7, 8 | 15 | 7.50 |
| 11 | Sam, Ted | 7, 9 | 16 | 8.00 |
| 12 | Sue, Bob | 8, 8 | 16 | 8.00 |
| 13 | Sue, Jan | 8, 7 | 15 | 7.50 |
| 14 | Sue, Art | 8, 8 | 16 | 8.00 |
| 15 | Sue, Ted | 8, 9 | 17 | 8.50 |
| 16 | Bob, Jan | 8, 7 | 15 | 7.50 |
| 17 | Bob, Art | 8, 8 | 16 | 8.00 |
| 18 | Bob, Ted | 8, 9 | 17 | 8.50 |
| 19 | Jan, Art | 7, 8 | 15 | 7.50 |
| 20 | Jan, Ted | 7, 9 | 16 | 8.00 |
| 21 | Art, Ted | 8, 9 | 17 | 8.50 |

---

[2]Note that there are 21 possible samples (combinations), found by applying formula (5–11) for combinations, namely:

$$_nC_r = \frac{n!}{r!(n - r)!} = \frac{7!}{2!(7 - 2)!} = 21$$

## TABLE    8-4

### Sampling Distribution of the Means for $n = 2$

| Sample mean | Number of Means | Probability |
|---|---|---|
| $7.00 | 3 | .1429 |
| 7.50 | 9 | .4285 |
| 8.00 | 6 | .2857 |
| 8.50 | 3 | .1429 |
|  | 21 | 1.0000 |

3. The mean of the distribution of sample means is obtained by summing the various sample means and dividing the sum by the number of samples. The mean of all the sample means is usually written $\mu_{\bar{x}}$. The $\mu$ reminds us that it is a population value, because we have considered all possible samples. The subscript $\bar{x}$ indicates that it is a sampling distribution of means.

$$\mu_{\bar{x}} = \frac{\text{Sum of all sample means}}{\text{Total number of samples}} = \frac{\$7.00 + \$7.50 + \cdots + \$8.50}{21}$$

$$= \frac{\$162}{21} = \$7.7143$$

Refer to Chart 8-1. What observations can be made?

## CHART    8-1

### Population Values and Sample Means

Population mean is equal to the mean of the sample means

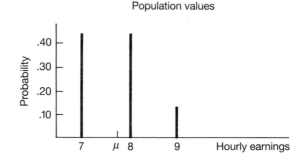

Population values

Sample means approximate a normal distribution

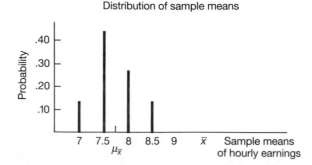

Distribution of sample means

4. These observations can be made:

   a. The mean of the sample means ($7.7143) is equal to the mean of the population: $\mu = \mu_{\bar{x}}$. This is always true if all possible samples of a given size are selected from the population of interest.

   b. Note from Chart 8-1 that the dispersion in the distribution of sample means is less than the dispersion in the population. The sample means vary from $7.00 to $8.50, whereas the population values vary from $7.00 to $9.00.

   c. The graph representing the distribution of the population and that of the sample means shows the change in shape from the population to the sample.

## Self-Review 8-3

*The answers are at the end of the chapter.*

The lengths of service of all the executives employed by Standard Chemicals are:

| Name | Years |
|------|-------|
| Mr. Snow | 20 |
| Ms. Tolson | 22 |
| Mr. Kraft | 26 |
| Ms. Irwin | 24 |
| Mr. Jones | 28 |

1. Using the combination formula, how many samples of size 2 are possible?
2. Select all possible samples of size 2 from the population, and compute their means.
3. Organize the means into a sampling distribution.
4. Compare the population mean and the mean of the sample means.
5. Compare the dispersion in the population with that of the distribution of sample means.

6. Following is a chart portraying the population values. Is the distribution of population values normally distributed (bell-shaped) or is it nonnormal?

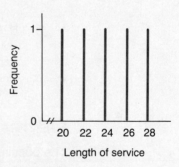

7. Is the distribution of sample means starting to show some tendency toward being bell-shaped?

## EXERCISES

*The answers to the odd-numbered exercises are at the end of the book.*

7. A population consists of the following four values: 12, 12, 14, 16.

   a. How many samples of size 2 are possible?
   b. List all possible samples of size 2, and compute the mean of each sample.
   c. Compute the mean of the sample means and the population mean. Compare the two values.
   d. Compare the dispersion in the population with that of the sample means.

8. A population consists of the following 5 values: 2, 2, 4, 4, 8.

   a. How many samples of size 2 are possible?
   b. List all possible samples of size 2, and compute the mean of each sample.

  c.  Compute the mean of the sample means and the population mean. Compare the two values.

  d.  Compare the dispersion in the population with that of the sample means.

9.  In your "Introduction to College Mathematics" class last semester, the instructor gave four tests. You received scores of 90, 86, 70, and 80. Suppose the instructor offered you the option of randomly selecting two scores and basing your course grade on the mean of those two tests.

  a.  How many different samples are possible?

  b.  List all the possible samples, and compute the mean of each.

  c.  Compare the mean of all the sample means with the mean of the population.

  d.  Compare the dispersion of the sample means with that of the population by drawing a graph.

  e.  Would you accept the instructor's grade offer? Explain.

10.  There are five sales representatives at Mid-Motors Ford. Below are listed the five representatives and the number of cars they sold last week.

| Sales representative | Cars sold |
|---|---|
| Pete Hankish | 8 |
| Connie Stallter | 6 |
| Ron Eaton | 4 |
| Jean Twenge | 10 |
| Andy Treese | 6 |

  a.  How many different samples of size 2 are possible?

  b.  List all possible samples of size 2, and compute the mean of each sample.

  c.  Compare the mean of the sample means with that of the population.

  d.  On a chart similar to Chart 8–1, compare the dispersion of the sample means with that of the population.

## CENTRAL LIMIT THEOREM

The population and the sample size in the preceding example and self-review were intentionally kept small in order to emphasize two concepts: first, that the mean of the sample means is exactly equal to the mean of the population, and second, that the shape of the distribution of sample means is not necessarily the same as that of the population.

• Refer to Chart 8–1. Notice the shape of the population compared to that of the sampling distribution of the means. The sampling distribution of the means more closely approximates the normal distribution.

*If the population is not normally distributed, the sampling distribution will be somewhat normal*

• Refer to Self-Review 8–3, where the lengths of service of executives at Standard Chemicals were reported. The sampling distribution of the means moves toward a normal distribution from a uniform distribution. See the comparison below.

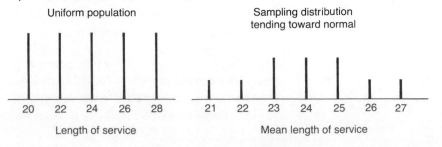

If population is normally distributed, so is the distribution of sample means

- If the population itself is normally distributed, the sampling distribution of the means is also normally distributed. The example below shows the hourly earnings of the six employees at Fulton Industries. The overtime hours are normally distributed. All possible samples of size 4 were selected from the population and the mean of each sample computed. Notice that the sampling distribution is also normal.

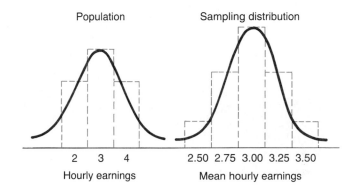

Why is this tendency toward the normal distribution so important? This is the basis of the **central limit theorem,** one of the most important theorems in statistics.

---

Central limit theorem   For a population with a mean $\mu$ and a variance $\sigma^2$, the sampling distribution of the means of all possible samples of size $n$ generated from the population will be approximately normally distributed—with the mean of the sampling distribution equal to $\mu$ and the variance equal to $\sigma^2/n$—assuming that the sample size is sufficiently large.

---

The important facets of the central limit theorem bear repeating.

1. If the sample size $n$ is sufficiently large, the sampling distribution of the means will be approximately normal. This is true whether or not the population is normally distributed. That is, whether the population is normally distributed, skewed, or uniform, the theorem will apply.

2. As shown earlier, the mean of the population, $\mu$, and the mean of all possible sample means, $\mu_{\bar{x}}$, are equal. If the population is large and a large number of samples are selected from that population, then the mean of the sample means will be close to the population mean.

3. The variance of the distribution of sample means is determined by $\sigma^2/n$.

There is no common agreement as to what constitutes a "sufficiently large" sample size. Some statisticians say 30; others go as low as 12. The example concerning the hourly earnings of all the employees at Tartus Industries worked quite well with a sample of 2. However, unless the population is approximately normal, such small sample sizes generally do not result in a sampling distribution that is normal. As the sample size becomes larger and larger, the distribution of the sample means becomes closer and closer to the bell-shaped normal distribution.

## COMPUTER SIMULATION 1

A computer simulation will be used to further demonstrate the central limit theorem. Chart 8–2 is an exponential probability distribution. This distribution is a continuous distribution, and, as you can see, it is positively skewed. The range of the data is from 1 to about 20, with the concentration of the data in the left-hand side of the curve. The mean of this distribution is 5.

---

### CHART 8–2

**Exponential Distribution with a Mean of 5**

```
MTB > set c1
DATA> 1:20
DATA> end
MTB > pdf c1 c2;
SUBC> exponential b=5.
MTB > name c1 'X-value' c2 'Prob'
MTB > plot c2 vs c1
           -
    0.180 +
           -  *
Prob       -
           -
           -    *
    0.120 +
           -      *
           -
           -       *
           -        *
    0.060 +          *
           -           *
           -            *   *
           -                *  *  *
           -                          *  *  *  *  *
    0.000 +                                           *  *  *
         -------+---------+---------+---------+---------+--------- X-value
             3.5       7.0      10.5      14.0      17.5
```

---

Using the MINITAB statistical software system, 50 random samples of size 10 were selected and the mean of each sample computed. The 50 sample means are summarized in a histogram, in Chart 8–3. The sample means range from about 2.683 up to 8.467 (as indicated in the data below the chart). The shape of the sampling distribution as shown in the histogram is approaching normal. The mean of the 50 samples of size 10 is 4.787, which is close to the population mean of 5.00.

---

### CHART 8–3

**Sampling Distribution of the Means for 50 Samples of Size 10**

```
MTB > random 50 c1-c10;
SUBC> exponential b=5.
MTB > rmean c1-c10 c11
MTB > name c11 'S-Mean'
MTB > hist c11

Histogram of S-Mean   N = 50

Midpoint   Count
     2.5       1    *
     3.0       3    ***
     3.5      10    **********
     4.0       3    ***
     4.5      10    **********
     5.0       7    *******
     5.5       4    ****
     6.0       4    ****
     6.5       5    *****
     7.0       1    *
     7.5       0
     8.0       1    *
     8.5       1    *

MTB > describe c11

              N     MEAN   MEDIAN   TRMEAN   STDEV   SEMEAN
S-Mean       50    4.787    4.608    4.709   1.291   0.183

            MIN      MAX       Q1       Q3
S-Mean    2.683    8.467    3.673    5.660
```

> Computer simulation:
> Exponential distribution
> with mean of 5, 50
> samples of size 10

---

Refer to the population in Chart 8–2. We will again take 50 random samples from that skewed population, but this time each sample will consist of 30 observations. The sample means are plotted in the form of a MINITAB histogram in Chart 8–4. Notice that the minimum and maximum values for the means of samples of size 30 are closer to the population mean than those for the samples of size 10 in Chart 8–3. Note too that the shape of the sampling distribution in Chart 8–4 is more nearly normal, and the mean of the sample means is 5.159. Most important is that as the sample size increases (from 10 to 30) in this computer simulation, the distribution of sample means becomes more and more normal despite the fact that the population is highly skewed.

## COMPUTER SIMULATION 2

The preceding simulation dealt with a skewed population. We pointed out that as the size of a sample taken from a skewed distribution becomes larger and larger, the sampling distribution of the means tends toward a normal distribution.

What about a normal population? Chart 8–5 depicts a normal distribution. This population has a mean of 50 and a standard deviation of 5. The population ranges from about 32 to 72.

## Chart 8—4

### Sampling Distribution of the Means for 50 Samples of Size 30

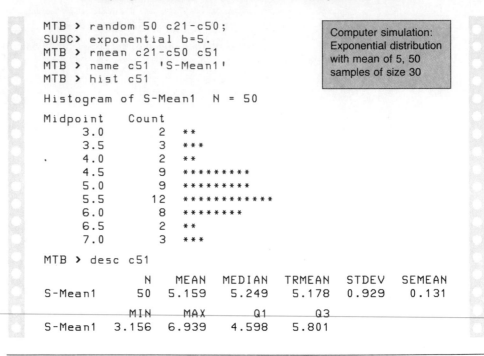

```
MTB > random 50 c21-c50;
SUBC> exponential b=5.
MTB > rmean c21-c50 c51
MTB > name c51 'S-Mean1'
MTB > hist c51

Histogram of S-Mean1   N = 50

Midpoint    Count
      3.0       2   **
      3.5       3   ***
      4.0       2   **
      4.5       9   *********
      5.0       9   ********
      5.5      12   ************
      6.0       8   ********
      6.5       2   **
      7.0       3   ***

MTB > desc c51

                N    MEAN   MEDIAN   TRMEAN   STDEV   SEMEAN
S-Mean1        50   5.159    5.249    5.178   0.929    0.131

              MIN     MAX       Q1       Q3
S-Mean1     3.156   6.939    4.598    5.801
```

Computer simulation: Exponential distribution with mean of 5, 50 samples of size 30

## Chart 8—5

### Normal Distribution with $\mu = 50$ and $\sigma = 5$

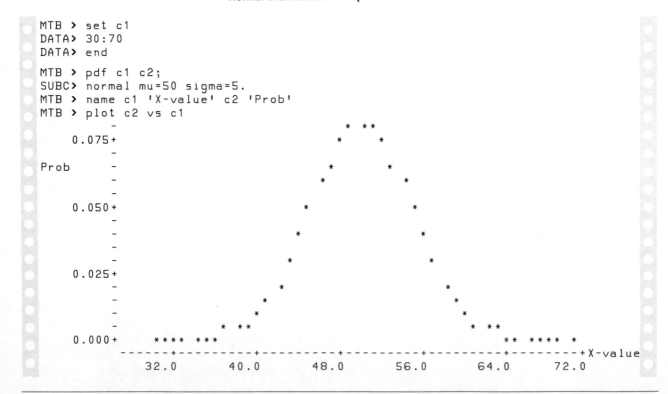

```
MTB > set c1
DATA> 30:70
DATA> end

MTB > pdf c1 c2;
SUBC> normal mu=50 sigma=5.
MTB > name c1 'X-value' c2 'Prob'
MTB > plot c2 vs c1
          -                              * **
    0.075+                            *       *
          -
Prob      -                        *       *
          -                      *           *
          -
    0.050+                   *              *
          -
          -               *                  *
          -
          -            *                       *
    0.025+
          -         *                            *
          -       *                                *
          -     *                                   *
          -   * **                               ** **
    0.000+  ****  ***                    ** **** *
          ------+--------+--------+--------+--------+--------+X-value
              32.0     40.0     48.0     56.0     64.0     72.0
```

Fifty random samples of size 10 are selected from this population and the mean of each of the 50 samples computed. The sampling distribution of the means ranges from about 45.628 to 51.416, and the sampling distribution, as shown in the histogram, appears normal. The mean of the sample means is 49.906, compared with the population value of 50. (See Chart 8–6.)

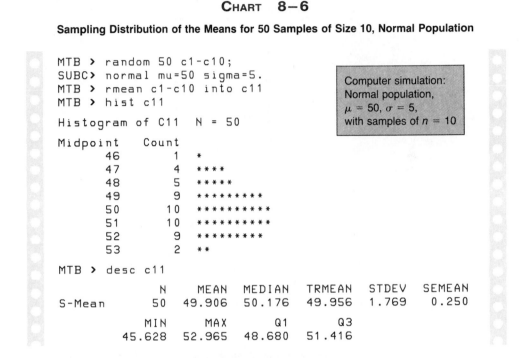

## CHART 8–6

**Sampling Distribution of the Means for 50 Samples of Size 10, Normal Population**

```
MTB > random 50 c1-c10;
SUBC> normal mu=50 sigma=5.
MTB > rmean c1-c10 into c11
MTB > hist c11

Histogram of C11  N = 50

Midpoint    Count
     46        1    *
     47        4    ****
     48        5    *****
     49        9    *********
     50       10    **********
     51       10    **********
     52        9    *********
     53        2    **

MTB > desc c11

                  N     MEAN    MEDIAN   TRMEAN   STDEV   SEMEAN
S-Mean           50   49.906   50.176   49.956   1.769   0.250

               MIN      MAX       Q1       Q3
            45.628   52.965   48.680   51.416
```

Computer simulation: Normal population, $\mu = 50$, $\sigma = 5$, with samples of $n = 10$

When the sample size for this normal population is increased from 10 to 50, the sampling distribution of the means is even more nearly normal, the range is smaller, and the mean of the sample means is 50.009—even closer to the population mean. (See Chart 8–7 on the next page.)

There are two very important observations evident from the computer simulations:

1. The shape of the sampling distribution of means approaches normal, regardless of the shape of the population.
2. The mean of the sample means is close to the mean of the population.

**Central limit theorem: Foundation for estimation and hypothesis testing**

The central limit theorem provides the theoretical foundation for statistical inference. Statistical inference is concerned with *estimation* (introduced in this chapter) and *hypothesis testing* (to be discussed starting with Chapter 9).

Managers in business, education, social work, and other fields make decisions without complete information. Automobile manufacturers do not know *exactly* how many people will purchase new cars next year. The college registrar does not know *exactly* how many students will enroll next fall. The sales manager for an automobile manufacturer, for example, must *estimate* the forthcoming sales of the new compact, the Firengia GT. She might estimate sales to be 325,000 units, but there is consid-

---

**CHART 8-7**

**Sampling Distribution of the Means for a Population, 50 Samples of Size 30**

```
MTB > random 50 c21-c50;
SUBC> normal mu=50 sigma=5.
MTB > rmean c21-c50 c51
MTB > hist c51

Histogram of C51   N = 50

Midpoint    Count
    48.5        1    *
    49.0        7    *******
    49.5       12    ************
    50.0        9    *********
    50.5       15    ***************
    51.0        4    ****
    51.5        1    *
    52.0        1    *

MTB > desc c51

                 N     MEAN    MEDIAN   TRMEAN   STDEV   SEMEAN
S-Mean          50   50.009    50.017   49.985   0.763    0.108

               MIN      MAX       Q1       Q3
            48.283   52.139   49.473   50.457
```

---

erable uncertainty about consumer reaction to the GT's new styling, the economic climate of the United States and foreign countries, and what competitors will introduce. Two kinds of estimates are *point estimates* and *interval estimates*.

# POINT ESTIMATES AND INTERVAL ESTIMATES

## POINT ESTIMATE

*Point estimate defined*

Fish and game wardens estimate the average weight and other characteristics of the fish or game population by using creel checks and other devices. Based on these sample data, a warden might estimate that the mean weight of Coho salmon caught in Lake Michigan is 2½ pounds. A sample of five financial "experts" might result in an estimate of 11.9 percent yield on certificates of deposit by the year's end. These single numbers (2½ pounds and 11.9 percent) are estimates of an unknown population parameter and are called **point estimates.**

---

> **Point estimate**   One number (called a *point*) that is used to estimate a population parameter.

---

*Sample mean used as an estimate of population mean*

The sample mean, $\overline{X}$, is the best estimator of the population mean, $\mu$. Recall that the sample mean is computed by formula (3–1):

$$\overline{X} = \frac{\Sigma X}{n}$$

where $X$ is the value of an observation and $n$ is the total number of observations.

## ■ EXAMPLE

A study of the cold cranking power of 12-volt Longlast automobile batteries is to be conducted to estimate the number of times a 440-cubic-inch displacement engine will start before the battery fails. A sample of 40 randomly selected batteries revealed these numbers of starts:

| | | | | | | | |
|---|---|---|---|---|---|---|---|
| 26 | 27 | 26 | 20 | 21 | 42 | 30 | 22 |
| 22 | 21 | 26 | 9 | 21 | 22 | 28 | 26 |
| 19 | 16 | 20 | 32 | 18 | 23 | 32 | 28 |
| 21 | 41 | 19 | 31 | 21 | 22 | 16 | 23 |
| 30 | 21 | 37 | 28 | 39 | 30 | 21 | 23 |

What is the best estimate of the population mean number of starts?

## ☑ SOLUTION

The sum of the 40 observations is 1,000. The mean number of starts before the battery fails is 25, found by

Best estimate of population mean is 25 starts

$\bar{p}$: The sample proportion—a statistic

$$\bar{X} = \frac{\Sigma X}{n} = \frac{1,000}{40} = 25 \text{ starts}$$

Likewise, the proportion of the population favoring more strict environmental protection measures can be estimated using a sample proportion. Letting $p$ be the unknown population proportion and $\bar{p}$ be the sample proportion, the point estimate for the population proportion is:

$$\bar{p} = \frac{\text{Number of successes in sample}}{\text{Number sampled}}$$

$$= \frac{X}{n}$$

where $X$ stands for the number of successes in the sample and $n$ the size of the sample.

## ■ EXAMPLE

Of 2,000 persons sampled, 1,600 favored more strict environmental protection measures. What is the estimated population proportion?

## ☑ SOLUTION

$$\bar{p} = \frac{\text{Number of successes in sample}}{\text{Number sampled}}$$

$$= \frac{1,600}{2,000} = .80$$

Eighty percent is an estimate of the proportion in the population that favor more strict measures.

In summary, based on the sampling distribution of the means and the central limit theorem, the sample mean can be used as a good estimator of the population mean. We assume, of course, that the size of the sample is sufficiently large. The same can be said for a population proportion (which is a special case of the sample mean), the population variance, the population standard deviation, and other population parameters. Each of these estimators is a point estimate.

## INTERVAL ESTIMATE

We now turn to the other type of estimate, the **interval estimate.**

---

Interval estimate   States the range within which a population parameter probably lies.

---

Mean is in this interval

The interval within which a population parameter is expected to lie is usually referred to as the *confidence interval.* For example, the confidence interval for the population mean is the interval that has a high probability of containing the population mean, $\mu$. Two confidence intervals are used extensively: the 95 percent confidence interval and the 99 percent confidence interval. Other confidence intervals may also be used, such as 80 percent, 90 percent, or even a value such as 87.6 percent.

How do we interpret a 95 percent confidence interval, for example? A 95 percent confidence interval means that about 95 percent of the similarly constructed intervals will contain the parameter being estimated. If we use the 99 percent level of confidence, then we expect about 99 percent of the intervals to contain the parameter being estimated. Notice two important features of this definition. First, not *every* interval constructed includes the parameter. Second, if we construct 100 intervals and use the 95 percent level, not *exactly* 95 of the intervals will include the parameter.

Another interpretation of the 95 percent confidence interval is that 95 percent of the sample means for a specified sample size will lie within 1.96 standard deviations of the hypothesized population mean. Similarly, for a 99 percent confidence interval, 99 percent of the sample means will lie within 2.58 standard deviations of the hypothesized population mean.

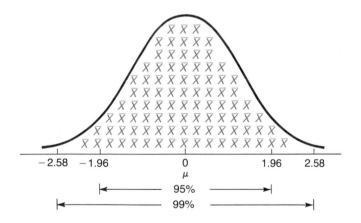

Where do the values 1.96 and 2.58 come from? The middle 95 percent of the sample means lie equally on either side of the mean and, logically, .95/2 = .4750, or 47.5 percent. Thus, the area to the right of the mean is .4750, and the area to the left of the mean is also .4750. Since these areas refer to the normal curve, we can use Appendix D to find the number of standard deviations (z values) from the mean of .4750. First, find .4750 in the body of Appendix D. Then move to the left margin and the appropriate column to find z. It is 1.96. The z to the right of the mean is designated as +1.96, and the z to the left is −1.96. Shown in a diagram:

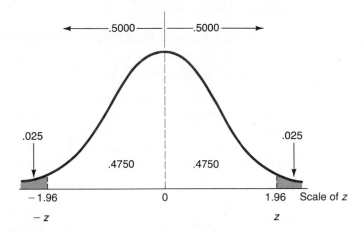

The same procedure is used to find the z of 2.58.

To expand on the confidence interval concept, suppose we had time to select 100 samples of size 256 from a population and we computed the sample means and confidence intervals for each sample. We would discover that about 95 of the 100 confidence intervals would contain the population mean, and about 5 of the intervals would not. Shown schematically:

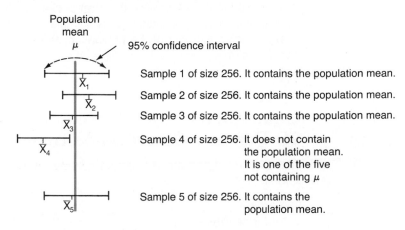

Of the intervals, 95 percent contain $\mu$

How is a confidence interval constructed? First we need to compute the *standard error of the mean.*

## STANDARD ERROR OF THE MEAN

Standard error of the mean defined

> **Standard error of the mean**   The standard deviation of the sampling distribution of the sample means.

Formula for standard error of mean

The standard error of the mean is computed by:

$$\sigma_{\bar{x}} = \frac{\sigma}{\sqrt{n}}$$

(8–1)

where:

$\sigma_{\bar{x}}$  is the symbol for the standard error of the mean.
$\sigma$  is the standard deviation of the population.
$n$  is the size of the sample.

Formula (8–1) for the standard error of the mean assumes that the population standard deviation, $\sigma$, is known. If it is not known and $n = 30$ or more (considered a large sample), the standard deviation of the sample, designated by $s$, is used to approximate the population standard deviation, $\sigma$. The formula for the standard error then becomes ($s_{\bar{x}}$ is substituted for $\sigma_{\bar{x}}$ to indicate that the standard error is based on sample statistics):

**Alternative formula for standard error of mean**

$$s_{\bar{x}} = \frac{s}{\sqrt{n}}$$                        (8–2)

Note that the standard error of the mean will vary according to the size of the sample (the denominator). As the sample size, $n$, gets larger and larger, the variability of the sample means gets smaller and smaller. Logically, an estimate of the population mean based on a large sample is more reliable than an estimate made using a small sample. To put it another way, the error in estimating the population mean decreases as the sample size increases. If the sample size kept getting larger and larger and finally equaled the size of the population, there would be no error in predicting the population mean because the sample size and the size of the population would be the same!

## CONSTRUCTING THE 95 PERCENT AND THE 99 PERCENT CONFIDENCE INTERVALS

The 95 percent and the 99 percent confidence intervals are constructed as follows when $n \geq 30$.

**95 percent confidence interval:**          $\bar{X} \pm 1.96 \dfrac{s}{\sqrt{n}}$                  (8–3)

**99 percent confidence interval:**          $\bar{X} \pm 2.58 \dfrac{s}{\sqrt{n}}$                  (8–4)

As discussed earlier, the values 1.96 and 2.58 refer to the $z$ values corresponding to the middle 95 percent or 99 percent of the observations.

Other levels of confidence can be used. For those cases, the $z$ value changes accordingly. For example, if we want to construct the 92 percent confidence interval, the formula becomes

$$\bar{X} \pm 1.75 \frac{s}{\sqrt{n}}$$

The value 1.75 comes from Appendix D. The table is based on half the normal distribution, so $.9200/2 = .4600$. The closest number in the body of the table is .4599, and the corresponding z value is 1.75. Try looking up the following z values, and check your answers against those on the right.

| Confidence interval | Closest number | z value |
|---------------------|----------------|---------|
| 90 percent | .4505 | 1.65 |
| 96 percent | .4798 | 2.05 |

## ◼ EXAMPLE

An experiment involves selecting a random sample of 256 middle managers for study. One item of interest is annual income. The sample mean is computed to be $35,420, and the sample standard deviation is $2,050.

1. What is the estimated mean income of all middle managers (the population)? That is, what is the point estimate?
2. What is the 95 percent confidence interval (rounded to the nearest $10)?
3. What are the 95 percent confidence limits?
4. What degree of confidence is being used?
5. Interpret the findings.

## ◪ SOLUTION

1. The sample mean is $35,420.
2. The confidence interval is between $35,170 and $35,670, found by:

$$\bar{X} \pm 1.96 \frac{s}{\sqrt{n}} = \$35,420 \pm 1.96 \frac{\$2,050}{\sqrt{256}}$$

Constructing the confidence interval

$$= \$35,420 \pm 1.96 \frac{\$2,050}{16}$$

$$= \$35,168.875 \text{ and } \$35,671.125$$

These endpoints are frequently rounded and, in this case, would be written as $35,170 and $35,670.

3. The endpoints of the confidence interval are called the *confidence limits.* In this example, $35,170 and $35,670 are the confidence limits.
4. The measure of confidence a person has is referred to as the *degree of confidence.* In this case it is .95.
5. Interpretation: If we had time to select 100 samples of size 256 from the population of middle managers and compute the sample means and confidence intervals, the population mean annual income would be found in about 95 out of the 100 confidence intervals. Either an interval contains the population mean or it does not. About 5 out of the 100 confidence intervals would *not* contain the population mean annual income, $\mu$.

## COMPUTER SIMULATION 3

The following computer simulation example reemphasizes the concept that the level of confidence represents the approximate percent of similarly constructed intervals that include the parameter being estimated.

# ■ EXAMPLE

Chart 8–5 presented a normal distribution with a population mean of 50 and a standard deviation of 5. We will select 30 random samples of size 50 from that population and develop the 95 percent confidence interval for each sample mean. We want to find out what proportion of those intervals include the population mean of 50. Interpret the result.

## ☑ SOLUTION

The first step is to generate the 30 random samples of size 50. This is accomplished in the same manner as the simulations for the skewed and the normal distributions presented in simulations 1 and 2. The MINITAB procedure used to develop the confidence interval is called ZINTERVAL. This procedure requires as input the level of confidence (95 percent in this case), the value of the population standard deviation (5 in this case), and the location of the samples. The 30 samples are stored in columns 21 through 50, and each sample is of size 50.

```
MTB > random 50 c21-c50;
SUBC> normal mu=50 sigma=5.
MTB > zinterval level of confidence 95 sigma=5 c21-c50

THE ASSUMED SIGMA =5.00

        N     MEAN    STDEV   SE MEAN    95.0 PERCENT C.I.
C21    50    50.153   5.542    0.707   ( 48.765, 51.541)
C22    50    48.922   4.984    0.707   ( 47.534, 50.310)
C23    50    49.711   4.822    0.707   ( 48.324, 51.099)
C24    50    49.737   4.373    0.707   ( 48.349, 51.125)
C25    50    49.286   5.084    0.707   ( 47.898, 50.673)
C26    50    50.695   5.341    0.707   ( 49.307, 52.083)
C27    50    50.357   6.021    0.707   ( 48.969, 51.745)
C28    50    48.429   4.516    0.707   ( 47.041, 49.817)*
C29    50    51.489   4.916    0.707   ( 50.101, 52.877)*
C30    50    50.658   5.394    0.707   ( 49.270, 52.046)
C31    50    50.188   5.119    0.707   ( 48.800, 51.576)
C32    50    50.853   4.460    0.707   ( 49.465, 52.241)
C33    50    50.231   4.149    0.707   ( 48.843, 51.618)
C34    50    49.925   5.016    0.707   ( 48.537, 51.313)
C35    50    51.271   4.508    0.707   ( 49.883, 52.659)
C36    50    51.629   4.363    0.707   ( 50.241, 53.017)*
C37    50    49.921   4.863    0.707   ( 48.534, 51.309)
C38    50    49.196   4.838    0.707   ( 47.808, 50.584)
C39    50    49.670   4.967    0.707   ( 48.282, 51.058)
C40    50    49.430   4.101    0.707   ( 48.042, 50.818)
C41    50    49.823   4.570    0.707   ( 48.435, 51.211)
C42    50    50.070   4.598    0.707   ( 48.682, 51.458)
C43    50    49.784   4.414    0.707   ( 48.396, 51.172)
C44    50    50.533   4.841    0.707   ( 49.145, 51.921)
C45    50    50.257   5.823    0.707   ( 48.869, 51.645)
C46    50    48.506   5.618    0.707   ( 47.118, 49.894)*
C47    50    49.586   4.354    0.707   ( 48.198, 50.973)
C48    50    50.359   5.178    0.707   ( 48.971, 51.747)
C49    50    49.427   4.220    0.707   ( 48.039, 50.815)
C50    50    50.179   4.060    0.707   ( 48.791, 51.566)
```

*Intervals that do not include the population mean of 50.

Out of a total of 30 confidence intervals produced, 4 or about 13 percent, do not include the population mean of 50. Another set of 30 intervals would have a different percentage of intervals that do not include the population mean.

For the 50 sample observations in column C21, the sample mean is 50.153, and the population standard deviation is 5.0. The interval 48.765 to 51.541 is determined as follows, using formula (8−3) (but using $\sigma$ instead of $s$). There is a difference of 0.002 between the calculated interval below and that of the MINITAB system. This difference is due to rounding.

$$\bar{X} \pm 1.96 \frac{\sigma}{\sqrt{n}} = 50.153 \pm 1.96 \frac{5}{\sqrt{50}}$$
$$= 50.153 \pm 1.386$$
$$= [48.767, 51.539]$$

## Self-Review 8−4

*The answers are at the end of the chapter.*

The wildlife department has been feeding a special food to rainbow trout fingerlings in a pond. A sample of the weights of 40 trout revealed that the mean weight is 402.7 grams and the standard deviation 8.8 grams.

1. What is the estimated mean weight of the population? What is that estimate called?

2. What is the 99 percent confidence interval?

3. What are the 99 percent confidence limits?

4. What degree of confidence is being used?

5. Interpret your findings.

## EXERCISES

*The answers to the odd-numbered exercises are at the end of the book.*

11. A sample of 49 observations is taken from a normal population. The sample mean is 55, and the standard deviation of the sample is 10. Determine the 99 percent confidence interval for the population mean.

12. A sample of 81 observations is taken from a normal population. The sample mean is 40, and the standard deviation of the sample is 5. Determine the 95 percent confidence interval for the population mean.

13. A sample of 10 observations is selected from a normal population for which the population standard deviation is known to be 5. The sample mean is 20.
    a. Determine the standard error of the mean.
    b. Explain why we can use formula (8−3) to determine the 95 percent confidence interval even though the sample is less than 30.
    c. Determine the 95 percent confidence interval for the population mean.

14. Suppose you wanted to use a 90 percent confidence level instead of the 95 percent and 99 percent intervals used in formulas (8−3) and (8−4). What value would you use to multiply the standard error of the mean?

15. Suppose a research firm conducted a survey to determine the average (mean) amount of money steady smokers spend on cigarettes during a week. A sample of 49 steady smokers revealed that $\bar{X} = \$20$ and $s = \$5$.
    a. What is the point estimate? Explain what it indicates.
    b. Using the .95 degree of confidence, determine the confidence interval for $\mu$.

16. Refer to Exercise 15. Suppose that 64 smokers (instead of 49) had been surveyed, and the sample mean and the sample standard deviation remained the same ($20 and $5, respectively).

    a.   What is the 95 percent confidence interval estimate of $\mu$?

    b.   Explain why this confidence interval is narrower than the one determined in Exercise 15.

17. Al Fishhaber is the owner of Al's Marathon gas station. Al would like to estimate the mean number of gallons of gasoline sold to his customers. From his records he selects a sample of 60 sales and finds that the mean number of gallons sold is 8.60 and the standard deviation is 2.30 gallons.

    a.   What is the estimate of the population mean?

    b.   Develop a 99 percent confidence interval for the population mean.

    c.   Interpret the meaning of part b.

18. An English professor counted the number of misspelled words on an essay he recently assigned. For his class of 40 students, the mean number of misspelled words was 6.05 and the standard deviation 2.44. Construct a 95 percent confidence interval for the mean number of misspelled words in the population of students.

## CONFIDENCE INTERVAL FOR A POPULATION PROPORTION

The theory and procedure for determining a point estimator and an interval estimator for a *population proportion* are quite similar to those described in the previous section. Therefore, the following discussion regarding point estimates and interval estimates will be rather brief.

As noted previously, a point estimate for the population proportion is found by dividing the number of successes in the sample by the total number sampled. Suppose 100 of 400 sampled said they liked a new cola they tested better than their regular cola. The best estimate of the population proportion favoring the new cola is .25, or 25 percent, found by 100/400. Note that a proportion is based on a *count* of the number of successes relative to the total number sampled.

Constructing confidence interval for a population proportion

How is the *confidence interval* for a population proportion estimated?

$$\bar{p} \pm z\sigma_{\bar{p}} \qquad (8\text{--}5)$$

where $\sigma_{\bar{p}}$ is the standard error of the proportion:

$$\sigma_{\bar{p}} = \sqrt{\frac{\bar{p}(1 - \bar{p})}{n}} \qquad (8\text{--}6)$$

Therefore, the confidence interval is constructed by:

$$\boxed{\bar{p} \pm z \sqrt{\frac{\bar{p}(1 - \bar{p})}{n}}} \qquad (8\text{--}7)$$

where:

$\bar{p}$   is the sample proportion.

$z$   is the z value for the degree of confidence selected.

$n$   is the sample size.

## EXAMPLE

Suppose 1,600 of 2,000 union members sampled said they plan to vote for the proposal to merge with the UMA. Using the .95 degree of confidence, what is the interval estimate for the population proportion? Based on the confidence interval, what conclusion can be drawn?

## SOLUTION

Using formula (8–7), the interval is computed as follows.

$$\bar{p} \pm z \sqrt{\frac{\bar{p}(1-\bar{p})}{n}} = .80 \pm 1.96 \sqrt{\frac{.80(1-.80)}{2,000}}$$

$$= .80 \pm 1.96 \sqrt{.00008}$$

Confidence limits: 78.2 and 81.8 percent

$$= .78247 \text{ and } .81753, \text{ rounded to } .782 \text{ and } .818.$$

Assume that at least 50 percent of the union members must approve of the merger. Based on the sample results, when all 2,000 union members vote, the proposal will probably pass because .50 does not lie in the interval between .782 and .818.

### Self-Review 8–5

*The answers are at the end of the chapter.*

A market survey was conducted to estimate the proportion of homemakers who could recognize the brand name of a cleanser based on the shape and color of the container. Of the 1,400 homemakers, 420 were able to identify the brand name.

1. Using the .99 degree of confidence, the population proportion lies within what interval?
2. What are the confidence limits?
3. Interpret your findings.

## EXERCISES

*The answers to the odd-numbered exercises are at the end of the book.*

19. In Exercise 17, the owner of Al's Marathon determined the mean number of gallons of gasoline purchased by his customers. He is also interested in the proportion of women who pump their own gasoline. He surveyed 100 women and found that 80 indicated they pump their own gasoline.
    a. What is the estimated proportion of women in the population that pump their own gasoline?
    b. Develop a 95 percent confidence interval for the proportion of women who pump their own gasoline. Interpret.

20. Ms. Maria Wilson is considering running for mayor of the town of Bear Gulch, Montana. Before completing the petitions, she decides to conduct a survey of voters in Bear Gulch. A sample of 400 voters revealed that 300 would support her in the November election.
    a. What proportion of the voters in Bear Gulch do you estimate would support Ms. Wilson?
    b. Develop a 99 percent confidence interval for the proportion of voters in the population that would support Ms. Wilson.
    c. In part b, note that both of the endpoints of the confidence interval are greater than .50. What importance would she attach to this?

21. Suppose that the NBC TV network is considering replacing one of its prime-time shows with a new family-oriented comedy. Before a final decision is made, a random sample of 400 prime-time viewers is conducted. After seeing a preview of the comedy, 250 indicated that they would watch it.

    a. What is your estimate of the proportion of viewers in the population who will watch the new show?

    b. Develop a 95 percent confidence interval for the proportion of viewers who will watch the new show.

22. A silkscreen printer purchases plastic cups on which to print logos for sporting events and other special occasions. The printer received a large shipment this morning and would like to estimate the percent defective. A sample of 200 revealed 30 of the cups to be defective.

    a. What proportion of the shipment is estimated to be defective?

    b. Develop a 95 percent confidence interval for the proportion of defective cups.

# FINITE-POPULATION CORRECTION FACTOR

The populations we have sampled so far have been very large, or assumed to be *infinite*. What happens if the sampled population is not infinite, or not even very large? In such instances we need to make some adjustments in the standard error of the mean and the standard error of the proportion.

*Infinite population*

*Finite population*

A population that has a fixed upper bound is said to be *finite*. For example, there are 21,376 students enrolled at Eastern Illinois University, and the Chrysler-Jeep Corp. manufactured 917 units at the Arkansas plant last year. A finite population can be rather small; it could be all the students registered for this class. It can also be very large, such as all senior citizens living in Florida. Note in the latter example that the number of senior citizens is large. We don't know exactly what the count is, but it is a number that in theory could be determined by a statewide census.

For a finite population, where the total number of objects is $N$ and the size of the sample is $n$, the following adjustment is made to the standard errors of the mean and the proportion:

Standard error of the mean:

$$\sigma_{\bar{x}} = \frac{\sigma}{\sqrt{n}} \sqrt{\frac{N-n}{N-1}} \qquad (8-8)$$

Standard error of the proportion:

$$\sigma_{\bar{p}} = \sqrt{\frac{\bar{p}(1-\bar{p})}{n}} \sqrt{\frac{N-n}{N-1}} \qquad (8-9)$$

*Finite-population correction factor*

This adjustment is called the **finite-population correction factor.** Why is it necessary to apply a factor, and what is its effect? Logically, if the sample is a substantial percentage of the population, then we would expect any estimates to be more precise than those for a smaller sample. Note the effect of the term $(N-n)/(N-1)$. Suppose the population is 1,000 and the sample is 100. Then this ratio is $(1,000 - 100)/(1,000 - 1)$, or 900/999. Taking the square root gives the correction factor, .9492. Multiplying by the standard error reduces the error by about 5 percent $(1 - .9492 \cong .05)$. This reduction in the size of the standard error yields a smaller range of values in estimating the population mean. If the sample is 200, the correction factor is .8949, meaning that the standard error has been reduced by more than 10 percent. Table 8−5 shows the effects of various sizes of samples on the correction factor. Note that when the sample is less than about 5 percent of the population, the impact of the correction factor is quite small. The usual rule is that if the ratio $n/N$ is less than .05, the finite-population correction factor is ignored.

## TABLE 8−5

**Computation of the Finite-Population Correction Factor for Various Sample Sizes When the Population Is 1,000**

| Sample size | Fraction of population | Correction factor |
|:---:|:---:|:---:|
| 10 | .010 | .9955 |
| 25 | .025 | .9879 |
| 50 | .050 | .9752 |
| 100 | .100 | .9492 |
| 200 | .200 | .8949 |
| 500 | .500 | .7075 |

## ◼ EXAMPLE

There are 250 families in the small town of Scandia. A poll of 40 families revealed that the mean annual church contribution is $450 with a standard deviation of $75. Construct a 95 percent confidence interval for the mean annual contribution.

## ☑ SOLUTION

First note that the population is finite. That is, there is a limit to the number of people in Scandia. Second, note that the sample constitutes more than 5 percent of the population; that is, $n/N = 40/250 = .16$. Hence, the finite-population correction factor is used. The 95 percent confidence interval is constructed as follows, using formulas (8−3) and (8−8).

$$\bar{X} \pm z \frac{s}{\sqrt{n}} \left( \sqrt{\frac{N-n}{N-1}} \right) = \$450 \pm 1.96 \frac{\$75}{\sqrt{40}} \left( \sqrt{\frac{250-40}{250-1}} \right)$$

$$= \$450 \pm \$23.24(\sqrt{.8433})$$

$$= \$450 \pm \$21.34$$

$$= [\$428.66, \$471.34]$$

### Self-Review 8−6

*The answers are at the end of the chapter.*

The same study of church contributions in Scandia revealed that 15 of the 40 families sampled attend church regularly. Construct the 95 percent confidence interval for the proportion of families attending church regularly. Should the finite-population correction factor be applied? Why or why not?

## EXERCISES

*The answers to the odd-numbered exercises are at the end of the book.*

23.  A population consists of 300 items. A sample of size 36 is selected, and the mean is 35 and the standard deviation 5. Develop a 95 percent confidence interval for the population mean.

24.  A population consists of 500 items. A sample of size 49 is selected. The mean is 40 and the standard deviation 9. Develop a 99 percent confidence interval for the population mean.

25.  The attendance at the Durham Bulls minor league baseball game last night was 400. A random sample of 50 of those in attendance revealed that the mean number of soft drinks consumed was 3.24 with a standard deviation of 0.50. Develop a 99 percent confidence interval for the number of soft drinks consumed.

Courtesy Durham Convention and Visitors Bureau

26.  There are 300 welders employed at the Maine Shipyards Corporation. A sample of 30 welders revealed that 18 graduated from a registered welding course. Construct the 95 percent confidence interval for the proportion of all welders who graduated from a registered welding course.

## SELECTING A SAMPLE SIZE

*Size of sample must be determined scientifically*

The sample sizes in the previous problems were always given. Now we are going to determine an appropriate sample size. Care must be taken not to select a sample too large or too small. For example, if we arbitrarily selected 400 items or individuals, and if that sample size were too large, time and money would be expended unnecessarily. If 400 were not large enough, the conclusions drawn about the population might be incorrect. Using an extreme example, suppose two persons were selected from the voting population and each asked his or her preference for president. If both persons selected for the sample were members of the Communist party, one might erroneously conclude that the next president of the United States would be a Communist.

*Misconceptions about how many to sample*

There are several misconceptions about the number to sample. One fallacy is that a sample consisting of 5 percent (or a similar constant percentage) is adequate for all problems. However, a sample of 3 from a population of 60 might be too small, and a sample of size 50,000 from a population of 1 million too large. Another misconception is that a larger sample of consumers or voters, for example, must be selected from a heavily populated state, such as California, than from a small state, such as New Hampshire.

There are three factors that determine the size of the sample, *none of which have any direct relationship to the size of the population.* They are:

1. **The degree of confidence selected.** This is usually .95 or .99, but it may be any level. You, the researcher, specify the degree of confidence.
2. **The maximum allowable error.** You must decide on this, too. It is the maximum error you will tolerate at a specified level of confidence.
3. **The variation of the population.** The variation of the population is measured by the standard deviation. (Of course, a population with little variation requires smaller samples.)

The role each of these factors plays in determining the sample size is now examined.

## DEGREE OF CONFIDENCE

Researcher must specify degree of confidence

Recall that the purpose of taking a sample is to estimate a population parameter. Suppose the parameter to be estimated is the arithmetic mean, and the degree of confidence selected is .90. Based on a sample, it was estimated that the population mean is in the interval between $89,050 and $91,050. Logically, if the degree of confidence were increased to .95 or .99, the sample size would have to be increased (assuming the interval remained the same). Carrying this to the extreme, if you wanted to be 100 percent sure that the true mean was in the interval between $89,050 and $91,050, you would have to survey the entire population—that is, take a 100 percent sample. Thus, one of the factors related to the sample size is the *degree of confidence.* The higher the degree of confidence, the larger the sample required to give a certain precision.

## MAXIMUM ERROR ALLOWED

Researcher must specify allowable error

Suppose that a developer is considering building a shopping mall near several subdivisions. One important statistic needed is the mean income in the area. A leisurely drive through the subdivisions indicated that the family incomes range from a probable low of $9,000 to a high of about $29,000. On the assumption that these are reasonable estimates, does it seem likely that the developer would be satisfied with this statement resulting from a sample of area residents: "The population mean is between $13,000 and $25,000"? Probably not! Confidence limits that wide indicate little or nothing about the population mean. Instead, the developer stated: "Using the .95 probability, the total error in predicting the population mean should not exceed $200." The developer is essentially saying this: "Based on a sample of size *n,* if the estimate of the population mean is computed to be $25,000, then you will assure me that the population mean is in the interval between $24,800 and $25,200—found by $25,000 + $200 and $25,000 − $200."

For the .95 degree of confidence selected by the developer, the maximum error of ±$200 in terms of $z$ is 1.96. To determine the value of *one* standard error of the mean, $\sigma_{\bar{x}}$, simply divide the total error of $200 by 1.96. It is $102.04.

$$\sigma_{\bar{x}} = \frac{\$200}{1.96}$$

$$= \$102.04$$

Shown schematically:

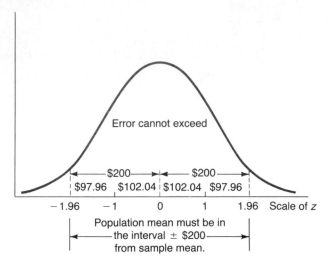

The size of the sample is computed by solving for *n* in the formula (note that since we are using a sample, $s_{\bar{x}}$ is substituted for $\sigma_{\bar{x}}$ and *s* for $\sigma$):

$$s_{\bar{x}} = \frac{s}{\sqrt{n}} \qquad (8-10)$$

where:

$s_{\bar{x}}$   is the standard error of the mean.
$s$   is the standard deviation of the sample.
$n$   is the sample size.

Thus far:

$$s_{\bar{x}} = \frac{s}{\sqrt{n}}$$

$$\frac{\text{Total allowable error}}{z \text{ standard deviations}} = \frac{\text{Sample standard deviation}}{\sqrt{\text{Sample size}}}$$

Letting *E* represent the total allowable error:

$$\frac{E}{z} = \frac{s}{\sqrt{n}}$$

$$\frac{\$200}{1.96} = \frac{s}{\sqrt{n}}$$

$$\$102.04 = \frac{s}{\sqrt{n}}$$

## VARIATION IN THE POPULATION

Pilot survey conducted to estimate variation in population

There are still two unknowns, *s* and *n*. To solve for the number to be sampled, we need to estimate the variation in the population. The standard deviation is a measure of variation. Thus, the standard deviation of the population must be estimated. This can be done either (1) by taking a small pilot survey (say, 50) and using the standard deviation of the pilot sample as an estimate of the population standard deviation or (2) by estimating the standard deviation based on knowledge of the population. Suppose a pilot survey is conducted and the sample standard deviation is computed to be $3,000. The number to be sampled can now be estimated:

$$s_{\bar{x}} = \frac{s}{\sqrt{n}}$$

$$\frac{E}{z} = \frac{s}{\sqrt{n}}$$

$$\frac{\$200}{1.96} = \frac{\$3,000}{\sqrt{n}}$$

$$\$102.04 \sqrt{n} = \$3,000$$

$$\sqrt{n} = \frac{\$3,000}{\$102.04}$$

$$n = 864.36$$

A more convenient computational formula for determining $n$ is:

$$\boxed{n = \left(\frac{z \cdot s}{E}\right)^2} \qquad (8\text{--}11)$$

where:

　　$E$　is the allowable error.
　　$z$　is the $z$ score associated with the degree of confidence selected.
　　$s$　is the sample deviation of the pilot survey.

For this problem:

$$n = \left(\frac{z \cdot s}{E}\right)^2$$

$$= \left(\frac{1.96 \times \$3,000}{\$200}\right)^2$$

$$= \left(\frac{\$5,880}{\$200}\right)^2$$

$$= 864.36$$

which is the same answer as before. We would round it up to 865.

The sample of size 865 may or may not give the developer what he wants—an estimate of the true mean within $200. The sample of 865 may be the correct sample size, or it may prove to be too small or too large. If it proves to be too large, the cost of surveying all 865 families was not warranted. If the sample of size 865 is too small, more families must be contacted if the error is to be reduced to within $200 (as originally specified by the developer).

Sample size seldom correct

Why isn't the sample size computed using the formula always the correct one? One reason is that it is highly unlikely for the standard deviation of the sample of 865 families to be exactly $3,000 (the same as for the pilot survey of about 50 families). If the standard deviation of the sample proved to be $2,500, the correct sample size should have been 600. This is found by solving for $n$ in the following: $\$200/1.96 = \$2,500/\sqrt{n}$, or $n = [(1.96 \times \$2,500)/\$200]^2$. Obviously, the sample of 865 was too large.

### Self-Review 8–7

*The answers are at the end of the chapter.*

Will you assist the college registrar in determining how many transcripts to study? The registrar wants to estimate the arithmetic mean final grade point average of all graduating seniors during the past 10 years. GPAs range between 2.0 and 4.0. The mean grade point average is to be estimated within plus and minus .05 of the population mean.

The .99 degree of confidence is to be used. Thus, the registrar wants to report something like this (hypothetical): "With a probability of .99, the mean grade point average of graduating seniors is in the interval between 2.45 and 2.55." The standard deviation of a small pilot survey is .279. How many transcripts should be sampled?

## EXERCISES

*The answers to the odd-numbered exercises are at the end of the book.*

27. A population is estimated to have a standard deviation of 10. We want to estimate the population mean within 2, with a 95 percent level of confidence. How large a sample is required?

28. We want to estimate the population mean within 5, with a 99 percent level of confidence. The population standard deviation is estimated to be 15. How large a sample is required?

29. A survey is being planned to determine the mean amount of time corporation executives watch television. A pilot survey indicated that the mean time per week is 12 hours, with a standard deviation of 3 hours. It is desired to estimate the mean viewing time within one-quarter hour. The .95 degree of confidence is to be used. How many executives should be surveyed?

30. A processor of carrots cuts the green top off each carrot, washes the carrots, and inserts six to a package. Twenty packages are inserted in a box for shipment. To test the weight of the boxes, a few were checked. The mean weight was 20.4 pounds, the standard deviation 0.5 pounds. How many boxes must the processor sample to be 95 percent confident that the sample mean does not differ from the population mean by more than 0.2 pounds?

## SAMPLE SIZE FOR PROPORTIONS

The procedure just used is applicable to determining the sample size when proportions are involved. Three things must be specified: (1) You, the researcher, must decide on the level of confidence—usually .95 or .99. (2) You must indicate how precise the estimate of the population proportion must be. (3) The population proportion, $\bar{p}$, must be either approximated from past experience (such as past elections) or approximated from a small pilot survey of, say, 50 or 100.

Proportions: Formula for sample size

The formula for determining the sample size in the case of a proportion is:

$$n = \bar{p}(1 - \bar{p})\left(\frac{z}{E}\right)^2$$

(8–12)

where:

$\bar{p}$   is the estimated proportion, based on past experience or a pilot survey.

$z$   is the $z$ value associated with the degree of confidence selected.

$E$   is the maximum allowable error the researcher will tolerate.

## ■ EXAMPLE

A member of Congress wants to determine her popularity in a certain part of the state. She indicates that the proportion of voters who will vote for her must be estimated within ±2 percent of the population proportion. Further, the .95 degree of confidence is to be used. In past elections she received 40 percent of the popular vote in that area of the state. She doubts whether it has changed much. How many registered voters should be sampled?

## ☑ SOLUTION

The sample size should be 2,305, found by using formula (8−12):

$$n = \bar{p}(1 - \bar{p}) \left[ \frac{z}{E} \right]^2$$
$$= .40(1 - .40) \left[ \frac{1.96}{.02} \right]^2$$
$$= .24[98]^2$$
$$= 2{,}304.96$$

Again, the sample size of 2,305 might be too large, too small, or exactly correct, depending on the accuracy of $\bar{p} = .40$.

*Note:* If there is no logical estimate of $\bar{p}$, the sample size can be estimated by letting $\bar{p} = .50$. (The size of the sample will never be larger than the one obtained for $n$ when $\bar{p} = .50$.)

### Self-Review 8−8

*The answers are at the end of the chapter.*

The following statements refer to the example regarding the popularity of the representative. For each statement, indicate whether it is true or false, and give supporting evidence. Suppose 2,305 registered voters were surveyed.

1. If 922 of the 2,305 registered voters surveyed said they plan to vote for the representative, the sample of size 2,305 was exactly correct.

2. If 461 of the 2,305 registered voters surveyed said they planned to vote for the representative, the sample size of 2,305 was too large.

## EXERCISES

*The answers to the odd-numbered exercises are at the end of the book.*

31. The estimate of the population proportion is to be within ±.05, with a 95 percent level of confidence. The best estimate of the population proportion is .15. How large a sample is required?

32. The estimate of the population proportion is to be within ±.10, with a 99 percent level of confidence. The best estimate of the population proportion is .45. How large a sample is required?

33. Suppose the president wants an estimate of the proportion of the population that support his current policy toward Honduras. The president wants the estimate to be within .04 of the true proportion. Assume a 95 percent level of confidence. The secretary of state estimated the proportion supporting current policy to be .60.

    a. How large a sample is required?
    b. How large would the sample have to be if the estimate by the secretary of state were not available?

34. Past surveys revealed that 30 percent of the tourists going to Las Vegas to gamble during a weekend spent more than $1,000. Management wants to update that percentage.

    a. Using the .90 degree of confidence, management wants to estimate the percentage of the tourists spending more than $1,000 within 1 percent. What sample size should be employed?
    b. Management said that the sample size suggested in part a is much too large. Suggest something that could be done to reduce the sample size. Based on your suggestion, recalculate the sample size.

## CHAPTER OUTLINE

I. There are many reasons for sampling a population.
   A. Often, testing destroys the sampled item, and it cannot be returned to the population.
   B. It may be impossible to check or locate all the members of the population.
   C. The cost of studying all items in the population may be prohibitive.
   D. The results of a sample may adequately estimate the population parameter, thus saving time and money.
   E. It may be too time-consuming to contact all the members of the population.

II. There are two types of samples: probability and nonprobability.
   A. In a probability sample all members of the population have a chance of being selected for the sample. There are several probability sampling methods.
      1. In a *simple random sample* all members of the population have the same chance of being selected for the sample.
      2. In a *systematic sample* a random starting point is selected, and then every $k$th item is selected for the sample.
      3. In a *stratified sample* the population is divided into several groups, or strata, and then a sample is selected from each stratum.
      4. In *cluster sampling* the population is divided into primary units, and then samples are drawn from the primary units.
   B. In nonprobability sampling, inclusion in the sample is based on the judgment of the person conducting the sample. Nonprobability samples may lead to biased results.

III. The difference between the population parameter and the sample statistic is called the *sampling error.*

IV. The *sampling distribution of the means* is a probability distribution showing all possible sample means and their probabilities of occurrence.
   A. For a given sample size, the mean of all possible sample means selected from the population is exactly equal to the population mean.
   B. There is less dispersion in the sampling distribution of the means than in the population. The variation in a sampling distribution, called the standard error of the mean, is computed by

$$\sigma_{\bar{x}} = \frac{\sigma}{\sqrt{n}}$$

(8–1)

   C. The *central limit theorem* states that if the population is normal, then the sampling distribution of the means is also normal. If the population is not normal, the sampling distribution of the means approaches normal as the size of the sample increases.

V. A *point estimate* is a single value used to estimate a population value.

VI. An *interval estimate* is a range of values within which the population parameter is expected to occur.

    A. The factors that make up a confidence interval for a mean are:

        1. The number of observations in the sample ($n$).

        2. The variability in the population, usually estimated by the sample standard deviation ($s$).

        3. The level of confidence. It is represented by the $z$ value.

    B. A 95 percent confidence interval for the mean is obtained using the formula

$$\bar{X} \pm 1.96 \frac{s}{\sqrt{n}} \tag{8-3}$$

    C. The factors that make up a confidence interval for a proportion are:

        1. The number of observations in the sample.

        2. The value of $\bar{p}$, which is obtained by dividing the number of successes in the sample ($X$) by the number of observations in the sample ($n$).

        3. The level of confidence. It is represented by the $z$ value.

    D. A confidence interval for a proportion is obtained using the formula

$$\bar{p} \pm z \sqrt{\frac{\bar{p}(1 - \bar{p})}{n}} \tag{8-7}$$

VII. The required size of a sample can be determined for both means and proportions.

    A. The factors that determine the size of the sample for a mean are:

        1. The desired level of confidence ($z$).

        2. The maximum allowable error ($E$).

        3. The variation in the population (usually estimated by $s$).

    B. The formula for sample size for a mean is:

$$n = \left(\frac{z \cdot s}{E}\right)^2 \tag{8-11}$$

    C. The factors that determine the size of the sample for a proportion are:

        1. The desired level of confidence ($z$).

        2. The maximum allowable error ($E$).

        3. An estimate of the population proportion. If no estimate is available, then .50 is used.

    D. The formula for sample size for a proportion is:

$$n = \bar{p}(1 - \bar{p})\left(\frac{z}{E}\right)^2 \tag{8-12}$$

    E. The finite-population correction factor is applied if $n/N$ is more than .05. The correction factor is

$$\sqrt{\frac{N - n}{N - 1}}$$

# EXERCISES

*The answers to the odd-numbered exercises are at the end of the book.*

35. Briefly explain:

    a. The purpose of sampling.

    b. Some of the reasons for using a sample instead of contacting, enumerating, or testing the entire population.

36. Identify each of the following types of sampling.

   a. Auditors may select every 20th file starting with, say, the 5th file in the top drawer. Then file numbers 25, 45, 65, 85, . . . are audited.

   b. Manufacturers were subdivided into groups by volume of sales. Those with more than $100 million in sales were classified as class A large, those from $50 to $100 million as class A medium, those between $25 and $50 million . . . , and so on. Samples were then selected from each of these groups.

37. Explain the statement: "If nonprobability sampling methods are used, the results may be biased."

38. Explain what is meant by sampling error.

39. Cite a situation in which cluster sampling might be used.

40. Briefly explain a nonprobability type of sampling called panel sampling.

41. The following is a list of family-practice physicians. Three physicians are to be randomly selected and contacted regarding their charge for a routine office visit. The 39 physicians have been coded from 00 to 38. Also noted is whether they are in practice by themselves (S), have a partner (P), or are in a group practice (G).

| Random number | Physician | Type of practice | Random number | Physician | Type of practice |
|---|---|---|---|---|---|
| 00 | R. E. Scherbarth, M.D. | S | 20 | Gregory Yost, M.D. | P |
| 01 | Crystal R. Goveia, M.D. | P | 21 | J. Christian Zona, M.D. | P |
| 02 | Mark D. Hillard, M.D. | P | 22 | Larry Johnson, M.D. | P |
| 03 | Jeanine S. Huttner, M.D. | P | 23 | Sanford Kimmel M.D. | P |
| 04 | Francis Aona, M.D. | P | 24 | Harry Mayhew M.D. | S |
| 05 | Janet Arrowsmith, M.D. | P | 25 | Leroy Rodgers M.D. | S |
| 06 | David DeFrance, M.D. | S | 26 | Thomas Tafelski M.D. | S |
| 07 | Judith Furlong, M.D. | S | 27 | Mark Zilkoski M.D. | G |
| 08 | Leslie Jackson, M.D. | G | 28 | Ken Bertka, M.D. | G |
| 09 | Paul Langenkamp, M.D. | S | 29 | Mark DeMichiei, M.D. | G |
| 10 | Philip Lepkowski, M.D. | S | 30 | John Eggert, M.D. | P |
| 11 | Wendy Martin, M.D. | S | 31 | Jeanne Fiorito, M.D. | P |
| 12 | Denny Mauricio, M.D. | P | 32 | Michael Fitzpatrick, M.D. | P |
| 13 | Hasmukh Parmar, M.D. | P | 33 | Charles Holt, D.O. | P |
| 14 | Ricardo Pena, M.D. | P | 34 | Richard Koby, M.D. | P |
| 15 | David Reames, M.D. | P | 35 | John Meier, M.D. | P |
| 16 | Ronald Reynolds, M.D. | G | 36 | Douglas Smucker, M.D. | S |
| 17 | Mark Steinmetz, M.D. | G | 37 | David Weldy, M.D. | P |
| 18 | Geza Torok, M.D. | S | 38 | Cheryl Zaborowski, M.D. | P |
| 19 | Mark Young, M.D. | P | | | |

   a. If the random numbers 31, 94, 43, 36, 03, 24, 17, and 09 are obtained, which physicians should be contacted?

   b. Select a random sample of size 4 using the table of random numbers (Appendix E).

42. Refer to Exercise 41. A sample is to consist of every fifth physician. The number 04 is selected as the starting point. Which physicians will be contacted?

43. Refer to Exercise 41. A sample is to consist of two physicians in solo practice (S), two in partnership (P), and one in group practice (G). Select a sample accordingly. Explain your procedure.

44. A study of motel facilities in a metropolitan area showed there were 25 facilities. The city's convention and visitors bureau is studying the number of rooms at each location. The results are as follows: 90, 72, 75, 60, 75, 72, 84, 72, 88, 74, 105, 115, 68, 74, 80, 64, 104, 82, 48, 58, 60, 80, 48, 58, and 108.

   a. Using a table of random numbers (Appendix E), select a random sample of size 5 from this population.

    b.   Obtain a systematic sample by selecting a random starting point among the first five motels, and then select every fifth motel.

    c.   Suppose the last five motels listed are "cut-rate" motels. Describe how you would select a random sample of three regular motels and two cut-rate motels.

45. Dr. Lamberg has five students doing special independent study with him this semester. To evaluate their reading progress, Dr. Lamberg gave the students a five-question true/false test. The number of correct answers for each student is given below.

| Student | Number correct |
|---|---|
| Tayor | 4 |
| Hurley | 3 |
| Fowler | 5 |
| Rousche | 3 |
| Telatko | 2 |

    a.   How many samples of size 2 are possible from this population?

    b.   List all possible samples of size 2, and compute the sample means.

    c.   Organize the sample means into a probability distribution.

    d.   Compute the mean of the sample means, and compare it with the population mean.

    e.   Compare the shape of the population and the shape of the distribution of the sample means.

46. The commercial banks in region III are to be surveyed. Some of them are very large, with assets of more than $500 million; others are medium-size, with assets between $100 million and $500 million; and the remaining banks have assets of less than $100 million. Explain how you would select a sample of these banks.

47. Plastic Products is concerned about the inside diameter of the plastic PVC pipe it produces. A machine extrudes the pipe, which is then cut into 10-foot lengths. About 720 pipes are produced per machine during a two-hour period. How would you go about taking a sample from the two-hour production period?

48. The ages of the six executives of the Ace Manufacturing Company (considered the population) are:

| Name | Age |
|---|---|
| Mr. Jones | 54 |
| Ms. Smith | 50 |
| Mr. Kirk | 52 |
| Ms. Small | 48 |
| Mr. Hugh | 50 |
| Mr. Sioto | 52 |

    a.   How many samples of size 2 are possible?

    b.   Select all possible samples of size 2 from the population of executives, and compute the means.

    c.   Organize the means into a sampling distribution.

    d.   What is the mean of the population? Of the sample means?

    e.   What is the shape of the population?

    f.   What is the shape of the sampling distribution?

49. A random sample of 85 group leaders, supervisors, and similar personnel at Amana revealed that, on the average, a person spent 6.5 years on the job before being promoted. The standard deviation of the sample was 1.7 years. Using the .95 degree of confidence, construct the confidence interval within which the population mean lies.

50. Of 900 consumers surveyed, 414 said they were very enthusiastic about a new home decor scheme. Construct the 99 percent confidence interval for the population proportion.

51. It is estimated that 60 percent of U.S. households now can get cable TV. You would like to verify this statement for your class in mass communications. If you want your estimate to be with ±5 percentage points with a 95 percent level of confidence, how large a sample is required? (Source: "Hot Media Businesses Are Cooling," *USA Today,* June 22, 1991, p. B2.)

52. There are 20,000 eligible voters in the fifth precinct. A sample of 500 voters is selected. Of the 500 surveyed, 350 said they are going to vote for the Democratic incumbent. Using the .99 degree of confidence, set the confidence limits for the proportion who plan to vote for the Democratic incumbent.

53. The mean number of travel days per year for the outside salespeople employed by Hardware Distributors is to be estimated. The .90 degree of confidence is to be used. The mean of a small pilot study was 150 days, with a standard deviation of 14 days. If the population mean is to be estimated within 2 days, how many outside salespeople should be sampled?

54. Ten passengers are to be selected at random from the New York–Los Angeles Delta flight and interviewed in depth regarding airport facilities, service, food, and so on. Each passenger boarding the aircraft was given a number. The numbers started with 001 and ended with 250.

    a.  Select 10 numbers at random using the table of random numbers in Appendix E.

    b.  The sample of 10 could have been chosen using a systematic sample. Choose the first number using Appendix E, and then list the numbers to be interviewed.

    c.  Evaluate the two methods by giving the advantages and possible disadvantages.

    d.  In what other way could a random sample be selected from the 250 passengers?

55. The Iowa state meat inspector has been given the assignment of estimating the actual mean net weight of packages of ground chuck labeled "3 pounds." Of course, he realizes that the weights cannot be precisely 3 pounds. A sample of 36 packages revealed the mean weight to be 3.01 pounds with a standard deviation of 0.03 pounds.

    a.  What is the estimated population mean?

    b.  Using the .95 degree of confidence, what are the confidence limits for the population mean?

    c.  Summarize your findings.

56. Police Chief Kress of River City reports that 500 traffic citations were issued last month. A sample of 35 of these citations showed the mean amount to be $54 with a standard deviation of $4.50. Construct a 95 percent confidence interval for the mean amount of a citation in River City.

57. The First National Bank of Wilson has 650 checking account customers. A recent sample of 50 of these customers showed 26 to have a MasterCard with the bank. Construct the 99 percent confidence interval for the proportion of checking account customers that have a MasterCard with the bank.

58. A recent study of 50 self-service gasoline stations in the Cincinnati, Ohio, area revealed that the mean price of unleaded gas was $1.179 per gallon and the standard deviation was $0.03 per gallon. Determine a 99 percent confidence interval for the mean price per gallon of unleaded gasoline.

59. In a survey of 1,200 voters in Oklahoma, 792 were able to name their two U.S. Senators. Develop a 95 percent confidence interval for the proportion of voters in Oklahoma that can identify their senators.

60. The Badik Construction Company limits its business to repairing driveways, installing patios, and building decks. The mean time for all three jobs is 12 hours, but the standard deviation is 3 hours for repairing a driveway, 6 hours for a patio, and 8 hours for a deck. This information is based on samples of 40 of each type of job.

    a.  Before you do any calculation, which of the three types of jobs will have the smallest range of values for a 99 percent confidence interval for mean construction time?

b.   Construct a confidence interval for the mean construction time for each type of job.

61. In Nantucket, Massachusetts, according to an article in *The Wall Street Journal,* it is estimated that 82 percent of the homes are vacation homes. A sample of 140 homes showed that 110 were actually vacation homes. Comment on the statement in the *Journal.* (Source: "Broken Homes," *The Wall Street Journal,* June 21, 1991, p. 1.)

62. A sample survey of the 256 largest companies in the United States found that 23 percent had told their employees how the economic downturn in early 1991 would affect the organization. Determine a 99 percent confidence interval for the proportion of all firms that will tell their employees the effects of the downturn. (Source: "Managing," *The Wall Street Journal,* June 20, 1991, p. B1.)

63. The proportion of junior executives leaving large manufacturing companies within three years is to be estimated within 3 percent. The .95 degree of confidence is to be used. A study conducted several years ago revealed that the percent of junior executives leaving within three years was 21.

a.   To update this study, the files of how many junior executives should be studied?

b.   How many junior executives would be contacted if no previous estimate were available?

64. The Hunington National Bank, like most other large banks, found that the use of automatic teller machines (ATMs) reduces the cost of routine bank transactions. Hunington installed an ATM in the corporate offices of the Fun Toy company. The ATM is for the exclusive use of Fun's 605 employees. After several months of operation, a sample of 100 employees revealed the following use of the ATM machine by Fun employees in a month.

| Number of times ATM used | Frequency |
|:---:|:---:|
| 0 | 25 |
| 1 | 30 |
| 2 | 20 |
| 3 | 10 |
| 4 | 10 |
| 5 | 5 |
| Total | 100 |

a.   What is the estimate of the proportion of employees that do not use the ATM in a month?

b.   Develop a 95 percent confidence interval for this estimate. Can Hunington be sure that at least 40 percent of the employees of Fun Toy Company will use the ATM?

c.   How many transactions does the average Fun employee make per month?

d.   Develop a 95 percent confidence interval for the mean number of transactions per month.

e.   Is it possible that the population mean is 0? Explain.

## COMPUTER DATA EXERCISES

65. Refer to data set 1, which reports information on homes sold in Florida during 1990.

a.   Determine the 95 percent confidence interval for the mean selling price.

b.   Determine the 95 percent confidence interval for the mean distance from the center of the city.

c.   Determine the 95 percent confidence interval for the proportion of homes with a garage.

66. Refer to data set 2, which reports information on 200 corporations in the United States.
    a.   Determine the 95 percent confidence interval for the mean return on investment.
    b.   Determine the 95 percent confidence interval for the mean share price.
    c.   After computing the 95 percent confidence limits in part b, you noticed that the share price of Berkshine Hathaway was $7,900. (It is #60 on the data set 2.) Assuming this to be an error, you decided to recalculate the confidence limits, using a share price of just $79. What will happen to the mean price and the confidence limits? (You need not recompute the confidence limits based on the adjusted share price of $79.) By the way, the $7,900 is not in error. The actual share price is $7,900.

# CHAPTER 8 EXAMINATION

*The answers are at the end of the chapter.*

For Questions 1 through 10, indicate whether the statement is true or false. If the statement is false, correct it.

1. A sample is a part of the population.
2. In a probability sample each member of the population has a chance of being selected as part of the sample.
3. The difference between a sample statistic and the corresponding population parameter is called the sampling error.
4. The mean of all the sample means is always larger than the population mean.
5. If a population is normal, the sampling distribution of the means is also normal.
6. A value used to estimate a population parameter is called a sample statistic.
7. An interval estimate always contains the population parameter.
8. If the sample size for estimating a population mean is increased, the width of the interval will decrease.
9. The finite-population correction factor is used when $n/N$ is greater than .80.
10. Suppose we want to determine the confidence interval for a population proportion. If the level of confidence is increased, say, from 95 percent to 99 percent, the width of the interval will decrease.
11. It has been discovered that some of the small steel shafts stored in warehouse E have rusted and will have to be cleaned before they can be sold. In order to approximate the percent that need cleaning, a sample of 200 was selected at random. It was found that 80 out of the 200 need cleaning. Using a degree of confidence of .90, set confidence limits between which the population proportion should fall.
12. A random sample of size 200 was selected to estimate the average (mean) amount of time adults over 65 years old, retired, and living in Florida listened to the radio during the day. The sample mean was calculated to be 110 minutes, and the standard deviation of the sample was 30 minutes. What are the 95 percent confidence limits for the population mean listening time?
13. A sample survey is to be conducted to determine the mean family income in an area. The question is, how many families should be sampled? In order to get more information about the area, a small pilot survey was conducted, and the standard deviation of the sample was computed to be $500. The sponsor of the survey wants you to use the .95 degree of confidence. The estimate is to be within $100. How many families should be interviewed?
14. You plan to conduct a survey to find out what proportion of the work force have two or more jobs. You decide on the .95 degree of confidence and state that the estimated proportion must be within 2 percent of the population proportion. A pilot survey reveals that 5 out of the 50 sampled hold two or more jobs. How many in the work force should be interviewed to meet your requirements?

# ANSWERS

8–1  1. Students selected are Price, Detlev, and Molter. You could have chosen any three numbers at random, such as 44, 17, and 32. The number 59 would be ignored and another number chosen.

2. Answers will vary.

3. Drop it, and move to the next random number.

8–2  The students selected are: Berry, Francis, Kopp, Poteau, and Swetye.

8–3  1. 10, found by:

$$\frac{5!}{2!(5-2)!}$$

2.

| | Service | Sample mean |
|---|---|---|
| Snow, Tolson | 20, 22 | 21 |
| Snow, Kraft | 20, 26 | 23 |
| Snow, Irwin | 20, 24 | 22 |
| Snow, Jones | 20, 28 | 24 |
| Tolson, Kraft | 22, 26 | 24 |
| Tolson, Irwin | 22, 24 | 23 |
| Tolson, Jones | 22, 28 | 25 |
| Kraft, Irwin | 26, 24 | 25 |
| Kraft, Jones | 26, 28 | 27 |
| Irwin, Jones | 24, 28 | 26 |

3.

| Means | Number | Probability |
|---|---|---|
| 21 | 1 | .10 |
| 22 | 1 | .10 |
| 23 | 2 | .20 |
| 24 | 2 | .20 |
| 25 | 2 | .20 |
| 26 | 1 | .10 |
| 27 | 1 | .10 |
| | 10 | 1.00 |

4. Identical: population mean, $\mu$, is 24, and mean of sample means is also 24.

5. Sample means range from 21 to 27. Population values go from 20 to 28.

6. Nonnormal.

7. Yes.

8–4  1. 402.7 grams. The point estimate.

2. The interval is between 399.11 and 406.29 grams, found by:

$$\bar{X} \pm 2.58 \frac{s}{\sqrt{n}} = 402.7 \pm 2.58 \frac{8.8}{\sqrt{40}}$$

3. 399.11 and 406.29 grams.

4. .99.

5. If we were to construct 100 similar intervals, about 99 should include the population mean.

8–5  1. .268 and .332, found by:

$$.30 \pm 2.58 \sqrt{\frac{.30[1-.30]}{1,400}} = .30 \pm 2.58(.0122474)$$

2. .268 and .332.

3. If we were to construct 100 similar intervals, about 99 should include the population proportion.

8–6  About 23.7 and 51.3 percent, found by:

$$.375 \pm 1.96 \sqrt{\frac{.375(.625)}{40}} \sqrt{\frac{250-40}{250-1}}$$

$$= .375 \pm 1.96(.0765466)(.9183537)$$

$$= .375 \pm .138$$

$$= [.237, .513]$$

The correction factor was applied because 40/250 > .05.

8–7  208, found by:

$$n = \left[\frac{(2.58)(.279)}{.05}\right]^2$$

$$= 207.26, \text{ which is rounded up to 208.}$$

8–8  1. True. $\bar{p} = 922/2,305 = .40$. Substituting:

$$n = .40(1-.40)\left[\frac{1.96}{.02}\right]^2 = 2,304.96$$

$$= 2,305$$

2. True. $\bar{p} = 461/2,305 = .20$. Substituting:

$$.20(1-.20)\left[\frac{1.96}{.02}\right]^2 = .16[98]^2$$

$$= 1,537$$

The sample of 2,305 was too large. Only 1,537 voters needed to be surveyed.

# Answers

## CHAPTER 8 EXAMINATION

1. True.
2. True.
3. True.
4. False. The mean of the sample means and the population mean are equal.
5. True.
6. True.
7. False. The parameter will be included in the interval about the same percent of times as the confidence interval.
8. True.
9. False. It is used when $n/N > .05$.
10. False. The width of the interval will be increased.
11. Between 34.3 and 45.7 percent, found by:

$$.40 \pm 1.645 \sqrt{\frac{.40(1 - .40)}{200}}$$

$$= .40 \pm 1.645 \sqrt{.0012}$$

$$= .40 \pm .057$$

12. Between 105.84 and 114.16 minutes, found by:

$$110 \pm 1.96 \left(\frac{30}{\sqrt{200}}\right) = 110 \pm 1.96(2.12)$$

$$= 110 \pm 4.16$$

13. 97, found by:

$$n = \left(\frac{1.96 \times \$500}{\$100}\right)^2 = 96.04$$

rounded up to 97.

14. 865, found by

$$(.10)(.90)\left[\frac{1.96}{.02}\right]^2 = .09[98]^2 = 864.36$$

Health Care—Courtesy Schering-Plough Corporation, photograph by Mark Tuschman

# TESTS OF HYPOTHESES: LARGE SAMPLES

When you have completed this chapter, you will be able to:

1. Define what is meant by a hypothesis and hypothesis testing.

2. Describe the five-step hypothesis-testing procedure.

3. Distinguish between a one-tailed and a two-tailed test.

4. Conduct a test of hypothesis about a population mean.

5. Conduct a test of hypothesis about the difference between two population means.

6. Describe the statistical errors that might result in testing a hypothesis.

7. Define a Type I error.

8. Define a Type II error.

9. Compute the probability of a Type II error.

C hapter 8 dealt with one aspect of statistical inference—estimation. Estimation involves estimating, or predicting, the value of an unknown population parameter, such as the population mean or the population proportion.

This chapter begins our study of another aspect of statistical inference, namely, **hypothesis testing.** Some types of questions to be dealt with are:

1. Is the mean impact strength of the plate glass being produced on the production line 70 pounds per square inch?
2. Are more than 10 percent of the 50-millimeter shells in storage defective?
3. Is there a difference in the proportion of consumers who purchased Smell Sweet soap before our television advertising campaign and after the campaign?
4. Is there a difference in the mean usable life between Always Ready and Hotshot type-C batteries?

This chapter and five of the following chapters are concerned with hypothesis testing. We will first examine what is meant by a *hypothesis* and *hypothesis testing*. Then we will outline the steps followed to test a hypothesis. We will conduct tests with respect to one population mean and two population means. Finally, the possible statistical errors in testing a hypothesis will be explored.

## WHAT IS A HYPOTHESIS?

| Hypothesis    A statement about the value of a population parameter. |
| --- |

Examples of hypotheses

Examples of hypotheses, or statements, made about a population parameter are:

- The mean monthly income from all sources for senior citizens is $993.
- Twenty percent of juvenile offenders ultimately are caught and sentenced to prison.
- The mean outside diameter of ball bearings produced during the day is 1.000 inches.
- Ninety percent of the federal income tax forms are filled out correctly.
- The mean impact strengths of the windshields produced by the Delaware Glass Company and Stabler-Pittsburgh Glass are the same.

May not be feasible to study entire population

All these hypotheses have one thing in common. The populations of interest are so large that for various reasons it would not be feasible to study all the items, or persons, in the population. For example, it would be almost impossible to contact every senior citizen in the United States to find out his or her monthly income. Likewise, the quality-assurance department does not have the personnel to check every ball bearing produced during the day to determine whether the mean outside diameter is in fact exactly 1.000 inches.

Sample imperative in many problems

As noted in Chapter 8, an alternative to measuring or interviewing the entire population is to take a sample from the population of interest. We can, therefore, test a statement to determine whether the empirical evidence does or does not support the statement.

# WHAT IS HYPOTHESIS TESTING?

Hypothesis: Statement about a population parameter

The terms *hypothesis testing* and *testing a hypothesis* are used interchangeably. Hypothesis testing starts with a statement, or assumption, about a population parameter—such as the population mean. As noted, this statement is referred to as a *hypothesis.* A hypothesis might be that the mean monthly commission of salespeople in retail computer stores, such as Computerland, is $2,000. We cannot contact all these salespeople to ascertain that the mean is in fact $2,000. The cost of locating and interviewing every computer salesperson in the United States would be exorbitant. To test the validity of the assumption (population mean = $2,000), we must select a sample from the population consisting of all computer salespeople, calculate sample statistics, and based on certain decision rules accept or reject the hypothesis. A sample mean of $1,000 for the computer salespeople would certainly cause rejection of the hypothesis. However, suppose the sample mean is $1,995. Is that close enough to $2,000 for us to accept the assumption that the population mean is $2,000? Can we attribute the difference of $5 between the two means to sampling error, or is that difference statistically significant?

Hypothesis testing defined

> Hypothesis testing    A procedure based on sample evidence and probability theory used to determine whether the hypothesis is a reasonable statement and should not be rejected, or is unreasonable and should be rejected.

# FIVE-STEP PROCEDURE FOR TESTING A HYPOTHESIS

A systematic procedure

There is a five-step procedure that systematizes hypothesis testing; when we get to step 5, we are ready to make a decision to reject or not reject the hypothesis. However, hypothesis testing as used by statisticians does not provide proof that something is true, in the manner in which a mathematician "proves" a statement. It does provide a kind of "proof beyond a reasonable doubt," in the manner of an attorney. Hence, there are specific rules of evidence, or a procedure, that are followed. The steps are:

## STEP 1: THE NULL HYPOTHESIS AND THE ALTERNATE HYPOTHESIS

The systematic procedure

The first step is to state the hypothesis to be tested. It is called the *null hypothesis,* designated $H_0$, and read "*H* sub-zero." The capital letter *H* stands for hypothesis, and the subscript zero implies "no difference." There is usually a *not* or a *no* term in the null hypothesis, meaning there is "no change." The null hypothesis for question 1 in the introduction would be, "The mean impact strength of the glass is *not* significantly different from 70 psi." This is the same as saying the mean ($\mu$) impact strength of the glass is equal to 70 psi. The null hypothesis $H_0$ would then be written $H_0: \mu = 70$. For question 3 in the introduction, the null hypothesis would be, "There is *no* difference in the proportion of consumers who purchased Smell Sweet before and after the television advertising campaign." This is the same as saying that the two proportions are equal, written $H_0: p_1 = p_2$. Generally speaking, *the null hypothesis is set up for the purpose of either accepting or rejecting it.* To put it another way, the null hypothesis is a statement that will be accepted if our sample data fail to provide us with convincing evidence that it is false.

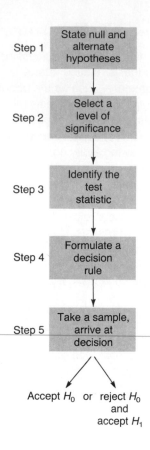

Accept $H_0$   or   reject $H_0$
and
accept $H_1$

We should emphasize at this point that if the null hypothesis is accepted based on sample data, in effect we are saying that the evidence does not allow us to reject it. We cannot state, however, that the null hypothesis is true. To put it another way, accepting the null hypothesis does not prove that $H_0$ is true. To prove without any doubt that the null hypothesis is true, the population parameter would have to be known. To actually determine it, we would have to test, survey, or count every item in the population. This is usually not feasible. The alternative is to take a sample from the population.

It should also be noted that we often begin the null hypothesis by stating "There is no *significant* difference between . . . ," or "The mean impact strength of the glass is not *significantly* different from. . . ." When we select a sample from a population, the sample statistic is usually different from the hypothesized population parameter. As an illustration, suppose that the hypothesized impact strength of a glass plate is 70 psi, and the mean impact strength of a sample of 12 glass plates is 69.5 psi. We must make a judgment about the difference of 0.5 psi. Is it a true difference, that is, a significant difference, or is the difference between the sample statistic (69.5) and the hypothe- sized population parameter (70.0) due to chance (sampling)? As noted, to answer this question we conduct a test of significance, commonly referred to as a test of hypothesis.

Identify $H_0$

---

Null hypothesis   A tentative assumption made about the value of a population parameter. Usually, it is a statement that the population parameter has a specific value.

*Identify $H_1$*

The *alternate hypothesis* describes what you will believe if you reject the null hypothesis. It is often called the research hypothesis, designated $H_1$, and read "H sub-one." The alternate hypothesis will be accepted if the sample data provide us with evidence that the null hypothesis is false.

> **Alternate hypothesis**  A statement that will be accepted if our sample data provide us with ample evidence that the null hypothesis is false.

## STEP 2: THE LEVEL OF SIGNIFICANCE

*Select a level of significance or risk*

After setting up the null hypothesis and alternate hypothesis, the next step is to state the level of significance. It is the *probability of rejecting the null hypothesis when it is actually true.*

> **Level of significance**  The risk we assume of rejecting the null hypothesis when it is actually true.

The level of significance is designated $\alpha$, the Greek letter alpha. It is also referred to as the *level of risk.* This may be a more appropriate term because it is the risk you take of rejecting the null hypothesis when it is really true.

There is no one level of significance that is applied to all studies involving sampling. A decision must be made to use the .05 level (often stated as the 5 percent level), the .01 level, the .10 level, or any other level between 0 and 1. Traditionally, the .05 level is selected for consumer research projects, .01 for quality assurance, and .10 for political polling. You, the researcher, must decide on the level of significance *before* formulating a decision rule and collecting sample data.

To illustrate how it is possible to reject a true hypothesis, suppose a firm manufacturing home computers uses a large number of printed circuit boards.

Courtesy Hewlett-Packard Company

Suppliers bid on the boards, and the one with the lowest bid is awarded a sizable contract. Suppose the contract specifies that the computer manufacturer's quality-assurance department will sample all incoming shipments of circuit boards. If more than 6 percent of the boards sampled are substandard, the shipment will be rejected. (The null hypothesis is that the incoming shipment of boards contains 6 percent or less substandard boards.) The alternate hypothesis is that more than 6 percent of the boards are defective.

A sample of 50 circuit boards received July 21 revealed that 4 boards, or 8 percent, were substandard. The shipment was rejected because it exceeded the maximum of 6 percent substandard printed circuit boards. If the shipment was actually substandard, then the decision to return the boards to the supplier was correct. However, suppose the 4 substandard printed circuit boards selected in the sample of 50 were the only substandard boards in the shipment of 4,000 boards. Only $1/10$ of 1 percent were defective ($4/4,000 = .001$). In that case, less than 6 percent of the entire shipment were substandard, and rejecting the shipment was an error. In terms of hypothesis testing, we rejected the null hypothesis that the shipment was not substandard when we should have accepted the null hypothesis. By rejecting a true hypothesis, we committed a
Type I error     *Type I error.* A Type I error is designated by the Greek letter alpha ($\alpha$).

| Type I error   Rejecting the null hypothesis, $H_0$, when it is actually true. |
|---|

Type II error          The probability of committing another type of error, called a *Type II error,* is designated by the Greek letter beta ($\beta$). A Type II error is accepting $H_0$ when it is actually false.

| Type II error   Accepting the null hypothesis when it is actually false. |
|---|

The firm manufacturing home computers would commit a Type II error if, unknown to the manufacturer, an incoming shipment of printed circuit boards contained 15 percent substandard boards, yet the shipment was accepted. How could this happen? Suppose 2 of the 50 boards in the sample (4 percent) tested were substandard, and 48 of the 50 were good boards. According to the stated procedure, because the sample contained less than 6 percent substandard boards, the shipment was accepted. It could be that *by chance* the 48 good boards selected in the sample were the only acceptable ones in the entire shipment consisting of thousands of boards!

In retrospect, the researcher cannot study every item or individual in the population. Thus, there is a possibility of two types of error—a Type I error, wherein the null hypothesis is rejected when it should have been accepted, and a Type II error, wherein the null hypothesis is accepted when it should have been rejected.
Alpha error          We often refer to these two possible errors as the *alpha error,* $\alpha$, and the *beta*
Beta error          *error,* $\beta$. Alpha ($\alpha$) is the probability of making a Type I error, and beta ($\beta$) is the probability of making a Type II error.

The following table summarizes the decisions the researcher could make and the possible consequences:

| Null hypothesis | Researcher | |
|---|---|---|
| | Accepts $H_0$ | Rejects $H_0$ |
| If $H_0$ is true and | Correct decision | Type I error |
| If $H_0$ is false and | Type II error | Correct decision |

## STEP 3: THE TEST STATISTIC

There are many test statistics. This chapter and the following one use $z$ as the test statistic. Other chapters will use such test statistics as $t$, $F$, and $\chi^2$, called chi-squared.

> Test statistic  A value, determined from sample information, used to accept or reject the null hypothesis.

Use of $z$ as the test statistic

In hypothesis testing, the test statistic $z$ is computed by:

$$z = \frac{\overline{X} - \mu}{\frac{\sigma}{\sqrt{n}}}$$

(9–1)

## STEP 4: THE DECISION RULE

Decision rule: States condition of rejection or nonrejection

A decision rule is a statement of the conditions under which the null hypothesis is rejected and the conditions under which it is not rejected. The region or area of rejection defines the location of all those values that are so large or so small that the probability of their occurrence under a true null hypothesis is rather remote.

Chart 9–1 on the following page portrays the rejection region for a test of significance that will be conducted later in the chapter.

Note in Chart 9–1:

1. The area where the null hypothesis is not rejected includes the area to the left of 1.645.
2. The area of rejection is to the right of 1.645.
3. A one-tailed test is being applied. (This will be explained later.)
4. The .05 level of significance was chosen.
5. The sampling distribution of the statistic $z$ is normally distributed.
6. The value 1.645 separates the regions where the null hypothesis is rejected and where it is not rejected.
7. The value 1.645 is called the **critical value.**

> Critical value  The dividing point between the region where the null hypothesis is rejected and the region where it is not rejected.

---

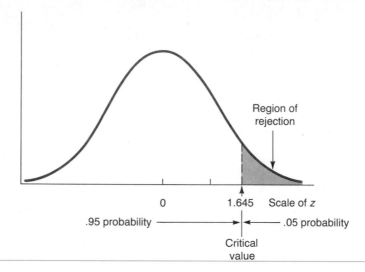

### CHART 9–1

**Sampling Distribution for the Statistic z for a One-Tailed Test, .05 Level of Significance**

Region of rejection

0   1.645   Scale of z

.95 probability ——————→|←—— .05 probability

Critical value

---

## STEP 5: MAKING A DECISION

The fifth and final step in hypothesis testing is making a decision to reject or not to reject the null hypothesis. Referring to Chart 9–1, if, based on sample information, z is computed to be 2.34, the null hypothesis is rejected at the .05 level of significance. The decision to reject $H_0$ was made because 2.34 lies in the region of rejection, that is, beyond 1.645. We would reject the null hypothesis reasoning that it is highly improbable that a computed z value this large is due to sampling variation (chance).

Had the computed value been 1.645 or less, say 0.71, the null hypothesis would not be rejected. It would be reasoned that such a small computed value could be attributed to chance, that is, sampling variation.

As noted, one of two decisions is possible in hypothesis testing—either accept or reject the null hypothesis. Instead of "accepting" the null hypothesis, $H_0$, some researchers prefer to phrase the decision as: "Do not reject $H_0$," "We fail to reject $H_0$," or "The sample results do not allow us to reject $H_0$." We will use these phrases interchangeably.

It should be reemphasized that there is a possibility that the null hypothesis will be rejected when it should not have been rejected (a Type I error). Also, there is a definable chance that the null hypothesis will be accepted when it should have been rejected (a Type II error).

It should also be noted that the decision whether or not to reject is one made by the statistician conducting the research. That person could be a professional statistician, an accountant, a marketing manager, a quality-control engineer, or an executive. He or she states the null and alternate hypotheses, decides on the level of significance, selects a sample, and makes a decision whether or not to reject the null hypothesis. The statistician makes a recommendation based on this sample evidence, however, unless it is a routine decision, top management usually makes the final decision.

Before actually conducting a test of hypothesis, we will differentiate between a one-tailed test of significance and a two-tailed test.

## ONE-TAILED AND TWO-TAILED TESTS OF SIGNIFICANCE

One-tailed test

Refer to Chart 9–1. It indicates that a one-tailed test is being applied. The region of rejection is only in the right (upper) tail of the curve. To illustrate, suppose that the packaging department at General Foods Corporation is concerned that some boxes of Grape Nuts are significantly overweight. The cereal is packaged in 453 gram boxes so the null hypothesis is $H_0$: $\mu = 453$. The alternate hypothesis is therefore $H_1$: $\mu > 453$. Note that the inequality sign $>$ points to the region of rejection in the upper tail. (See Chart 9–1.)

Chart 9–2 below portrays a situation where the rejection region is in the left (lower) tail of the normal curve. As an illustration, consider the problem of automobile manufacturers, large automobile leasing companies, and other organizations that purchase large quantities of tires. They want the tires to average, say, 40,000 miles of wear under normal usage. They will therefore reject a shipment of tires if accelerated-life tests reveal that the life of the tires is significantly below 40,000 miles on the average. They gladly accept a shipment if the mean life is greater than 40,000 miles. They are not concerned with this possibility, however. They are only concerned if they have sample evidence to conclude that the tires will average less than 40,000 miles of useful life. Thus, the test is set up to satisfy the concern of the automobile manufac-turers and others that *the mean life of the tires is less than 40,000 miles.* The null and alternate hypotheses are written $H_0$: $\mu = 40,000$ and $H_1$: $\mu < 40,000$.

Test is one-tailed if $H_1$ states $\mu >$ or $\mu <$

One way to determine the location of the rejection region is to look at the direction the inequality sign in the alternate hypothesis is pointing (either $<$ or $>$). In this problem it is pointing to the left, and the rejection region is therefore in the left tail.

---

### CHART   9–2

**Sampling Distribution for the Statistic z, One-Tailed Test, .05 Level of Significance**

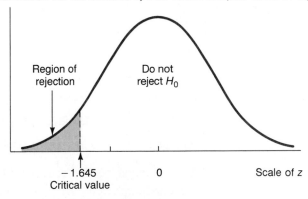

---

If $H_1$ states a direction, test is one-tailed

In summary, a test is one-tailed when the alternate hypothesis, $H_1$, states a direction, such as:

$H_0$:   There is *no* difference between the mean income of males and the mean in-come of females.

$H_1$:   The mean income of males is *greater than* the mean income of females.

Two-tailed test

Test is two-tailed if $H_1$
does not state a direction

If no direction is specified under the alternate hypothesis, a *two-tailed test* is being applied. Changing the previous alternate hypothesis to illustrate:

$H_0$:  There is *no* difference between the mean income of males and the mean income of females.

$H_1$:  There *is* a difference in the mean incomes of males and the mean incomes of females.

If the null hypothesis is rejected and $H_1$ accepted, the mean income of males could be greater than that of females, or vice versa. To accommodate these two possibilities, the 5 percent representing the area of rejection is divided equally into the two tails of the sampling distribution (2.5 percent each). Chart 9–3 shows the two areas and the critical values. Note that the total area under the normal curve is 1.000, found by .95 + .025 + .025.

---

## CHART 9–3

### Regions of Nonrejection and Rejection for a Two-Tailed Test, .05 Level of Significance

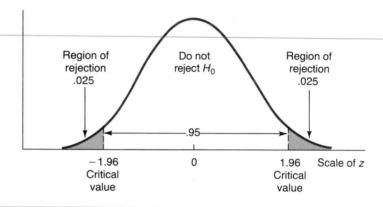

---

We will now test a hypothesis about the mean of a population by taking a large sample from that population. Recall that a sample of 30 or more is considered large.

## TESTING FOR THE POPULATION MEAN: LARGE SAMPLE, POPULATION STANDARD DEVIATION KNOWN

Answering these questions involves a population mean:

- Is the mean income of top executives in manufacturing $325,000?
- Is the mean length of the slugs being sheared 2.0000 inches?
- Is the mean age of the inmates of federal prisons less than 40 years?
- Is the mean amount owed by credit card holders greater than $1,000?
- Is the mean efficiency rating of the production employees at Boeing, Inc. equal to 200?

We will use the five-step hypothesis-testing procedure to test the last question. The phrasing of the question suggests a two-tailed test.

## A Two-Tailed Test

### ▮ Example

The efficiency ratings of Boeing employees at the Seattle plant have been normally distributed over a period of many years. The arithmetic mean ($\mu$) of the distribution is 200, and the standard deviation ($\sigma$) is 16. Recently, however, young employees have been hired and new training and production methods inaugurated. Using the .01 level of significance, we want to test the hypothesis that the mean is still 200. (Note that the population standard deviation is known, namely, 16.)

### ☑ Solution

*Step 1*  The null hypothesis is: "The population mean is 200." The alternate hypothesis is: "The mean is different from 200" or "The mean is not 200." The two hypotheses are written as:

$$H_0: \mu = 200$$
$$H_1: \mu \neq 200$$

Why a two-tailed test?

This is a *two-tailed test* because the alternate hypothesis does not state the direction of the difference. That is, it does not state whether the mean is greater than or less than 200.

*Step 2*  As noted, the .01 level of significance is to be used. This is $\alpha$, the probability of committing a Type I error. That is, it is the probability of rejecting a true hypothesis.

*Step 3*  The test statistic for this type of problem is *z*. It was discussed at length in Chapter 7. Transforming the efficiency rating data to standard units (*z* values) permits their use not only in this problem but also in other hypothesis-testing problems. Formula (9–1) for *z* is repeated below with the various letters identified.

Formula for the test statistic

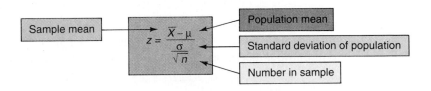

*Step 4*  The decision rule is formulated by finding the critical value of *z* from Appendix D. Since this is a two-tailed test, half of .01, or .005, is in each tail. The area where $H_0$ is not rejected, located between the two tails, is therefore .99. Appendix D is based on just half of the area under the curve, or .5000. Then, .5000 − .005 is .4950, so .4950 is the area between 0 and the critical value. Locate .4950 in the body of the table. The value nearest to .4950 is .4951. Then read the critical value in the row and column corresponding to .4951. It is 2.58. For your convenience Appendix D, Areas under the Normal Curve, is repeated in the inside back cover.

All the facets of this problem are shown in the form of a diagram in Chart 9–4.

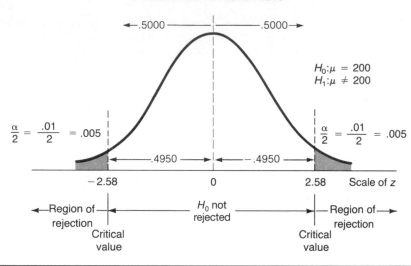

## Chart 9—4

### Decision Rule for the .01 Level

$$\frac{\alpha}{2} = \frac{.01}{2} = .005 \qquad\qquad \frac{\alpha}{2} = \frac{.01}{2} = .005$$

$$H_0: \mu = 200$$
$$H_1: \mu \neq 200$$

.5000 ───── │ ───── .5000

.4950 ───── │ ───── .4950

−2.58            0            2.58       Scale of $z$

←Region of─ ─ ─ ─    $H_0$ not    ─ ─ ─ ─ ─Region of→
rejection              rejected                   rejection
Critical                                              Critical
value                                                 value

**Accept $H_0$ if computed value is between −2.58 and +2.58**

The decision rule is therefore: Reject the null hypothesis and accept the alternate hypothesis (which states that the population mean is not 200) if the computed value of $z$ does not fall in the region between −2.58 and +2.58. Otherwise, do not reject the null hypothesis.

**STEP 5** Take a sample from the population (efficiency ratings); compute $z$; and, based on the decision rule, arrive at a decision to reject $H_0$ or not to reject $H_0$.

The efficiency ratings of 100 production employees were analyzed. The mean of the sample, $\overline{X}$, was computed to be 203.5. Computing $z$ using formula 9−1:

$$z = \frac{\overline{X} - \mu}{\dfrac{\sigma}{\sqrt{n}}} = \frac{203.5 - 200}{\dfrac{16}{\sqrt{100}}} = \frac{3.5}{1.6} = 2.19$$

**$H_0$ accepted because 2.19 is less than the critical value 2.58**

Since 2.19 does not fall in the rejection region, $H_0$ is not rejected; that is, it is accepted. So we conclude that the population mean is not different from 200. The difference between 203.5 and 200 can be attributed to chance variation.

### Self-Review 9—1

*The answers are at the end of the chapter.*

The mean annual turnover rate of a brand of allopurinol is 6.0. (This indicates that the stock of the medicine turns over on the shelf of West Pharmacy an average of six times a year.) The standard deviation is 0.5. It is suspected that the average turnover is not 6.0. The .05 level of significance is to be used to test this hypothesis.

1. State $H_0$ and $H_1$.
2. What is the probability of a Type 1 error?
3. Give the formula for the test statistic.
4. State the decision rule.
5. A random sample of 64 bottles of allopurinol was selected. The mean turnover rate was computed to be 5.84. Shall we reject the null hypothesis at the .05 level? Interpret.

We are concluding that our sample data *does not allow us to reject the null hypothesis.* We therefore assume that the null hypothesis is true.

We did not reject the null hypothesis that the population mean efficiency rating is 200 based on sample evidence. However, we did not prove beyond doubt that $H_0$ is true. The only way to prove beyond any doubt that it is 200 is to check every efficiency rating in the population—that is, take a 100 percent sample.

One further note about the hypothesis-testing procedure. This chapter has stressed the importance of selecting the level of significance *before* setting up the decision rule and sampling the population. In the example, the null hypothesis that $\mu = 200$ was *accepted* at the 1 percent level. You could have biased the later decision by not initially selecting the .01 level. Instead, you could have waited until *after* the sampling and selected a level of significance that would cause the null hypothesis to be *rejected.* You could have chosen, for example, the .05 level. The critical values for that level are plus and minus 1.96. Since the computed value of z (2.19) lies beyond 1.96, the null hypothesis would be rejected, and you would conclude that the mean efficiency rating is *not* 200. This decision would be just the opposite of our earlier conclusion!

Reason for selecting level of significance before choosing sample

## A ONE-TAILED TEST

We emphasized previously that if the alternate hypothesis states a direction (either "greater than" or "less than"), the test is *one-tailed.* The hypothesis-testing procedure is generally the same as for a two-tailed test, except that the critical value is different. Let us change the alternate hypothesis in the previous problem, involving the efficiency rating of the production workers at Boeing, from:

$$H_1: \mu \neq 200 \text{ (a two-tailed test)}$$

to

$$H_1: \mu > 200 \text{ (a one-tailed test)}$$

The critical values for the two-tailed test were $-2.58$ and $+2.58$ (see Chart 9–5). The region of rejection for a one-tailed test is in the right tail (the inequality sign, $>$, points to the rejection region). For a one-tailed test, the critical value is equal to $+2.33$, found by: (1) subtracting .01 from .5000 and (2) finding the z value associated with .4900 in Appendix D.

## CHART    9–5

### Rejection Regions for Two-Tailed and One-Tailed Tests, $\alpha = .01$

Critical values for a two-tailed and a one-tailed test, where $\alpha = .01$

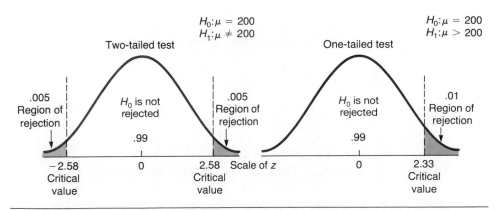

## p-VALUES IN HYPOTHESIS TESTING

In testing a hypothesis, we compare the test statistic to a critical value. A decision is made to either reject the null hypothesis or not reject it. So, for example, if the critical value of z is 1.96 and the computed value of the test statistic is 2.19, the decision is made to reject the null hypothesis. Likewise, if the value of z is 3.08, $H_0$ is still rejected.

In recent years, spurred by the availability of computer software, additional information is often reported on the "strength" of the rejection, or how confident we are in rejecting the null hypothesis. This method reports the probability (assuming that the null hypothesis is true) of getting a value of the test statistic at least as extreme as that obtained. This procedure compares the probability, called the **p-value,** with the significance level. If the p-value is smaller than the significance level, $H_0$ is rejected. If it is larger than the significance level, $H_0$ is not rejected. This procedure not only results in a decision regarding $H_0$, but it gives us insight into the strength of the decision. A very small p-value, say, .001, means that there is very little likelihood that $H_0$ is true. On the other hand, a p-value of .40 means that $H_0$ is not rejected, and we did not come very close to rejecting it.

To explain further, recall that for the efficiency ratings at Boeing, the computed value of z was 2.19. The decision was not to reject $H_0$ because the z of 2.19 fell in the nonrejection region between $-2.58$ and $+2.58$. The probability of obtaining a z-value of 2.19 or more is .0143, found by $.5000 - .4857$. To compute the p-value, we need to be concerned with values less than $-2.19$ and values greater than $+2.19$ (because there are rejection regions in both tails). The p-value is .0286, found by 2(.0143). The p-value of .0286 is greater than the significance level (.01), decided upon initially, so $H_0$ is not rejected.

### Self-Review 9–2

*The answers are at the end of the chapter.*

Refer to Self-Review 9–1.

1. Suppose this hypothesis-testing problem was changed to a one-tailed test. How would the null hypothesis be written symbolically if it read: "The population mean is equal to 6.0?"

2. How would the alternate hypothesis be written symbolically if it read: "The population mean is less than 6.0?"

3. Show the decision rule graphically. Show the regions of acceptance and rejection, and indicate the critical value.

### EXERCISES

*The answers to the odd-numbered exercises are at the end of the book.*

1. The following information has been released.

$$H_0: \mu = 50$$
$$H_1: \mu \neq 50$$

The sample mean is 49, and the sample size is 36. The population standard deviation is 5. Use the .05 significance level.

a. Is this a one-tailed or a two-tailed test?
b. State the decision rule.
c. Compute the value of the test statistic.
d. What is your decision regarding $H_0$?
e. Determine the p-value.

2.   The following information is available.

$$H_0: \mu = 10$$
$$H_1: \mu > 10$$

The sample mean is 12 for a sample of 36. The population standard deviation is 3. Use the .02 significance level.

   a.   Is this a one-tailed or a two-tailed test?
   b.   State the decision rule.
   c.   Compute the value of the test statistic.
   d.   What is your decision regarding $H_0$?
   e.   Determine the $p$-value.

3.   The manufacturer of the X-15 steel belted radial truck tire claims that the mean mileage the tire can be driven before the tread wears out is 60,000 miles. The standard deviation of the mileages is 5,000 miles. The Crosset Truck Company bought 48 tires and found that the mean mileage for their trucks is 59,500 miles. Is Crosset's experience different from that claimed by the manufacturer at the .05 significance level?

   a.   State the null hypothesis and the alternate hypothesis.
   b.   State the decision rule.
   c.   Compute the value of the test statistic.
   d.   What is your decision regarding $H_0$? Interpret the result. What is the $p$-value?

4.   The MacBurger restaurant chain claims that the mean waiting time of customers for service is normally distributed with a mean of 3 minutes and a standard deviation of 1 minute. The quality-assurance department found in a sample of 50 customers at the Warren Road MacBurger that the mean waiting time was 2.75 minutes. At the .05 significance level, is the mean waiting time less than 3 minutes?

   a.   State the null hypothesis and the alternate hypothesis.
   b.   State the decision rule.
   c.   Compute the value of the test statistic.
   d.   What is your decision regarding $H_0$? Interpret the result. What is the $p$-value?

## TESTING FOR THE POPULATION MEAN: LARGE SAMPLE, POPULATION STANDARD DEVIATION UNKNOWN

In the preceding problems, we knew $\sigma$, the population standard deviation. In most cases, however, it is unlikely that the population standard deviation would be known. Thus, $\sigma$ must be based on prior studies or estimated using the sample standard deviation, $s$. The population standard deviation in the following example is not known, so the sample standard deviation must be used to estimate $\sigma$. Formula (9–1) is revised slightly, with $s$ substituted for $\sigma$.

$$z = \frac{\bar{X} - \mu}{\dfrac{s}{\sqrt{n}}}$$

$$(9-2)$$

### ■ EXAMPLE

The Thompson's Discount Store chain issues its own credit card. The credit manager wants to find out if the mean monthly unpaid balance is $400. The level of significance is set at .05. A random check of 172 unpaid balances revealed the sample mean to be $407 and the standard deviation of the sample $38. Should the credit manager conclude that the population mean is greater than $400, or is it reasonable to assume that the difference of $7 ($407 − $400 = $7) is due to chance?

## ☑ SOLUTION

The null and alternate hypotheses are stated as:

$$H_0: \mu = \$400$$
$$H_1: \mu > \$400$$

Because the alternate hypothesis states a direction, a one-tailed test is applied. The critical value of $z$ is 1.645. The computed value of $z$ is 2.42, found by using formula (9–2):

$$z = \frac{\overline{X} - \mu}{\dfrac{s}{\sqrt{n}}} = \frac{\$407 - \$400}{\dfrac{\$38}{\sqrt{172}}} = \frac{\$7}{\$2.8975} = 2.42$$

The decision rule is portrayed graphically in the following chart.

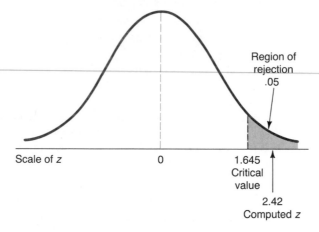

A value this large will occur less than 5 percent of the time. So the credit manager would reject the null hypothesis, $H_0$, that the mean unpaid balance is $400, in favor of $H_1$, which states that the mean is greater than $400.

The $p$-value in this case is the one-tailed probability that $z$ is greater than 2.42. It is .0078, found by .5000 − .4922.

## EXERCISES

*The answers to the odd-numbered exercises are at the end of the book.*

5.  A sample of 36 observations is selected from a normal population. The sample mean is 21, and the sample standard deviation is 5. Conduct the following test of hypothesis using the .05 significance level.

$$H_0: \mu = 20$$
$$H_1: \mu > 20$$

  a.  Is this a one-tailed or a two-tailed test?
  b.  State the decision rule.
  c.  Compute the value of the test statistic.
  d.  What is your decision regarding $H_0$?
  e.  What is the $p$-value?

6. A sample of 64 observations is selected from a normal population. The sample mean is 215, and the sample standard deviation is 15. Conduct the following test of hypothesis using the .03 significance level.

$$H_0: \mu = 220$$
$$H_1: \mu < 220$$

   a. Is this a one-tailed or a two-tailed test?
   b. State the decision rule.
   c. Compute the value of the test statistic.
   d. What is your decision regarding $H_0$?
   e. What is the $p$-value?

7. A recent national survey found that high school students watched an average (mean) of 6.8 videos per month. Do college students watch fewer videos per month? A random sample of 36 college students revealed that the mean number of videos watched last month was 6.2, with a standard deviation of 0.5. At the .05 significance level, can we conclude that college students watch fewer videos than high school students?
   a. State the null hypothesis and the alternate hypothesis.
   b. What is the decision rule?
   c. Compute the value of the test statistic.
   d. What is your decision regarding the null hypothesis? Interpret the result.
   (Source: "Students: 8.4 Hours of TV, Tunes, Talk," *USA Today,* June 25, 1991, p. A1.)

8. At the time she was hired as a server at the Grumney Family Restaurant, Beth Brigden was told, "You can average more than $20 a day in tips." Over the first 35 days she was employed at the restaurant, the mean daily amount of her tips was $24.85, with a standard deviation of $3.24. At the .01 significance level, can Ms. Brigden conclude that she is earning more than $20 in tips?
   a. State the null hypothesis and the alternate hypothesis.
   b. What is the decision rule?
   c. Compute the value of the test statistic.
   d. What is your decision regarding the null hypothesis? Interpret the result.

# HYPOTHESIS TESTING: TWO POPULATION MEANS

*This problem involves two means*

The following illustration, involving a test of significance between two population means, typifies a practical industrial problem.

Concrete blocks are to be used in the foundations of several buildings. The specifications state that the minimum arithmetic mean compressive strength of a sample of blocks must be 1,000 pounds per square inch (psi). If two companies submit samples of blocks that have mean compressive strengths over the minimum (1,000 psi), then the specifications state that one of two actions will be taken: (1) If a statistical test applied to the sampling results indicates that both samples could have come from the same, or identical, populations, the contract for the blocks will be divided equally. (2) If the sample statistics indicate that there are two populations involved, the company submitting the blocks having the higher compression strength will be awarded the contract.

A large construction project requires a large number of concrete blocks. The Stanblock Company and the Hicompressive Company have supplied blocks to the builder in the past, and both are interested in providing blocks for the new construction project. Before the blocks are tested for compressive strength, null and alternate hypotheses will be stated, a level of significance selected, an appropriate statistical test decided upon, and a decision rule formulated.

Follow the usual five-step testing procedure

**STEP 1. THE NULL HYPOTHESIS**  The null hypothesis is that there is *no* difference between the mean compressive strength of the concrete blocks manufactured by the Stanblock Company and the mean compressive strength of the concrete blocks manufactured by the Hicompressive Company. Thus, they constitute a single, overlapping population of concrete blocks. The alternate hypothesis, $H_1$, is that there *is* a significant difference between the two mean compressive strengths. Symbolically:

State $H_0$ and $H_1$

$$H_0: \mu_1 = \mu_2$$
$$H_1: \mu_1 \neq \mu_2$$

Since the alternative hypothesis does not specify direction (such as that the mean compressive strength of the blocks from Stanblock is greater than the mean of the Hicompressive blocks), a two-tailed test will be used.

$\alpha = .01$

**STEP 2. THE LEVEL OF SIGNIFICANCE**  The .01 level of significance has been chosen. This is the same as saying that the probability of committing a Type I error is .01.

**STEP 3. THE STATISTICAL TEST**  At least 30 blocks ($n_1$) will be selected at random from the Stanblock Company, and at least 30 will be selected from Hicompressive ($n_2$). As noted previously, when $n_1$ and $n_2$ are 30 or more, the samples are considered large, and the $z$ test can be applied as the test of significance. The selection process also meets one other assumption underlying the $z$ test, namely, independence. This means that the selection of one concrete block in no way affects the selection of another block. The $z$ test assumes that the data are at least interval-scaled. Of course, either of the two populations could be called number 1. However, once you have labeled a particular population number 1, you must continue to call it that.

The theory underlying the sampling distribution of $z$ (the critical value) will be examined briefly. It states in part:

> If a large number of independent random samples are selected from the two populations, the distribution of the differences between the two means divided by the standard error of the difference between the two means (the critical value) will approximate a normal distribution.

The corresponding formula for $z$ is:

$$z = \frac{\overline{X}_1 - \overline{X}_2}{\sqrt{\dfrac{s_1^2}{n_1} + \dfrac{s_2^2}{n_2}}} \qquad (9-3)$$

The test statistic

$$z = \frac{\overline{X}_1 - \overline{X}_2}{\sqrt{\dfrac{s_1^2}{n_1} + \dfrac{s_2^2}{n_2}}}$$

Difference between two sample means

Standard error of the difference between the two means

To illustrate this theory, assume that many samples of size 100 were taken from the Stanblock Company, and many samples of 100 blocks were taken from the Hicompressive Company. For the sake of simplicity, assume that the standard deviation for each sample was computed to be 20 psi. Then compute the $z$ values:

| Sample | $\bar{X}_1$ | $\bar{X}_2$ | $\bar{X}_1 - \bar{X}_2$ | $\dfrac{\bar{X}_1 - \bar{X}_2}{\sqrt{\dfrac{s_1^2}{n_1} + \dfrac{s_2^2}{n_2}}}$ | $z$ |
|---|---|---|---|---|---|
| 1 | 1,020 | 1,020 | 0 | $\dfrac{0}{2.8} =$ | 0 |
| 2 | 1,022 | 1,020 | +2 | $\dfrac{+2}{2.8} =$ | +0.71 |
| 3 | 1,030 | 1,021 | +9 | $\dfrac{+9}{2.8} =$ | +3.21 |
| 4 | 1,018 | 1,021 | −3 | $\dfrac{-3}{2.8} =$ | −1.07 |

Thus, in theory, if the two population means are equal and if the $z$ values of 0, +0.71, +3.21, −1.07, and so on were plotted, the distribution of these $z$ values would approximate a normal distribution.

Reference to the areas under the normal curve (Appendix D) reveals that about 68 percent of the $z$ values would fall within $0 \pm 1.0$; about 95 percent would fall within $0 \pm 1.96$; and about 99 percent would fall within $0 \pm 2.58$. (See Chart 9−6.)

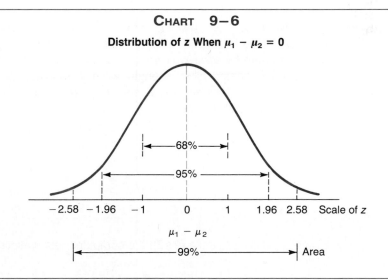

CHART   9−6

Distribution of z When $\mu_1 - \mu_2 = 0$

**STEP 4. THE DECISION RULE** Recall that the .01 level of significance was selected. A two-tailed test will be used (because the alternate hypothesis, $H_1$, does not state that the mean compressive strength of the blocks of one company is greater than the mean compressive strength of the other firm's blocks). It was noted in step 3 that about 99 percent of the computed $z$ values will be between −2.58 and

+2.58 under the assumption that there is no difference between the means of the two populations. So if the computed $z$ value does fall within the region between plus and minus 2.58, the null hypothesis is not rejected. Thus, it would be concluded that the difference between the two sample means is due to chance.

If the computed $z$ value is greater than 2.58, the null hypothesis is *rejected*. The null hypothesis would be rejected on the basis that it is highly unlikely that a computed $z$ value could be 2.58 or greater *by chance*. Of course, $H_0$ is also rejected if the computed $z$ is to the left of $-2.58$. This decision rule is portrayed in Chart 9–7.

---

### CHART 9–7

**Two-Tailed Test, Areas of Nonrejection and Rejection, with a Level of Risk of .01**

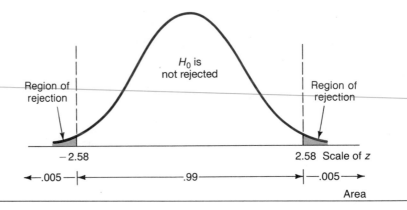

---

**STEP 5. THE SAMPLE RESULTS AND THE DECISION** A total of 81 blocks were selected at random from the Stanblock Company production, and the compressive strength of each was determined. The standard deviation of the sample and the mean compressive strength were computed. Sixty-four blocks from the Hicompressive Company were selected, and the same procedure was followed. The sample statistics are:

*Select samples from the two populations*

| Stanblock Company | Hicompressive Company |
|---|---|
| $\overline{X}_1 = 1{,}070$ psi | $\overline{X}_2 = 1{,}020$ psi |
| $n_1 = 81$ | $n_2 = 64$ |
| $s_1 = 63$ psi | $s_2 = 57$ psi |

Using formula (9–3), the computed test statistic ($z$) is 5.01. The calculations are:

$$z = \frac{\overline{X}_1 - \overline{X}_2}{\sqrt{\dfrac{s_1^2}{n_1} + \dfrac{s_2^2}{n_2}}}$$

$$= \frac{1{,}070 - 1{,}020}{\sqrt{\dfrac{(63)^2}{81} + \dfrac{(57)^2}{64}}} = \frac{50}{9.98827} = 5.01$$

Finally, a decision

The computed $z$ value of 5.01 falls in the area of rejection. The null hypothesis, $H_0$, is *rejected* at the .01 level, and the alternate hypothesis, $H_1$, is accepted. This indicates that $\mu_1 \neq \mu_2$. Thus, it is concluded that the population mean compressive strength of the blocks of the Stanblock Company is *not* equal to the population mean of the blocks of the Hicompressive Company. The difference in the sample means (1,070 and 1,020) is *not* due to chance. It is the function of the statistician to report the results of this test to management.

In this case the $p$-value is virtually 0, because the likelihood of a $z$-value greater than 5.01 or less than $-5.01$ is also virtually 0.

### Self-Review 9-3

*The answers are at the end of the chapter.*

Corngrow is a chemical specifically designed to add weight to corn during the growing season. Alternate acres were treated with Corngrow during the growing season. In order to determine whether or not Corngrow was effective, 400 ears of corn receiving the Corngrow treatment were selected at random. Each was weighed, and the mean weight was computed to be 16 ounces, with a standard deviation of 1 ounce. Likewise, 100 ears of untreated corn were weighed. The mean was 15.2 ounces, and the standard deviation was 1.2 ounces.

1. Using a one-tailed test and the .05 level, can we say that Corngrow was effective in adding weight to the corn?
2. Show the decision rule graphically.

## EXERCISES

*The answers to the odd-numbered exercises are at the end of the book.*

9. A sample of 40 observations is selected from one somewhat normal population. The sample mean is 102, and the sample standard deviation is 5. A sample of 50 observations is selected from a second somewhat normal population. The sample mean is 99, and the sample standard deviation is 6. Conduct the following test of hypothesis using the .04 significance level.

$$H_0: \mu_1 = \mu_2$$
$$H_1: \mu_1 \neq \mu_2$$

   a.   Is this a one-tailed or a two-tailed test?
   b.   State the decision rule.
   c.   Compute the value of the test statistic.
   d.   What is your decision regarding $H_0$?
   e.   What is the $p$-value?

10. A sample of 65 observations is selected from one somewhat normal population. The sample mean is 2.67, and the sample standard deviation is 0.75. A sample of 50 observations is selected from a second somewhat normal population. The sample mean is 2.59, and the sample standard deviation is 0.66. Conduct the following test of hypothesis using the .08 significance level.

$$H_0: \mu_1 = \mu_2$$
$$H_1: \mu_1 > \mu_2$$

    a.   Is this a one-tailed or a two-tailed test?

    b.   State the decision rule.

    c.   Compute the value of the test statistic.

    d.   What is your decision regarding $H_0$?

    e.   What is the $p$-value?

11.  The Metro Real Estate Association is preparing a pamphlet that they feel might be of interest to prospective home buyers in the Rossford and Northwood areas of the city. One item of interest is the length of time the seller occupied the home. A sample of 40 homes sold recently in Rossford revealed that the mean length of ownership was 7.6 years, with a standard deviation of 2.3 years. A sample of 55 homes in Northwood revealed that the mean length of ownership was 8.1 years with a standard deviation of 2.9 years. At the .05 significance level, can we conclude that the Rossford residents owned their homes for a shorter period of time? Use the five-step hypothesis-testing procedure.

12.  A study is made comparing the cost to rent a one-bedroom apartment in Cincinnati with the corresponding cost in Pittsburgh. A sample of 35 apartments in Cincinnati showed the mean rental rate to be $370 with a standard deviation of $30. A sample of 40 apartments in Pittsburgh showed the mean rate to be $380 with a standard deviation of $26. At the .05 significance level, is there a difference in mean rental rate between Cincinnati and Pittsburgh? Use the five-step hypothesis-testing procedure.

13.  A financial analyst is interested in comparing the turnover rates, in percent, for shares of oil-related stocks versus other stocks, such as GE and IBM. She referred to data set 2, column 7, in the back of this book and randomly selected 32 oil-related stocks and 49 other stocks. The mean turnover rate of oil-related stocks is 31.4 percent and the standard deviation 5.1 percent. For the other stocks, the mean rate was computed to be 34.9 percent and the standard deviation 6.7 percent. Is there a significant difference in the turnover rates of the two types of stock? The null and alternate hypotheses are:

$$H_0: \mu_1 = \mu_2$$
$$H_1: \mu_1 \neq \mu_2$$

    a.   Is this a one-tailed or a two-tailed test? What is your reasoning?

    b.   Using the .01 level of significance, what is the decision rule?

    c.   Determine the value of the test statistic, and arrive at a decision regarding $H_0$. Explain the meaning of your decision.

# Type II Errors, Operating Characteristic Curves, and Power Curves

## Type II Errors

Recall that the risk of a Type I error, also called the alpha risk of a statistical test, is *the probability of rejecting the null hypothesis when it is really true.* This risk is the same as the level of significance selected. As noted, the most commonly used levels are .05, .01, and .10.

$P(\text{Type II error}) = \beta$

    The risk of a Type II error, designated by $\beta$, is *the probability of accepting the null hypothesis as true when it is really not true.* To illustrate the computation of the probability of committing a Type II error, suppose a manufacturer purchases steel bars to make cotter pins. Past experience revealed that the true mean tensile strength of all incoming shipments is 10,000 psi and the standard deviation ($\sigma$) 400 psi.

    In order to make a decision about incoming shipments of steel bars, the manufacturer set up this rule for the quality-control inspector to follow: "Take a sample of 100 pieces of steel bars. If the mean ($\bar{X}$) strength falls between 9,922 psi and 10,078 psi, accept the lot. Otherwise the lot is to be rejected." Refer to Chart 9–8 and the graph labeled A. It shows the region where each lot is rejected and where it is not rejected. The mean of this distribution is designated $\mu_0$. The tails of the curve represent the probability of making a Type I error, that is, rejecting the incoming lot of steel bars when in fact it is a good lot, with a mean of 10,000 psi.

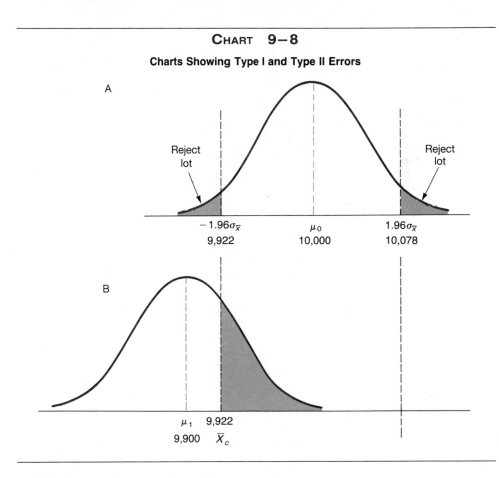

### CHART  9–8

**Charts Showing Type I and Type II Errors**

How is the probability of a Type II error computed? (Recall it is the probability of accepting an incoming lot as a "good lot" when in fact the mean is not 10,000 psi.)

### ◼ EXAMPLE

Suppose the unknown mean of an incoming lot, designated $\mu_1$, is really 9,900 psi. What is the probability that the quality-control inspector will fail to reject the shipment (a Type II error)?

### ☑ SOLUTION

Computations for $\beta$ (Type II error)

The probability of committing a Type II error, as represented by the colored area in Chart 9–8 in the graph labeled B, can be computed by determining the area under the normal curve that lies above 9,922 pounds. The calculation of the areas under the normal curve was discussed in Chapter 7. Reviewing briefly, it is necessary first to determine the probability of the sample mean falling between 9,900 and 9,922. Then this probability is subtracted from .5000 (which represents all the area beyond the mean of 9,900) to arrive at the probability of making a Type II error.

The number of standard units ($z$ values) between the mean of the incoming lot (9,900), designated $\mu_1$, and $\overline{X}_c$, representing the critical value for 9,922, is computed by:

$$z = \frac{\overline{X}_c - \mu_1}{\frac{\sigma}{\sqrt{n}}}$$

(9–4)

With $n = 100$ and $\sigma = 400$, the value of $z$ is 0.55:

$$z = \frac{\overline{X}_c - \mu_1}{\frac{\sigma}{\sqrt{n}}}$$

$$= \frac{9,922 - 9,900}{\frac{400}{\sqrt{100}}} = \frac{22}{40} = 0.55$$

The area under the curve between 9,900 and 9,922 (a $z$ of 0.55) is .2088 (from Appendix D).

The area under the curve beyond 9,922 pounds is .5000 − .2088, or .2912; this is the probability of making a Type II error—that is, accepting an incoming lot of steel bars when the population mean is 9,900 psi.

Using the methods illustrated by Charts 9–8B and 9–9C, the probability of accepting a hypothesis as true when it is actually false can be determined for any particular value of $\mu_1$.

Type II error probabilities are shown in the center column of Table 9–1 for selected values of $\mu$, given in the left column. The right column gives the probability of not making a Type II error.

---

### TABLE 9–1

**Probabilities of a Type II Error and Power Functions for $\mu_0 = 10,000$ Pounds and Selected Alternative Means, .05 Level of Significance**

| Selected alternative means (pounds) | Probability of Type II error ($\beta$) | Probability of not making a Type II error $(1 - \beta)$ |
|---|---|---|
| 9,820 | .0054 | .9946 |
| 9,880 | .1469 | .8531 |
| 9,900 | .2912 | .7088 |
| 9,940 | .6736 | .3264 |
| 9,980 | .9265 | .0735 |
| 10,000 | —* | — |
| 10,020 | .9265 | .0735 |
| 10,060 | .6736 | .3264 |
| 10,100 | .2912 | .7088 |
| 10,120 | .1469 | .8531 |
| 10,180 | .0054 | .9946 |

*It is not possible to make a Type II error when $\mu = \mu_0$.

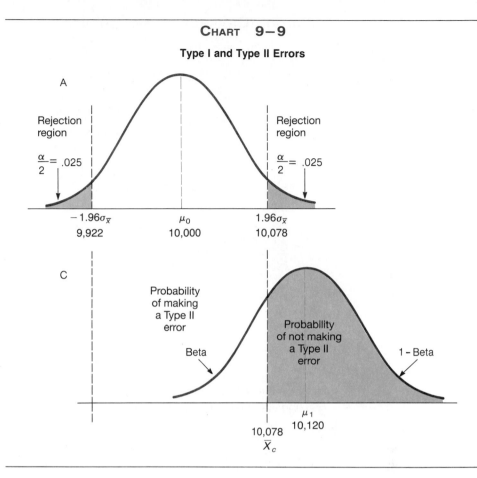

### CHART 9–9

**Type I and Type II Errors**

A

Rejection region

Rejection region

$\frac{\alpha}{2} = .025$

$\frac{\alpha}{2} = .025$

$-1.96\sigma_{\bar{x}}$     $\mu_0$     $1.96\sigma_{\bar{x}}$
9,922     10,000     10,078

C

Probability of making a Type II error

Beta

Probability of not making a Type II error

1 – Beta

10,078   $\mu_1$ 10,120
$\bar{X}_c$

Courtesy Republic Engineered Steels, Inc.

## Self-Review 9–4

*The answers are at the end of the chapter.*

Suppose the true mean of an incoming lot of steel bars is 10,120 psi. What is the probability that the quality control inspector will accept the bars as having a mean of 10,000 psi? (It sounds inconsistent that steel bars will be rejected if the tensile strength is higher than specified. However, it may be that the cotter pin has a dual function in an outboard motor. It many be designed not to shear off if the motor hits a small object, but to shear off if it hits a rock. Therefore, the steel should not be *too* strong.)

The white area in Chart 9–9C represents the probability of falsely accepting the hypothesis that the mean tensile strength of the incoming lot of steel is 10,000 psi. What is the probability of committing a Type II error?

## EXERCISES

*The answers to the odd-numbered exercises are at the end of the book.*

14. Refer to Table 9–1 and the example just completed. With $n = 100$, $\sigma = 400$, $\bar{X}_c = 9,922$, and $\mu_1 = 9,880$, verify that the probability of a Type II error is .1469.

15. Refer to Table 9–1 and the example just completed. With $n = 100$, $\sigma = 400$, $\bar{X}_c = 9,922$, and $\mu_1 = 9,940$, verify that the probability of a Type II error is .6736.

## OPERATING CHARACTERISTIC CURVES

The beta probabilities in Table 9–1 are used to plot an *operating characteristic curve* (see Chart 9–10).

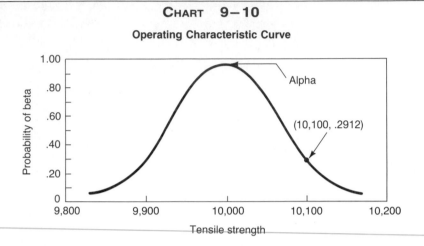

### CHART   9–10

**Operating Characteristic Curve**

The operating characteristic (OC) curve is a convenient way of showing graphically the probability of accepting a false hypothesis when it should have been rejected. The OC curves vary according to the sample size, the standard error of the mean, and the level of significance selected.

## POWER CURVES

Power curve

Referring to Table 9–1, the third column simply represents the probability of *not* committing a Type II error—that is, $1 - \beta$. These probabilities are the basis for the *power curve* shown in Chart 9–11.

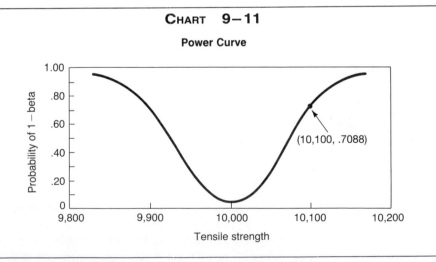

### CHART   9–11

**Power Curve**

What a power curve shows

The power curve is a graphic presentation of the probabilities of not committing a Type II error. The set of $1 - \beta$ probabilities in column 3 of Table 9–1 is called the *power function* of the test. The higher the probabilities, the greater the discriminatory power of the test. To explain, suppose the mean tensile strength of an incoming shipment of steel bars is 9,880 pounds per square inch. If a large number of samples of 100 bars were tested for tensile strength, about 85.31 percent of the samples would yield the correct decision to reject the incoming shipment. It should be noted that when the mean decreases or increases slightly, we cannot detect the change as readily as we can for a substantial change in the mean.

If management wishes to be more discriminatory, one possibility is to increase the size of the sample. Suppose the sample size were increased from 100 to 200 and the probability of $1 - \beta$ computed to be .9200. It can be said that the sample of size 200 yields more power to discover that the mean of the incoming shipment is not 10,000 psi (because .9200 > .8531).

## Chapter Outline

I. The objective of hypothesis testing is to check the validity of statements about a population parameter.
II. The procedures used in *hypothesis testing* are:
    A. State the null hypothesis $H_0$ and the alternate hypothesis $H_1$.
    B. Select the level of significance. The levels .10, .05, and .01 are three of the levels most commonly used. It is the probability of rejecting a true hypothesis and is the Type I error.
    C. Decide on the test statistic. The standard normal distribution using the test statistic $z$ is applied for large-sample tests of means.
    D. State the decision rule. Based on the sampling distribution, an area of acceptance and an area of rejection can be identified.
    E. Take a sample; make a decision. If the computed test statistic $z$ falls in the area of acceptance, do not reject $H_0$. Otherwise reject $H_0$ and accept $H_1$.
    F. The *p*-value is the probability that the test statistic in a hypothesis test is as extreme as the one obtained.
III. Testing a hypothesis about the population mean.
    A. *Example.* The 1990 census revealed that the mean age of the state's population is 41.3 years. Has the mean age changed since then?
    B. *Formula for z.* If the standard deviation of the population, $\sigma$, is known:

$$z = \frac{\overline{X} - \mu}{\dfrac{\sigma}{\sqrt{n}}}$$

(9–1)

    If $\sigma$ is unknown, substitute the sample standard deviation, $s$, when $s$ can reasonably be expected to approximate $\sigma$.
IV. Hypothesis testing: two means, large samples.
    A. *Objective.* Using the usual hypothesis-testing procedures, determine whether or not there is a difference between two population means using large samples (30 or more).
    B. *Formula for z:*

$$z = \frac{\overline{X}_1 - \overline{X}_2}{\sqrt{\dfrac{s_1^2}{n_1} + \dfrac{s_2^2}{n_2}}}$$

(9–3)

V.  Type I and Type II errors.
   A.  The probability of a Type I error, designated by $\alpha$, is the same as the level of significance selected. A Type I error probability of .05 is the probability that a true null hypothesis will be rejected.
   B.  The probability of a Type II error, designated by $\beta$, is the probability of accepting the null hypothesis as true when it is really not true.
   C.  The probability of a Type II error is computed from the following formula:

$$z = \frac{\bar{X}_c - \mu_1}{\dfrac{\sigma}{\sqrt{n}}}$$

# Exercises

*The answers to the odd-numbered exercises are at the end of the book.*

*Note:* It is suggested that the five-step hypothesis-testing procedure be followed for these exercises.

16.  A new weight-watching company, Weight Reducers International, advertises that those who join will lose, on the average, 10 pounds the first two weeks ($H_0: \mu = 10$, $H_1: \mu < 10$). A random sample of 50 people who joined the new weight reduction program revealed the mean loss to be 9 pounds. The standard deviation of the sample was computed to be 2.8 pounds. At the .05 level of significance, can we conclude that those joining Weight Reducers on average will lose less than 10 pounds? Determine the *p*-value.

Courtesy Dole® Food Company, Inc.

17.  Dole is concerned that the 16-ounce can of sliced pineapple is being overfilled. The quality-control department took a random sample of 50 cans and found that the arithmetic mean weight was 16.05 ounces, with a sample standard deviation of 0.03 ounces. At the 5 percent level of significance, can we conclude that the mean weight is greater than 16 ounces? Determine the *p*-value.

18.  The Peoria Board of Education wants to consider a new academic program funded by the U.S. Department of Education. In order to be eligible for the federal grant, the arithmetic mean income per household must not be more than $15,000. The board hired a research firm to gather the required data. In its report the firm indicated that the arithmetic mean income in the district is $17,000. They further reported that 75 households were surveyed and that the standard deviation of the sample was $3,000. Can the board argue that the difference between the mean income resulting from the sample survey and the mean specified by the Department of Education is due to chance (sampling)? Use the .05 level.

19.  A statewide real estate sales agency, Farm Associates, specializes in selling farm property in the state of Nebraska. Their records indicate that the mean selling time of farm property is 90 days. Because of recent drought conditions, they believe that the mean selling time is now greater than 90 days. A statewide study of 100 farms sold recently by the real estate agency is to be conducted in order to update their estimates. The random sample of 100 transactions revealed that the mean selling time was 94 days with a standard deviation of 22 days. At the .10 significance level, can we conclude that the selling time has increased?

20.  The mean gross annual incomes of certified tack welders are normally distributed with a mean of $30,000 and a standard deviation of $3,000. The shipbuilding association wishes to find out whether their tack welders earn more or less than $30,000 annually. The alternate hypothesis is that the mean is *not* $30,000. The .10 level of significance is to be used.

A sample of 120 welders employed in shipbuilding was selected. The sample mean was computed to be $30,500. Should $H_0$ be rejected?

21. The new director of the local office of the Utah state unemployment service thought the mean wait in line of 28 minutes to file a claim was much too long. Therefore, she instituted a number of changes to speed up the filing process. Three weeks later a sample of size 127 was selected. As each of the 127 unemployed people entered the office to file a claim, he or she was given a number with the time of arrival stamped on it. When the claim was filed, the time was again recorded. The mean wait was computed to be 26.9 minutes, and the standard deviation of the sample was 8 minutes. Shall we reject the null hypothesis of $\mu = 28$ in favor of the alternate hypothesis of $\mu < 28$ at the .02 level of significance?

22. The air force trains enlisted computer personnel at two bases—Cass AFB and Kingston AFB. A common final examination is administered. As part of an ongoing study of the training program, a comparison of the final test scores is to be made. Is there any significant difference in the final results of the two educational programs? Use the .04 significance level. Determine the $p$-value. Explain your decision to the committee studying the program.

|                          | Cass AFB | Kingston AFB |
|--------------------------|----------|--------------|
| Number sampled           | 40       | 50           |
| Mean score               | 114.6    | 117.9        |
| Sample standard deviation | 9.1      | 10.4         |

23. Corrigan Industries has been awarded a large contract to supply pipeline parts to Angus Oil, a company drilling in the Scotland-Ireland area. In the past, two subcontractors specializing in steel products have provided Corrigan Industries with high-quality supplies such as nuts, bolts, steel bars, and casing. One of the concerns of Corrigan is the delivery time of the two subcontractors, Jackson Steel and Alabama Distributors. The question to be explored is whether there is a difference in the delivery times of the two subcontractors.

Random samples from the files of Corrigan Industries revealed these statistics about delivery times:

|                                 | Jackson Steel | Alabama Distributors |
|---------------------------------|---------------|----------------------|
| Number in sample                | 45            | 50                   |
| Mean delivery time (days)       | 20            | 21                   |
| Sample standard deviation (days) | 4             | 3                    |

At the .05 significance level, is there a difference in the delivery times? Determine the $p$-value.

24. The Smith-Green motor for use in power tools is assembled on both the first and second shifts and requires critical attention and painstaking care to provide the motor with optimum operating conditions. Due to increasing complaints concerning motor performance, a review is made of the quality-control records for the motor rpms inspected on both shifts during the previous week. The records indicate that 64 units from the first shift had an average rpm value of 2,175, with a standard deviation of 12, and that 36 units from the second shift had an average value of 2,050, with a standard deviation of 20. Since the company wishes to spend its analysis efforts in the most productive way possible, it is interested in determining whether or not there is enough of a difference between the first and second shift values to concentrate efforts in this area. The company is willing to take a 10 percent risk of not recognizing when there is a significant difference.

25. A study was conducted of the annual incomes of beginning probation officers in metropolitan areas of less than 100,000 population and in metropolitan areas having more than 500,000 population. Some sample statistics:

| Sample statistic | Population less than 100,000 | Population more than 500,000 |
|---|---|---|
| Sample size | 45 | 60 |
| Sample mean | $31,290 | $31,330 |
| Sample standard deviation | $ 1,060 | $ 1,900 |

Test the hypothesis that the annual incomes of beginning probation officers in areas having more than 500,000 population are significantly greater than those paid in areas of less than 100.000. Use the 5 percent level of risk.

26. During the past several years, frequent checks of U.S. citizens returning from vacations abroad (of 21 days or less) indicated that they spend, on the average, $1,010 on such items as souvenirs, meals, and travel. A recent survey of size 400 by a nationally known research organization resulted in a sample mean of $1,250 and a sample standard deviation of $205. Test the hypothesis that $\mu = \$1,010$; that is, can the difference in the two means be attributed to sampling, or has there been a recent shift upward in the mean amount spent? Test at the .01 level.

27. The U.S. Public Health Service publishes the annual data tabulations, *Continuous Air Monitoring Projects,* which indicates that a large midwestern city has an annual mean level of sulfur dioxide of 0.12 (concentration in parts per million). Suppose that in order to reduce this excessively high concentration, many steel mills and others installed antipollution equipment. In 900 random checks made throughout the past year, it was found that the sample mean was 0.09 and the sample standard deviation 0.03. Assess the efforts of these industries. Use the .05 level.

28. After extensive tests, Tropico was adopted as the official paint for tropical rainy regions. Continuous tests are made in the laboratory by spraying water on test panels painted with Tropico. Records indicate that, on the average, the paint will withstand 200,000 tons of water before it loses its color. The standard deviation of the many panels tested was computed to be 12,000 tons of water. The Painto Manufacturing Company claims that its tropical paint (Painto II) is as good as the official paint, if not better. Painto II was tested by painting 144 test strips and giving them the usual water test. The arithmetic mean amount of water sprayed on the panels before they lost color was 190,000 tons. Although Painto II did not quite withstand the average of 200,000 tons, the manufacturers of Painto II claim that this difference was probably due to sampling. Using the .05 level, accept or reject their claim.

29. In a recent national survey the mean weekly allowance for a nine-year-old child from his or her parents was reported to be $3.65. A random sample of 45 nine-year-olds in northwestern Ohio revealed the mean allowance to be $3.69 with a standard deviation of $0.24. At the .05 significance level, is there a difference in the mean allowance nationally and the mean allowance in northwestern Ohio for nine-year-olds? (Source: "Making Allowances," *Vitality Digest,* June 1991, p. 16.)

30. The *fog index* is used to measure the reading difficulty of written text. Calculating the index involves the following steps: (1) Find the mean number of words per sentence. (2) Find the percent of words with three or more syllables. (3) The fog index is 40 percent of the sum of 1 and 2.

The fog index for a sample of 36 articles from a scientific journal showed a sample mean of 11.0 and a standard deviation of 2.65. A sample of 40 articles from trade publications showed a mean of 8.9 and a standard deviation of 1.64. At the .01 significance level, is the fog index in the scientific journals significantly higher? (Source: F. K. Shuptrine and D. D. McVicker, "Readability Levels of Magazine Advertisements," *Journal of Advertising Research,* vol. 21, no. 5, 1981, pp. 45–50.)

31. Clark Heter is an industrial engineer at Lyons Products. He would like to determine if there are more units produced on the afternoon shift than on the day shift. A sample of 54 day-shift workers showed that the mean number of units produced was 345 with a standard deviation of 21. A sample of 60 afternoon-shift workers showed that the mean number of units produced was 351 with a standard deviation of 28 units. At the .05 significance level, is the number of units produced on the afternoon shift larger?

32. One of the major U.S. automakers is studying its two-year/24,000-mile warranty policy. The warranty covers the engine, transmission, and drive train of all new cars for up to two years or 24,000 miles, whichever comes first. The manufacturer's quality-assurance department believes that the mean number of miles driven by owners is more than 24,000. A sample of 35 cars revealed that the mean number of miles driven was 24,421 with a standard deviation of 1,944 miles.

   a.  At the .05 significance level, conduct the following hypothesis test.

$$H_0: \mu = 24,000$$
$$H_1: \mu > 24,000$$

   b.  Using the .05 significance level, what is the largest sample mean for which $H_0$ is not rejected?

   c.  The population mean shifts to 25,000 miles. What is the probability that this change will not be detected?

33. A cola-dispensing machine is set to dispense 9.00 ounces of cola per cup, and a standard deviation of 1.00 ounces. The manufacturer of the machine would like to set it in such a way that for samples of 36, 5 percent of the sample means will be greater than the upper control limit, and 5 percent of the sample means will be less than the lower control limit.

   a.  At what value should the control limit be set?

   b.  What is the probability that if the population mean shifts to 8.9, this change will not be detected?

   c.  What is the probability that if the population mean shifts to 9.3, this change will not be detected?

34. The owners of the Franklin Park Mall are studying the shopping habits of their customers. From earlier studies the owners are under the impression that a typical shopper spends 0.75 hours at the mall, with a standard deviation of 0.10 hours. Recently the mall owners have added some specialty restaurants designed to keep shoppers in the mall longer. A consulting firm, Brunner and Swanson Marketing Enterprises, has been hired to evaluate the effects of the restaurants. A sample of 45 shoppers by Brunner and Swanson revealed that the mean time spent in the mall had increased to .80 hours.

   a.  Develop a test of hypothesis to determine if the mean time spent in the mall is more than 0.75 hours. Use the .05 significance level.

   b.  Suppose the mean shopping time actually increased from 0.75 hours to 0.77 hours. What is the probability this increase would not be detected?

   c.  When Brunner and Swanson reported the information in part b to the mall owners, they were upset with the statement that a survey could not detect a change from 0.75 to 0.77 hours of shopping time. How could this probability be reduced?

35. The following null and alternate hypotheses are given.

$$H_0: \mu = 50$$
$$H_1: \mu > 50$$

Suppose the population standard deviation is 10. The probability of a Type I error is set at .01 and the probability of a Type II error at .30. Assume the population mean shifts from 50 to 55. How large a sample is necessary to meet these requirements?

## COMPUTER DATA EXERCISES

36. Refer to the data set 1, which reports information on homes sold in Florida during 1990.

    a.  A recent article in an Arizona newspaper indicated that the mean selling price of homes in that state was $180,000. At the .05 significance level, can we conclude that homes sell for less than a mean of $180,000 in Florida? Determine the $p$-value.

    b.  The same article indicated that the mean size of the homes in Arizona is 2,000 square feet. Does this indicate that the homes in Florida are more than 2,000 square feet on the average? Use the .05 significance level.

37. Refer to data set 2, which reports information on 200 corporations in the United States.

    a.  If we consider this to be sample information, can we conclude that the mean corporation value of 10,304 ($ millions) came from a population with a mean of 12,000? Use a two-tailed test and $\alpha = .05$. Determine the $p$-value.

    b.  If we consider this to be sample information, can we conclude that the mean sales of 11,141 ($ millions) came from a population with a mean of 15,000? Use a two-tailed test and $\alpha = .05$. Determine the $p$-value.

## CHAPTER 9  EXAMINATION

*The answers are at the end of the chapter.*

For Questions 1–10, fill in the correct answer.

1.  A statement about the value of a population parameter is called a _____.

2.  If the null hypothesis is rejected, then the _____ hypothesis is accepted.

3.  The level of significance is equal to the probability of a Type _____ error.

4.  The probability that a false null hypothesis is accepted is called a Type _____ error.

5.  A value calculated from the sample information and used to make a decision regarding the null hypothesis is called the _____.

6.  The value that separates the region where the null hypothesis is rejected from the area where it is not rejected is called a _____.

7.  If the rejection region is all in the upper right tail, a _____-tailed test in applied.

8.  An operating characteristic curve is a graphic representation of the likelihood of accepting a _____ $H_0$.

9.  The equality sign in a test of hypothesis always occurs in the _____ hypothesis.

10. A sample of 50 observations is selected from a normal population, but the population standard deviation is not known. The _____ is substituted for the population standard deviation to conduct a test of hypothesis.

11. The Department of Agriculture reports that the mean weekly amount spent on food by families of four in the United States with children less than 12 years of age is $95 with a standard deviation of $20. The distribution of the amounts spent is normal. A sample of 50 families in rural Indiana revealed that the mean amount spent was $90 per week. At the .05 significance level, is the mean amount spent less in rural Indiana?

    a.  State the null hypothesis and the alternate hypothesis.

    b.  State the decision rule.

    c.  Compute the value of the test statistic.

    d.  State your decision regarding the null hypothesis. Interpret.

12. An official for the Iowa Department of Highways wants to compare the useful life, in months, of two brands of paint used for striping roads. The mean number of months that Cooper Paint lasted was 36.2 with a standard deviation of 1.14 months. The sample size was 35 road stripes. For King Paint, the mean number of months was 37.0 with a

standard deviation of 1.3 months. The sample size was 40 stripes. At the .01 significance level, is there a difference in the useful lives of the two paints?

a.  State the null hypothesis and the alternate hypothesis.

b.  State the decision rule.

c.  Compute the value of the test statistic.

d.  State your decision regarding the null hypothesis. Interpret.

13.  The Cains Pretzel Company sells its pretzels in 1-pound bags. The process that inserts the pretzels in the bags is normally distributed with a mean of 1.00 pounds and a standard deviation of 0.3 pounds. The quality-assurance department insists that the production line be stopped if the mean of a sample of 36 bags is greater than 1.098 pounds. What is the probability that if the population mean shifts from 1.00 pounds to 1.04 pounds, this change is not detected?

9–1   1. $H_0: \mu = 6.0,\ H_1: \mu \neq 6.0$.

   2. .05.

   3. $z = \dfrac{\bar{X} - \mu}{\dfrac{\sigma}{\sqrt{n}}}$

   4. Do not reject the null hypothesis if the computed $z$ value falls between $-1.96$ and $+1.96$.

   5. Yes. Computed $z = -2.56$, found by:

$$\frac{5.84 - 6.0}{\dfrac{.5}{\sqrt{64}}} = \frac{-.16}{.0625} = -2.56$$

   Reject $H_0$ at the .05 level. Accept $H_1$. The mean turnover rate is not equal to 6.0.

9–2   1. $H_0: \mu = 6.0$.

   2. $H_1: \mu < 6.0$.

   3. Note that the inequality sign ($<$) in the alternate hypothesis points in the direction of the region of rejection. To determine the critical value: $.5000 - .05 = .4500$. $z$ from Appendix D is about 1.645.

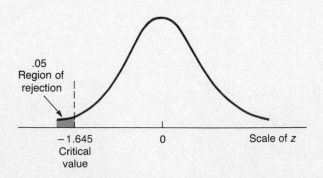

   .05
   Region of
   rejection

   $-1.645$
   Critical
   value

   0

   Scale of $z$

9–3   1. $H_0: \mu_1 = \mu_2,\ H_1: \mu_1 > \mu_2$. $H_0$ is rejected if computed $z$ is $>1.645$.

   Corngrow is effective. Computed $z$ is 6.15, found by:

$$z = \frac{16.0 - 15.2}{\sqrt{\dfrac{(1)^2}{400} + \dfrac{(1.2)^2}{100}}}$$

$$= \frac{0.8}{\sqrt{.0025 + .0144}}$$

$$= \frac{0.8}{0.13}$$

$$= 6.15$$

Since $6.15 > 1.645$ (critical value), the null hypothesis of $\mu_1 = \mu_2$ is rejected; the alternate, $\mu_1 > \mu_2$, is accepted.

   2.

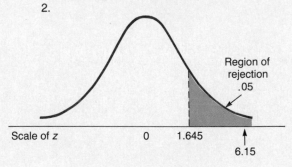

   Region of
   rejection
   .05

   Scale of $z$

   0   1.645

   6.15

9–4   .1469, found by determining the area under the curve between 10,078 and 10,120 (Chart 9–9C).

$$z = \frac{\bar{X}_c - \mu_1}{\dfrac{\sigma}{\sqrt{n}}}$$

$$= \frac{10,078 - 10,120}{\dfrac{400}{\sqrt{100}}}$$

$$= -1.05$$

The area under the curve for a $z$ of $-1.05$ is .3531 (Appendix D), and $.5000 - .3531 = .1469$, which is the area between 10,078 and 10,120.

**Answers**

## CHAPTER 9 EXAMINATION

1. Hypothesis.
2. Alternate.
3. I.
4. II.
5. Test statistic.
6. Critical value.
7. One.
8. False.
9. Null.
10. Sample standard deviation.
11. a. $H_0: \mu = 95$, $H_1: \mu < 95$.
    b. $H_0$ is rejected if $z < -1.645$.

    c. $z = \dfrac{90 - 95}{\dfrac{20}{\sqrt{50}}} = -1.77$

    d. $H_0$ is rejected. Those living in rural Indiana spend less than the national average.

12. a. $H_0: \mu_c = \mu_k$, $H_1: \mu_c \neq \mu_k$.
    b. $H_0$ is rejected if $z$ is less than $-2.58$ or greater than 2.58.

    c. $z = \dfrac{36.2 - 37.0}{\sqrt{\dfrac{(1.14)^2}{35} + \dfrac{(1.30)^2}{40}}} = \dfrac{-0.8}{.02817} = -2.84$

    d. The null hypothesis is rejected. There is a difference in the lengths of time the two brands of paint last.

13. $z = \dfrac{1.098 - 1.040}{\dfrac{0.3}{\sqrt{36}}} = \dfrac{0.058}{0.050} = 1.16$

    The probability that $z$ is less than 1.16 is .8770, found by .3770 + .5000. So the probability of a Type II error is .8770.

Communications—Courtesy Motorola Corporation

# TESTS OF HYPOTHESES: PROPORTIONS

When you have completed this chapter, you will be able to:

1. Define a proportion.

2. Test a hypothesis about a population proportion.

3. Test a hypothesis about two population proportions.

**C**hapter 9 began our study of hypothesis testing. Recall that a *hypothesis* is a statement, or assumption, made about an unknown population parameter, such as the population mean. The procedure followed to ultimately make a decision about the null hypothesis is called *hypothesis testing*. The procedure includes stating the null and alternate hypotheses; selecting a level of significance; choosing the test statistic; stating the decision rule; taking a sample from the population, or populations; computing sample statistics; and, based on these sample statistics, making a decision to reject or not to reject the null hypothesis. Testing a hypothesis using sample data is necessary because rarely can we study the entire population. The importance of the hypothesis-testing procedure is evident when, for example, we hypothesize the population mean to be 210 pounds, and the mean of the sample is 208 pounds. The test answers the question "Is the sample mean close enough to the hypothesized population mean so that we do not reject the null hypothesis?"

Chapter 9 dealt with interval and ratio levels of measurement—such variables as incomes, weights, and ages. This chapter will ask such questions as: Will 60 percent of the registered voters cast their votes for the Republican candidate? Are 10 percent of the electronic relays just received defective? Do 15 percent of the people 18 and older plan to purchase a new automobile this year? Is there a difference in the proportion of male executives and female executives willing to move to gain a promotion?

Note that a proportion is the result of counting something. We count the number of defectives, and we count the number of registered voters who plan to vote for the Republican candidate. Thus, hypothesis testing in this chapter involves the nominal level of measurement. We will first test a hypothesis about a single population proportion and then conduct a test of hypothesis about two population proportions.

## A TEST INVOLVING ONE POPULATION PROPORTION

> **Proportion**   A fraction, ratio, or percentage that indicates the part of the population or sample having a particular trait of interest.

As an example of a proportion, suppose 92 out of 100 surveyed favor daylight savings time during the summer. The sample proportion is 92/100, or .92, or 92 percent. If we let $\bar{p}$ stand for the sample proportion, then:

$$\bar{p} = \frac{\text{Number of successes in the sample}}{\text{Number sampled}} \qquad (10\text{-}1)$$

Some assumptions must be made and conditions met before testing a population proportion. To test a hypothesis about a population proportion, a random sample is chosen from the population. This is called the experiment. It is assumed that the binomial assumptions discussed in Chapter 6 are met: (1) the sample data collected are the result of counts; (2) an outcome of an experiment is classified into one of two mutually exclusive categories—a "success" or a "failure"; (3) the probability of a success stays the same for each trial; and (4) the trials are independent, meaning that the outcome of one trial does not affect the outcome of any other trial.

The test we will conduct shortly is appropriate when both $np$ and $n(1 - p)$ are greater than 5. $n$ is the sample size, and $p$ is the population proportion. In addition, $n$

*$np$ and $n(1 - p)$ must be greater than 5*

should be large. Researchers disagree on how large $n$ should be; some say 30, some say 50, and others say 100. For the purposes of this book, the sample size should be at least 50.

This test is introduced here because it is a special extension of the test presented in the previous chapter and also is widely used. This test is a good example of the case wherein the normal probability distribution is applied to approximate a binomial probability distribution with a great deal of accuracy.

## A ONE-TAILED TEST

### ■ EXAMPLE

Suppose prior elections in a state indicated that it is necessary for a candidate for governor to receive at least 80 percent of the vote in the northern section of the state to be elected. The incumbent governor is interested in assessing his chances of returning to office and plans to have a survey conducted consisting of 2,000 registered voters in the northern section of the state.

*Will the incumbent governor be reelected?*

Using the hypothesis-testing procedure, assess the governor's chances of reelection.

### ☑ SOLUTION

The following test of hypothesis can be conducted because both $np$ and $n(1 - p)$ exceed 5. Also, $n$ is greater than 50. In this problem $n = 2,000$ and $p = .80$ ($p$ is the percent of the vote in the northern part of the state, or 80 percent, needed to be elected). Thus, $np = 2,000 (.80) = 1,600$, and $n(1 - p) = 2,000(1 - .80) = 400$. Both 1,600 and 400 are greater than 5.

*Five-step hypothesis-testing procedure*

The five-step hypothesis-testing procedures developed in Chapter 9 will be followed to arrive at a decision, namely:

1. Statements regarding the null hypothesis and alternate hypothesis are made.
2. The level of significance is given.
3. A statistical test is chosen.
4. A decision rule is stated.
5. A sample is selected, and, based on the sample results, the null hypothesis is either rejected or not rejected.

*Hypotheses*

**STEP 1** The null hypothesis, $H_0$, is that the population proportion $p$ is .80 (or more). The alternate hypothesis, $H_1$, is that the proportion is less than .80. From a practical standpoint, the incumbent governor is concerned only when the sample proportion is less than .80. If it is equal to or greater than .80, he will have no problem; that is, the sample data would indicate he will probably be reelected. These hypotheses are written symbolically as:

$$H_0: p = .80$$
$$H_1: p < .80$$

$H_1$ states a direction. Thus, the test is one-tailed, with the inequality sign pointing to the tail of the curve containing the region of rejection.

*Level of significance*

**STEP 2** The level of significance is .05. This is the likelihood of committing a Type I error—that is, it is the probability that a true hypothesis will be rejected.

Test statistic is z

**STEP 3**   z is the appropriate statistic, found by:

$$z = \frac{\bar{p} - p}{\sigma_p}$$
                                                        (10–2)

where:

    $p$    is the population proportion.

    $\bar{p}$    is the sample proportion.

    $\sigma_p$    is the standard error of the population proportion. It is computed by $\sqrt{p(1 - p)/n}$, so the formula for z becomes:

$$z = \frac{\bar{p} - p}{\sqrt{\dfrac{p(1 - p)}{n}}}$$
                                                        (10–3)

where $n$ is the sample size.

Critical value

**STEP 4**   The critical value or values of z form the dividing point or points between the regions where $H_0$ is rejected and where it not rejected. Since the alternate hypothesis states a direction, this is a one-tailed test. The sign of inequality points to the left, so only the left half of the curve is used. (See Chart 10–1.) Alpha was given as .05 in step 2. This probability is in the left tail and determines the region of rejection. The area between zero and the critical value is .4500, found by .5000 – .0500. Referring to Appendix D and searching for .4500, we find the critical value of z to be about 1.645. The decision rule is therefore: Reject the null hypothesis and accept the alternate hypothesis if the computed value of z falls to the left of –1.645; otherwise do not reject $H_0$.

## CHART   10–1

**Rejection and Nonrejection Regions for the .05 Level of Significance, One-Tailed Test**

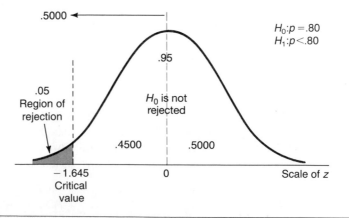

Sample, then accept or reject $H_0$

**STEP 5**   Sample and make a decision with respect to $H_0$. The sample survey of 2,000 potential voters in the northern part of the state revealed that 1,550 planned to vote for the incumbent governor. Is the proportion of .775 (found by 1,550/2,000) "close enough" to .80 to conclude that the difference is due to chance?

In this problem:

$\bar{p}$   is .775, the proportion in the sample who plan to vote for the governor.

$n$   is 2,000, the number of voters surveyed.

$p$   is .80, the hypothesized population proportion.

$z$   is a normally distributed test statistic when the hypothesis is true and the other assumptions are true.

$\bar{p}$ = sample proportion;
$p$ = population proportion

Using formula (10–3) and computing $z$:

$$z = \frac{\bar{p} - p}{\sqrt{\dfrac{p(1 - p)}{n}}} = \frac{\dfrac{1,550}{2,000} - .80}{\sqrt{\dfrac{.80(1 - .80)}{2,000}}} = \frac{.775 - .80}{\sqrt{.00008}} = \frac{-.025}{.0089443} = -2.80$$

Sample survey reveals incumbent won't be reelected.

The computed value of $z$ $(-2.80)$ is in the rejection region, so the null hypothesis is rejected at the .05 level. The difference of 2.5 percentage points between the sample percent (77.5 percent) and the hypothesized population percent in the northern part of the state necessary to carry the state (80 percent) is statistically significant. It is probably not due to sampling variation. To put it another way, the evidence at this point does not support the claim that the incumbent governor will return to the governor's mansion for another four years.

As pointed out in Chapter 9, this is a "statistical" decision. The incumbent governor may agree with this decision. He may also disagree with the findings and call for another survey of voters—or take some other action.

## A TWO-TAILED TEST

### ■ EXAMPLE

Test at the .01 level the statement that 55 percent of those families who plan to purchase a vacation residence in Florida want a condominium. The null hypothesis is $p = .55$, and the alternate is $p \neq .55$. A random sample of 400 families who said they planned to buy a vacation residence reveals that 228 families want a condominium. What decision should be made regarding the null hypothesis?

Courtesy Florida Department of Commerce, Division of Tourism

### ☑ SOLUTION

The $z$ test can be used because both $np$ and $n(1 - p)$ exceed 5: $np = 400(.55) = 220$, and $n(1 - p) = 400(1 - .55) = 180$.

Since no direction was given in the alternate hypothesis, the test is two-tailed. The decision rule is shown graphically in Chart 10–2.

In this problem:

$\bar{p}$   is .57, the proportion is the sample who want a condo $(228/400 = .57)$.

$n$   is 400, the number in the sample.

$p$   is .55, the claimed percent of the population who want a condominium.

Computing $z$:

$$z = \frac{\bar{p} - p}{\sqrt{\dfrac{p(1 - p)}{n}}} = \frac{.57 - .55}{\sqrt{\dfrac{.55(1 - .55)}{400}}} = \frac{.02}{.0248747} = .80$$

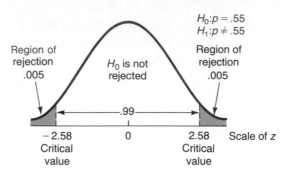

CHART    10–2

**Areas of Rejection and Nonrejection, .01 Level of Significance, for a Two-Tailed Test**

Chart showing decision rule, two-tailed test, $\alpha = .01$

$H_0: p = .55$
$H_1: p \neq .55$

Region of rejection .005

$H_0$ is not rejected

Region of rejection .005

.99

−2.58
Critical value

0

2.58
Critical value

Scale of $z$

Do not reject $H_0$, because 0.80 does not fall in the rejection region

The null hypothesis that the true proportion is .55 is not rejected at the .01 level. Although there is a difference between the hypothesized proportion (.55) and the sample proportion (.57), it can be attributed to sampling error. We conclude that, of the families who plan to buy a vacation residence in Florida, 55 percent plan to buy a condominium.

### Self-Review 10–1

*The answers are at the end of the chapter.*

This claim is to be investigated at the .02 level: "Forty percent of those persons who retired from an industrial job before the age of 60 would return to work if a suitable job were available." Seventy-four persons out of the 200 sampled said they would return to work.

1. Can the $z$ test be used? Why or why not?
2. State the null and alternate hypotheses.
3. Show the decision rule graphically.
4. Compute $z$, and arrive at a decision.

## EXERCISES

*The answers to the odd-numbered exercises are at the end of the book.*

1. The following hypotheses are given.

$$H_0: p = .70$$
$$H_1: p > .70$$

A sample of 100 observations revealed $\bar{p} = .75$. At the .05 significance level, can the null hypothesis be rejected?

   a.  State the decision rule.
   b.  Compute the value of the test statistic.
   c.  What is your decision regarding the null hypothesis?

2. The following hypotheses are given.

$$H_0: p = .40$$
$$H_1: p \neq .40$$

A sample of 120 observations revealed $\bar{p} = .30$. At the .05 significance level, can the null hypothesis be rejected?

a.   State the decision rule.

b.   Compute the value of the test statistic.

c.   What is your decision regarding the null hypothesis?

*Note:* It is recommended that the five-step hypothesis-testing procedure be used in solving the following problems.

3.   The National Safety Council reports that 52 percent of American turnpike drivers are men. A sample of 300 cars traveling eastbound on the Ohio Turnpike yesterday revealed that 170 were driven by men. At the .01 significance level, can we conclude that a larger proportion of men were driving on the Ohio Turnpike than the national statistics indicate? (Source: "Who Does the Driving," *Vitality,* June 1991, p. 7.)

4.   A recent article in *USA Today* reported that a job awaits only one in three new college graduates. The major reasons given were an overabundance of college graduates and a weak economy. A survey of 200 recent graduates from your school revealed that 80 students had jobs. At the .02 significance level, can we conclude that a larger proportion of students at your school have jobs? (Source: "Jobs Await 1 in 3 New Grads," *USA Today,* June 24, 1991, p. A1.)

5.   Chicken Delight claims that 90 percent of its orders are delivered within 30 minutes of the time the order is placed. A sample of 100 orders revealed that 82 were delivered within the promised time. Is Chicken Delight's claim valid at the .10 level of significance? Let $H_1$ be $p < .90$.

6.   Research at the University of Toledo indicates that 50 percent of the students change their major area of study after their first year in the program. A random sample of 100 students in the College of Business revealed that 48 had changed their major area of study after their first year of the program. Has there been a significant decrease in the proportion of students who change their major after the first year in the program? Test at the .05 level of significance. (Source: Unpublished study, Office of Institutional Research, University of Toledo.)

# A TEST INVOLVING THE DIFFERENCE BETWEEN TWO POPULATION PROPORTIONS

Cases involving two proportions

Several typical cases involving two population proportions follow.

A mock model of a proposed new automobile was shown to two groups of 150 persons each. One group consisted of a random sample of people between 18 and 25 years of age, and the other group consisted of a random sample of persons more than 50 years old. Eighty percent of the younger group rated the styling satisfactory, but only 50 percent of the older group gave it a similar rating. In evaluating the market potential of this proposed automobile, is it reasonable to expect that it would appeal primarily to younger persons? Or is it possible that this difference of 30 percentage points could be due to sampling, that is, might not the two age groups in the population like the proposed automobile equally well?

Two new high-speed machines designed by different companies are being considered for purchase. One factor in the final choice is the percent defective that each machine produces. A sample of the output of one of the machines revealed that 6 percent were defective. A sample of the output of the other machine indicated that 10 percent of the total were defective. Is the machine with the 6 percent scrap significantly better than the one with the 10 percent scrap? Or is there a chance that the two machines are producing an equal percent defective?

An agricultural example

Comstock hybrid corn seed was divided into two piles before planting. The seeds in one pile were soaked with a chemical claimed to significantly reduce corn borers. The other pile was not treated. The two types of seed corn were planted in alternate rows and clearly identified. Samples from each row were selected at random during the harvest season, and it was discovered that 20 percent of the treated corn had corn borers and 80 percent of the untreated sample had borers. Was the treatment effective?

*A marketing example*

Manelli has developed a new perfume named Heavenly. A number of comparison tests indicate that the perfume has a good market potential. The marketing and advertising departments, however, want to plan their strategy so as to reach and impress the largest possible segment of the buying public. One of the questions is whether the perfume is preferred by a larger proportion of younger women or a larger proportion of older women. There are two populations, therefore—a population consisting of young women and one consisting of older women. A standard smell test is used. Women selected at random are asked to sniff several perfumes in succession, including the one they most frequently use and, of course, Heavenly. The names of the perfumes are known only to the person administering the test. Each woman selects the perfume she likes best.

## A TWO-TAILED TEST

The procedures followed in making a statistical decision involving the difference between two proportions will now be examined. The perfume problem has been selected.

*The usual five steps*

**STEP 1: A STATEMENT OF $H_0$ AND $H_1$**   In this problem the null hypothesis is: "There is no difference between the proportion of young women who prefer Heavenly and the proportion of older women who prefer it." If the proportion of young women in the population is designated as $p_1$ and the proportion of older women is $p_2$, then the null hypothesis is $p_1 = p_2$. The alternate hypothesis is that the two proportions are not equal, or $p_1 \neq p_2$. (Note again that the lower-case letter $p$ represents the population proportions.)

**STEP 2: THE LEVEL OF SIGNIFICANCE**   It was decided to use the .05 level.

**STEP 3: THE STATISTICAL TEST**   Plans are to take a random sample of 100 young women, designated $n_1$, and a sample of 200 older women, designated $n_2$. Thus, both $np$ and $n(1 - p)$ for the two groups are greater than 5. Also, each of the two sample sizes is greater than 50. Hence, the $z$ distribution is the appropriate test statistic. It approximates the standard normal distribution and is computed by:

$$z = \frac{\bar{p}_1 - \bar{p}_2}{\sqrt{\dfrac{\bar{p}_c(1 - \bar{p}_c)}{n_1} + \dfrac{\bar{p}_c(1 - \bar{p}_c)}{n_2}}} \qquad (10-4)$$

where:

$n_1$   is the number of young women selected in the sample.

$n_2$   is the number of older women selected in the sample.

$\bar{p}_c$   is the *weighted* mean of the two sample proportions, computed by:

$$\bar{p}_c = \frac{\text{Total number of successes}}{\text{Total number in samples}} = \frac{X_1 + X_2}{n_1 + n_2} \qquad (10-5)$$

$X_1$ is the number of young women (sample 1) who prefer Heavenly.

$X_2$ is the number of older women (sample 2) who prefer Heavenly.

$\bar{p}_c$ = combined (pooled) estimate

$\bar{p}_c$ is generally referred to as the *pooled estimate of the population proportion*. This is the best estimate of the proportion of women in the population who prefer Heavenly, and it does not consider whether they are old or young. Hence, it is a "pooled," or "combined," estimate.

**STEP 4: THE DECISION RULE**  Recall that the null hypothesis, $H_0$, states that $p_1 = p_2$, and the alternate hypothesis, $H_1$, is $p_1 \neq p_2$. Since $H_1$ does not state any direction (such as $p_1 < p_2$), the test is *two-tailed*. Thus, the critical values for the .05 level are $-1.96$ and $+1.96$. As before, if the computed $z$ value falls in the region between $+1.96$ and $-1.96$, the null hypothesis is not rejected. If that does occur, it is assumed that any difference between the two sample proportions is due to chance variation (see Chart 10–3).

---

CHART   10–3

**Two-Tailed Test, Areas of Rejection and Nonrejection, .05 Level of Significance**

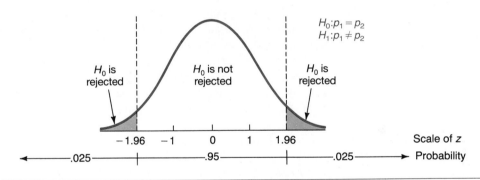

---

**STEP 5: THE DECISION**  A total of 100 young women were selected at random, and each was given the standard smell test. Twenty of the 100 young women chose Heavenly as the perfume they liked best.

Twenty percent of younger women prefer Heavenly

$X_1$ is the number preferring Heavenly = 20.

$n_1$ is the number in sample = 100.

$$\bar{p}_1 = \frac{X_1}{n_1} = \frac{20}{100} = .20$$

Two hundred older women were selected at random, and each was given the same standard smell test. Of the 200 older women, 100 preferred Heavenly.

Fifty percent of older women prefer Heavenly

$X_2$ is the number preferring Heavenly = 100.

$n_2$ is the number in sample = 200.

$$\bar{p}_2 = \frac{X_2}{n_2} = \frac{100}{200} = .50$$

The pooled or weighted proportion, $\bar{p}_c$, is computed using formula (10−5).

$$\bar{p}_c = \frac{X_1 + X_2}{n_1 + n_2} = \frac{20 + 100}{100 + 200} = \frac{120}{300} = .40$$

**Pooled estimate is .40**

Note the weighted proportion of .40 is closer to .50 than to .20. (More older women than younger women were sampled.)

Computing $z$ using formula (10−4):

$$z = \frac{\bar{p}_1 - \bar{p}_2}{\sqrt{\dfrac{\bar{p}_c(1 - \bar{p}_c)}{n_1} + \dfrac{\bar{p}_c(1 - \bar{p}_c)}{n_2}}}$$

$$= \frac{.20 - .50}{\sqrt{\dfrac{.40(1 - .40)}{100} + \dfrac{.40(1 - .40)}{200}}}$$

$$= \frac{-.30}{.06} = -5.00$$

**Reject $H_0$**

The computed $z$ of −5.00 falls in the area of rejection, that is, to the left of −1.96. Therefore, the null hypothesis is rejected at the .05 level of significance. To put it another way, the hypothesis that the proportion of young women in the population who prefer Heavenly is equal to the proportion of older women in the population who prefer Heavenly is rejected at the .05 level. It is highly unlikely that such a large difference between the two sample proportions (.30) could be due to chance (sampling).

**Unlikely that difference between .20 and .50 is due to sampling error**

The probability of committing a Type I error is .05, which is the same as the level of significance selected before the project started. This indicates there is a 5 percent risk of rejecting the true hypothesis that $p_1 = p_2$.

## A ONE-TAILED TEST

### ■ EXAMPLE

Guymon, Inc. is testing two high-speed shearing machines. One is manufactured by Sushi Industries, the other by Cordell. Sushi claims that its machine produces a lower percent of defective pieces. To investigate this claim, 200 sheared pieces of copper were selected at random from the output of the Sushi machine. A count revealed that 14 were defective. A similar experiment with the Cordell machine revealed that 10 of the 100 selected at random were defective. At the .05 level, does the statistical evidence support Sushi's claim?

### ☑ SOLUTION

The null hypothesis is: The percent defective for the Sushi machine, $p_1$, is equal to the Cordell percent defective, $p_2$. This is written $H_0$: $p_1 = p_2$. The alternate hypothesis is that $p_1$ is less than $p_2$, written $H_1$: $p_1 < p_2$. Since the alternate hypothesis states a direction, the test is one-tailed. The inequality points to the direction of the region of rejection. Use the .05 level of significance.

Using the same procedure as before, the decision rule would be: Reject the null hypothesis if the computed value of $z$ falls in the area of the curve to the left of −1.645. Otherwise, do not reject the null hypothesis.

$\bar{p}_c = .08$

The pooled estimate of the proportion, $\bar{p}_c$, is .08, found by using formula (10–5):

$$\bar{p}_c = \frac{\text{Total number of successes}}{\text{Total number sampled}} = \frac{X_1 + X_2}{n_1 + n_2} = \frac{14 + 10}{200 + 100} = .08$$

where:

$X_1$  is the number of defective pieces produced by the Sushi machine in the sample (14).

$n_1$  is the number of pieces produced by the Sushi machine in the sample (200).

$X_2$  is the total number of defective pieces produced by the Cordell machine in the sample (10).

$n_2$  is the total number of pieces produced by the Cordell machine in the sample (100).

If, in fact, there is no difference between the machines, this pooled estimate of 8 percent is the best estimate of the proportion defective.

Applying formula (10–4) to compute $z$:

$$z = \frac{\bar{p}_1 - \bar{p}_2}{\sqrt{\dfrac{\bar{p}_c(1 - \bar{p}_c)}{n_1} + \dfrac{\bar{p}_c(1 - \bar{p}_c)}{n_2}}}$$

$$= \frac{.07 - .10}{\sqrt{\dfrac{.08(1 - .08)}{200} + \dfrac{.08(1 - .08)}{100}}}$$

$$= \frac{-.03}{\sqrt{.001104}} = -.90$$

Since $-.90$ is to the right of $-1.645$ the null hypothesis is not rejected at the .05 level of significance. The difference of .03 between the two sample proportions can be attributed to chance. Based on these sample data, Sushi cannot claim that its shearing machine produces fewer defectives.

---

### Self-Review 10–2

*The answers are at the end of the chapter.*

Of 150 adults who tried Smack Smack, a new candy, 87 rated it excellent. Of 200 children sampled, 123 rated it excellent. Using the .10 level of significance, can we conclude that there is a difference in the proportion of adults versus children who rate the candy excellent?

1. What is the null hypothesis? What is the alternate hypothesis?

2. What is the probability of a Type I error?

3. Is this a one-tailed test or a two-tailed test?

4. What is the critical value?

5. Should the null hypothesis be rejected or not rejected?

# EXERCISES

*The answers to the odd-numbered exercises are at the end of the book.*

7. The stated hypotheses are:

$$H_0: p_1 = p_2$$
$$H_1: p_1 > p_2$$

A sample of 100 observations from the first population indicated that $X_1$ is 70. A sample of 150 observations from the second population revealed $X_2$ to be 90. Use the .05 significance level to test the hypothesis.

  a. State the decision rule.

  b. Compute the pooled proportion.

  c. Compute the value of the test statistic.

  d. What is your decision regarding the null hypothesis?

8. The hypotheses $H_0$ and $H_1$ are:

$$H_0: p_1 = p_2$$
$$H_1: p_1 \neq p_2$$

A sample of 200 observations from the first population revealed $X_1$ to be 170. A sample of 150 observations from the second population resulted in an $X_2$ of 110. Use the .05 significance level.

  a. State the decision rule.

  b. Compute the pooled proportion.

  c. Compute the value of the test statistic.

  d. What is you decision regarding the null hypothesis?

*Note:* It is recommended that the five-step hypothesis-testing procedure be used in solving the following problems

9. The Damon family owns a large grape vineyard in western New York state. The grapevines must be sprayed at the beginning of the growing season to protect against various insects and diseases. Two new insecticides have just been marketed: Pernod 5 and Action. To test their effectiveness, three long rows were selected and sprayed with Pernod 5, and three others were sprayed with Action. When the grapes ripened, 400 of the vines treated with Pernod 5 were checked for infestation. Likewise, a sample of 400 vines sprayed with Action were checked. The results are:

| Insecticide | Number of vines checked (sample size) | Number of infested vines |
|---|---|---|
| Pernod 5 | 400 | 24 |
| Action | 400 | 40 |

At the .05 significance level, can we say that there is a difference in the proportion of vines infested using Pernod 5 as opposed to Action?

10. The Roper Organization conducted identical surveys in 1970 and 1990. One question asked women was, "Are most men basically kind, gentle, and thoughtful?" The 1970 survey revealed that out of the 3,000 women surveyed 2,010 said that they were. In 1990 1,530 out of the 3,000 women surveyed thought that men were kind, gentle, and thoughtful. At the .05 level, can we conclude that women think men are less kind, gentle, and thoughtful in 1990 compared with 1970? (Source: "Men Rate Less," *Detroit Free Press*, April 26, 1990, 15.)

11. A nationwide sample of influential Republicans and Democrats were asked as a part of a comprehensive survey whether they favored lowering the environmental standards so that high-sulfur coal could be burned in coal-fired power plants. The results were:

| | Republicans | Democrats |
|---|---|---|
| Number sampled | 1,000 | 800 |
| Number in favor | 200 | 168 |

At the .02 level of significance, can we conclude that there is a larger proportion of Democrats in favor of lowering the standards?

12. The research department at the home office of New Hampshire Insurance conducts ongoing research on the causes of automobile accidents, the characteristics of the drivers, and so on. A random sample of 400 policies written on single persons was selected. It was discovered that in the previous three-year period, 120 of them had at least one accident. Similarly, a sample of 600 policies written on married persons revealed that 150 had been in at least one accident. At the .05 level, is there a significant difference in the proportions of single and married persons having an accident during a three-year period?

Courtesy Insurance Institute for Highway Safety

# CHAPTER OUTLINE

I.  Procedure for testing a hypothesis involving a proportion.
   A.  In order to safely use this particular test for one proportion, make sure that $np$ and $n(1 - p)$ are greater than 5. For two proportions, $np$ and $n(1 - p)$ for both samples must exceed 5.
   B.  Follow the usual five-step hypothesis-testing procedure.
      1. State the null and alternate hypotheses.
      2. Decide on the level of significance.
      3. Choose an appropriate statistical test.
      4. Formulate a decision rule.
      5. Take a sample, or samples, and based on the computed $z$ value(s), arrive at a decision to reject or fail to reject the null hypothesis.
II. To test a population proportion:
   A.  State the null hypothesis, $H_0$. For example, it might be $p = .42$. The alternate hypothesis, $H_1$, could be either $p \neq .42$, $p < .42$, or $p > .42$, where $p$ is the population proportion. Summarizing the possibilities:

$$H_0: p = .42 \qquad H_0: p = .42 \qquad H_0: p = .42$$
$$H_1: p \neq .42 \qquad H_1: p < .42 \qquad H_1: p > .42$$

B.    Compute $z$:

$$z = \frac{\bar{p} - p}{\sqrt{\dfrac{p(1 - p)}{n}}}$$

(10–3)

where:

$\bar{p}$   is the proportion in the sample possessing the trait.

$n$   is the size of the sample.

$p$   is the hypothesized population proportion.

III.   A test for the difference between two population proportions involves:
A.    Stating the null hypothesis, $H_0: p_1 = p_2$. The alternate hypothesis, $H_1$, could be either $p_1 \neq p_2$, $p_1 < p_2$, or $p_1 > p_2$.
B.    Computing $z$:

$$z = \frac{\bar{p}_1 - \bar{p}_2}{\sqrt{\dfrac{\bar{p}_c(1 - \bar{p}_c)}{n_1} + \dfrac{\bar{p}_c(1 - \bar{p}_c)}{n_2}}}$$

(10–4)

where:

$n_1$   is the total number in the first sample.

$n_2$   is the total number in the second sample.

$\bar{p}_c$   is the pooled estimate of the population proportion, found by:

$$\bar{p}_c = \frac{X_1 + X_2}{n_1 + n_2}$$

(10–5)

$X_1$   is the number possessing the trait in the first sample.

$X_2$   is the number possessing the trait in the second sample.

# Exercises

*The answers to the odd-numbered exercises are at the end of the book.*

*Note:* It is recommended that the five-step hypothesis-testing procedure be used in solving the following problems.

13.   Tina Dennis is the chief accountant for Meek Industries. She believes that the current cash-flow problems of MI are due to the slow collection of accounts receivable. She believes that more than 60 percent of the accounts are in arrears more than three months. A sample of 200 accounts showed that 140 were more than three months old. At the .01 significance level, can we conclude that more than 60 percent of the accounts are in arrears for more than three months?

14.   The policy of the Suburban Transit Authority is to add a bus route if more than 55 percent of the potential commuters indicate they would use the particular route. A sample of 70 commuters revealed that 42 would use a proposed route from Bowman Park to the downtown area. Does the Bowman-to-downtown route meet the STA criteria? Use the .05 significance level.

15.   In order to attract substantial advertising money, a new morning television soap opera must guarantee advertising agencies that 20 percent of the viewing audience watch it. "Ways of Our Children," a new soap opera, had a marketing research firm conduct a survey of 2,000 viewers. Out of the 2,000 surveyed, 390 watch "Ways of Our Children"

Courtesy Chicago Transit Authority

at least once a week. At the .05 level of significance, can it be concluded that less than 20 percent of the viewing audience watch the soap? Or is the sample proportion close enough to the required proportion (20 percent) to state that the difference between the two percentages could be due to sampling error?

16. Past experience at Wills Travel Agency indicated that 44 percent of those persons who wanted the agency to plan a vacation for them wanted to go to Europe. During the most recent busy season, a sampling of 1,000 plans was selected at random from the files. It was found that 480 persons wanted to go to Europe on vacation. Has there been a significant shift upward in the percentage of persons who want to go to Europe? Test at the .05 level.

Courtesy Southern California Edison Company

17. Brayfeld Pharmaceuticals, the manufacturer of *New* Go-Away, a tablet claimed to prevent headaches, is convinced that it is more effective than the old Go-Away, which it will replace. To evaluate the manufacturer's conviction, 200 persons were asked to take *New* Go-Away. During the trial period, 180 of them did not have a headache. A different group of 300 took the old Go-Away, and 261 had no headaches during the trial period. Test the manufacturer's conviction that *New* Go-Away is more effective at the .05 level.

18. Suppose a random sample of 1,000 American-born citizens revealed that 198 favored resumption of diplomatic relations with Cuba. Similarly, 117 of a sample of 500 foreign-born citizens favored it. Test at the .05 level that there is no difference in the proportion of American-born citizens and the proportion of foreign-born citizens who favor resumption of diplomatic relations with Cuba. $H_1$ states that there is a difference, that is, the two proportions are not equal.

19. Fisher, a manufacturer of stereophonic equipment, introduces the new models of receivers, tape cassettes, and other audio components in the fall. Retail dealers are surveyed immediately after the Christmas selling season regarding their stock on hand of each piece of equipment. It has been discovered that unless 40 percent of the new equipment ordered by the retailers in the fall had been sold by Christmas, immediate production cutbacks are needed.

   The manufacturer has found contacting all of the dealers after Christmas by mail rather frustrating because many of them never respond. This year the manufacturer selected 80 dealers at random and telephoned them regarding the new Model TX 3040 receiver. It was discovered that 38 percent of those receivers had been sold. Since 38 percent is less than 40 percent, does this mean that immediate production cutbacks are needed—or can this difference of 2 percent be attributed to sampling? Test at the .05 level.

20. The Ottawa Restaurant Association is studying the dining habits of married couples. A sample of 100 couples in which the wife is employed full-time outside the home revealed that 70 went out for at least one dinner meal last week. A sample of 150 couples in which the wife does not work full-time outside the home revealed that 90 went out for at least one dinner meal last week. At the .05 significance level, can the association conclude that a higher percentage of couples in which the wife works full-time eat the dinner meal out?

21. Is there a difference in the proportion of college men versus college women who smoke at least a pack of cigarettes a day? A sample of 500 men at Northern State University revealed that 70 smoked at least a pack of cigarettes a day. A sample of 400 women revealed that 72 smoked at least one pack of cigarettes a day. At the .05 significance level is there a difference between the proportion of men and the proportion of women that smoke at least a pack of cigarettes a day, or can the difference in the proportions be attributed to sampling error?

22. A newly developed breakfast cereal is to be test-marketed by a sample of consumers. After several weeks, 795 consumers out of the 1,060 consumers in the test group said they planned to purchase the cereal if it is marketed.

a.  The marketing department discovered that 76 percent of the test group must state that they will purchase the cereal, or other newly developed product, for the cereal or product to be profitable. Do the sample results indicate that the cereal will be profitable, if marketed? Use an alpha risk of .01.

b.  There is also interest in determining whether there is any significant difference in the preference for the cereal by those living on the east coast and those living on the west coast. The responses were tabulated as follows:

|                   | East Coast | West Coast |
|-------------------|------------|------------|
| Total responses   | 632        | 428        |
| Plan to purchase  | 468        | 327        |

Using the .01 significance level, conduct a test of hypothesis. State the null and alternate hypotheses, the alpha risk, and so on. Transmit your decision to management.

## COMPUTER DATA EXERCISE

23.  Refer to data set 1, which reports information on homes sold in Florida during 1990.

a.  Determine the proportion of homes that have a pool. At the .05 significance level, can we conclude that more than half of the homes sold have a pool?

b.  Determine the proportion of homes that have an attached garage. At the .05 significance level, can we conclude that more than 60 percent of the homes sold have a garage?

## CHAPTER 10  EXAMINATION

*The answers are at the end of the chapter.*

For Questions 1 through 5, indicate whether the statement is true or false. If it is false, correct the statement.

1.  The proportion of successes in a sample is designated $p$.

2.  To conduct a test of hypothesis about a proportion, the assumptions of the normal distribution must be met.

3.  To conduct a test of hypothesis about a proportion, both $np$ and $n(1 - p)$ must be greater than 5.

4.  A pooled or weighted sample proportion is determined by adding the number of successes in both samples and dividing by the total number of items sampled.

5.  Tests of proportions must be one-tailed.

Use the five-step hypothesis-testing procedure for problems 6 and 7.

6.  The high-speed automatic Walden machine mass-produces a small washer. Past experience reveals that 70 percent of each day's production is perfect. Most of the remaining washers have a rough burr, which must be filed off before the washers can be inserted in the assembly. In an attempt to increase the percent of production that is perfect, the machine was modified somewhat. A sample of 100 washers was then checked, and it was found that 72 percent were perfect. The boss thinks that there has been no change. The plant manager, however, believes that the production of the modified machine has definitely improved product quality; that is, the percent of perfect washers is greater than 70. Is the plant manager correct? Test at the .02 level.

7.  A committee studying employer-employee relations at Carson Industries proposed that a rating system be adopted. Each employee would rate his or her immediate supervisor; in

turn, the supervisor would rate each employee. In order to find out if there is a difference between the reactions of the office personnel and those of plant personnel regarding the proposal, 120 office personnel and 160 plant personnel were selected at random. Seventy-eight of the office personnel and 90 of the plant personnel were in favor of the proposal. Is there sufficient evidence to support the belief that the proportion of office personnel in favor of the proposal is greater than that of the plant personnel? Use the .05 level.

# Answers

10–1 1. Yes, because both $np$ and $n(1-p)$ exceed 5: $np = 200(.40) = 80$, and $n(1-p) = 200(.60) = 120$.

2. $H_0: p = .40$.
   $H_1: p \neq .40$.

3.

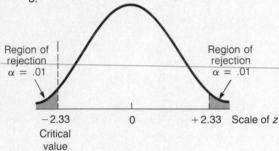

Region of rejection $\alpha = .01$

Region of rejection $\alpha = .01$

−2.33    0    +2.33    Scale of $z$

Critical value

4. $z = -0.87$, found by:

$$z = \frac{.37 - .40}{\sqrt{\dfrac{.40(1 - .40)}{200}}}$$

$$= \frac{-.03}{\sqrt{.0012}} = -0.866$$

Do not reject the null hypothesis at the .02 level.

10–2 1. $H_0: p_1 = p_2$; $H_1: p_1 \neq p_2$
   2. .10.
   3. Two-tailed.
   4. −1.645 and +1.645.
   5. Not rejected. Computed $z = -0.66$.

$$\bar{p}_c = \frac{87 + 123}{150 + 200} = \frac{210}{350} = .60$$

Then:

$$z = \frac{.58 - .615}{\sqrt{\dfrac{.60(.40)}{150} + \dfrac{.60(.40)}{200}}}$$

$$= \frac{-.035}{\sqrt{.0028}} = -0.66$$

# Answers

# Chapter 10 Examination

1. True.
2. False. The binomial assumptions must be met.
3. True.
4. True.
5. False. They can be either one-tailed or two-tailed.
6. $H_0: p = .70$, $H_1: p > .70$. $H_0$ is rejected if $z > 2.05$. The computed value of $z$ is 0.44, found by

$$z = \frac{.72 - .70}{\sqrt{\dfrac{(.70)(.30)}{100}}} = \frac{.02}{\sqrt{.0021}}$$

$H_0$ is not rejected. The difference of .02 is due to chance. The boss is correct.

7. $H_0: p_1 = p_2$; $H_1: p_1 > p_2$. Critical value is 1.645. Computed $z$ is 1.48, found by:

$$z = \frac{.65 - .5625}{\sqrt{\dfrac{.60(1 - .60)}{120} + \dfrac{.60(1 - .60)}{160}}}$$

Pooled estimate is .60, found by $(78 + 90)/(120 + 160)$. Since 1.48 is less than 1.645, $H_0$ is not rejected.

## Section Three

# A Review of Chapters 8—10

Why sampling is often imperative

This section is a review of the major concepts and terms introduced in Chapters 8 through 10. Chapter 8 explored why it is almost impossible to study every item, or individual, in some populations. It would be too expensive and time-consuming, for example, to contact and record the annual incomes of all U.S. bank officers. To estimate a population parameter, therefore, we sample the population. A sample is just part of the population. Care must be taken to ensure that every member of our population has a chance of being selected; otherwise the conclusions might be biased.

Sampling methods

A number of probability-type sampling methods can be used, including *simple random, systematic, stratified,* and *cluster sampling.*

Sampling error

Regardless of the sampling method selected, it is unlikely that a sample mean will be exactly the same as the population mean. The difference between this sample statistic and the population parameter is the *sampling error.* If the means of all possible samples of a specified size selected from a population are organized in a distribution, called the *sampling distribution of the means,* the mean of the sampling distribution will be equal to the population mean. If the sample size is large enough, the distribution of sample means is approximately normally distributed.

These concepts are the essence of the *central limit theorem,* which is the theoretical foundation of *statistical inference.* Briefly, statistical inference is concerned with inferring something about a population parameter based on a sample statistic. Chapter 8 discussed one facet of statistical inference—*estimation.* Chapters 9 and 10 concentrated on the other facet of statistical inference—*hypothesis testing.*

Point estimate

We may want to estimate a particular population parameter. For example, if, based on a sample, we estimate that the mean annual income of all professional house painters (the population) is $35,300, that estimate is called a *point estimate.* If we state that the population mean is probably in the interval between $35,200 and $35,400, that estimate is called an *interval estimate.* The two end points ($35,200 and $35,400) are called the *confidence limits* for the population mean.

Interval estimate
Confidence limits

Hypothesis testing: A systematic procedure followed to arrive at a decision

A *hypothesis* is a statement about a population parameter or parameters. One such statement is: "The mean net weight of Campbell's canned green pea soup is 319 grams." Using a systematic procedure called *hypothesis testing,* we decide whether or not to reject this hypothesis. The procedure calls for stating the null hypothesis and the alternate hypothesis, selecting a level of significance and the appropriate test statistic, formulating a decision rule, taking a sample, and (based on the sample results) not rejecting or rejecting the null hypothesis. Chapter 9 presented tests of hypotheses about one population mean and two population means. Chapter 10 presented tests about one population proportion and two population proportions.

# GLOSSARY

## CHAPTER 8

**Bias**   A possible consequence if certain members of the population are denied the chance to be selected for the sample. As a result, the sample may not be representative of the population.

**Central limit theorem**   If the size of the sample is sufficiently large, the distribution of the sample means will approximate a normal distribution regardless of the shape of the population. Further, the mean of the sampling distribution will equal the population mean.

**Cluster sampling**   A method often used to lower the cost of sampling if the population is dispersed over a wide geographic area. The area is divided in some way into smaller units (counties, precincts, blocks, etc.) called primary units. Then a few primary units are chosen, and a random sample is selected from each unit.

**Interval estimate**   The interval within which a population parameter probably lies, based on sample information. Example: Based on sample data, we might state that the population mean probably lies in the interval between 1.9 and 2.0 pounds.

**Point estimate**   A single number computed from a sample and used to estimate a population parameter. Example: If the sample mean is 1,020 psi, it is the best estimate of the tensile strength of the population.

**Probability sample**   A sample of items or individuals chosen so that each member of the population has a known chance of being included in the sample.

**Sampling distribution of the means**   A probability distribution consisting of all possible sample means of a given size selected from the population and their corresponding probabilities of occurrence.

**Sampling error**   The difference between a sample statistic and the corresponding population parameter. Example: The sample mean income is $22,100; the population mean is $22,000. The sampling error is $22,100 − $22,000 = $100. This error can be attributed to sampling, that is, chance.

**Simple random sampling**   A sampling scheme in which every member of the population has the same chance of being selected.

**Stratified random sampling**   A population is first divided into subgroups called strata. A sample is then chosen from each stratum. If, for example, the population of interest consisted of all undergraduate students, the sample design might call for sampling 62 freshmen, 51 sophmores, 40 juniors, and 39 seniors.

**Systematic random sampling**   Assuming that the population is arranged in some way, such as alphabetically, by height, or in a file drawer, a starting point is selected. Then every $k$th member becomes a member of the sample. If a sample design called for interviewing every ninth household on Main Street starting with 932 Main, the sample would consist of households at 932 Main, 941 Main, 950 Main, . . . .

## CHAPTERS 9 AND 10

**Critical value**   A number, designated $z$, that is the dividing point between the region where the null hypothesis is not rejected and the region where it is rejected. For a one-tailed test, there is only one critical value, such as −1.96. For a two-tailed test, there are two critical values—one in each tail—such as −1.96 and +1.96.

**Hypothesis**   A statement about the value of a population parameter. Examples: 40.7 percent of all persons 65 years old and older live alone. The mean number of persons per family is 3.33.

**Hypothesis testing**   A procedure based on sample evidence and probability theory used to determine whether the hypothesis stated is a reasonable statement and cannot be rejected or is unreasonable and should be rejected.

**One-tailed test**   Used when the alternate hypothesis states a direction, such as $H_1$: $\mu > 40$. Rejection region is only in one tail (the right tail).

**Proportion**   A fraction or percentage of a sample or a population having a particular trait. If 5 out of 50 in a sample liked a new cereal, the proportion is 5/50, or .10.

**Two-tailed test**   Used when the alternate hypothesis does not state a direction, such as $H_1$: $\mu \neq \$75$, read "the population mean is not equal to \$75." There is a region of rejection in each tail.

# EXERCISES

*The answers to the odd-numbered exercises are at the end of the book.*

## PART I—MULTIPLE CHOICE

1. Each new employee is given an identification number. The personnel files are arranged sequentially starting with employee number 0001. To sample the employees, the number 0153 was first selected. Then numbers 0253, 0353, 0453, and so on became members of the sample. This type of sampling is called:
   a. Simple random sampling.
   b. Systematic sampling.
   c. Stratified random sampling.
   d. Cluster sampling.
   e. None of these is correct.

2. You divide a precinct into blocks. Then you select 12 blocks at random and concentrate your sampling efforts in those 12 blocks. This type of sampling is called:
   a. Simple random sampling.
   b. Systematic random sampling.
   c. Stratified random sampling.
   d. Cluster sampling.
   e. Nonprobability sampling.

3. "Sampling error" as used in statistical inference:
   a. Indicates that a Type I error has been made.
   b. Indicates that a Type II error has been made.
   c. Is the difference between a sample statistic and its corresponding population parameter.
   d. Indicates that the $z$ test must be used.
   e. None of these is correct.

4. Of 180 calculators sampled, 5 were defective. The proportion of successes is found by:
   a. $\dfrac{\text{Number of successes in sample}}{\text{Number sampled}}$
   b. $n = \left(\dfrac{z \cdot s}{E}\right)^2$
   c. $\dfrac{s}{\sqrt{n}}$
   d. $\dfrac{X_1 + X_2}{n_1 + n_2}$
   e. None of these is correct.

5. The endpoints of a confidence interval are called:
   a. Confidence levels.
   b. The test statistics.

   c.    The degrees of confidence.

   d.    The confidence limits.

   e.    None of these is correct.

6.  If a one-tailed test is used, and if the level of significance is .01, the critical value is either:

   a.    −1.96 or +1.96.

   b.    −1.645 or +1.645.

   c.    −2.58 or +2.58

   d.    0 or 1.

   e.    None of these is correct.

7.  A Type II error is committed if we:

   a.    Reject a true null hypothesis.

   b.    Accept a true null hypothesis.

   c.    Reject a true alternate hypothesis.

   d.    Accept both the null and alternate hypotheses at the same time.

   e.    None of these is correct.

8.  The hypotheses are $H_0$: $\mu = 240$ inches of pressure; $H_1$: $\mu \neq 240$ inches of pressure.

   a.    A one-tailed test is being applied.

   b.    A two-tailed test is being applied.

   c.    A three-tailed test is being applied.

   d.    The wrong test is being applied.

   e.    None of these is correct.

9.  The .01 level is used in an experiment, and a one-tailed test is applied. Computed z is −1.8. This indicates:

   a.    $H_0$ should not be rejected.

   b.    We should reject $H_0$ and accept $H_1$.

   c.    We should take a larger sample.

   d.    We should have used the .05 level of significance.

   e.    None of these is correct.

10.  To test a hypothesis involving proportions, both $np$ and $n(1 - p)$ should:

   a.    Exceed 30.

   b.    Exceed 5.

   c.    Lie in the range from 0 to 1.

   d.    Be at least −2.58.

   e.    None of these is correct.

## PART II—PROBLEMS

11.  A machine is programmed to produce tennis balls so that the mean bounce is 36 inches when the ball is dropped from a platform. The supervisor suspects that the mean bounce has changed and is less than 36 inches. An experiment is to be conducted using 42 tennis balls. The 5 percent significance level is to be used to test the hypothesis. The sample mean was computed to be 35.5 inches and the standard deviation of the sample 0.9 inches. Is the supervisor correct?

12.  Research by the Illinois Banking Corp. home office revealed that only 8 percent of the corporation's customers wait more than five minutes to do their banking during rush hours. They consider this a reasonable percent and will add no new part-time tellers unless the proportion becomes significantly greater than 8 percent. One branch manager believes that more than 8 percent of customers wait more than five minutes, and she requested additional help during rush hours. The home office decided to test the

hypothesis at the 1 percent level. A random sample of 100 incoming customers were timed, and it was found that 10 waited more than five minutes.

   a.   State the null and alternate hypotheses.
   b.   State the level of significance.
   c.   Give the formula for the test statistic.
   d.   State the decision rule.
   e.   Do the necessary calculations, and arrive at a decision with respect to the null hypothesis.
   f.   Explain the difference between the sample proportion and the hypothesized population proportion.

13. You are interested in updating a study of the errors in the company's invoices. The study made several years ago revealed that 5 percent of the invoices contained at least one error. You decide to use the .05 level, and the error in your prediction is not to exceed plus or minus 2 percent of the population proportion.

   a.   How many invoices should be examined?
   b.   Suppose the sample size you computed in part a would be too time-consuming. What could you do to reduce the sample size?

14. You want to determine the mean amount sports fans spend on snacks and drinks at a professional football game. You decide to use the .01 level and estimate the mean within plus or minus 20 cents. How many fans should be sampled if the standard deviation of a pilot survey was computed to be 50 cents?

15. A firm with plants in two metropolitan areas adjusts the hourly wages paid their employees in one area if there is a significant difference between the two population mean hourly wages. Based on the following sample data, is there a difference between the two mean wages? To solve, answer these questions:

   a.   What are the null and alternate hypotheses?
   b.   Is this a one-tailed or a two-tailed test? Why?
   c.   What is the formula for the test statistic?
   d.   Using the .05 level, what is the critical value or values?
   e.   What is your decision regarding the null hypothesis?

| Metropolitan area | Sample mean hourly wage | Sample standard deviation | Number in sample |
|---|---|---|---|
| Cartersville | $10.92 | $0.78 | 180 |
| Kingston | $11.05 | $0.39 | 200 |

16. A wholesale automobile parts distributor has warehouses in Chicago and Dallas. Although perpetual inventories are taken, the number of items on the shelves and the number stored in the computer records are sometimes off by a few items. For example, if computer records indicate there are 122 boxes of GE #5 headlight bulbs on the shelf, but a count revealed 124, the computer record for that item is in error. An experiment is to be conducted to find out if there is a difference between the proportion of items in error in Chicago and the proportion of items in error in the Dallas warehouse.

   a.   State the null and alternate hypotheses.
   b.   Is this a one-tailed or a two-tailed test? Why?
   c.   Give the formula for the test statistic.
   d.   Using the .05 level, state the decision rule.
   e.   A sample of 200 automotive items in the Chicago warehouse revealed that the computer records and the count did not differ for 180 of the 200 items. A random sample of 100 items in the Dallas warehouse revealed that the computer records and the shelf count did not differ for 87 of the 100 items. What decision should be made regarding the null hypothesis? Explain.

*Aerospace—Courtesy Martin Marietta Corporation*

# STUDENT'S *t* TEST: SMALL SAMPLES

When you have completed this chapter, you will be able to:

GOALS

1. Describe the major characteristics of Student's *t* distribution.

2. Test a hypothesis involving one population mean, given that the population standard deviation is unknown and the sample size is small.

3. Test a hypothesis involving the difference between two population means where the population standard deviations are unknown and the sample sizes are small.

4. Conduct a test of hypothesis for the difference between a set of paired observations, given that the sample sizes are small.

**C**hapter 9 began our study of hypothesis testing. In that chapter the five-step hypothesis-testing procedure was described. The standard normal distribution—the $z$ distribution—was used as the test statistic. To employ the $z$ distribution, the population must be normal and the population standard deviation known. In many real-world situations, the population is approximately normal, but the population standard deviation is not known. In this case $s$, the sample standard deviation, is substituted for $\sigma$. If the size of the sample is at least 30, the results are deemed satisfactory.

What if the sample size is less than 30 observations and $\sigma$ is unknown? For these research projects, the $z$ distribution is not the appropriate test statistic. The Student $t$, or the **t distribution,** as it is usually called, is used as the test statistic.

We will first examine the characteristics of the $t$ distribution. Then three hypothesis-testing situations will be discussed.

## CHARACTERISTICS OF STUDENT'S $t$ DISTRIBUTION

The characteristics of Student's $t$ distribution will be examined before its application in testing a hypothesis is considered. It was developed by William S. Gossett, a brewmaster for the Guinness Brewery in Ireland, who published it in 1908 using the pen name "Student." Gossett was concerned with the behavior of

$$\frac{\overline{X} - \mu}{\dfrac{s}{\sqrt{n}}}$$

when $s$ had to be used as an estimator of $\sigma$. He was especially worried about the discrepancy between $s$ and $\sigma$ when $s$ was calculated from a very small sample. The $t$ distribution and the standard normal distribution are shown graphically in Chart 11–1. Note particularly that the $t$ distribution is flatter, more "spread out," than the normal $z$ distribution.

The following characteristics of the $t$ distribution are based on the assumption that the population of interest is normal, or nearly normal.

---

### CHART   11–1

**The Standard Normal Distribution and Student's $t$ Distribution**

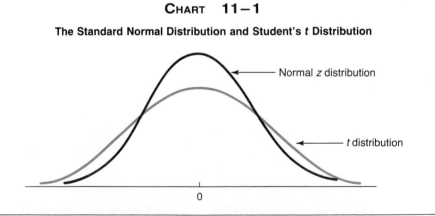

Normal $z$ distribution

$t$ distribution

0

---

Similarities between
$t$ and $z$

1. It is, like the $z$ distribution, a continuous distribution.
2. It is, like the $z$ distribution, bell-shaped and symmetrical.

3. There is not one *t* distribution, but rather a "family" of *t* distributions. All have the same mean of zero, but their standard deviations differ according to the sample size, *n*. There is a *t* distribution for a sample size of 20, another for a sample size of 22, and so on.

*Difference between t and z*

4. The *t* distribution is more spread out and flatter at the center than is the standard normal distribution (see Chart 11–1). However, as the sample size increases, the curve representing the *t* distribution approaches the standard normal distribution.

*t distribution spread out more and flatter at the peak than z*

As noted, Student's *t* distribution has a greater spread than the *z* distribution. As a result, the critical values of *t* for a given level of significance are larger in magnitude than the corresponding *z* critical values. Chart 11–2 shows the rejection region for a one-tailed test using the .05 level of significance. The critical value for the *z* test is 1.645, but for *t* it is 2.132. (Determining the critical *t* value of 2.132 will be discussed shortly.)

---

CHART    11–2

**Regions of Rejection for the *z* and *t* Distributions, .05 Level, One-Tailed Test**

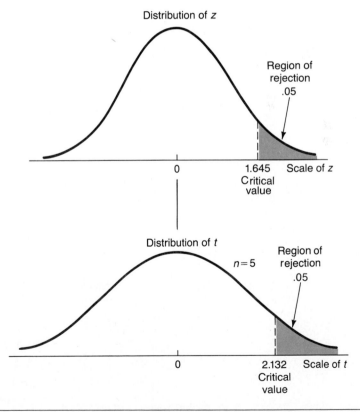

---

Of what importance is the fact that the critical value for a given level of significance is greater for small samples than for large samples? The following statements hold true for small samples (which employ the *t* distribution): (1) The confidence interval will be wider than for large samples using the *z* distribution. (2) The region where $H_0$ is not rejected is wider than for large samples using the $z$ distribution. (3) A larger computed $t$ value will be needed to reject the null hypothesis than for large samples using $z$. In other words, because there is more variability in sample means computed from smaller samples, we have less confidence in the resulting estimates and are less apt to reject the null hypothesis.

# A TEST FOR THE POPULATION MEAN

## ■ EXAMPLE

Question: Has there been a reduction in cost?

Experience in investigating accident claims by the McFarland Insurance Company revealed that it costs $60 on the average to handle the paperwork, pay the investigator, and make a decision. This cost compared with that of other insurance firms was deemed exorbitant, and cost-cutting measures were instituted. In order to evaluate the impact of these new measures, a sample of 26 recent claims was selected at random, and cost studies were made. It was found that the sample mean, $\bar{X}$, and the standard deviation, $s$, of the sample were $57 and $10, respectively. At the .01 level, is there a reduction in the average cost, or can the difference of $3 ($57 − $60) be attributed to chance?

## ☑ SOLUTION

The usual five-step hypothesis-testing procedure is used.

**STEP 1: STATE THE NULL AND THE ALTERNATE HYPOTHESES** The null hypothesis, $H_0$, is that the population mean is $60. The alternate hypothesis, $H_1$, is that the population mean is less than $60. This is written:

$$H_0 : \mu = \$60$$
$$H_1 : \mu < \$60$$

A left-tail test

The test is *one-tailed* because there is interest only in whether or not there has been a *reduction* in cost. The inequality in the alternate hypothesis points to the region of rejection in the left tail of the distribution.

**STEP 2: SELECT THE LEVEL OF SIGNIFICANCE** The .01 level is to be used.

**STEP 3: GIVE THE TEST STATISTIC** The test statistic is Student's $t$ distribution because (1) the population standard deviation is unknown, and (2) the sample size is small (under 30). The formula for $t$ is:

$$t = \frac{\bar{X} - \mu}{\dfrac{s}{\sqrt{n}}} \qquad (11-1)$$

**STEP 4: FORMULATE THE DECISION RULE** The critical values of $t$ are given in Appendix F, and a portion of that appendix is shown in Table 11−1. (Appendix F is also repeated on the back inside cover of the text.) The far left column of the table is labeled "Degrees of freedom, $df$." For this test there are $n - 1$ degrees of freedom.[1] Move down that column to 25 ($n - 1$, or $26 - 1 = 25$). The critical value for $df = 25$, a one-tailed test, and the .01 level is 2.485.

---

## TABLE 11-1

### A Portion of the *t* Distribution Table

Critical values of *t*

| Degrees of freedom, *df* | Level of significance for one-tailed test | | | | | |
|---|---|---|---|---|---|---|
| | .10 | .05 | .025 | .01 | .005 | .0005 |
| | Level of significance for two-tailed test | | | | | |
| | .20 | .10 | .05 | .02 | .01 | .001 |
| 21 | 1.323 | 1.721 | 2.080 | 2.518 | 2.831 | 3.819 |
| 22 | 1.321 | 1.717 | 2.074 | 2.508 | 2.819 | 3.792 |
| 23 | 1.319 | 1.714 | 2.069 | 2.500 | 2.807 | 3.767 |
| 24 | 1.318 | 1.711 | 2.064 | 2.492 | 2.797 | 3.745 |
| 25 | 1.316 | 1.708 | 2.060 | 2.485 | 2.787 | 3.725 |
| 26 | 1.315 | 1.706 | 2.056 | 2.479 | 2.779 | 3.707 |
| 27 | 1.314 | 1.703 | 2.052 | 2.473 | 2.771 | 3.690 |
| 28 | 1.313 | 1.701 | 2.048 | 2.467 | 2.763 | 3.674 |

---

Rejection area only in left tail

Shown schematically in Chart 11–3, the decision rule for this one-tailed test is to reject the null hypothesis if the computed value of *t* falls in any part of the tail to the left of $-2.485$. Otherwise, do not reject the null hypothesis that the population mean is $60.

---

## CHART 11-3

### Rejection Region, *t* Distribution, .01 Significance Level

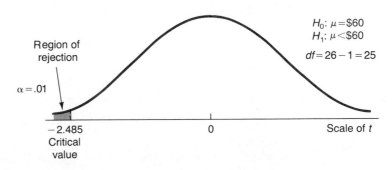

$H_0: \mu = \$60$
$H_1: \mu < \$60$

$df = 26 - 1 = 25$

Region of rejection

$\alpha = .01$

$-2.485$
Critical value

0

Scale of *t*

---

[1] In brief summary, because sample statistics are being used, it is necessary to determine the number of variables that are *free to vary*. To illustrate: If the sum of four numbers is 20, various combinations of *three* numbers can be written down, but the *fourth* number is restricted. If you select 7, 4, and 1 as three of the numbers, the fourth number *must be* 8 so that the sum of all is 20. Because of this restriction, it is said that "1 degree of freedom is lost."

For example, assume that the mean of four numbers is known to be 5. The four numbers are 7, 4, 1, and 8. The deviations of these numbers from the mean must total 0. The deviations of $+2$, $-1$, $-4$, and $+3$ do total 0. If the deviations of $+2$, $-1$, and $-4$ are known, then the value of $+3$ is fixed (restricted) in order to satisfy the condition that the sum of the deviations must equal 0. Thus, 1 degree of freedom is lost in a sampling problem involving the standard deviation of the sample because one number (the arithmetic mean) is known.

**STEP 5: COMPUTE t, AND ARRIVE AT A DECISION**   Recall that $t$ is computed by using formula (11−1):

$$t = \frac{\bar{X} - \mu}{\dfrac{s}{\sqrt{n}}}$$

with $n - 1$ degrees of freedom, where:

$\bar{X}$   is the mean of the small sample.

$\mu$   is the hypothesized population mean.

$s$   is the standard deviation of the sample.

$n$   is the sample size.

*Computing test statistic*

In this problem:

$\bar{X} = \$57$, the sample mean.

$\mu = \$60$, the hypothesized population mean.

$s = \$10$, the sample standard deviation.

$n = 26$, the number of items in the sample.

The value of $t$ is $-1.530$, found by:

$$t = \frac{\bar{X} - \mu}{\dfrac{s}{\sqrt{n}}} = \frac{\$57 - \$60}{\dfrac{\$10}{\sqrt{26}}} = -1.530$$

*No reduction in the mean cost*

Because $-1.530$ lies in the region to the right of the critical value of $-2.485$, the null hypothesis is not rejected at the .01 significance level. This indicates that the cost-cutting measures have not reduced the mean cost per claim to less than $60 based on the sample results.

---

### Self-Review 11−1

*The answers are at the end of the chapter.*

From past records it is known that the average life of a battery used in a digital clock is 305 days. The lives of the batteries are normally distributed. The battery was recently modified to last longer. A sample of 20 modified batteries were tested. It was discovered that the mean life was 311 days, and the sample standard deviation was 12 days. At the .05 level of significance, did the modification increase the mean life of the battery?

1. State the null and alternate hypotheses.
2. Show the decision rule graphically.
3. Compute $t$, and reach a decision. Briefly summarize your findings.

## EXERCISES

*The answers to the odd-numbered exercises are at the end of the book.*

1. The following hypotheses are given:

$$H_0: \mu = 10$$
$$H_1: \mu > 10$$

For a random sample of 10 observations the sample mean was 12 and the sample standard deviation 3. Using the .05 significance level:

a. State the decision rule.

b. Compute the value of the test statistic.

c. What is your decision regarding the null hypothesis?

2. You are given the following hypotheses:

$$H_0: \mu = 400$$
$$H_1: \mu \neq 400$$

For a random sample of 12 observations, the sample mean was 407 and the sample standard deviation 6. Using the .01 significance level:

a. State the decision rule.

b. Compute the value of the test statistic.

c. What is your decision regarding the null hypothesis?

*Note:* It is recommended that the five-step hypothesis-testing procedure be used in solving the following problems.

3. The Rocky Mountain district sales manager of John C. Rath, Inc., a college book publishing company, claims that each of his sales representatives makes 40 calls on professors per week. Several reps said that this estimate is too low. To research the claim, a random sample of 28 sales representatives revealed that the mean number of calls made last week was 42. The standard deviation of the sample was computed to be 2.1 calls. At the .05 level of significance, can we conclude that more than 40 calls are made, on the average, in a week?

4. The management of White Industries is considering a new method of assembling its three-wheel golf cart. The present method requires 42.3 minutes, on the average, to assemble a cart. The new method was introduced, and a time and motion study was conducted on a random sample of 24 carts. The mean assembly time was computed to be 40.6 minutes. The standard deviation of the sample was 2.7 minutes. Using the .10 level of significance, can it be said that the assembly time under the new method is significantly less than before?

5. The records of Yellowstone Trucks revealed that the mean life of a set of spark plugs is 22,100 miles. The distribution of the life of the plugs is approximately normally distributed. A spark plug manufacturer claimed that its plugs have a mean life in excess of 22,100 miles. The fleet owner purchased a large number of sets. A sample of 18 sets revealed that the sample mean life was 23,400 miles and the sample standard deviation was 1,500 miles. Is there enough evidence to substantiate the manufacturer's claim at the .05 level?

Champion Spark Plug, a division of Cooper Industries, Inc.

6. Fast Service, a chain of automotive tune-up shops, advertises that its personnel can change oil, replace the oil filter, and lubricate any standard automobile in 15 minutes, on the average. The National Business Bureau received complaints from customers that service takes considerably longer. To check the Fast Service claim, the bureau had service done on 21 unmarked cars. The mean service time was 18 minutes, and the standard deviation of the sample was 1 minute. Use the .05 level to check the reasonableness of the Fast Service claim.

Compute sample standard deviation

In the previous examples, the mean and standard deviation of the sample were given. The following example requires that they be computed from the sample observations.

### ■ EXAMPLE

The mean length of a small counterbalance bar is 43 millimeters. There is concern that the adjustments of the machine producing the bars have changed. The null hypothesis is that there has been no change in the mean length ($\mu = 43$). The alternate hypothesis is that there has been a change ($\mu \neq 43$). Test at the .02 level.

Twelve bars ($n = 12$) were selected at random and their lengths recorded. The lengths are (in millimeters) 42, 39, 42, 45, 43, 40, 39, 41, 40, 42, 43, and 42. Has there been a statistically significant change in the mean length of the bars?

### ✓ SOLUTION

Note that $H_1$ indicates two-tailed test must be used

The null and alternate hypotheses are:

$$H_0 : \mu = 43$$
$$H_1 : \mu \neq 43$$

The alternate hypothesis does not state a direction, so the test is two-tailed. There are 11 degrees of freedom, found by $n - 1 = 12 - 1 = 11$. Then—referring to Appendix F for a two-tailed test at the .02 level with 11 degrees of freedom—the critical value is 2.718. The critical values for the .02 level are shown in Chart 11−4. The decision rule is therefore to reject the null hypothesis if the computed $t$ is to the left of $-2.718$ or to the right of 2.718.

---

### CHART  11−4

**Regions of Rejection, Two-Tailed Test, Student's $t$ Distribution, $\alpha = .02$**

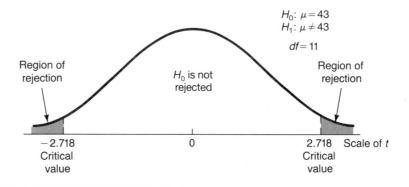

---

The standard deviation of the sample can be determined either by squaring the deviations from the mean or by an equivalent formula using the squares of the actual values. The two formulas from Chapter 4, (4−8) and (4−9), are:

<table>
<tr><th>Using squared deviations from mean</th><th>Using squares of actual values</th></tr>
<tr><td>$$s = \sqrt{\frac{\Sigma(X - \overline{X})^2}{n - 1}}$$</td><td>$$s = \sqrt{\frac{\Sigma X^2 - \frac{(\Sigma X)^2}{n}}{n - 1}}$$</td></tr>
</table>

The necessary calculations for these two methods are shown in Table 11−2. The mean ($\overline{X}$) is 41.5 millimeters, and the standard deviation ($s$) is 1.78 millimeters.

### TABLE 11−2

Sample standard deviation computed using two methods

**Calculations Needed for the Sample Standard Deviation**

| $X$ (mm) | $X - \bar{X}$ | $(X - \bar{X})^2$ | $X^2$ |
|---|---|---|---|
| 42 | 0.5 | 0.25 | 1,764 |
| 39 | −2.5 | 6.25 | 1,521 |
| 42 | 0.5 | 0.25 | 1,764 |
| 45 | 3.5 | 12.25 | 2,025 |
| 43 | 1.5 | 2.25 | 1,849 |
| 40 | −1.5 | 2.25 | 1,600 |
| 39 | −2.5 | 6.25 | 1,521 |
| 41 | −0.5 | 0.25 | 1,681 |
| 40 | −1.5 | 2.25 | 1,600 |
| 42 | 0.5 | 0.25 | 1,764 |
| 43 | 1.5 | 2.25 | 1,849 |
| 42 | 0.5 | 0.25 | 1,764 |
| 498 | 0 | 35.0 | 20,702 |

$$\bar{X} = \frac{498}{12} = 41.5 \text{ mm}$$

**Squared deviation method:**

$$s = \sqrt{\frac{\Sigma(X - \bar{X})^2}{n - 1}} = \sqrt{\frac{35}{12 - 1}} = 1.78$$

**Squaring actual values:**

$$s = \sqrt{\frac{\Sigma X^2 - \frac{(\Sigma X)^2}{n}}{n - 1}} = \sqrt{\frac{20,702 - \frac{(498)^2}{12}}{12 - 1}}$$

$$= 1.78$$

Now we are ready to compute *t*, using formula (11−1).

$$t = \frac{\bar{X} - \mu}{\frac{s}{\sqrt{n}}} = \frac{41.5 - 43.0}{\frac{1.78}{\sqrt{12}}} = -2.92$$

The null hypothesis that the population mean is 43 millimeters is rejected at the .02 level (because the computed *t* of − 2.92 lies in the area of the tail beyond the critical value of −2.718). The alternate hypothesis that the mean is not 43 millimeters is accepted. Based on the sample results, we can say that the machine is out of adjustment. Report this to the quality-assurance engineer and to the production manager.

## A COMPUTER SOLUTION

The MINITAB statistical software system, used extensively in earlier chapters, provides an efficient way of conducting a one-sample test of hypothesis for a population mean. First the sample observations are entered into the system, using the SET command. Next, the column of data is given the identification "Length," using the NAME command. Finally, the procedure TTEST is used. The procedure TTEST requires as input the value of the null hypothesis and the column in which the data are located. Note that *t* (−2.91) is approximately the same as the value determined using formula (11−1) (−2.92). The slight difference is due to rounding.

```
MTB > set c1
DATA> 42,39,42,45,43,40,39,41,40,42,43,42
DATA> end
MTB > name c1 'Length'
MTB > ttest mu=43, c1

TEST OF MU = 43.000 VS MU N.E. 43.000

              N      MEAN     STDEV    SE MEAN       T   P VALUE
Length       12    41.500     1.784     0.515    -2.91    0.014
```

An additional feature of MINITAB, and most other statistical software packages, is to output the *p*-value, which gives additional information on the null hypothesis. The *p*-value is the probability of a *t* value as large or larger than that computed, given that the null hypothesis is true. In this case, the *p*-value of .014 is the likelihood of a *t* value of −2.91 or less plus the likelihood of a *t* value of 2.91 or larger, given a population mean of 43. Thus, comparing the *p*-value to the significance level tells us whether the null hypothesis was close to being rejected, barely rejected, and so on.

To explain further, refer to the following diagram, in which the *p*-value of .014 is shown in green and the significance level in purple. Because the *p*-value of .014 is less than the significance level of .02, the null hypothesis is rejected. Had the *p*-value been larger than the significance level—say, .06, .19, or .57—the null hypothesis would not be rejected. If the significance level had initially been selected as .01, the null hypothesis would not be rejected.

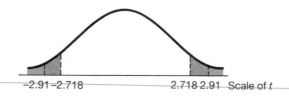

In the preceding example the alternate hypothesis was two-tailed, so there were rejection areas in both the upper and the lower tails. To determine the *p*-value, it was necessary to determine the area to the left of −2.91 for a *t* distribution with 11 degrees of freedom and add to it the value to the right of 2.91, also with 11 degrees of freedom.

What if we were conducting a one-tailed test, so that the entire rejection region would be in either the upper or the lower tail? In that case, we would report the area from only the one tail. In the counterbalance example, if $H_1$ were stated as $\mu < 43$, the inequality would point to the left. Thus, we would have reported the *p*-value as the area to the left of −2.91. This value is .007, found by .014/2. Thus, the *p*-value for a one-tailed test would be .007.

A computer software package such as MINITAB has extensive tables to estimate *p*-value accurately. How can we estimate a *p*-value without a computer? For the example just completed, go to Appendix F and the row for 11 degrees of freedom. Assume we are conducting the one-tailed test discussed in the above paragraph. Look in the row for the one-tailed test. The *t* value of 2.91 is located between 2.718 and 3.106. The one-tailed significance level corresponding to 2.718 is .01, and for 3.106 it is .005. Therefore, the one-tailed *p*-value is estimated to be between .01 and .005. This agrees with the MINITAB value of .007.

### Self-Review 11–2

*The answers are at the end of the chapter.*

A Corkill machine is set to fill a small bottle with 9.0 grams of medicine. It is claimed that the mean weight is less than 9.0 grams. The hypothesis is to be tested at the .01 level. A sample revealed these weights (in grams): 9.2, 8.7, 8.9, 8.6, 8.8, 8.5, 8.7, and 9.0.

1. State the null and alternate hypotheses.
2. Many degrees of freedom are there?
3. Give the decision rule.
4. Compute *t,* and arrive at a decision.
5. Estimate the *p*-value.

# EXERCISES

*The answers to the odd-numbered exercises are at the end of the book.*

7. The following null and alternate hypotheses are being considered:

$$H_0: \mu = 20$$
$$H_1: \mu < 20$$

A random sample of five observations was selected: 18, 15, 12, 19, and 21. At the .01 significance level, can we conclude that the population mean is less than 20?

   a.   State the decision rule.
   b.   Compute the value of the test statistic.
   c.   What is your decision regarding the null hypothesis?
   d.   Estimate the *p*-value.

8. The following hypotheses are given:

$$H_0: \mu = 100$$
$$H_1: \mu \neq 100$$

The following random sample of six observations was selected: 118, 105, 112, 119, 105, and 111. At the .05 significance level, can we conclude that the population mean is different from 100?

   a.   State the decision rule.
   b.   Compute the value of the test statistic.
   c.   What is your decision regarding the null hypothesis?
   d.   Estimate the *p*-value.

*Note:* It is recommended that the five-step hypothesis-testing procedure be used in solving the following problems.

9. Experience with raising New Jersey Red chickens revealed the average weight of the chickens at age five months to be 4.35 pounds. The weights are normally distributed. In an effort to increase their weight, a special additive was mixed with the chicken feed. The subsequent weights of a sample of five-month-old chickens were (in pounds): 4.41, 4.37, 4.33, 4.35, 4.30, 4.39, 4.36, 4.38, 4.40, and 4.39. At the .01 level, has the special additive increased the weight of the chickens?

10. The liquid chlorine added to swimming pools to combat algae has a relatively short shelf life before it loses it effectiveness. Past records indicate that the average shelf life of a 5-gallon jug of chlorine is 2,160 hours (90 days). As an experiment, Holdlonger was added to the chlorine to find out if it would increase the shelf life. A sample of nine jugs of chlorine gave these shelf lives (in hours): 2,159, 2,170, 2,180, 2,179, 2,160, 2,167, 2,171, 2,181, and 2,185. At the .025 level, has Holdlonger increased the shelf life of the chlorine?

11. Wyoming fisheries contend that the average number of cutthroat trout caught during a full day of fly-fishing on the Snake, Buffalo, and other rivers and streams in the Jackson Hole area is 4.0. To make their yearly update, the fishery personnel asked a sample of fly-fishermen to keep a count of the number caught during the day. The numbers were: 4, 4, 3, 2, 6, 8, 7, 1, 9, 3, 1, and 6. At the .05 level, is there convincing evidence that the number of trout caught daily has increased?

12. Hugger Polls contends that an agent conducts an average of 53 in-depth home surveys every week. A streamlined survey form has been introduced, and Hugger wants to evaluate its effectiveness. The number of in-depth surveys conducted during a week by a random sample of agents are: 53, 57, 50, 55, 58, 54, 60, 52, 59, 62, 60, 60, 51, 59, and 56. At the .05 level of significance, what do you conclude about the number of in-depth surveys completed during the week using the new form?

# COMPARING TWO POPULATIONS MEANS

A test using the $t$ distribution can also be applied to compare two sample means to determine if the samples were obtained from normal populations with the same mean. To conduct this test, three assumptions are required.

1. The populations must be normally distributed (or approximately normally distributed).
2. The populations must be independent.
3. The population variances must be equal.

The $t$ statistic for the two-sample case is similar to that employed in Chapter 9, formula (9–3), for the $z$ statistic, except that an additional calculation is required. The two sample variances must be "pooled" to form a single estimate of the unknown population variance. Why do we pool these variances? In most cases when the samples have fewer than 30 observations, the population standard deviations are not known. So we calculate $s^2$ and substitute it for $\sigma^2$. Because we assume that the two populations have equal variances, the best estimate we can make of that value is to combine or pool all the information we have with respect to the population variance.

The following formula is used to pool the sample variances. Notice that two factors make up the weights: the number of observations in each sample and the sample variances themselves.

$$s_p^2 = \frac{(n_1 - 1)s_1^2 + (n_2 - 1)s_2^2}{n_1 + n_2 - 2} \qquad (11\text{--}2)$$

where:

$s_1^2$   is the variance in the first sample.
$s_2^2$   is the variance in the second sample.

The value of $t$ is then determined by formula (11–3).

$$t = \frac{\bar{X}_1 - \bar{X}_2}{\sqrt{s_p^2\left(\frac{1}{n_1} + \frac{1}{n_2}\right)}} \qquad (11\text{--}3)$$

where:

$\bar{X}_1$   is the mean of the first sample.
$\bar{X}_2$   is the mean of the second sample.
$n_1$   is the number in the first sample.
$n_2$   is the number in the second sample.
$s_p^2$   is the pooled estimate of the population variance.

The number of degrees of freedom in the test is equal to the total number of items sampled minus the number of samples. Since there are two samples, there are $n_1 + n_2 - 2$ degrees of freedom.

## ■ EXAMPLE

O'Keane Products, Inc. manufactures and assembles lawnmowers, which are shipped to dealers throughout the United States and Canada. Two different procedures have been proposed for mounting the engine on the frame of the lawnmower. The question is: Is there a difference in the mean time to mount the engines on the frames of the lawnmowers? The first procedure was developed by Welles (designated as procedure

1), and the other procedure was developed by Atkins (designated as procedure 2). To evaluate the two proposed methods, it was decided to conduct a time and motion study. A sample of five employees were timed using procedure 1, and six were timed using procedure 2. The results, in minutes, are shown below. Is there a difference in the mean mounting times? Use the .10 significance level.

| Procedure 1 (minutes) | Procedure 2 (minutes) |
| --- | --- |
| 2 | 3 |
| 4 | 7 |
| 9 | 5 |
| 3 | 8 |
| 2 | 4 |
|   | 3 |

## ☑ SOLUTION

The null hypothesis states that there is no difference in mean mounting time between the Welles procedure and the Atkins procedure.

$$H_0 : \mu_1 = \mu_2$$
$$H_1 : \mu_1 \neq \mu_2$$

The required assumptions are: (1) The observations in the Welles sample are *independent* of those observations in the Atkins sample, and of each other. (2) The two populations are approximately normal. (3) The two populations have equal variances.

Is there a difference between the assembly times using the Welles and the Atkins methods? The way the problem is stated suggests a two-tailed test. Recall that the degrees of freedom are determined by $n_1 + n_2 - 2$. Five assemblers used the Welles method and six the Atkins method. Thus, there are 9 degrees of freedom, found by $5 + 6 - 2$. The critical values of *t*, from Appendix F for $df = 9$, a two-tailed test, and the .10 level of significance, are $+1.833$ and $-1.833$. The decision rule is portrayed graphically in Chart 11–5. We do not reject the null hypothesis if the computed *t* value falls between $-1.833$ and $+1.833$. Otherwise $H_0$ is rejected.

---

CHART    11–5

**Regions of Rejection, Two-Tailed Test (9 degrees of freedom, $\alpha = .10$)**

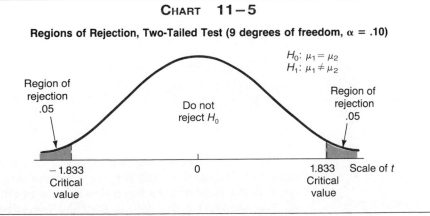

---

Determining Student's *t* is accomplished in three steps.

### STEP 1: CALCULATE THE SAMPLE VARIANCES

| Procedure 1 | | Procedure 2 | |
|---|---|---|---|
| $X_1$ | $X_1^2$ | $X_2$ | $X_2^2$ |
| 2 | 4 | 3 | 9 |
| 4 | 16 | 7 | 49 |
| 9 | 81 | 5 | 25 |
| 3 | 9 | 8 | 64 |
| 2 | 4 | 4 | 16 |
| 20 | 114 | 3 | 9 |
| | | 30 | 172 |

$$s_1^2 = \frac{\sum X_1^2 - \frac{(\sum X_1)^2}{n_1}}{n-1} \qquad s_2^2 = \frac{\sum X_2^2 - \frac{(\sum X_2)^2}{n_2}}{n-1}$$

$$= \frac{114 - \frac{(20)^2}{5}}{5-1} \qquad = \frac{172 - \frac{(30)^2}{6}}{6-1}$$

$$= 8.5 \qquad = 4.4$$

### STEP 2: POOL THE VARIANCES    Applying formula (11–2),

$$s_p^2 = \frac{(n_1 - 1)s_1^2 - (n_2 - 1)s_2^2}{n_1 + n_2 - 2}$$

$$= \frac{(5 - 1)(8.5) + (6 - 1)(4.4)}{5 + 6 - 2}$$

$$= 6.2222$$

### STEP 3: DETERMINE t    Using formula (11–3) with $\bar{X}_1 = 20/5 = 4$ and $\bar{X}_2 = 30/6 = 5$,

$$t = \frac{\bar{X}_1 - \bar{X}_2}{\sqrt{s_p^2 \left(\frac{1}{n_1} + \frac{1}{n_2}\right)}}$$

$$= \frac{4 - 5}{\sqrt{6.2222 \left(\frac{1}{5} + \frac{1}{6}\right)}} = -0.6620$$

The decision is not to reject the null hypothesis because $-0.6620$ falls in the region between $-1.833$ and $+1.833$. We conclude that there is no difference in the mean time to mount the engine on the frame between the two methods.

The MINITAB output for the O'Keane Products example is given below. The procedure is TWOSAMPLE, and the subcommand POOLED is required.

```
MTB > set c1
DATA> 2,4,9,3,2
DATA> end
MTB > set c2
DATA> 3,7,5,8,4,3
DATA> end
MTB > name c1 'Welles' c2 'Atkins'
MTB > twosample c1 c2;
SUBC> pooled.
TWOSAMPLE T FOR Welles VS Atkins
            N       MEAN      STDEV    SE MEAN
WELLES      5       4.00      2.92       1.3
ATKINS      6       5.00      2.10      0.86
95 PCT CI FOR MU Welles - MU Atkins: (-4.4, 2.42)
TTEST MU Welles = MU Atkins (VS NE): T= -0.66  P=0.52    DF=9
POOLED STDEV =      2.49
```

— *p*-value
— Test statistic

The *t* value of −0.66 is the same as that computed using formulas (11−1) and (11−2). Note that the *p*-value is .52. This is the probability that given the null hypothesis is true, namely, that there is no difference between the two mounting times, we could find a *t* value of −0.66 or less or a *t* value of 0.66 or larger with 9 degrees of freedom. The *p*-value is larger than the significance level, confirming that the null hypothesis should not be rejected.

## Self-Review 11−3

*The answers are at the end of the chapter.*

The net weights of a sample of bottles filled by a machine manufactured by Edne, and the net weights of a sample filled by a similar machine manufactured by Orno, Inc., are (in grams):

At the .05 level, is the mean weight of the bottles filled by the Orno machine greater than the mean weight of the bottles filled by the Edne machine?

Edne:   5, 8, 7, 6, 9, and 7
Orno:   8, 10, 7, 11, 9, 12, 14, and 9

# EXERCISES

*The answers to the odd-numbered exercises are at the end of the book.*

13. The following hypotheses are given.

$$H_0: \mu_1 = \mu_2$$
$$H_1: \mu_1 \neq \mu_2$$

A random sample of 10 observations from the first population revealed a sample mean of 23 and a sample standard deviation of 4. A random sample of 8 observations from the second population revealed a mean of 26 with a standard deviation of 5. At the .05 significance level is there a difference in the population means?

a.   State the decision rule.

b.   Compute the pooled estimate of the population variance.

c.   Compute the value of the test statistic.

d.   What is your decision regarding the null hypothesis?

14. The following hypotheses are to be tested.

$$H_0: \mu_1 = \mu_2$$
$$H_1: \mu_1 \neq \mu_2$$

A random sample of 15 observations from the first population revealed a sample mean of 350 and a sample standard deviation of 12. A random sample of 17 observations from the second population revealed a mean of 342 with a standard deviation of 15. At the .10 significance level, is there a difference in the population means?

a. State the decision rule.

b. Compute the pooled estimate of the population variance.

c. Compute the value of the test statistic.

d. What is your decision regarding the null hypothesis?

15. A sample of the scores on an examination given to both males and females in Statistics 201 are:

Males: 72, 69, 98, 66, 85, 76, 79, 80, and 77
Females: 81, 67, 90, 78, 81, 80, and 76

At the .01 significance level, is the mean grade of the females higher than that of the males?

16. The scores of two groups of inmates at Southard Prison on a rehabilitation test are:

|  | First offenders | Repeat offenders |
|---|---|---|
| Mean score | 300 | 305 |
| Sample variance | 20 | 18 |
| Sample size | 16 | 13 |

Test at the .05 level that there is no difference between the mean scores of the two groups. The alternate hypothesis is that there is a difference.

17. As an experiment, the weather bureau made 22 pollen counts in the valley surrounding Wilson, Wyoming (altitude 6,200 feet). Similarly, 25 counts were made in the Teton Mountains surrounding Wilson (altitude 7,800 feet). The findings were:

|  | Valley | Mountains |
|---|---|---|
| Mean pollen count | 89 | 87 |
| Sample standard deviation | 4 | 6 |
| Sample size | 22 | 25 |

At the .10 significance level, can we conclude that there is a higher pollen count in the valley around Wilson than in the nearby mountains?

18. The Kentucky Highway Department is considering a new four-lane highway. A number of questions have been raised. One of them involves the speed of trucks on a four-lane highway with a median strip over 50 feet versus a highway with a median strip under 50 feet.

To research the matter further, the speeds of a random sample of trucks traveling on the two types of highway were measured (speeds are in miles per hour).

| Under 50 feet | Over 50 feet | |
|---|---|---|
| 55 | 64 | 65 |
| 70 | 68 | 75 |
| 68 | 70 | 63 |
| 67 | 70 | 66 |
| 70 | 65 | 49 |

Based on this preliminary sample information and using the .01 level, can we say there is a significant difference in the speeds of the trucks on the two different highways? What action, if any, would you suggest the highway department take?

# HYPOTHESIS TESTING INVOLVING PAIRED OBSERVATIONS

In the previous example the difference between two population means was tested. The difference in the times required to mount the engine using the Welles method and using the Atkins method was given as an illustration. The samples were *independent,* meaning that the sample of assembly times using the Welles method was in no way related to the sample of assembly times using the Atkins method.

What to do when samples are not independent

There are situations, however, in which the samples are *not* independent. As an example, suppose the training director wishes to find out whether or not a unique training program will increase employee efficiency. He plans to take a random sample of 10 employees registered for the program and record their efficiency ratings before the training starts. After completion of the program, the efficiency ratings of the *same* sample of employees will be recorded. Thus, there will be a pair of efficiency ratings for each member of the sample. The set of sample pairs is aptly called a *paired sample.* The test of hypothesis to be conducted to find out if there is a difference between the ratings before and after the training program is called a *paired difference test.* Note that the two samples (a "before" sample and an "after" sample) depend on each other because the same employees are in both samples. Thus, they are not independent.

The paired difference test

For the test of hypothesis to be conducted now, there is essentially only one sample, not two. We are testing the hypothesis that the distribution of the differences has a mean of 0. The sample is made up of the *differences* between the efficiency ratings before the training program and the ratings after the program. If production methods before and after the training program remain the same, one could logically expect some employees to benefit from the training program and to become more efficient. Other employees would prefer the method used before the training program, and their efficiency would remain the same or even decrease. Thus, the mean of the differences in efficiency ratings, designated $\mu_d$, would "balance out" and equal zero.

As noted, before adopting the new production techniques presented in the training program, the training director wants to know whether or not it will affect efficiency. If it does, one would reasonably assume that most of the differences would be positive—that is, increased efficiency. The null hypothesis to be tested is therefore $H_0$: $\mu_d = 0$. The alternate hypothesis is that the mean of the differences is greater than 0, written $H_1$: $\mu_d > 0$, signifying that the differences are positive.

$H_0$ and $H_1$

The .05 level

The .05 level of significance is to be used, and the test statistic is the Student *t,* determined by:

Test statistic for the paired difference test

$$t = \frac{\bar{d}}{\dfrac{s_d}{\sqrt{n}}} \qquad (11-4)$$

with $n - 1$ degrees of freedom, where:

$\bar{d}$  is the mean difference between the paired observations.

$s_d$  is the standard deviation of the differences between the paired observations.

$n$  is the number of paired observations.

The standard deviation of the differences is computed using formula (4−9) except that $d$ is substituted for $X$.

$$s_d = \sqrt{\frac{\Sigma d^2 - \dfrac{(\Sigma d)^2}{n}}{n - 1}}$$

The decision rule

The critical value of $t$ for this one-tailed test of paired differences is 1.833, found by going to Appendix F and reading down the left column to $n - 1 = 10 - 1 = 9$ degrees of freedom.

The sample and needed calculations

These calculations are needed to determine $t$:

| Sample member | Efficiency rating Before | Efficiency rating After | Difference, $d$ | Difference squared, $d^2$ |
|---|---|---|---|---|
| 1 | 128 | 135 | 7 | 49 |
| 2 | 105 | 110 | 5 | 25 |
| 3 | 119 | 131 | 12 | 144 |
| 4 | 140 | 142 | 2 | 4 |
| 5 | 98 | 105 | 7 | 49 |
| 6 | 123 | 130 | 7 | 49 |
| 7 | 127 | 131 | 4 | 16 |
| 8 | 115 | 110 | −5 | 25 |
| 9 | 122 | 125 | 3 | 9 |
| 10 | 145 | 149 | 4 | 16 |
| | | | 46 | 386 |

$$\overline{d} = \frac{\Sigma d}{n} = \frac{46}{10} = 4.60$$

$$s_d = \sqrt{\frac{\Sigma d^2 - \frac{(\Sigma d)^2}{n}}{n - 1}} = \sqrt{\frac{386 - \frac{(46)^2}{10}}{10 - 1}} = 4.40$$

Using formula (11–4), the value of $t$ is 3.30, found by:

$$t = \frac{\overline{d}}{\frac{s_d}{\sqrt{n}}} = \frac{4.6}{\frac{4.40}{\sqrt{10}}} = 3.30$$

Because the value of $t$ (3.30) lies in the rejection region, that is, beyond the critical value of 1.833, the null hypothesis is rejected. We conclude that the distribution of the differences has a mean greater than 0. The training director has convincing evidence that the unique training program will be effective in increasing efficiency.

The MINITAB system can be used to conduct the paired difference test. First, the efficiency ratings before and after the special program are entered. Next, the differences in the ratings before and after the training program are determined by your computer. The MINITAB procedure is TTEST, with MU = 0 and the data located in column C3. The subcommand ALTERNATE = 1 is used to report the one-tailed $p$-value.

```
MTB > set c1
DATA> 128,105,119,140,98,123,127,115,122,145
DATA> end
MTB > set c2
DATA> 135,110,131,142,105,130,131,110,125,149
DATA> end
MTB > let c3=c2-c1
MTB > name c1 'before' c2 'after' c3 'diff'
MTB > ttest mu=0 c3;
SUBC> alternate =1.

TEST OF MU = 0.000 VS MU G.T. 0.000

              N     MEAN    STDEV   SE MEAN       T    P VALUE
diff         10    4.600    4.402     1.392    3.30     0.0046
```

The MINITAB output reports the same *t* value (3.30) as we computed using formula (11 4). The *p*-value is also given. By using the MINITAB subcommand ALTERNATE = 1, we are able to determine the one-tailed *p*-value. Because we set up a one-tailed test we are interested in the probability of a *t* value beyond 3.30, with 9 degrees of freedom. That value is .0046. Thus, the likelihood that we could find a *t* value of 3.30 or more with 9 degrees of freedom, given that the null hypothesis is true, is less than 0.5 percent.

The following self-review and chapter exercises suggest some other uses of the paired difference test of hypothesis.

### Self-Review 11–4

*The answers are at the end of the chapter.*

An Iowa agriculture experimental station plans to test the effectiveness of two presoak solutions for corn seeds. The purpose of the experiment is to determine if there is a difference in effectiveness of the two solutions, designated solution A and solution B. Various corn seeds, such as Iowa Whopper and Tyson Gold, are to be used in the experiment. A pair of Iowa Whopper seeds is selected; one is soaked in Solution A, the other in Solution B. Then they are planted, and the germination and growth times (in days) are recorded. This procedure is repeated for Tyson Gold and the other seeds. The number of days needed for germination and growth to six inches are indicated for each pair in the table below.

1. State the null and alternate hypotheses symbolically.

2. Using the .05 level, show the critical values graphically.

3. Using the following nine pairs of sample data, compute *t*, and arrive at a decision.

| Solution | Pair | | | | | | | | |
|---|---|---|---|---|---|---|---|---|---|
| | 1 | 2 | 3 | 4 | 5 | 6 | 7 | 8 | 9 |
| Solution A | 16 | 9 | 21 | 14 | 26 | 27 | 18 | 14 | 30 |
| Solution B | 18 | 7 | 26 | 11 | 26 | 22 | 19 | 20 | 28 |

## EXERCISES

*The answers to the odd-numbered exercises are at the end of the book.*

19. The hypotheses are:

$$H_0: \mu_d = 0$$
$$H_1: \mu_d > 0$$

The following paired sample observations were obtained. The numbers represent the scores on a mechanical aptitude test before and after a special review session.

| | Pair | | | |
|---|---|---|---|---|
| | 1 | 2 | 3 | 4 |
| Before | 10 | 12 | 15 | 19 |
| After | 8 | 9 | 12 | 15 |

At the .05 significance level, can we conclude that the mean of the distribution of the differences is greater than 0?

a. State the decision rule.

b. Compute the mean and the standard deviation of differences in the "before" and "after" scores.

c. Compute the value of the test statistic.

d. What is your decision regarding the null hypothesis? Was the review session effective?

20. The following hypotheses are given.

$$H_0: \mu_d = 0$$
$$H_1: \mu_d \neq 0$$

The following paired sample observations represent the intelligence scores for five disadvantaged children chosen at random. The "before" scores represent their knowledge of the outdoors before they were shown a special movie on the subject. The "after" scores are their scores after seeing the movie.

| | Pair | | | | |
|---|---|---|---|---|---|
| | 1 | 2 | 3 | 4 | 5 |
| Before | 30 | 22 | 25 | 19 | 26 |
| After | 26 | 19 | 20 | 15 | 19 |

At the .05 significance level, can we conclude that the mean of the distribution of the differences is different from 0?

a. State the decision rule.

b. Compute the mean and the standard deviation of differences in the "before" and the "after" scores.

c. Compute the value of the test statistic.

d. What is your decision regarding the null hypothesis? What does this indicate?

21. A survey is to be conducted at North Central University to measure the effect of the change in environment on foreign students. One of the facets of the study is a comparison of student weights upon arrival on campus with weights one year later. It is hypothesized that the richer American food will cause an increase in weight. The alternate hypothesis is that there has been an increase in weight. The .01 level is to be used. A random sample of 11 foreign students is chosen for the study. What is your conclusion?

| Name | Weight on arrival | Weight one year later |
|---|---|---|
| Nassar | 124 | 142 |
| O'Toole | 157 | 157 |
| Obie | 98 | 96 |
| Silverman | 190 | 212 |
| Kim | 103 | 116 |
| Gross | 135 | 134 |
| Farouk | 149 | 150 |
| Thatcher | 176 | 184 |
| Sambul | 200 | 209 |
| Onassis | 180 | 180 |
| Pierre | 256 | 269 |

22. The management of Discount Furniture, a chain of discount furniture stores in the Northeast, designed an incentive plan for salespeople. To evaluate this innovative plan, 12 salespeople were selected at random, and their weekly incomes before and after the plan were recorded.

| Salesperson | Weekly income Before | After | Salesperson | Weekly income Before | After |
|---|---|---|---|---|---|
| Sid Mahone | $320 | $340 | Peg Mancuso | $625 | $631 |
| Carol Quick | 290 | 285 | Anita Loma | 560 | 560 |
| Tom Jackson | 421 | 475 | John Cuso | 360 | 365 |
| Andy Jones | 510 | 510 | Carl Utz | 431 | 431 |
| Jean Sloan | 210 | 210 | A. S. Kushner | 506 | 525 |
| Jack Walker | 402 | 500 | Fern Lawton | 505 | 619 |

Was there a significant increase in the average salesperson's weekly income due to the innovative Incentive plan? Use the .05 significance level. Estimate the *p*-value, and interpret it.

23. Calorie Watchers, a national chain of exercise and diet centers, has a new weight-reduction program designed to produce dramatic results within three weeks. As a result of their advertisements, over one thousand signed up. Each was weighed before and after the initial three-week period. The results of a sample of 10 enrollees are:

| Name | Weight Before | Weight After | Name | Weight Before | Weight After |
|------|--------|-------|------|--------|-------|
| Evie Gorky | 190 | 196 | Pat O'Leary | 126 | 129 |
| Bob Mack | 250 | 240 | Kim Dennis | 186 | 189 |
| Lou Brandon | 345 | 345 | Connie Kaye | 116 | 115 |
| Karl Unger | 210 | 212 | Tom Dama | 196 | 194 |
| Sue Koontz | 114 | 113 | Maxine Sims | 125 | 124 |

At the .01 level of significance, we can say that the new weight-reduction program is a success?

24. A study of more than 100 high-crime locations in Miami, Florida, was conducted. The number of crimes in each of eight sample areas during a one-year period was recorded. Then a neighborhood watch program was inaugurated. The number of crimes before and after the watch are indicated in the table that follows. Has there been a decrease in the number of crimes since the program was inaugurated?

| | Number of crimes by area | | | | | | | |
|---|---|---|---|---|---|---|---|---|
| | A | B | C | D | E | F | G | H |
| Before watch | 14 | 7 | 4 | 5 | 17 | 12 | 8 | 9 |
| After watch | 2 | 7 | 3 | 6 | 8 | 13 | 3 | 5 |

Use the .01 significance level. Estimate the *p*-value.

Courtesy Florida Department of Commerce, Division of Tourism

# CHAPTER OUTLINE

I. The objective of tests of hypotheses using small samples is to check the validity of quantitative statements.

II. Student's *t* distribution.
   A. It is used when:
      1. The sample size is less than 30.
      2. The population or populations are normally or nearly normally distributed.
   B. Characteristics of the Student *t*.
      1. It is a continuous distribution.
      2. It is bell-shaped and symmetrical.
      3. There is a family of *t* distributions. All have the same mean—zero—but different standard deviations, depending on the sample size.
      4. It is spread out more than the standard normal distribution and is flatter at the apex of the curve.

III. The formula for a test of hypothesis about a population mean using Student's *t* distribution.

$$t = \frac{\bar{X} - \mu}{\frac{s}{\sqrt{n}}} \qquad (11-1)$$

with $n - 1$ degrees of freedom, where:

$\overline{X}$   is the sample mean.

$\mu$   is the hypothesized population mean.

$s$   is the sample standard deviation.

$n$   is the number in the sample.

IV.   Assumptions and formulas for a test of hypothesis involving the difference between two population means.
     A.   Assumptions
         1.   The observations in one sample are independent of those in the other sample and independent of each other.
         2.   The two populations are normal.
         3.   The two populations have equal variances.
     B.   Formulas.
         1.   The formula for pooling the variances.

$$s_p^2 = \frac{(n_1 - 1)(s_1^2) + (n_2 - 1)(s_2^2)}{n_1 + n_2 - 2} \qquad (11\text{–}2)$$

where:

$n_1$   is the number of observations in the first sample.

$n_2$   is the number of observations in the second sample.

$s_1^2$   is the variance of the first sample.

$s_2^2$   is the variance of the second sample.

         2.   The formula for the test statistic $t$.

$$t = \frac{\overline{X}_1 - \overline{X}_2}{\sqrt{s_p^2\left(\dfrac{1}{n_1} + \dfrac{1}{n_2}\right)}} \qquad (11\text{–}3)$$

V.   If the samples are dependent (paired):

$$t = \frac{\overline{d}}{\dfrac{s_d}{\sqrt{n}}} \qquad (11\text{–}4)$$

where:

$$\overline{d} = \frac{\Sigma d}{n} \qquad s_d = \sqrt{\frac{\Sigma d^2 - \dfrac{(\Sigma d)^2}{n}}{n - 1}}$$

VI.   A $p$-value is the likelihood of a value of $t$ as large, or larger, than computed when the null hypothesis is true.

# EXERCISES

*The answers to the odd-numbered exercises are at the end of the book.*

25.   The manufacturer of the Ososki motorcycle advertises that the cycle will average 87 miles per gallon on long trips. The mileages on eight long trips were 88, 82, 81, 87, 80, 78, 79, and 89. Test at the .05 level that the mean mileage is less than advertised.

26. The football coach at Southeastern University said that, based on past records, the mean weight of the defensive linemen is 235 pounds. A sample of 10 defensive linemen this year revealed that the mean weight is 240 pounds, and the standard deviation of the sample is 11 pounds. At the .01 level, is this sufficient evidence that the mean weight has increased?

27. The Myers Summer Casual Furniture Store tells customers that a special order will take six weeks (42 days). During recent months the owner has received several complaints that the special orders are taking longer than 42 days. A sample of 12 special orders delivered in the last month showed the mean waiting time was 51 days with a standard deviation of 8 days. At the .05 significance level, are customers waiting an average of more than 42 days?

28. A recent article in *The Wall Street Journal* reported that the prime rate for large banks now exceeds 9 percent. A sample of eight small banks in the midwest revealed the following prime rates: 10.1, 9.3, 9.2, 10.2, 9.3, 9.6, 9.4, and 8.8. At the .01 significance level, can we conclude that the prime rate for small banks also exceeds 9 percent?

29. A typical college student drinks an average of 27 gallons of coffee each year, or 2.25 gallons per month. A sample of 12 students at Northwestern State University revealed the following amounts of coffee consumed last month.

| 1.75 | 1.96 | 1.57 | 1.82 | 1.85 | 1.82 |
| 2.43 | 2.65 | 2.60 | 2.24 | 1.69 | 2.66 |

(Source: "The Typical College Student," *Vitality,* vol. 7, no. 7, July 1991, p. 3.)
At the .05 significance level, is there a significant difference between the average amount consumed at Northwestern and the national average?

30. A study of the health benefits packages for employees of large and small firms was recently completed by Pohlman Associates, a management consulting firm. Among the 15 large firms studied the benefits package costs an average of 17.6 percent of salary with a standard deviation of 2.6 percent. Among the 12 small firms studied the benefits package averaged 16.2 percent of salary with a standard deviation of 3.3 percent. Is there a significant difference between the mean percent of the employees' salaries spent by large firms and by small firms and health benefits? Use the .05 level of significance.

31. The Commercial Bank and Trust Company is studying the use of its automatic teller machines (ATMs). Of particular interest is whether young adults (under 25 years) use the machine more than senior citizens. To investigate further, samples of customers under 25 years of age and customers over 60 years of age were selected. The number of ATM transactions last month was determined for each selected individual, and the results are shown below. At the .01 significance level, can bank management conclude that younger customers use the ATMs more?

| Number of Transactions | |
| --- | --- |
| Under 25 years of age | Over 60 years of age |
| 10 | 4 |
| 10 | 8 |
| 11 | 7 |
| 15 | 7 |
| 7 | 4 |
| 11 | 5 |
| 10 | 1 |
| 9 | 7 |
| | 4 |
| | 10 |
| | 5 |

32. Two equal groups of seedlings were selected for an experiment. All the seedlings were of equal height. One group of seedlings was fed with a 10−10−40 fertilizer, the other with a 20−20−20 fertilizer. The mean heights of the two groups of seedlings after a period of time and pertinent information follow.

| Fertilizer | Sample mean height (inches) | Sample standard deviation (inches) | Sample size |
|---|---|---|---|
| 10−10−40 | 12.92 | 0.25 | 15 |
| 20−20−20 | 12.63 | 0.20 | 13 |

At the .025 level, determine whether or not the group of seedlings fed with 10−10−40 fertilizer has a greater mean height than the group fed with 20−20−20 fertilizer.

33. Samples of efficiency ratings of employees at Allied Chemicals in plant number 1 and plant number 2 are:

| Plant no. 1 | Plant no. 2 |
|---|---|
| 160 | 163 |
| 158 | 161 |
| 162 | 160 |
| 161 | 162 |
| 160 | 163 |
| 160 | 162 |
| 161 | 164 |
| 159 | 163 |
| 159 | 165 |
| 160 | 162 |
|  | 159 |
|  | 160 |

At the .02 level, test $H_0 : \mu_1 = \mu_2$ against the alternate hypothesis $H_1 : \mu_1 \neq \mu_2$.

34. A drill press operator has to do several safety checks before actually drilling holes in a steel plate. The START switch has to be held closed with one hand, and the safety checks have to be done with the other hand. The operators are on piece work and therefore want to do the job in the most efficient way. Twelve right-handed operators selected at random participated in an experiment. During a one-week period operators used the left hand to hold the START switch closed. The second week the right hand held the switch closed. The number of holes drilled each week is shown below.

| | Production, by operator number |
|---|---|

| | 1 | 2 | 3 | 4 | 5 | 6 | 7 | 8 | 9 | 10 | 11 | 12 |
|---|---|---|---|---|---|---|---|---|---|---|---|---|
| Left hand | 1,240 | 1,137 | 942 | 1,105 | 846 | 1,216 | 1,190 | 840 | 892 | 1,115 | 1,260 | 550 |
| Right hand | 1,248 | 1,130 | 940 | 1,105 | 849 | 1,221 | 1,180 | 841 | 890 | 1,120 | 1,257 | 551 |

Do the paired sample results give us evidence to reject the statement that there is no difference between use of the left hand and use of the right hand in holding the start switch closed and doing the safety checks with the other hand? Use the .05 level.

35. A number of minor automobile accidents occur at various high-risk intersections in Teton County despite traffic lights. The traffic department claims that a modification in the type of light will reduce these accidents. The county commissioners have agreed to a proposed experiment. Eight intersections were chosen at random, and the lights at those intersections were modified. The number of minor accidents during a six-month period before and after the modifications was:

| | Number of accidents, by intersection | | | | | | | |
|---|---|---|---|---|---|---|---|---|
| | A | B | C | D | E | F | G | H |
| Before modification | 5 | 7 | 6 | 4 | 8 | 9 | 8 | 10 |
| After modification | 3 | 7 | 7 | 0 | 4 | 6 | 8 | 2 |

Did the modification reduce the number of minor accidents at high-risk intersections? Test at the 1 percent level.

36. The manager of Fred's Grocery is making a study of the amount customers spend in the store. A sample of 10 weekday morning shoppers and 15 Saturday morning shoppers revealed the following amounts spent:

| Weekday | Saturday |
|---------|----------|
| $18.88 | $21.54 |
| 24.33 | 34.76 |
| 27.26 | 45.78 |
| 35.79 | 46.87 |
| 42.31 | 56.78 |
| 53.77 | 66.04 |
| 62.94 | 68.45 |
| 73.59 | 70.98 |
| 76.51 | 72.67 |
| 88.09 | 76.89 |
| | 81.65 |
| | 85.61 |
| | 91.87 |
| | 94.71 |
| | 95.80 |

Owner Fred Snead contends that Saturday morning shoppers spend an average of $10 more than weekday shoppers. Do these data substantiate his claim? Use the .05 significance level.

37. During recent seasons major league baseball has been criticized for the length of the games. A report indicated that the average game lasts 3 hours and 30 minutes. A sample of 17 games played during the week from July 12 to July 19, 1991, revealed the following times to completion. (Note that the minutes have been changed to fractions of hours, so that a game that lasted 2 hours and 24 minutes is reported at 2.40 hours.)

| 2.98 | 2.40 | 2.70 | 2.25 | 3.23 | 3.17 | 2.93 |
| 3.18 | 2.80 | 2.38 | 3.75 | 3.20 | 3.27 | 2.52 |
| 2.58 | 4.45 | 2.45 | | | | |

Do these sample data support the contention that baseball games take an average of 3½ hours to complete? Use the .05 significance level. (Source: "Basecrawl," *Toledo Blade*, June 18, 1991, p. 20.)

38. The following numbers indicate the years that the chief justice of the United States Supreme Court held the position.

| 5 | 0 | 4 | 34 | 28 | 8 | 14 |
| 21 | 10 | 8 | 11 | 4 | 7 | 15 |
| 17 | | | | | | |

If you were describing the tenure of these justices, would you be willing to make the statement that the typical justice spends more than 10 years on the bench? Use the .05 level of significance.

## COMPUTER DATA EXERCISES

39. Refer to data set 1, which reports information on homes sold in Florida during 1990.

   a. At the .05 significance level, can we conclude that the mean selling price for a home with a pool is different from the mean selling price of a home without a pool?

   b. At the .05 significance level, can we conclude that the mean selling price for a home with a garage is different from the mean selling price of a home without a garage?

    c.    At the .05 significance level, can we conclude that there is a difference in the mean selling price for a home in Township 1 versus one in Township 2?

40. Refer to data set 3, which reports information on the 26 major league baseball teams for the 1991 season.

    a.    At the .05 significance level, can we conclude that teams with turf home fields hit more home runs than those with grass fields?

    b.    At the .05 significance level, can we conclude that the mean number of stolen bases per team was higher for National League teams than for American League teams.

    c.    At the .05 significance level, is there a difference in the mean salary for the American League versus the National League?

    d.    At the .05 significance level, is there a difference in the mean attendance for American League teams versus National League teams?

# CHAPTER 11 EXAMINATION

*The answers are at the end of the chapter.*

For Questions 1 through 10, indicate whether the statement is true or false. If false, give the correct answer.

1. To apply the Student $t$ to a problem involving two means, the two populations must be normal, or nearly normal.

2. A test was made about a population mean. A sample of 22 pieces of steel were selected at random. There are 22 degrees of freedom.

3. As the sample size increases, the $t$ distribution tends to approximate the standard normal distribution.

4. There is only one $t$ distribution, and it has a mean of zero.

5. Generally speaking, Student's $t$ distribution is used when the sample size is less than 30.

6. In a test of the difference between two population means, the degrees of freedom are $n_1 + n_2 - 2$.

7. The $t$ test assumes that the variances of the two populations are equal, or approximately equal.

Questions 8–10 are based on the following:

$$H_0 : \mu_1 = \mu_2 \qquad H_1 : \mu_1 \neq \mu_2$$

Sample sizes are 12 and 11. The .05 level of risk is to be used.

8. The test is two-tailed.

9. The critical values of $t$ are $-2.069$ and $+2.069$.

10. If $t$ were computed to be $-0.999$, the null hypothesis would not be rejected.

11. A radical new treatment for repairing broken leg bones has been introduced. The claim is that the amount of time a patient spends in a cast and on crutches has been reduced. Extensive records revealed that using the old method, a patient, on the average, requires 20 days to recover from a leg break. A random sample of 16 individuals receiving the new treatment revealed that the mean length of time needed to recover was 18 days; the standard deviation of the sample was 2.5 days. Is the claim made for the new treatment supported at the .05 level? State the null and alternate hypotheses, give the critical value, and reach a decision.

12. The offense of the SU football team uses a large number of complicated plays that must be learned quickly at the start of the season. The offensive coordinator wants to experiment with two methods of memorizing the plays—the Pow Wow method and the Ding Ding method. To test them, 10 pairs of players were selected at random. He paired

two quarterbacks, two tight ends, and so on. One of each pair learned the plays using the Pow Wow method; the other used the Ding Ding method. Just prior to the first game against State, the 10 pairs were tested on their execution of the plays, with these results:

| Method | \multicolumn{10}{c}{Test scores by pair} |
| | A | B | C | D | E | F | G | H | I | J |
| --- | --- | --- | --- | --- | --- | --- | --- | --- | --- | --- |
| Pow Wow method | 100 | 86 | 82 | 70 | 82 | 77 | 80 | 99 | 86 | 91 |
| Ding Ding method | 91 | 86 | 94 | 65 | 91 | 86 | 60 | 98 | 89 | 90 |

Does this sample information at the .05 level of significance indicate a difference between the two methods? Answer by stating $H_0$ and $H_1$, giving the critical values, computing the appropriate statistics, and arriving at a decision to either reject or not reject $H_0$.

13. Two suppliers of bearings are being considered by Midland Manufacturing. Is there a difference in the quality of the bearings sold by the two suppliers? A sample of seven recent shipments from New York Supply revealed that the mean number of defects per shipment was 12 with a standard deviation of 2. A sample of six recent shipments from Discount Supply revealed the mean number of defects per shipment to be 9 with a standard deviation of 3. Use the .05 significance level to explore whether there is a difference in the quality of the bearings supplied by New York and those supplied by Discount.

11–1  1.  $H_0: \mu = 305, H_1: \mu > 305.$

2.  $df = 19$

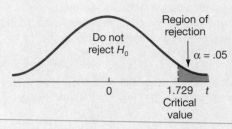

Do not
reject $H_0$

Region of
rejection

$\alpha = .05$

0        1.729  $t$
Critical
value

3.  $t = \dfrac{\overline{X} - \mu}{\dfrac{s}{\sqrt{n}}} = \dfrac{311 - 305}{\dfrac{12}{\sqrt{20}}}$

$= 2.236$

Reject $H_0$ because $2.236 > 1.729$. Accept $H_1$, that the mean is greater than 305 days. It is concluded that the modification increased battery life.

11–2  1.  $H_0 : \mu = 9.0, H_1 : \mu < 9.0.$

2.  7, found by $n - 1 = 8 - 1 = 7.$

3.  Do not reject the null hypothesis if the computed value of $t$ falls to the right of $-2.998$. Otherwise reject $H_0$ and accept $H_1$.

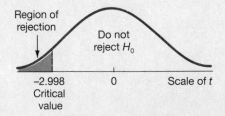

Region of
rejection

Do not
reject $H_0$

$-2.998$     0      Scale of $t$
Critical
value

4.  $t = -2.494$, found by:

| $X$ | $X - \overline{X}$ | $(X - \overline{X})^2$ | $X^2$ |
|---|---|---|---|
| 9.2 | 0.4 | 0.16 | 84.64 |
| 8.7 | −0.1 | 0.01 | 75.69 |
| 8.9 | 0.1 | 0.01 | 79.21 |
| 8.6 | −0.2 | 0.04 | 73.96 |
| 8.8 | 0.0 | 0.00 | 77.44 |
| 8.5 | −0.3 | 0.09 | 72.25 |
| 8.7 | −0.1 | 0.01 | 75.69 |
| 9.0 | 0.2 | 0.04 | 81.00 |
| 70.4 | 0.0 | 0.36 | 619.88 |

$\overline{X} = \dfrac{70.4}{8} = 8.8$

$s = \sqrt{\dfrac{.36}{8 - 1}} = 0.2268$

or

$s = \sqrt{\dfrac{619.88 - \dfrac{(70.4)^2}{8}}{8 - 1}} = 0.2268$

Then,

$t = \dfrac{8.8 - 9.0}{\dfrac{0.2268}{\sqrt{8}}} = -2.494$

Since $-2.494$ lies to the right of $-2.998$, $H_0$ is not rejected. We have not shown that the mean is less than 9.0.

5.  The $p$-value is between .025 and .010.

11–3  $H_0: \mu_1 = \mu_2, H_1: \mu_1 < \mu_2.$ $H_0$ is rejected if $t < -1.782.$ There are 12 degrees of freedom, found by $n_1 + n_2 - 2 = 6 + 8 - 2.$

|  | Edne | Orno |
|---|---|---|
| Mean | 7.00 | 10.00 |
| Standard deviation | 1.4142 | 2.2678 |
| $n$ | 6 | 8 |

$s_p^2 = \dfrac{(6 - 1)(1.4142)^2 + (8 - 1)(2.2678)^2}{6 + 8 - 2} = 3.8334$

$t = \dfrac{7.00 - 10.00}{\sqrt{3.8334\left(\dfrac{1}{6} + \dfrac{1}{8}\right)}} = \dfrac{-3.00}{1.0574} = -2.837$

Since $-2.837$ falls in the left tail beyond $-1.782$, the null hypothesis is rejected at the .05 level. Orno's mean weight is greater than Edne's mean weight.

11–4  1.  $H_0 : \mu_d = 0, H_1 : \mu_d \neq 0.$

2.  Two-tailed test; $n - 1 = 9 - 1 = 8$ degrees of freedom; critical values are $-2.306$ and $+2.306$.

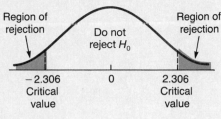

Region of rejection

Do not reject $H_0$

Region of rejection

−2.306
Critical value

0

2.306
Critical value

$$\bar{d} = \frac{\Sigma d}{n} = \frac{2}{9} = .22$$

$$s_d = \sqrt{\frac{108 - \frac{(2)^2}{9}}{9 - 1}} = 3.667$$

$$t = \frac{\bar{d}}{\frac{s_d}{\sqrt{n}}} = \frac{0.22}{\frac{3.667}{\sqrt{9}}} = \frac{0.22}{1.222} = 0.180$$

3.

| Pair | A | B | $d = B - A$ | $d^2$ |
|------|----|----|------|------|
| 1 | 16 | 18 | 2 | 4 |
| 2 | 9 | 7 | −2 | 4 |
| 3 | 21 | 26 | 5 | 25 |
| 4 | 14 | 11 | −3 | 9 |
| 5 | 26 | 26 | 0 | 0 |
| 6 | 27 | 22 | −5 | 25 |
| 7 | 18 | 19 | 1 | 1 |
| 8 | 14 | 20 | 6 | 36 |
| 9 | 30 | 28 | −2 | 4 |
| | | | 2 | 108 |

Since 0.180 lies between −2.306 and 2.306, the null hypothesis is not rejected. There is no difference between the effectiveness of solutions A and B.

## Answers

# CHAPTER 11  EXAMINATION

1. True.
2. False. 21 degrees of freedom, found by $n - 1 = 22 - 1$.
3. True.
4. False. There are many *t* distributions, each with a mean of zero. The shapes of the *t* distributions vary with the sample size.
5. True.
6. True.
7. True.
8. True.
9. False, $t = 2.080$. There are $n_1 + n_2 - 2 = 12 + 11 - 2 = 21$ degrees of freedom. From Appendix F, two-tailed test, .05 level, 21 degrees of freedom, the critical value of *t* is 2.080.
10. True.
11. $H_0 : \mu = 20$ days, $H_1 : \mu < 20$ days. $df = 15$. Computed $t = -3.20$, found by:

$$t = \frac{18 - 20}{\frac{2.5}{\sqrt{16}}}$$

Reject null hypothesis at the .05 level because computed *t* of −3.20 is in the region of rejection beyond

−1.753. The new method significantly reduces the healing time.

12. $H_0 : \mu_d = 0$, $H_1 : \mu_d \neq 0$. $df = 9$. $n = 10$. Critical values of *t* are −2.262 and +2.262 (.05 level, two-tailed values). Computed $t = 0.099$. $\bar{d} = 3/10 = 0.3$. $s_d = 9.56$. Then

$$t = \frac{0.3}{\frac{9.56}{\sqrt{10}}} = 0.099$$

Do not reject $H_0$. There is no significant difference between the two methods.

13. $H_0 : \mu_1 = \mu_2$, $H_1 : \mu_1 \neq \mu_2$. $df = 7 + 6 - 2 = 11$. $H_0$ is rejected if $t < -2.201$ or $t > 2.201$.

$$s_p^2 = \frac{(7 - 1)(2)^2 + (6 - 1)(3)^2}{7 + 6 - 2} = 6.2727$$

$$t = \frac{12.0 - 9.0}{\sqrt{6.2727\left(\frac{1}{7} + \frac{1}{6}\right)}} = \frac{3.0}{1.3934} = 2.153$$

$H_0$ is not rejected. There is no difference in the mean number of defects.

# CHAPTER

# 12

# ANALYSIS OF VARIANCE

## GOALS

When you have completed this chapter, you will be able to:

1. Discuss the general idea of analysis of variance.

2. Give the characteristics of the $F$ distribution.

3. Conduct a test of hypothesis to determine if two sample variances came from the same or equal populations.

4. Set up and organize data into an ANOVA table.

5. Conduct a test for a difference among three or more treatment means.

6. Conduct a test of hypothesis to determine if there is a difference between block means.

In this chapter we continue our discussion of hypothesis testing. Recall that in Chapter 9 we examined the general theory of hypothesis testing and applied it to situations where a large sample was selected from a normal population. We used the standard normal distribution as a basis for testing whether a sample mean came from a hypothesized population and whether two samples means were obtained from the same or equal populations. In Chapter 10 we conducted both one- and two-sample tests for proportions, again using the standard normal distribution as the test statistic. In Chapter 11 we described methods for conducting tests of means where the populations are normal but the samples are small.

## THE *F* DISTRIBUTION

In this chapter we describe the *F* distribution. This probability distribution is used as the test statistic for several situations. It is used to test whether two sample variances are from the same or equal populations, and it is also applied when we want to compare two or more population means simultaneously. The simultaneous comparison of several population means is called *analysis of variance (ANOVA)*. In both of these situations, the populations must be normal, and the data must be at least interval-scale. What are the major characteristics of the *F* distribution?

*Characteristics of the F distribution*

1. There is a "family" of *F* distributions. A particular member of the family is determined by two parameters: the degrees of freedom in the numerator and the degrees of freedom in the denominator. This is illustrated by the following graph. There is one *F* distribution for the combination of 29 degrees of freedom in the numerator and 28 degrees of freedom in the denominator. There is another *F* distribution for 19 degrees in the numerator and 6 degrees of freedom in the denominator. Note that the shape of the curves changes as the degrees of freedom change.
2. *F* cannot be negative and it is a continuous distribution.
3. The curve representing an *F* distribution is positively skewed.
4. Its values range from 0 to $\infty$. As the values of *F* increase, the curve approaches the *X*-axis, but it never touches it.

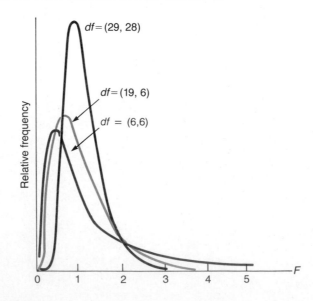

## COMPARING TWO POPULATION VARIANCES

The $F$ distribution is used in this section to test the hypothesis that the variance of one normal population equals the variance of another normal population, Thus, this test is useful for determining whether or not one normal population has more variation than another. The following examples show the use of this test:

Two Barth shearing machines are set to produce steel bars of the same length. The bars, therefore, should have the same mean length. We want to ensure that in addition to having the same mean length, they have similar variation.

The mean rate of return on investment of two types of stocks may be the same, but there may be more variation in the return of one than the other. A sample of 10 aerospace stocks and 10 utility stocks might show the same mean rate of return, but it is likely there is more variation in the rate of return of aerospace stocks.

## VALIDATING ASSUMPTIONS

The $F$ test can also be used to validate assumptions with respect to certain statistical tests. As an example, recall that the $t$ test described in Chapter 11 is used to determine whether two population means differ. To employ that test, it is necessary to assume that the two population variances are the same.

*First state null hypothesis*

Regardless of whether we want to determine if one population has more variation than another population or validate an assumption with respect to a statistical test, we first state the null hypothesis. For either investigation, the null hypothesis is that the variance of one normal population, $\sigma_1^2$, equals the variance of the other normal population, $\sigma_2^2$. To conduct the test, a random sample of $n_1$ observations is obtained from one population, and a sample of $n_2$ observations is obtained from the second population. The test statistic is $s_1^2/s_2^2$, where $s_1^2$ and $s_2^2$ are the respective sample variances. If the null hypothesis is true ($H_0 : \sigma_1^2 = \sigma_2^2$), the test statistic follows the $F$ distribution with $n_1 - 1$ and $n_2 - 1$ degrees of freedom. The *larger* sample variance is placed in the numerator; hence, the $F$ ratio is always positive and larger than 1.00. Thus, the upper-tail critical value is the only one required. The critical value of $F$ is found by dividing the significance level in half ($\alpha/2$) and then referring to the appropriate number of degrees of freedom in Appendix G.

## ■ EXAMPLE

Lammers Limos offers limousine service from city hall in Toledo, Ohio, to Metro Airport in Detroit. Sean Lammers, president of the company, is considering two routes. One is via U.S. 25 and the other via I-75. He wants to conduct a study of both routes and then compare the results. He recorded the following data. Using the .10 significance level, is there a difference in the variation in the two routes?

| Route | Mean time (minutes) | Standard deviation (minutes) | Sample size |
|---|---|---|---|
| U.S. 25 | 56 | 12 | 7 |
| I-75 | 59 | 5 | 8 |

## ☑ SOLUTION

Lammers noted that the mean times seem very similar, but there is more variation, as measured by the standard deviation, in the U.S. 25 route than in the I-75 route. This is somewhat consistent with his knowledge of the two routes; the U.S. 25 route contains more stoplights, whereas I-75 is a limited-access highway. However, the I-75 route is several miles longer. It is important that the service offered be both timely and consistent, so he decides to conduct a statistical test to determine if there really is a difference in the variation of the two routes.

The usual five-step hypothesis-testing procedure will be employed.

**STEP 1** The null hypothesis and the alternate hypothesis are stated. The test is two-tailed because we are looking for a difference in the variation of the two routes. We are not trying to show that one route has more variation than the other.

$$H_0 : \sigma_1^2 = \sigma_2^2$$
$$H_1 : \sigma_1^2 \neq \sigma_2^2$$

**STEP 2** A significance level of .10 is selected.

**STEP 3** The appropriate test statistic is the $F$ distribution.

**STEP 4** The decision rule is obtained from Appendix G, a portion of which is reproduced as Table 12–1. Because we are using a two-tailed test, the significance level is .05, found by $\alpha/2 = .10/2 = .05$. There are $n_1 - 1 = 7 - 1 = 6$ degrees of freedom in the numerator, and $n_2 - 1 = 8 - 1 = 7$ degrees of freedom in the denominator. To obtain the critical value, move horizontally across the top portion of the $F$ Table (Table 12–1 or Appendix G) for the .05 significance level to 6 degrees of freedom in the numerator. Then move down that column to the critical value opposite 7 degrees of freedom in the denominator. The critical value is 3.87. If the ratio of the sample variances, $s_1^2/s_2^2$, exceeds 3.87, the null hypothesis is rejected.

### TABLE 12–1

**Critical Values of the $F$ Distribution, $\alpha = .05$**

| Degrees of freedom for denominator | Degrees of freedom for numerator | | | |
|---|---|---|---|---|
| | 5 | 6 | 7 | 8 |
| 1 | 230 | 234 | 237 | 239 |
| 2 | 19.3 | 19.3 | 19.4 | 19.4 |
| 3 | 9.01 | 8.94 | 8.89 | 8.85 |
| 4 | 6.26 | 6.16 | 6.09 | 6.04 |
| 5 | 5.05 | 4.95 | 4.88 | 4.82 |
| 6 | 4.39 | 4.28 | 4.21 | 4.15 |
| 7 | 3.97 | 3.87 | 3.79 | 3.73 |
| 8 | 3.69 | 3.58 | 3.50 | 3.44 |
| 9 | 3.48 | 3.37 | 3.29 | 3.23 |
| 10 | 3.33 | 3.22 | 3.14 | 3.07 |
| 11 | 3.20 | 3.09 | 3.01 | 2.95 |
| 12 | 3.11 | 3.00 | 2.91 | 2.85 |
| 13 | 3.03 | 2.92 | 2.83 | 2.77 |
| 14 | 2.96 | 2.85 | 2.76 | 2.70 |
| 15 | 2.90 | 2.79 | 2.71 | 2.64 |

**STEP 5** The computed value of the test statistic is 5.76, found by $s_1^2/s_2^2 = (12)^2/(5)^2$. The null hypothesis is rejected and the alternate hypothesis accepted. The variation is not the same in the two populations.

As noted, the usual procedure is to determine the $F$ ratio by putting the larger variance in the numerator. This will force the $F$ ratio to be larger than the 1.00. Why is this necessary? It allows us to always use the upper tail of the $F$ statistic, thus avoiding the need for more extensive $F$ tables.

A question arises regarding *one-tailed tests.* How are they handled? Again, arrange the $F$ ratio so that it is always greater than 1.00. Under these conditions it is not necessary to divide the level of significance in half. We are therefore restricted to the .05 or .01 significance levels (for one-tailed tests) in Appendix G.

## Self-Review 12–1

*The answers are at the end of the chapter.*

The Treece Company assembles electrical components. For the last 10 days Mark Treece has averaged 9 rejects per day, with a standard deviation of 2 rejects. Debbie Thorton averaged 8.5 rejects per day with standard deviation of 1.5 rejects over the same period. At the .05 significance level, can we conclude that there is more variation in the number of rejects per day attributed to Mark?

## EXERCISES

*The answers to the odd-numbered exercises are at the end of the book.*

1. Using a two-tailed test and the .10 significance level, what is the critical $F$ value for a sample of six observations in the numerator and four in the denominator?

2. Using a one-tailed test and the .01 significance level, what is the critical $F$ value for a sample of four observations in the numerator and seven in the denominator?

3. The following hypotheses are given.

$$H_0 : \sigma_1^2 = \sigma_2^2$$
$$H_1 : \sigma_1^2 \neq \sigma_2^2$$

A random sample of eight observations from the first sample resulted in a standard deviation of 10. A random sample of six observations from the second sample gave a standard deviation of 7. At the .02 significance level, is there a difference in the variation of the two populations?

4. The following hypotheses are given.

$$H_0 : \sigma_1^2 = \sigma_2^2$$
$$H_1 : \sigma_1^2 > \sigma_2^2$$

A random sample of five observations from the first sample resulted in a standard deviation of 12. A random sample of seven observations from the second sample showed a standard deviation of 7. At the .01 significance level, is there more variation in the first population?

5. Macklin Research Associates conducted a study of the radio listening habits of men and women. One facet of the study involved the mean listening time. It was discovered that the mean listening time for men is 35 minutes per day. The standard deviation of the sample of the 10 men studied was 10 minutes per day. The mean listening time for the 12 women studied was 32 minutes and the standard deviation of the sample was 12 minutes. At the .05 significance level, can we conclude that there is a difference in the variation in the number of minutes men and women listen to the radio?

6.  A stockbroker at Columbus Securities reported that the mean rate of return on a sample of 10 oil stocks was 12.6 percent with a standard deviation of 3.9 percent. The mean rate of return on a sample of 8 utility stocks was 10.9 percent with a standard deviation of 3.5 percent. At the .05 significance level, can we conclude that there is more variation in the oil stocks?

# ANOVA: THE GENERAL IDEA

*What is the effect of different treatments?*

*Definition of treatment*

The second use of the $F$ distribution involves the **analysis of variance** technique, abbreviated **ANOVA**. Basically, analysis of variance uses sample information to determine whether or not three or more **treatments** produce different results. The use of the word *treatment* has its origin in agricultural research. Fields were treated with different fertilizers, or sprays, to determine whether or not there was an overall difference in the yields. We will test whether or not five gasoline additives (the treatments) result in a difference in mileage per gallon. We will also explore the question, "Are four different training methods (the treatments) equally effective?"

> **Treatment**   A cause, or specific source, of variation in a set of data.

Following are several cases to expand on the meaning of a treatment.

## CASE 1

*Do different treatments of fertilizer affect yield?*

Hydroponics, Inc. is a research firm that grows tomatoes and other plants in water. The question is how often to treat newly developed tomatoes with soluble plant food. For maximum growth, should they receive a full treatment of food at the beginning of the growing season and none thereafter? Or should the plants be given one-half dose at the beginning and the other half in the middle of the four-month growing season? Or should one quarter of the soluble solution be fed to the plants every month?

As an experiment, one tank was given the full treatment, another tank received the two half-treatments, and a third tank got monthly doses. Samples of the ripe tomatoes from each of three tanks were weighed, and the weights were recorded. A few results are shown in tabular form.

| | Weight (grams) | | |
| --- | --- | --- | --- |
| Sample number | Full treatment | Half-treatment | Monthly treatment |
| 1 | 12.3 | 15.6 | 13.8 |
| 2 | 25.8 | 11.4 | 15.2 |

The question is, is there a difference in the mean weights of the tomatoes grown under the different treatments?

## CASE 2

*Do different grades of gasoline affect performance?*

For an automobile manufacturer, the different "treatments" may be four different grades of gasoline. Suppose, for example, that an automobile manufacturer designed a radical new lightweight engine and wants to recommend the grade of gasoline to use. The four unleaded grades, the treatments, are: below regular, regular, premium, and super premium. The test car made three trial runs on the test track using each of the four grades. The results are:

| Trial run number | Kilometers per liter | | | |
|---|---|---|---|---|
| | Below regular | Regular | Premium | Super premium |
| 1 | 39.31 | 36.69 | 38.99 | 40.04 |
| 2 | 39.87 | 40.00 | 40.02 | 39.89 |
| 3 | 39.87 | 41.01 | 39.99 | 39.93 |

The question to be answered by applying ANOVA is: Are the treatments (grades of gasoline) producing the same results (the same mean number of kilometers per liter)?

### CASE 3

Do four different assembly methods result in different population means?

The "treatments" might be four different ways of doing a job. Suppose, for illustration, that four employees at BMD Electronics have submitted different methods of assembling a subassembly. Some sample data for each of the four treatments are:

| Sample number | Minutes required for assembly | | | |
|---|---|---|---|---|
| | Utz method | Lock method | Sass method | Corbea method |
| 1 | 16.6 | 22.4 | 31.4 | 18.4 |
| 2 | 17.0 | 21.5 | 33.4 | 19.6 |

Applying the analysis of variance technique to the sample observations, we might conclude that there is no difference in the mean assembly time required and, hence, that the differences in the sample data are due to chance (sampling).

Why do we need to study ANOVA? Why can't we just use the $t$ distribution, discussed in Chapter 11, to compare the treatment means two at a time? The major reason is the unsatisfactory buildup of Type I or $\alpha$ error. To explain further, suppose we have four different methods (A, B, C, and D) of training new recruits to be fire fighters. We randomly assign each of the 40 recruits in this year's class to one of the four methods. At the end of the training program, a common test to measure understanding of fire-fighting techniques is given to the four groups. The question to be explored is: Is there a difference in the mean test scores among the four groups? An answer to this question will allow us to compare the four training methods.

Using the $t$ distribution to compare the four sample means, we would have to run six different $t$ tests. That is, we would need to compare the mean scores for the four methods as follows: A versus B, A versus C, A versus D, B versus C, B versus D, and C versus D. If we set $\alpha$ at .05, the probability of a correct statistical decision is .95, found by a 1 − .05. The probability that we do not make an incorrect decision due to sampling in any of the six independent tests is $(.95)^6 = .735$. Thus, the probability of at least one incorrect decision due to sampling is 1 − .735 = 265. So if we conduct six independent tests using the $t$ distribution, the likelihood of at least one sampling error is increased from .05 to an unsatisfactory level of .265. It is obvious that we need a better method than conducting six $t$ tests. ANOVA will allow us to compare the treatment means simultaneously and avoid the buildup of the Type I or $\alpha$ error.

## ASSUMPTIONS UNDERLYING THE ANOVA TEST

Before we actually conduct a test using the ANOVA technique, the assumptions underlying the test will be examined. If any of the following assumptions cannot be met, another analysis of variance technique (developed by Kruskal and Wallis and presented in Chapter 17) may be applied.

1. The three or more populations of interest are normally distributed.
2. The populations have equal standard deviations.
3. The samples we select from each of the populations are random and independent—that is, they are not related.

## ANALYSIS OF VARIANCE PROCEDURE

**Does difference between these sample means indicate unequal population means?**

The ANOVA procedure can best be illustrated using an example. Suppose the manager of the west-end branch of Appliance Stores, Inc. resigned, and three salespeople at the branch are being considered for the position. All three have about the same length of service, education, and so on. In order to make a decision, it was suggested that each of their monthly sales records be examined. The sample results of their monthly sales are shown in Table 12–2. The "treatments" in this problem are the salespeople.

TABLE   12–2

**Monthly Sales of Appliances of Three Salespeople**

|  | Monthly sales ($000) | | |
|---|---|---|---|
|  | Ms. Mapes | Mr. Sonnar | Mr. Mafee |
|  | 15 | 15 | 19 |
|  | 10 | 10 | 12 |
|  | 9 | 12 | 16 |
|  | 5 | 11 | 16 |
|  | 16 | 12 | 17 |
| Treatment means | 11 | 12 | 16 |

The ANOVA procedure calls for the same hypothesis-testing procedure outlined in Chapter 9 and used in Chapters 10 and 11.

**Null hypothesis**

**STEP 1: THE NULL HYPOTHESIS AND THE ALTERNATE HYPOTHESIS** $H_0$ states that there is no significant difference among the mean sales of the three salespeople; that is, $\mu_1 = \mu_2 = \mu_3$. $H_1$ states that at least one mean is different. As before, if $H_0$ is rejected, $H_1$ will be accepted. So,

$$H_0: \mu_1 = \mu_2 = \mu_3$$
$$H_1: \text{The treatment means are not the same.}$$

**Level of significance**

**STEP 2: THE LEVEL OF SIGNIFICANCE** The .05 level was selected.

**STEP 3: THE TEST STATISTIC** The appropriate test statistic is the $F$ distribution. Underlying this procedure are several assumptions: (1) The data must be at least interval-level. (2) The actual selection of the sales must be chosen using a probability-type procedure. (3) The distribution of the monthly sales for each of the populations is normal. (4) The variance of the three populations are equal, i.e., $\sigma_1^2 = \sigma_2^2 = \sigma_3^2$.

**The test statistic**

$F$ is the ratio of two variances:

$$F = \frac{\text{Estimated population variance based on variation between the sample means}}{\text{Estimated population variance based on variation within samples}}$$

The common terminology for the numerator is *"between-sample variance."* For the denominator, it is *"within-sample variance."* The numerator has $k - 1$ degrees of freedom and the denominator $N - k$ degrees of freedom, where $k$ is the number of treatments and $N$ is the total number of observations.

**The decision rule**

**STEP 4: THE DECISION RULE** As noted previously, the $F$ distribution and accompanying curve are positively skewed and dependent on (1) the number of treatments, $k$, and (2) the total number of observations, $N$. For this problem involving a new store manager, there are three treatments (salespeople), so there are $k - 1 = 3 - 1 = 2$ degrees of freedom in the numerator. There are 15 observations (three samples of five each). Therefore, there are $N - k = 15 - 3 = 12$ degrees of freedom in the denominator.

**Two degrees of freedom needed**

The critical value of $F$, which is the dividing point between the region where we do not reject $H_0$ and the region of rejection, is found by referring to Appendix G. (*Note:* There is one page for the .05 significance level and another for the .01 significance level.) The degrees of freedom for the numerator are listed at the top of the columns. The degrees of freedom for the denominator are in the left column. Referring to the previous paragraph, we see that there are 2 degrees of freedom in the numerator and 12 degrees of freedom in the denominator. To locate the critical value of $F$, refer to the portion of Appendix G shown in Table 12−3 for the .05 level. Move horizontally to 2 degrees of freedom in the numerator. Then go down that column until the number opposite 12 degrees of freedom in the left column is reached. That number is 3.89 and is the critical value of $F$ for the .05 level.

**TABLE 12−3**

**Critical Values of the $F$ Statistic (.05 level of significance)**

| Degrees of freedom in denominator | Degrees of freedom in numerator | | | | | | | | | |
|---|---|---|---|---|---|---|---|---|---|---|
| | 1 | 2 | 3 | 4 | 5 | 6 | 7 | 8 | 9 | 10 |
| 11 | 4.84 | 3.98 | 3.59 | 3.36 | 3.20 | 3.09 | 3.01 | 2.95 | 2.90 | 2.85 |
| 12 | 4.75 | 3.89 | 3.49 | 3.26 | 3.11 | 3.00 | 2.91 | 2.85 | 2.80 | 2.75 |
| 13 | 4.67 | 3.81 | 3.41 | 3.18 | 3.03 | 2.92 | 2.83 | 2.77 | 2.71 | 2.67 |
| 14 | 4.60 | 3.74 | 3.34 | 3.11 | 2.96 | 2.85 | 2.76 | 2.70 | 2.65 | 2.60 |
| 15 | 4.54 | 3.68 | 3.29 | 3.06 | 2.90 | 2.79 | 2.71 | 2.64 | 2.59 | 2.54 |
| 16 | 4.49 | 3.63 | 3.24 | 3.01 | 2.85 | 2.74 | 2.66 | 2.59 | 2.54 | 2.49 |

In using the predetermined .05 level, the decision rule is not to reject the null hypothesis $H_0$ if the computed $F$ value is less than or equal to 3.89; we reject $H_0$ and accept $H_1$ if the computed $F$ value is greater than 3.89. The decision rule is shown diagrammatically in Chart 12–1.

### CHART 12–1

**Distribution of $F$ for a $k$ of 3 and an $N$ of 15, $\alpha = .05$**

Do not reject $H_0$

Reject $H_0$

$\alpha = .05$

3.89
Critical value

$F$ scale

Make a decision

An ANOVA table

**STEP 5:** **COMPUTE F, AND ARRIVE AT A DECISION** To help us compute $F$ an *ANOVA table* is constructed. It is a convenient form to record the sum of squares and other computations. The general format for a one-way analysis of variance problem is shown in Table 12–4.

### TABLE 12–4

**General Format for Analysis of Variance Table**

| Source of variation | (1) Sum of squares | (2) Degrees of freedom | (3) Mean square (1)/(2) |
|---|---|---|---|
| Between treatments | SST | $k - 1$ | $\dfrac{\text{SST}}{k - 1} = \text{MSTR}$ |
| Error (within treatments) | SSE | $N - k$ | $\dfrac{\text{SSE}}{N - k} = \text{MSE}$ |
| Total | SS total | | |

Formula for $F$

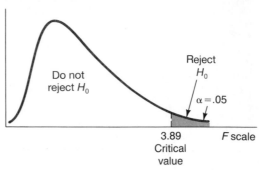

$$F = \frac{\dfrac{\text{SST}}{k - 1}}{\dfrac{\text{SSE}}{N - k}} = \frac{\text{MSTR}}{\text{MSE}}$$

Table 12–4 uses some unfamiliar abbreviations. MSTR is the *mean square between treatments.* MSE is the *mean square due to error.* It is also referred to as the *mean square within treatments.* SST is the abbreviation for *sum of squares treatment* and is found by:

SST

$$SST = \Sigma \left[ \frac{T_c^2}{n_c} \right] - \frac{(\Sigma X)^2}{N} \qquad (12-1)$$

where:

$T_c^2$   directs one to square each column total (subscript $c$ refers to a column).

$n_c$   is the number of observations for each respective treatment (column). There are five sales figures for Ms. Mapes, five for Mr. Sonnar, and five for Mr. Mafee.

$\Sigma X$   is the sum of all the observations (sales). It is $195 (see Table 12−5).

$k$   is the number of treatments (salespeople). There are three.

$N$   is the *total* number of observations. There are 15.

Table 12−5 gives the needed calculations.

## TABLE 12−5

### Monthly Appliance Sales: Data Required for ANOVA Table

| | Ms. Mapes | | Mr. Sonnar | | Mr. Mafee | | |
|---|---|---|---|---|---|---|---|
| | Sales ($000), $X_1$ | Sales squared, $X_1^2$ | Sales ($000), $X_2$ | Sales squared, $X_2^2$ | Sales ($000), $X_3$ | Sales squared, $X_3^2$ | |
| | 15 | 225 | 15 | 225 | 19 | 361 | |
| | 10 | 100 | 10 | 100 | 12 | 144 | |
| | 9 | 81 | 12 | 144 | 16 | 256 | |
| | 5 | 25 | 11 | 121 | 16 | 256 | |
| | 16 | 256 | 12 | 144 | 17 | 289 | Total |
| Column total: $T_c$ | 55 | | 60 | | 80 | | 195 |
| Sample size: $n_c$ | 5 | | 5 | | 5 | | 15 |
| Sum of squares: $x^2$ | | 687 | | 734 | | 1,306 | 2,727 |

Source: Table 12−2.

Computing SST:

$$SST = \Sigma \left[ \frac{T_c^2}{n_c} \right] - \frac{(\Sigma X)^2}{N}$$

$$= \left[ \frac{(55)^2}{5} + \frac{(60)^2}{5} + \frac{(80)^2}{5} \right] - \frac{(195)^2}{15}$$

$$= 2,605 - 2,535$$

$$= 70$$

SSE          Now to compute SSE, which is the abbreviation for *sum of squares error:*

$$SSE = \Sigma(X^2) - \Sigma \left[ \frac{T_c^2}{n_c} \right] \qquad (12-2)$$

where $\Sigma(X^2)$ directs one to square each monthly sales figure and then sum the squares.

$$SSE = (15)^2 + (10)^2 + (9)^2 + \cdots + (17)^2 - \left[ \frac{(55)^2}{5} + \frac{(60)^2}{5} + \frac{(80)^2}{5} \right]$$

$$= 2{,}727 - 2{,}605$$

$$= 122$$

Total variation (SS total) is the sum of the between-columns and the between-rows variation; that is, SS total = SST + SSE = 70 + 122 = 192. It is computed as follows:

$$\boxed{SS\ total = \Sigma(X^2) - \frac{(\Sigma X)^2}{N}} \qquad (12\text{--}3)$$

As a check:

$$SS\ total = \Sigma(X^2) - \frac{(\Sigma X)^2}{N}$$

$$= 2{,}727 - \frac{(195)^2}{15}$$

$$= 2{,}727 - 2{,}535$$

$$= 192$$

The three sums of squares and the calculations needed for $F$ are transferred to the ANOVA table (Table 12–6).

---

### TABLE   12–6

**ANOVA Table for the Store Managers Problem**

| Source of variation | (1) Sum of squares | (2) Degrees of freedom | (3) Mean square (1)/(2) | |
|---|---|---|---|---|
| Between treatments | SST = 70 | $k - 1 = 3 - 1 = 2$ | $\dfrac{SST}{k - 1} = \dfrac{70}{2} = 35$ | MSTR |
| Error (within treatments) | SSE = 122 | $N - k = 15 - 3 = 12$ | $\dfrac{SSE}{N - k} = \dfrac{122}{12} = 10.17$ | MSE |
| SS total | 192 | | | |

*k is the number of treatments (3), N is the total number of observations (15)*

---

Computing $F$:

$$F = \frac{\dfrac{SST}{k - 1}}{\dfrac{SSE}{N - k}} = \frac{MSTR}{MSE} = \frac{35}{10.17} = 3.44 \qquad (12\text{--}4)$$

The decision rule states that if the computed value of $F$ is less than or equal to the critical value of 3.89, the null hypothesis is not rejected. If the $F$ value is greater than 3.89, $H_0$ is rejected and $H_1$ accepted. Since 3.44 < 3.89, the null hypothesis is not rejected at the .05 level. To put it another way, the differences in the mean monthly sales ($11,000, $12,000, and $16,000) are attributed to chance (sampling). From a practical standpoint, the levels of sales of the three salespeople being considered for store manager are the same. No decision with respect to the position can be made on the basis of monthly sales.

## EXERCISES

*The answers to the odd-numbered exercises are at the end of the book.*

7. The following is sample information. Test the hypothesis that the treatment means are equal. Use the .05 significance level.

| Treatment 1 | Treatment 2 | Treatment 3 | Treatment 4 |
|:-----------:|:-----------:|:-----------:|:-----------:|
| 8 | 3 | 3 | 5 |
| 6 | 2 | 4 | 4 |
| 10 | 4 | 5 | 4 |
| 9 | 3 | 4 | 5 |

    a. State the null hypothesis and the alternate hypothesis.
    b. What is the decision rule?
    c. Compute SST, SSE, and SS total.
    d. Complete an ANOVA table.
    e. State your decision regarding the null hypothesis.

8. The following is sample information. Test the hypothesis that the treatment means are equal. Use the .05 significance level.

| Treatment 1 | Treatment 2 | Treatment 3 |
|:-----------:|:-----------:|:-----------:|
| 9 | 13 | 10 |
| 7 | 20 | 9 |
| 11 | 14 | 15 |
| 9 | 13 | 14 |
| 12 | 12 | 15 |
| 10 | 14 | 12 |

    a. State the null hypothesis and the alternate hypothesis.
    b. What is the decision rule?
    c. Compute SST, SSE, and SS total.
    d. Complete an ANOVA table.
    e. State your decision with respect to the null hypothesis.

9. A real estate developer is considering investing in a shopping mall on the outskirts of Atlanta, Georgia. Three parcels of land are being evaluated. Of particular importance is the income in the area surrounding the proposed mall. A random sample of four families is selected near each proposed mall. Following are the sample results. At the .05 significance level, can the developer conclude there is a difference in the mean income? Use the usual five-step hypothesis-testing procedure. (Of course, in actual practice more than four families would be selected.)

| Southwyck area ($000) | Franklin Park ($000) | Old Orchard ($000) |
|:---------------------:|:--------------------:|:------------------:|
| 34 | 44 | 45 |
| 38 | 41 | 50 |
| 40 | 39 | 46 |
| 30 | 40 | 48 |

Courtesy International
Business Machines Corporation

10. The manager of a computer software company is studying the number of hours top executives spend at their computer terminals by type of industry. A sample of five executives from each of three industries is obtained. At the .05 significance level, can the manager conclude there is a difference in the mean number of hours spent at a terminal per week by industry?

| Banking | Retail | Insurance |
|:---:|:---:|:---:|
| 12 | 8 | 10 |
| 10 | 8 | 8 |
| 10 | 6 | 6 |
| 12 | 8 | 8 |
| 10 | 10 | 10 |

The previous example and exercises had the same number of observations in each treatment. The following example of the one-way analysis of variance does not have the same number of observations in each treatment. There are four observations in rating group 1, five in rating group 2, seven in group 3, and six in group 4. However, the procedure and the formulas are the same.

## ■ EXAMPLE

A colleague had students in a large marketing class rate his performance as either 1 (excellent), 2 (good), 3 (fair), or 4 (poor). A graduate assistant collected the ratings and assured the students that the professor would not receive them until after the course grades had been filed in the office of the registrar. The rating (the treatment) a student gave the professor was matched with his or her final course grade. Logically, one might expect that in general the group of students who thought the professor was excellent would have a final average course grade significantly higher than those who rated him good, fair, or poor. It would also seem that those who rated him poor would have the lowest course grades on the average. Samples from each rating group were selected. The results are:

Note unequal number of observations among treatments (ratings)

| Course Grades | | | |
|:---:|:---:|:---:|:---:|
| Rating group 1 (excellent) | Rating group 2 (good) | Rating group 3 (fair) | Rating group 4 (poor) |
| 94 | 75 | 70 | 68 |
| 90 | 68 | 73 | 70 |
| 85 | 77 | 76 | 72 |
| 80 | 83 | 78 | 65 |
|  | 88 | 80 | 74 |
|  |  | 68 | 65 |
|  |  | 65 |  |

The question is whether or not there is a statistical difference among the mean scores of the four groups. Use the .01 significance level.

## ☑ SOLUTION

As before, the null hypothesis states that there is no difference among the four treatment means.

$H_0$:   $\mu_1 = \mu_2 = \mu_3 = \mu_4$
$H_1$:   The treatment means are not equal.

The decision rule is that the null hypothesis, which states that there is no difference among the means, will not be rejected if the computed value of $F$ is less than the critical value. Otherwise, the null hypothesis will be rejected and $H_1$ accepted.

Recall that the degrees of freedom in the numerator of the $F$ ratio are found by $k - 1$, where $k$ is the number of treatments (groups of faculty ratings, in this problem). There are four treatments, so there are $4 - 1 = 3$ degrees of freedom. The degrees of freedom in the denominator total 18, found by $N - k$, where $N$ is the total number of students sampled. There were 22 students, so there are $22 - 4 = 18$ degrees of freedom.

The decision rule is portrayed diagrammatically in Chart 12–2. Note that the critical value of $F$ is 5.09. To determine it, refer to Appendix G and the page for the .01 level of significance. Move horizontally at the top of the table to 3 degrees of freedom in the numerator. Then move down that column to the critical value opposite 18 degrees of freedom in the denominator. Do not reject the null hypothesis at the .01 level if the computed value of $F$ is less than or equal to 5.09, but reject it if the computed value is greater than 5.09.

## CHART   12–2

### Areas of Rejection and Nonrejection, .01 Level of Significance

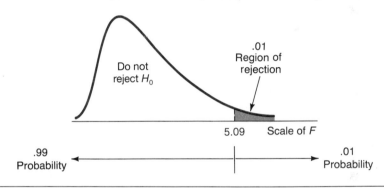

The calculations needed for the completion of the ANOVA table and the $F$ ratio are shown in Table 12–7.

## TABLE   12–7

### Calculations Needed for the F Ratio

|  | Group 1 (excellent) | | Group 2 (good) | | Group 3 (fair) | | Group 4 (poor) | |
|---|---|---|---|---|---|---|---|---|
|  | $X_1$ | $X_1^2$ | $X_2$ | $X_2^2$ | $X_3$ | $X_3^2$ | $X_4$ | $X_4^2$ |
|  | 94 | 8,836 | 75 | 5,625 | 70 | 4,900 | 68 | 4,624 |
|  | 90 | 8,100 | 68 | 4,624 | 73 | 5,329 | 70 | 4,900 |
|  | 85 | 7,225 | 77 | 5,929 | 76 | 5,776 | 72 | 5,184 |
|  | 80 | 6,400 | 83 | 6,889 | 78 | 6,084 | 65 | 4,225 |
|  |  |  | 88 | 7,744 | 80 | 6,400 | 74 | 5,476 |
|  |  |  |  |  | 68 | 4,624 | 65 | 4,225 |
|  |  |  |  |  | 65 | 4,225 |  |  |
| Column total: $T_c$ | 349 |  | 391 |  | 510 |  | 414 |  |
| Sample size: $n_c$ | 4 |  | 5 |  | 7 |  | 6 |  |
| Sum of squares: $X^2$ |  | 30,561 |  | 30,811 |  | 37,338 |  | 28,634 |

Note that the sum of the column totals ($\Sigma X$) is 1,664; the total of the sample size ($N$) is 22; and the sum of the squares ($\Sigma X^2$) is 127,344.

Computing SST, SSE, and SS total using formulas (12−1) and (12−2), we get:

$$SST = \Sigma \left[ \frac{T_c^2}{n_c} \right] - \frac{(\Sigma X)^2}{N}$$

$$= \left[ \frac{(349)^2}{4} + \frac{(391)^2}{5} + \frac{(510)^2}{7} + \frac{(414)^2}{6} \right] - \frac{(1,664)^2}{22}$$

$$= 890.68$$

$$SSE = \Sigma(X^2) - \Sigma \frac{T_c^2}{n_c}$$

$$= (94)^2 + (90)^2 + \cdots + (65)^2 - \frac{(349)^2}{4} + \frac{(391)^2}{5} + \frac{(510)^2}{7} + \frac{(414)^2}{6}$$

$$= 594.41$$

$$SS\ total = SST + SSE = 890.68 + 594.41 = 1,485.09$$

As a check, using formula (12−3):

$$SS\ total = \Sigma(X^2) - \frac{(\Sigma X)^2}{N}$$

$$= 127,344 - \frac{(1,664)^2}{22}$$

$$= 1,485.09$$

These values are inserted in the ANOVA table. (See Table 12−8.)

## TABLE   12−8

**ANOVA Table for the Faculty Evaluation Problem**

| Source of variation | (1) Sum of squares | (2) Degrees of freedom | (3) Mean square (1)/(2) |
|---|---|---|---|
| Treatment (between columns) | SST = 890.68 | $k - 1 = 4 - 1 = 3$ | $\frac{SST}{k-1} = \frac{890.68}{3} = 296.89$ |
| Error (between rows) | SSE = 594.41 | $N - k = 22 - 4 = 18$ | $\frac{SSE}{N-k} = \frac{594.41}{18} = 33.02$ |

Numerator of the $F$ ratio = 296.89. Denominator of the $F$ ratio is 33.02

Inserting the mean squares into formula (12−4) for $F$, we get:

$$F = \frac{MSTR}{MSE} = \frac{296.89}{33.02} = 8.99$$

The decision: Since the computed $F$ value of 8.99 is greater than the critical value of 5.09 (from Appendix G), the null hypothesis that there is no difference among the means is rejected at the .01 level. This indicates that it is likely that the observed differences among the means are not due to chance. From a practical standpoint, it suggests that the grades students earn in a course are related to the opinions they have of the overall competency and classroom performance of the instructor.

Use MINITAB

As you noted from the previous example, the calculations become very tedious if the number of observations in each treatment is large. The MINITAB solution to the same problem is shown below. The output is in the form of an ANOVA table. To employ the MINITAB system, first enter the data. Each treatment is entered in its own column.

This is accomplished using the SET command. The MINITAB procedure used is AOVONEWAY.

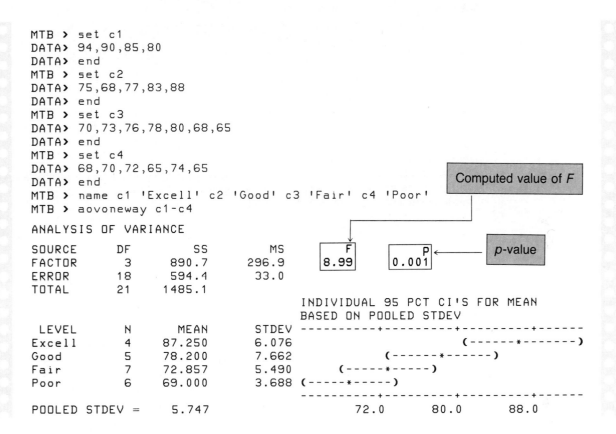

```
MTB > set c1
DATA> 94,90,85,80
DATA> end
MTB > set c2
DATA> 75,68,77,83,88
DATA> end
MTB > set c3
DATA> 70,73,76,78,80,68,65
DATA> end
MTB > set c4
DATA> 68,70,72,65,74,65
DATA> end
MTB > name c1 'Excell' c2 'Good' c3 'Fair' c4 'Poor'
MTB > aovoneway c1-c4
```

Computed value of $F$

```
ANALYSIS OF VARIANCE

SOURCE      DF        SS        MS          F          P
FACTOR       3      890.7     296.9       8.99      0.001
ERROR       18      594.4      33.0
TOTAL       21     1485.1
```

$p$-value

```
                                   INDIVIDUAL 95 PCT CI'S FOR MEAN
                                   BASED ON POOLED STDEV
 LEVEL      N      MEAN     STDEV  ----------+---------+---------+------
Excell      4    87.250     6.076                         (------*------)
Good        5    78.200     7.662               (------*------)
Fair        7    72.857     5.490        (-----*-----)
Poor        6    69.000     3.688  (-----*-----)
                                   ----------+---------+---------+------
POOLED STDEV =    5.747               72.0      80.0      88.0
```

The results reported in the MINITAB output are the same as in Table 12–8. The MINITAB system uses the term *factor* instead of *treatment,* with the same intended meaning. The value of $F$ is the same as that reported in Table 12–8. The *p*-value is also reported. The value is located under the heading "p" and in this case is .001. How do we interpret this value? It is the probability of finding an $F$ value to the right of 8.99 with 3 degrees of freedom in the numerator and 18 degrees of freedom in the denominator, given that $H_0$ is true. So the likelihood of committing a Type I error by rejecting a true $H_0$ is 0.1 percent—a very small likelihood indeed!

Before continuing, do Self-Review 12–2 on the top of following page.

## INFERENCES ABOUT TREATMENT MEANS

Suppose in carrying out the ANOVA procedure, we make the decision to reject the null hypothesis. This allows us to conclude that all the treatment means are not the same. Sometimes we may be satisfied with this conclusion, but in other instances we may want to know which treatment means differ. This section provides the details for such a test.

Recall in the monthly appliance sales data that there was no difference in the treatment means. In this case further analysis of the treatment means is not warranted.

### Self-Review 12–2

*The answers are at the end of the chapter.*

In an effort to determine the most effective way to teach safety principles to a group of employees at Weedco, four different methods were tried. A sample of 20 employees were randomly assigned to one of four groups. The first group was given programmed instruction booklets and worked through the course at their own pace. The second group attended lectures. The third group watched television presentations, and the fourth was divided into small discussion groups. At the end of the sessions, a test was given to the four groups. A high of 10 points was possible.

The results were:

| Test grades | | | |
| --- | --- | --- | --- |
| Programmed instruction | Lecture | TV | Group discussion |
| 6 | 8 | 7 | 8 |
| 7 | 5 | 9 | 5 |
| 6 | 8 | 6 | 6 |
| 5 | 6 | 8 | 6 |
| 6 | 8 | 5 | 5 |

Test at the .05 level that there is no difference among the four means.

However, in the example regarding student opinions and grades there was a difference in the treatment means. That is, the null hypothesis was rejected and the alternate hypothesis accepted. If the student opinions do differ, the question is: Between which groups do the treatment means differ?

Several procedures are available to answer this question. Perhaps the simplest is through the use of confidence intervals. From the computer output of the previous example (see page 439), note that the mean score for those students rating the instruction excellent is 87.250, and for those rating the instruction poor it is 69.000. Thus, those students who rated the instruction excellent seemingly obtained higher grades than those who rated the instruction poor. Is this enough difference to justify the conclusion that there is a difference in the mean scores of the two groups?

The $t$ distribution, described in Chapter 11, is used as the basis for this test. Recall that one of the basic assumptions of ANOVA is that the population variances are the same for all treatments. As noted, this common population value is called the *mean square error,* or MSE, obtained by $SSE/(N - k)$. A confidence interval for the difference between two population means is found by:

$$(\bar{X}_1 - \bar{X}_2) \pm t \sqrt{MSE\left(\frac{1}{n_1} + \frac{1}{n_2}\right)} \tag{12–5}$$

where:

$\bar{X}_1$   is the mean of the first treatment.

$\bar{X}_2$   is the mean of the second treatment.

$t$   is obtained from the $t$ table. The degrees of freedom is equal to $N - k$.

MSE   is the mean square error term obtained from the ANOVA table [$SSE/(N - k)$].

$n_1$   is the number of observations in the first treatment.

$n_2$   is the number of observations in the second treatment.

If the confidence interval includes 0, we conclude there is no difference in the pair of treatment means. However, if both endpoints of the confidence interval are *of the same sign,* it indicates that the treatment means differ.

Using the previous student opinion example and the .95 level of confidence, the endpoints of the confidence interval are 10.46 and 26.04, found by:

$$(\bar{X}_1 - \bar{X}_2) \pm t \sqrt{MSE\left(\frac{1}{n_1} + \frac{1}{n_2}\right)} = (87.25 - 69.00) \pm 2.101 \sqrt{33.0\left(\frac{1}{4} + \frac{1}{6}\right)}$$

$$= 18.25 \pm 7.79$$
$$= [10.46, 26.04]$$

where:

$$\bar{X}_1 = 87.25$$
$$\bar{X}_2 = 69.00$$
$$t = 2.101 \text{ from Appendix F } (N - k = 22 - 4 = 18 \text{ degrees of freedom})$$
$$MSE = 33.0, \text{ from the ANOVA table}$$
$$n_1 = 4$$
$$n_2 = 6$$

We found that the 95 percent confidence interval ranges from 10.46 up to 26.04. Both endpoints are positive; hence, we can conclude these treatment means differ significantly. That is, students who rated the instructor excellent have significantly higher grades than those who rated the instructor as poor.

Likewise, approximate results can be obtained directly from the MINITAB output on page 439. On the bottom of the MINITAB output a confidence interval for each mean is provided. The endpoints of the dotted line indicate the endpoints of a confidence interval for each treatment mean. These endpoints are identified by the symbols ( and ). In those instances where the intervals overlap (that is, contain a common area) the treatment means do not differ. However, where there is not a common area, the treatment means differ. In this example, the students who rated the instructor excellent had a significantly different mean grade from that of those who rated him fair. Also, the mean grade of those who rated the instruction excellent differed from the mean of those rating it poor.

*Caution:* The investigation of differences in treatment means is a sequential process. The initial step is to conduct the ANOVA test. Only if the null hypothesis that the treatment means are equal is rejected should any analysis of the treatment means be attempted.

### Self-Review 12–3

*The answers are at the end of the chapter.*

The following data represent the tuition charges (in thousands of dollars) for a sample of private colleges in various regions of the United States. At the .05 significance level, can we conclude there is a difference in the mean tuition charge?

| Northeast ($000) | Southeast ($000) | West ($000) |
|---|---|---|
| 10 | 8 | 7 |
| 11 | 9 | 8 |
| 12 | 10 | 6 |
| 10 | 8 | 7 |
| 12 | | 6 |

1. State the null and alternate hypotheses.
2. What is the decision rule?
3. What is the computed value of the test statistic?
4. What is your decision regarding the null hypothesis?
5. Could there be a significant difference between the mean tuition in the Northeast and that in the West? If so, develop a confidence interval for that difference.

# EXERCISES

*The answers to the odd-numbered exercises are at the end of the book.*

11. The following sample information is given. Test the hypothesis that the treatment means are equal at the .05 significance level.

| Treatment 1 | Treatment 2 | Treatment 3 |
|:---:|:---:|:---:|
| 8 | 3 | 3 |
| 11 | 2 | 4 |
| 10 | 1 | 5 |
| | 3 | 4 |
| | 2 | |

a. State the null hypothesis and the alternate hypothesis.

b. What is the decision rule?

c. Compute SST, SSE, and SS total.

d. Complete an ANOVA table.

e. State your decision about the null hypothesis.

f. If $H_0$ is rejected, can we conclude that treatment 1 and treatment 2 differ? Use the 95 percent level of confidence.

12. The following is sample information. Test the hypothesis that the treatment means are equal at the .05 significance level.

| Treatment 1 | Treatment 2 | Treatment 3 |
|:---:|:---:|:---:|
| 3 | 9 | 6 |
| 2 | 6 | 3 |
| 5 | 5 | 5 |
| 1 | 6 | 5 |
| 3 | 8 | 5 |
| 1 | 5 | 4 |
| | 4 | 1 |
| | 7 | 5 |
| | 6 | |
| | 4 | |

a. State the null hypothesis and the alternate hypothesis.

b. What is the decision rule?

c. Compute SST, SSE, and SS total.

d. Complete an ANOVA table.

e. State your decision regarding the null hypothesis.

f. If $H_0$ is rejected, can we conclude that treatment 2 and treatment 3 differ? Use the 95 percent level of confidence.

13. A senior accounting major at Midsouth State University has job offers from four CPA firms. To explore the offers further, she asked a sample of recent trainees how many weeks each worked for the firm before receiving a raise in salary. The sample information is:

| Number of weeks before first raise in salary | | | |
|:---:|:---:|:---:|:---:|
| CPA, Inc. | AB Intl. | Acct Ltd. | Pfisters |
| 12 | 14 | 18 | 12 |
| 10 | 12 | 12 | 14 |
| 14 | 10 | 16 | 16 |
| 12 | 10 | | |

At the .05 level of significance, can it be concluded that there is no difference in the mean number of weeks before a raise was granted among the four CPA firms?

14. A stock analyst wants to determine if there is a difference in the mean rate of return for three types of stock: utility, retail, and banking stocks. The following sample information is collected.

| Rates of return | | |
|---|---|---|
| Utility | Retail | Banking |
| 14.3 | 11.5 | 15.5 |
| 18.1 | 12.0 | 12.7 |
| 17.8 | 11.1 | 18.2 |
| 17.3 | 11.9 | 14.7 |
| 19.5 | 11.6 | 18.1 |
|  |  | 13.2 |

a. Using the .05 level of significance, is there a difference in the mean rate of return among the three types of stock?

b. Suppose the null hypothesis is rejected. Can the analyst conclude there is a difference between the mean rates of return for the utility and the retail stocks? Explain.

# TWO-FACTOR ANALYSIS OF VARIANCE

In the appliance store example earlier in the chapter, we were unable to show that a difference exists among the mean sales of the three salespeople. In the computation of the $F$ statistic, variation was considered from two sources. First, variation *among* the differences in the treatments means was considered. Second, variation *within* each of the treatments was considered. Thus, the variation either originated from the treatments or was considered random. There are many other sources of variation, such as the type of training the salespeople had, the days of the week on which the sample data were obtained, perhaps their gender, and so on. A two-factor analysis of variance will allow us to consider a second factor.

## ■ EXAMPLE

WARTA, the Warren Area Regional Transit Authority, is expanding bus service from the suburb of Starbrick into the central business district of Warren. There are four routes being considered from Starbrick into downtown Warren: via U.S. 6, via the west end, via the Hickory Street bridge, and via Rte. 59. WARTA conducted test runs to determine if there is a difference in the mean travel times along the four routes. The travel times, in minutes, along each of the four routes are given below.

| Driver | Travel time from Starbrick to Warren (minutes) | | | |
|---|---|---|---|---|
|  | U.S. 6 | West end | Hickory St. | Rte. 59 |
| Piper | 18 | 20 | 20 | 22 |
| Sanders | 21 | 22 | 24 | 24 |
| McLain | 20 | 23 | 25 | 23 |
| Hammons | 25 | 21 | 28 | 25 |
| Hoffman | 26 | 24 | 28 | 25 |

At the .05 significance level, can it be concluded that there is a difference among the four routes? Is there a difference among the drivers?

### ☑ SOLUTION

Blocking variable

If the null hypothesis is that the mean travel time is the same along the four routes, this requires the one-factor ANOVA approach. The variation that occurs because of differences in the drivers is considered random and is included in the MSE term. Thus, the $F$ ratio is reduced. If the variation due to the drivers can be removed, the denominator of the $F$ ratio will be reduced. In this case the driver is called a *blocking variable*. Hence, we have variation due to treatment and due to blocks. The sum of squares due to blocks (SSB) is computed as follows:

$$\text{SSB} = \Sigma \left[ \frac{B_r^2}{k} \right] - \frac{(\Sigma X)^2}{N} \qquad (12-6)$$

where $B_r$ refers to the block total, that is, the total for each row, and $k$ refers to the number of items in each block.

The same format is used for the two-factor ANOVA table as was used for the one-factor ANOVA case. SST and SS total are computed as before. SSE is obtained by subtraction (SSE = SS total − SST − SSB). Table 12−9 shows the necessary calculations.

---

### TABLE   12−9

**Calculations Needed for Two-Way ANOVA**

| Driver | U.S. 6 | West end | Hickory St. | Rte. 59 | Row sum, $B_r$ | |
|---|---|---|---|---|---|---|
| Piper | 18 | 20 | 20 | 22 | 80 | |
| Sanders | 21 | 22 | 24 | 24 | 91 | |
| McLain | 20 | 23 | 25 | 23 | 91 | |
| Hammons | 25 | 21 | 28 | 25 | 99 | |
| Hoffman | 26 | 24 | 28 | 25 | 103 | *Total* |
| Column total, $T_c$ | 110 | 110 | 125 | 119 | | 464 |
| Sum of squares | 2,466 | 2,430 | 3,169 | 2,839 | | 10,904 |
| Number of blocks, $b$ | 5 | 5 | 5 | 5 | | |

*Travel time, by route (minutes)*

---

Analogous to the ANOVA table for a one-factor analysis, the two-factor general format is:

| Source | (1) Sum of squares | (2) Degrees of freedom | (3) Mean square (1)/(2) |
|---|---|---|---|
| Treatments | SST | $k - 1$ | $\dfrac{\text{SST}}{k - 1} = \text{MSTR}$ |
| Blocks | SSB | $b - 1$ | $\dfrac{\text{SSB}}{b - 1} = \text{MSB*}$ |
| Error | SSE | $(k - 1)(b - 1)$ | $\dfrac{\text{SSE}}{(k - 1)(b - 1)} = \text{MSE}$ |
| Total | SS total | | |

*MSB = Mean square for blocks

As before, we compute SST using formula (12–1), but changing $n_c$ to $b$ to represent the number of blocks.

$$\text{SST} = \Sigma \left[ \frac{T_c^2}{b} \right] - \frac{(\Sigma X)^2}{N}$$

$$= \left[ \frac{(110)^2}{5} + \frac{(110)^2}{5} + \frac{(125)^2}{5} + \frac{(119)^2}{5} \right] - \frac{(464)^2}{20}$$

$$= 32.4$$

SSB is found by using formula (12–6):

$$\text{SSB} = \Sigma \left[ \frac{B_r^2}{k} \right] - \frac{(\Sigma X)^2}{N}$$

$$= \frac{(80)^2}{4} + \frac{(91)^2}{4} + \frac{(91)^2}{4} + \frac{(99)^2}{4} + \frac{(103)^2}{4} - \frac{(464)^2}{20}$$

$$= 78.2$$

The remaining sum-of-squares terms are, using formula (12–3):

$$\text{SS total} = \Sigma X^2 - \frac{(\Sigma X)^2}{N}$$

$$= 10{,}904 - \frac{(464)^2}{20}$$

$$= 139.2$$

$$\text{SSE} = \text{SS total} - \text{SST} - \text{SSB}$$

$$= 139.2 - 32.4 - 78.2$$

$$= 28.6$$

The values for the various components of the ANOVA table are computed as follows:

| Source of variation | (1) Sum of squares | (2) Degrees of freedom | (3) Mean square (1)/(2) |
|---|---|---|---|
| Treatments | 32.4 | 3 | 10.8 |
| Blocks | 78.2 | 4 | 19.55 |
| Error | 28.6 | 12 | 2.38 |
| Total | 139.2 | | |

There are two sets of hypotheses being tested.

1. $H_0$ : The treatment means are the same ($\mu_1 = \mu_2 = \mu_3 = \mu_4$).
   $H_1$ : The treatment means are not the same.
2. $H_0$: The block means are the same ($\mu_1 = \mu_2 = \mu_3 = \mu_4 = \mu_5$).
   $H_1$ : The block means are not the same.

First we will test the hypothesis concerning the treatment means. There are $k - 1 = 4 - 1 = 3$ degrees of freedom in the numerator and $(b - 1)(k - 1) = (5 - 1)(4 - 1) = 12$ degrees of freedom in the denominator. Using the .05 significance level, the critical value of $F$ is 3.49. The null hypothesis that the mean times for the four routes are the same is rejected if the $F$ ratio exceeds 3.49. Using formula (12–4) $F$ is 4.54.

$$F = \frac{\text{MSTR}}{\text{MSE}} = \frac{10.8}{2.38} = 4.54$$

The null hypothesis is rejected and the alternate accepted. It is concluded that the mean travel time is not the same for all routes. WARTA will want to conduct some tests to determine which treatment means differ.

Next, we test to find out if the travel time is the same for the various drivers. The degrees of freedom in the numerator for blocks is $b - 1 = 5 - 1 = 4$. The degrees of freedom for the denominator is the same as before: $(b - 1)(k - 1) = (5 - 1)(4 - 1) = 12$. The null hypothesis that the block means are the same is rejected if the $F$ ratio exceeds 3.26.

$$F = \frac{\text{MSB}}{\text{MSE}} = \frac{19.55}{2.38} = 8.21$$

The null hypothesis is rejected, and the alternate is accepted. The mean time is not the same for the various drivers.

Thus, WARTA management can conclude, based on the sample results, that there is a difference in the routes and in the drivers.

A two-factor procedure called ANOVA is available on the MINITAB system. For the WARTA example of Table 12–9, the travel times are entered in column C1. The times are entered by going down the columns. So the first five values in C1 refer to the times along U.S. 6, the next five refer to the west end, and so on. We use columns C2 and C3 in MINITAB to identify the routes (C2) and the drivers (C3). We code the times along U.S. 6 as 1s, those via the west end as 2s, those via Hickory Street as 3s, and those for Rte. 59 as 4s. Therefore, the first five values in C2 are 1s, because these times were along U.S. 6. The next five times are all via the west end, so they are coded as 2s, and so on. Column C3 refers to the drivers. Driver Piper is coded as 1, so we place a 1 in the first position in C3. Next is a 2, representing driver Sanders, followed by a 3, representing driver McLain, and so on. The results are shown below.

```
MTB > set c1
DATA> 18,21,20,25,26,20,22,23,21,24,20,24,25,28,28,22,24,23,25,25
DATA> end
MTB > set c2
DATA> 1,1,1,1,1,2,2,2,2,2,3,3,3,3,3,4,4,4,4,4
MTB > set c3
DATA> 1,2,3,4,5,1,2,3,4,5,1,2,3,4,5,1,2,3,4,5
DATA> end
MTB > name c1 'Time' c2 'Routes' c3 'Drivers'
MTB > anova c1=c2 c3

Analysis of Variance for Time

Source    DF       SS       MS      F       P
Routes     3   32.400   10.800   4.53   0.024
Drivers    4   78.200   19.550   8.20   0.002
Error     12   28.600    2.383
Total     19  139.200
```

These are the same results reported earlier. An additional feature of the MINITAB output is to report the $p$-values of .024 for routes and .002 for drivers.

### Self-Review 12—4

*The answers are at the end of the chapter.*

Rudduck Shampoo sells three shampoos— for dry, normal, and oily hair. Sales, in millions of dollars, for the past five months are given in the following table.

|  | Sales ($ millions) | | |
|---|---|---|---|
| Month | Dry | Normal | Oily |
| June | 7 | 9 | 12 |
| July | 11 | 12 | 14 |
| August | 13 | 11 | 8 |
| September | 8 | 9 | 7 |
| October | 9 | 10 | 13 |

Using the .05 level, apply the ANOVA procedure to test whether:

1. The mean sales for dry, normal, and oily hair are the same.

2. The mean sales are the same for each of the five months.

## EXERCISES

*The answers to the odd-numbered exercises are at the end of the book.*

15. The following data are given for a two-factor ANOVA.

|  | Treatment | |
|---|---|---|
| Block | 1 | 2 |
| A | 46 | 31 |
| B | 37 | 26 |
| C | 44 | 35 |

Conduct a test of hypothesis to determine if the block and the treatment means differ, $\alpha = .05$:

a. State the null and alternate hypotheses for treatments.

b. State the decision rule for treatments.

c. State the null and alternate hypotheses for blocks. Also, state the decision rule for blocks.

d. Compute SST, SSB, SS total, and SSE.

e. Complete an ANOVA table.

f. What is you decision regarding the two sets of hypotheses?

16. The following data are given for a two-factor ANOVA. It is a completely randomized design.

|  | Treatment | | |
|---|---|---|---|
| Block | 1 | 2 | 3 |
| A | 12 | 14 | 8 |
| B | 9 | 11 | 9 |
| C | 7 | 8 | 8 |

Conduct a test of hypothesis to determine if the block and the treatment means differ, $\alpha = .05$.

a. State the null and alternate hypotheses for treatments.

b. State the decision rule for treatments.

c. State the null and alternate hypotheses for blocks. Also, state the decision rule for blocks.

d. Compute SST, SSB, SS total, and SSE.

e. Complete an ANOVA table.

f. What is your decision regarding the two sets of hypotheses?

17. The Brunner Manufacturing Company operates 24 hours a day, five days a week. The workers rotate shifts each week. Management is interested in whether there is a difference in the number of units produced when the employees work on various shifts. A sample of five workers is selected and their output recorded on each shift. At the .05 significance level, can we conclude there is a difference in the mean production by shift and in the mean production by employee?

| | Units produced | | |
| Employee | Day | Afternoon | Night |
| --- | --- | --- | --- |
| Skaff | 31 | 25 | 35 |
| Lum | 33 | 26 | 33 |
| Clark | 28 | 24 | 30 |
| Treece | 30 | 29 | 28 |
| Morgan | 28 | 26 | 27 |

18. There are three hospitals in the Tulsa area. The following data show the number of outpatient surgeries performed at each hospital last week. At the .05 significance level, can we conclude that there is a difference in the mean number of surgeries performed among the three hospitals and in the mean number of surgeries by day of the week?

| | Number of surgeries performed | | |
| Day | St. Luke's | St. Vincent | Mercy |
| --- | --- | --- | --- |
| Monday | 14 | 18 | 24 |
| Tuesday | 20 | 24 | 14 |
| Wednesday | 16 | 22 | 14 |
| Thursday | 18 | 20 | 22 |
| Friday | 20 | 28 | 24 |

## CHAPTER OUTLINE

I. Characteristics of the $F$ distribution.
   A. It is continuous.
   B. Its values cannot be negative.
   C. It is positively skewed.
   D. There is a family of $F$ distributions. Each time the degrees of freedom in either the numerator or the denominator change, a new distribution is created.
II. The $F$ distribution is used to test whether two sample variances come from the same or equal populations.
   A. The sampled populations must be normal.
   B. The ratio of the two sample variances is computed and the result compared to the critical value of $F$.
   C. The larger of the two sample variances is placed in the numerator, forcing the ratio to always be greater than 1.00.
III. One-way ANOVA is used to compare three or more treatment means to determine if they came from the same or equal populations. A *treatment* is a source of variation.
   A. Assumptions underlying ANOVA.
      1. The samples are obtained from normal populations.
      2. The populations have equal standard deviations.
      3. The populations are independent.
   B. An ANOVA table is developed, which uses SS total, SST, and SSE. These values are computed as follows, where $N$ is the total number of observations, $T_c$ is a column total, and $n_c$ is the number of observations in each treatment (column).
      1. SS total, the total sum of squares:

$$\text{SS total} = \Sigma X^2 - \frac{(\Sigma X)^2}{N} \tag{12-3}$$

2. SST, the sum of squares treatment:

$$\text{SST} = \Sigma\left[\frac{T_c^2}{n_c}\right] - \frac{(\Sigma X)^2}{N} \tag{12-1}$$

3. SSE, the sum of squares error:

$$\text{SSE} = \text{SS total} - \text{SST}$$

IV. Treatment means are compared to determine if they differ significantly, using the following relationship.

$$(\bar{X}_1 - \bar{X}_2) \pm t\ \sqrt{\text{MSE}\left(\frac{1}{n_1}+\frac{1}{n_2}\right)} \tag{12-5}$$

where:

$\bar{X}_1$ is the mean of the first treatment.
$\bar{X}_2$ is the mean of the second treatment.
$t$ is the value obtained from the $t$ table, where the degrees of freedom equal $N - k$.
MSE is the mean square error, found by $\text{SSE}/(N - k)$.
$n_1$ is the number of observations in the first treatment.
$n_2$ is the number of observations in the second treatment.

V. Two-way ANOVA considers variation due to both treatments and blocks.
A. The same format is used as for one-way ANOVA.
B. A blocking variable is a second source of variation. It is computed from the following formula:

$$\text{SSB} = \Sigma\left[\frac{B_r^2}{k}\right] - \frac{(\Sigma X)^2}{N} \tag{12-6}$$

# EXERCISES

*The answers to the odd-numbered exercises are at the end of the book.*

19. A physician who specializes in weight control has three different diets she recommends. As an experiment, she randomly selected 15 patients and then assigned 5 to each diet. After three weeks the following weight losses, in pounds, were noted. At the .05 significance level, can she conclude that there is a difference in the mean amount of weight loss among the three diets?

| Plan A | Plan B | Plan C |
|---|---|---|
| 5 | 6 | 7 |
| 7 | 7 | 8 |
| 4 | 7 | 9 |
| 5 | 5 | 8 |
| 4 | 6 | 9 |

20. The City of Maumee comprises four districts. Chief of Police Andy North wants to determine if there is a difference in the mean number of crimes committed among the

four districts. He recorded the number of crimes reported in each district for a sample of six days. At the .05 significance level, can the chief of police conclude there is a difference in the mean number of crimes?

| Number of crimes | | | |
| --- | --- | --- | --- |
| Rec center | Key Street | Monclova | Whitehouse |
| 13 | 21 | 12 | 16 |
| 15 | 13 | 14 | 17 |
| 14 | 18 | 15 | 18 |
| 15 | 19 | 13 | 15 |
| 14 | 18 | 12 | 20 |
| 15 | 19 | 15 | 18 |

21. The personnel director of Cander Machine Products is investigating "perfectionism" on the job. A test designed to measure perfectionism was administered to a random sample of 18 employees. The scores ranged from 20 to about 40. One of the facets of the study involved the early bakcground of each employee. Did the employee come from a rural background, a small city, or a large city? The scores are:

| Rural area | Small urban area | Large urban area |
| --- | --- | --- |
| 35 | 28 | 24 |
| 30 | 24 | 28 |
| 36 | 25 | 26 |
| 38 | 30 | 30 |
| 29 | 32 | 34 |
| 34 | 28 | |
| 31 | | |

a. At the .05 level, can it be concluded that there is a difference in the three mean scores?

b. If the null hypothesis is rejected, can you state that the mean score of those with a rural background is different from the score of those with a large-city background?

22. Family Surveys, a consumer testing firm based in Dallas, was hired to investigate the service times of three restaurants in the Giorgio chain. (Service time is the difference, in minutes, between the time a customer places an order and the time the food is received.) The sample results are:

| Service time (minutes) | | |
| --- | --- | --- |
| Giorgio East | Giorgio West | Giorgio South |
| 2.3 | 3.2 | 4.0 |
| 3.3 | 1.9 | 4.3 |
| 3.6 | 2.4 | 3.8 |
| 3.0 | | 4.1 |
| | | 5.0 |

a. At the .05 level, is there a difference in the mean service times?

b. Do any pairs differ significantly?

23. Following is a partial ANOVA table.

| Source | Sum of squares | df | Mean square | F |
| --- | --- | --- | --- | --- |
| Treatment | | 2 | | |
| Error | | | 20 | |
| Total | 500 | 11 | | |

Complete the table, and answer the following questions. Use the .05 significance level.

a. How many treatments are there?

b. What was the total sample size?

c. What is the critical value of $F$?

d. Write out the null and alternate hypotheses.

e. What is your conclusion regarding the null hypothesis?

24. It can be shown that when only two treatments are involved, ANOVA and the Student $t$ test (Chapter 11) result in the same conclusions. Also, $t^2 = F$. As an example, suppose that 14 randomly selected students were divided into two groups, one consisting of 6 students and the other of 8. One group was taught using a combination of lecture and programmed instruction, the other using a combination of lecture and television. At the end of the course, each group was given a 50-item test. The following is a list of the number correct for each of the two groups.

| Lecture and programmed instruction | Lecture and television |
|:---:|:---:|
| 19 | 32 |
| 17 | 28 |
| 23 | 31 |
| 22 | 26 |
| 17 | 23 |
| 16 | 24 |
|  | 27 |
|  | 25 |

a. Using analysis of variance techniques, test $H_0$ that the two mean test scores are equal; $\alpha = .05$.

b. Using the $t$ test from Chapter 11, compute $t$.

c. Interpret the results.

25. There are four radio stations in Midland. The stations have different formats (hard rock, classical, country/western, and easy listening), but each is concerned with the number of minutes of music played per hour. From a sample of 10 hours from each station, the following sample means were obtained.

$$\bar{X}_1 = 51.32 \qquad \bar{X}_2 = 44.64 \qquad \bar{X}_3 = 47.2 \qquad \bar{X}_4 = 50.85$$
$$\text{SS total} = 650.75$$

a. Determine SST.

b. Determine SSE.

c. Complete an ANOVA table.

d. At the .05 significance level, is there a difference in the treatment means?

e. Is there a difference in the mean amount of music time between station 1 and station 4? Use the .05 significance level.

26. Sports Management International owns the concession operations at Joe Louis Arena, home of the Detroit Red Wings hockey team. The management of Sports Management International wants some information about the mean amount spent at the concession stand by hockey fans. Four groups of respondents were surveyed: students under 21 years of age, students 21 years old or over, blue-collar workers, and professional people. At the .05 significance level, is there a difference in the mean amount spent among the four groups?

| Students under 21 years | Students 21 years old or older | Professional | Blue-collar |
|---|---|---|---|
| $4.19 | $5.49 | $5.36 | $3.64 |
| 3.81 | 8.11 | 6.99 | 1.23 |
| 1.77 | 6.55 | 3.91 | 5.03 |
| 2.83 | 3.39 | 3.04 | 2.64 |
| 3.45 | 9.12 | 1.90 | 2.86 |
| 4.16 | 2.46 | 3.93 | 5.75 |
| 2.89 | 4.11 | 1.04 | 3.17 |
| 2.33 | | 3.98 | 1.09 |
| | | 3.09 | 4.90 |
| | | 2.45 | 5.14 |
| | | 1.42 | |
| | | 2.19 | |

27. Martin Motors has in stock three cars of the same make and model. The president would like to compare the gas consumption of the three cars (labeled car A, car B, and car C) using four different types of gasoline. For each trial, a gallon of gasoline was added to an empty tank, and the car was driven until it ran out of gas. The following table shows the number of miles driven in each trial.

| | Distance (miles) | | |
|---|---|---|---|
| Types of gasoline | Car A | Car B | Car C |
| Regular | 22.4 | 20.8 | 21.5 |
| Super regular | 17.0 | 19.4 | 20.7 |
| Unleaded | 19.2 | 20.2 | 21.2 |
| Premium unleaded | 20.3 | 18.6 | 20.4 |

Using the .05 level of significance:
a. Is there a difference among types of gasoline?
b. Is there a difference in the cars?

28. Shank's, Inc., a nationwide advertising firm, wants to know if the size of an advertisement and the color of the advertisement make a difference in the response of magazine readers. A random sample of readers are shown ads of four different colors and three different sizes. Each reader is asked to give the particular combination of size and color a rating between 1 and 10. The rating for each combination is shown in the following table (for example, the rating for a small red ad is 2).

| | Color of ad | | | |
|---|---|---|---|---|
| Size of ad | Red | Blue | Orange | Green |
| Small | 2 | 3 | 3 | 8 |
| Medium | 3 | 5 | 6 | 7 |
| Large | 6 | 7 | 8 | 8 |

Is there a difference in the effectiveness of an advertisement by color and by size? Use the .05 level of significance.

29. There are four McBurger restaurants in the Columbus, Georgia, area. The numbers of burgers sold at the respective restaurants for each of the last six weeks are shown below. At the .05 significance level, is there a difference in the number sold among the four restaurants, when the factor of week is considered?

| Week | Restaurant | | | |
|---|---|---|---|---|
| | Metro | Interstate | University | River |
| 1 | 124 | 160 | 320 | 190 |
| 2 | 234 | 220 | 340 | 230 |
| 3 | 430 | 290 | 290 | 240 |
| 4 | 105 | 245 | 310 | 170 |
| 5 | 240 | 205 | 280 | 180 |
| 6 | 310 | 260 | 270 | 205 |

a. Is there a difference in the treatment means?

b. Is there a difference in the block means?

30. The city of Tucson, Arizona, employs people to assess the value of homes for the purpose of establishing real estate tax. The city manager routinely sends each assessor to five homes and then compares the results. The information is given below, in thousands of dollars. Can we conclude that there is a difference in the assessors, at $\alpha = .05$?

| Home | Assessor | | | |
|---|---|---|---|---|
| | Zawodny | Norman | Cingle | Holiday |
| A | $53.0 | $55.0 | $49.0 | $45.0 |
| B | 50.0 | 51.0 | 52.0 | 53.0 |
| C | 48.0 | 52.0 | 47.0 | 53.0 |
| D | 70.0 | 68.0 | 65.0 | 64.0 |
| E | 84.0 | 89.0 | 92.0 | 86.0 |

a. Is there a difference in the treatment means?

b. Is there a difference in the block means?

31. One reads that a business school graduate with an undergraduate degree earns more than a high school graduate with no additional education, and a person with a master's degree or a doctorate earns even more. To test this, a random sample of 25 executives from companies with assets over $1 million was selected. Their incomes, classified by highest level of education, follow.

| Incomes ($000) | | |
|---|---|---|
| High school or less | Undergraduate degree | Master's degree or more |
| 45 | 49 | 51 |
| 47 | 57 | 73 |
| 53 | 85 | 82 |
| 62 | 73 | 59 |
| 39 | 81 | 94 |
| 43 | 84 | 89 |
| 54 | 89 | 89 |
| | 92 | 95 |
| | 62 | 73 |

Test at the .05 level of significance that there is no difference in the arithmetic mean salaries of the three groups. If a difference is found between a pair of means, conduct further tests to determine which groups differ.

32. A sample survey of the annual incomes of in-training probation aides was conducted. The annual incomes of those selected in the sample, by size of the city, are (in thousands of dollars):

| Less than 100,000 | 100,000 to 250,000 | 250,000 to 500,000 | Greater than 500,000 |
|---|---|---|---|
| $14.2 | $11.7 | $16.0 | $13.2 |
| 16.9 | 15.8 | 17.2 | 19.0 |
| 12.3 | 21.3 | 11.6 | 25.5 |
| 15.6 | 13.3 | 14.9 | 11.8 |
| 11.5 | 11.4 | 15.9 | 17.1 |
| 24.7 | 13.0 | 11.6 | 16.9 |
| 12.2 | 15.9 | 13.2 | |
| 10.2 | 11.7 | 12.9 | |
| 13.3 | 10.8 | 25.3 | |
| 13.1 | 16.2 | | |
| | 15.6 | | |
| | 13.7 | | |
| | 21.4 | | |

The question to be explored is whether or not there is a significant difference among the four city sizes with respect to the mean annual income of an in-training probation aide.

a. State the null hypothesis and alternate hypothesis.

b. Using the .05 level, state the decision rule.

c. What is the computed $F$ value?

d. What conclusion can be drawn?

33. Suppose that a sample of sophomore students at five small colleges revealed these ages:

| Landon | Adrian | Jackson | Saint Mark | Diaz |
|---|---|---|---|---|
| 24 | 19 | 21 | 23 | 22 |
| 21 | 20 | 23 | 19 | 20 |
| 18 | 21 | 20 | 16 | 19 |
| 20 | 16 | 17 | 18 | 17 |
| 23 | 22 | 22 | 21 | 21 |
| 19 | 20 | 19 | 20 | 18 |
| 21 | 23 | 24 | 22 | 20 |
| 15 | 18 | 18 | 15 | 18 |
| 22 | 21 | 21 | 21 | 21 |
| 17 | 15 | 15 | 21 | 19 |

Test the hypothesis that there is no significant difference with respect to the mean age of the sophomore students enrolled in the five colleges. Use the .01 level of significance.

## COMPUTER DATA EXERCISES

34. Refer to data set 1, which reports information on homes sold in Florida during 1990.

a. At the .02 significance level, is there a difference in the variability of the selling prices of homes that have a pool versus those that do not have a pool?

b. At the .02 significance level, is there a difference in the variability of the selling prices of homes that have a garage versus those that do not have a garage?

c. At the .05 significance level, is there a difference in the mean selling price of a home among the five townships?

35. Refer to data set 2, which reports information on 200 corporations in the United States.

a. Create a variable that divides the 200 companies into those that lost money, those that made between $0 and $750, and those that made more than $750 (million). Is there a difference in their mean assets? Use the .05 significance level.

36. Refer to data set 3, which reports information on the 26 major league baseball teams for the 1991 season.

a. Create a variable that divides a team's total attendance into three groups: those with less than 1.5 (million), those with 1.5 up to 2.5, and those with 2.5 or more. At the .05 significance level, is there a difference in the mean winning percent among the three groups?

b. Using the attendance groups in part a, compare the number of home runs hit.

c. Using the attendance groups in part a, compare the number of stolen bases.

# CHAPTER 12 EXAMINATION

*The answers are at the end of the chapter.*

For Questions 1 through 10, indicate whether the statement is true or false. If it is false, correct the statement.

1. The $F$ distribution is positively skewed.

2. The $F$ distribution is based on two sets of degrees of freedom.

3. A treatment is a source of variation in the data.

4. For the ANOVA procedure, the populations should be positively skewed.

5. Rejecting the null hypothesis in an ANOVA procedure indicates that all pairs of means differ.

6. If the significance level is .05 and there are 3 degrees of freedom in the numerator and 12 in the denominator, the critical value of $F$ is 3.49.

7. If there are four treatments, the number of degrees of freedom in the numerator of $F$ is also 4.

8. If there are four treatments and five observations in each treatment, the number of degrees of freedom in the denominator is 19.

9. A blocking variable is a source of variation similar to a treatment variable.

10. There is a "family" of $F$ distributions. There is one distribution for $df$ 17, 14, another for $df$ 6, 4, etc.

11. A sample of eight observations are chosen at random from population 1, and six observations are chosen from population 2. The following is the sample information. At the .10 significance level, can we conclude that there is a difference between the two population variances?

|  | Population 1 | Population 2 |
|---|---|---|
| Mean | 15 | 12 |
| Variance | 10 | 15 |
| Sample size | 8 | 6 |

12. The Exact Machine Company uses precision grinders manufactured by four different firms. There is interest in determining if there is any overall difference in the performance of the four grinders. Sample measurements, to the nearest ten-thousandth of an inch, obtained from each of the four machines follow. At the .05 significance level, is there a difference among the four grinders? Apply the usual five-step hypothesis-testing procedure.

| Machine | | | |
|---|---|---|---|
| Deitz | Arvis | Milcron | Hunt |
| 8 | 8 | 9 | 6 |
| 7 | 9 | 9 | 7 |
| 9 | 6 | 6 | 9 |
|  | 5 | 4 | 4 |
|  |  | 7 |  |

13. The following is a two-way ANOVA table.

| Source | Sum of squares | Degrees of freedom | Mean square |
|--------|--------|--------|--------|
| Treatment | 50 | 2 | 25 |
| Blocks | 24 | 3 | 8 |
| Error | 48 | 6 | 8 |
| Total | 122 | 11 | |

   a.   How many treatments are there?

   b.   How many blocks are there?

   c.   How many samples are there in the problem?

   d.   Conduct a test for treatments. Is there a significant difference among the treatment means? Use the .05 significance level.

   e.   Conduct a test for blocks. Is there a significant difference among the block means? Use the .05 significance level.

# ANSWERS

**12–1** Let Mark's assemblies be population 1. Then $H_0$: $\sigma_1^2 = \sigma_2^2$; $H_1$: $\sigma_1^2 > \sigma_2^2$; $df_1 = 10 - 1 = 9$; and $df_2$ also equals 9. $H_0$ is rejected if $F > 3.18$.

$$F = \frac{(2.0)^2}{(1.5)^2} = 1.78$$

$H_0$ is not rejected. The variation is the same for both employees.

**12–2**
$$F = \frac{1.667}{1.625} = 1.026$$

Do not reject $H_0$ because 1.026 is less than the critical value of 3.24. The ANOVA table is computed as follows:

$$\text{SS total} = 876 - \frac{(130)^2}{20} = 31$$

$$\text{SST} = \frac{(30)^2}{5} + \frac{(35)^2}{5} + \frac{(35)^2}{5} + \frac{(30)^2}{5}$$

$$- \frac{(130)^2}{20} = 5$$

$$\text{SSE} = 31 - 5 = 26$$

| Treatments | Sum of squares | Degrees of freedom | Mean square |
|---|---|---|---|
| Between columns | 5 | 3 | 1.667 |
| Between rows | 26 | 16 | 1.625 |
| Total | 31 | 19 | |

**12–3** 1. $H_0$: $\mu_1 = \mu_2 = \mu_3$
$H_1$: Not all means are equal.
2. $H_0$ is rejected if $F > 3.98$.

3. $$\text{SS total} = 1,152 - \frac{(124)^2}{14} = 53.71$$

$$\text{SST} = \frac{(55)^2}{5} + \frac{(35)^2}{4} + \frac{(34)^2}{5}$$

$$- \frac{(124)^2}{14} = 44.16$$

$$\text{SSE} = 53.71 - 44.16 = 9.55$$

| Source | Sum of Squares | df | Mean square | F |
|---|---|---|---|---|
| Treatment | 44.16 | 2 | 22.08 | 25.43 |
| Error | 9.55 | 11 | 0.8682 | |
| Total | 53.71 | 13 | | |

4. $H_0$ is rejected. The treatment means differ.

5. $(11.0 - 6.8) \pm 2.201 \sqrt{0.8682\left(\frac{1}{5} + \frac{1}{5}\right)} = 4.2 \pm 1.30 = 2.90$ and 5.50.

These treatment means differ because both endpoints of the confidence interval are of the same sign—positive in this problem.

**12–4** For types:

$$H_0: \mu_1 = \mu_2 = \mu_3$$

$$H_1: \text{The treatment means are not equal.}$$

Reject $H_0$ if $F > 4.46$.
For months:

$$H_0: \mu_1 = \mu_2 = \mu_3 = \mu_4 = \mu_5$$

$$H_1: = \text{The block means are not equal.}$$

Reject $H_0$ if $F > 3.84$.
The analysis of variance table is as follows:

| Source | df | SS | MS | F |
|---|---|---|---|---|
| Types | 2 | 3.60 | 1.80 | 0.39 |
| Months | 4 | 31.73 | 7.93 | 1.71 |
| Error | 8 | 37.07 | 4.63 | |
| Total | 14 | 72.40 | | |

The null hypothesis cannot be rejected for either types or months. There is no difference in the mean sales among types or by months.

# CHAPTER 12 EXAMINATION

1. True.
2. True.
3. True.
4. False. The populations should be normally distributed.
5. False. At least one pair of means is different.
6. True.
7. False. The number of degrees of freedom is equal to $k$, the number of treatments, minus 1. There are 3 degrees of freedom.
8. False. The number of degrees of freedom is equal to $N - k = 20 - 4 = 16$.
9. True.
10. True.

11.
$$H_0: \sigma_2^2 = \sigma_1^2$$
$$H_1: \sigma_2^2 \neq \sigma_1^2$$

There are 5 degrees of freedom in the numerator and 7 in the denominator. Note that to make $F$ greater than 1.00, the variance in population 2 is placed in the numerator. $H_0$ is rejected if $F > 3.97$.

$$F = \frac{15}{10} = 1.5$$

$H_0$ is not rejected. There is no difference in the population variances.

12. $H_0: \mu_1 = \mu_2 = \mu_3 = \mu_4$
$H_1$: Not all means are the same.
$H_0$ is rejected if the computed $F > 3.49$.

$$\text{SS total} = 845 - \frac{(113)^2}{16} = 46.9375$$

$$\text{SST} = \frac{(24)^2}{3} + \frac{(28)^2}{4} + \frac{(35)^2}{5} + \frac{(26)^2}{4}$$

$$-\frac{(113)^2}{16} = 3.9375$$

$$\text{SSE} = 46.9375 - 3.9375 = 43.0000$$

| Source | SS | df | MS | F |
|--------|-----|-----|------|------|
| Treatments | 3.9375 | 3 | 1.3125 | 0.3663 |
| Error | 43.000 | 12 | 3.5833 | |
| Total | 46.9375 | 15 | | |

$H_0$ is not rejected. There is no difference in the overall performance of the four grinders.

13.  a.  3 treatments.
 b.  4 blocks.
 c.  12 samples.
 d.  $H_0: \mu_1 = \mu_2 = \mu_3$
 $H_1$: Not all treatment means are the same.
 $H_0$ is rejected if $F > 5.14$ (using the .05 significance level).

$$F = \frac{25}{8} = 3.125$$

$H_0$ is not rejected. There is no difference in the treatment means.
 e.  $H_0: \mu_1 = \mu_2 = \mu_3 = \mu_4$
 $H_1$: Not all block means are the same.
 $H_0$ is rejected if $F > 4.76$.

$$F = \frac{8.0}{8.0} = 1.00$$

$H_0$ is not rejected. There is no difference in the block means.

# A Review of Chapters 11 and 12

**T**his section is a review of the major concepts and terms introduced in Chapters 11 and 12. Chapter 11 continued the subject of hypothesis testing started in Chapter 9. Chapter 9 dealt with large samples (30 and more).

*Less than 30—a small sample*

Chapter 11 was concerned with small samples (less than 30). In the small-sample case, it is assumed that the standard deviation of the population is unknown. The major difference between the testing procedures for large samples (Chapter 9) and small samples (Chapter 11) is the test statistic used. For large samples it is $z$, and for small samples it is the *Student t*.

*Paired difference test used for dependent samples*

Testing for the reasonableness of a mean involving a small sample, or the difference between two means, also requires that the samples be *independent*. For *dependent* samples, we applied the *paired difference test,* which also uses $t$ as the test statistic. One typical paired sample problem calls for recording an individual's blood pressure before administering antihypertensive medication and then again afterward in order to evaluate the effectiveness of the medication. Another typical problem using the paired difference test involves recording the production of an individual using method A and then using method B. The purpose of the experiment is to find out whether or not the difference in production between method A and method B is statistically significant.

*The ANOVA procedure*

Chapters 9, 10, and 11 dealt with either one mean or the difference between two means. Chapter 12 presented a procedure called the *analysis of variance, or ANOVA,* used to simultaneously determine whether or not three or more populations have identical means. This is accomplished by comparing the variances of the random samples selected from these populations. The usual five-step hypothesis-testing procedure is applied, but we use a probability distribution called the $F$ distribution as the test statistic. Before beginning the calculations for $F$, we set up an ANOVA table to organize the calculations into a convenient form.

As an example of the application of the analysis of variance, a test could be conducted to find out if there is any difference in effectiveness among five fertilizers on the weight of popcorn ears. This type of analysis is referred to as *one-factor ANOVA* because we are able to draw conclusions about only one factor, called a *treatment.* If we want to draw a conclusion about the simultaneous effects of more than one factor or variable, the *two-factor ANOVA* technique is applied. Both the one-factor and two-factor tests use the *F distribution* as the test statistic. The $F$ distribution is also the test statistic used to find out if one normal population has more variation than another. In addition, it is applied when we want to test the assumption that the variances of two populations are equal.

# GLOSSARY

## CHAPTER 11

**Degrees of freedom**   The number of items in a sample that are free to vary. Suppose there are two items in a sample, and we know the mean. We are free to specify only one of the two values because the other value is automatically determined (since the two values total twice the mean). Example: If the mean is $6, we are free to choose only one value. Choosing $4 makes the other value $8 because $4 + $8 = 2($6). So there is 1 degree of freedom in this illustration. It could have been determined by $n - 1 = 2 - 1 = 1$ degree of freedom. If $n$ is 4, then there are 3 degrees of freedom, found by $n - 1 = 4 - 1 = 3$.

**Dependent samples**   Samples chosen from several populations in such a way that they are not independent of each other. Paired samples are dependent because the same individual or item is a member of both samples. Example: If the test scores of 10 individuals were recorded before a new teaching method was introduced, and then their test scores after using the new method were recorded, the two paired samples would be considered dependent.

**Independent samples**   The samples chosen at random are in no way related to each other. A sample of the ages of 28 inmates in the Auburn maximum security prison and a sample of the ages of 19 students at Mid-South University are examples of independent samples.

**Paired difference test**   A test of hypothesis conducted using paired samples. It is especially useful for "before" and "after" problems and to test whether Method A and Method B are equally effective.

*t distribution*   Investigated and reported by William S. Gossett in 1908 and published under the pseudonym *Student,* it is similar to the normal distribution in Chapter 7. The major characteristics of *t* are:
1. It is a continuous distribution.
2. It can assume values between $-\infty$ and $\infty$.
3. It is symmetrical about its mean of zero. However, it is more spread out and flatter at the apex than the normal distribution.
4. It approaches the standard normal distribution as $n$ gets larger.
5. There is a "family" of *t* distributions. One *t* distribution exists for a sample of 15, another for a sample of 16, and so on.

## CHAPTER 12

**Analysis of variance (ANOVA)**   A technique used to test simultaneously whether or not the means of three or more populations are equal. It uses the *F* distribution as the test statistic.

**F distribution**   Used as the test statistic for ANOVA problems, it has the following characteristics:
1. The value of *F* is always positive.
2. The *F* distribution is a continuous distribution approaching the *X*-axis but never touching it.
3. It is positively skewed.
4. Like the *t* distribution, there is a "family" of *F* distributions. There is one distribution for 17 degrees of freedom in the numerator and 9 degrees of freedom in the denominator, there is another *F* distribution for 7 degrees of freedom in the numerator and 12 degrees of freedom in the denominator, and so on.

**Treatment**   A cause, or specific source of variation in the data.

# EXERCISES

*The answers to the odd-numbered exercises are at the end of the book.*

## PART I—MULTIPLE-CHOICE

For Exercises 1 through 12, give the letter representing the correct answer.

1. The test statistic for testing a hypothesis for small samples when the population standard deviation is not known is:
   a.  $z$.
   b.  $t$.
   c.  $F$.
   d.  $A > B$.
   e.  None of these is correct.

2. We want to test a hypothesis for the difference between two population means. The null and alternate hypotheses are stated as $H_0$: $\mu_1 = \mu_2$ and $H_1$: $\mu_1 \neq \mu_2$.
   a.  A left-tailed test should be applied.
   b.  A two-tailed test should be applied.
   c.  A right-tailed test should be applied.
   d.  We cannot determine whether a left-, right-, or two-tailed test should be applied based on the information given.
   e.  None of these is correct.

3. The $F$ distribution:
   a.  Cannot be negative.
   b.  Cannot be positive.
   c.  Is the same as the $t$ distribution.
   d.  Is the same as the $z$ distribution.
   e.  None of these is correct.

4. As the sample size increases, the $t$ distribution approaches:
   a.  ANOVA.
   b.  The standard normal distribution.
   c.  The Poisson distribution.
   d.  Zero.
   e.  None of these is correct.

5. To conduct a paired difference test, the samples must be:
   a.  Infinitely large.
   b.  Equal to ANOVA.
   c.  Independent.
   d.  Dependent.
   e.  None of these is correct.

6. An ANOVA test was conducted with respect to the population means. The null hypothesis was rejected. This indicates that:
   a.  There were too many degrees of freedom.
   b.  There is no difference between the population means.
   c.  There is a difference between at least one pair of population means.
   d.  A larger sample should be selected.
   e.  None of these is correct.

Use the following information for Exercises 7, 8, and 9. The Rochester Builders Association stated that the mean cost of erecting a multistory apartment building in the area is $80 per square foot. A building contractor claims that the mean cost per square foot is more than $80. A sample of 21 apartment buildings resulted in the sample mean of $81.

7. The alternate hypothesis is:

    a.   $H_1: \mu < \$80$.

    b.   $H_1: \mu \neq \$80$.

    c.   $H_1: \mu \geq \$81$.

    d.   $H_1: \mu > \$81$.

    e.   None of these is correct.

8. The number of degrees of freedom for this problem is:

    a.   80.

    b.   0.

    c.   21.

    d.   20.

    e.   None of these is correct.

9. $t$ was computed to be 1.90. At the .05 level, the null hypothesis is:

    a.   Not rejected.

    b.   Rejected.

    c.   Both accepted and rejected.

    d.   None of these is correct.

Exercises 10, 11, and 12 are based on the following. A preliminary study of the hourly wages paid unskilled employees in three metropolitan areas was conducted. Seven employees were included from area A, 9 from area B, and 12 from area C. The objective of the study is to find out whether there is a significant difference in the mean hourly wage in the three areas. The .01 level of significance is to be applied. The test statistic was computed to be 4.91.

10. For this type of problem we would use as the test statistic the:

    a.   $z$ distribution.

    b.   $t$ distribution.

    c.   $X^2$ distribution.

    d.   $F$ distribution.

    e.   None of these is correct.

11. At the .01 level, the critical value is:

    a.   1.96.

    b.   −1.96.

    c.   5,000.

    d.   5.00.

    e.   None of these is correct.

12. We would conclude that:

    a.   The mean hourly wages of unskilled employees in the three areas are equal.

    b.   The mean hourly wages in at least two metropolitan areas are different.

    c.   More degrees of freedom are needed.

    d.   None of these is correct.

## PART II—PROBLEMS

13. It was hypothesized that university clerical employees did not engage in productive work 20 minutes on the average out of every hour. Some claimed the time lost was greater than 20 minutes. An actual study was conducted at a midwestern university using a stopwatch and other ways of checking the work habits of the clerical employees. A random check of the employees revealed the following unproductive times, in minutes, during a one-hour period (exclusive of regularly scheduled breaks): 10, 25, 17, 20, 28, 30, 18, 23, and 18. Test at the .05 level that the mean unproductive time is 20 minutes, against the alternate hypothesis that it is greater than 20 minutes.

14. A test of significance is to be conducted involving the mean holding power of two glues designed for plastic. First, a small plastic hook was coated at one end with Epox glue and fastened to a sheet of plastic. After it dried, weight was added to the hook until it separated from the sheet of plastic. The weight was then recorded. This was repeated until 12 hooks were tested. The same procedure was followed for Holdtite glue, but only 10 hooks were used. The sample results, in pounds, were:

|  | Epox | Holdtite |
|---|---|---|
| Sample mean | 250 | 252 |
| Sample standard deviation | 5 | 8 |
| Number in sample | 12 | 10 |

At the .01 level is there a difference between the holding power of Epox and that of Holdtite?

15. An additive formulated to add to the life of paints used in the South is to be tested. The top half of a piece of wood was painted using the regular paint. The bottom half was painted with the paint including the additive. The same procedure was followed for a total of 10 pieces. Then each piece was subjected to high-pressure water and brilliant light. The data, number of hours each piece lasted before it faded beyond a certain point, follow:

| | Number of hours by sample | | | | | | | | | |
|---|---|---|---|---|---|---|---|---|---|---|
| | A | B | C | D | E | F | G | H | I | J |
| Without additive | 325 | 313 | 320 | 340 | 318 | 312 | 319 | 330 | 333 | 319 |
| With additive | 323 | 313 | 326 | 343 | 310 | 320 | 313 | 340 | 330 | 315 |

Using the .05 level, determine if the additive is effective in prolonging the life of the paint.

16. The Buffalo, N.Y., cola distributor is featuring a super-special sale on 12-packs. She wonders where to place the cola for maximum attention. Should it be near the front door of the grocery stores, in the cola section, at the checkout registers, or near the milk and other dairy products? Four stores with similar total sales cooperated in an experiment. In one store the 12-packs were stacked near the front door, in another they were placed near the checkout registers, and so on. Sales were checked at specified times in each store for exactly four minutes. The results were:

| Cola at door | Cola in cola section | Cola near registers | Cola near dairy products |
|---|---|---|---|
| $6 | $ 5 | $ 7 | $10 |
| 8 | 10 | 10 | 9 |
| 3 | 12 | 9 | 6 |
| 7 | 4 | 4 | 11 |
| | 9 | 5 | |
| | | 7 | |

The Buffalo distributor wants to find out if there is a difference in the mean sales for cola stacked at the four locations in the store. Use the .05 significance level.

17. An agriculture economist wants to determine whether soil condition and type of fertilizer have an effect on the yield of blueberries. The following results were obtained, in boxes per acre, from a study of 15 combinations of soil conditions and fertilizer types. Use the .05 significance level.

| Soil conditions | Yield (boxes) by fertilizer type | | | | |
|---|---|---|---|---|---|
| | A | B | C | D | E |
| Dry | 15 | 13 | 7 | 16 | 9 |
| Moderate | 10 | 11 | 8 | 15 | 10 |
| Moist | 18 | 14 | 6 | 19 | 12 |

18. A recent study by the dean of students at Napa Valley College showed that the mean number of hours attempted by a sample of 28 engineering majors was 12.2, and the standard deviation was 2.85 hours. A study of 23 nursing arts majors at Napa Valley showed the mean number of hours attempted was nearly the same—12.8—but the standard deviation was much larger—3.9 hours. The dean speculated that this was because many nursing students were able to find part-time work at nights and weekends at a local hospital and elected to take fewer hours. Also, some of the nursing students apparently were anxious to complete their program because jobs were plentiful in the field and took an excessive number of hours. At the .05 significance level, can the dean conclude that there is more variation in the number of hours attempted by nursing majors compared with engineering majors?

Advertising—Courtesy of Jordache Enterprises, Inc.

# SIMPLE CORRELATION ANALYSIS

When you have completed this chapter, you will be able to:

## GOALS

1. Draw a scatter diagram.
2. Calculate Pearson's coefficient of correlation and explain its use.
3. Test for the significance of the coefficient of correlation.

4. Calculate and explain the use of the coefficients of determination and nondetermination.
5. Explain the purpose of the coefficient of rank-order correlation and compute its value.

C hapters 2 through 4 dealt with *descriptive statistics.* We organized raw data into a frequency distribution and computed several averages and measures of dispersion in order to describe the major characteristics of the data. Chapter 5 started the study of *statistical inference.* The main emphasis was on inferring something about a population parameter, such as the population mean, based on a sample statistic. We tested for the reasonableness of a population mean or proportion, the difference between two population means, and (in Chapter 12) whether more than two population means are equal. All these tests involved just *one* interval- or ratio-level variable, such as income, job efficiency, or length.

We shift our emphasis in this chapter to the *relationship between two or more variables.* We will explore such questions as these: Is there a relationship between high school and college grade point averages? Is there a relationship between the amount a firm spends on advertising and its sales? Is there a relationship between the number of years on the job and productivity? Note that there are *two* variables—number of years on the job and productivity, for example.

We will first examine the meaning and intent of correlation analysis and then look at a chart designed to portray the relationship between two variables—a *scatter diagram.* The measures available to describe the degree of relationship will be presented, including the correlation coefficient and the coefficient of determination.

## What Is Simple Correlation Analysis?

An example best describes what is meant by *correlation analysis.* Suppose we are interested in a group of sophomore students in college. We want to determine the relationship between their grade point averages in high school and their corresponding grade point averages after the first year in college. The GPAs for a sample of four students are:

Relationship between high school performance and college performance

| Student | High school GPA | College GPA |
|---|---|---|
| Frank Rousos | 3.0 | 2.9 |
| Sue Navchek | 2.1 | 2.3 |
| Art Seiple | 4.0 | 3.9 |
| Carma Lopez | 3.8 | 1.9 |

There does seem to be some relationship between academic performance in high school and in college. That is, those with high grades in high school seem to have high college GPAs. The relationship is not "perfect" or exact, however. Carma Lopez, for example, had a very high GPA in high school, but her 1.9 performance in college is well below average.

Instead of talking in generalities, as we have been doing up to this point, we will now use several statistical measures to portray and explain more precisely the relationship between the two variables—high school GPA and college GPA. This group of statistical techniques is referred to as *correlation analysis.*

What is correlation analysis?

> Correlation analysis   A group of statistical techniques used to measure the strength of the relationship (correlation) between two variables.

The basic purpose of correlation analysis is to find how strong the relationship is between two variables. One measure of this relationship is the *coefficient of correlation*. It may assume any value on a scale from $-1$ to $+1$ inclusive. We will apply these measures to interval- and ratio-scaled data first. However, before doing this, we will portray the two sets of data in a *scatter diagram*.

## SCATTER DIAGRAM

Scatter diagram—a chart that may look like this:

| Scatter diagram    A chart that portrays the relationship between the two variables of interest. |
| --- |

### ▮ EXAMPLE

The human resource director of Intrepid, Inc., which has a large sales force, has to interview and select new salespeople. He has designed a test that he hopes will help select the best possible applicants for the sales force. In order to check the validity of the test as a predictor of weekly sales, he randomly chose five experienced salespeople and administered the test to each one. (Of course, in actual practice, to determine the validity of the test, a much larger group would be selected. The size of the group was intentionally kept at a minimum to simplify the calculations.) The test score of each salesperson was then paired with his or her weekly sales. (See Table 13–1.) How are these paired data portrayed in a scatter diagram?

Paired data (test score and sales)

### TABLE   13–1

**Test Scores and Weekly Sales of Five Salespeople at Intrepid, Inc.**

| Salesperson | Test score | Weekly sales |
| --- | --- | --- |
| Mr. J. A. Amber | 4 | $ 5,000 |
| Mr. B. N. Archer | 7 | 12,000 |
| Ms. G. D. Smith | 3 | 4,000 |
| Mr. A. B. Malcolm | 6 | 8,000 |
| Ms. A. Goodwin | 10 | 11,000 |

### ☑ SOLUTION

One variable is the dependent variable. The other is the independent variable

Based on the paired data in Table 13–1, the human resource director suspects that the test scores are in fact good predictors of weekly sales. Ms. Goodwin, for example, has the highest test score, and her weekly sales are relatively high. Ms. Smith's test score was low, and her sales are relatively low. This implies that her weekly sales *depend* on her test score. Thus, sales is referred to as the *dependent* variable. The test score is called the *independent* variable.

Dependent variable on the Y-axis; independent variable on the X-axis

It is common practice to put the dependent variable (sales, in this example) on the vertical axis (Y-axis) and the independent variable—test score—on the horizontal axis (X-axis). The paired data for Mr. Amber from Table 13–1 are $X = 4$, $Y = \$5,000$. To plot, move right on the X-axis to 4; then go vertically to $5,000, and place a dot at that

Plot $X = 4$, $Y = 5,000$ like this:

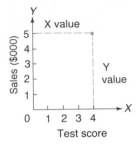

A scatter diagram

intersection. (See Chart 13–1.) This process is continued until all the paired data are plotted.

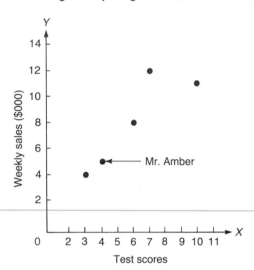

CHART    13–1

Scatter Diagram Depicting Test Scores and Sales

Note from the scatter diagram that as test scores increase, so do sales. It does appear that there is a rather strong relationship (correlation) between test scores and weekly sales. The following section will measure that relationship by computing the *coefficient of correlation.*

## THE COEFFICIENT OF CORRELATION

Interval or ratio data

An $r$ can assume any value between $-1$ and $+1$ inclusive

An $r$ can assume any value between $-1$ and $+1$ inclusive

Coefficients of $-.87$ and $+.87$ have equal strength

Originated by Karl Pearson about 1900, the **coefficient of correlation** describes the strength of the relationship between two sets of interval-scaled or ratio-scaled variables. Designated $r$, it is often referred to as *Pearson's r* and as the *Pearson product-moment correlation coefficient.* It can assume any value from $-1.00$ to $+1.00$ inclusive. A correlation coefficient of $-1.00$ or $+1.00$ indicates *perfect correlation.* For example, a correlation coefficient for the preceding example computed to be $+1.00$ would indicate that test scores were perfect predictors of weekly sales. That is, the scores and sales are perfectly related in a positive linear sense. A computed value of $-1.00$ reveals that the independent variable $X$ and the dependent variable $Y$ are perfectly related in a negative linear way. How the scatter diagrams would appear if the relationship between the two sets of data were linear and perfect is shown in Chart 13–2.

If there is absolutely no relationship between the two sets of variables, Pearson's $r$ will be zero. A coefficient of correlation $r$ close to 0 (say, .08) shows that the relationship is quite weak. The same conclusion is drawn if $r = -.08$. Coefficients of $-.91$ and $+.91$ have equal strength; both indicate very strong correlation between the two sets of variables. Thus, *the strength of the correlation does not depend on the direction (either $-$ or $+$).*

## Chart 13–2

**Scatter Diagrams Showing Perfect Negative Correlation and Perfect Positive Correlation**

An *r* of −1.00 indicates an inverse relationship

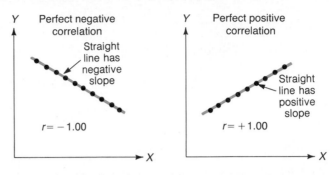

Scatter diagrams for *r* = 0, a weak *r* (say, −.23), and a strong *r* (say, +.87) are shown in Chart 13–3. Note that if the correlation is weak, there is considerable scatter about a straight line drawn through the center of the data. For the scatter diagram representing a strong relationship, there is very little scatter about the straight line. This indicates that high school GPA is a very good predictor of performance in college.

Relationship strength can be "strong," "weak," etc.

## Chart 13–3

**Scatter Diagrams Depicting Zero, Weak, and Strong Correlation**

Examples of degrees of correlation

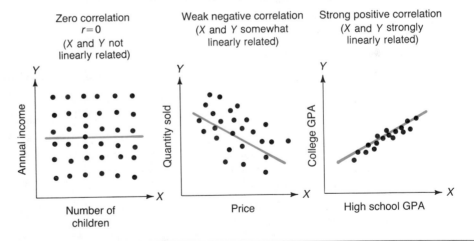

The following drawing summarizes the strength and direction of the coefficient of correlation.

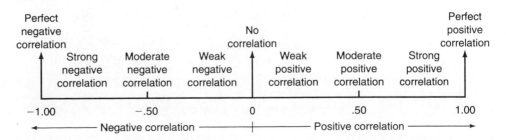

Correlation coefficient defined

> Coefficient of correlation   A measure of the strength of the linear relationship between two sets of variables.

Convenient formula for $r$

The formula for $r$ is:

$$r = \frac{n(\Sigma XY) - (\Sigma X)(\Sigma Y)}{\sqrt{[n(\Sigma X^2) - (\Sigma X)^2][n(\Sigma Y^2) - (\Sigma Y)^2]}} \qquad (13-1)$$

where:

   $n$   is the number of paired observations.

   $\Sigma X$   is the $X$ variable summed.

   $\Sigma Y$   is the $Y$ variable summed.

   $(\Sigma X^2)$   is the $X$ variable squared and the squares summed.

   $(\Sigma X)^2$   is the $X$ variable summed and the sum squared.

   $(\Sigma Y^2)$   is the $Y$ variable squared and the squares summed.

   $(\Sigma Y)^2$   is the $Y$ variable summed and the sum squared.

## ■ EXAMPLE

The data for the problem involving weekly sales and test scores and the calculations needed for the correlation coefficient are given in Table 13–2. What is the coefficient of correlation?

TABLE   13–2

**Calculations Needed for the Correlation Coefficient**

Calculations needed for $r$

| Salesperson | Test score, $X$ | Weekly sales ($000), $Y$ | $X^2$ | $XY$ | $Y^2$ |
|---|---|---|---|---|---|
| Mr. Amber | 4 | 5 | 16 | 20 | 25 |
| Mr. Archer | 7 | 12 | 49 | 84 | 144 |
| Ms. Smith | 3 | 4 | 9 | 12 | 16 |
| Mr. Malcolm | 6 | 8 | 36 | 48 | 64 |
| Ms. Goodwin | 10 | 11 | 100 | 110 | 121 |
| Total | 30 | 40 | 210 | 274 | 370 |

## ☑ SOLUTION

The coefficient of correlation is .88, found by using formula 13–1.

$$\begin{aligned}
r &= \frac{n(\Sigma XY) - (\Sigma X)(\Sigma Y)}{\sqrt{[n(\Sigma X^2) - (\Sigma X)^2][n(\Sigma Y^2) - (\Sigma Y)^2]}} \\
&= \frac{5(274) - (30)(40)}{\sqrt{[5(210) - (30)^2][5(370) - (40)^2]}} \\
&= \frac{170}{\sqrt{[150][250]}} \\
&= .88
\end{aligned}$$

An *r* of .88 indicates a
very strong relationship

The usual practice is to round *r* to the nearest hundredth; in this problem it is .88, indicating a very strong relationship between the test scores and weekly sales. It does appear that the human resource director's test has a potential for predicting weekly sales.

## Self-Review 13–1

*The answers are at the end of the chapter.*

Self-review: A valuable
learning tool

An agronomist employed by Agrico experimented with different amounts of liquid fertilizer on a sample of equal-size plots. The amounts of fertilizer and the yields are:

| Plot | Amount of fertilizer (tons) | Yield (hundreds of bushels) |
|------|------|------|
| A | 2 | 7 |
| B | 1 | 3 |
| C | 3 | 8 |
| D | 4 | 10 |

1. The agronomist is interested in predicting yield. What is the dependent variable? The independent variable?
2. Draw a scatter diagram.
3. Determine the coefficient of correlation.
4. Interpret the strength of *r*.

## EXERCISES

*The answers to the odd-numbered exercises are at the end of the book.*

1. The following sample observations were selected.

$$X: \quad 4 \quad 5 \quad 3 \quad 6 \quad 10$$
$$Y: \quad 4 \quad 6 \quad 5 \quad 7 \quad 7$$

Determine the coefficient of correlation. Interpret.

2. The following sample observations were selected.

$$X: \quad 5 \quad 3 \quad 6 \quad 3 \quad 4 \quad 4 \quad 6 \quad 8$$
$$Y: \quad 13 \quad 15 \quad 7 \quad 12 \quad 13 \quad 11 \quad 9 \quad 5$$

Determine the coefficient of correlation. Interpret.

3. Bi-lo Appliance Stores has outlets in several large metropolitan areas. The general sales manager plans to air a camcorder television commercial on selected local stations at least twice prior to a gigantic sale starting on Saturday and ending Sunday. She plans to get the figures for Saturday-Sunday camcorder sales at the various outlets and pair them with the number of times the advertisement was shown on the local TV stations. The basic purpose of the research is to find out if there is any relationship between the number of times the advertisement was aired and camcorder sales. The pairings are:

| Location of TV station | Number of airings | Saturday-Sunday sales ($000) |
|------|------|------|
| Buffalo | 4 | 15 |
| Albany | 2 | 8 |
| Erie | 5 | 21 |
| Syracuse | 6 | 24 |
| Rochester | 3 | 17 |

a. What is the dependent variable?
b. Draw a scatter diagram.

c. Does there appear to be any relationship between the number of airings and sales? Explain.

d. Determine the coefficient of correlation.

e. Evaluate the strength of the relationship between $X$ and $Y$.

4. Sabin Motorcycle Works plans to develop a brochure for its revolutionary new X2B cycle. One of the facets to be explored and reported on is the speed-mileage question: Is there a linear relationship between the cycle's speed and miles per gallon? Tests on their track revealed the following:

| Constant speed (miles per hour), $X$ | Miles per gallon, $Y$ |
|---|---|
| 40 | 54 |
| 30 | 60 |
| 70 | 37 |
| 50 | 46 |
| 60 | 48 |

To explore the relationship:

a. Draw a scatter diagram.

b. Does there appear to be a relationship between the two variables? Describe it.

c. Compute the coefficient of correlation, and evaluate its strength.

5. A research project at Grumann Plastics was undertaken to determine if there is a relationship between years of service and the efficiency rating of an employee. The objective of the study was to predict the efficiency rating of an employee based on years of service. The sample results were:

| Employee | Years of service | Efficiency rating |
|---|---|---|
| Jones | 1 | 6 |
| Orlando | 20 | 5 |
| Ireland | 6 | 3 |
| Smith | 8 | 5 |
| Kordel | 2 | 2 |
| Harper | 1 | 2 |
| Lopez | 15 | 4 |
| Sobecki | 8 | 3 |

a. What is the dependent variable?

b. Draw a scatter diagram.

c. Based on the scatter diagram, does there appear to be any relationship between years of service and efficiency?

d. Compute the coefficient of correlation.

e. Evaluate the strength of the relationship.

6. The production department of NDB Electronics wants to explore the relationship between the number of employees who assemble a subassembly and the number produced. As an experiment, two employees were assigned to assemble the subassembly. They produced 15 during a one-hour period. Then four employees assembled it. They produced 25 during a one-hour period. The complete set of paired observations follows.

| Number of assemblers | One-hour production (units) |
|---|---|
| 2 | 15 |
| 4 | 25 |
| 1 | 10 |
| 5 | 40 |
| 3 | 30 |

The dependent variable is production; that is, it is assumed that the level of production depends upon the number of employees.

a. Draw a scatter diagram.
b. Based on the scatter diagram, does there appear to be any relationship between the number of assemblers and production? Explain.
c. Compute the coefficient of correlation.
d. Evaluate the strength of the relationship.

# THE COEFFICIENT OF DETERMINATION

Coefficient of determination has a more exact meaning

Meaning of $r^2$

In the previous example regarding the relationship of test scores and weekly sales, the correlation coefficient .88 was interpreted as being "very strong." The terms *weak, moderate,* and *strong,* however, do not have precise meaning. A measure that has a more exact meaning is the **coefficient of determination.** It is computed by squaring the coefficient of correlation. In the example, the coefficient of determination, $r^2$, is .77, found by $(.88)^2$. This is a proportion or percent; we can say that 77 percent of the total variation in weekly sales is explained, or accounted for, by the variation in the test scores.

> Coefficient of determination   The proportion of the total variation in the dependent variable $Y$ that is explained, or accounted for, by the variation in the independent variable $X$.

Further discussion and use of the coefficient of determination is found in Chapter 14.

# THE COEFFICIENT OF NONDETERMINATION

Coefficient of nondetermination defined

The **coefficient of nondetermination,** logically, is the proportion of the total variation in $Y$ that is *not* explained by the variation in $X$. It is computed by $1 - r^2$. In the test score–weekly sales problem, $1 - r^2 = 1 - (.88)^2 = 1 - .77 = .23$. This means that 23 percent of the total variation in weekly sales is not accounted for by the variation in the test scores.

Value of $r^2$ can only be between 0 and +1 inclusive:

|←————→|
0      +1

The coefficients of determination and nondetermination can only be positive (because squaring a negative $r$ results in a positive number). The coefficients can assume any number between 0 and 1.00 inclusive. Note that the coefficient of determination is always smaller than the coefficient of correlation. For example, a correlation coefficient of .80 squared gives a coefficient of determination of .64. Some statisticians would prefer to use the more conservative measure of .64—reasoning that the .80 correlation coefficient may overstate the relationship between the two sets of variables.

## Self-Review 13–2

*The answers are at the end of the chapter.*

1. What are the coefficient of determination and the coefficient of nondetermination for the fertilizer yield problem?

2. Interpret the meaning of the two coefficients.

# EXERCISES

*The answers to the odd-numbered exercises are at the end of the book.*

7. Refer to Exercise 1. Determine the coefficient of determination and the coefficient of nondetermination.

8. Refer to Exercise 2. Determine the coefficient of determination and the coefficient of nondetermination.

9. Refer to Exercise 3.
   a. What are the coefficient of determination and the coefficient of nondetermination for the TV commercial–sales problem?
   b. Interpret the meaning of the two coefficients.

10. Refer to Exercise 4.
    a. What are the coefficient of determination and the coefficient of nondetermination for the motorcycle speed problem?
    b. Interpret the meaning of the two coefficients.

11. Refer to Exercise 5.
    a. What are the coefficient of determination and the coefficient of nondetermination for the efficiency rating problem?
    b. Interpret the meaning of the two coefficients.

12. Refer to Exercise 6.
    a. What are the coefficient of determination and the coefficient of nondetermination for the assembly problem?
    b. Interpret the meaning of the two coefficients.

# TESTING THE SIGNIFICANCE OF THE COEFFICIENT OF CORRELATION

Recall that the human resources director at Intrepid, Inc. designed a test to predict weekly sales. The coefficient of correlation between the test scores and weekly sales was computed to be .88. This indicates a strong relationship between the two sets of variables. However, only five salespeople were included in the experiment. Therefore, one might ask whether or not (because of the small sample size) the correlation in the population might actually be 0. Perhaps the strong relationship of .88 between test scores and sales is due to chance. The population in this example is all the salespeople employed by the firm.

*Could the correlation in the population be zero?*

Resolving this dilemma requires a test to answer the obvious question: Is there zero correlation in the population from which the sample was selected? To put it another way, did the computed $r$ come from a population of paired observations with zero correlation? To continue our convention of allowing Greek letters to represent a population value, we will let $\rho$ represent the correlation in the population. It is pronounced "rho."

## SMALL SAMPLES

We will continue with the test scores–weekly sales illustration. The null hypothesis and the alternate hypothesis are:

$H_0$: $\rho = 0$   (The correlation in the population is zero.)
$H_1$: $\rho \neq 0$   (The correlation in the population is different from zero.)

From the way $H_1$ is stated, we know that the test is two-tailed.
The formula for $t$ is:

$$t = \frac{r\sqrt{n-2}}{\sqrt{1-r^2}}$$     with $n-2$ degrees of freedom     (13-2)

Using the .10 level of significance, the decision rule states that if the computed $t$ falls in the area between plus 2.353 and minus 2.353, the null hypothesis will not be rejected. To locate the critical value of 2.353, refer to Appendix F for $df = n - 2 = 5 - 2 = 3$. Shown schematically:

Critical values of $t$ are
$-2.353$ and 2.353

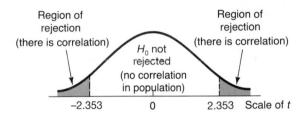

Region of rejection
(there is correlation)

$H_0$ not rejected
(no correlation in population)

Region of rejection
(there is correlation)

$-2.353$       0       2.353    Scale of $t$

Applying formula (13-2) to the test scores-weekly sales problem:

$$t = \frac{r\sqrt{n-2}}{\sqrt{1-r^2}} = \frac{.88\sqrt{5-2}}{\sqrt{1-(.88)^2}} = 3.21$$

The computed value of $t$ falls in the rejection region. Thus, $H_0$ is rejected at the .10 significance level. This means that the correlation in the population is not zero. From a practical standpoint, it indicates to the human resource director that there is correlation in the population of salespeople with respect to test scores and weekly sales.

## AN APPLICATION USING THE MINITAB SYSTEM

The computer offers substantial savings in time and greatly reduces the likelihood of a computational error. Most packages also have available some type of plot routine. The MINITAB system was used to solve the following problem.

### ■ EXAMPLE

The principal at Oil City High School in Pennsylvania surveyed a sample of 20 students in the 1980 graduating class. She recorded the number of years of education beyond high school and the individual's yearly income last year. She wants to know if there is an association between the two variables. The sample findings are listed in Table 13-3.

## TABLE 13–3

**Number of Years of Education beyond High School and Annual Income**

| Years beyond high school | Yearly income ($000) | Years beyond high school | Yearly income ($000) |
|---|---|---|---|
| 0 | 31.6 | 4 | 35.6 |
| 0 | 28.0 | 4 | 50.2 |
| 1 | 34.0 | 4 | 31.7 |
| 1 | 30.5 | 5 | 48.0 |
| 1 | 27.8 | 5 | 36.5 |
| 2 | 29.5 | 6 | 50.6 |
| 2 | 26.8 | 6 | 63.9 |
| 2 | 31.2 | 7 | 57.6 |
| 3 | 34.2 | 7 | 61.2 |
| 3 | 39.8 | 7 | 54.9 |

### ✓ SOLUTION

As a first step, the principal plotted the data using MINITAB. Note that the relationship is not exact—that is, all the points are not on a straight line—but it does appear that as the years of education increase, so does the yearly income. The MINITAB plot follows, and the coefficient of correlation is given.

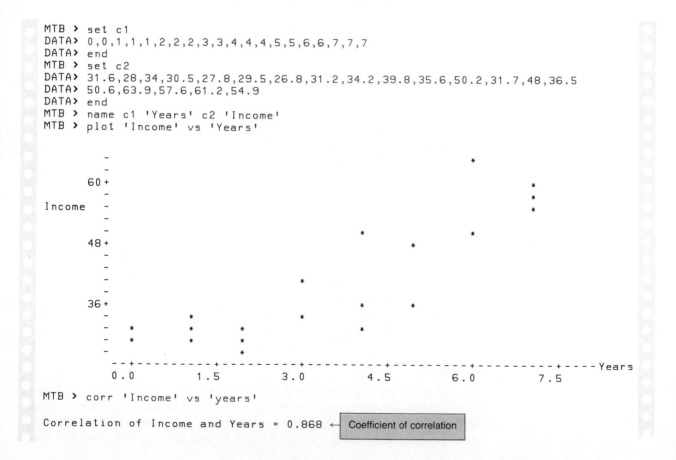

```
MTB > set c1
DATA> 0,0,1,1,1,2,2,2,3,3,4,4,4,5,5,6,6,7,7,7
DATA> end
MTB > set c2
DATA> 31.6,28,34,30.5,27.8,29.5,26.8,31.2,34.2,39.8,35.6,50.2,31.7,48,36.5
DATA> 50.6,63.9,57.6,61.2,54.9
DATA> end
MTB > name c1 'Years' c2 'Income'
MTB > plot 'Income' vs 'Years'
```

```
          -                                                       *
          -
     60 + 
          -                                                          *
 Income   -                                                          *
          -                                                          *
          -
          -                                 *              *
     48 +                                            *
          -
          -
          -
          -                          *
     36 +                                   *        *
          -           *         *
          -        *      *        *               *
          -        *      *             *
          -                          *
          - --+---------+---------+---------+---------+---------+----Years
            0.0       1.5       3.0       4.5       6.0       7.5
```

```
MTB > corr 'Income' vs 'years'

Correlation of Income and Years = 0.868 ← Coefficient of correlation
```

The normal hypothesis-testing procedure can be used to determine if the association in the population is greater than zero. In this instance, assume that the principal wants to determine if there is a positive association between years of education and yearly income. The null and alternate hypotheses would be:

$$H_0: \rho = 0$$

$$H_1: \rho > 0$$

The sample size is 20, so there are $n - 2 = 20 - 2 = 18$ degrees of freedom. Using the .05 level and a one-tailed test, the decision rule is to reject the null hypothesis if the computed value of $t$ is greater than 1.734. The computed test statistic $t$ is 7.42, found by using formula (13–2):

$$t = \frac{r\sqrt{n-2}}{\sqrt{1-r^2}}$$

$$= \frac{.868\sqrt{20-2}}{\sqrt{1-(.868)^2}} = 7.42$$

Since the computed $t$ value of 7.42 exceeds the critical value, the null hypothesis is rejected and the alternate hypothesis accepted. Yearly income does increase as the number of years of education increases. There is a positive association in the population between these two variables.

### Self-Review 13–3

*The answers are at the end of the chapter.*

A sample of 25 mayoral campaigns in cities with populations larger than 50,000 showed that the correlation between the percent of the vote received and the amount spent on the campaign by the candidate was .43. At the .05 significance level, is there a positive association between the variables?

## EXERCISES

*The answers to the odd-numbered exercises are at the end of the book.*

13. The following hypotheses are given.

$$H_0: \rho = 0$$

$$H_1: \rho > 0$$

A sample of 12 paired observations indicated a correlation of .32. Can we conclude that the correlation in the population is greater than zero? Use the .05 significance level.

14. $H_0$ and $H_1$ are:

$$H_0: \rho = 0$$

$$H_1: \rho < 0$$

A sample of 15 paired observations have a correlation of $-.46$. Can we conclude that the correlation in the population is zero? Use the .05 significance level.

15. The Pennsylvania Refining Company is studying the relationship between the pump price of gasoline and the number of gallons sold at a particular gasoline station. For a sample of 20 stations last Tuesday, the correlation was .78. At the .01 significance level, is the correlation in the population greater than zero?

16. A study of 20 worldwide financial institutions showed the correlation between their assets and pretax profit, to be .86. At the .05 significance level, can we conclude that there is positive correlation in the population?

Courtesy Amoco Corporation

# RANK-ORDER CORRELATION

*Use Spearman's coefficient for ordinal data*

Pearson's product-moment correlation coefficient, $r$, discussed in the previous section, requires that the data be interval- or ratio-scaled, such as incomes and weights. Charles Spearman, a British statistician, introduced a measure of correlation for ordinal-level data—that is, data that are, or can be, ranked from either low to high or vice versa. The measure is referred to as **Spearman's rank-order correlation coefficient.** Symbolized by $r_s$, it measures the degree of relationship between two sets of ranked observations.

*Formula for Spearman's coefficient*

The formula for $r_s$ is:

$$r_s = 1 - \frac{6\Sigma d^2}{n(n^2 - 1)} \qquad (13-3)$$

where:

$d$  is the difference between the ranks for each pair.

$n$  is the number of paired observations.

*$r_s$ can be between −1 and +1 inclusive*

Like Pearson's $r$, Spearman's rank-order correlation coefficient can assume any value from −1.00 to +1.00 inclusive, with −1.00 indicating perfect negative correlation, +1.00 indicating perfect positive correlation, and 0 indicating no relationship between the two sets of data. Remember, values of −.14 and +.14 have the same strength; both indicate a very weak relationship. The value −.14 reveals that the relationship is inverse; as the independent variable $X$ increases, the dependent variable $Y$ decreases. A positive rank-order correlation signifies that as $X$ increases, so does $Y$.

Now we will determine the rank-order correlation coefficient for two sets of ordinal-level data.

## ■ EXAMPLE

The paired data in Table 13–4 and the following scatter diagram illustrate the case of perfect correlation between the rank a worker has within the sample group of workers on a finger dexterity test and his or her rank with respect to weekly production. Both finger dexterity scores and production level have been ranked from high (1) to low (5). However, as long as both groups are treated the same, there is no reason the scores and production cannot be ranked from high (5) to low (1): $r_s$ will be the same (+1.00) in either case. Note from the table that Joe had the highest test score, and he also ranked first with respect to production. Sue's performances ranked 2 and 2 within the group, and so on.

## TABLE 13–4

**Finger Dexterity Test Scores and Weekly Production**

| Name of worker | Finger dexterity test score | Weekly production index | Rank Dexterity | Rank Production |
|---|---|---|---|---|
| Pete | 62 | 800 | 4 | 4 |
| Joe | 92 | 900 | 1 | 1 |
| Dee | 70 | 840 | 3 | 3 |
| Sam | 50 | 775 | 5 | 5 |
| Sue | 86 | 875 | 2 | 2 |

It does appear that $r_s$, when computed, will be +1.00

Portraying the ranks in a scatter diagram:

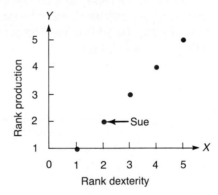

Scatter diagram also reveals that $r_s$ will be +1.00

It should be emphasized that $r_s$ is being used as the measure of correlation in this problem (instead of Pearson's $r$) because there is interest in the degree of relationship between two sets of *ranked* data.

For the data in the Table 13–4, what is Spearman's rank-order correlation coefficient?

## ☑ SOLUTION

In this problem $n$ is the total number of workers in the sample, or 5, and $d$ is the difference between ranks for each pair. In part, formula (13–3) directs one to square each difference and then sum the squares.

The calculations for $r_s$ are shown in Table 13–5.

## TABLE 13–5

**Calculations Needed for Spearman's Rank-Order Coefficient**

| Worker | Finger dexterity | Weekly production | $d$ | $d^2$ |
|---|---|---|---|---|
| Pete | 4 | 4 | 0 | 0 |
| Joe | 1 | 1 | 0 | 0 |
| Dee | 3 | 3 | 0 | 0 |
| Sam | 5 | 5 | 0 | 0 |
| Sue | 2 | 2 | 0 | 0 |
| Total | | | | 0 |

From these data we find that, as expected, Spearman's rank-order correlation coefficient is 1.00. (See the following calculations.)

$$r_s = 1 - \frac{6\Sigma d^2}{n(n^2 - 1)} = 1 - \frac{6(0)}{5(5^2 - 1)} = 1.00$$

$r_s = 1.00$

Thus, we can say that there is perfect (positive) correlation between the ranks.
    Now for a case involving less-than-perfect rank-order correlation.

### ■ EXAMPLE

This problem involves a composite rating given by executives to each college graduate joining a plastic manufacturing firm. The executive rating is an expression of the future potential of the college graduate. (The ratings represent, of course, ordinal level of measurement.) The recent college graduate then enters an in-plant training program and is given another composite rating (based on tests, opinions of group leaders, training officers, and so on). The executive ratings and the in-plant training ratings are given in Table 13–6.

### TABLE 13–6

**Executive Ratings and In-Plant Training Ratings for a Selected Group of College Graduates**

| Graduate | Executive rating, X | Training rating, Y |
|----------|:-------------------:|:------------------:|
| A | 8 | 4 |
| B | 10 | 4 |
| C | 9 | 4 |
| D | 4 | 3 |
| E | 12 | 6 |
| F | 11 | 9 |
| G | 11 | 9 |
| H | 7 | 6 |
| I | 8 | 6 |
| J | 13 | 9 |
| K | 10 | 5 |
| L | 12 | 9 |

    The problem is to determine the relationship between the ratings college graduates received from the executives before they entered the in-plant training program ($X$) and the ratings they received in the training program ($Y$). That is, what is the coefficient of rank correlation?

### ☑ SOLUTION

Dealing with ties

It was decided to rank the variables from low (1) to high. The lowest rating given by the executives was 4, so it was ranked 1. The next lowest was 7, ranked 2. Then there were two graduates rated 8. The tie is resolved by giving each a rank of 3.5, which is the average of ranks 3 and 4. The same procedure is followed when there are more than two ratings tied. For example, note that the lowest training rating is 3, and it is given a rank of 1. Then there are three ratings of 4. The average of the three tied ranks is 3.00, found by $(2 + 3 + 4)/3$. This is illustrated along with the necessary calculations for $r_s$ in Table 13–7.

---

### TABLE 13–7

**Calculations Needed for $r_s$**

| Graduate | Executive rating, X | Training rating, Y | Rank Executive | Rank Training | Difference between ranks, d | Difference squared, $d^2$ |
|---|---|---|---|---|---|---|
| A | 8 | 4 | 3.5 | 3.0 | 0.5 | 0.25 |
| B | 10 | 4 | 6.5 | 3.0 | 3.5 | 12.25 |
| C | 9 | 4 | 5.0 | 3.0 | 2.0 | 4.00 |
| D | 4 | 3 | 1.0 | 1.0 | 0 | 0 |
| E | 12 | 6 | 10.5 | 7.0 | 3.5 | 12.25 |
| F | 11 | 9 | 8.5 | 10.5 | −2.0 | 4.00 |
| G | 11 | 9 | 8.5 | 10.5 | −2.0 | 4.00 |
| H | 7 | 6 | 2.0 | 7.0 | −5.0 | 25.00 |
| I | 8 | 6 | 3.5 | 7.0 | −3.5 | 12.25 |
| J | 13 | 9 | 12.0 | 10.5 | 1.5 | 2.25 |
| K | 10 | 5 | 6.5 | 5.0 | 1.5 | 2.25 |
| L | 12 | 9 | 10.5 | 10.5 | 0 | 0 |
|  |  |  |  |  | 0.0* | 78.50 |

*Sum of deviations must equal 0.

---

A value of .73 indicates a rather strong relationship between the paired data

$r_s$ is computed to be .73, found by:

$$r_s = 1 - \frac{6\Sigma d^2}{n(n^2 - 1)} = 1 - \frac{6(78.50)}{12(143)} = .73$$

This problem may also be solved on the MINITAB system. The first step is to enter the data in the usual fashion. Next the ranks for each column of data are determined, and then the correlation of the ranks is determined. (Note there is a small difference between the two answers. This is due to using different forms of the equation and rounding.)

```
MTB > set c1
DATA> 8,10,9,4,12,11,11,7,8,13,10,12
DATA> end
MTB > set c2
DATA> 4,4,4,3,6,9,9,6,6,9,5,9
DATA> end
MTB > rank c1, put in c10
MTB > rank c2, put in c11
MTB > name c1 'Exec' c2 'Train' c10 'Rank-ex' c11 'Rank-tr'
MTB > corr c10 c11

Correlation of Rank-ex and Rank-tr = 0.715
```

## Self-Review 13—4

*The answers are at the end of the chapter.*

A small sample of individuals revealed the following scores on an eye perception test (X) and a mechanical aptitude test (Y):

| Subject | Eye perception | Mechanical aptitude |
|---|---|---|
| 001 | 805 | 23 |
| 002 | 777 | 62 |
| 003 | 820 | 60 |
| 004 | 682 | 40 |
| 005 | 777 | 70 |
| 006 | 810 | 28 |
| 007 | 805 | 30 |
| 008 | 840 | 42 |
| 009 | 777 | 55 |
| 010 | 820 | 51 |

1. Draw a scatter diagram (using ranks).
2. Based on the scatter diagram, what can be said about the rank correlation between the two variables?
3. Compute $r_s$.
4. Interpret $r_s$.

## EXERCISES

*The answers to the odd-numbered exercises are at the end of the book.*

17. The ABC network television research staff wants to pretest a questionnaire to be mailed to several thousand viewers. One question involves the ranking of male and female senior citizens with respect to the popularity of certain prime-time programs. The composite rankings of a small group of senior citizens are:

| Program | Ranking by males | Ranking by females |
|---|---|---|
| "Monday Night Football' | 1 | 5 |
| "Robin Crest" | 4 | 1 |
| "Simon and Sandor" | 3 | 2 |
| Evening News | 2 | 4 |
| "Our Hero" | 5 | 3 |

a. Draw a scatter diagram. Let the rankings by males be X.

b. Compute Spearman's rank-order correlation coefficient. Interpret.

18. Far West University offers both day and evening classes in business administration. An extensive survey is to be conducted. One question involves sophomore students and how they perceive the prestige associated with certain careers, such as accounting. Each student was asked to rank the careers from 1 to 8, with 1 having the most prestige and 8 the least prestige. The composite results were:

| Career | Ranking by day students | Ranking by evening students |
|---|---|---|
| Accountant | 6 | 3 |
| Computer programmer | 7 | 2 |
| Branch bank manager | 2 | 6 |
| Hospital administrator | 5 | 4 |
| Statistician | 1 | 7 |
| Marketing researcher | 4 | 8 |
| Stock analyst | 3 | 5 |
| Production manager | 8 | 1 |

a. Portray the rankings in a scatter diagram. Let the rankings by day students be $X$.

b. Compute Spearman's correlation coefficient. Interpret.

19. New representatives for the John Ford Metal and Wheel Company attend a brief training program before being assigned to a regional office. At the end of such a program, each representative was ranked with respect to future sales potential. At the end of the first sales year, their rankings were paired with their annual sales:

| Representative | Annual sales ($000) | Ranking in training program |
|----------------|---------------------|-----------------------------|
| Kitchen | 319 | 3 |
| Bond | 150 | 9 |
| Gross | 175 | 6 |
| Arbuckle | 460 | 1 |
| Greene | 348 | 4 |
| Arden | 300 | 10 |
| Crane | 280 | 5 |
| Arthur | 200 | 2 |
| Keene | 190 | 7 |
| Knopf | 300 | 8 |

a. Compute Spearman's rank correlation coefficient.

b. Interpret $r_s$.

20. The University of Winston has five scholarships available for the women's basketball team. The coach provided two scouts with the names of 10 high school players with potential. Each scout attended at least three games and then ranked the players with respect to potential.

| Player | Rank, by scout Jean Cann | Rank, by scout John Cannelli |
|--------|-----------|---------------|
| Cora Jean Seiple | 7 | 5 |
| Bette Jones | 2 | 4 |
| Jeannie Black | 10 | 10 |
| Norma Tidwell | 1 | 3 |
| Kathy Marchal | 6 | 6 |
| Candy Jenkins | 3 | 1 |
| Rita Rosinski | 5 | 7 |
| Anita Lockes | 4 | 2 |
| Brenda Towne | 8 | 9 |
| Denise Ober | 9 | 8 |

a. Determine Spearman's rank correlation coefficient.

b. Comment on the association of the ranks.

## TESTING THE SIGNIFICANCE OF $r_s$

Testing whether correlation in the population is zero

Earlier we tested the significance of Pearson's $r$. For ranked data using a small sample, the question also arises whether the correlation in the population is actually zero. For instance, there were only 12 executives sampled in the preceding example and only 10 individuals in Self-Review 13–4. In the solution to the example, the rank correlation coefficient of .73 indicates a rather strong relationship between the two sets of ranks. Is it possible that the correlation of .73 is due to chance and that the correlation in the population is really 0? We will now conduct a test of significance to answer that question.

The test for small samples differs somewhat from the test for large samples. However, the first step for either size is to state the null and alternate hypotheses.

$H_0$: The correlation in the population is zero.

$H_1$: The correlation in the population is greater than zero.

### SMALL SAMPLES

"Small" samples—less than 10

For a sample of less than 10, the critical value is determined by referring to Appendix H. If, based on the sample results, the computed value of $r_s$ is less than the critical value, the null hypothesis is not rejected. Otherwise, it is rejected and $H_1$ accepted.

Note that Appendix H actually extends from an $n$ of 4 to 30, indicating that it may be used for any sample size in that range. As an example, in Self-Review 13–4, involving eye perception and mechanical aptitude, $r_s$ was computed to be $-.17; n = 10$. The critical value at the .05 level is .564. Since .17 is less than .564, the null hypothesis is not rejected. There is no relationship between eye perception and mechanical aptitude in the population; that is, the value of .17 is probably due to chance.

### LARGE SAMPLES

"Large" samples—10 or more

For a sample of 10 or more, the significance of $r_s$ is determined by either (1) referring to Appendix H for the critical value or (2) computing Student's $t$, that is, using formula (13–2), but replacing $r$ with $r_s$. In this regard, the sampling distribution of $r_s$ follows the $t$ distribution with $n - 2$ degrees of freedom. The computed value of $t$ is found by:

$$t = r_s \sqrt{\frac{n - 2}{1 - r_s^2}}$$                    (13–4)

with $n - 2$ degrees of freedom.

Both methods will be applied to our result of .73 computed in the example involving executive ratings and in-plant training ratings (Table 13–6). First, using Appendix H, the critical value for an $n$ of 12 and the .05 level is .506. Since the computed value (.73) falls beyond this critical value, the null hypothesis is rejected at the .05 level, and $H_1$ is accepted. This means that the rank-order correlation in the population is greater than zero.

The decision rule for the second method, using Student's $t$, calls for not rejecting $H_0$ if the computed value of $t$ is less than the critical value of 1.812 (Appendix F, .05 level, one-tailed test, and $df = 10$ found by $n - 2 = 12 - 2 = 10$).

The computed value of $t$ is 3.38:

$$t = r_s \sqrt{\frac{n - 2}{1 - r_s^2}} = .73 \sqrt{\frac{12 - 2}{1 - (.73)^2}} = 3.38$$

The decision is the same as before, namely, the null hypothesis is rejected at the .05 level (because 3.38 is beyond the critical value of 1.812). To repeat, it is highly unlikely that the relationship between the two variables in the population is zero.

# EXERCISES

*The answers to the odd-numbered exercises are at the end of the book.*

21. A series of questions on sports and world events was asked a randomly selected group of male senior citizens. The results were translated into a "knowledge" score. The scores were:

| Citizen | Sports | World events |
|---|---|---|
| Mr. J. C. McCarthy | 47 | 49 |
| Mr. A. N. Baker | 12 | 10 |
| Mr. B. B. Beebe | 62 | 76 |
| Mr. L. D. Gaucet | 81 | 92 |
| Mr. C. A. Jones | 90 | 86 |
| Mr. J. N. Narko | 35 | 42 |
| Mr. A. F. Nissen | 61 | 61 |
| Mr. L. M. Zaugg | 87 | 75 |
| Mr. J. B. Simon | 59 | 86 |
| Mr. J. Goulden | 40 | 61 |
| Mr. A. A. Davis | 87 | 18 |
| Mr. A. M. Carbo | 16 | 75 |
| Mr. A. O. Smithy | 50 | 51 |
| Mr. J. J. Pascal | 60 | 61 |

a. Draw a scatter diagram. Let sports be the *X* variable.

b. Determine the degree of association between how the senior citizens ranked with respect to knowledge of sports and how they ranked on world events.

c. At the .05 significance level is the rank correlation in the population greater than zero?

22. A physical inventory accounting program was conducted at an ordnance depot containing about 186,000 different items.[1] One objective was to determine how accurate were the inventory data stored in the computer. If, for example, the inventory figure on a certain size of snow tire indicated that 1,000 were on hand, but an actual count revealed only 800, obviously the record would be 20 percent inaccurate. (The discrepancies were due to paperwork errors, stealing, and so on.)

The question to be examined here is: Are the active warehouses more inaccurate than the less active warehouses? A warehouse containing hardware such as nuts, bolts, and cotter pins is considered "active" because these items are always being shipped out to military installations. A warehouse containing antifreeze and similar slow-moving items is considered "inactive."

In order to measure the degree of activity, an *activity score* was computed for each warehouse. The *error rate* for each warehouse was also calculated. Note from the following table that warehouse number 2 was the most active, with an activity score of 328.6. The error rate for that warehouse was 42.3 percent, meaning that, on the average, there was a discrepancy of 42.3 percent between the computer records and the actual inventory for the items in that warehouse.

Specifically, the problem involves determining the relationship (correlation) between the ranking the warehouses have on the activity score and the corresponding ranking with respect to error rate. That is, do the warehouses that rank high in activity also have high error rates? Conversely, are the inactive warehouses ranked low in error rate?

---

[1]Source: Marion R. Bryson and Robert D. Mason, *Physical Inventory Accounting Program,* Technical Report no. 1, Office of Ordnance Research.

| Warehouse number | Activity score | Error rate | Warehouse number | Activity score | Error rate |
|---|---|---|---|---|---|
| 2 | 328.6 | 42.3 | 9 | 181.5 | 28.8 |
| 3 | 324.5 | 45.6 | 8 | 180.3 | 30.9 |
| 26 | 288.4 | 45.3 | 10 | 178.2 | 29.2 |
| 24 | 281.3 | 33.2 | 20 | 174.5 | 20.5 |
| 14 | 238.5 | 41.4 | 6 | 169.1 | 15.9 |
| 23 | 230.7 | 44.3 | 18 | 166.9 | 19.6 |
| 19 | 209.5 | 31.3 | 27 | 166.4 | 20.6 |
| 5 | 207.1 | 33.2 | 21 | 164.4 | 16.6 |
| 25 | 193.7 | 16.9 | 17 | 160.7 | 33.3 |
| 4 | 192.0 | 41.3 | 7 | 158.1 | 26.4 |
| 1 | 188.3 | 35.6 | 11 | 150.4 | 29.9 |
| 15 | 188.2 | 29.2 | 12 | 140.0 | 23.2 |
| 16 | 184.6 | 31.3 | 13 | 124.2 | 27.1 |
| 22 | 183.5 | 21.4 | | | |

a.  Rank the activity scores. Then rank the error rates. (Watch the ties.)

b.  Plot the paired rankings in the form of a scatter diagram. The $Y$ variable is the error rate, and the $X$ variable is the activity score.

c.  Interpret the scatter diagram.

d.  Compute Spearman's rank correlation coefficient.

e.  Is there a relationship between the activity score and error rate? Use $\alpha = .05$.

f.  Interpret your findings.

## A WORD OF CAUTION

If there is a strong relationship (say, .91) between two sets of variables, we are tempted to assume that an increase or decrease in the independent variable *causes* a change in the dependent variable. For example, it can be shown that the consumption of Georgia peanuts and the consumption of aspirin have moved together. However, this does not indicate that an increase in the consumption of peanuts *caused* the consumption of aspirin to increase. (Nor does it indicate that there is any other relationship between the two variables.) Likewise, the incomes of professors and the number of inmates in mental institutions have increased proportionately. Further, as the population of donkeys decreased, there was a proportional increase in the number of Ph.D.s. Relationships like this are called *spurious* or *nonsense correlation*. The foregoing illustrations show that the independent variable ($X$) used to predict the $Y$ variable must be selected with discretion.

## CHAPTER OUTLINE

I.  Correlation analysis—interval or ratio level of measurement.

   A.  The purpose is to find the degree of association between the dependent and independent variables.

   B.  There are three measures of association.

      1. The correlation coefficient, $r$, measures the degree of linear association between $X$ and $Y$. It can assume any value between $-1$ and $+1$. The formula for $r$ is:

$$r = \frac{n(\Sigma XY) - (\Sigma X)(\Sigma Y)}{\sqrt{[n(\Sigma X^2) - (\Sigma X)^2][n(\Sigma Y^2) - (\Sigma Y)^2]}} \tag{13-1}$$

      2. The coefficient of determination, $r^2$, is the proportion of the variation in $Y$ explained by $X$. It can assume any value between 0 and 1 inclusive.

3. The coefficient of nondetermination, $1 - r^2$, is the proportion of the variation in the dependent variable not accounted for by the independent variable.

C. Testing significance of $r$: Is the correlation in the population zero? For small samples student's $t$ distribution is the test statistic.

$$t = \frac{r\sqrt{n - 2}}{\sqrt{1 - r^2}} \qquad (13-2)$$

II. Correlation analysis—ordinal level of measurement.

A. The rank-order correlation coefficient is used to explain the degree of relationship between two sets of data that are at least ordinal level. The formula is:

$$r_s = 1 - \frac{6\Sigma d^2}{n(n^2 - 1)} \qquad (13-3)$$

$r_s$ can assume any value between $-1$ and $+1$ inclusive. A $-1$ or $+1$ indicates perfect correlation between the ranks.

B. Testing the significance of $r_s$.
1. State null and alternate hypotheses.

$H_0$: Rank correlation in population is 0.

$H_1$: Rank correlation in population is not 0.

2. For an $n$ of less than 10, refer to Appendix H for the critical value. If $r_s$ is less than the critical value, do not reject $H_0$; otherwise reject it.
3. If $n$ is between 10 and 30, either use Appendix H for the critical value or use Student's $t$ and Appendix F.
4. For sample size over 30, use $t$.

$$t = r_s \sqrt{\frac{n - 2}{1 - r_s^2}} \qquad (13-4)$$

# EXERCISES

*The answers to the odd-numbered exercises are at the end of the book.*

23. What is the relationship between the amount spent per week on food and the size of the family? Do larger families spend more on food? A sample of 10 families in the Chicago area revealed the following figures for family size and the amount spent on food last week.

| Family size | Amount spent on food |
|---|---|
| 3 | $ 99 |
| 6 | 104 |
| 5 | 151 |
| 6 | 129 |
| 6 | 142 |
| 3 | 111 |
| 4 | 74 |
| 4 | 91 |
| 5 | 119 |
| 3 | 91 |

a. Compute the coefficient of correlation.
b. Determine the coefficient of determination.
c. Can we conclude that there is a positive association between the amount spent on food and the family size? Use the .05 significance level.

24. A sample of 12 homes sold last week in St. Paul, Minnesota, is selected. Can we conclude that as the size of the home (reported below in hundreds of square feet) increases, the selling price (reported in $000) also increases?

| Home size (hundreds of square feet) | Selling price ($000) |
|:---:|:---:|
| 1.4 | 100 |
| 1.3 | 110 |
| 1.2 | 105 |
| 1.1 | 120 |
| 1.4 | 80 |
| 1.0 | 105 |
| 1.3 | 110 |
| 0.8 | 85 |
| 1.2 | 105 |
| 0.9 | 75 |
| 1.1 | 70 |
| 1.1 | 95 |

a. Compute the coefficient of correlation.

b. Determine the coefficient of determination.

c. Can we conclude that there is a positive association between the size of the home and the selling price? Use the .05 significance level.

25. A sample of 30 used cars sold by Northcut Motors in 1992 revealed that the correlation between the selling price and the number of miles driven was −.45. At the .05 significance level, can we conclude that there is a negative association in the population between the two variables?

26. For a sample of 32 large U.S. cities, the correlation between the mean number of square feet per office worker and the mean monthly rental rate in the central business district is −.363. At the .05 significance level, can we conclude that there is a negative association in the population between the two variables?

27. Is there a relationship between the length of a toll road and the cost per mile to drive the toll road? The following information was recently reported.

| Toll road | Length (miles) | Cost per mile (cents) |
|:---|:---:|:---:|
| Massachusetts Turnpike | 123.0 | 4.15 |
| Pennsylvania (east−west) | 358.9 | 4.10 |
| Pennsylvania (northeast) | 111.1 | 3.74 |
| New Jersey Turnpike | 118.0 | 3.89 |
| Florida Turnpike | 265.0 | 3.75 |
| New York Thruway (Mainline) | 390.0 | 3.10 |
| New York Thruway (Erie) | 67.0 | 3.13 |
| New York Thruway (Saratoga) | 24.0 | 3.13 |
| Kansas Turnpike | 236.0 | 2.97 |
| Indiana | 156.9 | 2.96 |
| Maine Turnpike | 106.0 | 2.92 |
| Oklahoma (Turner Turnpike) | 86.0 | 2.33 |
| Oklahoma (Will Rogers) | 88.5 | 2.26 |
| Ohio | 241.2 | 2.03 |

a. Determine the coefficient of correlation.

b. Determine the coefficient of determination.

(Source: The Tale of the Tolls," *USA Today*, March 22, 1991, p. A3.)

28. The United Nations released these annual birth rates and suicide rates for selected countries:

| Country | Birth rate (per 1,000 population) | Suicide rate (per 1,000 population) |
|---|---|---|
| Australia | 15.7 | 11.1 |
| Czechoslovakia | 18.4 | 21.9 |
| Finland | 13.5 | 25.1 |
| Germany | 13.9 | 30.5 |
| Italy | 12.5 | 5.8 |
| Mexico | 35.3 | 2.1 |
| Poland | 19.0 | 12.1 |
| Singapore | 17.0 | 11.3 |
| Spain | 17.2 | 4.0 |
| United States | 15.3 | 12.7 |

To explore the relationship between birth rate and suicide rate:

a. Draw a scatter diagram. Let birth rate be the X variable.

b. Evaluate the relationship between birth rate and suicide rate based on your scatter diagram.

c. Compute the coefficient of correlation and the coefficients of determination and nondetermination.

d. Evaluate the strength of the relationship.

e. Test the significance of the coefficient of correlation. Use the 1 percent level. Explain your findings.

29. The paralegal program offered at the University of Toledo is career-oriented, and many of those enrolled are older people considering the possibility of a new career. Did these older people earn higher grades than the younger persons in the program? That is, based on the following information, is there a strong correlation between age and GPA?

| Age | GPA | Age | GPA | Age | GPA |
|---|---|---|---|---|---|
| 17 | 2.6 | 22 | 4.0 | 25 | 3.0 |
| 17 | 2.3 | 28 | 3.7 | 34 | 3.7 |
| 54 | 3.3 | 17 | 2.7 | 22 | 4.0 |
| 18 | 3.1 | 18 | 3.2 | 18 | 2.7 |
| 30 | 2.4 | 22 | 3.0 | 29 | 2.8 |
| 41 | 2.3 | 27 | 2.3 | 17 | 2.8 |
| 16 | 3.1 | 23 | 3.0 | 25 | 2.8 |
| 24 | 3.6 | 17 | 2.3 | 18 | 2.5 |
| 50 | 3.2 | 21 | 2.0 | 31 | 3.0 |
| 28 | 3.0 | 19 | 2.3 | 33 | 3.4 |
| 26 | 3.2 | 20 | 3.3 | 17 | 2.0 |
| 35 | 3.9 | 17 | 3.4 | 42 | 3.5 |
| 23 | 4.0 | 26 | 2.6 | 18 | 2.8 |
| 29 | 3.6 | 20 | 2.8 | 18 | 2.5 |
| 19 | 3.2 | 20 | 3.2 | 17 | 2.3 |

a. Compute the coefficient of correlation.

b. At the .05 significance level, is there a positive association between the two variables in the population?

30. A large number of New Mexico College graduates are employed by an internationally known computer company. The director of recruiting for the company is conducting an extensive study of these graduates and their progress in the company in hopes of improving his recruiting. One facet of the investigation involves determining the relationship between how the college graduates ranked academically in college and how they ranked in the company for advancement.

| Employee | Academic performance (1 = top fifth of class) | Rating for advancement |
|----------|----------------------------------------------|------------------------|
| D. M. | 1 (high) | 1 (high) |
| S. A. | 4 | 4 |
| N. W. | 3 | 1 |
| T. R. | 2 | 2 |
| E. F. | 5 | 3 |
| U. M. | 4 | 2 |
| Q. F. | 1 | 2 |
| I. B. | 1 | 2 |
| A. A. | 3 | 4 |

An academic rank of 1 indicates that the graduate ranked in the top fifth of the class in college; a rank of 5 indicates the lowest fifth. For advancement, each employee was rated on a scale from 1 (high) to 4 (low). D. M., for example, was in the highest fifth of her graduating class and in the group next in line for advancement.

a. Rank the academic performance and the ratings for advancement (watch the many ties).
b. Draw a scatter diagram using academic performance as the X variable.
c. Based on the scatter diagram, evaluate the strength of the correlation between the two sets of ranked data.
d. Compute the rank-order correlation coefficient.
e. Test the significance of $r_s$ at $\alpha = .05$ and at $\alpha = .01$.
f. Summarize your findings.

31. Members of a large politically active group were asked to rank the prestige associated with 10 elected or appointed positions in federal or state government. Their rankings were averaged to give one composite ranking. The president of the United States was ranked 1, a U.S. ambassador ranked 2, and so on. The same procedure was followed for a large group of individuals not active in politics. The rankings are:

| Position | Composite rank Active | Nonactive |
|----------|-----------------------|-----------|
| U.S. ambassador | 2 | 4 |
| U.S. president | 1 | 1 |
| Cabinet member | 3 | 6 |
| State governor | 9 | 3 |
| U.S. vice president | 4 | 2 |
| Supreme Court justice | 5 | 5 |
| U.S. senator | 8 | 7 |
| U.S. representative | 6 | 8 |
| Secretary of state | 7 | 9 |
| FBI director | 10 | 10 |

a. Draw a scatter diagram. Let the ranking of the active group be X.
b. Based on the scatter diagram, evaluate the relationship between the two sets of ranks.
c. Compute the rank-order correlation coefficient.
d. Test the significance of the rank-order correlation coefficient at $\alpha = .01$ and $\alpha = .05$.
e. Summarize your findings.

32. The following table lists figures on the qualifying speed, the starting position, and the finishing position for drivers in the 1991 Indianapolis 500 race.

a. What is the relationship (correlation) between the starting position rank and the driver's rank at the finish of the race?

b. What is the correlation between how a driver ranked with regard to qualifying speed and his rank at the finish of the race?

c. Conduct, using the .05 level of significance, tests of hypotheses for part a and part b.

d. Interpret the results of your investigation.

| Driver | Speed (mph) | Starting position | Finishing position |
|---|---|---|---|
| Mears, Rick | 224.113 | 1 | 1 |
| Foyt, A. J. | 222.443 | 2 | 28 |
| Andretti, Mario | 221.818 | 3 | 7 |
| Rahal, Bobby | 221.401 | 4 | 19 |
| Andretti, Michael | 220.943 | 5 | 2 |
| Unser, Al | 219.823 | 6 | 4 |
| Andretti, John | 219.059 | 7 | 5 |
| Crawford, Jim | 218.947 | 8 | 26 |
| Sullivan, Danny | 218.343 | 9 | 10 |
| Cheever, Eddie | 218.122 | 10 | 31 |
| Andretti, Jeff | 217.632 | 11 | 15 |
| Goodyear, Scott | 216.751 | 12 | 27 |
| Bettenhausen, Gary | 224.468 | 13 | 22 |
| Luyendyk, Arie | 223.881 | 14 | 3 |
| Fitipaldi, Emerson | 223.064 | 15 | 11 |
| Cogan, Kevin | 222.844 | 16 | 29 |
| Fox, Stan | 219.501 | 17 | 8 |
| Groff, Michael | 219.015 | 18 | 24 |
| Brayton, Scott | 218.627 | 19 | 17 |
| Bettenhausen, Tony | 218.188 | 20 | 9 |
| Jourdain, Bernard | 216.683 | 21 | 18 |
| Brabham, Geof | 214.859 | 22 | 20 |
| Lazier, Buddy | 218.692 | 23 | 33 |
| Matsushita, Hiro | 218.351 | 24 | 16 |
| Paul, John, Jr. | 217.952 | 25 | 25 |
| Palmroth, Tero | 215.648 | 26 | 23 |
| Pruett, Scott | 214.814 | 27 | 12 |
| Guerrero, Roberto | 214.027 | 28 | 30 |
| Ribbs, Willy T. | 217.997 | 29 | 32 |
| Dobson, Dominic | 215.326 | 30 | 13 |
| Lewis, Randy | 215.043 | 31 | 14 |
| Carter, Pancho | 214.012 | 32 | 21 |
| Johncock, Gordon | 213.812 | 33 | 6 |

Source: *Toledo Blade,* May 26, 1991, p. D2.

Courtesy International Business Machines Corporation

33. Mr. Lewis Gibson is the sales manager of Betts Manufacturing Company. He is preparing for an upcoming sales meeting and would like to show the sales force how the number of sales calls relates to the annual value of purchase orders received. From his records he gathered the following sample information for last year. From these sample data, can he conclude that as the number of sales calls is increased, the annual amount of purchase orders will also increase? Conduct an appropriate statistical test. Use the .05 significance level.

| Number of calls | Orders ($000) | Number of calls | Orders ($000) |
|---|---|---|---|
| 5 | 4.8 | 2 | 2.2 |
| 4 | 6.1 | 4 | 7.1 |
| 6 | 12.3 | 4 | 8.7 |
| 7 | 13.7 | 8 | 13.7 |
| 8 | 15.7 | 1 | 2.3 |
| 1 | 2.2 | 3 | 4.6 |
| 3 | 7.3 | 9 | 16.7 |
| 4 | 5.8 | 3 | 6.1 |
| 1 | 1.9 | 4 | 7.5 |
| 3 | 6.7 | 8 | 15.1 |

## COMPUTER DATA EXERCISES

34. Refer to data set 1, which reports information on homes sold in Florida during 1990.
    a.  Determine the correlation between selling price and the size of the home. At the .05 level, can you conclude that there is a positive relationship?
    b.  Determine the correlation between the selling price and the distance from the center of the city. At the .05 significance level, is there a negative relationship?
    c.  Would it be meaningful to determine the correlation between selling price and township? Why or why not?

35. Refer to data set 2, which reports information on 200 corporations in the United States.
    a.  Determine the correlation between profit and sales. Is it significant at the .05 level?
    b.  Determine the correlation between profit and market share. Is it significant at the .05 level?
    c.  What other relationships might be important? Determine the correlations in those variables.

36. Refer to data set 3, which reports information on the 26 major league baseball teams.
    a.  Determine the correlation between attendance and total salary. Would you expect this relationship to be positive? Is it significant at the .05 level?
    b.  Determine the relationship between the proportion of games won and both attendance and salary. Plot the relationships. What, if any, important results stand out? Use the .05 significance level in any tests.
    c.  Is pitching more important than hitting in terms of winning? This point has been argued by baseball managers, team owners, sports writers, and fans for many years. Let team ERA represent the pitching component, and let both team batting average and number of home runs represent the hitting component. Which of the variables has the strongest association with the proportion of games won? (For those less familiar with baseball, ERA stands for *earned run average,* which is the number of runs scored per game, without the benefit of errors. A low ERA generally means the team has good pitching. The batting average is determined by dividing the number of base hits by the number of times at bat.) Comment on your findings for the 1991 major league season.

## CHAPTER 13 EXAMINATION

*The answers are at the end of the chapter.*

For Questions 1 through 10, fill in the correct answer.
Questions 1 through 3 refer to the following chart.

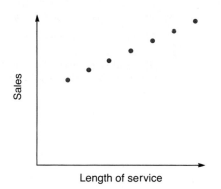

Length of service

1. This chart is called a _____.
2. The relationship between sales and length of service is _____ (positive or negative).
3. If the coefficient of correlation were computed, it would be about _____.

Questions 4 through 6 are based on the following chart.

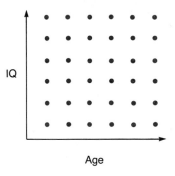

Age

4. If the coefficient of correlation were computed, it would be about _____.
5. The dependent variable is _____.
6. If computed, the coefficient of nondetermination would be about _____.

Questions 7 through 9 are based on the following chart.

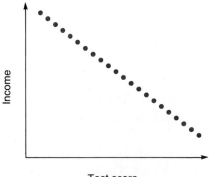

Test score

7. In this particular problem, the independent variable is _____.
8. If computed, the coefficient of determination would be about _____.

9. Based on this chart, as test score increases, income can be expected to _____.

10. The square of the coefficient of correlation is called the _____.

11. Sales of toothpaste seem to be heavily dependent on the level of advertisement. In order to explore this observation further, the annual advertising expenditures for several well-known brands and their annual sales were obtained.

| Brand | Annual advertising expenditures ($ millions) | Annual sales ($ millions) |
|---|---|---|
| Glint | 2 | 5 |
| Pearl One | 4 | 7 |
| Shine On | 3 | 6 |
| Number 1 | 1 | 2 |

   a.   Draw a scatter diagram.

   b.   Compute Pearson's product-moment correlation coefficient. Interpret.

   c.   Compute the coefficient of determination. Interpret.

   d.   Compute the coefficient of nondetermination. Interpret.

12. The football coaches rate the performance of the players on a scale of 0 to 100 both during the weekly practice and during the game on Saturday. A sample of the players who played in the big game against Carson College revealed these ratings:

| Player | Rating In practice | During game |
|---|---|---|
| Art | 80 | 80 |
| Bob | 20 | 10 |
| Jim | 100 | 90 |
| Abe | 65 | 50 |
| Arch | 50 | 35 |
| John | 40 | 30 |
| Dean | 90 | 95 |
| Jimmie | 60 | 35 |

   a.   Determine the degree of relationship between how the players ranked in performance during the practice and how they ranked during the game by computing the rank-order correlation coefficient.

   b.   Test the significance of the coefficient of rank correlation. Use $\alpha = .01$.

   c.   Interpret your findings.

13–1  1.  Yield is the dependent variable. The amount of fertilizer is the independent variable.

2.

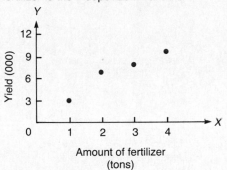

Amount of fertilizer
(tons)

3.

| $X$ | $Y$ | $XY$ | $X^2$ | $Y^2$ |
|---|---|---|---|---|
| 2 | 7 | 14 | 4 | 49 |
| 1 | 3 | 3 | 1 | 9 |
| 3 | 8 | 24 | 9 | 64 |
| 4 | 10 | 40 | 16 | 100 |
| 10 | 28 | 81 | 30 | 222 |

$r = .96$, found by

$$r = \frac{4(81) - (10)(28)}{\sqrt{[4(30) - (10)^2][4(222) - (28)^2]}}$$

$$= \frac{44}{\sqrt{2080}} = \frac{44}{45.607017} = .9648$$

4.  A very strong (almost perfect) correlation between the amount of fertilizer applied and yield is indicated by .96.

13–2  1.  $r^2 = (.96)^2 = .92$

$1 - r^2 = 1 - .92 = .08$

2.  Ninety-two percent of the variation in yield is explained by the amount of fertilizer applied; 8 percent is not.

13–3  $H_0: \rho = 0$, $H_1: \rho > 0$. $H_0$ is rejected if $t > 1.714$.

$$t = \frac{.43\sqrt{25 - 2}}{\sqrt{1 - (.43)^2}} = 2.284$$

$H_0$ is rejected. There is a positive correlation between the percent of the vote received and the amount spent on the campaign.

13–4  1.

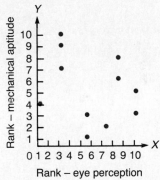

Rank – eye perception

2.  There seems to be a rather low correlation between the two sets of ranks—perhaps negative.

3.

$$r_s = 1 - \frac{6\Sigma d^2}{n(n^2 - 1)}$$

$$= 1 - \frac{6(193)}{10(99)} = -.17$$

| | | Rank | | | |
|---|---|---|---|---|---|
| $X$ | $Y$ | $X$ | $Y$ | $d$ | $d^2$ |
| 805 | 23 | 5.5 | 1 | 4.5 | 20.25 |
| 777 | 62 | 3.0 | 9 | −6.0 | 36.00 |
| 820 | 60 | 8.5 | 8 | 0.5 | 0.25 |
| 682 | 40 | 1.0 | 4 | −3.0 | 9.00 |
| 777 | 70 | 3.0 | 10 | −7.0 | 49.00 |
| 810 | 28 | 7.0 | 2 | 5.0 | 25.00 |
| 805 | 30 | 5.5 | 3 | 2.5 | 6.25 |
| 840 | 42 | 10.0 | 5 | 5.0 | 25.00 |
| 777 | 55 | 3.0 | 7 | −4.0 | 16.00 |
| 820 | 51 | 8.5 | 6 | 2.5 | 6.25 |
| | | | | 0 | 193.00 |

4.  As expected, the correlation of −.17 is quite weak, indicating that there is little correlation between eye perception and mechanical aptitude.

# Answers

## CHAPTER 13 EXAMINATION

1. Scatter diagram.
2. Positive.
3. 1.00.
4. Zero.
5. IQ.
6. 1.00.
7. Test score.
8. 1.00.
9. Decrease.
10. Coefficient of determination.
11. a.

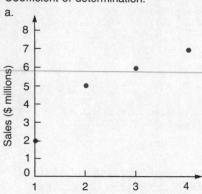

Advertising expenditures ($ millions)

  b. Pearson's r is about .96, indicating that there is an almost perfect relationship between advertising expenditures and sales:

$$r = \frac{4(58) - (10)(20)}{\sqrt{[4(30) - (10)^2][4(114) - (20)^2]}}$$

$$= \frac{32}{\sqrt{1120}} = .96$$

  c. The coefficient of determination is about .92,

found by $(.96)^2$. About 92 percent of the variation in sales is explained by advertising expenditures.

  d. The coefficient of nondetermination is .08, found by $1 - .92$. About 8 percent of the variation in sales is not explained by advertising expenditures.

12. a. $r_s$ is about .97, found by:

| Player | Rank In practice | Rank In game | Difference $d$ | $d^2$ |
|--------|-----------------|--------------|----------------|-------|
| Art | 6 | 6.0 | 0 | 0 |
| Bob | 1 | 1.0 | 0 | 0 |
| Jim | 8 | 7.0 | +1.0 | 1.00 |
| Abe | 5 | 5.0 | 0 | 0 |
| Arch | 3 | 3.5 | −0.5 | 0.25 |
| John | 2 | 2.0 | 0 | 0 |
| Dean | 7 | 8.0 | −1.0 | 1.00 |
| Jimmie | 4 | 3.5 | +0.5 | 0.25 |
| | | | 0 | 2.50 |

$$r_s = 1 - \frac{6\Sigma d^2}{n(n^2 - 1)} = 1 - \frac{6(2.50)}{8[(8)^2 - 1]} = .97$$

  b. At the .01 level, the null hypothesis that there is no relationship between the two rankings in the population is rejected. It is rejected because the computed value of the rank correlation coefficient (.97) is greater than the critical value of .833 (from Appendix H).

  c. There is a very high degree of relationship between how the players ranked in performance during the practice and how they ranked in performance during the Carson College game. If all the players were included in this study, it is highly unlikely that the rank correlation coefficient would be zero.

Construction—Courtesy Southern California Edison Company

# SIMPLE REGRESSION ANALYSIS

When you have completed this chapter, you will be able to:

1. Discuss the purpose of simple linear regression.

2. Determine an equation that can be used for prediction.

3. Measure the error in your prediction.

4. Give the assumptions underlying regression analysis.

5. Construct confidence intervals for your predictions.

**C** hapter 13 was concerned with. determining the relationship between two sets of data. We drew a scatter diagram to portray the relationship graphically and computed such measures as the coefficient of correlation and the coefficients of determination and nondetermination. Pearson's product-moment correlation coefficient is used to measure the strength of the relationship between sets of interval- and ratio-level data. Spearman's rank-order correlation coefficient is applied to ordinal (ranked) data. We explored such questions as these: What is the degree of association between a score on a test designed by the human resource director and weekly sales? What is the relationship between the advertising expenditures of a firm and its sales?

We will continue our study of the relationship between two sets of data in this chapter by developing a mathematical equation designed to describe the relationship between two variables. The equation will allow us to predict the value of the dependent variable $Y$ based on a value of the independent variable $X$. We will (1) reintroduce the scatter diagram, (2) determine the equation for the straight line that best fits the data, (3) predict a value of $Y$ based on a selected value of $X$, (4) measure the error in our prediction, and (5) establish confidence intervals for our prediction.

## REGRESSION ANALYSIS

As noted in the introduction, we are going to develop an equation to express the relationship between two variables and estimate the value of the dependent variable $Y$ based on a selected value of the independent variable $X$. The technique used to develop the equation for the straight line and make these predictions is called **regression analysis.**[1]

In order to visualize the form of the regression, we can draw a scatter diagram. Remember from Chapter 13 that the dependent variable is scaled on the $Y$-axis, and the independent variable is scaled on the $X$-axis. Recall the test developed by the human resource director. The paired data from that test are shown in Table 14−1 and the accompanying scatter diagram in Chart 14−1. Each point on the scatter diagram represents the test score and weekly sales of one salesperson. For example, the plot

### TABLE 14−1

#### Test Scores and Weekly Sales of Five Salespeople

| Salesperson | Test score | Weekly sales |
|-------------|------------|--------------|
| Mr. J. A. Amber | 4 | $ 5,000 |
| Mr. B. N. Archer | 7 | 12,000 |
| Ms. G. D. Smith | 3 | 4,000 |
| Mr. A. B. Malcolm | 6 | 8,000 |
| Ms. A. Goodwin | 10 | 11,000 |

---

[1]The word *regression* was introduced by Sir Francis Galton in 1877 in his study of heredity. He found that the heights of descendants of tall parents tended to regress (i.e., to go back) toward the average height of the population. The mathematical line he developed was called the line of regression. The term *line of regression* is commonly used even though *predictive equation* or *estimating equation* seems to be more appropriate.

To plot $X = 4$, $Y = 5,000$, do this:

for Mr. Amber is located by going to 4 on the *X*-axis and then moving vertically to $5,000.

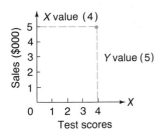

---

### CHART 14−1

**A Scatter Diagram**

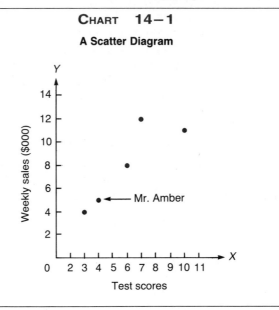

---

What the scatter diagram reveals

The scatter diagram shows: (1) As test scores increase, so do sales. (2) A straight line seems to best describe the average path of the points. (3) Any prediction of sales based on test scores cannot be 100 percent accurate but can be fairly precise.

## THE REGRESSION EQUATION

Since a straight line appears to best describe the relationship between test scores and weekly sales, we will now develop a mathematical equation for that line. The human resource director could then use the equation to predict the weekly sales of an applicant for a sales position based on the applicant's test score (should the applicant be hired). The equation for that straight line is referred to as the **regression equation.** It is alternatively called an *estimating equation* and a *predicting equation.*

Regression equation used to estimate *Y* based on *X*

> Regression equation   A mathematical equation that defines the relationship between two variables.

Straight line drawn by hand to fit scatter plots

The scatter diagram in the Chart 14−1 is reproduced in Chart 14−2, with a line drawn with a ruler through the dots to illustrate that a straight line would probably fit the data best. However, the line drawn using a straight edge has one disadvantage: Its position is based on the judgment of the person drawing the line. The hand-drawn lines in Chart 14−3 represent the judgments of four people. All the lines except line A seem to be reasonable. Each would, however, give a different prediction of sales.

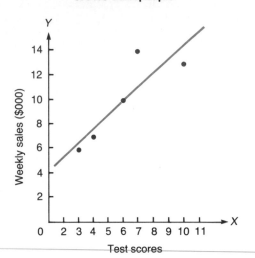

**CHART  14−2**

**Test Scores and Weekly Sales
of Five Salespeople**

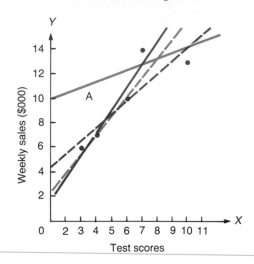

**CHART  14−3**

**Many Freehand Lines Superimposed
on the Scatter Diagram**

## LEAST SQUARES PRINCIPLE

Least squares line gives
"best" fit; freehand
method is unreliable

Judgment is eliminated by determining the regression line using a mathematical method called the **least squares principle.** This method gives what is commonly referred to as the "best-fitting" straight line. It *minimizes the sum of the squares of the vertical deviations about the line.* To illustrate this concept, the same data are plotted in the three charts that follow. The regression line in Chart 14−4 was determined using the least squares method. It is the best-fitting line because the sum of the squares of the vertical deviations about it is at a minimum. The first plot ($X = 3$, $Y = 8$) deviates by 2 from the line, found by $10 - 8$. The deviation squared is 4. The squared deviation for the plot $X = 4$, $Y = 18$ is 16. The squared deviation for the plot $X = 5$, $Y = 16$ is 4. The sum of the squared deviations is 24, found by $4 + 16 + 4$.

Assume that the straight lines in Charts 14−5 and 14−6 were drawn using a straight edge. The sum of the squared vertical deviations in Chart 14−5 is 44. For Chart 14−6 it is 132. Both sums are greater than the one in Chart 14−4 found using the least squares method.

> Least squares principle    A technique used to arrive at the regression equation by minimizing the sum of the squares of the vertical distances between the actual $Y$ values and the predicted values of $Y$.

The general form of the regression equation is:

General form of the linear
equation

$$Y' = a + bX \qquad (14-1)$$

| CHART 14–4 | CHART 14–5 | CHART 14–6 |
|---|---|---|
| **The Least Squares Line** | **Line Drawn Using a Straight Edge** | **Line Drawn Using a Straight Edge** |
| 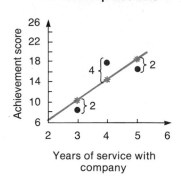 | 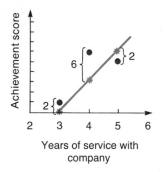 |  |

where

$Y'$  read $Y$ prime, is the predicted value of the $Y$ variable for a selected $X$ value.

$a$  is the $Y$-intercept. It is the estimated value of $Y$ when $X = 0$. Another way to put it is: $a$ is the estimated value of $Y$ where the regression line crosses the $Y$-axis when $X$ is zero.

$b$  is the slope of the line, or the average change in $Y'$ for each change of one unit (either increase or decrease) in the independent variable $X$.

$X$  is any value of the independent variable that is selected.

It should be noted that the linear regression equation for the sample of salespeople is just an estimate of the relationship between the two variables in the population. Thus, the values of $a$ and $b$ in the regression equation are usually referred to as the *estimated regression coefficients,* or just the *regression coefficients.*

The formulas for $b$ and $a$ are:

How to solve for $b$ and $a$

$$b = \frac{n(\Sigma XY) - (\Sigma X)(\Sigma Y)}{n(\Sigma X^2) - (\Sigma X)^2} \qquad (14-2)$$

$$a = \frac{\Sigma Y}{n} - b\frac{\Sigma X}{n} \qquad (14-3)$$

where:

$X$  is a value of the independent variable.

$Y$  is a value of the dependent variable.

$n$  is the number of items in the sample.

### ■ EXAMPLE

Calculations needed for $b$ and $a$

Returning to the test scores and weekly sales of the five salespeople, the sums and other essential figures needed to solve for $a$ and $b$ are given in Table 14–2.

## TABLE   14−2

### Calculations Needed for Determining the Regression Equation

| Salesperson | Test score, X | Weekly sales ($000), Y | X² | XY | Y² |
|---|---|---|---|---|---|
| Mr. Amber | 4 | 5 | 16 | 20 | 25 |
| Mr. Archer | 7 | 12 | 49 | 84 | 144 |
| Ms. Smith | 3 | 4 | 9 | 12 | 16 |
| Mr. Malcolm | 6 | 8 | 36 | 48 | 64 |
| Ms. Goodwin | 10 | 11 | 100 | 110 | 121 |
| Total | 30 | 40 | 210 | 274 | 370 |

What is the regression equation?

## ☑ SOLUTION

The sums from Table 14−2 and equations (14−2) and (14−3) are used to illustrate the computations for $a$ and $b$ in the regression equation:

$$b = \frac{n(\Sigma XY) - (\Sigma X)(\Sigma Y)}{n(\Sigma X^2) - (\Sigma X)^2} \qquad a = \frac{\Sigma Y}{n} - b\frac{\Sigma X}{n}$$

$$= \frac{5(274) - (30)(40)}{5(210) - (30)^2} \qquad = \frac{40}{5} - 1.133\left(\frac{30}{5}\right)$$

$$= 1.133 \qquad = 8 - 6.798$$

$$= 1.202$$

$$Y' = 1.202 + 1.133X \text{ (in \$000)}$$

*This is the regression equation*

Thus, the regression equation is $Y' = 1.202 + 1.133X$ (in thousands of dollars). Predicted sales for an applicant for a sales position who scored 6 on the human resource director's test is $8,000, found by $Y' = a + bX = 1.202 + 1.133(6) = 1.202 + 6.798 = 8.000$ (in $000).

## DRAWING THE LINE OF REGRESSION

The least squares regression equation $Y' = 1.202 + 1.133X$ is used to determine the least squares line of regression to be drawn on the scatter diagram. When $X = 3$, $Y' = 4.601$, found by: $Y' = a + bX = 1.202 + 1.133(3)$. Other points on the straight line can be determined by substituting particular values of $X$ into the equation:

*One point on the straight line is $X = 3$, $Y' = 4.601$*

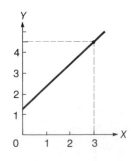

| Test score, X | Predicted weekly sales ($000), Y' | Solution |
|---|---|---|
| 3 | 4.601 | $Y' = 1.202 + 1.133(3)$ |
| 4 | 5.734 | $= 1.202 + 1.133(4)$ |
| 6 | 8.000 | $= 1.202 + 1.133(6)$ |
| 7 | 9.133 | $= 1.202 + 1.133(7)$ |
| 10 | 12.532 | $= 1.202 + 1.133(10)$ |

The plot for $X = 3$, $Y' = 4.601$ is located by moving to 3 on the $X$-axis and then going vertically to 4.601. The next plot is $X = 4$, $Y' = 5.734$. All the points are connected to give the straight line. (See Chart 14−7.)

This straight line has some interesting features. As we have discussed, there is no straight line through the data where the sum of the squared deviations, $\Sigma(Y - Y')^2$, is less. In addition, this line will always pass through the points representing the mean of the X values and the mean of the Y values, that is, $\overline{X}$ and $\overline{Y}$. In this example, $\overline{X} = 6.0$ and $\overline{Y} = 8.0$

CHART   14–7

**The Line of Regression Drawn on the Scatter Diagram**

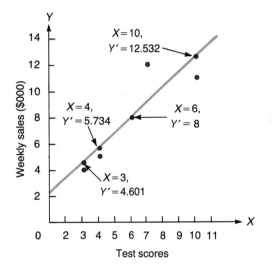

Self-Review 14–1

*The answers are at the end of the chapter.*

(*Note:* This problem is a continuation of one used in Chapter 13.)

An agronomist experimented with different amounts of liquid fertilizer on a sample of equal-size plots. The amounts of fertilizer and the corresponding yields are:

| Plot | Amount of fertilizer (tons) | Yield (hundreds of bushels) |
|------|------|------|
| A | 2 | 7 |
| B | 1 | 3 |
| C | 3 | 8 |
| D | 4 | 10 |

1. The agronomist is interested in predicting yield. What is the dependent variable? The independent variable?

2. Draw a scatter diagram.

3. Determine the regression equation.

# EXERCISES

*The answers to the odd-numbered exercises are at the end of the book.*

*Note:* It is suggested that you save your values for $\Sigma X$, $\Sigma X^2$, $\Sigma XY$, $\Sigma Y$, and $\Sigma Y^2$, as these problems will be referred to later in the chapter.

1. The following sample observations were selected.

| X | Y |
|---|---|
| 4 | 4 |
| 5 | 6 |
| 3 | 5 |
| 6 | 7 |
| 10 | 7 |

    a. Determine the regression equation.

    b. Determine the value of $Y'$ when $X$ is 7.

2. The following sample observations were selected.

| X | Y |
|---|----|
| 5 | 13 |
| 3 | 15 |
| 6 | 7 |
| 3 | 12 |
| 4 | 13 |
| 4 | 11 |
| 6 | 9 |
| 8 | 5 |

    a. Determine the regression equation.

    b. Determine the value of $Y'$ when $X$ is 7.

3. The Bradford Electric Illuminating Company is studying the relationship between kilowatt-hours (thousands) and the number of rooms in a private single-family residence. A random sample of 10 homes yielded the following.

| Number of rooms | Kilowatt-hours (thousands) |
|-----------------|----------------------------|
| 12 | 9 |
| 9 | 7 |
| 14 | 10 |
| 6 | 5 |
| 10 | 8 |
| 8 | 6 |
| 10 | 8 |
| 10 | 10 |
| 5 | 4 |
| 7 | 7 |

    a. Determine the regression equation.

    b. Determine the number of kilowatt-hours, in thousands, for a six-room house.

4. Mr. James McWhinney, president of Daniel-James Financial Services, believes there is a relationship between the number of client contacts and the dollar amount of sales. To document this assertion, Mr. McWhinney gathered the following sample information. The $X$ column indicates the number of client contacts last month, and the $Y$ column shows the value of sales ($000) last month for each client sampled.

| Number of contacts, X | Sales ($000), Y |
|---|---|
| 14 | 24 |
| 12 | 14 |
| 20 | 28 |
| 16 | 30 |
| 46 | 80 |
| 23 | 30 |
| 48 | 90 |
| 50 | 85 |
| 55 | 120 |
| 50 | 110 |

a. Determine the regression equation.

b. Determine the estimated sales if 40 clients are contacted.

# THE STANDARD ERROR OF ESTIMATE

Note in the preceding scatter diagram (Chart 14–7) that all of the points do not lie on the regression line. If they all were on the line, and if the number of observations were sufficiently large, there would be no error in predicting weekly sales. To put it another way, if all the points were on the regression line, sales could be predicted with 100 percent accuracy. Thus, there would be no error in predicting the $Y$ variable based on an $X$ variable. This is true in the following hypothetical case (see Chart 14–8). Theoretically, if $X = 6$, then an exact $Y$ of 200 could be predicted with 100 percent confidence. Or if $X = 10$, then $Y = 800$. There is no error in this estimate.

---

CHART   14–8

**Example of Perfect Prediction: Horsepower of Motor and Cost of Electricity**

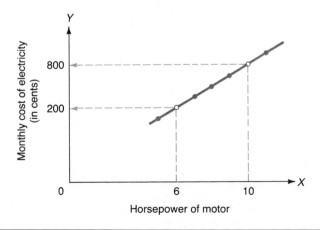

---

Perfect prediction unrealistic in business

Perfect prediction in problems involving economics and business is practically impossible. For example, the revenue for the year from gasoline sales ($Y$) based on the number of automobile registrations ($X$) as of a certain date could no doubt be approximated fairly closely, but the prediction would not be exact to the nearest dollar, or probably even to the nearest thousand dollars. Even predictions of tensile strengths of steel wires based on the outside diameters of the wires are not always exact (due to slight differences in the composition of the steel).

What is needed, then, is a measure that would indicate how precise the prediction of Y is based on X or, conversely, how inaccurate the prediction might be. This measure is called the **standard error of estimate.** The standard error of estimate, symbolized by $s_{y \cdot x}$, is the same concept as the standard deviation discussed in Chapter 4. The standard deviation measures this dispersion about an average, such as the mean. The standard error of estimate measures the dispersion about an average line, the regression line.

Standard error of estimate defined

> Standard error of estimate    Measures the scatter, or dispersion, of the observed values around the line of regression.

The standard error of estimate is found by the following equation. (Note that the equation is quite similar to the one for the standard deviation of a sample.)

Formula for the standard error

$$s_{y \cdot x} = \sqrt{\frac{\Sigma(Y - Y')^2}{n - 2}} \tag{14-4}$$

## ■ EXAMPLE

The symbol for the standard error of estimate ($s_{y \cdot x}$) represents the standard deviation of the Ys based on the Xs. Returning to the problem involving test scores and weekly sales, the first step is to determine each value of Y' (the point on the straight line) for each X value. These Y' points were computed previously in order to plot the straight line on the scatter diagram (Chart 14-7). The next step is to subtract each Y' value from its corresponding Y value. These differences are squared and then summed. (See Table 14-3.)

### TABLE    14-3

#### Computations Needed for Standard Error of Estimate

| Salesperson | Test score, X | Sales ($000) Actual, Y | Predicted Y' | Deviations, Y − Y' | Deviations squared (Y − Y')² |
|---|---|---|---|---|---|
| Mr. Amber | 4 | 5 | 5.734 | −0.734 | 0.5388 |
| Mr. Archer | 7 | 12 | 9.133 | +2.867 | 8.2200 |
| Ms. Smith | 3 | 4 | 4.601 | −0.601 | 0.3612 |
| Mr. Malcolm | 6 | 8 | 8.000 | 0.000 | 0.0000 |
| Ms. Goodwin | 10 | 11 | 12.532 | −1.532 | 2.3470 |
| Total | 30 | 40 | 40.000 | 0.000 | 11.4670 |

What is the standard error of estimate?

## ☑ SOLUTION

The standard error of estimate is 1.955 determined by applying formula (14−4).

$$s_{y\cdot x} = \sqrt{\frac{\Sigma(Y - Y')^2}{n - 2}}$$

$$= \sqrt{\frac{11.467}{5 - 2}}$$

$$= 1.955 \text{ (in \$000)}$$

The figure 1.955 is really $1,955 (because the sales are in thousands of dollars).

The deviations $(Y - Y')$ are vertical deviations from the regression line. To illustrate, the five deviations from Table 14−3 are shown in Chart 14−9. Note in Table 14−3 that the sum of the deviations is equal to zero, indicating that the positive deviations (above the regression line on the scatter diagram) are offset by the negative deviations (below the line).

---

## CHART 14−9

**Vertical Distances between Scatter Points and Line of Regression**

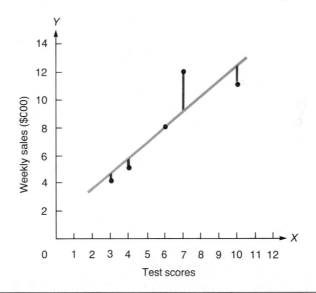

---

Formula (14−4) for the standard error of estimate is used to show the similarity in concept and computation between the standard deviation and the standard error of estimate. Suppose a large number of observations are being studied, and the numbers are large. Computing each $Y'$ point on the regression line and then squaring the differences—that is, $(Y - Y')^2$—would be rather tedious. The following formula is algebraically equivalent to formula (14−4) but is much easier to use.

More convenient formula for the standard error

$$s_{y\cdot x} = \sqrt{\frac{\Sigma Y^2 - a(\Sigma Y) - b(\Sigma XY)}{n - 2}} \qquad (14-5)$$

The squares, sums, and other numbers for the test score–weekly sales problem were calculated in Table 14–2. Inserting these values into the formula:

$$s_{y \cdot x} = \sqrt{\frac{370 - 1.202(40) - 1.133(274)}{5 - 2}}$$

$$= 1.955 \text{ (in \$000)}$$

This is the same standard error of estimate as computed previously.

For a better understanding of the application of the standard error of estimate of $1,955 in regression analysis, the underlying assumptions about linear regression should be stated.

## ASSUMPTIONS UNDERLYING LINEAR REGRESSION

*Assumptions required to apply linear regression analysis*

1. For each value of $X$, there is a group of $Y$ values, and these $Y$ values are *normally distributed*.
2. The *means* of these normal distributions of $Y$ values all lie on the straight line of regression.
3. The *standard deviations* of these normal distributions are *equal*.
4. The $Y$ values are statistically *independent.* This means that in the selection of a sample, the $Y$ values chosen for a particular $X$ value do not depend on the $Y$ values for any other $X$ value.

Chart 14–10 illustrates these assumptions. Note that these statements are true for each of the three $X$ values: (1) The $Y$ values are normally distributed. (2) The means are all on the line of regression. (3) The standard deviations, as represented by the standard error of estimate $s_{y \cdot x}$, are equal.

---

### CHART   14–10

**Assumptions Underlying Regression Depicted Graphically**

*Visual presentation of the assumptions*

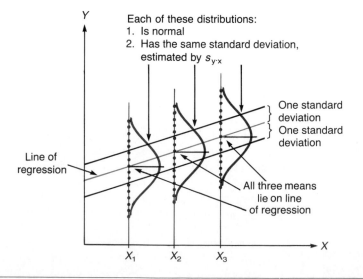

---

Recall from Chapter 7 that if the values are somewhat normally distributed:

$\overline{X} \pm 1s$ encompasses approximately the middle 68 percent of the values.
$\overline{X} \pm 2s$ encompasses approximately the middle 95.5 percent of the values.
$\overline{X} \pm 3s$ encompasses approximately the middle 99.7 percent of the values.

If the distribution is highly skewed, these relationships will not hold.

The same relationships exist between the average predicted value, $Y'$, and the standard error of estimate, $s_{y \cdot x}$. Again, if the scatter about the regression line is somewhat normally distributed and the sample is large, then:

$Y' \pm 1s_{y \cdot x}$ encompasses the middle 68 percent of the observed values.
$Y' \pm 2s_{y \cdot x}$ encompasses the middle 95.5 percent of the observed values.
$Y' \pm 3s_{y \cdot x}$ encompasses the middle 99.7 percent of the observed values.

We can now relate these assumptions and the standard error of estimate to our test score–weekly sales experiment. The difference between predicted sales, $Y'$, and actual sales would be less than one standard error ($1,955) for 68 percent of the salespeople. Further, 95 percent of the predictions would not vary more than 2($1,955). More than 99 percent of weekly sales predictions would be "off" by no more than 3($1,955).

---

### Self-Review 14–2

*The answers are at the end of the chapter.*

Refer to Self-Review 14–1.

1. Determine the standard error of estimate.
2. Suppose a large number of plots were included in the experiment (instead of just four). Ninety-five percent of our predictions of yield would lie between what two values?

## EXERCISES

*The answers to the odd-numbered exercises are at the end of the book.*

5. Refer to Exercise 1.
   a. Determine the standard error of estimate.
   b. Suppose a large sample is selected (instead of just five). About 68 percent of the predictions would be between what two values?
6. Refer to Exercise 2.
   a. Determine the standard error of estimate.
   b. Suppose a large sample is selected (instead of just eight). About 95 percent of the predictions would be between what two values?
7. Refer to Exercise 3.
   a. Determine the standard error of estimate.
   b. Suppose a large sample is selected (instead of just 10). About 95 percent of the predictions regarding kilowatt-hours would occur between what two values?
8. Refer to Exercise 4.
   a. Determine the standard error of estimate.

b.    Suppose a large sample is selected (instead of just 10). About 95 percent of the predictions regarding sales would occur between what two values?

## CONFIDENCE-INTERVAL ESTIMATES

The standard error of estimate is a valid measure to use in setting *confidence intervals* when the sample size is large and the scatter about the regression line is somewhat normally distributed. Neither of these assumptions is valid in the problem involving the weekly sales. The sample size of five, for example, is very small. Therefore, a correction factor for a small sample must be introduced.

Two kinds of confidence intervals

A confidence interval can be determined for:

1. The *mean* value of Y for a given value of X.
2. An *individual* value of Y for a given value of X.

To determine the confidence interval for the *mean* value of Y for a given value of X, the formula is:

How to determine the confidence interval for the mean of Y, given X

$$Y' \pm t(s_{y \cdot x}) \sqrt{\frac{1}{n} + \frac{(X - \bar{X})^2}{\Sigma X^2 - \frac{(\Sigma X)^2}{n}}} \qquad (14-6)$$

where, in this problem:

Y'   is the predicted value for any selected X value. For example, Y' is $8,000 for an X value of 6. (See Table 14–3.)

X   is any selected value of X.

$\bar{X}$   is the mean of the Xs (6 in this case), found by $\Sigma X/n$.

n   is the number of observations. There are five.

$s_{y \cdot x}$   is the standard error of estimate (computed previously to be 1.955).

t   is the value of t from Appendix F for $n - 2 = 5 - 2 = 3$ degrees of freedom.

It is sufficient to again note that the concept of t was developed by William Gossett in the early 1900s. He noticed that $\bar{X} \pm z(s)$ was not precisely correct for small samples. He observed, for example, for samples of size 120, that 95 percent of the items fell within $\bar{X} \pm 1.98s$ instead of $\bar{X} \pm 1.96s$. This is not too critical, but note what happens as the sample size becomes smaller:

| df  | t     |
|-----|-------|
| 120 | 1.980 |
| 60  | 2.000 |
| 21  | 2.080 |
| 10  | 2.228 |
| 3   | 3.182 |

This is logical. The smaller the sample, the larger the possible error. The increase in the t value compensates for this possibility. The Student t value for a confidence level of 95 percent and $n - 2$ degrees of freedom is 3.182. What he found for the standard deviation ($s$) is directly applicable to the standard error of estimate ($s_{y \cdot x}$).

The 95 percent confidence limits for the $Y'$ value of 8.0 are 5.218 and 10.782. (See Table 14-4 for some of the essential computations.) Substituting the values for $n$, $t$, and other variables in formula (14-6), we find:

95 percent confidence interval for mean of 8.0 when $X = 6$

$$Y' \pm t(s_{y \cdot x}) \sqrt{\frac{1}{n} + \frac{(X - \overline{X})^2}{\Sigma X^2 - \frac{(\Sigma X)^2}{n}}}$$

$$= 8.0 \pm 3.182(1.955) \sqrt{\frac{1}{5} + \frac{(6 - 6)^2}{210 - \frac{(30)^2}{5}}}$$

$$= 8.0 \pm 3.182(1.955)\sqrt{0.20}$$

$$= 5.218 \text{ and } 10.782, \text{ or } \$5,218 \text{ and } \$10,782$$

---

### TABLE 14-4

**Calculations Needed for the Confidence Limits**

| $X$ | $Y$ | $X^2$ | $XY$ |
|-----|-----|-------|------|
| 4 | $ 5 | 16 | 20 |
| 7 | 12 | 49 | 84 |
| 3 | 4 | 9 | 12 |
| 6 | 8 | 36 | 48 |
| 10 | 11 | 100 | 110 |
| 30 | 40 | 210 | 274 |

---

**INTERPRETATION** For a group of applicants whose test scores are exactly 6, the probability is .95 that their average weekly sales will be in the interval between $5,218 and $10,782.

As another example of the construction of confidence limits for the mean value of $Y$ for a given value of $X$, suppose a group of applicants had test scores of exactly 7. The essential numbers to compute the .95 confidence limits for $X = 7$ are entered as follows (when $X = 7$, $Y' = 9.133$ from Table 14-3):

$$9.133 \pm 3.182(1.955) \sqrt{\frac{1}{5} + \frac{(7 - 6)^2}{210 - \frac{(30)^2}{5}}}$$

$$= 9.133 \pm 3.182(1.955) \sqrt{0.20 + 0.0333}$$

$$= 9.133 \pm 3.182(1.955)(0.483)$$

$$= 6.128 \text{ and } 12.138, \text{ or } \$6,128 \text{ and } \$12,138$$

Now to determine the confidence interval for an *individual* value of $Y$ for a given value of $X$. The formula is modified slightly: A 1 is added to the number under the radical. The formula becomes:

Formula for the confidence interval for an individual $Y$, given $X$

$$Y' \pm t(s_{y \cdot x}) \sqrt{1 + \frac{1}{n} + \frac{(X - \overline{X})^2}{\Sigma X^2 - \dfrac{(\Sigma X)^2}{n}}} \qquad (14-7)$$

The weekly sales of Mr. Archer are used for illustration. He scored 7 on the test. (See Table 14–3.) The 95 percent confidence limits are found by:

$$9.133 \pm 3.182(1.955) \sqrt{1 + \frac{1}{5} + \frac{(7 - 6)^2}{210 - \dfrac{(30)^2}{5}}}$$

$$= 9.133 \pm 3.182(1.955)(1.111)$$
$$= 2.224 \text{ and } 16.042, \text{ or } \$2,224 \text{ and } \$16,042$$

We conclude that the probability is .95 that the weekly sales for Mr. Archer will be between $2,224 and $16,042. This interval is quite large. What can be done to make it smaller? We can decrease the level of confidence from 95 percent to 90 percent, or, as we would be more likely to do, we could increase the sample size.

Again, there is an important distinction between these two types of confidence intervals. The first interval is for the mean of all sales for a given value of $X$, and the second interval is for the sales of an individual with a given value of $X$. In the first case we were interested in an interval estimate for *all* salespeople with a test score of 7. In the second case we were interested in an interval estimate of the sales for a *particular* salesperson, Mr. Archer, who had a test score of 7. It is logical to find, as we did, that the interval is wider for a particular $X$ than for a mean of $X$.

### Self-Review 14–3

*The answers are at the end of the chapter.*

Sample data for Self-Reviews 14–1 and 14–2 are repeated below.

| Plot | Amount of fertilizer (tons), $X$ | Yield (hundreds of bushels), $Y$ |
|------|------|------|
| A | 2 | 7 |
| B | 1 | 3 |
| C | 3 | 8 |
| D | 4 | 10 |

The regression equation was computed to be $Y' = 1.5 + 2.2X$ (in hundreds of bushels). The standard error was computed to be 0.9487 (in hundreds of bushels).

1. Keeping in mind that this is a small sample, set the .90 confidence limits for a group of plots that received exactly three tons of fertilizer each.

2. Interpret your findings.

## EXERCISES

*The answers to the odd-numbered exercises are at the end of the book.*

9. Refer to Exercise 1.
   a. Determine the .95 confidence interval for the mean predicted value of 7.
   b. Determine the .95 confidence interval for an individual predicted value of 7.
10. Refer to Exercise 2.
   a. Determine the .95 confidence interval for the mean predicted value of 7.
   b. Determine the .95 confidence interval for an individual predicted value of 7.

11. Refer to Exercise 3.
    a. Determine the .95 confidence interval, in thousands of kilowatt-hours, for the mean of all six-room homes.
    b. Determine the .95 confidence interval, in thousands of kilowatt-hours, for a particular six-room home.
12. Refer to Exercise 4.
    a. Determine the .95 confidence interval, in thousands of dollars, for the mean of all sales personnel who make 40 contacts.
    b. Determine the .95 confidence interval, in thousands of dollars, for a particular salesperson who makes 40 contacts.

# WHAT DID THE HUMAN RESOURCE DIRECTOR CONCLUDE?

Summary of the test score–sales problem

The same sales problem has been continued for two chapters. Recall that the human resource director of a firm hiring a large number of salespeople began a search for a more objective way of determining which applicant to hire for a sales opening. He designed a test to predict weekly sales. Before using it, plans were made to find out its reliability. The test was administered to five experienced salespeople, and their test scores were paired with their weekly sales. (The number of salespeople in the experiment was kept small to keep the calculations at a minimum.)

First, the paired data were plotted in a scatter diagram, as shown in Chart 14–11.

---

## CHART 14–11

### Scatter Diagram Showing Test Scores and Sales

Paired data—test scores and weekly sales

| Salesperson | Test score | Weekly sales |
|---|---|---|
| Mr. J. A. Amber | 4 | $ 5,000 |
| Mr. B. N. Archer | 7 | 12,000 |
| Ms. G. D. Smith | 3 | 4,000 |
| Mr. A. B. Malcolm | 6 | 8,000 |
| Ms. A. Goodwin | 10 | 11,000 |

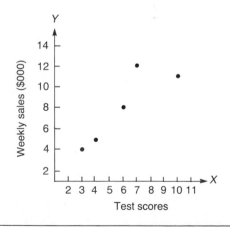

---

It appears from the scatter diagram that there is a fairly strong relationship between test scores (the independent variable, $X$) and sales (the dependent variable, $Y$). To measure that relationship, we computed the coefficient of correlation, $r$. Its value is .88, indicating, as suspected, a strong relationship between the two variables. The meaning of $r$, however, is not as explicit as that of the coefficient of determination. Because Pearson's $r$ tends to overstate the degree of relationship between the $X$ and $Y$ variables, some statisticians prefer the coefficient of determination: $r^2 = (.88)^2 = .77$. The number .77 indicates that 77 percent of the total variation in weekly sales is accounted for by the variation in the test scores. The coefficient of nondetermination, .23 (found by $1 - r^2 = 1 - .77 = .23$), gives the proportion of the variation in sales not accounted for by the variation in test scores.

At this point, the human resource director probably would have concluded (had a sample of more than 30 been used) that his test, although not a perfect predictor of weekly sales, could be used to predict sales with a fairly high degree of success. To predict sales, the linear regression equation $Y' = a + bX = 1.202 + 1.133X$ was determined. To illustrate its use, suppose an applicant for a sales position scored 6 on the test. The average applicant's weekly sales would be $8,000, found by: $Y' = 1.202 + 1.133(6)$ (in $000).

Had the coefficient of correlation been a perfect 1.00, there would be no error in the estimated weekly sales of $8,000. The coefficient of correlation was .88, signifying there will be an error in any prediction made using the regression equation. This error is measured by the standard error of estimate. We found it to be $1,955. The human resource director would conclude: (1) 68 percent of the weekly sales predictions will not be off by more than 1($1,955), (2) 95 percent will not be off by more than 2($1,955), and (3) 99.7 percent of the predictions will not be off by more than 3($1,955).

In summary, the human resource director would probably conclude that the test has great potential as an objective instrument for estimating the weekly sales of applicants for openings in the sales department.

Before concluding our discussion of simple correlation and regression, we need to expand on the coefficient of determinatioin and examine the relationship between the coefficient of correlation, the coefficient of determination, and the standard error of estimate.

## More on the Coefficient of Determination

In Chapter 13 we used a convenient computational formula to determine the coefficient of correlation, $r$. The coefficient of determination was found by squaring the coefficient of correlation.

To further examine the basic concept of the coefficient of determination, suppose there is interest in the relationship between years on job, $X$, and weekly production, $Y$. Sample data revealed:

| Employee | Years on job, $X$ | Weekly production, $Y$ |
|----------|-------------------|------------------------|
| Gordon   | 14                | 6                      |
| James    | 7                 | 5                      |
| Ford     | 3                 | 3                      |
| Salter   | 15                | 9                      |
| Artes    | 11                | 7                      |

The sample data were plotted in a scatter diagram. Since the relationship between $X$ and $Y$ appears to be linear, a straight line was drawn through the plots (see Chart 14–12). The equation is $Y' = a + bX = 2 + 0.4X$.

Note in Chart 14–12 that if we were to use that straight line to predict weekly production for an employee, in no case would our prediction be exact. That is, there would be some error in each of our predictions. As an example, for Gordon, who has been with the company 14 years, we would predict weekly production to be 7.6 units; however, he only produces 6 units.

## CHART 14-12

### Observed Data and Straight Line

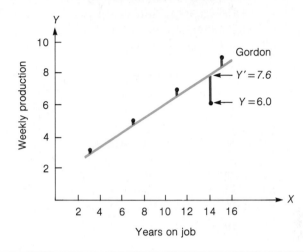

To measure the overall error in our prediction, every deviation from the straight line is squared and the squares summed. The predicted point on the straight line is designated $Y'$, read $Y$ prime, and the observed point is designated $Y$. For Gordon, $(Y - Y')^2 = (6 - 7.6)^2 = (-1.6)^2 = 2.56$. Logically, this variation cannot be explained by the independent variable, so it is referred to as the *unexplained variation.* Specifically, we cannot explain why Gordon's production of 6 units is 1.6 units below his predicted production of 7.6 units, based on the number of years he has been on the job.

**Unexplained variation**

The sum of the squared deviations, $\Sigma(Y - Y')^2$, is 4.00. (See Table 14-5.) The term $\Sigma(Y - Y')^2 = 4.00$ is the variation in $Y$ (production) that cannot be predicted from $X$. It is the "unexplained" variation in $Y$.

## TABLE 14-5

### Computations Needed for the Unexplained Variation

|  | $X$ | $Y$ | $Y'$ | $Y - Y'$ | $(Y - Y')^2$ |
|---|---|---|---|---|---|
| Gordon | 14 | 6 | 7.6 | −1.6 | 2.56 |
| James | 7 | 5 | 4.8 | 0.2 | 0.04 |
| Ford | 3 | 3 | 3.2 | −0.2 | 0.04 |
| Salter | 15 | 9 | 8.0 | 1.0 | 1.00 |
| Artes | 11 | 7 | 6.4 | 0.6 | 0.36 |
| Total | 50 | 30 |  | 0.0* | 4.00 |

*Must be 0.

Now suppose *only* the Y values (weekly production, in this problem) are known and we want to predict production for every employee. The actual production figures for the employees are 6, 5, 3, 9, and 7 (from Table 14-5). To make these predictions, we could assign the mean weekly production (6 units, found by $\Sigma Y/n = 30/5 = 6$) to each employee. This would keep the sum of the squared prediction errors at a minimum.

(Recall from Chapter 3 that the sum of the squared deviations from the arithmetic mean for a set of numbers is smaller than the sum of the squared deviations from any other value, such as the median.) Table 14−6 shows the necessary calculations. The sum of the squared deviations is 20, as shown in Table 14−6. The 20 is referred to as the *total variation in Y.*

*Total variation in Y* (margin)

---

### TABLE   14−6

**Calculations Needed for the Total Variation in Y**

| Name | Weekly production, $Y$ | Mean weekly production, $\bar{Y}$ | $Y - \bar{Y}$ | Mean squared, $(Y - \bar{Y})^2$ |
|------|------|------|------|------|
| Gordon | 6 | 6 | 0 | 0 |
| James | 5 | 6 | −1 | 1 |
| Ford | 3 | 6 | −3 | 9 |
| Salter | 9 | 6 | 3 | 9 |
| Artes | 7 | 6 | 1 | 1 |
| Total |   |   | 0* | 20 |

---

*Must be 0.

What we did to arrive at the total variation in $Y$ is shown diagrammatically in Chart 14−13.

---

### CHART   14−13

**Plots Showing Deviations from the Mean of Y**

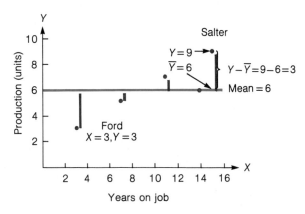

---

*Explained variation* (margin)

Logically, the total variation in $Y$ can be subdivided into unexplained variation and explained variation. To arrive at the explained variation, knowing the total variation and unexplained variation, we simply subtract: Explained variation = Total variation −

Coefficient of
determination

Unexplained variation. Dividing the explained variation by the total variation gives the coefficient of determination, $r^2$, which is a percentage. In terms of a formula:

$$r^2 = \frac{\text{Total variation} - \text{Unexplained variation}}{\text{Total variation}} \qquad (14-8)$$

$$= \frac{\Sigma(Y - \overline{Y})^2 - \Sigma(Y - Y')^2}{\Sigma(Y - \overline{Y})^2}$$

In this problem:

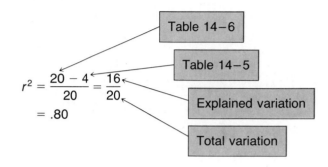

$$r^2 = \frac{20 - 4}{20} = \frac{16}{20}$$

$$= .80$$

Table 14-6

Table 14-5

Explained variation

Total variation

As mentioned, .80 is a percentage. We say that 80 percent of the variation in weekly production, $Y$, is determined, or accounted for, by its linear relationship with $X$ (years on the job).

As a check, the computational formula for the coefficient of correlation, $r$, in Chapter 13 could be used. Squaring $r$ gives the coefficient of determination. Exercise 13 offers a check on the preceding problem.

# EXERCISES

*The answers to the odd-numbered exercises are at the end of the book.*

13. Using the preceding problem, involving years on the job and weekly production, verify that the coefficient of determination is in fact .80.

14. The number of shares of Icom, Inc. that turned over during a month, and the price at the end of the month, are listed in the following table. Also, the $Y'$ plots on the straight line going through observed data are given.

| Turnover (thousands of shares), $X$ | Actual price, $Y$ | Estimated price $Y'$ |
|---|---|---|
| 4 | $2 | 2.7 |
| 1 | 1 | 0.6 |
| 5 | 4 | 3.4 |
| 3 | 2 | 2.0 |
| 2 | 1 | 1.3 |

a.  Draw a scatter diagram. Plot a straight line through the dots.

b.  Compute the coefficient of determination using formula (14-8).

c.  As a check, use the computational formula for $r$ (from Chapter 13).

d.  Interpret the coefficient of determination.

# THE RELATIONSHIP AMONG THE COEFFICIENT OF CORRELATION, THE COEFFICIENT OF DETERMINATION, AND THE STANDARD ERROR OF ESTIMATE

In an earlier section, we discussed the standard error of estimate, which measures how close the actual values are to the regression line. When the standard error is small, it indicates that the two variables are closely related. In the calculation of the standard error, the key term is $\Sigma(Y - Y')^2$. If the value of this term is "small," then the standard error will also be small.

Recall from Chapter 13 that the correlation coefficient measures the strength of the association between two variables. When the dots on the scatter diagram appear close to the straight line, we note that the correlation coefficient tends to be "large." Thus, the standard error of estimate and the coefficient of correlation relate the same information but use a different scale to report the strength of the association. However, both measures involve the term $\Sigma(Y - Y')^2$.

We also noted that the square of the correlation coefficient is called the coefficient of determination. The coefficient of determination measures the percent of the variation in $Y$ that is explained by the variation in $X$.

A convenient vehicle for showing the relationship between these three measures is an ANOVA table. This table is similar to the analysis of variance table developed in Chapter 12. In that chapter, the variation was divided into two components: that due to the *treatments* and that due to *random error.* The concept is similar in regression analysis. The total variation, $\Sigma(Y - \overline{Y})^2$, is divided into two components: (1) that explained by the *regression* (explained by the independent variable) and (2) the *error,* or unexplained variation. These two categories are identified in the column of the ANOVA table that follows. The column headed "DF" refers to the degrees of freedom associated with each category. The total number of degrees of freedom is found by $n - 1$. The number of degrees of freedom in the regression is 1, since there is only one independent variable. The number of degrees of freedom associated with the error term is $n - 2$. The term SS located in the middle of the ANOVA table refers to the sum of squares—the variation. The terms are computed as follows:

$$\text{Total variation} = \text{SS total} = \Sigma(Y - \overline{Y})^2$$
$$\text{Error variation} = \quad \text{SSE} = \Sigma(Y - Y')^2$$
$$\text{Regression} = \quad \text{SSR} = \Sigma(Y' - \overline{Y})^2$$

The format for the ANOVA table is:

| Source | DF | SS | MS |
|--------|-----|---------|-------------|
| Regression | 1 | SSR | SSR/1 |
| Error | $n - 2$ | SSE | SSE/$(n - 2)$ |
| Total | $n - 1$ | SS total* | |

*SS total = SSR + SSE.

The coefficient of determination, $r^2$, can be obtained directly from the ANOVA table by:

$$r^2 = \frac{\text{SSR}}{\text{SS total}} = 1 - \frac{\text{SSE}}{\text{SS total}}$$

The term "SSR/SS total" is the percent of the variation in *Y explained* by the independent variable, *X*. Note the effect of the term SSE on $r^2$. As SSE decreases, $r^2$ will increase. Conversely, as the standard error decreases, the $r^2$ term increases.

The standard error of estimate can also be obtained from the ANOVA table using the following equation.

$$s_{y \cdot x} = \sqrt{\frac{SSE}{n-2}}$$

The sales and test score problem started in Chapter 13 and continued in this chapter is used to illustrate the computations of the coefficient of determination and the standard error of estimate from an ANOVA table.

## ✓ EXAMPLE

The test scores and weekly sales of a sample of five salespeople is repeated from Table 14-1.

| Salesperson | Test score | Weekly sales |
|---|---|---|
| Mr. J. A. Amber | 4 | $ 5,000 |
| Mr. B. N. Archer | 7 | 12,000 |
| Ms. G. D. Smith | 3 | 4,000 |
| Mr. A. B. Malcolm | 6 | 8,000 |
| Ms. A. Goodwin | 10 | 11,000 |

The following ANOVA table is part of the regression output obtained from the MINITAB system. It reports the regression equation and the coefficient of determination.

```
MTB > set c1
DATA> 4,7,3,6,10
DATA> end
MTB > set c2
DATA> 5,12,4,8,11
DATA> end
MTB > name c1 'Score' c2 'Sales'
MTB > regr c2 1 c1

The regression equation is
Sales = 1.20 + 1.13 Score  ← Regression equation

Predictor        Coef        Stdev      t-ratio          p
Constant        1.200        2.313         0.52      0.640
Score          1.1333       0.3569         3.18      0.050

s = 1.955      R-sq = 77.1%        R-sq(adj) = 69.4%

Analysis of Variance            Coefficient of determination

SOURCE          DF          SS          MS          F          p
Regression       1      38.533      38.533      10.08      0.050
Error            3      11.467       3.822
Total            4      50.000
```

What is the coefficient of determination? What is the standard error of estimate?

## ☑ SOLUTION

The coefficient of determination is .771, found by:

$$r^2 = \frac{SSR}{SS\ total} = \frac{38.533}{50.000} = .771$$

This is the same value as computed on page 473 in Chapter 13. Again, we can say that about 77.1 percent of the total variation in the dependent variable (sales) is explained, or accounted for, by the variation in the independent variable (test score). If we had needed the coefficient of correlation, $r$, we would take the square root of the coefficient of determination: $\sqrt{r^2} = \sqrt{.771} = .88$, indicating a strong relationship between test scores and sales. (This value is also the same as computed in Chapter 13.)

The standard error of estimate is determined as follows:

$$s_{y \cdot x} = \sqrt{\frac{SSE}{n - 2}} = \sqrt{\frac{11.467}{5 - 2}} = 1.955$$

It is the same as computed on page 508 of this chapter.

Again, we see how efficient a computer system is for supplying us with essential statistical measures.

## CHAPTER OUTLINE

I. Regression analysis.
  A. Its purpose is to arrive at the regression equation to predict the value of one variable (designated by $Y$ and called the dependent variable) based on another variable (denoted by $X$ and called the independent variable).
  B. The procedure.
    1. Select a sample from the population, and list the paired data ($X$ and $Y$) for each observation.
    2. Draw a scatter diagram to give a visual portrayal of the relationship.
    3. Determine the regression equation mathematically, which has the form $Y' = a + bX$, where:

      $Y'$    is the average predicted value of the $Y$ variable for any $X$ value.

      $a$    is the $Y$-intercept, or the estimated value of $Y$ when $X = 0$.

      $b$    called the slope of the line, is the average change in $Y'$ for each change of one unit in $X$.

      $X$    is any value of $X$.

    4. The computations for $a$ and $b$ can be accomplished by:

    $$b = \frac{n(\Sigma XY) - (\Sigma X)(\Sigma Y)}{n(\Sigma X^2) - (\Sigma X)^2} \tag{14-2}$$

    $$a = \frac{\Sigma Y}{n} - b\left(\frac{\Sigma X}{n}\right) \tag{14-3}$$

    5. The standard error of estimate measures the variation around the regression line. Two formulas used to determine the standard error are:

    $$s_{y \cdot x} = \sqrt{\frac{\Sigma Y^2 - a(\Sigma Y) - b(\Sigma XY)}{n - 2}} \tag{14-5}$$

    $$s_{y \cdot x} = \sqrt{\frac{\Sigma (Y - Y')^2}{n - 2}} \tag{14-4}$$

6. The confidence limits for the mean value of $Y$ for a given value of $X$ are found by:

$$Y' \pm t(s_{y \cdot x}) \sqrt{\frac{1}{n} + \frac{(X - \bar{X})^2}{\Sigma X^2 - \frac{(\Sigma X)^2}{n}}} \qquad (14-6)$$

To set confidence limits for an individual value of $Y$ for a given value of $X$:

$$Y' \pm t(s_{y \cdot x}) \sqrt{1 + \frac{1}{n} + \frac{(X - \bar{X})^2}{\Sigma X^2 - \frac{(\Sigma X)^2}{n}}} \qquad (14-7)$$

## EXERCISES

*The answers to the odd-numbered exercises are at the end of the book.*

15. A research project was undertaken to determine if there is a relationship between years of service and the efficiency ratings of employees. The objective of the study is to predict the efficiency rating of an employee based on years of service. The sample results are:

| Employee | Years of service | Efficiency rating |
|---|---|---|
| Jones | 1 | 6 |
| Orlando | 20 | 5 |
| Ireland | 6 | 3 |
| Smith | 8 | 5 |
| Kordel | 2 | 2 |
| Harper | 1 | 2 |
| Lopez | 15 | 4 |
| Sobecki | 8 | 3 |

a. What is the dependent variable?

b. Draw a scatter diagram.

c. Based on the scatter diagram, does there appear to be any relationship between years of service and efficiency?

d. Compute the regression equation.

e. For eight years of service, what is the predicted efficiency rating?

f. Compute any three points for the straight line, and plot the line on the scatter diagram.

16. The production department at National Sheet and Metal wants to explore the relationship between the number of employees who assemble a subassembly and the number produced. As an experiment, two employees were assigned to assemble the subassembly. They produced 15 during a one-hour period. Then four employees assembled it. They produced 25 during a one-hour period. The complete set of paired observations is as follows.

| Number of assemblers | One-hour production (units) |
|---|---|
| 2 | 15 |
| 4 | 25 |
| 1 | 10 |
| 5 | 40 |
| 3 | 30 |

The dependent variable is production; that is, it is assumed that the level of production depends on the number of assemblers.

a.   Draw a scatter diagram.

b.   Based on the scatter diagram, does there appear to be any relationship between the number of assemblers and production? Explain.

c.   Compute the regression equation.

d.   For three assemblers, what is the predicted hourly production?

e.   Determine any three points for the straight line, and plot the line on the scatter diagram.

*Note: Exercises 17 through 24 use large samples. It is suggested, therefore, that a computer be used.*

Courtesy The Kroger Company

17.   What is the relationship between the amount spent per week on food and the size of the family? Do larger families spend more on food? A sample of 10 families in the Chicago area revealed the following family sizes and amounts spent on food last week.

| Family size | Amount spent on food |
|---|---|
| 3 | $ 99 |
| 6 | 104 |
| 5 | 151 |
| 6 | 129 |
| 6 | 142 |
| 3 | 111 |
| 4 | 74 |
| 4 | 91 |
| 5 | 119 |
| 3 | 91 |

a.   Determine the regression equation. Interpret the equation.

b.   Determine the standard error of estimate.

c.   Estimate the amount that a family of four will spend on food.

d.   Develop a 95 percent confidence interval for the mean amount spent by families of four.

e. Develop a 95 percent confidence interval for the amount spent by a particular family of four.

18. A sample of 12 homes sold last week in St. Paul, Minnesota, was selected. Can we conclude that as the size of the home (reported in hundreds of square feet) increases, selling price (reported in $000) also increases?

| Home size (hundreds of square feet), X | Selling price ($000), Y |
|---|---|
| 14 | $100 |
| 13 | 110 |
| 12 | 105 |
| 11 | 120 |
| 14 | 80 |
| 10 | 105 |
| 13 | 110 |
| 8 | 85 |
| 12 | 105 |
| 9 | 75 |
| 11 | 70 |
| 11 | 95 |

a. Determine the regression equation. Interpret the equation.
b. Determine the standard error of estimate.
c. Estimate the selling price for a home of 10 (hundreds of square feet).
d. Develop a 95 percent confidence interval for the mean selling price of all homes of size 10.
e. Develop a 95 percent confidence interval for the selling price of a particular home of size 10.

19. The following regression equation was computed from a sample of 20 observations.

$$Y' = 15 - 5X$$

SSE was found to be 100 and SS total 400.
a. Determine the standard error of estimate.
b. Determine the coefficient of determination.
c. Determine the coefficient of correlation. (Caution: Watch the sign!)

20. An ANOVA table is:

| SOURCE | DF | SS | MS | F |
|---|---|---|---|---|
| Regression | 1 | 50 | | |
| Error | | | | |
| Total | 24 | 500 | | |

a. Complete the ANOVA table.
b. How large was the sample?
c. Determine the standard error of estimate.
d. Determine the coefficient of determination.

21. Following is a regression equation.

$$Y' = 17.08 + 0.16X$$

This information is also available: $s_{y \cdot x} = 4.05$, $\Sigma X = 210$, $\Sigma X^2 = 9,850$, and $n = 5$.
a. Estimate the value of $Y'$ when $X = 50$.
b. Develop a 95 percent confidence interval for an individual value of Y for $X = 50$.

22. The National Highway Association is studying the relationship between the number of bidders on a highway project and the winning (lowest) bid for the project. Of particular interest is whether the number of bidders increases or decreases the amount of the winning bid.

| Project | Number of bidders, X | Winning bid ($ millions), Y |
|---|---|---|
| 1 | 5 | 4.0 |
| 2 | 8 | 6.9 |
| 3 | 5 | 4.8 |
| 4 | 4 | 3.9 |
| 5 | 4 | 4.2 |
| 6 | 3 | 2.7 |
| 7 | 9 | 7.8 |
| 8 | 4 | 4.1 |
| 9 | 7 | 6.1 |
| 10 | 4 | 4.4 |
| 11 | 5 | 4.8 |
| 12 | 5 | 5.9 |
| 13 | 3 | 3.6 |
| 14 | 4 | 3.9 |
| 15 | 5 | 4.8 |

a.  Determine the regression equation. Interpret the equation. Do more bidders tend to increase or decrease the amount of the winning bid?

b.  Estimate the amount of the winning bid if there were seven bidders.

c.  A new turnpike entrance is to be constructed on the Ohio Turnpike at the junction of I-75. There are seven bidders on the project. Develop a 95 percent confidence interval for the winning bid.

d.  Determine the coefficient of determination. Interpret its value.

23. Mr. William Profit is studying companies going public for the first time. He is particularly interested in the relationship between the size of the offering and the price per share. A sample of 15 companies that recently went public revealed the following information.

| Company | Size ($ millions), X | Price per share, Y |
|---|---|---|
| 1 | 9.0 | 10.8 |
| 2 | 94.4 | 11.3 |
| 3 | 27.3 | 11.2 |
| 4 | 179.2 | 11.1 |
| 5 | 71.9 | 11.1 |
| 6 | 97.9 | 11.2 |
| 7 | 93.5 | 11.0 |
| 8 | 70.0 | 10.7 |
| 9 | 160.7 | 11.3 |
| 10 | 96.5 | 10.6 |
| 11 | 83.0 | 10.5 |
| 12 | 23.5 | 10.3 |
| 13 | 58.7 | 10.7 |
| 14 | 93.8 | 11.0 |
| 15 | 34.4 | 10.8 |

a.  Determine the regression equation.

b.  Determine the coefficient of determination. Do you think Mr. Profit should be satisfied with using the size of the offering as the independent variable?

24. Suppose the owners of the 26 major league baseball teams would like to know the relationship between the proportion of games won and attendance. Just before Labor Day 1991 figures for the proportion of games won and the number of people attending home games, in millions, were obtained. They are reported below. Use proportion of games won as the independent variable.

| Team | Proportion of games won | Home attendance (millions) |
|------|-------------------------|----------------------------|
| Pittsburgh | .603 | 1.51 |
| St. Louis | .543 | 1.88 |
| Chicago Cubs | .508 | 1.82 |
| New York Mets | .487 | 1.85 |
| Philadelphia | .466 | 1.51 |
| Montreal | .402 | 0.86 |
| Los Angeles | .559 | 2.44 |
| Atlanta | .543 | 1.50 |
| Cincinnati | .491 | 1.87 |
| San Diego | .487 | 1.47 |
| San Francisco | .487 | 1.39 |
| Houston | .419 | 0.97 |
| Toronto | .546 | 3.00 |
| Detroit | .521 | 1.25 |
| Boston | .500 | 1.93 |
| Milwaukee | .466 | 1.23 |
| New York Yankees | .457 | 1.46 |
| Baltimore | .407 | 1.87 |
| Cleveland | .325 | 0.86 |
| Minnesota | .597 | 1.52 |
| Chicago White Sox | .568 | 2.15 |
| Oakland | .557 | 1.93 |
| Seattle | .534 | 1.50 |
| Kansas City | .526 | 1.60 |
| Texas | .517 | 1.75 |
| California | .496 | 1.85 |

a. Determine the regression equation. Does attendance increase with an increase in the winning proportion?

b. If a team wins 60 percent of its games, how many fans will attend?

c. Determine and interpret the coefficient of determination.

25. Refer to Exercise 33 in Chapter 13.

a. Plot the relationship between number of calls and the value of orders. Assume that the number of calls is the independent variable.

b. Develop a regression equation for predicting the value of orders from the number of calls.

c. What is the forecast value of orders if five calls are made?

d. Develop a 95 percent confidence interval for the value of orders received from Hammond Iron Works, Inc. if five calls are made.

e. What percent of the variation in the value of orders is explained by the variation in the number of calls?

## COMPUTER DATA EXERCISES

26. Refer to data set 1, which reports information on homes sold in Florida during 1990.

a. Let selling price be the dependent variable and size of the home the independent variable. Determine the regression equation. Estimate the selling price of a home with an area of 2,200 square feet. Determine the 95 percent confidence interval for the mean selling price of all 2,200-square-foot homes and the 95 percent confidence interval for a particular home of 2,200 square feet.

b.   Let selling price be the dependent variable and distance from the home to the center of the city the independent variable. Determine the regression equation. Estimate the selling price of a home 20 miles from the center of the city. Determine the 95 percent confidence interval for the mean selling price of all homes and for the selling price of an individual home 20 miles from the center of the city.

27.   Refer to data set 2, which reports information on 200 corporations in the United States.

a.   Let profit be the dependent variable and sales the independent variable. Determine the regression equation. Estimate the profit on $12,000 (million) sales. Determine the 95 percent confidence interval for the mean profit for all firms selling $12,000. Determine the 95 percent confidence interval for a particular firm with sales of $12,000.

b.   Let profit be the dependent variable and share price the independent variable. Determine the regression equation. Estimate the profit for a share price of 60. Determine the 95 percent confidence interval for the mean profit for all firms with a share price of 60. Determine the 95 percent confidence interval for a particular firm with a share price of 60.

28.   Refer to data set 3, which reports information on the 26 major league baseball teams for the 1991 season.

a.   Let the proportion of games won be the dependent variable and team batting average the independent variable. Determine the regression equation. Estimate the proportion of games won by a team with a batting average of .270. If the Texas Rangers batted .270, determine the 95 percent confidence interval for their proportion of games won. Does it appear that a .270 batting average will result in a winning season? (*Hint:* Is .5000 in the interval?)

b.   Let the proportion of games won be the dependent variable and team ERA the independent variable. Determine the regression equation. Estimate the proportion of games won by a team with an ERA of 3.00. If the San Diego Padres had a team ERA of 3.00, determine the 95 percent confidence interval for their proportion of games won. Does it appear that an ERA of 3.00 will result in a winning season? (*Hint:* Is .5000 in the interval?)

# CHAPTER 14   EXAMINATION

*The answers are at the end of the chapter.*

Questions 1 through 6 are based on the following picture.

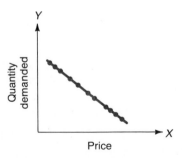

1.   The picture is called a:

a.   Dotted-swiss chart.

b.   Bar chart.

    c.    Scatter diagram.

    d.    Straight-line chart.

    e.    None of these is correct.

2. The equation for the line going through the points would take the form of:
   a. $Y' = a + b + c$.
   b. $Y' = a + bX$, or $Y' = a - bX$.
   c. $Y' = X - 1$.
   d. $Y' = a + bX^2$.
   e. None of these is correct.

3. In this particular problem, the researcher is trying to predict:
   a. Quantity demanded based on price.
   b. Price based on quantity demanded.
   c. Both price and quantity demanded.
   d. None of these is correct.

4. If computed, the sign of $b$ in the equation would be:
   a. Either positive or negative.
   b. Positive.
   c. Negative.
   d. Infinity.
   e. None of these is correct.

5. The standard error of estimate, if computed, would be:
   a. Infinity.
   b. $+1.00$.
   c. $-1.00$.
   d. 0
   e. None of these is correct.

6. Any predictions based on this picture would:
   a. Have no error.
   b. Be of little or no use.
   c. None of these is correct.

7. The variable used to predict another variable is called the:
   a. Dependent variable.
   b. Independent variable.
   c. Correlation variable.
   d. Student's $t$ variable.
   e. None of these is correct.

8. The method used to arrive at the "best-fitting" straight line in regression analysis is referred to as the:
   a. Freehand method.
   b. Nondetermination method.
   c. Least squares method.
   d. Correlation method.
   e. None of these is correct.

Questions 9 and 10 are based on the following chart.

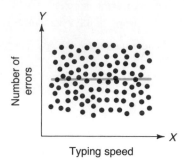

9. In the regression equation for the straight line, the value of $b$ would be about:

    a.   −1.00.

    b.   +1.00.

    c.   0.

    d.   None of these is correct.

10. The independent variable is scaled on the:

    a.   $Y$-axis.

    b.   $X$-axis.

Sales of toothpaste seem to be heavily dependent on the level of advertisement. The annual advertising expenditures for several well-known brands and their annual sales are:

| Brand | Annual advertising expenditures ($ millions) | Annal sales ($ millions) |
| --- | --- | --- |
| Glint | 2 | 5 |
| Pearl One | 4 | 7 |
| Shine On | 3 | 6 |
| Number 1 | 1 | 2 |

11. a.   Draw a scatter diagram.

    b.   Compute the least squares regression equation.

    c.   Based on the regression equation, an advertising expenditure of $1.9 million should produce what amount of sales on the average?

    d.   Compute three points, and plot the straight line on the scatter diagram.

12. a.   Determine the standard error of estimate.

    b.   For a group of toothpastes whose annual advertising expenditures are exactly $1.9 million, what is the 95 percent confidence interval for their arithmetic mean annual sales?

    c.   Interpret these limits.

## ANSWERS

**14–1**  **1.**  Yield is the dependent variable. The amount of fertilizer is the independent variable.

**2.**

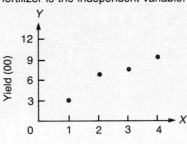

Amount of fertilizer
(tons)

**3.**

| X | Y | XY | X² | Y² |
|---|---|----|----|----|
| 2 | 7 | 14 | 4 | 49 |
| 1 | 3 | 3 | 1 | 9 |
| 3 | 8 | 24 | 9 | 64 |
| 4 | 10 | 40 | 16 | 100 |
| 10 | 28 | 81 | 30 | 222 |

$$b = \frac{4(81) - (10)(28)}{4(30) - (10)^2}$$

$$= \frac{324 - 280}{120 - 100} = 2.2$$

$$a = \frac{28}{4} - 2.2\left(\frac{10}{4}\right)$$

$$= 7 - 5.5 = 1.5$$

The equation is: $Y' = 1.5 + 2.2X$ (in hundreds of bushels).

**14–2**  **1.**  0.9487 (in hundreds of bushels), found by:

$$s_{y \cdot x} = \sqrt{\frac{\Sigma Y^2 - a(\Sigma Y) - b(\Sigma XY)}{n - 2}}$$

$$= \sqrt{\frac{222 - 1.5(28) - 2.2(81)}{4 - 2}}$$

$$= \sqrt{\frac{1.8}{2}}$$

$$= 0.9487 \text{ or } 94.87 \text{ bushels}$$

**2.**  189.74 bushels, found by 2(94.87).

**14–3**  **1.**  6.58 and 9.52, since $Y'$ for an $X$ of 3 is 8.1, found by $Y' = 1.5 + 2.2(3) = 8.1$. $\bar{X} = 2.5$. Then $\Sigma X^2 = 30$ and $\Sigma X = 10$.
$t$ from Appendix F for $4 - 2 = 2$ degrees of freedom at the .10 level is 2.920.

$$Y' \pm t(s_{y \cdot x}) \sqrt{\frac{1}{n} + \frac{(X - \bar{X})^2}{\Sigma X^2 - \frac{(\Sigma X)^2}{n}}}$$

$$= 8.1 \pm 2.920(0.9487) \sqrt{\frac{1}{4} + \frac{(3 - 2.5)^2}{30 - \frac{(10)^2}{4}}}$$

$$= 8.1 \pm 2.920(0.9487)(0.5477)$$

$$= 6.58 \text{ and } 9.62 \text{ (in hundreds of bushels),}$$
or 658 and 962 bushels

**2.**  For a group of plots receiving exactly three tons of fertilizer, the probability is .90 that the mean yield is in the interval between 658 and 962 bushels.

# Answers

## CHAPTER 14 EXAMINATION

1. c.
2. b.
3. a.
4. c.
5. d.

6. a.
7. b.
8. c.
9. c.
10. b.

11. a.

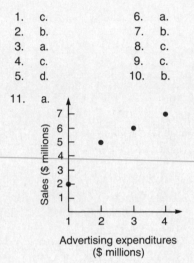

Advertising expenditures
($ millions)

b. $Y' = a + bX = 1 + 1.6X$ (in $ millions)

$$b = \frac{4(58) - 10(20)}{4(30) - (10)^2} = \frac{32}{20} = 1.6$$

$$a = \frac{20}{4} - 1.6\left(\frac{10}{4}\right) = 5 - 4 = 1$$

c. $4.04 million, found by $Y' = 1 + 1.6(1.9)$.

d.

| $X$ | $Y'$ |
|---|---|
| 1 | 2.6 |
| 2 | 4.2 |
| 3 | 5.8 |
| 4 | 7.4 |

12. a. 0.77 (in $ millions), found by:

$$\sqrt{\frac{114 - 1(20) - 1.6(58)}{4 - 2}} = \sqrt{\frac{1.2}{2}} = 0.77$$

b. $2.16 and $5.92 (in $ millions), found by:

$$4.04 \pm 4.303(0.77) \sqrt{\frac{1}{4} + \frac{(1.9 - 2.5)^2}{5.0}}$$

$$= 4.04 \pm 4.303(0.77)(0.5674504)$$

$$= 4.04 \pm 1.88$$

c. For a group of toothpastes with advertising expenditures of exactly $1.9 million, the probability is .95 that the mean sales amount is in the interval between $2.16 million and $5.92 million.

Transportation—Courtesy American Airlines

# MULTIPLE REGRESSION AND CORRELATION

When you have completed this chapter, you will be able to:

1. Describe the relationship between two or more independent variables and a dependent variable using a multiple regression equation.

2. Describe the error in the prediction using the multiple standard error of estimate.

3. Describe the strength of the relationship between the independent variables and the dependent variable using the multiple coefficients of correlation, determination, and nondetermination.

4. Explain a stepwise multiple regression and correlation computer output.

5. Conduct a global test to determine whether or not the multiple regression model is useful.

6. Evaluate individual regression coefficients.

T he previous two chapters dealt with the relationship between two sets of interval- or ratio-scaled measurements. One is designated the independent variable, and the other is the dependent variable. We noted that if the relationship between the two sets of variables is linear, the regression equation $Y' = a + bX$ is used to predict the dependent variable, $Y$, based on the independent variable, $X$. Further, Pearson's product-moment coefficient of correlation is one measure we examined that reveals whether the relationship is strong, moderate, or weak. A coefficient near plus or minus 1.00 indicates a very strong relationship between $X$ and $Y$. A coefficient near 0 (say, $-.12$ or $+.12$) would mean that the relationship is quite weak.

   Use of only one independent variable to predict the dependent variable ignores the relationship of other variables to the dependent variable. This chapter expands our study of correlation and regression by examining the influence of *two or more* independent variables on the dependent variable. This approach is referred to as **multiple regression and correlation analysis.** We will present multiple regression analysis first by developing and explaining the use of the multiple regression equation and the multiple standard error of estimate. Then the strength of the relationship between the independent variables and the dependent variable will be measured using the multiple coefficient of correlation and the multiple coefficients of determination and nondetermination. Finally, several computer applications using MINITAB will be presented.

## MULTIPLE REGRESSION ANALYSIS

Recall from Chapter 14 that the simple linear regression equation encompassing one independent variable and one dependent variable has the form $Y' = a + bX$. The multiple regression case merely extends the equation to include additional independent variables. For two independent variables, the general form of the **multiple regression equation** is:

$$Y' = a + b_1X_1 + b_2X_2 \qquad (15-1)$$

where:

*b* is called a regression coefficient

$X_1, X_2$    are the two independent variables.
   $a$    is the $Y$-intercept, that is, the point of intercept with the $Y$-axis.
   $b_1$    is the net change in $Y$ for each unit change in $X_1$, *holding $X_2$ constant* (unchanged). It is called a *partial regression coefficient,* a *net regression coefficient,* or just a *regression coefficient.*
   $b_2$    is the net change in $Y$ for each single unit change in $X_2$, *holding $X_1$ constant* (unchanged). It is also referred to as a partial regression coefficient, or just a regression coefficient.

   To illustrate the interpretation of $a$ and the two regression coefficients, suppose a vehicle's mileage per gallon of gasoline is directly related to the octane rating of the gasoline being used ($X_1$) and inversely related to the weight of the automobile ($X_2$). Assume that the multiple regression equation was computed to be $Y' = 6.3 + 0.2X_1 + (-0.001)X_2$. The $a$ value of 6.3 indicates that the regression plane intercepts the $Y$-axis at 6.3 when both $X_1$ and $X_2$ are zero. Of course, it does not make any sense to own an automobile that has no (zero) weight and to use gasoline with no octane. It is important to keep in mind that a regression equation is not effective outside the range of the sample values for the dependent variable.

**Negative $b$ indicates inverse relationship**

The $b_1$ of 0.2 indicates that for each increase of 1 in the octane rating of the gasoline, the automobile would travel two tenths of a mile more per gallon, *regardless of the weight of the vehicle.* That is, the vehicle's weight is held constant. The $b_2$ value of $-0.001$ reveals that for each increase of one pound in the vehicle's weight, the number of miles traveled per gallon decreases by 0.001, *regardless of the octane of the gasoline being used.*

As an example, an automobile with 92-octane gasoline in the tank and weighing 2,000 pounds would travel on the average 22.7 miles per gallon, found by:

$$Y' = a + b_1X_1 + b_2X_2$$
$$= 6.3 + 0.2(92) + (-0.001)2,000$$
$$= 22.7 \text{ miles per gallon}$$

For three independent variables designated $X_1$, $X_2$, and $X_3$, the general multiple regression equation is:

$$\boxed{Y' = a + b_1X_1 + b_2X_2 + b_3X_3} \tag{15-2}$$

**General form of the multiple regression equation**

This can be extended for any number of independent variables ($k$), with the general multiple regression equation being:

$$\boxed{Y' = a + b_1X_1 + b_2X_2 + b_3X_3 + \cdots + b_kX_k} \tag{15-3}$$

**Need computer to solve these**

As was demonstrated in Chapter 14, the least squares method minimizes the sum of the squares of the vertical deviations about the straight line. The same applies to multiple regression. To arrive at $a$, $b_1$, and $b_2$ in the multiple regression equation, however, the many calculations are very tedious—even using a hand calculator. As an example, for two independent variables, three equations must be solved simultaneously, namely:

$$\Sigma Y = na + b_1\Sigma X_1 + b_2\Sigma X_2$$
$$\Sigma X_1Y = a\Sigma X_1 + b_1\Sigma X_1^2 + b_2\Sigma X_1X_2$$
$$\Sigma X_2Y = a\Sigma X_2 + b_1\Sigma X_1X_2 + b_2\Sigma X_2^2$$

There are many computer software packages available, and most outputs provide a fairly standard set of results. MINITAB, SPSS, and SAS are three of the most widely used packages. Before presenting the MINITAB multiple regression package, we will examine the meaning of the intercept term, $a$, and the partial regression coefficients, $b_1$ and $b_2$. To do this, the two-variable sales problem from Chapter 14 will be reintroduced and another independent variable added. Thus, we will have a multiple regression problem involving one dependent variable, $Y$, and two independent variables, $X_1$ and $X_2$.

## ■ EXAMPLE

Recall from Chapter 14 that a small sample of experienced salespeople were given a test by the human resource director, and the test scores were paired with their weekly sales. Now a second independent variable—their achievement ratings in phase 1 of the initial training program—is introduced in an effort to improve the predictive process. Note in Table 15–1 that weekly sales (the dependent variable) are designated by $Y$. The test scores and achievement ratings (independent variables) are designated by $X_1$ and $X_2$, respectively.

### TABLE 15–1

**Weekly Sales, Test Scores, and Achievement Ratings for the Sample of Salespeople**

| Salesperson | Weekly sales ($000), $Y$ | Test score, $X_1$ | Achievement rating, $X_2$ |
|---|---|---|---|
| Mr. Amber | 5 | 4 | 2 |
| Mr. Archer | 12 | 7 | 5 |
| Ms. Smith | 4 | 3 | 1 |
| Mr. Malcolm | 8 | 6 | 4 |
| Ms. Goodwin | 11 | 10 | 6 |

1. What is the multiple regression equation?

*Predicting Y*

2. Suppose that an applicant for an opening in the sales department scored 6.0 on the test and earned an achievement rating of 3.8 in phase 1 of the training program. What is the applicant's estimated weekly sales?

## ☑ SOLUTION

1. The general form is $Y' = a + b_1X_1 + b_2X_2$. For this problem, suppose the regression equation was found to be $Y' = 3.5 + (-0.975)X_1 + 2.875X_2$.
2. The applicant's estimated weekly sales would be $8,575, found by:

$$Y' = 3.5 + (-0.975)6.0 + 2.875(3.8)$$
$$= 3.5 - 5.85 + 10.925$$
$$= 8.575 \text{ (in \$000)}$$

## Self-Review 15–1

*The answers are at the end of the chapter.*

The quality control engineer at Bethel Steel is interested in predicting the tensile strength of steel wire based on its outside diameter and the amount of molybdenum in the steel. As an experiment, she selected four pieces of wire, measured the outside diameters, and determined the molybdenum content. Then she measured the tensile strength of each piece. The results were:

| Piece | Tensile strength (psi), $Y$ | Outside diameter (cm), $X_1$ | Amount of molybdenum (units), $X_2$ |
|-------|------|------|------|
| A | 11 | 3 | 6 |
| B | 9 | 2 | 5 |
| C | 16 | 4 | 8 |
| D | 12 | 3 | 7 |

Suppose the multiple regression equation is: $Y' = -0.5 + 2X_1 + 1X_2$.

1. Based on the equation, what is the predicted tensile strength of a steel wire having an outside diameter of 3.5 cm and 6.4 units of molybdenum?

2. Explain what the value $b_1$ in the equation means.

# EXERCISES

*The answers to the odd-numbered exercises are at the end of the book.*

1. The director of marketing at Reeves Wholesale Products is studying the monthly sales of his company's six regions. Three independent variables were selected as predictors of sales: regional population, per-capita income, and regional unemployment rate. The regression equation was computed to be (in dollars):

$$Y' = 64,100 + 0.394X_1 + 9.6X_2 - 11,600X_3$$

   a. What is the full name of the equation?

   b. Explain what the number 64,100 is.

   c. What is the estimated monthly sales total for region IV? The region has a population of 796,000, per-capita income of $6,940, and an unemployment rate of 6.0 percent.

2. Thompson Machine Works purchased several new, highly sophisticated machines. The production department needed some guidance with respect to qualifications needed by an operator. Is age a factor? Is the length of service as a machine operator important? In order to explore further the factors needed to predict performance on the new machines, four variables were listed:

   $X_1$ = Length of time employee was a machinist.
   $X_2$ = Mechanical aptitude test score.
   $X_3$ = Prior on-the-job rating.
   $X_4$ = Age.

Performance on the new machine is designated $Y$.

   Twelve machinists were selected at random. Data were collected for each, and their performances on the new machines were recorded. A few results are:

| Name | Performance on new machine, $Y$ | Length of time as a machinist, $X_1$ | Mechanical aptitude score, $X_2$ | Prior on-the-job performance, $X_3$ | Age, $X_4$ |
|------|------|------|------|------|------|
| Andy Kosin | 112 | 12 | 312 | 121 | 52 |
| Sue Annis | 113 | 2 | 380 | 123 | 27 |

Suppose the equation is:

$$Y' = 11.6 + 0.4X_1 + 0.286X_2 + 0.112X_3 + 0.002X_4$$

a. What is the full designation of the equation?

b. How many dependent variables are there? Independent variables?

c. What is the number 0.286 called?

d. As age increases by one year, how much does estimated performance on the new machine increase?

e. Carl Knox applied for a job on a new machine. He has been a machinist for six years, and he scored 280 on the mechanical aptitude test. Carl's prior on-the-job performance rating is 97, and he is 35 years old. Estimate Carl's performance on the new machine.

3. A sample of widowed senior citizens was studied to determine their degree of satisfaction with their present life. A special index, called the index of satisfaction, was used to measure satisfaction. Six factors were studied, namely, age at the time of first marriage ($X_1$), annual income ($X_2$), number of children living ($X_3$), value of all assets ($X_4$), status of health in the form of an index ($X_5$), and the average number of social activities per week—such as bowling, and dancing ($X_6$). Suppose the multiple regression equation is:

$$Y' = -16.24 + 0.017X_1 + 0.0028X_2 + 42X_3 + 0.0012X_4 + 0.19X_5 + 26.8X_6$$

a. What is the estimated index of satisfaction for a person who first married at 18, has an annual income of $26,500, has three children living, has assets of $156,000, has an index of health status of 141, and has 2.5 social activities a week on the average?

b. Which would add more to satisfaction, an additional income of $10,000 a year or two more social activities a week?

4. Cellulon, a manufacturer of a new type of home insulation, wants to develop guidelines for builders and consumers regarding the effects on natural gas consumption (1) of the thickness of the insulation in the attic of a home and (2) of the outdoor temperature. In the laboratory they varied the insulation thickness and temperature. A few of the findings are:

| Monthly natural gas consumption (cubic feet), $Y$ | Thickness of insulation (inches), $X_1$ | Outdoor temperature (Fahrenheit), $X_2$ |
|------|------|------|
| 30.3 | 6 | 40 |
| 26.9 | 12 | 40 |
| 22.1 | 8 | 49 |

Based on the sample results, the regression equation is:

$$Y' = 62.65 - 1.86X_1 - 0.52X_2$$

a. How much natural gas can homeowners expect to use per month if (1) they install 6 inches of insulation and (2) the outdoor temperature is 40 degrees F?

b. What effect would installing 7 inches of insulation instead of 6 have on the monthly natural gas consumption (assuming the outdoor temperature remains at 40 degrees F)?

c. Why are the regression coefficients $b_1$ and $b_2$ negative? Is this logical?

## MULTIPLE STANDARD ERROR OF ESTIMATE

Standard error of estimate measures dispersion around multiple regression plane

Returning to the weekly sales example, it was determined that an applicant scoring 6.0 on the test and having an achievement rating of 3.8 in phase 1 of the training program should have weekly sales of $8,575. Obviously, for some weeks sales will be more than this amount, and for some weeks they will be less. The error in this estimate can be measured by the **multiple standard error of estimate,** denoted by $s_{y \cdot 12}$. (The subscripts indicate that two independent variables are being used to estimate the error in $Y$.)

Recall from Chapter 14 that the standard error of estimate in regression analysis measures the variation about the straight line. Likewise, the standard error of estimate in multiple regression analysis measures the error for values of $Y$ about the regression plane. Note that formula (15–4) for the standard error of estimate is almost the same as that used previously in the simple case when just two variables are being studied.

$$s_{y \cdot 12} = \sqrt{\frac{\Sigma(Y - Y')^2}{n - (k + 1)}} \qquad (15-4)$$

where $n$ is the number of observations and $k$ is the number of *independent* variables.

The weekly sales problem is used to illustrate. The first salesperson selected at random was Mr. Amber. His test score was 4; this is $X_1$. His achievement rating was 2; this is $X_2$. His estimated sales ($Y'$) are $5,350, found by: $Y' = 3.5 + (-0.975)4 + 2.875(2) = 5.35$ (in $000). The sales, estimated sales, and calculations needed for the standard error are given in Table 15–2. It shows that Mr. Amber's actual weekly sales total was $5,000, but his predicted sales were $5,350. Thus, the prediction error, or **residual,** is −$350, found by $Y - Y'$, or $5,000 − $5,350.

---

### TABLE 15–2

**Calculations Needed for the Multiple Standard Error of Estimate**

| Salesperson | Test score, $X_1$ | Achievement rating, $X_2$ | Weekly sales ($000), $Y$ | Predicted weekly sales ($000), $Y'$ | $(Y - Y')$ | $(Y - Y')^2$ |
|---|---|---|---|---|---|---|
| Mr. Amber | 4 | 2 | $ 5 | $ 5.35 | $−0.35 | 0.1225 |
| Mr. Archer | 7 | 5 | 12 | 11.05 | 0.95 | 0.9025 |
| Ms. Smith | 3 | 1 | 4 | 3.45 | 0.55 | 0.3025 |
| Mr. Malcolm | 6 | 4 | 8 | 9.15 | −1.15 | 1.3225 |
| Ms. Goodwin | 10 | 6 | 11 | 11.00 | 0.00 | 0.0000 |
| | | | | | $ 0.00* | 2.6500 |

---

*Must equal 0.

In this problem, $n = 5$ (five salespeople) and $k = 2$ (two independent variables). Solving for the multiple standard error of estimate:

$$s_{y \cdot 12} = \sqrt{\frac{\Sigma(Y - Y')^2}{n - (k + 1)}} = \sqrt{\frac{2.65}{5 - 2 - 1}} = 1.151 \text{ (in \$000)}$$

The standard error of estimate computed in Chapter 14 involving only sales and test scores was \$1,955. Adding one additional independent variable (achievement rating) reduced the error in making a prediction to \$1,151. Of course, this signifies that adding a second independent variable made the sales predictions more precise.

### INTERPRETATION

If the weekly sales are distributed normally about the multiple regression plane, approximately 68 percent of the sales would fall within \$1,151 of their estimated $Y'$ value. And 95.5 percent of the weekly sales would be within $2s_{y \cdot 12}$, that is, within 2(\$1,151) of the $Y'$ value predicted by the equation. Further, approximately 99.7 percent of the sales would be within $\pm 3s_{y \cdot 12}$.

Chapter 14 used the standard error of estimate to construct confidence intervals. The procedure for constructing these intervals in the multiple regression case is somewhat similar to that followed in simple regression and will not be detailed here.

### Self-Review 15–2

*The answers are at the end of the chapter.*

The multiple regression equation for Exercise 4 was given as $Y' = 62.65 - 1.86X_1 - 0.52X_2$, where $X_1$ is the amount of insulation installed in the attic and $X_2$ is the outdoor temperature.

1. For a home installing 8 inches of insulation and for an outdoor temperature of 45 degrees F, what is the estimated natural gas consumption?

2. For the Goldman home, with 8 inches of insulation and an outdoor temperature of 45 degrees F, the actual natural gas consumption was 22.0 cubic feet. What is the difference between the actual consumption and the best estimate of natural gas consumption for the Goldman home? What is this difference called?

## ASSUMPTIONS ABOUT MULTIPLE REGRESSION AND CORRELATION

Before beginning our discussion of multiple correlation, we will list the assumptions underlying both multiple regression and multiple correlation. As noted in several previous chapters, we need to identify the assumptions because if they are not fully met, the results might be biased. For instance, in selecting a sample, we assume that all the items in the population have a chance of being selected. If our research involves surveying all those who ski, but we ignore those over 40 because we believe they are "too old," we would be biasing the responses toward the younger skiers. It should be mentioned, however, that in actual practice strict adherence to the following assumptions is not always possible in multiple regression and correlation problems involving the ever-changing business climate. But the statistical techniques discussed in this chapter appear to work well even when one or more of the following assumptions are violated. Even if the values in the multiple regression equation are "off" slightly, our estimates based on the equation will be closer than any that could otherwise be made.

Courtesy Wyoming Division of Tourism

Each of the following assumptions will be discussed in more detail as we progress through the chapter.

1. The independent variables and the dependent variable have a linear, or straight-line, relationship.
2. The dependent variable must be continuous and at least interval-scale.

**Homoscedasticty**

3. The variation in the difference between the actual and the predicted values must be the same for all fitted values of Y. That is, $(Y - Y')$ must be approximately the same for all values of $Y'$. When this is the case, differences exhibit **homoscedasticity.** Further, the residuals, computed by $Y - Y'$, should be normally distributed with a mean of 0.

**Autocorrelation**

4. Successive observations of the dependent variable must be uncorrelated. Violation of this assumption is called **autocorrelation.** Autocorrelation often happens when data are collected over periods of time.

**Multicollinearity**

5. The independent variables should not be highly correlated with each other. When the independent variables are highly correlated, it is called **multicollinearity.**

Statistical tests are available to detect homoscedasticity, autocorrelation, and multicollinearity. For those interested, these tests are covered in more advanced textbooks such as *Applied Linear Regression Models* by Neter, Wasserman, and Kutner (2nd ed., 1989, published by Richard D. Irwin, Inc.).

## MULTIPLE CORRELATION ANALYSIS

Three coefficients describe relationship between the Xs and Y

The same three coefficients cited in simple correlation analysis (Chapter 13) to describe the relationship between the dependent and independent variables are used in multiple correlation analysis. They are the *coefficient of multiple correlation,* the *coefficient of multiple determination,* and the *coefficient of multiple nondetermination.*

## COEFFICIENT OF MULTIPLE CORRELATION

> **Coefficient of multiple correlation**   A measure of the strength of the association between the dependent variable and two or more independent variables.

*R ranges between 0 and 1 inclusive*

The coefficient of multiple correlation can have any value between 0 and $+1.00$ inclusive and is designated $R$. Multiple $R$ is always positive. A coefficient of .94 indicates a very strong association between the dependent and independent variables. A coefficient of .09 reveals a very weak relationship.

*Is the relationship weak, moderate, or strong?*

## COEFFICIENT OF MULTIPLE DETERMINATION

$R^2$ *measures proportion of total variation in Y accounted for by the Xs*

The coefficient of multiple correlation permits us to say that the coefficient .94 indicates a "very strong" association between the dependent and independent variables. A more meaningful and precise measure of association is the *coefficient of multiple determination, $R^2$*. (Note that it is found by squaring the coefficient of multiple correlation.) Obviously, if we know the coefficient of multiple determination, $R^2$, the coefficient of correlation $R$ can be found by taking its square root.

> **Coefficient of multiple determination**   The proportion (percent) of the total variation in the dependent variable $Y$ that is explained by the set of independent variables.

## COEFFICIENT OF MULTIPLE NONDETERMINATION

Logically, the *coefficient of multiple nondetermination* measures the proportion of the total variation in the dependent variable $Y$ that is *not* accounted for by the independent variables. It is found by $1 - R^2$.

### ■ EXAMPLE

Exercise 4 involved the relationship between the amount of natural gas consumed ($Y$) and the two independent variables—the thickness of the attic insulation and the outdoor temperature. Suppose the coefficient of multiple determination is computed to be .81.

1. Interpret the coefficient of multiple determination.
2. What is the coefficient of nondetermination? Interpret.
3. What is the coefficient of multiple correlation? Interpret.
4. The two independent variables do not explain all (100 percent) of the variation in natural gas consumption. What other factors might be affecting natural gas usage?

### ☑ SOLUTION

1. Of the variation in natural gas consumption, 81 percent is explained by the thickness of the attic insulation and the outdoor temperature.
2. Therefore, 19 percent of the variation in natural gas consumption is *not* explained by the thickness of the insulation and outdoor temperature: $1 - R^2 = 1 - .81 = .19$.
3. .90, found by $\sqrt{.81}$. This indicates a very strong association between natural gas consumption and the two independent variables (insulation thickness and outdoor temperature).
4. How many times a month the outside doors are opened and closed and the strength of the wind may be other factors affecting natural gas consumption.

## THE ANOVA TABLE

As mentioned previously, the calculations involved in multiple regression are lengthy. Fortunately, many computer programs are available. Most of them output the information in fairly standard format. The following, from the MINITAB system for the weekly sales data in Table 15–1, is typical. It includes the regression equation and the analysis of variance table. We have described the meaning of the terms in the regression equation $Y' = 3.500 - 0.9750X_1 + 2.875X_2$. We will discuss the "Coef," "Stdev," and "t-ratio" columns later.

```
MTB > set c1
DATA> 5,12,4,8,11
DATA> end
MTB > set c2
DATA> 4,7,3,6,10
DATA> end
MTB > set c3
DATA> 2,5,1,4,6,
DATA> end
MTB > name c1 'sales' c2 'score' c3 'rating'
MTB > regr c1 2 c2 c3

The regression equation is
sales =3.50 - 0.975 score + 2.87 rating

Predictor        Coef      Stdev     t-ratio
Constant        3.500      1.628       2.15
score         -0.9750     0.8439      -1.16
rating          2.875      1.115       2.58

s=1.151       R-sq=94.7%        R-sq(adj)=89.4%

Analysis of Variance

SOURCE        DF        SS         MS
Regression     2     47.350     23.675
Error          2      2.650      1.325
Total          4     50.000
```

ANOVA table

Let's focus on the ANOVA table. How is it calculated? It is similar to the ANOVA table described in Chapter 12. In that chapter the variation was divided into two components—that due to the *treatments* and that due to random *error*. Here the total variation is also divided into two components—that explained by the regression, i.e., the independent variables, and the error, or unexplained variation. These two categories (regression and error) are identified in the "source" column. The column headed "DF" indicates the degrees of freedom. In this example there are five observations, so $n = 5$. The *total* number of degrees of freedom is $n - 1$. In this case $n - 1 = 5 - 1 = 4$ degrees of freedom. The degrees of freedom in the "regression" row of the ANOVA table is equal to the number of independent variables. We use $k$ to represent the number of independent variables, so $k = 2$. The degrees of freedom in the "error" row is $n - (k + 1) = 5 - (2 + 1) = 2$ degrees of freedom.

SS

The term SS (middle column of the ANOVA table) refers to the sum of squares, or the variation. These terms are computed as follows:

$$\text{Total variation} = \text{SS total} = \Sigma(Y - \overline{Y})^2 = 50.00$$
$$\text{Error variation} = \text{SSE} = \Sigma(Y - Y')^2 = 2.650$$
$$\text{Regression variation} = \text{SSR} = \text{SS total} - \text{SSE} = 50.000 - 2.650 = 47.350$$

MS

The right column, headed MS (mean square), is obtained by dividing the SS term by the DF term. Thus, MSR, the mean square regression, is found by SSR / $k$ and MSE by SSE / $[n - (k + 1)]$.

ANOVA table

The general format of the analysis of variance table, therefore, is:

| Source | df | SS | MS |
|---|---|---|---|
| Regression | $k$ | SSR | MSR = SSR / $k$ |
| Error | $n - (k + 1)$ | SSE | MSE = SSE / $[n - (k + 1)]$ |
| Total | $n - 1$ | SS total | |

The coefficient of multiple determination, $R^2$, can be arrived at from the ANOVA table. Recall that the coefficient of determination is the percent of the variation explained by the regression. It is the variation explained by the regression divided by the total variation.

$$R^2 = \frac{\text{SSR}}{\text{SS total}} = \frac{47.350}{50.000} = .947$$

This procedure was discussed at length near the end of Chapter 14. The multiple standard error of estimate may also be obtained directly from the analysis of variance table:

$$s_{y \cdot 12} = \sqrt{\frac{\text{SSE}}{n - (k + 1)}} = \sqrt{\frac{2.650}{5 - (2 + 1)}} = 1.151$$

The computation of the standard error of estimate from an ANOVA table was also examined near the end of Chapter 14. These values, $R^2 = .947$ and $s_{y \cdot 12} = 1.151$, are included in the preceding MINITAB output.

## A CASE STUDY

To cite an example of the use of multiple regression and correlation, and to show the universal application of a computer in problem solving, we will expand on an earlier exercise. Suppose a large, nationwide real estate firm wants to develop some guidelines for prospective buyers of small, single-family houses the firm lists. One of the most common questions prospective buyers ask is: If we purchased this home, what would we probably pay for heat during the winter months? The agent considered four variables important in predicting heating costs: (1) average daily minimum outside temperature, (2) number of inches of insulation in the attic, (3) number of windows in the house, and (4) age of the furnace.

The agent had 20 local offices in various sections of the country gather information on the small houses they had listed. (See Table 15–3.)

## TABLE 15–3

### Cost of Heating and Other Characteristics about Small Houses

| Small home | Heating cost (in dollars), $Y$ | Minimum outside temperature, $X_1$ | Inches of insulation, $X_2$ | Number of windows, $X_3$ | Age of furnace, $X_4$ |
|---|---|---|---|---|---|
| 1 | 250 | 35 | 3 | 10 | 6 |
| 2 | 360 | 29 | 4 | 1 | 10 |
| 3 | 165 | 36 | 7 | 9 | 3 |
| 4 | 43 | 60 | 6 | 8 | 9 |
| 5 | 92 | 65 | 5 | 8 | 6 |
| 6 | 200 | 30 | 5 | 9 | 5 |
| 7 | 355 | 10 | 6 | 14 | 7 |
| 8 | 290 | 7 | 10 | 9 | 10 |
| 9 | 230 | 21 | 9 | 11 | 11 |
| 10 | 120 | 55 | 2 | 9 | 5 |
| 11 | 73 | 54 | 12 | 11 | 4 |
| 12 | 205 | 48 | 5 | 10 | 1 |
| 13 | 400 | 20 | 5 | 12 | 15 |
| 14 | 320 | 39 | 4 | 10 | 7 |
| 15 | 72 | 60 | 8 | 8 | 6 |
| 16 | 272 | 20 | 5 | 10 | 8 |
| 17 | 94 | 58 | 7 | 10 | 3 |
| 18 | 190 | 40 | 8 | 11 | 11 |
| 19 | 235 | 27 | 9 | 14 | 8 |
| 20 | 139 | 30 | 7 | 9 | 5 |

Four independent variables, one dependent variable

There are four independent variables, designated $X_1$, $X_2$, $X_3$, and $X_4$. The dependent variable, the cost of heating, is $Y$. In order to visualize the relationship between some of the independent variables and the dependent variable (cost), scatter diagrams have been drawn.

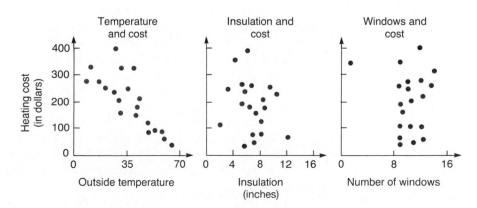

Of the three independent variables shown, it does appear that the strongest correlation exists between minimum outside temperature and heating cost. Observing the wide scatter, one might conclude that there is practically no relationship between the number of windows in the house and heating cost.

### CORRELATION MATRIX

Correlation matrix

As a first step in analyzing the factors involved in the cost of heating a home, we develop a **correlation matrix.** A correlation matrix shows the simple correlation coefficients among all the variables. The output from MINITAB is as follows:

```
MTB > C1-C5
                 cost         temp        insul       window
temp           -0.812
insul          -0.257       -0.103
window          0.097       -0.256        0.307
age             0.537       -0.486        0.064        0.030
```

Cost is the dependent variable, $Y$. We are particularly interested in which independent variable has the strongest correlation with cost. As indicated in the output, temperature has the strongest correlation ($-.812$) with cost. The negative sign indicates that as temperature increases, the cost to heat the home decreases. The independent variable $X_3$, number of windows, has a very weak association with cost (.097). It is likely this variable will be dropped from further analysis.

Multicollinearity

A second use of the correlation matrix is to check for multicollinearity. Multicollinearity occurs when the independent variables are themselves correlated. This distorts the standard error of estimate and may lead to incorrect conclusions regarding which variables are significant and which are not. In this example, the correlation between the age of the furnace and outside temperature is $-.486$. This is not large enough to cause a problem. A common rule of thumb is that correlations among the independent variables from $-.70$ to .70 do not cause problems.

## GLOBAL TEST: TESTING WHETHER OR NOT THE MULTIPLE REGRESSION MODEL IS VALID

The overall ability of the independent variables $X_1$, $X_2$, . . . , $X_k$ to explain the behavior of the dependent variable $Y$ can be tested. To put this in question form: Can the dependent variable be estimated without relying on the independent variables? The

Global test

test used is referred to as the **global test.** Basically, it investigates whether all the independent variables have zero net regression coefficients. To put it another way, could the amount of explained variation, $R^2$, occur by chance?

To relate this question to the heating cost problem, we will test whether the independent variables (amount of insulation in the attic, minimum daily temperature, age of furnace, and number of windows) are capable of predicting home heating costs.

Null hypothesis

Recall that in testing a hypothesis, we first state the null hypothesis and the alternate hypothesis. In the heating cost problem, there are four independent variables. Recall that $b_1$, $b_2$, $b_3$, and $b_4$ are sample net regression coefficients. The corresponding coefficients in the population are given the symbols $\beta_1$, $\beta_2$, $\beta_3$, and $\beta_4$. We now test whether the net regression coefficients in the population are zero. The null hypothesis is:

$$H_0 : \beta_1 = \beta_2 = \beta_3 = \beta_4 = 0$$

Alternate hypothesis

The alternate hypothesis is:

$$H_1: \text{Not all the } \beta\text{s are 0.}$$

If the null hypothesis is true, it implies that the regression coefficients are all zero and, logically, are of no use in predicting the dependent variable (heating cost). Should that be the case, we would have to search for some other independent variables—or take a different approach—to predict home heating costs.

F test applied

To test the null hypothesis that the multiple regression coefficients are all zero, we apply the $F$ test introduced in Chapter 12. We will use the .05 level of significance. Recall these characteristics of the $F$ distribution:

1. It is positively skewed, with the critical value for the .05 level located in the right tail. The critical value is the point that separates the region where $H_0$ is not rejected from the region of rejection.
2. It is constructed by knowing the number of degrees of freedom in the numerator and the number of degrees of freedom in the denominator.

The degrees of freedom for the numerator and the denominator may be found in the computer summary. That portion of the table is included below. The top number in the column marked "DF" is 4, indicating that there are 4 degrees of freedom in the numerator. The middle number in the "DF" column (15) indicates that there are 15 degrees of freedom in the denominator. The number 15 is found by $n - (k + 1) = 20 - (4 + 1) = 15$. The number 4 corresponds to the number of independent variables.

```
Analysis of Variance

SOURCE          DF        SS        MS
Regression       4    171227     42807  =  MSR
Error           15     41689      2779  =  MSE
Total           19    212916
```

The value of $F$ is computed by dividing the MSR term by MSE.

$$F = \frac{\dfrac{SSR}{k}}{\dfrac{SSE}{n - (k + 1)}} = \frac{MSR}{MSE} = \frac{42,807}{2,779} = 15.40$$

Diagram showing regions of acceptance and rejection

The critical value of $F$ is found in Appendix G. Using the table for the .05 level, move horizontally to 4 degrees of freedom in the numerator, read down to 15 degrees of freedom in the denominator, and read the critical value. It is 3.06. The region where $H_0$ is not rejected and the region where $H_0$ is rejected are shown in the following diagram.

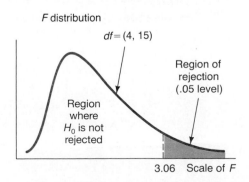

F distribution

$df = (4, 15)$

Region of rejection (.05 level)

Region where $H_0$ is not rejected

3.06   Scale of F

Decision rule    Continuing with the global test, the decision rule is: Do not reject the null hypothesis that all the regression coefficients are 0 if the computed value of $F$ is less than or equal to 3.06. If computed $F$ is greater than 3.06, reject $H_0$ and accept the alternate hypothesis, $H_1$.

The decision    The computed value of $F$ is 15.40, which is in the rejection region. The null hypothesis that all the multiple regression coefficients are zero is therefore rejected. The alternate hypothesis is accepted, indicating that not all the regression coefficients are zero. From a practical standpoint, this means that the independent variables (amount of insulation, etc.) do have the ability to explain the variation in the dependent variable (heating cost). We expected this decision. Logically, the outside temperature, the amount of insulation, and so on have a great bearing on heating costs. The global test assures us that they do.

## EVALUATING INDIVIDUAL REGRESSION COEFFICIENTS

In the heating cost problem, we showed that some, but not necessarily all, of the regression coefficients are not equal to zero. The next step is to test the variables *individually* to determine which ones are not zero.

Why is it important to find out if it is possible that any of the $\beta$s equal 0? If a $\beta$ does equal 0, it implies that this particular independent variable is of no value in explaining any variation in the dependent variable. If there are coefficients for which $H_0$ cannot be rejected, we may want to eliminate them from the regression equation.

We will now test four separate hypotheses—for temperature, for insulation, for windows, and for furnace.

| For temperature: | For insulation: | For windows: | For furnace: |
|---|---|---|---|
| $H_0: \beta_1 = 0$ | $H_0: \beta_2 = 0$ | $H_0: \beta_3 = 0$ | $H_0: \beta_4 = 0$ |
| $H_1: \beta_1 \neq 0$ | $H_1: \beta_2 \neq 0$ | $H_1: \beta_3 \neq 0$ | $H_1: \beta_4 \neq 0$ |

We will test the hypotheses at the .05 level. The way the alternate hypothesis is stated indicates that the test is two-tailed.

The test statistic is the Student $t$ distribution with $n - (k + 1)$ degrees of freedom. The number of sample observations is $n$. There are 20 homes in the study, so $n = 20$. The number of independent variables is $k$, which is 4. Thus, there are $n - (k + 1) = 20 - (4 + 1) = 15$ degrees of freedom.

The critical value for $t$ is in Appendix F. For a two-tailed test with 15 degrees of freedom and using the .05 significance level, $H_0$ is rejected if $t$ is less than $-2.131$ or greater than 2.131. The MINITAB system produced the following output.

```
The regression equation is
cost = 425 - 4.57 temp - 14.9 insul + 0.24 window + 6.13 age

Predictor        Coef      Stdev    t-ratio    p-value
Constant        424.74     79.23       5.36      0.000
temp            -4.5719    0.8272     -5.53      0.000
insul          -14.906     5.140      -2.90      0.011
window           0.244     4.953       0.05      0.961
age              6.126     4.175       1.47      0.163

s = 52.72      R-sq = 80.4%      R-sq(adj) = 75.2%
```

The column headed "Coef" gives the multiple regression equation:

$$Y' = 424.74 - 4.5719X_1 - 14.906X_2 + 0.244X_3 + 6.126X_4$$

Interpreting the term $-4.5719X_1$ in the equation: For each degree the temperature increases, it is expected that the heating cost will decrease about $4.57, holding the other three variables constant.

The column on the MINITAB output labeled "Stdev" indicates the standard deviation of the sample regression coefficient. Recall that we selected a sample of heating costs in various sections of the country. If we were to select a second sample at random and compute the regression coefficients of that sample, the values would not be exactly the same. If we were to repeat the sampling process many times, however, we could design a sampling distribution of the regression coefficients. The column labeled "Stdev" estimates the variability of these regression coefficients. The sampling distribution of Coef/Stdev follows the $t$ distribution with $n - (k + 1)$ degrees of freedom. Hence, we are able to test the independent variables individually to determine if the net regression coefficients differ from zero. The computed $t$ ratio is $-5.53$ for temperature and $-2.90$ for insulation. Both of these $t$ values are in the rejection region to the left of $-2.131$. Thus, we conclude that the regression coefficients for the temperature and insulation variables are *not* zero. The computed $t$ ratios for window (0.05) and age (1.47) are in the region between 0 and 2.131. Therefore, these two independent variables are not significant predictors. In Chapter 11, we described how a $p$-value is used to interpret the strength of the rejection. $p$-values are also reported on this output. The value .011 in the $p$-value column and insulation row is the two-tailed probability of a $t$-value less than $-2.90$ or greater than 2.90, given a true $H_0$. In summary, we recommend that the independent variables windows and furnace age be removed from the study and variables temperature and insulation retained.

*p*-value

## Self-Review 15–3

*The answers are at the end of the chapter.*

The multiple regression and correlation data for the preceding heating cost problem were rerun on the computer using only the two significant independent variables—temperature and insulation. (See MINITAB output.)

1. What is the new multiple regression equation? (Temperature is $X_1$ and insulation $X_2$.)

2. What is the coefficient of multiple determination? Interpret.

3. What is the coefficient of nondetermination? Interpret.

4. How can you tell that these two independent variables are of value in predicting heating costs?

5. What is the $p$-value of insulation? Interpret.

```
The regression equation is
cost = 490 - 5.15 temp - 14.7 insul

Predictor        Coef      Stdev    t-ratio   p-value
Constant       490.29      44.41      11.04     0.000
temp          -5.1499     0.7019      -7.34     0.000
insul         -14.718      4.934      -2.98     0.008

s = 52.98      R-sq =77.6%      R-sq(adj) = 74.9%

Analysis of Variance

SOURCE        DF        SS       MS       F    p-value
Regression     2    165195    82597   29.42     0.000
Error         17     47721     2807
Total         19    212916
```

As noted in Self-Review 15–3 and the accompanying output, the multiple regression problem was run again using MINITAB but only two variables—"temperature" and "insulation" were included. These two variables explained 77.6 percent of the variation in heating cost. Using all four variables—temperature, insulation, windows, and age—a total of 80.4 percent of the variation is explained. The additional two variables have increased $R^2$ by only 2.8 percent—a rather small increase for the addition of two independent variables. It probably would not be worth the cost to count the windows in a home and determine the age of the furnace since these two factors explain very little variation in heating cost.

## QUALITATIVE VARIABLES IN REGRESSION

**Qualitative variables**

So far the variables used to estimate the cost of heating a home have been *quantitative;* that is, they have been numerical in nature. Frequently, we wish to use variables that are not numerical in nature. These variables are called **qualitative variables** or **dummy variables.**

For example, we might be interested in estimating an executive's salary based on years of job experience and whether or not he or she graduated from college. We surmise that a graduate will earn a larger salary than someone who did not graduate. "Graduation from college" can take on only one of two conditions—yes or no. Thus, it is considered a qualitative variable.

Suppose in the heating cost study the independent variable "stories" is added. For those homes with one story a 0 is used; for homes with two stories a 1 is used. Assume that all the homes in the study have either one or two stories. We will refer to the "stories" variable as $X_5$. The data from Table 15–4 are entered into the MINITAB system.

---

### TABLE 15–4

**Home Heating Costs, Temperature, Insulation, and Number of Stories for a Sample of 20 Homes**

| Cost, $Y$ | Temperature, $X_1$ | Insulation, $X_2$ | Stories, $X_5$ |
|---|---|---|---|
| 250 | 35 | 3 | 0 |
| 360 | 29 | 4 | 1 |
| 165 | 36 | 7 | 0 |
| 43 | 60 | 6 | 0 |
| 92 | 65 | 5 | 0 |
| 200 | 30 | 5 | 0 |
| 355 | 10 | 6 | 1 |
| 290 | 7 | 10 | 1 |
| 230 | 21 | 9 | 0 |
| 120 | 55 | 2 | 0 |
| 73 | 54 | 12 | 0 |
| 205 | 48 | 5 | 1 |
| 400 | 20 | 5 | 1 |
| 320 | 39 | 4 | 1 |
| 72 | 60 | 8 | 0 |
| 272 | 20 | 5 | 1 |
| 94 | 58 | 7 | 0 |
| 190 | 40 | 8 | 1 |
| 235 | 27 | 9 | 0 |
| 139 | 30 | 7 | 0 |

---

The output from MINITAB is:

```
MTB > NAME C6 'STORIES'
MTB > REGR C1 3 C2 C3 C6

The regression equation is
cost = 394 - 3.96 temp - 11.3 insul + 77.4 stories

Predictor        Coef      Stdev    t-ratio    p-value
Constant       393.67      45.00       8.75      0.000
temp          -3.9628     0.6527      -6.07      0.000
insul         -11.334      4.002      -2.83      0.012
stories         77.43      22.78       3.40      0.004

s = 41.62       R-sq = 87.0%      R-sq(adj) = 84.5%

Analysis of Variance

SOURCE         DF        SS        MS       F    p-value
Regression      3    185202     61734   35.64      0.000
Error          16     27713      1732
Total          19    212916
```

What is the effect of the variable "stories"? Should it be included in the analysis? To show the effect of the variable, suppose we have a one-story house and a two-story house next to each other in Buffalo, New York. Both homes have 3 inches of insulation, and the mean January temperature in Buffalo is 20 degrees. For the single-story house, a 0 is substituted for $X_5$ in the regression equation. The estimated heating cost is $280.90, found by:

$$Y' = 394 - 3.96X_1 - 11.3X_2 + 77.4X_5$$
$$= 394 - 3.96(20) - 11.3(3) + 77.4(0) = 280.90$$

For the two-story house, a 1 is substituted for $X_5$ in the regression equation. The estimated heating cost is $358.30, found by:

$$Y' = 394 - 3.96X_1 - 11.3X_2 + 77.4X_5$$
$$= 394 - 3.96(20) - 11.3(3) + 77.4(1) = 358.30$$

The difference between the estimated heating costs is $77.40 ($358.30 − $280.90). Hence, we can expect the cost to heat the two-story house to be $77.40 more than the cost for an equivalent single-story house.

We have shown the difference between the two types of homes to be $77.40, but is the difference significant? We conduct the following test of hypothesis.

$$H_0: \beta_5 = 0$$
$$H_1: \beta_5 \neq 0$$

The information necessary to answer the above question can be found in the MINITAB output given above. The computed $t$ ratio is 3.40. There are three independent variables in the analysis, so there are $n - (k + 1) = 20 - (3 + 1) = 16$ degrees of freedom. The critical value from Appendix F is 2.120. The decision rule, using a two-tailed test and the .05 significance level, is to reject $H_0$ if the computed $t$ is to the left of −2.120 or to the right of 2.120. Since the computed value of 3.40 is to the right of 2.120, the null hypothesis is rejected. It is concluded that the regression coefficient is not zero. The independent variable "stories" should be included in the analysis.

# STEPWISE REGRESSION

The regression equation we developed for the heating cost problem included three independent variables: minimum average temperature, inches of insulation, and number of stories the home has. To obtain this equation, we first ran a global or "all at once" test to determine if any of the regression coefficients were significant. When we found at least one to be significant, we then tested the coefficients individually to determine which were significant. We dropped those that were not significant and retained the others. We argued that by retaining the significant coefficients, we found the regression equation that used the fewest independent variables possible, making it easy to interpret and explaining as much of the variation in the dependent variable as possible. We are now going to describe a technique called **stepwise regression,** which is more efficient in building the equation.

*The stepwise technique*

In the stepwise method, a sequence of equations is developed. The first equation contains only one independent variable. However, this independent variable is the one from the set of proposed variables that explains the most variation in the dependent variable. Stated differently, if all the simple correlations between each independent variable and the dependent variable are computed, the stepwise method selects the independent variable with the largest correlation with the dependent variable.

Next, the stepwise method looks at the remaining independent variables and selects the one that will explain the largest percentage of the variation yet unexplained. This process is continued until all the independent variables with significant net regression coefficients are included in the equation. The advantages to the stepwise method are: (1) Only significant regression coefficients are included in the equation, (2) the steps involved in building the equation are clearly seen, and (3) the step-by-step changes in the standard error of estimate and the coefficient of determination are shown.

The stepwise MINITAB output for the heating problem follows. Note that the final equation includes the same three variables we obtained using the preceding global test. The variables with nonsignificant regression coefficients have been eliminated.

```
MTB > STEP C1 C2 - C6
STEPWISE REGRESSION OF COST ON 5 PREDICTORS, WITHIN N = 20
      STEP          1          2          3
CONSTANT        388.8      300.3      393.7

temp            -4.93      -3.56      -3.96
T-RATIO         -5.89      -4.70      -6.07

stories                       93         77
T-RATIO                     3.56       3.40

insul                                -11.3
T-RATIO                              -2.83

S                63.6       49.5       41.6
R-SQ            65.85      80.46      86.98
```

Reviewing the steps: The regression equation after the first step is:

$$Y' = 388.8 - 4.93X_1$$

The independent variable "temperature" explains 65.85 percent of the variation in heating cost. The standard error of estimate is $63.60.

The next independent variable to enter the equation is the variable for the number of stories. Including the two independent variables "temperature" and "stories," the $R$-square term is increased from 65.85 percent to 80.46 percent. That is, by adding the second variable, "stories," $R^2$ increased 14.61 percentage points. This increase is larger than the increase would have been if any other independent variable had been added. The regression equation after step 2 is:

$$Y' = 300.3 - 3.56X_1 + 93.0X_5$$

Usually the regression coefficients will change from one step to the next. In this case the coefficient for temperature has retained its negative sign, but it changed from $-4.93$ to $-3.56$. This change is reflective of the added influence of the independent variable "stories." Why did the stepwise method select the variable for stories instead of the variable for insulation? Again, it is because the increase in $R^2$ (the coefficient of determination) is larger if stories is used than if insulation were used.

After the third step the regression equation is:

$$Y' = 393.7 - 3.96X_1 - 11.3X_2 + 77.0X_5$$

This is the same equation we obtained using the global test followed by the individual test on each of the regression coefficients. The $R^2$ value is 86.98 percent, the same as calculated earlier. Thus, with the stepwise method we have developed the same regression equation, and it consists of the same variables. However, the stepwise method offers a more direct route to the optimal equation.

## ANALYSIS OF RESIDUALS

In an earlier section we described the basic assumptions required for regression and correlation analysis. These assumptions are:

1. There is a linear (straight-line) relationship between the dependent variable and the independent variables.
2. The dependent variable is interval- or ratio-scale.
3. The independent variables are not correlated.
4. Successive observations of the dependent variable are not correlated.
5. The differences between the actual values and the estimated values are approximately normally distributed, and they are the same for all estimated values.

Residuals

The last assumption can be verified by plotting the **residuals.** A residual is the difference between the actual value of $Y$ and the predicted value of $Y$, namely, $(Y - Y')$.

| |
|---|
| Residual    The difference between the actual value of $Y$ and the predicted value of $Y$. |

The MINITAB system is useful for investigating if the residuals are normally distributed and also if they have a constant variance around the values of $Y'$. Table 15–5 presents the data necessary for further analysis of the heating cost problem. Column 1 shows the actual heating costs, originally presented in Table 15–3. Column

2 presents the fitted or estimated value of $Y$; this is $Y'$. The $Y'$ value can be obtained by substituting the actual values of the three independent variables into the regression equation. For example, the first fitted value is 221.08, found by:

$$Y' = 393.67 - 3.96(35) - 11.33(3) + 77.43(0) = 221.08$$

(The difference between 221.08 and the value 220.964 in Table 15−5 is due to rounding in the computer software.) The residual in column 3 is 29.0358, found by 250.00 − 220.96. The residuals for the other 19 observations are computed similarly.

---

### TABLE 15−5

**Summary of Actual Costs, Estimated Costs, and Residuals for Heating Cost Problem**

| Home | Actual cost, $Y$ | Estimated cost, $Y'$ | Residual, $Y - Y'$ |
|------|------|------|------|
| 1  | 250 | 220.964 | 29.0358 |
| 2  | 360 | 310.839 | 49.1606 |
| 3  | 165 | 171.665 | −6.6655 |
| 4  | 43  | 87.891  | −44.8911 |
| 5  | 92  | 79.411  | 12.5892 |
| 6  | 200 | 218.110 | −18.1105 |
| 7  | 355 | 363.466 | −8.4656 |
| 8  | 290 | 330.018 | −40.0183 |
| 9  | 230 | 208.440 | 21.5597 |
| 10 | 120 | 153.041 | −33.0412 |
| 11 | 73  | 43.664  | 29.3355 |
| 12 | 205 | 224.211 | −19.2113 |
| 13 | 400 | 335.171 | 64.8289 |
| 14 | 320 | 271.211 | 48.7891 |
| 15 | 72  | 65.223  | 6.7768 |
| 16 | 272 | 335.171 | −63.1711 |
| 17 | 94  | 84.483  | 9.5171 |
| 18 | 190 | 221.912 | −31.9123 |
| 19 | 235 | 184.663 | 50.3368 |
| 20 | 139 | 195.443 | −56.4426 |

---

The fitted values and the residuals can be computed by MINITAB. The following statements are required to place the fitted values in C11 and the residuals in C20 of the MINITAB output. (The information in C10 is not described here but is required to obtain the fitted values from MINITAB.) The ";" at the end of the first line and the "." at the end of the second line are required.

```
MTB> regr c1 3 c2 c3 c6, c10 c11;
SUBC> residuals c20.
```

The MINITAB system also develops both a stem-and-leaf display, introduced in Chapter 2 (see Chart 15−1), and a histogram (see Chart 15−2) for the residuals. Both charts indicate that the distribution of the residuals is somewhat normal, as required in the assumptions. To interpret the histogram in Chart 15–2, note that it is constructed so the residuals are tallied in classes: −50 through −69, with a midpoint of −60; −30 through −59, with a midpoint of −40; and so on. Some of the classes are:

| Class | Midpoint | Residuals | Count |
|---|---|---|---|
| −50 through −69 | −60 | −63.1711, −56.4426 | 2 |
| −30 through −49 | −40 | −44.8911, −40.0183 | 4 |
|  |  | −33.0142, −31.9123 |  |
| −10 through −29 | −20 | −18.1105, −19.2113 | 2 |

## CHART 15−1

**Stem-and-Leaf Display of Residuals**

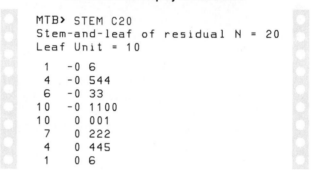

```
MTB> STEM C20
Stem-and-leaf of residual N = 20
Leaf Unit = 10

 1   -0 6
 4   -0 544
 6   -0 33
10   -0 1100
10    0 001
 7    0 222
 4    0 445
 1    0 6
```

## CHART 15−2

**Histogram of Residuals**

MTB > GHISTOGRAM C20

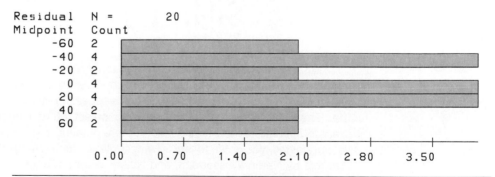

| Residual Midpoint | Count |
|---|---|
| −60 | 2 |
| −40 | 4 |
| −20 | 2 |
| 0 | 4 |
| 20 | 4 |
| 40 | 2 |
| 60 | 2 |

N = 20

0.00    0.70    1.40    2.10    2.80    3.50

**Homoscedasticity**

The assumptions for regression analysis also require that the residuals remain constant for all values of $Y'$. Recall that this condition is called **homoscedasticity.** To check for homoscedasticity, the residuals are plotted against the fitted values of $Y$ (see Chart 15–3). Because there is no more variation around large values of $Y'$ than around small values of $Y'$, we can conclude this assumption is met.

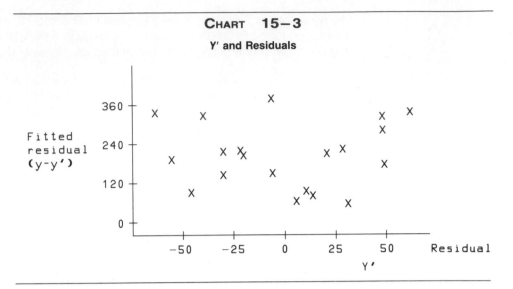

**CHART 15–3**

**Y' and Residuals**

Following are two examples where the homoscedasticity requirement is not met. Note that in the first example, the residuals are funnel-shaped. That is, as the fitted $Y$ values increase, so does the variation in the residuals. In the second example, there is a pattern to the residuals. The residuals seem to take the shape of a polynomial, or second-degree equation.

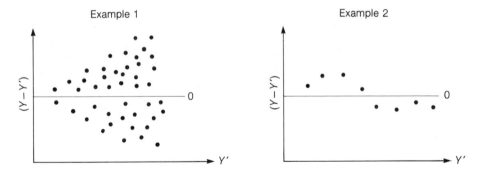

What problems are caused by residuals that fail to show homoscedasticity? The standard deviations of the regression coefficients will be understated (too small), causing potential independent variables to appear to be significant when they may not be. The remedy for this condition is to select other independent variables or to transform some of the variables. For a more detailed discussion of residual analysis, it is suggested you refer to an advanced text, such as *Applied Linear Regression Models* by Neter, Wasserman, and Kutner (Irwin, 1989).

## CHAPTER OUTLINE

I. Multiple regression and correlation analysis is based on these assumptions.
   A. There is a linear relationship between the independent variables and the dependent variable.
   B. The dependent variable is continuous and of interval scale.

    C.   The residual variation is the same for all fitted values of $Y$, and these residuals are normally distributed.

    D.   Successive observations of the dependent variable are uncorrelated.

    E.   The independent variables are not highly correlated.

II. The general form of the sample multiple regression equation is:

$$Y' = a + b_1X_1 + b_2X_2 + \cdots + b_kX_k$$

where $Y'$ is the estimated value, $a$ is the $Y$-intercept, the $b$s are the sample regression coefficients, and the $X$s represent the values of the various independent variables.

    A.   There can be an unlimited number of independent variables.

    B.   The least squares criterion is used to develop the equation.

    C.   A computer is needed to determine $a$ and the various $b$ values.

III. There are three measures of the effectiveness of the regression equation.

    A.   The multiple standard error of estimate is similar to the standard deviation.

        1. It is measured in the same units as the dependent variable.

        2. It is difficult to determine what is a large value and what is a small value of the standard error.

    B.   The coefficient of multiple correlation is similar to the simple correlation coefficient.

        1. It ranges from 0 to 1 inclusive.

        2. Strong associations are close to 1; weak ones are close to 0.

    C.   The coefficient of determination may range from 0 to 1.

        1. It shows the fraction of the variation in $Y$ that is explained by the set of independent variables.

        2. It is the square of the coefficient of multiple correlation.

IV. The ANOVA table gives the variation in the dependent variable that is explained by the regression equation, as well as that which is not explained.

V. A correlation matrix is used to show all possible simple correlation coefficients between all the variables.

VI. A global test is used to investigate whether any of the independent variables have significant regression coefficients.

    A.   The null hypothesis is: All the regression coefficients are zero.

    B.   The alternate hypothesis is: At least one regression coefficient is not zero.

    C.   The test statistic is the $F$ distribution with $k$ (the number of independent variables) and $n - (k + 1)$ degrees of freedom, where $n$ is the sample size.

VII. The test for individual variables is used to determine which independent variables have nonzero regression coefficients.

    A.   The variables that have zero regression coefficients are usually dropped from the analysis.

    B.   The test statistic is the $t$ distribution with $n - (k + 1)$ degrees of freedom.

VIII. Qualitative variables are nonnumeric.

    A.   They are also called dummy variables.

    B.   There are only two possible outcomes for a qualitative variable—such as male or female.

IX. A stepwise regression leads directly to the most efficient regression equation.

    A.   Only independent variables with significant regression coefficients are entered into the analysis.

    B.   Variables are entered in the order in which they increase the $R^2$ term the greatest amount.

X. A residual is the difference between the actual value of $Y$ and the predicted value of $Y$.

    A.   Residuals should be approximately normally distributed. Histograms and stem-and-leaf charts are useful in checking this requirement.

    B.   A plot of the residuals and their corresponding $Y'$ values is useful for showing that there are no trends or patterns in the residuals.

# EXERCISES

*The answers to the odd-numbered exercises are at the end of the book.*

5. The district manager of Jasons, a large discount retail chain, is investigating why certain stores in her region are performing better than others. She believes that three factors are related to total sales: the number of competitors in the region, the population in the surrounding area, and the amount spent on advertising. From her district, consisting of several hundred stores, she selects a random sample of 30 stores. For each store she gathered the following information.

$Y$ = total sales last year (in $000).
$X_1$ = number of competitors in the region.
$X_2$ = population (in millions).
$X_3$ = advertising expense (in $000).

The sample data were run on the MINITAB software package with the following results.

Analysis of variance

| Source | DF | SS | MS |
|---|---|---|---|
| Regression | 3 | 3050.00 | 762.50 |
| Error | 26 | 2200.00 | 84.62 |
| Total | 29 | 5250.00 | |

| Predictor | Coef | Stdev | t-ratio |
|---|---|---|---|
| Constant | 14.00 | 7.00 | 2.00 |
| $X_1$ | -1.00 | 0.70 | -1.43 |
| $X_2$ | 30.00 | 5.20 | 5.77 |
| $X_3$ | 0.20 | 0.08 | 2.50 |

a. What is the estimated sales for the Bryne Store, which has four competitors, population of 0.4 (400,000), and advertising expense of 30 ($30,000)?
b. Compute the $R^2$ value.
c. Compute the multiple standard error of estimate.
d. Conduct a global test of hypothesis to determine if any of the regression coefficients are not equal to zero. Use the .05 level of significance.
e. Conduct tests of hypotheses to determine which of the independent variables have significant regression coefficients. Which variables would you consider eliminating? Use the .05 significance level.

6. In a multiple regression equation $k$ = 5 and $n$ = 20, the MSE value is 5.10, and SS total is 519.68. At the .05 significance level, can we conclude that any of the regression coefficients are not equal to 0?

7. A multiple regression equation yields the following partial results.

| Source | Sum of squares | df |
|---|---|---|
| Regression | 750 | 4 |
| Error | 500 | 35 |

a. What is the total sample size?
b. How many independent variables are being considered?
c. Compute the coefficient of determination.

    d.   Compute the standard error of estimate.

    e.   Test the hypothesis that none of the regression coefficients is equal to zero. Let $\alpha = .05$.

8.  In a multiple regression equation two independent variables are considered, and the total sample size is 25. The regression coefficients and the standard errors are as follows.

$$b_1 = \phantom{-}2.676 \qquad s_{b1} = 0.56$$
$$b_2 = -0.880 \qquad s_{b2} = 0.71$$

Conduct a test of hypothesis to determine if either independent variable has a coefficient equal to zero. Would you consider deleting either variable from the regression equation? Use the .05 significance level.

9.  The following MINITAB output was obtained.

```
Analysis of variance

Source          DF          SS          MS
Regression       5         100          20
Error           20          40           2
Total           25         140

Predictor      Coef      Stdev     t-ratio
Constant       3.00       1.50        2.00
  X₁           4.00       3.00        1.33
  X₂           3.00       0.20       15.00
  X₃           0.20       0.05        4.00
  X₄          -2.50       1.00       -2.50
  X₅           3.00       4.00        0.75
```

    a.   What is the total sample size?

    b.   Compute the value of $R^2$.

    c.   Compute the multiple standard error of estimate.

    d.   Conduct a global test of hypothesis to determine if any of the regression coefficients are significant. Use the .05 significance level.

    e.   Test the regression coefficients individually. Would you consider omitting any variable(s)? If so, which one(s)? Use the .05 significance level.

10.  Suppose that the sales manager of a large automotive parts distributor wants to develop an objective tool to predict as early as April the total annual sales of a region. Based on regional sales, the total sales for the company can also be estimated. If, based on past experience, it is found that the April estimates of annual sales are reasonably accurate, then in future years the April forecast could be used to revise production schedules and maintain the correct inventory at the retail outlets.

    Several factors appear to be related to sales, including the number of retail outlets in the region stocking the company's parts, the number of automobiles in the region registered as of April 1, and the total personal income for the first quarter of the year. A total of five independent variables were finally selected as being the most important (according to the sales manager). Then the data were gathered for a recent year. The total annual sales for that year for each region were also recorded. Note in the following table that for region 1 there were 1,739 retail outlets stocking the company's automotive parts, there were 9,270,000 registered automobiles in the region as of April 1, and sales for that year were $37,702,000.

Courtesy Dana Corporation

| Annual sales ($ millions), Y | Number of retail outlets, $X_1$ | Number of automobiles registered (millions), $X_2$ | Personal income ($ billions), $X_3$ | Average age of automobiles (years), $X_4$ | Number of supervisors, $X_5$ |
|---|---|---|---|---|---|
| 37.702 | 1,739 | 9.27 | 85.4 | 3.5 | 9.0 |
| 24.196 | 1,221 | 5.86 | 60.7 | 5.0 | 5.0 |
| 32.055 | 1,846 | 8.81 | 68.1 | 4.4 | 7.0 |
| 3.611 | 120 | 3.81 | 20.2 | 4.0 | 5.0 |
| 17.625 | 1,096 | 10.31 | 33.8 | 3.5 | 7.0 |
| 45.919 | 2,290 | 11.62 | 95.1 | 4.1 | 13.0 |
| 29.600 | 1,687 | 8.96 | 69.3 | 4.1 | 15.0 |
| 8.114 | 241 | 6.28 | 16.3 | 5.9 | 11.0 |
| 20.116 | 649 | 7.77 | 34.9 | 5.5 | 16.0 |
| 12.994 | 1,427 | 10.92 | 15.1 | 4.1 | 10.0 |

The MINITAB software system was used to generate the following output.

a.  Consider the following correlation matrix. Which variable has the strongest correlation with the dependent variable? The correlations between the independent variables "outlets" and "income" and between "cars" and "outlets" is fairly strong. Could this be a problem? What is this condition called?

```
             sales    outlets     cars     income      age
  outlets    0.899
  cars       0.605      0.775
  income     0.964      0.825    0.409
  age       -0.323     -0.489   -0.447    -0.349
  bosses     0.286      0.183    0.395     0.155    0.291
```

b.  The following regression equation was obtained using the five independent variables. What percent of the variation is explained by the regression equation?

```
The regression equation is
sales = -19.7 - 0.00063 outlets + 1.74 cars + 0.410 income
        + 2.04 age - 0.034 bosses

         Predictor         Coef        Stdev      t-ratio
         Constant       -19.672        5.422        -3.63
         outlets      -0.000629     0.002638        -0.24
         cars           1.7399       0.5530         3.15
         income        0.40994      0.04385         9.35
         age            2.0357       0.8779         2.32
         bosses        -0.0344       0.1880        -0.18

Analysis of Variance

SOURCE         DF          SS           MS
Regression      5     1593.81       318.76
Error           4        9.08         2.27
Total           9     1602.89
```

c.  Conduct a global test of hypothesis to determine if any of the regression coefficients are not zero.

d.  Conduct a test of hypothesis on each of the independent variables. Would you consider eliminating "outlets" and "bosses"?

e. The regression has been rerun below, eliminating "outlets" and "bosses." Compute the coefficient of determination. How much has $R^2$ changed from the previous analysis?

```
The regression equation is
       sales = -18.9 + 1.61 cars + 0.400 income + 1.96 age

              Predictor          Coef        Stdev      t-ratio
              Constant        -18.924        3.636        -5.20
              Cars             1.6129       0.1979         8.15
              Income          0.40031      0.01569        25.52
              Age              1.9637       0.5846         3.36

              Analysis of Variance

              SOURCE         DF          SS          MS
              Regression      3     1593.66      531.22
              Error           6        9.23        1.54
              Total           9     1602.89
```

f. Following is a histogram and a stem-and-leaf chart of the residuals. Does the normality assumption appear reasonable?

```
Histogram of residual N = 10          Stem-and-leaf of residual N = 10
                                      Leaf Unit = 0.10
Midpoint   Count
    -1.5      1    *                     1   -1  7
    -1.0      1    *                     2   -1  2
    -0.5      2    **                    2   -0
     0.0      2    **                    5   -0  440
     0.5      2    **                    5    0  24
     1.0      1    *                     3    0  68
     1.5      1    *                     1    1
                                         1    1  7
```

g. Following is a plot of the fitted value of Y (i.e., Y') and the residuals. Do you see any violations of the assumptions?

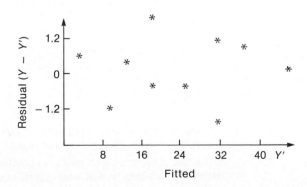

11. The administrator of a new paralegal program at a community and technical college wants to predict the grade point average in the new program. He thought that high school

GPA, the verbal score on the Scholastic Aptitude Test (SAT), and the mathematics score on the SAT would be good predictors of paralegal GPA. The data on nine students are:

| Student | High school GPA | SAT verbal | SAT math | Paralegal GPA |
|---|---|---|---|---|
| 1 | 3.25 | 480 | 410 | 3.21 |
| 2 | 1.80 | 290 | 270 | 1.68 |
| 3 | 2.89 | 420 | 410 | 3.58 |
| 4 | 3.81 | 500 | 600 | 3.92 |
| 5 | 3.13 | 500 | 490 | 3.00 |
| 6 | 2.81 | 430 | 460 | 2.82 |
| 7 | 2.20 | 320 | 490 | 1.65 |
| 8 | 2.14 | 530 | 480 | 2.30 |
| 9 | 2.63 | 469 | 440 | 2.33 |

Source: Plan Administrator, Community and Technical College, University of Toledo, Ohio.

The MINITAB software system was used to generate the following output.

a. The following correlation matrix was obtained. Which variable has the strongest correlation with the dependent variable? Some of the correlations among the independent variables are strong. Does this appear to be a problem?

```
              legal        gpa        verbal
gpa          0.911
verbal       0.616      0.609
math         0.487      0.636        0.599
```

b. Consider the following output. Compute the coefficient of multiple determination.

```
The regression equation is
legal =-0.411 + 1.20 gpa + 0.00163 verbal -0.00194 math

Predictor          Coef       Stdev    t-ratio
Constant        -0.4111      0.7823      -0.53
gpa              1.2014      0.2955       4.07
verbal         0.001629    0.002147       0.76
math          -0.001939    0.002074      -0.94

Analysis of Variance

SOURCE         DF          SS         MS
Regression      3      4.3595     1.4532
Error           5      0.7036     0.1407
Total           8      5.0631
```

c. Conduct a global test of hypothesis from the preceding output. Does it appear that any of the regression coefficients are not equal to zero?

d. Conduct a test of hypothesis on each independent variable. Would you consider eliminating the variables "verbal" and "math"? Let $\alpha = .05$.

e. The analysis has been rerun without "verbal" and "math." See the following output. Compute the coefficient of determination. How much has $R^2$ changed from the previous analysis?

```
The regression equation is
legal = -0.454 + 1.16 gpa

Predictor        Coef       Stdev     t-ratio
Constant      -0.4542      0.5542      -0.82
gpa            1.1589      0.1977       5.86

Analysis of Variance

SOURCE          DF        SS          MS
Regression       1     4.2061      4.2061
Error            7     0.8570      0.1224
Total            8     5.0631
```

f.  Following are a histogram and a stem-and-leaf diagram of the residuals. Does the normality assumption for the residuals seem reasonable?

```
Histogram of residual N = 9

Midpoint   Count
   -0.4       1 *
   -0.2       3 ***
    0.0       3 ***
    0.2       1 *
    0.4       0
    0.6       1 *

Stem-and-leaf of residual N = 9
Leaf Unit = 0.10

  1      -0 4
  2      -0 2
 (3)     -0 110
  4       0 00
  2       0 2
  1       0
  1       0 6
```

g.  Following is a plot of the residuals and the $Y'$ values. Do you see any violation of the assumptions?

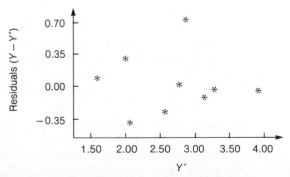

The following problems require the MINITAB system or a similar software package.

12. Mr. Mike Wilde is president of the teachers' union for the Otsego School District. In preparing for the upcoming negotiations, he would like to investigate the salary structure

of classroom teachers in the district. He believes there are three factors that affect a teacher's salary: years of experience, a rating of teaching effectiveness given by the principal, and whether or not the teacher has a master's degree. A sample of 20 teachers resulted in the following data.

| Salary ($000), $Y$ | Years of experience, $X_1$ | Principal's rating, $X_2$ | Master's degree,* $X_3$ |
|---|---|---|---|
| 21.1 | 8 | 35 | 0 |
| 23.6 | 5 | 43 | 0 |
| 19.3 | 2 | 51 | 1 |
| 33.0 | 15 | 60 | 1 |
| 28.6 | 11 | 73 | 0 |
| 35.0 | 14 | 80 | 1 |
| 32.0 | 9 | 76 | 0 |
| 26.8 | 7 | 54 | 1 |
| 38.6 | 22 | 55 | 1 |
| 21.7 | 3 | 90 | 1 |
| 15.7 | 1 | 30 | 0 |
| 20.6 | 5 | 44 | 0 |
| 41.8 | 23 | 84 | 1 |
| 36.7 | 17 | 76 | 0 |
| 28.4 | 12 | 68 | 1 |
| 23.6 | 14 | 25 | 0 |
| 31.8 | 8 | 90 | 1 |
| 20.7 | 4 | 62 | 0 |
| 22.8 | 2 | 80 | 1 |
| 32.8 | 8 | 72 | 0 |

*1 = yes, 0 = no.

a. Develop a correlation matrix. Which independent variable has the strongest correlation with the dependent variable? Does it appear that there will be any problems with multicollinearity?

b. Determine the regression equation. What salary would you estimate for a teacher with five years' experience, a rating by the principal of 60, and no master's degree?

c. Conduct a global test of hypothesis to determine if any of the net regression coefficients differ from zero.

d. Conduct a test of hypothesis for the individual regression coefficients. Would you consider deleting any of the independent variables?

e. If your conclusion in part d was to delete one or more independent variables, run the analysis again without those variables.

f. Determine the residuals for the equation of part e. Use a stem-and-leaf chart or a histogram to verify that the distribution of the residuals is approximately normal.

g. Plot the residuals computed in part f in a scatter diagram with the residuals on the $Y$-axis and the $Y'$ values on the $X$-axis. Does the plot reveal any violations of the assumptions of regression?

13. The district sales manager for a major automobile manufacturer is studying car sales. Specifically, he would like to determine what factors affect the number of cars sold at a dealership. To investigate, he randomly selects 12 dealers. From these dealers he obtains the number of cars sold last month, the minutes of radio advertising purchased last month, the number of full-time salespeople employed in the dealership, and whether the dealer is located in the city or not. The information is as follows:

| Cars sold last month, $Y$ | Advertising, $X_1$ | Sales force, $X_2$ | City, $X_3$ |
|---|---|---|---|
| 127 | 18 | 10 | Yes |
| 138 | 15 | 15 | No |
| 159 | 22 | 14 | Yes |
| 144 | 23 | 12 | Yes |
| 139 | 17 | 12 | No |
| 128 | 16 | 12 | Yes |
| 161 | 25 | 14 | Yes |
| 180 | 26 | 17 | Yes |
| 102 | 15 | 7 | No |
| 163 | 24 | 16 | Yes |
| 106 | 18 | 10 | No |
| 149 | 25 | 11 | Yes |

a. Develop a correlation matrix. Which independent variable has the strongest correlation with the dependent variable? Does it appear that there will be any problems with multicollinearity?

b. Determine the regression equation. How many cars would you expect to be sold by a dealership employing 20 salespeople, purchasing 15 minutes of advertising, and located in a city?

c. Conduct a global test of hypothesis to determine if any of the net regression coefficients differ from zero. Let $\alpha = .05$.

d. Conduct a test of hypothesis for the individual regression coefficients. Would you consider deleting any of the independent variables? Let $\alpha = .05$.

e. If your conclusion in part d was to delete one or more independent variables, run the analysis again without those variables.

f. Determine the residuals for the equation of part e. Use a stem-and-leaf chart or a histogram to verify that the distribution of the residuals is approximately normal.

g. Plot the residuals computed in part f in a scatter diagram with the residuals on the $Y$-axis and the $Y'$ values on the $X$-axis. Does the plot reveal any violations of the assumptions of regression?

14. Dr. Thomas Klein, an agricultural economist, is studying the relationship between the per-capita income in a county (the dependent variable) and the percent of the population that is employed in agriculture, and the mean number of years of education for people over 25 years of age. Nineteen rural midwestern counties are randomly selected.

| Per-capita income ($000), $Y$ | Percent employed in agriculture, $X_1$ | Education (years), $X_2$ | Per-capita income ($000), $Y$ | Percent employed in agriculture, $X_1$ | Education (years), $X_2$ |
|---|---|---|---|---|---|
| 19.6 | 10.2 | 10.6 | 21.4 | 12.6 | 16.0 |
| 19.4 | 13.4 | 16.9 | 19.2 | 12.8 | 10.4 |
| 16.0 | 10.2 | 15.1 | 26.4 | 9.7 | 13.7 |
| 19.8 | 10.8 | 14.9 | 25.8 | 9.5 | 14.0 |
| 21.8 | 10.3 | 15.0 | 20.2 | 10.5 | 10.2 |
| 18.2 | 13.3 | 16.0 | 15.2 | 13.0 | 13.8 |
| 18.2 | 11.3 | 16.0 | 19.8 | 10.6 | 13.0 |
| 21.4 | 10.3 | 15.1 | 24.8 | 8.4 | 15.2 |
| 15.2 | 12.7 | 12.9 | 13.3 | 9.6 | 13.8 |
| 24.8 | 8.5 | 10.1 | | | |

a. Develop a correlation matrix. Which independent variable has the strongest correlation with the dependent variable? Does it appear that there will be any problems with multicollinearity?

b.    Determine the regression equation. Warren County is located in Illinois. It has 12 percent of the work force employed in agriculture, and the mean number of years of education is 15. What is the estimated income for the county?

c.    Conduct a global test of hypothesis to determine if any of the net regression coefficients differ from zero. Let $\alpha = .05$.

d.    Conduct a test for the individual regression coefficients. Would you consider deleting any of the independent variables? Let $\alpha = .05$.

e.    If your conclusion in part d was that one or more variables should be deleted, rerun the analysis, deleting those variables.

f.    Determine the residuals for the equation of part e. Use a stem-and-leaf chart or a histogram to verify that the distribution of the residuals is approximately normal.

g.    Plot the residuals computed in part f in a scatter diagram with the residuals on the $Y$-axis and the $Y'$ values on the $X$-axis. Does the plot reveal any violations of the assumptions of regression?

h.    Do you have any suggestions about the analysis?

15.   Mr. Steve Douglas recently graduated from a large university with a degree in finance. He has been hired as a management trainee by a large brokerage firm. As his first project, he is asked to study the gross profit of firms in the chemical industry. What factors affect profitability in that industry? Steve selects a sample of 16 firms and obtains data on the number of employees, number of consecutive common stock dividends paid, the total value of inventory at the start of the current year, and the gross profit for each firm. His findings are:

| Company | Gross profit ($000), $Y$ | Number of employees, $X_1$ | Consecutive dividends, $X_2$ | Beginning inventory ($000), $X_3$ |
|---|---|---|---|---|
| 1 | 2,800 | 140 | 12 | 1,800 |
| 2 | 1,300 | 65 | 21 | 320 |
| 3 | 1,230 | 130 | 42 | 820 |
| 4 | 1,600 | 115 | 80 | 76 |
| 5 | 4,500 | 390 | 120 | 3,600 |
| 6 | 5,700 | 670 | 64 | 8,400 |
| 7 | 3,150 | 205 | 43 | 508 |
| 8 | 640 | 40 | 14 | 870 |
| 9 | 3,400 | 480 | 88 | 5,500 |
| 10 | 6,700 | 810 | 98 | 9,875 |
| 11 | 3,700 | 120 | 44 | 6,500 |
| 12 | 6,440 | 590 | 110 | 9,130 |
| 13 | 1,280 | 440 | 38 | 1,200 |
| 14 | 4,160 | 280 | 24 | 890 |
| 15 | 3,870 | 650 | 60 | 1,200 |
| 16 | 980 | 150 | 24 | 1,300 |

a.    Determine the regression equation. The Master Chemical Company employs 220 people, has paid 64 consecutive common stock dividends, and has an inventory valued at $1,500,000 at the start of the year. What is the estimate of the gross profit?

b.    Conduct a global test of hypothesis to determine if any of the net regression coefficients differ from zero.

c.    Conduct a test of hypothesis for the individual regression coefficients. Would you consider deleting any of the independent variables?

d.    If your conclusion in part c was to delete one or more independent variables, run the analysis again, deleting those variables.

e. Determine the residuals for the equation of part d. Use a stem-and-leaf chart or a histogram to verify that the distribution of the residuals is approximately normal.

f. Plot the residuals computed in part e in a scatter diagram with the residuals on the Y-axis and the Y' values on the X-axis. Does the plot reveal any violations of the assumptions of regression?

16. The *Times-Observer* is a daily newspaper in Metro City. Like many city newspapers, the *Times-Observer* is suffering through difficult financial times. The circulation manager is interested in studying other papers in similar cities in the United States and Canada. She is particularly interested in what variables relate to the circulation of the paper. She is able to obtain the following sample information on 25 newspapers in similar cities. The following notation is used:

$$Sub = \text{Number of subscriptions (in thousands).}$$
$$Popul = \text{The metropolitan population (in thousands).}$$
$$Adv = \text{The advertising budget of the paper (in hundreds of dollars).}$$
$$Income = \text{The median family income in the metropolitan area (in \$000).}$$

| Paper | Sub | Popul | Adv | Income |
|---|---|---|---|---|
| 1 | 37.95 | 588.9 | 13.2 | 35.1 |
| 2 | 37.66 | 585.3 | 13.2 | 34.7 |
| 3 | 37.55 | 566.3 | 19.8 | 34.8 |
| 4 | 38.78 | 642.9 | 17.6 | 35.1 |
| 5 | 37.67 | 624.2 | 17.6 | 34.6 |
| 6 | 38.23 | 603.9 | 15.4 | 34.8 |
| 7 | 36.90 | 571.9 | 11.0 | 34.7 |
| 8 | 38.28 | 584.3 | 28.6 | 35.3 |
| 9 | 38.95 | 605.0 | 28.6 | 35.1 |
| 10 | 39.27 | 676.3 | 17.6 | 35.6 |
| 11 | 38.30 | 587.4 | 17.6 | 34.9 |
| 12 | 38.84 | 576.4 | 22.0 | 35.4 |
| 13 | 38.14 | 570.8 | 17.6 | 35.0 |
| 14 | 38.39 | 586.5 | 15.4 | 35.5 |
| 15 | 37.29 | 544.0 | 11.0 | 34.9 |
| 16 | 39.15 | 611.1 | 24.2 | 35.0 |
| 17 | 38.29 | 643.3 | 17.6 | 35.3 |
| 18 | 38.09 | 635.6 | 19.8 | 34.8 |
| 19 | 37.83 | 598.9 | 15.4 | 35.1 |
| 20 | 39.37 | 657.0 | 22.0 | 35.3 |
| 21 | 37.81 | 595.2 | 15.4 | 35.1 |
| 22 | 37.42 | 520.0 | 19.8 | 35.1 |
| 23 | 38.83 | 629.6 | 22.0 | 35.3 |
| 24 | 38.33 | 680.0 | 24.2 | 34.7 |
| 25 | 40.24 | 651.2 | 33.0 | 35.8 |

a. Determine the regression equation.

b. Conduct a global test of hypothesis to determine if any of the net regression coefficients are not equal to zero.

c. Conduct a test for the individual regression coefficients. Would you consider deleting any coefficients?

d. Determine the residuals, and plot them against the fitted values. Do you see any problems?

e. Develop a histogram of the residuals. Do you see any problems with the normality assumption?

## Computer Data Exercises

17. Refer to data set 1, which reports information on homes sold in Florida during 1990.
    a. Use price as the dependent variable, and determine the regression equation with bedrooms, size of the house, whether there is a pool, whether there is an attached garage, distance from the city, and number of bathrooms as independent variables.
    b. Determine the $R^2$ value.
    c. Conduct a global test of hypothesis on the set of independent variables.
    d. Conduct a test of hypothesis on each of the independent variables. Would you consider deleting any variables?
    e. Rerun the regression equation using the following independent variables: size of the home, distance from the center of the city, whether there is an attached garage, and number of bathrooms.
    f. Plot the residuals against the fitted values using the regression equation developed in part e. Does it appear that the requirement of homoscedasticity is met?
    g. Develop a histogram of the residuals using the regression equation from part e. Does it appear that the normality assumption is met?

18. Refer to data set 2, which reports information on 200 corporations in the United States.
    a. Let corporate profits be the dependent variable, and use the following as independent variables: value, sales, assets, share price, turnover rate, and the percent return on investment. Determine the regression equation.
    b. Determine the $R^2$ value.
    c. Conduct a global test of hypothesis on the set of independent variables.
    d. Conduct a test of hypothesis on each of the independent variables. Would you consider deleting any variables?
    e. Rerun the regression equation using the following independent variables: value, sales, and assets. Determine the regression equation.
    f. Plot the residuals against the fitted values using the regression equation developed in part e. Does it appear that the requirement of homoscedasticity is met?
    g. Developa histogram of the residuals using the regression equation from part e. Does it appear that the normality assumption is met?

19. Refer to data set 3, which reports information on the 26 major league baseball teams for the 1991 season.
    a. Determine a regression equation using the proportion of games won as the dependent variable and the following five variables as independent variables: team batting average, number of home runs hit by the team, the team ERA, the number of stolen bases, and the number of errors committed by the team.
    b. Determine the $R^2$ value.
    c. Conduct a global test of hypothesis on the set of independent variables.
    d. Conduct a test of hypothesis on each of the independent variables. Would you consider deleting any variables?
    e. Rerun the regression equation using the following independent variables: team batting average, home runs, and ERA.
    f. Plot the residuals against the fitted values using the regression equation developed in part e. Does it appear that the requirement of homoscedasticity is met?
    g. Develop a histogram of the residuals using the regression equation from part e. Does it appear that the normality assumption is met?

# CHAPTER 15  EXAMINATION

*The answers are at the end of the chapter.*

1. What is the general form of a multiple regression equation having two independent variables?

Questions 2 through 7 refer to the following multiple regression output.

```
Analysis of Variance

Source              DF      SS        MS          F
Regression           3      75
Error               25      25
Total

Predictor                 Coef    Stdev     t-ratio
Constant                  6.00    3.35
        X₁                0.70    0.50
        X₂               -9.00    4.00
        X₃                5.00    2.00
```

2. How many independent variables are there in this analysis?
3. What is the total number of observations, $n$?
4. Compute the value of $R^2$.
5. Compute the multiple standard error of estimate.
6. Conduct the following global test of hypothesis.

$$H_0: \beta_1 = \beta_2 = \beta_3 = 0$$
$$H_1: \text{The } \beta_i\text{s are not all equal to zero.}$$

   a.   What is the decision rule for this test? Use the .05 significance level.
   b.   What is your decision regarding the null hypothesis?

7. Conduct the three tests of hypotheses stated below. Use the .05 significance level.

$$H_0: \beta_1 = 0 \quad H_0: \beta_2 = 0 \quad H_0: \beta_3 = 0$$
$$H_1: \beta_1 \neq 0 \quad H_1: \beta_2 \neq 0 \quad H_1: \beta_3 \neq 0$$

   a.   What is the decision rule for this test?
   b.   Which independent variables have significant regression coefficients, and which do not? Which variable or variables would you consider eliminating?

# ANSWERS

15–1 1. 12.9 psi, found by $Y' = -0.5 + 2(3.5) + 1(6.4)$.
  2. The $b_1$ of 2 indicates that the tensile strength of the wire will increase 2 psi for each increase of 1 cm in outside diameter, with the amount of molybdenum held constant. That is, tensile strength will increase 2 psi regardless of the amount of molybdenum in the wire.

15–2 1. 24.37 cubic feet, found by $Y' = 62.65 + (-1.86)8 + (-0.52)45$.
  2. 2.37 cubic feet, found by $24.37 - 22.00$. Fuel consumption is 2.37 cubic feet less than anticipated. This is called the *residual*.

15–3 1. $Y' = 490 - 5.15X_1 - 14.7X_2$
  2. .776. A total of 77.6% of the variation in heating cost is explained by temperature and insulation.

3. $1 - .776 = .224$. A total of 22.4 percent of the variation is not explained by temperature and insulation.
4. The results of the global test indicate that at least one of the regression coefficients is not zero. To arrive at that conclusion, we first stated the null hypothesis as $H_0: \beta_1 = \beta_2 = 0$. The critical value of $F$ is 3.59, and the computed value 29.4, found by 82,597/2,807. Since 29.4 lies in the region of rejection beyond 3.59, we reject $H_0$.
5. The *p*-value is .008. The probability of a *t*-value less than $-2.98$ or greater than 2.98, with 17 degrees of freedom, is .008.

# Answers

## CHAPTER 15 EXAMINATION

1. $Y' = a + b_1X_1 + b_2X_2$
2. Three independent variables.
3. $n = 29$
4. $R^2 = 75/100 = .75$
5. $s_{y \cdot 123} = \sqrt{1.00} = 1.00$
6. a. $H_0$ is rejected if $F > 2.99$.

  b. $F = \dfrac{75/3}{25/25} = 25.00$

  $H_0$ is rejected. At least one regression coefficient is not zero.

7. a. $H_0$ is rejected if $t < -2.060$ or $t > 2.060$.

  $t = \dfrac{0.70}{0.50} = 1.40$ for $\beta_1$

  $t = \dfrac{-9.00}{4.00} = -2.25$ for $\beta_2$

  $t = \dfrac{5.00}{2.00} = 2.50$ for $\beta_3$

  b. Drop $X_1$, and keep $X_2$ and $X_3$.

# A Review of Chapters 13–15

Simple regression and correlation examines the relationship between two variables

This section is a review of the major concepts and terms introduced in Chapters 13, 14, and 15. Chapter 13 noted that the strength of the relationship between the independent variable and the dependent variable can be measured by the *coefficient of correlation.* Developed by Karl Pearson, *Pearson's r* can assume any value between $-1.00$ and $+1.00$ inclusive. Coefficients of $-1.00$ and $+1.00$ indicate perfect relationship, and 0 indicates no relationship. A value near 0, such as $-.14$ or $.14$, indicates a weak relationship. A value near $-1$ or $+1$, such as $-.90$ or $+.90$, indicates a strong relationship. Squaring $r$ gives the *coefficient of determination.* It indicates the proportion of the total variation in the dependent variable explained by the independent variable.

Multiple regression and correlation concerned with relationship between two or more independent variables and the dependent variable

Likewise, the strength of the relationship between a group of many independent variables and a dependent variable is measured by the *coefficient of multiple correlation, R* (Chapter 15). It is always positive and can assume any value between 0 and $+1.00$ inclusive. The *coefficient of multiple determination, $R^2$,* measures the proportion of the variation in $Y$ explained by the two or more independent variables.

The linear relationship in the simple case involving one independent variable and one dependent variable is described by the equation $Y' = a + bX$. For three independent variables, $X_1$, $X_2$, and $X_3$, the sample multiple regression equation is

$$Y' = a + b_1X_1 + b_2X_2 + b_3X_3$$

Computer invaluable in multiple regression and correlation

Solving for $b_1, b_2, b_3, \ldots, b_k$ would involve hours of tedious calculations. Fortunately, this type of problem can be quickly solved using one of the many statistical packages available for the computer. Commonly used are MINITAB and SPSS. One program uses a stepwise procedure. The independent variable most highly correlated with the dependent variable is brought in first. Various measures, such as the coefficient of determination, are given. Next, the variable is entered along with the remaining independent variables that results in the greatest proportional reduction in the unexplained variation. Then a new set of measures ($R$, $R^2$, etc.) is computed. This process is continued until all the significant independent variables are brought into the regression equation.

## Glossary

### Chapter 13

**Coefficient of correlation**  A measure developed by Karl Pearson that gives the strength of association between the independent variable and the dependent variable. The formula is:

$$r = \frac{n(\Sigma XY) - (\Sigma X)(\Sigma Y)}{\sqrt{[n(\Sigma X^2) - (\Sigma X)^2][n(\Sigma Y^2) - (\Sigma Y)^2]}}$$

**Coefficient of determination**   The proportion of the total variation in the dependent variable that is explained by the independent variable. It can assume any value between 0 and +1.00 inclusive. A coefficient of .82 indicates that 82 percent of the variation in $Y$ is accounted for by $X$. This coefficient is computed by squaring $r$ (for simple correlation) or $R$ (for multiple correlation).

**Coefficient of nondetermination**   Measures the proportion of the total variation in $Y$ that is not explained by $X$. It is computed by $1 - r^2$ for two variables, or $1 - R^2$ for the multiple case.

**Correlation analysis**   A group of statistical techniques used to measure the strength of the relationship between two variables.

**Rank-order coefficient of correlation**   Developed by Charles Spearman in the early 1900s, a measure of strength of the association between two sets of ordinal-level data, that is, data that can be ranked from low to high or vice versa. The formula for Spearman's rank-order coefficient of correlation is:

$$r_s = 1 - \frac{6\Sigma d^2}{n(n^2 - 1)}$$

**Scatter diagram**   A chart that visually depicts the relationship between two variables.

**Test for significance of $r$**   A formula to answer the question: Is the correlation in the population from which the sample was selected zero? The test statistic is $t$, and the number of degrees of freedom is $n - 2$.

$$t = \frac{r\sqrt{n - 2}}{\sqrt{1 - r^2}}$$

**Test for significance of $r_s$**   A formula to answer the question: Is the correlation among the ranks in the population from which the sample was selected zero? For samples less than 10, use Appendix H. For samples between 10 and 30, use either Appendix H or Student's $t$ distribution. For sample size over 30, use $t$:

$$t = r_s \sqrt{\frac{n - 2}{1 - r_s^2}}$$

with $n - 2$ degrees of freedom.

## CHAPTER 14

**Least squares method**   A technique used to arrive at the regression equation.

**Linear regression equation**   A mathematical equation that defines the relationship between two variables. It has the form $Y' = a + bX$. It is used to predict $Y$ based on a selected $X$ value.

**Standard error of estimate**   Measures the dispersion of the actual $Y$ values about the linear regression line. It tells us how far off our prediction might be.

## CHAPTER 15

**Autocorrelation**   Correlation of successive residuals. This condition frequently occurs when time is involved in the analysis.

**Coefficient of multiple correlation**   A measure of the strength of the relationship between two or more independent variables and the dependent variable.

**Correlation matrix**   A listing of all possible simple coefficients of correlation. A correlation matrix includes the correlations between each of the independent variables and the dependent variable, as well as those among all the independent variables.

**Homoscedasticity**   The standard error of estimate is the same for all fitted values of the dependent variable.

**Multicollinearity**   A condition that occurs in multiple regression analysis if the independent variables are themselves correlated.

**Multiple regression equation**   The relationship in the form of a mathematical equation between many independent variables and a dependent variable. The general form is $Y' = a + b_1X_1 + b_2X_2 + b_3X_3 + \cdots + b_kX_k$. It is used to estimate $Y$ given selected $X$ values.

**Qualitative variable**   A nominal-scale variable that is nonnumeric. For example, a person is considered either employed or unemployed.

**Residual**   The difference between the actual value of the dependent variable and the estimated value of the dependent variable.

**Stepwise regression**   A method for determining the order in which independent variables enter a multiple regression equation. Independent variables enter the regression equation in the order in which they will increase $R^2$ by the largest amount. Only independent variables whose regression coefficients are significantly different from zero are entered into the equation.

# EXERCISES

*The answers to the odd-numbered exercises are at the end of the book.*

## PART I—FILL IN THE BLANKS AND DISCUSSION

1. The strength of the relationship between a set of independent variables $X$ and a dependent variable $Y$ is measured by the _____.
2. A rank-order coefficient of correlation was computed to be $-.90$. Comment.
3. Pearson's $r$ for a problem involving 60 pairs of data was computed to be .40. Comment. Is the correlation in the population zero? Give evidence.
4. The coefficient of nondetermination was computed to be .04 in a problem involving one independent and one dependent variable. What does this mean?
5. Explain the function of the "stepwise" procedure followed in MINITAB.

Exercises 6 through 10 are based on the following table. The accounting division for a large chain of department stores is trying to predict the net profit for each of the chain's many stores based on the number of employees in the store, overhead cost, and so on. A few statistics from some of the stores are:

| Store | Net profit ($000) | Number of employees | Overhead cost ($000) | Average markup rate (percent) | Loss from theft ($000) |
|-------|--------|--------|--------|--------|--------|
| 1 | 846 | 143 | 79 | 69 | 52 |
| 2 | 513 | 110 | 64 | 50 | 45 |

6. The dependent variable is _____.
7. The general equation for this problem is _____.
8. The multiple regression equation was computed to be $Y' = 67 + 8X_1 - 10X_2 + 0.004X_3 - 3X_4$. What is predicted sales for a store with 112 employees, an overhead cost of $65,000, a markup rate of 50 percent, and a loss from theft of $50,000?
9. Suppose $R$ was computed to be .86. What is the coefficient of determination? Explain.

10. Suppose that the multiple standard error of estimate was computed to be 3 (in $000). Explain what this means in this problem.

## PART II—PROBLEMS

11. Quick-print firms in a large downtown business area spend most of their advertising dollars on advertisements on bus benches. A research project involves predicting monthly sales based on the annual amount spent on placing ads on bus benches. A sample of quick-print firms revealed these advertising expenses and sales:

| Firm | Annual amount spent on bus bench advertisements ($000) | Monthly sales ($000) |
|------|--------------------------------------------------------|----------------------|
| A | 2 | 10 |
| B | 4 | 40 |
| C | 5 | 30 |
| D | 7 | 50 |
| E | 3 | 20 |

   a.   Draw a scatter diagram.

   b.   Determine the coefficient of correlation.

   c.   What are the coefficients of determination and nondetermination?

   d.   Compute the regression equation.

   e.   Predict the monthly sales of a quick-print firm that spends $4,500 on bus bench advertisements.

   f.   Summarize your findings.

12. Two states offered a special incentive to professional bowlers to bowl one night only in various cities in the state over a period of two weeks. To create interest and stimulate competition, points were awarded for a 300 game, for the highest score each night, and so on. The points earned for each bowler are:

| Bowler | Points earned in Florida | Points earned in Georgia |
|--------|--------|---------|
| Thompson | 81 | 76 |
| Sobecki | 18 | 36 |
| Lopez | 41 | 46 |
| Arnold | 91 | 88 |
| Rollins | 50 | 42 |
| Cresent | 29 | 36 |
| Adrian | 62 | 60 |
| Cork | 77 | 36 |
| Adami | 81 | 87 |
| Marchal | 56 | 72 |

The statistician attached to the Professional Bowlers Association is interested in evaluating the ranks of the bowlers in the two states.

   a.   Rank the points earned in each state (watch ties).

   b.   Compute Spearman's rank-order correlation coefficient to evaluate the consistency of the bowlers in each state. Interpret your findings.

13. The following ANOVA output is given.

```
Source          Sum of Squares      DF              MS
Regression         1050.8            4            262.70
Error                83.8           20              4.19
Total              1134.6           24

      Predictor              Coef     St.Dev.      t-ratio
      Constant              70.06      2.13         32.89
         X₁                  0.42      0.17          2.47
         X₂                  0.27      0.21          1.29
         X₃                  0.75      0.30          2.50
         X₄                  0.42      0.07          6.00
```

a.   Compute the coefficient of determination.

b.   Compute the multiple standard error of estimate.

c.   Conduct a test of hypothesis to determine if any of the net regression coefficients are different from zero.

d.   Conduct a test of hypothesis on the individual regression coefficients. Can any of the variables be deleted?

*Government—Jeffrey M. Spielman/The Image Bank*

# ANALYSIS OF NOMINAL-LEVEL DATA: THE CHI-SQUARE DISTRIBUTION

When you have completed this chapter, you will be able to:

1. List the characteristics of the chi-square distribution.

2. Conduct a test of hypothesis involving the difference between a set of observed frequencies and a corresponding set of expected frequencies.

3. Conduct a test for normality using chi-square.

4. Conduct a test of hypothesis to determine whether two criteria of classification are related.

C hapters 8 through 12 dealt with data that were at least interval-scale, such as weights, incomes, and ages. We conducted a number of tests of hypotheses about a population mean and two or more population means. For these tests it was assumed that the population was normal. Can tests of hypotheses be made if the data are not interval-scale, but are nominal- or ordinal-scale, and if no assumptions are made about the shape of the parent population?

To answer this question, there are tests for nominal and ordinal levels of measurement, and no assumptions need be made about the shape of the population. Recall from Chapter 1 that *nominal*-level data are the "lowest" type of data. This type of data can only be classified into categories, such as Republican, Democrat, and "all others," or male and female. *Ordinal* level of measurement assumes that one category is ranked higher than the next one. As an example, a sample of joggers are asked by Marketing Research Associates to rate a newly developed shoe as either outstanding, good, fair, or unsatisfactory. It is implied that a ranking of outstanding is higher than good, good is higher than fair, and so on.

Tests of hypotheses concerned with nominal or ordinal levels of measurement are called **nonparametric,** or **distribution-free, tests.** The latter name implies that these tests are free of assumptions regarding the distribution of the parent population. These distribution-free tests are relatively easy to apply, and the computations are generally easy to perform.

## CHI-SQUARE GOODNESS-OF-FIT TEST: EQUAL EXPECTED FREQUENCIES

The **chi-square goodness-of-fit test** is one of the most commonly used nonparametric tests. Developed by Karl Pearson in the early 1900s, it is appropriate for both nominal and ordinal levels of data. It can also be used for interval- and ratio-level data. The first test of significance involves *equal expected frequencies.*

### ▮ EXAMPLE

Has the slot machine been altered?

As the full name implies, the purpose of the chi-square goodness-of-fit test is to determine how well an *observed* set of data fits an *expected* set. An illustration can best describe the hypothesis-testing procedure. Suppose there is some doubt that one of the slot machines in Nero's Palace in Las Vegas is true; that is, there is suspicion that the mechanism behind one of the windows in the slot machine has been altered.

---

### TABLE    16–1

**Results of Operating the Slot Machine 120 Times**

| Fruit in left window (cell) | Number of times fruit appeared, $f_o$ |
|---|---|
| Banana | 13 |
| Cherry | 33 |
| Orange | 14 |
| Peach | 7 |
| Lemon | 36 |
| Pear | 17 |
| Total | 120 |

---

As an experiment, the handle of this one-armed bandit, as it is affectionately called, is pulled down 120 times and the results recorded. They are listed in Table 16–1. The question to be answered is: Has the slot machine been tampered with?

### ✅ SOLUTION

The same systematic five-step hypothesis-testing procedure followed in Chapters 8 through 12 will be used.

State $H_0$ and $H_1$

**STEP 1** The null hypothesis and the alternate hypothesis are stated. The null hypothesis, $H_0$, is that the mechanism has not been tampered with. To put it another way, there is no difference between the set of observed frequencies and the set of expected frequencies; that is, any differences can be attributed to chance. The alternate hypothesis, $H_1$, is that there is a difference between the two sets of frequencies—that is, the machine has been altered. If $H_0$ is rejected and $H_1$ accepted, it means that the mechanism has been altered to allow a fruit, or fruits, to appear in the window more frequently than other fruits.

Alpha is .05

**STEP 2** A level of significance is chosen. We selected the .05 level, which is the same as the Type I error probability. Thus, the probability is .05 that a true null hypothesis will be rejected.

The test statistic

**STEP 3** The test statistic is selected. It is the chi-square distribution, designated as $\chi^2$.

$$\chi^2 = \sum \left[ \frac{(f_0 - f_e)^2}{f_e} \right] \qquad (16-1)$$

with $k - 1$ degrees of freedom, where $k$ is the number of categories, and

$f_0$   is an observed frequency in a particular category.
$f_e$   is an expected frequency in a particular category.

We will examine the characteristics of the chi-square distribution in more detail shortly.

The decision rule

The critical value

**STEP 4** The *decision rule* is formulated. Recall that the decision rule in hypothesis testing requires finding a number that separates the region where we do not reject $H_0$ from the region of rejection. This number is called the *critical value*. As we will soon see, the chi-square distribution is really a family of distributions. Each distribution has a different shape, depending on the number of degrees of freedom. This number is found by $k - 1$, where $k$ stands for the number of categories. In this problem there are six fruits that appear in the left window of the slot machine under suspicion, namely, banana, cherry, orange, peach, lemon, and pear. Since there are six categories, there are $k - 1 = 6 - 1 = 5$ degrees of freedom. A category is called a *cell*, so there are six cells. The critical value for 5 degrees of freedom and the .05 level of significance is found in Appendix I. A portion of that table is shown in Table 16–2. The critical value is 11.070, found by locating 5 degrees of freedom in the left margin, and then moving horizontally (to the right) and reading the critical value in the .05 column.

---

### TABLE 16–2

**A Portion of the Chi-Square Table**

| Degrees of freedom, df | Right-tail area | | | |
|:---:|:---:|:---:|:---:|:---:|
| | .10 | .05 | .02 | .01 |
| 1 | 2.706 | 3.841 | 5.412 | 6.635 |
| 2 | 4.605 | 5.991 | 7.824 | 9.210 |
| 3 | 6.251 | 7.815 | 9.837 | 11.345 |
| 4 | 7.779 | 9.488 | 11.668 | 13.277 |
| 5 | 9.236 | 11.070 | 13.388 | 15.086 |

---

The decision rule, therefore, is: Do not reject the null hypothesis if the computed value of chi-square is less than or equal to 11.070. If it is greater than 11.070, reject $H_0$ and accept the alternate hypothesis, $H_1$. Chart 16–1 shows the two regions.

---

### CHART 16–1

**Chi-Square Probability Distribution for 5 Degrees of Freedom, Showing the Region of Rejection, .05 Level of Significance**

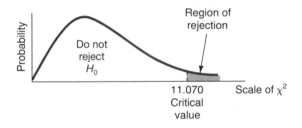

---

In essence, the decision rule indicates that if there are large differences between the observed and expected frequencies, resulting in a computed $\chi^2$ of more than 11.070, the null hypothesis should be rejected. However, if the differences between $f_0$ and $f_e$ are small, the computed $\chi^2$ value will be 11.070 or less, and the null hypothesis should not be rejected. The reasoning is that such small differences between the observed and expected frequencies are probably due to chance.

Take a sample, and arrive at a decision

**STEP 5**  A sample is selected, a chi-square value is computed, and a decision is made to reject or not to reject the null hypothesis. We decided to pull down the handle of the slot machine under investigation 120 times and count the number of bananas, cherries, and other fruits appearing. The counts (observed frequencies) for each of the six cells were reported in Table 16–1.

How do we determine the expected frequencies? Assume the slot machine is set so that each fruit has an equal chance of appearing in the window. Suppose we operated the slot machine six times. Theoretically, one would expect one banana, one cherry, one orange, one peach, one lemon, and one pear to appear in the window of the slot machine. If the experiment called for 12 operations, logically we would expect each of the six fruits to appear twice (determined by 12 divided by 6). Since we operated the machine 120 times, we expect each fruit to appear 120 divided by 6, or 20 times (provided the slot machine has not been tampered with).

Equal expected
frequencies

The set of observed frequencies from Table 16–1 and the set of expected frequencies are shown in Table 16–3. Note again that the expected frequencies are *all equal* (20 in each cell).

---

TABLE   16–3

**Observed and Expected Frequencies for 120 Operations of the Slot Machine**

| Fruit | Observed frequencies, $f_0$ | Expected frequencies, $f_e$ |
|---|---|---|
| Banana | 13 | 20 |
| Cherry | 33 | 20 |
| Orange | 14 | 20 |
| Peach | 7 | 20 |
| Lemon | 36 | 20 |
| Pear | 17 | 20 |
| Total | 120 | 120 |

---

An examination of Table 16–3 indicates that a peach seldom appeared in the left window, and a lemon appeared much more frequently than expected. Should we conclude that the slot machine has been tampered with? No. Perhaps the differences between the observed and expected frequencies can reasonably be attributed to chance. Computing chi-square and comparing it with the critical value will resolve the dilemma.

Recall that the test statistic, $\chi^2$, is computed by formula (16–1).

$$\chi^2 = \sum \left[ \frac{(f_0 - f_e)^2}{f_e} \right]$$

Calculations needed
for $\chi^2$

Referring to the following computations, the steps required to determine chi-square are:

*Column 1:*   The difference between each paired $f_0$ and $f_e$ is calculated. (*Note:* The sum of the differences must equal zero.)

*Column 2:*   The differences are squared.

*Column 3:*   Each squared difference is divided by the appropriate frequency expected, $f_e$. These quotients are then summed. The sum (34.40) is the computed value of chi-square.

| Fruit | $f_0$ | $f_e$ | (1) $f_0 - f_e$ | (2) $(f_0 - f_e)^2$ | (3) $\dfrac{(f_0 - f_e)^2}{f_e}$ |
|---|---|---|---|---|---|
| Banana | 13 | 20 | −7 | 49 | 49/20 =  2.45 |
| Cherry | 33 | 20 | 13 | 169 | 169/20 =  8.45 |
| Orange | 14 | 20 | −6 | 36 | 36/20 =  1.80 |
| Peach | 7 | 20 | −13 | 169 | 169/20 =  8.45 |
| Lemon | 36 | 20 | 16 | 256 | 256/20 = 12.80 |
| Pear | 17 | 20 | −3 | 9 | 9/20 =  0.45 |
| | | | 0 | | 34.40 |

must be ➔

$\chi^2$ ➔

The decision

The computed $\chi^2$ of 34.40 is in the rejection region, beyond the critical value of 11.070. The decision, therefore, is to reject $H_0$ at the .05 level. $H_1$, which states that the mechanism behind the left window of the slot machine has been tampered with, is accepted. In essence, rejecting $H_0$ means that it is highly unlikely that such large discrepancies between the observed frequencies and the expected frequencies would appear if the slot machine were true (unaltered). To repeat, the conclusion is that the mechanism has been altered.

## Self-Review 16–1

*The answers are at the end of the chapter.*

The personnel manager is concerned about absenteeism. She decides to sample the records to determine if absenteeism is distributed evenly throughout the six-day workweek. The null hypothesis to be tested is: Absenteeism is distributed evenly throughout the week. The .01 level is to be used. The sample results are:

|  | Number absent |
|---|---|
| Monday | 12 |
| Tuesday | 9 |
| Wednesday | 11 |
| Thursday | 10 |
| Friday | 9 |
| Saturday | 9 |

1. What kind of frequencies are the numbers 12, 9, 11, 10, 9, and 9 called?
2. How many categories (cells) are there?
3. What is the *expected* frequency for each day?
4. How many degrees of freedom are there?
5. What is the chi-square critical value at the 1 percent level?
6. Using the chi-square test of significance, compute $\chi^2$.
7. Is the null hypothesis rejected?
8. Specifically, what does this indicate to the personnel manager?

Both the slot machine example and the example in the self-review involved *equal* expected frequencies. Before considering problems with *unequal* expected frequencies, we will look briefly at the characteristics of the chi-square distribution.

## CHARACTERISTICS OF THE CHI-SQUARE DISTRIBUTION

$\chi^2$ is always positive

1. The computed value of chi-square is *always positive* because the difference between $f_0$ and $f_e$ is squared, that is, $(f_0 - f_e)^2$.

Shape of chi-square distribution depends on number of cells

2. There is a family of chi-square distributions. There is a chi-square distribution for 1 degree of freedom, another for 2 degrees of freedom, another for 3 degrees of freedom, and so on. The number of degrees of freedom is determined by $k - 1$, where $k$ is the number of categories. Therefore, the shape of the chi-square distribution does *not* depend on the size of the sample. For example, if 200 employees of an airline were classified into one of three categories—flight personnel, ground support, and administrative personnel—there would be $k - 1 = 3 - 1 = 2$ degrees of freedom.

Chi-square distribution is positively skewed

3. The chi-square distribution is *positively skewed*. However, as the number of degrees of freedom increases, the distribution begins to approximate the normal distribution. Chart 16–2 shows the distributions for selected degrees of freedom. Notice that for 10 degrees of freedom, the curve is approaching a normal curve.

## Chart 16—2

**Chi-Square Distributions for Selected Degrees of Freedom**

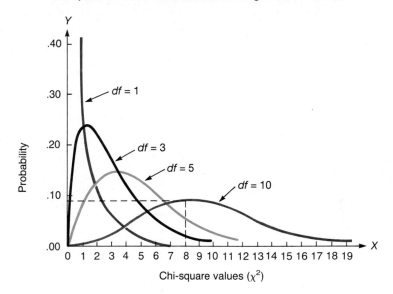

Shape of $\chi^2$ distribution approaches normal curve as *df* becomes larger

# Goodness-of-Fit Test: Unequal Expected Frequencies

Expected frequencies not equal in this problem

The expected frequencies ($f_e$) in the slot machine experiment were all equal; that is, for 120 trials, theoretically it is expected that a picture of a banana will appear 20 times in the left window of the slot machine, a cherry will appear 20 times, and so on. Chi-square can also be used if the expected frequencies are not equal. The following example illustrates the case of unequal frequencies and also gives a practical use of chi-square—namely, to find out if a local experience differs from the national experience.

### ▊ Example

A national study of hospital admissions during a two-year period revealed these statistics concerning senior citizens who resided in care centers and who were hospitalized during the period: Forty percent were admitted only once in the two-year period. Twenty percent were admitted twice. Fourteen percent were admitted three times, and so on. The complete percentage distribution is given in Table 16—4.

The administrator of the local hospital is anxious to compare her Bartow County Hospital experience with the national experience. She selected 400 senior citizens in local care centers who needed hospitalization and determined the number of times during a two-year period that each was admitted to her hospital. The observed frequencies are listed in Table 16—5.

Chi-square is used to compare this local experience with the national experience. How can the locally observed frequencies in Table 16–5 be compared with the national percentages in Table 16–4? We will use the .05 level of significance.

---

### TABLE 16–4

**Admission of Senior Citizens to the Hospital**

| Number of admissions in a two-year period | Percent of total |
|:---:|:---:|
| 1 | 40 |
| 2 | 20 |
| 3 | 14 |
| 4 | 10 |
| 5 | 8 |
| 6 | 6 |
| 7 | 2 |
|  | 100 |

---

### TABLE 16–5

**Number of Admissions to the Local Hospital during a Two-Year Period**

| Number of admissions | Number of senior citizens, $f_0$ |
|:---:|:---:|
| 1 | 165 |
| 2 | 79 |
| 3 | 50 |
| 4 | 44 |
| 5 | 32 |
| 6 | 20 |
| 7 | 10 |
|  | 400 |

---

### ☑ SOLUTION

Determining expected frequencies

Obviously, the *number* of observed frequencies resulting from the study of local senior citizens cannot be compared directly with the *percentages* given for the nation's hospitals. However, the percentages for the nation in Table 16–4 can be converted to expected frequencies, $f_e$. Table 16–4 shows that 40 percent of the senior citizens who required hospitalization only went once in a two-year period. Thus, if there is *no* difference between the experience at Bartow County Hospital and the national experience, then 40 percent of the 400 sampled by the hospital administrator (160 senior citizens) would have been admitted just once in the period. Further, 20 percent of the 400 sampled (80 people) would have been admitted twice, and so on. The observed local frequencies and the expected local frequencies based on the national study are given in Table 16–6.

## TABLE   16–6

### Observed and Expected Frequencies for Bartow County Hospital

Expected frequencies unequal

| Number of times admitted | Observed number of admissions, $f_0$ | Expected number of admissions, $f_e$ | | |
|---|---|---|---|---|
| 1 | 165 | 160 | ← | 40% × 400 |
| 2 | 79 | 80 | ← | 20% × 400 |
| 3 | 50 | 56 | ← | 14% × 400 |
| 4 | 44 | 40 | ← | 10% × 400 |
| 5 | 32 | 32 | ← | 8% × 400 |
| 6 | 20 | 24 | ← | 6% × 400 |
| 7 | 10 | 8 | ← | 2% × 400 |
| | 400 | 400 | | |

Must be equal

The null and alternate hypotheses are:

$H_0$: No difference between local and national experience

$H_0$:  There is no difference between the local experience and the national experience.

$H_1$:  There is a difference between the local experience and the national experience.

The decision rule is portrayed graphically in Chart 16–3.

## CHART   16–3

### Decision Criteria for the Bartow County Hospital Research Study

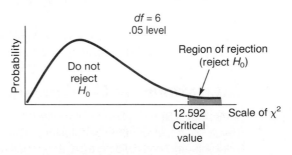

To determine the critical value, note in Table 16–6 that there are seven cells. Thus, there are $k - 1 = 7 - 1 = 6$ degrees of freedom. Referring to Appendix I and the .05 significance level, the critical value is 12.592. The decision rule is: Do not reject the null hypothesis if the computed value of chi-square is less than or equal to 12.592. Otherwise, reject $H_0$ and accept $H_1$.

Decision rule

The computations for chi-square are:

| Number of times admitted | $f_0$ | $f_e$ | $f_0 - f_e$ | $(f_0 - f_e)^2$ | $\dfrac{(f_0 - f_e)^2}{f_e}$ |
|---|---|---|---|---|---|
| 1 | 165 | 160 | +5 | 25 | 0.156 |
| 2 | 79 | 80 | −1 | 1 | 0.013 |
| 3 | 50 | 56 | −6 | 36 | 0.643 |
| 4 | 44 | 40 | +4 | 16 | 0.400 |
| 5 | 32 | 32 | 0 | 0 | 0.000 |
| 6 | 20 | 24 | −4 | 16 | 0.667 |
| 7 | 10 | 8 | +2 | 4 | 0.500 |
|   |   |   | 0 |   | $\chi^2 = 2.379$ |

No difference between local and national experience

The computed value of chi-square (2.379) lies to the left of 12.592 and is therefore in the region where we cannot reject $H_0$. The null hypothesis, that there is no difference between the local experience at Bartow County Hospital and the national experience, is therefore not rejected. The hospital administrator would conclude that the local situation with respect to the hospitalization of senior citizens in care centers is like that in other parts of the country.

The MINITAB system can be used to compute the value of chi-square. The first step is to enter the observed set of frequencies into the system. Next, the expected frequencies are input. The value of chi-square is then computed using the LET command. The final step is to print the value of chi-square, which is called K1.

```
MTB > set c1
DATA > 165, 79, 50, 44, 32, 20, 10
DATA > end
MTB > set c2
DATA > 160, 80, 56, 40, 32, 24, 8
DATA > end
MTB > name c1 'observed' c2 'expected'
MTB > let k1=sum((c1-c2)**2 / c2)
MTB > print k1
K1          2.37827
```

Note that the value computed by the MINITAB system is the same as computed earlier (except for a slight discrepancy due to rounding).

## LIMITATIONS OF CHI-SQUARE

Be careful in applying $\chi^2$ to some problems

If there is an unusually small expected frequency in a cell, chi-square (if applied) might result in an erroneous conclusion. This can happen because $f_e$ appears in the denominator, and dividing by a very small number makes the quotient quite large! Two generally accepted rules regarding small cell frequencies are:

1. If there are only two cells, the *expected* frequency in each cell should be 5 or more. The computation of chi-square would be permissible in the following problem, involving a minimum $f_e$ of 6.

| Individual | $f_0$ | $f_e$ |
|---|---|---|
| Literate | 643 | 642 |
| Illiterate | 7 | 6 |

2. For more than two cells, $x^2$ should not bc applied if more than 20 percent of the $f_e$ cells have expected frequencies less than 5. According to this rule, it would be permissible to compute $x^2$ for the management data in the left-hand table below. Only one out of six cells, or 17 percent, contains a frequency less than 5.

| Level of management | Number $f_0$ | $f_e$ | Level of management | Number $f_0$ | $f_e$ |
|---|---|---|---|---|---|
| Foreman | 18 | 16 | Foreman | 30 | 32 |
| Supervisor | 39 | 37 | Supervisor | 110 | 113 |
| Manager | 8 | 13 | Manager | 86 | 87 |
| Middle management | 6 | 4 | Middle management | 23 | 24 |
| Assistant vice president | 82 | 78 | Assistant vice president | 5 | 2 |
| Vice president | 10 | 15 | Vice president | 5 | 4 |
|  | 163 | 163 | Senior vice president | 4 | 1 |

Chi-square should not be used for the management data in the right-hand table because three of the seven expected frequencies, or 43 percent, are less than 5.

Using this example to develop the reasoning behind the rule, note that most of the paired observed and expected frequencies are almost equal. The largest difference is just 3. One might conclude, therefore, that there is no significant difference between the observed set and the expected set of frequencies. However, actually computing chi-square and evaluating it against the appropriate critical value will refute that conclusion. Instead, it would be concluded that there is a difference between the frequencies observed in the sample and the expected frequencies. This conclusion, however, does not seem logical. Verify this by solving the self-review that follows.

## Self-Review 16–2

*The answers are at the end of the chapter.*

Using the management data shown in the preceding right-hand table, test the null hypothesis at the .05 level that there is no significant difference between the observed set and the expected set of frequencies.

The dilemma can be resolved if the data are such that some of the categories can be combined. This seems to be the case in the management problem above. The three vice-presidential levels were combined into one category in order to satisfy the 20 percent rule.

| Level of management | Number in sample, $f_0$ | Expected number, $f_e$ |
|---|---|---|
| Foreman | 30 | 32 |
| Supervisor | 110 | 113 |
| Manager | 86 | 87 |
| Middle management | 23 | 24 |
| Vice president | 14 | 7 |

The computed value of chi-square for the revised set of frequencies is 7.26. This is less than the critical value of 9.488 for the .05 level. The null hypothesis is therefore not rejected at the .05 level of significance. This indicates that there is no difference between the observed sample results and the expected results. The small differences between the observed and expected observations can be attributed to sampling. This is, of course, a more logical conclusion.

### Self-Review 16–3

*The answers are at the end of the chapter.*

Refer to the preceding discussion.

1. Verify that computed chi-square is in fact 7.26.

2. Using the same level of significance (.05), what is the decision rule? (*Caution:* The data have been reorganized.)

3. Do you agree that the null hypothesis should not be rejected at the .05 level?

## EXERCISES

*The answers to the odd-numbered exercises are at the end of the book.*

1. The null and alternate hypotheses are:

    $H_0$:  The cell categories are equal.

    $H_1$:  The cell categories are not equal.

    | Category | $f_0$ |
    |----------|-------|
    | A | 10 |
    | B | 20 |
    | C | 30 |

    a.  Use the .05 significance level, and state the decision rule.
    b.  Compute the value of chi-square.
    c.  What is your decision regarding $H_0$?

2. The following hypotheses are given.

    $H_0$:  Forty percent of the observations are in category A, 40 percent are in B, and 20 percent are in C.

    $H_1$:  The observations are not as described in $H_0$.

    The sample results are:

    | Category | $f_0$ |
    |----------|-------|
    | A | 30 |
    | B | 20 |
    | C | 10 |

    a.  State the decision rule using the .01 significance level.
    b.  Compute the value of chi-square.
    c.  What is your decision regarding $H_0$?

3. The chief of security of a large shopping mall was directed to study the problem of missing goods. He selected a sample of 100 boxes that had been tampered with and ascertained that for 60 of the boxes the missing pants, shoes, and so on were attributed

to shoplifting. For 30 other boxes employees had stolen the goods, and for the remaining 10 boxes he blamed poor inventory control.

In his report to the mall management, can he say that shoplifting is *twice* as likely to be the cause of the loss as compared with employee theft or poor inventory control? Use the .02 level.

4. The director of human resources collected the following data on absenteeism by day of the week. At the .05 significance level, can she conclude that there is a difference in the absence rate by day of the week?

| Day | Frequency |
|-----|-----------|
| Monday | 124 |
| Tuesday | 74 |
| Wednesday | 104 |
| Thursday | 98 |
| Friday | 120 |

5. A group of department store buyers viewed a new line of dresses and gave their opinions of them. The results were:

| Opinion | Number of buyers |
|---------|------------------|
| Outstanding | 47 |
| Excellent | 45 |
| Very good | 40 |
| Good | 39 |
| Fair | 35 |
| Undesirable | 34 |

Source: Unpublished study, Office of Institutional Research, University of Toledo.

Because the largest number (47) indicated the new line is outstanding, the head designer thinks that this is a mandate to go into mass production of the dresses. The head sweeper (who somehow became involved in this) believes that there is not a clear mandate and claims that the opinions are evenly distributed among the six categories. He further says that the slight differences among the various counts are probably due to chance. Test the null hypothesis that there is no significant difference among the opinions of the buyers. Test at the .01 level of risk. Follow a formal approach; that is, state the null hypothesis, the alternate hypothesis, and so on.

6. The safety director of Honda USA took samples at random from the file of minor accidents and classified them according to the time the accident took place.

| Time | Number of accidents |
|------|---------------------|
| 8–9 A.M. | 6 |
| 9–10 A.M. | 6 |
| 10–11 A.M. | 20 |
| 11–12 A.M. | 8 |
| 1–2 P.M. | 7 |
| 2–3 P.M. | 8 |
| 3–4 P.M. | 19 |
| 4–5 P.M. | 6 |

Using the chi-square test and the .01 level of significance, determine whether or not the accidents are evenly distributed throughout the day. Write a brief explanation of your conclusion.

7. Column 1 of the following table gives the number of students enrolled, by college, at a midwestern university during the fall quarter.

| College | (1) Number enrolled | (2) Number responding |
|---|---|---|
| Arts and sciences | 4,700 | 90 |
| Business administration | 2,450 | 45 |
| Education | 3,250 | 60 |
| Engineering | 1,300 | 30 |
| Law | 850 | 15 |
| Pharmacy | 1,250 | 15 |
| University college | 3,400 | 45 |

The editor of the student newspaper selected names at random from each college and mailed the students chosen questionnaires dealing with campus activities, fees, the sports program, and so on. The numbers responding, by college, are in column 2. Using the .05 level, determine whether or not the sample response is representative of the student population.

8. A national study was conducted with respect to the major leisure indoor activity of males. The percent of the total for each activity is shown in the center column of the following table. The results of a similar study of a sample of males older than 60 living in the Rocky Mountain area are given in the right column.

| Major indoor activity | National results (percent of total) | Rocky Mountain study (number) |
|---|---|---|
| Photography | 22 | 337 |
| Stamp and coin collecting | 19 | 293 |
| Needlework, crocheting, and sewing | 6 | 82 |
| Greenhouse and indoor gardening | 9 | 128 |
| Metalworking and woodworking | 12 | 182 |
| Gourmet cooking | 4 | 54 |
| Painting and sculpture | 7 | 99 |
| Chess, checkers, and all others | 21 | 325 |

Test at the .05 level that there is no difference between the national results and those of males older than 60 in the Rocky Mountain area.

9. Did you ever purchase a bag of M&M Peanut candies and wonder about the distribution of the colors? A recent article in the *Lansing State Journal* reported that 30 percent of the candies are brown, 20 percent yellow, 20 percent red, 20 percent green, and 10 orange. On September 11, 1991, a one-pound bag of M&M peanut candies was purchased at the Anderson's in Maumee, Ohio. A total of 188 candies were in the bag, with 67 brown, 22 yellow, 51 red, 24 green, and 24 orange. At the .05 significance level, can we conclude that this agrees with the expected distribution?

# USING THE GOODNESS-OF-FIT TEST TO TEST FOR NORMALITY

We can also use the goodness-of-fit test to determine whether a set of observed frequencies matches a set of expected frequencies that conforms to a normal distribution. To put it another way, do the observed values in a frequency distribution coincide with the theoretical expected values based on a normal distribution?

## ◼ EXAMPLE

The North Carolina Testing Institute designs tests for college entrance, tests for selection of applicants for high-level industrial positions, tests for disadvantaged children, and so on. Clients who purchase a test generally require that the test scores follow a normal pattern, that is, a normal distribution. The institute has been commissioned by a large international company to formulate a test to evaluate certain characteristics of applicants for high-level executive positions. The test designed by the institute was given to a sample of 300 executives, and the results were organized into the following frequency distribution.

| Score | Number of executives |
|---|---|
| Under 50 | 0 |
| 50 up to 60 | 24 |
| 60 up to 70 | 64 |
| 70 up to 80 | 120 |
| 80 up to 90 | 73 |
| 90 up to 100 | 19 |
| 100 and over | 0 |

Do these observed frequencies conform to a theoretical normal distribution?

## ☑ Solution

Basically, we want to find out whether the observed frequency in each class matches the theoretical expected frequency based on the normal probability distribution.

**Step 1**    The institute stated that the mean score for this particular test is 75. That is, $\mu = 75$. Further, the institute indicated that the standard deviation ($\sigma$) of the distribution of population scores is 15.

**Step 2**   We first use the mean of 75 and the standard deviation of 15 to compute the $z$ value for the lower class limit and the upper class limit for each class. To illustrate the computation of the two $z$ values, we selected the "80 up to 90" class.
   To determine $z$, we use formula (7–1).

$$z = \frac{X - \mu}{\sigma}$$

where $X$ is a particular test score, such as 80, $\mu$ is the mean of the population (75), and $\sigma$ is the standard deviation of the population (15).
   The $z$ value for 80, the lower limit of the "80 up to 90" class, is 0.33, found by

$$z = \frac{X - \mu}{\sigma} = \frac{80 - 75}{15} = 0.33$$

This indicates that 80 is $0.33\sigma$ from the mean of 75.
   For the upper limit of the "80 up to 90" class, $z = 1.00$, found by

$$z = \frac{X - \mu}{\sigma} = \frac{90 - 75}{15} = 1.00$$

Thus, 90 is $1.00\sigma$ from the mean of 75.
   Now to determine the area from the mean designated as 0 and $0.33\sigma$ we refer to Appendix D or the back cover. Reading down the left margin to 0.3 and horizontally to 0.03, we find that the area is .1293. This is the area between 75 and 80. Likewise, the

area between 75 and 90, or between 0 and 1.00$\sigma$, is .3413. Subtracting, .3413 − .1293 gives .2120, which is the area between 80 and 90. Shown schematically:

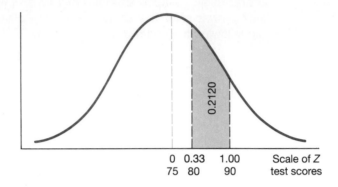

| | 0 | 0.33 | 1.00 | Scale of $Z$ |
| | 75 | 80 | 90 | test scores |

## Self-Review 16−4

*The answers are at the end of the chapter.*

Referring to the test score problem above, what is the area under the normal curve between the scores 90 and 100?

The areas under the normal curve for the remaining categories are computed in a similar manner. They are portrayed in the following chart.

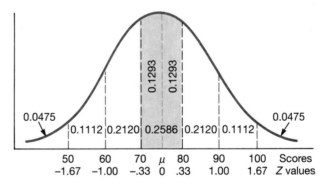

|  | 50 | 60 | 70 $\mu$ | 80 | 90 | 100 | Scores |
|  | −1.67 | −1.00 | −.33  0 | .33 | 1.00 | 1.67 | $Z$ values |

*STEP 3* Determine the expected frequency ($f_e$) for each category. For example, we found the area between the test scores 80 and 90 to be .2120. Logically, we expect 21.20 percent of the total number of executives who took the test (300) to be in the interval 80 to 90. So, .2120 × 300 = 63.6 executives are expected to score between 80 and 90 on the test.

## Self-Review 16−5

*The answers are at the end of the chapter.*

1. Refer again to the test score problem above. Determine the area under the normal curve in the category "100 and over." Show essential calculations.

2. How many executives would you expect to score 100 or more on the test?

Since we are dealing with a normal curve, the mean divides the curve into two equal parts. Thus, the area under the normal curve between 80 and 90 (.2120) is the same as the area between 60 and 70. The areas between the test scores 90 and 100 and between the scores 50 and 60 are also equal (.1112), and the areas in the two tails are the same (.0475).

Recall that the total area under the normal curve is 1.0000. Logically, the total area to the left of the mean score of 75 is .5000 and is identical to the total area to the right of the mean (.5000). Adding .5000 and .5000 gives us the total area under the normal curve of 1.0000.

All the expected frequencies ($f_e$) are shown in Table 16−7 along with the test scores, the z values, and the areas under the normal curve. As noted, the expected frequencies are based on the assumption that the test scores are normally distributed.

---

### TABLE   16−7

**Test Scores, z Values, and Areas under the Normal Curve**

| Test score | z value | Area | Expected frequency |
|---|---|---|---|
| Under 50 | Under −1.67 | .0475 | 14.25 ←—— .0475 × 300 |
| 50 up to 60 | −1.67 to −1.00 | .1112 | 33.36 ←—— .1112 × 300 |
| 60 up to 70 | −1.00 to −0.33 | .2120 | 63.60 ←—— .2120 × 300 |
| 70 up to 80 | −0.33 to 0.33 | .2586 | 77.58 ←—— .2586 × 300 |
| 80 up to 90 | 0.33 to 1.00 | .2120 | 63.60 ←—— .2120 × 300 |
| 90 up to 100 | 1.00 to 1.67 | .1112 | 33.36 ←—— .1112 × 300 |
| 100 and over | Over 1.67 | .0475 | 14.25 ←—— .0425 × 300 |
| | | 1.0000 | 300.00 |

---

**STEP 4**   We will now use the chi-square goodness-of-fit test to find out whether the observed set of executive test scores ($f_0$) coincides with the expected set ($f_e$), which theoretically comes from a normal distribution. That is, can we conclude that the set of executive scores is normally distributed?

As usual, the null and alternate hypotheses are stated first.

$H_0$:   The observed executive test scores are normally distributed with the mean $\mu = 75$ and standard deviation $\sigma = 15$.

$H_1$:   The observed executive test scores are not normally distributed with a mean of 75 and a standard deviation of 15.

If the null hypothesis is not rejected, we conclude that the executive test scores are normally distributed with a mean of 75 and a standard deviation of 15, as stated by the testing institute. The .05 level of significance is to be used.

The chi-square test statistic is calculated using formula (16−1).

$$\chi^2 = \sum \left[ \frac{(f_0 - f_e)^2}{f_e} \right]$$

There are seven categories (classes). The number of degrees of freedom is 6, found by $k - 1 = 7 - 1 = 6$. Referring to Appendix I, the .05 level of significance, and 6 degrees of freedom, we find that the critical value is 12.592. The calculations for chi-square are presented in Table 16−8.

## TABLE 16–8

### Calculations for Chi-square

| Test score | $f_o$ | $f_e$ | $f_o - f_e$ | $(f_o - f_e)^2$ | $\dfrac{(f_o - f_e)^2}{f_e}$ |
|---|---|---|---|---|---|
| Under 50 | 0 | 14.25 | −14.25 | 203.06 | 14.25 |
| 50 up to 60 | 24 | 33.36 | −9.36 | 87.60 | 2.63 |
| 60 up to 70 | 64 | 63.60 | 0.40 | 0.16 | 0.00 |
| 70 up to 80 | 120 | 77.58 | 42.42 | 1,799.46 | 23.19 |
| 80 up to 90 | 73 | 63.60 | 9.40 | 88.36 | 1.39 |
| 90 up to 100 | 19 | 33.36 | −14.36 | 206.21 | 6.18 |
| 100 and over | 0 | 14.25 | −14.25 | 203.06 | 14.25 |
| | 300 | 300 | 0 | | 61.89 |

Must be equal   Must be 0   $\chi^2$

The computed value of chi-square (61.89) is greater than the critical value of 12.592. Thus, we reject the null hypothesis. We conclude that the executive test scores do not come from a normal distribution with a mean of 75 and a standard deviation of 15. The North Carolina Testing Institute cannot inform the client that the executive test scores are normally distributed with a mean of 75 and a standard deviation of 15. Apparently, the institute needs to redesign their test.

Some closing comments: Recall that 1 degree of freedom is lost in this problem, found by the number of categories minus 1: $k - 1 = 7 - 1 = 6$. The North Carolina Testing Institute stated that for this executive test score problem $\mu = 75$ and $\sigma = 15$. Since these are population parameters, no degrees of freedom are to be subtracted for those two parameters. Had the mean and standard deviation been estimated from a sample, 1 degree of freedom would be subtracted for the sample mean, $\overline{X}$, and 1 for the sample standard deviation, $s$. Had this been the case, letting $m$ stand for the degree of freedom lost for the mean plus the one for the standard deviation, we would have only 4 degrees of freedom, found by $k - 1 - m = 7 - 1 - 2$. The critical value at the .05 level and $df = 4$ would be 9.488 instead of 12.592.

In conclusion, it should noted that the expected frequencies were all over 5. We mentioned in the previous section that if more than 20 percent of the categories have expected frequencies of less than 5, it is imperative to combine some of the categories. If, for example, the expected frequencies in the lower and upper tails of the distribution of executive test scores were less than 5, we could combine the "under 50" cell with the "50 up to 60" cell and the "100 and over" cell with the "90 up to 100" category.

## EXERCISES

*The answers to the odd-numbered exercises are at the end of the book.*

10. The manufacturer of a computer terminal reports in its advertising material that the mean life of the terminal, under normal use, is 6 years with a standard deviation of 1.4 years. A sample of 90 units sold 10 years ago revealed the following distribution of the lengths of life. At the .05 significance level, can the manufacturer conclude that the terminal lives are normally distributed with $\mu = 6$ and $\sigma = 1.4$?

| Length of life (years) | Frequency |
|---|---|
| Up to 4 | 7 |
| 4 to 5 | 14 |
| 5 to 6 | 25 |
| 6 to 7 | 22 |
| 7 to 8 | 16 |
| 8 or more | 6 |

11. The commissions for sales of new cars are reported to average $1,500 per month with a standard deviation of $300. A sample of 500 sales representatives in the Northwest revealed the following distribution of commissions. At the .01 significance level, can we conclude that the population is normally distributed with a mean of $1,500 and a standard deviation of $300?

| Commission ($) | Frequency |
|---|---|
| Less than 900 | 9 |
| 900 to 1,200 | 63 |
| 1,200 to 1,500 | 165 |
| 1,500 to 1,800 | 180 |
| 1,800 to 2,100 | 71 |
| 2,100 or more | 12 |
| Total | 500 |

## CONTINGENCY TABLE ANALYSIS

The goodness-of-fit test applied in the previous section was concerned with only a single variable and a single trait. The chi-square test can also be used for a research project involving *two* traits. These are examples:

- Does a male released from federal prison make a better adjustment to civilian life if he returns to his hometown or if he goes elsewhere to live? The two traits are adjustment to civilian life and place of residence. Note that both traits are measured on the nominal scale.

- Is there any relationship between the grade point average students earn in college and their income 10 years after graduation? The two traits measured for each individual are grade point average and income.

### ▪ EXAMPLE

Suppose the Federal Correction Agency wants to investigate the first question cited above: Does a male released from federal prison make better adjustment to civilian life if he returns to his hometown or if he goes elsewhere to live? To put it another way, is there a relationship between adjustment to civilian life and place of residence after release from prison?

### ☑ SOLUTION

As before, the first step in hypothesis testing is to state the null and alternate hypotheses.

$H_0$: There is no relationship between adjustment to civilian life and where the individual lives after being released from prison.

$H_1$: There is a relationship between adjustment to civilian life and where the individual lives after being released from prison.

The .01 level of significance will be used to test the hypothesis. Recall that this is the probability of a Type I error (i.e., the probability is .01 that a true null hypothesis is rejected).

The agency's psychologists interviewed 200 randomly selected former prisoners. Using the series of questions, the psychologists classified the adjustment of each individual to civilian life as outstanding, good, fair, or unsatisfactory. The classifications for the 200 former prisoners were tallied as follows. Joseph Camden, for example, returned to his hometown and has shown outstanding adjustment to civilian life. His case is one of the 27 tallies in the upper left box.

| Residence after release from prison | Adjustment to civilian life | | | |
|---|---|---|---|---|
| | Outstanding | Good | Fair | Unsatisfactory |
| Hometown | ‖‖ ‖‖ ‖‖ ‖‖ ‖‖ ‖‖ ‖ ‖ | ‖‖ ‖‖ ‖‖ ‖‖ ‖‖ ‖‖ ‖‖ | ‖‖ ‖‖ ‖‖ ‖‖ ‖‖ ‖‖ ‖‖ ‖ ‖ ‖ | ‖‖ ‖‖ ‖‖ ‖‖ ‖‖ ‖‖ |
| Not hometown | ‖‖ ‖‖ ‖ ‖ ‖ ‖ | ‖‖ ‖‖ ‖‖ ‖‖ | ‖‖ ‖‖ ‖‖ ‖‖ ‖‖ ‖‖ ‖ ‖ ‖ | ‖‖ ‖‖ ‖‖ ‖‖ ‖‖ ‖‖ |

**Contingency table consists of count data**

The tallies in each box, or *cell,* were counted. The counts are given in the following **contingency table.** (See Table 16–9.) In this case, the Federal Correction Agency wondered whether or not adjustment to civilian life is *contingent on* where the prisoner goes after released from prison.

## Table 16–9

**Adjustment to Civilian Life and Place of Residence**

| Residence after release from prison | Adjustment to civilian life | | | | Total |
|---|---|---|---|---|---|
| | Outstanding | Good | Fair | Unsatisfactory | |
| Hometown | 27 | 35 | 33 | 25 | 120 |
| Not hometown | 13 | 15 | 27 | 25 | 80 |
| Total | 40 | 50 | 60 | 50 | 200 |

**Contingency table has rows and columns**

Once we know how many rows (2) and how many columns (4) there are in the contingency table, the critical value and the decision rule can be determined. For a chi-square test of significance where two traits are cross-classified in a contingency table, one finds the degrees of freedom by:

**df found by $(r - 1)(c - 1)$**

$$df = \text{(number of rows} - 1)\text{(number of columns} - 1)$$
$$= (r - 1)(c - 1)$$

In this problem:

$$df = (r - 1)(c - 1)$$
$$= (2 - 1)(4 - 1)$$
$$= 3$$

The decision rule

To find the critical value for 3 degrees of freedom and the .01 level (selected earlier), refer to Appendix I. It is 11.345. The decision rule is therefore: Do not reject the null hypothesis if the computed value of $\chi^2$ is equal to or less than 11.345; reject $H_0$ and accept $H_1$ if it is greater than 11.345. The decision rule is portrayed graphically in Chart 16–4.

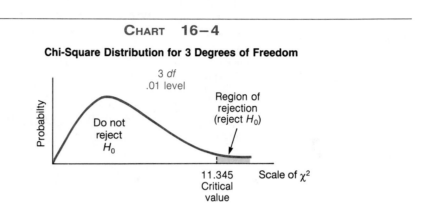

CHART   16–4

**Chi-Square Distribution for 3 Degrees of Freedom**

Now to find the computed value of $\chi^2$. The observed frequencies, $f_0$, are shown in Table 16–9. How are the corresponding expected frequencies, $f_e$, determined? Note in the "Total" column of Table 16–9 on the previous page, that 120 of the 200 former prisoners (60 percent) returned to their hometowns. *If there were no relationship whatsoever* between adjustment and residency after release from prison, we would expect 60 percent of the 40 ex-prisoners who made outstanding adjustment to civilian life to reside in their hometowns. Thus, the expected frequency $f_e$ for the upper left cell is .60 × 40, or 24. Likewise, if there were no relationship between adjustment and present residence, we would expect 60 percent of the 50 ex-prisoners (30) who had "good" adjustment to civilian life to reside in their hometowns.

Further, notice that 80 of the 200 ex-prisoners studied (40 percent) did not return to their hometowns to live. Thus, of the 60 considered by the psychologists to have made "fair" adjustment to civilian life, .40 × 60, or 24, would be expected not to return to their hometowns.

Convenient formula for determining expected frequency

The expected frequency for any cell can be determined by

$$\text{Expected frequency for a cell} = \frac{(\text{Row total})(\text{Column total})}{\text{Grand total}} \qquad (16-2)$$

Using that formula, the expected frequency for the upper left cell in Table 16–9 is:

$$\text{Expected frequency} = \frac{(\text{Row total})(\text{Column total})}{\text{Grand total}}$$
$$= \frac{(120)(40)}{200}$$
$$= 24$$

The observed frequencies, $f_0$, and the expected frequencies, $f_e$, for all of the cells in the contingency table are listed in Table 16–10.

---

### TABLE 16–10

**Observed Frequencies and Expected Frequencies**

| Residence after release from prison | Adjustment to civilian life | | | | | | | | | |
|---|---|---|---|---|---|---|---|---|---|---|
| | Outstanding | | Good | | Fair | | Unsatisfactory | | Total | |
| | $f_0$ | $f_e$ | $f_0$ | $f_e$ | $f_0$ | $f_e$ | $f_0$ | $f_e$ | $f_0$ | $f_e$ |
| Hometown | 27 | 24 | 35 | 30 | 33 | 36 | 25 | 30 | 120 | 120 |
| Not hometown | 13 | 16 | 15 | 20 | 27 | 24 | 25 | 20 | 80 | 80 |
| Total | 40 | 40 | 50 | 50 | 60 | 60 | 50 | 50 | 200 | 200 |

Must be equal

$$\frac{(80)(50)}{200}$$

Must be equal

---

**What to do if $\Sigma f_e$ and $\Sigma f_0$ in a column are not equal**

Due to rounding, the total of the expected frequencies for a column may not be exactly equal to the total of the observed frequencies for that column. If this does happen, the totals can be made equal by adjusting one or more of the expected frequencies in that column.

Recall that the computed value of chi-square using formula (16–1) is found by:

$$\chi^2 = \Sigma \left[ \frac{(f_0 - f_e)^2}{f_e} \right]$$

**Computed $\chi^2 = 5.729$**

Starting with the upper-left cell:

$$\chi^2 = \frac{(27 - 24)^2}{24} + \frac{(35 - 30)^2}{30} + \frac{(33 - 36)^2}{36} + \frac{(25 - 30)^2}{30}$$
$$+ \frac{(13 - 16)^2}{16} + \frac{(15 - 20)^2}{20} + \frac{(27 - 24)^2}{24} + \frac{(25 - 20)^2}{20}$$
$$= 0.375 + 0.833 + 0.250 + 0.833 + 0.563 + 1.250 + 0.375 + 1.250$$
$$= 5.729$$

**Conclusion: No relationship between adjustment and residence**

Since the computed value of chi-square (5.729) lies in the region to the left of 11.345, the null hypothesis is not rejected at the .01 level. We conclude that there is no relationship between adjustment to civilian life and where the prisoner resides after being released from prison. For the Federal Correction Agency's advisement program, adjustment to civilian life is not related to where the ex-prisoner lives.

The MINITAB output for this problem follows. The READ command was used to input the data instead of the usual SET command. The command used to compute chi-square is CHISQUARE.

```
MTR > read c1 c2 c3 c4
DATA > 27, 35, 33, 25
DATA > 13, 15, 27, 25
DATA > end
MTB > chisquare c1-c4
MTB > name c1 'outstand' c2 'good' c3 'fair' c4 'poor'
MTB > chisquare c1-c4

Expected counts are printed below observed counts

              outstand      good      fair      poor      Total
         1          27        35        33        25        120
                  24.0      30.0      36.0      30.0

         2          13        15        27        25         80
                  16.0      20.0      24.0      20.0

     Total          40        50        60        50        200

    ChiSq=        0.37+     0.83+     0.25+     0.83+
                  0.56+     1.25+     0.37+     1.25=5.73 ← x²

    df=3
```

Observe that the computed value of chi-square (5.73) is the same as that found earlier.

## Self-Review 16–6

*The answers are at the end of the chapter.*

A sociologist was researching this question: Is there any relationship between the level of education and social activities of an individual? She decided on three levels of education: attended or completed college, attended or completed high school, and attended or completed grade school or less. Each individual kept a record of his or her social activities, such as bowling with a group, dancing, and church functions. The sociologist divided them into above-average frequency, average frequency, and below-average frequency.

| | Social activity | | |
| Education | Above average | Average | Below average |
|---|---|---|---|
| College | 20 | 10 | 10 |
| High school | 30 | 50 | 80 |
| Grade school | 10 | 60 | 130 |

1. What is the table called?
2. State the null hypothesis. It is to be tested at the .05 level.
3. Should the null hypothesis be rejected? Cite figures to substantiate your decision.
4. What specifically does this indicate in this problem?

## EXERCISES

*The answers to the odd-numbered exercises are at the end of the book.*

12. A survey of industrial salespeople who are either self-employed or work for small, medium-size, or large firms revealed the following with respect to incomes:

Of those who earn less than $20,000 a year, 9 are self-employed, and 12 are employed by small firms, 40 by medium-size firms, and 89 by large firms.

Of those who earn $20,000–$39,999, 11 are self-employed, and 10 are employed by small firms, 45 by medium-sized firms, and 104 by large firms.

Of those who earn $40,000 or more, 10 are self-employed, and 13 are employed by small firms, 50 by medium-size firms, and 107 by large firms.

Examine the hypothesis that there is no relationship between the income level of the industrial salespeople and their employment status (self-employed or employed by small, medium-size, or large firms). Test at the .05 level.

13. The survey mentioned in Exercise 12 included questions on the age of the respondent and the degree of pressure the industrial salesperson felt in connection with the job. Ages and amounts of job pressure were cross-classified in the following table.

| Age (years) | Degree of pressure (number of salespeople) | | |
|---|---|---|---|
| | Low | Medium | High |
| Less than 25 | 20 | 18 | 22 |
| 25–39 | 50 | 46 | 44 |
| 40–59 | 58 | 63 | 59 |
| 60 and older | 34 | 43 | 43 |

Examine whether there is any relationship between age and the degree of job pressure. Use the .01 level.

14. The marketing director for a metropolitan daily newspaper is studying the relationship between the type of community the reader lives in and the portion of the paper he or she reads first. For a sample of 500 readers the following information was collected.

| | National news | Sports | Comics |
|---|---|---|---|
| Urban | 170 | 124 | 90 |
| Rural | 120 | 112 | 100 |
| Farm | 130 | 90 | 88 |

At the .05 significance level, can we conclude that there is a relationship between the type of community where the person resides and the portion of the paper read first?

15. Four different brands of light bulbs are being considered for use in a large manufacturing plant. The director of purchasing asked for samples of 100 from each manufacturer. The numbers of acceptable and unacceptable bulbs from each manufacturer are shown below. At the .05 significance level, is there a difference in the quality of the bulbs?

| | Manufacturer | | | |
|---|---|---|---|---|
| | A | B | C | D |
| Acceptable | 12 | 8 | 5 | 11 |
| Unacceptable | 88 | 92 | 95 | 89 |
| Total | 100 | 100 | 100 | 100 |

## CHAPTER OUTLINE

I. Goodness-of-fit test.
   A. A goodness-of-fit test is applied to find out if a set of observed frequencies fits a set of matching expected frequencies. It can be used for all levels of data—nominal, ordinal, interval, and ratio. No assumptions about the shape of the parent population are required.
   B. The procedure is:
      1. State $H_0$ and $H_1$.
      2. Select a level of risk—usually .10, .05, or .01.
      3. The formula for chi-square is:

$$\chi^2 = \sum \left[ \frac{(f_0 - f_e)^2}{f_e} \right] \tag{16-1}$$

      with $k - 1$ degrees of freedom, where $k$ is the number of categories.
      4. The decision rule is based on $k - 1$ degrees of freedom and the level of significance selected.

5. A sample from the population is chosen, $\chi^2$ is computed, and its magnitude is compared with the critical value in order to reach a decision regarding $H_0$.
6. The goodness-of-fit test is also used to find out whether a set of observed frequencies conforms to a normal distribution.

II. Contingency table analysis.
   A. It is used to test whether or not two traits are related. Two traits an individual possesses might be political affiliation and view of current policy aimed at reducing the federal deficit.
   B. The procedure is:
      1. Cross-classify the two traits in a contingency table.
      2. Determine the expected frequency, $f_e$, for a particular cell:

$$\text{Expected frequency} = \frac{(\text{Row total})(\text{Column total})}{\text{Grand total}} \qquad (16\text{-}2)$$

      3. Find the degrees of freedom for the contingency table by: (rows − 1)(columns − 1).
      4. Compute chi-square, and arrive at a decision.

III. Characteristics of the chi-square distribution:
   A. The value of chi-square is always positive.
   B. There is a family of chi-square distributions. The shape of the distribution changes for each number of degrees of freedom.
   C. The distributions of the chi-square statistic are positively skewed, but as the number of degrees of freedom increases, the distributions approach normality.

## EXERCISES

*The answers to the odd-numbered exercises are at the end of the book.*

16. A sample of the employees of Carter Industries regarding acceptance of a new pension plan revealed the following:

| | Opinion regarding new pension plan | | | | |
|---|---|---|---|---|---|
| Age | Superior | Very good | Good | Fair | Unsatisfactory |
| 20–29 | 19 | 27 | 25 | 52 | 81 |
| 30–39 | 10 | 17 | 15 | 29 | 41 |
| 40–49 | 51 | 40 | 31 | 21 | 27 |
| 50 and older | 142 | 81 | 16 | 9 | 8 |

Is there a relationship between age and an employee's opinion of the new plan? Test at the .05 level. Use the five-step hypothesis-testing procedure.

17. A sample of unpaid balances on Southwestern charge accounts as of September 1 was organized into the following frequency distribution.

| Size of unpaid balance | Number of accounts |
|---|---|
| Less than $20 | 13 |
| $20 to under $40 | 10 |
| $40 to under $60 | 15 |
| $60 to under $80 | 14 |
| $80 to under $100 | 9 |
| $100 to under $150 | 12 |
| $150 and over | 11 |

The hypothesis that the unpaid balances are evenly distributed among the seven categories is to be tested at the .01 level of risk.
   a. State the null and alternate hypotheses.
   b. Show the decision rule graphically.
   c. Arrive at a decision.

18. Suppose that there is interest in testing if there is any relationship between the scholastic achievement (final grade point average in college) of a business administration graduate and his or her level of income. The null hypothesis is: There is no relationship between scholastic achievement and level of income. $H_1$ states that there is a relationship. For this test, the .05 level of significance was selected.

It was decided to classify the scholastic achievement levels of the business administration graduates into three groups: above average, average, and below average, represented by final grade point scores of 3.0–4.0, 2.5–2.9999, and 2.0–2.4999, respectively (2.0 is needed for graduation, and 4.0 indicates that an alumnus had all A grades when in college).

The incomes of the 751 respondents were classified into four levels: low, lower middle, upper middle, and high. The responses of the 751 graduates were tallied into a table.

| Scholastic achievement | Income level | | | | |
|---|---|---|---|---|---|
| | Low | Lower middle | Upper middle | High | Total |
| Above average | 22 | 31 | 31 | 8 | 92 |
| Average | 67 | 80 | 73 | 17 | 237 |
| Below average | 124 | 161 | 122 | 15 | 422 |

Source: Robert D. Mason, *Alumni Study* (Toledo, Ohio: University of Toledo, College of Business Administration).

Is there a relationship between scholastic achievement and level of income? Use the five-step hypothesis-testing procedure.

19. In 1969 the Selective Service System conducted a lottery to determine the sequence in which young men would be drafted into the armed services of the United States. The Selective Service System developed elaborate measures to ensure that birthdays were randomly selected and a sequence number assigned. Since that time many critics have alleged that the lottery was not random. They contend that those with birthdays late in the year tended to have lower lottery numbers and hence were more likely to be drafted.

The following table gives the results of the 1969 lottery. The left column gives the day of the month; the 12 months are listed across the top. The numbers in the body of the table indicate the draft sequence. Note that the number 001 appears in row 14 in the September column—all those born on September 14 were drafted first. When that pool of men was exhausted, those born on April 24 were drafted (because they had the number 002). Then those born on December 30 were drafted, and so on.

| Date | Jan. | Feb. | Mar. | Apr. | May | Jun. | Jul. | Aug. | Sep. | Oct. | Nov. | Dec. |
|---|---|---|---|---|---|---|---|---|---|---|---|---|
| 1 | 305 | 086 | 108 | 032 | 330 | 249 | 093 | 111 | 225 | 359 | 019 | 129 |
| 2 | 159 | 144 | 029 | 271 | 298 | 228 | 350 | 045 | 161 | 125 | 034 | 328 |
| 3 | 251 | 297 | 267 | 083 | 040 | 301 | 115 | 261 | 049 | 244 | 348 | 157 |
| 4 | 215 | 210 | 275 | 081 | 276 | 020 | 279 | 145 | 232 | 202 | 266 | 165 |
| 5 | 101 | 214 | 293 | 269 | 364 | 028 | 188 | 054 | 082 | 024 | 310 | 056 |
| 6 | 224 | 347 | 139 | 253 | 155 | 110 | 327 | 114 | 006 | 087 | 076 | 010 |
| 7 | 306 | 091 | 122 | 147 | 035 | 085 | 050 | 168 | 008 | 234 | 051 | 012 |
| 8 | 199 | 181 | 213 | 312 | 321 | 366 | 013 | 048 | 184 | 283 | 097 | 105 |
| 9 | 194 | 338 | 317 | 219 | 197 | 335 | 277 | 106 | 263 | 342 | 080 | 043 |
| 10 | 325 | 216 | 323 | 218 | 065 | 206 | 284 | 021 | 071 | 220 | 282 | 041 |
| 11 | 329 | 150 | 136 | 014 | 037 | 134 | 248 | 324 | 158 | 237 | 046 | 039 |
| 12 | 221 | 068 | 300 | 346 | 133 | 272 | 015 | 142 | 242 | 072 | 066 | 314 |
| 13 | 318 | 152 | 259 | 124 | 295 | 069 | 042 | 307 | 175 | 138 | 126 | 163 |
| 14 | 238 | 004 | 354 | 231 | 178 | 356 | 331 | 198 | 001 | 294 | 127 | 026 |
| 15 | 017 | 089 | 169 | 273 | 130 | 180 | 322 | 102 | 113 | 171 | 131 | 320 |
| 16 | 121 | 212 | 166 | 148 | 055 | 274 | 120 | 044 | 207 | 254 | 107 | 096 |
| 17 | 235 | 189 | 033 | 260 | 112 | 073 | 098 | 154 | 255 | 288 | 143 | 304 |
| 18 | 140 | 292 | 332 | 090 | 278 | 341 | 190 | 141 | 246 | 005 | 146 | 128 |
| 19 | 058 | 025 | 200 | 336 | 075 | 104 | 227 | 311 | 177 | 241 | 203 | 240 |
| 20 | 280 | 302 | 239 | 345 | 183 | 360 | 187 | 344 | 063 | 192 | 185 | 135 |

| Date | Jan. | Feb. | Mar. | Apr. | May | Jun. | Jul. | Aug | Sep. | Oct. | Nov. | Dec. |
|------|------|------|------|------|-----|------|------|-----|------|------|------|------|
| 21 | 186 | 363 | 334 | 062 | 250 | 060 | 027 | 291 | 204 | 243 | 156 | 070 |
| 22 | 337 | 290 | 265 | 316 | 326 | 247 | 153 | 339 | 160 | 117 | 009 | 053 |
| 23 | 118 | 057 | 256 | 252 | 319 | 109 | 172 | 116 | 119 | 201 | 182 | 162 |
| 24 | 059 | 236 | 258 | 002 | 031 | 358 | 023 | 036 | 195 | 196 | 230 | 095 |
| 25 | 052 | 179 | 343 | 351 | 361 | 137 | 067 | 286 | 149 | 176 | 132 | 084 |
| 26 | 092 | 365 | 170 | 340 | 357 | 022 | 303 | 245 | 018 | 007 | 309 | 173 |
| 27 | 355 | 205 | 268 | 074 | 296 | 064 | 289 | 352 | 233 | 264 | 047 | 078 |
| 28 | 077 | 299 | 223 | 262 | 308 | 222 | 088 | 167 | 257 | 094 | 281 | 123 |
| 29 | 349 | 285 | 362 | 191 | 226 | 353 | 270 | 061 | 151 | 229 | 099 | 016 |
| 30 | 164 | | 217 | 208 | 103 | 209 | 287 | 333 | 315 | 038 | 174 | 003 |
| 31 | 211 | | 030 | | 313 | | 193 | 011 | | 079 | | 100 |

To continue, men born on October 8 had the lottery number 283. This meant that the nationwide supply of men born on 282 other days would have to be exhausted before those born on October 8 were drafted.

A cursory examination of the lottery numbers does seem to indicate that the men with birthdays in the last three or four months of the year did have low lottery numbers and were more likely to be drafted. To examine this contention further, you may want to organize the lottery numbers into a 3 × 4 contingency table. The lottery numbers could be grouped as low, medium, and high. The months could be separated into quarters. Interpret your findings.

20. The lengths of service for each of the associate justices of the Supreme Court of the United States were given in an earlier chapter. These raw data have been organized into the following frequency distribution. The population mean number of years of service is 15.68, and the standard deviation is 9.57 years. Could these data be from a normal population? Conduct an appropriate test using the .05 level of significance.

| Years of service | Frequency |
|------------------|-----------|
| Up to 5 | 12 |
| 5 up to 10 | 18 |
| 10 up to 15 | 12 |
| 15 up to 20 | 16 |
| 20 up to 25 | 11 |
| 25 up to 30 | 7 |
| 30 or more | 9 |
| Total | 85 |

Courtesy Office of the Curator, Supreme Court of the United States, photograph by Joe Bailey and Larry Kinney. © National Geographic Society

## COMPUTER DATA EXERCISES

21. Refer to data set 1, which reports information on homes sold in Florida during 1990.

    a. Develop a contingency table that shows whether or not a home has a pool according to the township in which the home is located. Is there any association between the variables pool and township? Use the .05 significance level.

    b. Develop a contingency table that shows whether or not a home has an attached garage according to the township in which the home is located. Is there any association between the variables pool and township? Use the .05 significance level.

    c. Develop a frequency distribution for the number of bedrooms in a home. Is it reasonable to conclude that this distribution is normal? Use the .01 significance level.

22. Refer to data set 3, which reports information on the 26 major league baseball teams for the 1991 season. Set up a variable that divides the teams into two groups: those that had a winning season and those that did not. That is, create a variable to count the cases where the variable "Fraction" is less than .500 and those where it is .500 or more. We'll call this variable "Winning". Next create a new variable for attendance, where there are two categories: less than 2.0 million, and 2.0 or more millions. Is there an association between winning and team attendance? Use the .05 significance level.

# CHAPTER 16 EXAMINATION

*The answers are at the end of the chapter.*

1. In recent years, 55 percent of the American-made automobiles sold in the United States were manufactured by General Motors, 25 percent by Ford, 15 percent by Chrysler, and 5 percent by all others (Honda USA, etc.). A sample of the sales of American-made automobiles conducted last week revealed that 174 were manufactured by Chrysler, 275 by Ford, 330 by GM, and 21 by all others. Test the hypothesis at the .05 level that there has been no change in the sales pattern.

2. Two hundred men selected at random from various levels of management were interviewed regarding their concern about environmental issues. The response of each person was tallied into one of three categories: no concern, some concern, and great concern. The results were:

| Level of management | No concern | Some concern | Great concern |
|---|---|---|---|
| Top management | 15 | 13 | 12 |
| Middle management | 20 | 19 | 21 |
| Supervisor | 7 | 7 | 6 |
| Group leader | 28 | 21 | 31 |

Using the .01 level, determine if there is any difference in the responses with respect to the level of management.

16–1  1. Observed frequencies.
2. Six (six days of the week).
3. 10. Total observed frequencies ÷ 6 = 60/6 = 10.
4. 5; $k - 1 = 6 - 1 = 5$.
5. 15.086 (from the chi-square table in Appendix I).
6. Computed:

$$\chi^2 = \sum \left[ \frac{(f_0 - f_e)^2}{f_e} \right] = \frac{(12 - 10)^2}{10}$$
$$+ \frac{(9 - 10)^2}{10} + \frac{(11 - 10)^2}{10}$$
$$+ \frac{(10 - 10)^2}{10} + \frac{(9 - 10)^2}{10}$$
$$+ \frac{(9 - 10)^2}{10} = 0.8$$

7. No. We do not reject $H_0$.
8. Absenteeism is distributed evenly throughout the week. The observed differences are due to sampling variation.

16–2  $\chi^2$ was computed to be 14.01, found by:

| $f_0$ | $f_e$ | $f_0 - f_e$ | $(f_0 - f_e)^2$ | $\dfrac{(f_0 - f_e)^2}{f_e}$ |
|---|---|---|---|---|
| 30 | 32 | −2 | 4 | 4/32 = 0.13 |
| 110 | 113 | −3 | 9 | 9/113 = 0.08 |
| 86 | 87 | −1 | 1 | 1/87 = 0.01 |
| 23 | 24 | −1 | 1 | 1/24 = 0.04 |
| 5 | 2 | 3 | 9 | 9/2 = 4.50 |
| 5 | 4 | 1 | 1 | 1/4 = 0.25 |
| 4 | 1 | 3 | 9 | 9/1 = 9.00 |
| | | 0 | | 14.01 |

The critical value of $\chi^2$ for $k - 1 = 7 - 1 = 6$ degrees of freedom and the .05 level is 12.592. The computed $\chi^2$ (14.01) is greater than this critical value, so the null hypothesis is rejected. There is a difference between the set of observed frequencies and the set of expected frequencies.

16–3  1. $\chi^2 = 7.26$, found by:

| $f_0$ | $f_e$ | $f_0 - f_e$ | $(f_0 - f_e)^2$ | $\dfrac{(f_0 - f_e)^2}{f_e}$ |
|---|---|---|---|---|
| 30 | 32 | −2 | 4 | 0.13 |
| 110 | 113 | −3 | 9 | 0.08 |
| 86 | 87 | −1 | 1 | 0.01 |
| 23 | 24 | −1 | 1 | 0.04 |
| 14 | 7 | 7 | 49 | 7.00 |
| | | 0 | | 7.26 |

2. The critical value of $\chi^2$ for $k - 1 = 5 - 1 = 4$ degrees of freedom and the .05 level is 9.488. The computed value of 7.26 is less than 9.488, so the null hypothesis of no difference between the sample results and the expected results is not rejected at the .05 level of significance.
3. Yes.

16–4  .1112, found by: z for 90 = 1.00, and z for 100 = 1.67. Then, the area for 1.67 is .4525 and for 1.00 it is .3413. Subtracting, .4525 − .3413 = .1112.

16–5  1. .0475, found by .5000 − .4525.
2. 14.25, found by .0475 × 300.

16–6  1. Contingency table.
2. There is no relationship between the level of education and the frequency of social activity.
3. Computing chi-square:

| Above average | | Average | | Below average | | | |
|---|---|---|---|---|---|---|---|
| $f_0$ | $f_e$ | $f_0$ | $f_e$ | $f_0$ | $f_e$ | Total | Percent |
| 20 | 6 | 10 | 12 | 10 | 22 | 40 | 10 |
| 30 | 24 | 50 | 48 | 80 | 88 | 160 | 40 |
| 10 | 30 | 60 | 60 | 130 | 110 | 200 | 50 |
| 60 | 60 | 120 | 120 | 220 | 220 | 400 | 100 |

$$\chi^2 = \frac{(20-6)^2}{6} + \frac{(10-12)^2}{12} +$$
$$\cdots + \frac{(130-110)^2}{110}$$
$$= 32.67 + 0.33 + \cdots + 3.64$$
$$= 58.83$$

The computed value of chi-square is 58.83. Because it is greater than the critical value of 9.488, the null hypothesis is rejected at the .05 level.

4. There is a relationship between the level of education and the frequency of social activity.

## Answers

## CHAPTER 16 EXAMINATION

1. $H_0$: There has been no change in the pattern of sales.
$H_1$: There has been a change.
The computed value of chi-square (88.950) is in the region of rejection (to the right of 7.815).

| | $f_0$ | $f_e$ | $f_0 - f_e$ | $\frac{(f_0 - f_e)^2}{f_e}$ |
|---|---|---|---|---|
| GM | 330 | 440 | −110 | 27.500 |
| Ford | 275 | 200 | 75 | 28.125 |
| Chrysler | 174 | 120 | 54 | 24.300 |
| All others | 21 | 40 | −19 | 9.025 |
| | 800 | 800 | 0 | 88.950 |

2. As indicated by the following computations, the computed value of chi-square is about 1.550, which is less than the critical value of 16.812. Thus, the null hypothesis, which states that there is no significant difference in the responses with regard to the level of management, is not rejected. To put it another way, there is no relationship between the degree of concern about environmental issues and the level of management. The critical value of 16.812 was determined by referring to Appendix I for (rows − 1)(columns − 1) = (4 − 1) × (3 − 1) = 6 degrees of freedom.

| Level of management | No concern $f_0$ | $f_e$ | Some concern $f_0$ | $f_e$ | Very concerned $f_0$ | $f_e$ | Total Number | Percent |
|---|---|---|---|---|---|---|---|---|
| Top management | 15 | (14) | 13 | (12) | 12 | (14) | 40 | 20 |
| Middle management | 20 | (21) | 19 | (18) | 21 | (21) | 60 | 30 |
| Supervisor | 7 | (7) | 7 | (6) | 6 | (7) | 20 | 10 |
| Group leader | 28 | (28) | 21 | (24) | 31 | (28) | 80 | 40 |
| | 70 | (70) | 60 | (60) | 70 | (70) | 200 | 100 |

$$\chi^2 = \frac{(15-14)^2}{14} + \frac{(13-12)^2}{12} + \frac{(12-14)^2}{14} + \frac{(20-21)^2}{21} + \cdots = 1.550$$

# NONPARAMETRIC METHODS: ANALYSIS OF RANKED DATA

When you have completed this chapter, you will be able to:

GOALS

1. Conduct a sign test and explain its applications.

2. Describe and apply the Mann-Whitney $U$ test to ordinal-level data.

3. Apply the Kruskal-Wallis one-way analysis of variance by ranks test to ordinal-level data.

4. Describe the Wilcoxon matched-pair signed rank test and its applications.

C hapter 16 introduced nonparametric, or distribution-free, tests of hypotheses. We stressed that the chi-square goodness-of-fit test is especially useful for *nominal* level of measurement. Its purpose is to determine whether or not an observed set of frequencies, $f_o$, is significantly different from a corresponding set of expected frequencies, $f_e$. Likewise, if we are interested in the relationship between two characteristics—such as the age of an individual and his or her music preference—we would tally the data into a contingency table and use the chi-square distribution as the test statistic. For both these types of problems, no assumptions need to be made about the shape of the parent population. We do not have to assume, for example, that the population of interest is normally distributed, as was done with tests of hypotheses in Chapters 8 through 12.

This chapter is a continuation of tests of hypotheses designed especially for nonparametric data. However, instead of being applicable to nominal-level data, as is the chi-square test, these tests require that the responses be at least *ordinal-level.* That is, it is imperative that the responses can be ranked from low to high. An example of ranking is the executive title. Executives are ranked assistant vice president, vice president, senior vice president, and president. A vice president is ranked higher than an assistant vice president, a senior vice president is ranked higher than a vice president, and so on.

Five distribution-free tests requiring ranking will be considered in this chapter: the sign test, the median test, the Mann-Whitney $U$ test, the Kruskal-Wallis analysis of variance by ranks test, and the Wilcoxon matched-pair signed rank test.

## THE SIGN TEST

Sign test

The **sign test** is one of the simplest nonparametric tests. As the name suggests, it is based on the sign of a difference—a plus sign for a positive difference and a minus sign for a negative difference. If, for example, sales increased from $34,698 million in October to $51,276 million in November, we record a plus sign. If production dropped from 98,000 computers in the first quarter to 51,000 in the second quarter, a minus sign is recorded. For a sign test, we are not concerned with the magnitude of the difference.

The sign test has many applications. One is for "before/after" experiments. To illustrate, suppose an evaluation is to be made on a new tune-up program for automobiles. The number of miles traveled per gallon of gasoline is recorded before the tune-up and again after the tune-up. If the tune-up is not effective, that is had no effect on performance, theoretically about half of the automobiles tested would show an increase in miles per gallon and the other half a decrease. A "+" sign is assigned to an increase, a "−" sign to a decrease.

A product-preference experiment illustrates another use of the sign test. Taster's Choice markets two kinds of coffee in a 4-ounce jar: decaffeinated and regular. Their market research department wants to determine whether coffee drinkers prefer decaffeinated or regular coffee. Coffee drinkers are given two small, unmarked cups of coffee, and each is asked his or her preference. Preference for decaffeinated could be coded "+" and preference for regular "−". In a sense the data are ordinal-level because the coffee drinker gives his/her preferred coffee the higher rank; the other kind is ranked below it. Here again, if the consumers do not have a preference, we would expect half of the coffee drinkers to prefer decaffeinated and the other half regular coffee.

We can best show the application of the sign test by an example. We will use a "before/after" experiment.

# EXAMPLE

Top management at Samuelson Chemicals recommended that an in-plant computer training program be instituted for managers, with the objective of improving their knowledge of computer usage in accounting, procurement, production, and so on. Some managers thought it would be a worthwhile program; others resisted it, saying it would be of no value. Despite these objections, it was announced that the computer sessions would commence the first of the month.

A sample of 15 managers was selected at random. The general level of competence of each manager with respect to the computer was determined by a panel of experts before the program started. Their competence and understanding were rated as being either outstanding, excellent, good, fair, or poor. (See Table 17–1.) After the three-month training program, the same panel of computer experts rated each manager again. The two ratings (before and after) are shown along with the sign of the difference. A "+" sign indicates improvement, and a "−" sign indicates that the manager's competence on the computer had declined after the training program.

## TABLE 17–1

### Competence before and after the Computer Training Program

| Name | Before | After | Sign of difference |
|------|--------|-------|--------------------|
| T. J. Bowers | Good | Outstanding | + |
| Sue Jenkins | Fair | Excellent | + |
| James Brown | Excellent | Good | − |
| Tad Jackson | Poor | Good | + |
| Andy Love | Excellent | Excellent | 0 |
| Sarah Truett | Good | Outstanding | + |
| John Sinshi | Poor | Fair | + |
| Jean Unger | Excellent | Outstanding | + |
| Coy Farmer | Good | Poor | − |
| Troy Archer | Poor | Good | + |
| V. A. Jones | Good | Outstanding | + |
| Coley Casper | Fair | Excellent | + |
| Candy Fry | Good | Fair | − |
| Arthur Seiple | Good | Outstanding | + |
| Sandy Gumpp | Poor | Good | + |

(Dropped from Analysis — Andy Love)

We are interested in finding out whether the in-plant computer training program was effective in increasing the competence of the managers on the computer. That is, are the managers more competent after the training program than before?

## SOLUTION

**STEP 1** As is the usual procedure, the null and alternate hypotheses are stated. Following are the hypotheses to be tested.

| Hypothesis | Meaning |
|------------|---------|
| Null—$H_0:p = .50$ | There is no change in competence as a result of the in-plant computer training program. |
| Alternate—$H_1:p > .50$ | The computer competence of the managers has increased. |

If we *do not reject* the null hypothesis, it will indicate that the skeptics are correct: the training program has produced no change in the level of computer competence. If we *reject* the null hypothesis, it will mean that the computer competence of the managers has increased as a result of the training program.

The binomial distribution discussed in Chapter 6 is used as the test statistic. It is appropriate because the sign test meets all the binomial assumptions, namely:

1. There are only two outcomes: a "success" or a "failure." A manager either increased his or her computer competence (a success) or did not.
2. For each trial the probability of a success is assumed to be .50. The probability of a failure is also .50. Thus, $H_0$ is $p = .50$.
3. The total number of trials is fixed (15 in this experiment).
4. Each trial is independent. This means, for example, that Arthur Seiple's performance in the three-month course is unrelated to Sandy Gumpp's performance.

**STEP 2**  Select a level of significance. We chose the .10 level.

**STEP 3**  Decide on the test statistic. It is *the number of plus signs* resulting from the experiment (11).

**STEP 4**  Formulate a decision rule. Fifteen managers were enrolled in the computer course, but Andy Love showed no increase or decrease in competence. (See Table 17–1.) He was therefore eliminated from the test, so $n = 14$. Going to the binomial probability distribution in Appendix A, for an $n$ of 14 and a probability of .50, we have the binomial probability distribution shown in Table 17–2. The number of successes is in column 1, the probability of success in column 2, and the cumulative probabilities in column 3. To arrive at the cumulative probabilities, we

### TABLE 17–2

**Binomial Probability Distribution for $n = 14$, $p = .50$**

| (1) Number of successes | (2) Probability of success | (3) Cumulative probability |
|---|---|---|
| 0 | .000 | 1.000* |
| 1 | .001 | .999 |
| 2 | .006 | .998 |
| 3 | .022 | .992 |
| 4 | .061 | .970 |
| 5 | .122 | .909 |
| 6 | .183 | .787 |
| 7 | .209 | .604 |
| 8 | .183 | .395 |
| 9 | .122 | .212 |
| 10 | .061 | .090 |
| 11 | .022 | .029 ←——.000 + .001 + |
| 12 | .006 | .007    .006 + .022 |
| 13 | .001 | .001 |
| 14 | .000 | .000 |

*Slight discrepancy due to rounding.

*add up* the probabilities of success in column 2 from the bottom. For illustration, to get the cumulative probability of 11 or more successes we add .000 + .001 + .006 + .022 = .029.

This is a one-tailed test because the alternate hypothesis gives a direction. The inequality (>) points to the right. Thus, the region of rejection is in the upper tail. If the inequality sign pointed toward the left tail (<), the region of rejection would be in the lower tail. If that were the case, we would add the probabilities in column 2 *down* to get the cumulative probabilities in column 3.

Recall that the .10 level of significance was selected. To arrive at the decision rule for this problem, we go to the cumulative probabilities in (Table 17−2) column 3. We read up from the bottom until we come to the *cumulative probability nearest to but not exceeding the level of significance (.10)*. That cumulative probability is .090: The number of successes (pluses) corresponding to .090 in column 1 is 10. Therefore, the decision rule is: If the number of pluses in the sample is 10 or more, the null hypothesis will be rejected and the alternate hypothesis accepted.

To repeat: We add the probabilities up from the bottom because the direction of the inequality (>) is toward the right, indicating that the region of rejection is in the upper tail. If the number of plus signs in the sample is 10 or more, we reject the null hypothesis; otherwise, we do not reject $H_0$. The region of rejection is portrayed in Chart 17−1.

## CHART 17−1

### Region of Rejection, *n = 14, p = .05*

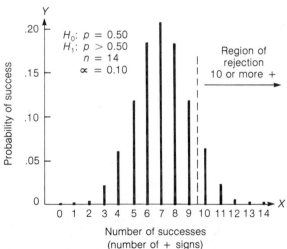

What procedure is followed for a two-tailed test? We combine (add) the probabilities of success in the two tails until we come as close to $\alpha$ as possible without exceeding it. In this example, $\alpha$ is .10. The probability of 3 or fewer successes is .029, found by .000 + .001 + .006 + .022. The probability of 11 or more successes is also .029. Adding the two probabilities gives .058. This is the closest we can come to .10 without exceeding it. (Had we included the probabilities of 4 and 10 successes, the total would be .180, which exceeds .10.) Hence, the decision rule for a two-tailed test would be to reject the null hypothesis if there are 3 or fewer plus signs, or 11 or more plus signs.

**STEP 5** Eleven out of the 14 managers in the computer course increased their computer competency. The number 11 is in the rejection region, which starts at 10, so $H_0$ is rejected. The three-month computer course did increase the computer competency of the managers. The course was effective. In effect, we are saying that 11 out of 14 improved their competency, and that this large number of successes is *probably not due to chance.*

It should be noted again that if the alternate hypothesis does not give a direction—for example, $H_0 : p = .50$ and $H_1 : p \neq .50$—the test of hypothesis is *two-tailed.* In such cases there will be two rejection regions—one in the lower tail and one in the upper tail. If $\alpha = .10$ and the test is two-tailed, the area in each tail is .05 ($\alpha/2 = .10/2 = .05$). Self-Review 17–1 illustrates this.

---

### Self-Review 17–1

*The answers are at the end of the chapter.*

Returning to the Taster's Choice problem, involving a consumer test to determine the preference for decaffeinated versus regular coffee:

$$H_0 : p = .50 \qquad n = 12$$
$$H_1 : p \neq .50 \qquad \alpha = .10$$

1. Is this a one-tailed or a two-tailed test of hypothesis?

2. Show the decision rule in a chart.

3. Letting consumer preference for decaffeinated coffee be a "+" and preference for regular coffee a "−," it was found that two consumers preferred decaffeinated. What is your decision? Explain.

---

## EXERCISES

*The answers to the odd-numbered exercises are at the end of the book.*

1. The following hypothesis-testing situation is given.

$$H_0: p = .50$$
$$H_1: p > .50$$

The significance level is .10, and the sample size is 12.

a. What is the decision rule?

b. There were nine successes. What is your decision regarding the null hypothesis? Explain.

2. The following hypothesis-testing situation is given.

$$H_0: p = .50$$
$$H_1: p \neq .50$$

The significance level is .05, and the sample size is 9.

a. What is the decision rule?

b. There were five successes. What is your decision regarding the null hypothesis?

3. Calorie Watchers has low-calorie breakfasts, lunches, and dinners. If you join the club, you receive two packaged meals a day. CW claims that you can eat anything you want

for the third meal and still lose at least five pounds the first month. As a member, you are weighed before commencing the program and again at the end of the first month. The experiences of a random sample of 11 enrollees are:

| Name | Weight change |
|------|---------------|
| Foster | Lost |
| Taoka | Lost |
| Lange | Gained |
| Rousos | Lost |
| Stephens | No change |
| Cantrell | Lost |
| Hercher | Lost |
| Camder | Lost |
| Hinckle | Lost |
| Hinkley | Lost |
| Justin | Lost |

We are interested in finding out whether there has been a weight loss as a result of the Calorie Watchers program.

a. State $H_0$ and $H_1$.

b. Using the .05 level of significance, what is the decision rule?

c. What is your conclusion about the Calorie Watchers program?

4. Many new stockbrokers resist giving presentations to senior citizens, bankers, and certain other groups. Sensing this lack of self-confidence, management arranged to have a confidence-building seminar for a sample of new stockbrokers and enlisted Career Boosters for a three-week course. Before the first session, Career Boosters measured the level of confidence of each participant. It was measured again after the three-week seminar. The "before" and "after" levels of self-confidence for the 14 in the course are shown below. Self-confidence was classified as being either negative, low, high, or very high.

| Stockbroker | Before seminar | After seminar |
|-------------|----------------|---------------|
| J. M. Martin | Negative | Low |
| T. D. Jagger | Negative | Negative |
| A. D. Hammer | Low | High |
| T. A. Jones, Jr. | Very high | Low |
| J. J. Cornwall | Low | High |
| D. A. Skeen | Low | High |
| C. B. Simmer | Negative | High |
| F. M. Orphey | Low | Very high |
| C. C. Ford | Low | High |
| A. R. Utz | Negative | Low |
| M. R. Murphy | Low | High |
| P. A. Arms | Negative | Low |
| B. K. Pierre | Low | High |
| N. S. Walker | Low | Very high |

The purpose of this study is to find out if Career Boosters was effective in raising the self-confidence of the new stockbrokers. That is, was the level of self-confidence higher after the seminar than before it?

a. State the null and alternate hypotheses.

b. Using the .05 level of significance, state the decision rule—either in words or in chart form.

c. Draw conclusions about the seminar offered by Career Boosters.

## Using the Normal Approximation

If the total number of usable pairs in the sample is larger than 20, the sample is considered "large." Some researchers consider a sample of 11 or more large, but we will use a limit of 20.

Instead of applying the binomial distribution to problems involving large samples and the sign test, we use the normal probability distribution. Both $np$ and $n(1 - p)$ must be greater than 5 for the test to be applied.

The mean of a normal distribution is

$$\mu = .50n$$

The standard deviation is

$$\sigma = .50 \sqrt{n}$$

The test statistic $z$ is

$$z = \frac{(X \pm .50) - \mu}{\sigma} \tag{17-1}$$

If the number of pluses or minuses *is more than* $n/2$, we use the following form as the test statistic:

$$z = \frac{(X - .50) - \mu}{\sigma} = \frac{(X - .50) - .50n}{.50\sqrt{n}} \tag{17-2}$$

If the number of pluses or minuses is *less than* $n/2$, the test statistic $z$ is:

$$z = \frac{(X + .50) - \mu}{\sigma} = \frac{(X + .50) - .50n}{.50\sqrt{n}} \tag{17-3}$$

In the preceding formulas, $X$ is the number of plus (or minus) signs. The value $+.50$ or $-.50$ is the *continuity correction factor,* discussed in Chapter 7. Briefly, it is applied when a continuous distribution such as the normal distribution (which we are using) is used to approximate a discrete distribution (the binomial).

Courtesy Alcoa

## ■ Example

The market research department of Cola, Inc. has been given the assignment of testing a new soft drink. Two versions of the drink are considered—a rather sweet drink and a somewhat bitter one. A preference test is to be conducted consisting of a sample of 64 consumers. Each will taste both the sweet cola (labeled A) and the bitter one (labeled B) and indicate a preference. How will the test of hypothesis be conducted, and what cola, if any, should be marketed?

## ☑ Solution

**Step 1**   State the null and alternate hypotheses.

$$H_0: p = .50 \qquad \text{There is no preference.}$$
$$H_1: p \neq .50 \qquad \text{There is a preference.}$$

**Step 2**   Select a level of significance. It is the .05 level.

**STEP 3**   The test statistic is selected. It is $z$, introduced in formula (17–1).

$$z = \frac{(X \pm .50) - \mu}{\sigma}$$

where $\mu = .50n$ and $\sigma = .50\sqrt{n}$.

**STEP 4**   Arrive at a decision rule. Referring to Appendix D, Areas under the Normal Curve, for a two-tailed test, the critical values are $+1.96$ and $-1.96$. To explain, for a two-tailed test we split alpha in half and place one half in each tail. That is, $\alpha/2 = .05/2 = .025$. Continuing, $.5000 - .025 = .4750$. Searching for $.4750$ in the body of the table and reading the $z$ value in the left margin gives 1.96, the critical value. Therefore, do not reject $H_0$ if the computed $z$ value is between $+1.96$ and $-1.96$. Otherwise, reject $H_0$ and accept $H_1$.

**STEP 5**   Compute $z$, and then compare the computed value with the critical value of $-1.96$ or 1.96. Arrive at a decision regarding $H_0$.

Preference for cola A was given a "+" sign and preference for B a "−" sign. Out of the 64 in the sample, 46 preferred the sweet cola, A. Therefore, there are 46 pluses. Since 46 is *more than* $n/2 = 64/2 = 32$, we use formula (17–2) for $z$:

$$z = \frac{(X - .50) - .50n}{.50\sqrt{n}}$$

$$= \frac{(46 - .50) - .50(64)}{.50\sqrt{64}} = 3.375$$

The computed $z$ of 3.375 is in the region beyond 1.96. Therefore, the null hypothesis of no difference is rejected at the .05 level. We conclude that there is a difference in consumer preference. That is, we conclude that consumers prefer one cola over the other.

---

### Self-Review 17–2

*The answers are at the end of the chapter.*

$$H_0: p = .50 \qquad H_1: p > .50 \qquad .05 \text{ level} \qquad n = 100$$

For a "before/after" test, a "+" indicates that an athlete gained weight after taking extremely large doses of selected vitamins. A "−" indicates a loss in weight. Eighty athletes gained weight. Can we say that the vitamins were effective in adding weight to the athletes? Explain your procedure and your decision.

## EXERCISES

*The answers to the odd-numbered exercises are at the end of the book.*

5.   A sample of 45 overweight men participated in an exercise program. A total of 32 showed a loss of weight at the completion of the program. At the .05 significance level, can we conclude that the program is effective?

    a.   State the null hypothesis and the alternate hypothesis.

    b.   State the decision rule.

    c.   Compute the value of the test statistic.

    d.   What is your decision regarding the null hypothesis?

6. A sample of 60 college students was given a special training program designed to improve their study and time management skills. One month after completing the course the students were contacted and asked if the skills learned in the program were effective. A total of 42 responded yes. At the .05 significance level, can we conclude that the program is effective?
   a. State the null hypothesis and the alternate hypothesis.
   b. State the decision rule.
   c. Compute the value of the test statistic.
   d. What is your decision regarding the null hypothesis?
7. Pierre's Restaurant announced that on Thursday night the menu would consist of unusual gourmet items, such as squid, rabbit, snails from Scotland, and dandelion greens. As part of a larger survey, a sample of 81 regular customers were asked if they preferred the regular menu or the gourmet menu. Forty-three preferred the gourmet menu. Using the sign test and the .02 level, test whether his customers liked the gourmet menu better than the regular menu. Justify your conclusion.
8. Assembly workers at Computer Associates assemble just one or two subassemblies and insert them in a frame. The executives at CA think that the employees would have more pride in their work if they assembled all of the subassemblies and tested the complete computer. The null hypothesis is that the employees have no preference. A sample of 25 employees was selected to experiment with the idea. After a training program, each was asked his or her preference. Twenty liked assembling the entire unit and testing it. At the .05 level, use the sign test to arrive at a decision regarding employee preference. Explain the steps you used to arrive at your decision.

## Testing a Hypothesis about a Median

Most of the tests of hypothesis we have conducted so far involved the population mean or a proportion. The sign test is one of the few tests that can be used to test the value of a median. Recall from Chapter 3 that the median is the value above which half of the observations lie and below which the other half lie. For hourly wages of \$7, \$9, \$11, and \$18, the median is \$10. Half of the wages are above \$10 an hour and the other half below \$10.

To conduct a test of hypothesis, *a value above the median is assigned a plus sign.* A value below the median is assigned a minus sign. If a value is the same as the median, it is dropped from further analysis. The procedure is identical to that followed in the small-sample and large-sample cases just discussed.

### Example

The district manager of Superior Grocers hypothesized that the median grocery bill of the customers in his region is \$23.00. He wants to investigate his hypothesis. The null hypothesis to be tested is $H_0$: Median = \$23.00. If the median is exactly \$23.00, half of the bills will be less than \$23.00, and the other half will be more than \$23.00. If that happens, we would definitely agree with the district manager that the median grocery bill is in fact \$23.00. Suppose, however, that the manager randomly selected 102 grocery bills and found that 50 were over the median and 52 were under the median of \$23.00. Is that sufficient evidence to reject the null hypothesis that the median is \$23.00, or could this slight imbalance be due to sampling error? What if the sample survey revealed that 55 grocery bills were greater than the median and 47 were less than the median? Should we reject $H_0$?

When the district manager did randomly select 102 grocery bills, he found that 60 of them were above his hypothesized median of \$23.00, 40 were below \$23.00, and 2 were exactly \$23.00. Based on these sample results, should we refrain from rejecting the null hypothesis that the median bill is $23.00? Or is this imbalance (60 above, 40 below the median) so great that we need to reject $H_0$ and accept $H_1$, which states that the median is not equal to $23.00? We will use the .10 significance level.

### ✓ SOLUTION

The null and alternate hypotheses are:

$$H_0: \text{Median} = \$23.00$$
$$H_1: \text{Median} \neq \$23.00$$

This is a two-tailed test because the alternate hypothesis does not state a direction (either less than or more than $23.00).

The critical values are ±1.645, found by $\alpha/2 = .10/2 = .05$. Then $.5000 - .05 = .4500$. Find .4500 in Appendix D, and read the critical value of $z$ in the left margin. It is 1.645.

As noted previously, the district manager selected 102 grocery bills. Since 2 were exactly $23.00 (the hypothesized median), they are omitted. Thus, $102 - 2 = 100$, which is $n$. Substituting 100 for $n$ and solving for the mean, $\mu$, and the standard deviation, $\sigma$:

$$\mu = .50n = .50(100) = 50$$
$$\sigma = .50\sqrt{n} = .50\sqrt{100} = 5$$

We use formula (17–2) for $z$ because 60 is greater than $n/2$ (100/2 = 50).

$$z = \frac{(X - .50) - .50n}{.50\sqrt{n}} = \frac{(60 - .50) - .50(100)}{.50\sqrt{100}} = 1.90$$

Since 1.90 is in the area beyond 1.645, the null hypothesis is rejected at the .10 level. The median is not $23.00.

### A MINITAB SOLUTION

Arranging the values from low to high and then determining whether each value is above, below, or equal to the hypothesized median is rather tedious—especially if the sample size is quite large. Instead, MINITAB can quickly tell us how many observations are above, below, or equal to the hypothesized median.

Suppose a local store manager wanted to check the district manager's hypothesis that the median bill is $23.00. She selected a sample of 64 grocery bills and entered them in her MINITAB software package, with the following results:

```
MTB > set c1
DATA> 27.5,103,41.62,214.25,16.26,91.3,18.52,89.18,19.31,106.01,8.5
DATA> 4.8,87.52,26.4,41.61,1.87,52.91,56.4,52.9,86.14,71.16,36.18,291.67
DATA> 23,11.12,12.91,28,15,3.96,3.8,29.81,9.26,7.14,23,62.14,39.03,47.16
DATA> 103.62,99.91,15.14,71,46.18,11.9,41.6,37.42,88.18,91.65,18.19,46.8
DATA> 14.22,19.67,39.05,5.6,49.09,103.2,97.62,77.8,39.16,46,21,32.18,61.03
DATA> 77.16,27.14
DATA> end
MTB > name c1 'Amount'
MTB > stest median=23 data in c1

SIGN TEST OF MEDIAN = 23.00 VERSUS  N.E.   23.00

            N  BELOW  EQUAL  ABOVE  P-VALUE     MEDIAN
Amount     64     20      2     42   0.0077      39.10
```

Assist the local grocery store manager by doing Self-Review 17–3.

---

**Self-Review 17–3**

*The answers are at the end of the chapter.*

Referring to the preceding MINITAB output:

1. What is the hypothesized null hypothesis? Assuming that the local manager is going to conduct a two-tailed test, what is the alternate hypothesis?

2. How many bills were below the hypothesized median of $23.00? Above it? Equal to it?

3. What is $n$?

4. Using the .10 level of significance, what is the critical value of $z$?

5. What is the computed value of $z$?

6. What action should the local manager take regarding the null hypothesis? Explain your decision.

7. What is the actual median grocery bill based on her sample results?

8. Based on the sample results, isn't the actual median bill close enough to the hypothesized median to say that the difference could be due to sampling?

---

# EXERCISES

*The answers to the odd-numbered exercises are at the end of the book.*

9. It is claimed that the median annual income of computer programmers with at least five years of experience is $40,000. The claim is being challenged by the programmers, who say the median annual income is greater than $40,000. To resolve the controversy, a random sample of 205 programmers was selected. It was found that 170 had incomes above $40,000, 5 earned exactly $40,000, and the remaining number had incomes under $40,000.

   a. State the null and alternate hypotheses.

   b. Using the .05 level, state the decision rule in words.

   c. Do the necessary computations, and write out your conclusions.

10. Central Airlines claims that the median price of a round-trip ticket to Jackson Hole, Wyoming, is $503. This claim is being challenged by the Association of Travel Agents. To resolve the issue, a random sample of 400 round-trip tickets was selected. Of these, 160 tickets were below $503. None of the tickets were exactly $503. Let $\alpha = .05$.

   a. Decide on the null and alternate hypotheses, level of significance, and so on.

   b. Reach a decision regarding the controversy.

# MANN-WHITNEY $U$ TEST

Mann-Whitney test requires independent samples and ranked data

The **Mann-Whitney test** of significance is an especially appropriate test when *two independent* and randomly selected sets of sample observations are at least *ordinal-level;* that is, the data must be such that they can be ranked from low to high (or high to low). The express purpose of the Mann-Whitney test is *to determine whether or not the two independent samples come from the same population.*

In addition to applying it to problems involving ordinal-level data, many researchers prefer to use the Mann-Whitney test instead of the Student $t$ test (1) when there is some doubt whether the population is normal, and (2) when the population variances are not equal.

Small sample: 20 or less

If the larger of the two samples has 20 or fewer observations, a *small-sample* approach is followed. Otherwise, the samples are considered large.

## SMALL SAMPLES

Why use Mann-Whitney test?

Suppose there is interest in determining whether there is a difference in mechanical aptitude between male and female assembly-line workers. To resolve the issue, nine males and five females were selected at random, and each was given a mechanical aptitude test. The nonparametric Mann-Whitney test (proposed by Mann and Whitney in 1947) is used in this problem (instead of the parametric Student $t$ test discussed in Chapter 11). The reason? We are unwilling to assume (1) that the mechanical aptitude test scores are normally distributed, or (2) that the population variances are equal.

The usual five steps are followed in arriving at a decision regarding the differences in mechanical aptitude of the two groups.

State $H_0$ and $H_1$

### STEP 1: THE NULL AND ALTERNATE HYPOTHESES

$H_0$:  The distributions of the mechanical aptitudes of the males and the females are the same.

$H_1$:  The distributions are not the same.

We know by the way the alternate hypothesis is stated that a two-tailed test is to be applied.

.05 level

### STEP 2: THE LEVEL OF SIGNIFICANCE  It was decided that $\alpha = .05$.

$U$ is the test statistic

### STEP 3: THE STATISTICAL TEST  The Mann-Whitney $U$ test is the appropriate test because the data (mechanical aptitude test scores) can be converted to ranks for the purpose of the test. Also, it should be noted that the samples are independent—a prerequisite for the use of the Mann-Whitney $U$ test. That is, the mechanical aptitude of a male in no way influences the mechanical aptitude of a female.

### STEP 4: THE DECISION RULE  The critical values for the statistic $U$ are given in Appendix J. A portion of that appendix table follows.

It should be noted that Appendix J is divided into two tables. The top table is for the .025 level (one-tailed) or the .05 level (two-tailed). The bottom table is for the .05 level (one-tailed) or the .10 level (two-tailed test). We are therefore somewhat limited in the selection of our $\alpha$ value.

Recall that nine men and five women were given the mechanical aptitude test, so $n_1 = 9$ and $n_2 = 5$. Move horizontally across the top of the table until the number 9 is located. Then go down that column until the number opposite 5 is reached. It is 7, the critical value.

| $n_1$ / $n_2$ | 1 | 2 | 3 | 4 | 5 | 6 | 7 | 8 | 9 | 10 | 11 | 12 | 13 | 14 | 15 | 16 | 17 | 18 | 19 | 20 |
|---|---|---|---|---|---|---|---|---|---|---|---|---|---|---|---|---|---|---|---|---|
| 1 | | | | | | | | | | | | | | | | | | | | |
| 2 | | | | | | | | 0 | 0 | 0 | 0 | 1 | 1 | 1 | 1 | 1 | 2 | 2 | 2 | 2 |
| 3 | | | | 0 | 1 | 1 | 2 | 2 | 3 | 3 | 4 | 4 | 5 | 5 | 6 | 6 | 7 | 7 | 8 |
| 4 | | | 0 | 1 | 2 | 3 | 4 | 4 | 5 | 6 | 7 | 8 | 9 | 10 | 11 | 11 | 12 | 13 | 13 |
| 5 | | 0 | 1 | 2 | 3 | 5 | 6 | 7 | 8 | 9 | 11 | 12 | 13 | 14 | 15 | 17 | 18 | 19 | 20 |
| 6 | | 1 | 2 | 3 | 5 | 6 | 8 | 10 | 11 | 13 | 14 | 16 | 17 | 19 | 21 | 22 | 24 | 25 | 27 |
| 7 | | 1 | 3 | 5 | 6 | 8 | 10 | 12 | 14 | 16 | 18 | 20 | 22 | 24 | 26 | 28 | 30 | 32 | 34 |

Now for the decision rule. The null hypothesis will be *rejected* if the computed value, designated as *U,* is 7 *or less.* Otherwise, it will not be rejected. Note that this is just the opposite of the decision-making procedure followed for most other tests of significance. That is, the table value (7) is in the rejection region, which is from 0 to 7 inclusive. The decision rule shown schematically:

Rejection region | Region of nonrejection

0                 7
Critical value

*Be careful formulating the decision rule*

**STEP 5: THE DECISION** The nine men and five women were administered a mechanical aptitude test, and the raw test scores ranged from a high of 1,600 to a low of 600. (See Table 17–3.) The highest score (1,600) was earned by a man and ranked 1. The second highest score was 1,500, also earned by a man, and it was ranked 2. The next highest score, 1,400, was earned by a woman, and it was ranked 3. A woman ranked fourth, a man fifth, a woman sixth, and so on. It does appear that the ranks are about evenly distributed between the two sexes. (The scores could have been ranked from low to high, instead of high to low.) Note that there are two scores of 800. Theoretically, these would be ranked 10 and 11. The tie is resolved by giving each score the arithmetic mean rank of 10.5. Had there been a tie for ranks 6, 7, and 8, each number would be awarded the rank of 7.

As a test, assume that the numbers are to be ranked from high to low. Give the rank for the tied numbers in each of the following groups. Check your answers against the ones given on the right.

| Numbers | Rank for tied numbers |
|---|---|
| 103, 86, 86, 52 | 2.5 |
| 81, 44, 44, 44, 16, 9 | 3 |
| 23, 77, 8, 77 | 1.5 |

---

## TABLE 17–3

### Raw Scores and Ranks of Males and Females on the Mechanical Aptitude Test

| | Men | | Women | |
|---|---|---|---|---|
| | Raw score | Rank | Raw score | Rank |
| | 1,500 | 2 | 1,400 | 3 |
| | 1,600 | 1 | 1,200 | 6 |
| | 670 | 13 | 780 | 12 |
| | 800 | 10.5 | 1,350 | 4 |
| | 1,100 | 8 | 890 | 9 |
| | 800 | 10.5 | | 34 |
| | 1,320 | 5 | | |
| | 1,150 | 7 | | |
| | 600 | 14 | | |
| | | 71 | | |

*Watch for ties when ranking data*

---

*Formulas for U and U′*

Two statistics are computed, *U* and *U′*, found by:

$$U = n_1 n_2 + \frac{n_1(n_1 + 1)}{2} - \Sigma R_1 \qquad (17\text{–}4)$$

$$U' = n_1 n_2 + \frac{n_2(n_2 + 1)}{2} - \Sigma R_2 \qquad (17\text{–}5)$$

where:

$n_1$    is the size of one sample. There are nine men, so $n_1 = 9$.

$n_2$    is the size of the other sample. There are five women, so $n_2 = 5$.

$\Sigma R_1$    is the sum of the ranks for the sample of men, designated as 1. The sum of the ranks for the men is 71.

$\Sigma R_2$    is the sum of the ranks for the sample of women, designated as 2. The sum of the ranks for the women is 34.

Substituting the appropriate values in formulas (17−4) and (17−5), we get:

$$U = n_1 n_2 + \frac{n_1(n_1 + 1)}{2} - \Sigma R_1 \qquad U' = n_1 n_2 + \frac{n_2(n_2 + 1)}{2} - \Sigma R_2$$

$$= (5)(9) + \frac{9(9 + 1)}{2} - 71 \qquad\qquad = (5)(9) + \frac{5(5 + 1)}{2} - 34$$

$$= 19 \qquad\qquad\qquad\qquad\qquad = 26$$

**Suggestion: Check your computations**

As a check:

$$U' = n_1 n_2 - U$$
$$= (5)(9) - 19$$
$$= 26 \text{ (same as computed previously)}$$

**Use the smaller computed value of $U$ or $U'$**

The smaller computed $U$ value, 19 in this problem, is used in arriving at the decision to either reject or not reject the null hypothesis—namely, that there is no difference in the distribution of high and low ranks between the two samples. The computed $U$ value of 19 is greater than the critical value of 7, so the decision rule directs that the null hypothesis not be rejected at the .05 level. There is no difference between the mechanical aptitudes of the male and female assembly-line workers.

The following illustrates a clear-cut case where the null hypothesis would be rejected. Suppose that the mechanical aptitude test scores had resulted in the sets of scores shown in Table 17−4. A cursory examination of the rankings (which have been ordered from high to low) would lead one to conclude that these are two separate populations—one male and the other female. All the low ranks are associated with the scores of the men, and all the women are ranked high. Either the computed $U$ or $U'$ will be decidedly less than the critical value, causing, as expected, $H_0$ to be rejected. (You might want to verify that statement.)

---

### TABLE    17−4

**Raw Scores and Ranks of Males and Females of the Mechanical Aptitude Test**

| Males | | Females | |
|---|---|---|---|
| Raw score | Rank | Raw score | Rank |
| 1,200 | 8 | 1,600 | 1 |
| 1,190 | 9 | 1,580 | 2 |
| 1,175 | 10 | 1,450 | 3 |
| 1,160 | 11 | 1,310 | 4 |
| 1,097 | 12 | 1,275 | 5 |
| 940 | 13 | 1,250 | 6 |
| 800 | 14 | 1,230 | 7 |
| 790 | 15 | | |
| 670 | 16 | | |
| 650 | 17 | | |
| 620 | 18 | | |

---

## Self-Review 17—4

*The answers are at the end of the chapter.*

A company-sponsored course at Stein's Clothiers on the principles of management was taken jointly by a group of middle managers and a group of supervisors. Random samples of the scores earned are:

*Group 1: Middle managers.* 121, 180, 122, 160, 141, 97, 212, 186.

*Group 2: Supervisors.* 128, 197, 180, 126, 167, 99, 147.

It is known that the population of scores is not normally distributed. The Student $t$ therefore cannot be applied. Using the Mann-Whitney $U$ test, a two-tailed test, and the .05 level:

1. State $H_0$ and $H_1$.
2. What is the critical value? Show the region of rejection (be careful).
3. Rank the scores from low to high (watch for ties), compute $U$ and $U'$, and make a decision.

# EXERCISES

*The answers to the odd-numbered exercises are at the end of the book.*

11. The following sample observations were selected from populations that were not normally distributed. Use the .05 significance level, a two-tailed test, and the Mann-Whitney $U$ test to determine if the populations are the same.

| Sample 1 | Sample 2 |
|----------|----------|
| 38 | 26 |
| 45 | 31 |
| 56 | 35 |
| 57 | 42 |
| 61 | 51 |
| 69 | |

    a. State the null hypothesis and the alternate hypothesis.
    b. State the decision rule.
    c. Compute the value of $U$.
    d. What is your decision regarding the null hypothesis?

12. The following sample observations were selected from populations with unequal standard deviations. Use the .05 significance level, a two-tailed test, and the Mann-Whitney $U$ test to determine if the populations are the same.

| Sample 1 | Sample 2 |
|----------|----------|
| 12 | 13 |
| 14 | 16 |
| 15 | 19 |
| 19 | 21 |
| 23 | 22 |
| 29 | 33 |
| 33 | |
| 45 | |
| 51 | |

    a. State the null hypothesis and the alternate hypothesis.
    b. State the decision rule.
    c. Compute the value of $U$.
    d. What is your decision regarding the null hypothesis?

13. Two groups of professional musicians—rock musicians and country western musicians—are being studied. One facet of the study involves the ages of those in the two groups. It cannot be assumed that the two populations of ages are normal. Thus, the Mann-Whitney $U$ test is to be applied to the sample of ages. The ages of rock musicians selected at random for study are: 28, 16, 42, 29, 31, 22, 50, 42, 23, and 25. The ages of the country-western musicians are: 26, 42, 65, 38, 29, 32, 59, 42, 27, 41, 46, and 18.

   Test at the .05 level that the country-western musicians are older than the rock musicians. (The word *older* implies a one-tailed test. Be sure to use the lower table in Appendix J for the critical value, which is for a one-tailed test using the .05 level.)

14. One group was taught an assembly procedure using the usual sequence of steps. Another group was taught using an experimental technique. The times (in seconds) required to assemble the unit for two samples are:

   Group using usual steps: 41, 36, 42, 39, 36, 48.
   Group using experimental technique: 21, 27, 36, 20, 19, 21, 39, 24, 22.

   Using the Mann-Whitney $U$ test and the .05 level of risk, test the statement that the experimental group required less time to assemble the unit. As usual, state the null and alternate hypotheses and the decision rule, compute $U$ and $U'$, and arrive at a decision.

## LARGE SAMPLES

*Use large-sample approach if one sample exceeds 20 observations*

As the sizes of the two independent samples increase, the sampling distribution of the statistic $U$ tends to become normally distributed. Thus, if one of the samples exceeds 20 observations, a form of the $z$ test is applied. (Some researchers use the normal approximation if both sample sizes are equal to or greater than 10.) The test statistic $z$ is found by:

$$z = \frac{\Sigma R_1 - \Sigma R_2 - \left[(n_1 - n_2)\dfrac{n_1 + n_2 + 1}{2}\right]}{\sqrt{n_1 n_2 \left[\dfrac{n_1 + n_2 + 1}{3}\right]}} \qquad (17-6)$$

### ◼ EXAMPLE

*Since 25 exceeds 20, large-sample approach is used*

Continuing with the same type of problem, suppose 25 women and 15 men were given a mechanical aptitude test. The test scores were ranked as follows.

| Female ranks | | | | | Male ranks | | |
|---|---|---|---|---|---|---|---|
| 7 | 33 | 39 | 16 | 19 | 26 | 6 | 38 |
| 20 | 1 | 2 | 37 | 29 | 10 | 14 | 24 |
| 27 | 9 | 5 | 23 | 31 | 30 | 17 | 40 |
| 28 | 13 | 36 | 15 | 18 | 3 | 22 | 25 |
| 4 | 21 | 8 | 11 | 35 | 32 | 34 | 12 |

Is there a significant difference in mechanical aptitude between the women and men?

### ☑ SOLUTION

$H_0$ states that there is no difference in mechanical aptitude between the women and the men. A two-tailed test and the .05 level are to be used. The critical values of $z$ are $-1.96$ and $1.96$ from Appendix D. The two regions of rejection would appear as:

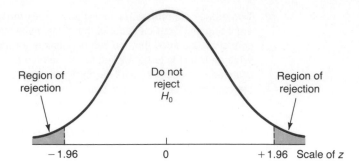

The number in each sample and the sums of the ranks are:

| Female ranks | | | | | Male ranks | | |
|---|---|---|---|---|---|---|---|
| 7 | 33 | 39 | 16 | 19 | 26 | 6 | 38 |
| 20 | 1 | 2 | 37 | 29 | 10 | 14 | 24 |
| 27 | 9 | 5 | 23 | 31 | 30 | 17 | 40 |
| 28 | 13 | 36 | 15 | 18 | 3 | 22 | 25 |
| 4 | 21 | 8 | 11 | 35 | 32 | 34 | 12 |
| $n_1 = 25$ | | $\Sigma R_1 = 487$ | | | $n_2 = 15$ | $\Sigma R_2 = 333$ | |

Substituting the appropriate values in formula (17–6) for $z$, we get

$$z = \frac{\Sigma R_1 - \Sigma R_2 - \left[(n_1 - n_2)\dfrac{n_1 + n_2 + 1}{2}\right]}{\sqrt{n_1 n_2 \left[\dfrac{n_1 + n_2 + 1}{3}\right]}}$$

$$= \frac{487 - 333 - \left[(25 - 15)\dfrac{25 + 15 + 1}{2}\right]}{\sqrt{(25)(15)\left[\dfrac{25 + 15 + 1}{3}\right]}}$$

$$= -0.71$$

The computed value of $z$ (−0.71) falls between −1.96 and +1.96, so the null hypothesis is not rejected at the .05 level. This indicates that there is no difference in aptitude between the male and female employees at the .05 level.

## CAN TESTS REQUIRING ORDINAL MEASUREMENT BE APPLIED TO HIGHER-LEVEL DATA?

Recall that the Mann-Whitney test requires the ordinal level of measurement (data capable of being ranked). Before discussing two other tests requiring ordinal measurement, it should be noted that these and other such tests (not covered in this text) can also be applied to interval- and ratio-level data. This is because interval- and ratio-level data can be converted to ordinal-level measurement by ordering them in ascending order and assigning each number a rank, starting with 1. For example, these are the weights in pounds of four defensive linemen: 260, 311, 255, 288. The weights can be rearranged from low to high (255, 260, 288, 311) and assigned rank orders 1, 2, 3, and 4. Then the Mann-Whitney and other tests (to follow) can be applied.

It is not permissible, however, to perform parametric tests that require at least interval-level data (such as the Student *t* and ANOVA) on ordinal-level data. This is because ranks 1, 2, 3, 4, . . . cannot be converted to the interval or ratio level of measurement. We cannot, for example, convert the order of finish 1, 2, and 3 in the Indianapolis 500 race to miles per hour.

In summary:

*When to apply nonparametric and parametric tests*

1. We can apply tests that require ordinal level of measurement, such as the Mann-Whitney test, to problems involving interval- or ratio-level data.
2. We cannot apply parametric tests, such as the *t* test, to the ordinal (ranked) level of measurement.
3. If we have interval or ratio level of measurement, and if certain specified assumptions are met, such as normality of the population, a parametric test should be performed.
4. If we have interval or ratio level of measurement, and if the assumption of normality and other assumptions cannot be met, a distribution-free test, such as the ones presented in this chapter should be used.

## KRUSKAL-WALLIS TEST: ANALYSIS OF VARIANCE BY RANKS

*Kruskal-Wallis test less restrictive than ANOVA*

The analysis of variance (ANOVA) procedure discussed in Chapter 12 was concerned with whether three or more population means are equal. The data were interval- or ratio-level, and it was assumed the populations were normally distributed and the standard deviations of those populations were equal. What if the data are ordinal-scaled and/or the populations are not normal? Fortunately, W. H. Kruskal and W. A. Wallis reported a nonparametric test of significance in 1952 requiring only ordinal-level (ranked) data. No assumptions about the shape of the populations are required by that test. The test is referred to as the **Kruskal-Wallis one-way analysis of variance by ranks.**

For the Kruskal-Wallis test to be applied, the samples selected from the populations must be *independent.* For example, if samples from three groups—executives, staff, and supervisors—are to be selected and interviewed, the responses of one group (say, the executives) must in no way influence the responses of the others.

*Kruskal-Wallis: All sample values combined, then ranked*

For the Kruskal-Wallis test, (1) all the sample values are combined, (2) the combined values are ordered from low to high, and (3) the ordered values are *replaced by ranks starting with 1 for the smallest value.* An example will clarify the procedure.

### ■ EXAMPLE

A management seminar consisting of a large number of executives from manufacturing, finance, and trade is to be conducted. Before scheduling the seminar sessions, the seminar leader is interested in finding out whether the three groups are equally knowledgeable about management principles. Plans are to take samples of the executives in manufacturing, in finance, and in trade and to administer a test to each executive. If there is no difference among the three distributions, the seminar leader will conduct just one session. However, if there is a difference in the scores, separate sessions will be given.

We will use the Kruskal-Wallis test instead of ANOVA because the seminar leader is unwilling to assume that (1) the populations of management scores are normally distributed or (2) the population variances are the same.

## ☑ SOLUTION

The first step in hypothesis testing is to state the null and the alternate hypotheses.

*$H_0$ and $H_1$ same as for ANOVA*

$H_0$:  The distributions of the management scores for the populations of executives in manufacturing, finance, and trade are equal.

$H_1$:  The distributions are not all equal

The seminar leader selected the .05 level of risk.

The test statistic used for the Kruskal-Wallis test is designated $H$. Its formula is:

*Formula for the $H$ statistic*

$$H = \frac{12}{N(N+1)}\left[\frac{(\Sigma R_1)^2}{n_1} + \frac{(\Sigma R_2)^2}{n_2} + \cdots + \frac{(\Sigma R_k)^2}{n_k}\right] - 3(N+1) \qquad (17\text{--}7)$$

with $k - 1$ degrees of freedom ($k$ is the number of populations), where

$\Sigma R_1, \Sigma R_2, \ldots, \Sigma R_k$  are the sums of the ranks of samples 1, 2, . . . , $k$.

$n_1, n_2, \ldots, n_k$  are the sizes of samples 1, 2, . . . , $k$.

$N$  is the combined number of observations for all samples.

*Chi-square used if every sample is at least 5*

The distribution of the sample $H$ statistic is very close to the chi-square distribution with $k - 1$ degrees of freedom *if every sample size is at least 5.* Therefore, we will use chi-square in formulating the decision rule. In this problem there are three populations—a population of executives in manufacturing, another for executives in finance, and a third population of trade executives. So there are $k - 1$, or $3 - 1 = 2$ degrees of freedom. Refer to the chi-square table of critical values in Appendix I. The critical value for 2 degrees of freedom and the .05 level of risk is 5.991. Chart 17–2 portrays the decision rule graphically. Do not reject $H_0$ if the computed value of the test statistic $H$ is less than or equal to 5.991. Reject $H_0$ if the computed value of $H$ is greater than 5.991, and accept $H_1$.

---

## CHART   17–2

### Region of Rejection, 2 Degrees of Freedom, .05 Level

*Decision rule portrayed graphically*

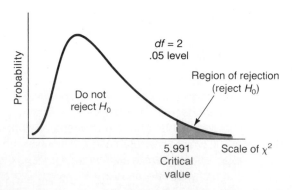

The next step is to select samples from the three populations. A sample of seven manufacturing, eight finance, and six trade executives were selected. Their scores on the test are recorded in Table 17–5.

### TABLE 17–5

**Management Test Scores for the Manufacturing, Finance, and Trade Executives**

Lowest score is 14, ranked 1

| Manufacturing executives | | Finance executives | Trade executives |
|---|---|---|---|
| 51 | lowest⟶ | 14 | 89 |
| 32 | | 31 | 20 |
| 17 | ⟵second | 68 tie | 60 |
| 69 | lowest | 87 | 72 |
| 86 | | 20 | 56 |
| 62 | | 28 | 22 |
| 96 | | 77 | |
| | | 97 | |

Tie for third rank resolved by giving each score a rank of 3.5

Considering the scores as a single population, *the score of 14 is the lowest, and it is ranked 1.* The score of 17 is the second lowest, and it is ranked 2. There are two scores of 20. To resolve the tie, each score is given the rank 3.5, found by $(3 + 4)/2$. The next score, 22, is ranked 5. This process is continued until all the scores are ranked. The scores, the ranks, and the sum of the ranks for each of three samples are given in Table 17–6.

### TABLE 17–6

**Scores, Ranks, and Sum of Ranks of Management Test Scores**

| Manufacturing executives | | Finance executives | | Trade executives | |
|---|---|---|---|---|---|
| Score | Rank | Score | Rank | Score | Rank |
| 51 | 9 | 14 | 1 | 89 | 19 |
| 32 | 8 | 31 | 7 | 20 | 3.5 |
| 17 | 2 | 68 | 13 | 60 | 11 |
| 69 | 14 | 87 | 18 | 72 | 15 |
| 86 | 17 | 20 | 3.5 | 56 | 10 |
| 62 | 12 | 28 | 6 | 22 | 5 |
| 96 | 20 | 77 | 16 | | |
| | | 97 | 21 | | |
| $\Sigma R_1 = 82$ | | $\Sigma R_2 = 85.5$ | | $\Sigma R_3 = 63.5$ | |
| $n_1 = 7$ | | $n_2 = 8$ | | $n_3 = 6$ | |

Computed $H = 0.14$

Solving for $H$:

$$H = \frac{12}{N(N+1)}\left[\frac{(\Sigma R_1)^2}{n_1} + \frac{(\Sigma R_2)^2}{n_2} + \frac{(\Sigma R_3)^2}{n_3}\right] - 3(N+1)$$

$$= \frac{12}{21(21+1)}\left[\frac{(82)^2}{7} + \frac{(85.5)^2}{8} + \frac{(63.5)^2}{6}\right] - 3(21+1)$$

$$= \frac{12(2546.394)}{462} - 66$$

$$= 0.14$$

Decision: distributions are
equal

Since the computed value of $H$ (0.14) is less than the critical value of 5.991, the null hypothesis is not rejected at the .05 level. There is no difference among the executives from manufacturing, finance, and trade with respect to their knowledge of management principles. From a practical standpoint, the seminar leader should consider offering only one seminar session including executives from all three areas.

The Kruskal-Wallis test is available on the MINITAB system. The data for all three groups of executives are entered in column C1 and the code identifying the executive's group in C2. The level "1" refers to manufacturing, "2" to finance, and "3" to trade executives. Note in the following output that the value of $H$ (0.14) is the same as computed before.

```
MTB > set c1
DATA> 51,32,17,69,86,62,96,14,31,68,87,20,28,77,97,89,20,60,72,56,22
DATA> end
MTB > set c2
DATA> 1,1,1,1,1,1,1,2,2,2,2,2,2,2,2,3,3,3,3,3,3
DATA> end
MTB > kruskal c1 c2

LEVEL      NOBS     MEDIAN    AVE. RANK    Z VALUE
   1          7      62.00        11.7       0.37
   2          8      49.50        10.7      -0.18
   3          6      58.00        10.6      -0.19
OVERALL      21                   11.0

H = 0.14   d.f. = 2   p = 0.932
H = 0.14   d.f. = 2   p = 0.932 (adj. for ties)
```

Recall from Chapter 12 that for the analysis of variance technique to apply, it is assumed that: (1) the three or more populations of interest are normally distributed, (2) these populations have equal standard deviations, and (3) the samples selected from the populations are random and independent—that is, they are not related. If these assumptions are met, we use the $F$ distribution as the test statistic. If these three assumptions cannot be met, the distribution-free test by Kruskal and Wallis is applied.

To show the similarity between the two approaches, a problem will be solved using MINITAB. First we will solve it using the analysis of variance (ANOVA) and then using Kruskal-Wallis. To illustrate, Micom Electronic uses a performance rating system at the end of the year. All the managers and executives are included. Key employees rate their performance as being excellent, good, fair, or poor.

The research department plans to conduct an in-depth study of the rating system and make recommendations on how to improve it. One of the questions to be explored is: Does the salary increase awarded a key employee affect his or her end-of-year rating? Logically, one might expect that, in general, employees who received a substantial salary increase would rate the manager or executive "excellent." It would also seem that those who rated the performance of the executive or manager "poor" would probably have the lowest salary increases.

The performance ratings of President Micom were selected for study. A random sample of 42 employees was chosen. Six employees rated his performance excellent, 19 rated it good, and so on. His ratings (excellent, good, fair, and poor) and the weekly salary increases for the 42 in the sample are given in the following table. The number in the upper left corner of the table, for example, indicates that the key employee received a raise of $85 a week and rated the performance of President Micom as excellent.

| Ratings of 42 employees and their weekly salary increases | | | | |
|---|---|---|---|---|
| Excellent | Good | | Fair | Poor |
| $85 | $80 | $78 | $73 | $81 |
| 77 | 70 | 75 | 71 | 85 |
| 74 | 78 | 73 | 70 | 76 |
| 77 | 72 | 80 | 79 | 81 |
| 70 | 74 | 82 | 73 | 79 |
| 74 | 77 | 73 | 76 | 70 |
| | 79 | 74 | 76 | 79 |
| | 78 | 76 | 68 | |
| | 82 | 91 | 80 | |
| | | 78 | 78 | |

The question to be explored is whether the salary increases awarded the employees are related to the opinions they have of the manager or executive being rated. Assuming the assumptions underlying the ANOVA test have been met, a graphic portrayal of the decision rule for the $F$ test and the .01 level of significance follows.

Areas of acceptance and rejection, .01 level of significance

Critical value is 4.31

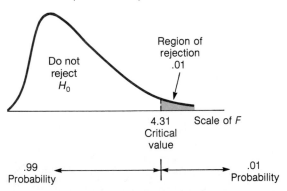

Thus, we will not reject the null hypothesis that the ratings are not related to the salary increases awarded to employees if the computed valued of $F$ is 4.31 or less. From the following MINITAB output we see that the computed value of $F$ is 1.44. It lies in the region below 4.31, so we cannot reject $H_0$. Since we cannot reject the null hypothesis, we conclude that the ratings of the employees and the weekly raises awarded them are unrelated. Apparently, the magnitude of the weekly raise did not influence an employee's evaluation of the performance of President Micom.

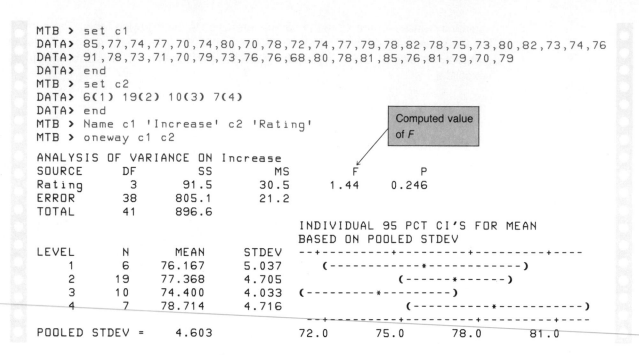

```
MTB > set c1
DATA> 85,77,74,77,70,74,80,70,78,72,74,77,79,78,82,78,75,73,80,82,73,74,76
DATA> 91,78,73,71,70,79,73,76,76,68,80,78,81,85,76,81,79,70,79
DATA> end
MTB > set c2
DATA> 6(1) 19(2) 10(3) 7(4)
DATA> end
MTB > Name c1 'Increase' c2 'Rating'
MTB > oneway c1 c2
```

Computed value of $F$

```
ANALYSIS OF VARIANCE ON Increase
SOURCE      DF        SS        MS         F        P
Rating       3      91.5      30.5      1.44     0.246
ERROR       38     805.1      21.2
TOTAL       41     896.6
                                    INDIVIDUAL 95 PCT CI'S FOR MEAN
                                    BASED ON POOLED STDEV
LEVEL        N      MEAN     STDEV   --+---------+---------+---------+----
    1        6    76.167     5.037      (-------------*-------------)
    2       19    77.368     4.705               (------*------)
    3       10    74.400     4.033   (---------*--------)
    4        7    78.714     4.716                    (----------*-----------)
                                    --+---------+---------+---------+----
POOLED STDEV =       4.603           72.0      75.0      78.0      81.0
```

Suppose, however, that we concluded that some or all of the assumptions for the ANOVA test cannot be met. Under these circumstances, the nonparametric Kruskal-Wallis test is applied. For the .01 level of significance, the decision rule is portrayed in the following diagram (the critical value of 11.345 is found in Appendix I for the .01 level and $k - 1$ degrees of freedom, where $k$ is the number of populations; $k - 1 = 4 - 1 = 3$ degrees of freedom).

Decision rule portrayed graphically

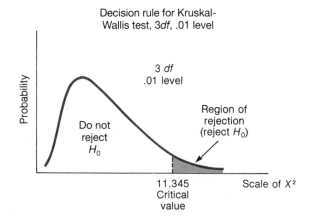

Decision rule for Kruskal-Wallis test, 3*df*, .01 level

Recall from our earlier discussion that the Kruskal-Wallis test uses the chi-square distribution as the test statistic, and the computed value is referred to as *H*. After adjusting for ties, *H* was computed to be 4.73 (see the following MINITAB output).

```
MTB > kruskal c1 c2
    LEVEL        NOBS      MEDIAN   AVE. RANK      Z VALUE
      1            6       75.50        19.2        -0.50
      2           19       78.00        22.9         0.66
      3           10       74.50        15.7        -1.71
      4            7       79.00        28.1         1.55
    OVERALL       42                    21.5

    H = 4.70   d.f. = 3   p = 0.196
    H = 4.73   d.f. = 3   p = 0.194 (adj. for ties)
```

Computed value
of $H$

Again, we would not reject the null hypothesis because $4.73 < 11.345$. This reaffirms the earlier statement that the four populations (ratings of excellent, good, fair, and poor) are identical. Repeating, the job performance ratings are unrelated to the magnitude of the salary increases of the employees.

### Self-Review 17–5

*The answers are at the end of the chapter.*

The regional bank manager of Statewide Financial is interested in the turnover rate of personal checking accounts in four of the large branch banks. He is wondering whether or not there is a difference in the turnover rates among the four branch banks. (Turnover rate is the speed at which the money in an account is deposited and withdrawn. An extremely active account may have a rate of 300; it only one or two checks were written, the rate could be about 30.) The turnover rates of the samples selected from the four branch banks are:

Using the .01 level and the Kruskal-Wallis test, determine if there is a difference in the turnover rates of the personal checking accounts among the four branches.

| Englewood branch | West Side branch | Great Northern branch | Sylvania branch |
|---|---|---|---|
| 208 | 91 | 302 | 99 |
| 307 | 62 | 103 | 116 |
| 199 | 86 | 319 | 189 |
| 142 | 91 | 340 | 103 |
| 91 | 80 | 180 | 100 |
| 296 |  |  | 131 |

## EXERCISES

*The answers to the odd-numbered exercises are at the end of the book.*

15. Under what conditions should the Kruskal-Wallis test be used instead of analysis of variance?

16. Under what conditions should the Kruskal-Wallis test be used instead of the Mann-Whitney test?

17. The following sample data were obtained from three populations that were not normal.

| Sample 1 | Sample 2 | Sample 3 |
|---|---|---|
| 50 | 48 | 39 |
| 54 | 49 | 41 |
| 59 | 49 | 44 |
| 59 | 52 | 47 |
| 65 | 56 | 51 |
|  | 57 |  |

a.    State the null hypothesis.

b.    Using the .05 level of risk, state the decision rule.

c.    Compute the value of the test statistic.

d.    What is your decision on the null hypothesis?

18.  The following sample data were obtained from three populations where the variances were not equal.

| Sample 1 | Sample 2 | Sample 3 |
|----------|----------|----------|
| 21 | 15 | 38 |
| 29 | 17 | 40 |
| 35 | 22 | 44 |
| 45 | 27 | 51 |
| 56 | 31 | 53 |
| 71 | | |

a.    State the null hypothesis.

b.    Using the .01 level of risk, state the decision rule.

c.    Compute the value of the test statistic.

d.    What is your decision on the null hypothesis?

19.  An outboard motor manufacturer has developed an epoxy painting process for corrosion protection on exhaust components. The engineers want to determine if the distributions of the lengths of life for the paint are equal for three different conditions—salt water, fresh water without weeds, and fresh water with a heavy concentration of weeds. Accelerated-life tests were conducted in the laboratory, and the number of hours the paint lasted before peeling was recorded.

| Salt water | Fresh water | Fresh water with weeds |
|------------|-------------|------------------------|
| 167.3 | 160.6 | 182.7 |
| 189.6 | 177.6 | 165.4 |
| 177.2 | 185.3 | 172.9 |
| 169.4 | 168.6 | 169.2 |
| 180.3 | 176.6 | 174.7 |

Use the Kruskal-Wallis test and the .01 level to determine whether the lasting quality of the paint is the same for the three water conditions.

20.  The National Turkey Association wants to experiment with three different food mixtures for very young turkeys. Since no experience exists regarding the three food mixtures, no assumptions can be made about the shape of the distribution of weights. The Kruskal-Wallis test must be used to test if the turkeys are equal in weight after eating the food for a specified length of time. Five young turkeys were given food A, six were given food B, and five were given food C. Test at the .05 level whether the mean weights of the turkeys who ate food A, food B, and food C are equal.

| Weight (in pounds) | | |
|--------------------|--------------------|--------------------|
| Food mixture A | Food mixture B | Food mixture C |
| 11.2 | 12.6 | 11.3 |
| 12.1 | 10.8 | 11.9 |
| 10.9 | 11.3 | 12.4 |
| 11.3 | 11.0 | 10.6 |
| 12.0 | 12.0 | 12.0 |
| | 10.7 | |

# WILCOXON MATCHED-PAIR SIGNED RANK TEST OF DIFFERENCES

Wilcoxon test replaces paired *t* test when assumptions for *t* cannot be met

The paired *t* test in Chapter 11 is used if it can be assumed that the differences between two sets of *paired observations* approximate a normal distribution. If this assumption cannot be met, a nonparametric test developed by Frank Wilcoxon (1945) should be applied. It is known as the **Wilcoxon matched-pair signed rank test of differences.** It requires that the data be at least ordinal-scaled and that the two samples be related (paired).

## ■ EXAMPLE

Suppose that a radical new experimental word processor has been developed by the engineering section of Computer Technologies. A vice president is somewhat skeptical, however, that even after a period of transition the number of words per minute a data entry clerk can achieve will differ significantly from that achieved using the current model. Plans are to randomly select a group of data entry clerks and check their performance on the current model. Then each will be provided with the newly developed word processor, and after a few weeks their performance will be again recorded. Thus, for each operator there will be a matched pair of data. For this type of experiment, it is said that each person is *acting as his/her own control.* How can the Wilcoxon matched-pair signed rank test be used to test for the difference in performance between the old and new models by data entry clerks?

## ☑ SOLUTION

Null and alternate hypotheses stated

As usual, the first step in hypothesis testing is to state the null and alternate hypotheses.

$H_0$:  There is no difference between the performance using the current model and that using the new model.

$H_1$:  There is a difference in the two typing speeds.

Since no direction is specified (such as "the speed attained on the new data processor is greater than that on the old model"), a two-tailed test will be applied.

Level of significance

The null hypothesis is to be tested at the .01 level. To test the hypothesis, 29 operators selected at random were first given a test on the current model. Then each operator was assigned to one of the experimental word processors. After a period of training, the operators were given another test. Table 17−7 shows the results and the differences.

The steps necessary to ultimately reject or not reject the null hypothesis are:

1. Compute the difference between the number of words per minute typed on the current model and the number typed on the experimental model for each of the 29 operators. The differences are shown in column 4 of Table 17−7.

2. Only the positive and negative changes are considered further. That is, if the difference between the words per minute typed on the current model and the words per minute typed on the newly developed processor is zero, those data will be ignored (because there is only interest in ranking actual differences). Seven of the 29 operators showed no change in typing speed. Therefore, $N = 22$, found by 29 − 7.

## TABLE 17−7

**Number of Words per Minute Typed on Current Word Processor and on a Newly Developed Model (29 typists)**

| (1)<br>Operator<br>number | (2)<br>Speed on<br>current<br>word processor | (3)<br>Speed on<br>experimental<br>word processor | (4)<br>Difference<br>(3) − (2) |
|:---:|:---:|:---:|:---:|
| 1 | 43 | 49 | 6 |
| 2 | 91 | 92 | 1 |
| 3 | 33 | 32 | −1 |
| 4 | 54 | 54 | — |
| 5 | 45 | 65 | 20 |
| 6 | 55 | 90 | 35 |
| 7 | 65 | 64 | −1 |
| 8 | 90 | 85 | −5 |
| 9 | 53 | 56 | 3 |
| 10 | 70 | 70 | — |
| 11 | 76 | 74 | −2 |
| 12 | 87 | 87 | — |
| 13 | 32 | 64 | 32 |
| 14 | 99 | 104 | 5 |
| 15 | 87 | 87 | — |
| 16 | 80 | 77 | −3 |
| 17 | 88 | 88 | — |
| 18 | 23 | 32 | 9 |
| 19 | 75 | 90 | 15 |
| 20 | 54 | 51 | −3 |
| 21 | 43 | 49 | 6 |
| 22 | 23 | 90 | 67 |
| 23 | 56 | 78 | 22 |
| 24 | 56 | 57 | 1 |
| 25 | 70 | 70 | — |
| 26 | 76 | 78 | 2 |
| 27 | 45 | 60 | 15 |
| 28 | 76 | 80 | 4 |
| 29 | 54 | 54 | — |

Calculate difference between each pair of values

Order absolute differences (column 1)

Rank absolute differences (column 2)

Resolve ties and insert correct sign (column 3)

3. Now order the *absolute differences* in column 4 of Table 17−7. That is, ignore the fact that some differences are positive and others negative. The 22 ordered differences are shown in column 1 of Table 17−8.

4. Now we rank the absolute differences in column 1, starting with 1 and ending with 22. (See column 2 of Table 17−8.)

5. Note in column 1 of Table 17−8 that there are four differences of 1. These differences have been ranked 1, 2, 3, and 4. (See column 2.) To resolve this tie, the arithmetic mean of these four ranks is determined: $(1 + 2 + 3 + 4)/4 = 10/4 = 2.5$. (See column 3.) To continue with the ranking process, there are two differences of 2 in the first column. These differences are ranked 5 and 6 in column 2. The mean of those ranks is 5.5, recorded in column 3.

6. Each assigned rank in column 3 is given the sign of the original difference. For example, two out of the four differences of 1 are negative. Therefore, two out of the four assigned ranks of 2.5 are given a negative sign. The rank of 10 is positive because the corresponding difference of 4 is positive.

### TABLE 17−8

**Computations for the Computed *T* Value for the Wilcoxon Test**

| (1) Absolute differences ordered from smallest to largest | (2) Rank | (3) Assigned ranks correctly signed | |
|---|---|---|---|
| 1 | 1 | −2.5 | |
| 1 | 2 | −2.5 | |
| 1 | 3 | 2.5 | |
| 1 | 4 | 2.5 | |
| 2 | 5 | −5.5 | |
| 2 | 6 | 5.5 | |
| 3 | 7 | −8 | |
| 3 | 8 | −8 | |
| 3 | 9 | 8 | |
| 4 | 10 | 10 | Sum of negative ranks |
| 5 | 11 | −11.5 | is −38. |
| 5 | 12 | 11.5 | Sum of positive ranks |
| 6 | 13 | 13.5 | is +215. |
| 6 | 14 | 13.5 | |
| 9 | 15 | 15 | |
| 15 | 16 | 16.5 | |
| 15 | 17 | 16.5 | |
| 20 | 18 | 18 | |
| 22 | 19 | 19 | |
| 32 | 20 | 20 | |
| 35 | 21 | 21 | |
| 67 | 22 | 22 | |

Sum negative ranks (−38) and positive ranks (+215)

7. All the negative ranks in column 3 are summed (−38), and all the positive ranks are summed (+215). *The smaller of the two sums* (disregarding signs) is 38. *The value of 38 is called the computed* T. It was not really necessary to sum the positive ranks, since it could be seen that the sum of the negative ranks is smaller than the sum of the positive ranks. However, a check on the accuracy of the computations can be made by summing the negative assigned ranks and the positive assigned ranks. This sum (disregarding signs) must equal the sum of the ranks in column 2. In this case 38+ 215 = 253, which is the same as the sum of column 2.

Recall that the sum of the negative ranks is 38, and the sum of the positive ranks is 215. If any improvement in proficiency were exactly offset by a loss in proficiency, each of the two rank sums would have been about 126.5, found by 253/2.

Decision rule

The Wilcoxon critical value in Appendix K for *N* = 22 at the .01 level of significance and a two-tailed test is 48. This indicates that a computed *T* value greater than 48 up to (and including) 126.5 could result by chance; that is, a computed *T* value greater than 48 but equal to or less than 126.5 would indicate that the sum of the positive and negative ranks do *not* depart significantly from zero.

The decision rule is shown schematically as follows:

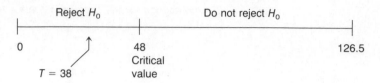

Since the computed $T$ value of 38 is less than the critical $T$ value of 48, the null hypothesis—which states that there is no difference in the typing speeds using the current model and the experimental model—is *rejected* at the .01 level. $H_1$ is accepted. Because of the large imbalance ($-38$ and $+215$), the null hypothesis is rejected.

### Self-Review 17–6

*The answers are at the end of the chapter.*

A record of the production for each machine operator was kept over a period of time. Certain changes in the production procedure were suggested, and 11 operators were picked as an experimental test group to determine whether or not the new procedures were worthwhile. Their productions before and after the new procedures were established are as follows:

| Operator | Production before | Production after |
|---|---|---|
| S. M. | 17 | 18 |
| D. J. | 21 | 23 |
| M. D. | 25 | 22 |
| B. B. | 15 | 25 |
| M. F. | 10 | 28 |
| A. A. | 16 | 16 |
| U. Z. | 10 | 22 |
| Y. U. | 20 | 19 |
| U. T. | 17 | 20 |
| Y. H. | 24 | 30 |
| Y. Y. | 23 | 26 |

1. How many usable pairs are there? That is, what is $N$?

2. Using the Wilcoxon signed rank test, determine whether or not the new procedures actually increased production. Use the .05 level and a one-tailed test.

## EXERCISES

*The answers to the odd-numbered exercises are at the end of the book.*

21. A random sample of seven young urban professional (yuppie) couples that own their own homes is selected. The size of the yuppies' home is compared with that of their parents, in terms of square feet. At the .05 significance level, can we conclude that the yuppies live in larger homes?

| Couple name | Yuppie | Parent |
|---|---|---|
| Gordon | 1,725 | 1,175 |
| Sharkey | 1,310 | 1,120 |
| Uselding | 1,670 | 1,420 |
| Bell | 1,520 | 1,640 |
| Kulhman | 1,290 | 1,360 |
| Welch | 1,880 | 1,750 |
| Anderson | 1,530 | 1,440 |

22. One of the major car manufacturers is studying the effect of regular versus high-octane gasoline in its economy cars. Ten executives are selected and asked to maintain records on mileage during their trips to and from work. The results are as follows.

| Executive | Regular | High-octane |
|---|---|---|
| Bowers | 25 | 28 |
| Demars | 33 | 31 |
| Grasser | 31 | 35 |
| DeToto | 45 | 44 |
| Kleg | 42 | 47 |
| Rau | 38 | 40 |
| Greolke | 29 | 29 |
| Burns | 42 | 37 |
| Snow | 41 | 44 |
| Lawless | 30 | 44 |

At the .05 significance level, is there a difference between the regular and the high-octane?

23. A new assembly-line procedure has been suggested by Mr. Mump. In order to test whether or not the new procedure is superior to the old procedure, a sample group of 15 men was selected at random. First their production under the old system was determined. Then the new Mump procedure was introduced. After an appropriate break-in period, their production was measured again. The results were:

| Employee | Production Old system | Mump method |
|---|---|---|
| A | 60 | 64 |
| B | 40 | 52 |
| C | 59 | 58 |
| D | 30 | 37 |
| E | 70 | 71 |
| F | 78 | 83 |
| G | 43 | 46 |
| H | 40 | 52 |
| I | 87 | 84 |
| J | 80 | 80 |
| K | 56 | 57 |
| L | 21 | 21 |
| M | 99 | 108 |
| N | 50 | 56 |
| O | 56 | 62 |

Test by applying the Wilcoxon signed rank test and the .05 level that production using the new Mump method is greater than production under the old method.

a. State the null and alternate hypotheses.

b. State the decision rule.

c. Arrive at a decision regarding the null hypothesis.

24. It has been suggested that the daily production of a subassembly would be increased if better portable lighting were installed and background music and free coffee and doughnuts were provided during the day. Management agreed to try the scheme for a limited time. The numbers of subassemblies produced per week by a small test group of employees are as follows.

| Employee | Past production record | Production after installing lighting, music, etc. |
|---|---|---|
| JD | 23 | 33 |
| SB | 26 | 26 |
| MD | 24 | 30 |
| RCF | 17 | 25 |
| MF | 20 | 19 |
| UHH | 24 | 22 |
| IB | 30 | 29 |
| WWJ | 21 | 25 |
| OP | 25 | 22 |
| CD | 21 | 23 |
| PA | 16 | 17 |
| RRT | 20 | 15 |
| AT | 17 | 9 |
| QQ | 23 | 30 |

Using the Wilcoxon signed rank test, determine whether or not the suggested changes are worthwhile—that is, whether or not they increased production.

a. State the null hypothesis.
b. You decide on the alternate hypothesis.
c. You decide on the level of significance.
d. State the decision rule.
e. Compute $T$, and arrive at a decision.

# CHAPTER OUTLINE

I. Sign test.
   A. No assumptions need be made about the shape of the two populations.
   B. It is especially useful for "before/after" experiments, product-preference tests, and testing a hypothesis about the median.
   C. Both small and large samples use plus and minus signs. For small samples the number of plus or minus signs is the test statistic, and the binomial distribution is referred to for the critical value. Large samples and a test for the median use the normal distribution as the test statistic. The formula for $z$ is:

$$z = \frac{(X \pm .50) - .50n}{.50 \sqrt{n}} \tag{17-1}$$

II. Mann-Whitney $U$ test.
   A. At least ordinal level of measurement and two independent and randomly selected samples are required.
   B. Small samples.
      1. Samples are designated as small if the larger of two samples has 20 or fewer observations.
      2. The procedure is: Rank all the data from low to high, or vice versa. Then compute $U$ and $U'$.

$$U = n_1 n_2 + \frac{n_1(n_1 + 1)}{2} - \Sigma R_1 \qquad (17-4)$$

$$U' = n_1 n_2 + \frac{n_2(n_2 + 1)}{2} - \Sigma R_2 \qquad (17-5)$$

where:

$n_1$ and $n_2$    are the two sample sizes.

$\Sigma R_1$    is the sum of the ranks for one sample.

$\Sigma R_2$    is the sum of the ranks for the other sample.

The *smaller* computed value, $U$ or $U'$, is used in reaching a decision about whether to accept or reject the null hypothesis. Appendix J gives critical values.

C. Large samples.
   1. Samples are designated as large if the larger of two samples has 21 or more observations.
   2. The procedure is: Rank all the data from low to high, or vice versa. Then compute $z$.

$$z = \frac{\Sigma R_1 - \Sigma R_2 - \left[ (n_1 - n_2)\dfrac{n_1 + n_2 + 1}{2} \right]}{\sqrt{n_1 n_2 \left[ \dfrac{n_1 + n_2 + 1}{3} \right]}} \qquad (17-6)$$

III. Kruskal-Wallis one-way analysis of variance by ranks.
   A. No assumptions about the shape of the populations are required. To apply the test, the data must be capable of being ranked, and samples must be independent.
   B. It is used to test if three or more populations are identical.
   C. Combine all the values, and rank them starting with the lowest value, which is given the rank of 1. Sum the ranks for each sample, and insert them in the following formula:

$$H = \frac{12}{N(N + 1)} \left[ \frac{(\Sigma R_1)^2}{n_1} + \frac{(\Sigma R_2)^2}{n_2} + \cdots + \frac{(\Sigma R_k)^2}{n_k} \right] - 3(N + 1) \qquad (17-7)$$

IV. Wilcoxon matched-pair signed rank test.
   A. Data must be at least ordinal-scaled, and the two samples must be related. One way to accomplish this is to have each person act as his or her own control, meaning that the same person (or item) is in both sample 1 and sample 2.
   B. It is used extensively in "before/after" situations.
   C. Procedure.
      1. Rank absolute differences between old method and new method.
      2. Recognize ties, and give ranks appropriate signs.
      3. Sum negative ranks and positive ranks.
      4. Disregarding signs, the smaller of the two sums is the computed $T$ value.
      5. Refer to Appendix K for the critical value, and reject or do not reject $H_0$.

# EXERCISES

*The answers to the odd-numbered exercises are at the end of the book.*

25. Suppose NBC-TV is considering two western series for the forthcoming season. One is "Loner," the other "Cattleman." Only one will be aired. To assess whether there is a preference, 20 critics selected at random were shown a preview of an episode of each program. The null hypothesis to be tested is: There is no difference in preference for one

show over the other. The alternate hypothesis is: There is a preference for one show over the other. The hypothesis is to be tested at the .10 level.

    a.    Will a one-tailed or two-tailed sign test be used?

    b.    When the preferences were tallied, a "+" sign was recorded if the critic preferred "Loner," and "−" sign was recorded if the preference was for "Cattleman." A count of the pluses revealed that 12 critics preferred "Loner," 7 liked "Cattleman," and 1 was undecided. State the decision rule in words. Picture it in a chart.

    c.    What conclusion would you forward to NBC-TV? Explain.

26.    Suppose Merrill Lynch wants to award a substantial contract for fine-line pens to be used nationally in their offices. Two suppliers, Bic and Pilot, have submitted the lowest bids. To determine the preference of office employees, brokers, and others, a personal preference test is to be conducted using a randomly selected sample of 20 employees. The .05 level of significance is to be used.

    a.    If the alternate hypothesis states that Bic is preferred over Pilot, is the sign test to be conducted as a one-tailed test or a two-tailed test? Explain.

    b.    As each of the sample members told the researchers his or her preference, a "+" was recorded if it was Bic and a "−" if it was the Pilot fine-line pen. A count of the pluses revealed that 12 employees preferred Bic, 5 preferred Pilot, and 3 were undecided. What is $n$?

    c.    What is the decision rule in words? Show it in a chart.

    d.    What conclusion did you reach regarding pen preference? Explain.

27.    A research project involving community responsibility is to be conducted. The objective is to find out if women are more community-conscious before marriage or after five years of marriage. A test to measure community consciousness was administered to a sample of women before marriage, and the same test was given to them five years after marriage. The test scores are:

| Name | Before marriage | After marriage |
|------|-----------------|----------------|
| Beth | 110 | 114 |
| Jean | 157 | 159 |
| Sue | 121 | 120 |
| Cathy | 96 | 103 |
| Mary | 130 | 139 |
| Carol | 186 | 196 |
| Lisa | 116 | 116 |
| Sandy | 160 | 140 |
| Petra | 149 | 142 |

Test at the .05 level. $H_0$ is: There is no difference in community consciousness before and after marriage. $H_1$ is: There is a difference.

28.    Is there a difference in the annual divorce rates in predominantly rural counties among three geographic regions, namely, the Southwest, the Southeast, and the Northwest? Test at the .05 level. Annual divorce rates per 1,000 population for randomly selected counties are:

    Southwest: 5.9, 6.2, 7.9, 8.6, 4.6

    Southeast: 5.0, 6.4, 7.3, 6.2, 8.1, 5.1

    Far west: 6.7, 6.2, 4.9, 8.0, 5.5

29.    The idle times during the eight-hour day shift and the night shift are to be compared. A time study revealed the following numbers of minutes of idle time for eight-hour periods.

    Day shift: 92, 103, 116, 81, 89

    Night shift: 96, 114, 80, 82, 88, 91

Is there a difference in the idle time between the two shifts? Test at the .05 level.

30. The mobility of executives in stock exchanges, in service, in heavy construction, and in air transportation is to be researched. Samples from each of these industries were selected, and the number of times an executive moved during a 10-year period was converted to an index. An index of 0 would indicate no movement, whereas 100 would indicate almost constant movement from one location to another or one firm to another. The indexes for the four groups are:

| Stock exchange | Service | Heavy construction | Air transportation |
|---|---|---|---|
| 4 | 3 | 62 | 30 |
| 17 | 12 | 40 | 38 |
| 8 | 40 | 81 | 46 |
| 20 | 17 | 96 | 40 |
| 16 | 31 | 76 | 21 |
|  | 19 |  |  |

We cannot assume that the indexes are normally distributed. Thus, we must use a nonparametric test. Using the .05 level, determine whether the four populations of mobility indexes are identical.

31. The South Carolina Real Estate Association claims that the median rental for three-bedroom condominiums in the metropolitan area is $1,200 a month. To check this, a random sample of 149 units was selected. Of the 149, 5 rented for exactly $1,200 a month, and 75 rented for more than $1,200. At the .05 level, test the statement that the median rental is $1,200.

   a. State $H_0$ and $H_1$.

   b. Give the decision rule.

   c. Do the necessary calculations, and arrive at a decision.

32. The Citrus Council wants to find out if consumers prefer plain orange juice or juice with some orange pulp in it. A random sample of 212 consumers was selected. Each member of the sample tasted a small, unlabeled cup of one kind and then tasted the other kind. Twelve consumers said they had no preference, 40 preferred plain juice, and the remainder liked the juice with pulp better. Test at the .05 level that the preferences for plain juice and for orange juice with pulp are equal.

33. Cornwall and Hudson, a large department store chain, wants to handle just one brand of high-quality stereo components. The list has been narrowed to two brands: Sony and Pioneer. To help make a decision, a panel of 16 audio experts met. A passage using Sony components (labeled A) was played. Then the same passage was played using

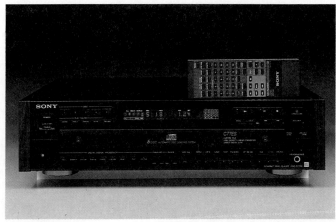

Courtesy Sony Corporation

Pioneer components (labeled B). A "+" in the following table indicates an individual's preference for the Sony components, a "−" indicates preference for Pioneer, and a 0 signifies no preference.

| | Expert | | | | | | | | | | | | | | | |
|---|---|---|---|---|---|---|---|---|---|---|---|---|---|---|---|
| 1 | 2 | 3 | 4 | 5 | 6 | 7 | 8 | 9 | 10 | 11 | 12 | 13 | 14 | 15 | 16 |
| + | − | + | − | + | + | − | 0 | − | + | − | + | + | − | + | − |

Conduct a test of hypothesis at the .10 significance level to determine if there is a difference in preference between the two brands.

34. In Exercise 19 in Chapter 16, some information on the 1969 draft lottery was given. Assume each month is a treatment and the lottery numbers are ranks. Use the Kruskal-Wallis test to determine if the lottery numbers were random. Comment on your results.

35. In Exercise 32 in Chapter 12, data on the annual incomes of probation aides were given. Suppose we cannot assume that the information was from normal populations. Conduct an appropriate test to determine if the populations of incomes are identical

## COMPUTER DATA EXERCISES

36. Refer to data set 1, which reports information on homes sold in Florida during 1990. Use the .05 significance level.

  a. Use an appropriate nonparametric method to determine if there is a difference in the price of the homes among the various townships.

  b. Combine the homes with six or more bedrooms, and determine if there is a difference in the prices of the homes by the number of bedrooms. Assume that the prices of homes are not normally distributed.

  c. Use nonparametric methods to determine if the distribution of the distances from the center of the city is different between homes that have a pool and those that do not have a pool.

# CHAPTER 17 EXAMINATION

*The answers are at the end of the chapter.*

For Questions 1–11, record the letter in front of the correct answer.

1. If the assumptions for the paired *t* test (Chapter 11) cannot be met, the nonparametric alternative is:
   a. The Mann-Whitney test.
   b. The Kruskal-Wallis test.
   c. The Wilcoxon test.
   d. The sign test.

2. The nonparametric tests presented in this chapter require that the populations of interest be normally distributed and that the observations be at least interval-scale.
   a. True.
   b. False.

3. The Mann-Whitney *U* test requires that the observations be paired. (An example of paired data would be the score an applicant had before attending the police academy and the score at the end of the course.)
   a. True.
   b. False.

4. Which one of the nonparametric tests presented in this chapter requires at least five samples from each population and ordinal level of measurement?
   a. Mann-Whitney test.
   b. Kruskal-Wallis test.
   c. Wilcoxon test.
   d. The sign test.

5. Which of the following is not a distribution-free test?
   a. Mann-Whitney test.
   b. The Student $t$ test.
   c. Kruskal-Wallis test.
   d. Wilcoxon test.
   e. None of these is correct.

6. The region of rejection for the Kruskal-Wallis test:
   a. Is in the upper tail only.
   b. Is in the lower tail only.
   c. Can be in the upper or lower tail.
   d. Is identified in none of these statements.

7. If the null hypothesis for the Kruskal-Wallis test is rejected, it indicates:
   a. There is no difference between the two groups.
   b. There is no difference between the set of "before" observations and the set of "after" observations.
   c. The distributions are not equal.
   d. None of these.

8. The test statistic for the Mann-Whitney test is:
   a. $z$.
   b. $t$.
   c. $H$.
   d. $U$.
   e. None of these.

9. For the Kruskal-Wallis test, the rankings are determined by combining all the groups and ranking all the values starting with 1.
   a. True.
   b. False.

10. For the Wilcoxon test:
    a. There must be an expected set of frequencies, $f_e$, and an observed set of frequencies, $f_o$.
    b. Paired data are required.
    c. There must be three or more populations.
    d. The data must be at least interval-scaled.
    e. None of these is correct.

11. The sign test is an appropriate nonparametric test for "before/after" experiments and consumer preference tests.
    a. True.
    b. False.

12. The hourly production of a sample of employees before attending a special course and after completing the course are:

| | Production | |
|---|---|---|
| Employee | Before course | After course |
| Frank Unati | 21 | 26 |
| Sue Marker | 29 | 28 |
| Arthur Noble | 20 | 20 |
| Jean Sobecki | 39 | 47 |
| Agnes Locker | 25 | 30 |
| George Taoka | 44 | 48 |
| Dan Obet | 18 | 27 |
| Mirmie Gladen | 33 | 36 |
| Yando Larkin | 31 | 34 |
| Nastir Ufasse | 45 | 48 |
| Gladys Rollins | 36 | 41 |

Test at the .05 level that the special course significantly increased production.

13. The murder rates in large cities, small cities, and rural areas are to be compared. Samples were selected from the three areas. The rates given are per 10,000 population.

| Large cities | Small cities | Rural areas |
|---|---|---|
| 6.7 | 7.8 | 12.6 |
| 5.2 | 7.1 | 8.4 |
| 11.2 | 12.2 | 8.2 |
| 8.6 | 9.6 | 4.9 |
| 5.5 | 5.2 | 11.7 |
| | 6.8 | 7.1 |

Assuming that the rates are not normally distributed, apply a nonparametric test. Use the .01 level to find out if there is a difference among the distributions of the murder rates for the three groups.

14. We want to test whether there has been a decrease in the median age of international flight travelers. The null hypothesis is $H_0$: Median = 37.0 years. A sample of 410 travelers revealed that 208 were younger than 37 years, 10 were exactly 37, and the remainder were over 37 years. Using the .10 level, has the median age of international travelers decreased?

# ANSWERS

17–1 1. Two-tailed because $H_1$ does not state a direction.

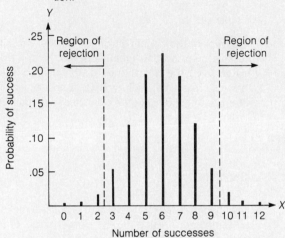

3. Reject $H_0$; accept $H_1$. There is a preference. Adding down, .000 + .003 + .016 = .019. This is the largest cumulative probability up to but not exceeding .050, which is half of the level of significance.

17–2 Since 80 is more than $n/2 = 100/2 = 50$, we use:

$$z = \frac{(80 - .50) - .50(100)}{.50 \sqrt{100}} = \frac{29.5}{5} = 5.9$$

Since 5.9 lies in the tail beyond 1.645 (Appendix D), $H_0$ is rejected. The vitamins were effective.

17–3 1. $H_0$: The median is 23.
   $H_1$: The median is not 23.
2. Twenty bills were below $23.00, 42 were above $23.00, and 2 were exactly equal to $23.00.
3. $n = 62$
4. Reject $H_0$ if $z < -1.645$ or $z > 1.645$.
5. 2.67, found by $[(42 - .50) - .50(62)]/.50\sqrt{62}$
6. Reject $H_0$ because computed $z$ of 2.67 is in the rejection region beyond 1.645.
7. The median is $39.10.
8. No. The median is *not* $23.00. The difference between $23.00 and $39.10 is not due to chance.

17–4 1. $H_0$: There is no difference between the two distributions of scores.
   $H_1$: There is a difference between the distributions of the scores.
2. 10.

| Region of rejection | Do not reject $H_0$ |
|---|---|
| 0 | 10 |

3.

| Group 1 | | Group 2 | |
|---|---|---|---|
| Score | Rank | Score | Rank |
| 121 | 3 | 128 | 6 |
| 180 | 11.5 | 197 | 14 |
| 122 | 4 | 180 | 11.5 |
| 160 | 9 | 126 | 5 |
| 141 | 7 | 167 | 10 |
| 97 | 1 | 99 | 2 |
| 212 | 15 | 147 | 8 |
| 186 | 13 | | 56.5 |
| | 63.5 | | |

$$U = (8)(7) + \frac{8(8 + 1)}{2} - 63.5$$
$$= 28.5$$
$$U' = (8)(7) + \frac{7(7 + 1)}{2} - 56.5$$
$$= 56 + 28 - 56.5$$
$$= 27.5$$

The smaller of the two values (27.5) falls in the region above 10. Do not reject $H_0$. There is no difference between the distributions of the two groups of scores. As a check:

$$U' = (8)(7) - 28.5 = 27.5$$

17–5

| | | Ranks | |
|---|---|---|---|
| | | Great | |
| Englewood | West Side | Northern | Sylvania |
| 17 | 5 | 19 | 7 |
| 20 | 1 | 9.5 | 11 |
| 16 | 3 | 21 | 15 |
| 13 | 5 | 22 | 9.5 |
| 5 | 2 | 14 | 8 |
| 18 | | | 12 |

$\Sigma R_1 = 89$   $\Sigma R_2 = 16$   $\Sigma R_3 = 85.5$   $\Sigma R_4 = 62.5$
$n_1 = 6$       $n_2 = 5$       $n_3 = 5$           $n_4 = 6$

$H_0$: The distributions are the same.
$H_1$: The distributions are not the same.

$$H = \frac{12}{22(22+1)}\left[\frac{(89)^2}{6} + \frac{(16)^2}{5} + \frac{(85.5)^2}{5} + \frac{(62.5)^2}{6}\right]$$
$$- 3(22+1)$$
$$= 0.0237154(3484.459) - 69$$
$$= 13.635$$

The critical value of chi-square for $k - 1 = 4 - 1 = 3$ degrees of freedom is 11.345. Since the computed value of 13.635 is greater than 11.345, the null hypothesis is rejected. We conclude that the distributions are not the same.

17–6   1.   $N = 10$.

2.

| Before | After | Differ-ence | Absolute difference ordered | Ranks | Signed ranks |
|--------|-------|--------|--------|-------|-------|
| 17 | 18 | +1 | 1 | 1 | −1.5 |
| 21 | 23 | +2 | 1 | 2 | +1.5 |
| 25 | 22 | −3 | 2 | 3 | +3 |
| 15 | 25 | +10 | 3 | 4 | −5 |
| 10 | 28 | +18 | 3 | 5 | +5 |
| 16 | 16 | — | 3 | 6 | +5 |
| 10 | 22 | +12 | 6 | 7 | +7 |
| 20 | 19 | −1 | 10 | 8 | +8 |
| 17 | 20 | +3 | 12 | 9 | +9 |
| 24 | 30 | +6 | 18 | 10 | +10 |
| 23 | 26 | +3 | | | |

The sum of the negative signed ranks is −6.5; the positive sum is 48.5. From Appendix K, one-tailed test, $N = 10$, the critical value is 10. Since 6.5 is less than 10, reject the null hypothesis and accept the alternate. New procedures did increase production.

## Answers

# CHAPTER 17 EXAMINATION

1.  c.
2.  False. Only ordinal scale needed. No assumptions about normality required.
3.  False. Samples must be independent.
4.  b.
5.  b.
6.  a.
7.  c.
8.  d.
9.  a.
10. b.
11. a.
12. $H_0$:   There is no difference in production before the course and after the course.
    $H_1$:   The course significantly increased production (a one-tailed test).

| Before course | After course | Difference | Absolute differences ranked | Assigned ranks correctly signed |
|-------|-------|--------|--------|--------|
| 21 | 26 | −5 | 1 | +1 |
| 29 | 28 | +1 | 3 | −3 |
| 20 | 20 | 0 | 3 | −3 |
| 39 | 47 | −8 | 3 | −3 |
| 25 | 30 | −5 | 4 | −5 |
| 44 | 48 | −4 | 5 | −7 |
| 18 | 27 | −9 | 5 | −7 |
| 33 | 36 | −3 | 5 | −7 |
| 31 | 34 | −3 | 8 | −9 |
| 45 | 48 | −3 | 9 | −10 |
| 36 | 41 | −5 | | |

Sum of negative ranks = −54, sum of positive ranks = +1. Computed $T$ value = +1. Critical value at .05 level = 10, where $N = 10$. Reject $H_0$. The course has significantly increased production.

13. $H_0$:   There is no difference in the distributions of the murder rates for the three groups.
    $H_1$:   There is a difference in the distributions of the murder rates.

| Large cities | | Small cities | | Rural areas | |
|-------|-------|-------|-------|-------|-------|
| Rates | Rank | Rates | Rank | Rates | Rank |
| 6.7 | 5 | 7.8 | 9.0 | 12.6 | 17.0 |
| 5.2 | 2.5 | 7.1 | 7.5 | 8.4 | 11.0 |
| 11.2 | 14.0 | 12.2 | 16.0 | 8.2 | 10.0 |
| 8.6 | 12.0 | 9.6 | 13.0 | 4.9 | 1.0 |
| 5.5 | 4.0 | 5.2 | 2.5 | 11.7 | 15.0 |
| $\Sigma R_1 = 37.5$ | | 6.8 | 6.0 | 7.1 | 7.5 |
| | | $\Sigma R_2 = 54.0$ | | $\Sigma R_3 = 61.5$ | |
| $n_1 = 5$ | | $n_2 = 6$ | | $n_3 = 6$ | |

$$H = \frac{12}{17(17+1)}\left[\frac{(37.5)^2}{5} + \frac{(54)^2}{6} + \frac{(61.5)^2}{6}\right] - 3(17+1)$$
$$= \frac{12}{306}[281.25 + 486 + 630.375] - 54$$
$$= .0392157[1397.625] - 54$$
$$= 0.79$$

$N = 17$; critical value of chi-square at .01 level and 2 degrees of freedom is 9.210. Computed value of $H$ is

0.81. Since 0.81 is less than 9.210, the null hypothesis is not rejected.

14. $H_0$: Median = 37; $H_1$: Median < 37. Critical value of $z$ is 1.28 (one-tailed test; search Appendix D for .5000 − .10 = .4000). Since 208 is greater than $n/2 = 400/2 = 200$, use

$$z = \frac{(208 - .50) - .50(400)}{.50\sqrt{400}} = \frac{7.50}{10} = 0.75$$

Since 0.75 is in the area of the standard normal curve between 0 and 1.28, we do not reject $H_0$. Median age hasn't changed. It is still 37.

# A Review of Chapters 16 and 17

This section is a review of the major concepts and terms introduced in Chapters 16 and 17. Chapter 16 began the study of *nonparametric,* or *distribution-free,* tests by discussing the *chi-square goodness-of-fit test.* This test is applied to a set of observed frequencies, $f_o$, and a corresponding expected set of frequencies, $f_e$, to test how well the sets fit. This test involves only one characteristic possessed by an individual, such as education. If we are interested in two characteristics, such as a relationship between education level and income, the data are cross-classified into a contingency table, and the chi-square test is applied. For these two tests, no assumption about the shape of the population is needed; they require only that the data be nominal-level. The chi-square goodness-of-fit test is also used to determine if a set of observed frequencies is normally distributed.

*Goodness-of-fit test and contingency table analysis applicable to nominal-level data*

Chapter 17 presented four nonparametric tests, but these tests require that the data be at least ordinal-level. That is, the data must be ranked from low to high. The tests discussed were the *sign test,* the *Mann-Whitney U test,* the *Kruskal-Wallis analysis of variance test,* and the *Wilcoxon signed rank test.*

*Four tests for ordinal-level data*

## Glossary

### Chapter 16

**Chi-square distribution**   A distribution with these characteristics: (1) Its value can only be positive. (2) There is a family of chi-square distributions, a different one for each different degree of freedom. (3) The distributions are positively skewed, but as the number of degrees of freedom increases, the distribution approaches the normal distribution.

**Chi-square goodness-of-fit test**   A test with the objective of determining how good an observed set of frequencies fits an expected set of frequencies. It is concerned with only one characteristic, such as the age of an individual or the color of a car.

**Contingency table**   If two characteristics, such as education and income, are cross-classified into a table, the table is called a contingency table. The chi-square test statistic is applied to find out if the two characteristics are related.

**Nominal level of measurement**   The "lowest" level of measurement. Such data can only be classified into categories, and there is no particular order for the categories. For example, it makes no difference whether the categories "male" and "female" are listed in that order, or female first and male second. The categories are mutually exclusive—meaning, in this illustration, that a person cannot be a male and a female at the same time.

**Nonparametric or distribution-free tests**   Hypothesis tests involving nominal- and ordinal-level data. No assumptions need be made about the shape of the parent population; that is, we do not have to assume that the population is normally distributed.

### Chapter 17

**Kruskal-Wallis one-way analysis of variance by ranks**   A test used when the assumptions for the parametric analysis of variance (ANOVA) cannot be met. Its purpose is to test whether or not three or more populations are equal. Again, the data must be at least ordinal-scaled.

**Mann-Whitney *U* test**   A nonparametric test requiring that the data be at least ordinal level of measurement. That is, the data must be capable of being ranked. The test is used when the assumptions for the parametric Student *t* test cannot be met. The objective of the test is to find out if two independent samples can be considered as coming from the same population.

**Sign test**   A test that can be used for nominal data. The calculations for both the small-sample and the large-sample cases are minimal. The sign test is used to find out if there is a brand preference for two products and to determine whether performance after an experiment is greater than before the experiment. Also, the sign test is used to test a hypothesis about the median.

**Wilcoxon matched-pair signed rank test**   Another nonparametric test requiring at least ordinal-level data. Its purpose is to find out if there is any difference between two sets of paired (related) observations. It is used if the assumptions required for the paired $t$ test cannot be met.

# EXERCISES

*The answers to the odd-numbered exercises are at the end of the book.*

1.  For a chi-square test, what do $f_o$ and $f_e$ stand for?
2.  The following is an example of what?

| Political affiliation | Amount contributed to campaign | | |
|---|---|---|---|
| | $1–$99 | $100–$1,000 | $1,000 and more |
| Republican | 42 | 87 | 342 |
| Democrat | 596 | 302 | 116 |
| Socialist | 42 | 49 | 36 |
| All others | 19 | 17 | 11 |

3.  Refer to Exercise 2. What test statistic would be used to find out if there is any relationship between political affiliation and the amount contributed?
4.  Refer to Exercise 2. How many degrees of freedom are there?
5.  Refer to Exercise 2. Suppose the computed value of $\chi^2$ is 11.248, and the .05 level is being used. Should the null hypothesis be rejected?
6.  For a goodness-of-fit test, the computed value of chi-square is 8.403, and the critical value is 5.991. The .05 level is being used. Is the null hypothesis rejected?
7.  Refer to Exercise 6. What is the null hypothesis?
8.  What level of measurement is required for the parametric tests of hypotheses discussed in Chapters 11 and 12?
9.  What level of measurement is required for the goodness-of-fit test?
10.  What level of measurement is required for the Mann-Whitney $U$ test?
11.  What is the purpose of the Mann-Whitney $U$ test?
12.  What assumptions are made about the shape of the populations in using the Kruskal-Wallis test?
13.  What is the objective of the Kruskal-Wallis test?
14.  What is the objective of the Wilcoxon signed rank test?
15.  Of the four nonparametric tests in Chapter 17 (sign test, Mann-Whitney, Kruskal-Wallis, and Wilcoxon), which one deals with three or more samples?
16.  Refer to Exercise 15. Which test deals with paired data?
17.  Refer to Exercise 15. Can these tests be applied to interval- and ratio-level data?
18.  For a Mann-Whitney $U$ test, the alternate hypothesis is: The women have better eye perception than the men. Would a one-tailed or a two-tailed test be applied?
19.  The chi-square distribution for 5 degrees of freedom is approximately normally distributed. Is that statement true?
20.  How are the degrees of freedom for a goodness-of-fit test determined?
21.  Describe the steps followed, using a simple example, to test a hypothesis involving the median.

Publishing—Courtesy of R. R. Donnelley and Sons Company

# INDEX NUMBERS

When you have completed this chapter, you will be able to:

1. Tell why millions of dollars are spent yearly constructing and publishing indexes.

2. Construct unweighted and weighted indexes.

3. Construct a price, quality, value, and special-purpose index.

4. Explain how the Consumer Price Index is constructed and used.

5. Cite the special applications of the Consumer Price Index in determining real income, deflating sales, and determining the purchasing power of the dollar.

n this chapter we will examine a very useful statistical tool called an **index.** Many indexes, such as the Consumer Price Index, the New York Stock Exchange Composite, the Standard & Poor's 500 indexes, and the index of leading economic indicators, compiled and published by the federal government, receive considerable attention on the nightly television news, on the front pages of newspapers such as *USA Today* and *The Wall Street Journal,* and in government publications including the *Monthly Labor Review* and the *Federal Reserve Bulletin.* As examples:

- A 6.1 percent rise in the Consumer Price Index for all urban consumers during the year largely reflected price rises in energy, apparel commodities, and most services. The increase was the largest since 1981.[1]
- Stocks rallied strongly Tuesday after the Federal Reserve Board moved to lower interest rates. The Dow Jones Industrial Average rose 38.24 points to 3027.28. Broader indexes also rose. Both the New York Stock Exchange Composite and Standard & Poor's 500 indexes hit new highs.[2]

Other nations are equally concerned with price rises. As an illustration, the September 27, 1991, headline in the *South China Morning Post* was "Price Rises Hit Inflation Battle Plan."[3] A passage from the accompanying article emphasizes the concern for the high inflation rate in Hong Kong.

The Government's fight against inflation is continuing to spin off course with the latest monthly figures showing a mild acceleration in price rises. Strong increases in the cost of fresh food, services and housing all pushed the main indicator of retail inflation, the Consumer Price Index (A) which covers low income families, up by 12.7 percent in August. Drought and flooding in China is blamed for the extra cost of foodstuffs. However, in terms of CPI (A) alcoholic drinks and tobacco recorded the single largest year-on-year increase at 42.1 percent.

Consumer Price Index (B), which covers households with slightly higher incomes, rose by 12.0 percent during August. The Hang Seng Consumer Price Index, which covers high income households, rose by 10.9 percent.

## THE MEANING OF INDEX NUMBERS

What is an index?

> Index number  A percent that measures the change in price, quantity, value, or some other item of interest from one time period to another.

### ■ EXAMPLE

The main use of an index number in business is to show the percent change from one time period to another. To illustrate this, the average hourly earnings in manufacturing in 1980 was $7.27, according to the Bureau of Labor Statistics. In March 1991 it was $11.08.[4] What is the index of hourly earnings in manufacturing for March 1991 based on 1980?

[1]U.S. Department of Labor, *Monthly Labor Review,* May 1991, p. 10.
[2]*USA Today,* August 7, 1991, p. 3B.
[3]*South China Morning Post,* September 27, 1991, p. 1.
[4]U.S. Department of Labor, *Monthly Labor Review,* May 1991, p. 70.

### ✓ SOLUTION

Wages increased

It is 152.4, found by:

$$\frac{\text{Hourly earnings in March 1991}}{\text{Hourly earnings in 1980}} \times 100 = \frac{\$11.08}{\$7.27} \times 100 = 152.4$$

indicating that hourly earnings in manufacturing in 1991 compared with 1980 were 152.4 percent, or they increased 52.4 percent during that period—found by 152.4 − 100.

### ■ EXAMPLE

The Bureau of the Census reported that farm population dropped from 30,529,000 in 1930 to an estimated 5,100,000 in 1992.[5] What is the index of farm population for 1992 based on 1930?

Reprinted with permission of Del Monte Corporation

### ✓ SOLUTION

The index is 16.7, found by

$$\frac{\text{1992 population}}{\text{1930 population}} \times 100 = \frac{5,100,000}{30,529,000} \times 100 = 16.7$$

This indicates that the farm population in 1992 compared with 1930 was 16.7 percent, or it decreased 83.3 percent during the period, found by 100.0 − 16.7.

    An index can also be used to compare one thing with another. For example, the population of the Canadian province of British Columbia is estimated to be 3,044,200, and for Ontario it is 9,546,200.[6] What is the population of British Columbia compared with that of Ontario?

---

[5]U.S: Bureau of the Census, *Current Population Reports,* series P−27, no. 56.
[6]*World Almanac and Book of Facts,* 1991, p. 696.

As a second example, the number of passengers arriving and departing at Chicago's O'Hare International Airport, the largest in the United States, is 59,130,000 a year; for the fifth largest, JFK in New York, the number is 30,323,000.[7] What is the arrival and departure rate for O'Hare compared with that of JFK, expressed as an index?

The index of population for British Columbia is 31.9, found by:

$$\frac{\text{Population of British Columbia}}{\text{Population of Ontario}} \times 100 = \frac{3,044,200}{9,546,200} \times 100 = 31.9$$

This indicates that the population of British Columbia is 31.9 percent (about one third) of the population of Ontario, or the population of British Columbia is 68.1 percent less than the population of Ontario (100.0 − 31.9 = 68.1).

The index for O'Hare is 195.0, found by:

$$\frac{\text{Arrive/depart O'Hare}}{\text{Arrive/depart JFK}} \times 100 = \frac{59,130,000}{30,323,000} \times 100 = 195.0$$

This indicates that the number of arrivals and departures from Chicago's O'Hare is 195.0 percent of that of New York's JFK; that is, O'Hare's arrival and departure rate is 95.0 percent greater than that for JFK.

Note from the previous discussion that:

1.  The index of hourly earnings in manufacturing (152.4) and the index of farm population (16.7) are actually percents. The percent sign, however, is usually omitted.

**Base period**

2.  Each index number has a **base.** Until recently the **base period** for most indexes compiled and published by the federal government was 1967, written "1967 = 100." However, this policy has changed, and indexes now have various base periods. As examples, the Consumer Price Index now has a 1982−84 base period. The U.S. import and export price indexes have 1977 as the base period. The Producers Price Index uses 1982 = 100, and the parity ratio, which is an index—the ratio of prices received by farmers to prices paid by the farmers—still has 1910−14 as the base period.

**Base number for most indexes is 100.0**

3.  The **base number** of most indexes is 100.0. Thus, when we computed the index of hourly earnings in manufacturing for 1991 based on 1980, we divided $11.08 by $7.27 and then multiplied the quotient of 1.524 by 100. This gave us the index of 152.4, which is easy to interpret: the average hourly earnings in manufacturing increased 52.4 percent from 1980 to 1991. There is no reason, however, why 10, 50, 1,000, or any other number cannot be used as the base number. In fact, the New York Stock Exchange index has December 31, 1965 = 50. Standard & Poor's Corporation Index uses 1941−43 as the base period and 10 as the base, written 1941−43 = 10. And the American Stock Exchange uses August 31, 1973 = 50.

4.  Most business and economic indexes are carried either to the nearest whole percent, such as 312 or 96, or to the nearest tenth of a percent, such as 97.5 or 178.6.

---

[7]Air Transport Association of America.

## Self-Review 18-1

*The answers are at the end of the chapter.*

1. The average hourly earnings in mining in March 1991 were \$14.12. In 1979 they were \$8.49[8] Express the average hourly earnings in 1991 as an index using the 1979 average as the base (denominator). Interpret.

2. According to *Fortune,* the annual sales of a few selected industrial corporations are:

| Rank | Company | Sales ($ millions) |
|------|---------|--------------------|
| 1 | GM | 101,781.9 |
| 2 | Exxon | 76,416.0 |
| 3 | Ford | 71,643.4 |
| 4 | IBM | 54,217.0 |
| 10 | Chrysler | 26,257.7 |

a. Express the annual sales of General Motors as an index using the sales of International Business Machines as the base (denominator). Interpret.

b. Express the annual sales of Chrysler as an index using the sales of IBM as the base. Interpret.

# WHY CONVERT DATA TO INDEXES?

Indexes allow us to express a change in price, quantity, or value as a percent

Compiling index numbers is not a recent innovation. An Italian, G. R. Carli, has been credited with originating the first index numbers in 1764. They were incorporated in a report he made regarding price fluctuations in Europe from 1500 to 1750. No systematic approach to collecting and reporting data in index form was evident in the United States until about 1900. The cost-of-living index (now called the Consumer Price Index) was introduced in 1913, and the list of indexes has increased steadily since then.

Why convert data to indexes? An index is a convenient way of expressing a change in a heterogeneous group of items. The Consumer Price Index (CPI), for example, encompasses about 400 items—including golf balls, lawn mowers, hamburgers, funeral services, and dentists' fees. Prices are expressed in dollars per pound, box, yard, and many other different units. Only by converting the prices of these many diverse goods and services to one index number every month can the federal government and others concerned with inflation keep informed of the overall movement of consumer prices.

Converting data to indexes also makes it easier to assess the trend in a series composed of exceptionally large numbers. For example, suppose 1992 retail sales were \$185,679,432,621.87 and 1982 sales were \$185,500,000,000.00. The increase of \$179,432,621.87 appears significant. Yet if the 1992 sales total were expressed as an index based on 1982 sales, the increase would be less than one tenth of 1 percent!

$$\frac{\text{Total retail sales in 1992}}{\text{Total retail sales in 1982}} = \frac{\$185,679,432,621.87}{\$185,500,000,000.00} \times 100 = 100.09$$

---

[8]U.S. Department of Labor, *Monthly Labor Review,* June 1988, p. 87; and May 1991, p. 70.

# Types of Index Numbers

An index can be classified as a **price index,** a **quantity index,** a **value index,** or a **special-purpose index.** A few examples of the four types of indexes published on a regular basis follow.

## Price Indexes

Some important indexes

*Consumer Price Index.* Actually, there are two consumer price indexes, one for all urban consumers and the other for urban wage earners and clerical workers. Also, there are separate indexes to show the changes in the price of food, transportation, and so on (1982–84 = 100).

*Producers Price Index.* This measures the average change in prices received in the primary markets of the United States by producers of commodities in all stages of processing (1982 = 100).

*U.S. import and export price indexes.* These are published in the *Monthly Labor Review* (1977 = 100).

## Quantity Indexes

*Federal Reserve Board indexes of quantity output.* In addition, there are output indexes by market grouping and industry grouping. They are published monthly in the *Survey of Current Business* (1977 = 100).

## Value Indexes

*Value-of-construction contracts awarded in 50 states.*

*McCann-Erickson Advertising Index.* Subdivided into network TV, spot TV, magazine, and newspaper, this index is reported monthly in the *Survey of Current Business.*

## Special-Purpose Indexes

There are several indexes that reflect the overall economic activity in the United States. The federal government puts out an index of leading economic indicators. It includes such diverse economic indicators as stock prices, new orders for plant and equipment, and building permits issued. Another such index, the Forbes index, combines production, department store sales, and several other business indicators. *Business Week* has what it calls a "leading index." It consists of such business and economic indicators as stock prices, bond yields, material prices, number of business failures, and real estate loans.

# Construction of Index Numbers

There are two methods used in constructing indexes—the *unweighted* method and the *weighted* method.

## Unweighted Indexes

An **unweighted index** is also referred to as a *simple index.* It is the most elementary type of index. Basically, it describes the percent change in one item over a period of time. The item might be a VCR, a robot, a cellular telephone, or the total number of persons employed at Occidental Petroleum. The index may involve the price, quantity, or value of the item.

> Unweighted index   A percent that describes one item in a given period compared with a base period.

Unweighted price index

To illustrate the construction of a simple price index, the prices of a golf cart tire for selected years are given in Table 18–1. We want to convert the price for each year to an index using 1970 as the base period, that is, 1970 = 100. To arrive at the index for 1992 we divide the price ($38) by the base period price of $20 and multiply the result by 100 to convert it to a percent: ($38/$20) × 100 = 190.0. The result 190.0 is often referred to as a *relative*.

---

### TABLE 18–1

**Price Indexes for Golf Cart Tire, 1965–92**

| Year | Price of tire | Index (1970 = 100) |
|------|------|------|
| 1965 | $18 | $\dfrac{18}{20} \times 100 = 90.0$ |
| 1970 | 20 | $\dfrac{20}{20} \times 100 = 100.0$ |
| 1971 | 22 | $\dfrac{22}{20} \times 100 = 110.0$ |
| 1972 | 23 | $\dfrac{23}{20} \times 100 = 115.0$ |
| 1992 | 38 | $\dfrac{38}{20} \times 100 = 190.0$ |

---

The base-period price is designated as $p_0$, and a price other than the base period is often referred to as the *given period* or *selected period* and designated $p_t$. To calculate the simple price index (relative) $P$ for any given period:

$$P = \frac{p_t}{p_0}(100)$$

(18–1)

For 1992 the price index for the golf cart tire is 190.0.

$$P = \frac{p_t}{p_0}(100) = \frac{\$38}{\$20}(100) = 190.0$$

Interpreting, one could say that the price of the tire increased 90 percent from the base period of 1970 to 1992 (190.0 − 100.0 = 90.0).

Had the years 1970–71 been selected as the base period (i.e., 1970–71 = 100), the arithmetic mean of the two prices ($20 and $22) would be the representative value in the base year. The prices $20, $22, and $23 would be averaged if 1970–72 had been selected as the base. The mean price would be $21.67. The indexes constructed using the three different base periods are presented in Table 18–2. (Note that when 1970–72 = 100, logically the index numbers for 1970, 1971, and 1972 average 100.0.)

### TABLE 18–2

**Prices of the Golf Cart Tire Converted to Indexes Using Three Different Base Periods**

| Year | Price of tire | Price index (1970 = 100) | Price index (1970–71 = 100) | Price index (1970–72 = 100) |
|------|------|------|------|------|
| 1965 | $18 | 90.0 | $\frac{18}{21} \times 100 = 85.7$ | $\frac{18}{21.67} \times 100 = 83.1$ |
| 1970 | 20 | 100.0 | $\frac{20}{21} \times 100 = 95.2$ | $\frac{20}{21.67} \times 100 = 92.3$ |
| 1971 | 22 | 110.0 | $\frac{22}{21} \times 100 = 104.8$ | $\frac{22}{21.67} \times 100 = 101.5$ |
| 1972 | 23 | 115.0 | $\frac{23}{21} \times 100 = 109.5$ | $\frac{23}{21.67} \times 100 = 106.1$ |
| 1992 | 38 | 190.0 | $\frac{38}{21} \times 100 = 181.0$ | $\frac{38}{21.67} \times 100 = 175.4$ |

### Self-Review 18–2

*The answers are at the end of the chapter.*

The average hourly earnings in retail trade for selected periods are:

| Year | Average hourly earnings |
|------|------|
| 1968 | $2.16 |
| 1969 | 2.30 |
| 1970 | 2.44 |
| 1991 (Mar.) | 6.94 |

Source: U.S. Department of Labor, *Monthly Labor Review*, June 1988, p. 85; and May, 1991, p. 70.

1. Using 1968 as the base period, determine an index number for March 1991 that might aptly be called the index of average hourly earnings in retail trade. Interpret.

2. Using the average of 1968 and 1969 (that is, 1968–69 = 100), determine the index for March 1991.

3. What is the index for 1968 using 1970 = 100? Interpret.

A slightly more complex problem is to determine an index of food prices for 1992. Assume for this illustration that the typical family eats only three food items: milk, bread, and avocados. Using the foregoing procedure for calculating simple indexes, we find that the unweighted index of food prices for 1992 (see Table 18–3) would be 122.9 (1977 = 100). The index for 1992 was computed by dividing the total of the prices for 1992 by the total of the 1977 prices.

The index of price, using formula (18–1) and adjusting it to include all items, is:

$$P = \frac{\Sigma p_t}{\Sigma p_0}(100) = \frac{\$2.20}{\$1.79}(100) = 122.9$$

### TABLE    18–3

**Computation of an Index of Food Prices for 1992**
**Using the Simple Unweighted Method**

| Item | 1977 price $p_0$ | 1992 price, $p_t$ |
|------|------------------|-------------------|
| Milk (quart) | $0.64 | $0.61 |
| Bread (loaf) | 0.65 | 0.59 |
| Avocado (each) | 0.50 | 1.00 |
| Total | $1.79 | $2.20 |

The unweighted price index of 122.9, however, seems illogical because the two major food items *declined* in price from 1977 to 1992; only the price of avocados increased. Avocados are eaten only infrequently by most consumers. It seems, therefore, that the prices of bread and milk should be given more weight (importance) than the price of avocados.

Also, the simple method of computing an index illustrated in the preceding problem does not meet the *units test.* This means that if the items were quoted in different units, the answer would be different from 122.9. For example, if the price of milk were quoted in gallons instead of quarts, and if avocados were quoted by the box instead of singly, the price index would probably not be 122.9. Because of these inadequacies, the simple aggregative method is seldom used in actual practice for this type of problem. Instead the weighted method, described in the following section, is applied.

## WEIGHTED INDEXES

Two methods of computing a **weighted price index** are the **Laspeyres** method and the **Paasche** method. They differ only with respect to the period used for weighting. The Laspeyres method uses *base-period weights;* that is, the original prices and quantities of the items bought are used to find the percent change over a period of time in either price or quantity consumed, depending on the problem. The Paasche method uses *current-year weights* for the denominator of the weighted index.

### LASPEYRES' PRICE INDEX

Etienne Laspeyres developed a method in the latter part of the 18th century to determine a weighted index using base-period weights. Applying his method, a weighted price index is computed by:

$$P = \frac{\Sigma p_t q_0}{\Sigma p_0 q_0} (100) \qquad (18–2)$$

where:

    $P$   is the price index.

    $p_t$   is the current price.

    $p_0$   is the price in the base period.

    $q_0$   is the quantity consumed in the base period.

## ▮ EXAMPLE

Laspeyres method uses base-period weights

The prices of three foods for 1977 and 1992 and the quantities consumed by a typical consumer in 1977 are:

| Item | 1977 price $p_0$ | 1977 amount consumed, $q_0$ | 1992 price, $p_t$ |
|------|------------------|------------------------------|-------------------|
| Milk (quart) | $0.64 | 100 | $0.61 |
| Bread (loaf) | 0.65 | 1,000 | 0.59 |
| Avocado (each) | 0.50 | 1 | 1.00 |

What is the weighted index of price for 1992 using 1977 = 100?

## ☑ SOLUTION

The total amount spent for food by the typical consumer in the base period, 1977, is determined first. The total amount spent on the three food items was $714.50 (see Table 18−4). In measuring the effect of price, *it is assumed that the amount of food consumed did not change between the base period (1977) and 1992.* Thus, to find how much the typical consumer spent on food in 1992, the 1992 prices are multiplied by the corresponding quantities consumed in the original year of 1977. The total is $652.00.

---

### TABLE 18−4

**Computation of a Weighted Price Index for 1992
Using the Laspeyres Method (1977 = 100)**

| Item | 1977 price $p_0$ | 1977 amount consumed, $q_0$ | $p_0 q_0$ | 1992 price, $p_t$ | $p_t q_0$ |
|------|------------------|------------------------------|-----------|-------------------|-----------|
| Milk (quart) | $0.64 | 100 | $ 64.00 | $0.61 | $ 61.00 |
| Bread (loaf) | 0.65 | 1,000 | 650.00 | 0.59 | 590.00 |
| Avocado (each) | 0.50 | 1 | 0.50 | 1.00 | 1.00 |
| | | | $714.50 | | $652.00 |

---

The weighted index of price for 1992 is 91.3, found by:

$$P = \frac{\Sigma p_t q_0}{\Sigma p_0 q_0} (100) = \frac{\$652.00}{\$714.50} (100) = 91.3$$

Index of 91.3 means overall price declined 8.7 percent from 1977 to 1992

**INTERPRETATION**　The average price of food *declined* about 8.7 percent from 1977 to 1992. The weighted method results in a more logical answer (91.3) than the unweighted index (122.9), which indicated an *increase* of about 23 percent in the price of food.

Both prices weighted by amount consumed in base period (1977)

　　　Note that the weighted method, alternatively called the *weighted aggregative method,* uses the amounts consumed in the base period ($q_0$) as weights. It assumes that the eating habits of the typical consumer did not change from 1977 to 1992. Thus, *only price* fluctuated, causing a decrease in the index from 100 in the base period to 91.3 in 1992.

### Self-Review 18-3

*The answers are at the end of the chapter.*

An index of clothing prices for 1993 based on 1982 is to be constructed. The prices for 1982 and 1993 and the quantity consumed in 1982 are shown below.

| Item | 1982 price | 1982 amount sold | 1993 price |
|------|------------|------------------|------------|
| Dress (each) | $35 | 500 | $65 |
| Shoes (pair) | 40 | 1,200 | 90 |

1. Assuming that the number sold remained constant—that is, the same number were sold in 1993 as in 1982—what is the weighted index of price for 1993 using 1982 as the base?

2. Interpret.

## EXERCISES

*The answers to the odd-numbered exercises are at the end of the book.*

1. The average purchase prices and loan amounts on conventional mortgages on new homes for a recent four-year period are:

| Year | Purchase price | Amount of loan |
|------|----------------|----------------|
| 1981 | $ 90,400 | $65,300 |
| 1982 | 94,600 | 69,800 |
| 1983 | 92,800 | 69,500 |
| 1991 (Apr.) | 115,500 | 87,200 |

Source: *Federal Reserve Bulletin,* February 1985, p. A32; June 1991, p. A52.

   a. Using 1981 as the base period, what is the index of the purchase price of a new home for 1991? Interpret.

   b. Using 1981–82 = 100, what is the index of the amount of the loan on conventional mortgages for 1991? Interpret.

2. The hourly earnings in selected durable-goods manufacturing groups for December 1979 and March 1991 are:

| | Hourly earnings | |
|------|------------------|-------------|
| Manufacturing group | December 1979 | March 1991 |
| Lumber and wood products | $6.24 | $ 9.14 |
| Furniture and fixtures | 5.26 | 8.70 |
| Stone, clay, and glass | 7.11 | 11.25 |
| Instruments and related products | 6.50 | 11.73 |

Source: U.S. Department of Labor, *Monthly Labor Review,* February 1981, Table 17; and May 1991, p. 70.

   a. Convert the hourly earnings for March 1991 to indexes for each of the four groups, using December 1979 = 100.

   b. Interpret your findings.

3. Fruit prices and the amounts of fruit consumed for 1983 and 1992 are:

| Fruit | Price 1983 | Amount consumed 1983 | Price 1992 |
|-------|------------|----------------------|------------|
| Bananas (pound) | $0.23 | 100 | $0.35 |
| Grapefruit (each) | 0.29 | 50 | 0.27 |
| Apples (pound) | 0.35 | 85 | 0.35 |
| Strawberries (basket) | 1.02 | 8 | 1.69 |
| Oranges (bag) | 0.89 | 6 | 0.99 |

a.  Assuming that the amounts of fruit consumed did not change between 1983 and 1992, determine the weighted index of price using the Laspeyres method for 1992 (1983 = 100).

b.  Interpret your findings.

4.  The prices and numbers of various items produced by a small machine and stamping plant for January 1985 and the prices of these items for January 1992 are:

|  | January 1985 | | January 1992 |
| Item | Price | Number produced | price |
| --- | --- | --- | --- |
| Washer | $0.07 | 17,000 | $0.10 |
| Cotter pin | 0.04 | 125,000 | 0.03 |
| Stove bolt | 0.15 | 40,000 | 0.15 |
| Hex nut | 0.08 | 62,000 | 0.05 |

a.  Assuming that the numbers produced did not change between January 1985 and January 1992, determine the weighted index of price for January 1992 using the Laspeyres method and January 1985 as the base period.

b.  Interpret your findings.

## LASPEYRES' QUANTITY INDEX

The Laspeyres method of weighting is also used to compute a *weighted quantity index*. The procedure is similar to the method of constructing a weighted price index, except that the original *base-year prices* are used as weights instead of base-year quantities. The formula for a weighted quantity index, designated $Q$, is:

$$Q = \frac{\Sigma p_0 q_t}{\Sigma p_0 q_0} (100)$$

(18–3)

where:

$Q$  is the weighted quantity index.

$p_0$  is the original price in the base period.

$q_0$  is the original quantity consumed in the base period.

$q_t$  is the current quantity consumed.

### ■ EXAMPLE

The prices of selected commodities for 1983 and the quantities mined in 1983 and 1992 follow.

| Commodity | 1983 price, $p_0$ | 1983 quantity mined, $q_0$ | 1992 quantity mined, $q_t$ |
| --- | --- | --- | --- |
| Oil (barrels) | $ 2 | 100 | 110 |
| Coal (ton) | 20 | 10 | 9 |
| Sulfur (tank car) | 15 | 90 | 80 |
| Granite (block) | 60 | 5 | 5 |

What is the index of the quantity mined in 1992 using 1983 as the base period?

## ◪ SOLUTION

One might be tempted to add the quantities in 1992 and divide this total by the total of the 1983 quantities. Of course, it is impossible to add barrels, tons, tank cars, and blocks. The quantities, therefore, have to be converted to a common denominator using 1983 prices.

Quantity mined dropped 7.3 percent from 1983 to 1992

In computing the quantity index it is assumed that 1983 prices still prevailed in 1992—that is, the price of each commodity is held constant. Thus, any change in the quantity index is *due only to the quantity mined.* In this problem the quantity of minerals mined declined 7.3 percent from 1983 to 1992. See Table 18–5 for computations. Using formula (18–3):

$$Q = \frac{\Sigma p_0 q_t}{\Sigma p_0 q_0} (100) = \frac{\$1,900}{\$2,050} (100) = 92.7$$

---

### TABLE    18–5

Quantities mined in 1983 and 1992 weighted by price in base period (1983)

**Computation of Weighted Index of the Quantity of Minerals Mined for 1992 Using the Laspeyres Method (1983 = 100)**

| Commodity | 1983 price $p_0$ | 1983 quantity mined, $q_0$ | $p_0 q_0$ | 1992 quantity mined, $q_t$ | $p_0 q_t$ |
|---|---|---|---|---|---|
| Oil (barrels) | $ 2 | 100 | $   200 | 110 | $   220 |
| Coal (ton) | 20 | 10 | 200 | 9 | 180 |
| Sulfur (tank car) | 15 | 90 | 1,350 | 80 | 1,200 |
| Granite (block) | 60 | 5 | 300 | 5 | 300 |
| | | | $2,050 | | $1,900 |

---

### Self-Review 18–4

*The answers are at the end of the chapter.*

The wholesale prices and the numbers produced for selected agricultural items are:

1. Using the Laspeyres method, compute an index of the quantity of agricultural production for 1991 (1975 = 100).
2. Interpret the index.

| | Price | | Production | |
|---|---|---|---|---|
| Item | 1975 | 1991 | 1975 | 1991 |
| Wheat (bushel) | $ 2.00 | $ 4.00 | 100 | 700 |
| Egg (dozen) | 0.30 | 0.20 | 1,000 | 800 |
| Pork (cwt.) | 60.00 | 70.00 | 50 | 110 |

### PAASCHE PRICE INDEX

Paasche method uses present-year weights

Several years after Laspeyres introduced the concept of using base-period figures as weights, Paasche suggested a similar procedure—except that present-year weights were substituted for the original base-period weights. The Paasche formula for a weighted price index using present-year figures as weights is:

$$P = \frac{\Sigma p_t q_t}{\Sigma p_0 q_t} (100) \qquad (18-4)$$

The calculations needed for the weighted price index using the Paasche formula is illustrated in Table 18−6. The data are the same as used in Table 18−4, but the quantities consumed in 1992 have been added. Using formula (18−4):

$$P = \frac{\Sigma p_t q_t}{\Sigma p_0 q_t} (100) = \frac{\$655}{\$714} (100) = 91.7$$

---

### TABLE   18−6

**Computation of a Weighted Price Index for 1992
Using the Paasche Formula (1977 = 100)**

| Commodity | 1977 price, $p_0$ | 1992 price, $p_t$ | 1992 quantity consumed, $q_t$ | $p_0 q_t$ | $p_t q_t$ |
|---|---|---|---|---|---|
| Milk (quart) | $0.64 | $0.61 | 200 | $128 | $122 |
| Bread (loaf) | 0.65 | 0.59 | 900 | 585 | 531 |
| Avocado (each) | 0.50 | 1.00 | 2 | 1 | 2 |
| | | | | $714 | $655 |

---

The interpretation of the index of price (91.7) using the Paasche method is as follows: A market basket of food selected in 1992 costs 8.3 percent less than the same food cost at 1977 prices, found by 100.0 − 91.7.

The Paasche method has the advantage of using current consumption figures as weights; that is, the consumption pattern is always up to date. However, the method poses a practical problem. The index must be revised every year using new present-year weights. If the Paasche method were used to compute the producer price indexes, for example, the consumption of approximately 2,800 wholesale items would have to be determined every year in order to weight the present-year prices. The Laspeyres method of using base-period weights, therefore, is the most commonly used (with some modification).

*Advantages and disadvantages of Paasche method*

# VALUE INDEX

*Value index measures percent change in value*

A **value index,** such as the index of department store sales, needs the original base-year prices, the original base-year quantities, the present-year prices, and the present-year quantities for its construction. Its formula is:

$$V = \frac{\Sigma p_t q_t}{\Sigma p_0 q_0} (100) \qquad (18-5)$$

## ▮ EXAMPLE

Suppose the prices and quantities sold for various items of apparel for 1982 and 1991 are:

| Item | 1982 price $p_0$ | 1982 quantity sold (000), $q_0$ | 1991 price, $p_t$ | 1991 quantity sold (000), $q_t$ |
|---|---|---|---|---|
| Ties (each) | $ 1 | 1,000 | $ 2 | 900 |
| Suits (each) | 30 | 100 | 40 | 120 |
| Shoes (pair) | 10 | 500 | 8 | 500 |

What is the index of value for 1991 using 1982 as the base period?

## ☑ SOLUTION

Total sales in 1991 were $10,600,000, and the comparable figure for 1982 is $9,000,000 (see Table 18–7). Thus, the index of value for 1991 using 1982 = 100 is 117.8. The value of apparel sales in 1991 was 117.8 percent of the 1982 sales. To put it another way, apparel sales increased 17.8 percent from 1982 to 1991.

$$V = \frac{\Sigma p_t q_t}{\Sigma p_0 q_0} (100) = \frac{\$10,600,000}{\$9,000,000} (100) = 117.8$$

---

### TABLE 18–7

**Construction of a Value Index for 1991 (1982 = 100)**

| Item | 1982 price $p_0$ | 1982 quantity sold (000), $q_0$ | $p_0 q_0$ (000) | 1991 price, $p_t$ | 1991 quantity sold (000), $q_t$ | $p_t q_t$ (000) |
|---|---|---|---|---|---|---|
| Ties (each) | $ 1 | 1,000 | $1,000 | $ 2 | 900 | $ 1,800 |
| Suits (each) | 30 | 100 | 3,000 | 40 | 120 | 4,800 |
| Shoes (pair) | 10 | 500 | 5,000 | 8 | 500 | 4,000 |
| | | | $9,000 | | | $10,600 |

---

### Self-Review 18–5

*The answers are at the end of the chapter.*

The number of items produced by Houghton Products for 1983 and 1990 and the wholesale prices for the two periods are:

1. Find the index of the value of production for 1990 using 1983 as the base period.
2. Interpret the index.

| Item produced | Price 1983 | Price 1990 | Number produced 1983 | Number produced 1990 |
|---|---|---|---|---|
| Shear pins (box) | $ 3 | $4 | 10,000 | 9,000 |
| Cutting compound (pound) | 1 | 5 | 600 | 200 |
| Tie rods (each) | 10 | 8 | 3,000 | 5,000 |

# EXERCISES

*The answers to the odd-numbered exercises are at the end of the book.*

5. The prices and production levels of grains for 1977 and 1992 are:

| Grain | 1977 price | 1977 quantity produced (millions of bushels) | 1992 price | 1992 quantity produced (millions of bushels) |
|---|---|---|---|---|
| Oats | $1.52 | 200 | $1.87 | 214 |
| Wheat | 2.10 | 565 | 2.05 | 489 |
| Corn | 1.48 | 291 | 1.48 | 203 |
| Barley | 3.05 | 87 | 3.29 | 106 |

a. Using 1977 as the base period and the Laspeyres method, determine the weighted index of the quantity of grains produced for 1992. Interpret.

b. Using 1977 as the base period, find the index of the value of grains produced for 1992. Interpret.

6. The Johnson Wholesale Company manufactures a variety of products. The prices and quantities produced for 1974 and 1991 are:

| Product | 1974 price | 1991 price | 1974 quantity produced | 1991 quantity produced |
|---|---|---|---|---|
| Small motor (each) | $23.60 | $28.80 | 1,760 | 4,259 |
| Scrubbing compound (gallon) | 2.96 | 3.08 | 86,450 | 62,949 |
| Nails (pound) | 0.40 | 0.48 | 9,460 | 22,370 |

a. Using 1974 as the base period and the Laspeyres method, determine the weighted index of the quantity produced for 1991. Interpret.

b. Using 1974 as the base period, find the index of the value of goods produced for 1991.

# SPECIAL-PURPOSE INDEX

**Special-purpose indexes** usually employ a combination of business and economic indicators, such as sales, employment, and stock prices. As mentioned, the federal government compiles and publishes an index of leading economic indicators. So do *Forbes* and *Business Week*. The Forbes Index is a measure of U.S. economic activity composed of eight equally weighted elements: total industrial production, new claims for unemployment compensation, the cost of services relative to all consumer prices, the level of new orders for durable goods compared with manufacturers' inventories, total retail sales, new housing starts, personal income, and total consumer installment credit. To measure these eight elements, *Forbes* monitors 10 series of U.S. government data, including the Consumer Price Index and consumer installment credit released by the Federal Reserve Board.

One of the uses of an index of leading economic indicators is to predict possible changes in the direction of our economy. If the index declines steadily for three or four time periods, it may lead many economists to forecast that a recession is imminent. History, however, indicates that these forecasts are not infallible. For example, in the 20-year period from 1950 to 1970, the forecast based on the trend of the leading indexes was incorrect three times. However, most economists consider the federal index of leading economic indicators and others as rough guides to the future trend of our economy.

Most special-purpose indexes designed to monitor economy

The data needed for the construction of a special-purpose index designed to measure general business activity is shown in Table 18–8. Note that weights, based on the judgments of the statistician, are assigned to each series, and the series are in different units—dollars, freight car loadings, and so on. This weighting is somewhat different from the *Forbes* weighting, which applies equal weights to the elements.

---

TABLE   18-8

**Data for the Computation of the Index of General Business Activity**

|  | Department store sales ($ billions) | Index of employment (1967 = 100) | Freight car loadings (millions) | Exports (thousands of tons) |
|--------|--------|--------|--------|--------|
| Weight | (.40) | (.30) | (.10) | (.20) |
| 1986 | 20 | 100 | 50 | 500 |
| 1991 | 41 | 110 | 30 | 900 |
| 1992 | 44 | 125 | 18 | 700 |

---

To compute the index of general business activity for 1992 using 1986 = 100, each 1992 figure is first expressed as a relative using the base-period figure as the denominator. For illustration, department store sales for 1992 are converted to a relative by ($44/$20) × 100 = 220. The relatives are then adjusted by the appropriate weights. For the department store relative, 220 × .40 = 88.0. (See the calculations below.)

Business activity up 57.1 percent from 1986 to 1992

The index of general business activity for 1992 is 157.1. Interpreting, business activity increased 57.1 percent from the base period (arbitrarily selected as 1986) to 1992.

$$\text{Department store sales:} \quad \left(\frac{\$44}{\$20}\right) 100 \times .40 = 88.0$$

$$\text{Employment:} \quad \left(\frac{125}{100}\right) 100 \times .30 = 37.5$$

$$\text{Freight car loadings:} \quad \left(\frac{18}{50}\right) 100 \times .10 = 3.6$$

$$\text{Exports:} \quad \left(\frac{700}{500}\right) 100 \times .20 = \underline{28.0}$$
$$157.1$$

---

## Self-Review 18-6

*The answers are at the end of the chapter.*

As chief statistician for the county, you want to compute and publish every year a special-purpose index, which you plan to call the *Index of County Business Activity*. Three series seem to hold promise as the basis for the index, namely, the price of cotton, the number of new automobiles sold, and the rate of money turnover for the county (published by a local bank). Arbitrarily you decide that money turnover should have a weight of 60 percent, the number of new automobiles sold 30 percent, and the price of cotton 10 percent.

1. Construct the *Index of County Business Activity* for 1981 (the base period) and 1992.

| Year | Price of cotton (per pound) | Number of automobiles sold | Rate of money turnover (an index) |
|------|------|------|------|
| 1981 | $0.20 | 100,000 | 80 |
| 1992 | 0.50 | 80,000 | 120 |

2. Interpret the indexes.

# EXERCISES

*The answers to the odd-numbered exercises are at the end of the book.*

7. The index of leading economic indicators compiled and published by the U.S. National Bureau of Economic Research is composed of 12 time series, such as the average work hours of production in manufacturing, manufacturers' new orders, and money supply. This index and similar indexes are designed to move up or down before the economy begins to move the same way. Thus, an economist has statistical evidence to forecast future trends.

    You want to construct a leading indicator for your own use. Because of the time and work involved, you decide to use only four time series. As an experiment, you select these four series: unemployment, stock prices, producer prices, and exports. Here are the figures for 1989 and 1991:

| | 1989 | 1991 |
|---|---|---|
| Unemployment rate (percent) | 5.3 | 6.8 |
| Index of stock prices, Standard & Poor's (1941–43 = 10) | 265.88 | 362.26 |
| Producers Price Index (1984 = 100) | 109.6 | 115.2 |
| Exports ($ millions) | 529,917 | 622,864 |

Source: U.S. Department of Labor, *Monthly Labor Review,* May 1991, pp. A24, 66, 88, and 790.

    The weights you arbitrarily assigned are: unemployment rate 20 percent, stock prices 40 percent, Producers Price Index 25 percent, and exports 15 percent.

    a. Using 1989 as the base period, construct a leading economic indicator for 1991.

    b. Interpret your leading index.

8. You are employed by the state bureau of economic development. There is a demand for a leading economic index to review past economic activity and to forecast future economic trends in the state. You decide that several key factors should be included in the index: number of new businesses started during the year, number of business failures, state income tax receipts, college enrollment, and the state sales tax receipts. The data for 1987 and the present year are:

| | 1987 | Present year |
|---|---|---|
| New businesses | 1,088 | 1,162 |
| Business failures | 627 | 520 |
| State income tax receipts ($ millions) | 191.7 | 162.6 |
| College student enrollment | 242,119 | 290,841 |
| State sales tax ($ millions) | 41.6 | 39.9 |

    a. Decide on the weights to be applied to each item going into the leading index.

    b. Compute the leading economic indicator for the present year.

    c. Interpret the indexes for 1987 and the present year.

# CONSUMER PRICE INDEX

There are two consumer price indexes

Frequent mention has been made of the Consumer Price Index (CPI) in the preceding pages. It measures the change in price of a fixed market basket of goods and services from one period to another. In January 1978 the Bureau of Labor Statistics began publishing CPIs for two groups of the population. One index, for all urban consumers, covers about 80 percent of the total population. The other index is for urban wage earners and clerical workers and covers about 32 percent of the population.

    In brief, the CPI serves several major functions. It allows consumers to determine the degree to which their purchasing power is being eroded by price increases. In that respect, it is a yardstick for revising wages, pensions, and other income payments to keep pace with changes in price. Equally important, it is an economic indicator of the rate of inflation in the United States.

The index includes about 400 items, and about 250 part-time and full-time agents collect price data monthly. Prices are collected from more than 21,000 retail establishments and 60,000 housing units in 91 urban areas across the country. The prices of baby cribs, bread, beer, cigars, gasoline, haircuts, mortgage interest rates, physicians' fees, taxes, and operating-room charges are just a few of the items included in what is often termed a typical "market basket" of goods and services that you purchase.

The CPI originated in 1913 and has been published regularly since 1921. The standard reference period (the base period) has been updated periodically. The base periods prior to the present (1982–84) base were 1967, 1957–59, 1947–49, 1935–39, and 1925–29. The need for this rather frequent rebasing is somewhat obvious. Consumption patterns have changed drastically. The automobile has replaced the horse as a mode of transportation. In the 1910s and 1920s a relatively small proportion of the income of wage earners and clerical workers was spent on higher education. Now the typical family spends a sizable amount on the higher education of its children, and the CPI reflects any changes in costs of tuition, books, and home computers.[9]

In addition to changing the base period periodically, the Bureau of Labor Statistics conducts an extensive consumer expenditure survey from time to time to determine the items to be included in the CPI and the relative weights to be put on stereo cassettes, bananas, gasoline, rent, and so on.

The CPI is not just one index. There are consumer price indexes for New York City, Chicago, and a number of other large cities. There are price indexes for food, apparel, medical care, and other items. A few of them are shown below for March 1991 (1982–84 = 100).

| Items | March 1991 |
| --- | --- |
| All items | 135.0 |
| Food and beverages | 136.3 |
| Apparel and upkeep | 128.8 |
| Transportation | 122.3 |
| Medical care | 173.7 |
| Entertainment | 136.7 |
| Housing | 132.6 |

Source: U.S. Department of Labor, *Monthly Labor Review,* May 1991, p. 82.

A perusal of this listing shows that the weighted price of all items combined increased 35.0 percent since 1982–84; medical care increased the most (73.7 percent), and transportation went up the least (22.3 percent) during the eight-year period.

## Special Uses of the Consumer Price Index

In addition to measuring changes in the prices of goods and services, both consumer price indexes have a number of other applications. The CPI is used to determine real disposable personal income, to deflate sales or other series, to find the purchasing power of the dollar, and to establish cost-of-living increases. We discuss first the use of the CPI in determining real income.

---

[9]For a discussion of the general method for computing the CPI, see *BLS Handbook of Methods,* Bulletin 2285 (Bureau of Labor Statistics, 1988). An overview of the recently introduced revised CPI, reflecting 1982–84 expenditure patterns, is contained in *The Consumer Price Index: 1987 Revision,* Report 736 (Bureau of Labor Statistics, 1987).

### REAL INCOME

Real income

As an example of the meaning and computation of *real income,* assume for the sake of simplicity that the Consumer Price Index is presently 200 with 1982–84 = 100. Also, assume that Ms. Watts earned $20,000 in the base period of 1982, 1983, and 1984.

Money income

She has a current income of $40,000. Note that although her *money income* has doubled since the base period of 1982–84, the prices she paid for food, gasoline, clothing, and other items has also doubled. Thus, Ms. Watts' standard of living has remained the same from the base period to the present time. Price increases have exactly offset an increase in income, so her present buying power (real income) is still $20,000. (See Table 18–9 for computations.)

In general:

Formula for real income

$$\text{Real income} = \frac{\text{Money income}}{\text{CPI}} \times 100 \qquad (18\text{–}6)$$

### TABLE 18–9

**Computation of Real Income for 1982–84 and Present Year**

| Year | Money income | Consumer Price Index (1982–84 = 100) | Real income | Computation of real income |
|------|--------------|--------------------------------------|-------------|----------------------------|
| 1982–84 | $20,000 | 100 | $20,000 | $\dfrac{\$20,000}{100}(100)$ |
| Present year | 40,000 | 200 | 20,000 | $\dfrac{\$40,000}{200}(100)$ |

Deflated income and real income are the same

The concept of real income is sometimes called *deflated income,* and the CPI is called the *deflator.* Also, a popular term for deflated income is *income expressed in constant dollars.* Thus, in Table 18–9, in order to determine whether or not Ms. Watts' standard of living was raised, money income was converted to constant dollars. It was found that her purchasing power, expressed in 1982–84 dollars (constant dollars), remained at $20,000.

### Self-Review 18–7

*The answers are at the end of the chapter.*

The take-home pay of Jon Greene and the CPI for 1986 and 1992 are:

1. What was Jon's real income in 1986?
2. What was his real income in 1992?
3. Interpret your findings.

| Year | Take-home pay | CPI (1982–84 = 100) |
|------|---------------|---------------------|
| 1986 | $25,000 | 109.60 |
| 1992 | 41,200 | 140.00 |

### DEFLATING SALES

Deflated sales important for showing the trend in "real" sales

A price index can also be used to "deflate" sales or similar money series. Deflated sales are determined by

$$\text{Deflated sales} = \frac{\text{Actual sales}}{\text{An appropriate index}} (100) \qquad (18\text{–}7)$$

### ■ EXAMPLE

The sales of Eugene Enterprises, a small manufacturer, increased from $1,482,000 in 1982 to $1,502,000 in 1992. Eugene Enterprises knows that the price of raw materials used in production has also risen since 1982, so EE wants to deflate the 1992 sales to account for the rise in raw material prices. What are the deflated sales for 1992? That is, what are the 1992 sales expressed in constant 1982 dollars?

### ☑ SOLUTION

"Sales in constant dollars" same as deflated sale

The Producers Price Index (PPI) is an index released every month and published in the *Monthly Labor Review.* The prices included in the PPI reflect the prices charged the manufacturer for the metals, rubber, and other items purchased. So the PPI seems an appropriate index to use to deflate the manufacturer's sales. The manufacturer's sales are listed in the first column of Table 18–10, and the PPI is in the second column. The next column shows sales divided by the Producers Price Index, and the deflated sales are in the extreme right column.

### TABLE   18–10

**Computations for Deflating Sales**

| Year | Sales | PPI* (1982 = 100) | Computation of deflated sales | Sales in constant 1982 dollars |
|------|-------|-------------------|-------------------------------|--------------------------------|
| 1982 | $1,482,000 | 100.0 | $\frac{\$1,482,000}{100.0} \times 100 =$ | $1,482,000 |
| 1990 | 1,491,000 | 119.2 | $\frac{\$1,491,000}{119.2} \times 100 =$ | $1,250,839 |
| 1992 | 1,502,000 | 121.00† | $\frac{\$1,502,000}{121.0} \times 100 =$ | $1,241,322 |

*Source: U.S. Department of Labor, *Monthly Labor Review,* May 1991, p. 88.
†Estimated.

The conclusion is that although the actual dollar sales of Eugene Enterprises increased from 1982 to 1992, sales deflated for the rise in prices the company paid for raw materials actually declined (from about $1,482,000 down to about $1,241,322). This is so because the prices Eugene paid for raw materials increased at a more rapid rate than did sales.

What has happened to the purchasing power of the dollar?

## PURCHASING POWER OF THE DOLLAR

The Consumer Price Index is also used to determine the *purchasing power of the dollar.*

$$\text{Purchasing power of dollar} = \frac{\$1}{\text{CPI}} \times 100 \qquad (18-8)$$

### ■ EXAMPLE

Suppose the Consumer Price Index this month is 200.0 (1982−84 = 100). What is the purchasing power of the dollar?

### ☑ SOLUTION

Using formula (18−8), it is 50 cents, found by:

$$\text{Purchasing power of dollar} = \frac{\$1}{200.0} (100) = \$0.50$$

*INTERPRETATION* The CPI of 200.0 indicates that prices have doubled from the years 1982−84 to this month. Thus, the purchasing power of a dollar has been cut in half. That is, a 1982−84 dollar is worth only 50 cents this month. To put it another way, if you lost $1,000 in the period 1982−84 and just found it, the $1,000 could only buy half of what it could have bought in the years 1982, 1983, and 1984.

The Bureau of Labor Statistics still cites the CPI on the previous base period (1967) for those who still need to use it on that base. Table 18−11 shows the computation of the purchasing power of the dollar for a few actual periods using 1967 = 100. Note that the purchasing power of the dollar for March 1991 was 24.7 cents. Theoretically, if $1,000 could purchase 1,000 porterhouse steaks at $1 each in 1967, by March 1991 the same $1,000 could buy only 247 steaks.

---

### TABLE   18−11

**Computing the Purchasing Power of the Dollar**

| Year | Consumer Price Index* (1967 = 100) | Computations: $\frac{\$1}{\text{CPI}}(100)$ | Purchasing power of the dollar (1967 = $1) |
|------|---------|---------------------|-------------|
| 1967 | 100.0 | $\frac{\$1}{100.0}(100) =$ | $1.000 |
| 1989 | 371.3 | $\frac{\$1}{371.3}(100) =$ | 0.269 |
| 1990 | 391.4 | $\frac{\$1}{391.4}(100) =$ | 0.255 |
| 1991 (Mar.) | 404.3 | $\frac{\$1}{404.3}(100) =$ | 0.247 |

---

*Source: U.S. Department of Labor, *Monthly Labor Review*, May 1991, p. 82.

Suppose the Consumer Price Index for the latest month is 145.6 (1982–84 = 100). What is the purchasing power of the dollar? Interpret.

### COST-OF-LIVING ADJUSTMENTS

*CPI used to adjust wages, pensions, and so on*

The Consumer Price Index is also the basis for so-called cost-of-living adjustments in many management-union contracts. The specific clause in the contract is often referred to as the "escalator clause." About 31 million Social Security beneficiaries, 2.5 million retired military and federal civil service employees and survivors, and 600,000 postal workers have their incomes or pensions pegged to the Consumer Price Index.

The CPI is also used to adjust alimony and child support payments; attorneys' fees; workers' compensation payments; rentals on apartments, homes, and office buildings; welfare payments; and so on.

## SHIFTING THE BASE

If two or more series have the same base period, they can be compared directly. As an example, suppose we are interested in the trend in the prices of food and beverages, housing, medical care, and so on since the base period, 1982–84. Note in Table 18–12 that all of the consumer price indexes use the same base. Thus, it can be said that the price of all consumer items combined increased 35.0 percent from the base period (1982–84) to 1991. Likewise, housing prices increased 32.6 percent, medical care 73.7 percent, and so on.

### TABLE 18-12

**Trend in Consumer Prices, 1982–84 to Present Year (1982–84 = 100)**

| Year | All items | Food and beverages | Housing | Apparel and upkeep | Medical care |
|------|-----------|--------------------|---------|--------------------| -------------|
| 1982–84 | 100.0 | 100.0 | 100.0 | 100.0 | 100.0 |
| 1986 | 109.6 | 109.1 | 110.9 | 105.9 | 122.0 |
| 1987 | 113.6 | 113.5 | 114.2 | 110.6 | 130.1 |
| 1991 (Mar.) | 135.0 | 136.3 | 132.6 | 128.8 | 173.7 |

Source: U.S. Department of Labor, *Monthly Labor Review,* May 1991, p. 82.

However, a problem arises when two or more series being compared do not have the same base period.

### ◼ EXAMPLE

We want to compare the price changes on the New York Stock Exchange and the American Stock Exchange since 1985. The two price indexes are as follows.

|  | Year | | | |
|---|---|---|---|---|
| Index | 1985 | 1986 | 1987 | 1991 |
| New York Stock Exchange (Dec. 31, 1965 = 10) | 108.09 | 136.00 | 161.70 | 197.75(Feb.) |
| American Stock Exchange (Aug. 31, 1973 = 50) | 229.10 | 264.38 | 316.61 | 338.11(Feb.) |

Source: *Federal Reserve Bulletin,* July 1988, p. A25; and May 1991, p. A24.

Compare the price changes on the two stock exchanges.

## ☑ SOLUTION

Price indexes are on different base years and cannot be compared directly

Note again that the two price indexes have different base periods—the New York base period is 1965, and the American base is 1973. Thus, a direct comparison of 338.11 and 197.75 is meaningless. We want to compare the movement of price since 1985, so the logical thing to do is to let the base period be 1985 for both series. For the New York price series 108.09 becomes the base, and for the American series the base is 229.10.

The calculations for the 1991 American Stock Exchange price index using 1985 = 100 are:

$$\frac{338.11}{229.10} \times 100 = 147.6$$

The complete set of indexes using 1985 = 100 is:

|  | Year | | | |
|---|---|---|---|---|
| Index | 1985 | 1986 | 1987 | 1991 |
| New York Stock Exchange | 100.0 | 125.8 | 149.6 | 182.9 |
| American Stock Exchange | 100.0 | 115.4 | 138.2 | 147.6 |

We can now conclude that common stock prices on both the New York Stock Exchange and the American Stock Exchange since 1985 have risen, with the rise on the New York Stock Exchange being significantly greater (82.9 percent compared with 47.6 percent on the American exchange).

### Self-Review 18–9

*The answers are at the end of the chapter.*

1. In the preceding example, verify that the New York Stock Exchange price index for 1991, using 1985 as the base period, is 182.9.

2. The changes in industrial production and in the prices manufacturers have paid for raw materials since 1982 are to be compared. Unfortunately, the index of industrial production, which measures changes in production, and the Producers Price Index, which measures the change in the prices of raw materials, have different base periods. The production index has a 1977 base period, and the Producers Price Index uses 1982 as the base period.

| Year | Industrial production index (1977 =100) | Producers Price Index (1982 =100) |
|---|---|---|
| 1982 | 115.3 | 100.0 |
| 1987 | 129.8 | 105.4 |
| 1990 | 142.8 | 119.2 |

Sources: *Survey of Current Business,* August 1988, p. A47; U.S. Department of Labor, *Monthly Labor Review,* May 1991, p. 88.

a. Shift the base to make the two series comparable.

b. Interpret.

# EXERCISES

*The answers to the odd-numbered exercises are at the end of the book.*

9. *USA Today* reported that in 1991 the average salary for experienced bedside nurses was $32,000. The Consumer Price Index for that year was 135.0 (1982−84 = 100). A nurse's average annual money income for the 1982−84 period was $19,800. What was the real income of a bedside nurse in 1991? What was a nurse's real income in the 1982−84 period? Compare the two real incomes; that is, indicate what happened to a nurse's purchasing power between the two periods.

10. The Sarasota (Florida) *Herald Tribune* cited Chrysler chairman Lee Iacocca's compensation since 1980 in the form of a bar chart.

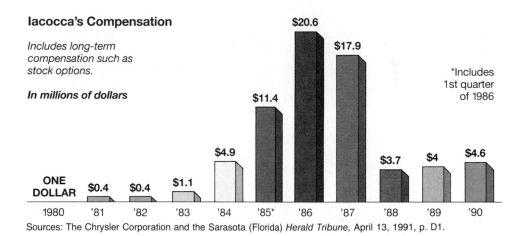

**Iacocca's Compensation**

*Includes long-term compensation such as stock options.*

**In millions of dollars**

*Includes 1st quarter of 1986

Sources: The Chrysler Corporation and the Sarasota (Florida) *Herald Tribune,* April 13, 1991, p. D1.

The Consumer Price Index figures for selected years are:

| Year | CPI | Year | CPI |
|------|-----|------|-----|
| 1980 | 82.4 | 1987 | 113.6 |
| 1982−84 | 100.0 | 1988 | 118.3 |
| 1985 | 107.6 | 1989 | 124.0 |
| 1986 | 109.6 | 1990 | 130.7 |

Source: Bureau of Labor Statistics, U.S. Labor Department.

a. During the period 1982−84, what was Iacocca's real income? What was his real income in 1990 based on the 1982−84 period? Compare the two real incomes for Iacocca, and explain the difference.

b. Using 1985 as the base period, compare his real income for 1985 with that for 1990.

c. Explain the CPI for 1980.

11. The Consumer Price Index values for 1989, 1990, and 1991 and the average weekly earnings for selected industries are:

| Year | CPI (1982−84 = 100) | Mining | Apparel | Printing and publishing | Retail trade |
|------|---------------------|--------|---------|-------------------------|--------------|
| 1989 | 124.0 | $569.75 | $234.34 | $412.35 | $188.72 |
| 1990 | 130.7 | 600.60 | 239.88 | 426.38 | 195.26 |
| 1991 | 135.0 | 621.28 | 240.73 | 427.89 | 195.01 |

Source: U.S. Department of Labor, *Monthly Labor Review,* May 1991, pp. 71, 82.

a. Trace the trend in real income for each of the four industries for 1989, 1990, and 1991.

b. Compare and interpret the trends in real weekly income for these selected industries.

# CHAPTER OUTLINE

I. Index numbers.
   A. The purpose of an index is to show the change in price, quantity, or value from one period to another.
   B. Characteristics.
      1. An index number, such as 185.0, is a percent, but the percent sign is usually ommitted.
      2. An index number has a base period. The base period for the CPI is 1982−84; for the index of industrial production it is 1977. Other base periods are 1982, 1984, and 1965.
      3. The base number of most indexes is 100. Thus, a price index of 185.0 for last month, using 1982 = 100, means that prices increased 85 percent from 1982 to last month.
      4. Most indexes are carried to the nearest whole percent, such as 164 or 96, or to the nearest tenth of a percent, such as 185.6 or 83.2.
   C. The reasons for computing indexes.
      1. Indexes facilitate a comparison of unlike series.
      2. An index is a convenient way to express the change in the total of a heterogeneous group of items.
      3. A percent change is sometimes easier to comprehend than actual numbers, especially when the numbers are extremely large.
   D. Types of index numbers.
      1. Price: Its purpose is to measure the change in prices from a selected base period to another period, such as this year.
      2. Quantity: Portrays the change in quantity consumed from the base period to another period.
      3. Value: Shows the change in value from, say, 1977 to 1992. The value for 1992, found by Price × Quantity, is divided by the value in 1977 to give a value index for 1992.
      4. A special-purpose index combines and weights a heterogeneous group of series, such as employment, prices, production, and bank debits, to arrive at an overall index showing the change in business activity from the base period to the present.
II. Construction of index numbers.
   A. Unweighted index numbers.
      1. The formulas for unweighted price and quantity indexes are similar:

$$P = \frac{p_t}{p_0}(100)$$

$$Q = \frac{q_t}{q_0}(100)$$

(18−1)

where

   $p_t$ is the price of an item in the present time period.
   $p_0$ is the price in the base period.
   $q_t$ is the quantity consumed in the present period.
   $q_0$ is the quantity consumed in the base period.

      2. An unweighted index is used to show the change in a single price or a single commodity from one period to another.
      3. To determine the change in the quantity of a group of items, such as food items, it is impossible to add quarts of milk, pounds of coffee, and heads of lettuce.
   B. Weighted index numbers.
      1. Formulas.
         a. Price:

**Laspeyres method:**  $P = \dfrac{\Sigma p_t q_0}{\Sigma p_0 q_0}(100)$ (18−2)

**Paasche method:** $P = \dfrac{\Sigma p_t q_t}{\Sigma p_0 q_t}(100)$ (18−4)

b. Quantity:

**Laspeyres method:** $Q = \dfrac{\Sigma p_0 q_t}{\Sigma p_0 q_0}(100)$ (18−3)

c. Value: $V = \dfrac{\Sigma p_t q_t}{\Sigma p_0 q_0}(100)$ (18−5)

   2. Using the weighted aggregative method, (1) a price index reflects the change in the price paid *only* (because the quantity consumed is held constant), and (2) a quantity index reflects the change in the quantity consumed *only* (because price is held constant).
III. Consumer Price Index.
   A. Starting in 1978 two consumer price indexes were published. One was designed for urban wage earners and clerical workers. It covers about one third of the population. Another was designed for all urban households. It covers about 80 percent of the population.
   B. The uses of the CPI.
      1. It allows consumers to determine the effect of price increases on their purchasing power.
      2. It is a yardstick for revising wages, pensions, alimony payments, and so on.
      3. It is an economic indicator of the rate of inflation in the United States.
   C. Other uses of the Consumer Price Index.
      1. Computing real income:

$$\text{Real income} = \frac{\text{Money income}}{\text{CPI}}(100)$$ (18−6)

      2. Deflating sales:

$$\text{Deflated sales} = \frac{\text{Actual sales}}{\text{An appropriate index}}(100)$$ (18−7)

      3. Determining the purchasing power of the dollar compared with its value for the base period:

$$\text{Purchasing power of dollar} = \frac{\$1}{\text{CPI}}(100)$$ (18−8)

      4. Millions of employees in automobile, steel, and other industries have their wages adjusted upward when the CPI increases. The specifics are in the management-union contracts.
   D. Shifting the base.
      1. It is necessary when two or more series of index numbers to be compared do not have the same base period.
      2. First select a common base period for all series. Then use the respective base numbers as the denominators, and convert each series to the new base period.

# EXERCISES

*The answers to the odd-numbered exercises are at the end of the book.*

12. Cash dividends per common share declared by NCR for selected years are:

| Year | Cash dividends |
|------|----------------|
| 1979 | $0.40 |
| 1980 | 0.50 |
| 1981 | 0.55 |
| 1982 | 0.60 |
| 1989 | 1.32 |
| 1990 | 1.40 |

Source: NCR, *1987 Annual Report,* pp. 7, 37; and *1990 Annual* Report, p. 1.

   a. Using 1980 as the base period, determine the index of cash dividends for 1990. Interpret.
   b. Using 1979–80 as the base period, determine the index of cash dividends for 1990.

13. The number of employees and other data for NCR since 1979 are:

| Year | Number of employees | Long-term debt | Revenue |
|------|---------------------|----------------|---------|
| 1979 | 67,000 | $344,568,000 | $3,002,640,000 |
| 1980 | 68,000 | 321,540,000 | 3,322,370,000 |
| 1981 | 65,000 | 299,658,000 | 3,432,701,000 |
| 1982 | 63,000 | 311,298,000 | 3,526,217,000 |
| 1989 | 56,000 | 233,000,000 | 5,956,000,000 |
| 1990 | 55,000 | 236,000,000 | 6,285,000,000 |

Source: NCR, *1987 Annual Report,* pp. 15, 32; *1990 Annual Report* p. 26.

    Determine the index of employment for 1990 using 1979 = 100. Interpret.

14. Refer to Exercise 13. Determine the index of long-term debt for 1990 using 1979 = 100. Interpret.

15. Refer to Exercise 13. Determine the index of revenue for 1990 using 1979–80 as the base period. Interpret.

16. The average weekly earnings of production or nonsupervisory workers on nonagricultural payrolls for selected industries follow. Use 1979 equals 100.

| Year | Construction | Finance insurance, and real estate | Wholesale trade | Transportation and public utilities |
|------|--------------|------------------------------------|-----------------|-------------------------------------|
| 1979 | $342.99 | $190.77 | $247.93 | $325.56 |
| 1983 | 442.97 | 263.90 | 329.18 | 420.81 |
| 1987 | 477.28 | 317.11 | 367.10 | 469.59 |
| 1991 (Mar.) | 512.45 | 369.81 | 418.82 | 503.26 |

Source: U.S. Department of Labor, *Monthly Labor Review,* June 1988, pp. 86, 88; and May 1991, p. 71.

    Compare, using index numbers, the percent change in the average weekly wages of construction workers and of those working in finance, insurance, and real estate.

17. Refer to Exercise 16. Compare, using index numbers, the percent change in the average weekly wages of those in wholesale trade and of those working in transportation and public utilities from 1979 to 1991.

18. The Consumer Price Index and the average hourly earnings in selected industries are:

| | CPI (all items) (1982−84 = 100) | Hourly earnings | | |
|---|---|---|---|---|
| Year | | Services | Retail trade | Manufacturing |
| 1982−84 | 100.0 | $ 7.27 | $5.69 | $ 8.84 |
| 1986 | 109.6 | 8.16 | 6.03 | 9.73 |
| 1987 | 113.6 | 8.47 | 6.12 | 9.73 |
| 1991 (Mar.) | 135.0 | 10.20 | 6.94 | 11.08 |

Source: U.S. Department of labor, *Monthly Labor Review,* June 1988, pp. 86, 88, 94 and May 1991, pp. 70, 71.

What happened to the real hourly earnings of a "typical" employee in each of the three selected industries between the 1982−84 period and March 1991? Explain.

19. Refer to Exercise 18. What happened to the purchasing power of the dollar between the years 1982, 1983, and 1984 and the month of March 1991? Explain.

20. Refer to Exercise 18. Jose Gomez's monthly income in 1986 was $2,040. By March 1991 it had risen to $2,090. Explain what happened to his real monthly income.

21. A special-purpose index is to be designed to monitor the overall economy of the Southwest. Four key series were selected. After considerable deliberation it was decided to weight retail sales 20 percent, total bank deposits 10 percent, industrial production in the area 40 percent, and nonagricultural employment 30 percent. The data for 1983, 1986, and 1992 are:

| Year | Retail sales ($ millions) | Bank deposits ($ billions) | Industrial production (1977 = 100) | Employment |
|---|---|---|---|---|
| 1983 | 1,159.0 | 87 | 110.6 | 1,214,000 |
| 1986 | 1,467.0 | 85 | 111.1 | 1,316,000 |
| 1992 | 1,971.0 | 91 | 114.7 | 1,501,000 |

   a. Construct a special-purpose index for 1992 using 1983 as the base period.
   b. Interpret.

22. We are making a historical study of certain facets of the American economy from 1950 to 1980. Data on prices, the labor force, productivity, and the GNP were collected. Note in the following table that the CPI is on a 1967 base, employment is in millions of persons, and so on. A direct comparison, therefore, is not feasible.
   a. Make whatever calculations are necessary to compare the trend in the four series from 1950 to 1980.
   b. Interpret.

| Year | Consumer Price Index (1967 = 100) | Total labor force (millions) | Index of productivity in manufacturing (1967 = 100) | Gross national product ($ billions) |
|---|---|---|---|---|
| 1950 | 72.1 | 64 | 64.9 | 286.2 |
| 1967 | 100.0 | 81 | 100.0 | 789.6 |
| 1971 | 121.3 | 87 | 110.3 | 1,063.4 |
| 1975 | 161.2 | 95 | 114.9 | 1,516.3 |
| 1980 | 246.8 | 107 | 146.6 | 2,626.0 |

Sources: U.S. Department of Labor, *Monthly Labor Review,* April 1977, pp. 91, 103, 109; *National Income and Products Accounts of the United States; Survey of Current Business,* March 1981, p. S−1.

23. Prices of selected foods for 1977 and 1992 are given in the following table.

|  | 1977 | | 1992 | |
|---|---|---|---|---|
| Item | Price | Amount produced | Price | Amount produced |
| Cabbage (pound) | $0.06 | 2,000 | $0.05 | 1,500 |
| Carrots (bunch) | 0.10 | 200 | 0.12 | 200 |
| Peas (quart) | 0.20 | 400 | 0.18 | 500 |
| Endive (bunch) | 0.15 | 100 | 0.15 | 200 |

a. Using the Laspeyres formula, calculate a weighted index of price for 1992 (1977 = 100). Interpret.

b. Using the Paasche formula, calculate a weighted index of price for 1992. Interpret.

c. Explain the difference between the price index for 1992 using the Laspeyres method and the Paasche method.

d. Using the Laspeyres formula, determine a weighted index of quantity for 1992 (1977 = 100). Interpret.

e. Calculate an index of value for 1992 (1977 = 100). Interpret.

24. The prices of selected items for 1980 and 1991 follow. Production figures for those two periods are also given.

| Items | 1980 price* | 1991 price** | 1980 production | 1991 production |
|---|---|---|---|---|
| Aluminum (cents per lb.) | $ 0.287 | $ 0.76 | 1,000 | 1,200 |
| Natural gas (1,000 cu. ft.) | 0.17 | 2.50 | 5,000 | 4,000 |
| Petroleum, crude (barrel) | 3.18 | 26.00 | 60,000 | 60,000 |
| Platinum (troy ounce) | 133 | 490 | 500 | 600 |

*Source: Statistical Abstract of the United States.
**Estimated.

a. Using 1980 as the base period, determine the weighted index of price for 1991 using the Laspeyres method. Interpret.

b. Using 1980 as the base period, determine the weighted index of the quantity produced for 1991 using the Laspeyres method. Interpret.

25. Refer to Exercise 24.

a. Using the Paasche method and 1980 as the base period, determine a weighted index of price for 1991.

b. Determine a value index for 1991 using 1980 as the base period. Interpret.

26. Discuss the main features of the two consumer price indexes that are compiled and published, including what they measure, the base period, and so on.

27. Discuss the escalator clause (also called the cost-of-living clause) found in many management-union contracts.

28. If a management-union contract is available, cite any provisions that pertain to changes in wages resulting from changes in the Consumer Price Index.

# CHAPTER 18 EXAMINATION

*The answers are at the end of the chapter.*

1. The prices of aluminum scrap for three years are:

| Year | Price of aluminum scrap (per ton) |
|---|---|
| 1977 | $40.00 |
| 1982 | 50.00 |
| 1992 | 80.65 |

a. Using 1982 as the base period, determine price indexes for 1977 and for 1992.

b. Interpret.

Questions 2–5 are based on the following prices and quantities consumed for 1983 and 1992.

| | 1983 | | 1992 | |
| | Price (bushel) | Amount consumed (millions of bushels) | Price (bushel) | Amount consumed (millions of bushels) |
| Item | | | | |
| --- | --- | --- | --- | --- |
| Corn | $2 | 10 | $4 | 12 |
| Wheat | 3 | 6 | 1 | 8 |
| Oats | 7 | 2 | 5 | 9 |

2. Using the Laspeyres formula and 1983 as the base period, determine a weighted price index for 1992.

3. Using the Laspeyres formula and 1983 as the base period, determine a weighted quantity index for 1992.

4. Compute a value index for 1992 using 1983 = 100.

5. a. Using a Paasche formula and 1983 as the base period, determine a weighted price index for 1992.

   b. Why is this price index different from the one found in Question 2? Which one is the more commonly used?

Questions 6 and 7 are based on the following.

| Year | Consumer Price Index (1982–84 = 100) | Mr. Martin's monthly take-home pay |
| --- | --- | --- |
| 1982–84 | 100.0 | $ 600 |
| 1986 | 109.6 | 700 |
| 1991 (Mar.) | 135.0 | 2,000 |

6. What is the purchasing power of the dollar for March 1991 based on the period 1982–84?

7. a. Determine Mr. Martin's "real" monthly income for each of the three time periods.

   b. Interpret.

8. Suppose that the Producers Price Index and the sales of Hoskin's Wholesale Distributors for 1983 and 1992 are:

| Year | Producers Price Index | Sales |
| --- | --- | --- |
| 1983 | 120.0 | $2,400,000 |
| 1992 | 265.9 | 3,500,000 |

   a. What are Hoskin's real sales (also called deflated sales) for the two years?

   b. Interpret.

9. The management of Ingalls Super Discount stores, with several stores in the Oklahoma City area, wants to construct an index of economic activity for the metropolitan area. Management contends that if the index reveals that the economy is slowing down, inventory should be kept at a low level.

   Three series seem to hold promise as predictors of economic activity—area retail sales, bank deposits, and employment. All of these data can be secured monthly from the U.S. government. Retail sales is to be weighted 40 percent, bank deposits 35 percent, and employment 25 percent. Seasonally adjusted data for the first three months of the year are:

| Month | Retail sales ($ millions) | Bank deposits ($ billions) | Employment (thousands) |
|---|---|---|---|
| January | 8.0 | 20 | 300 |
| February | 6.8 | 23 | 303 |
| March | 6.4 | 21 | 297 |

a.  Construct an index of economic activity for each of the three months using January as the base period.

b.  Send a recommendation to management.

# ANSWERS

18–1  1.  166.3, found by ($14.12/$8.49)100. Hourly earnings increased 66.3 percent from 1979 to March 1991.

2.  a.  187.7, found by ($101,781.9/$54,217.0) × 100. Sales of GM are 87.7 percent greater than sales of IBM.

  b.  48.4, found by ($26,257.7/$54,217.0)100. Sales of Chrysler are 51.6 percent below IBM sales.

18–2  1.  321.3, found by ($6.94/$2.16)100. Earnings increased 221.3 percent in the period.

2.  311.2, found by ($6.94/$2.23)100.

3.  88.5, found by ($2.16/$2.44)100. Earnings in 1968 were 11.5 percent less than in 1970, found by 100.0 − 88.5.

18–3  1.  214.5, found by $P = ($140,500/$65,500)100$.

| $p_0$ | $q_0$ | $p_0q_0$ | $p_t$ | $p_tq_0$ |
|-------|-------|----------|-------|----------|
| $35 | 500 | $17,500 | $65 | $ 32,500 |
| 40 | 1,200 | 48,000 | 90 | 108,000 |
|  |  | $65,500 |  | $140,500 |

2.  The price of clothing in 1993 was 214.5 percent of the price in 1982. Or the price of clothing increased 114.5 percent from 1982 to 1993.

18–4  1.  235.4, found by $Q = ($8,240/$3,500)100$.

| $p_0q_0$ | $p_0q_t$ |
|----------|----------|
| $ 200 | $1,400 |
| 300 | 240 |
| 3,000 | 6,600 |
| $3,500 | $8,240 |

2.  Quantity produced between 1975 and 1991 increased 135.4 percent.

18–5  1.  127.1, found by $V = ($77,000/$60,600)100$.

| $p_0q_0$ | $p_tq_t$ |
|----------|----------|
| $30,000 | $36,000 |
| 600 | 1,000 |
| 30,000 | 40,000 |
| $60,600 | $77,000 |

2.  Value of sales up 27.1 percent from 1983 to 1990.

18–6  1.  1981 = 100
1992 = 139, found by:

|  | Weight |
|--|--------|
| ($0.50/$0.20)(100) × .10 = | 25 |
| (80,000/100,000)(100) × .30 = | 24 |
| (120/80)(100) × .60 = | 90 |
|  | 139 |

2.  Business activity in 1992 was 139 percent of the activity in 1981. Or business activity in 1992 was 39 percent higher than in 1981.

18–7  1.  $22,810.22, found by ($25,000/109.6)100.

2.  $29,428.57, found by ($41,200/140.0)100.

3.  Jon's real income increased from about $22,810 in 1986 to $29,429 in 1992. This indicates that his take-home pay increased at a faster rate than the prices he paid for food, transportation, etc.

18–8  68.7 cents, found by:

$$\frac{\$1}{145.6} \times 100$$

18–9  1.  (197.75/108.09)100 = 182.9

2.  a.

|  | Industrial Production Index | Producers' Price Index |
|--|------------------------------|------------------------|
| 1982 | 100.0 | 100.0 |
| 1987 | 112.6 | 105.4 |
| 1990 | 142.8 | 119.2 |

Using 1982 as the base period for both series:

|  | Production Index | Price Index |
|--|------------------|-------------|
| 1982 | 100.0 | 100.0 |
| 1987 | 112.6 | 105.4 |
| 1990 | 123.9* | 119.2 |

*(142.8/115.3)100 = 123.9

b.  From the base period of 1982 to 1990, industrial production increased at a faster rate (23.9 percent) than prices (19.2 percent).

# Answers

## CHAPTER 18 EXAMINATION

1. a. For 1977, 80.0; for 1992, 161.3, found by (80.65/ 50.00)100.
   b. In 1977 the price of aluminum scrap was 80 percent of the 1982 price, or it was 20 percent below the 1982 price. In 1992 the price was 61.3 percent above the 1982 price, or the price of aluminum scrap increased 61.3 percent from 1982 to 1992.

Questions 2–5 are based on the following sums:

|        | $p_0q_0$ | $p_tq_0$ | $p_0q_t$ | $p_tq_t$ |
|--------|----------|----------|----------|----------|
| Corn   | $20      | $40      | $ 24     | $ 48     |
| Wheat  | 18       | 6        | 24       | 8        |
| Oats   | 14       | 10       | 63       | 45       |
|        | $52      | $56      | $111     | $101     |

2. 107.7, found by ($56/$52)100.
3. 213.5, found by ($111/$52)100.
4. 194.2, found by ($101/$52)100.
5. a. 91.0, found by (101/$111)100.
   b. The difference is explained by the two different weighting systems. The Laspeyres system is used extensively.
6. $0.741, found by ($1/135.0)100.

7. a.

| Year       | Real income | Calculations        |
|------------|-------------|---------------------|
| 1992–84    | $ 600       | ($600/100.0)100     |
| 1986       | 639         | ($700/109.6)100     |
| 1991 (Mar.)| 1,481       | ($2,000/135.0)100   |

   b. Mr. Martin's purchasing power increased almost 2½ times from the period 1982–84 to 1991. His real income increased from $600 a month to $1,481.
8. a. 1983 deflated sales are $2,000,000, found by ($2,400,000/120.0)100. For 1992 real sales are $1,316,284, found by ($3,500,000/265.9)100.
   b. Real sales dropped from $2,000,000 in 1983 to $1,316,284 in 1992, caused by a sharp increase in the price of raw materials.
9. a. The three indexes of economic activity are: January, 100.0; February 99.5; March, 93.5. The calculations for February are:

Retail sales    (6.8/8.0)100   =  85. Then  85 × .40 = 34.00
Bank deposits (23/20)100   = 115. Then 115 × .35 = 40.25
Employment   (303/300)100 = 101. Then 101 × .25 = <u>25.25</u>
                                                         99.50

   b. The overall economic level declined 6.5 percent during the first three months (found by 100.0 − 93.5). Management might be advised to carefully regulate the size of the inventories at their stores.

*Real Estate—Scott Barrow/Superstock*

# TIME SERIES AND FORECASTING

When you have completed this chapter, you will be able to:

**What is a time series?**

$T$he emphasis in this chapter is on time series analysis and forecasting. A **time series** is a collection of data recorded over a period of time—usually weekly, monthly, quarterly, or yearly. Two examples of time series are (1) a department store's sales by quarter since opening in 1962 and (2) the annual production of sulfuric acid since 1970.

An analysis of past history—a time series—can be used by management to make current decisions and for long-term forecasting and planning. Long-term forecasts usually extend more than 1 year into the future; 5-, 10-, 15-, and 20-year projections are common. Long-range predictions are considered essential in order to allow sufficient time for the procurement, manufacturing, sales, finance, and other departments of a company to develop plans for possible new plants, financing, development of new products, and new methods of assembling.

Forecasting the level of sales, both short-term and long-term, is practically dictated by the very nature of business organizations in the United States. Competition for the consumer's dollar, stress on earning a profit for the stockholders, a desire to procure a larger and larger share of the market, and the ambitions of executives are some of the prime motivating forces in business. Thus, a forecast (a statement of the goals of management) is considered necessary in order to have the raw materials, production facilities, and staff available to meet the projected demand.

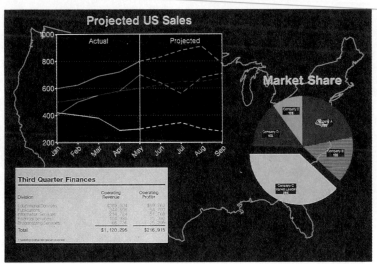

Many computer programs such as SPSS have become popular in visually depicting time series data

*Courtesy SPSS, Inc.*

This chapter deals with the use of past data to forecast future events. First we look at the components of a time series, then we examine some of the techniques used in analyzing past data, and finally we project future events.

## COMPONENTS OF A TIME SERIES

### SECULAR TREND

**Secular or long-term trend**

One component of a times series is referred to as the **secular trend.** It is the smooth long-term trend of the data. Long-term trends of sales, employment, stock prices, and other business and economic series follow various patterns. Some move steadily upward, others decline, and others stay the same over a period of time. A few of these are depicted graphically in the following charts.

- Chart 19–1 shows the revenues of the International Business Machine Corporation and subsidiary companies since 1986. Note that there has been a rather smooth upward trend in IBM revenues since 1986.
- Chart 19–2 also depicts an upward trend. Note that the population of the United States has increased rather steadily, from about 76 million in 1900 to approximately 250 million in 1990.
- Chart 19–3 portrays the downward trend in employment since 1980 for the NCR Corporation. It decreased steadily in the 10 years depicted, from 68,000 in 1980 to 55,000 in 1990.
- Chart 19–4 pictures a series that remained relatively constant. It shows Chevron's total worldwide gross production of crude oil and natural-gas liquids since 1984.

### CHART  19–1

**Total Revenues of IBM, 1986–90**

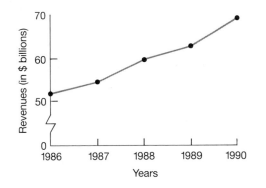

Source: IBM, *1990 Annual Report,* p. 59.

### CHART  19–2

**Population of the United States, 1900–90**

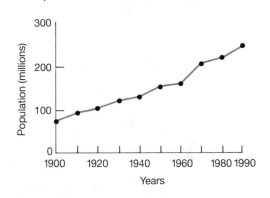

Source: U.S. Bureau of the Census, *Current Population Reports,* series P-25, nos. 802, 1023, and 1046.

### CHART  19–3

**Employment at the NCR Corporation, 1980–90**

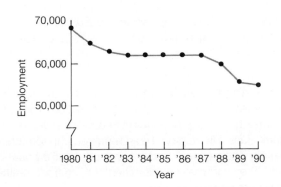

Source: NCR Corporation, *1990 Annual Report,* p. 26.

### CHART  19–4

**Chevron's Gross Worldwide Production of Crude Oil and Natural-Gas Liquids, 1984–90 (in thousands of barrels per day)**

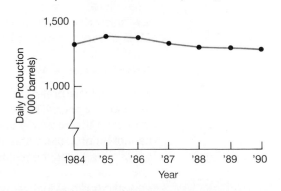

Source: Chevron Corporation, *1990 Annual Report,* p. 70.

## CYCLICAL VARIATION

Cyclical variation:
Prosperity, recession,
depression, expansion

**Cyclical variation** is another component of a time series. A typical business cycle consists of a period of prosperity followed by periods of recession, depression, and recovery (see Chart 19–5). There are sizable fluctuations, representing more than one year in time, above and below the secular trend. In a recession, for example, employment, production, the Dow Jones Industrial Average, and many other business and economic series are below their long-term trend lines. Conversely, in periods of prosperity they are above their long-term trend lines.

---

### CHART 19–5

**A Typical Business Cycle**

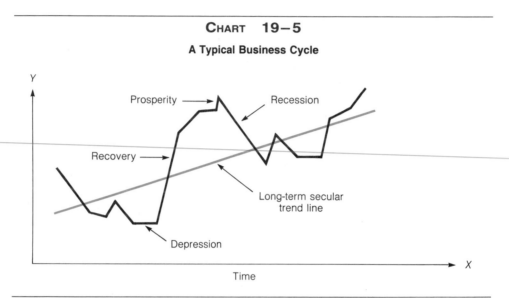

---

## SEASONAL VARIATION

Seasonal variation: A
short-term pattern
repeated yearly

Another component of a time series is **seasonal variation.** Many sales, production, and other series fluctuate with the seasons. The unit of time may be either quarterly, monthly, weekly, or even daily.

Practically all business and economic series have recurring seasonal patterns. A few exceptions are found in certain electronic and aircraft firms under contract to the federal government to supply aerospace and military parts. Sales of men's and boys' wear stores, for example, have extremely high sales prior to Christmas and relatively low sales after Christmas and in the summer. As reported in the *Survey of Current Business,* department store sales have a similar pattern, as shown in Chart 19–6.

## IRREGULAR VARIATION

Many analysts prefer to subdivide the **irregular variation** into *episodic* and *residual* variations. Episodic fluctuations are unpredictable, but they can be identified. The initial impact on the economy of a major strike or a war can be identified, but a strike or war cannot be predicted. After the episodic fluctuations have been removed, the remaining variation is called the residual variation. The residual fluctuations, often called chance fluctuations, are unpredictable, and they cannot be identified. Of course, neither episodic nor residual variation can be projected into the future.

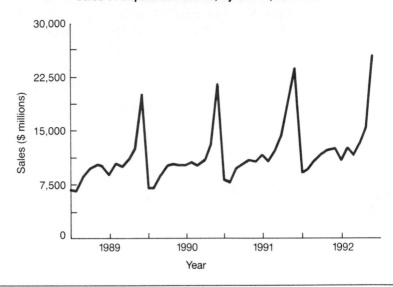

## CHART 19—6

**Sales of Department Stores, by Month, 1989—92**

We will begin our study of the components of a time series with linear trend.

## LINEAR TREND

Linear trend equation

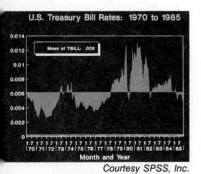

*Courtesy SPSS, Inc.*

Slope of trend line is *b*

The long-term trend of many business series, such as sales, exports, and production, often approximates a straight line. If so, the equation to describe this growth is:

$$Y' = a + bt \qquad (19-1)$$

where:

*Y′*  read *Y* prime, is the projected value of the *Y* variable for a selected value of *t*.

*a*  is the *Y*-intercept. It is the estimated value of *Y* when *t* = 0. Another way to put it is: *a* is the estimated value of *Y* where the straight line crosses the *Y*-axis when *t* is zero.

*b*  is the slope of the line, or the average change in *Y′* for each change of one unit (either increase or decrease) in *t*.

*t*  is any value of time that is selected.

To illustrate further the meaning of *Y′*, *a, b,* and *t* in a time series problem, a straight line has been drawn in Chart 19—7 to represent the typical trend of sales. Assume that this company started in business in 1983. This beginning year (1983) has been arbitrarily designated as year 0. Note that sales increased $2 million on the average every year; that is, based on the straight line drawn through the sales data, sales increased from $3 million in 1983, to $5 million in 1984, to $7 million in 1985, to $9 million in 1986, and so on. The slope, or *b,* is therefore 2. Note too that the line intercepts the Y-axis (when $t = 0$) at $3 million. This point (3) is *a*. Another way of determining *b* is to locate the starting place of the straight line in year 0. It is 3 for 1983 in this problem. Then locate the value on the straight line for the last year. It is 19 for 1991. Sales went up $19 million − $3 million, or $16 million, in eight years (1983 to 1991). Thus, 16 ÷ 8 = 2, which is the slope of the line, or *b*.

CHART 19–7

**A Straight Line Fitted to the Sales Data**

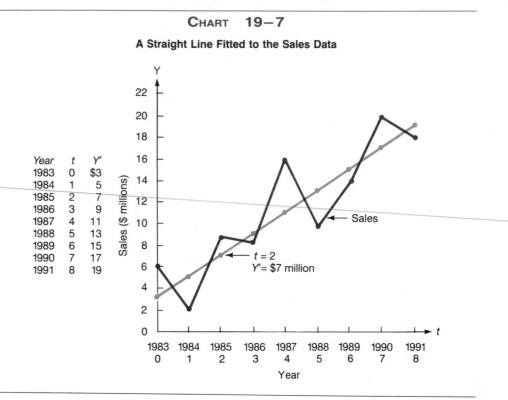

| Year | t | Y′ |
|------|---|-----|
| 1983 | 0 | $3 |
| 1984 | 1 | 5 |
| 1985 | 2 | 7 |
| 1986 | 3 | 9 |
| 1987 | 4 | 11 |
| 1988 | 5 | 13 |
| 1989 | 6 | 15 |
| 1990 | 7 | 17 |
| 1991 | 8 | 19 |

The equation for the line in Chart 19–7 is:

$$Y' = 3 + 2t \text{ (in \$ millions)}$$

where:

Sales are in $ millions.
The origin, or year 0, is 1983.
*t* increases by one unit for each year.

In Chapter 14 we drew a straight line through points on a scatter diagram to approximate the regression line. We stressed, however, that this method for determining the regression equation has a serious drawback—namely, the position of the line depends on the judgment of the individual who drew the line. Three people would probably draw three different lines through the scatter plots. Likewise, the line we drew through the sales data in Chart 19–7 might not be the "best-fitting" line.

Such lines usually inaccurate

Because of the subjective judgment involved, this method should be used only when a quick approximation of the straight-line equation is needed, or to check the reasonableness of the least squares line, which is discussed next.

# LEAST SQUARES METHOD

We could solve these two equations simultaneously

The **least squares method** of computing the equation for a straight line through the data of interest gives the "best-fitting" line. Two equations may be solved simultaneously to arrive at the least squares trend equation. They are:

$$\Sigma Y = na + b\Sigma t$$
$$\Sigma tY = a\Sigma t + b\Sigma t^2$$

(19–2)

You may recognize these as the normal equations discussed in Chapter 14, with $t$ replacing $X$ in the equations. As we described in Chapter 14, using the normal equations to determine $a$ and $b$ can be tedious. A better approach is to use the following computational equations.

$$b = \frac{\Sigma tY - (\Sigma Y)(\Sigma t)/n}{\Sigma t^2 - (\Sigma t)^2/n}$$

(19–3)

$$a = \frac{\Sigma Y}{n} - b\left(\frac{\Sigma t}{n}\right)$$

(19–4)

If the number of years is large—say, 15 or more—and the magnitude of the numbers is also large, a computer software package is recommended.

## ■ EXAMPLE

The sales of Jensen Foods, a small grocery chain, since 1987 are:

| Year | Sales ($ millions) |
|------|--------------------|
| 1987 | 7 |
| 1988 | 10 |
| 1989 | 9 |
| 1990 | 11 |
| 1991 | 13 |

Determine the least squares trend line equation.

## ☑ SOLUTION

To simplify the calculations, the years are replaced by *coded* values. That is, we let 1987 be 0, 1988 be 1, and so forth. This reduces the size of the values of $\Sigma t$, $\Sigma t^2$, and $\Sigma tY$. (See Table 19–1.) This is often referred to as the **coded method.**

---

### TABLE 19–1

**Computations Needed for Determining the Trend Equation**

| Year | Sales ($ millions), $Y$ | $t$ | $tY$ | $t^2$ |
|------|-------------------------|-----|------|-------|
| 1987 | 7 | 0 | 0 | 0 |
| 1988 | 10 | 1 | 10 | 1 |
| 1989 | 9 | 2 | 18 | 4 |
| 1990 | 11 | 3 | 33 | 9 |
| 1991 | 13 | 4 | 52 | 16 |
|      | 50 | 10 | 113 | 30 |

---

Determining $a$ and $b$ using formulas (19–3) and (19–4):

$$b = \frac{\Sigma tY - (\Sigma Y)(\Sigma t)/n}{\Sigma t^2 - (\Sigma t)^2/n} = \frac{113 - 50(10)/5}{30 - (10)^2/5} = 1.30$$

$$a = \frac{\Sigma Y}{n} - b\left(\frac{\Sigma t}{n}\right) = \frac{50}{5} - 1.30\left(\frac{10}{5}\right) = 7.40$$

The trend equation is therefore $Y' = 7.40 + 1.30t$, where:

Sales are in millions of dollars.

The origin, or year 0, is in the middle of 1987 (i.e., July 1, 1987), and $t$ increases by one unit for each year.

How do we interpret the equation? The value of 1.30 indicates that sales increased at a rate of $1.3 million per year. The value 7.40 is the estimated sales when $t = 0$. That is, the estimated sales amount for 1987 (the zero year) is $7.4 million.

## PLOTTING THE STRAIGHT LINE

The least squares equation can be used to find the points on the straight line going through the middle of the data. The sales data from Table 19–1 are repeated in Table 19–2 to show the procedure. The equation determined earlier is $Y' = 7.40 + 1.30t$. To get the coordinates of the point on the straight line for 1990, for example, insert the $t$ value of 3 in the equation. Then $Y' = 7.40 + 1.30(3) = 11.3$.

TABLE 19–2

**Calculations Needed for Determining the Points on the Straight Line Using the Coded Method**

| Year | Sales ($ millions), Y | t | Y' | Found by |
|------|------|---|-----|----------|
| 1987 | $ 7 | 0 | 7.4 | ← 7.40 + 1.30(0) |
| 1988 | 10 | 1 | 8.7 | ← 7.40 + 1.30(1) |
| 1989 | 9 | 2 | 10.0 | ← 7.40 + 1.30(2) |
| 1990 | 11 | 3 | 11.3 | ← 7.40 + 1.30(3) |
| 1991 | 13 | 4 | 12.6 | ← 7.40 + 1.30(4) |

The actual sales and the trend in sales as represented by the straight line are shown in Chart 19–8. The first point on the straight line has the coordinates $t = 0$, $Y' = 7.4$. Another point is $t = 2$, $Y' = 10$.

## ESTIMATION

If the sales, production, or other data over a period of time tend to approximate a straight-line trend, the equation developed by the least squares method can be used to estimate sales for some future period.

## ■ EXAMPLE

Refer to the sales data in Table 19–1. Note that the origin, or year 0, is 1987. The year 1988 is coded 1, and 1989 is coded 2. What is the sales forecast for 1994?

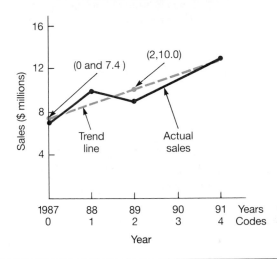

**CHART   19–8**

**Actual Sales and Straight-Line Trend**

## SOLUTION

Estimating sales for 1994

The year 1989 is coded 2; 1990 is logically coded 3; 1991 is coded 4; 1992 is coded 5; 1993 is coded 6; and 1994 is coded 7. So in 1994, $t = 7$. Substituting the period 7 in the straight-line equation [formula (19–1)]:

$$Y' = a + bt = 7.40 + 1.30(7) = 16.5$$

Thus, based on past sales, the sales estimate for 1994 is $16.5 million.

In this time series problem, there were five years of sales data. Based on those five sales figures, we estimated sales for 1994. Many researchers suggest that we do not project sales, production, and other business and economic series more than $n/2$ time periods into the future. If, for example, there are 10 years of past data, we would make estimates only up to 5 years into the future ($n/2 = 10/2 = 5$). Others suggest that the forecast be for no longer than 2 years, especially in rapidly changing economic times.

### Self-Review 19–1

*The answers are at the end of the chapter.*

Annual production of king-size rockers by Wood Products, Inc. since 1984 follows:

| Year | Production (000s) |
|------|------|
| 1984 | 4 |
| 1985 | 8 |
| 1986 | 5 |
| 1987 | 8 |
| 1988 | 11 |
| 1989 | 9 |
| 1990 | 11 |
| 1991 | 14 |

1. Plot the production data.
2. Determine the least squares equation.
3. Determine the points on the straight line for 1984 and 1990. Connect the two points to arrive at the straight line.
4. Based on the equation for the straight line, what is the estimated production for 1994?

# EXERCISES

*The answers to the odd-numbered exercises are at the end of the book.*

1.  The total number of bank failures for the years 1987 to 1991 are given below. Determine the least squares equation, and estimate the number of failures in 1994.

    | Year | Code | Number of failures |
    |------|------|--------------------|
    | 1987 | 0 | 79 |
    | 1988 | 1 | 120 |
    | 1989 | 2 | 138 |
    | 1990 | 3 | 184 |
    | 1991 | 4 | 200 |

2.  The personal consumption expenditures for telephone and telegraph, in billions of dollars, in the United States for the years 1986 to 1991 are given below. Determine the least squares equation, and estimate the expenditure for 1994.

    | Year | Code | Expenditures ($ billions) |
    |------|------|---------------------------|
    | 1986 | 0 | 37.9 |
    | 1987 | 1 | 39.8 |
    | 1988 | 2 | 40.4 |
    | 1989 | 3 | 42.7 |
    | 1990 | 4 | 44.1 |
    | 1991 | 5 | 47.1 |

3.  The following table gives the annual amount of scrap produced by Machine Products, Inc.

    | Year | Code | Scrap (tons) |
    |------|------|--------------|
    | 1988 | 0 | 2.0 |
    | 1989 | 1 | 4.0 |
    | 1990 | 2 | 3.0 |
    | 1991 | 3 | 5.0 |
    | 1992 | 4 | 6.0 |

    Determine the least squares trend equation. Estimate the amount of scrap for the year 1994.

4.  The amounts spent in vending machines in the United States, in billions of dollars, for the years 1988 through 1992 are given below. Determine the least squares equation, and estimate vending sales for 1994.

    | Year | Code | Vending machine sales ($ billions) |
    |------|------|------------------------------------|
    | 1988 | 0 | 17.5 |
    | 1989 | 1 | 19.0 |
    | 1990 | 2 | 21.0 |
    | 1991 | 3 | 22.7 |
    | 1992 | 4 | 24.5 |

# THE MOVING-AVERAGE METHOD

*Moving-average method smooths out fluctuations*

The **moving-average method** is not only useful in smoothing out a time series; it is the basic method used in measuring the seasonal fluctuation described later in the chapter. In contrast to the least squares method, which expresses the trend in terms of a mathematical equation ($Y' = a + bt$), the moving-average method merely smooths out the fluctuations in the data. This is accomplished by "moving" the arithmetic mean values through the time series.

To apply the moving-average method to a time series, the data should follow a fairly linear trend and have a definite rhythmic pattern of fluctuations (repeating, say, every three years). The data in the following example have three components—trend, cycle, and irregular, abbreviated *T, C,* and *I.* There is no seasonal variation because the data are recorded annually. What the moving-average method does, in effect, is average out *C* and *I.* The residual is trend.

If the duration of the cycles is constant, and if the amplitudes of the cycles are equal, the cyclical and irregular fluctuations can be removed entirely using the moving-average method. The result is a straight line. For example, in the following time series the cycle repeats itself every seven years, and the amplitude of each cycle is 4; that is, there are exactly four units from the trough (lowest time period) to the peak. The seven-year moving average, therefore, averages out the cyclical and irregular fluctuations perfectly, and the residual is a straight-line trend.

**Compute mean of first seven years**

The first step in computing the seven-year moving average is to determine the seven-year moving totals. The total sales for the first seven years (1967–73 inclusive) are $22 million, found by 1 + 2 + 3 + 4 + 5 + 4 + 3. (See Table 19–3.) The total of $22 million is divided by 7 to determine the arithmetic mean sales per year. This amount ($3.134 million) is positioned opposite the middle year of 1970. Then the total sales for the next seven years (1968–74 inclusive) are determined. [A convenient way of doing this is to subtract the sales for 1967 ($1 million) from the first seven-year total ($22 million) and add the sales for 1974 ($2 million), to give the new total of $23

## TABLE   19–3

**Exhibit of the Computations for the Seven-Year Moving Average**

| Year | Sales ($ millions) | Seven-year moving total | Seven-year moving average |
|------|------|------|------|
| 1967 | $1 | | |
| 1968 | 2 | | |
| 1969 | 3 | | |
| 1970 | 4 | 22 | 3.143 |
| 1971 | 5 | 23 | 3.286 |
| 1972 | 4 | 24 | 3.429 |
| 1973 | 3 | 25 | 3.571 |
| 1974 | 2 | 26 | 3.714 |
| 1975 | 3 | 27 | 3.857 |
| 1976 | 4 | 28 | 4.000 |
| 1977 | 5 | 29 | 4.143 |
| 1978 | 6 | 30 | 4.286 |
| 1979 | 5 | 31 | 4.429 |
| 1980 | 4 | 32 | 4.571 |
| 1981 | 3 | 33 | 4.714 |
| 1982 | 4 | 34 | 4.857 |
| 1983 | 5 | 35 | 5.000 |
| 1984 | 6 | 36 | 5.143 |
| 1985 | 7 | 37 | 5.286 |
| 1986 | 6 | 38 | 5.429 |
| 1987 | 5 | 39 | 5.571 |
| 1988 | 4 | 40 | 5.714 |
| 1989 | 5 | 41 | 5.857 |
| 1990 | 6 | | |
| 1991 | 7 | | |
| 1992 | 8 | | |

million.] The mean of this total, $3.286 million, is positioned opposite the middle year, 1971.

This procedure is repeated until all possible seven-year totals and their means are found. (Note that there are no totals for the first three years and the last three years.) See Table 19–3 and Chart 19–9.

---

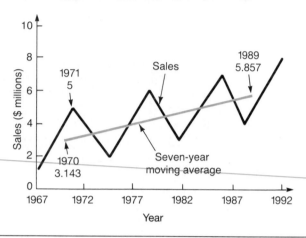

## CHART 19–9

### Sales and Seven-Year Moving Average

---

A three-year and a five-year moving average are shown in Table 19–4 and depicted in Chart 19–10.

---

## TABLE 19–4

### Exhibit of a Three-Year Moving Average and a Five-Year Moving Average

| Year | Production, Y | Three-year moving total | Three-year moving average | Five-year moving total | Five-year moving average |
|------|------|------|------|------|------|
| 1973 | 5 | | | | |
| 1974 | 6 | 19 | 6.3 | | |
| 1975 | 8 | 24 | 8.0 | 34 | 6.8 |
| 1976 | 10 | 23 | 7.7 | 32 | 6.4 |
| 1977 | 5 | 18 | 6.0 | 33 | 6.6 |
| 1978 | 3 | 15 | 5.0 | 35 | 7.0 |
| 1979 | 7 | 20 | 6.7 | 37 | 7.4 |
| 1980 | 10 | 29 | 9.7 | 43 | 8.6 |
| 1981 | 12 | 33 | 11.0 | 49 | 9.8 |
| 1982 | 11 | 32 | 10.7 | 55 | 11.0 |
| 1983 | 9 | 33 | 11.0 | 60 | 12.0 |
| 1984 | 13 | 37 | 12.3 | 66 | 13.2 |
| 1985 | 15 | 46 | 15.3 | 70 | 14.0 |
| 1986 | 18 | 48 | 16.0 | 72 | 14.4 |
| 1987 | 15 | 44 | 14.7 | 73 | 14.6 |
| 1988 | 11 | 40 | 13.3 | 75 | 15.0 |
| 1989 | 14 | 42 | 14.0 | 79 | 15.8 |
| 1990 | 17 | 53 | 17.7 | | |
| 1991 | 22 | | | | |

---

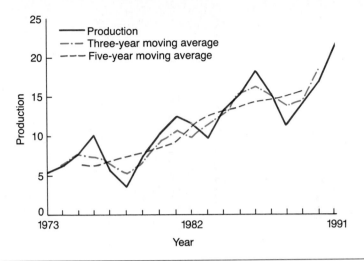

CHART   19-10

**Exhibit of a Three-Year Moving Average and a Five-Year Moving Average**

Moving-average method does not result in straight line

Sales, production, and other economic and business series usually do not have (1) periods of oscillation that are of equal length or (2) oscillations that have identical amplitudes. Thus, in actual practice, the application of the moving-average method to data does not result precisely in a straight line. For example, the production series in Table 19–4 repeats about every five years, but the amplitude of the data varies from one oscillation to another. The trend appears to be upward and somewhat linear. Both moving averages—the three-year and the five-year—seem to adequately describe the trend in production since 1973.

Three-year and five-year moving averages

The MINITAB system can be used to compute the moving average. The production data in Table 19–4 are used to show the MINITAB procedure for a three-year moving average. The first step is to lag each of the production values one period. The data in column C2 are the yearly production figures from column C1 lagged one year. Column C3 is the yearly production lagged two years. Next, the three columns are averaged, creating the moving average. Note that the moving averages are the same as the ones in Table 19–4 (except for rounding).

```
MTB>   set c1
DATA>  5,6, * * *, 17, 22
DATA>  end
MTB>   lag 1 c1 c2
MTB>   lag 2 c1 c3
MTB>   let c4= (c1+c2+c3)/3
MTB>   name c1 'Prod' c2 'lag-1' c3 'lag-2' c4 'Mov-avg'
MTB>   print c1 c2 c3 c4
```

*(continued)*

*(continued from 695)*

Three-year moving
average using MINITAB

```
ROW   Prod     lag-1     lag-2  Mov-avg
  1    5         *          *         *
  2    6         5          *         *
  3    8         6          5    6.3333
  4   10         8          6    8.0000
  5    5        10          8    7.6667
  6    3         5         10    6.0000
  7    7         3          5    5.0000
  8   10         7          3    6.6667
  9   12        10          7    9.6667
 10   11        12         10   11.0000
 11    9        11         12   10.6667
 12   13         9         11   11.0000
 13   15        13          9   12.3333
 14   18        15         13   15.3333
 15   15        18         15   16.0000
 16   11        15         18   14.6667
 17   14        11         15   13.3333
 18   17        14         11   14.0000
 19   22        17         14   17.6667
```

Determining a moving
average for an
even-numbered period,
such as four years

Four-year, six-year, and other even-numbered-year moving averages present one minor problem regarding the centering of the moving totals and moving averages. Note in Table 19−5 that there is no center time period, so the moving totals are positioned *between* two time periods. The total for the first four years ($42) is positioned between 1985 and 1986. The total for the next four years is $43. The averages of the first four years and the second four years ($10.50 and $10.75, respectively) are averaged, and the resulting figure is centered on 1986. This procedure is repeated until all possible four-year averages are computed.

---

## Table 19−5

### Exhibit of a Four-Year Moving Average

| Year | Sales, Y | Four-year moving total | Four-year moving average | Centered four-year moving average |
|------|----------|------------------------|--------------------------|-----------------------------------|
| 1984 | $ 8 | | | |
| 1985 | 11 | | | |
| | | $42 (8 + 11 + 9 + 14) | $10.50 ($42 ÷ 4) | |
| 1986 | 9 | | | 10.625 |
| | | 43 (11 + 9 + 14 + 9) | 10.75 ($43 ÷ 4) | |
| 1987 | 14 | | | 10.625 |
| | | 42 | 10.50 | |
| 1988 | 9 | | | 10.625 |
| | | 43 | 10.75 | |
| 1989 | 10 | | | 10.000 |
| | | 37 | 9.25 | |
| 1990 | 10 | | | 9.625 |
| | | 40 | 10.00 | |
| 1991 | 8 | | | |
| 1992 | 12 | | | |

---

Furthermore, also note that the averages tend to dampen or smooth out the fluctuations.

In summary of the technique using moving averages, its purpose is to help identify the long-term trend in a time series (because it smooths out short-term fluctuations). It is used to reveal any cyclical and seasonal fluctuations. It is usually applied to weekly, quarterly, or annual data.

### Self-Review 19–2

*The answers are at the end of the chapter.*

1. Complete a three-year moving average for the following production series.
2. Plot both the original data and the moving average.
3. Comment on the fit.

| Year | Number produced (000) |
|------|------------------------|
| 1987 | 2 |
| 1988 | 6 |
| 1989 | 4 |
| 1990 | 5 |
| 1991 | 3 |
| 1992 | 10 |

## NONLINEAR TRENDS

The emphasis in the previous discussion was on a time series whose growth or decline approximated a straight line. A straight-line trend equation is used to represent the time series when it is believed that the data are increasing (or decreasing) by *equal amounts,* on the average, from one period to another.

*A straight line will not be the "best" fit for these data*

Data that increase (or decrease) by *increasing amounts* over a period of time appear *curvilinear* when plotted on paper having an arithmetic scale. To put it another way, data that increase (or decrease) by *equal percents or proportions* over a period of time appear curvilinear on arithmetic paper. (See Chart 19–11.)

---

### CHART 19–11

**Imports on an Arithmetic Scale**

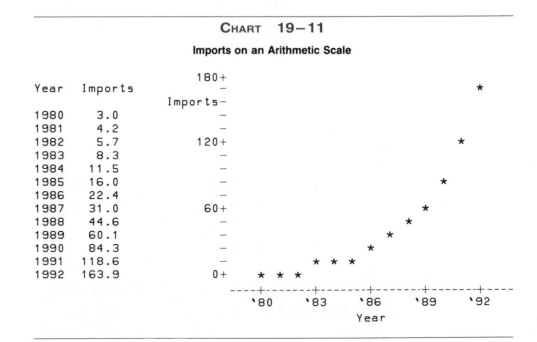

| Year | Imports |
|------|---------|
| 1980 | 3.0 |
| 1981 | 4.2 |
| 1982 | 5.7 |
| 1983 | 8.3 |
| 1984 | 11.5 |
| 1985 | 16.0 |
| 1986 | 22.4 |
| 1987 | 31.0 |
| 1988 | 44.6 |
| 1989 | 60.1 |
| 1990 | 84.3 |
| 1991 | 118.6 |
| 1992 | 163.9 |

---

Formula for logarithmic
trend equation

The trend equation for a time series that does approximate a curvilinear trend, such as the one portrayed in Chart 19–11, can be computed by using the logarithms of the data and the least squares method.

The general equation for the logarithmic trend equation is:

$$\log Y' = \log a + \log b(t) \tag{19-5}$$

The logarithmic equation can be determined for the import data given in Chart 19–11 using the MINITAB system. The first step is to enter the years and the codes for the years. The import data are entered next. The LET command is used to determine the log to the base 10 for each import value. Finally, the regression procedure is used, with the log of the imports as the dependent variable and the coded years as the independent variable. The output is as follows.

```
MTB > set c1
DATA> 1980:1992
DATA> end
MTB > set c2
DATA> 0:12
DATA> end
MTB > set c3
DATA> 3,4.2,5.7,8.3,11.5,16,22.4,31,44.6,60.1,84.3,118.6,163.9
DATA> end
MTB > let c4=logten(c3)
MTB > name c1 'Year' c2 'Code' c3 'Imports' c4 'Logs'
MTB > Print c1-c4

  ROW    Year    Code    Imports      Logs
    1    1980       0        3.0    0.47712
    2    1981       1        4.2    0.62325
    3    1982       2        5.7    0.75587
    4    1983       3        8.3    0.91908
    5    1984       4       11.5    1.06070
    6    1985       5       16.0    1.20412
    7    1986       6       22.4    1.35025
    8    1987       7       31.0    1.49136
    9    1988       8       44.6    1.64933
   10    1989       9       60.1    1.77887
   11    1990      10       84.3    1.92583
   12    1991      11      118.6    2.07408
   13    1992      12      163.9    2.21458

MTB > regr c4 1 c2

The regression equation is
Logs = 0.478 + 0.145 Code

Predictor        Coef        Stdev      t-ratio         p
Constant     0.477618     0.003012       158.57     0.000
Code         0.145069     0.000426       340.56     0.000
```

The regression (trend) equation is:

$$\log Y' = \log a + \log b(t)$$
$$= 0.478 + 0.145t$$

or, more precisely,

$$\log Y' = 0.477618 + 0.145069t$$

What we now have is the trend equation in terms of percent change. That is, the value 0.145 represents a percent change in $Y'$. This value is similar in concept and computation to the geometric mean, discussed in Chapter 3, which gives the percent change in $Y$ (sales, production, and so on) from one time period to another.

The log of $b$ is 0.145, and its antilog is about 1.3964. Subtracting 1 from this value, as we did in Chapter 3, indicates that the imports increased at a rate of about 39.64 percent per year from 1980 to 1992.

The logarithmic straight line is also used to make estimates. Suppose we wanted to estimate imports for 1997. The first step is to determine the coded year for 1997, which is 17. How did we get the value of 17? The year 1992 has a code of 12, 1997 is five years later, so $12 + 5 = 17$. The log of imports for 1997 is

$$Y' = 0.477618 + 0.145069t$$
$$= 0.477618 + 0.145069(17) = 2.943791$$

To obtain the estimated imports for 1997 we need to take the antilog of 2.943791, which is 878.6. This is our estimate of imports for 1997. Recall that the original data are in thousands of dollars, so the actual value is $878,600.

## Self-Review 19–3

*The answers are at the end of the chapter.*

Sales at Tomlin Manufacturing since 1988 are:

| Year | Sales ($ millions) |
|------|--------------------|
| 1988 | 2.13 |
| 1989 | 18.10 |
| 1990 | 39.80 |
| 1991 | 81.40 |
| 1992 | 112.00 |

1. Determine the logarithmic straight-line equations for the sales data.
2. Sales increased by what percent annually?
3. What is the projected sales amount for 1993?

## EXERCISES

*The answers to the odd-numbered exercises are at the end of the book.*

5. Sally's Software, Inc. is a rapidly growing supplier of computer software to the Sarasota area. Sales for the last five years are given below.

| Year | Sales ($000) |
|------|--------------|
| 1987 | 1.1 |
| 1988 | 1.5 |
| 1989 | 2.0 |
| 1990 | 2.4 |
| 1991 | 3.1 |

   a. Determine the logarithmic straight-line equation.
   b. By what percent did sales increase, on the average, during the period?
   c. Estimate sales for the year 1994.

6. It appears that the imports of carbon black have been increasing by about 10 percent annually.

|  Year | Imports of carbon black (thousands of tons) |
|---|---|
| 1984 | 92.0 |
| 1985 | 101.0 |
| 1986 | 112.0 |
| 1987 | 124.0 |
| 1988 | 135.0 |
| 1989 | 149.0 |
| 1990 | 163.0 |
| 1991 | 180.0 |

a. Determinethe logarithmic straight-line equation.

b. By what percent did imports increase, on the average, during the period?

c. Estimate sales for the year 1994.

# Seasonal Variation

We mentioned that *seasonal variation* is another of the components of a time series. Business series, such as automobile sales, shipments of soft-drink bottles, and residential construction, have periods of above-average and below-average activity during the year.

In the area of production, one of the reasons for analyzing seasonal fluctuations is to have a sufficient supply of raw materials on hand to meet the varying seasonal demand. The glass container division of a large glass company, for example, manufactures nonreturnable beer bottles, returnable beer bottles, iodine bottles, aspirin bottles, bottles for rubber cement, and so on. The production scheduling department must know how many bottles to produce and when to produce each kind. A run of too many bottles of one kind may cause a serious storage problem. Production cannot be based entirely on orders on hand because many orders are telephoned in for immediate shipment. Since the demand for many of the bottles varies according to the season, a forecast a year or two in advance, by month, is essential to good scheduling.

An analysis of seasonal fluctuations over a period of years can also be of help in evaluating current sales. The typical sales of department stores in the United States, excluding mail-order sales, are expressed as indexes in Table 19–6. Each index represents the average sales for a period of seven years. The actual sales for some months were above average (which is represented by an index of 100.0 or more), and the sales for other months were below average. The index of 126.8 for December indicates that, typically, sales for December are 26.8 percent above the average for the year; the index of 86.0 for July indicates that department store sales for July are typically 14 percent below the average for the year.

## Table 19–6

**Typical Seasonal Indexes for U.S. Department Store Sales, Excluding Mail-Order Sales**

| Month | Index | Month | Index |
|---|---|---|---|
| January | 87.0 | July | 86.0 |
| February | 83.2 | August | 99.7 |
| March | 100.5 | September | 101.4 |
| April | 106.5 | October | 105.8 |
| May | 101.6 | November | 111.9 |
| June | 89.6 | December | 126.8 |

Source: Computed from data in the *Survey of Current Business*.

Suppose that an enterprising store manager, in an effort to stimulate sales during December, introduced a number of unique promotions, including bands of carolers strolling through the store singing holiday songs, large mechanical exhibits, and clerks dressed in Santa Claus costumes. When the index of sales was computed for that December, it was 150.0. Compared with the typical sales of 126.8, it was concluded that the promotional program was a huge success.

## DETERMINING A SEASONAL INDEX

Objective: To determine a set of "typical" seasonal indexes

A typical set of monthly indexes consists of 12 indexes that are representative of the data for a 12-month period. Logically, there are four typical seasonal indexes for data reported quarterly. Each index is a percent, with the average for the year equal to 100.0; that is, each monthly index indicates the level of sales, production, or other variable in relation to the annual average of 100.0. A typical index of 96.0 for January indicates that sales (or whatever the variable is) are usually 4 percent below the average for the year. An index of 107.2 for October means that the variable is typically 7.2 percent above the annual average.

Ratio-to-moving-average method

Several methods have been developed to measure the typical seasonal fluctuation in a time series. The method most commonly used to compute the typical seasonal pattern is called the **ratio-to-moving-average method.** It eliminates the trend, cyclical, and irregular components from the original data ($Y$). In the following discussion, $T$ refers to trend, $C$ to cyclical, $S$ to seasonal, and $I$ to irregular variation. The numbers that result are called the *typical seasonal index.*

We will discuss in detail the steps followed in arriving at typical seasonal indexes using the ratio-to-moving-average method. As before, simple figures are used to illustrate.

The data of interest might be monthly or quarterly. To illustrate, we have chosen the quarterly sales of Toys International. First we will show the steps needed to arrive at a set of typical quarterly indexes. Then we will apply a procedure by Hall and Adelman from their *Computerized Business Statistics,* a statistical software package published by Richard D. Irwin, Inc.

### ■ EXAMPLE

Toys International takes an inventory of its dolls, mechanical toys, and other products on hand every quarter. The value of the inventory, in millions of dollars, at the beginning of each quarter since 1987 is indicated in Table 19–7.

#### TABLE 19–7

#### Quarterly Inventory of Toys International (in $ millions)

| Year | Winter | Spring | Summer | Fall |
|------|--------|--------|--------|------|
| 1987 | $6.7 | $4.9 | $10.0 | $12.7 |
| 1988 | 6.5 | 4.8 | 9.8 | 13.6 |
| 1989 | 6.9 | 4.3 | 10.4 | 13.1 |
| 1990 | 7.0 | 5.5 | 10.8 | 15.0 |
| 1991 | 7.1 | 4.4 | 11.1 | 14.5 |
| 1992 | 8.0 | 4.2 | 11.4 | 14.9 |

What are the typical quarterly indexes using the ratio-to-moving-average method?

## ☑ SOLUTION

***STEP 1*** Refer to Table 19–8. Determine a four-quarter moving total. Starting with the winter quarter of 1987, we add $6.7, $4.9, $10.0, and $12.7. The total is $34.3 million (see column 2).

---

### TABLE  19–8

**Computations Needed for the Specific Seasonal Indexes**

| | | (1) Inventory ($ millions) | (2) Four-quarter moving total | (3) Four-quarter moving average | (4) Centered moving average | (5) Specific seasonal |
|---|---|---|---|---|---|---|
| Year | Quarter | | | | | |
| 1987 | Winter | $ 6.7 | | | | |
| | Spring | 4.9 | | | | |
| | | | $34.3 | 8.575 | | |
| | Summer | 10.0 | | | 8.550 | 117.0 |
| | | | 34.1 | 8.525 | | |
| | Fall | 12.7 | | | 8.513 | 149.2 |
| | | | 34.0 | 8.500 | | |
| 1988 | Winter | 6.5 | | | 8.475 | 76.7 |
| | | | 33.8 | 8.450 | | |
| | Spring | 4.8 | | | 8.563 | 56.1 |
| | | | 34.7 | 8.675 | | |
| | Summer | 9.8 | | | 8.725 | 112.3 |
| | | | 35.1 | 8.775 | | |
| | Fall | 13.6 | | | 8.713 | 156.1 |
| | | | 34.6 | 8.650 | | |
| 1989 | Winter | 6.9 | | | 8.725 | 79.1 |
| | | | 35.2 | 8.800 | | |
| | Spring | 4.3 | | | 8.738 | 49.2 |
| | | | 34.7 | 8.675 | | |
| | Summer | 10.4 | | | 8.688 | 119.7 |
| | | | 34.8 | 8.700 | | |
| | Fall | 13.1 | | | 8.850 | 148.0 |
| | | | 36.0 | 9.000 | | |
| 1990 | Winter | 7.0 | | | 9.050 | 77.3 |
| | | | 36.4 | 9.100 | | |
| | Spring | 5.5 | | | 9.338 | 58.9 |
| | | | 38.3 | 9.575 | | |
| | Summer | 10.8 | | | 9.588 | 112.6 |
| | | | 38.4 | 9.600 | | |
| | Fall | 15.0 | | | 9.463 | 158.5 |
| | | | 37.3 | 9.325 | | |
| 1991 | Winter | 7.1 | | | 9.363 | 75.8 |
| | | | 37.6 | 9.400 | | |
| | Spring | 4.4 | | | 9.338 | 47.1 |
| | | | 37.1 | 9.275 | | |
| | Summer | 11.1 | | | 9.388 | 118.2 |
| | | | 38.0 | 9.500 | | |
| | Fall | 14.5 | | | 9.475 | 153.0 |
| | | | 37.8 | 9.450 | | |
| 1992 | Winter | 8.0 | | | 9.488 | 84.3 |
| | | | 38.1 | 9.525 | | |
| | Spring | 4.2 | | | 9.575 | 43.9 |
| | | | 38.5 | 9.625 | | |
| | Summer | 11.4 | | | | |
| | Fall | 14.9 | | | | |

The four-quarter total in column 2 is "moved along" by adding the spring, summer, and fall inventories of 1987 and the 1988 winter inventory. That total is $34.1 million, found by $4.9 + 10.0 + 12.7 + 6.5$. Instead of adding the four inventory values on a hand calculator, we can subtract the winter 1987 inventory (6.7) from the initial total of $34.3 million and add the winter 1988 inventory (6.5). This gives $34.1 million. This procedure is continued until all the quarterly inventories are accounted for. Those four-quarter moving totals are given in column 2 in Table 19−8. Note that the first moving total (34.3) is positioned between the spring and summer of 1987. The next total (34.1) is positioned between summer and fall of 1987, and so on. Frequent checks of the totals should be made. For example, a check of the 1989 total inventory (34.7) positioned between spring and summer 1989 is made by adding the four figures for 1989 ($6.9 + 4.3 + 10.4 + 13.1 = 34.7$). It checks.

**STEP 2** Each quarterly moving total in column 2 is divided by 4 to give the four-quarter moving average. (See column 3.) All the moving averages are still positioned between quarters. For example, the first moving average (8.575) is positioned between spring and summer 1987.

**STEP 3** The moving averages are then centered. To determine the first centered moving average: $(8.575 + 8.525)/2 = 8.550$. The second is found by $(8.525 + 8.500)/2 = 8.513$, and so forth. Note in column 4 that a centered moving average is now positioned on a particular quarter.

**STEP 4** A *specific seasonal* for each quarter is then computed by dividing the value of the inventory in column 1 by the centered moving average in column 4. Each quotient is multiplied by 100.0 to convert it to an index. The first specific seasonal is 117.0, found by $(10.0/8.550)(100)$.

**STEP 5** The specific seasonals are organized in a table. (See Table 19−9.) Then either the mean, modified mean, or median is determined for each of the four quarters. We selected the mean.

**STEP 6** The four quarterly means (78.64, 51.04, 115.96, and 152.96 in Table 19−9) should theoretically total 400.0 because the average is set at 100.0. The total may not equal 400.0 due to rounding. In this problem the total of the means is 398.6. A *correction factor* is therefore applied to each of the four means to force them to total 400.

## TABLE 19−9

**Calculations Needed for the Typical Quarterly Indexes**

| Year | Quarter | | | | |
|---|---|---|---|---|---|
| | Winter | Spring | Summer | Fall | |
| 1987 | | | 117.0 | 149.2 | |
| 1988 | 76.7 | 56.1 | 112.3 | 156.1 | |
| 1989 | 79.1 | 49.2 | 119.7 | 148.0 | |
| 1990 | 77.3 | 58.9 | 112.6 | 158.5 | |
| 1991 | 75.8 | 47.1 | 118.2 | 153.0 | |
| 1992 | 84.3 | 43.9 | | | |
| Total | 393.2 | 255.2 | 579.80 | 764.8 | *Total* |
| Mean | 78.64 | 51.04 | 115.96 | 152.96 | 398.60 |
| Typical index | 78.92 | 51.22 | 116.37 | 153.50 | |

$$\text{Correction factor} = \frac{400}{\text{Total of the four means}} \qquad (19-6)$$

In this problem using formula (19−6):

$$\text{Correction factor} = \frac{400.0}{398.6} = 1.00351$$

To adjust the fall quarterly index, (1.00351)(152.96) = 153.50.

Each of the means has been adjusted upward. The four typical seasonal indexes are shown in Table 19−9 and plotted on the following chart.

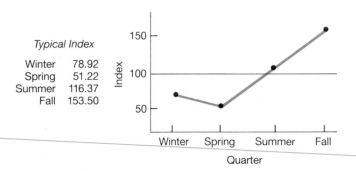

| Typical Index | |
|---|---|
| Winter | 78.92 |
| Spring | 51.22 |
| Summer | 116.37 |
| Fall | 153.50 |

Interpreting the fall index of 153.50, the toy inventory at the beginning of the fall quarter (about October 1) is typically 53.50 percent above the average for the year. Inventory is necessarily high in order to meet the impending shipments for the Christmas selling period.

Now to briefly discuss the reasoning underlying the preceding calculations. The original data in column 1 contain trend (*T*), cycle (*C*), seasonal (*S*) and irregular (*I*) components. The ultimate objective is to remove seasonal (*S*) from the original inventory valuation.

Columns 2 and 3 in Table 19−8 were concerned with deriving the centered moving average given in column 4. Basically, we "averaged out" the seasonal and irregular fluctuations from the original data in column 1. Thus, in column 4 we have only trend and cycle (*TC*).

Next we divided the inventory data in column 1 (*TCSI*) by the centered four-month moving average in column 4 (*TC*) to arrive at the specific seasonals in column 5 (*SI*). In terms of letters, *TCSI/TC = SI*. We multiplied *SI* by 100.0 in order to express the typical seasonal in index form.

Finally, we took the mean of all the winter typical indexes, all the spring indexes, and so on. This averaging eliminates most of the irregular fluctuations from the seasonals, and the resulting four indexes indicate the typical seasonal inventory pattern.

### A COMPUTER SOLUTION

As noted previously, a statistical software package called *Computerized Business Statistics,* developed by Hall and Adelman, has a routine for computing seasonal indexes. The following is the output obtained for the previous example. Much of the same information on the trend and seasonal-irregular components is shown. The final answers differ slightly, due to rounding, from those in Table 19−9. Use of a package such as Hall and Adelman's will greatly reduce computational time and the possibility of an error in arithmetic. The seasonal values obtained from the Hall and Adelman software package will be used in the analyses later in the chapter.

```
Model Type:                Classical - Seasonal Analysis
Number of Periods:              6
                    Classical Time Series (Seasonal)
Period    Quarter         Value           Trend          S-I
  1          1           6.7000           --            --
             2           4.9000           --            --
             3          10               8.5500        1.1696
             4          12.7000          8.5125        1.4919
  2          1           6.5000          8.4750        0.7670
             2           4.8000          8.5625        0.5606
             3           9.8000          8.7250        1.1232
             4          13.6000          8.7125        1.5610
  3          1           6.9000          8.7250        0.7908
             2           4.3000          8.7375        0.4921
             3          10.4000          8.6875        1.1971
             4          13.1000          8.8500        1.4802
  4          1           7               9.0500        0.7735
             2           5.5000          9.3375        0.5890
             3          10.8000          9.5875        1.1265
             4          15               9.4625        1.5852
  5          1           7.1000          9.3625        0.7583
             2           4.4000          9.3375        0.4712
             3          11.1000          9.3875        1.1824
             4          14.5000          9.4750        1.5303
  6          1           8               9.4875        0.8432
             2           4.2000          9.5750        0.4386
             3          11.4000           --            --
             4          14.9000           --            --
                   Seasonal Index by Quarter
                         Average SI      Seasonal
           Quarter       Component        Index
              1           0.7866         0.7905
              2           0.5103         0.5129
              3           1.1598         1.1656
              4           1.5297         1.5374
                   END OF ANALYSIS
```

Multiply by 100 to obtain index

## Self-Review 19-4

*The answers are at the end of the chapter.*

Teton Village, Wyoming, near Grand Teton Park and Yellowstone Park, contains shops, restaurants, and motels. They have two peak seasons—winter, for skiing on the 10,000-foot slopes, and summer, for tourists visiting the parks. The specific seasonals with respect to the total sales volume for recent years are:

1. Develop the typical seasonal sales pattern for Teton Village using the ratio-to-moving-average method.

2. Explain the typical index for the winter season.

| Year | Winter | Spring | Summer | Fall |
|------|--------|--------|--------|------|
| 1986 | 117.0 | 80.7 | 129.6 | 76.1 |
| 1987 | 118.6 | 82.5 | 121.4 | 77.0 |
| 1988 | 114.0 | 84.3 | 119.9 | 75.0 |
| 1989 | 120.7 | 79.6 | 130.7 | 69.6 |
| 1990 | 125.2 | 80.2 | 127.6 | 72.0 |

# EXERCISES

*The answers to the odd-numbered exercises are at the end of the book.*

7. Victor Anderson, the owner of Anderson Belts, Inc., is studying absenteeism among his employees. His work force is very small, consisting of only five employees. For the last three years he recorded the following number of employee absences, in days, for each quarter.

| | Quarter | | | |
|---|---|---|---|---|
| Year | I | II | III | IV |
| 1990 | 4 | 10 | 7 | 3 |
| 1991 | 5 | 12 | 9 | 4 |
| 1992 | 6 | 16 | 12 | 4 |

Determine a typical seasonal index for each of the four quarters.

8. The Appliance Center sells a variety of electronic equipment and home appliances. For the last four years the following quarterly sales (in $ millions) were reported.

| | Quarter | | | |
|---|---|---|---|---|
| Year | I | II | III | IV |
| 1989 | 5.3 | 4.1 | 6.8 | 6.7 |
| 1990 | 4.8 | 3.8 | 5.6 | 6.8 |
| 1991 | 4.3 | 3.8 | 5.7 | 6.0 |
| 1992 | 5.6 | 4.6 | 6.4 | 5.9 |

Determine a typical seasonal index for each of the four quarters.

# DESEASONALIZING DATA

A set of typical indexes is very useful in adjusting a sales series, for example, for seasonal fluctuations. The resulting sales series is called **deseasonalized sales** or **seasonally adjusted sales.** The reason for deseasonalizing the sales series is to remove the seasonal fluctuations so that the trend and cycle can be studied. To illustrate the procedure, the quarterly inventory totals of Toys International from Table 19−9 are repeated in column 1 of Table 19−10. It is difficult to determine if the inventory of Toys International is increasing, decreasing, or remaining the same, because of the seasonal effects.

To remove the effect of seasonal variation, the inventory for each quarter (which contains trend, cyclical, irregular, and seasonal variations) is divided by the seasonal index for that quarter, that is, $TSCI/S = TCI$. For example, the actual inventory for the first quarter of 1987 was $6.7 million. The seasonal index for the first quarter is 79.05, using the Hall and Adelman results on page 705. The index of 79.05 indicates that inventory in the first quarter is typically 20.95 percent below the average for a typical quarter. By dividing the actual inventory of $6.7 million by 79.05 and multiplying the result by 100, the deseasonalized value of inventory, $8,475,600, is obtained for the first quarter of 1987. Since the seasonal component has been removed (divided out) from the quarterly inventory, the deseasonalized inventory contains only trend (*T*), cyclical (*C*), and irregular (*I*) components. Scanning the deseasonalized inventory in column 3 of Table 19−10, we see that the inventory of toys has remained somewhat constant over the six-year period.

## TADLE 19-10

### Inventory and Deseasonalized Inventory for Toys International

| Year | Period | Quarter | (1) Inventory | (2) Seasonal index | (3) Deseasonalized inventory |
|------|--------|---------|-----------|---------|---------------|
| 1987 | 1 | Winter | 6.7 | 79.05 | 8.4756 |
| | 2 | Spring | 4.9 | 51.29 | 9.5535 |
| | 3 | Summer | 10.0 | 116.56 | 8.5793 |
| | 4 | Fall | 12.7 | 153.74 | 8.2607 |
| 1988 | 5 | Winter | 6.5 | 79.05 | 8.2226 |
| | 6 | Spring | 4.8 | 51.29 | 9.3586 |
| | 7 | Summer | 9.8 | 116.56 | 8.4077 |
| | 8 | Fall | 13.6 | 153.74 | 8.8461 |
| 1989 | 9 | Winter | 6.9 | 79.05 | 8.7287 |
| | 10 | Spring | 4.3 | 51.29 | 8.3837 |
| | 11 | Summer | 10.4 | 116.56 | 8.9224 |
| | 12 | Fall | 13.1 | 153.74 | 8.5209 |
| 1990 | 13 | Winter | 7.0 | 79.05 | 8.8552 |
| | 14 | Spring | 5.5 | 51.29 | 10.7233 |
| | 15 | Summer | 10.8 | 116.56 | 9.2656 |
| | 16 | Fall | 15.0 | 153.74 | 9.7567 |
| 1991 | 17 | Winter | 7.1 | 79.05 | 8.9817 |
| | 18 | Spring | 4.4 | 51.29 | 8.5787 |
| | 19 | Summer | 11.1 | 116.56 | 9.5230 |
| | 20 | Fall | 14.5 | 153.74 | 9.4315 |
| 1992 | 21 | Winter | 8.0 | 79.05 | 10.1202 |
| | 22 | Spring | 4.2 | 51.29 | 8.1887 |
| | 23 | Summer | 11.4 | 116.56 | 9.7804 |
| | 24 | Fall | 14.9 | 153.74 | 9.6917 |

### USING DESEASONALIZED DATA TO FORECAST

The procedure for identifying trend and the seasonal adjustments can be combined to yield seasonally adjusted forecasts. To identify the trend we determine the least squares trend equation on the historical data. Then we project this trend into future periods, and finally we adjust these trend values to account for the seasonal factors. The following example will help to clarify.

### ◼ EXAMPLE

Toys International would like to forecast their inventory for each quarter of 1993. Use the information in Table 19-10 to determine the forecast.

### ☑ SOLUTION

The first step is to use the deseasonalized data in column 3 of Table 19-10 to determine the least squares trend equation. The deseasonalized trend equation is:

$$Y' = a + bt$$

where:

$Y'$  is the estimated trend for Toys International inventory in period $t$.

$a$  is the intercept of the trend line at time 0.

$b$  is the slope of the trend line.

The winter quarter of 1987 is the period $t = 1$, and $t = 24$ corresponds to the fourth quarter of 1992. (See Column 1 in Table 19–11.) The sums needed to compute $a$ and $b$ are also shown in Table 19–11.

---

**TABLE 19–11**

**Deseasonalized Inventory for Toys International and Data for Determining Trend Line**

| Year | Quarter | (1) $t$ | (2) $Y$ | (3) $tY$ | (4) $t^2$ |
|------|---------|-----|-------|---------|------|
| 1987 | Winter | 1 | 8.4756 | 8.4756 | 1 |
| | Spring | 2 | 9.5535 | 19.1070 | 4 |
| | Summer | 3 | 8.5793 | 25.7379 | 9 |
| | Fall | 4 | 8.2607 | 33.0428 | 16 |
| 1988 | Winter | 5 | 8.2226 | 41.1130 | 25 |
| | Spring | 6 | 9.3586 | 56.1516 | 36 |
| | Summer | 7 | 8.4077 | 58.8539 | 49 |
| | Fall | 8 | 8.8461 | 70.7688 | 64 |
| 1989 | Winter | 9 | 8.7287 | 78.5583 | 81 |
| | Spring | 10 | 8.3837 | 83.8370 | 100 |
| | Summer | 11 | 8.9224 | 98.1464 | 121 |
| | Fall | 12 | 8.5209 | 102.2508 | 144 |
| 1990 | Winter | 13 | 8.8552 | 115.1176 | 169 |
| | Spring | 14 | 10.7233 | 150.1262 | 196 |
| | Summer | 15 | 9.2656 | 138.9840 | 225 |
| | Fall | 16 | 9.7567 | 156.1072 | 256 |
| 1991 | Winter | 17 | 8.9817 | 152.6889 | 289 |
| | Spring | 18 | 8.5787 | 154.4166 | 324 |
| | Summer | 19 | 9.5230 | 180.9370 | 361 |
| | Fall | 20 | 9.4315 | 188.6300 | 400 |
| 1992 | Winter | 21 | 10.1202 | 212.5242 | 441 |
| | Spring | 22 | 8.1887 | 180.1514 | 484 |
| | Summer | 23 | 9.7804 | 224.9492 | 529 |
| | Fall | 24 | 9.6917 | 232.6008 | 576 |
| | | 300 | 217.1565 | 2,763.2762 | 4,900 |

---

Determining $a$ and $b$ from formulas (19–3) and (19–4):

$$b = \frac{\Sigma tY - (\Sigma Y)(\Sigma t)/n}{\Sigma t^2 - (\Sigma t)^2/n} = \frac{2,763.2762 - 217.1565(300)/24}{4,900 - (300)^2/24}$$

$$= 0.0425$$

$$a = \frac{\Sigma Y}{n} - b\left(\frac{\Sigma t}{n}\right) = \frac{217.1565}{24} - 0.0425\left(\frac{300}{24}\right)$$

$$= 8.5169$$

The trend equation is

$$Y' = 8.5169 + 0.0425t$$

The slope of the trend line is 0.0425. This indicates that over the 24 quarters the deseasonalized inventory growth rate is 0.0425 ($ millions), or $42,500 per quarter. The value 8.5169 is the intercept of the trend line on the $Y$-axis when $t = 0$.

If we assume that the past 24 periods are a reasonably good indicator of future inventory, we can use the trend equation to estimate the future inventory. For example, in the winter quarter of 1993 $t = 25$, so the estimated inventory for that period is $9,579,400, found by

$$Y' = 8.5169 + 0.0425(25) = 9.5794$$

Using the trend equation, we can forecast inventories for the other quarters of 1993. These are shown in Table 19–12.

Now that we have the forecasts for the four quarters of 1993, we can seasonally adjust them. The seasonal index for the winter quarter is 79.05 (see the Hall and Adelman computer solution earlier in this chapter), so we can estimate inventory in this quarter by 9.5794(79.05)/100 = 7.5725. The estimates for the quarters are reported in the last column of Table 19–12. Notice how the seasonal adjustments drastically increase the inventory estimates for the last two quarters of the year.

### TABLE   19–12

#### Quarterly Forecasts for Toys International for 1993

| Quarter | $t$ | (1)<br>Estimated<br>inventory | (2)<br>Seasonal<br>index | (3)<br>Quarterly<br>forecast |
|---|---|---|---|---|
| Winter | 25 | 9.5794 | 79.05 | 7.5725 |
| Spring | 26 | 9.6219 | 51.29 | 4.9351 |
| Summer | 27 | 9.6644 | 116.56 | 11.2648 |
| Fall | 28 | 9.7069 | 156.74 | 15.2146 |

### Self-Review 19–5

*The answers are at the end of the chapter.*

The Westberg Electric Company sells electric motors to customers in the Jamestown, New York, area. The monthly trend equation, based on five years of monthly data is

$$Y' = 4.40 + 0.50t$$

The seasonal factor for the month of January is 120, and it is 95 for February. Determine the seasonally adjusted forecast for January and February of the sixth year.

## EXERCISES

*The answers to the odd-numbered exercises are at the end of the book.*

9. The planning department of Padget and Kure Shoes, the manufacturer of an exclusive brand of women's shoes, developed the following trend equation, in millions of pairs, based on five years of quarterly data.

$$Y' = 3.30 + 1.75t$$

*Courtesy Ametek*

The following table gives the seasonal factors for each quarter.

|        | Quarter |       |       |       |
|--------|---------|-------|-------|-------|
|        | I       | II    | III   | IV    |
| Index  | 110.0   | 120.0 | 80.0  | 90.0  |

Determine the seasonally adjusted forecast for each of the four quarters of the sixth year.

10. Team Sports, Inc. sells sporting goods to high schools and colleges via a nationally distributed catalog. Management at Team Sports estimates they will sell 2,000 Wilson Model A2000 catcher's mitts next year. The deseasonalized sales are projected to be the same for each of the four quarters next year. The seasonal factor for the second quarter is 145. Determine the seasonally adjusted sales for the second quarter of next year.

11. Refer to Exercise 7, regarding the absences at Anderson Belts, Inc. Use the seasonal indexes you computed to determine the deseasonalized absences. Determine the trend equation based on the quarterly data for the three years. Forecast the seasonally adjusted absences for 1993.

12. Refer to Exercise 8, regarding sales at the Appliance Center. Use the seasonal indexes you computed to determine the deseasonalized sales. Determine the trend equation based on the quarterly data for the four years. Forecast the seasonally adjusted sales for 1993.

# CHAPTER OUTLINE

I. A time series is a collection of data over a period of time.
   A. The trend is the long-run direction of the time series.
   B. The cyclical component is the fluctuation above and below the trend line.
   C. The seasonal variation is the pattern in a time series within a year. These patterns tend to repeat themselves from year to year for most businesses.
   D. The irregular variation is divided into two components.
      1. The episodic variations are unpredictable, but they can usually be identified. A flood is an example.
      2. The residual variations are random in nature.
II. The long-run trend equation is $Y' = a + bt$, where $a$ is the $Y$-intercept, $b$ is the slope of the line, and $t$ is time.
   A. The trend equation is determined using the least squares principle.
   B. If the trend is not linear, but rather the increases tend to be of a constant percent, the $Y$ values are converted to logarithms, and a least squares equation is determined using the logs.
III. A moving average is used to smooth the trend in a time series.
IV. A seasonal factor can be estimated using the ratio-to-moving-average method.
   A. The six-step procedure yields a seasonal index for each period.
      1. Seasonal factors are usually computed on a monthly or a quarterly basis.
      2. The seasonal factor is used to adjust forecasts, taking into account the effects of the season.

# EXERCISES

*The answers to the odd-numbered exercises are at the end of the book.*

13. Refer to the diagram on the top of page 711.

   a. Estimate the linear equation for the following production series by drawing a straight line through the data. Use 1970 as the origin.
   b. What is the average annual decrease in production?
   c. Based on the trend equation, what is the forecast for 1995?

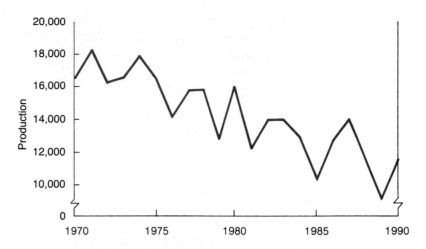

14. a. Estimate the trend equation for the following personal income series. Use 1978 as the origin, or year 0.

b. What is the average annual increase in personal income?

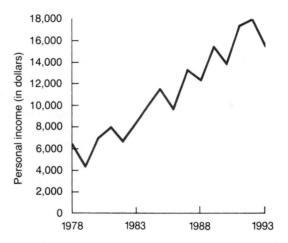

15. The asset turnovers, excluding cash and short-term investments, for the RNC Company from 1980 to 1990 are:

| 1980 | 1981 | 1982 | 1983 | 1984 | 1985 | 1986 | 1987 | 1988 | 1989 | 1990 |
|------|------|------|------|------|------|------|------|------|------|------|
| 1.11 | 1.28 | 1.17 | 1.10 | 1.06 | 1.14 | 1.24 | 1.33 | 1.38 | 1.50 | 1.65 |

a. Plot the data.

b. Determine the least squares trend equation.

c. Calculate the points on the trend line for 1983 and 1989, and plot the line on the graph.

d. Estimate the asset turnover for 1995.

e. How much did the asset turnover increase per year, on the average, from 1980 to 1990?

16. A historical study conducted on the Kiesier Corporation's dividends on preferred stocks from 1980 to 1989 showed:

| 1980 | 1981 | 1982 | 1983 | 1984 | 1985 | 1986 | 1987 | 1988 | 1989 |
|------|------|------|------|------|------|------|------|------|------|
| $2.90 | $2.80 | $2.60 | $2.60 | $2.40 | $1.80 | $0.90 | $0.70 | $0.70 | $1.40 |

    a.    Plot the data.

    b.    Determine the least squares trend equation.

    c.    Calculate the points on the trend line for 1982 and 1989, and plot the line on the graph.

    d.    Estimate the dividends for 1994.

    e.    How much did the dividends increase (or decrease) on the average, from 1980 to 1990?

17. The sales of paper and paper products (in millions of dollars) by Cascade, Inc. since 1982 are:

| 1982 | 1983 | 1984 | 1985 | 1986 | 1987 | 1988 | 1989 | 1990 | 1991 | 1992 |
|------|------|------|------|------|------|------|------|------|------|------|
| 841 | 829 | 1,042 | 1,256 | 1,405 | 1,314 | 1,412 | 1,660 | 1,874 | 1,853 | 2,156 |

    a.    Plot the data.

    b.    Determine the least squares trend equation.

    c.    Calculate the points on the straight line for 1984 and 1990. Then plot the line on the graph.

    d.    By how much did the sales volume increase per year, on the average, during the period?

    e.    Predict the sales for 1997.

18. The sales of building products by Cascade, Inc. since 1982 (in millions of dollars) are:

| 1982 | 1983 | 1984 | 1985 | 1986 | 1987 | 1988 | 1989 | 1990 | 1991 | 1992 |
|------|------|------|------|------|------|------|------|------|------|------|
| 1,114 | 1,288 | 1,360 | 1,250 | 1,084 | 921 | 1,268 | 1,278 | 957 | 986 | 1,030 |

    a.    Plot the data in a chart.

    b.    Determine the least squares trend equation.

    c.    Calculate the points on the line for 1983 and 1989. Then plot the line on the chart.

    d.    Predict the sales for 1998.

    e.    What is the average annual increase (or decrease) in sales during the period?

19. If plotted on arithmetic paper, the following sales series would appear curvilinear. This indicates that sales are increasing at a somewhat constant annual rate (percent). To fit the sales, therefore, a logarithmic straight-line equation should be used.

| Year | Sales ($ millions) |
|------|------|
| 1982 | 8.0 |
| 1983 | 10.4 |
| 1984 | 13.5 |
| 1985 | 17.6 |
| 1986 | 22.8 |
| 1987 | 29.3 |
| 1988 | 39.4 |
| 1989 | 50.5 |
| 1990 | 65.0 |
| 1991 | 84.1 |
| 1992 | 109.0 |

    a.    Determine the logarithmic straight-line equation.

    b.    Determine the coordinates of the points on the logarithmic straight line for 1985 and 1990.

    c.    By what percent did sales increase per year, on the average, during the period from 1982 to 1992?

    d.    Based on the equation, what are the estimated sales for 1993?

20. Reported below are the amounts spent on advertising ($ billions) from 1984 to 1990.

| Year | Amount |
|------|--------|
| 1984 | 88.1 |
| 1985 | 94.7 |
| 1986 | 102.1 |
| 1987 | 109.8 |
| 1988 | 118.1 |
| 1989 | 125.6 |
| 1990 | 132.6 |

   a. Determine the logarithmic straight-line equation.

   b. Estimate the advertising expenses for 1993.

   c. By what percent did advertising expense increase during the period?

21. The numbers of households (in millions) in the United States with videocassette recorders (VCRs) for each year from 1980 to 1989 are shown below.

| Year | Number |
|------|--------|
| 1980 | 0.8 |
| 1981 | 1.4 |
| 1982 | 3.0 |
| 1983 | 4.6 |
| 1984 | 8.9 |
| 1985 | 17.6 |
| 1986 | 30.9 |
| 1987 | 42.6 |
| 1988 | 51.4 |
| 1989 | 58.4 |

   a. Determine the logarithmic straight-line equation.

   b. Estimate the number of households with VCRs in 1993.

   c. By what percent did the number of households with VCRs increase during the period?

22. The production of the Reliable Manufacturing Company for 1988 and part of 1989 follows.

| Month | 1988 production (000) | 1989 production (000) |
|-------|-----------------------|-----------------------|
| January | 6 | 7 |
| February | 7 | 9 |
| March | 12 | 14 |
| April | 8 | 9 |
| May | 4 | 5 |
| June | 3 | 4 |
| July | 3 | 4 |
| August | 5 | |
| September | 14 | |
| October | 6 | |
| November | 7 | |
| December | 6 | |

   a. Using the ratio-to-moving-average method, determine the specific seasonals for July, August, and September 1988.

   b. Assume the specific seasonal indexes in the following table are correct. Insert in the table the specific seasonals you computed in part a for July, August, and September 1988, and determine the 12 typical seasonal indexes.

| Year | Jan. | Feb. | Mar. | Apr. | May | June | July | Aug. | Sept. | Oct. | Nov. | Dec. |
|------|------|------|------|------|------|------|------|------|-------|------|------|------|
| 1988 | | | | | | | ? | ? | ? | 92.1 | 106.5 | 92.9 |
| 1989 | 88.9 | 102.9 | 178.9 | 118.2 | 60.1 | 43.1 | 44.0 | 74.0 | 200.9 | 90.0 | 101.9 | 90.9 |
| 1990 | 87.6 | 103.7 | 170.2 | 125.9 | 59.4 | 48.6 | 44.2 | 77.2 | 196.5 | 89.6 | 113.2 | 80.6 |
| 1991 | 79.8 | 105.6 | 165.8 | 124.7 | 62.1 | 41.7 | 48.2 | 72.1 | 203.6 | 80.2 | 103.0 | 94.2 |
| 1992 | 89.0 | 112.1 | 182.9 | 115.1 | 57.6 | 56.9 | | | | | | |

    c.   Interpret the typical seasonal index.

23. The sales of Andre's Boutique for 1988 and part of 1989 are:

| Month | 1988 sales ($000) | 1989 sales ($000) |
|-------|-------------------|-------------------|
| January | 78 | 65 |
| February | 72 | 60 |
| March | 80 | 72 |
| April | 110 | 97 |
| May | 92 | 86 |
| June | 86 | 72 |
| July | 81 | 65 |
| August | 85 | 61 |
| September | 90 | 75 |
| October | 98 | |
| November | 115 | |
| December | 130 | |

    a.   Using the ratio-to-moving-average method, determine the specific seasonals for July, August, September, and October 1988.

    b.   Assume the specific seasonals in the following table are correct. Insert in the table the specific seasonals you computed in part a for July, August, September, and October 1988, and determine the 12 typical seasonal indexes.

| Year | Jan. | Feb. | Mar. | Apr. | May | June | July | Aug. | Sept. | Oct. | Nov. | Dec. |
|------|------|------|------|------|------|------|------|------|-------|------|------|------|
| 1988 | | | | | | | ? | ? | ? | ? | 123.6 | 150.9 |
| 1989 | 83.9 | 77.6 | 86.1 | 118.7 | 99.7 | 92.0 | 87.0 | 91.4 | 97.3 | 105.4 | 124.9 | 140.1 |
| 1990 | 86.7 | 72.9 | 86.2 | 121.3 | 96.6 | 92.0 | 85.5 | 93.6 | 98.2 | 103.2 | 126.1 | 141.7 |
| 1991 | 85.6 | 65.8 | 89.2 | 125.6 | 99.6 | 94.4 | 88.9 | 90.2 | 100.2 | 102.7 | 121.6 | 139.6 |
| 1992 | 77.3 | 81.2 | 85.8 | 115.7 | 100.3 | 89.7 | | | | | | |

    c.   Interpret the typical seasonal index.

24. The quarterly production of pine lumber, in millions of board feet, by Northwest Lumber since 1986 is:

| | Quarter | | | |
|------|--------|--------|--------|------|
| Year | Winter | Spring | Summer | Fall |
| 1986 | 7.8 | 10.2 | 14.7 | 9.3 |
| 1987 | 6.9 | 11.6 | 17.5 | 9.3 |
| 1988 | 8.9 | 9.7 | 15.3 | 10.1 |
| 1989 | 10.7 | 12.4 | 16.8 | 10.7 |
| 1990 | 9.2 | 13.6 | 17.1 | 10.3 |

    a.   Determine the typical seasonal pattern for the production data using the ratio-to-moving-average method.

    b.   Interpret the pattern.

    c.    Deseasonalize the data, and determine the trend equation.

    d.    Project the seasonally adjusted production for the four quarters of 1991.

25. Work Gloves Corp. is reviewing its quarterly sales of Toughie, the most durable glove they produce. The numbers of pairs produced (in thousands) by quarter are:

| | Quarter | | | |
|---|---|---|---|---|
| | I | II | III | IV |
| Year | Jan.–Mar. | Apr.–June | July–Sept. | Oct.–Dec. |
| 1987 | 142 | 312 | 488 | 208 |
| 1988 | 146 | 318 | 512 | 212 |
| 1989 | 160 | 330 | 602 | 187 |
| 1990 | 158 | 338 | 572 | 176 |
| 1991 | 162 | 380 | 563 | 200 |
| 1992 | 162 | 362 | 587 | 205 |

    a.    Using the ratio-to-moving-average method, determine the four typical quarterly indexes.

    b.    Interpret the typical seasonal pattern.

26. Sales of aluminum, by quarter, since 1985 are shown below (in $ millions).

| | Quarter | | | |
|---|---|---|---|---|
| Year | I | II | III | IV |
| 1985 | 210 | 180 | 60 | 246 |
| 1986 | 214 | 216 | 82 | 230 |
| 1987 | 246 | 228 | 91 | 280 |
| 1988 | 258 | 250 | 113 | 298 |
| 1989 | 279 | 267 | 116 | 304 |
| 1990 | 302 | 290 | 114 | 310 |
| 1991 | 321 | 291 | 120 | 320 |

    a.    Determine the typical seasonal patterns for sales using the ratio-to-moving average method.

    b.    Deseasonalize the data, and determine the trend equation.

    c.    Project the sales for 1992, and then seasonally adjust each quarter.

27. The inventory turnover rates for Bassett Wholesale Enterprises, by quarter, are:

| | Quarter | | | |
|---|---|---|---|---|
| Year | I | II | III | IV |
| 1988 | 4.4 | 6.1 | 11.7 | 7.2 |
| 1989 | 4.1 | 6.6 | 11.1 | 8.6 |
| 1990 | 3.9 | 6.8 | 12.0 | 9.7 |
| 1991 | 5.0 | 7.1 | 12.7 | 9.0 |
| 1992 | 4.3 | 5.2 | 10.8 | 7.6 |

    a.    Arrive at the four typical quarterly turnover rates for the Bassett Company using the ratio-to-moving-average method.

    b.    Deseasonalize the data, and determine the trend equation.

    c.    Project the turnover rates for 1993, and seasonally adjust each quarter.

28. The following is the enrollment at the University of Toledo from 1967 until 1991. Develop both a linear and a logarithmetic trend equation. Estimate the enrollment for 1993 using both equations. Which trend equation would you recommend? Why?

| Year | Enrollment | Year | Enrollment |
|------|-----------|------|-----------|
| 1967 | 12,755 | 1980 | 20,270 |
| 1968 | 13,501 | 1981 | 21,117 |
| 1969 | 14,489 | 1982 | 21,386 |
| 1970 | 15,158 | 1983 | 21,589 |
| 1971 | 14,903 | 1984 | 21,039 |
| 1972 | 14,669 | 1985 | 21,238 |
| 1973 | 14,343 | 1986 | 21,176 |
| 1974 | 15,730 | 1987 | 21,740 |
| 1975 | 17,109 | 1988 | 22,806 |
| 1976 | 17,204 | 1989 | 23,928 |
| 1977 | 17,498 | 1990 | 24,781 |
| 1978 | 17,257 | 1991 | 24,969 |
| 1979 | 18,246 | | |

29. Ray Anderson, owner of the Anderson Ski Lodge in upstate New York, is interested in forecasting the number of visitors for the upcoming year. The following data are available, by quarter since 1986. Develop a seasonal index for each quarter. How many visitors would you expect for each quarter of 1993, if Ray projects that there will be a 10 percent increase from the total number of visitors in 1992? Determine the trend equation, project the number of visitors for 1993, and seasonally adjust the forecast. Which forecast would you choose?

| Year | Quarter | Visitors | Year | Quarter | Visitors |
|------|---------|----------|------|---------|----------|
| 1986 | I | 86 | 1990 | I | 188 |
| | II | 62 | | II | 172 |
| | III | 28 | | III | 128 |
| | IV | 94 | | IV | 198 |
| 1987 | I | 106 | 1991 | I | 208 |
| | II | 82 | | II | 202 |
| | III | 48 | | III | 154 |
| | IV | 114 | | IV | 220 |
| 1988 | I | 140 | 1992 | I | 246 |
| | II | 120 | | II | 240 |
| | III | 82 | | III | 190 |
| | IV | 154 | | IV | 252 |
| 1989 | I | 162 | | | |
| | II | 140 | | | |
| | III | 100 | | | |
| | IV | 174 | | | |

30. The enrollment in the College of Business at Midwestern University by quarter since 1988 is:

| | Quarter | | | |
|------|--------|--------|--------|------|
| Year | Winter | Spring | Summer | Fall |
| 1988 | 2,033 | 1,871 | 714 | 2,318 |
| 1989 | 2,174 | 2,069 | 840 | 2,413 |
| 1990 | 2,370 | 2,254 | 927 | 2,704 |
| 1991 | 2,625 | 2,478 | 1,136 | 3,001 |
| 1992 | 2,803 | 2,668 | — | — |

Using the ratio-to-moving-average method:

a. Determine the four quarterly indexes.

b. Interpret the quarterly pattern of enrollment. Does the seasonal variation surprise you?

c. Compute the trend equation, and forecast the 1993 enrollment by quarter.

# Chapter 19 Examination

*The answers are at the end of the chapter.*

1. The numbers of computers sold by P. C. Modem Computers, Inc. by year for the last four years are:

   | Year | Sales (hundreds) |
   |------|------------------|
   | 1988 | 10.1 |
   | 1989 | 17.5 |
   | 1990 | 25.0 |
   | 1991 | 31.3 |

   Determine the least squares equation, and estimate sales for 1993 and 1994. Code 1988 as 1.

2. Following are the quarterly sales for a time series.

   | Year | Quarter | Sales |
   |------|---------|-------|
   | 1992 | I | 26 |
   |      | II | 14 |
   |      | III | 6 |
   |      | IV | 10 |
   | 1993 | I | 34 |
   |      | II | 20 |

   a. Determine the trend and cyclical components for the third and fourth quarters of 1992.

   b. Determine the seasonal and irregular components for the third and fourth quarters of 1992.

3. The trend equation describing the monthly sales, in thousands of units, for a large manufacturer of snow blowers is

   $$Y' = 2.50 + 4.56t$$

   a. The equation was developed using five years of monthly data. Determine the projected number of snow blowers sold in April of the sixth year. Code the first quarter as 1.

   b. The seasonal index for the month of April is 75.0. Determine the seasonally adjusted sales forecast for April of the sixth year.

# Answers

19–1  1.

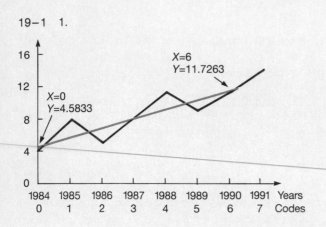

2.  $Y' = a + bt = 4.5833 + 1.1905t$ (in thousands)

$$b = \frac{295 - (28)(70)/8}{140 - (28)^2/8} = \frac{50}{42} = 1.1905$$

$$a = \frac{70}{8} - 1.1905\left(\frac{28}{8}\right) = 4.5833$$

3.  For 1984:

$$Y' = 4.5833 + 1.1905(0) = 4.5833$$

for 1990:

$$Y' = 4.5833 + 1.1905(6) = 11.7263$$

4.  For 1994, $t = 10$, so

$$Y' = 4.5833 + 1.1905(10) = 16.488$$

or 16,488 king-size rockers.

19–2  1.

| Year | Production (000) | Three-year moving total | Three-year moving average |
|------|------------------|-------------------------|---------------------------|
| 1987 | 2  | —  | —  |
| 1988 | 6  | 12 | 4  |
| 1989 | 4  | 15 | 5  |
| 1990 | 5  | 12 | 4  |
| 1991 | 3  | 18 | 6  |
| 1992 | 10 | —  | —  |

2.

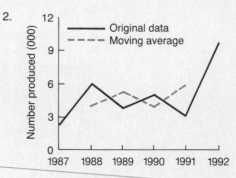

3.  Comment: The three-year moving average is not a good fit. The statistician must search for a better-fitting line.

19–3  1.

| Year | $Y$ | $\log Y$ | $t$ | $t \log Y$ | $t^2$ |
|------|------|---------|-----|-----------|-------|
| 1988 | 2.13 | 0.3284 | 0 | 0 | 0 |
| 1989 | 18.10 | 1.2577 | 1 | 1.2577 | 1 |
| 1990 | 39.80 | 1.5999 | 2 | 3.1998 | 4 |
| 1991 | 81.40 | 1.9106 | 3 | 5.7318 | 9 |
| 1992 | 112.00 | 2.0492 | 4 | 8.1968 | 16 |
|      |       | 7.1458 | 10 | 18.3861 | 30 |

$$b = \frac{18.3861 - (10)(7.1458)/5}{30 - (10)^2/5} = \frac{4.0945}{10}$$

$$= 0.40945$$

$$a = \frac{7.1458}{5} - 0.40945\left(\frac{10}{5}\right) = 0.61026$$

$\log Y' = 0.61026 + 0.40945t$

2.  About 156.7 percent. The antilog of 0.40945 is 2.567, and subtracting 1 yields 1.567.

3.  About 454.5, found by $\log Y' = 0.61026 + 0.40945(5) = 2.65751$. The antilog of 2.65751 is 454.5.

19–4  1.  The following values are from the Hall and Adelman package. Due to rounding, your figures might be slightly different.

|  | Winter | Spring | Summer | Fall |
|--|--------|--------|--------|------|
| Mean | 119.35 | 81.66 | 125.31 | 74.24 |
| Typical seasonal | 119.35 | 81.66 | 125.31 | 74.24 |

No correction is needed.

2. Total sales at Teton Village for the winter season are typically 19.35 percent above the annual average.

19–5    The forecast value for January of the sixth year is 34.9, found by

$$Y' - 4.40 + 0.50(61) = 34.9$$

Seasonally adjusting the forecast, $34.9(120)/100 = 41.88$. For February, $Y' = 4.40 + 0.50(62) = 35.4$. Then $(35.4)95/100 = 33.63$.

## Answers

# CHAPTER 19 EXAMINATION

1.

| Year | $t$ | Sales | $tY$ | $t^2$ |
|------|-----|-------|------|-------|
| 1988 | 1 | 10.1 | 10.1 | 1 |
| 1989 | 2 | 17.5 | 35.0 | 4 |
| 1990 | 3 | 25.0 | 75.0 | 9 |
| 1991 | 4 | 31.3 | 125.2 | 16 |
|      | 10 | 83.9 | 245.3 | 30 |

$$b = \frac{245.30 - 10(83.9)/4}{30 - (10)^2/4} = \frac{35.55}{5} = 7.11$$

$$a = \frac{83.9}{4} - 7.11\left(\frac{10}{4}\right) = 3.20$$

The estimates for 1993 and 1994 in hundreds, respectively, are:

$$Y' = 3.20 + 7.11(6) = 45.86$$
$$Y' = 3.20 + 7.11(7) = 52.97$$

2.

| Year | Quarter | Sales | Total | Moving average | Centered average |
|------|---------|-------|-------|----------------|------------------|
| 1992 | I | 26 | | | |
|      | II | 14 | | | |
|      |   |   | 56 | 14.0 | |
|      | III | 6 | | | 15.00 |
|      |   |   | 64 | 16.0 | |
|      | IV | 10 | | | 16.75 |
|      |   |   | 70 | 17.5 | |
| 1993 | I | 34 | | | |
|      | II | 20 | | | |

a. The trend and cyclical components for the third and fourth quarters of 1992 are 15.00 and 16.75.

b. The contribution of the seasonal and irregular components for the third quarter of 1992 is 0.40, found by 6/15. For the fourth quarter it is 0.597, found by 10/16.75.

3. a. April of the sixth year is the 64th month of the study, found by 5 years times 12 months, plus 4 months into the sixth year. The estimated number of snow blowers sold during that month is

$$Y' = 2.50 + 4.56(64) = 294.34$$

b. The seasonally adjusted forecast is 220.755, found by 291.84(75.0)/100.

*Energy—Courtesy Saab Scania*

# CHAPTER

# 20

# AN INTRODUCTION TO DECISION MAKING UNDER UNCERTAINTY

When you have completed this chapter, you will be able to:

**A** new branch of statistics, called *statistical decision theory,* has developed rapidly since the early 1950s. The term *Bayesian statistics* is also used to indicate this branch of statistics. It is given this name in honor of Reverend Thomas Bayes for his work in the 1700s. As the name implies, the major focus of statistical decision theory is on the process of making decisions. In contrast, classical statistics focuses on estimating a parameter, such as the population mean, constructing confidence intervals, or hypothesis testing.

Statistical decision theory is concerned with determining which decision, from a set of possible decisions, is optimal for a particular set of conditions. Consider the following examples of statistical decision theory problems.

- Ford Motor Company must decide whether to purchase assembled door locks for the new model Ford Escort or to manufacture and assemble the parts at their Sandusky, Ohio, plant. If sales of the Escort continue to increase, it will be more profitable to manufacture and assemble the parts. If sales level off or decline, it will be more profitable to purchase the door locks assembled. Which decision should be made?

- Haggar slacks has just developed new wool slacks that are very popular in the cold-weather regions of the country. Haggar would like to purchase commercial television time during the upcoming Super Bowl. If both teams that play in the Super Bowl are from warm parts of the country, Haggar estimates that only a small proportion of the viewers will be interested in the wool slacks. However, a match-up between the Cleveland Browns and the Chicago Bears, who come from cold climates, would reach a large proportion of viewers who wear wool slacks. What decision should Haggar make?

- General Electric is considering three options regarding the prices of refrigerators for next year. GE could (1) raise the prices 5 percent, (2) raise the prices 2.5 percent, or (3) leave the prices as they are. The final decision will be based on sales estimates and on GE's knowledge of what other refrigerator manufacturers might do.

In each of these cases note that the decision was characterized by several courses of action and several factors not under the control of the decision maker. For example, Haggar has no control over which teams reach the Super Bowl. These cases characterize the nature of decision making. Possible decision alternatives can be listed, possible future events determined, and even probabilities established, but *the decisions are made in the face of uncertainty.*

## ELEMENTS OF A DECISION

There are three components to any decision-making situation: (1) the choices available, or alternatives; (2) the states of nature, which are not under the control of the decision maker; and (3) the payoffs. These concepts will be explained in the following paragraphs.

Acts or alternatives

The **alternatives,** or acts, are the choices available to the decision maker. Ford can decide to manufacture and assemble the door locks in Sandusky, or they can decide to purchase them. To simplify our presentation, we are going to assume that the decision maker can select from a rather small number of outcomes. However, with the help of computers, the decision alternatives can be expanded to a large number of possibilities.

States of nature

Payoff

The **states of nature** are the uncontrollable future events. The state of nature that actually happens is outside the control of the decision maker. Ford does not know whether demand will remain high for the Escort. Haggar cannot determine whether warm-weather or cold-weather teams will play in the Super Bowl.

A **payoff** is needed for each combination of decision alternative and state of nature. Ford may estimate that if they assemble door locks at their Sandusky Plant and the demand for Escorts is low, the payoff will be $40,000. Conversely, if they purchase the door locks assembled and the demand is high, the payoff is estimated to be $22,000.

The main elements of the decision problem under conditions of uncertainty are identified schematically:

Explanatory statements

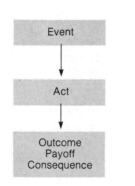

Uncertainty regarding future demand.
State of nature (future demand) unknown.
Decision maker has no control over state of nature.

Two or more courses of action open to decision maker.
Decision maker must evaluate alternatives.
Decision maker selects a course of action based on certain criteria. Depending on the set of circumstances, these criteria may be quantitative, psychological, sociological, and so on.

Profit.
Break even.
Loss.

In many cases we can make better decisions if we establish probabilities for the various states of nature. These probabilities may be based on historical data or subjective estimates. Ford may estimate the probability of continued high demand as .70. GE may estimate the probability to be .25 that Sears and other manufacturers will raise the prices of their refrigerators.

# A Case Involving Decision Making under Conditions of Uncertainty

At the outset it should be emphasized that this case description includes only the fundamental concepts found in a decision-making problem. The purpose of examining the case is to explain the logical procedure that might be followed in the simplest of problems. In most real-world problems, there would be many other variables to consider.

The first step is to set up a payoff table.

## Payoff Table

Bob Hill, a small investor, has $1,100 to invest. He has studied the performance of several common stocks and narrowed his choice to three, namely, Kayser Chemicals, Rim Homes, and Texas Electronics. He estimated that if his $1,100 were invested in Kayser Chemicals and a strong bull market developed by the end of the year (that is, stock prices increased drastically), the value of his Kayser stock would more than double, to $2,400. However, if there were a bear market (i.e., stock prices declined), the value of his Kayser stock could conceivably drop to $1,000 by the end of the year.

Payoff table

His predictions regarding the value of his $1,100 investment for the three stocks for a bull market and for a bear market are shown in Table 20–1. This table is a **payoff table.**

---

### TABLE 20–1

**Payoff Table for Three Common Stocks under Two Market Conditions**

| Purchase | Bull market $S_1$ | Bear market $S_2$ |
|---|---|---|
| Kayser Chemicals ($A_1$) | $2,400 | $1,000 |
| Rim Homes ($A_2$) | 2,200 | 1,100 |
| Texas Electronics ($A_3$) | 1,900 | 1,150 |

---

Decision alternatives

The various choices are called the **decision alternatives.** There are three in this problem. Let $A_1$ be the purchase of Kayser Chemicals, $A_2$ the purchase of Rim Homes, and $A_3$ the purchase of Texas Electronics. Whether the market turns out to be bear or bull is not under the control of Bob Hill. These uncontrolled future events are the states of nature. Let the bull market be represented by $S_1$ and the bear market by $S_2$.

## EXPECTED PAYOFF

If the payoff table were the only information available, the investor might take a conservative action and buy Texas Electronics in order to be assured of at least $1,150 at the end of the year (a slight profit). A speculative venture, however, might be to buy Kayser Chemicals, with the possibility of more than doubling the $1,100 investment.

Any decision regarding the purchase of one of the three common stocks made solely on the information in the payoff table would ignore the valuable historical records kept by Moody's, Value Line, and other investment services relative to stock price movements over a long period. A study of these records, for example, revealed that during the past 10 years stock market prices increased six times and declined only four times. Thus, it can be said that the probability of a market rise is .60 and the probability of a market decline is .40.

Expected payoff

Assuming that these historical frequencies are somewhat typical, we see that the payoff table and the probability estimates (.60 and .40) can be combined to arrive at the *expected payoff* of buying each of the three stocks. Expected payoff is also called *expected monetary value,* shortened to EMV. The calculations needed to arrive at the expected payoff for the act of purchasing Kayser Chemical are shown in Table 20–2.

---

### TABLE 20–2

Computing expected profit

**Expected Payoff for the Act of Buying Kayser Chemicals, EMV($A_1$)**

| State of nature | Payoff | Probability of state of nature | Expected value |
|---|---|---|---|
| Market rise, $S_1$ | $2,400 | .60 | $1,440 |
| Market decline, $S_2$ | 1,000 | .40 | 400 |
| | | | $1,840 |

---

To explain one expected monetary value calculation, note that if the investor had purchased Kayser Chemicals and the market prices declined, the value of the stock would be only $1,000 at the end of the year (from Table 20–1). Past experience, however, revealed that this event (a market decline) occurred only 40 percent of the time. In the long run, therefore, a market decline would contribute $400 to the total expected payoff from the stock, found by $1,000 × .40. Adding the $400 to the $1,400 expected under rising market conditions gives $1,840, the total payoff in the long run.

These calculations are summarized as follows.

$$EMV(A_i) = \Sigma P(S_j) \cdot V(A_i, S_j) \tag{20-1}$$

where:

$EMV(A_i)$   refers to the expected monetary value of the various decision alternatives. There may be many decisions possible. We will let 1 stand for the first decision, 2 for the second, and so on. The lower-case letter $i$ represents the entire set of decisions.

$P(S_j)$   refers to the probability of the various states of nature. There can be an unlimited number, so we will let $j$ represent the various possible outcomes.

$V(A_i, S_j)$   refers to the value of the various payoffs. Note that each payoff is the result of a combination of a decision alternative and a state of nature.

$EMV(A_1)$, the expected monetary value for the decision alternative of purchasing Kayser Chemical stock, is computed by:

$$EMV(A_1) = P(S_1) \cdot V(A_1, S_1) + P(S_2) \cdot V(A_1, S_2)$$
$$= .60(\$2,400) + .40(\$1,000) = \$1,840$$

Purchasing Kayser Chemicals stock is only one possible choice. The expected payoffs in the long run for the acts of buying Kayser Chemicals, Rim Homes, and Texas Electronics are given in Table 20–3.

### TABLE 20–3

**Expected Payoffs for Three Stocks**

| Purchase | Expected payoff |
|----------|-----------------|
| Kayser Chemicals | $1,840 |
| Rim Homes | 1,760 |
| Texas Electronics | 1,600 |

Kayser Chemicals—highest expected payoff

An analysis of the expected payoffs in Table 20–3 indicates that purchasing Kayser Chemicals would yield the greatest expected profit. This outcome is based upon (1) the investor's estimated future value of the stocks and (2) historical experience with respect to the rise and decline of stock prices. It should be emphasized that although the purchase of Kayser stock represents the best action under the expected-value criterion, the investor might decide to buy Texas Electronics stock in order to minimize the risk of losing some of the $1,100 investment.

## Self-Review 20–1

*The answers are at the end of the chapter.*

Verify the conclusion, shown in Table 20–3, that the expected payoff for the act of purchasing Rim Homes stock is $1,760.

## EXERCISES

*The answers to the odd-numbered exercises are at the end of the book.*

1. The following payoff table was developed. Compute the expected value for each of the three decisions. Let $P(S_1) = .30$, $P(S_2) = .50$, and $P(S_3) = .20$. Compute the expected monetary value for each of the alternatives. What decision would you recommend?

|  | State of nature | | |
| --- | --- | --- | --- |
| Alternative | $S_1$ | $S_2$ | $S_3$ |
| $A_1$ | $50 | $70 | $100 |
| $A_2$ | 90 | 40 | 80 |
| $A_3$ | 70 | 60 | 90 |

2. The Wilhelms Cola Company plans to market a new pineapple-flavored cola this coming summer. The decision is whether to package the cola in returnable or in no-return bottles. Currently, the state legislature is considering the elimination of no-return bottles. Tybo Wilhelms, president of Wilhelms Cola Company, has discussed the problem with his state representative and estimated the probability to be .70 that no-return bottles will be eliminated. The following table shows the estimated monthly profits (in thousands of dollars) if the pineapple cola is bottled in returnable versus no-return bottles. Of course, if the law is passed and the decision is to bottle the cola in no-return bottles, all profits would be from out-of-state sales. Compute the expected profit for both bottling decisions. Which decision do you recommend?

| Alternative | Law is passed ($S_1$) | Law is not passed ($S_2$) |
| --- | --- | --- |
| Returnable bottle | 80 | 40 |
| No-return bottle | 25 | 60 |

## OPPORTUNITY LOSS

Another way of arriving at a decision regarding which common stock to purchase is to determine the profit that might be lost because the exact state of nature (the market behavior) was not known at the time the investor bought the stock. This potential loss is called *opportunity loss* or *regret*. To illustrate, suppose the investor had purchased the common stock of Rim Homes, and a bull market developed. Further, suppose the value of his Rim Homes stock increased from $1,100 to $2,200, as anticipated. But had the investor bought Kayser Chemicals stock and market values increased, the value of his Kayser stock would be $2,400 (from Table 20–1). Thus, the investor missed making an extra profit of $200 by buying Rim Homes instead of Kayser Chemicals. To put it another way, the $200 represents the opportunity loss for not knowing the correct state of nature. If market prices did increase, the investor would have *regretted* buying Rim Homes. However, had the investor bought Kayser Chemicals and market prices increased, he would have had no regret, that is, no opportunity loss.

*Opportunity loss or regret*

The opportunity losses corresponding to this example are given in Table 20–4. Each amount is the outcome (opportunity loss) of a particular combination of acts and a state of nature, that is, stock purchase and market reaction.

It is apparent that the stock of Kayser Chemicals would be a good investment choice in a rising (bull) market, Texas Electronics would be the best buy in a declining (bear) market, and Rim Homes is somewhat of a compromise.

---

### TABLE 20–4

**Opportunity Losses for Various Combinations of Stock Purchase and Market Movement**

| | Opportunity loss | |
| Purchase | Market rise | Market decline |
| --- | --- | --- |
| Kayser Chemicals | $ 0 | $150 |
| Rim Homes | 200 | 50 |
| Texas Electronics | 500 | 0 |

---

### Self-Review 20–2

*The answers are at the end of the chapter.*

Refer to Table 20–4. Verify that:

1. The opportunity loss for Rim Homes given a market decline is $50.

2. The opportunity loss for Texas Electronics given a market rise is $500.

## EXERCISES

*The answers to the odd-numbered exercises are at the end of the book.*

3. Refer to Exercise 1. Develop an opportunity loss table. Determine the opportunity loss for each decision.

4. Refer to Exercise 2, involving the Wilhelms Cola Company. Develop an opportunity loss table, and determine the opportunity loss for each decision.

## EXPECTED OPPORTUNITY LOSS

Expected opportunity loss

The opportunity losses in Table 20–4 again ignore the historical experience of market movements. Recall that the probability of a market rise is .60 and that of a market decline .40. These probabilities and the opportunity losses are combined to determine the *expected opportunity loss*. The essential calculations are shown in Table 20–5 for the decision to purchase Rim Homes. The expected opportunity loss was found to be $140.

Interpreting, the expected opportunity loss of $140 means that, in the long run, the investor would lose the opportunity to make an additional profit of $140 if he decided to buy Rim Homes stock. This expected loss would be incurred because the investor was unable to accurately predict the trend of the stock market. In a bull market he could earn an additional $200 by purchasing the common stock of Kayser Chemicals, but in a bear market an investor could earn an additional $50 by buying Texas Electronics stock. When weighted by the probability of the event, the opportunity loss is $140.

## TABLE 20–5

**Expected Opportunity Loss for the Act of Buying Rim Homes Stock**

| State of nature | Opportunity loss | Probability of state of nature | Expected opportunity loss |
|---|---|---|---|
| Market rise, $S_1$ | $200 | .60 | $120 |
| Market decline, $S_2$ | 50 | .40 | 20 |
| | | | $140 |

These calculations are summarized as follows:

$$EOL(A_i) = P(S_j) \cdot R(A_i, S_j) \qquad (20-2)$$

where:

EOL($A_i$)   refers to the expected opportunity loss for a particular decision alternative.

$P(S_j)$   refers to the probability associated with the various states of nature.

$R(A_i, S_j)$   refers to the regret or loss for a particular combination of a state of nature and a decision alternative.

EOL($A_2$), the regret or opportunity loss for selecting Rim Homes, is computed as follows:

$$EOL(A_2) = P(S_1) \cdot R(A_2, S_1) + P(S_2) \cdot R(A_2, S_2)$$
$$= .60(\$200) + .40(\$50) = \$140$$

The expected opportunity losses for the three decision alternatives are given in Table 20–6. The lowest expected opportunity loss is $60, meaning that the investor would experience the least regret in the long run if he purchased Kayser Chemicals.

## TABLE 20–6

**Expected Opportunity Losses for the Three Stocks**

| Purchase | Expected opportunity loss |
|---|---|
| Kayser Chemicals | $ 60 |
| Rim Homes | 140 |
| Texas Electronics | 300 |

Incidentally, note that the decision to purchase Kayser Chemicals stock, based on the fact that it offers the lowest expected opportunity loss, reinforces the decision made previously, that Kayser stock would ultimately result in the highest payoff ($1,840). These two approaches (lowest expected opportunity loss and highest expected payoff) will always lead to the same decision concerning which course of action to follow.

### Self-Review 20-3

*The answers are at the end of the chapter.*

Referring to Table 20-6, verify that the expected opportunity loss for the act of purchasing Texas Electronics is $300.

## EXERCISES

*The answers to the odd-numbered exercises are at the end of the book.*

5. Refer to Exercises 1 and 3. Compute the expected opportunity losses.
6. Refer to Exercises 2 and 4. Compute the expected opportunity losses.

## MAXIMIN, MAXIMAX, AND MINIMAX REGRET STRATEGIES

Maximin strategy

Several financial advisors consider the purchase of Kayser Chemicals stock too risky. They note that the payoff might not be $1,840, but only $1,000 (from Table 20-1). Arguing that the stock market is too unpredictable, they urge the investor to take a more conservative position and buy Texas Electronics. This is called a **maximin strategy:** it maximizes the minimum gain. Based on the payoff table (Table 20-1), they reason that the investor would be assured of at least a $1,150 return, that is, a small profit. Those who subscribe to this somewhat pessimistic strategy are sometimes called **maximiners.**

Maximax strategy

At the other extreme are the optimistic *maximaxers.* If their **maximax strategy** were followed, the investor would purchase Kayser Chemicals stock. These extreme optimists stress that there is a possibility of selling the stock in the future for $2,400 instead of only $1,150, as advocated by the maximiners.

Minimax strategy

Another possible strategy is the **minimax regret strategy.** Financial advisors advocating this would scan the opportunity losses in Table 20-4 and select the stock that minimizes the maximum regret. In this example it would be Kayser Chemicals stock, with a maximum opportunity loss of $150.

## VALUE OF PERFECT INFORMATION

How much is "perfect" information worth?

Before deciding on a stock and purchasing it, the investor might want to consider ways of predicting the movement of the stock market in the near future. If he knew precisely what the market would do, he could maximize profit by always purchasing the correct stock. The question is: What is this advance information worth? The dollar value of this information is called the **expected value of perfect information,** written EVPI. In this problem, it would mean that Bob Hill knew beforehand whether the stock market would rise or decline in the near future.

An acquaintance who is an analyst with a large brokerage firm said that he would be willing to supply Bob with information that he might find quite valuable in predicting market rises and declines. Of course, there would be a fee, as yet undertermined, for this information, regardless of whether or not the investor used it. What is the maximum amount that Bob should pay for this special service? $10? $100? $500?

The value of the information from the analyst is in essence the expected value of perfect information, because the investor would then be assured of buying the most profitable stock. The value of perfect information is defined as the *difference between the maximum payoff under conditions of certainty and the maximum payoff under uncertainty.* In this problem it is the difference between the maximum value of the stock at the end of the year under conditions of certainty and the value associated with the optimum decision using the expected-value criterion.

From a practical standpoint, the maximum expected value under conditions of certainty means that the investor would buy Kayser Chemicals if a market rise were predicted and Texas Electronics if a market decline were imminent. The expected payoff in the long run under conditions of certainty is $1,900. (See Table 20−7.)

---

### TABLE   20−7

**Calculations for the Expected Payoff under Conditions of Certainty**

| State of nature | Payoff | Probability of state of nature | Expected payoff |
|---|---|---|---|
| Market rise, $S_1$ | $2,400 | .60 | $1,440 |
| Market decline, $S_2$ | 1,150 | .40 | 460 |
| | | | $1,900 |

---

Recall that if the actual behavior of the stock market were unknown (conditions of uncertainty), the stock to buy would be Kayser Chemicals; its expected value at the end of the period was computed to be $1,840 (from Table 20−3). The value of perfect information is therefore $60, found by:

$1,900   Expected value of stock purchase under conditions of certainty

−1,840   Expected value of purchase (Kayser) under conditions
          of uncertainty

$   60   Expected value of perfect information

In general, the expected value of perfect information is computed as follows:

$$\text{EVPI} = \text{Expected value under conditions of certainty} \qquad (20-3)$$
$$- \text{ Optimal decision under conditions of uncertainty}$$

Perfect information worth
$60

It would be worth up to $60 for the information the stock analyst might supply. In essence, the analyst would be "guaranteeing" a selling price in the long run of $1,900, and if the analyst asked $40 for the information, the investor would be assured of a $1,860 payoff, found by $1,900 − $40. Thus, it would be worthwhile for the investor to agree to this fee ($40) because the expected outcome ($1,860) would be greater than the expected value under conditions of uncertainty ($1,840). However, if his acquaintance wanted a fee of $100 for the service, the investor would realize only $1,800 in the long run, found by $1,900 − $100. Logically, the service would not be worth $100 because the investor could expect $1,840 in the long run without agreeing to this financial arrangement.

It should be noted that the expected value of perfect information ($60) is the same as the minimum of the expected regrets (Table 20−6).

The calculations in the preceding investment problem were mainly kept at a minimum to emphasize the new terms and the decision-making procedures. When the number of decision alternatives and the number of states of nature become large, a computer package is recommended. The output for the investment problem using *Computerized Business Statistics,* developed by Hall and Adelman and described in the previous chapter, is used as an example. The required inputs are: the decision alternatives, the states of nature and the corresponding probabilities, and the payoffs.

```
CBS-Decision Analysis          I-TBL20.1    O-TBL20.1  9-01-1991 - 07:44:46
                             Information Entered
                    Decision Making under Risk - Maximization
       Number of Decision Alternatives:        3
       Number of States of Nature:             2

          State Probabilities

       1  =    0.6
       2  =    0.4

             Kayser  Rim     Texas

       1  =   2400   2200    1900
       2  =   1000   1100    1150

                                       Results
                           Decision Alternatives

       Criteria              Kayser      Rim       Texas

         EMV                  1840      1760       1600
         EOL                    60       140        300
         EPPI                 1900      1900       1900
```

Note that the results for EMV are the same as in Table 20−3, the EOL figures are the same as in Table 20−6, and EPPI (EVPI) is the same as in Table 20−7.

## SENSITIVITY ANALYSIS

*Expected payoffs are not highly sensitive*

Recall that in the foregoing stock selection problem, the set of probabilities applied to the payoff values was derived from historical experience with similar market conditions. Objections may be voiced, however, that future market behavior may be different from past experiences. Despite these differences, *the expected payoffs are not highly sensitive to any changes within a plausible range.* As an example, suppose the investor's brother believes that instead of a 60 percent chance of a market rise and a 40 percent chance of a decline, the reverse is true—that is, there is a .40 probability that the stock market will rise and a .60 probability of a decline. Further, the investor's cousin thinks the probability of a market rise is .50 and that of a decline is .50. A comparison of the original expected payoffs (left column), the expected payoffs for the set of probabilities suggested by the investor's brother (center column), and those cited by the cousin (right column) is shown in Table 20−8. The decision is the same in all three cases—purchase Kayser Chemicals.

### TABLE  20−8

**Expected Payoffs for Three Sets of Probabilities**

| | Expected payoffs | | |
|---|---|---|---|
| Purchase | Historical experience* (probability of .60 rise, .40 decline) | Brother's estimate (probability of .40 rise, .60 decline) | Cousin's estimate (probability of .50 rise, .50 decline) |
| Kayser Chemicals | $1,840 | $1,560 | $1,700 |
| Rim Homes | 1,760 | 1,540 | 1,650 |
| Texas Electronics | 1,600 | 1,450 | 1,525 |

*From Table 20−3.

## Self-Review 20–4

*The answers are at the end of the chapter.*
Referring to Table 20–8, verify that:

1. The expected payoff for Texas Electronics for the brother's set of probabilities is $1,450.

2. The expected payoff for Kasyer Chemicals for the counsin's set of probabilities is $1,700.

A comparison of the three sets of expected payoffs in Table 20–8 reveals that the best alternative would still be to purchase Kayser Chemicals. As might be expected, there are some differences in the expected future values for each of the three stocks.

If there are any drastic changes in the assigned probabilities, the expected values and the optimal decision may in fact change. As an example, suppose the prognostication for a market rise was .20 and for a market decline .80. The expected payoffs would be as shown in Table 20–9. In the long run, the best alternative would be to buy Rim Homes stock.

---

### TABLE   20–9

#### Expected Values for Purchasing the Three Stocks

| Purchase | Expected payoff |
|---|---|
| Kayser Chemicals | $1,280 |
| Rim Homes | 1,320 |
| Texas Electronics | 1,300 |

---

## Self-Review 20–5

*The answers are at the end of the chapter.*

Is there any choice of probabilities for which the best alternative would be to purchase Texas Electronics stock? (*Hint:* this can be arrived at algebraically or using a trial-and-error method. Try a somewhat extreme probability for a market rise.)

## EXERCISES

*The answers to the odd-numbered exercises are at the end of the book.*

7. Refer to Exercises 1, 3, and 5. Compute the expected value of perfect information.

8. Refer to Exercises 2, 4, and 6. Compute the expected value of perfect information.

9. Refer to Exercise 1. Revise the probabilities as follows: $P(S_1) = .50$, $P(S_2) = .20$, and $P(S_3) = .30$. Does this change the decision?

10. Refer to Exercise 2. Reverse the probabilities; that is, let $P(S_1) = .30$ and $P(S_2) = .70$. Does this alter your decision?

# DECISION TREES

Decision tree: A picture of all possible outcomes

An analytic tool introduced in Chapter 5 that is very useful for studying a decision situation is a *decision tree.* Basically, it is a picture of all the possible courses of action and the consequent possible outcomes. A box is used to indicate the point at which a decision must be made, and the branches going out from the box indicate the alternatives under consideration. Referring to Chart 20−1, on the left is the box with three branches radiating from it, representing the acts of purchasing Kayser Chemicals, Rim Homes, and Texas Electronics.

The three nodes, numbered 1, 2, and 3, represent the expected payoff of each of the three stocks. The branches going out to the right of the nodes show the chance events (market rise or decline) and their corresponding probabilities in parentheses. The numbers at the extreme ends of the branches are the estimated future values of stopping the decision process at those points. This is sometimes called the *conditional payoff* to denote that the payoff depends on a particular choice of action and a particular chance outcome. Thus, if the investor purchased Rim Homes stock and the market rose, the estimated value of the stock would be $2,200.

After the decision tree has been constructed, the optimal decision strategy can be found by what is termed *backward induction.* Suppose, for example, that the investor is considering the act of purchasing Texas Electronics. Starting at the lower right in Chart 20−1 with the anticipated payoff given a market rise ($1,900) versus a market decline ($1,150) and going backward (moving left), the appropriate probabilities are applied to give the expected payoff of $1,600 [found by .60($1,900) + .40($1,150)]. The investor would mark the expected value of $1,600 above circled node 3 as shown in Chart 20−1. Similarly, the investor would determine the expected values for Rim Homes and Kayser Chemicals.

## CHART 20−1

**Decision Tree for the Investor's Decision**

Decision tree shows Kayser Chemicals best buy

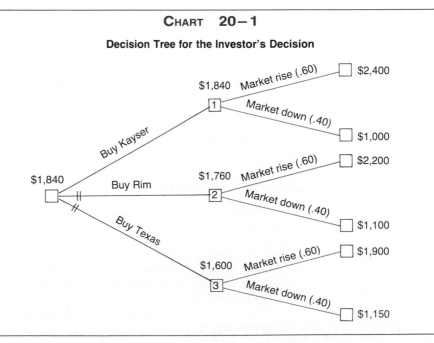

Assuming that the investor wants to maximize the expected future value of his stock purchase, $1,840 would be preferred over $1,760 or $1,600. Continuing to the left toward the box, the investor would draw a double bar across branches representing the two alternatives he rejected (numbers 2 and 3, representing Rim Homes and Texas Electronics). The unmarked branch that leads to the box is clearly the best action to follow, namely, buy Kayser Chemicals stock.

The expected value under *conditions of certainty* can also be portrayed via a decision tree analysis (see Chart 20–2). Recall that under conditions of certainty the investor would know *before the stock is purchased* whether the stock market will rise or decline in the near future. Hence, he would purchase Kayser Chemicals in a rising market and Texas Electronics in a falling market, and in the long run the expected payoff would be $1,900. Again, backward induction would be used to arrive at the expected payoff of $1,900.

---

### CHART   20–2

**Decision Tree Given Perfect Information**

If perfect information available: Buy Kayser in rising market; buy Texas in declining market

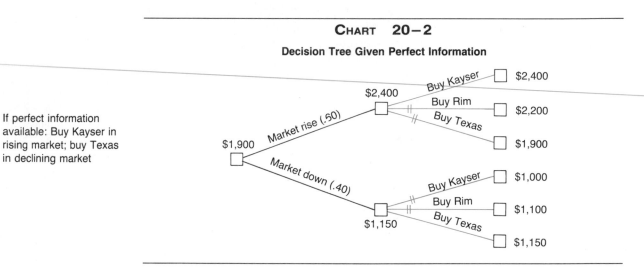

---

The monetary difference based on the perfect information in Chart 20–2 and the decision based on imperfect information in Chart 20–1 is $60, found by $1,9000 – $1,840. Recall that the $60 is the value of perfect information.

Decision tree analysis merely provides an alternative way to perform the same calculations presented earlier in the chapter. Some managers find that these graphic sketches help them in following the decision path.

## CHAPTER OUTLINE

   I.  Statistical decision theory is concerned with making decisions from a set of possible alternatives.
      A.  The various courses of action are called the acts or alternatives.
      B.  The uncontrollable future events are called the states of nature. Probabilities are usually assigned to the various states of nature.
      C.  The combination of a particular decision alternative and state of nature is called the payoff.
      D.  All possible combinations of decision alternatives and states of nature result in a payoff table.

II. There are several criteria for selecting the optimal decision.
   A. In the expected monetary value (EMV) criterion, the expected value for each decision alternative is computed, and the optimal (largest if profits, smallest if cost) is selected.
   B. An opportunity loss table can be developed.
      1. An opportunity loss table is constructed by taking the difference between the optimal decision for each state of nature and the other decision alternatives.
      2. The difference between the optimal decision and any other decision is the opportunity loss or regret due to making a decision other than the optimum.
      3. The expected opportunity loss (EOL) is similar to the expected monetary value. The opportunity loss is combined with the probabilities of the various states of nature for each decision alternative to determine the expected opportunity loss.
   C. The strategy of maximizing the minimum gain is referred to as maximin.
   D. The strategy of maximizing the maximum gain is called maximax.
   E. The strategy that minimizes the maximum regret is designated minimax.
III. The expected value of perfect information (EVPI) is the difference between the expected payoff if the state of nature is known and the optimal decision under conditions of uncertainty.
IV. Sensitivity analysis examines the effects of various probabilities for the states of nature on the expected values.
V. Decision trees are useful for structuring the various alternatives. They present a picture of the various courses of action and the possible states of nature.

# Exercises

*The answers to the odd-numbered exercises are at the end of the book.*

11. The Twenge Manufacturing Company is considering the introduction of two new products. The company can add both to the current line, neither, or just one of the two. The success of these products depends on the general economy and on the consumer's reaction to the products. These reactions can be summarized as "good," $P(S_1) = .30$; "fair," $P(S_2) = .50$; or "poor," $P(S_3) = .20$. The company's revenues, in thousands of dollars, are estimated in the following payoff table.

| | State of nature | | |
| Decision | $S_1$ | $S_2$ | $S_3$ |
|---|---|---|---|
| Neither | 0 | 0 | 0 |
| Product 1 only | 125 | 65 | 30 |
| Product 2 only | 105 | 60 | 30 |
| Both | 220 | 110 | 40 |

   a. Compute the expected monetary value for each decision.
   b. What decision would you recommend?
   c. Develop an opportunity loss table.
   d. Compute the expected opportunity loss for each decision.
   e. Compute the expected value of perfect information.

12. A financial executive lives in Boston but frequently must travel to New York. She can go to New York by car, train, or plane. The cost for a plane ticket from Boston to New York is $100, and it is estimated that the trip takes 30 minutes in good weather and 45 minutes in bad weather. The cost for a train ticket is $50, and the trip takes an hour in good weather and two hours in bad weather. The cost to drive her own car from Boston to New York is $20, and this trip takes three hours in good weather and four in bad weather. The executive places a cost of $30 per hour on her time. The weather forecast is for a 60 percent chance of bad weather tomorrow.
   What decision would you recommend? (*Hint:* Set up a payoff table, and remember that you want to minimize costs.) What is the expected value of perfect information?

13. The Thomas Manufacturing Company has $100,000 available to invest. Doctor Thomas, the president and CEO of the company, would like to either expand his production, invest the money in stocks, or purchase a certificate of deposit from the bank. Of course, the unknown is whether the economy will continue at a high level or there will be a recession. He estimates the likelihood of a recession at .20. Whether there is a recession or not, the certificate of deposit will result in a gain of 6 percent. If there is a recession, he predicts a 10 percent loss if he expands his production and a 5 percent loss if he invests in stocks. If there is not a recession, an expansion of production will result in a 15 percent gain, and stock investment will produce a 12 percent gain.

    a.    What decision should he make if he uses the maximin strategy?

    b.    What decision should Doctor Thomas make if the maximax strategy is used?

    c.    What decision would be made if he uses the expected-monetary-value criterion?

    d.    What is the expected value of perfect information? Explain.

14. The quality-assurance department at Malcomb Products must either inspect each part in a lot or not inspect any of the parts. That is, there are two decision alternatives: inspect all the parts or inspect none of the parts. The proportion of parts defective in the lot, $S_i$, is known from historical data to assume the following probability distribution.

| State of nature, $S_i$ | Probability, $P(S_i)$ |
|---|---|
| .02 | .70 |
| .04 | .20 |
| .06 | .10 |

For the decision not to inspect any parts the cost of quality is

$$C = NS_iK$$

For inspecting all the items in the lot it is

$$C = Nk$$

where:

$$N = 20 \text{ (lot size)}$$
$$K = \$18.00 \text{ (the cost of finding a defect)}$$
$$k = \$0.50 \text{ (the cost of sampling one item)}$$

    a.    Develop a payoff table.

    b.    What decision should be made if the expected-value criterion is used?

    c.    What is the expected value of perfect information?

15. Dude Ranches Incorporated was founded on the idea that many families in the eastern and southern areas of the United States do not have a sufficient amount of vacation time to drive to the dude ranches in the Southwest and Rocky Mountain areas for their vacations. Various surveys indicated, however, that there was a considerable interest in this type of family vacation, which includes horseback riding, cattle drives, swimming, fishing, and the like. Dude Ranches Incorporated bought a large farm near several eastern cities and constructed a lake, a swimming pool, and other facilities. However, to build a number of family cottages on the ranch would have required a considerable amount of investment. Further, they reasoned that most of this investment would be lost should the ranch-farm complex be a financial failure. Instead, they decided to enter into an agreement with the Mobile Homes Manufacturing Company to supply a very attractive authentic ranch-type mobile home. Mobile Homes agreed to deliver a mobile home on Saturday for $300 a week. Mobile Homes must know early Saturday morning how many mobile homes Dude Ranches Incorporated wants for the forthcoming week. They have

other customers to supply and can only deliver the homes on Saturday. This presents a problem. Dude Ranches will have some reservations by Saturday, but indications are that many families do not make them. Instead, they prefer to examine the facilities before making a decision. An analysis of the various costs involved indicated that $350 a week should be charged for a ranch home, including all privileges. The basic problem is how many mobile ranch homes to order from Mobile Homes each week. Should Dude Ranches Incorporated order 10 (considered the minimum), 11, 12, 13, or 14 (considered the maximum)?

Any decision made solely on the information in the payoff table would ignore, however, the valuable experience that Dude Ranches Incorporated has acquired in the past four years (about 200 weeks) actually operating a dude ranch in the Southwest. Their records showed that they always had nine advance reservations. Also, they never had a demand for 15 or more cottages. The occupancy of 10, 11, 12, 13, or 14 ranch cottages, in part, represented families who drove in and inspected the facilities before renting. A frequency distribution showing the number of weeks in which 10, 11, . . ., 14 ranch cottages were rented during the 200-week period is found in the following table.

| Number of cottages rented | Number of weeks |
|---|---|
| 10 | 26 |
| 11 | 50 |
| 12 | 60 |
| 13 | 44 |
| 14 | 20 |
| | 200 |

a. Construct a payoff table.

b. Determine the expected payoffs, and arrive at a decision.

c. Set up an opportunity loss table.

d. Compute the expected opportunity losses, and arrive at a decision.

e. Determine the value of perfect information.

16. The proprietor of the newly built Ski and Swim Lodge has been considering the purchase or lease of several snowmobiles for the use of guests. The owner found that other financial obligations made it impossible to purchase the machines. Snowmobiles Incorporated (SI) will lease a machine for $20 a week, including any needed maintenance. According to SI, the usual rental charge to the guests of the lodge is $25 a week. Gasoline and oil are extra. Snowmobiles Incorporated only leases a machine for the full season. The proprietor of Ski and Swim, knowing that leasing an excessive number of snowmobiles might cause a net loss for the lodge, investigated the records of other resort owners. The combined experience at several other lodges was found to be:

| Number of snowmobiles demanded by guests | Number of weeks |
|---|---|
| 7 | 10 |
| 8 | 25 |
| 9 | 45 |
| 10 | 20 |

a. Design a payoff table.

b. Compute the expected profits for leasing 7, 8, 9, and 10 snowmobiles based on the cost of leasing of $20, a rental charge of $25, and the experience at other lodges.

c. Which alternative is the most profitable?

d. Design an opportunity loss table.

e.   Find the expected oppportunity losses for leasing 7, 8, 9, and 10 snowmobiles.

f.   Which act would give the least expected opportunity loss?

g.   Determine the value of perfect information.

h.   Suggest a course of action to the proprietor of the Ski and Swim Lodge, and include in your explanation the various figures, such as expected profit.

17.   A furniture store has had numerous inquiries regarding the availability of furniture and equipment that could be rented for large outdoor summer parties. This includes such items as folding chairs and tables, a deluxe grill, propane gas, and lights. No rental equipment of this nature is available locally, and the management of the furniture store is considering forming a subsidiary to handle rentals.

An investigation revealed that most people interested in renting wanted a complete group of party essentials (about 12 chairs, four tables, a deluxe grill, a bottle of propane gas, tongs, etc.). Management decided not to buy a large number of complete sets because of the financial risk involved. That is, if the demand for the rental groups was not as large as anticipated, a large financial loss might be incurred. Further, outright purchase would mean that the equipment would have to be stored during the off-season.

It was then discovered that a firm in Boston leased a complete party set for $560 for the summer season. This amounts to about $5 a day. In the promotional literature from the Boston firm, a rental fee of $15 was suggested. For each set rented, a profit of $10 would thus be earned. It was then decided to lease from the Boston firm, at least for the first season.

The Boston firm suggested that, based on the combined experience of similar rental firms in other cities, either 41, 42, 43, 44, 45, or 46 complete sets be leased for the season. Based on this suggestion, management must now decide on the most profitable number of complete sets to lease for the season.

The leasing firm in Boston also made available some additional information gathered from several rental firms similar to the newly formed subsidiary. Note in the following table (which is based on the experience of other rental firms) that for 360 days of the total of 6,000 days' experience—or about 6 percent of the days—these rental firms rented out 41 complete party sets. On 10 percent of the days during a typical summer, they rented 42 complete sets, and so on.

| Number of sets rented | Number of days out of the total (6,000 days) |
|:---:|:---:|
| 40 | 0 |
| 41 | 360 |
| 42 | 600 |
| 43 | 840 |
| 44 | 2,400 |
| 45 | 1,500 |
| 46 | 300 |
| 47 | 6 |

a.   Construct a payoff table. (As a check figure, for the act of having 41 complete sets available and the event of renting 41, the payoff is $410.)

b.   The expected daily profit for leasing 43 complete sets from the Boston firm is $426.70; for 45 sets, $431.70; and for 46 sets, $427.45. Organize these expected daily profits into a table, and complete the table by finding the expected daily profit for leasing 41, 42, and 44 sets from the Boston firm.

c.   Based on the expected daily profit, what is the most profitable action to take?

d.   The expected opportunity loss for leasing 43 party sets from the Boston firm is $11.60; for 45 sets, $6.60; for 46 sets, $10.85. Organize these into an expected opportunity loss table, and complete the table by computing the expected opportunity loss for 41, 42, and 44.

e.  Based on the expected opportunity loss table, what is the most profitable course of action to take? Does this agree with your decision for part c?

f.  Determine the value of perfect information. Explain what it indicates in this problem.

18. Kevin Waltzer owns and operates Rent A Wreck, a discount car rental agency near the Cleveland Hopkins International Airport. He rents a wreck for $20 a day. He has an arrangement with Landrum Leasing to purchase used cars at $6,000 each. His cars receive only needed maintenance and, as a result, are worth only $2,000 at the end of the first year of operation. Kevin has decided to sell all his wrecks every year and purchase a complete set of used cars from Landrum Leasing.

His clerk-accountant provided him with a probability distribution with respect to the number of cars rented per day.

|  | Average number of cars rented per day | | | |
|---|---|---|---|---|
|  | 20 | 21 | 22 | 23 |
| Probability | .10 | .20 | .50 | .20 |

Kevin is an avid golfer and tennis player. He is either on the golf course on weekends or playing tennis indoors. Thus, his car rental agency is only open weekdays. Also, he closes for two weeks during the summer and goes on a golfing tour.

The clerk-accountant estimated that it cost $1.50 per car rental for minimal maintenance and cleaning.

a.  How many cars should he purchase every year to maximize profit?

b.  What is the expected value of perfect information?


# CHAPTER 20   EXAMINATION

*The answers are at the end of the chapter.*

For Questions 1 through 10, fill in the blank.

1.  The choices available to the decision maker are called the _____.

2.  The future events that cannot be controlled are called the _____.

3.  The combination of a particular state of nature and a particular decision alternative is called the _____.

4.  All possible combinations of states of nature and decision alternatives is called a _____.

5.  The difference between the expected payoff when the state of nature is known and the optimal decision under conditions of uncertainty is called the _____.

6.  The EVPI and the expected opportunity loss are always _____.

7.  The strategy of maximizing the minimum gain is called _____.

8.  The EMV is computed by multiplying the payoff for a particular decision alternative and the probability of the _____.

9.  The difference between the optimal decision and any other decision is the _____.

10. The strategy of maximizing the maximum gain is called _____.

11. A manufacturer has $100,000 available to make either lightweight or heavy jackets for winter wear. A decision must be made in the summer in order to have the jackets available fo early fall shipments. Of course, the manufacturer is unable to predict whether the winter will be mild or severe. If lightweight jackets are manufactured and the winter is mild, the payoff will be $120,000; but if weather is severe, the payoff will only be $105,000 (because consumers will purchase heavy jackets from competitors). If heavy jackets are produced, the payoffs for mild and severe winters are $110,000 and

$125,000, respectively. Past records showed that 70 percent of the winters were mild and 30 percent were severe.

a. Construct a payoff table.
b. Determine the two expected payoffs, and arrive at a decision.
c. Construct an opportunity loss table, and determine the expected opportunity losses.
d. Compute the value of perfect information.
e. Design a decision tree for this problem.

# ANSWERS

20-1

| Event | Payoff | Probability of event | Expected value |
|---|---|---|---|
| Market rise | $2,200 | .60 | $1,320 |
| Market decline | 1,100 | .40 | 440 |
| | | | $1,760 |

20-2 1. Suppose the investor purchased Rim Homes stock, and the value of the stock in a bear market dropped to $1,100 as anticipated (Table 20-1). Instead, had the investor purchased Texas Electronics and the market declined, the value of the Texas Electronics stock would be $1,150. The difference of $50, found by $1,150 − $1,100, represents the investor's regret for buying RIm Homes stock.

2. Suppose the investor purchased Texas Electronics stock, and then a bull market developed. The stock rose to $1,900, as anticipated (Table 20-1). However, had the investor bought Kayser Chemicals stock and the market value increased to $2,400 as anticipated, the difference of $500 represents the extra profit the investor could have made by purchasing Kayser Chemicals stock.

20-3

| Event | Opportunity loss | Probability of event | Expected opportunity loss |
|---|---|---|---|
| Market rise | $500 | .60 | $300 |
| Market decline | 0 | .40 | 0 |
| | | | $300 |

20-4 1.

| Event | Payoff | Probability of event | Expected value |
|---|---|---|---|
| Market rise | $1,900 | .40 | $ 760 |
| Market decline | 1,150 | .60 | 690 |
| | | | $1,450 |

2.

| Event | Payoff | Probability of event | Expected value |
|---|---|---|---|
| Market rise | $2,400 | .50 | $1,200 |
| Market decline | 1,000 | .50 | 500 |
| | | | $1,700 |

20-5 For probabilities of a market rise (or decline) down to .333, Kayser Chemicals stock would provide the largest expected profit in the long run. For probabilities .333 to .143, Rim Homes would be the best buy. For .143 and below, Texas Electronics would give largest expected profit. Algebraic solutions:

Kayser: $2,400P + (1 − P)1,000$
Rim: $2,200P + (1 − P)1,100$
$1,400P + 1,000 = 1,100P + 1,100$
$P = .333$

Rim: $2,200P + (1 − P)1,100$
Texas: $1,900P + (1 − P)1,150$
$1,100P + 1,100 = 750P + 1,150$
$P = .143$

## CHAPTER 20 EXAMINATION

1. Alternatives.
2. States of nature.
3. Payoff.
4. Payoff table.
5. Expected value of perfect information (EVPI).
6. The same.
7. Maximin.
8. State of nature.
9. Opportunity loss.
10. Maximax.
11.

a.

| Manufacture | Payoff | |
|---|---|---|
| | Mild winter | Severe winter |
| Lightweight jacket | $120,000 | $105,000 |
| Heavy jacket | 110,000 | 125,000 |

b. $EMV(A_1) = .70(\$120,000) + .30(\$105,000)$
$= \$115,500$

$EMV(A_2) = .70(\$110,000) + .30(\$125,000)$
$= \$114,500$

c. Expected payoffs: lightweight, $115,500; heavy, $114,500. Decision: Manufacture lightweight jackets because payoff is greater.

| Manufacture | Opportunity loss | |
|---|---|---|
| | Mild winter | Severe winter |
| Lightweight jacket | $    0 | $20,000 |
| Heavy jacket | 10,000 | 0 |

$EOL(A_1) = .70(0) + .30(\$20,000)$
$= \$6,000$

$EOL(A_2) = .70(\$10,000) + .30(0)$
$= \$7,000$

The expected opportunity loss for lightweight jackets is $6,000; for heavy jackets it is $7,000. Decision: Manufacture lightweight jackets.

d. The value of perfect information is $6,000, found by:

| $121,500 | Expected payoff under conditions of certainty. |
|---|---|
| − 115,500 | Expected payoff under conditions of uncertainty. |
| $6,000 | Value of perfect information. |

*Note:* This is the same as the minimum expected opportunity loss.

e. The decision tree is:

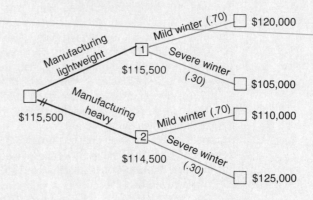

*Services—Courtesy Airborne Express*

# STATISTICAL QUALITY CONTROL

When you have completed this chapter, you will be able to:

1. Discuss the role of statistical quality control in evaluating the quality of production in a manufacturing plant.

2. Define several terms unique to quality control, including *chance causes, assignable causes, in control,* and *out of control.*

3. Construct two charts for variables— a mean chart and a range chart.

4. Construct two charts for attributes— a percent defective chart and a chart for the number of defects per unit.

5. Construct an operating characteristic curve for various sampling plans.

Interest in quality has accelerated dramatically in the United States during the past 10 years. We need only to turn on the television and watch the commercials sponsored by GM, Ford, and Chrysler to verify that there is tremendous emphasis on quality control on the assembly line. It is now the "in" topic in all facets of business. Quoting from just a few recently published articles in business magazines such as *Business Week,* speeches, and books written on the subject: "Quality is entering a new dimension." "Quality: the way to export success." "Quality starts with design." "Futuristic agile factories must be based on work performed with quality foremost." "Quality first." "Lumbering corporate hierarchies must be streamlined in order to focus on teamwork, quality, and speed." To emphasize the need for better quality, V. Daniel Hunt, president of Technology Research Corporation, stated in his book *Quality in America* that in America, 20 to 25 percent of production costs is currently spent finding and correcting mistakes. And, he added, the additional cost incurred in repairing or replacing faulty products in the field drives the total cost of poor quality to nearly 30 percent. In Japan, he said, it is about 3 percent.[1]

Courtesy Ford Motor Company

What is quality? There is no commonly agreed upon definition of quality. To cite a few diverse definitions: From Westinghouse, "Total quality is performance leadership in meeting customer requirements by doing the right things right the first time." From AT&T, "Quality is meeting customer expectations." "Quality is achieving or reaching the highest standard as against being satisfied with the sloppy or fraudulent," said Barbara W. Tuchman.

---

[1]V. Daniel Hunt, *Quality in America* (Homewood, Ill.: Business One Irwin, 1992), p. 9.

The need for better-quality American products is underscored by a statement by Hioshi Kashiwagi, the director general of Japan's most prestigious research laboratory, when he said, "If the U.S. giants started making better use of their vast storehouse of technology, we [Japan] would not be able to compete with them."[2]

To challenge American industry, a number of awards have been established in recent years. The most prestigious is the Malcolm Baldrige National Quality Award. On August 20, 1987, President Reagan signed an act aimed toward promoting quality awareness. Since then, the Federal Express Corporation, Globe Metallurgical, Motorola, IBM, and the Cadillac Motor Car Division of GM have won the award. (See Chapter 5 in the Hunt book mentioned above for the criteria used and a capsule report on how the companies qualified for the award.)

There are many facets to an overall quality control program. This chapter will focus only on one part of the program, namely, the control of production on the assembly line. We will try to identify when production becomes "out of control," that is, the point where an excessive number of defective parts are being produced. We will address such questions as: "Are an excessively large number of cola bottles being overfilled?" "Is 3 percent defective too high?" "Are six defects in a car door unreasonable?"

A brief background of quality control follows. Prior to the early 1900s, American industry was largely characterized by small shops making such relatively simple products as buggies, furniture, plows, and stoves. In these shops, the individual worker was generally a crafter who was completely responsible for the "quality" of the work and could ensure it through personal selection of material, skillful manufacture, and selective fitting and adjustment.

With the spread of the Industrial Revolution in the early 1900s, factories sprang up. People with only limited training were formed into long assembly lines. Products became more complex. The individual worker no longer had complete control over the quality of the product. A semiprofessional staff was developed (the inspection department), which became responsible for the quality. This responsibility was fulfilled by a 100 percent evaluation of all characteristics deemed important, with corrective action on discrepancies being handled by notifying the production department supervisors. During this period, quality was obtained by "inspecting it into the product."

During the 1920s, the concepts of statistical quality control were developed, primarily through the work of Dr. Walter A. Shewhart of the Bell Telephone Laboratories. Shewhart introduced the concept of "controlling" the quality rather than inspecting it into the part. For the purpose of controlling the quality, the *Shewhart control chart technique* was developed for in-process manufacturing operations. In addition, he introduced the concept of *statistical sampling inspection* to estimate whether manufactured lots were good or bad, replacing the old method of inspecting every part.

Statistical quality control, with its emphasis on in-process control of the quality, came into its own during World War II. The need for mass-produced, intricate bomb sights, accurate radar, and other electronic equipment at lowest cost accelerated the use of control charts and statistical sampling. These statistical techniques were retained, refined, and added to both during and after the war. Most manufacturers now utilize control charts and/or sampling plans for evaluating production. High-quality imports from Japan, Germany, and other industrialized countries have in recent years revitalized quality-assurance programs in the automobile industry and in other high-technology industries.

---

[2]"Learning from Japan," *Business Week,* January 27, 1992, p. 52.

This chapter will be concerned with only two statistical techniques used in quality control: **control charts** and **acceptance sampling.**

# THE CONTROL CHART

Production varies slightly

Courtesy ABB Robotics, Inc.

Variation is a basic law of nature. The amount of rainfall each year will vary, the heights of college freshmen will vary, and the parts produced by a manufacturing process will vary.

On the production line, a most important concept is that *there is no such thing as two identical parts.* The difference from one part to the next is minute (perhaps one millionth of an inch), but they are different. One automobile engine block is different from the next one, and any one valve is different from the next one produced. Even the tensile strength of a roll of steel wire varies throughout the length of the wire. This variation is recognized in the tolerances and limits specified on blueprints. For example, a roll of steel wire may be acceptable if it tests between 14,000 and 14,500 psi tensile strength.

To illustrate the pattern of variation inherent in quantitative data, the weights of a sample of 23 incoming freshmen football players were recorded (see Table 21−1). Note that the weights tend to cluster about an arithmetic mean weight of 210 pounds. Some weigh more, some less. Practically all of them weigh between 150 and 270 pounds. If all freshmen players were weighed, however, it is quite possible that a few might weigh less than 140 or more than 280 pounds.

---

### TABLE   21−1

**Variations in the Weights of Football Players**

| Weight (in pounds) | | Number of players |
|---|---|---|
| 140 up to 160 | / | 1 |
| 160 up to 180 | // | 2 |
| 180 up to 200 | ⊬⊬ | 5 |
| 200 up to 220 | ⊬⊬ // | 7 |
| 220 up to 240 | ⊬⊬ | 5 |
| 240 up to 260 | // | 2 |
| 260 up to 280 | / | 1 |
| Total | | 23 |

---

Machined parts cluster about the average

Machined parts follow somewhat this inherent pattern. Suppose a gang drill drilling holes in bushings is set for 2.9870 inches diameter. A sample of bushings from this machine might reveal the results shown in Chart 21−1.

---

### CHART   21−1

**Variations in the Inside Diameters of Bushings**

| Inside diameter | | Number of bushings |
|---|---|---|
| 2.9873 | ○ | 1 |
| 2.9872 | ○ ○ | 2 |
| 2.9871 | ○ ○ ○ ○ | 4 |
| 2.9870 | ○ ○ ○ ○ ○ ○ | 6 |
| 2.9869 | ○ ○ ○ ○ | 4 |
| 2.9868 | ○ ○ | 2 |
| 2.9867 | ○ | 1 |

---

The inside diameters of the bushings can be considered to be approximately normally distributed. The normal distribution has the familiar form of a bell-shaped curve, and its characteristics are generally described by measures of central tendency, discussed in Chapter 3, and measures of dispersion and areas under the curve from Chapters 4 and 7.

The average most commonly used in quality control is the arithmetic mean. The range and the standard deviation are the two most often used measures of dispersion. The relationship between the mean ($\mu$) and the standard deviation ($\sigma$) is portrayed graphically in Chart 21–2.

---

### Chart 21–2

**Areas under the Normal Curve within $\mu \pm \sigma$, $\mu \pm 2\sigma$, and $\mu \pm 3\sigma$**

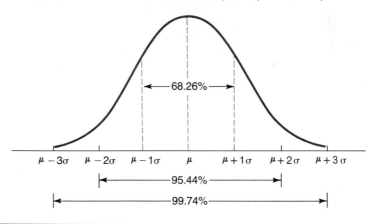

---

To understand why control charts are a basic tool in quality control, the following two questions must be answered:

1. What causes the basic pattern of variation in a manufacturing process?
2. What is the purpose of control charts?

## Causes of Variation

*Variation may be due to chance*

There are two general causes of variation in a manufacturing process: **chance** and **assignable variation.** Chance variations are usually large in number and random in nature, and they cannot be eliminated unless, for example, there is a major change in equipment or material. Internal machine friction, slight variations in materials or process conditions (such as the temperature of a mold being used to make glass bottles), atmospheric conditions (such as temperature, humidity, and the dust content of the air), and vibrations transmitted to a machine from a passing forklift are a few examples of sources of chance variation.

*Variation may be assignable*

Assignable variation is usually nonrandom in nature and can be eliminated or reduced. If the hole drilled in a piece of steel is much too large due to a dull drill, the drill may be sharpened or a new drill inserted. An operator who continually sets up the machine incorrectly can be replaced. If the roll of steel to be used in the process does not have the correct tensile strength, it can be rejected.

Why be concerned with the causes of variation?

1. Variation can (and will) change the shape, dispersion, and central tendency of the distribution of the product characteristic being measured.
2. Assignable variation is usually correctable, whereas chance variation usually cannot be corrected or stabilized economically.

To illustrate the effect of variation, the frequency distribution of the inside diameters of the bushings noted previously (Chart 21–1) has been smoothed out to approximate a normal distribution curve and plotted in Chart 21–3A. Assuming that the upper and lower blueprint specifications match the inherent pattern of variation, 99.74 percent of the bushings would be acceptable. This indicates that 997 bushings out of 1,000 would be expected to fall between the specified tolerances.

---

## CHART  21–3

### The Usual Pattern of Variation and the Effects of Upward and Downward Shifts in the Arithmetic Mean Inside Diameter

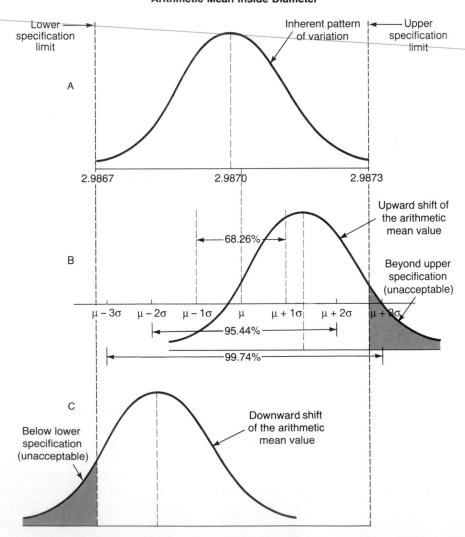

Larger mean inside diameter

Smaller mean inside diameter

Chart 21–3B shows graphically the effect of an upward shift in the arithmetic mean inside diameter; that is, the mean inside diameter of the bushings has become much larger. This may be due to excessive vibration of the drill as it bites through the steel. Chart 21–3C shows the effect of a downward shift in the arithmetic mean diameter. The mean inside diameter has become much smaller, perhaps due to excessive drill wear. In both cases a large proportion of the output would be unacceptable.

In summary, if specifications have been established on the basis of the inherent pattern, then a shift in the arithmetic mean value results in defective parts. Chart 21–3A represents the pattern of *chance* variation. The areas above and below the upper and lower specifications in Chart 21–3B and C represent *assignable* causes of variation.

Again, assuming that the upper and lower specifications of the bushings match the inherent pattern of variation, then any change in the range $R$ of the distribution of bushings will cause a proportion of the bushings to be beyond the upper or lower specification, even though the arithmetic mean inside diameter stays the same, at 2.9870. A change in the range indicates that some very small and/or very large

CHART 21–4

**The Usual Pattern of Variation and the Effects of an Increase in the Range of the Inside Diameters**

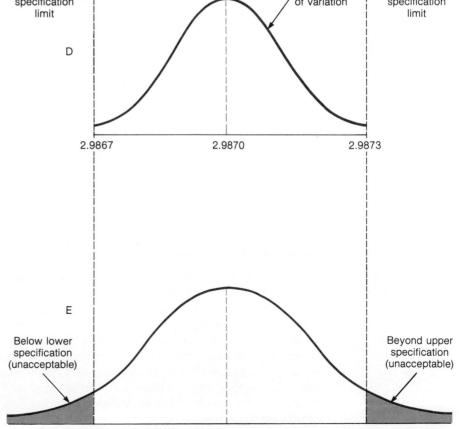

bushings are being produced. The large inside diameters may be caused by one of the gang drills expanding due to excessive heat. Chart 21−4D on page 749 shows the usual normal pattern of production, and Chart 21−4E illustrates the effect of an increased range.

In summary, if specifications have been established on the basis of the inherent pattern, then an increase in the range results in defective parts. Chart 21−4D shows the pattern of chance variation. The areas above and below the upper and lower specifications in Chart 21−4E represent assignable causes of variation.

## PURPOSE AND TYPES OF QUALITY-CONTROL CHARTS

*Purpose of QC charts*

What is the purpose of a statistical quality-control chart? Fundamentally, the purpose is to identify *when* assignable causes of variation or changes in process level have entered the production system. It is important to know when these changes have occurred so that the cause may be identified and corrected before a large number of defective items are produced.

Statistical quality-control charts may be compared to a football scoreboard. By looking at the scoreboard, the fans, coaches, and players can tell which team is ahead. The scoreboard can do nothing to win or lose the game; it is merely a signal to the losing coach to try to do something about the situation. Changing the quarterback, for example, might turn the tide. Quality-control charts are similar in function. These charts indicate to the workers, group leaders, quality-control engineers, and management whether the production of a part or parts is **in control** or **out of control.** If production is out of control, the quality-control chart cannot correct the situation; it is just a piece of paper with figures and dots on it. Instead, the person responsible will adjust the machine manufacturing the part or do whatever is necessary to return production to "in control" status. "In control" means satisfactory production; "out of control" indicates unsatisfactory production. Unsatisfactory production might mean that the part being produced is too heavy, too light, too large, too small, or that it has other manifestations of poor, unacceptable production.

Control charts have been developed for both *variables* and *attributes*. A variable chart deals with and portrays graphically actual measurements, such as the outside diameter of a piston ring or the net weight of a can of tomato juice. An attribute chart is based on a product being classified as either acceptable or unacceptable. An electric light bulb coming off the production line is either acceptable (it lights) or unacceptable (it does not light).

## CHARTS FOR VARIABLES

*Outside diameter, length, and weight are variables*

As has been pointed out previously, parts vary in length, inside diameter, outside diameter, tensile strength, and so on. One group of statistical quality-control charts is used for these variables. Two charts will be studied—*X bar charts* (alternately called *mean charts*) and *range charts.*

Statistical quality-control charts utilize the theoretical concepts with respect to sampling developed in the foregoing chapters. Suppose that a small sample of, say, five pieces is selected from the population, and the arithmetic mean is computed. Many additional samples of five pieces are then selected and the means computed. The means of these samples could be designated $\bar{X}_1$, $\bar{X}_2$, $\bar{X}_3$, and so on. The mean of these sample means is denoted by $\bar{\bar{X}}$. We use $k$ for the number of sample means.

$$\overline{\overline{X}} = \frac{\text{Sum of the means of the subgroups (samples)}}{\text{Number of sample means}}$$

$$= \frac{\Sigma \overline{X}}{k}$$

(21–1)

The standard error of the distribution of the individual sample (subgroup) means is designated $\sigma_{\overline{x}}$ and found by:

$$\sigma_{\overline{x}} = \frac{\sigma}{\sqrt{n}}$$

If all the sample means were plotted in a frequency distribution, the plot would approximate the bell-shaped curve in Chart 21–5. The plot distribution of sample means superimposed on the distribution of the actual measurements might appear as shown in the chart.

---

### CHART 21–5

**Distribution of Sample means and Population Values**

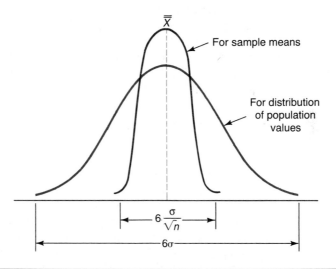

---

The arithmetic mean of a population is equal to the mean of all the means of the random samples selected from that population. Also, the total dispersion in the population is greater than that of the distribution of sample means by the factor $\sqrt{n}$. It also should be noted that even if the population is only approximately normal, inferences regarding the distribution of sample means can be made based on the normal distribution. They are:

68.26 percent of the subgroup averages will be within plus or minus 1 standard error of the population mean.

95.44 percent of the subgroup averages will be within plus or minus 2 standard errors of the population mean.

99.74 percent of the subgroup averages will be within plus or minus 3 standard errors of the population mean.

Mean chart used to control mean outside diameter, weight, and length

Courtesy George J. Meyer Manufacturing, a Figgie International Company

These relationships allow limits to be set up around the subgroup averages to show how much variation can be expected for subgroup samples of a given size. These expected limits are called the *upper control limits,* usually abbreviated UCL, and the *lower control limits* (LCL).

## MEAN CHART

The first chart designed for variables is called a **mean chart.** Its purpose is to portray the fluctuation in the sample means.

### ■ EXAMPLE

Suppose a new bottle-making machine has just been installed. The machine is set to produce 41-ounce bottles, but variation in the weights of these bottles is expected. This expected variation is due to a number of factors, namely, the temperature of the glass, temperature of the molds, and the composition of the glass mixture. The quality control design calls for taking a sample of five bottles every hour, weighing them, and computing the arithmetic mean weight.

How is a mean chart constructed?

### ☑ SOLUTION

UCL is upper control limit

LCL is lower control limit

A mean chart has two limits, an upper control limit (UCL), and a lower control limit (LCL). The meaning of these two limits will be discussed shortly. We will first construct a mean chart and plot the sample data on the chart.

The upper control limit (UCL) and the lower control limit (LCL) may be computed by:

$$UCL = \overline{\overline{X}} + 3\,\frac{\hat{\sigma}}{\sqrt{n}} \qquad LCL = \overline{\overline{X}} - 3\,\frac{\hat{\sigma}}{\sqrt{n}}$$

where $\hat{\sigma}$ is an estimate of the standard deviation of the population, $\sigma$. (The symbol ^ is called a "hat.") Notice that in the calculation of the upper and lower control limits, the number 3 represents the 99.74 percent confidence limits. However, it should be pointed out that although the 99.74 percent confidence level is commonly used, other confidence levels (90 percent, 95 percent, etc.) can be used, depending on the risk one is willing to assume of being out of control. This will become clearer as we progress through the chapter. The calculations for UCL and LCL have been simplified by using:[3]

$$\boxed{UCL = \overline{\overline{X}} + A_2\overline{R} \qquad LCL = \overline{\overline{X}} - A_2\overline{R}} \qquad (21-2)$$

where:

$A_2$ is a factor used in the computation of the upper and lower control limits based on the range, $\overline{R}$. The factors for various sample sizes can be found in Appendix L. (*Note: n* in the table refers to the number in the sample.) A partial table is shown below. To find the factor, first locate the sample size, *n*

[3]For this conversion, see Acheson J. Duncan, *Quality Control and Industrial Statistics,* 5th ed. (Homewood, Ill.: Richard D. Irwin, 1986), pp. 479–87.

(5 in this example), in the left margin. Then move horizontally to the $A_2$ column, and read the factor. It is 0.577.

Factors for control charts

| Number of Items in Sample | Chart for Averages | Chart for Ranges | | |
|---|---|---|---|---|
| | Factors for Control Limits | Factors for Central Line | Factors for Control Limits | |
| $n$ | $A_2$ | $d_2$ | $D_3$ | $D_4$ |
| 2 | 1.880 | 1.128 | 0 | 3.267 |
| 3 | 1.023 | 1.693 | 0 | 2.575 |
| 4 | .729 | 2.059 | 0 | 2.282 |
| 5 | .577 | 2.326 | 0 | 2.115 |
| 6 | .483 | 2.534 | 0 | 2.004 |

$\overline{\overline{X}}$ is the mean of the sample means

$\overline{R}$ is the mean of the ranges

$\overline{\overline{X}}$   is the mean of the sample means, computed by $\Sigma\overline{X}/k$, where $k$ is the number of samples selected. In this problem a sample will be taken every hour for four hours, so $k = 4$.

$\overline{R}$   is the mean of the ranges of the sample, computed by $\Sigma R/k$. (Recall that a sample range is the difference between the largest and smallest values in the sample.)

The quality-control inspector recorded the weight of each of the five bottles she selected. The data for the samples, taken at 8, 9, 10, and 11 A.M., are given in Table 21−2.

## TABLE   21−2

### Weights of Five Bottles Selected at Random, 8−11 A.M. (in ounces)

| Time | Bottle | | | | | Arithmetic mean, $\overline{X}$ | Range, $R$ |
|---|---|---|---|---|---|---|---|
| | 1 | 2 | 3 | 4 | 5 | | |
| 8 A.M. | 41 | 43 | 42 | 41 | 43 | 42 | 2 |
| 9 A.M. | 39 | 40 | 40 | 39 | 42 | 40 | 3 |
| 10 A.M. | 41 | 44 | 43 | 46 | 41 | 43 | 5 |
| 11 A.M. | 38 | 39 | 40 | 39 | 39 | 39 | 2 |
| Total | | | | | | 164 | 12 |

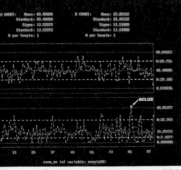

Computer software, such as CSS: STATISTICA, is an important tool in the improvement of quality
Courtesy StatSoft, Inc.

The centerline ($\overline{\overline{X}}$) for the mean chart is 41, found by 164/4. The mean of the range ($\overline{R}$) is 3, found by 12/4. Thus, the upper control limit (UCL) of the $X$ bar chart is:

$$\overline{\overline{X}} + A_2\overline{R} = 41 + 0.577(3)$$
$$= 42.731$$

The lower control limit (LCL) of the $X$ bar chart is:

$$\overline{\overline{X}} - A_2\overline{R} = 41 - 0.577(3)$$
$$= 39.269$$

$\overline{\overline{X}}$, UCL, LCL, and the means of the samples are portrayed in Chart 21−6.

The 10 A.M. and 11 A.M. checks are "out of control"

### CHART 21–6

**Mean Chart for the Weights of Bottles**

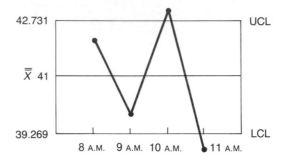

There is considerable variation in the process mean. In fact, both the 10 A.M. and the 11 A.M. samples indicate that the process is out of control. It is the responsibility of the QC inspector to inform the production department so that an adjustment can be made as soon as possible. In this case, it is essential that the process mean be returned to about 41 ounces.

*INTERPRETATION* Based on just the first four hours of experience with this new bottling machine: (1) If a sample of five bottles is picked at random and weighed, the arithmetic mean weight will fall between 39.269 and 42.731 ounces about 99.74 percent of the time. (2) If many samples of five bottles are taken and the arithmetic means computed, the mean of 41 ounces will appear more than any other. This figure (41 ounces) is the grand mean of the subgroup means. UCL and LCL represent $\overline{\overline{X}} \pm 3\hat{\sigma}/\sqrt{n}$.

Generally, quality-control charts should be developed after the process has stabilized. One rule of thumb is to design a chart after at least 25 samples have been selected. In this example, the mean chart was drawn after only four samples were chosen.

### Self-Review 21–1

*The answers are at the end of the chapter.*

Every half hour the quality-control inspector checks four pieces and records the outside diameters of each of the four pieces. The results are shown in the following table.

Compute the overall mean, determine the control limits, and show the limits and the mean of a mean chart. Then plot the sample means.

|  | Sample Piece |  |  |  |
|---|---|---|---|---|
| Time | 1 | 2 | 3 | 4 |
| 9:00 A.M. | 1 | 4 | 5 | 2 |
| 9:30 A.M. | 2 | 3 | 2 | 1 |
| 10:00 A.M. | 1 | 7 | 3 | 5 |

The MINITAB system has a procedure for computing the control limits for the mean and the range. The output is shown below. There are some slight differences in the limits, which are due to rounding and to a slightly different formula.

```
MTB > set c1
DATA> 41,43,42,41,43,39,40,40,39,42,41,44,43,46,41,38,39,40,39,39
DATA> end
MTB > name c1 'Weights'
MTB > gxbarchart c1 5;
MTB ' title 'Mean Chart for Bottle Weights';
MTB > rbar.
```

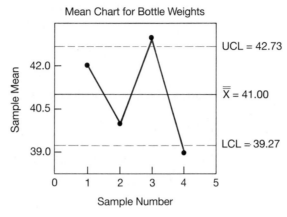

Mean Chart for Bottle Weights

### RANGE CHART

A **range chart** shows variation in the ranges of the samples. If the dots representing the ranges fall within the upper and lower limits, it is concluded that production is in control. According to chance, 997 times out of 1,000 the range of the samples will fall between the two limits. If a range should fall above or below the limits, it is concluded that some *assignable* cause affected the production, resulting in some individual pieces being too large, too small, too heavy, or too light, depending on what is being measured. UCL and LCL represent $\bar{R} \pm 3\sigma_R$. The upper and lower control limits for the range chart can be quickly determined by:

How to compute UCL and LCL of range chart

$$\boxed{UCL = D_4\bar{R}} \qquad \boxed{LCL = D_3\bar{R}} \qquad (21-3)$$

where $D_3$ and $D_4$ are factors from Appendix L (also given in the partial table on page 753).

### ■ EXAMPLE

The weights of the samples of five bottles from Table 21−2 are repeated below.

| Time | Weights (in ounces) | | | | |
|---|---|---|---|---|---|
| | 1 | 2 | 3 | 4 | 5 |
| 8 A.M. | 41 | 43 | 42 | 41 | 43 |
| 9 A.M. | 39 | 40 | 40 | 39 | 42 |
| 10 A.M. | 41 | 44 | 43 | 46 | 41 |
| 11 A.M. | 38 | 39 | 40 | 39 | 39 |

How is a range chart for these weights constructed?

### ☑ SOLUTION

The first step is to find the mean range, $\bar{R}$. The range of the 8 A.M. sample is 2, found by $43 - 41$. The range of the 9 A.M. sample is 3, found by $42 - 39$. The ranges for the 10 A.M. and 11 A.M. samples are 5 and 2, respectively. The mean range, $\bar{R}$, is 3, found by $(2 + 3 + 5 + 2)/4 = 12/4 = 3$.

*Locating $D_3$ and $D_4$*

Referring to Appendix L for $D_3$ and $D_4$ and a sample size of 5, we get $D_4 = 2.115$ and $D_3 = 0$. Determining the upper and lower control limits for the range chart:

$$\text{UCL} = D_4\bar{R} \qquad\qquad \text{LCL} = D_3\bar{R}$$
$$= 2.115(3) \qquad\qquad = (0)(3)$$
$$= 6.345 \qquad\qquad = 0$$

Construction of the range chart and plotting of the 8–11 A.M. ranges is shown in Chart 21–7.

---

### CHART   21–7

*Ranges of weights of bottles are "in control"*

**Range Chart for the Weights of Bottles**

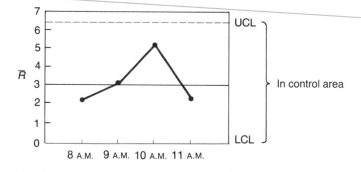

---

The lower control limit of 0 for the range chart is really not needed. No doubt management would be very pleased if there were no variation in the bottle weights.

Note that all the ranges lie in the "in control" area, indicating that the fluctuations in the weights of the bottles are as expected. That is, there are no unusual fluctuations in the weights. No adjustments to the process are needed.

---

### Self-Review 21–2

*The answers are at the end of the chapter.*

1. Using the data from Self-Review 21–1 (repeated here), construct a range chart showing the control limits. Plot the ranges.
2. Is the process in control?

| | Sample piece | | | |
|---|---|---|---|---|
| Time | 1 | 2 | 3 | 4 |
| 9:00 A.M. | 1 | 4 | 5 | 2 |
| 9:30 A.M. | 2 | 3 | 2 | 1 |
| 10:00 A.M. | 1 | 7 | 3 | 5 |

MINITAB also has a procedure for producing a range chart. using the same weights of bottles:

```
MTB > grchart c1 5;
SUBC> title 'Range Chart for Bottle Weights';
SUBC> rbar.
```

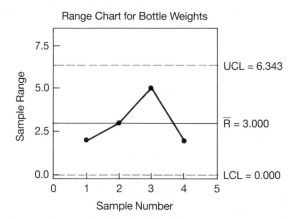

Range Chart for Bottle Weights

Some means are "out of control"

Some ranges are "out of control"

The following illustration is an actual combination mean and range chart (only the name of the grinder has been changed). To plot the chart, a quality-control inspector checks five pieces for inside diameter every three hours. The Sun Grinder in this operation is set to grind an inside diameter of 3.87525 inches. The gauge the inspector uses is calibrated to the nearest ten-thousandth of an inch. He inserts the gauge in part

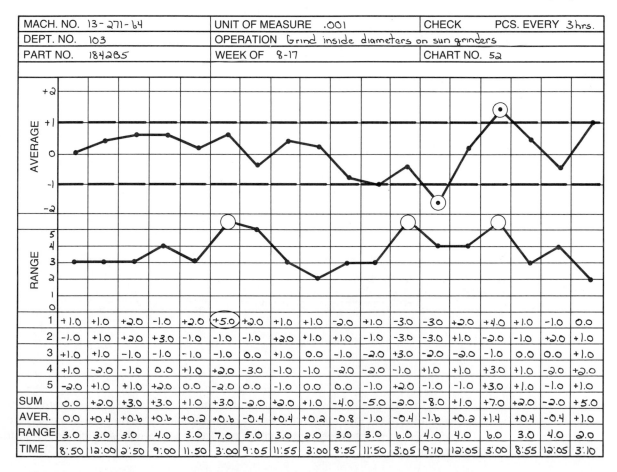

| MACH. NO. 13-271-64 | | | | | UNIT OF MEASURE .001 | | | | | | CHECK | PCS. EVERY 3 hrs. | | | | |
|---|---|---|---|---|---|---|---|---|---|---|---|---|---|---|---|---|
| DEPT. NO. 103 | | | | | OPERATION Grind inside diameters on sun grinders | | | | | | | | | | | |
| PART NO. 184285 | | | | | WEEK OF 8-17 | | | | | | CHART NO. 52 | | | | | |

| | | | | | | | | | | | | | | | | |
|---|---|---|---|---|---|---|---|---|---|---|---|---|---|---|---|---|
| 1 | +1.0 | +1.0 | +2.0 | -1.0 | +2.0 | +5.0 | +2.0 | +1.0 | +1.0 | -2.0 | +1.0 | -3.0 | -3.0 | +2.0 | +4.0 | +1.0 | -1.0 | 0.0 |
| 2 | -1.0 | +1.0 | +2.0 | +3.0 | -1.0 | -1.0 | -1.0 | +2.0 | +1.0 | +1.0 | -1.0 | -3.0 | -3.0 | +1.0 | -2.0 | -1.0 | +2.0 | +1.0 |
| 3 | +1.0 | +1.0 | -1.0 | -1.0 | -1.0 | -1.0 | 0.0 | +1.0 | 0.0 | -1.0 | -2.0 | +3.0 | -2.0 | -2.0 | -1.0 | 0.0 | 0.0 | +1.0 |
| 4 | +1.0 | -2.0 | -1.0 | 0.0 | +1.0 | +2.0 | -3.0 | -1.0 | -1.0 | -2.0 | -2.0 | -1.0 | +1.0 | +1.0 | +3.0 | +1.0 | -2.0 | +2.0 |
| 5 | -2.0 | +1.0 | +1.0 | +2.0 | 0.0 | -2.0 | 0.0 | -1.0 | 0.0 | 0.0 | -1.0 | +2.0 | -1.0 | -1.0 | +3.0 | +1.0 | -1.0 | +1.0 |
| SUM | 0.0 | +2.0 | +3.0 | +3.0 | +1.0 | +3.0 | -2.0 | +2.0 | +1.0 | -4.0 | -5.0 | -2.0 | -8.0 | +1.0 | +7.0 | +2.0 | -2.0 | +5.0 |
| AVER. | 0.0 | +0.4 | +0.6 | +0.6 | +0.2 | +0.6 | -0.4 | +0.4 | +0.2 | -0.8 | -1.0 | -0.4 | -1.6 | +0.2 | +1.4 | +0.4 | -0.4 | +1.0 |
| RANGE | 3.0 | 3.0 | 3.0 | 4.0 | 3.0 | 7.0 | 5.0 | 3.0 | 2.0 | 3.0 | 3.0 | 6.0 | 4.0 | 4.0 | 6.0 | 3.0 | 4.0 | 2.0 |
| TIME | 8:50 | 12:00 | 2:50 | 9:00 | 11:50 | 3:00 | 9:05 | 11:55 | 3:00 | 8:55 | 11:50 | 3:05 | 9:10 | 12:05 | 3:00 | 8:55 | 12:05 | 3:10 |

number 1842B5 and records the reading on the chart, such as −1.0. He sums the five sample readings and computes the arithmetic mean and the range. (The gauge reading of −1.0 indicates that the part was one ten-thousandth of an inch below the mean. A +2.0 reading would indicate that the part was two ten-thousandths above the mean.)

## SOME IN-CONTROL AND OUT-OF-CONTROL SITUATIONS

Following are three illustrations of in-control and out-of-control production processes.

Everything OK

1.   The mean chart and the range chart together indicate that the process is in control. Note that the sample means and sample ranges are clustered close to the centerlines. Some are above and some below the centerlines, indicating that the process is quite stable. That is, there is no visible tendency for the means and ranges to move toward the "out of control" areas.

Mean Chart

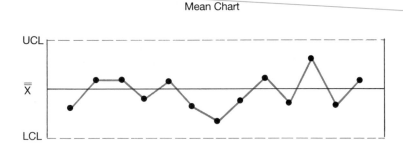

Range Chart

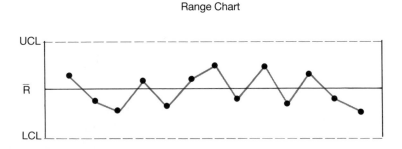

Considerable variation in ranges

2.   The sample means are in control, but the ranges of the last two samples are out of control. This indicates that there is considerable variation from piece to piece. Some pieces are extremely large; others are extremely small. An adjustment in the process is necessary.

Mean Chart

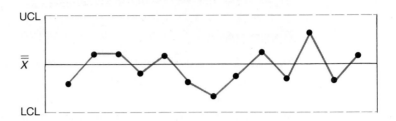

Range Chart

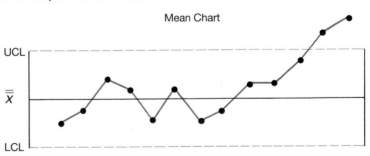

Mean measurement mean getting larger and larger

3. The arithmetic mean weight was in control for the first samples, but there was an upward trend toward UCL. The mean weights of the last two were out of control. An adjustment in the process is indicated.

Mean Chart

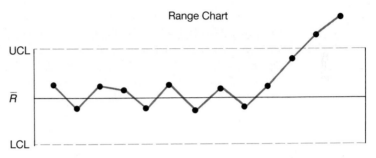

Range Chart

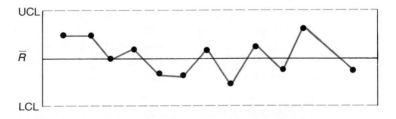

The above chart for the mean is an example in which the control chart offers some additional information. Note the direction of the last five observations of the mean. They are all above $\overline{\overline{X}}$ and increasing, and, in fact, the last two observations are out of control.

The fact that the sample means were increasing for seven consecutive observations is an indication that the process is out of control.

## EXERCISES

*The answers to the odd-numbered exercises are at the end of the book.*

1. Describe the difference between assignable variation and chance variation.

2. Describe the difference between a variable control chart and an attribute control chart.

3. Samples of size $n = 4$ are selected hourly from a production line.
   a. What is the value of the $A_2$ factor used to determine the upper and lower control limits for the mean?
   b. What are the values of the $D_3$ and $D_4$ factors used to determine the upper and lower control limits for the range?

4. Samples of size 5 are selected from a manufacturing process. The mean of the sample ranges is 0.25. What is the estimated standard deviation of the population?

5. A new industrial oven has just been installed. In order to develop experience regarding the temperature of the oven, the inspector reads the temperature in the oven at four different places every half hour. The first reading, taken at 8 A.M., was 2,040 degrees Fahrenheit. (Only the last two digits are given in the following table to facilitate computations.)

|  | Reading | | | |
| --- | --- | --- | --- | --- |
| Time | 1 | 2 | 3 | 4 |
| 8:00 A.M. | 40 | 50 | 55 | 39 |
| 8:30 A.M. | 44 | 42 | 38 | 38 |
| 9:00 A.M. | 41 | 45 | 47 | 43 |
| 9:30 A.M. | 39 | 39 | 41 | 41 |
| 10:00 A.M. | 37 | 42 | 46 | 41 |
| 10:30 A.M. | 39 | 40 | 39 | 40 |

   a. Based on this initial experience, set up a mean chart. Mark the upper and lower control limits and the grand mean. Then plot the 8:00–10:30 experience.
   b. Interpret the chart.

6. a. Design a range chart for the data from Exercise 5, and plot it immediately below the mean chart. Indicate the upper and lower control limits and mean range.
   b. Interpret the chart.

## CHARTS FOR ATTRIBUTES

Attribute charts—used mainly to show percent or number defective

A weld either has a crack in it or it doesn't; a relay works or it doesn't; a radiator leaks or it doesn't; the lock on a car door works or it doesn't; a tire fits on the rim or it doesn't. These are examples of *attributes*. If a part leaks, doesn't fit, won't lock, or doesn't work, it is said to be *defective*. Go/no-go gauges are one type of inspection tool for attributes; X-ray is another. Two types of quality-control charts for attributes will be examined. A **percent defective chart** shows the percent of production that is defective. A **c̄ chart** shows the number of defects per unit.

### PERCENT DEFECTIVE CHART

*Percent defective charts* are also known as *P charts or p̄ charts;* the latter is pronounced "*p* bar charts." The percent defective chart shows graphically the proportion of the production that is not acceptable.

## EXAMPLE

Percent defective

A new shearing machine is set to cut off a piece of steel from a long bar. For various reasons, the machine at times cuts off a piece that is too long or too short. These unacceptable pieces are automatically dropped in a box, and the operator of the shearing machine must count these defectives after every 100 pieces are sheared off. The record after the first day of operation is:

| Number sheared off | Number defective | Proportion defective |
|---|---|---|
| 100 | 5 | .05 |
| 100 | 6 | .06 |
| 100 | 7 | .07 |
| 100 | 4 | .04 |
| 100 | 8 | .08 |
| | | .30 |

How is a percent defective chart constructed?

## SOLUTION

Mean percent defective = 6 percent

The arithmetic mean proportion defective ($\bar{p}$) is .06, found by:

$$\bar{p} = \frac{\text{Sum of the percent defectives}}{\text{Number of samples}}$$

$$= \frac{.30}{5}$$

$$= .06 \qquad\qquad (21-4)$$

The upper control limit and the lower control limit are computed as the mean percent defective plus and minus three times the standard error of the percents.

$$\text{UCL and LCL} = \bar{p} \pm 3\sqrt{\frac{\bar{p}(1-\bar{p})}{n}} \qquad\qquad (21-5)$$

For this example:

UCL = 13.12 percent, LCL = 0

$$\text{UCL and LCL} = \bar{p} \pm 3\sqrt{\frac{\bar{p}(1-\bar{p})}{n}}$$

$$= .06 \pm 3\sqrt{\frac{(.06)(.94)}{100}}$$

$$= .06 \pm .0712$$

$$= .1312 \text{ and } -.0112$$

The upper control limit is .1312, and the lower control limit is 0, since there cannot be less than 0 percent defective.

Note in Chart 21–8 that the average percent defective ($\bar{p}$) of .06 along with UCL and LCL are shown. To complete the chart, the percent defective for each sample is plotted—namely, .05, .06, .07, .04, and .08, respectively.

## CHART 21–8

**Percent Defective Chart for Shearing Machine**

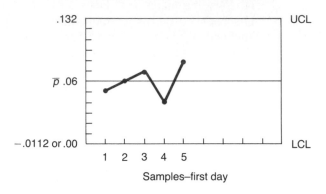

Samples–first day

Several observations can be made after the first day of operation: (1) The arithmetic mean percent defective is 6 percent. (2) About 99.7 percent of the time there will be between 0 percent and 13.1 percent defective pieces. (3) Only in 3 out of 1,000 samples of size 100 (1,000 − 997) will the percent defective either exceed 13.1 percent or, theoretically, be below 0 percent. (4) The first few samples revealed that the process is in control. No adjustments are warranted.

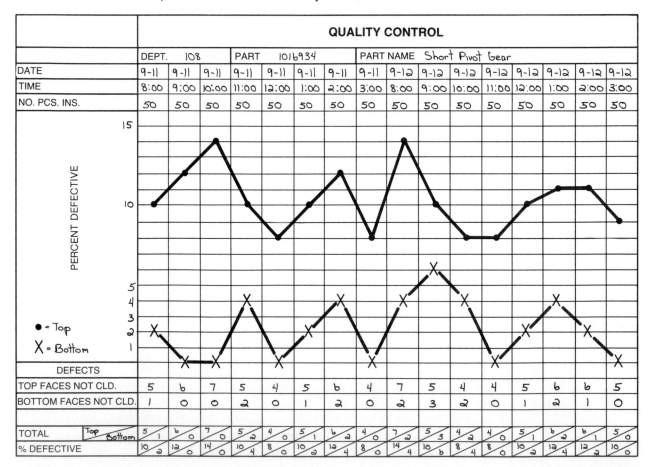

| | | QUALITY CONTROL | | | | | | | | | | | | | | |
|---|---|---|---|---|---|---|---|---|---|---|---|---|---|---|---|---|
| | DEPT. 108 | PART 1016934 | | PART NAME Short Pivot Gear | | | | | | | | | | | | |
| DATE | 9-11 | 9-11 | 9-11 | 9-11 | 9-11 | 9-11 | 9-11 | 9-11 | 9-12 | 9-12 | 9-12 | 9-12 | 9-12 | 9-12 | 9-12 | 9-12 |
| TIME | 8:00 | 9:00 | 10:00 | 11:00 | 12:00 | 1:00 | 2:00 | 3:00 | 8:00 | 9:00 | 10:00 | 11:00 | 12:00 | 1:00 | 2:00 | 3:00 |
| NO. PCS. INS. | 50 | 50 | 50 | 50 | 50 | 50 | 50 | 50 | 50 | 50 | 50 | 50 | 50 | 50 | 50 | 50 |
| DEFECTS | | | | | | | | | | | | | | | | |
| TOP FACES NOT CLD. | 5 | 6 | 7 | 5 | 4 | 5 | 6 | 4 | 7 | 5 | 4 | 4 | 5 | 6 | 6 | 5 |
| BOTTOM FACES NOT CLD. | 1 | 0 | 0 | 2 | 0 | 1 | 2 | 0 | 2 | 3 | 2 | 0 | 1 | 2 | 1 | 0 |
| TOTAL  Top/Bottom | 5/1 | 6/0 | 7/0 | 5/2 | 4/0 | 5/1 | 6/2 | 4/0 | 7/2 | 5/3 | 4/2 | 4/0 | 5/1 | 6/2 | 6/1 | 5/0 |
| % DEFECTIVE | 10/2 | 12/0 | 14/0 | 10/4 | 8/0 | 10/2 | 12/4 | 8/0 | 14/4 | 10/6 | 8/4 | 8/0 | 10/2 | 12/4 | 12/2 | 10/0 |

● = Top
X = Bottom

Management might or might not be satisfied with an average of 6 percent scrap or scrap as high as 13.1 percent. The chart cannot make a decision; that is management's responsibility. The $\bar{p}$ chart merely sets limits based on actual experience.

**Actual percent defective chart**

An actual $\bar{p}$ chart from an automobile manufacturing plant appears on page 762. (The name of the part has been changed slightly, but the data have not been altered.)

---

### Self-Review 21–3

*The answers are at the end of the chapter.*

Samples of 200 parts were taken every day. The numbers of defectives were counted.

Set up a percent defective chart, and plot the sample percents.

| Day | Number checked | Number defective |
|-----|----------------|------------------|
| 1 | 200 | 4 |
| 2 | 200 | 3 |
| 3 | 200 | 5 |
| 4 | 200 | 4 |

MINITAB has a system for generating a percent defective chart. Using the previous data:

```
MTB > set c10
DATA> 5,6,7,4,8
DATA> end
MTB > set c11
DATA> 5(100)
DATA> end
MTB > name c10 'Defects' c11 'Sample'

MTB > pchart c10 c11;
SUBC> Title 'Proportion Defective Chart'.
                    Proportion Defective Chart
        0.150+
             -
             -     ---------------------------------------------   UCL=0.1312
     P       -
     r       -
     o  0.100+
     p       -
     o       -                                          +
     r       -
     t       -     -----------+---------------------------------   P=0.06000
     i  0.050+     +
     o       -
     n       -                                    +
             -
             -
        0.000+     ---------------------------------------------   LCL=0.000
             -
             -
             +--------+--------+--------+--------+--------+----
             0        1        2        3        4        5
                              Sample Number
```

# EXERCISES

*The answers to the odd-numbered exercises are at the end of the book.*

7. The number of defectives in each of 10 samples of $n = 50$ is given below.

| Sample | Number defective | Sample | Number defective |
|--------|------------------|--------|------------------|
| 1 | 2 | 6 | 2 |
| 2 | 1 | 7 | 2 |
| 3 | 0 | 8 | 4 |
| 4 | 2 | 9 | 3 |
| 5 | 3 | 10 | 5 |

   a. Design a percent defective chart. Indicate the upper and lower control limits.

   b. The 11th sample of $n = 50$ contained 10 defects. Does this indicate the process is out of control?

8. A new high-speed machine appears to be producing a large percentage of defective bolts. A frequent check of its output on Tuesday resulted in the following:

| Sample number | Sample size | Number of defects | Sample number | Sample size | Number of defects |
|---------------|-------------|-------------------|---------------|-------------|-------------------|
| 1 | 50 | 4 | 11 | 50 | 2 |
| 2 | 50 | 0 | 12 | 50 | 3 |
| 3 | 50 | 3 | 13 | 50 | 6 |
| 4 | 50 | 5 | 14 | 50 | 4 |
| 5 | 50 | 6 | 15 | 50 | 5 |
| 6 | 50 | 4 | 16 | 50 | 7 |
| 7 | 50 | 1 | 17 | 50 | 6 |
| 8 | 50 | 6 | 18 | 50 | 5 |
| 9 | 50 | 7 | 19 | 50 | 10 |
| 10 | 50 | 8 | 20 | 50 | 2 |

   a. Design a percent defective chart. Indicate the upper and lower control limits and $\bar{p}$ on the chart. Plot Tuesday's experience.

   b. Interpret the chart.

## $\bar{c}$ BAR CHART

$\bar{c}$ bar chart for number of defects per unit

The $\bar{c}$ **chart** is alternatively called a $\bar{c}$ **bar chart.** It portrays the *number of defects per unit.* A glass bottle might be considered defective if there are "stones" or imperfections $\frac{1}{32}$ inch in size or more. If eight stones are found in a bottle picked at random from the assembly line, then the number of defects per unit is eight. In an automotive assembly plant, the number of defects per car door are counted. The defects might be two open seams, three slivers of steel that might scratch the new owner, one wavy section, and three small areas not completely painted. Thus, on this one car door there would be nine defects.

The purpose of a $\bar{c}$ chart, therefore, is to show graphically how many defects appear in a unit of production. $\bar{c}$ charts on subassemblies and the final assembly show management weak areas in the construction process. Remedial action can be taken, including shift of personnel or closer supervision of certain subassemblies.

## ■ EXAMPLE

A high-fidelity tuner is subjected to a final inspection. It is plugged in and tested by tuning to a local radio station. The tuners that work are packed and shipped. The others must be repaired before being released for sale. Possible defects might lie in the soldering or in the omission of parts. The quality-control inspector checks these defective tuners and counts the number of defects per tuner. Checks on 10 new-model tuners revealed the following number of defects per tuner: 8, 5, 6, 4, 3, 8, 8, 10, 9, and 9.

How is a $\bar{c}$ bar chart constructed?

## ☑ SOLUTION

**Formula for UCL and LCL for $\bar{c}$ chart**

The formula for the upper and lower control limits of a $\bar{c}$ bar chart is:

$$\boxed{\text{UCL and LCL} = \bar{c} \pm 3\sqrt{\bar{c}}} \qquad (21-6)$$

The total number of defects in the 10 new-model tuners is 70, found by $8 + 5 + 6 + 4 + 3 + 8 + 8 + 10 + 9 + 9$.

The arithmetic mean number of defects per tuner ($\bar{c}$) is:

$$\bar{c} = \frac{\text{Sum of the defects}}{\text{Total number of tuners}}$$

$$= \frac{70}{10}$$

$$= 7$$

The upper control limit and the lower control limit are:

$$\text{UCL and LCL} = \bar{c} \pm 3\sqrt{\bar{c}}$$

$$= 7 \pm 3\sqrt{7}$$

$$= 7 \pm 7.94$$

$$\text{UCL} = 14.94$$

$$\text{LCL} = 0 \text{ (since the number of defects per unit cannot be less than 0)}$$

Again, a lower control limit for a $\bar{c}$ chart is of no value. No doubt the assembly line workers, and management, would be very pleased if a tuner had no defects!

**Production "in control"**

The number of defects per tuner is plotted in Chart 21–9.

---

**CHART    21–9**

**C Bar Chart for High-Fidelity Tuner**

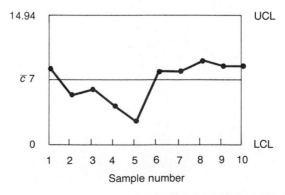
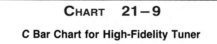

---

***INTERPRETATION*** The mean number of defects per unit is 7. In the long run, about 997 out of 1,000 tuners would have between 0 and 15 defects. UCL and LCL represent $\bar{c} \pm 3\sigma_c$.

The $\bar{c}$ chart would no doubt be revised after more samples were taken. It is reasoned that during the production of the first units of a new model, the machine operators and group leaders are somewhat unfamiliar with the process. Days or weeks are usually necessary before the process is stabilized.

Following is the MINITAB $\bar{c}$ bar chart for the high-fidelity tuner.

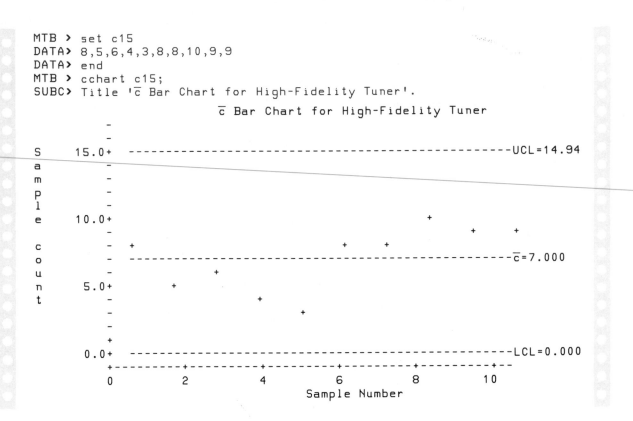

```
MTB > set c15
DATA> 8,5,6,4,3,8,8,10,9,9
DATA> end
MTB > cchart c15;
SUBC> Title 'c̄ Bar Chart for High-Fidelity Tuner'.
```

The following actual $\bar{c}$ chart from an automobile manufacturing plant might be of interest. (The name of the part has been changed, but the data have not been altered.)

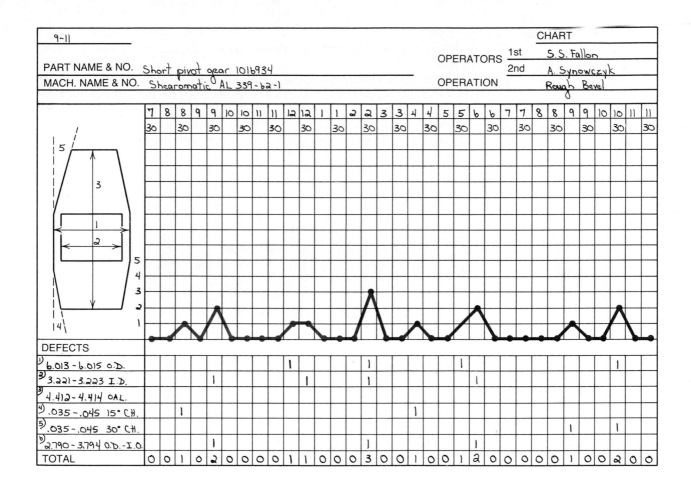

## Self-Review 21–4

*The answers are at the end of the chapter.*

A subassembly is thoroughly inspected, and the number of defects is recorded. A new group of assemblers began work Monday morning. The numbers of defects per subassembly for the first 10 they produced were: 3, 2, 0, 5, 4, 6, 0, 7, 7, and 6.

1. Set up a control chart for the average number of defects per subassembly, and plot the number of defects per subassembly.

2. Does it appear that the process is in control?

## EXERCISES

*The answers to the odd-numbered exercises are at the end of the book.*

9. The number of defectives per unit in each of 10 samples is given below.

| Unit | Number of defects | Unit | Number of defects |
|------|-------------------|------|-------------------|
| 1 | 2 | 6 | 2 |
| 2 | 1 | 7 | 2 |
| 3 | 0 | 8 | 4 |
| 4 | 2 | 9 | 3 |
| 5 | 3 | 10 | 5 |

a. Design a $\bar{c}$ bar chart. Indicate the upper and lower control limits.

b. The 11th unit sampled contained 6 defects. Does this indicate the process is out of control?

10. The manufacturer of a newly designed metal storage cabinet ships the cabinet unassembled, and the purchaser assembles it. An increasing number of complaints have been received regarding missing parts, sharp edges, hinges that did not align properly, imperfections in the enamel, and so on. In order to eliminate these complaints as far as possible, starting with Monday's production, each cabinet was fully assembled at the factory and the defects corrected before it was disassembled for shipment. A record of the number of defects per cabinet for the first 12 cabinets checked follows.

| Cabinet designation | Number of defects | Cabinet designation | Number of defects |
|---|---|---|---|
| OA1 | 7 | OA7 | 9 |
| OA2 | 6 | OA8 | 3 |
| OA3 | 8 | OA9 | 4 |
| OA4 | 10 | OA10 | 6 |
| OA5 | 8 | OA11 | 5 |
| OA6 | 4 | OA12 | 2 |

a. Design a chart to show the number of defects per unit. Show the upper and lower control limits and other essential data. Plot the experience for the first 12 cabinets inspected.

b. Interpret the chart.

## ACCEPTANCE SAMPLING

The previous section was concerned with maintaining the *quality of the product as it is being produced.* In many business situations we are also concerned with the *quality of the incoming finished product.* What do the following cases have in common?

- Sims Software, Inc. purchased diskettes from Diskettes International. The normal purchase order is for 100,000 diskettes, packaged in lots of 1,000. Todd Sims, president, does not expect each diskette to be perfect. In fact, he has agreed to accept lots of 1,000 with up to 10 percent defective. He would like to develop a plan to inspect incoming lots, to ensure that the quality standard is met. The purpose of the inspection procedure is to separate the acceptable from the unacceptable lots.

- Zenith Electric purchases magnetron tubes from Bono Electronics for use in their new microwave oven. The tubes are shipped to Zenith in lots of 10,000. Zenith allows the incoming lots to contain up to 5 percent defective tubes. They would like to develop a sampling plan to determine which lots meet the criterion and which do not.

- General Motors purchases windshields from many suppliers. GM insists that the windshields be in lots of 1,000. They are willing to accept 50 or fewer defects in each lot, i.e., 5 percent defective. They would like to develop a sampling procedure to verify that incoming shipments meet the criterion.

The common thread in these cases is a need to verify that incoming products meet the stipulated requirements. The situation can be likened to a screen door, which allows the warm summer air to enter the room while keeping the bugs out. Acceptance sampling lets the lots of acceptable quality into the manufacturing area and screens out lots that are not acceptable.

Of course, the situation in modern business is more complex. The buyer wants protection against accepting lots that are below the quality standard. The best protection against inferior quality is 100 percent inspection. Unfortunately, the cost of 100 percent inspection is often prohibitive. Another problem with checking each item is that the test may be destructive. If all light bulbs were tested until burning out before they were shipped, there would be none left to sell. Also, 100 percent inspection may not lead to the identification of all defects due to boredom and the consequent loss of perception on the part of the inspectors. Thus, complete inspection is rarely employed in practical situations.

The usual procedure is to screen the quality of incoming parts by use of a statistical sampling plan. According to this plan a sample of $n$ units is randomly selected from the lots of $N$ units (the population). This is called **acceptance sampling.** The inspection will determine the number of defects in the sample. This number is compared with a predetermined number called the **critical number** or the **acceptance number.** The acceptance number is usually designated **c.** If the number of defects in the sample of size $n$ is less than or equal to **c,** the lot is accepted. If the number of defects exceeds **c,** the lot is rejected and returned to the supplier, or perhaps submitted to 100 percent inspection.

Acceptance sampling is a decision-making process. There are two possible decisions: accept or reject the lot. In addition, there are two situations under which the decision is made: the lot is good or the lot is bad. These are the states of nature. If the lot is good and the sample inspection reveals the lot to be good, or if the lot is bad and the sample inspection indicates it is bad, then a correct decision is made. However, there are two other possibilities. The lot may actually contain more defects than it should, but it is accepted. This is called *consumer's risk,* or the *beta error.* Similarly, the lot may be within the agreed-upon limits, but it is rejected during the sample inspection. This is called the *producer's risk* or the *alpha error.* The following summary table for acceptance decisions shows these possibilities.

*Margin notes:*
100 percent inspection not feasible

Acceptance sampling

Acceptance number

States of nature

Consumer's risk

Producer's risk

|  | States of nature | |
|---|---|---|
| Decision | Good lot | Bad lot |
| Accept lot | Correct | Beta error |
| Reject lot | Alpha error | Correct |

*Margin notes:*
OC curve

Binomial distribution

To evaluate a sampling plan and determine that it is fair to both the producer and the consumer, the usual procedure is to develop an **operating characteristic curve,** or an **OC curve,** as it is usually called. An OC curve reports the percent defective along the horizontal axis and the probability of accepting that percent defective along the vertical axis. A smooth curve is usually drawn connecting all the possible levels of quality. The binomial distribution is used to develop the probabilities for an OC curve.

### ■ EXAMPLE

Sims Software, as mentioned earlier, purchases diskettes from Diskettes International. The diskettes are packaged in lots of 1,000 each. Todd Sims, president of Sims Software, has agreed to accept lots with 10 percent or fewer defective diskettes. Todd has directed his inspection department to select a sample of 20 diskettes and examine them carefully. He will accept the lot if it has two or fewer defectives in the sample. Develop an OC curve for this inspection plan. What is the probability of accepting a lot that is 20 percent defective?

### ☑ SOLUTION

Attribute sampling

This type of sampling is called **attribute sampling** because the sampled item, a diskette in this case, is classified as acceptable or unacceptable. No "reading" or "measurement" is obtained on the diskette. Let's structure the problem in terms of the states of nature. Let $p$ represent the actual proportion defective in the population.

> The lot is good if $p \leq .10$.
> The lot is bad if $p > .10$.

Decision rule

Let $X$ be the number of defects in the sample. The decison rule is:

> Reject the lot if $X \geq 3$.
> Accept the lot if $X \leq 2$.

Here the acceptable lot is one with 10 percent or fewer defective diskettes. If the lot is acceptable when it has exactly 10 percent defectives, it would be even more acceptable if it contained fewer than 10 percent defective. Hence, it is the usual practice to work with the upper limit of the percent of defectives.

The binomial distribution is used to compute the various values on the OC curve. Recall that for us to use the binomial, there are four requirements.

1. There are only two possible outcomes. Here the diskette is either acceptable or unacceptable.
2. There are a fixed number of trials. In this instance the number of trials is the sample size of 20.
3. There is a constant probability of success. A success is the probability of finding a defective part. It is assumed to be .10.
4. The trials are independent. The probability of obtaining a defective diskette on the third one selected is not related to the likelihood of finding a defect on the fourth diskette selected.

Appendix A gives the various binomial probabilities. We need to convert the acceptance sampling nomenclature to that used in Chapter 6 for discrete probability distributions. Let $p = .10$, the probability of a success, and $n = 20$, the number of trials. **c** is the number of defects allowed—two in this case. We will now determine the probability of accepting an incoming lot that is 10 percent defective using a sample size of 20 and allowing zero, one, or two defects. First, locate within Appendix A the case where $n = 20$ and $p = .10$. Find the row where $r$, the number of defects, is 0. The probability is .122. Next find the probability of one defect, that is, where $r = 1$. It is .270. Similarly, the probability of $r = 2$ is .285. To find the probability of two or fewer defects, we need to add these three probabilities. The total is .677. Hence, the probability of accepting a lot that is 10 percent defective, that is, containing two or fewer defects in a sample of 20, is .677. The probability of rejecting this lot is .323, found by $1 - .677$. This result is usually written in shorthand notation as follows (the bar, |, means "given that"):

$$P(X \leq 2 \mid p = .10 \text{ and } n = 20) = .677$$

The probability can also be obtained directly from Appendix B. Appendix B is a *cumulative binomial table*. It gives the values less than or equal to $X$. The table is structured the same as Appendix A for locating a probability. Go to $n = 20$, and find the column where $p = .10$ and the row where $r = 2$. Read the value. It is .677, the same as we found earlier.

To obtain other values on the OC curve, we assume other values for $p$. For example, to compute the probability of accepting a lot that is actually 20 percent defective, we can read the value directly from Appendix B:

$$P(X \le 2 \mid p = .20 \text{ and } n = 20) = .206$$

The OC curve in Chart 21–10 shows various values of $p$ and the corresponding probabilities of accepting a lot of that quality. Management of Sims Software wil be able to quickly evaluate the probabilities of various quality levels. Note that only a small number of values for $n$ and $p$ are given in Appendix B. Other values may be obtained by using the normal approximation of the binomial.

---

CHART   21–10

**OC Curve for Sampling Plan ($n = 20$, $c = 2$)**

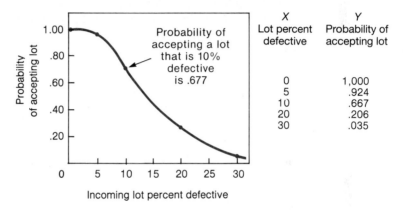

| X<br>Lot percent<br>defective | Y<br>Probability of<br>accepting lot |
|:---:|:---:|
| 0 | 1,000 |
| 5 | .924 |
| 10 | .667 |
| 20 | .206 |
| 30 | .035 |

Incoming lot percent defective

---

## Self-Review 21–5

*The answers are at the end of the chapter.*

Compute the probability of accepting a lot of diskettes that is actually 30 percent defective, using the sampling plan for Sims Software. Use Appendix B.

## EXERCISES

*The answers to the odd-numbered exercises are at the end of the book.*

11. Determine the probability of accepting lots that are 10 percent, 20 percent, 30 percent, and 40 percent defective using a sample of size 12 and an acceptance number of 2.

12. Determine the probability of accepting lots that are 10 percent, 20 percent, 30 percent, and 40 percent defective using a sample of size 14 and an acceptance number of 3.

13. Warren Electric manufactures fuses for many customers. To ensure the quality of the outgoing product, they test 10 fuses each hour. If no more than one fuse is defective, they package the fuses and prepare them for shipment. Develop an OC curve for this sampling plan. Compute the probabilities of accepting lots that are 10 percent, 20 percent, 30 percent, and 40 percent defective. Draw the OC curve for this sampling plan using the four quality levels.

14. Grills Radio Products purchases transistors from Mira Electronics. According to his sampling plan, Art Grills, owner of Grills Radio, will accept a shipment of transistors if three or fewer are defective in a sample of 25. Develop an OC curve for these percents defective: 10 percent, 20 percent, 30 percent, and 40 percent.

## CHAPTER OUTLINE

I. The objective of statistical quality control is to control the quality of a manufacturing or service operation using sampling techniques.

II. Control chart.
    A. There are two causes of variation in production.
        1. Chance causes: Few in number, random in nature, cannot be entirely eliminated.
        2. Assignable causes: Few in number, nonrandom, can be reduced or eliminated.
    B. The purpose of quality-control charts is to determine and portray graphically just when an assignable cause enters the production system so that it can be identified and corrected. This is accomplished by selecting a very small random sample from current production periodically.
    C. Types of charts.
        1. Mean charts, also called $X$ bar charts, are designed to control variables, such as weights, lengths, and tensile strengths. The upper control limit (UCL) and lower control limit (LCL) are found by $\overline{\overline{X}} \pm A_2\overline{R}$ [formula (21–2)], where $\overline{\overline{X}}$ is the mean of the sample means, $A_2$ is a factor from Appendix L, and $\overline{R}$ is the mean of the sample ranges. The chart on the left indicates that production is "in control." The one on the right is an "out of control" situation, with the outside diameter of the part in question much too large and unacceptable at the last two checks.

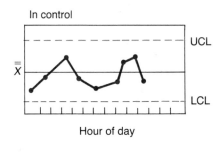
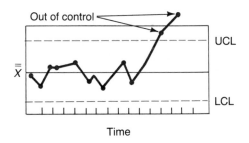

        2. A range chart is another chart for variables. It shows whether the overall range of measurement is in or out of control. UCL and LCL are found by $D_4\overline{R}$ and $D_3\overline{R}$, respectively. The factors $D_4$ and $D_3$ are given in Appendix L. $\overline{R}$ is the mean of the sample ranges.
        3. The percent defective chart is a chart for an attribute. An example of an attribute is: Ball bearing is either good or defective. UCL and LCL are found by:

$$\overline{p} \pm 3\sqrt{\frac{\overline{p}(1 - \overline{p})}{n}} \tag{21–5}$$

        where $\overline{p}$ is the mean proportion defective based on samples taken from the production line.
        4. The $\overline{c}$ chart is another attribute chart designed to control the number of defects per unit. UCL and LCL are found by:

$$\overline{c} \pm 3\sqrt{\overline{c}} \tag{21–6}$$

        where $\overline{c}$ is the mean number of defects per unit.

III. Acceptance sampling is a method of determining whether an incoming lot of a product meets specified standards.
   A. It is based on random sampling techniques.
   B. A random sample of $n$ units is obtained from the entire lot.
   C. **c** is the maximum number of defective units that may be found in the sample for the lot to still be considered acceptable.
   D. An OC, or operating characteristic, curve is developed using the binomial probability distribution, in order to determine the probabilities of accepting lots of various quality levels.

# EXERCISES

*The answers to the odd-numbered exercises are at the end of the book.*

15. McBurger fast food restaurants fill their soft drinks with an automatic machine that works based on the weight of the soft drink. When the process is in control, the machine fills each cup so that the grand mean is 10.0 ounces and the mean range is 0.25 ounce for samples of size 5.
   a. Determine the upper and lower control limits for the process.
   b. The manager of the I-280 store tested five soft drinks served last hour and found the mean was 10.16 ounces and the range was 0.35 ounces. Is the process in control? Should action be taken?

16. The Clean City Police Department maintains records on crimes per 1,000 residents in its various precincts. The mean is 4.00 crimes per 1,000 residents.
   a. Determine a control chart limits for the number of crimes per precinct.
   b. Last month there were 11.3 crimes committed per 1,000 residents in Willoughby Hills. Does crime seem to be out of control in Willoughby Hills?

17. The Early Morning delivery service guarantees delivery of its packages by 10:30 A.M. Of course, all packages do not meet this standard. For a sample of 200 packages delivered each of the last 15 working days, the following numbers were delivered after 10:30: 9, 14, 2, 13, 9, 5, 9, 3, 4, 3, 4, 3, 3, 8, 4.
   a. Determine the mean proportion of packages delivered after 10:30 A.M.
   b. Determine the upper and lower control limits for the proportion of packages delivered after 10:30 A.M.
   c. If 10 packages out of 200 were delivered after 10:30 A.M. today, does this exceed the usual standard?

18. Eric's Cookie House sells chocolate chip cookies in shopping malls. Of concern is the number of chocolate chips in each cookie. Eric, the owner and president, would like to establish a control chart for the number of chocolate chips per cookie. He selected a sample of 10 cookies from today's production and counted the number of chocolate chips in each of the sampled cookies. The results are: 15, 18, 15, 4, 14, 18, 9, 17, 12, 15. What are the appropriate control limits?

19. A mean chart and a range chart are to be designed. Every hour a quality-control technician measures the thickness of the part and records the measurements. She also computes the mean thickness of the four parts and determines the range. After 30 hours had elapsed, the sum of the 30 means was computed to be 1,356 inches and the sum of the ranges 375 inches. Assume that the process is in control.
   a. Determine the centerline, the upper control limit, and the lower control limit for the X bar chart.
   b. Determine the centerline, the upper control limit, and the lower control limit for the range chart.

20. A glass manufacturer installed a new furnace and automatic equipment to make clear glass bowls. One of the problems associated with glassmaking is the appearance of unwanted stones. (Stones are small bubbles in the glass, which are considered imperfections if over a specified diameter.)

    In order to monitor the number of stones per bowl, a quality-control inspector selected 15 bowls at random and counted the number of stones over 1.5 millimeters in diameter in each bowl. The number of stones per bowl were 14, 15, 10, 10, 14, 13, 12, 10, 11, 12, 9, 12, 12, 8, and 21.

    a. Construct a chart specifically designed to monitor the number of defects per unit. Show essential figures on the chart.

    b. Plot the number of imperfections for the 15 bowls selected at random.

    c. Interpret your chart.

21. An automatic machine produces 5.0-millimeter bolts at a high rate of speed. A quality-control program has been started to control the number of defectives. The quality-control inspector selects 50 bolts at random and determines how many are defective. The numbers defective for the first 10 samples follow.

| Sample number | Size of sample | Number of defects |
|---|---|---|
| 1 | 50 | 3 |
| 2 | 50 | 5 |
| 3 | 50 | 0 |
| 4 | 50 | 4 |
| 5 | 50 | 1 |
| 6 | 50 | 2 |
| 7 | 50 | 6 |
| 8 | 50 | 5 |
| 9 | 50 | 7 |
| 10 | 50 | 7 |

    a. Design a percent defective chart. Insert $\bar{p}$, LCL, and the percents defective on the chart.

    b. Plot the number of defects for the first 10 samples on the chart.

    c. Interpret the chart.

22. A new machine has just been installed to cut and rough-shape large slugs. The slugs are then transferred to a precision grinder. One critical measurement is the outside diameter. The quality-control inspector was instructed to select five slugs at random every half hour from the output of the new machine, measure the outside diameter, and record the results. The measurements (in millimeters) for the period from 8:00 A.M. to 10:30 A.M. follow.

| Time | Outside diameter (in millimeters) | | | | |
|---|---|---|---|---|---|
| | 1 | 2 | 3 | 4 | 5 |
| 8:00 A.M. | 87.1 | 87.3 | 87.9 | 87.0 | 87.0 |
| 8:30 A.M. | 86.9 | 88.5 | 87.6 | 87.5 | 87.4 |
| 9:00 A.M. | 87.5 | 88.4 | 86.9 | 87.6 | 88.2 |
| 9:30 A.M. | 86.0 | 88.0 | 87.2 | 87.6 | 87.1 |
| 10:00 A.M. | 87.1 | 87.1 | 87.1 | 87.1 | 87.1 |
| 10:30 A.M. | 88.0 | 86.2 | 87.4 | 87.3 | 87.8 |

    a. Design a mean chart. Insert the control limits and other essential figures on the chart.

    b. Plot the means on the chart.

    c. Immediately below the mean chart, draw a range chart. plot the ranges on the chart.

    d. Interpret the two charts.

23. The numbers of near misses recorded for the last 20 months at the Lima International Airport are shown below. Develop an appropriate control chart. What would you conclude from a general upward trend, even though the upper control limit was not reached?

| Month | Near misses | Month | Near misses |
|-------|-------------|-------|-------------|
| 1 | 3 | 11 | 5 |
| 2 | 2 | 12 | 2 |
| 3 | 1 | 13 | 3 |
| 4 | 4 | 14 | 1 |
| 5 | 5 | 15 | 1 |
| 6 | 0 | 16 | 3 |
| 7 | 1 | 17 | 3 |
| 8 | 3 | 18 | 2 |
| 9 | 0 | 19 | 3 |
| 10 | 2 | 20 | 3 |

24. At the beginning of each football season Team Sports, the local sporting goods store, purchases 5,000 footballs. A sample of 25 balls is selected, and they are inflated, tested, and then deflated. If more than two balls are found defective, the lot of 5,000 is returned to the manufacturer. Develop an OC curve for this sampling plan.

    a. What are the probabilities of accepting lots that are 10 percent, 20 percent, and 30 percent defective?

    b. Estimate the probability of accepting a lot that is 15 percent defective.

    c. John Brennen, owner of Team Sports, would like the probability of accepting a lot that is 5 percent defective to be more than 90 percent. Does this appear to be the case with this sampling plan?

25. Marchal Screen Door Manufacturing Company purchases door latches from a number of vendors. The purchasing department is responsible for inspecting the incoming latches. Marchal purchases 10,000 door latches per month and inspects 20 latches selected at random. Develop an OC curve for the sampling plan if three latches can be defective and the incoming lot is still accepted.

# CHAPTER 21 EXAMINATION

*The answers are at the end of the chapter.*

For Questions 1 through 3 fill in the blank with the correct answer.

1. Percent defective and $\bar{c}$ bar charts are examples of _____ (attribute or variable) control charts.

2. In a percent defective chart the underlying distribution is the _____.

3. In a $\bar{c}$ bar chart the underlying distribution is the _____.

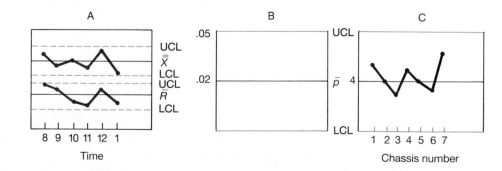

Questions 4 through 10 are based on Charts A, B, and C, on the bottom of the previous page.

4. Chart A combines which two charts?

5. For Chart A, is the process in control or out of control?

6. What will Chart B be called when its construction is completed?

7. Referring again to Chart B, what is the lower control limit?

8. Referring to Chart C, based on past experience, how many defects are there per chassis on the average?

9. What is Chart C called?

10. What are the upper and lower control limits of Chart C?

11. The quality-control inspector checks five pieces of the output of a shearing machine every hour. She measures and records each piece to the nearest hundredth of an inch. The record for the first four hours is:

| Time | 1 | 2 | 3 | 4 | 5 |
|------|------|------|------|------|------|
| 8 A.M. | 6.04 | 6.01 | 6.05 | 6.02 | 6.06 |
| 9 A.M. | 6.01 | 6.02 | 6.03 | 6.02 | 6.02 |
| 10 A.M. | 6.01 | 6.05 | 6.07 | 6.03 | 6.04 |
| 11 A.M. | 6.02 | 6.04 | 6.04 | 6.03 | 6.02 |

a. Design an $X$ bar chart, and plot the essential data for the four hours.

b. Design a range chart, and plot the essential data for the four hours.

12. The quality-control inspector from the previous problem goes to another operation, where she checks 200 pieces. The piece is either good or defective. The record for nine hours is:

| Time | Number of pieces checked | Number of defects |
|------|------|------|
| 8 A.M. | 200 | 0 |
| 9 A.M. | 200 | 3 |
| 10 A.M. | 200 | 4 |
| 11 A.M. | 200 | 0 |
| 12 A.M. | 200 | 5 |
| 1 P.M. | 200 | 2 |
| 2 P.M. | 200 | 0 |
| 3 P.M. | 200 | 1 |
| 4 P.M. | 200 | 3 |

a. Design a percent defective chart, and plot the essential data.

b. Interpret the chart.

13. A new assembly operation has just been started. A small group of assembly-line employees inserts parts, solders, and performs other tasks to produce a radio chassis. The completed chassis is checked, and all defects must be repaired. The numbers of defects per chassis for the first 10 produced are:

| Chassis number | Number of defects |
|------|------|
| 1 | 0 |
| 2 | 1 |
| 3 | 0 |
| 4 | 2 |
| 5 | 3 |
| 6 | 0 |
| 7 | 1 |
| 8 | 1 |
| 9 | 2 |
| 10 | 4 |

    a.    Design a $\bar{c}$ chart, and plot the essential data.

    b.    Interpret the chart.

14. Seiko purchases watch stems for their watches in lots of 10,000. Seiko's sampling plan calls for checking 20 stems, and if 3 or fewer stems are defective, the lot is accepted.

    a.    Based on their sampling plan, what is the probability that a lot of 40 percent defective will be accepted?

    b.    Design an OC curve for incoming lots that have zero, 10 percent, 20 percent, 30 percent, and 40 percent defective stems.

21–1

| Sample piece | | | | | | |
|---|---|---|---|---|---|---|
| 1 | 2 | 3 | 4 | Total | Average | Range |
| 1 | 4 | 5 | 2 | 12 | 3 | 4 |
| 2 | 3 | 2 | 1 | 8 | 2 | 2 |
| 1 | 7 | 3 | 5 | 16 | 4 | 6 |
| | | | | | 9 | 12 |

$$\bar{\bar{X}} = \frac{9}{3} = 3$$

$$\bar{R} = \frac{12}{3} = 4$$

$$\text{UCL and LCL} = \bar{\bar{X}} \pm A_2\bar{R}$$

$$= 3 \pm 0.729(4)$$

$$\text{UCL} = 5.916$$

$$\text{LCL} = 0.084$$

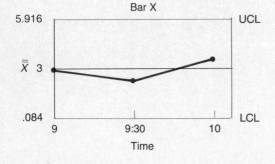

2. Yes. Both the mean chart (Self-Review 21–1) and the range chart indicate that the process is in control.

21–3

| Day | Number checked | Number defective | Percent defective |
|---|---|---|---|
| 1 | 200 | 4 | .020 |
| 2 | 200 | 3 | .015 |
| 3 | 200 | 5 | .025 |
| 4 | 200 | 4 | .020 |
| | | | .080 |

$$\bar{p} = \frac{.08}{4} = .02$$

$$\text{UCL and LCL} = .02 \pm 3\sqrt{\frac{.02(.98)}{200}}$$

$$= .02 \pm .0297$$

$$= .0497 \text{ and } 0$$

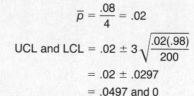

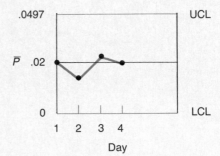

21–2  1.    $$\text{LCL} = \bar{R} - 3\sigma_R \quad \text{UCL} = \bar{R} + 3\sigma_R$$

$$= D_3\bar{R} \qquad\qquad = D_4\bar{R}$$

$$= 0(4) \qquad\qquad = 2.282(4)$$

$$= 0 \qquad\qquad = 9.128$$

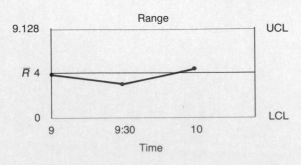

21–4  1.    $$\bar{c} = \frac{40}{10} = 4$$

$$\text{UCL and LCL} = \bar{c} \pm 3\sqrt{\bar{c}} = 4 \pm 3\sqrt{4}$$

$$= 10, -2 \text{ (or 0)}$$

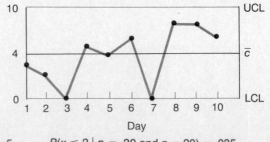

21–5    $$P(x \le 2 \mid p = .30 \text{ and } n = 20) = .035$$

# CHAPTER 21 EXAMINATION

1. Attribute.
2. Binomial.
3. Poisson.
4. A mean chart and a range chart.
5. In control.
6. A percent defective chart.
7. Zero.
8. 4.
9. A chart for the number of defects per unit, called a $C$ bar chart.
10. 10 and 0, found by $4 \pm 3\sqrt{4}$
11. a. UCL and LCL are 6.0531375 inches and 6.0098625 inches, respectively, found by $\bar{\bar{X}} \pm A_2\bar{R} = 6.0315 \pm 0.577(0.0375)$. Plots are 6.036, 6.020, 6.04, and 6.03, respectively.

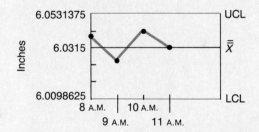

b. UCL and LCL for the range chart are 0.0793125 and 0, found by $D_4\bar{R} = (2.115)(0.0375)$ and $D_3\bar{R} = (0)(0.0375)$. Plots are .05, .02, .06, and .02, respectively.

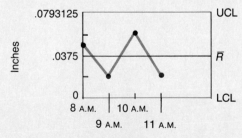

12. a. UCL and LCL are 3.1108 and 0 percent, found by:

$$.01 \pm 3\sqrt{\frac{(.01)(.99)}{200}}$$

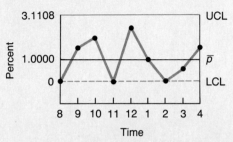

b. If production continues, as evidenced by the nine samples of 200 pieces selected at random, then the average percent defective will be 1.0 percent. More than 99 percent of the samples of 200 will contain between 0 percent and 3.1108 percent defectives.

13. a. UCL and LCL for the $\bar{c}$ chart are 4.949648 and 0, found by $\bar{c} \pm 3\sqrt{\bar{c}} = 1.4 \pm 3(1.83216)$.

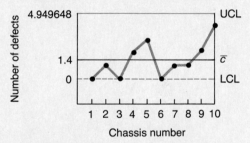

b. If the assembly process continues as evidenced by the first 10 produced, more than 99 percent of the chassis will have between 0 and 4.949648 defects. The mean will be 1.4 defects per chassis.

14. a. .016, from Appendix B.

b.

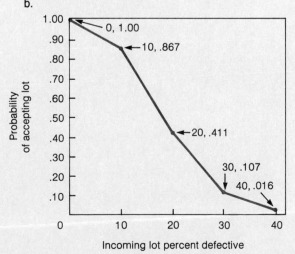

# Appendixes

## TABLES AND DATA SETS

# Binomial Probability Distribution

### $n = 1$
PROBABILITY

| r | 0.05 | 0.10 | 0.20 | 0.30 | 0.40 | 0.50 | 0.60 | 0.70 | 0.80 | 0.90 | 0.95 |
|---|------|------|------|------|------|------|------|------|------|------|------|
| 0 | 0.950 | 0.900 | 0.800 | 0.700 | 0.600 | 0.500 | 0.400 | 0.300 | 0.200 | 0.100 | 0.050 |
| 1 | 0.050 | 0.100 | 0.200 | 0.300 | 0.400 | 0.500 | 0.600 | 0.700 | 0.800 | 0.900 | 0.950 |

### $n = 2$
PROBABILITY

| r | 0.05 | 0.10 | 0.20 | 0.30 | 0.40 | 0.50 | 0.60 | 0.70 | 0.80 | 0.90 | 0.95 |
|---|------|------|------|------|------|------|------|------|------|------|------|
| 0 | 0.903 | 0.810 | 0.640 | 0.490 | 0.360 | 0.250 | 0.160 | 0.090 | 0.040 | 0.010 | 0.003 |
| 1 | 0.095 | 0.180 | 0.320 | 0.420 | 0.480 | 0.500 | 0.480 | 0.420 | 0.320 | 0.180 | 0.095 |
| 2 | 0.003 | 0.010 | 0.040 | 0.090 | 0.160 | 0.250 | 0.360 | 0.490 | 0.640 | 0.810 | 0.903 |

### $n = 3$
PROBABILITY

| r | 0.05 | 0.10 | 0.20 | 0.30 | 0.40 | 0.50 | 0.60 | 0.70 | 0.80 | 0.90 | 0.95 |
|---|------|------|------|------|------|------|------|------|------|------|------|
| 0 | 0.857 | 0.729 | 0.512 | 0.343 | 0.216 | 0.125 | 0.064 | 0.027 | 0.008 | 0.001 | 0.000 |
| 1 | 0.135 | 0.243 | 0.384 | 0.441 | 0.432 | 0.375 | 0.288 | 0.189 | 0.096 | 0.027 | 0.007 |
| 2 | 0.007 | 0.027 | 0.096 | 0.189 | 0.288 | 0.375 | 0.432 | 0.441 | 0.384 | 0.243 | 0.135 |
| 3 | 0.000 | 0.001 | 0.008 | 0.027 | 0.064 | 0.125 | 0.216 | 0.343 | 0.512 | 0.729 | 0.857 |

### $n = 4$
PROBABILITY

| r | 0.05 | 0.10 | 0.20 | 0.30 | 0.40 | 0.50 | 0.60 | 0.70 | 0.80 | 0.90 | 0.95 |
|---|------|------|------|------|------|------|------|------|------|------|------|
| 0 | 0.815 | 0.656 | 0.410 | 0.240 | 0.130 | 0.063 | 0.026 | 0.008 | 0.002 | 0.000 | 0.000 |
| 1 | 0.171 | 0.292 | 0.410 | 0.412 | 0.346 | 0.250 | 0.154 | 0.076 | 0.026 | 0.004 | 0.000 |
| 2 | 0.014 | 0.049 | 0.154 | 0.265 | 0.346 | 0.375 | 0.346 | 0.265 | 0.154 | 0.049 | 0.014 |
| 3 | 0.000 | 0.004 | 0.026 | 0.076 | 0.154 | 0.250 | 0.346 | 0.412 | 0.410 | 0.292 | 0.171 |
| 4 | 0.000 | 0.000 | 0.002 | 0.008 | 0.026 | 0.063 | 0.130 | 0.240 | 0.410 | 0.656 | 0.815 |

### $n = 5$
PROBABILITY

| r | 0.05 | 0.10 | 0.20 | 0.30 | 0.40 | 0.50 | 0.60 | 0.70 | 0.80 | 0.90 | 0.95 |
|---|------|------|------|------|------|------|------|------|------|------|------|
| 0 | 0.774 | 0.590 | 0.328 | 0.168 | 0.078 | 0.031 | 0.010 | 0.002 | 0.000 | 0.000 | 0.000 |
| 1 | 0.204 | 0.328 | 0.410 | 0.360 | 0.259 | 0.156 | 0.077 | 0.028 | 0.006 | 0.000 | 0.000 |
| 2 | 0.021 | 0.073 | 0.205 | 0.309 | 0.346 | 0.313 | 0.230 | 0.132 | 0.051 | 0.008 | 0.001 |
| 3 | 0.001 | 0.008 | 0.051 | 0.132 | 0.230 | 0.313 | 0.346 | 0.309 | 0.205 | 0.073 | 0.021 |
| 4 | 0.000 | 0.000 | 0.006 | 0.028 | 0.077 | 0.156 | 0.259 | 0.360 | 0.410 | 0.328 | 0.204 |
| 5 | 0.000 | 0.000 | 0.000 | 0.002 | 0.010 | 0.031 | 0.078 | 0.168 | 0.328 | 0.590 | 0.774 |

### $n = 6$
PROBABILITY

| r | 0.05 | 0.10 | 0.20 | 0.30 | 0.40 | 0.50 | 0.60 | 0.70 | 0.80 | 0.90 | 0.95 |
|---|------|------|------|------|------|------|------|------|------|------|------|
| 0 | 0.735 | 0.531 | 0.262 | 0.118 | 0.047 | 0.016 | 0.004 | 0.001 | 0.000 | 0.000 | 0.000 |
| 1 | 0.232 | 0.354 | 0.393 | 0.303 | 0.187 | 0.094 | 0.037 | 0.010 | 0.002 | 0.000 | 0.000 |
| 2 | 0.031 | 0.098 | 0.246 | 0.324 | 0.311 | 0.234 | 0.138 | 0.060 | 0.015 | 0.001 | 0.000 |
| 3 | 0.002 | 0.015 | 0.082 | 0.185 | 0.276 | 0.313 | 0.276 | 0.185 | 0.082 | 0.015 | 0.002 |
| 4 | 0.000 | 0.001 | 0.015 | 0.060 | 0.138 | 0.234 | 0.311 | 0.324 | 0.246 | 0.098 | 0.031 |
| 5 | 0.000 | 0.000 | 0.002 | 0.010 | 0.037 | 0.094 | 0.187 | 0.303 | 0.393 | 0.354 | 0.232 |
| 6 | 0.000 | 0.000 | 0.000 | 0.001 | 0.004 | 0.016 | 0.047 | 0.118 | 0.262 | 0.531 | 0.735 |

## Appendix A

## BINOMIAL PROBABILITY DISTRIBUTION (continued)

### n = 7
PROBABILITY

| r | 0.05 | 0.10 | 0.20 | 0.30 | 0.40 | 0.50 | 0.60 | 0.70 | 0.80 | 0.90 | 0.95 |
|---|------|------|------|------|------|------|------|------|------|------|------|
| 0 | 0.698 | 0.478 | 0.210 | 0.082 | 0.028 | 0.008 | 0.002 | 0.000 | 0.000 | 0.000 | 0.000 |
| 1 | 0.257 | 0.372 | 0.367 | 0.247 | 0.131 | 0.055 | 0.017 | 0.004 | 0.000 | 0.000 | 0.000 |
| 2 | 0.041 | 0.124 | 0.275 | 0.318 | 0.261 | 0.164 | 0.077 | 0.025 | 0.004 | 0.000 | 0.000 |
| 3 | 0.004 | 0.023 | 0.115 | 0.227 | 0.290 | 0.273 | 0.194 | 0.097 | 0.029 | 0.003 | 0.000 |
| 4 | 0.000 | 0.003 | 0.029 | 0.097 | 0.194 | 0.273 | 0.290 | 0.227 | 0.115 | 0.023 | 0.004 |
| 5 | 0.000 | 0.000 | 0.004 | 0.025 | 0.077 | 0.164 | 0.261 | 0.318 | 0.275 | 0.124 | 0.041 |
| 6 | 0.000 | 0.000 | 0.000 | 0.004 | 0.017 | 0.055 | 0.131 | 0.247 | 0.367 | 0.372 | 0.257 |
| 7 | 0.000 | 0.000 | 0.000 | 0.000 | 0.002 | 0.008 | 0.028 | 0.082 | 0.210 | 0.478 | 0.698 |

### n = 8
PROBABILITY

| r | 0.05 | 0.10 | 0.20 | 0.30 | 0.40 | 0.50 | 0.60 | 0.70 | 0.80 | 0.90 | 0.95 |
|---|------|------|------|------|------|------|------|------|------|------|------|
| 0 | 0.663 | 0.430 | 0.168 | 0.058 | 0.017 | 0.004 | 0.001 | 0.000 | 0.000 | 0.000 | 0.000 |
| 1 | 0.279 | 0.383 | 0.336 | 0.198 | 0.090 | 0.031 | 0.008 | 0.001 | 0.000 | 0.000 | 0.000 |
| 2 | 0.051 | 0.149 | 0.294 | 0.296 | 0.209 | 0.109 | 0.041 | 0.010 | 0.001 | 0.000 | 0.000 |
| 3 | 0.005 | 0.033 | 0.147 | 0.254 | 0.279 | 0.219 | 0.124 | 0.047 | 0.009 | 0.000 | 0.000 |
| 4 | 0.000 | 0.005 | 0.046 | 0.136 | 0.232 | 0.273 | 0.232 | 0.136 | 0.046 | 0.005 | 0.000 |
| 5 | 0.000 | 0.000 | 0.009 | 0.047 | 0.124 | 0.219 | 0.279 | 0.254 | 0.147 | 0.033 | 0.005 |
| 6 | 0.000 | 0.000 | 0.001 | 0.010 | 0.041 | 0.109 | 0.209 | 0.296 | 0.294 | 0.149 | 0.051 |
| 7 | 0.000 | 0.000 | 0.000 | 0.001 | 0.008 | 0.031 | 0.090 | 0.198 | 0.336 | 0.383 | 0.279 |
| 8 | 0.000 | 0.000 | 0.000 | 0.000 | 0.001 | 0.004 | 0.017 | 0.058 | 0.168 | 0.430 | 0.663 |

### n = 9
PROBABILITY

| r | 0.05 | 0.10 | 0.20 | 0.30 | 0.40 | 0.50 | 0.60 | 0.70 | 0.80 | 0.90 | 0.95 |
|---|------|------|------|------|------|------|------|------|------|------|------|
| 0 | 0.630 | 0.387 | 0.134 | 0.040 | 0.010 | 0.002 | 0.000 | 0.000 | 0.000 | 0.000 | 0.000 |
| 1 | 0.299 | 0.387 | 0.302 | 0.156 | 0.060 | 0.018 | 0.004 | 0.000 | 0.000 | 0.000 | 0.000 |
| 2 | 0.063 | 0.172 | 0.302 | 0.267 | 0.161 | 0.070 | 0.021 | 0.004 | 0.000 | 0.000 | 0.000 |
| 3 | 0.008 | 0.045 | 0.176 | 0.267 | 0.251 | 0.164 | 0.074 | 0.021 | 0.003 | 0.000 | 0.000 |
| 4 | 0.001 | 0.007 | 0.066 | 0.172 | 0.251 | 0.246 | 0.167 | 0.074 | 0.017 | 0.001 | 0.000 |
| 5 | 0.000 | 0.001 | 0.017 | 0.074 | 0.167 | 0.246 | 0.251 | 0.172 | 0.066 | 0.007 | 0.001 |
| 6 | 0.000 | 0.000 | 0.003 | 0.021 | 0.074 | 0.164 | 0.251 | 0.267 | 0.176 | 0.045 | 0.008 |
| 7 | 0.000 | 0.000 | 0.000 | 0.004 | 0.021 | 0.070 | 0.161 | 0.267 | 0.302 | 0.172 | 0.063 |
| 8 | 0.000 | 0.000 | 0.000 | 0.000 | 0.004 | 0.018 | 0.060 | 0.156 | 0.302 | 0.387 | 0.299 |
| 9 | 0.000 | 0.000 | 0.000 | 0.000 | 0.000 | 0.002 | 0.010 | 0.040 | 0.134 | 0.387 | 0.630 |

# Appendix A

## BINOMIAL PROBABILITY DISTRIBUTION (*continued*)

### n = 10
PROBABILITY

| r | 0.05 | 0.10 | 0.20 | 0.30 | 0.40 | 0.50 | 0.60 | 0.70 | 0.80 | 0.90 | 0.95 |
|----|------|------|------|------|------|------|------|------|------|------|------|
| 0 | 0.599 | 0.349 | 0.107 | 0.028 | 0.006 | 0.001 | 0.000 | 0.000 | 0.000 | 0.000 | 0.000 |
| 1 | 0.315 | 0.387 | 0.268 | 0.121 | 0.040 | 0.010 | 0.002 | 0.000 | 0.000 | 0.000 | 0.000 |
| 2 | 0.075 | 0.194 | 0.302 | 0.233 | 0.121 | 0.044 | 0.011 | 0.001 | 0.000 | 0.000 | 0.000 |
| 3 | 0.010 | 0.057 | 0.201 | 0.267 | 0.215 | 0.117 | 0.042 | 0.009 | 0.001 | 0.000 | 0.000 |
| 4 | 0.001 | 0.011 | 0.088 | 0.200 | 0.251 | 0.205 | 0.111 | 0.037 | 0.006 | 0.000 | 0.000 |
| 5 | 0.000 | 0.001 | 0.026 | 0.103 | 0.201 | 0.246 | 0.201 | 0.103 | 0.026 | 0.001 | 0.000 |
| 6 | 0.000 | 0.000 | 0.006 | 0.037 | 0.111 | 0.205 | 0.251 | 0.200 | 0.088 | 0.011 | 0.001 |
| 7 | 0.000 | 0.000 | 0.001 | 0.009 | 0.042 | 0.117 | 0.215 | 0.267 | 0.201 | 0.057 | 0.010 |
| 8 | 0.000 | 0.000 | 0.000 | 0.001 | 0.011 | 0.044 | 0.121 | 0.233 | 0.302 | 0.194 | 0.075 |
| 9 | 0.000 | 0.000 | 0.000 | 0.000 | 0.002 | 0.010 | 0.040 | 0.121 | 0.268 | 0.387 | 0.315 |
| 10 | 0.000 | 0.000 | 0.000 | 0.000 | 0.000 | 0.001 | 0.006 | 0.028 | 0.107 | 0.349 | 0.599 |

### n = 11
PROBABILITY

| r | 0.05 | 0.10 | 0.20 | 0.30 | 0.40 | 0.50 | 0.60 | 0.70 | 0.80 | 0.90 | 0.95 |
|----|------|------|------|------|------|------|------|------|------|------|------|
| 0 | 0.569 | 0.314 | 0.086 | 0.020 | 0.004 | 0.000 | 0.000 | 0.000 | 0.000 | 0.000 | 0.000 |
| 1 | 0.329 | 0.384 | 0.236 | 0.093 | 0.027 | 0.005 | 0.001 | 0.000 | 0.000 | 0.000 | 0.000 |
| 2 | 0.087 | 0.213 | 0.295 | 0.200 | 0.089 | 0.027 | 0.005 | 0.001 | 0.000 | 0.000 | 0.000 |
| 3 | 0.014 | 0.071 | 0.221 | 0.257 | 0.177 | 0.081 | 0.023 | 0.004 | 0.000 | 0.000 | 0.000 |
| 4 | 0.001 | 0.016 | 0.111 | 0.220 | 0.236 | 0.161 | 0.070 | 0.017 | 0.002 | 0.000 | 0.000 |
| 5 | 0.000 | 0.002 | 0.039 | 0.132 | 0.221 | 0.226 | 0.147 | 0.057 | 0.010 | 0.000 | 0.000 |
| 6 | 0.000 | 0.000 | 0.010 | 0.057 | 0.147 | 0.226 | 0.221 | 0.132 | 0.039 | 0.002 | 0.000 |
| 7 | 0.000 | 0.000 | 0.002 | 0.017 | 0.070 | 0.161 | 0.236 | 0.220 | 0.111 | 0.016 | 0.001 |
| 8 | 0.000 | 0.000 | 0.000 | 0.004 | 0.023 | 0.081 | 0.177 | 0.257 | 0.221 | 0.071 | 0.014 |
| 9 | 0.000 | 0.000 | 0.000 | 0.001 | 0.005 | 0.027 | 0.089 | 0.200 | 0.295 | 0.213 | 0.087 |
| 10 | 0.000 | 0.000 | 0.000 | 0.000 | 0.001 | 0.005 | 0.027 | 0.093 | 0.236 | 0.384 | 0.329 |
| 11 | 0.000 | 0.000 | 0.000 | 0.000 | 0.000 | 0.000 | 0.004 | 0.020 | 0.086 | 0.314 | 0.569 |

### n = 12
PROBABILITY

| r | 0.05 | 0.10 | 0.20 | 0.30 | 0.40 | 0.50 | 0.60 | 0.70 | 0.80 | 0.90 | 0.95 |
|----|------|------|------|------|------|------|------|------|------|------|------|
| 0 | 0.540 | 0.282 | 0.069 | 0.014 | 0.002 | 0.000 | 0.000 | 0.000 | 0.000 | 0.000 | 0.000 |
| 1 | 0.341 | 0.377 | 0.206 | 0.071 | 0.017 | 0.003 | 0.000 | 0.000 | 0.000 | 0.000 | 0.000 |
| 2 | 0.099 | 0.230 | 0.283 | 0.168 | 0.064 | 0.016 | 0.002 | 0.000 | 0.000 | 0.000 | 0.000 |
| 3 | 0.017 | 0.085 | 0.236 | 0.240 | 0.142 | 0.054 | 0.012 | 0.001 | 0.000 | 0.000 | 0.000 |
| 4 | 0.002 | 0.021 | 0.133 | 0.231 | 0.213 | 0.121 | 0.042 | 0.008 | 0.001 | 0.000 | 0.000 |
| 5 | 0.000 | 0.004 | 0.053 | 0.158 | 0.227 | 0.193 | 0.101 | 0.029 | 0.003 | 0.000 | 0.000 |
| 6 | 0.000 | 0.000 | 0.016 | 0.079 | 0.177 | 0.226 | 0.177 | 0.079 | 0.016 | 0.000 | 0.000 |
| 7 | 0.000 | 0.000 | 0.003 | 0.029 | 0.101 | 0.193 | 0.227 | 0.158 | 0.053 | 0.004 | 0.000 |
| 8 | 0.000 | 0.000 | 0.001 | 0.008 | 0.042 | 0.121 | 0.213 | 0.231 | 0.133 | 0.021 | 0.002 |
| 9 | 0.000 | 0.000 | 0.000 | 0.001 | 0.012 | 0.054 | 0.142 | 0.240 | 0.236 | 0.085 | 0.017 |
| 10 | 0.000 | 0.000 | 0.000 | 0.000 | 0.002 | 0.016 | 0.064 | 0.168 | 0.283 | 0.230 | 0.099 |
| 11 | 0.000 | 0.000 | 0.000 | 0.000 | 0.000 | 0.003 | 0.017 | 0.071 | 0.206 | 0.377 | 0.341 |
| 12 | 0.000 | 0.000 | 0.000 | 0.000 | 0.000 | 0.000 | 0.002 | 0.014 | 0.069 | 0.282 | 0.540 |

## Appendix A

## BINOMIAL PROBABILITY DISTRIBUTION (*continued*)

### n = 13
PROBABILITY

| r | 0.05 | 0.10 | 0.20 | 0.30 | 0.40 | 0.50 | 0.60 | 0.70 | 0.80 | 0.90 | 0.95 |
|---|------|------|------|------|------|------|------|------|------|------|------|
| 0 | 0.513 | 0.254 | 0.055 | 0.010 | 0.001 | 0.000 | 0.000 | 0.000 | 0.000 | 0.000 | 0.000 |
| 1 | 0.351 | 0.367 | 0.179 | 0.054 | 0.011 | 0.002 | 0.000 | 0.000 | 0.000 | 0.000 | 0.000 |
| 2 | 0.111 | 0.245 | 0.268 | 0.139 | 0.045 | 0.010 | 0.001 | 0.000 | 0.000 | 0.000 | 0.000 |
| 3 | 0.021 | 0.100 | 0.246 | 0.218 | 0.111 | 0.035 | 0.006 | 0.001 | 0.000 | 0.000 | 0.000 |
| 4 | 0.003 | 0.028 | 0.154 | 0.234 | 0.184 | 0.087 | 0.024 | 0.003 | 0.000 | 0.000 | 0.000 |
| 5 | 0.000 | 0.006 | 0.069 | 0.180 | 0.221 | 0.157 | 0.066 | 0.014 | 0.001 | 0.000 | 0.000 |
| 6 | 0.000 | 0.001 | 0.023 | 0.103 | 0.197 | 0.209 | 0.131 | 0.044 | 0.006 | 0.000 | 0.000 |
| 7 | 0.000 | 0.000 | 0.006 | 0.044 | 0.131 | 0.209 | 0.197 | 0.103 | 0.023 | 0.001 | 0.000 |
| 8 | 0.000 | 0.000 | 0.001 | 0.014 | 0.066 | 0.157 | 0.221 | 0.180 | 0.069 | 0.006 | 0.000 |
| 9 | 0.000 | 0.000 | 0.000 | 0.003 | 0.024 | 0.087 | 0.184 | 0.234 | 0.154 | 0.028 | 0.003 |
| 10 | 0.000 | 0.000 | 0.000 | 0.001 | 0.006 | 0.035 | 0.111 | 0.218 | 0.246 | 0.100 | 0.021 |
| 11 | 0.000 | 0.000 | 0.000 | 0.000 | 0.001 | 0.010 | 0.045 | 0.139 | 0.268 | 0.245 | 0.111 |
| 12 | 0.000 | 0.000 | 0.000 | 0.000 | 0.000 | 0.002 | 0.011 | 0.054 | 0.179 | 0.367 | 0.351 |
| 13 | 0.000 | 0.000 | 0.000 | 0.000 | 0.000 | 0.000 | 0.001 | 0.010 | 0.055 | 0.254 | 0.513 |

### n = 14
PROBABILITY

| r | 0.05 | 0.10 | 0.20 | 0.30 | 0.40 | 0.50 | 0.60 | 0.70 | 0.80 | 0.90 | 0.95 |
|---|------|------|------|------|------|------|------|------|------|------|------|
| 0 | 0.488 | 0.229 | 0.044 | 0.007 | 0.001 | 0.000 | 0.000 | 0.000 | 0.000 | 0.000 | 0.000 |
| 1 | 0.359 | 0.356 | 0.154 | 0.041 | 0.007 | 0.001 | 0.000 | 0.000 | 0.000 | 0.000 | 0.000 |
| 2 | 0.123 | 0.257 | 0.250 | 0.113 | 0.032 | 0.006 | 0.001 | 0.000 | 0.000 | 0.000 | 0.000 |
| 3 | 0.026 | 0.114 | 0.250 | 0.194 | 0.085 | 0.022 | 0.003 | 0.000 | 0.000 | 0.000 | 0.000 |
| 4 | 0.004 | 0.035 | 0.172 | 0.229 | 0.155 | 0.061 | 0.014 | 0.001 | 0.000 | 0.000 | 0.000 |
| 5 | 0.000 | 0.008 | 0.086 | 0.196 | 0.207 | 0.122 | 0.041 | 0.007 | 0.000 | 0.000 | 0.000 |
| 6 | 0.000 | 0.001 | 0.032 | 0.126 | 0.207 | 0.183 | 0.092 | 0.023 | 0.002 | 0.000 | 0.000 |
| 7 | 0.000 | 0.000 | 0.009 | 0.062 | 0.157 | 0.209 | 0.157 | 0.062 | 0.009 | 0.000 | 0.000 |
| 8 | 0.000 | 0.000 | 0.002 | 0.023 | 0.092 | 0.183 | 0.207 | 0.126 | 0.032 | 0.001 | 0.000 |
| 9 | 0.000 | 0.000 | 0.000 | 0.007 | 0.041 | 0.122 | 0.207 | 0.196 | 0.086 | 0.008 | 0.000 |
| 10 | 0.000 | 0.000 | 0.000 | 0.001 | 0.014 | 0.061 | 0.155 | 0.229 | 0.172 | 0.035 | 0.004 |
| 11 | 0.000 | 0.000 | 0.000 | 0.000 | 0.003 | 0.022 | 0.085 | 0.194 | 0.250 | 0.114 | 0.026 |
| 12 | 0.000 | 0.000 | 0.000 | 0.000 | 0.001 | 0.006 | 0.032 | 0.113 | 0.250 | 0.257 | 0.123 |
| 13 | 0.000 | 0.000 | 0.000 | 0.000 | 0.000 | 0.001 | 0.007 | 0.041 | 0.154 | 0.356 | 0.359 |
| 14 | 0.000 | 0.000 | 0.000 | 0.000 | 0.000 | 0.000 | 0.001 | 0.007 | 0.044 | 0.229 | 0.488 |

# Appendix A

## BINOMIAL PROBABILITY DISTRIBUTION (*continued*)

### $n = 15$
PROBABILITY

| r | 0.05 | 0.10 | 0.20 | 0.30 | 0.40 | 0.50 | 0.60 | 0.70 | 0.80 | 0.90 | 0.95 |
|---|------|------|------|------|------|------|------|------|------|------|------|
| 0 | 0.463 | 0.206 | 0.035 | 0.005 | 0.000 | 0.000 | 0.000 | 0.000 | 0.000 | 0.000 | 0.000 |
| 1 | 0.366 | 0.343 | 0.132 | 0.031 | 0.005 | 0.000 | 0.000 | 0.000 | 0.000 | 0.000 | 0.000 |
| 2 | 0.135 | 0.267 | 0.231 | 0.092 | 0.022 | 0.003 | 0.000 | 0.000 | 0.000 | 0.000 | 0.000 |
| 3 | 0.031 | 0.129 | 0.250 | 0.170 | 0.063 | 0.014 | 0.002 | 0.000 | 0.000 | 0.000 | 0.000 |
| 4 | 0.005 | 0.043 | 0.188 | 0.219 | 0.127 | 0.042 | 0.007 | 0.001 | 0.000 | 0.000 | 0.000 |
| 5 | 0.001 | 0.010 | 0.103 | 0.206 | 0.186 | 0.092 | 0.024 | 0.003 | 0.000 | 0.000 | 0.000 |
| 6 | 0.000 | 0.002 | 0.043 | 0.147 | 0.207 | 0.153 | 0.061 | 0.012 | 0.001 | 0.000 | 0.000 |
| 7 | 0.000 | 0.000 | 0.014 | 0.081 | 0.177 | 0.196 | 0.118 | 0.035 | 0.003 | 0.000 | 0.000 |
| 8 | 0.000 | 0.000 | 0.003 | 0.035 | 0.118 | 0.196 | 0.177 | 0.081 | 0.014 | 0.000 | 0.000 |
| 9 | 0.000 | 0.000 | 0.001 | 0.012 | 0.061 | 0.153 | 0.207 | 0.147 | 0.043 | 0.002 | 0.000 |
| 10 | 0.000 | 0.000 | 0.000 | 0.003 | 0.024 | 0.092 | 0.186 | 0.206 | 0.103 | 0.010 | 0.001 |
| 11 | 0.000 | 0.000 | 0.000 | 0.001 | 0.007 | 0.042 | 0.127 | 0.219 | 0.188 | 0.043 | 0.005 |
| 12 | 0.000 | 0.000 | 0.000 | 0.000 | 0.002 | 0.014 | 0.063 | 0.170 | 0.250 | 0.129 | 0.031 |
| 13 | 0.000 | 0.000 | 0.000 | 0.000 | 0.000 | 0.003 | 0.022 | 0.092 | 0.231 | 0.267 | 0.135 |
| 14 | 0.000 | 0.000 | 0.000 | 0.000 | 0.000 | 0.000 | 0.005 | 0.031 | 0.132 | 0.343 | 0.366 |
| 15 | 0.000 | 0.000 | 0.000 | 0.000 | 0.000 | 0.000 | 0.000 | 0.005 | 0.035 | 0.206 | 0.463 |

### $n = 16$
PROBABILITY

| r | 0.05 | 0.10 | 0.20 | 0.30 | 0.40 | 0.50 | 0.60 | 0.70 | 0.80 | 0.90 | 0.95 |
|---|------|------|------|------|------|------|------|------|------|------|------|
| 0 | 0.440 | 0.185 | 0.028 | 0.003 | 0.000 | 0.000 | 0.000 | 0.000 | 0.000 | 0.000 | 0.000 |
| 1 | 0.371 | 0.329 | 0.113 | 0.023 | 0.003 | 0.000 | 0.000 | 0.000 | 0.000 | 0.000 | 0.000 |
| 2 | 0.146 | 0.275 | 0.211 | 0.073 | 0.015 | 0.002 | 0.000 | 0.000 | 0.000 | 0.000 | 0.000 |
| 3 | 0.036 | 0.142 | 0.246 | 0.146 | 0.047 | 0.009 | 0.001 | 0.000 | 0.000 | 0.000 | 0.000 |
| 4 | 0.006 | 0.051 | 0.200 | 0.204 | 0.101 | 0.028 | 0.004 | 0.000 | 0.000 | 0.000 | 0.000 |
| 5 | 0.001 | 0.014 | 0.120 | 0.210 | 0.162 | 0.067 | 0.014 | 0.001 | 0.000 | 0.000 | 0.000 |
| 6 | 0.000 | 0.003 | 0.055 | 0.165 | 0.198 | 0.122 | 0.039 | 0.006 | 0.000 | 0.000 | 0.000 |
| 7 | 0.000 | 0.000 | 0.020 | 0.101 | 0.189 | 0.175 | 0.084 | 0.019 | 0.001 | 0.000 | 0.000 |
| 8 | 0.000 | 0.000 | 0.006 | 0.049 | 0.142 | 0.196 | 0.142 | 0.049 | 0.006 | 0.000 | 0.000 |
| 9 | 0.000 | 0.000 | 0.001 | 0.019 | 0.084 | 0.175 | 0.189 | 0.101 | 0.020 | 0.000 | 0.000 |
| 10 | 0.000 | 0.000 | 0.000 | 0.006 | 0.039 | 0.122 | 0.198 | 0.165 | 0.055 | 0.003 | 0.000 |
| 11 | 0.000 | 0.000 | 0.000 | 0.001 | 0.014 | 0.067 | 0.162 | 0.210 | 0.120 | 0.014 | 0.001 |
| 12 | 0.000 | 0.000 | 0.000 | 0.000 | 0.004 | 0.028 | 0.101 | 0.204 | 0.200 | 0.051 | 0.006 |
| 13 | 0.000 | 0.000 | 0.000 | 0.000 | 0.001 | 0.009 | 0.047 | 0.146 | 0.246 | 0.142 | 0.036 |
| 14 | 0.000 | 0.000 | 0.000 | 0.000 | 0.000 | 0.002 | 0.015 | 0.073 | 0.211 | 0.275 | 0.146 |
| 15 | 0.000 | 0.000 | 0.000 | 0.000 | 0.000 | 0.000 | 0.003 | 0.023 | 0.113 | 0.329 | 0.371 |
| 16 | 0.000 | 0.000 | 0.000 | 0.000 | 0.000 | 0.000 | 0.000 | 0.003 | 0.028 | 0.185 | 0.440 |

# Appendix A

## BINOMIAL PROBABILITY DISTRIBUTION (*continued*)

### *n* = 17
PROBABILITY

| r | 0.05 | 0.10 | 0.20 | 0.30 | 0.40 | 0.50 | 0.60 | 0.70 | 0.80 | 0.90 | 0.95 |
|---|------|------|------|------|------|------|------|------|------|------|------|
| 0 | 0.418 | 0.167 | 0.023 | 0.002 | 0.000 | 0.000 | 0.000 | 0.000 | 0.000 | 0.000 | 0.000 |
| 1 | 0.374 | 0.315 | 0.096 | 0.017 | 0.002 | 0.000 | 0.000 | 0.000 | 0.000 | 0.000 | 0.000 |
| 2 | 0.158 | 0.280 | 0.191 | 0.058 | 0.010 | 0.001 | 0.000 | 0.000 | 0.000 | 0.000 | 0.000 |
| 3 | 0.041 | 0.156 | 0.239 | 0.125 | 0.034 | 0.005 | 0.000 | 0.000 | 0.000 | 0.000 | 0.000 |
| 4 | 0.008 | 0.060 | 0.209 | 0.187 | 0.080 | 0.018 | 0.002 | 0.000 | 0.000 | 0.000 | 0.000 |
| 5 | 0.001 | 0.017 | 0.136 | 0.208 | 0.138 | 0.047 | 0.008 | 0.001 | 0.000 | 0.000 | 0.000 |
| 6 | 0.000 | 0.004 | 0.068 | 0.178 | 0.184 | 0.094 | 0.024 | 0.003 | 0.000 | 0.000 | 0.000 |
| 7 | 0.000 | 0.001 | 0.027 | 0.120 | 0.193 | 0.148 | 0.057 | 0.009 | 0.000 | 0.000 | 0.000 |
| 8 | 0.000 | 0.000 | 0.008 | 0.064 | 0.161 | 0.185 | 0.107 | 0.028 | 0.002 | 0.000 | 0.000 |
| 9 | 0.000 | 0.000 | 0.002 | 0.028 | 0.107 | 0.185 | 0.161 | 0.064 | 0.008 | 0.000 | 0.000 |
| 10 | 0.000 | 0.000 | 0.000 | 0.009 | 0.057 | 0.148 | 0.193 | 0.120 | 0.027 | 0.001 | 0.000 |
| 11 | 0.000 | 0.000 | 0.000 | 0.003 | 0.024 | 0.094 | 0.184 | 0.178 | 0.068 | 0.004 | 0.000 |
| 12 | 0.000 | 0.000 | 0.000 | 0.001 | 0.008 | 0.047 | 0.138 | 0.208 | 0.136 | 0.017 | 0.001 |
| 13 | 0.000 | 0.000 | 0.000 | 0.000 | 0.002 | 0.018 | 0.080 | 0.187 | 0.209 | 0.060 | 0.008 |
| 14 | 0.000 | 0.000 | 0.000 | 0.000 | 0.000 | 0.005 | 0.034 | 0.125 | 0.239 | 0.156 | 0.041 |
| 15 | 0.000 | 0.000 | 0.000 | 0.000 | 0.000 | 0.001 | 0.010 | 0.058 | 0.191 | 0.280 | 0.158 |
| 16 | 0.000 | 0.000 | 0.000 | 0.000 | 0.000 | 0.000 | 0.002 | 0.017 | 0.096 | 0.315 | 0.374 |
| 17 | 0.000 | 0.000 | 0.000 | 0.000 | 0.000 | 0.000 | 0.000 | 0.002 | 0.023 | 0.167 | 0.418 |

### *n* = 18
PROBABILITY

| r | 0.05 | 0.10 | 0.20 | 0.30 | 0.40 | 0.50 | 0.60 | 0.70 | 0.80 | 0.90 | 0.95 |
|---|------|------|------|------|------|------|------|------|------|------|------|
| 0 | 0.397 | 0.150 | 0.018 | 0.002 | 0.000 | 0.000 | 0.000 | 0.000 | 0.000 | 0.000 | 0.000 |
| 1 | 0.376 | 0.300 | 0.081 | 0.013 | 0.001 | 0.000 | 0.000 | 0.000 | 0.000 | 0.000 | 0.000 |
| 2 | 0.168 | 0.284 | 0.172 | 0.046 | 0.007 | 0.001 | 0.000 | 0.000 | 0.000 | 0.000 | 0.000 |
| 3 | 0.047 | 0.168 | 0.230 | 0.105 | 0.025 | 0.003 | 0.000 | 0.000 | 0.000 | 0.000 | 0.000 |
| 4 | 0.009 | 0.070 | 0.215 | 0.168 | 0.061 | 0.012 | 0.001 | 0.000 | 0.000 | 0.000 | 0.000 |
| 5 | 0.001 | 0.022 | 0.151 | 0.202 | 0.115 | 0.033 | 0.004 | 0.000 | 0.000 | 0.000 | 0.000 |
| 6 | 0.000 | 0.005 | 0.082 | 0.187 | 0.166 | 0.071 | 0.015 | 0.001 | 0.000 | 0.000 | 0.000 |
| 7 | 0.000 | 0.001 | 0.035 | 0.138 | 0.189 | 0.121 | 0.037 | 0.005 | 0.000 | 0.000 | 0.000 |
| 8 | 0.000 | 0.000 | 0.012 | 0.081 | 0.173 | 0.167 | 0.077 | 0.015 | 0.001 | 0.000 | 0.000 |
| 9 | 0.000 | 0.000 | 0.003 | 0.039 | 0.128 | 0.185 | 0.128 | 0.039 | 0.003 | 0.000 | 0.000 |
| 10 | 0.000 | 0.000 | 0.001 | 0.015 | 0.077 | 0.167 | 0.173 | 0.081 | 0.012 | 0.000 | 0.000 |
| 11 | 0.000 | 0.000 | 0.000 | 0.005 | 0.037 | 0.121 | 0.189 | 0.138 | 0.035 | 0.001 | 0.000 |
| 12 | 0.000 | 0.000 | 0.000 | 0.001 | 0.015 | 0.071 | 0.166 | 0.187 | 0.082 | 0.005 | 0.000 |
| 13 | 0.000 | 0.000 | 0.000 | 0.000 | 0.004 | 0.033 | 0.115 | 0.202 | 0.151 | 0.022 | 0.001 |
| 14 | 0.000 | 0.000 | 0.000 | 0.000 | 0.001 | 0.012 | 0.061 | 0.168 | 0.215 | 0.070 | 0.009 |
| 15 | 0.000 | 0.000 | 0.000 | 0.000 | 0.000 | 0.003 | 0.025 | 0.105 | 0.230 | 0.168 | 0.047 |
| 16 | 0.000 | 0.000 | 0.000 | 0.000 | 0.000 | 0.001 | 0.007 | 0.046 | 0.172 | 0.284 | 0.168 |
| 17 | 0.000 | 0.000 | 0.000 | 0.000 | 0.000 | 0.000 | 0.001 | 0.013 | 0.081 | 0.300 | 0.376 |
| 18 | 0.000 | 0.000 | 0.000 | 0.000 | 0.000 | 0.000 | 0.000 | 0.002 | 0.018 | 0.150 | 0.397 |

# Appendix A

## BINOMIAL PROBABILITY DISTRIBUTION (*continued*)

### n = 19
PROBABILITY

| r | 0.05 | 0.10 | 0.20 | 0.30 | 0.40 | 0.50 | 0.60 | 0.70 | 0.80 | 0.90 | 0.95 |
|---|------|------|------|------|------|------|------|------|------|------|------|
| 0 | 0.377 | 0.135 | 0.014 | 0.001 | 0.000 | 0.000 | 0.000 | 0.000 | 0.000 | 0.000 | 0.000 |
| 1 | 0.377 | 0.285 | 0.068 | 0.009 | 0.001 | 0.000 | 0.000 | 0.000 | 0.000 | 0.000 | 0.000 |
| 2 | 0.179 | 0.285 | 0.154 | 0.036 | 0.005 | 0.000 | 0.000 | 0.000 | 0.000 | 0.000 | 0.000 |
| 3 | 0.053 | 0.180 | 0.218 | 0.087 | 0.017 | 0.002 | 0.000 | 0.000 | 0.000 | 0.000 | 0.000 |
| 4 | 0.011 | 0.080 | 0.218 | 0.149 | 0.047 | 0.007 | 0.001 | 0.000 | 0.000 | 0.000 | 0.000 |
| 5 | 0.002 | 0.027 | 0.164 | 0.192 | 0.093 | 0.022 | 0.002 | 0.000 | 0.000 | 0.000 | 0.000 |
| 6 | 0.000 | 0.007 | 0.095 | 0.192 | 0.145 | 0.052 | 0.008 | 0.001 | 0.000 | 0.000 | 0.000 |
| 7 | 0.000 | 0.001 | 0.044 | 0.153 | 0.180 | 0.096 | 0.024 | 0.002 | 0.000 | 0.000 | 0.000 |
| 8 | 0.000 | 0.000 | 0.017 | 0.098 | 0.180 | 0.144 | 0.053 | 0.008 | 0.000 | 0.000 | 0.000 |
| 9 | 0.000 | 0.000 | 0.005 | 0.051 | 0.146 | 0.176 | 0.098 | 0.022 | 0.001 | 0.000 | 0.000 |
| 10 | 0.000 | 0.000 | 0.001 | 0.022 | 0.098 | 0.176 | 0.146 | 0.051 | 0.005 | 0.000 | 0.000 |
| 11 | 0.000 | 0.000 | 0.000 | 0.008 | 0.053 | 0.144 | 0.180 | 0.098 | 0.017 | 0.000 | 0.000 |
| 12 | 0.000 | 0.000 | 0.000 | 0.002 | 0.024 | 0.096 | 0.180 | 0.153 | 0.044 | 0.001 | 0.000 |
| 13 | 0.000 | 0.000 | 0.000 | 0.001 | 0.008 | 0.052 | 0.145 | 0.192 | 0.095 | 0.007 | 0.000 |
| 14 | 0.000 | 0.000 | 0.000 | 0.000 | 0.002 | 0.022 | 0.093 | 0.192 | 0.164 | 0.027 | 0.002 |
| 15 | 0.000 | 0.000 | 0.000 | 0.000 | 0.001 | 0.007 | 0.047 | 0.149 | 0.218 | 0.080 | 0.011 |
| 16 | 0.000 | 0.000 | 0.000 | 0.000 | 0.000 | 0.002 | 0.017 | 0.087 | 0.218 | 0.180 | 0.053 |
| 17 | 0.000 | 0.000 | 0.000 | 0.000 | 0.000 | 0.000 | 0.005 | 0.036 | 0.154 | 0.285 | 0.179 |
| 18 | 0.000 | 0.000 | 0.000 | 0.000 | 0.000 | 0.000 | 0.001 | 0.009 | 0.068 | 0.285 | 0.377 |
| 19 | 0.000 | 0.000 | 0.000 | 0.000 | 0.000 | 0.000 | 0.000 | 0.001 | 0.014 | 0.135 | 0.377 |

### n = 20
PROBABILITY

| r | 0.05 | 0.10 | 0.20 | 0.30 | 0.40 | 0.50 | 0.60 | 0.70 | 0.80 | 0.90 | 0.95 |
|---|------|------|------|------|------|------|------|------|------|------|------|
| 0 | 0.358 | 0.122 | 0.012 | 0.001 | 0.000 | 0.000 | 0.000 | 0.000 | 0.000 | 0.000 | 0.000 |
| 1 | 0.377 | 0.270 | 0.058 | 0.007 | 0.000 | 0.000 | 0.000 | 0.000 | 0.000 | 0.000 | 0.000 |
| 2 | 0.189 | 0.285 | 0.137 | 0.028 | 0.003 | 0.000 | 0.000 | 0.000 | 0.000 | 0.000 | 0.000 |
| 3 | 0.060 | 0.190 | 0.205 | 0.072 | 0.012 | 0.001 | 0.000 | 0.000 | 0.000 | 0.000 | 0.000 |
| 4 | 0.013 | 0.090 | 0.218 | 0.130 | 0.035 | 0.005 | 0.000 | 0.000 | 0.000 | 0.000 | 0.000 |
| 5 | 0.002 | 0.032 | 0.175 | 0.179 | 0.075 | 0.015 | 0.001 | 0.000 | 0.000 | 0.000 | 0.000 |
| 6 | 0.000 | 0.009 | 0.109 | 0.192 | 0.124 | 0.037 | 0.005 | 0.000 | 0.000 | 0.000 | 0.000 |
| 7 | 0.000 | 0.002 | 0.055 | 0.164 | 0.166 | 0.074 | 0.015 | 0.001 | 0.000 | 0.000 | 0.000 |
| 8 | 0.000 | 0.000 | 0.022 | 0.114 | 0.180 | 0.120 | 0.035 | 0.004 | 0.000 | 0.000 | 0.000 |
| 9 | 0.000 | 0.000 | 0.007 | 0.065 | 0.160 | 0.160 | 0.071 | 0.012 | 0.000 | 0.000 | 0.000 |
| 10 | 0.000 | 0.000 | 0.002 | 0.031 | 0.117 | 0.176 | 0.117 | 0.031 | 0.002 | 0.000 | 0.000 |
| 11 | 0.000 | 0.000 | 0.000 | 0.012 | 0.071 | 0.160 | 0.160 | 0.065 | 0.007 | 0.000 | 0.000 |
| 12 | 0.000 | 0.000 | 0.000 | 0.004 | 0.035 | 0.120 | 0.180 | 0.114 | 0.022 | 0.000 | 0.000 |
| 13 | 0.000 | 0.000 | 0.000 | 0.001 | 0.015 | 0.074 | 0.166 | 0.164 | 0.055 | 0.002 | 0.000 |
| 14 | 0.000 | 0.000 | 0.000 | 0.000 | 0.005 | 0.037 | 0.124 | 0.192 | 0.109 | 0.009 | 0.000 |
| 15 | 0.000 | 0.000 | 0.000 | 0.000 | 0.001 | 0.015 | 0.075 | 0.179 | 0.175 | 0.032 | 0.002 |
| 16 | 0.000 | 0.000 | 0.000 | 0.000 | 0.000 | 0.005 | 0.035 | 0.130 | 0.218 | 0.090 | 0.013 |
| 17 | 0.000 | 0.000 | 0.000 | 0.000 | 0.000 | 0.001 | 0.012 | 0.072 | 0.205 | 0.190 | 0.060 |
| 18 | 0.000 | 0.000 | 0.000 | 0.000 | 0.000 | 0.000 | 0.003 | 0.028 | 0.137 | 0.285 | 0.189 |
| 19 | 0.000 | 0.000 | 0.000 | 0.000 | 0.000 | 0.000 | 0.000 | 0.007 | 0.058 | 0.270 | 0.377 |
| 20 | 0.000 | 0.000 | 0.000 | 0.000 | 0.000 | 0.000 | 0.000 | 0.001 | 0.012 | 0.122 | 0.358 |

## Appendix A

# Binomial Probability Distribution (concluded)

$n = 25$
PROBABILITY

| r | 0.05 | 0.10 | 0.20 | 0.30 | 0.40 | 0.50 | 0.60 | 0.70 | 0.80 | 0.90 | 0.95 |
|---|------|------|------|------|------|------|------|------|------|------|------|
| 0 | 0.277 | 0.072 | 0.004 | 0.000 | 0.000 | 0.000 | 0.000 | 0.000 | 0.000 | 0.000 | 0.000 |
| 1 | 0.365 | 0.199 | 0.024 | 0.001 | 0.000 | 0.000 | 0.000 | 0.000 | 0.000 | 0.000 | 0.000 |
| 2 | 0.231 | 0.266 | 0.071 | 0.007 | 0.000 | 0.000 | 0.000 | 0.000 | 0.000 | 0.000 | 0.000 |
| 3 | 0.093 | 0.226 | 0.136 | 0.024 | 0.002 | 0.000 | 0.000 | 0.000 | 0.000 | 0.000 | 0.000 |
| 4 | 0.027 | 0.138 | 0.187 | 0.057 | 0.007 | 0.000 | 0.000 | 0.000 | 0.000 | 0.000 | 0.000 |
| 5 | 0.006 | 0.065 | 0.196 | 0.103 | 0.020 | 0.002 | 0.000 | 0.000 | 0.000 | 0.000 | 0.000 |
| 6 | 0.001 | 0.024 | 0.163 | 0.147 | 0.044 | 0.005 | 0.000 | 0.000 | 0.000 | 0.000 | 0.000 |
| 7 | 0.000 | 0.007 | 0.111 | 0.171 | 0.080 | 0.014 | 0.001 | 0.000 | 0.000 | 0.000 | 0.000 |
| 8 | 0.000 | 0.002 | 0.062 | 0.165 | 0.120 | 0.032 | 0.003 | 0.000 | 0.000 | 0.000 | 0.000 |
| 9 | 0.000 | 0.000 | 0.029 | 0.134 | 0.151 | 0.061 | 0.009 | 0.000 | 0.000 | 0.000 | 0.000 |
| 10 | 0.000 | 0.000 | 0.012 | 0.092 | 0.161 | 0.097 | 0.021 | 0.001 | 0.000 | 0.000 | 0.000 |
| 11 | 0.000 | 0.000 | 0.004 | 0.054 | 0.147 | 0.133 | 0.043 | 0.004 | 0.000 | 0.000 | 0.000 |
| 12 | 0.000 | 0.000 | 0.001 | 0.027 | 0.114 | 0.155 | 0.076 | 0.011 | 0.000 | 0.000 | 0.000 |
| 13 | 0.000 | 0.000 | 0.000 | 0.011 | 0.076 | 0.155 | 0.114 | 0.027 | 0.001 | 0.000 | 0.000 |
| 14 | 0.000 | 0.000 | 0.000 | 0.004 | 0.043 | 0.133 | 0.147 | 0.054 | 0.004 | 0.000 | 0.000 |
| 15 | 0.000 | 0.000 | 0.000 | 0.001 | 0.021 | 0.097 | 0.161 | 0.092 | 0.012 | 0.000 | 0.000 |
| 16 | 0.000 | 0.000 | 0.000 | 0.000 | 0.009 | 0.061 | 0.151 | 0.134 | 0.029 | 0.000 | 0.000 |
| 17 | 0.000 | 0.000 | 0.000 | 0.000 | 0.003 | 0.032 | 0.120 | 0.165 | 0.062 | 0.002 | 0.000 |
| 18 | 0.000 | 0.000 | 0.000 | 0.000 | 0.001 | 0.014 | 0.080 | 0.171 | 0.111 | 0.007 | 0.000 |
| 19 | 0.000 | 0.000 | 0.000 | 0.000 | 0.000 | 0.005 | 0.044 | 0.147 | 0.163 | 0.024 | 0.001 |
| 20 | 0.000 | 0.000 | 0.000 | 0.000 | 0.000 | 0.002 | 0.020 | 0.103 | 0.196 | 0.065 | 0.006 |
| 21 | 0.000 | 0.000 | 0.000 | 0.000 | 0.000 | 0.000 | 0.007 | 0.057 | 0.187 | 0.138 | 0.027 |
| 22 | 0.000 | 0.000 | 0.000 | 0.000 | 0.000 | 0.000 | 0.002 | 0.024 | 0.136 | 0.226 | 0.093 |
| 23 | 0.000 | 0.000 | 0.000 | 0.000 | 0.000 | 0.000 | 0.000 | 0.007 | 0.071 | 0.266 | 0.231 |
| 24 | 0.000 | 0.000 | 0.000 | 0.000 | 0.000 | 0.000 | 0.000 | 0.001 | 0.024 | 0.199 | 0.365 |
| 25 | 0.000 | 0.000 | 0.000 | 0.000 | 0.000 | 0.000 | 0.000 | 0.000 | 0.004 | 0.072 | 0.277 |

# Appendix B

## CUMULATIVE BINOMIAL PROBABILITY DISTRIBUTION

### $n = 1$
PROBABILITY

| r | 0.1 | 0.2 | 0.3 | 0.4 | 0.5 | 0.6 | 0.7 | 0.8 | 0.9 |
|---|-----|-----|-----|-----|-----|-----|-----|-----|-----|
| 0 | 0.900 | 0.800 | 0.700 | 0.600 | 0.500 | 0.400 | 0.300 | 0.200 | 0.100 |
| 1 | 1.000 | 1.000 | 1.000 | 1.000 | 1.000 | 1.000 | 1.000 | 1.000 | 1.000 |

### $n = 2$
PROBABILITY

| r | 0.1 | 0.2 | 0.3 | 0.4 | 0.5 | 0.6 | 0.7 | 0.8 | 0.9 |
|---|-----|-----|-----|-----|-----|-----|-----|-----|-----|
| 0 | 0.810 | 0.640 | 0.490 | 0.360 | 0.250 | 0.160 | 0.090 | 0.040 | 0.010 |
| 1 | 0.990 | 0.960 | 0.910 | 0.840 | 0.750 | 0.640 | 0.510 | 0.360 | 0.190 |
| 2 | 1.000 | 1.000 | 1.000 | 1.000 | 1.000 | 1.000 | 1.000 | 1.000 | 1.000 |

### $n = 3$
PROBABILITY

| r | 0.1 | 0.2 | 0.3 | 0.4 | 0.5 | 0.6 | 0.7 | 0.8 | 0.9 |
|---|-----|-----|-----|-----|-----|-----|-----|-----|-----|
| 0 | 0.729 | 0.512 | 0.343 | 0.216 | 0.125 | 0.064 | 0.027 | 0.008 | 0.001 |
| 1 | 0.972 | 0.896 | 0.784 | 0.648 | 0.500 | 0.352 | 0.216 | 0.104 | 0.028 |
| 2 | 0.999 | 0.992 | 0.973 | 0.936 | 0.875 | 0.784 | 0.657 | 0.488 | 0.271 |
| 3 | 1.000 | 1.000 | 1.000 | 1.000 | 1.000 | 1.000 | 1.000 | 1.000 | 1.000 |

### $n = 4$
PROBABILITY

| r | 0.1 | 0.2 | 0.3 | 0.4 | 0.5 | 0.6 | 0.7 | 0.8 | 0.9 |
|---|-----|-----|-----|-----|-----|-----|-----|-----|-----|
| 0 | 0.656 | 0.410 | 0.240 | 0.130 | 0.063 | 0.026 | 0.008 | 0.002 | 0.000 |
| 1 | 0.948 | 0.819 | 0.652 | 0.475 | 0.313 | 0.179 | 0.084 | 0.027 | 0.004 |
| 2 | 0.996 | 0.973 | 0.916 | 0.821 | 0.688 | 0.525 | 0.348 | 0.181 | 0.052 |
| 3 | 1.000 | 0.998 | 0.992 | 0.974 | 0.938 | 0.870 | 0.760 | 0.590 | 0.344 |
| 4 | 1.000 | 1.000 | 1.000 | 1.000 | 1.000 | 1.000 | 1.000 | 1.000 | 1.000 |

### $n = 5$
PROBABILITY

| r | 0.1 | 0.2 | 0.3 | 0.4 | 0.5 | 0.6 | 0.7 | 0.8 | 0.9 |
|---|-----|-----|-----|-----|-----|-----|-----|-----|-----|
| 0 | 0.590 | 0.328 | 0.168 | 0.078 | 0.031 | 0.010 | 0.002 | 0.000 | 0.000 |
| 1 | 0.919 | 0.737 | 0.528 | 0.337 | 0.188 | 0.087 | 0.031 | 0.007 | 0.000 |
| 2 | 0.991 | 0.942 | 0.837 | 0.683 | 0.500 | 0.317 | 0.163 | 0.058 | 0.009 |
| 3 | 1.000 | 0.993 | 0.969 | 0.913 | 0.813 | 0.663 | 0.472 | 0.263 | 0.081 |
| 4 | 1.000 | 1.000 | 0.998 | 0.990 | 0.969 | 0.922 | 0.832 | 0.672 | 0.410 |
| 5 | 1.000 | 1.000 | 1.000 | 1.000 | 1.000 | 1.000 | 1.000 | 1.000 | 1.000 |

### $n = 6$
PROBABILITY

| r | 0.1 | 0.2 | 0.3 | 0.4 | 0.5 | 0.6 | 0.7 | 0.8 | 0.9 |
|---|-----|-----|-----|-----|-----|-----|-----|-----|-----|
| 0 | 0.531 | 0.262 | 0.118 | 0.047 | 0.016 | 0.004 | 0.001 | 0.000 | 0.000 |
| 1 | 0.886 | 0.655 | 0.420 | 0.233 | 0.109 | 0.041 | 0.011 | 0.002 | 0.000 |
| 2 | 0.984 | 0.901 | 0.744 | 0.544 | 0.344 | 0.179 | 0.070 | 0.017 | 0.001 |
| 3 | 0.999 | 0.983 | 0.930 | 0.821 | 0.656 | 0.456 | 0.256 | 0.099 | 0.016 |
| 4 | 1.000 | 0.998 | 0.989 | 0.959 | 0.891 | 0.767 | 0.580 | 0.345 | 0.114 |
| 5 | 1.000 | 1.000 | 0.999 | 0.996 | 0.984 | 0.953 | 0.882 | 0.738 | 0.469 |
| 6 | 1.000 | 1.000 | 1.000 | 1.000 | 1.000 | 1.000 | 1.000 | 1.000 | 1.000 |

## Appendix B

# CUMULATIVE BINOMIAL PROBABILITY DISTRIBUTION
### (continued)

### n = 7
PROBABILITY

| r | 0.1 | 0.2 | 0.3 | 0.4 | 0.5 | 0.6 | 0.7 | 0.8 | 0.9 |
|---|-----|-----|-----|-----|-----|-----|-----|-----|-----|
| 0 | 0.478 | 0.210 | 0.082 | 0.028 | 0.008 | 0.002 | 0.000 | 0.000 | 0.000 |
| 1 | 0.850 | 0.577 | 0.329 | 0.159 | 0.063 | 0.019 | 0.004 | 0.000 | 0.000 |
| 2 | 0.974 | 0.852 | 0.647 | 0.420 | 0.227 | 0.096 | 0.029 | 0.005 | 0.000 |
| 3 | 0.997 | 0.967 | 0.874 | 0.710 | 0.500 | 0.290 | 0.126 | 0.033 | 0.003 |
| 4 | 1.000 | 0.995 | 0.971 | 0.904 | 0.773 | 0.580 | 0.353 | 0.148 | 0.026 |
| 5 | 1.000 | 1.000 | 0.996 | 0.981 | 0.938 | 0.841 | 0.671 | 0.423 | 0.150 |
| 6 | 1.000 | 1.000 | 1.000 | 0.998 | 0.992 | 0.972 | 0.918 | 0.790 | 0.522 |
| 7 | 1.000 | 1.000 | 1.000 | 1.000 | 1.000 | 1.000 | 1.000 | 1.000 | 1.000 |

### n = 8
PROBABILITY

| r | 0.1 | 0.2 | 0.3 | 0.4 | 0.5 | 0.6 | 0.7 | 0.8 | 0.9 |
|---|-----|-----|-----|-----|-----|-----|-----|-----|-----|
| 0 | 0.430 | 0.168 | 0.058 | 0.017 | 0.004 | 0.001 | 0.000 | 0.000 | 0.000 |
| 1 | 0.813 | 0.503 | 0.255 | 0.106 | 0.035 | 0.009 | 0.001 | 0.000 | 0.000 |
| 2 | 0.962 | 0.797 | 0.552 | 0.315 | 0.145 | 0.050 | 0.011 | 0.001 | 0.000 |
| 3 | 0.995 | 0.944 | 0.806 | 0.594 | 0.363 | 0.174 | 0.058 | 0.010 | 0.000 |
| 4 | 1.000 | 0.990 | 0.942 | 0.826 | 0.637 | 0.406 | 0.194 | 0.056 | 0.005 |
| 5 | 1.000 | 0.999 | 0.989 | 0.950 | 0.855 | 0.685 | 0.448 | 0.203 | 0.038 |
| 6 | 1.000 | 1.000 | 0.999 | 0.991 | 0.965 | 0.894 | 0.745 | 0.497 | 0.187 |
| 7 | 1.000 | 1.000 | 1.000 | 0.999 | 0.996 | 0.983 | 0.942 | 0.832 | 0.570 |
| 8 | 1.000 | 1.000 | 1.000 | 1.000 | 1.000 | 1.000 | 1.000 | 1.000 | 1.000 |

### n = 9
PROBABILITY

| r | 0.1 | 0.2 | 0.3 | 0.4 | 0.5 | 0.6 | 0.7 | 0.8 | 0.9 |
|---|-----|-----|-----|-----|-----|-----|-----|-----|-----|
| 0 | 0.387 | 0.134 | 0.040 | 0.010 | 0.002 | 0.000 | 0.000 | 0.000 | 0.000 |
| 1 | 0.775 | 0.436 | 0.196 | 0.071 | 0.020 | 0.004 | 0.000 | 0.000 | 0.000 |
| 2 | 0.947 | 0.738 | 0.463 | 0.232 | 0.090 | 0.025 | 0.004 | 0.000 | 0.000 |
| 3 | 0.992 | 0.914 | 0.730 | 0.483 | 0.254 | 0.099 | 0.025 | 0.003 | 0.000 |
| 4 | 0.999 | 0.980 | 0.901 | 0.733 | 0.500 | 0.267 | 0.099 | 0.020 | 0.001 |
| 5 | 1.000 | 0.997 | 0.975 | 0.901 | 0.746 | 0.517 | 0.270 | 0.086 | 0.008 |
| 6 | 1.000 | 1.000 | 0.996 | 0.975 | 0.910 | 0.768 | 0.537 | 0.262 | 0.053 |
| 7 | 1.000 | 1.000 | 1.000 | 0.996 | 0.980 | 0.929 | 0.804 | 0.564 | 0.225 |
| 8 | 1.000 | 1.000 | 1.000 | 1.000 | 0.998 | 0.990 | 0.960 | 0.866 | 0.613 |
| 9 | 1.000 | 1.000 | 1.000 | 1.000 | 1.000 | 1.000 | 1.000 | 1.000 | 1.000 |

## Appendix B

# CUMULATIVE BINOMIAL PROBABILITY DISTRIBUTION
*(continued)*

### $n = 10$
PROBABILITY

| r | 0.1 | 0.2 | 0.3 | 0.4 | 0.5 | 0.6 | 0.7 | 0.8 | 0.9 |
|---|-----|-----|-----|-----|-----|-----|-----|-----|-----|
| 0 | 0.349 | 0.107 | 0.028 | 0.006 | 0.001 | 0.000 | 0.000 | 0.000 | 0.000 |
| 1 | 0.736 | 0.376 | 0.149 | 0.046 | 0.011 | 0.002 | 0.000 | 0.000 | 0.000 |
| 2 | 0.930 | 0.678 | 0.383 | 0.167 | 0.055 | 0.012 | 0.002 | 0.000 | 0.000 |
| 3 | 0.987 | 0.879 | 0.650 | 0.382 | 0.172 | 0.055 | 0.011 | 0.001 | 0.000 |
| 4 | 0.998 | 0.967 | 0.850 | 0.633 | 0.377 | 0.166 | 0.047 | 0.006 | 0.000 |
| 5 | 1.000 | 0.994 | 0.953 | 0.834 | 0.623 | 0.367 | 0.150 | 0.033 | 0.002 |
| 6 | 1.000 | 0.999 | 0.989 | 0.945 | 0.828 | 0.618 | 0.350 | 0.121 | 0.013 |
| 7 | 1.000 | 1.000 | 0.998 | 0.988 | 0.945 | 0.833 | 0.617 | 0.322 | 0.070 |
| 8 | 1.000 | 1.000 | 1.000 | 0.998 | 0.989 | 0.954 | 0.851 | 0.624 | 0.264 |
| 9 | 1.000 | 1.000 | 1.000 | 1.000 | 0.999 | 0.994 | 0.972 | 0.893 | 0.651 |
| 10 | 1.000 | 1.000 | 1.000 | 1.000 | 1.000 | 1.000 | 1.000 | 1.000 | 1.000 |

### $n = 11$
PROBABILITY

| r | 0.1 | 0.2 | 0.3 | 0.4 | 0.5 | 0.6 | 0.7 | 0.8 | 0.9 |
|---|-----|-----|-----|-----|-----|-----|-----|-----|-----|
| 0 | 0.314 | 0.086 | 0.020 | 0.004 | 0.000 | 0.000 | 0.000 | 0.000 | 0.000 |
| 1 | 0.697 | 0.322 | 0.113 | 0.030 | 0.006 | 0.001 | 0.000 | 0.000 | 0.000 |
| 2 | 0.910 | 0.617 | 0.313 | 0.119 | 0.033 | 0.006 | 0.001 | 0.000 | 0.000 |
| 3 | 0.981 | 0.839 | 0.570 | 0.296 | 0.113 | 0.029 | 0.004 | 0.000 | 0.000 |
| 4 | 0.997 | 0.950 | 0.790 | 0.533 | 0.274 | 0.099 | 0.022 | 0.002 | 0.000 |
| 5 | 1.000 | 0.988 | 0.922 | 0.753 | 0.500 | 0.247 | 0.078 | 0.012 | 0.000 |
| 6 | 1.000 | 0.998 | 0.978 | 0.901 | 0.726 | 0.467 | 0.210 | 0.050 | 0.003 |
| 7 | 1.000 | 1.000 | 0.996 | 0.971 | 0.887 | 0.704 | 0.430 | 0.161 | 0.019 |
| 8 | 1.000 | 1.000 | 0.999 | 0.994 | 0.967 | 0.881 | 0.687 | 0.383 | 0.090 |
| 9 | 1.000 | 1.000 | 1.000 | 0.999 | 0.994 | 0.970 | 0.887 | 0.678 | 0.303 |
| 10 | 1.000 | 1.000 | 1.000 | 1.000 | 1.000 | 0.996 | 0.980 | 0.914 | 0.686 |
| 11 | 1.000 | 1.000 | 1.000 | 1.000 | 1.000 | 1.000 | 1.000 | 1.000 | 1.000 |

### $n = 12$
PROBABILITY

| r | 0.1 | 0.2 | 0.3 | 0.4 | 0.5 | 0.6 | 0.7 | 0.8 | 0.9 |
|---|-----|-----|-----|-----|-----|-----|-----|-----|-----|
| 0 | 0.282 | 0.069 | 0.014 | 0.002 | 0.000 | 0.000 | 0.000 | 0.000 | 0.000 |
| 1 | 0.659 | 0.275 | 0.085 | 0.020 | 0.003 | 0.000 | 0.000 | 0.000 | 0.000 |
| 2 | 0.889 | 0.558 | 0.253 | 0.083 | 0.019 | 0.003 | 0.000 | 0.000 | 0.000 |
| 3 | 0.974 | 0.795 | 0.493 | 0.225 | 0.073 | 0.015 | 0.002 | 0.000 | 0.000 |
| 4 | 0.996 | 0.927 | 0.724 | 0.438 | 0.194 | 0.057 | 0.009 | 0.001 | 0.000 |
| 5 | 0.999 | 0.981 | 0.882 | 0.665 | 0.387 | 0.158 | 0.039 | 0.004 | 0.000 |
| 6 | 1.000 | 0.996 | 0.961 | 0.842 | 0.613 | 0.335 | 0.118 | 0.019 | 0.001 |
| 7 | 1.000 | 0.999 | 0.991 | 0.943 | 0.806 | 0.562 | 0.276 | 0.073 | 0.004 |
| 8 | 1.000 | 1.000 | 0.998 | 0.985 | 0.927 | 0.775 | 0.507 | 0.205 | 0.026 |
| 9 | 1.000 | 1.000 | 1.000 | 0.997 | 0.981 | 0.917 | 0.747 | 0.442 | 0.111 |
| 10 | 1.000 | 1.000 | 1.000 | 1.000 | 0.997 | 0.980 | 0.915 | 0.725 | 0.341 |
| 11 | 1.000 | 1.000 | 1.000 | 1.000 | 1.000 | 0.998 | 0.986 | 0.931 | 0.718 |
| 12 | 1.000 | 1.000 | 1.000 | 1.000 | 1.000 | 1.000 | 1.000 | 1.000 | 1.000 |

## Appendix B

## CUMULATIVE BINOMIAL PROBABILITY DISTRIBUTION
### (continued)

### n = 13
#### PROBABILITY

| r | 0.1 | 0.2 | 0.3 | 0.4 | 0.5 | 0.6 | 0.7 | 0.8 | 0.9 |
|---|-----|-----|-----|-----|-----|-----|-----|-----|-----|
| 0 | 0.254 | 0.055 | 0.010 | 0.001 | 0.000 | 0.000 | 0.000 | 0.000 | 0.000 |
| 1 | 0.621 | 0.234 | 0.064 | 0.013 | 0.002 | 0.000 | 0.000 | 0.000 | 0.000 |
| 2 | 0.866 | 0.502 | 0.202 | 0.058 | 0.011 | 0.001 | 0.000 | 0.000 | 0.000 |
| 3 | 0.966 | 0.747 | 0.421 | 0.169 | 0.046 | 0.008 | 0.001 | 0.000 | 0.000 |
| 4 | 0.994 | 0.901 | 0.654 | 0.353 | 0.133 | 0.032 | 0.004 | 0.000 | 0.000 |
| 5 | 0.999 | 0.970 | 0.835 | 0.574 | 0.291 | 0.098 | 0.018 | 0.001 | 0.000 |
| 6 | 1.000 | 0.993 | 0.938 | 0.771 | 0.500 | 0.229 | 0.062 | 0.007 | 0.000 |
| 7 | 1.000 | 0.999 | 0.982 | 0.902 | 0.709 | 0.426 | 0.165 | 0.030 | 0.001 |
| 8 | 1.000 | 1.000 | 0.996 | 0.968 | 0.867 | 0.647 | 0.346 | 0.099 | 0.006 |
| 9 | 1.000 | 1.000 | 0.999 | 0.992 | 0.954 | 0.831 | 0.579 | 0.253 | 0.034 |
| 10 | 1.000 | 1.000 | 1.000 | 0.999 | 0.989 | 0.942 | 0.798 | 0.498 | 0.134 |
| 11 | 1.000 | 1.000 | 1.000 | 1.000 | 0.998 | 0.987 | 0.936 | 0.766 | 0.379 |
| 12 | 1.000 | 1.000 | 1.000 | 1.000 | 1.000 | 0.999 | 0.990 | 0.945 | 0.746 |
| 13 | 1.000 | 1.000 | 1.000 | 1.000 | 1.000 | 1.000 | 1.000 | 1.000 | 1.000 |

### n = 14
#### PROBABILITY

| r | 0.1 | 0.2 | 0.3 | 0.4 | 0.5 | 0.6 | 0.7 | 0.8 | 0.9 |
|---|-----|-----|-----|-----|-----|-----|-----|-----|-----|
| 0 | 0.229 | 0.044 | 0.007 | 0.001 | 0.000 | 0.000 | 0.000 | 0.000 | 0.000 |
| 1 | 0.585 | 0.198 | 0.047 | 0.008 | 0.001 | 0.000 | 0.000 | 0.000 | 0.000 |
| 2 | 0.842 | 0.448 | 0.161 | 0.040 | 0.006 | 0.001 | 0.000 | 0.000 | 0.000 |
| 3 | 0.956 | 0.698 | 0.355 | 0.124 | 0.029 | 0.004 | 0.000 | 0.000 | 0.000 |
| 4 | 0.991 | 0.870 | 0.584 | 0.279 | 0.090 | 0.018 | 0.002 | 0.000 | 0.000 |
| 5 | 0.999 | 0.956 | 0.781 | 0.486 | 0.212 | 0.058 | 0.008 | 0.000 | 0.000 |
| 6 | 1.000 | 0.988 | 0.907 | 0.692 | 0.395 | 0.150 | 0.031 | 0.002 | 0.000 |
| 7 | 1.000 | 0.998 | 0.969 | 0.850 | 0.605 | 0.308 | 0.093 | 0.012 | 0.000 |
| 8 | 1.000 | 1.000 | 0.992 | 0.942 | 0.788 | 0.514 | 0.219 | 0.044 | 0.001 |
| 9 | 1.000 | 1.000 | 0.998 | 0.982 | 0.910 | 0.721 | 0.416 | 0.130 | 0.009 |
| 10 | 1.000 | 1.000 | 1.000 | 0.996 | 0.971 | 0.876 | 0.645 | 0.302 | 0.044 |
| 11 | 1.000 | 1.000 | 1.000 | 0.999 | 0.994 | 0.960 | 0.839 | 0.552 | 0.158 |
| 12 | 1.000 | 1.000 | 1.000 | 1.000 | 0.999 | 0.992 | 0.953 | 0.802 | 0.415 |
| 13 | 1.000 | 1.000 | 1.000 | 1.000 | 1.000 | 0.999 | 0.993 | 0.956 | 0.771 |
| 14 | 1.000 | 1.000 | 1.000 | 1.000 | 1.000 | 1.000 | 1.000 | 1.000 | 1.000 |

## Appendix B

# CUMULATIVE BINOMIAL PROBABILITY DISTRIBUTION
*(continued)*

$n = 15$
PROBABILITY

| r | 0.1 | 0.2 | 0.3 | 0.4 | 0.5 | 0.6 | 0.7 | 0.8 | 0.9 |
|---|-----|-----|-----|-----|-----|-----|-----|-----|-----|
| 0 | 0.206 | 0.035 | 0.005 | 0.000 | 0.000 | 0.000 | 0.000 | 0.000 | 0.000 |
| 1 | 0.549 | 0.167 | 0.035 | 0.005 | 0.000 | 0.000 | 0.000 | 0.000 | 0.000 |
| 2 | 0.816 | 0.398 | 0.127 | 0.027 | 0.004 | 0.000 | 0.000 | 0.000 | 0.000 |
| 3 | 0.944 | 0.648 | 0.297 | 0.091 | 0.018 | 0.002 | 0.000 | 0.000 | 0.000 |
| 4 | 0.987 | 0.836 | 0.515 | 0.217 | 0.059 | 0.009 | 0.001 | 0.000 | 0.000 |
| 5 | 0.998 | 0.939 | 0.722 | 0.403 | 0.151 | 0.034 | 0.004 | 0.000 | 0.000 |
| 6 | 1.000 | 0.982 | 0.869 | 0.610 | 0.304 | 0.095 | 0.015 | 0.001 | 0.000 |
| 7 | 1.000 | 0.996 | 0.950 | 0.787 | 0.500 | 0.213 | 0.050 | 0.004 | 0.000 |
| 8 | 1.000 | 0.999 | 0.985 | 0.905 | 0.696 | 0.390 | 0.131 | 0.018 | 0.000 |
| 9 | 1.000 | 1.000 | 0.996 | 0.966 | 0.849 | 0.597 | 0.278 | 0.061 | 0.002 |
| 10 | 1.000 | 1.000 | 0.999 | 0.991 | 0.941 | 0.783 | 0.485 | 0.164 | 0.013 |
| 11 | 1.000 | 1.000 | 1.000 | 0.998 | 0.982 | 0.909 | 0.703 | 0.352 | 0.056 |
| 12 | 1.000 | 1.000 | 1.000 | 1.000 | 0.996 | 0.973 | 0.873 | 0.602 | 0.184 |
| 13 | 1.000 | 1.000 | 1.000 | 1.000 | 1.000 | 0.995 | 0.965 | 0.833 | 0.451 |
| 14 | 1.000 | 1.000 | 1.000 | 1.000 | 1.000 | 1.000 | 0.995 | 0.965 | 0.794 |
| 15 | 1.000 | 1.000 | 1.000 | 1.000 | 1.000 | 1.000 | 1.000 | 1.000 | 1.000 |

$n = 16$
PROBABILITY

| r | 0.1 | 0.2 | 0.3 | 0.4 | 0.5 | 0.6 | 0.7 | 0.8 | 0.9 |
|---|-----|-----|-----|-----|-----|-----|-----|-----|-----|
| 0 | 0.185 | 0.028 | 0.003 | 0.000 | 0.000 | 0.000 | 0.000 | 0.000 | 0.000 |
| 1 | 0.515 | 0.141 | 0.026 | 0.003 | 0.000 | 0.000 | 0.000 | 0.000 | 0.000 |
| 2 | 0.789 | 0.352 | 0.099 | 0.018 | 0.002 | 0.000 | 0.000 | 0.000 | 0.000 |
| 3 | 0.932 | 0.598 | 0.246 | 0.065 | 0.011 | 0.001 | 0.000 | 0.000 | 0.000 |
| 4 | 0.983 | 0.798 | 0.450 | 0.167 | 0.038 | 0.005 | 0.000 | 0.000 | 0.000 |
| 5 | 0.997 | 0.918 | 0.660 | 0.329 | 0.105 | 0.019 | 0.002 | 0.000 | 0.000 |
| 6 | 0.999 | 0.973 | 0.825 | 0.527 | 0.227 | 0.058 | 0.007 | 0.000 | 0.000 |
| 7 | 1.000 | 0.993 | 0.926 | 0.716 | 0.402 | 0.142 | 0.026 | 0.001 | 0.000 |
| 8 | 1.000 | 0.999 | 0.974 | 0.858 | 0.598 | 0.284 | 0.074 | 0.007 | 0.000 |
| 9 | 1.000 | 1.000 | 0.993 | 0.942 | 0.773 | 0.473 | 0.175 | 0.027 | 0.001 |
| 10 | 1.000 | 1.000 | 0.998 | 0.981 | 0.895 | 0.671 | 0.340 | 0.082 | 0.003 |
| 11 | 1.000 | 1.000 | 1.000 | 0.995 | 0.962 | 0.833 | 0.550 | 0.202 | 0.017 |
| 12 | 1.000 | 1.000 | 1.000 | 0.999 | 0.989 | 0.935 | 0.754 | 0.402 | 0.068 |
| 13 | 1.000 | 1.000 | 1.000 | 1.000 | 0.998 | 0.982 | 0.901 | 0.648 | 0.211 |
| 14 | 1.000 | 1.000 | 1.000 | 1.000 | 1.000 | 0.997 | 0.974 | 0.859 | 0.485 |
| 15 | 1.000 | 1.000 | 1.000 | 1.000 | 1.000 | 1.000 | 0.997 | 0.972 | 0.815 |
| 16 | 1.000 | 1.000 | 1.000 | 1.000 | 1.000 | 1.000 | 1.000 | 1.000 | 1.000 |

## Appendix B

# CUMULATIVE BINOMIAL PROBABILITY DISTRIBUTION
## (continued)

### n = 17
#### PROBABILITY

| r | 0.1 | 0.2 | 0.3 | 0.4 | 0.5 | 0.6 | 0.7 | 0.8 | 0.9 |
|---|-----|-----|-----|-----|-----|-----|-----|-----|-----|
| 0 | 0.167 | 0.023 | 0.002 | 0.000 | 0.000 | 0.000 | 0.000 | 0.000 | 0.000 |
| 1 | 0.482 | 0.118 | 0.019 | 0.002 | 0.000 | 0.000 | 0.000 | 0.000 | 0.000 |
| 2 | 0.762 | 0.310 | 0.077 | 0.012 | 0.001 | 0.000 | 0.000 | 0.000 | 0.000 |
| 3 | 0.917 | 0.549 | 0.202 | 0.046 | 0.006 | 0.000 | 0.000 | 0.000 | 0.000 |
| 4 | 0.978 | 0.758 | 0.389 | 0.126 | 0.025 | 0.003 | 0.000 | 0.000 | 0.000 |
| 5 | 0.995 | 0.894 | 0.597 | 0.264 | 0.072 | 0.011 | 0.001 | 0.000 | 0.000 |
| 6 | 0.999 | 0.962 | 0.775 | 0.448 | 0.166 | 0.035 | 0.003 | 0.000 | 0.000 |
| 7 | 1.000 | 0.989 | 0.895 | 0.641 | 0.315 | 0.092 | 0.013 | 0.000 | 0.000 |
| 8 | 1.000 | 0.997 | 0.960 | 0.801 | 0.500 | 0.199 | 0.040 | 0.003 | 0.000 |
| 9 | 1.000 | 1.000 | 0.987 | 0.908 | 0.685 | 0.359 | 0.105 | 0.011 | 0.000 |
| 10 | 1.000 | 1.000 | 0.997 | 0.965 | 0.834 | 0.552 | 0.225 | 0.038 | 0.001 |
| 11 | 1.000 | 1.000 | 0.999 | 0.989 | 0.928 | 0.736 | 0.403 | 0.106 | 0.005 |
| 12 | 1.000 | 1.000 | 1.000 | 0.997 | 0.975 | 0.874 | 0.611 | 0.242 | 0.022 |
| 13 | 1.000 | 1.000 | 1.000 | 1.000 | 0.994 | 0.954 | 0.798 | 0.451 | 0.083 |
| 14 | 1.000 | 1.000 | 1.000 | 1.000 | 0.999 | 0.988 | 0.923 | 0.690 | 0.238 |
| 15 | 1.000 | 1.000 | 1.000 | 1.000 | 1.000 | 0.998 | 0.981 | 0.882 | 0.518 |
| 16 | 1.000 | 1.000 | 1.000 | 1.000 | 1.000 | 1.000 | 0.998 | 0.977 | 0.833 |
| 17 | 1.000 | 1.000 | 1.000 | 1.000 | 1.000 | 1.000 | 1.000 | 1.000 | 1.000 |

### n = 18
#### PROBABILITY

| r | 0.1 | 0.2 | 0.3 | 0.4 | 0.5 | 0.6 | 0.7 | 0.8 | 0.9 |
|---|-----|-----|-----|-----|-----|-----|-----|-----|-----|
| 0 | 0.150 | 0.018 | 0.002 | 0.000 | 0.000 | 0.000 | 0.000 | 0.000 | 0.000 |
| 1 | 0.450 | 0.099 | 0.014 | 0.001 | 0.000 | 0.000 | 0.000 | 0.000 | 0.000 |
| 2 | 0.734 | 0.271 | 0.060 | 0.008 | 0.001 | 0.000 | 0.000 | 0.000 | 0.000 |
| 3 | 0.902 | 0.501 | 0.165 | 0.033 | 0.004 | 0.000 | 0.000 | 0.000 | 0.000 |
| 4 | 0.972 | 0.716 | 0.333 | 0.094 | 0.015 | 0.001 | 0.000 | 0.000 | 0.000 |
| 5 | 0.994 | 0.867 | 0.534 | 0.209 | 0.048 | 0.006 | 0.000 | 0.000 | 0.000 |
| 6 | 0.999 | 0.949 | 0.722 | 0.374 | 0.119 | 0.020 | 0.001 | 0.000 | 0.000 |
| 7 | 1.000 | 0.984 | 0.859 | 0.563 | 0.240 | 0.058 | 0.006 | 0.000 | 0.000 |
| 8 | 1.000 | 0.996 | 0.940 | 0.737 | 0.407 | 0.135 | 0.021 | 0.001 | 0.000 |
| 9 | 1.000 | 0.999 | 0.979 | 0.865 | 0.593 | 0.263 | 0.060 | 0.004 | 0.000 |
| 10 | 1.000 | 1.000 | 0.994 | 0.942 | 0.760 | 0.437 | 0.141 | 0.016 | 0.000 |
| 11 | 1.000 | 1.000 | 0.999 | 0.980 | 0.881 | 0.626 | 0.278 | 0.051 | 0.001 |
| 12 | 1.000 | 1.000 | 1.000 | 0.994 | 0.952 | 0.791 | 0.466 | 0.133 | 0.006 |
| 13 | 1.000 | 1.000 | 1.000 | 0.999 | 0.985 | 0.906 | 0.667 | 0.284 | 0.028 |
| 14 | 1.000 | 1.000 | 1.000 | 1.000 | 0.996 | 0.967 | 0.835 | 0.499 | 0.098 |
| 15 | 1.000 | 1.000 | 1.000 | 1.000 | 0.999 | 0.992 | 0.940 | 0.729 | 0.266 |
| 16 | 1.000 | 1.000 | 1.000 | 1.000 | 1.000 | 0.999 | 0.986 | 0.901 | 0.550 |
| 17 | 1.000 | 1.000 | 1.000 | 1.000 | 1.000 | 1.000 | 0.998 | 0.982 | 0.850 |
| 18 | 1.000 | 1.000 | 1.000 | 1.000 | 1.000 | 1.000 | 1.000 | 1.000 | 1.000 |

## Appendix B

# CUMULATIVE BINOMIAL PROBABILITY DISTRIBUTION
### (continued)

$n = 19$
PROBABILITY

| r | 0.1 | 0.2 | 0.3 | 0.4 | 0.5 | 0.6 | 0.7 | 0.8 | 0.9 |
|---|-----|-----|-----|-----|-----|-----|-----|-----|-----|
| 0 | 0.135 | 0.014 | 0.001 | 0.000 | 0.000 | 0.000 | 0.000 | 0.000 | 0.000 |
| 1 | 0.420 | 0.083 | 0.010 | 0.001 | 0.000 | 0.000 | 0.000 | 0.000 | 0.000 |
| 2 | 0.705 | 0.237 | 0.046 | 0.005 | 0.000 | 0.000 | 0.000 | 0.000 | 0.000 |
| 3 | 0.885 | 0.455 | 0.133 | 0.023 | 0.002 | 0.000 | 0.000 | 0.000 | 0.000 |
| 4 | 0.965 | 0.673 | 0.282 | 0.070 | 0.010 | 0.001 | 0.000 | 0.000 | 0.000 |
| 5 | 0.991 | 0.837 | 0.474 | 0.163 | 0.032 | 0.003 | 0.000 | 0.000 | 0.000 |
| 6 | 0.998 | 0.932 | 0.666 | 0.308 | 0.084 | 0.012 | 0.001 | 0.000 | 0.000 |
| 7 | 1.000 | 0.977 | 0.818 | 0.488 | 0.180 | 0.035 | 0.003 | 0.000 | 0.000 |
| 8 | 1.000 | 0.993 | 0.916 | 0.667 | 0.324 | 0.088 | 0.011 | 0.000 | 0.000 |
| 9 | 1.000 | 0.998 | 0.967 | 0.814 | 0.500 | 0.186 | 0.033 | 0.002 | 0.000 |
| 10 | 1.000 | 1.000 | 0.989 | 0.912 | 0.676 | 0.333 | 0.084 | 0.007 | 0.000 |
| 11 | 1.000 | 1.000 | 0.997 | 0.965 | 0.820 | 0.512 | 0.182 | 0.023 | 0.000 |
| 12 | 1.000 | 1.000 | 0.999 | 0.988 | 0.916 | 0.692 | 0.334 | 0.068 | 0.002 |
| 13 | 1.000 | 1.000 | 1.000 | 0.997 | 0.968 | 0.837 | 0.526 | 0.163 | 0.009 |
| 14 | 1.000 | 1.000 | 1.000 | 0.999 | 0.990 | 0.930 | 0.718 | 0.327 | 0.035 |
| 15 | 1.000 | 1.000 | 1.000 | 1.000 | 0.998 | 0.977 | 0.867 | 0.545 | 0.115 |
| 16 | 1.000 | 1.000 | 1.000 | 1.000 | 1.000 | 0.995 | 0.954 | 0.763 | 0.295 |
| 17 | 1.000 | 1.000 | 1.000 | 1.000 | 1.000 | 0.999 | 0.990 | 0.917 | 0.580 |
| 18 | 1.000 | 1.000 | 1.000 | 1.000 | 1.000 | 1.000 | 0.999 | 0.986 | 0.865 |
| 19 | 1.000 | 1.000 | 1.000 | 1.000 | 1.000 | 1.000 | 1.000 | 1.000 | 1.000 |

$n = 20$
PROBABILITY

| r | 0.1 | 0.2 | 0.3 | 0.4 | 0.5 | 0.6 | 0.7 | 0.8 | 0.9 |
|---|-----|-----|-----|-----|-----|-----|-----|-----|-----|
| 0 | 0.122 | 0.012 | 0.001 | 0.000 | 0.000 | 0.000 | 0.000 | 0.000 | 0.000 |
| 1 | 0.392 | 0.069 | 0.008 | 0.001 | 0.000 | 0.000 | 0.000 | 0.000 | 0.000 |
| 2 | 0.677 | 0.206 | 0.035 | 0.004 | 0.000 | 0.000 | 0.000 | 0.000 | 0.000 |
| 3 | 0.867 | 0.411 | 0.107 | 0.016 | 0.001 | 0.000 | 0.000 | 0.000 | 0.000 |
| 4 | 0.957 | 0.630 | 0.238 | 0.051 | 0.006 | 0.000 | 0.000 | 0.000 | 0.000 |
| 5 | 0.989 | 0.804 | 0.416 | 0.126 | 0.021 | 0.002 | 0.000 | 0.000 | 0.000 |
| 6 | 0.998 | 0.913 | 0.608 | 0.250 | 0.058 | 0.006 | 0.000 | 0.000 | 0.000 |
| 7 | 1.000 | 0.968 | 0.772 | 0.416 | 0.132 | 0.021 | 0.001 | 0.000 | 0.000 |
| 8 | 1.000 | 0.990 | 0.887 | 0.596 | 0.252 | 0.057 | 0.005 | 0.000 | 0.000 |
| 9 | 1.000 | 0.997 | 0.952 | 0.755 | 0.412 | 0.128 | 0.017 | 0.001 | 0.000 |
| 10 | 1.000 | 0.999 | 0.983 | 0.872 | 0.588 | 0.245 | 0.048 | 0.003 | 0.000 |
| 11 | 1.000 | 1.000 | 0.995 | 0.943 | 0.748 | 0.404 | 0.113 | 0.010 | 0.000 |
| 12 | 1.000 | 1.000 | 0.999 | 0.979 | 0.868 | 0.584 | 0.228 | 0.032 | 0.000 |
| 13 | 1.000 | 1.000 | 1.000 | 0.994 | 0.942 | 0.750 | 0.392 | 0.087 | 0.002 |
| 14 | 1.000 | 1.000 | 1.000 | 0.998 | 0.979 | 0.874 | 0.584 | 0.196 | 0.011 |
| 15 | 1.000 | 1.000 | 1.000 | 1.000 | 0.994 | 0.949 | 0.762 | 0.370 | 0.043 |
| 16 | 1.000 | 1.000 | 1.000 | 1.000 | 0.999 | 0.984 | 0.893 | 0.589 | 0.133 |
| 17 | 1.000 | 1.000 | 1.000 | 1.000 | 1.000 | 0.996 | 0.965 | 0.794 | 0.323 |
| 18 | 1.000 | 1.000 | 1.000 | 1.000 | 1.000 | 0.999 | 0.992 | 0.931 | 0.608 |
| 19 | 1.000 | 1.000 | 1.000 | 1.000 | 1.000 | 1.000 | 0.999 | 0.988 | 0.878 |
| 20 | 1.000 | 1.000 | 1.000 | 1.000 | 1.000 | 1.000 | 1.000 | 1.000 | 1.000 |

# Appendix B

## CUMULATIVE BINOMIAL PROBABILITY DISTRIBUTION
### (concluded)

$n = 25$

PROBABILITY

| r | 0.1 | 0.2 | 0.3 | 0.4 | 0.5 | 0.6 | 0.7 | 0.8 | 0.9 |
|---|-----|-----|-----|-----|-----|-----|-----|-----|-----|
| 0 | 0.072 | 0.004 | 0.000 | 0.000 | 0.000 | 0.000 | 0.000 | 0.000 | 0.000 |
| 1 | 0.271 | 0.027 | 0.002 | 0.000 | 0.000 | 0.000 | 0.000 | 0.000 | 0.000 |
| 2 | 0.537 | 0.098 | 0.009 | 0.000 | 0.000 | 0.000 | 0.000 | 0.000 | 0.000 |
| 3 | 0.764 | 0.234 | 0.033 | 0.002 | 0.000 | 0.000 | 0.000 | 0.000 | 0.000 |
| 4 | 0.902 | 0.421 | 0.090 | 0.009 | 0.000 | 0.000 | 0.000 | 0.000 | 0.000 |
| 5 | 0.967 | 0.617 | 0.193 | 0.029 | 0.002 | 0.000 | 0.000 | 0.000 | 0.000 |
| 6 | 0.991 | 0.780 | 0.341 | 0.074 | 0.007 | 0.000 | 0.000 | 0.000 | 0.000 |
| 7 | 0.998 | 0.891 | 0.512 | 0.154 | 0.022 | 0.001 | 0.000 | 0.000 | 0.000 |
| 8 | 1.000 | 0.953 | 0.677 | 0.274 | 0.054 | 0.004 | 0.000 | 0.000 | 0.000 |
| 9 | 1.000 | 0.983 | 0.811 | 0.425 | 0.115 | 0.013 | 0.000 | 0.000 | 0.000 |
| 10 | 1.000 | 0.994 | 0.902 | 0.586 | 0.212 | 0.034 | 0.002 | 0.000 | 0.000 |
| 11 | 1.000 | 0.998 | 0.956 | 0.732 | 0.345 | 0.078 | 0.006 | 0.000 | 0.000 |
| 12 | 1.000 | 1.000 | 0.983 | 0.846 | 0.500 | 0.154 | 0.017 | 0.000 | 0.000 |
| 13 | 1.000 | 1.000 | 0.994 | 0.922 | 0.655 | 0.268 | 0.044 | 0.002 | 0.000 |
| 14 | 1.000 | 1.000 | 0.998 | 0.966 | 0.788 | 0.414 | 0.098 | 0.006 | 0.000 |
| 15 | 1.000 | 1.000 | 1.000 | 0.987 | 0.885 | 0.575 | 0.189 | 0.017 | 0.000 |
| 16 | 1.000 | 1.000 | 1.000 | 0.996 | 0.946 | 0.726 | 0.323 | 0.047 | 0.000 |
| 17 | 1.000 | 1.000 | 1.000 | 0.999 | 0.978 | 0.846 | 0.488 | 0.109 | 0.002 |
| 18 | 1.000 | 1.000 | 1.000 | 1.000 | 0.993 | 0.926 | 0.659 | 0.220 | 0.009 |
| 19 | 1.000 | 1.000 | 1.000 | 1.000 | 0.998 | 0.971 | 0.807 | 0.383 | 0.033 |
| 20 | 1.000 | 1.000 | 1.000 | 1.000 | 1.000 | 0.991 | 0.910 | 0.579 | 0.098 |
| 21 | 1.000 | 1.000 | 1.000 | 1.000 | 1.000 | 0.998 | 0.967 | 0.766 | 0.236 |
| 22 | 1.000 | 1.000 | 1.000 | 1.000 | 1.000 | 1.000 | 0.991 | 0.902 | 0.463 |
| 23 | 1.000 | 1.000 | 1.000 | 1.000 | 1.000 | 1.000 | 0.998 | 0.973 | 0.729 |
| 24 | 1.000 | 1.000 | 1.000 | 1.000 | 1.000 | 1.000 | 1.000 | 0.996 | 0.928 |
| 25 | 1.000 | 1.000 | 1.000 | 1.000 | 1.000 | 1.000 | 1.000 | 1.000 | 1.000 |

## Appendix C

# POISSON DISTRIBUTION: PROBABILITY OF EXACTLY X OCCURRENCES

| X | $\mu$ | | | | | | | | |
|---|---|---|---|---|---|---|---|---|---|
|   | 0.1 | 0.2 | 0.3 | 0.4 | 0.5 | 0.6 | 0.7 | 0.8 | 0.9 |
| 0 | 0.9048 | 0.8187 | 0.7408 | 0.6703 | 0.6065 | 0.5488 | 0.4966 | 0.4493 | 0.4066 |
| 1 | 0.0905 | 0.1637 | 0.2222 | 0.2681 | 0.3033 | 0.3293 | 0.3476 | 0.3595 | 0.3659 |
| 2 | 0.0045 | 0.0164 | 0.0333 | 0.0536 | 0.0758 | 0.0988 | 0.1217 | 0.1438 | 0.1647 |
| 3 | 0.0002 | 0.0011 | 0.0033 | 0.0072 | 0.0126 | 0.0198 | 0.0284 | 0.0383 | 0.0494 |
| 4 | 0.0000 | 0.0001 | 0.0003 | 0.0007 | 0.0016 | 0.0030 | 0.0050 | 0.0077 | 0.0111 |
| 5 | 0.0000 | 0.0000 | 0.0000 | 0.0001 | 0.0002 | 0.0004 | 0.0007 | 0.0012 | 0.0020 |
| 6 | 0.0000 | 0.0000 | 0.0000 | 0.0000 | 0.0000 | 0.0000 | 0.0001 | 0.0002 | 0.0003 |
| 7 | 0.0000 | 0.0000 | 0.0000 | 0.0000 | 0.0000 | 0.0000 | 0.0000 | 0.0000 | 0.0000 |

| X | $\mu$ | | | | | | | | |
|---|---|---|---|---|---|---|---|---|---|
|   | 1.0 | 2.0 | 3.0 | 4.0 | 5.0 | 6.0 | 7.0 | 8.0 | 9.0 |
| 0 | 0.3679 | 0.1353 | 0.0498 | 0.0183 | 0.0067 | 0.0025 | 0.0009 | 0.0003 | 0.0001 |
| 1 | 0.3679 | 0.2707 | 0.1494 | 0.0733 | 0.0337 | 0.0149 | 0.0064 | 0.0027 | 0.0011 |
| 2 | 0.1839 | 0.2707 | 0.2240 | 0.1465 | 0.0842 | 0.0446 | 0.0223 | 0.0107 | 0.0050 |
| 3 | 0.0613 | 0.1804 | 0.2240 | 0.1954 | 0.1404 | 0.0892 | 0.0521 | 0.0286 | 0.0150 |
| 4 | 0.0153 | 0.0902 | 0.1680 | 0.1954 | 0.1755 | 0.1339 | 0.0912 | 0.0573 | 0.0337 |
| 5 | 0.0031 | 0.0361 | 0.1008 | 0.1563 | 0.1755 | 0.1606 | 0.1277 | 0.0916 | 0.0607 |
| 6 | 0.0005 | 0.0120 | 0.0504 | 0.1042 | 0.1462 | 0.1606 | 0.1490 | 0.1221 | 0.0911 |
| 7 | 0.0001 | 0.0034 | 0.0216 | 0.0595 | 0.1044 | 0.1377 | 0.1490 | 0.1396 | 0.1171 |
| 8 | 0.0000 | 0.0009 | 0.0081 | 0.0298 | 0.0653 | 0.1033 | 0.1304 | 0.1396 | 0.1318 |
| 9 | 0.0000 | 0.0002 | 0.0027 | 0.0132 | 0.0363 | 0.0688 | 0.1014 | 0.1241 | 0.1318 |
| 10 | 0.0000 | 0.0000 | 0.0008 | 0.0053 | 0.0181 | 0.0413 | 0.0710 | 0.0993 | 0.1186 |
| 11 | 0.0000 | 0.0000 | 0.0002 | 0.0019 | 0.0082 | 0.0225 | 0.0452 | 0.0722 | 0.0970 |
| 12 | 0.0000 | 0.0000 | 0.0001 | 0.0006 | 0.0034 | 0.0113 | 0.0263 | 0.0481 | 0.0728 |
| 13 | 0.0000 | 0.0000 | 0.0000 | 0.0002 | 0.0013 | 0.0052 | 0.0142 | 0.0296 | 0.0504 |
| 14 | 0.0000 | 0.0000 | 0.0000 | 0.0001 | 0.0005 | 0.0022 | 0.0071 | 0.0169 | 0.0324 |
| 15 | 0.0000 | 0.0000 | 0.0000 | 0.0000 | 0.0002 | 0.0009 | 0.0033 | 0.0090 | 0.0194 |
| 16 | 0.0000 | 0.0000 | 0.0000 | 0.0000 | 0.0000 | 0.0003 | 0.0014 | 0.0045 | 0.0109 |
| 17 | 0.0000 | 0.0000 | 0.0000 | 0.0000 | 0.0000 | 0.0001 | 0.0006 | 0.0021 | 0.0058 |
| 18 | 0.0000 | 0.0000 | 0.0000 | 0.0000 | 0.0000 | 0.0000 | 0.0002 | 0.0009 | 0.0029 |
| 19 | 0.0000 | 0.0000 | 0.0000 | 0.0000 | 0.0000 | 0.0000 | 0.0001 | 0.0004 | 0.0014 |
| 20 | 0.0000 | 0.0000 | 0.0000 | 0.0000 | 0.0000 | 0.0000 | 0.0000 | 0.0002 | 0.0006 |
| 21 | 0.0000 | 0.0000 | 0.0000 | 0.0000 | 0.0000 | 0.0000 | 0.0000 | 0.0001 | 0.0003 |
| 22 | 0.0000 | 0.0000 | 0.0000 | 0.0000 | 0.0000 | 0.0000 | 0.0000 | 0.0000 | 0.0001 |

## Appendix D

# AREAS UNDER THE NORMAL CURVE

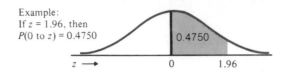

Example:
If $z = 1.96$, then
$P(0 \text{ to } z) = 0.4750$

0.4750

$z \longrightarrow$        0        1.96

| Z | 0.00 | 0.01 | 0.02 | 0.03 | 0.04 | 0.05 | 0.06 | 0.07 | 0.08 | 0.09 |
|-----|--------|--------|--------|--------|--------|--------|--------|--------|--------|--------|
| 0.0 | 0.0000 | 0.0040 | 0.0080 | 0.0120 | 0.0160 | 0.0199 | 0.0239 | 0.0279 | 0.0319 | 0.0359 |
| 0.1 | 0.0398 | 0.0438 | 0.0478 | 0.0517 | 0.0557 | 0.0596 | 0.0636 | 0.0675 | 0.0714 | 0.0753 |
| 0.2 | 0.0793 | 0.0832 | 0.0871 | 0.0910 | 0.0948 | 0.0987 | 0.1026 | 0.1064 | 0.1103 | 0.1141 |
| 0.3 | 0.1179 | 0.1217 | 0.1255 | 0.1293 | 0.1331 | 0.1368 | 0.1406 | 0.1443 | 0.1480 | 0.1517 |
| 0.4 | 0.1554 | 0.1591 | 0.1628 | 0.1664 | 0.1700 | 0.1736 | 0.1772 | 0.1808 | 0.1844 | 0.1879 |
| 0.5 | 0.1915 | 0.1950 | 0.1985 | 0.2019 | 0.2054 | 0.2088 | 0.2123 | 0.2157 | 0.2190 | 0.2224 |
| 0.6 | 0.2257 | 0.2291 | 0.2324 | 0.2357 | 0.2389 | 0.2422 | 0.2454 | 0.2486 | 0.2517 | 0.2549 |
| 0.7 | 0.2580 | 0.2611 | 0.2642 | 0.2673 | 0.2704 | 0.2734 | 0.2764 | 0.2794 | 0.2823 | 0.2852 |
| 0.8 | 0.2881 | 0.2910 | 0.2939 | 0.2967 | 0.2995 | 0.3023 | 0.3051 | 0.3078 | 0.3106 | 0.3133 |
| 0.9 | 0.3159 | 0.3186 | 0.3212 | 0.3238 | 0.3264 | 0.3289 | 0.3315 | 0.3340 | 0.3365 | 0.3389 |
| 1.0 | 0.3413 | 0.3438 | 0.3461 | 0.3485 | 0.3508 | 0.3531 | 0.3554 | 0.3577 | 0.3599 | 0.3621 |
| 1.1 | 0.3643 | 0.3665 | 0.3686 | 0.3708 | 0.3729 | 0.3749 | 0.3770 | 0.3790 | 0.3810 | 0.3830 |
| 1.2 | 0.3849 | 0.3869 | 0.3888 | 0.3907 | 0.3925 | 0.3944 | 0.3962 | 0.3980 | 0.3997 | 0.4015 |
| 1.3 | 0.4032 | 0.4049 | 0.4066 | 0.4082 | 0.4099 | 0.4115 | 0.4131 | 0.4147 | 0.4162 | 0.4177 |
| 1.4 | 0.4192 | 0.4207 | 0.4222 | 0.4236 | 0.4251 | 0.4265 | 0.4279 | 0.4292 | 0.4306 | 0.4319 |
| 1.5 | 0.4332 | 0.4345 | 0.4357 | 0.4370 | 0.4382 | 0.4394 | 0.4406 | 0.4418 | 0.4429 | 0.4441 |
| 1.6 | 0.4452 | 0.4463 | 0.4474 | 0.4484 | 0.4495 | 0.4505 | 0.4515 | 0.4525 | 0.4535 | 0.4545 |
| 1.7 | 0.4554 | 0.4564 | 0.4573 | 0.4582 | 0.4591 | 0.4599 | 0.4608 | 0.4616 | 0.4625 | 0.4633 |
| 1.8 | 0.4641 | 0.4649 | 0.4656 | 0.4664 | 0.4671 | 0.4678 | 0.4686 | 0.4693 | 0.4699 | 0.4706 |
| 1.9 | 0.4713 | 0.4719 | 0.4726 | 0.4732 | 0.4738 | 0.4744 | 0.4750 | 0.4756 | 0.4761 | 0.4767 |
| 2.0 | 0.4772 | 0.4778 | 0.4783 | 0.4788 | 0.4793 | 0.4798 | 0.4803 | 0.4808 | 0.4812 | 0.4817 |
| 2.1 | 0.4821 | 0.4826 | 0.4830 | 0.4834 | 0.4838 | 0.4842 | 0.4846 | 0.4850 | 0.4854 | 0.4857 |
| 2.2 | 0.4861 | 0.4864 | 0.4868 | 0.4871 | 0.4875 | 0.4878 | 0.4881 | 0.4884 | 0.4887 | 0.4890 |
| 2.3 | 0.4893 | 0.4896 | 0.4898 | 0.4901 | 0.4904 | 0.4906 | 0.4909 | 0.4911 | 0.4913 | 0.4916 |
| 2.4 | 0.4918 | 0.4920 | 0.4922 | 0.4925 | 0.4927 | 0.4929 | 0.4931 | 0.4932 | 0.4934 | 0.4936 |
| 2.5 | 0.4938 | 0.4940 | 0.4941 | 0.4943 | 0.4945 | 0.4946 | 0.4948 | 0.4949 | 0.4951 | 0.4952 |
| 2.6 | 0.4953 | 0.4955 | 0.4956 | 0.4957 | 0.4959 | 0.4960 | 0.4961 | 0.4962 | 0.4963 | 0.4964 |
| 2.7 | 0.4965 | 0.4966 | 0.4967 | 0.4968 | 0.4969 | 0.4970 | 0.4971 | 0.4972 | 0.4973 | 0.4974 |
| 2.8 | 0.4974 | 0.4975 | 0.4976 | 0.4977 | 0.4977 | 0.4978 | 0.4979 | 0.4979 | 0.4980 | 0.4981 |
| 2.9 | 0.4981 | 0.4982 | 0.4982 | 0.4983 | 0.4984 | 0.4984 | 0.4985 | 0.4985 | 0.4986 | 0.4986 |
| 3.0 | 0.4987 | 0.4987 | 0.4987 | 0.4988 | 0.4988 | 0.4989 | 0.4989 | 0.4989 | 0.4990 | 0.4990 |

# Appendix E

## TABLE OF RANDOM NUMBERS

| | | | | | | | | | |
|---|---|---|---|---|---|---|---|---|---|
| 02711 | 08182 | 75997 | 79866 | 58095 | 83319 | 80295 | 79741 | 74599 | 84379 |
| 94873 | 90935 | 31684 | 63952 | 09865 | 14491 | 99518 | 93394 | 34691 | 14985 |
| 54921 | 78680 | 06635 | 98689 | 17306 | 25170 | 65928 | 87709 | 30533 | 89736 |
| 77640 | 97636 | 37397 | 93379 | 56454 | 59818 | 45827 | 74164 | 71666 | 46977 |
| 61545 | 00835 | 93251 | 87203 | 36759 | 49197 | 85967 | 01704 | 19634 | 21898 |
| 17147 | 19519 | 22497 | 16857 | 42426 | 84822 | 92598 | 49186 | 88247 | 39967 |
| 13748 | 04742 | 92460 | 85801 | 53444 | 65626 | 58710 | 55406 | 17173 | 69776 |
| 87455 | 14813 | 50373 | 28037 | 91182 | 32786 | 65261 | 11173 | 34376 | 36408 |
| 08999 | 57409 | 91185 | 10200 | 61411 | 23392 | 47797 | 56377 | 71635 | 08601 |
| 78804 | 81333 | 53809 | 32471 | 46034 | 36306 | 22498 | 19239 | 85428 | 55721 |
| 82173 | 26921 | 28472 | 98958 | 07960 | 66124 | 89731 | 95069 | 18625 | 92405 |
| 97594 | 25168 | 89178 | 68190 | 05043 | 17407 | 48201 | 83917 | 11413 | 72920 |
| 73881 | 67176 | 93504 | 42636 | 38233 | 16154 | 96451 | 57925 | 29667 | 30859 |
| 46071 | 22912 | 90326 | 42453 | 88108 | 72064 | 58601 | 32357 | 90610 | 32921 |
| 44492 | 19686 | 12495 | 93135 | 95185 | 77799 | 52441 | 88272 | 22024 | 80631 |
| 31864 | 72170 | 37722 | 55794 | 14636 | 05148 | 54505 | 50113 | 21119 | 25228 |
| 51574 | 90692 | 43339 | 65689 | 76539 | 27909 | 05467 | 21727 | 51141 | 72949 |
| 35350 | 76132 | 92925 | 92124 | 92634 | 35681 | 43690 | 89136 | 35599 | 84138 |
| 46943 | 36502 | 01172 | 46045 | 46991 | 33804 | 80006 | 35542 | 61056 | 75666 |
| 22665 | 87226 | 33304 | 57975 | 03985 | 21566 | 65796 | 72915 | 81466 | 89205 |
| 39437 | 97957 | 11838 | 10433 | 21564 | 51570 | 73558 | 27495 | 34533 | 57808 |
| 77082 | 47784 | 40098 | 97962 | 89845 | 28392 | 78187 | 06112 | 08169 | 11261 |
| 24544 | 25649 | 43370 | 28007 | 06779 | 72402 | 62632 | 53956 | 24709 | 06978 |
| 27503 | 15558 | 37738 | 24849 | 70722 | 71859 | 83736 | 06016 | 94397 | 12529 |
| 24590 | 24545 | 06435 | 52758 | 45685 | 90151 | 46516 | 49644 | 92686 | 84870 |
| 48155 | 86226 | 40359 | 28723 | 15364 | 69125 | 12609 | 57171 | 86857 | 31702 |
| 20226 | 53752 | 90648 | 24362 | 83314 | 00014 | 19207 | 69413 | 97016 | 86290 |
| 70178 | 73444 | 38790 | 53626 | 93780 | 18629 | 68766 | 24371 | 74639 | 30782 |
| 10169 | 41465 | 51935 | 05711 | 09799 | 79077 | 88159 | 33437 | 68519 | 03040 |
| 81084 | 03701 | 28598 | 70013 | 63794 | 53169 | 97054 | 60303 | 23259 | 96196 |
| 69202 | 20777 | 21727 | 81511 | 51887 | 16175 | 53746 | 46516 | 70339 | 62727 |
| 80561 | 95787 | 89426 | 93325 | 86412 | 57479 | 54194 | 52153 | 19197 | 81877 |
| 08199 | 26703 | 95128 | 48599 | 09333 | 12584 | 24374 | 31232 | 61782 | 44032 |
| 98883 | 28220 | 39358 | 53720 | 80161 | 83371 | 15181 | 11131 | 12219 | 55920 |
| 84568 | 69286 | 76054 | 21615 | 80883 | 36797 | 82845 | 39139 | 90900 | 18172 |
| 04269 | 35173 | 95745 | 53893 | 86022 | 77722 | 52498 | 84193 | 22448 | 22571 |
| 10538 | 13124 | 36099 | 13140 | 37706 | 44562 | 57179 | 44693 | 67877 | 01549 |
| 77843 | 24955 | 25900 | 63843 | 95029 | 93859 | 93634 | 20205 | 66294 | 41218 |
| 12034 | 94636 | 49455 | 76362 | 83532 | 31062 | 69903 | 91186 | 65768 | 55949 |
| 10524 | 72829 | 47641 | 93315 | 80875 | 28090 | 97728 | 52560 | 34937 | 79548 |
| 68935 | 76632 | 46984 | 61772 | 92786 | 22651 | 07086 | 89754 | 44143 | 97687 |
| 89450 | 65665 | 29190 | 43709 | 11172 | 34481 | 95977 | 47535 | 25658 | 73898 |
| 90696 | 20451 | 24211 | 97310 | 60446 | 73530 | 62865 | 96574 | 13829 | 72226 |
| 49006 | 32047 | 93086 | 00112 | 20470 | 17136 | 28255 | 86328 | 07293 | 38809 |
| 74591 | 87025 | 52368 | 59416 | 34417 | 70557 | 86746 | 55809 | 53628 | 12000 |
| 06315 | 17012 | 77103 | 00968 | 07235 | 10728 | 42189 | 33292 | 51487 | 64443 |
| 62386 | 09184 | 62092 | 46617 | 99419 | 64230 | 95034 | 85481 | 07857 | 42510 |
| 86848 | 82122 | 04028 | 36959 | 87827 | 12813 | 08627 | 80699 | 13345 | 51695 |
| 65643 | 69480 | 46598 | 04501 | 40403 | 91408 | 32343 | 48130 | 49303 | 90689 |
| 11084 | 46534 | 78957 | 77353 | 39578 | 77868 | 22970 | 84349 | 09184 | 70603 |

## Appendix F

# STUDENT *t* DISTRIBUTION

| df | Level of significance for one-tailed test | | | | | |
|---|---|---|---|---|---|---|
|  | 0.100 | 0.050 | 0.025 | 0.010 | 0.005 | 0.0005 |
|  | Level of significance for two-tailed test | | | | | |
|  | 0.20 | 0.10 | 0.05 | 0.02 | 0.01 | 0.001 |
| 1 | 3.078 | 6.314 | 12.706 | 31.821 | 63.657 | 636.619 |
| 2 | 1.886 | 2.920 | 4.303 | 6.965 | 9.925 | 31.599 |
| 3 | 1.638 | 2.353 | 3.182 | 4.541 | 5.841 | 12.924 |
| 4 | 1.533 | 2.132 | 2.776 | 3.747 | 4.604 | 8.610 |
| 5 | 1.476 | 2.015 | 2.571 | 3.365 | 4.032 | 6.869 |
| 6 | 1.440 | 1.943 | 2.447 | 3.143 | 3.707 | 5.959 |
| 7 | 1.415 | 1.895 | 2.365 | 2.998 | 3.499 | 5.408 |
| 8 | 1.397 | 1.860 | 2.306 | 2.896 | 3.355 | 5.041 |
| 9 | 1.383 | 1.833 | 2.262 | 2.821 | 3.250 | 4.781 |
| 10 | 1.372 | 1.812 | 2.228 | 2.764 | 3.169 | 4.587 |
| 11 | 1.363 | 1.796 | 2.201 | 2.718 | 3.106 | 4.437 |
| 12 | 1.356 | 1.782 | 2.179 | 2.681 | 3.055 | 4.318 |
| 13 | 1.350 | 1.771 | 2.160 | 2.650 | 3.012 | 4.221 |
| 14 | 1.345 | 1.761 | 2.145 | 2.624 | 2.977 | 4.140 |
| 15 | 1.341 | 1.753 | 2.131 | 2.602 | 2.947 | 4.073 |
| 16 | 1.337 | 1.746 | 2.120 | 2.583 | 2.921 | 4.015 |
| 17 | 1.333 | 1.740 | 2.110 | 2.567 | 2.898 | 3.965 |
| 18 | 1.330 | 1.734 | 2.101 | 2.552 | 2.878 | 3.922 |
| 19 | 1.328 | 1.729 | 2.093 | 2.539 | 2.861 | 3.883 |
| 20 | 1.325 | 1.725 | 2.086 | 2.528 | 2.845 | 3.850 |
| 21 | 1.323 | 1.721 | 2.080 | 2.518 | 2.831 | 3.819 |
| 22 | 1.321 | 1.717 | 2.074 | 2.508 | 2.819 | 3.792 |
| 23 | 1.319 | 1.714 | 2.069 | 2.500 | 2.807 | 3.768 |
| 24 | 1.318 | 1.711 | 2.064 | 2.492 | 2.797 | 3.745 |
| 25 | 1.316 | 1.708 | 2.060 | 2.485 | 2.787 | 3.725 |
| 26 | 1.315 | 1.706 | 2.056 | 2.479 | 2.779 | 3.707 |
| 27 | 1.314 | 1.703 | 2.052 | 2.473 | 2.771 | 3.690 |
| 28 | 1.313 | 1.701 | 2.048 | 2.467 | 2.763 | 3.674 |
| 29 | 1.311 | 1.699 | 2.045 | 2.462 | 2.756 | 3.659 |
| 30 | 1.310 | 1.697 | 2.042 | 2.457 | 2.750 | 3.646 |
| 40 | 1.303 | 1.684 | 2.021 | 2.423 | 2.704 | 3.551 |
| 60 | 1.296 | 1.671 | 2.000 | 2.390 | 2.660 | 3.460 |
| 120 | 1.289 | 1.658 | 1.980 | 2.358 | 2.617 | 3.373 |
| $\infty$ | 1.282 | 1.645 | 1.960 | 2.326 | 2.576 | 3.291 |

## Appendix G

## CRITICAL VALUES OF THE *F* DISTRIBUTION AT A **5** PERCENT LEVEL OF SIGNIFICANCE, $\alpha = .05$

Degrees of freedom for the numerator

| | 1 | 2 | 3 | 4 | 5 | 6 | 7 | 8 | 9 | 10 | 12 | 15 | 20 | 24 | 30 | 40 | 60 | 120 | ∞ |
|---|---|---|---|---|---|---|---|---|---|---|---|---|---|---|---|---|---|---|---|
| 1 | 161 | 200 | 216 | 225 | 230 | 234 | 237 | 239 | 241 | 242 | 244 | 246 | 248 | 249 | 250 | 251 | 252 | 253 | 254 |
| 2 | 18.5 | 19.0 | 19.2 | 19.2 | 19.3 | 19.3 | 19.4 | 19.4 | 19.4 | 19.4 | 19.4 | 19.4 | 19.4 | 19.5 | 19.5 | 19.5 | 19.5 | 19.5 | 19.5 |
| 3 | 10.1 | 9.55 | 9.28 | 9.12 | 9.01 | 8.94 | 8.89 | 8.85 | 8.81 | 8.79 | 8.74 | 8.70 | 8.66 | 8.64 | 8.62 | 8.59 | 8.57 | 8.55 | 8.53 |
| 4 | 7.71 | 6.94 | 6.59 | 6.39 | 6.26 | 6.16 | 6.09 | 6.04 | 6.00 | 5.96 | 5.91 | 5.86 | 5.80 | 5.77 | 5.75 | 5.72 | 5.69 | 5.66 | 5.63 |
| 5 | 6.61 | 5.79 | 5.41 | 5.19 | 5.05 | 4.95 | 4.88 | 4.82 | 4.77 | 4.74 | 4.68 | 4.62 | 4.56 | 4.53 | 4.50 | 4.46 | 4.43 | 4.40 | 4.37 |
| 6 | 5.99 | 5.14 | 4.76 | 4.53 | 4.39 | 4.28 | 4.21 | 4.15 | 4.10 | 4.06 | 4.00 | 3.94 | 3.87 | 3.84 | 3.81 | 3.77 | 3.74 | 3.70 | 3.67 |
| 7 | 5.59 | 4.74 | 4.35 | 4.12 | 3.97 | 3.87 | 3.79 | 3.73 | 3.68 | 3.64 | 3.57 | 3.51 | 3.44 | 3.41 | 3.38 | 3.34 | 3.30 | 3.27 | 3.23 |
| 8 | 5.32 | 4.46 | 4.07 | 3.84 | 3.69 | 3.58 | 3.50 | 3.44 | 3.39 | 3.35 | 3.28 | 3.22 | 3.15 | 3.12 | 3.08 | 3.04 | 3.01 | 2.97 | 2.93 |
| 9 | 5.12 | 4.26 | 3.86 | 3.63 | 3.48 | 3.37 | 3.29 | 3.23 | 3.18 | 3.14 | 3.07 | 3.01 | 2.94 | 2.90 | 2.86 | 2.83 | 2.79 | 2.75 | 2.71 |
| 10 | 4.96 | 4.10 | 3.71 | 3.48 | 3.33 | 3.22 | 3.14 | 3.07 | 3.02 | 2.98 | 2.91 | 2.85 | 2.77 | 2.74 | 2.70 | 2.66 | 2.62 | 2.58 | 2.54 |
| 11 | 4.84 | 3.98 | 3.59 | 3.36 | 3.20 | 3.09 | 3.01 | 2.95 | 2.90 | 2.85 | 2.79 | 2.72 | 2.65 | 2.61 | 2.57 | 2.53 | 2.49 | 2.45 | 2.40 |
| 12 | 4.75 | 3.89 | 3.49 | 3.26 | 3.11 | 3.00 | 2.91 | 2.85 | 2.80 | 2.75 | 2.69 | 2.62 | 2.54 | 2.51 | 2.47 | 2.43 | 2.38 | 2.34 | 2.30 |
| 13 | 4.67 | 3.81 | 3.41 | 3.18 | 3.03 | 2.92 | 2.83 | 2.77 | 2.71 | 2.67 | 2.60 | 2.53 | 2.46 | 2.42 | 2.38 | 2.34 | 2.30 | 2.25 | 2.21 |
| 14 | 4.60 | 3.74 | 3.34 | 3.11 | 2.96 | 2.85 | 2.76 | 2.70 | 2.65 | 2.60 | 2.53 | 2.46 | 2.39 | 2.35 | 2.31 | 2.27 | 2.22 | 2.18 | 2.13 |
| 15 | 4.54 | 3.68 | 3.29 | 3.06 | 2.90 | 2.79 | 2.71 | 2.64 | 2.59 | 2.54 | 2.48 | 2.40 | 2.33 | 2.29 | 2.25 | 2.20 | 2.16 | 2.11 | 2.07 |
| 16 | 4.49 | 3.63 | 3.24 | 3.01 | 2.85 | 2.74 | 2.66 | 2.59 | 2.54 | 2.49 | 2.42 | 2.35 | 2.28 | 2.24 | 2.19 | 2.15 | 2.11 | 2.06 | 2.01 |
| 17 | 4.45 | 3.59 | 3.20 | 2.96 | 2.81 | 2.70 | 2.61 | 2.55 | 2.49 | 2.45 | 2.38 | 2.31 | 2.23 | 2.19 | 2.15 | 2.10 | 2.06 | 2.01 | 1.96 |
| 18 | 4.41 | 3.55 | 3.16 | 2.93 | 2.77 | 2.66 | 2.58 | 2.51 | 2.46 | 2.41 | 2.34 | 2.27 | 2.19 | 2.15 | 2.11 | 2.06 | 2.02 | 1.97 | 1.92 |
| 19 | 4.38 | 3.52 | 3.13 | 2.90 | 2.74 | 2.63 | 2.54 | 2.48 | 2.42 | 2.38 | 2.31 | 2.23 | 2.16 | 2.11 | 2.07 | 2.03 | 1.98 | 1.93 | 1.88 |
| 20 | 4.35 | 3.49 | 3.10 | 2.87 | 2.71 | 2.60 | 2.51 | 2.45 | 2.39 | 2.35 | 2.28 | 2.20 | 2.12 | 2.08 | 2.04 | 1.99 | 1.95 | 1.90 | 1.84 |
| 21 | 4.32 | 3.47 | 3.07 | 2.84 | 2.68 | 2.57 | 2.49 | 2.42 | 2.37 | 2.32 | 2.25 | 2.18 | 2.10 | 2.05 | 2.01 | 1.96 | 1.92 | 1.87 | 1.81 |
| 22 | 4.30 | 3.44 | 3.05 | 2.82 | 2.66 | 2.55 | 2.46 | 2.40 | 2.34 | 2.30 | 2.23 | 2.15 | 2.07 | 2.03 | 1.98 | 1.94 | 1.89 | 1.84 | 1.78 |
| 23 | 4.28 | 3.42 | 3.03 | 2.80 | 2.64 | 2.53 | 2.44 | 2.37 | 2.32 | 2.27 | 2.20 | 2.13 | 2.05 | 2.01 | 1.96 | 1.91 | 1.86 | 1.81 | 1.76 |
| 24 | 4.26 | 3.40 | 3.01 | 2.78 | 2.62 | 2.51 | 2.42 | 2.36 | 2.30 | 2.25 | 2.18 | 2.11 | 2.03 | 1.98 | 1.94 | 1.89 | 1.84 | 1.79 | 1.73 |
| 25 | 4.24 | 3.39 | 2.99 | 2.76 | 2.60 | 2.49 | 2.40 | 2.34 | 2.28 | 2.24 | 2.16 | 2.09 | 2.01 | 1.96 | 1.92 | 1.87 | 1.82 | 1.77 | 1.71 |
| 30 | 4.17 | 3.32 | 2.92 | 2.69 | 2.53 | 2.42 | 2.33 | 2.27 | 2.21 | 2.16 | 2.09 | 2.01 | 1.93 | 1.89 | 1.84 | 1.79 | 1.74 | 1.68 | 1.62 |
| 40 | 4.08 | 3.23 | 2.84 | 2.61 | 2.45 | 2.34 | 2.25 | 2.18 | 2.12 | 2.08 | 2.00 | 1.92 | 1.84 | 1.79 | 1.74 | 1.69 | 1.64 | 1.58 | 1.51 |
| 60 | 4.00 | 3.15 | 2.76 | 2.53 | 2.37 | 2.25 | 2.17 | 2.10 | 2.04 | 1.99 | 1.92 | 1.84 | 1.75 | 1.70 | 1.65 | 1.59 | 1.53 | 1.47 | 1.39 |
| 120 | 3.92 | 3.07 | 2.68 | 2.45 | 2.29 | 2.18 | 2.09 | 2.02 | 1.96 | 1.91 | 1.83 | 1.75 | 1.66 | 1.61 | 1.55 | 1.50 | 1.43 | 1.35 | 1.25 |
| ∞ | 3.84 | 3.00 | 2.60 | 2.37 | 2.21 | 2.10 | 2.01 | 1.94 | 1.88 | 1.83 | 1.75 | 1.67 | 1.57 | 1.52 | 1.46 | 1.39 | 1.32 | 1.22 | 1.00 |

Degrees of freedom for the denominator

# CRITICAL VALUES OF THE *F* DISTRIBUTION AT A 1 PERCENT LEVEL OF SIGNIFICANCE, $\alpha = .01$ *(concluded)*

Degrees of freedom for the numerator

| | 1 | 2 | 3 | 4 | 5 | 6 | 7 | 8 | 9 | 10 | 12 | 15 | 20 | 24 | 30 | 40 | 60 | 120 | ∞ |
|---|---|---|---|---|---|---|---|---|---|---|---|---|---|---|---|---|---|---|---|
| 1 | 4052 | 5000 | 5403 | 5625 | 5764 | 5859 | 5928 | 5981 | 6022 | 6056 | 6106 | 6157 | 6209 | 6235 | 6261 | 6287 | 6313 | 6339 | 6366 |
| 2 | 98.5 | 99.0 | 99.2 | 99.2 | 99.3 | 99.3 | 99.4 | 99.4 | 99.4 | 99.4 | 99.4 | 99.4 | 99.4 | 99.5 | 99.5 | 99.5 | 99.5 | 99.5 | 99.5 |
| 3 | 34.1 | 30.8 | 29.5 | 28.7 | 28.2 | 27.9 | 27.7 | 27.5 | 27.3 | 27.2 | 27.1 | 26.9 | 26.7 | 26.6 | 26.5 | 26.4 | 26.3 | 26.2 | 26.1 |
| 4 | 21.2 | 18.0 | 16.7 | 16.0 | 15.5 | 15.2 | 15.0 | 14.8 | 14.7 | 14.5 | 14.4 | 14.2 | 14.0 | 13.9 | 13.8 | 13.7 | 13.7 | 13.6 | 13.5 |
| 5 | 16.3 | 13.3 | 12.1 | 11.4 | 11.0 | 10.7 | 10.5 | 10.3 | 10.2 | 10.1 | 9.89 | 9.72 | 9.55 | 9.47 | 9.38 | 9.29 | 9.20 | 9.11 | 9.02 |
| 6 | 13.7 | 10.9 | 9.78 | 9.15 | 8.75 | 8.47 | 8.26 | 8.10 | 7.98 | 7.87 | 7.72 | 7.56 | 7.40 | 7.31 | 7.23 | 7.14 | 7.06 | 6.97 | 6.88 |
| 7 | 12.2 | 9.55 | 8.45 | 7.85 | 7.46 | 7.19 | 6.99 | 6.84 | 6.72 | 6.62 | 6.47 | 6.31 | 6.16 | 6.07 | 5.99 | 5.91 | 5.82 | 5.74 | 5.65 |
| 8 | 11.3 | 8.65 | 7.59 | 7.01 | 6.63 | 6.37 | 6.18 | 6.03 | 5.91 | 5.81 | 5.67 | 5.52 | 5.36 | 5.28 | 5.20 | 5.12 | 5.03 | 4.95 | 4.86 |
| 9 | 10.6 | 8.02 | 6.99 | 6.42 | 6.06 | 5.80 | 5.61 | 5.47 | 5.35 | 5.26 | 5.11 | 4.96 | 4.81 | 4.73 | 4.65 | 4.57 | 4.48 | 4.40 | 4.31 |
| 10 | 10.0 | 7.56 | 6.55 | 5.99 | 5.64 | 5.39 | 5.20 | 5.06 | 4.94 | 4.85 | 4.71 | 4.56 | 4.41 | 4.33 | 4.25 | 4.17 | 4.08 | 4.00 | 3.91 |
| 11 | 9.65 | 7.21 | 6.22 | 5.67 | 5.32 | 5.07 | 4.89 | 4.74 | 4.63 | 4.54 | 4.40 | 4.25 | 4.10 | 4.02 | 3.94 | 3.86 | 3.78 | 3.69 | 3.60 |
| 12 | 9.33 | 6.93 | 5.95 | 5.41 | 5.06 | 4.82 | 4.64 | 4.50 | 4.39 | 4.30 | 4.16 | 4.01 | 3.86 | 3.78 | 3.70 | 3.62 | 3.54 | 3.45 | 3.36 |
| 13 | 9.07 | 6.70 | 5.74 | 5.21 | 4.86 | 4.62 | 4.44 | 4.30 | 4.19 | 4.10 | 3.96 | 3.82 | 3.66 | 3.59 | 3.51 | 3.43 | 3.34 | 3.25 | 3.17 |
| 14 | 8.86 | 6.51 | 5.56 | 5.04 | 4.69 | 4.46 | 4.28 | 4.14 | 4.03 | 3.94 | 3.80 | 3.66 | 3.51 | 3.43 | 3.35 | 3.27 | 3.18 | 3.09 | 3.00 |
| 15 | 8.68 | 6.36 | 5.42 | 4.89 | 4.56 | 4.32 | 4.14 | 4.00 | 3.89 | 3.80 | 3.67 | 3.52 | 3.37 | 3.29 | 3.21 | 3.13 | 3.05 | 2.96 | 2.87 |
| 16 | 8.53 | 6.23 | 5.29 | 4.77 | 4.44 | 4.20 | 4.03 | 3.89 | 3.78 | 3.69 | 3.55 | 3.41 | 3.26 | 3.18 | 3.10 | 3.02 | 2.93 | 2.84 | 2.75 |
| 17 | 8.40 | 6.11 | 5.18 | 4.67 | 4.34 | 4.10 | 3.93 | 3.79 | 3.68 | 3.59 | 3.46 | 3.31 | 3.16 | 3.08 | 3.00 | 2.92 | 2.83 | 2.75 | 2.65 |
| 18 | 8.29 | 6.01 | 5.09 | 4.58 | 4.25 | 4.01 | 3.84 | 3.71 | 3.60 | 3.51 | 3.37 | 3.23 | 3.08 | 3.00 | 2.92 | 2.84 | 2.75 | 2.66 | 2.57 |
| 19 | 8.18 | 5.93 | 5.01 | 4.50 | 4.17 | 3.94 | 3.77 | 3.63 | 3.52 | 3.43 | 3.30 | 3.15 | 3.00 | 2.92 | 2.84 | 2.76 | 2.67 | 2.58 | 2.49 |
| 20 | 8.10 | 5.85 | 4.94 | 4.43 | 4.10 | 3.87 | 3.70 | 3.56 | 3.46 | 3.37 | 3.23 | 3.09 | 2.94 | 2.86 | 2.78 | 2.69 | 2.61 | 2.52 | 2.42 |
| 21 | 8.02 | 5.78 | 4.87 | 4.37 | 4.04 | 3.81 | 3.64 | 3.51 | 3.40 | 3.31 | 3.17 | 3.03 | 2.88 | 2.80 | 2.72 | 2.64 | 2.55 | 2.46 | 2.36 |
| 22 | 7.95 | 5.72 | 4.82 | 4.31 | 3.99 | 3.76 | 3.59 | 3.45 | 3.35 | 3.26 | 3.12 | 2.98 | 2.83 | 2.75 | 2.67 | 2.58 | 2.50 | 2.40 | 2.31 |
| 23 | 7.88 | 5.66 | 4.76 | 4.26 | 3.94 | 3.71 | 3.54 | 3.41 | 3.30 | 3.21 | 3.07 | 2.93 | 2.78 | 2.70 | 2.62 | 2.54 | 2.45 | 2.35 | 2.26 |
| 24 | 7.82 | 5.61 | 4.72 | 4.22 | 3.90 | 3.67 | 3.50 | 3.36 | 3.26 | 3.17 | 3.03 | 2.89 | 2.74 | 2.66 | 2.58 | 2.49 | 2.40 | 2.31 | 2.21 |
| 25 | 7.77 | 5.57 | 4.68 | 4.18 | 3.85 | 3.63 | 3.46 | 3.32 | 3.22 | 3.13 | 2.99 | 2.85 | 2.70 | 2.62 | 2.54 | 2.45 | 2.36 | 2.27 | 2.17 |
| 30 | 7.56 | 5.39 | 4.51 | 4.02 | 3.70 | 3.47 | 3.30 | 3.17 | 3.07 | 2.98 | 2.84 | 2.70 | 2.55 | 2.47 | 2.39 | 2.30 | 2.21 | 2.11 | 2.01 |
| 40 | 7.31 | 5.18 | 4.31 | 3.83 | 3.51 | 3.29 | 3.12 | 2.99 | 2.89 | 2.80 | 2.66 | 2.52 | 2.37 | 2.29 | 2.20 | 2.11 | 2.02 | 1.92 | 1.81 |
| 60 | 7.08 | 4.98 | 4.13 | 3.65 | 3.34 | 3.12 | 2.95 | 2.82 | 2.72 | 2.63 | 2.50 | 2.35 | 2.20 | 2.12 | 2.03 | 1.94 | 1.84 | 1.73 | 1.60 |
| 120 | 6.85 | 4.79 | 3.95 | 3.48 | 3.17 | 2.96 | 2.79 | 2.66 | 2.56 | 2.47 | 2.34 | 2.19 | 2.03 | 1.95 | 1.86 | 1.76 | 1.66 | 1.53 | 1.38 |
| ∞ | 6.63 | 4.61 | 3.78 | 3.32 | 3.02 | 2.80 | 2.64 | 2.51 | 2.41 | 2.32 | 2.18 | 2.04 | 1.88 | 1.79 | 1.70 | 1.59 | 1.47 | 1.32 | 1.00 |

Degrees of freedom for the denominator

## Appendix H

# CRITICAL VALUES OF RHO, THE SPEARMAN RANK CORRELATION COEFFICIENT

| N | Significance level (one-tailed test) | |
|---|---|---|
| | .05 | .01 |
| 4 | 1.000 | |
| 5 | .900 | 1.000 |
| 6 | .829 | .943 |
| 7 | .714 | .893 |
| 8 | .643 | .833 |
| 9 | .600 | .783 |
| 10 | .564 | .746 |
| 12 | .506 | .712 |
| 14 | .456 | .645 |
| 16 | .425 | .601 |
| 18 | .399 | .564 |
| 20 | .377 | .534 |
| 22 | .359 | .508 |
| 24 | .343 | .485 |
| 26 | .329 | .465 |
| 28 | .317 | .448 |
| 30 | .306 | .432 |

Sources: Adapted from E. G. Olds, "Distributions of Sums of Squares of Rank Differences for Small Numbers of Individuals," *Annals of Mathematical Statistics* 9 (1938), pp. 133–48; and from E. G. Olds, "The 5 Percent Significance Levels for Sums of Squares of Rank Differences and a Correction," *Annals of Mathematical Statistics* 20 (1949), pp. 117–18, with the kind permission of the author and publisher.

## Appendix I

# CRITICAL VALUES OF CHI-SQUARE

*This table contains the values of $\chi^2$ that correspond to a specific right tail area and specific numbers of degrees of freedom df.*

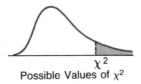

$\chi^2$
Possible Values of $\chi^2$

| DEGREES OF FREEDOM df | RIGHT-TAIL AREA | | | |
|---|---|---|---|---|
| | 0.10 | 0.05 | 0.02 | 0.01 |
| 1 | 2.706 | 3.841 | 5.412 | 6.635 |
| 2 | 4.605 | 5.991 | 7.824 | 9.210 |
| 3 | 6.251 | 7.815 | 9.837 | 11.345 |
| 4 | 7.779 | 9.488 | 11.668 | 13.277 |
| 5 | 9.236 | 11.070 | 13.388 | 15.086 |
| 6 | 10.645 | 12.592 | 15.033 | 16.812 |
| 7 | 12.017 | 14.067 | 16.622 | 18.475 |
| 8 | 13.362 | 15.507 | 18.168 | 20.090 |
| 9 | 14.684 | 16.919 | 19.679 | 21.666 |
| 10 | 15.987 | 18.307 | 21.161 | 23.209 |
| 11 | 17.275 | 19.675 | 22.618 | 24.725 |
| 12 | 18.549 | 21.026 | 24.054 | 26.217 |
| 13 | 19.812 | 22.362 | 25.472 | 27.688 |
| 14 | 21.064 | 23.685 | 26.873 | 29.141 |
| 15 | 22.307 | 24.996 | 28.259 | 30.578 |
| 16 | 23.542 | 26.296 | 29.633 | 32.000 |
| 17 | 24.769 | 27.587 | 30.995 | 33.409 |
| 18 | 25.989 | 28.869 | 32.346 | 34.805 |
| 19 | 27.204 | 30.144 | 33.687 | 36.191 |
| 20 | 28.412 | 31.410 | 35.020 | 37.566 |
| 21 | 29.615 | 32.671 | 36.343 | 38.932 |
| 22 | 30.813 | 33.924 | 37.659 | 40.289 |
| 23 | 32.007 | 35.172 | 38.968 | 41.638 |
| 24 | 33.196 | 36.415 | 40.270 | 42.980 |
| 25 | 34.382 | 37.652 | 41.566 | 44.314 |
| 26 | 35.563 | 38.885 | 42.856 | 45.642 |
| 27 | 36.741 | 40.113 | 44.140 | 46.963 |
| 28 | 37.916 | 41.337 | 45.419 | 48.278 |
| 29 | 39.087 | 42.557 | 46.693 | 49.588 |
| 30 | 40.256 | 43.773 | 47.962 | 50.892 |

## Appendix J

# CRITICAL VALUES OF *U* IN THE MANN-WHITNEY TEST

*In the first table the entries are the critical values of* U *for a one-tailed test at 0.025 or for a two-tailed test at 0.05; in the second, for a one-tailed test at 0.05 or for a two-tailed test at 0.10.*

| $n_2$ \ $n_1$ | 1 | 2 | 3 | 4 | 5 | 6 | 7 | 8 | 9 | 10 | 11 | 12 | 13 | 14 | 15 | 16 | 17 | 18 | 19 | 20 |
|---|---|---|---|---|---|---|---|---|---|---|---|---|---|---|---|---|---|---|---|---|
| 1 | | | | | | | | | | | | | | | | | | | | |
| 2 | | | | | | | | 0 | 0 | 0 | 0 | 1 | 1 | 1 | 1 | 1 | 2 | 2 | 2 | 2 |
| 3 | | | | | 0 | 1 | 1 | 2 | 2 | 3 | 3 | 4 | 4 | 5 | 5 | 6 | 6 | 7 | 7 | 8 |
| 4 | | | | 0 | 1 | 2 | 3 | 4 | 4 | 5 | 6 | 7 | 8 | 9 | 10 | 11 | 11 | 12 | 13 | 13 |
| 5 | | | 0 | 1 | 2 | 3 | 5 | 6 | 7 | 8 | 9 | 11 | 12 | 13 | 14 | 15 | 17 | 18 | 19 | 20 |
| 6 | | | 1 | 2 | 3 | 5 | 6 | 8 | 10 | 11 | 13 | 14 | 16 | 17 | 19 | 21 | 22 | 24 | 25 | 27 |
| 7 | | | 1 | 3 | 5 | 6 | 8 | 10 | 12 | 14 | 16 | 18 | 20 | 22 | 24 | 26 | 28 | 30 | 32 | 34 |
| 8 | | 0 | 2 | 4 | 6 | 8 | 10 | 13 | 15 | 17 | 19 | 22 | 24 | 26 | 29 | 31 | 34 | 36 | 38 | 41 |
| 9 | | 0 | 2 | 4 | 7 | 10 | 12 | 15 | 17 | 20 | 23 | 26 | 28 | 31 | 34 | 37 | 39 | 42 | 45 | 48 |
| 10 | | 0 | 3 | 5 | 8 | 11 | 14 | 17 | 20 | 23 | 26 | 29 | 33 | 36 | 39 | 42 | 45 | 48 | 52 | 55 |
| 11 | | 0 | 3 | 6 | 9 | 13 | 16 | 19 | 23 | 26 | 30 | 33 | 37 | 40 | 44 | 47 | 51 | 55 | 58 | 62 |
| 12 | | 1 | 4 | 7 | 11 | 14 | 18 | 22 | 26 | 29 | 33 | 37 | 41 | 45 | 49 | 53 | 57 | 61 | 65 | 69 |
| 13 | | 1 | 4 | 8 | 12 | 16 | 20 | 24 | 28 | 33 | 37 | 41 | 45 | 50 | 54 | 59 | 63 | 67 | 72 | 76 |
| 14 | | 1 | 5 | 9 | 13 | 17 | 22 | 26 | 31 | 36 | 40 | 45 | 50 | 55 | 59 | 64 | 67 | 74 | 78 | 83 |
| 15 | | 1 | 5 | 10 | 14 | 19 | 24 | 29 | 34 | 39 | 44 | 49 | 54 | 59 | 64 | 70 | 75 | 80 | 85 | 90 |
| 16 | | 1 | 6 | 11 | 15 | 21 | 26 | 31 | 37 | 42 | 47 | 53 | 59 | 64 | 70 | 75 | 81 | 86 | 92 | 98 |
| 17 | | 2 | 6 | 11 | 17 | 22 | 28 | 34 | 39 | 45 | 51 | 57 | 63 | 67 | 75 | 81 | 87 | 93 | 99 | 105 |
| 18 | | 2 | 7 | 12 | 18 | 24 | 30 | 36 | 42 | 48 | 55 | 61 | 67 | 74 | 80 | 86 | 93 | 99 | 106 | 112 |
| 19 | | 2 | 7 | 13 | 19 | 25 | 32 | 38 | 45 | 52 | 58 | 65 | 72 | 78 | 85 | 92 | 99 | 106 | 113 | 119 |
| 20 | | 2 | 8 | 13 | 20 | 27 | 34 | 41 | 48 | 55 | 62 | 69 | 76 | 83 | 90 | 98 | 105 | 112 | 119 | 127 |

| $n_2$ \ $n_1$ | 1 | 2 | 3 | 4 | 5 | 6 | 7 | 8 | 9 | 10 | 11 | 12 | 13 | 14 | 15 | 16 | 17 | 18 | 19 | 20 |
|---|---|---|---|---|---|---|---|---|---|---|---|---|---|---|---|---|---|---|---|---|
| 1 | | | | | | | | | | | | | | | | | | | 0 | 0 |
| 2 | | | | | 0 | 0 | 0 | 1 | 1 | 1 | 1 | 2 | 2 | 2 | 3 | 3 | 3 | 4 | 4 | 4 |
| 3 | | | 0 | 0 | 1 | 2 | 2 | 3 | 3 | 4 | 5 | 5 | 6 | 7 | 7 | 8 | 9 | 9 | 10 | 11 |
| 4 | | | 0 | 1 | 2 | 3 | 4 | 5 | 6 | 7 | 8 | 9 | 10 | 11 | 12 | 14 | 15 | 16 | 17 | 18 |
| 5 | | 0 | 1 | 2 | 4 | 5 | 6 | 8 | 9 | 11 | 12 | 13 | 15 | 16 | 18 | 19 | 20 | 22 | 23 | 25 |
| 6 | | 0 | 2 | 3 | 5 | 7 | 8 | 10 | 12 | 14 | 16 | 17 | 19 | 21 | 23 | 25 | 26 | 28 | 30 | 32 |
| 7 | | 0 | 2 | 4 | 6 | 8 | 11 | 13 | 15 | 17 | 19 | 21 | 24 | 26 | 28 | 30 | 33 | 35 | 37 | 39 |
| 8 | | 1 | 3 | 5 | 8 | 10 | 13 | 15 | 18 | 20 | 23 | 26 | 28 | 31 | 33 | 36 | 39 | 41 | 44 | 47 |
| 9 | | 1 | 3 | 6 | 9 | 12 | 15 | 18 | 21 | 24 | 27 | 30 | 33 | 36 | 39 | 42 | 45 | 48 | 51 | 54 |
| 10 | | 1 | 4 | 7 | 11 | 14 | 17 | 20 | 24 | 27 | 31 | 34 | 37 | 41 | 44 | 48 | 51 | 55 | 58 | 62 |
| 11 | | 1 | 5 | 8 | 12 | 16 | 19 | 23 | 27 | 31 | 34 | 38 | 42 | 46 | 50 | 54 | 57 | 61 | 65 | 69 |
| 12 | | 2 | 5 | 9 | 13 | 17 | 21 | 26 | 30 | 34 | 38 | 42 | 47 | 51 | 55 | 60 | 64 | 68 | 72 | 77 |
| 13 | | 2 | 6 | 10 | 15 | 19 | 24 | 28 | 33 | 37 | 42 | 47 | 51 | 56 | 61 | 65 | 70 | 75 | 80 | 84 |
| 14 | | 2 | 7 | 11 | 16 | 21 | 26 | 31 | 36 | 41 | 46 | 51 | 56 | 61 | 66 | 71 | 77 | 82 | 87 | 92 |
| 15 | | 3 | 7 | 12 | 18 | 23 | 28 | 33 | 39 | 44 | 50 | 55 | 61 | 66 | 72 | 77 | 83 | 88 | 94 | 100 |
| 16 | | 3 | 8 | 14 | 19 | 25 | 30 | 36 | 42 | 48 | 54 | 60 | 65 | 71 | 77 | 83 | 89 | 95 | 101 | 107 |
| 17 | | 3 | 9 | 15 | 20 | 26 | 33 | 39 | 45 | 51 | 57 | 64 | 70 | 77 | 83 | 89 | 96 | 102 | 109 | 115 |
| 18 | | 4 | 9 | 16 | 22 | 28 | 35 | 41 | 48 | 55 | 61 | 68 | 75 | 82 | 88 | 95 | 102 | 109 | 116 | 123 |
| 19 | 0 | 4 | 10 | 17 | 23 | 30 | 37 | 44 | 51 | 58 | 65 | 72 | 80 | 87 | 94 | 101 | 109 | 116 | 123 | 130 |
| 20 | 0 | 4 | 11 | 18 | 25 | 32 | 39 | 47 | 54 | 62 | 69 | 77 | 84 | 92 | 100 | 107 | 115 | 123 | 130 | 138 |

Source: Reproduced from the *Bulletin of the Institute of Educational Research at Indiana University,* vol 1, no. 2; with the permission of the author and the publisher.

## Appendix K

# WILCOXON *T* VALUES

*Critical values of* T, *the Wilcoxon signed rank statistic, where* T *is the largest integer such that* Pr(T ≤ t/N) ≤ α *the cumulative one-tail probability*

| N | 2 α .15 α.075 | .10 .050 | .05 .025 | .04 .020 | .03 .015 | .02 .010 | .01 .005 |
|----|------|------|------|------|------|------|------|
| 4  | 0   |     |     |     |     |     |     |
| 5  | 1   | 0   |     |     |     |     |     |
| 6  | 2   | 2   | 0   | 0   |     |     |     |
| 7  | 4   | 3   | 2   | 1   | 0   | 0   |     |
| 8  | 7   | 5   | 3   | 3   | 2   | 1   | 0   |
| 9  | 9   | 8   | 5   | 5   | 4   | 3   | 1   |
| 10 | 12  | 10  | 8   | 7   | 6   | 5   | 3   |
| 11 | 16  | 13  | 10  | 9   | 8   | 7   | 5   |
| 12 | 19  | 17  | 13  | 12  | 11  | 9   | 7   |
| 13 | 24  | 21  | 17  | 16  | 14  | 12  | 9   |
| 14 | 28  | 25  | 21  | 19  | 18  | 15  | 12  |
| 15 | 33  | 30  | 25  | 23  | 21  | 19  | 15  |
| 16 | 39  | 35  | 29  | 28  | 26  | 23  | 19  |
| 17 | 45  | 41  | 34  | 33  | 30  | 27  | 23  |
| 18 | 51  | 47  | 40  | 38  | 35  | 32  | 27  |
| 19 | 58  | 53  | 46  | 43  | 41  | 37  | 32  |
| 20 | 65  | 60  | 52  | 50  | 47  | 43  | 37  |
| 21 | 73  | 67  | 58  | 56  | 53  | 49  | 42  |
| 22 | 81  | 75  | 65  | 63  | 59  | 55  | 48  |
| 23 | 89  | 83  | 73  | 70  | 66  | 62  | 54  |
| 24 | 98  | 91  | 81  | 78  | 74  | 69  | 61  |
| 25 | 108 | 100 | 89  | 86  | 82  | 76  | 68  |
| 26 | 118 | 110 | 98  | 94  | 90  | 84  | 75  |
| 27 | 128 | 119 | 107 | 103 | 99  | 92  | 83  |
| 28 | 138 | 130 | 116 | 112 | 108 | 101 | 91  |
| 29 | 150 | 140 | 126 | 122 | 117 | 110 | 100 |
| 30 | 161 | 151 | 137 | 132 | 127 | 120 | 109 |
| 31 | 173 | 163 | 147 | 143 | 137 | 130 | 118 |
| 32 | 186 | 175 | 159 | 154 | 148 | 140 | 128 |
| 33 | 199 | 187 | 170 | 165 | 159 | 151 | 138 |
| 34 | 212 | 200 | 182 | 177 | 171 | 162 | 148 |
| 35 | 226 | 213 | 195 | 189 | 182 | 173 | 159 |
| 40 | 302 | 286 | 264 | 257 | 249 | 238 | 220 |
| 50 | 487 | 466 | 434 | 425 | 413 | 397 | 373 |
| 60 | 718 | 690 | 648 | 636 | 620 | 600 | 567 |
| 70 | 995 | 960 | 907 | 891 | 872 | 846 | 805 |
| 80 | 1318 | 1276 | 1211 | 1192 | 1168 | 1136 | 1086 |
| 90 | 1688 | 1638 | 1560 | 1537 | 1509 | 1471 | 1410 |
| 100 | 2105 | 2045 | 1955 | 1928 | 1894 | 1850 | 1779 |

Source: Abridged from Robert L. McCormack, "Extended Tables of the Wilcoxon Matched-Pair Signed Rank Statistic," *Journal of the American Statistical Association,* September 1965, pp. 866–67.

## Appendix L

# FACTORS FOR CONTROL CHARTS

| Number of Items in Sample, n | Chart for Averages | Chart for Ranges | | |
|---|---|---|---|---|
| | Factors for Control Limits | Factors for Central Line | Factors for Control Limits | |
| | $A_2$ | $d_2$ | $D_3$ | $D_4$ |
| 2 | 1.880 | 1.128 | 0 | 3.267 |
| 3 | 1.023 | 1.693 | 0 | 2.575 |
| 4 | .729 | 2.059 | 0 | 2.282 |
| 5 | .577 | 2.326 | 0 | 2.115 |
| 6 | .483 | 2.534 | 0 | 2.004 |
| 7 | .419 | 2.704 | .076 | 1.924 |
| 8 | .373 | 2.847 | .136 | 1.864 |
| 9 | .337 | 2.970 | .184 | 1.816 |
| 10 | .308 | 3.078 | .223 | 1.777 |
| 11 | .285 | 3.173 | .256 | 1.744 |
| 12 | .266 | 3.258 | .284 | 1.716 |
| 13 | .249 | 3.336 | .308 | 1.692 |
| 14 | .235 | 3.407 | .329 | 1.671 |
| 15 | .223 | 3.472 | .348 | 1.652 |

Source: Adapted from American Society for Testing and Materials, *Manual on Quality Control of Materials,* 1951, Table B2, p. 115. For a more detailed table and explanation, see Acheson J. Duncan, *Quality Control and Industrial Statistics,* 3d ed. (Homewood, Ill.: Richard D. Irwin, 1974), Table M, p. 927.

# Appendix M

# DATA SET 1 — REAL ESTATE

$x_1$ = Selling price in $000
$x_2$ = Number of Bedrooms
$x_3$ = Size of the house in square feet
$x_4$ = Pool (1 = yes, 0 = no)
$x_5$ = Distance in miles from center of city
$x_6$ = Township
$x_7$ = Garage (1 = yes, 0 = no)
$x_8$ = Number of bathrooms

| $x_1$ | $x_2$ | $x_3$ | $x_4$ | $x_5$ | $x_6$ | $x_7$ | $x_8$ | $x_1$ | $x_2$ | $x_3$ | $x_4$ | $x_5$ | $x_6$ | $x_7$ | $x_8$ |
|---|---|---|---|---|---|---|---|---|---|---|---|---|---|---|---|
| 194.9 | 4 | 2349 | 0 | 17 | 5 | 1 | 2.0 | 148.0 | 3 | 2069 | 1 | 19 | 3 | 1 | 2.0 |
| 135.1 | 4 | 2102 | 1 | 19 | 4 | 0 | 2.0 | 202.4 | 5 | 2182 | 1 | 16 | 2 | 1 | 3.0 |
| 179.3 | 3 | 2271 | 1 | 12 | 3 | 0 | 2.0 | 152.6 | 3 | 2090 | 0 | 9 | 3 | 0 | 1.5 |
| 158.2 | 2 | 2188 | 1 | 16 | 2 | 0 | 2.5 | 172.0 | 3 | 1928 | 0 | 16 | 1 | 1 | 1.5 |
| 103.6 | 2 | 2148 | 1 | 28 | 1 | 0 | 1.5 | 146.9 | 4 | 2056 | 0 | 19 | 1 | 1 | 1.5 |
| 181.8 | 2 | 2117 | 0 | 12 | 1 | 1 | 2.0 | 151.9 | 3 | 2012 | 0 | 20 | 4 | 0 | 2.0 |
| 242.4 | 6 | 2484 | 1 | 15 | 3 | 1 | 2.0 | 130.1 | 4 | 2262 | 0 | 24 | 4 | 1 | 2.0 |
| 201.3 | 2 | 2130 | 1 | 9 | 2 | 1 | 2.5 | 228.0 | 3 | 2431 | 0 | 21 | 2 | 1 | 3.0 |
| 163.8 | 3 | 2254 | 0 | 18 | 1 | 0 | 1.5 | 199.4 | 5 | 2217 | 1 | 8 | 5 | 1 | 3.0 |
| 197.5 | 4 | 2385 | 1 | 13 | 4 | 1 | 2.0 | 166.5 | 3 | 2157 | 1 | 17 | 1 | 1 | 2.5 |
| 216.6 | 4 | 2108 | 1 | 14 | 3 | 1 | 2.0 | 127.1 | 3 | 2014 | 0 | 16 | 4 | 0 | 2.0 |
| 154.8 | 2 | 1715 | 1 | 8 | 4 | 1 | 1.5 | 160.6 | 3 | 2221 | 1 | 15 | 1 | 1 | 2.0 |
| 200.6 | 6 | 2495 | 1 | 7 | 4 | 1 | 2.0 | 142.7 | 6 | 2236 | 0 | 14 | 1 | 0 | 2.0 |
| 182.3 | 4 | 2073 | 1 | 18 | 3 | 1 | 2.0 | 175.1 | 5 | 2189 | 1 | 20 | 3 | 1 | 2.0 |
| 144.0 | 2 | 2283 | 1 | 11 | 3 | 0 | 2.0 | 127.7 | 3 | 2218 | 1 | 23 | 3 | 0 | 2.0 |
| 208.4 | 3 | 2119 | 1 | 16 | 2 | 1 | 2.0 | 186.2 | 3 | 1937 | 1 | 12 | 2 | 1 | 2.0 |
| 127.9 | 4 | 2189 | 0 | 16 | 3 | 0 | 2.0 | 182.2 | 6 | 2296 | 1 | 7 | 3 | 1 | 3.0 |
| 153.7 | 5 | 2316 | 0 | 21 | 4 | 0 | 2.5 | 109.2 | 6 | 1749 | 0 | 12 | 1 | 0 | 2.0 |
| 147.3 | 3 | 2220 | 0 | 10 | 4 | 1 | 2.0 | 130.4 | 4 | 2230 | 1 | 15 | 1 | 1 | 2.0 |
| 155.0 | 6 | 1901 | 0 | 15 | 4 | 1 | 2.0 | 169.2 | 3 | 2263 | 1 | 17 | 5 | 1 | 1.5 |
| 186.9 | 4 | 2624 | 1 | 8 | 4 | 1 | 2.0 | 123.3 | 3 | 1593 | 0 | 19 | 3 | 0 | 2.5 |
| 142.9 | 4 | 1938 | 0 | 14 | 2 | 1 | 2.5 | 140.3 | 4 | 2221 | 1 | 24 | 1 | 1 | 2.0 |
| 155.0 | 5 | 2101 | 1 | 20 | 5 | 0 | 1.5 | 231.2 | 7 | 2403 | 1 | 13 | 3 | 1 | 3.0 |
| 255.8 | 8 | 2644 | 1 | 9 | 4 | 1 | 2.0 | 214.7 | 6 | 2036 | 1 | 21 | 3 | 1 | 3.0 |
| 241.7 | 6 | 2141 | 1 | 11 | 5 | 1 | 3.0 | 199.9 | 5 | 2170 | 0 | 11 | 4 | 1 | 2.5 |
| 128.2 | 2 | 2198 | 0 | 21 | 5 | 1 | 1.5 | 114.3 | 2 | 2007 | 1 | 13 | 2 | 0 | 2.0 |
| 138.5 | 2 | 1912 | 1 | 26 | 4 | 0 | 2.0 | 164.5 | 2 | 2054 | 1 | 9 | 5 | 1 | 2.0 |
| 190.5 | 2 | 2117 | 1 | 9 | 4 | 1 | 2.0 | 155.3 | 5 | 2247 | 0 | 13 | 2 | 1 | 2.0 |
| 172.6 | 3 | 2162 | 1 | 14 | 3 | 1 | 1.5 | 141.4 | 3 | 2190 | 0 | 18 | 3 | 1 | 2.0 |
| 133.6 | 2 | 2041 | 1 | 11 | 5 | 0 | 2.0 | 188.4 | 4 | 2495 | 0 | 15 | 3 | 1 | 2.0 |
| 173.3 | 2 | 1712 | 1 | 19 | 3 | 1 | 2.0 | 153.7 | 3 | 2080 | 0 | 10 | 2 | 0 | 2.0 |
| 153.4 | 2 | 1974 | 1 | 11 | 5 | 1 | 2.0 | 155.3 | 4 | 2210 | 0 | 19 | 2 | 1 | 2.0 |
| 183.5 | 5 | 2438 | 1 | 16 | 2 | 1 | 2.0 | 217.8 | 2 | 2133 | 1 | 13 | 2 | 1 | 2.5 |
| 123.1 | 3 | 2019 | 0 | 16 | 2 | 1 | 2.0 | 130.6 | 2 | 2037 | 0 | 17 | 3 | 0 | 2.0 |
| 131.2 | 2 | 1919 | 1 | 10 | 5 | 1 | 2.0 | 218.0 | 7 | 2448 | 1 | 8 | 4 | 1 | 2.0 |
| 135.3 | 4 | 2023 | 0 | 14 | 4 | 0 | 2.5 | 165.9 | 3 | 1900 | 0 | 6 | 1 | 1 | 2.0 |
| 160.0 | 4 | 2310 | 1 | 19 | 2 | 0 | 2.0 | 92.6 | 2 | 1871 | 1 | 18 | 4 | 0 | 1.5 |
| 231.2 | 6 | 2639 | 1 | 7 | 5 | 1 | 2.5 | | | | | | | | |

## Appendix N

# DATA SET 2 — 1990 CORPORATE DATA

$x_1$ = Market value in millions of $
$x_2$ = 1990 Sales in millions of $
$x_3$ = 1990 Profits in millions of $
$x_4$ = 1990 Return on invested capital %
$x_5$ = 1990 Assets in millions of $
$x_6$ = Recent share price
$x_7$ = Turnover %
$x_8$ = Dividends return on investment
$x_9$ = Company name

| $x_1$ | $x_2$ | $x_3$ | $x_4$ | $x_5$ | $x_6$ | $x_7$ | $x_8$ | $x_9$ |
|---|---|---|---|---|---|---|---|---|
| 74966 | 69018 | 6020 | 12.4 | 87568 | 131 | 72.5 | 29 | IBM |
| 68974 | 107197 | 5010 | * | 88000 | 55 | 24.1 | 23 | Exxon |
| 62158 | 46226 | 3540 | 15.4 | 46600 | 67 | 57.9 | 83 | Philip Morris |
| 58281 | 57662 | 4303 | 23.3 | 153884 | 67 | 47.0 | 13 | General Electric |
| 41034 | 7672 | 1781 | 41.8 | 7772 | 106 | 51.4 | 52 | Merck |
| 41024 | 32602 | 1291 | 21.7 | 11105 | 36 | 36.0 | 61 | Wal-Mart Stores |
| 40476 | 10300 | 1747 | 31.1 | 9129 | 77 | 49.5 | 48 | Bristol-Myers Squibb |
| 36041 | 37285 | 2735 | 13.9 | 43775 | 33 | 36.8 | -13 | AT&T |
| 34915 | 10236 | 1381 | 34.1 | 9278 | 52 | 37.7 | 51 | Coca-Cola |
| 30170 | 25848 | 1733 | 15.9 | 20607 | 87 | 47.6 | 30 | Procter & Gamble |
| 29887 | 11232 | 1268 | 22.7 | 9506 | 90 | 53.8 | 56 | Johnson & Johnson |
| 26973 | 28012 | 1913 | 11.8 | 31163 | 53 | 33.5 | -1 | Amoco |
| 26398 | 42600 | 2157 | 11.0 | 35089 | 75 | 37.8 | 17 | Chevron |
| 26149 | 64244 | 1928 | 10.5 | 40757 | 65 | 44.0 | 7 | Mobil |
| 25561 | 17803 | 1090 | 14.0 | 16483 | 33 | 55.7 | 70 | Pepsico |
| 25452 | 40047 | 2310 | 13.0 | 38128 | 38 | 34.4 | 0 | Du Pont |
| 24878 | 14345 | 1631 | 10.5 | 30207 | 52 | 19.0 | 4 | Bellsouth |
| 23991 | 12470 | -1985 | * | 180236 | 40 | 52.2 | -6 | General Motors |
| 22106 | 5192 | 1127 | 30.1 | 7143 | 83 | 68.1 | 34 | Eli Lilly |
| 21253 | 18374 | 1541 | 11.0 | 33769 | 32 | 37.2 | 7 | GTE |
| 20905 | 18808 | 1688 | 17.3 | 23037 | 130 | 49.6 | 19 | Atlantic Richfield |
| 20769 | 6034 | 709 | 11.5 | 9970 | 43 | 57.5 | 35 | Waste Mgt |
| 20331 | 6159 | 965 | 34.7 | 5563 | 47 | 42.8 | 47 | Abbott Labs |
| 20060 | 13021 | 1308 | * | 11079 | 91 | 55.1 | 14 | Minnesota Mining & Mfg |
| 19888 | 14932 | 1442 | * | 58000 | 94 | 46.5 | 17 | American International |
| 19021 | 12298 | 1312 | * | 27999 | 48 | 24.9 | 14 | Bell Atlantic |
| 17926 | 6775 | 1230 | * | 5991 | 57 | 35.9 | 19 | American Home Products |
| 17751 | 6406 | 801 | 17.2 | 9052 | 108 | 87.0 | 82 | Pfizer |
| 17082 | 10663 | 1253 | 12.4 | 21715 | 65 | 23.5 | 20 | Ameritech |
| 17008 | 27595 | 1385 | 19.4 | 14008 | 50 | 102.3 | 16 | Boeing |
| 16827 | 9716 | 1030 | 11.3 | 21471 | 42 | 28.8 | 0 | Pacific Telesis Group |
| 16718 | 41822 | 1450 | * | 25900 | 65 | 70.7 | 13 | Texaco |
| 16562 | 6048 | 820 | * | 8568 | 127 | 112.1 | 13 | Walt Disney |
| 16157 | 9113 | 1101 | 10.8 | 22195 | 54 | 30.7 | 3 | Southwestern Bell |
| 16085 | 97650 | 860 | 6.0 | 173662 | 34 | 51.5 | -23 | Ford |
| 15317 | 5306 | 570 | 18.4 | 5887 | 64 | 66.7 | 37 | Schlemberger |
| 15208 | 13592 | 949 | * | 26651 | 76 | 38.5 | -1 | NYNEX |
| 15100 | 9957 | 1199 | 10.3 | 27050 | 38 | 28.0 | 18 | US West |

## Appendix N

# DATA SET 2—1990 CORPORATE DATA (continued)

| $x_1$ | $x_2$ | $x_3$ | $x_4$ | $x_5$ | $x_6$ | $x_7$ | $x_8$ | $x_9$ |
|-------|-------|-------|-------|-------|-------|-------|-------|-------|
| 14810 | 18908 | 703 | 8.5 | 24125 | 46 | 80.4 | 22 | Eastman Kodak |
| 14310 | 19773 | 1384 | 13.8 | 23953 | 53 | 70.1 | -13 | Dow Chemical |
| 13374 | 10744 | 842 | 15.0 | 9634 | 47 | 39.6 | 37 | Anheuser-Busch |
| 12309 | 24332 | 338 | 24.2 | 137682 | 27 | 71.5 | -14 | American Express |
| 12209 | 6640 | 802 | 12.5 | 10668 | 34 | 66.1 | 1 | McDonalds |
| 12072 | 13538 | 771 | 13.2 | 11126 | 49 | 65.2 | 9 | Hewlett-Packard |
| 11757 | 1478 | 356 | 32.0 | 1366 | 103 | 229.2 | 110 | Microsoft |
| 11577 | 3323 | 565 | 25.9 | 4103 | 51 | 69.8 | 32 | Schering-Plough |
| 10979 | 55972 | 891 | 15.9 | 96300 | 32 | 45.4 | -19 | Sears, Roebuck |
| 10931 | 12720 | 1173 | 9.8 | 133112 | 46 | 137.3 | 29 | Federal National Mortgage |
| 10738 | 2462 | 487 | 35.8 | 2160 | 39 | 18.8 | 60 | Marion Merrell Dow |
| 10411 | 4687 | 485 | 32.0 | 3261 | 78 | 64.0 | 52 | Warner-Lambert |
| 10348 | 9470 | 987 | * | 21958 | 25 | 29.1 | 18 | Pacific Gas & Electric |
| 10280 | 3921 | 650 | 19.0 | 5118 | 52 | 242.6 | 19 | Intel |
| 9981 | 5181 | 502 | 24.4 | 3829 | 83 | 30.8 | 40 | Kellogg |
| 9916 | 13072 | -94 | * | 11584 | 82 | 139.9 | -7 | Digital Equipment |
| 9642 | 6503 | 547 | 21.0 | 5015 | 37 | 28.5 | 23 | H. J. Heinz |
| 9546 | 7728 | 618 | 20.0 | 6449 | 43 | 40.3 | 16 | Emerson Electric |
| 9267 | 13781 | 596 | 12.3 | 13835 | 46 | 53.5 | 43 | American Brands |
| 9245 | 8100 | 40 | 2.3 | 8517 | 33 | 73.8 | 28 | Baxter International |
| 9141 | 5254 | 398 | 19.9 | 2995 | 25 | 70.0 | 28 | The Limited |
| 9053 | 2283 | 380 | 7.4 | 9266 | 7900 | 3.5 | 12 | Berkshire Hathaway |
| 8982 | 6325 | 57 | 2.6 | 4281 | 71 | 38.4 | 52 | Campbell Soup |
| 8950 | 6896 | 417 | 25.1 | 3733 | 54 | 51.1 | 72 | General Mills |
| 8550 | 12184 | 500 | 12.5 | 7780 | 37 | 59.0 | 27 | Sara Lee |
| 8541 | 1686 | 393 | 37.9 | 1908 | 76 | 93.4 | 59 | Syntex |
| 8483 | 7975 | 719 | 7.3 | 22866 | 27 | 40.4 | 14 | Southern |
| 8478 | 10885 | 499 | 12.0 | 8774 | 64 | 136.7 | -2 | Motorola |
| 8449 | 12915 | 268 | 9.1 | 23300 | 29 | 70.9 | -21 | Westinghouse Electric |
| 8447 | 2993 | 614 | 17.3 | 11033 | 97 | 56.0 | 13 | General RE |
| 8279 | 5262 | 128 | 2.6 | 20496 | 39 | 53.8 | 17 | Commonwealth Edison |
| 8238 | 10465 | 775 | * | 93103 | 44 | 69.6 | 29 | J. P. Morgan |
| 8217 | 4818 | 508 | 24.1 | 4754 | 46 | 47.0 | 4 | Dun & Bradstreet |
| 8138 | 7199 | 831 | 10.6 | 17477 | 37 | 33.2 | 9 | Scecorp |
| 8092 | 5386 | 478 | 11.6 | 6315 | 480 | 47.1 | -9 | Capital Cities ABC |
| 8069 | 32070 | 756 | 12.5 | 13899 | 40 | 63.1 | 8 | K Mart |
| 7946 | 5510 | 326 | 18.7 | 4362 | 28 | 80.6 | 10 | Toys 'R' Us |
| 7826 | 20659 | 818 | 9.6 | 17268 | 31 | 78.0 | -10 | USX |
| 7784 | 12637 | 805 | 13.3 | 34736 | 108 | 45.8 | 2 | Loews |
| 7737 | 8995 | 546 | 11.6 | 9232 | 62 | 78.6 | 14 | Monsanto |
| 7630 | 3033 | 458 | 21.0 | 3668 | 43 | 111.1 | 37 | Upjohn |
| 7595 | 4345 | 368 | 24.2 | 3671 | 78 | 99.4 | 51 | Gillette |
| 7533 | 6964 | 618 | 11.0 | 13078 | 75 | 50.2 | 5 | Union Pacific |
| 7430 | 5741 | 501 | 32.4 | 3157 | 65 | 396.2 | 70 | Apple Computer |
| 7317 | 13603 | 541 | 12.7 | 12130 | 28 | 51.6 | 12 | Phillips Petroleum |
| 7116 | 4543 | 969 | 10.5 | 18651 | 36 | 110.4 | 16 | Texas Utilities |
| 7094 | 12323 | 877 | 14.0 | 110728 | 33 | 102.9 | 16 | Bankamerica |
| 6989 | 7680 | 299 | 7.9 | 7979 | 28 | 222.9 | -21 | MCI Communications |
| 6973 | 6407 | 432 | 16.8 | 5284 | 87 | 55.0 | 41 | Kimberly-Clark |

## Appendix N

# DATA SET 2—1990 CORPORATE DATA (continued)

| $x_1$ | $x_2$ | $x_3$ | $x_4$ | $x_5$ | $x_6$ | $x_7$ | $x_8$ | $x_9$ |
|---|---|---|---|---|---|---|---|---|
| 6923 | 4620 | 556 | 9.9 | 10523 | 45 | 42.7 | 21 | Norfolk Southern |
| 6826 | 8388 | 459 | 11.2 | 6073 | 23 | 64.4 | 12 | Archer Daniels Midland |
| 6803 | 12973 | 569 | 8.9 | 13669 | 62 | 95.7 | 25 | International Paper |
| 6732 | 12432 | 620 | 14.8 | 9562 | 29 | 34.6 | 29 | Rockwell International |
| 6704 | 10945 | 401 | 11.9 | 9707 | 29 | 67.8 | -9 | Unocal |
| 6682 | 10066 | 500 | 12.2 | 8056 | 54 | 54.1 | 16 | May Department Stores |
| 6493 | 20691 | 958 | 8.5 | 49043 | 57 | 62.6 | 5 | ITT |
| 6424 | 16365 | 577 | 10.6 | 12709 | 55 | 68.1 | -15 | J. C. Penney |
| 6419 | 3442 | 377 | 14.5 | 3826 | 40 | 44.4 | -1 | Gannett |
| 6335 | 6285 | 369 | 18.1 | 4547 | 98 | 146.0 | 42 | NCR |
| 6323 | 3423 | 187 | 11.3 | 7323 | 40 | 61.8 | 46 | Contel |
| 6265 | 11517 | -227 | * | 24666 | 109 | 87.9 | 14 | Time Warner |
| 6200 | 5781 | 374 | * | 4490 | 82 | 56.0 | 29 | CPC International |
| 6103 | 21783 | 751 | 11.4 | 15918 | 50 | 71.3 | 1 | United Technologies |
| 6099 | 14511 | 561 | 13.1 | 19034 | 50 | 75.2 | -23 | Tenneco |
| 6069 | 3599 | 454 | 25.2 | 2718 | 71 | 301.9 | 64 | Compaq Computer |
| 6067 | 7177 | 401 | 17.3 | 4519 | 54 | 56.8 | 33 | Ralston Purina |
| 6007 | 3815 | 163 | 15.3 | 1640 | 51 | 129.0 | 84 | Home Depot |
| 5827 | 2723 | 304 | 23.3 | 2411 | 79 | 43.3 | 0 | Marsh & McLennan |
| 5796 | 21694 | -1688 | -6.8 | 21085 | 20 | 60.8 | -20 | Occidental Petroleum |
| 5789 | 17454 | 264 | 10.1 | 9565 | 42 | 40.0 | 61 | Conagra |
| 5727 | 10710 | 295 | 9.6 | 11484 | 68 | 118.5 | 3 | Aluminum Co. of America |
| 5709 | 2917 | 1 | * | 4085 | 83 | 75.3 | 39 | Rhone-Poulenc Rorer |
| 5683 | 4294 | 522 | 14.1 | 12268 | 69 | 84.0 | 38 | Chubb |
| 5680 | 4800 | 571 | 9.7 | 14023 | 26 | 32.8 | 8 | Public Service Enterprise |
| 5634 | 6926 | 197 | 9.1 | 4544 | 53 | 106.4 | 22 | Halliburton |
| 5628 | 3044 | 288 | 16.8 | 2930 | 53 | 59.5 | 4 | Amp |
| 5607 | 3511 | -213 | * | 12277 | 16 | 92.3 | 4 | Tele-Communications |
| 5534 | 8345 | 308 | 8.9 | 10673 | 26 | 85.1 | -30 | United Technologies |
| 5525 | 11436 | 210 | 6.8 | 11951 | 55 | 95.8 | -8 | Caterpillar |
| 5501 | 6021 | 475 | 15.3 | 6108 | 52 | 39.1 | 37 | PPG Industries |
| 5488 | 2941 | 289 | 13.0 | 3512 | 60 | 46.6 | 25 | Corning |
| 5485 | 6222 | 361 | 10.3 | 7168 | 50 | 49.9 | 30 | Cooper Industries |
| 5470 | 8219 | 234 | 21.0 | 2014 | 41 | 34.0 | 51 | Albertson's |
| 5444 | 3681 | 538 | 9.5 | 10084 | 27 | 41.0 | 10 | Duke Power |
| 5437 | 5584 | 173 | 20.9 | 1559 | 17 | 13.4 | 41 | Food Lion |
| 5392 | 5739 | 572 | 8.9 | 10486 | 24 | 38.1 | -2 | Con Edison |
| 5382 | 17973 | 605 | * | 31500 | 58 | 90.7 | 16 | Xerox |
| 5349 | 3783 | 474 | 8.5 | 12374 | 21 | 27.9 | 4 | Pacificorp |
| 5321 | 3507 | 423 | 18.1 | 30336 | 34 | 44.8 | 12 | Bank One |
| 5282 | 5168 | 549 | 9.2 | 13758 | 29 | 39.1 | 1 | American Electric |
| 5227 | 8687 | 385 | * | 4078 | 51 | 49.4 | 10 | Melville |
| 5196 | 4570 | 108 | 5.3 | 5092 | 56 | 89.4 | 13 | American Cyanamid |
| 5191 | 9944 | 367 | * | 31089 | 84 | 12.2 | 17 | CNA Financial |
| 5110 | 38385 | 318 | -9.4 | 227560 | 15 | 133.2 | -33 | Citicorp |
| 5085 | 9268 | 557 | 22.7 | 6119 | 78 | 89.3 | 27 | Raytheon |
| 5059 | 299 | 4 | 1.2 | 444 | 126 | 490.3 | 217 | AMGEN |
| 5044 | 7633 | 364 | 15.1 | 5284 | 34 | 45.1 | 11 | Borden |
| 5019 | 1147 | 176 | 15.8 | 1606 | 24 | 29.5 | 29 | Chemical Waste Mgt |

# Appendix N

## DATA SET 2—1990 CORPORATE DATA (continued)

| $x_1$ | $x_2$ | $x_3$ | $x_4$ | $x_5$ | $x_6$ | $x_7$ | $x_8$ | $x_9$ |
|---|---|---|---|---|---|---|---|---|
| 5017 | 3922 | 231 | 6.9 | 6539 | 43 | 82.0 | 1 | Paramount Communications |
| 5014 | 5075 | 321 | 15.0 | 4159 | 48 | 75.2 | 22 | Humana |
| 5010 | 19021 | 614 | * | 89343 | 46 | 64.9 | -4 | Aetna Life & Casualty |
| 4995 | 5691 | 321 | 16.4 | 4158 | 75 | 78.6 | 33 | Colgate-Palmolive |
| 4972 | 9024 | 394 | 8.5 | 16401 | 25 | 44.0 | 0 | Weyerhaeuser |
| 4966 | 1871 | 208 | 6.6 | 6360 | 36 | 67.8 | -12 | Burlington Resources |
| 4894 | 14739 | 410 | 12.1 | 8808 | 69 | 99.0 | 13 | Dayton Hudson |
| 4889 | 3619 | 301 | 10.2 | 41124 | 52 | 101.9 | 21 | Student Loan Marketing |
| 4671 | 6289 | -374 | * | 12949 | 29 | 42.8 | -2 | FPL Group |
| 4635 | 1106 | 120 | 12.5 | 2091 | 43 | 20.2 | 24 | American TV & Communications |
| 4618 | 3560 | 504 | 9.1 | 10991 | 45 | 41.2 | 13 | Dominion Resources |
| 4585 | 1736 | 210 | 19.2 | 1604 | 67 | 62.2 | 25 | Automatic Data Processing |
| 4578 | 3965 | 414 | 17.3 | 40579 | 76 | 130.1 | 4 | Federal Home Loan Mortgage |
| 4539 | 765 | 223 | 46.7 | 623 | 43 | 44.2 | 64 | UST |
| 4502 | 4179 | 340 | 7.6 | 11877 | 35 | 58.3 | 20 | Houston Industries |
| 4489 | 3982 | 541 | 8.7 | 14817 | 24 | 52.9 | 19 | Entergy |
| 4357 | 9789 | 317 | 14.5 | 4305 | 34 | 80.5 | 13 | Woolworth |
| 4318 | 6309 | 372 | 19.0 | 4746 | 61 | 125.7 | 49 | Honeywell |
| 4304 | 5296 | 227 | 15.6 | 3087 | 57 | 56.2 | 25 | Quaker Oats |
| 4301 | 1037 | 371 | 9.1 | 8714 | 24 | 97.3 | -22 | McCaw Cellular Comm. |
| 4284 | 4481 | 562 | * | 33808 | 39 | 121.3 | 34 | American General |
| 4166 | 3072 | 248 | 12.3 | 3563 | 27 | 101.2 | -22 | Browning-Ferris |
| 4134 | 5960 | 712 | * | 56199 | 80 | 179.1 | -1 | Wells Fargo |
| 4114 | 3307 | 515 | 10.7 | 10573 | 28 | 49.1 | 23 | Detroit Edison |
| 4100 | 7328 | 137 | 15.8 | 2476 | 51 | 112.1 | 24 | Fluor |
| 4095 | 3705 | 106 | 4.1 | 12566 | 19 | 50.3 | 2 | Philadelphia Electric |
| 4077 | 643 | 142 | 24.4 | 713 | 39 | 19.8 | -31 | Newmont Gold |
| 4062 | 3196 | 207 | 13.5 | 6061 | 52 | 56.4 | 19 | Pitney Bowes |
| 4041 | 12343 | 462 | 12.4 | 10456 | 30 | 46.2 | -10 | Allied-Signal |
| 4030 | 7081 | 483 | 12.7 | 7895 | 50 | 76.1 | -1 | Amerada Hess |
| 4030 | 2194 | 185 | 24.8 | 1707 | 34 | 24.5 | 50 | Reader's Digest Assoc. |
| 3960 | 2669 | 288 | 30.8 | 1462 | 53 | 295.2 | 71 | Nike |
| 3948 | 7679 | 290 | 12.3 | 10941 | 52 | 139.5 | -24 | Deere |
| 3940 | 2744 | 386 | 10.4 | 9073 | 42 | 49.5 | 21 | Central & South West |
| 3938 | 6201 | 178 | 17.1 | 2022 | 32 | 51.2 | 56 | Walgreen |
| 3897 | 1729 | 206 | * | 985 | 46 | 198.7 | 122 | Liz Claiborne |
| 3884 | 2719 | 153 | 9.8 | 2906 | 28 | 102.4 | 18 | Baker Hughes |
| 3876 | 3606 | 183 | 11.6 | 3153 | 105 | 63.8 | 47 | Dillard Department Stores |
| 3822 | 3633 | 181 | 7.8 | 4193 | 30 | 30.8 | -15 | Times Mirror |
| 3815 | 12665 | 365 | 7.7 | 12060 | 44 | 81.9 | 1 | Georgia-Pacific |
| 3796 | 2967 | 241 | 11.1 | 4030 | 68 | 73.1 | 45 | Air Products & Chemicals |
| 3767 | 3498 | 226 | 10.3 | 3343 | 49 | 34.5 | 4 | R. R. Donnelley & Sons |
| 3731 | 6022 | 297 | 8.3 | 6280 | 63 | 111.0 | 18 | Reynolds Metals |
| 3726 | 2715 | 164 | 9.1 | 4586 | 43 | 25.3 | -5 | Consolidated Natural Gas |
| 3717 | 2617 | 280 | 9.8 | 7519 | 46 | 41.6 | 14 | Carolina Power & Light |
| 3712 | 7919 | 665 | 48.7 | 63596 | 46 | 80.3 | 23 | Bankers Trust New York |
| 3657 | 7863 | 145 | 12.3 | 2146 | 40 | 48.4 | 38 | SYSCO |
| 3649 | 1534 | 144 | 18.4 | 1114 | 46 | 31.9 | 36 | Rubbermaid |
| 3644 | 526 | 110 | * | 539 | 52 | 377.2 | 170 | Novell |

## Appendix N

### DATA SET 2—1990 CORPORATE DATA (concluded)

| $x_1$ | $x_2$ | $x_3$ | $x_4$ | $x_5$ | $x_6$ | $x_7$ | $x_8$ | $x_9$ |
|-------|-------|-------|-------|-------|-------|-------|-------|-------|
| 3637 | 13380 | 199 | 4.4 | 9000 | 34 | 26.9 | -13 | Sun |
| 3629 | 6567 | -39 | * | 5048 | 44 | 132.1 | 20 | Texas Instruments |
| 3621 | 11720 | -40 | * | 13341 | 58 | 211.0 | 0 | AMR |
| 3620 | 3742 | 260 | 12.2 | 3919 | 46 | 94.6 | 44 | National Medical Enterprises |
| 3585 | 10323 | 161 | 12.0 | 84731 | 29 | 109.7 | -23 | Security Pacific |
| 3581 | 8205 | 365 | 9.3 | 12494 | 36 | 45.0 | 11 | CSX |
| 3574 | 2716 | 216 | 16.5 | 2079 | 40 | 35.5 | 41 | Hershey Foods |
| 3559 | 4706 | 169 | 9.8 | 3119 | 26 | 91.6 | 20 | Dresser Industries |
| 3520 | 2514 | 232 | 15.9 | 6690 | 30 | 37.7 | 14 | Ethyl |
| 3517 | 977 | 124 | 24.2 | 973 | 118 | 93.0 | 80 | Medtronic |
| 3512 | 2830 | 308 | 14.1 | 3739 | 37 | 11.4 | 7 | Arco Chemical |
| 3510 | 18164 | 318 | 5.5 | 57800 | 49 | 59.7 | 2 | Cigna |
| 3496 | 1934 | 145 | 30.7 | 777 | 50 | 116.8 | 63 | The Gap |
| 3461 | 6194 | 373 | 14.1 | 20000 | 32 | 75.3 | 16 | Primerica |
| 3397 | 2519 | 297 | 30.7 | 26271 | 49 | 26.8 | 28 | First Wachovia |

## Appendix O

# DATA SET 3—1991 MAJOR LEAGUE BASEBALL

$x_1$ = Team
$x_2$ = Wins
$x_3$ = Losses
$x_4$ = Proportion of games won
$x_5$ = Team batting average
$x_6$ = Number of team home runs
$x_7$ = Team earned run average
$x_8$ = Team stolen bases
$x_9$ = Team errors
$x_{10}$ = Total player salary in millions of dollars
$x_{11}$ = Attendance in millions
$x_{12}$ = Home surface (1 = artificial, 0 = natural grass)
$x_{13}$ = League (1 = National, 0 = American)

| $x_1$ | $x_2$ | $x_3$ | $x_4$ | $x_5$ | $x_6$ | $x_7$ | $x_8$ | $x_9$ | $x_{10}$ | $x_{11}$ | $x_{12}$ | $x_{13}$ |
|---|---|---|---|---|---|---|---|---|---|---|---|---|
| Toronto | 91 | 71 | 0.562 | 0.257 | 133 | 3.50 | 148 | 127 | 27.5 | 4.00 | 1 | 0 |
| Boston | 84 | 78 | 0.519 | 0.268 | 126 | 4.01 | 59 | 116 | 32.7 | 2.56 | 0 | 0 |
| Detroit | 84 | 78 | 0.519 | 0.247 | 209 | 4.50 | 109 | 104 | 28.8 | 1.64 | 0 | 0 |
| Milwaukee | 83 | 79 | 0.512 | 0.271 | 116 | 4.14 | 106 | 118 | 24.4 | 1.48 | 0 | 0 |
| New York Yanks | 71 | 91 | 0.438 | 0.255 | 147 | 4.41 | 109 | 133 | 27.6 | 1.86 | 0 | 0 |
| Baltimore | 67 | 95 | 0.414 | 0.253 | 170 | 4.58 | 50 | 91 | 14.6 | 2.55 | 0 | 0 |
| Cleveland | 57 | 105 | 0.352 | 0.254 | 79 | 4.23 | 58 | 149 | 18.1 | 1.05 | 0 | 0 |
| Minnesota | 95 | 67 | 0.586 | 0.280 | 140 | 3.69 | 107 | 95 | 22.3 | 2.29 | 1 | 0 |
| Chicago White Sox | 87 | 75 | 0.537 | 0.261 | 139 | 3.78 | 134 | 116 | 16.6 | 2.93 | 0 | 0 |
| Texas | 85 | 77 | 0.525 | 0.269 | 177 | 4.46 | 102 | 134 | 19.2 | 2.30 | 0 | 0 |
| Oakland | 84 | 78 | 0.519 | 0.248 | 159 | 4.57 | 151 | 107 | 36.3 | 2.71 | 0 | 0 |
| Seattle | 83 | 79 | 0.512 | 0.254 | 126 | 3.78 | 97 | 110 | 16.2 | 2.15 | 1 | 0 |
| Kansas City | 82 | 80 | 0.506 | 0.264 | 117 | 3.92 | 119 | 125 | 28.1 | 2.16 | 1 | 0 |
| California | 81 | 81 | 0.500 | 0.255 | 115 | 3.68 | 94 | 102 | 31.8 | 2.42 | 0 | 0 |
| Pittsburgh | 98 | 64 | 0.605 | 0.262 | 126 | 3.44 | 124 | 120 | 23.1 | 2.07 | 1 | 1 |
| St. Louis | 84 | 78 | 0.519 | 0.254 | 68 | 3.68 | 202 | 107 | 21.4 | 2.45 | 1 | 1 |
| Philadelphia | 78 | 84 | 0.481 | 0.241 | 111 | 3.86 | 92 | 119 | 20.1 | 2.05 | 1 | 1 |
| Chicago Cubs | 77 | 83 | 0.481 | 0.252 | 159 | 4.03 | 64 | 113 | 26.8 | 2.31 | 0 | 1 |
| New York Mets | 77 | 84 | 0.478 | 0.243 | 117 | 3.55 | 153 | 143 | 32.6 | 2.28 | 0 | 1 |
| Montreal | 71 | 90 | 0.441 | 0.245 | 95 | 3.64 | 221 | 133 | 20.2 | 0.98 | 1 | 1 |
| Atlanta | 94 | 68 | 0.580 | 0.257 | 141 | 3.48 | 165 | 138 | 18.9 | 2.14 | 0 | 1 |
| Los Angles | 93 | 69 | 0.574 | 0.252 | 108 | 3.06 | 126 | 123 | 33.3 | 3.35 | 0 | 1 |
| San Diego | 84 | 78 | 0.519 | 0.244 | 121 | 3.57 | 101 | 113 | 22.6 | 1.80 | 0 | 1 |
| San Francisco | 75 | 87 | 0.463 | 0.246 | 141 | 4.03 | 95 | 109 | 30.8 | 1.74 | 0 | 1 |
| Cincinnati | 74 | 88 | 0.457 | 0.257 | 164 | 3.83 | 124 | 125 | 25.1 | 2.37 | 1 | 1 |
| Houston | 65 | 97 | 0.401 | 0.244 | 79 | 4.00 | 125 | 161 | 11.2 | 1.20 | 1 | 1 |

# Answers to Odd-Numbered Chapter Exercises

## Chapter 1  What Is Statistics?

1. The collection of facts and figures is often referred to in everyday usage as statistics. Examples are: Greg Norman shot 68 to take the lead of the USF&G Classic in New Orleans; the yearly low of IBM common stock is 104½, and the high is 130⅞.

   Here we define statistics as the science of collecting, organizing, analyzing, and interpreting numerical data in order to make more informed decisions. For example, to make a decision regarding a newly developed breakfast cereal, the Kellogg Company might have a sample of 270 persons selected at random try it and give their reactions. A sample of 10 pieces of steel wire randomly selected might be tested for tensile strength in order to make a decision about all the wire produced during the day.

3. We could use these random sample results to infer something about all the executives. In this case, it would be estimated that about 30 percent of all executives have some degree of hypertension, found by (60/200)100. This is just one illustration of the extensive use of sampling to infer something about a population.

5. In order to suggest several sites to management, you would probably first collect data on the population in the metropolitan areas of Orlando, Birmingham, Atlanta, and other cities in the Southeast. Data on the availability and the prices of land, utilities, and so on need to be collected and analyzed. After a location has been decided on, an in-depth survey of, say, 2,000 persons should be conducted to determine whether the park should be constructed to appeal to all ages, just children, or just adults.

7. a. Sample. The 112 stocks are just a portion of the total number of stocks listed on the New York Stock Exchange.
   b. Nominal. The data resulted from counts, and the order of the three movements is immaterial.
   c. Yes. A stock cannot increase, decrease, and stay the same at the same time.
   d. A statistic.

9. American consumers' confidence in the economy in November 1991 (50.6) fell below the lowest level recorded during the 1982 recession. That low confidence (50.6) reflects growing uneasiness over job security by the American workers. It is about 50 percent below normal.

## Chapter 2  Summarizing Data: Frequency Distributions and Graphic Presentation

1. An array is a listing of the values from the smallest to the largest, or vice versa.

3. *Mutually exclusive* means that a person or object cannot be in more than one category at the same time.

5. a. Using the formula $2^k \geq n$, we suggest four.
   b. Using formula (2−1) the suggested class interval is 1.5, found by (31−25)/4. But 2.0 would be better.
   c. 24
   d.

   |       | $f$ |
   |-------|-----|
   | 24−25 | 2   |
   | 26−27 | 8   |
   | 28−29 | 4   |
   | 30−31 | 2   |
   |       | 16  |

   e. The largest concentration is in the 26−27 class.

7. a. MINITAB gives this histogram:

   ```
   MTB > hist c1;
   SUBC> start 1;
   SUBC> increment 3.

   Histogram of C1    N = 51

   Midpoint   Count
      1.00       9    *********
      4.00      21    *********************
      7.00      13    *************
     10.00       4    ****
     13.00       3    ***
     16.00       1    *
   ```

   Thus, the frequency distribution would be:

   |       | $f$ |
   |-------|-----|
   | 0−2   | 9   |
   | 3−5   | 21  |
   | 6−8   | 13  |
   | 9−11  | 4   |
   | 12−14 | 4   |

b. Data cluster around 3, 4, or 5. Very few customers shop seven or more times.

c.

| | Relative frequency |
|---|---|
| 0–2 | 17.65 |
| 3–5 | 41.18 |
| 6–8 | 25.49 |
| 9–11 | 7.84 |
| 12–14 | 7.84 |
| Total | 100.00 |

9. The five values in that class are 621, 623, 623, 627, and 629.

11. From MINITAB:

```
MTB > stem c1;
SUBC> increment 10.

Stem-and-leaf of C1       N = 16
Leaf Unit = 1.0

     1      0  5
     3      1  28
     3      2
    (7)     3  0024789
     6      4  12366
     1      5  2
```

13. a. 50.
    b. 1.
    c. Using midpoints on X-axis: (stated or true limits could be used)

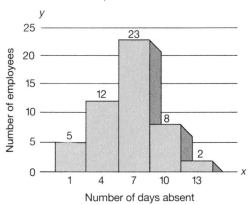

    d. $X \doteq 1, Y = 5$.
    e.

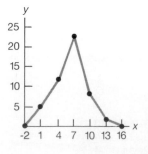

15. a.

| Time in minutes | Relative frequencies | |
|---|---|---|
| | Wilcox method | Lambert method |
| 5–7 | .060 | .080 |
| 8–10 | .213 | .220 |
| 11–13 | .530 | .500 |
| 14–16 | .143 | .140 |
| 17–19 | .054 | .060 |
| Total | 1.000 | 1.000 |

b.

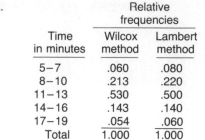

c. The distributions of times are almost identical.

17. a. 5, 17.

b.

| | CF |
|---|---|
| 0–2 inclusive | 5 |
| 3–5 inclusive | 17 |
| 6–8 inclusive | 40 |
| 9–11 inclusive | 48 |
| 12–14 inclusive | 50 |

c.

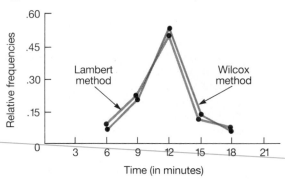

d. About 8.

19. a. 33.

b.

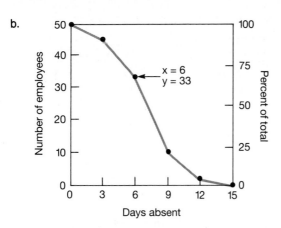

Days absent

c. More than 45 employees were absent more than 3 days, 2 employees were absent 12 days or more, and no employees were absent more than 15 days.

21.

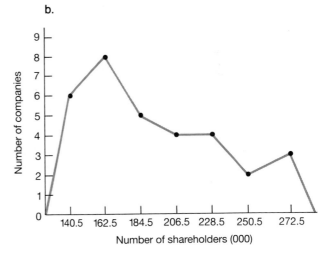

23.

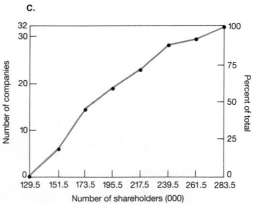

25. a. $36.60, found by ($265 − $82)/5.
   b. $40.

   c.

| | |
|---|---|
| $ 80–$119 | 8 |
| 120– 159 | 19 |
| 160– 199 | 10 |
| 200– 239 | 6 |
| 240– 279 | 1 |
| Total | 44 |

   d. The purchases ranged from a low of about $80 to a high of about $279. The concentration is in the $120–$159 class.

27. a. Class interval is 21 or 22, found by (282−133)/7. We selected 22.

| Shareholders (000) | Number of companies | Less-than CF |
|---|---|---|
| 130−151 | 6 | 6 |
| 152−173 | 8 | 14 |
| 174−195 | 5 | 19 |
| 196−217 | 4 | 23 |
| 218−239 | 4 | 27 |
| 240−261 | 2 | 29 |
| 262−283 | 3 | 32 |
| Total | 32 | |

d.   About 220,000, found by three fourths of 32 = 24. The 24th company has about 220,000 shareholders, found by drawing a line to the curve from 24 and down to the X-axis.

e.   The largest number of companies (8) have between 152,000 and 174,000 shareholders. The smallest number is about 130,000; the largest number is about 284,000.

29.  a.

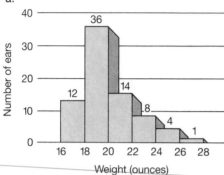

b.

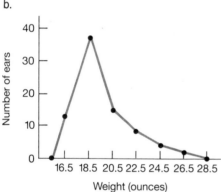

c.   The weights range from a low of about 16 ounces to a high of about 28 ounces. The concentration of weights is in the 18–19-ounce class.

31.

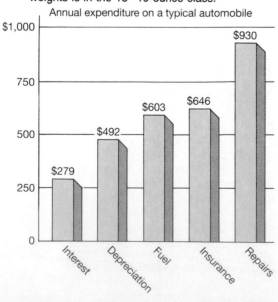

Annual expenditure on a typical automobile

33.  From MINITAB:

```
MTB > stem c1;
SUBC> increment 10.

Stem-and-leaf of C1      N = 26
Leaf Unit = 1.0
    2       6 57
  (12)      7 044555677779
   12        8 0355668
    5        9 1145
    1       10 3
```

35.

(bar chart)

261.93  United States
83.26  Switzerland
81.85  France
66.67  Italy
24.23  Japan
16.10  Canada

37.  a.   Using a class interval of $400,000, the salaries ($000) are:

|                    | f  |
|--------------------|----|
| $    0–$  399      | 14 |
| 400–     799       | 4  |
| 800–   1,199       | 3  |
| 1,200–  1,599      | 2  |
| 1,600 and over     | 4  |
| Total              | 27 |

b.   Fourteen out of the 27 players earn under $400,000. The others are scattered somewhat evenly from $400,000 upward, with 4 earning $1,600,000 or more.

c.   About 10 percent earn more than $2,000,000.

39.  a.

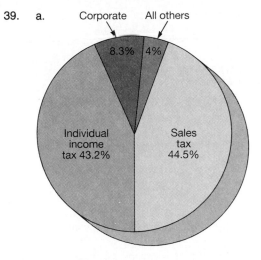

b.    44.5 percent

41.

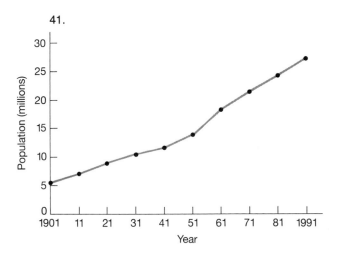

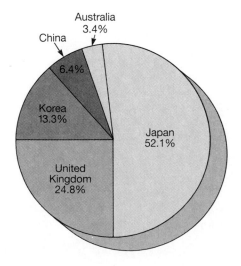

47.    Number with AIDS per 100,000 population

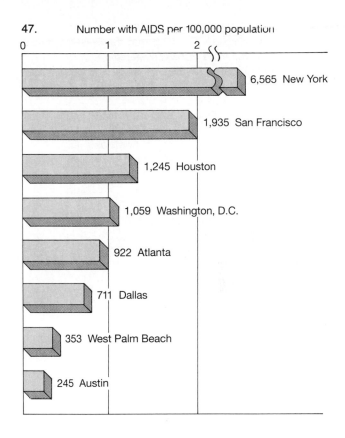

## CHAPTER 3    DESCRIBING DATA— MEASURES OF CENTRAL TENDENCY

1.    A sample mean is found by

$$\overline{X} = \frac{\text{Sums of all the values in a sample}}{\text{Number of values in the sample}}$$

Thus, it is a measurable characteristic of a sample. A population mean is found by

$$\mu = \frac{\text{Sum of all the values in a particular population}}{\text{Number of values in the population}}$$

Thus, it is a measurable characteristic of the population of interest. Note that the steps for computing the sample mean and the population mean are the same. Only the symbols are different.

3.    a.    Mean = 7.0, found by 28/4.
      b.    $(5 - 7) + (9 - 7) + (4 - 7) + (10 - 7) = 0$

5.    14.58, found by 43.74/3.

7.    a.    15.4, found by 154/10.
      b.    Population, since it includes all the salespersons at Midtown Ford.

9.  a.  $54.55, found by 1,091/20.
    b.  A sample—assuming that the power company serves more than 20 customers.
11. $0.775, found by ($10.00 + $37.50 + $30.00)/100.
13. $11.50, found by ($400 + $500 + $1,400)/200.
15. a.  Nominal.
    b.  Lecture, because it is the most frequently used method.
    c.  No. Data must be at least ordinal level.
    d.  No. Data must be at least interval level.
17. a.  $96.70.
    b.  No. It is the highest value.
    c.  $91.40.
    d.  $88.70, found by $620.90/7.
    e.  Either mean or median.
19. Mean or median. Mode of 10 too low. Mean of 15.4 or median of 16.5 almost equal. From MINITAB:

```
MTB > describe c1

     N   MEAN  MEDIAN  TRMEAN  STDEV  SEMEAN
C1   10  15.40  16.50   15.25   7.40    2.34

     MIN    MAX    Q1     Q3
C1  4.00  28.00  9.50  20.00
```

21. 11.18, found by:

|                         | Display |
|-------------------------|---------|
| 8 × 12 × 14 × 26 × 5    | 174720  |

Depress [2nd] [$y^x$]

Depress reciprocal of 5 (.20) =    11.180688

23. 62.5%, found by:

|                   | Display  |
|-------------------|----------|
| 926,429 ÷ 30,948  | 29.93502 |

Depress [2nd] [$y^x$]

Depress .1428571 =    1.6251099
Depress − 1 =    .625

25. Since the exact values in a frequency distribution are not known, the computed mean can only be an estimate.
27. 46.8, found by:

$$\bar{X} = \frac{\Sigma fx}{n} = \frac{3,275}{70} = 46.7857$$

29. 44.3 years of age found by 2,215/50.
31. 47.12, found by:

| Lower limit |      | f  | CF |
|-------------|------|----|----|
| 20–29       | 19.5 | 7  | 7  |
| 30–39       | 29.5 | 12 | 19 |
| 40–49       | 39.5 | 21 | 40 |
| 50–59       | 49.5 | 18 | 58 |
| 60–69       | 59.5 | 12 | 70 |
|             |      | 70 |    |

$$\text{Median} = 39.5 + \frac{\frac{70}{2} - 19}{21}(10)$$
$$= 39.5 + 7.619$$
$$= 47.119$$

Mode = 44.5

33. a.  17.9 miles per gallon, found by:

$$15.5 + \frac{\frac{30}{2} - 7}{10}(3)$$

    b.  17 miles per gallon. It is the midpoint of the 16–18 class.
35. a.  Half of the price-earnings are above the median of 10.8, the other half below the median of 10.8.
    b.  More price-earning ratios are 10.2 than any other value.
    c.  11.1
37. a.  81.0, found by [3(78.0) − 72]/2.
    b.

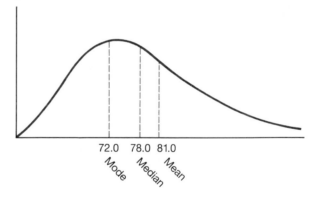

                       72.0  78.0  81.0
                       Mode  Median  Mean

39. a.  Mean = 21.71, median = 22.00
    b.  (23 − 21.71) + (19 − 21.71) + (26 − 21.71) + (24 − 21.71) + (22 − 21.71) = 0.
41. Mean = 70.53, found by 2,116/30.
43. Mean = $672,963, found by $18,170,000/27. Median = $345,000. A few very high salaries are pulling mean upward, so median seems to be a more representative average.

    From MINITAB:

```
MTB > describe c1

     N  MEAN  MEDIAN  TRMEAN  STDEV  SEMEAN
C1  27   673    345     623    729    140

     MIN   MAX   Q1    Q3
C1  100  2500  102  1150
```

45. 15.6 percent, found by

|  | Display |
|---|---|
| $165,470 \div 44,871$ | 3.6876825 |

Depress [2nd] $y^x$

Depress .1111111 $=$    1.1560393
Depress $-1=$        .1560393

47. 61.68 percent.
49. Arithmetic mean $= 60.1$ percent. Geometric mean $= 55.2$ percent, found by:

|  | Display |
|---|---|
| $32.2 \times 35.5 \times 80.0 \times 60.9 \times 92.1$ |  |

Depress [2nd] $y^x$

Depress reciprocal of 5 (.20) $=$    55.209044

51. 227.4667 pounds, found by

$$\frac{[7(240) + 4(212) + 3(190) + 1(314)]}{15}$$

53. a. No. The 3,333 pounds assumes that there are an equal number of containers weighing 1,000, 3,000, and 6,000 pounds, respectively. This is not the case.
    b. 2,500 pounds, found by [(60 × 1,000) + (40 × 3,000) + (20 × 6,000)]/120. Each of the three sizes is weighted by the number of containers.
55. 19.74 years, found by:

$$19.5 + \frac{\frac{515.6}{2} - 249.8}{168.6}(5)$$

Half of the unmarried mothers are under 19.74 years old and the other half over 19.74 years old.

57. a. $30,082.49, found by:

$$\$29,999.50 + \frac{\frac{100}{2} - 49.8}{24.1}(\$10,000)$$

Half of the incomes are below $30,082.49, the other half above it.
    b  $24,999.50, midpoint of $20,000–$29,999 class. Appears most frequently.
59. a. 45.84 years, found by:

$$44.5 + \frac{\frac{1,829}{2} - 854}{450}(10)$$

Half of the divorced males are younger than 45.84 years, the other half older than 45.84 years

b. 43.29 years, found by:

$$34.5 + \frac{\frac{2,827}{2} - 837}{656}(10)$$

Half of the divorced females are younger than 43.29 years; the other half are older than 43.29 years.
    c. Males, 49.5. Females: distribution bimodal (two modes), 39.5 and 49.5.

61. a. $3,330, found by [3($3,220) − $3,000]/2.
    b. Mean. It is being pulled up by extreme values.
    c. $3,000
    d. Positively skewed. The median and the mean are larger than the mode.
63. 8.7 percent, found by:

|  | Display |
|---|---|
| $17,000,000 \div 22,000$ | 772.72727 |

Depress [2nd] $y^x$

Depress 0.0125 $=$     1.0866766
Depress $-1=$         .0866766

65. 6.23%.
67. a. $\bar{X} = \$166,670$, median $= \$160,000$.
    b. 3.0 bedrooms (median).
    c. 2.0 baths.
    d. 14.9 miles (median $= 15.0$ miles).
69. a. $\bar{X} = \$24,240,000$, median $= \$23,750,000$.
    b. Either the mean or median.
    c. $\bar{X} = 2,186,000$
    median $= 2,220,000$
    d. Either the mean or median.

# CHAPTER 4   MEASURES OF DISPERSION AND SKEWNESS

1. a. 7, found by $10 - 3$.
    b. 6.
    c. 2.4, found by 12/5.
    d. difference between largest and smallest value
3. a. 30, found by $54 - 24$.
    b. 38, found by 380/10.
    c. 7.2, found by 72/10.
    d. On the average, the number of minutes required to install a door deviates 7.2 minutes from the mean.
5. a. 15, found by $41 - 26$.
    b. 33.9, found by $339 \div 10$.
    c. 4.12, found by $41.2 \div 10$. The ratings deviate 4.12 from the mean of 33.9, on the average.
    d. Since $8 < 15$ and $1.9 < 4.12$, we conclude that there is more dispersion in the first group.

7.  a.  4.4, found by 22/5.
    b.  4.4, found by 29.4 − 25.
9.  a.  $2.770, found by $13.85/5.
    b.  1.259, found by 44.6573/5 − (2.77)$^2$ = 1.25856.
11. a.  Range is 7.3, found by 11.6 − 4.3.
        Mean = 6.94, found by 34.7/5.
        Variance = 6.59, found by 273.79/5 − (6.94)$^2$.
        Standard deviation = 2.57, found by $\sqrt{6.59}$.
    b.  Arithmetic mean for Dennis Industries (11.76) considerably higher than that for Plywood, Inc. (6.94). There is more dispersion (spread) in the equity returns for Dennis Industries than for Plywood, Inc.

13. a.  2.35. (See the following partial MINITAB output.)

| N | MEAN | MEDIAN | TRMEAN | STDEV | SEMEAN |
|---|------|--------|--------|-------|--------|
| 5 | 4.00 | 3.00 | 4.00 | 2.35 | 1.05 |

    b.  5.52, found by (2.35)$^2$.
15. a.  82.667, found by 744/9.
    b.  82.667
    c.  9.09.
17. a.  7 grams, found by 127 − 120.
    b.  124 grams, found by 1,240 ÷ 10.
    c.  4.667, found by either 42/(10 − 1) or:

$$\frac{153,802 - \frac{(1,240)^2}{10}}{10 - 1}$$

    d.  2.1602 grams, found by $\sqrt{4.667}$.
19. a.  24, found by 24 − 0.
    b.  5.33, found by:

$$\sqrt{\frac{5,265 - \frac{(365)^2}{30}}{30 - 1}}$$

21. a.  17 minutes, using the stated class limits (18 − 1 = 17). Using the true class limits, the range is 18 minutes, found by 18.5 − 0.5.
    b.  3.8938 minutes, found by:

$$\sqrt{\frac{3,759 - \frac{(363)^2}{42}}{42 - 1}}$$

    c.  15.162, found by (3.8938)$^2$.
23. About 69 percent, found by:

$$1 - \frac{1}{k^2} = 1 - \frac{1}{(1.8)^2} = .691$$

25. a.  About 95 percent, found by .4750 + .4750.
    b.  About 47.5 percent. About 2.5 percent.
27. a.  8.429, found by:

$$4.5 + \frac{\frac{30}{4} - 2}{7}(5)$$

    b.  15.75, found by:

$$14.5 + \frac{\frac{3(30)}{4} - 21}{6}(5)$$

    c.  7.32, found by 15.75 − 8.43.
    d.  5.21, found by:

$$4.5 + \frac{\frac{10(30)}{100} - 2}{7}(5)$$

    e.  19.5, found by:

$$14.5 + \frac{\frac{90(30)}{100} - 21}{6}(5)$$

29. a.  About $1,281.32, found by:

$$\$1,199.5 + \frac{\frac{120}{4} - 21}{22}(\$200)$$

    b.  About $1,657.83, found by:

$$\$1,599.5 + \frac{\frac{(3)(120)}{4} - 83}{24}(\$200)$$

    c.  About $376.51, found by $1,657.83 − $1,281.32. It is the difference between the third and first quartiles.
    d.  $188.26, found by $376.51 ÷ 2. If is half the distance between the third and first quartiles.
31. a.  $Q_1$ = 40,422.33 miles, found by:

$$39,500 + \frac{\frac{570}{4} - 133}{103}(10,000)$$

    $Q_3$ = 66,722.22 miles

    Interquartile range = 26,299.89. The middle 50 percent of the mileages are between 66,722.22 and 40,422.3 miles.
    b.  Q.D. = 26,299.89/2 = 13,149.95.
    c.  32,350.147 miles. About 60 percent of the miles flown are between 69,640.845 and 37,290.698 miles. The 80th percentile is found by:

$$69,500 + \frac{\frac{80(570)}{100} - 455}{71}(10,000)$$

33. C.V. for domestic is 21.3 percent. C.V. for overseas is 19.2 percent. Although the mean weight of the luggage for overseas passengers is 31 pounds more than for the domestic passengers, there is less relative spread in the weights of overseas luggage.

35. a. The difference in the prices between the two sets of stocks is quite large.
    b. C.V. for low-priced stock is 29.0 percent, and for high-priced stock it is 5.7 percent (found by ($5.28/$92.50)(100). More relative dispersion in low-priced stocks because 29.0 > 5.7.

37.
$$Sk = \frac{3(\$673,000 - \$345,000)}{\$729,000} = 1.35$$

There is a moderate degree of positive skewness.

39. a. Negatively skewed.
    b. $-1.8$, found by $3(2.1 - 2.4)/0.5$. There is skewness.

41. For a sample, $n - 1$ is substituted for $N$ in the denominator of the formula for the sample variance. This substitution prevents underestimation of the population variance.

43. The distribution with the C.V. of 30 percent has more relative dispersion than the distribution with a 20 percent C.V.

45. a. 55, found by $72 - 17$.
    b. 14.4, found by $144/10$.
    c. 17.62, found by:

$$\sqrt{\frac{21,458 - \frac{(432)^2}{10}}{10 - 1}}$$

47. a. Population.
    b. 183.47, found by:

$$\text{Mean} = 193.3$$

$$\sigma = \sqrt{\frac{235,637.43}{7}}$$

    c. 94.9 percent, found by $(183.47 \div 193.3)(100)$.

49. a. $29, found by $109 - $80.
    b. Considering the distribution a sample, standard deviation = $6.51, found by:

$$\sqrt{\frac{1,109,345 - \frac{(10,565)^2}{110}}{110 - 1}}$$

MINITAB can give you the three essential numbers for the above formula, with C1 = midpoints, C2 = frequencies.

C1

| 82 | 87 | 92 | 97 | 102 | 107 |

C2

| 6 | 12 | 23 | 35 | 24 | 10 |

```
MTB > sum c2
   SUM      =        110.00
MTB > let c3 = c1 × C2
MTB > SUM C3
   SUM      =        10565
MTB > LET C4 = C1 × C3
MTB > SUM C4
   SUM      =       1019345
```

    c. $9.28, found by $Q_3 - Q_1 = \$100.85 - \$91.57$.
    d. $17.71, found by $104.29 - $86.58.

51. a. Mean = 28.16, found by $2,253 \div 80$. Median = 27.6, found by:

$$25.5 + \frac{\frac{80}{2} - 26}{20}(3)$$

    b. 5.76, found by:

$$\sqrt{\frac{66,069 - \frac{(2,253)^2}{80}}{80 - 1}}$$

    c. 20.44 percent, found by $(5.76/28.16)100$.
    d. Positively skewed, because the mean of 28.16 is greater than the mode of 27.

53. a.
55. b.
57. a. $Q_1 = 18.15$ pounds
       $Q_3 = 23.62$ pounds, found by:

$$19.5 + \frac{\frac{3(100)}{4} - 32.5}{51.6}(5)$$

    b. 2.74, found by $(23.62 - 18.15)/2$.

59. a. $Q_1 = \$13,113$, found by:

$$\$10,000 + \frac{25 - 18.4}{10.6}(\$5,000)$$

       $Q_3 = \$44,331$
    b. Q.D. = ($44,331 - $13,113)/2 = $15,609
    c. 20th = $10,755, found by:

$$\$10,000 + \frac{20 - 18.4}{10.6}(\$5,000)$$

    d. 80th = $48,692, found by:

$$\$35,000 + \frac{80 - 64.3}{17.2}(\$15,000)$$

d. 20th to 80th = $48,692 − $10,255 = $37,937.
e. 60 percent of the incomes lie between $10,255 and $48,192.

61. a. 0.556 or 55.6 percent, found by:

$$1 - \frac{1}{k^2} = 1 - \frac{1}{(1.5)^2}$$

b. 8.33 percent, found by (2/24)(100). The discounts are dispersed 8.33 percent from the mean.
c. −2.25, found by

$$\frac{3(24 - 25.5)}{2}$$

considerable negative skewness

63. a. s = 35.68, CV = 21.41, sk = 0.56.
b. s = 4.892, CV = 32.85, sk = −0.066.

65. a. s = 6.51, CV = 26.86, sk = .226.
b. s = .622, CV = 30.28, sk = −.154.

# CHAPTER 5   A SURVEY OF PROBABILITY CONCEPTS

1. An experiment is the observation of some activity or the act of taking some measurement, whereas an event is the collection of several outcomes from the experiment.

3. a. A probability may range from 0 to 1.00 inclusive.
b. It cannot be greater than 1.
c. It cannot be less than 0.
d. A probability close to 1.00 indicates the event is likely to occur.

5. a. The experiment is asking the 500 citizens whether they favor or oppose widening Indiana Avenue to three lanes.
b. Possible events include 321 favor the widening, 387 favor the widening, 444 favor the widening, and so on.
c. Answers will vary, but two possibilities are: (1) A majority favor the widening, which would be 251 or more. (2) More than 300 favor the widening.

7. a. Relative frequency.
b. Classical.
c. Classical.
d. Subjective, because this is someone's opinion.

9. a. 13/52 = .25
b. 1/52 = .019
c. Classical.

11. a. The survey of 40 people about abortion.
b. 26 or more favor, for example.
c. 10/40 = .25.
d. Relative frequency.
e. The events are not equally likely, but they are mutually exclusive.

13. $P(A \text{ or } B) = P(A) + P(B)$
   $= .30 + .20$
   $= .50$
   $P(\text{neither}) = 1 − .50 = .50$

15. a. 102/200 = .51
b. .49, found by 61/200 + 37/200 = .305 + .185. Special rule of addition.

17. $P(A \text{ or } B) = P(A) + P(B) − P(A \text{ and } B)$
   $= .20 + .30 − .15$
   $= .35$

19. When two events are mutually exclusive, it means that if one occurs the other event cannot occur. Therefore, the probability of their joint occurrence is zero.

21. a. .65, found by .35 + .40 − .10.
b. A joint probability.
c. No, an executive might read both magazines.

23. a. A joint probability is the occurrence of two events at the same time.
b. A conditional probability is the probability of one event occurring, given that another event has already occurred.

25. a. Venn diagram.
b. Sample space.
c. No. There is an overlapping of events D and H.
d. $P(D \text{ or } H) = P(D) + P(H) − P(D \text{ and } H)$

27. $P(X_1 \text{ and } Y_2) = P(X_1) \times P(Y_2|X_1)$
   $= .75 \times .40$
   $= .30$

29. a. 6/380 or .01579, found by 3/20 × 2/19.
b. 272/380 or .7158, found by 17/20 × 16/19.

31.

$$P(A_1|B_1) = \frac{P(A_1) \times P(B_1|A_1)}{P(A_1) \times P(B_1|A_1) + P(A_2) \times P(B_1|A_2)}$$

$$= \frac{.60 \times .05}{(.60 \times .05) + (.40 \times .10)} = .4286$$

33. .5645, found by:

$$P(\text{night}|\text{win}) = \frac{P(\text{night})\, P(\text{win}|\text{night})}{P(\text{night})\, P(\text{win}|\text{night}) + P(\text{day})\, P(\text{win}|\text{day})}$$

$$= \frac{(.70)(.50)}{[(.70)(.50)] + [(.30)(.90)]}$$

35.   .1053, found by:

$$P(\text{cash}|{>}\$50) = \frac{P(\text{cash})\,P({>}\$50|\text{cash})}{P(\text{cash})\,P({>}\$50|\text{cash}) + P(\text{check})\,P({>}\$50|\text{check}) + P(\text{charge})\,P({>}\$50|\text{charge})}$$

$$= \frac{(.30)(.20)}{[(.30)(.20)] + [(.30)(.90)] + [(.40)(.60)]}$$

37.   a.   A permutation is the number of arrangements of $r$ objects selected from $n$ possible objects.
      b.   A combination is the number of ways to select $r$ objects from a group of $n$ objects without regard to order.

39.   a.   6,840
      b.   504
      c.   21

41.   10,000, found by $(10)^4$.

43.   3,003, found by $_{15}C_{10} = (15 \times 14 \times 13 \times 12 \times 11)/(5 \times 4 \times 3 \times 2)$

45.   a.   Asking teenagers their reactions to a newly developed soft drink.
      b.   More than half like it.

47.   Subjective.

49.   3/6 or 1/2, found by 1/6 + 1/6 + 1/6. Classical.

51.   a.   The likelihood an event will occur, assuming that another event has already occurred.
      b.   The collection of one or more outcomes of an experiment.
      c.   A measure of the likelihood that two or more events will happen concurrently.

53.   a.   .81, found by $(.95)^4$, or $(.95)(.95)(.95)(.95)$.
      b.   Special rule of multiplication.
      c.   $P(A \text{ and } B \text{ and } C \text{ and } D) = P(A) \times P(B) \times P(C) \times P(D)$

67.   .0294, found by:

$$P(\text{poor}|\text{profit}) = \frac{P(\text{poor})\,P(\text{profit}|\text{poor})}{P(\text{poor})\,P(\text{profit}|\text{poor}) + P(\text{good})\,P(\text{profit}|\text{good}) + P(\text{fair})\,P(\text{profit}|\text{fair})}$$

$$= \frac{(.10)(.20)}{[(.10)(.20)] + [(.60)(.80)] + [(.30)(.60)]}$$

69.   45 matches, found by:

$$\frac{10!}{2!(10 - 2)!}$$

71.   .70, found by:

$$P(A) + P(B) - P(A \text{ and } B) = .60 + .40 - .30 = .70$$

73.   .5454, found by applying Bayes' theorem:

$$\frac{(.50)(.75)}{(.50)(.75) + (.50)(.625)}$$

75.   .40, found by applying Bayes' theorem:

$$\frac{(.50)(.25)}{(.50)(.25) + (.50)(.375)}$$

55.   a.   .08, found by .80 × .10.

| Sex | | College | | Joint |
|---|---|---|---|---|
| | .90 | Attended | .80 × .90 = | .72 |
| Female | | Not | | |
| .80 | .10 | attended | .80 × .10 = | .08 |
| | .78 | Attended | .20 × .78 = | .156 |
| .20 | Male | Not | | |
| | .22 | attended | .20 × .22 = | .044 |
| | | | Total | 1.000 |

      c.   Yes, because all the possible outcomes are shown on the tree diagram.

57.   a.   .062, found by 100/400 × 99/399.
      b.   .7538, found by 300/398.
      c.   .2462, found by 1 − .7538.

59.   a.   $P(A \text{ and } B) = P(A) \times P(B|A)$.
      b.   6/2,450 or .0024, found by 3/50 × 2/49.

61.   All hit = .4096, found by $(.80)^4$. None hit = .0016, found by $(.20)^4$.

63.   a.   .3818, found by (9/12)(8/11)(7/10).
      b.   .6182, found by 1 − .3818.

65.   a.   .5467, found by 82/150.
      b.   .76, found by (39/150) + (75/150).
      c.   .6267, found by 82/150 + 39/150 − 27/150. General rule.
      d.   .3293, found by 27/82.
      e.   .2972, found by (82/150)(81/149).

77.   Yes. 256 is found by $2^8$.

79.   2,520, found by:

$$_7P_5 = \frac{7!}{(7 - 5)!}$$

81.   .4437, found by $(.85)^5$.

83.   17,576,000, found by (26)(26)(26)(10)(10)(10).

85.   a.   .333, found by (6/10) × (5/9).
      b.   .9286, found by 1 − [(6/10)(5/9)(4/8)(3/7)].
      c.   Dependent.

87.   a.   2,024, found by:

$$_{24}C_3 = \frac{24!}{3!(24 - 3)!}$$

      b.   .125, found by 1 − [(23/24)(22/23)(21/22)].

89. a. .328, found by 220/670.
    b. .104, found by 70/670.
    c. .403, found by (220/670) + (70/670) − (20/670).
    d. .286, found by 20/70.
    e. .111, found by 50/450.

91.

| Supplier | Percent supplied | Percent defective |
|---|---|---|
| Tyson | 20.0 | 3.0 |
| Fuji | 30.0 | 4.0 |
| Kirkpatricks | 25.0 | 7.0 |
| Parts, Inc. | 25.0 | 6.5 |

a. The overall percent defective is 5.175, found by:

$E(X) = .20(.03) + .30(.04) + .25(.07) + .25(.065)$

$= .05175$

b. Using Bayes' theorem:

$P(\text{Tyson}|\text{defective}) = \dfrac{.20(.03)}{.20(.03) + .30(.04) + .25(.07) + .25(.065)}$

$= .1159$

c.

| Supplier | Joint probability | Revised |
|---|---|---|
| Tyson | .00600 | .1159 |
| Fuji | .01200 | .2319 |
| Kirkpatricks | .01750 | .3382 |
| Parts | .01625 | .3140 |
| Total | .05175 | 1.0000 |

93. Using the probabilities from Exercise 92, the probability both components fail is .01, found by (1.0 − .9)(1.0 − .9). The probability that at least one of the components work is .99.

95. The following diagram lists the probabilities.

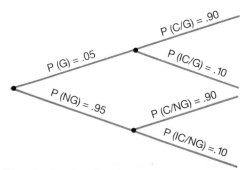

$P(G)$ = Probability of guilty = .05
$P(NG)$ = Probability of not guilty = .95.
$P(C|G)$ = Probability of correct assessment if guilty = .90
$P(C|NG)$ = Probability of correct assessment if not guilty = .90

a. George will fire all those who fail the lie detector test, whether they are guilty or not.

   $P(\text{Fire}) = .05(.90) + .95(.10) = .14$

b. $P(G|F) = \dfrac{.05(.90)}{.05(.90) + .95(.10)} = .3214$

c. $P(G|N) = \dfrac{.05(.10)}{.05(.10) + .95(.90)} = .0058$

   These are guilty but not fired.

d. George's policy is not very effective. About 2/3 of the time innocent people are fired (the complement of the answer to part b).

97. a. 1. 61.54%, found by 16/26.
       2. 65.38, found by 16/26 + 6/26 − 5/26.
       3. 83.33%, found by 5/6.
       4. 11.54%, found by (10/26)(3/10).
    b. 1. 38.46%, found by 10/26.
       2. Grass. 10/16 is larger than 6/16.
       3. 76.92% found by 10/26 + 10/26 − 6/26.

# CHAPTER 6    DISCRETE PROBABILITY DISTRIBUTIONS

1. A discrete distribution can assume only certain values and is usually found by a counting process. A continuous distribution can assume an infinite number of values within a given range. Continuous distributions are usually determined by some type of measurement.

3. $\mu = \Sigma XP(X) = 0(.20) + 1(.40) + 2(.30) + 3(.10) = 1.3$
   $\sigma^2 = \Sigma(X − \mu)^2 P(X)$
   $= (0 − 1.3)^2(.2) + (1 − 1.3)^2(.4) + (2 − 1.3)^2(.3) + (3 − 1.3)^2(.10)$
   $= .81$

5. $\mu = 0(.3) + 1(.4) + 2(.2) + 3(.1)$
   $= 1.1$
   $\sigma^2 = (0 − 1.1)^2(.3) + (1 − 1.1)^2(.4) + (2 − 1.1)^2(.2) + (3 − 1.1)^2(.1)$
   $= .89$
   $\sigma = .943$

7. The characteristics are: (1) There are only two possible outcomes. (2) The data collected are the result of counts. (3) The probability of success remains the same from one trial to another. (4) Each trial is independent of another trial.

9. a. $P(2) = \dfrac{4!}{2!(4 − 2)!}(.25)^2(.75)^{4−2} = .211$

   b. $P(3) = \dfrac{4!}{3!(4 − 3)!}(.25)^3(.75)^{4−3} = .0469$

11. a.

| r | P(r) |
|---|---|
| 0 | .064 |
| 1 | .288 |
| 2 | .432 |
| 3 | .216 |

b.  $\mu = np = 3(.6) = 1.8$
$\sigma^2 = np\ (1 - p) = 3(.6)(.4) - .72$
$\sigma = \sqrt{.72} = .8485$

13. a.  Number of production employees absent.
b.  Discrete, because the number absent can assume only certain values, such as 1, 2, 3, and so on. There cannot be a fractional number of employees absent on a particular day.
c.  .349, found by referring to Appendix A, $n = 10$, $r = 0$, and $p = .10$.

d.
| $r$ | $P(r)$ | $r$ | $P(r)$ |
|---|---|---|---|
| 0 | .349 | 6 | .000 |
| 1 | .387 | 7 | .000 |
| 2 | .194 | 8 | .000 |
| 3 | .057 | 9 | .000 |
| 4 | .011 | 10 | .000 |
| 5 | .001 | | |

e.  $\mu = 1.00$, found by $np = (10)(.10)$.
$\sigma^2 = .90$, found by $np(1 - p) = (10)(.10)(.90)$.
$\sigma = .949$, found by $\sqrt{.90}$.

f.
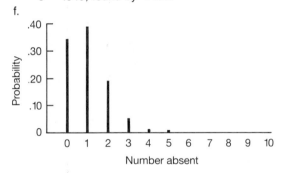

Number absent

g.  (1) The outcomes can be classified only as "absent" or "not absent"; (2) the number absent is the result of counts; (3) the probability of .10 remains the same; and (4) the daily number of absences are independent.

15. a.  .296, found by using Appendix A with $n = 8$, $p = .30$, and $r = 2$.
b.  .552, found by using Appendix B with $n = 8$, $p = .30$, and $r \leq 2$. It could also be determined by the special rule of addition and Appendix A. This is done by adding all the probability values of $r$ up to 7 in the .30 column for $p$.

17. a.  .387, found from Appendix A with $n = 9$, $p = .90$, and $r = 9$.
b.  .001, found in Appendix B with $n = 9$, $p = .90$, and $r \leq 4$.
c.  .992, found by $1 - .008$, which is probability that five or fewer have a color TV.
d.  .947, found by $1 - .053$, which is the probability that six or fewer have a color TV.

19. a.  .50
b.  About .40.
c.  .377, found by $1 - .623$.

21.  $P(2) = \dfrac{{}_6C_2\ {}_4C_1}{{}_{10}C_3} = \dfrac{15(4)}{120} = .50$

23.  .4667, found by:

$$\frac{\dfrac{7!}{2!5!} \times \dfrac{3!}{0!3!}}{\dfrac{10!}{2!8!}} = \frac{21}{45}$$

25.  .4196, found by:

$$\frac{\dfrac{9!}{6!3!} \times \dfrac{6!}{4!2!}}{\dfrac{15!}{5!10!}} = \frac{1,260}{3,003}$$

27. a.  .6703, found from Appendix C with $\mu = 0.4$ and $X = 0$.
b.  .3297, found from Appendix C with $\mu = 0.4$ and $X \geq 0$.

29. a.  .0613, where $n = 40$, $p = .025$, and $\mu = 1$. See Appendix C.
b.  .0803, found by $.0613 + .0153 + .0031 + .0005 + .0001$, from Appendix C.

31.  .7148, where $\mu = np = (.005)(1,200) = 6$. Adding, $.1606 + .1606 + .1377 + \cdots + .0001 = .7148$.

33.  The characteristics are: (1) There are only two possible outcomes. (2) The trials are not independent, so the probability of a success is not the same on each trial. (3) The distribution results from a count of the number of successes in a fixed number of trials.

35.  When $n$ is large and $p$ is small, the Poisson and binomial distributions will yield approximately the same results.

37.  Mean $= 2.0$ units, found by $0 + .20 + .60 + 1.20$. Standard deviation $= 1.00$, found by $\Sigma(X - \mu)^2 \times P(X) = .40 + .20 + 0 + .40 = 1\sqrt{1.0} = 1$.

39.  Mean $= 1.30$ accidents, found by $.00 + .20 + .40 + .30 + .40$. Variance $= 1.81$, found by $\Sigma(X - \mu)^2 P(X) = .676 + .018 + .098 + .289 + .729$. Standard deviation $= \sqrt{1.81} = 1.3454$ accidents.

41.  Yes. $\mu = .0025$, found by $-.03 + (-.03) + 0 + .0225 + .0200 + .0200$. $\sigma^2 = .02905$, found by $.00765 + .00390 + .00000 + .00270 + .00490 + .00990$.

43. a.  .0009765, found by:

$$P(5) = \frac{5!}{5!(5 - 5)!}(.25)^5\ (.75)^{5-5}$$
$$= (1)(.0009765)(1)$$

b.  .2373046, found by:

$$P(0) = \frac{5!}{0!(5 - 0)!}(.25)^0\ (.75)^{5-0}$$
$$= (1)(1)(.2373046)$$

c.  .7626954, found by $1 - .2373046$.

45. The probability of exactly two Spanish-speaking Americans on the jury is .168 (Appendix A, $n = 12$, $p = .3$, and $r = 2$). One might argue that this is a sufficiently large chance and agree with the government lawyer.

47. a. About 6,065 doors. From Appendix C, $\mu = .5$, $X = 0$. $P(0) = .6065$.
    b. About 902 doors, found by $1 - (.6065 + .3033)$ (Appendix C).

49. a. .8187, from Appendix C. $\mu = .2$, found by $100(.002)$.
    b. .9824, found by $.8187 + .1637$.
    c. No. The probability that three or more machines are broken down is only .0012, found by $.0011 + .0001$.

51. $\mu = 4.0$ from Appendix C.
    a. .0183
    b. .1954
    c. .6289
    d. .5665

53. a. .0498
    b. .7746, found by $(1 - .0498)^5$

55. a. .4506, found by:

$$\frac{20!}{3!17!} \times \frac{5!}{1!4!} \times \frac{4!21!}{25!}$$

    b. .410, found from Appendix A with $n = 4$, $p = .2$, and $r = 1$.
    c. .3595, found by $\mu = np = 4(.2) = .8$, with $X = 1$. .8409, where $N = 12$, $S = 5$, $n = 3$, $r = 0$.

57.

$$\left(\frac{5!}{0!5!}\right)\left(\frac{7!}{3!4!}\right)\left(\frac{3!9!}{12!}\right) = \frac{35}{220} = .1591$$

Then, $1 - .1591 = .8409$.

59. For NASA, $\mu = np = .0004$. As shown in the following MINITAB Poisson table for a $k$ of 1, 2, and so on, the total is .0004. This is the probability that NASA will have one or more disasters.

```
MTB > PDF;
SUBC> POISSON MU = .0004.

POISSON WITH MEAN = 0.000

K     P(X = K)

0     0.9996
1     0.0004
2     0.0000
```

For the Air Force: $\mu = np = .7143$, where $n = 25$ and $p = 1/35$. Referring to the following MINITAB Poisson table for a $k$ of 1 through 7, the probability is .5105 that the Air Force will have one or more disasters ($.3497 + .1249 + \cdots + .0001 = .5105$).

```
MTB > PDF;
SUBC> POISSON MU = 0.7143.

POISSON WITH MEAN = 0.714

K     P(X = K)

0     0.4895
1     0.3497
2     0.1249
3     0.0297
4     0.0053
5     0.0008
6     0.0001
7     0.0000
```

Thus, the probability of a disaster for NASA (.0004) is much less than for the Air Force (.5105).

61. a. $\bar{X} = 3.72$, $s = 1.4837$
    b. $\bar{X} = 2.0866$, $s = .3947$

# CHAPTER 7    THE NORMAL PROBABILITY DISTRIBUTION

1. The actual shape of a normal distribution depends on its mean and standard deviation. Thus, there is a normal distribution, and an accompanying normal curve, for a mean of 7 and a standard deviation of 2. There is another normal curve for a mean of $25,000 and a standard deviation of $1,742, and so on.

3. a. 490 and 510, found by $500 \pm 1(10)$.
   b. 480 and 520, found by $500 \pm 2(10)$.
   c. 470 and 530, found by $500 \pm 3(10)$.

5. a. 1.25, found by:

$$z = \frac{X - \mu}{\sigma} = \frac{25 - 20}{4.0} = 1.25$$

   b. .3944, found in Appendix D.
   c. .3085, found by:

$$z = \frac{18 - 20}{4.0} = -0.5$$

Find .1915 in Appendix D for $z = 0.5$; then $.5000 - .1915 = .3085$.

7. a. .3413, found by:

$$z = \frac{\$20 - \$16.50}{\$3.50} = 1.00$$

Then find .3413 in Appendix D for $z = 1$.
   b. .1587, found by $.5000 - .3413 = .1587$.
   c. .3336, found by:

$$z = \frac{\$15.00 - \$16.50}{\$3.50} = -0.43$$

Find .1664 in Appendix D for a $z = -0.43$; then $.5000 - .1664 = .3336$.

9.  a.  .8276. First, find $z = -1.5\ [(44 - 50)/4]$ and $z = 1.25\ [(55 - 50)/4]$. The area between $-1.5$ and 0 is .4332, and the area between 0 and 1.25 is .3944, both from Appendix D. Second, adding the two areas we find that $.4332 + .3944 = .8276$.

    b.  .1056, found by $.5000 - .3944$, where $z = 1.25$.

    c.  .2029. Recall that the area for $z = 1.25$ is .3944, and the area for $z = 0.5\ [(52 - 50)/4]$ is .1915. Then subtract $.3944 - .1915$ to find .2029.

    d.  $X = 56.58$, found by adding .5000 (the area left of the mean) and then finding a $z$ value that forces 45 percent of the data to fall inside the curve. That $z$ value is 1.645. $.5000 + .4500 = .9500$. Solving for $X$: $1.645 = (X - 50)/4 = 56.58$.

11. a.  .1525, found by subtracting $.4938 - .3413$, which are the areas associated with $z$ values of 2.5 and 1, respectively.

    b.  .0062, found by $.5000 - .4938$.

    c.  .9710. Recall that the area for the $z$ value of 2.5 is .4938. Then $z = -2.00$, found by $(6.8 - 7.0)/0.1$. Then add the area for $z = 2.5$ and $z = 2$. Thus, $.4938 + .4772 = .9710$.

    d.  7.233. Find the $z$ value such that .4900 of the area is between 0 and $z$. That value is $z = 2.33$. Then solve for $X$: $2.33 = (X - 7)/0.1$, $X = 7.233$.

13. a.  .0764, found by $z = (20 - 15)/3.5 = 1.43$. Then $.5000 - .4236 = .0764$.

    b.  .9236, found by $.5000 + .4236$, where $z = 1.43$.

    c.  .1185, found by $z = (12 - 15)/3.5 = -0.86$. The area under the curve is .3051. Then $z = (10 - 15)/3.5 = -1.43$. The area is .4236. Finally, $.4236 - .3051 = .1185$.

    d.  16.84 minutes, found by solving for $X$ where $z = 0.525$. This point forces .20 of the area to fall under the curve. First multiplying $0.525 \times 3.5$ and then adding 15, we find $X = 16.84$.

15. a.  $\mu = np = 50(.25) = 12.5$
        $\sigma^2 = np(1 - p) = 12.5(1 - .25) = 9.375$
        $\sigma = \sqrt{9.375} = 3.06$

    b.  .2578, found by $(14.5 - 12.5)/3.06 = 0.65$. The area is .2422. Then $.5000 - .2422 = .2578$.

    c.  .2578, found by $(10.5 - 12.5)/3.06 = -0.65$. The area is .2422. Then $.5000 - .2422 = .2578$.

17. a.  .0655, found by $(9.5 - 6)/2.32 = 1.51$. The area is .4345. Then $.5000 - .4345 = .1401$.

    b.  .1401, found by $(8.5 - 6)/2.32 = 1.08$. The area is .1401. Then $.5000 - .3599 = .1401$.

    c.  .0746, found by $.4345 - .3599 = .0746$. This is the probability of getting exactly nine errors.

19. a.  Yes. (1) There are two mutually exclusive outcomes: overweight and not overweight. (2) It is the result of counting the number of successes (overweight members). (3) Each trial is independent. (4) The probability of .30 remains the same for each trial.

    b.  .0084, found by $\mu = np = 500(.30) = 150$. Variance $= np(1 - p) = 105$. Standard deviation $= 10.24695$, found by $\sqrt{105}$.

$$z = \frac{X - \mu}{\sigma} = \frac{174.5 - 150}{10.24695} = 2.39$$

    Area under the curve for 2.39 is .4916. Then $.5000 - .4916 = .0084$.

    c.  .8461, found by:

$$z = \frac{139.5 - 150}{10.24695} = -1.02$$

    The area between 139.5 and 150 is .3461. Adding .3461 + .5000 = .8461.

21. a.  46.41 percent, found by $z = (20.27 - 20.00)/0.15 = 1.80$. The area under the curve is .4641.

    b.  3.59 percent, found by $.5000 - .4641$.

    c.  81.85 percent, found by $.3413 + .4772$.

    d.  27.43 percent. The area for $z = 0.60$ is .2257. Subtracting, $.5000 - .2257 = .2743$.

23. a.  $-0.4$ for net sales, found by $(170 - 180)/25$, and 2.92 for employees, found by $(1,850 - 1,500)/120$.

    b.  Net sales are $-0.4$ standard deviations below the mean. Employees are 2.92 standard deviations above the mean.

    c.  65.54 percent of the aluminum fabricators have greater net sales compared with Clarion, found by $.1554 + .5000$. Only 0.18 percent have more employees than Clarion, found by $.5000 - .4982$.

25. a.  15.87 percent, found by $(15 - 20)/5 = -1.0$. The area for $-1.0$ is .3413. Then $.5000 - .3413 = .1587$.

    b.  .5403. First, the area between 18 and 20 is .1554. The area between 20 and 26 is .3849. Adding, $.1554 + .3849 = .5403$.

    c.  About one person, found by $z = (7 - 20)/5 = -2.6$, for which the area is .4953. Then $.5000 - .4953 = .0047$. Finally, $200(.0047) = 0.94$, which is about 1.

27. 60.06 percent, found by $(\$42,000 - \$40,000)/\$5,000 = 0.40$. The area under the curve for 0.40 is .1554. Similarly, the area between \$32,000 and \$40,000 is .4452. Adding, $.1554 + .4452 = .6006$.

29. a.  39.44 percent, found by $(1,970 - 1,820)/120 = 1.25$. The area for a $z$ of 1.25 is .3944.

    b.  10.56 percent, found by $.5000 - .3944$.

    c.  3.36 percent, found by $.5000 - .4664 = .0336$.

31. a.  About 578, found by solving for $X$ in the equation $1.56 = (X - 500)/50$.

    b.  About 2.28 percent. $z = -2.00$, found by $(400 - 500)/50$. The area between 400 and 500 is .4772. Then $.5000 - .4772 = .0228$.

c. About 39.93 percent. The area between 500 and 400 is .4772, and the area between 500 and 485 is .1179. Subtracting, .4772 − .1179 = .3593. About 360.

33. a. About .47 percent. $(65,200 − 60,000)/2,000 = 2.60$. Then .5000 − .4953 = .0047.

     b. About 22 trucks. $(55,000 − 60,000)/2,000 = −2.50$. Then .5000 − .4938 = .0062. Multiplying, .0062 × 3,500 = 21.7.

     c. About 2,945. $(62,000 − 60,000)/2,000 = 1.00$. Then .5000 + .3413 = .8413. Multiplying, .8413 × 3,500 = 2,944.55.

35. a. 26.43 percent, found by $(30 − 35)/8 = −0.63$. Then .5000 − .2357 = .2643.

     b. 26.43 percent, found by $(40 − 35)/8 = 0.63$. Then .5000 − .2357 = .2643.

     c. The normal distribution is continuous. Thus, the probability of an exact value is very small.

     d. About 4.26 percent. You could find the probability of 39.5 and 40.5:

$z = (39.5 − 35)/8 = 0.56,$     area is .2123

$z = (40.5 − 35)/8 = 0.69,$     area is .2549

Subtracting, .2549 − .2123 = .0426.

     e. 45.24 minutes, found by solving for $X$: $1.28 = (X − 35)/8$.

37. a. 6.55, found by solving for $\sigma$:

$$0.84 = \frac{45 − 39.5}{\sigma}$$

$$\sigma = 6.55$$

     b. .3520, found by $(42 − 39.5)/6.55$. Then .5000 − .1480 = .3520.

     c. About 50.27 yards, found by solving for $X$: $1.645 = (X − 39.5)/6.55 = 50.27$.

     d. Mean would decrease, standard deviation would increase, distribution would become negatively skewed.

39. a. .9678, found by:

$$\mu = np = 60(.64) = 38.4$$

$$\sigma^2 = np(1 − p) = 60(.64)(.36) = 13.824$$

$$\sigma = \sqrt{13.824} = 3.72.$$

Then $(31.5 − 38.4)/3.72 = −1.85$, for which the area is .4678. Then .5000 + .4678 = .9678.

     b. .0853, found by $(43.5 − 38.4)/3.72 = 1.37$, for which the area is .4147. Then .5000 − .4147 = .0853.

     c. .8084, found by $(32.5 − 38.4)/3.72 = −1.59$. The area is .4441. And $(42.5 − 38.4)/3.72 = 1.10$. The area is .3643. Then add .4441 + .3643.

     d. .0348, by finding area for $<44.0$ $(44.5 − 38.4)/3.72 = 1.64$. The area is .4495. Recall the area for

43 or less was .4147. Then .4495 − .4147 = .0348.

41. a. .8106, where $\mu = 10$, variance = 8, standard deviation = 2.8284. $z = (7.5 − 10)/2.8284 = −0.88$. The area is = .3106. Then .5000 + .3106 = .8106.

     b. .1087, found by $z = (8.5 − 10)/2.8284 = −0.53$. Then .3106 − .2019 = .1087.

     c. .2981, found by .5000 − .2019.

43. .0968, found by:

$$\mu = np = 50(.40) = 20$$

$$\sigma^2 = np(1 − p) = 50(.40)(.60) = 12$$

$$\sigma = \sqrt{12} = 3.4641$$

$z = (24.5 − 20)/3.4641 = 1.30$. The area is .4032. Then for 25 or more, .5000 − .4032 = .0968.

45. a. 36.775 minutes, found by solving for $\mu$: $1.645 = (45 − \mu)/5 = 36.775$.

     b. 28.55 minutes, found by solving for $\mu$; $1.645 = (45 − \mu)/10 = 28.55$.

     c. 55.96 percent, found by $(30 − 28.55)/10 = 0.15$. The area is .0596. Then .5000 + .0596 = .5596.

47. a. .6687, found by: $z = (2.00 − 2.80)/.40 = −2.00$, $p = .4772$. And $(3.00 − 2.80)/.40 = .50$, $p = .1915$. Then .4772 + .1915 = .6687.

     b. .0228, found by $(2.00 − 2.80)/.40 = −2.00$, $p = .5000 − .4772 = .0228$.

     c. 122, found by $z = (3.70 − 2.80)/.40 = 2.25$, $p = .5000 − .4878 = .0122$. Then $10,000 × .0122 = 122$.

     d. 3.312, found by $1.28 = (X − 2.8)/.40 = 3.312$.

49. a. 21.19 percent, found by $z = (9.00 − 9.20)/.25 = −0.80$, $p = .5000 − .2881 = .2119$

     b. Increase the mean: $\sigma = (9.00 − 9.25)/.25 = 1.00$, $p = .5000 − .3413 = .1587$. Reduce the standard deviation: $\sigma = (9.00 − 9.20)/.15 = 1.33$, $p = .5000 − .4082 = .0918$. Reducing the standard deviation is better because a smaller percent of the hams will be below the limit.

51. a. Normal. 31.56 percent, found by .5000 −.1844. Actual = 30.5 percent. Difference insignificant.

     b. 22.06 percent, found by .5000 − .2794. Not very accurate because 8 out of 200, or 4 percent actually lost money.

# CHAPTER 8   SAMPLING METHODS AND SAMPLING DISTRIBUTIONS

1. a. 303 Louisiana, 5155 S. Main, 3501 Monroe, 2652 W. Central.

     b. Answers will vary.

3. 630 Dixie, 835 S. McCord, 4624 Woodville.

5. Answers will vary.

7.   a.   6, found by the combination $_4C_2$:

$$_4C_2 = \frac{4!}{2!(4-2)!} = \frac{4 \cdot 3 \cdot 2 \cdot 1}{(2 \cdot 1)(2 \cdot 1)} = 6$$

   b.

| Sample | Values | Sum | Mean |
|--------|--------|-----|------|
| 1 | 12, 12 | 24 | 12 |
| 2 | 12, 14 | 26 | 13 |
| 3 | 12, 16 | 28 | 14 |
| 4 | 12, 14 | 26 | 13 |
| 5 | 12, 16 | 28 | 14 |
| 6 | 14, 16 | 30 | 15 |

   c.   $\mu_{\overline{X}} = \dfrac{12 + 13 + 14 + 13 + 14 + 15}{6} = 13.5$

   $\mu = \dfrac{12 + 12 + 14 + 16}{4} = 13.5$

   They are equal.

   d.   The dispersion of the population is greater than that of the sample means. The sample means vary from 12 to 15, whereas the population varies from 12 to 16.

9.   a.   6, found by 4!/2!2!.

   b.

| Test scores | Mean |
|-------------|------|
| 90, 86 | 88 |
| 90, 70 | 80 |
| 90, 80 | 85 |
| 86, 70 | 78 |
| 86, 80 | 83 |
| 70, 80 | 75 |

   c.   $\mu_{\overline{X}} = \dfrac{88 + 80 + 85 + 78 + 83 + 75}{6} = 81.5$

   $\mu = \dfrac{90 + 86 + 70 + 80}{4} = 81.5$

   They are equal.

   d.

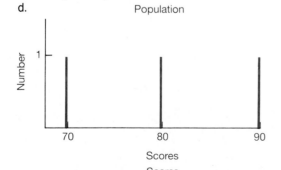

Population

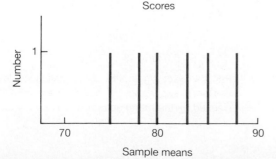

Sample means

11.   51.314 to 58.686, found by $55 \pm 2.58(10/\sqrt{49})$.

13.   a.   1.581, found by $\sigma_{\overline{X}} = \sigma/\sqrt{n} = 5/\sqrt{10} = 1.581$.

   b.   The population is normally distributed, and the population variance is known.

   c.   16.901 to 23.099, found by $20 \pm 3.099$.

15.   a.   $20. It is our best estimate of the population mean.

   b.   $18.60 to $21.40, found by $20 \pm 1.96(\$5/\sqrt{49})$.

17.   a.   8.60 gallons.

   b.   7.83 to 9.37, found by $8.60 \pm 2.58(2.30/\sqrt{60})$.

   c.   If 100 such intervals were determined, the population mean would lie in about 99 intervals.

19.   a.   .80, found by 80/100.

   b.   .7216 to .8784, found by $.80 \pm 1.96\sqrt{[(.80)(.20)]/100}$.
   If 100 such intervals were determined, the population mean would lie in about 95 intervals.

21.   a.   .625, found by 250/400.

   b.   .578 to .672, found by $.625 \pm 1.96\sqrt{[(.625)(.375)]/400}$.
   If 100 such intervals were determined, the population mean would lie in about 95 intervals.

23.   33.465 to 36.535, found by:

$$35 \pm 1.96(5/\sqrt{36})\sqrt{\frac{300 - 36}{300 - 1}}$$

   If 100 such intervals were determined, the population mean would lie in about 95 intervals.

25.   3.069 to 3.411, found by:

$$3.24 \pm 2.58(.50/\sqrt{50})\sqrt{\frac{400 - 50}{400 - 1}}$$

   If 100 such intervals were determined, the population mean would lie in about 99 intervals.

27.   97, found by $n = [(1.96 \times 10)/2]^2 = 96.04$.

29.   554, found by $n = [(1.96 \times 3)/.25]^2 = 553.19$.

31.   196, found by $n = .15(.85) \times [1.96/.05]^2 = 195.916$.

33.   a.   577, found by $n = .60(.40) \times [1.96/.04]^2 = 576.24$.

   b.   601, found by $n = .50(.50) \times [1.96/.04]^2 = 600.25$.

35.   a.   It is usually not feasible to study the entire population. Thus, if we want to infer something about a characteristic of a population, a part of the population—called a sample—is needed.

   b.   Contacting all the voters or all consumers would be too time-consuming and too costly. It is impossible to tag all the whales in the ocean for study. Checking all products for strength is destructive, and none would be available for sale.

37.   A nonprobability sample, such as a panel sample, may not give results that are representative of the popula-

tion because not every item or person has a chance of being selected for the sample.

39. The metropolitan area could be subdivided into precincts and four precincts selected for study. Suppose there are 74 mobile home parks in the area. Eight could be selected, and the persons conducting the survey would concentrate on the residents of those eight parks.

41. a. Jeanne Fiorito, Douglas Smucker, Jeanine S. Huttner, Harry Mayhew, Mark Steinmetz, and Paul Langenkamp.
   b. One randomly selected group of numbers is 05, 06, 74, 64, 66, 55, 27, 22. The members of the sample are Janet Arrowsmith, David DeFrance, Mark Zilkoski, and Larry Johnson.

43. Answers will vary.

45. a. 10, found by $5!/3!2!$.

   b.

   | Number correct | Mean | Number correct | Mean |
   |---|---|---|---|
   | 4, 3 | 3.5 | 3, 3 | 3.0 |
   | 4, 5 | 4.5 | 3, 2 | 2.5 |
   | 4, 3 | 3.5 | 5, 3 | 4.0 |
   | 4, 2 | 3.0 | 5, 2 | 3.5 |
   | 3, 5 | 4.0 | 3, 2 | 2.5 |

   c.

   | Sample mean | Frequency | Probability |
   |---|---|---|
   | 2.5 | 2 | .20 |
   | 3.0 | 2 | .20 |
   | 3.5 | 3 | .30 |
   | 4.0 | 2 | .20 |
   | 4.5 | 1 | .10 |
   | | 10 | 1.00 |

   d. $\mu_{\overline{X}} = \dfrac{3.5 + 4.5 + \cdots + 2.5}{10} = 3.4$

   $\mu = \dfrac{4 + 3 + 5 + 3 + 2}{5} = 3.4$

   The two means are equal.

   e. The population values are uniform in shape. The distribution of sample means tends toward normality.

47. A simple random sample would be appropriate, but this means that each 10-foot length would have to be numbered 1, 2, 3, . . ., 720. A faster method would be to (1) select a pipe from the first, say, 20 pipes produced and (2) select every 20th pipe produced thereafter and measure its inside diameter. Thus, the sample would include about 36 PVC pipes.

49. 6.14 years to 6.86 years, found by $6.5 \pm 1.96(1.7/\sqrt{85})$.

51. 369, found by $n = .60(1 - .60) \times (1.96/.05)^2 = 368.79$.

53. 133, found by $[(1.645 \times 14)/2]^2$.

55. a. 3.01 pounds.
   b. 3.0002 and 3.0198 pounds, found by $3.01 \pm 1.96(.03/\sqrt{36})$

   c. About 95 percent of similarly constructed intervals would include the population mean.

57. .345 to .695, found by:

$$.52 \pm 2.58 \sqrt{\frac{.52(.48)}{.50}} \sqrt{\frac{650 - 50}{650 - 1}}.$$

59. .633 and .687, found by:

$$.66 \pm 1.96 \sqrt{\frac{(.66)(.34)}{1,200}}$$

61. It is highly likely that the estimate is accurate. If we use the actual sample as $p$, the 82 percent estimate does fall within a 95 percent confidence interval:

$$.786 \pm 1.96\sqrt{[(.786)(.214)]/140}$$

$$.786 \pm .068$$

So the actual interval is from .718 to .854, and .82 is included in this interval.

63. a. 708.13, rounded up to 709, found by $.21(1 - .21)(1.96/.03)^2$.
   b. 1,068, found by $.50(.50)(1.96/.03)^2$.

65. a. $158.59 and $174.76 found by $166.67 $\pm$ 1.96 ($35.68/\sqrt{75}$)
   b. 13.78 miles and 16.00 miles, found by $14.8933 \pm 1.96(4.892/\sqrt{75})$
   c. $\overline{p} = 51/75 = .68$. Then $.68 \pm 1.96$

   $\sqrt{\left(\dfrac{(.68)(.32)}{75}\right)}$ gives 57.44 percent to 78.56 percent.

# CHAPTER 9 TESTS OF HYPOTHESES: LARGE SAMPLES

1. a. Two-tailed.
   b. Reject $H_0$ and accept $H_1$ if $z$ does not fall in the region from $-1.96$ to $1.96$. Otherwise, we fail to reject $H_0$.
   c. 1.2, found by:

   $$z = \frac{\overline{X} - \mu}{\sigma/\sqrt{n}} = \frac{49 - 50}{5/\sqrt{36}} = -1.2$$

   d. Fail to reject $H_0$.
   e. $p$-value is $2(.1151) = .2302$.

3. a. $H_0: \mu = 60,000$
      $H_1: \mu \neq 60,000$
   b. Reject $H_0$ if $z < -1.96$ or $z > 1.96$.
   c. $-0.69$, found by:

   $$z = \frac{59,500 - 60,000}{5,000/\sqrt{48}} = -0.69$$

   d. Fail to reject $H_0$ at the .05 significance level. Crosset's experience is not different from that claimed by the manufacturer. $p$-value is .4902.

5.  a.  One-tailed.
    b.  Reject $H_0$ and accept $H_1$ if $z > 1.645$.
    c.  1.2, found by:

$$z = \frac{\bar{X} - \mu}{s/\sqrt{n}} = \frac{21 - 20}{5/\sqrt{36}} = 1.2$$

    d.  Fail to reject $H_0$ at the .05 significance level.
    e.  $p$-value is .1151, found by $.5000 - .3849$.
7.  a.  $H_0: \mu = 6.8$
        $H_1: \mu < 6.8$
    b.  Reject $H_0$ if $z < -1.645$.
    c.  $-7.2$, found by:

$$z = \frac{6.2 - 6.8}{0.5/\sqrt{36}} = -7.2$$

    d.  Reject $H_0$ and conclude that the mean number of videos watched by college students is less than 6.8 at the .05 significance level.
9.  a.  Two-tailed test.
    b.  Reject $H_0$ if $z < -2.055$ or $z > 2.055$.
    c.  2.59, found by:

$$z = \frac{102 - 99}{\sqrt{\dfrac{5^2}{40} + \dfrac{6^2}{50}}} = 2.59$$

    d.  Reject $H_0$ and accept $H_1$.
    e.  $p$-value is $2(.0048) = .0096$.
11. *Step 1:* $H_0: \mu_1 = \mu_2$
        $H_1: \mu_1 < \mu_2$
    *Step 2:* The .05 significance level was chosen.
    *Step 3:* Reject $H_0$ and accept $H_1$ if $z < -1.645$.
    *Step 4:* $z = -0.94$ found by:

$$z = \frac{7.6 - 8.1}{\sqrt{\dfrac{(2.3)^2}{40} + \dfrac{(2.9)^2}{55}}} = -0.94$$

    *Step 5:* Fail to reject $H_0$. No difference in the mean length of time owner occupied his home.
13. a.  Two-tailed test, because we are trying to show that a difference exists between the two population means.
    b.  Reject $H_0$ if $z < -2.58$ or $z > 2.58$.
    c.  $-2.66$, found by:

$$z = \frac{31.4 - 34.9}{\sqrt{\dfrac{(5.1)^2}{32} + \dfrac{(6.7)^2}{49}}} = -2.66$$

    Reject $H_0$ at the .01 level. There is a difference in the mean turnover rate. $p$-value $= .0078$.
15. $z = (9{,}922 - 9{,}940)/(400/\sqrt{100}) = -0.45$. Then $.1736 + .5000 = .6736$, which is the probability of a Type II error.

17. $H_0: \mu = 16$
    $H_1: \mu > 16$. Reject $H_0$ if $z > 1.645$.
    Computed $z = 11.78$, found by:

$$z = \frac{16.05 - 16.0}{0.03/\sqrt{50}} = 11.78$$

    Reject $H_0$. The cans are being overfilled. $p$-value is .0000.
19. $H_0: \mu = 90$
    $H_1: \mu > 90$
    Reject $H_0$ if $z > 1.28$. Computed $z = 1.82$, found by:

$$z = \frac{94 - 90}{22/\sqrt{100}} = 1.82$$

    Reject $H_0$. The mean selling time has increased.
21. $H_0: \mu = 28$
    $H_1: \mu < 28$
    Reject $H_0$ if $z < -2.05$. Computed $z = -1.55$, found by:

$$z = \frac{26.9 - 28.0}{8/\sqrt{127}} = -1.55$$

    Fail to reject $H_0$. The change did not reduce the mean waiting time.
23. $H_0: \mu_1 = \mu_2$
    $H_1: \mu_1 \neq \mu_2$
    Reject $H_0$ if $z < -1.96$ or $z > 1.96$. Computed $z = -1.37$, found by:

$$z = \frac{20 - 21}{\sqrt{\dfrac{4^2}{45} + \dfrac{3^2}{50}}} = -1.37$$

    Do not reject $H_0$. There is no difference in delivery times. The $p$-value is .1706, found by $2(.5000 - .4147)$.
25. $H_0: \mu_1 = \mu_2$
    $H_1: \mu_1 < \mu_2$
    Reject $H_0$ if $z$ is $< -1.645$. Computed $z = -0.14$, found by:

$$z = \frac{\$31{,}290 - \$31{,}330}{\sqrt{\dfrac{(\$1{,}060)^2}{45} + \dfrac{(\$1{,}900)^2}{60}}} = -0.14$$

    Fail to reject $H_0$. There is no difference in the salaries.
27. $H_0: \mu = 0.12$
    $H_1: \mu < 0.12$
    Reject $H_0$ if $z < -1.645$. Computed $z = -30.0$, found by:

$$z = \frac{0.09 - 0.12}{0.03/\sqrt{900}} = -30.0$$

    Reject $H_0$. The pollution level has declined.

29.  $H_0: \mu = \$3.65$
$H_1: \mu \neq \$3.65$

Reject $H_0$ if $z$ does not fall in the range between $-1.96$ and $1.96$. Computed $z = 1.12$, found by:

$$z = \frac{3.69 - 3.65}{0.24/\sqrt{45}} = 1.12$$

Fail to reject $H_0$. There is no difference between northwestern Ohio and the rest of the United States.

31.  $H_0: \mu_1 = \mu_2$
$H_1: \mu_1 < \mu_2$
Reject $H_0$ if $z < -1.645$. Computed $z = -1.30$, found by:

$$z = \frac{345 - 351}{\sqrt{\dfrac{(21)^2}{54} + \dfrac{(28)^2}{60}}} = -1.30$$

Fail to reject $H_0$. There is not enough evidence to say that more units are produced on the afternoon shift.

33.  a.  $9.00 \pm 1.645(1/\sqrt{36}) = 9.00 \pm 0.274$, so the limits are 8.726 and 9.274.

b.  $z = (8.726 - 8.900)/(1/\sqrt{36}) = -1.04$, so the probability is $.3508 + .5000 = .8508$.

c.  $z = (9.274 - 9.300)/(1/\sqrt{36}) = -0.16$, so the probability is $.5000 - .0636 = .4364$.

35.  About 33 found by:

$$50 + 2.33\left(\frac{10}{\sqrt{n}}\right) = 55 - 0.525\left(\frac{10}{\sqrt{n}}\right)$$

$$\frac{10}{\sqrt{n}}(2.33 + 0.525) = 5$$

$$10(2.855) = 5\sqrt{n}$$

$$n = (2 \times 2.855)^2 = 32.6 \approx 33$$

37.  a.  Reject $H_0$ if $z < -1.96$ or $z > 1.96$
$z = -2.177$, found by

$$z = \frac{10{,}304 - 12{,}000}{\dfrac{11017.55}{\sqrt{200}}}$$

$p$-value is .0297

b.  Reject $H_0$ if $z < 1.96$ or $z > 1.96$. Computed $z = 3.793$. The mean sales are different from $15,000 million.

## CHAPTER 10   TESTS OF HYPOTHESES: PROPORTIONS

1.  a.  $H_0$ is rejected if $z > 1.645$.

b.  $$z = \frac{.75 - .70}{\sqrt{\dfrac{(.70)(.30)}{100}}} = \frac{.0500}{.0458} = 1.09$$

c.  $H_0$ is not rejected.

3.  a.  $H_0: p = .52$, $H_1: p > .52$
b.  $H_0$ is rejected if $z > 2.33$.

c.  $$z = \frac{.5667 - .52}{\sqrt{\dfrac{.52(.48)}{300}}} = \frac{.0467}{.0288} = 1.620$$

d.  $H_0$ is not rejected. The proportion of men driving on the Ohio Turnpike is not larger than .52.

5.  a.  $H_0: p = .90$, $H_1: p < .90$
b.  $H_0$ is rejected if $z < -1.28$.

c.  $$z = \frac{.82 - .90}{\sqrt{\dfrac{.90(.10)}{100}}} = \frac{-.08}{.03} = -2.667$$

d.  $H_0$ is rejected. The proportion of customers receiving their orders in less than 30 minutes is less than 90 percent.

7.  a.  $H_0$ is rejected if $z > 1.645$.

b.  $$\bar{p}_c = \frac{70 + 90}{100 + 150} = .64$$

c.  $$z = \frac{.70 - .60}{\sqrt{\dfrac{(.64)(.36)}{100} + \dfrac{(.64)(.36)}{150}}} = \frac{.10000}{.06197} = 1.614$$

d.  $H_0$ is not rejected.

9.  $H_0: p_1 = p_2$, $H_1: p_1 \neq p_2$. $H_0$ is rejected if $z < -1.96$ or $z > 1.96$.

$$\bar{p}_c = \frac{24 + 40}{400 + 400} = .08$$

$$z = \frac{.06 - .10}{\sqrt{\dfrac{(.08)(.92)}{400} + \dfrac{(.08)(.92)}{400}}} = \frac{-.04}{.01918} = -2.085$$

$H_0$ is rejected. The proportion infested is not the same in the two fields.

11.  $H_0: p_d = p_r$, $H_1: p_d > p_r$. $H_0$ is rejected if $z > 2.05$.

$$\bar{p}_c = \frac{168 + 200}{800 + 1{,}000} = .2044$$

$$z = \frac{.21 - .20}{\sqrt{\dfrac{(.2044)(.7956)}{800} + \dfrac{(.2044)(.7956)}{1{,}000}}} = \frac{.0100}{.0191} = 0.523$$

$H_0$ is not rejected. There is no difference in the proportion of Democrats and Republicans who favor lowering the standards.

13. $H_0: p = .60$, $H_1: p > .60$. $H_0$ is rejected if $z > 2.33$.

$$z = \frac{.70 - .60}{\sqrt{\frac{(.60)(.40)}{200}}} = \frac{.10}{.0346} = 2.887$$

$H_0$ is rejected. Ms. Dennis is correct. More than 60 percent of the accounts are more than three months old.

15. $H_0: p = .20$, $H_1: p < .20$. $H_0$ is rejected if $z < -1.645$.

$$z = \frac{.195 - .20}{\sqrt{\frac{(.20)(.80)}{2,000}}} = \frac{-.005}{.0089} = -0.56$$

$H_0$ is not rejected. We cannot conclude that less than 20 percent of the population will watch the show.

17. $H_0: p_n = p_o$, $H_1: p_n > p_o$. $H_0$ is rejected if $z > 1.645$.

$$\bar{p}_c = \frac{180 + 261}{200 + 300} = .882$$

$$z = \frac{.90 - .87}{\sqrt{\frac{(.882)(.118)}{200} + \frac{(.882)(.118)}{300}}} = \frac{.03}{.0294} = 1.019$$

$H_0$ is not rejected. There is no difference in the proportions that found relief from the new versus the old drugs.

19. $H_0: p = .40$, $H_1: p < .40$. $H_0$ is rejected if $z < -1.645$.

$$z = \frac{.38 - .40}{\sqrt{\frac{(.40)(.60)}{80}}} = \frac{-.02}{.0548} = -0.365$$

$H_0$ is not rejected. We conclude that the 2 percent difference could be due to chance. Production cutbacks are not needed.

21. $H_0: p_m = p_w$, $H_1: p_m \neq p_w$. $H_0$ is rejected if $z < -1.96$ or $z > 1.96$.

$$\bar{p}_c = \frac{70 + 72}{500 + 400} = .1578$$

$$z = \frac{.14 - .18}{\sqrt{\frac{(.1578)(.8422)}{500} + \frac{(.1578)(.8422)}{400}}} = -1.636$$

Do not reject $H_0$ because computed $z$ of $-1.636$ falls between 0 and $-1.96$. There is no difference in the proportions of men and women who smoke.

23. a. $H_0. \mu = .50$ $H_1: p > .50$. Reject $H_0$ if $z > 1.645$.

$$\bar{p} = 46/75 = .6133$$

$$z = \frac{.6133 - .50}{\sqrt{\frac{(.50)(.50)}{75}}} = 1.962$$

$H_0$ is rejected. More than half of the homes have a pool.

b. $H_0: p = .50$ $H_1: p > .50$. Reject $H_0$ if $z > 1.645$.

$$\bar{p} = 51/75 = .68$$

$$z = \frac{.68 - .50}{\sqrt{\frac{(.50)(.50)}{75}}} = 3.118$$

$H_0$ is rejected. More than half of the homes have a garage.

# CHAPTER 11   STUDENT'S $t$ TEST: SMALL SAMPLES

1. a. Reject $H_0$ if $t > 1.833$

b. $t = \dfrac{\bar{X} - \mu}{s/\sqrt{n}} = \dfrac{12 - 10}{3/\sqrt{10}} = 2.108$

c. Reject $H_0$. The mean is greater than 10.

3. $H_0: \mu = 40$
$H_1: \mu > 40$
Reject $H_0$ if $t > 1.703$.

$$t = \frac{42 - 40}{2.1/\sqrt{28}} = 5.04$$

Reject $H_0$ and conclude that the mean number of calls is greater than 40 per week.

5. $H_0: \mu = 22,100$
$H_1: \mu > 22,100$
Reject $H_0$ if $t > 1.740$

$$t = \frac{23,400 - 22,100}{1,500/\sqrt{18}} = 3.68$$

Reject $H_0$. The mean life of the spark plug is greater than 22,100 miles.

7. a. Reject $H_0$ if $t < -3.747$.

b. $\bar{X} = 17$ and $s = \sqrt{(1,495 - (85)^2/5)/(5 - 1)} = 3.536$

$$t = \frac{17 - 20}{3.536/\sqrt{5}} = -1.90$$

c. Do not reject $H_0$. We cannot conclude that the population mean is less than 20.

d. Between .05 and .10, about .065.

9. $H_0: \mu = 4.35$
   $H_1: \mu > 4.35$
   Reject $H_0$ if $t > 2.821$.

   $$t = \frac{4.368 - 4.35}{0.0339/\sqrt{10}} = 1.68$$

   Do not reject $H_0$. The additive did not increase the mean weight of the chickens.

11. a.  $H_0: \mu = 4.0$
        $H_1: \mu > 4.0$
        Reject $H_0$ if $t > 1.796$.

   $$t = \frac{4.50 - 4.0}{2.68/\sqrt{12}} = 0.65$$

   Do not reject $H_0$. The mean number of fish caught has not been shown to be greater than 4.0.

13. a.  Reject $H_0$ if $t < -2.120$ or $t > 2.120$.

   b.  $$s_p^2 = \frac{(10-1)4^2 + (8-1)5^2}{10+8-2}$$
       $$= 19.9375$$

   c.  $$t = \frac{23 - 26}{\sqrt{19.9375(1/10 + 1/8)}} = -1.416$$

   d.  Do not reject $H_0$.

15. $H_0: \mu_1 = \mu_2$
    $H_1: \mu_1 < \mu_2$
    Reject $H_0$ if $t < -2.624$.

   $$s_1^2 = \frac{55,476 - (702)^2/9}{9-1} \qquad s_2^2 = \frac{43,971 - (553)^2/7}{7-1}$$
   $$= 90 \qquad\qquad\qquad = 47.33$$

   $$s_p^2 = \frac{(9-1)(90) + (7-1)(47.33)}{9+7-2} = 71.7129$$

   $$t = \frac{78 - 79}{\sqrt{71.7129(1/9 + 1/7)}} = -0.234$$

   Do not reject $H_0$. There is no difference in the mean grades.

17. $H_0: \mu_1 = \mu_2$
    $H_1: \mu_1 > \mu_2$
    Reject $H_0$ if $t > 1.301$.

   $$t = \frac{89 - 87}{\sqrt{26.667(1/22 + 1/25)}} = 1.325$$

   Reject $H_0$. The mean pollen count in the valley is greater than in the mountains.

19. a.  Reject $H_0$ if $t > 2.353$.
    b.  $\bar{d} = 3.000$
        $s_d = 0.816$

   c.  $$t = \frac{\bar{d}}{s_d/\sqrt{n}} = \frac{3}{0.816/\sqrt{4}} = 7.353$$

   d.  Reject $H_0$. The review session was effective.

21. $H_0: \mu_d = 0$
    $H_1: \mu_d > 0$
    Reject $H_0$ if $t > 2.764$. $\bar{d} = 7.3636$, $s_d = 8.3699$.

   $$t = \frac{7.3636}{8.3699/\sqrt{11}} = 2.92$$

   Reject $H_0$. The weights have increased.

23. $H_0: \mu_d = 0$
    $H_1: \mu_d > 0$
    Reject $H_0$ if $t > 2.821$. $\bar{d} = 0.10$, $s_d = 4.28$.

   $$t = \frac{0.10}{4.28/\sqrt{10}} = 0.07$$

   Fail to reject $H_0$. There has been no reduction.

25. $H_0: \mu = 87$
    $H_1: \mu < 87$
    Reject $H_0$ if $t < -1.895$.

   $$s = \sqrt{\frac{55,244 - (664)^2/8}{8-1}} = 4.3425$$

   $$\bar{X} = \frac{664}{8} = 83.0$$

   $$t = \frac{83 - 87}{4.3425/\sqrt{8}} = -2.61$$

   Reject $H_0$. The mileage is less than advertised.

27. $H_0: \mu = 42$
    $H_1: \mu > 42$
    Reject $H_0$ if $t > 1.796$.

   $$t = \frac{51 - 42}{8/\sqrt{12}} = 3.90$$

   Reject $H_0$. The mean time for delivery is more than 42 days.

29. $H_0: \mu = 2.25$
    $H_1: \mu \neq 2.25$
    Reject $H_0$ if $t < -2.201$ or $t > 2.201$. $\bar{X} = 2.086$, $s = 0.4048$.

   $$t = \frac{2.087 - 2.25}{0.4048/\sqrt{12}} = -1.403$$

   Do not reject $H_0$. There is no difference in the amount of coffee consumed at Northwestern State compared to the national average.

31. $H_0: \mu_1 = \mu_2$
    $H_1: \mu_1 > \mu_2$
    Reject $H_0$ if $t > 2.567$

   $$s_p^2 = \frac{(8-1)(2.2638)^2 + (11-1)(2.4606)^2}{8+11-2} = 5.672$$

   $$t = \frac{10.375 - 5.636}{\sqrt{5.672(1/8 + 1/11)}} = 4.28$$

Reject $H_0$. The mean number of transactions by young adults is greater.

33. $H_0: \mu_1 = \mu_2$
$H_1: \mu_1 \neq \mu_2$
Reject $H_0$ if $t < -2.528$ or $t > 2.528$.

$$s_1^2 = 1.3333 \qquad s_2^2 = 3.0909$$

$$\overline{X}_1 = 160 \qquad \overline{X}_2 = 162 \qquad s_p^2 = 2.30$$

$$t = \frac{160 - 162}{\sqrt{2.30(1/10 + 1/12)}} = -3.08$$

Reject $H_0$. The mean ratings are not the same.

35. $H_0: \mu_d = 0$
$H_1: \mu_d < 0$
Reject $H_0$ if $t < -2.998$. $\overline{d} = -2.50$, $s_d = 2.928$.

$$t = \frac{-2.5}{2.928/\sqrt{8}} = -2.42$$

Do not reject $H_0$. The mean number of accidents has not changed.

37. $H_0: \mu = 3.5$, $H_1: \mu < 3.5$. Reject $H_0$ if $t < -1.746$.

$$t = -4.01, \text{ found by } \frac{2.9553 - 3.5}{.55955/\sqrt{16}}$$

Reject $H_0$. Games last less than 3.5 hours on the average.

39. a. $H_0: \mu_1 = \mu_2$, $H_1: \mu_1 \neq \mu_2$. Reject $H_0$ if $t < 2.00$ or $t > 2.00$. Computed $t = -2.817$ so we reject $H_0$. The mean selling price of a home with a pool is different from a home without a pool.
b. $t = 5.680$. Homes with a garage cost more.
c. $H_0: \mu_1 = \mu_2$, $H_1: \mu_1 \neq \mu_2$. Reject $H_0$ if $t < -2.060$ or $t > 2.060$
$s_p^2 = 924.94$, $t = -2.042$. $H_0$, therefore, is not rejected. The mean selling price in Township 1 and Township 2 is the same.

# CHAPTER 12   ANALYSIS OF VARIANCE

1. 9.01
3. Reject $H_0$ if $F > 10.5$, where $df$ in the numerator is 7 and is 5 in the denominator. Computed $F = 2.04$, found by:

$$F = \frac{s_1^2}{s_2^2} = \frac{(10)^2}{(7)^2} = 2.04$$

Do not reject $H_0$. There is no difference in the variation of the two populations.

5. $H_0: \sigma_1^2 = \sigma_2^2$
$H_1: \sigma_1^2 \neq \sigma_2^2$

Reject $H_0$ where $F > 3.10$. (3.10 is about halfway between 3.14 and 3.07.) Computed $F = 1.44$, found by:

$$F = \frac{(12)^2}{(10)^2} = 1.44$$

Do not reject $H_0$. There is no difference in the variation of the two populations.

7. a. $H_0: \mu_1 = \mu_2 = \mu_3 = \mu_4$
$H_1$: The treatment means are not the same.
b. Reject $H_0$ if $F > 3.49$.
c. SST $= 63.19$, SSE $= 13.75$, and SS total $= 76.94$.
d.

| Source | SS | df | MS | F |
|---|---|---|---|---|
| Treatment | 63.19 | 3 | 21.06 | 18.38 |
| Error | 13.75 | 12 | 1.15 | |

e. Reject $H_0$: $18.38 > 3.49$.

9. $H_0: \mu_1 = \mu_2 = \mu_3$; $H_1$: not all treatment means are the same. $H_0$ is rejected if $F > 4.26$.

$$\text{SS total} = 20{,}783 - \frac{(495)^2}{12} = 364.25$$

$$\text{SST} = \frac{(142)^2}{4} + \frac{(164)^2}{4} + \frac{(189)^2}{4} - \frac{(495)^2}{12} = 276.5$$

$$\text{SSE} = 364.25 - 276.50 = 87.75$$

| Source | SS | df | MS | F |
|---|---|---|---|---|
| Treatment | 276.50 | 2 | 138.25 | 14.18 |
| Error | 87.75 | 9 | 9.75 | |
| Total | 364.25 | 11 | | |

Since $14.18 > 4.26$, $H_0$ is rejected. The mean incomes differ.

11. a. $H_0: \mu_1 = \mu_2 = \mu_3$
$H_1$: Not all means are the same.
b. Reject $H_0$ if $F > 4.26$.
c. SST $= 107.20$, SSE $= 9.47$, SS total $= 116.67$.
d.

| Source | SS | df | MS | F |
|---|---|---|---|---|
| Treatment | 107.20 | 2 | 53.600 | 50.96 |
| Error | 9.47 | 9 | 1.052 | |
| Total | 116.67 | 11 | | |

e. Since $50.96 > 4.26$, $H_0$ is rejected. At least one of the means differs.
f. $\overline{X}_1 - \overline{X}_2 \pm t\sqrt{\text{MSE}(1/n_1 + 1/n_2)}$

$$= (9.667 - 2.20) \pm 2.262\sqrt{1.052(1/3 + 1/5)}$$

$$= 7.467 \pm 1.69 = [5.777, 9.157]$$

Yes, we conclude that treatments 1 and 2 are different.

13. $H_0: \mu_1 = \mu_2 = \mu_3 = \mu_4$; $H_1$: Not all means are equal. $H_0$ is rejected if $F > 3.71$.

$$SS\ total = 2{,}444 - \frac{(182)^2}{14} = 78.00$$

$$SST = \frac{(48)^2}{4} + \frac{(46)^2}{4} + \frac{(46)^2}{3} + \frac{(42)^2}{3}$$

$$-\frac{(182)^2}{14} = 32.33$$

$$SSE = 78.00 - 32.33 = 45.67$$

| Source | SS | df | MS | F |
|---|---|---|---|---|
| Treatment | 32.33 | 3 | 10.77 | 2.36 |
| Error | 45.67 | 10 | 4.567 | |
| Total | 78.00 | 13 | | |

Since 2.36 is less than 3.71, $H_0$ is not rejected. There is no difference in the mean number of weeks.

15. a. $H_0: \mu_1 = \mu_2$
   $H_1$: Not all treatment means are equal.
   b. Reject $H_0$ if $F > 18.5$.
   c. $H_0: \mu_1 = \mu_2 = \mu_3$
   $H_1$. Not all block means are equal. $H_0$ is rejected if $F > 19.0$.
   d. $$SST = \frac{(127)^2}{3} + \frac{(92)^2}{3} - \frac{(219)^2}{6} = 204.167$$

   $$SSB = \frac{(77)^2}{2} + \frac{(63)^2}{2} + \frac{(79)^2}{2} - \frac{(219)^2}{6} = 76$$

   $$SS\ total = 8{,}283 - (219)^2/6 = 289.5$$

   $$SSE = 289.5 - 204.167 - 76 = 9.333$$

   e.
   | Source | SS | df | MS | F |
   |---|---|---|---|---|
   | Treatment | 204.167 | 1 | 204.167 | 43.75 |
   | Blocks | 76.000 | 2 | 38.000 | 8.14 |
   | Error | 9.333 | 2 | 4.667 | |
   | Total | 289.5000 | 5 | | |

   f. For treatments, $43.75 > 18.5$, so reject $H_0$. There is a difference in the treatments. For blocks, $8.14 < 19.0$, so fail to reject $H_0$. There is no difference among blocks.

17.

| For treatments | For blocks |
|---|---|
| $H_0: \mu_1 = \mu_2 = \mu_3$ | $H_0: \mu_1 = \mu_2 = \mu_3 = \mu_4 = \mu_5$ |
| $H_1$: Not all means equal | $H_1$: Not all means equal |
| Reject if $F > 4.46$ | Reject if $F > 3.84$ |

SS total = 139.73, SST = 62.53, SSB = 33.73, SSE = 43.47.

| Source | SS | df | MS | F |
|---|---|---|---|---|
| Treatment | 62.53 | 2 | 31.265 | 5.75 |
| Blocks | 33.73 | 4 | 8.4325 | 1.55 |
| Error | 43.47 | 8 | 5.4338 | |
| Total | 139.73 | | | |

There is a difference by shifts not by employee.

19. $H_0: \mu_1 = \mu_2 = \mu_3$; $H_1$: Not all means are equal. $H_0$ is rejected if $F > 3.89$.
SS total = 37.73, SST = 26.13, SSE = 11.60.

| Source | SS | df | MS | F |
|---|---|---|---|---|
| Treatment | 26.13 | 2 | 13.067 | 13.52 |
| Error | 11.60 | 12 | 0.967 | |
| Total | 37.73 | 14 | | |

Reject $H_0$ since $13.52 > 3.89$. There is a difference in the mean weight loss among the three diets.

21. a. $H_0: \mu_1 = \mu_2 = \mu_3$; $H_1$: Not all means are equal. $H_0$ is rejected if $F > 3.68$.

   $$SS\ total = 16{,}608 - \frac{(542)^2}{18} = 287.7778$$

   $$SST = \frac{(233)^2}{7} + \frac{(167)^2}{6} + \frac{(142)^2}{5} - \frac{(542)^2}{18}$$

   $$= 116.3187$$

   $$SSE = 287.7778 - 116.3187 = 171.4591$$

   $F = 5.09$. Therefore, $H_0$ is rejected because $5.09 > 3.68$. Perfectionism scores differ depending on the size of the city.

   b. Yes, because both endpoints are positive:

   $$(33.29 - 28.4) \pm 2.131\sqrt{11.43(1/7 + 1/5)} =$$
   $$0.67\ and\ 9.11$$

   The mean perfectionism score for those from a rural background differs, from the score for those from urban areas.

23.
| Source | SS | df | MS | F |
|---|---|---|---|---|
| Treatment | 320 | 2 | 160 | 8.00 |
| Error | 180 | 9 | 20 | |
| Total | 500 | 11 | | |

   a. 3
   b. 12
   c. 4.26
   d. $H_0: \mu_1 = \mu_2 = \mu_3$; $H_1$: Not all means are equal.
   e. $H_0$ is rejected. The treatment means differ.

25. a. Recall that $\bar{X} = \Sigma X/n$, so $\bar{X}(n) = \Sigma X$. For the first treatment $\bar{X}(n) = 51.32(10)$, so $\Sigma X = 513.2$. SST is 300.65, found by:

   $$SST = \frac{(513.2)^2}{10} + \frac{(446.4)^2}{10} + \frac{(472.0)^2}{10} + \frac{(508.5)^2}{10} - \frac{(1{,}940.1)^2}{40}$$
   $$= 300.645$$

   b. $650.750 - 300.645 = 350.105$

   c.
   | Source | SS | df | MS | F |
   |---|---|---|---|---|
   | Treatment | 300.645 | 3 | 100.215 | 10.304 |
   | Error | 350.105 | 36 | 9.725 | |
   | Total | 650.750 | | | |

d.    10.304 > 2.89, so reject $H_0$. There is a difference in the treatment means.

e.    $(51.32 - 50.85) \pm 2.03\sqrt{9.725(1/10 + 1/10)}$
      $= 0.470 \pm 2.831$
      $= [-2.361, 3.301]$

We cannot conclude that the number of minutes of music differs between station 1 and station 4.

27.    SS total = 22.59, SST = 3.92, SSB = 10.21, SSE = 8.46.

| For cars | For gasoline |
|---|---|
| $H_0: \mu_1 = \mu_2 = \mu_3$ | $H_0: \mu_1 = \mu_2 = \mu_3 = \mu_4$ |
| $H_1$: Means not equal | $H_1$: Means not equal |
| $H_0$ is rejected if $F > 5.14$ | $H_0$ is rejected if $F > 4.76$ |

| Source | SS | df | MS | F |
|---|---|---|---|---|
| Treatment | 3.92 | 2 | 1.96 | 1.39 |
| Blocks | 10.21 | 3 | 3.40 | 2.41 |
| Error | 8.46 | 6 | 1.41 | |
| Total | 22.59 | 11 | | |

a.    There is no difference among the types of gasoline because 2.41 is less than 4.76.
b.    There is no difference among the cars because 1.39 is less than 5.14.

29.

| Source | SS | df | MS | F |
|---|---|---|---|---|
| Treatment | 31,533 | 3 | 10,511 | 2.86 |
| Blocks | 35,403 | 5 | 7,081 | 1.93 |
| Error | 55,034 | 15 | 3,669 | |
| | 121,969 | | | |

a.    $H_0: \mu_1 = \mu_2 = \mu_3 = \mu_4$
      $H_1$: Not all treatment means are equal.
      Reject $H_0$ if $F > 3.29$. Fail to reject $H_0$ because 2.86 < 3.29.
b.    $H_0: \mu_1 = \mu_2 = \mu_3 = \mu_4 = \mu_5 = \mu_6$
      $H_1$: Not all block means are equal.
      Reject $H_0$ if $F > 2.90$. Fail to reject $H_0$ because 1.93 < 2.90.

31.    $H_0: \mu_1 = \mu_2 = \mu_3$. $H_1$: At least one mean differs. Critical value of $F = 3.44$.
      From MINITAB:

ANALYSIS OF VARIANCE

| Source | df | SS | MS | F |
|---|---|---|---|---|
| Factor | 2 | 3872 | 1936 | 10.18 |
| Error | 22 | 4182 | 190 | |
| Total | 24 | 8054 | | |

Since the computed value of 10.18 exceeds the critical value, the null hypothesis is rejected and the alternate is accepted. At least one mean is different. The mean salary for those with high school education or less is $49,000. It is $74,670 for those with an undergraduate degree and $78,330 for those with a master's degree

or more. The salary for those with only high school differs from each of the other groups. The salaries for those with college work do not differ. The confidence interval for the difference between high school and undergraduate is computed as follows:

$$(49.00 - 74.67) \pm 2.074\sqrt{190\left(\frac{1}{7} + \frac{1}{9}\right)}$$
$$= -25.67 \pm 14.41$$

for $\overline{X}_1$ and $\overline{X}_3$: $-29.333 \pm 14.41$. So, this pair differs.

33.    $H_0: \mu_1 = \mu_2 = \mu_3 = \mu_4 = \mu_5$. $H_1$: At least one mean differs. $H_0$ is rejected if computed $F > 3.78$.

ANALYSIS OF VARIANCE

| Source | df | SS | MS | F |
|---|---|---|---|---|
| Factor | 4 | 2.68 | 0.67 | 0.11 |
| Error | 45 | 281.40 | 6.25 | |
| Total | 49 | 284.08 | | |

The null hypothesis is not rejected. There is no difference in the mean ages.

35.    $H_0: \mu_1 = \mu_2 = \mu_3$. $H_1$: Not all treatment means are equal. Reject if $F > 3.00$. Computed $F = 12.046$. Reject $H_0$.

# CHAPTER 13    SIMPLE CORRELATION ANALYSIS

1.

| X | Y | X² | XY | Y² |
|---|---|---|---|---|
| 4 | 4 | 16 | 16 | 16 |
| 5 | 6 | 25 | 30 | 36 |
| 3 | 5 | 9 | 15 | 25 |
| 6 | 7 | 36 | 42 | 49 |
| 10 | 7 | 100 | 70 | 49 |
| 28 | 29 | 186 | 173 | 175 |

$$r = \frac{5(173) - (28)(29)}{\sqrt{[5(186) - (28)^2][5(175) - (29)^2]}}$$
$$= \frac{53}{\sqrt{(146)(34)}} = .75$$

The .75 coefficient indicates a rather strong positive correlation between X and Y.

3.    a.    Sales.
      b.

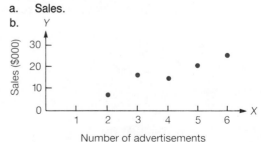

Number of advertisements

c.   Yes. There is a strong positive correlation.
d.   .93
e.   .93 indicates a strong positive correlation be-
     tween the number of times the advertisement was
     aired and sales.

5.  a.  Efficiency rating.
    b.

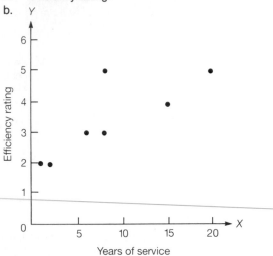

Years of service

c.   There appears to be a weak positive correlation.
d.   .35, found by:

$$\frac{8(254) - (61)(30)}{\sqrt{[8(795) - (61)^2][8(128) - (30)^2]}}$$

e.   .35 indicates a weak relationship.

7.  $r^2 = (.75)^2 = .56$
    $1 - r^2 = 1 - .56 = .44$

9.  a.  $r^2 = (.93)^2 = .86$
        $1 - r^2 = 1 - .86 = .14$
    b.  The coefficient of determination of .86 is the
        proportion of the variation in sales explained by
        the number of advertisements; .14 is the propor-
        tion of the variation in sales not explained by the
        number of advertisements.

11. a.  $r^2 = (.35)^2 = .12$
        $1 - r^2 = 1 - .12 = .88$
    b.  The coefficient .12 is the proportion of the varia-
        tion in the efficiency rating that is accounted for by
        years of service; .88 is the proportion of the
        variation not accounted for by years of service.

13. Reject $H_0$ if $t > 1.812$.

$$t = \frac{.32\sqrt{12 - 2}}{\sqrt{1 - (.32)^2}} = 1.07$$

Do not reject $H_0$.

15. $H_0: \rho = 0$
    $H_1: \rho > 0$

Reject $H_0$ if $t > 2.552$.

$$t = \frac{.78\sqrt{20 - 2}}{\sqrt{1 - (.78)^2}} = 5.28$$

Reject $H_0$. There is a positive correlation between
gallons sold and the pump price.

17. a.

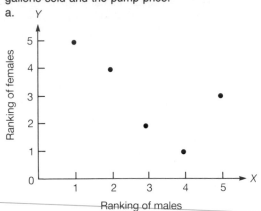

Ranking of males

b.   $-.70$, found by:

$$1 - \frac{(6)(34)}{5(5^2 - 1)}$$

There is a rather strong, but inverse, relationship.

19. a.  $r_s = -.488$, found by:

$$r_s = 1 - \frac{6(245.5)}{10(10^2 - 1)}$$

b.   There is a moderate, but inverse, relationship.

21. a.  $r_s$ is a sample statistic.

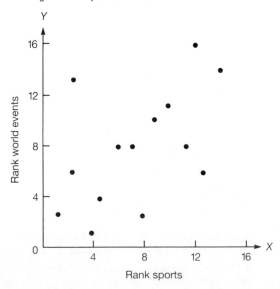

Rank sports

b.   .49, found by:

$$1 - \frac{6(234)}{14[(14)^2 - 1]}$$

c.   No, the correlation in the population is not 0. Computed $t = 1.95$, found by:

$$.49\sqrt{\frac{14 - 2}{1 - (.49)^2}}$$

Since 1.95 lies beyond the critical value of 1.782 (from Appendix F), the null hypothesis that the rank correlation in the population is 0 is rejected at the .05 level.

23.   a.   $r = .589$, found by MINITAB.
      b.   $r^2 = .347$
      c.   $H_0: \rho = 0$
           $H_1: \rho > 0$
           Reject $H_0$ if $t > 1.860$.

$$t = \frac{.589\sqrt{10 - 2}}{\sqrt{1 - .347}} = 2.06$$

Reject $H_0$. Larger families spend more money on food.

25.   $H_0: \rho = 0$
      $H_1: \rho < 0$
      Reject $H_0$ if $t < -1.701$.

$$t = \frac{-.45\sqrt{30 - 2}}{\sqrt{1 - .2025}} = -2.67$$

Reject $H_0$. There is a negative correlation between the selling price and the number of miles driven.

27.   a.   $r = .181$, found by MINITAB.
      b.   $r^2 = .0328$

29.   a.   $r = .291$
      b.   $H_0: \rho = 0$
           $H_1: \rho > 0$
           Reject $H_0$ if $t > 1.684$.

$$t = \frac{.291\sqrt{45 - 2}}{\sqrt{1 - .085}} = 1.995$$

Reject $H_0$. Positive correlation exists between age and GPA.

31.   a.

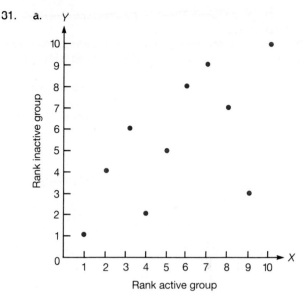

b.   There is a moderately strong relationship.
c.   .62, found by

$$1 - \frac{(6)(62)}{10[(10)^2 - 1]}$$

d.   At the .01 level we do not reject $H_0$ because .62 is less than .746. We conclude that the correlation is 0. At the .05 level we reject $H_0$ because .62 is greater than .564. We conclude that the rank correlation in the population is not 0.

e.   This illustrates that we accept $H_0$ at one level (.01), but we reject $H_0$ at the .05 level. The level of significance should be chosen before the experiment is conducted.

33.   The correlation of calls and orders is .956. There is extremely high correlation between the number of calls and the amount of purchase orders. Using the hypothesis-testing procedure, $H_0: \rho = 0$, $H_1: \rho > 0$. $H_0$ is rejected if $t > 1.734$ ($df = 18$).

$$t = \frac{.956\sqrt{20 - 2}}{\sqrt{1 - (.956)^2}} = 13.83$$

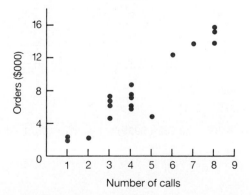

$H_0$ is rejected. There is positive correlation in the population.

35. a. The correlation between sales and profit is .681. $t = 13.09$. We conclude that sales and profit are related.

  b. The correlation between profit and share price is $-.011$. Do not reject the null hypothesis.

  c. Profit and value is .86. Otherwise, all other correlations are weak.

# CHAPTER 14   SIMPLE REGRESSION ANALYSIS

1. a. $Y' = 3.77 + 0.363X$, found by:

| X | Y | X² | XY | Y² |
|---|---|---|---|---|
| 4 | 4 | 16 | 16 | 16 |
| 5 | 6 | 25 | 30 | 36 |
| 3 | 5 | 9 | 15 | 25 |
| 6 | 7 | 36 | 42 | 49 |
| 10 | 7 | 100 | 70 | 49 |
| 28 | 29 | 186 | 173 | 175 |

$$b = \frac{5(173) - (28)(29)}{5(186) - (28)^2} \qquad a = \frac{29}{5} - (0.363)\frac{28}{5}$$

$$= \frac{53}{146} \qquad\qquad = 3.767$$

$$= 0.363$$

  b. 6.308, found by $Y' = 3.767 + 0.363(7)$.

3. a. Hours $= 1.33 + 0.667$(Rooms), found by MINITAB.

  b. 5.333

5. a. 0.9929, found by:

$$s_{y\cdot x} = \sqrt{\frac{175 - 3.767(29) - 0.363(173)}{5 - 2}}$$

  b. $Y' \pm 1s_{y\cdot x} = Y' \pm 1(0.9929)$

7. a. 0.913, found by:

$$s_{y\cdot x} = \sqrt{\frac{584 - 1.33(74) - 0.667(718)}{10 - 2}}$$

  b. $Y' \pm 2(0.913) = Y' \pm 1.826$

9. a.

$$6.308 \pm (3.182)(0.9929)\sqrt{0.2 + \frac{(7 - 5.6)^2}{186 - (784/5)}}$$

$$= 6.308 \pm 1.633$$

$$= [4.675, 7.941]$$

  b. $6.308 \pm (3.182)(.9929)\sqrt{1 + 1/5 + .0671}$

$$= 6.308 \pm 3.556$$

$$= [2.652, 9.864]$$

11. a. [4.294, 6.373], found by MINITAB.

  b. [2.985, 7.682], found by MINITAB.

13. Coefficient of correlation $r = .8944$, found by:

$$\frac{(5)(340) - (50)(30)}{\sqrt{[(5)(600) - (50)^2][(5)(200) - (30)^2]}}$$

Then, $(.8944)^2 = .80$, the coefficient of determination.

15. a. Efficiency rating.

  b.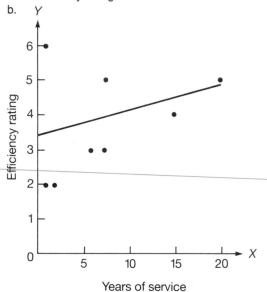

  c. Some, but a rather weak relationship.

  d. $Y' = a + bX = 3.166352 + 0.076544X$

$$b = \frac{8(254) - 61(30)}{8(795) - (61)^2} = 0.076544$$

$$a = \frac{30}{8} - 0.076544\left(\frac{61}{8}\right) = 3.166352$$

  e. 3.778704, found by $Y' = 3.166352 + 0.076544(8)$.

  f.

| X | Y' |
|---|---|
| 0 | 3.166352 |
| 6 | 3.625616 |
| 10 | 3.931792 |

17. Problem solved by MINITAB:

  a. Amount spent $= 60.4 + 11.3$(Size)

  b. 20.818, found by

$$s_{y\cdot x} = \sqrt{\frac{SSE}{n - 2}} = \sqrt{\frac{3,467.2}{8}}$$

  c. $105.46

  d. The 95 percent confidence interval for the mean amount spent by a family of four is $89.02 to $121.90.

  e. For a particular family of four: $54.70 to $156.22.

19. a. 2.357, found by:

$$\sqrt{\frac{SSE}{n-2}} = \sqrt{\frac{100}{20-2}}$$

b. $r^2 = .75$, found by:

$$r^2 = 1 - \frac{SSE}{SS\ total} = 1 - \frac{100}{400}$$

c. $-.87$, found by $\sqrt{.75} = \pm.87$. Use the negative sign because the sign of the slope is negative.

21. a. 25.08, found by $17.08 + 0.16(50)$

b. [10.92, 39.24], found by:

$$25.08 \pm 3.182(4.05) \sqrt{1 + 1/5 + \frac{(50 - 42)^2}{9,850 - 210^2/5}}$$

$$= 25.08 \pm 14.48$$

$$= [10.60, 39.56]$$

23. Problem solved by MINITAB:

a. Price = $10.7 + 0.00302$(Size)

b. $r^2 = .217$. No. By using size of the offering as the independent variable, the regression equation explains only 21.7 percent of the variation in price per share.

25. a.

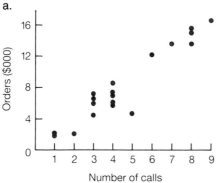

b. Using MINITAB:

```
MTB > regr c2 1 c1;
SUBC> predict 5.
```

The regression equation is

```
Orders = -0.105 + 1.85 Calls
Predictor    Coef   Stdev  t-ratio     p
Constant  -0.1046  0.6693   -0.16  0.878
Calls      1.8476  0.1331   13.89  0.000
         s = 1.450    R-sq = 91.5%
         R-sq(adj) = 91.0%
```

c. $Y' = -0.105 + 1.85(5) = 9.145$

d. $9.145 \pm (2.101)(1.450) \sqrt{1 + \dfrac{1}{20} + \dfrac{(5-4.4)^2}{506 - (88)^2/20}}$

$$= 9.145 \pm 3.126$$

e. About 91.5 percent of the variation in orders is explained by numbers of calls.

27. a. $Y' = 197.2238 + .03795\ X$ when $X = 12,000$,
$Y' = 652.6624$ for mean, $652.6624 \pm 81.828$ for individual, $652.6624 \pm 1158.05$

b. $Y' = 621.05 - .0155\ X$
$s_{y\cdot x} = 804.3\ r^2 = 0.0$
for mean: [508.2, 773.0]
for individual: [−969.9, 2211.1]
Caution: The $7900 share price for company #60 distorts the analysis.

# CHAPTER 15   MULTIPLE REGRESSION AND CORRELATION

1. a. Multiple regression equation.
   b. The $y$-intercept.
   c. $374,748, found by:

$$Y' = 64,100 + 0.394(796,000) + 9.6(6,940) - 11,600(6.0)$$

3. a. 465.256, found by:

$$Y' = -16.24 + 0.017(18)$$
$$+ 0.0028(26,500) + 42(3)$$
$$+ 0.0012(156,000)$$
$$+ 0.19(141) + 26.8(2.5)$$

b. Two more social activities. Income added only 28 to the index; social activities added 53.6.

5. a. $28,000 a day.
   b. .58, found by

$$R^2 = \frac{SSR}{SS\ total} = \frac{3,050}{5,250}$$

c. 9.20, found by $\sqrt{84.62}$.

d. $H_0$ is rejected if $F > 2.97$ (approximately).

$$\text{Computed } F = \frac{762.50}{84.62} = 9.01$$

$H_0$ is rejected. At least one regression coefficient is not zero.

e. If computed $t$ is to the left of $-2.056$ or to the right of 2.056, the null hypothesis in each of these cases is rejected. Computed $t$ for $X_2$ and $X_3$ exceed the critical value. Thus, "population" and "advertising expenses" should be retained and "number of competitors," $X_1$, dropped.

7. $n = 40$

b.   4

c.   $R^2 = \dfrac{750}{1,250} = .60$

d.   $s_{y.1234} = \sqrt{500/35} = 3.78$

e.   $H_0: \beta_1 = \beta_2 = \beta_3 = \beta_4 = 0$
$H_1:$ not all the $\beta_i$s are zero.
$H_0$ is rejected if $F > 2.65$.

$$F = \dfrac{750/4}{500/35} = 13.125$$

$H_0$ is rejected. At least one $\beta_i$ does not equal zero.

9.   a.   $n = 26$
b.   $R^2 = 100/140 = .71$
c.   1.41, found by $\sqrt{2}$
d.   $H_0: \beta_1 = \beta_2 = \beta_3 = \beta_4 = \beta_5 = 0$
$H_1:$ Not all the $\beta$s are 0.
$H_0$ is rejected if $F > 2.71$.
Computed $F = 10.0$. Reject $H_0$. At least one regression coefficient is not zero.
e.   $H_0$ is rejected in each case if $t < -2.086$ or $t > 2.086$. $X_1$ and $X_5$ should be dropped.

11.   a.   The strongest correlation is between GPA and legal. No problem with multicollinearity.

b.   $R^2 = \dfrac{4.3595}{5.0631} = .861$

c.   $H_0$ is rejected if $F > 5.41$.
$$F = \dfrac{1.4532}{0.1407} = 10.33$$

$H_0$ is rejected. At least one coefficient is not zero.

d.   Any $H_0$ is rejected if $t < -2.571$ or $t > 2.571$. It appears that only GPA is significant.

e.   $R^2 = \dfrac{4.2061}{5.0631} = .831$

$R^2$ has been reduced only .03,

f.   The residuals appear slightly skewed (positive) but acceptable.

g.   There does not seem to be a problem with the plot.

13.   a.   Using MINITAB, the correlation matrix is:

|       | cars  | adv   | sales |
|-------|-------|-------|-------|
| adv   | 0.808 |       |       |
| sales | 0.872 | 0.537 |       |
| city  | 0.639 | 0.713 | 0.389 |

Size of sales force (.872) has strongest correlation with cars sold. Fairly strong relationship between location of dealership and advertising (.713), which could be a problem.

b.

```
The regression equation is
cars = 31.1 + 2.15 adv + 5.01
sales + 5.67 city
```

$$Y' = 31.1 + 2.15(15) + 5.01(20) + 5.67(1)$$
$$= 169.22$$

c.   $H_0: \beta_1 = \beta_2 = \beta_3 = 0$; $H_1:$ Not all $\beta$s are 0. Reject $H_0$ if computed $F > 4.07$.

Analysis of Variance

| Source     | DF | SS     | MS     |
|------------|----|--------|--------|
| Regression | 3  | 5504.4 | 1834.8 |
| Error      | 8  | 420.2  | 52.5   |
| Total      | 11 | 5924.7 |        |

$F = 1,834.8/52.5 = 34.95$. Reject $H_0$. At least one regression coefficient is not 0.

d.

| Predictor | Coef   | Stdev  | t-ratio | P     |
|-----------|--------|--------|---------|-------|
| Constant  | 31.13  | 13.40  | 2.32    | 0.049 |
| adv       | 2.1516 | 0.8049 | 2.67    | 0.028 |
| sales     | 5.0140 | 0.9105 | 5.51    | 0.000 |
| city      | 5.665  | 6.332  | 0.89    | 0.397 |

$H_0$ is rejected in all cases if $t < -2.306$ or if $t > 2.306$. Advertising and sales force should be retained, and city dropped. (Note that dropping city removes the problem with multicollinearity.)

e.   The new output is

```
The regression equation is
cars = 25.3 + 2.62 adv + 5.02 sales
```

| Predictor | Coef   | Stdev  | t-ratio |
|-----------|--------|--------|---------|
| Constant  | 25.30  | 11.57  | 2.19    |
| adv       | 2.6187 | 0.6057 | 4.32    |
| sales     | 5.0233 | 0.9003 | 5.58    |

$s = 7.167$   $R\text{-}sq = 92.2\%$
$R\text{-}sq(adj) = 90.5\%$

Analysis of Variance

| Source     | DF | SS     | MS     |
|------------|----|--------|--------|
| Regression | 2  | 5462.4 | 2731.2 |
| Error      | 9  | 462.3  | 51.4   |
| Total      | 11 | 5924.7 |        |

f.

```
Stem-and-leaf of C12    N = 12
Leaf Unit = 1.0
  1    -1   6
  1    -1
  2    -0   5
  5    -0   110
 (5)    0   01224
  2     0   58
```

The normality assumption is reasonable.

g.

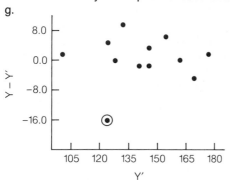

The circled value could be a problem. However, with a small sample the residual plot is acceptable.

15. a. Using MINITAB:

```
The regression equation is
profit = 965 + 2.87 workers + 6.8 divid +
0.287 inv
```

$2,461.1, found by

$$y' = 965 + 2.87(220) + 6.8(64) + 0.287(1,500).$$

b.

```
Analysis of Variance

Source       DF      SS        MS
Regression    3  45510096  15170032
Error        12  12215892   1017911
    Total    15  57725984
```

$$F = \frac{15{,}170{,}032}{1{,}017{,}991} = 14.9$$

$H_0$ is rejected because computed $F$ of 14.9 is greater than the critical value of 3.49. At least one of the regression coefficients is not zero.

c. $H_0: \beta_1 = 0 \quad \beta_2 = 0 \quad \beta_3 = 0$
$H_1: \beta_1 \neq 0 \quad \beta_2 \neq 0 \quad \beta_3 \neq 0$
The $H_0$s are rejected if $t < -2.179$ or $t > 2.179$. Both workers and dividends are not significant variables. Inventory is significant. Stepwise suggests inventory and workers be used.

d.

```
The regression equation is
profit = 1135 + 3.26 workers + 0.310 inv

Predictor    Coef     Stdev    t-ratio
Constant    1134.8    418.6      2.71
Workers      3.258    1.434      2.27
inv          0.3099   0.1033     3.00

  s = 986.7  R-sq = 78.1%
  R-sq(adj) = 74.7%
```

```
Analysis of Variance

  Source      DF       SS          MS
Regression     2   45070624    22535312
Error         13   12655356      973489
    Total     15   57725968
```

e.

```
MTB > hist c12

Histogram of C12    N = 16

Midpoint    Count

 -1500        1     .
 -1000        3     ...
  -500        1     .
     0        6     ......
   500        2     ..
  1000        2     ..
  1500        0
  2000        1     .
```

f.

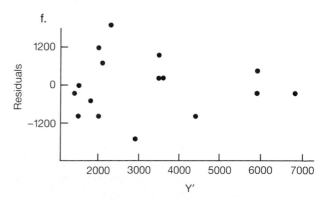

The plot of the residuals is acceptable.

17. a. Regression equation is:

Price = −8.9 + 3.90 bedrooms + 0.0500 size + 11.9 pool − 1.15 distance + 25.7 garage + 21.9 baths

b. $s = 22.24$, $R - sq = 64.3\%$, $R - sq(adj) = 61.2\%$

c. Reject $H_0$ if $F > 2.24$. Computed $F$ is 20.42. Reject $H_0$. Not all coefficients are 0.

d.  Reject $H_0$ if $t < -2.000$ or $t > 2.000$ computed $t = 1.85$ for bedrooms so we accept $H_0$. Reject all others.

e.  Regression equation is:

Price $= -29.3 + .0.0652$ size $- 1.28$ distance $+ 27.7$ garage $+ 26.7$ baths

19.  a.  Fraction $= 0.229 + 2.39$ average $+ 0.000843$ $HR - 0.100$ ERA $+ 0.000372$ SB $- 0.000849E$

b.  $s = 0.03410$, $R - sq = 73.9\%$, $R - sq(adj) = 67.4\%$

c.  $H_0$: all regression coefficients $= 0$. $H_1$ not all are 0. Reject $H_0$ if computed $F > 2.71$. $F = 11.33$, so we repeat $H_0$.

d.  Reject $H_0$ if $t > 2.086$ or $t < -2.086$. For stolen bases and errors computed $t$ values are 1.95 and $-1.82$ respectively. So we accept $H_0$.

e.  $Y' = .2292 + 2.3489$ average $+ .00098$ HR $- .1170$ERA.

# CHAPTER 16   ANALYSIS OF NOMINAL-LEVEL DATA: THE CHI-SQUARE DISTRIBUTION

1.  a.  There are $k - 1 = 3 - 1 = 2$ degrees of freedom. The critical value is 5.991. Reject $H_0$ if the computed value of $\chi^2$ is greater than 5.991. Otherwise, do not reject $H_0$.

b.  Computed value of $\chi^2$ is 10.

| $f_0$ | $f_e$ | $f_0 - f_e$ | $(f_0 - f_e)^2$ | $\dfrac{(f_0 - f_e)^2}{f_e}$ |
|---|---|---|---|---|
| 10 | 20 | −10 | 100 | 5 |
| 20 | 20 | 0 | 0 | 0 |
| 30 | 20 | 10 | 100 | 5 |
| 60 | 60 | 0 | | 10   ←$\chi^2$ |

c.  Since $10 > 5.991$, reject $H_0$ and accept $H_1$.

3.  $H_0$: Shoplifting accounts for half of the loss, employee theft 25 percent, and poor inventory control 25 percent.

$H_1$: Shoplifting does not account for 50 percent of the loss, employee theft does not account for 25 percent and poor inventory control does not account for 25 percent of the loss.

Computed $\chi^2 = 11.00$.

| $f_0$ | $f_e$ | $f_0 - f_e$ | $(f_0 - f_e)^2$ | $\dfrac{(f_0 - f_e)^2}{f_e}$ |
|---|---|---|---|---|
| 60 | 50 | 10 | 100 | 2.0 |
| 30 | 25 | 5 | 25 | 1.0 |
| 10 | 25 | −15 | 225 | 9.0 |
| 100 | 100 | 0 | | 12.0   ←$\chi^2$ |

12.0 is greater than the critical value of 7.824, so $H_0$ is rejected. Shoplifting does not account for twice the losses compared to theft or inventory control.

5.  $H_0$: There is no difference between the opinions.
    $H_1$: There is a difference between the opinions.
    $H_0$ is rejected if computed chi-square is greater than 15.086. There are 5 degrees of freedom, found by $6 - 1$.
    Computed chi-square is 3.400. $H_0$ is not rejected. The differences are due to chance.

7.  $H_0$: The sample responses are representative of the population.
    $H_1$: The responses are not representative of the population.
    There are $7 - 1 = 6$ degrees of freedom. The critical value of chi-square is 12.592. Reject $H_0$ if the computed value is greater than 12.592.

| College | $f_0$ | Proportion | $f_e$ | $\dfrac{(f_0 - f_e)^2}{f_e}$ |
|---|---|---|---|---|
| A & S | 90 | .27 | 81 | 1.00 |
| Business | 45 | .14 | 42 | .21 |
| Education | 60 | .19 | 57 | .16 |
| Engineering | 30 | .08 | 24 | 1.50 |
| Law | 15 | .05 | 15 | 0 |
| Pharmacy | 15 | .07 | 21 | 1.71 |
| University | 45 | .20 | 60 | 3.75 |
| | | | | 8.33 |

Computed $\chi^2 = 8.33$. $H_0$ is not rejected. The sample is representative of the population since $8.33 < 12.592$.

9.  There are $k - 1 = 5 - 1 = 4$ degrees of freedom. The critical value is 9.488, and computed chi-square is 19.60.

| $f_0$ | $f_e$ | $f_0 - f_e$ | $(f_0 - f_e)^2$ | $\dfrac{(f_0 - f_e)^2}{f_e}$ |
|---|---|---|---|---|
| 67 | 56.4 | 10.6 | 112.36 | 1.99 |
| 22 | 37.6 | −15.6 | 243.36 | 6.47 |
| 51 | 37.6 | 13.4 | 179.56 | 4.78 |
| 24 | 37.6 | −13.6 | 184.96 | 4.92 |
| 24 | 18.8 | 5.2 | 27.04 | 1.44 |
| 188 | 188 | 0 | | 19.60 |

Reject $H_0$ since $19.60 > 9.488$. The observed distribution of M&M colors does not match the expected distribution.

11.  To compute $f_e$:

| Commission | z value | Area | $f_e$ |
|---|---|---|---|
| Less than $900 | Under −2.00 | .0228 | 11.40 |
| $900 to $1,200 | −2.00 to −1.00 | .1359 | 67.95 |
| 1,200 to 1,500 | −1.00 to 0 | .3413 | 170.65 |
| 1,500 to 1,800 | 0 to 1.00 | .3413 | 170.65 |
| 1,800 to 2,100 | 1.00 to 2.00 | .1359 | 67.95 |
| $2,100 or more | Over 2.00 | .0228 | 11.40 |
| | | 1.000 | 500 |

To compute chi-square:

| $f_0$ | $f_e$ | $\dfrac{(f_0 - f_e)^2}{f_e}$ |
|-------|--------|------|
| 9 | 11.40 | 0.51 |
| 63 | 67.95 | 0.36 |
| 165 | 170.65 | 0.19 |
| 180 | 170.65 | 0.51 |
| 71 | 67.95 | 0.14 |
| 12 | 11.40 | 0.03 |
| 500 | 500.00 | 1.74 |

There are $k - 1 = 6 - 1 = 5$ degrees of freedom. Critical value is 15.086. Since $1.74 < 15.086$, we fail to reject $H_0$. The commissions are normally distributed.

13. $H_0$: Age is not related to the degree of pressure.
$H_1$: Age is related to the degree of pressure.
$df = (4 - 1)(3 - 1) = 6$. $H_0$ is rejected if $\chi^2 > 16.812$.
    Expected counts are printed below the observed counts.

| | Low | Medium | High | Total |
|---|-----|--------|------|-------|
| Less than 25 | 20 | 18 | 22 | 60 |
| | 19.44 | 20.40 | 20.16 | |
| 25–39 | 50 | 46 | 44 | 140 |
| | 45.36 | 47.60 | 47.04 | |
| 40–59 | 58 | 63 | 59 | 180 |
| | 58.32 | 61.20 | 60.48 | |
| 60 and older | 34 | 43 | 43 | 120 |
| | 38.88 | 40.80 | 40.32 | |
| Total | 162 | 170 | 168 | 500 |

$\chi^2 = 0.016 + 0.282 + 0.168 + \cdots + 0.178 = 2.191$

Since $2.191 < 16.812$, $H_0$ is not rejected. Age and pressure are not related.

15. $H_0$: There is no relationship between the manufacturer and the quality of the light bulbs.
$H_1$: There is a relationship between the quality of the light bulbs and the manufacturer:

$$df = (r - 1)(c - 1) = (2 - 1)(4 - 1) = 3$$

Reject $H_0$ if $\chi^2 > 7.815$.
$\chi^2 = 3.66$, found by:

$$(12 - 9)^2/9 + (8 - 9)^2/9 + \cdots + (89 - 91)^2/91$$
$$= 1.0 + 0.11 + 1.78 + 0.44 + 0.10 + 0.01 + 0.18 + 0.04$$

Do not reject $H_0$ because $3.66 < 7.815$.

17. $H_0$: Unpaid balances are uniformly distributed by size.
$H_1$: Unpaid balances are not uniformly distributed by size.
$df = 7 - 1 = 6$. $H_0$ is rejected if $\chi^2 > 16.812$.

Computed chi-square $= 2.332$, found by:

| Size | $f_0$ | $f_e$ | $\dfrac{(f_0 - f_e)^2}{f_e}$ |
|------|-------|-------|------|
| <$20 | 13 | 12 | 0.083 |
| $20 but under $40 | 10 | 12 | 0.333 |
| 40 but under 60 | 15 | 12 | 0.750 |
| 60 but under 80 | 14 | 12 | 0.333 |
| 80 but under 100 | 9 | 12 | 0.750 |
| 100 but under 150 | 12 | 12 | 0 |
| 150 and over | 11 | 12 | 0.083 |
| | | | 2.332 |

Since $2.332 < 16.812$, $H_0$ is not rejected. The unpaid balances are uniformly distributed by size.

19. The null and alternate hypotheses are as follows:

$H_0$: Quarter and group are not related.

$H_1$: Quarter and group are related.

Using MINITAB the following cell frequencies were developed:

| | Quarter | | | | |
|------------|-----|-----|-----|-----|-------|
| Group Rank | I | II | III | IV | Total |
| Low | 21 | 28 | 35 | 38 | 122 |
| Medium | 34 | 22 | 29 | 37 | 122 |
| High | 36 | 41 | 28 | 17 | 122 |
| Total | 91 | 91 | 92 | 92 | 366 |

There are 6 degrees of freedom, so $H_0$ is rejected if $\chi^2 > 12.592$. The computed value of $\chi^2$ is 20.680, so $H_0$ is rejected. Quarter and group are related. It is concluded that the draft order is not random.

21. a. $H_0$: No relationship between pool and township.
$H_1$: There is a relationship.
Reject $H_0$ if $\chi^2 > 9.488$. Computed $\chi^2 = 4.571$. $H_0$ is not rejected. No relationship between pool and township.

b. $H_0$: No relationship between garage and township.
$H_1$: There is a relationship.
Reject $H_0$ if computed $\chi^2 > 9.488$. Computed chi-square $= 1.768$. Do not reject $H_0$. No relationship between garage and township.

# CHAPTER 17  NONPARAMETRIC METHODS: ANALYSIS OF RANKED DATA

1. a. If the number of pluses (successes) in the sample is 9 or more, reject $H_0$.
b. Reject $H_0$ because the cumulative probability associated with nine successes (.073) does not exceed the significance level (.10).

3. a. $H_0$: $p = .50$, $H_1$: $p < .50$; $n = 10$.

b.  $H_0$ is rejected if there are nine or more plus signs. A "+" represents a loss.

c.  Reject $H_0$. It is an effective program, because there was only one person who gained weight.

5.  a.  $H_0: p = .50$ (There is no change in weight.)
    $H_1: p > .50$ (There is a loss of weight. The program was effective.)

    b.  Do not reject $H_0$ if the computed value of $z$ is between 0 and 1.645. Otherwise, reject $H_0$. (A weight loss is considered a "+".)

    c.  $$z = \frac{(32 - .50) - .50(45)}{.50\sqrt{45}}$$

    $$= \frac{31.5 - 22.5}{3.35}$$

    $$= 2.69$$

    d.  Reject $H_0$ because 2.69 falls to the right of 1.645. The weight loss program is effective.

7.  $H_0: p = .50, H_1: p > .50$
    $H_0$ is rejected if $z > 2.05$.

    $$\mu = 81(.50) = 40.5$$

    $$\sigma = \sqrt{81(.50)(.50)} = 4.5$$

    $$z = \frac{42.5 - 40.5}{4.5} = 0.44$$

    $H_0$ is not rejected. There is no decided preference for the gourmet or the regular menu.

9.  a.  $H_0$: Median = \$40,000, $H_1$: Median > \$40,000
    b.  $H_0$ is rejected if $z > 1.645$.

    c.  $$\mu = 200(.50) = 100$$

    $$\sigma = \sqrt{200(.50)(.50)} = 7.07$$

    $$z = \frac{170.0 - .50 - 100}{7.07} = 9.83$$

    $H_0$ is rejected. The median income is greater than \$40,000.

11. a.  $H_0$: The two distributions come from the same population.
    $H_1$: The two distributions do not come from the same population.

    b.  $n_1 = 6, n_2 = 5$. Using Appendix J, the critical value is 3. Reject $H_0$ if computed $U$ is 3 or less.

    c.  $$U = (6)(5) + \frac{6(6 + 1)}{2} - 48$$

    $$= 30 + 21 - 48 = 3$$

    $$U' = (6)(5) + \frac{5(5 + 1)}{2} - 18$$

    $$= 30 + 15 - 18$$

    $$= 27$$

The smaller of 3 and 27 is 3 (observations ranked from high to low).

d.  The computed value of $U$ is equal to or less than 3. Reject $H_0$ at the .05 significance level. There is a difference between the two groups. The distributions are not the same.

13. $H_0$: The distributions of ages of the two groups are the same.

$H_1$: The country-western musicians are older.

$n_1 = 10, n_2 = 12$. $H_0$ is rejected if the smaller of $U$ or $U' \leq 34$.

| Rock | | Country | |
|---|---|---|---|
| Age | Rank | Age | Rank |
| 28 | 8.0 | 26 | 6.0 |
| 16 | 1.0 | 42 | 16.5 |
| 42 | 16.5 | 65 | 22.0 |
| 29 | 9.5 | 38 | 13.0 |
| 31 | 11.0 | 29 | 9.5 |
| 22 | 3.0 | 32 | 12.0 |
| 50 | 20.0 | 59 | 21.0 |
| 42 | 16.5 | 42 | 16.5 |
| 23 | 4.0 | 27 | 7.0 |
| 25 | 5.0 | 41 | 14.0 |
| | 94.5 | 46 | 19.0 |
| | | 18 | 2.0 |
| | | | 158.5 |

$$U = 10(12) + \frac{10(11)}{2} - 94.5 = 80.5$$

$$U' = 10(12) + \frac{12(13)}{2} - 158.5 = 39.5$$

$H_0$ is not rejected (since 39.5 is greater than 34). There is no difference in the two age distributions.

15. ANOVA requires that we have three or more populations, the data are interval or ratio-level, the populations are normally distributed, and the population standard deviations are equal. Kruskal-Wallis requires only ordinal-level data, and no assumptions are made regarding the shape of the populations.

17. a.  $H_0$: The three population distributions are equal.
    b.  If the computed value of $H$ is greater than 5.991, reject $H_0$. If it is 5.991 or less, do not reject $H_0$. (Use Appendix I; the chi-square distribution.)
    c.  $H = 8.98$, found by:

| Rank | Rank | Rank |
|---|---|---|
| 8 | 5 | 1 |
| 11 | 6.5 | 2 |
| 14.5 | 6.5 | 3 |
| 14.5 | 10 | 4 |
| 16 | 12 | 9 |
| 64 | 13 | 19 |
| | 53 | |

$$H = \frac{12}{16(16+1)}\left[\frac{(64)^2}{5} + \frac{(58)^2}{6} + \frac{(19)^2}{5}\right] - 3(16+1)$$

$$= .0441176[1{,}359.6] - 51$$

$$= 59.98 - 51 = 8.98$$

d. Reject $H_0$ because $8.98 > 5.991$. The three distributions are not equal.

19. $H_0$: The distributions of the lengths of life are the same.
    $H_1$: The distributions of the lengths of life are not the same.
    $H_0$ is rejected if $H > 9.210$. (Refer to the $\chi^2$ table, Appendix I, for the critical value.)

| Salt | | Fresh | | Others | |
|---|---|---|---|---|---|
| Hours | Rank | Hours | Rank | Hours | Rank |
| 167.3 | 3 | 160.6 | 1 | 182.7 | 13 |
| 189.6 | 15 | 177.6 | 11 | 165.4 | 2 |
| 177.2 | 10 | 185.3 | 14 | 172.9 | 7 |
| 169.4 | 6 | 168.6 | 4 | 169.2 | 5 |
| 180.3 | 12 | 176.6 | 9 | 174.7 | 8 |
|  | 46 |  | 39 |  | 35 |

$H = 0.62$, found by:

$$\frac{12}{15(16)}\left[\frac{(46)^2}{5} + \frac{(39)^2}{5} + \frac{(35)^2}{5}\right] - 3(16)$$

$H_0$ is not rejected. There is no difference in the three distributions.

21.

| Absolute difference | Rank | Correctly signed |
|---|---|---|
| 70 | 1 | −1 |
| 90 | 2 | 2 |
| 120 | 3 | −3 |
| 130 | 4 | 4 |
| 190 | 5 | 5 |
| 250 | 6 | 6 |
| 550 | 7 | 7 |

Sums: $-4$, $+24$. So $T = 4$ (the smaller of the two sums.) From Appendix K, .05 level, one-tailed test, $N = 7$, the critical value is 3. Since the $T$ of $4 > 3$, do not reject $H_0$ (one-tailed test). There is no difference in square footage. Yuppies do not live in larger homes.

23. a. $H_0$: The production is the same for the two systems.
    $H_1$: Production using the Mump method is greater.
    b. $H_0$ is rejected if $T \le 21$, $N = 13$.
    c. The calculations for the first three employees are:

| Employee | Old | Mump | d | Rank | $R^+$ | $R^-$ |
|---|---|---|---|---|---|---|
| A | 60 | 64 | 4 | 6 | 6 | |
| B | 40 | 52 | 12 | 12.5 | 12.5 | |
| C | 59 | 58 | −1 | 2 | | 2 |
| . | | | | | | |
| . | | | | | | |
| . | | | | | | |

The sum of the negative ranks is 6.5, which is smaller than the sum of the positive ranks. Since 6.5 is less than 21, $H_0$ is rejected. Production using the Mump method is greater.

25. a. Two-tailed.
    b. $N = 19$. $H_0$ is rejected if there are either 5 or fewer "+" signs, or 14 or more. The total of 12 "+" signs falls in the acceptance region. $H_0$ is not rejected. There is no preference between the two shows.
    c. Both shows would be equally popular.

27. $H_0$: Community responsibility is the same before and after marriage.
    $H_1$: Community responsibility is not the same.
    $H_0$ is rejected if $T \le 3$, $N = 8$.
    The calculations for the first four women are:

| Name | Before | After | d | Rank | $R^+$ | $R^-$ |
|---|---|---|---|---|---|---|
| Beth | 110 | 114 | 4 | 3 | 3 | |
| Jean | 157 | 159 | 2 | 2 | 2 | |
| Sue | 121 | 120 | −1 | 1 | | 1 |
| Cathy | 96 | 103 | 7 | 4.5 | 4.5 | |

The smaller sum of ranks is 13.5, which is the computed $T$. It lies in the acceptance region beyond 3. Community responsibility is the same before and after marriage.

29. $H_0$: Idle minutes are same.
    $H_1$: Idle minutes are not the same.
    $n_1 = 5$, $n_2 = 6$. $H_0$ is rejected if $U$ or $U'$ is less than or equal to 3.

| Day | | Night | |
|---|---|---|---|
| Minutes | Rank | Minutes | Rank |
| 92 | 7 | 96 | 8 |
| 103 | 9 | 114 | 10 |
| 116 | 11 | 80 | 1 |
| 81 | 2 | 82 | 3 |
| 89 | 5 | 88 | 4 |
|  | 34 | 91 | 6 |
|  |  |  | 32 |

$$U = 5 \times 6 + \frac{5 \times 6}{2} - 34 = 11$$

$$U' = 5 \times 6 + \frac{6 \times 7}{2} - 32 = 19$$

$H_0$ is not rejected. There is no difference in the idle minutes.

31. $H_0$: Median $= \$1{,}200$
    $H_1$: Median $> \$1{,}200$
    $H_0$ is rejected if $z > 1.645$.

$$\mu = 144(.50) = 72$$

$$\sigma = .50\sqrt{144} = 6$$

$$z = \frac{74.5 - 72}{6} = 0.42$$

$H_0$ is not rejected. The median is not greater than $1,200.

33. $H_0$: $p = .50$
$H_1$: $p \neq .50$
$H_0$ is rejected if there are 12 or more or 3 or less plus signs. Since there are only 8 plus signs, $H_0$ is not rejected. There is no preference with respect to the two brands of components.

35. $H_0$: Incomes are the same.
$H_1$: Incomes are not the same.
$H_0$ is rejected if $\chi^2 > 7.815$. Computed $\chi^2 = 2.92$
$H_0$ is not rejected. There is no difference in the salaries.

# CHAPTER 18    INDEX NUMBERS

1. a. 127.8, found by ($115,500/$90,400)(100). Price increased by 27.8 percent from 1981 to 1991.
   b. 129.1, found by ($87,200/$67,550)(100). The loan amount increased 29.1 percent between 1981–82 and 1991.
3. a. 121.0, found by ($97.71/$80.75)(100).

| | Price 1983 | | Amount consumed | | Price 1992 | |
|---|---|---|---|---|---|---|
| Fruit | $p_0$ | | $q_0$ | $p_0 q_0$ | $p_t$ | $p_0 p_t$ |
| Bananas | $0.23 | | 100 | $23.00 | $0.35 | $35.00 |
| Grapefruit | 0.29 | | 50 | 14.50 | 0.27 | 13.50 |
| Apples | 0.35 | | 85 | 29.75 | 0.35 | 29.75 |
| Strawberries | 1.02 | | 8 | 8.16 | 1.69 | 13.52 |
| Oranges | 0.89 | | 6 | 5.34 | 0.99 | 5.94 |
| | | | | $80.75 | | $97.71 |

   b. Prices of fruits in 1992 were 21.0 percent more than they were in 1983.
5. a. $Q = 90.4$, found by ($1,975.92/$2,186.53)(100).
   b. $V = 93.8$, found by ($2,051.81/$2,186.53)(100).

| | $p_0$ | $q_0$ | $p_0 q_0$ | $p_t$ | $q_t$ | $p_0 q_t$ | $p_t q_t$ |
|---|---|---|---|---|---|---|---|
| Oats | $1.52 | 200 | $ 304.00 | $1.87 | 214 | $ 325.28 | $ 400.18 |
| Wheat | 2.10 | 565 | 1,186.50 | 2.05 | 489 | 1,026.90 | 1,002.45 |
| Corn | 1.48 | 291 | 430.68 | 1.48 | 203 | 300.44 | 300.44 |
| Barley | 3.05 | 87 | 265.35 | 3.29 | 106 | 323.30 | 348.74 |
| | | | $2,186.53 | | | $1,975.92 | $2,051.81 |

7. a. Unemployment rate: $\dfrac{6.8}{5.3}(100)(.20) = 25.66$

   Index of stock prices: $\dfrac{362.26}{265.88}(100)(.40) = 54.50$

   Producers Price Index: $\dfrac{115.2}{109.6}(100)(.25) = 26.28$

   Exports ($ millions): $\dfrac{\$622,864}{\$529,917}(100)(.15) = \dfrac{17.63}{124.07}$

   b. Business activity increased 24.07 percent from 1989 to 1991.

9.
| Period | Money income | CPI | Real income |
|---|---|---|---|
| 1982–84 | $19,800 | 100 | $19,800 |
| 1991 | $32,000 | 135 | $23,704 |

A nurse's purchasing power has increased since 1982–84. The amount of the increase is about $3,904.

11. a. Real incomes:

| | Mining | Apparel | Printing/publishing | Retail trade |
|---|---|---|---|---|
| 1989 | $459.48 | $188.98 | $332.54 | $152.19 |
| 1990 | 459.53 | 183.53 | 326.23 | 149.40 |
| 1991 | 460.21 | 178.32 | 316.96 | 144.45 |

   b. Only weekly mining wages remained virtually the same. All other real weekly wages decreased over time. In none of the industries have real wages increased in real terms.
13. 82.09, found by (55,000/67,000)(100). The number of employees has decreased by about 18 percent.
15. 198.73, found by ($6,285,000,000/$3,162,505,000) × (100). Revenue has increased by 98.73 percent since 1979–80.
17. Wholesale index = 168.93, found by ($418.82/$247.93)(100). This shows a 68.93 percent increase. Transportation and public utilities increased by 54.58 percent.
19. Purchasing power of the dollar in 1982–84 = $1.00. In March 1991 the purchasing power was $0.7407, found by ($1.00/135)(100). Purchasing power declined $0.2593 between 1982–84 and March 1991.
21. a. 1983 = 100.00
      1992 = 123.04

Retail sales:             ($1,971/1,159)(100)(.20) = 34.01
Bank deposits:            ($91/87)(100)(.10) = 10.46
Industrial production:   (114.7/110.6)(100)(.40) = 41.48
Employment:              (1,501/1,214)(100)(.30) = 37.09

  Adding: 34.01 + 10.46 + 41.48 + 37.09 = 123.04
b.  The economy is up 23.04 percent for 1992 compared with 1983.

23.

|        | 1977 $p_0q_0$ | 1977 $p_tq_t$ | 1992 $p_tq_0$ | 1992 $p_0q_t$ |
|--------|--------|--------|--------|--------|
| Cabbage | $120 | $75 | $100 | $90 |
| Carrots | 20 | 24 | 24 | 20 |
| Peas | 80 | 90 | 72 | 100 |
| Endive | 15 | 30 | 15 | 30 |
|        | $235 | $219 | $211 | $240 |

a.  $P$ = ($211/$235)100 = 89.8. Prices down 10.2 percent between 1977 and 1992.
b.  $P$ = ($219/$240)100 = 91.3. Prices down 8.7 percent.
c.  Laspeyres uses 1977 quantities for the base; Paasche uses 1992 quantities for the base.
d.  $Q$ = ($240/$235)100 = 102.1. Production increased 2.1 percent from 1977 to 1992.
e.  $V$ = ($219/$235)100 = 93.2. Value down 6.8 percent between 1977 and 1992.

25.  a.  Paasche price index = 686.6, found by ($1,864,912/$271,624.40)100.
   b.  Value index = 721.6, found by ($1,864,912/$258,437)(100). The value of sales increased 621.6 percent since 1980.

27.  Answers will vary, but a typical clause might state that if the CPI increases during a six-month period by 5 points (say, from 180.0 to 185.0), hourly wages will go up 5 cents.

# CHAPTER 19    TIME SERIES AND FORECASTING

1.

| Year | Failures | $t$ | $tY$ | $t^2$ |
|------|----------|-----|------|-------|
| 1987 | 79 | 0 | 0 | 0 |
| 1988 | 120 | 1 | 120 | 1 |
| 1989 | 138 | 2 | 276 | 4 |
| 1990 | 184 | 3 | 552 | 9 |
| 1991 | 200 | 4 | 800 | 16 |
|      | 721 | 10 | 1,748 | 30 |

$$b = \frac{\Sigma tY - (\Sigma Y)(\Sigma t)/n}{\Sigma t^2 - (\Sigma t)^2/n} = \frac{1,748 - 721(10)/5}{30 - (10)^2/5} = 30.6$$

$$a = \frac{\Sigma Y}{n} - b\left(\frac{\Sigma t}{n}\right) = \frac{721}{5} - 30.6\left(\frac{10}{5}\right) = 83$$

$Y' = 83 + 30.6t$

  For 1994, $Y'$ = 83 + 30.6(7) = 297.2.

3.

| Year | Scrap | Code | $Y_t$ | $t^2$ |
|------|-------|------|-------|-------|
| 1988 | 2.0 | 0 | 0 | 0 |
| 1989 | 4.0 | 1 | 4.0 | 1 |
| 1990 | 3.0 | 2 | 6.0 | 4 |
| 1991 | 5.0 | 3 | 15.0 | 9 |
| 1992 | 6.0 | 4 | 24.0 | 16 |
|      | 20.0 | 10 | 49.0 | 30 |

$$b = \frac{49 - (20(10)/5}{30 - (10)^2/5} = 0.90 \qquad a = \frac{20}{5} - 0.90\left(\frac{10}{5}\right) = 2.2$$

$Y'$ = 2.2 + 0.90t
  = 2.2 + 0.90(6) = 7.60 tons

5.  a.  $Y'$ = 0.0572 + 0.110t, found by MINITAB. 1987 = 0.
   b.  28.82 percent, found by antilog of 0.110, which is 1.2882. Then, 1.2882 − 1 = 0.2882. This is the percent by which sales increased on average during the period.
   c.  Estimated sales for 1994 are 6.717, found by:

   $Y'$ = 0.0572 + 0.110(7)
      = 0.8272

   The antilog of 0.8272 is 6.717.

7.  The output from the CBS system is as follows.

Classical Seasonal Indices

| Period | Quarter | Value | Trend | S-I |
|--------|---------|-------|-------|-----|
| 1 | 1 | 4 | - | - |
|   | 2 | 10 | - | - |
|   | 3 | 7 | 6.1250 | 1.1429 |
|   | 4 | 3 | 6.5000 | 0.4615 |
| 2 | 1 | 5 | 7 | 0.7143 |
|   | 2 | 12 | 7.3750 | 1.6271 |
|   | 3 | 9 | 7.6250 | 1.1803 |
|   | 4 | 4 | 8.2500 | 0.4848 |
| 3 | 1 | 6 | 9.1250 | 0.6575 |
|   | 2 | 16 | 9.5000 | 1.6842 |
|   | 3 | 12 | - | - |
|   | 4 | 4 | - | - |

Seasonal Index by Quarter

| Quarter | Average SI Component | Seasonal Index |
|---------|---------------------|----------------|
| 1 | 0.6859 | 0.6911 |
| 2 | 1.6557 | 1.6682 |
| 3 | 1.1616 | 1.1704 |
| 4 | 0.4732 | 0.4768 |

9.  Forecast in millions.

| $t$ | Estimated pairs | Seasonal index | Quarterly forecast |
|-----|-----------------|----------------|--------------------|
| 21 | 40.05 | 110.0 | 44.055 |
| 22 | 41.80 | 120.0 | 50.160 |
| 23 | 43.55 | 80.0 | 34.840 |
| 24 | 45.30 | 90.0 | 40.770 |

11.   *Note:* The first period of 1990 is coded 1. The last quarter of 1992 therefore is coded 12.

| Row | Quarter | Index | Absent | Deseason | Time |
|-----|---------|-------|--------|----------|------|
| 1 | 1 | 0.6911 | 4 | 5.7879 | 1 |
| 2 | 2 | 1.6682 | 10 | 5.9945 | 2 |
| 3 | 3 | 1.1704 | 7 | 5.9809 | 3 |
| 4 | 4 | 0.4768 | 3 | 6.2919 | 4 |
| 5 | 1 | 0.6911 | 5 | 7.2348 | 5 |
| 6 | 2 | 1.6682 | 12 | 7.1934 | 6 |
| 7 | 3 | 1.1704 | 9 | 7.6897 | 7 |
| 8 | 4 | 0.4768 | 4 | 8.3893 | 8 |
| 9 | 1 | 0.6911 | 6 | 8.6818 | 9 |
| 10 | 2 | 1.6682 | 16 | 9.5912 | 10 |
| 11 | 3 | 1.1704 | 12 | 10.2529 | 11 |
| 12 | 4 | 0.4768 | 4 | 8.3893 | 12 |

Using MINITAB the results are as follows:

```
MTB > regr c4 1 c5;

The regression equation is
Deseason = 5.17 + 0.378 Time

Predictor      Coef      Stdev    t-ratio       p
Constant     5.1658     0.3628      14.24   0.000
Time        0.37805    0.04930       7.67   0.000

               Index   Seasonally adjusted

10.008        0.6911         6.966
10.458        1.6682        17.446
10.837        1.1704        12.836
11.215        0.4768         5.347
```

13.   a.   $Y' = 18,000 - 400t$, assuming the straight line starts at 18,000 in 1970 and goes down to 10,000 in 1990.
    b.   400
    c.   8,000, found by $18,000 - 400(25)$.

15.   a.   `MTB > plot c3 vs C1`

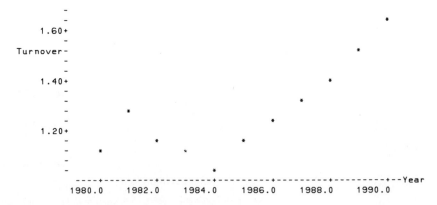

b. Using MINITAB, the year 1980 is coded as 0, 1981 as 1, and so on.

```
MTB > regr c3 1 c2

The regression equation is
Turnover = 1.05 + 0.0441 Code

Predictor        Coef        Stdev     t-ratio         p
Constant      1.04864      0.06665       15.73     0.000

Code          0.04409      0.01127        3.91     0.004

               Y' = 1.05 + 0.0441t
```

c. 1983: $Y' = 1.05 + 0.0441(3) = 1.1823$
   1989: $Y' = 1.05 + 0.0441(9) = 1.4469$

d. 1995: $Y' = 1.05 + 0.0441(15) = 1.7115$

e. 0.0441 per year.

17. a. *Note:* In this problem 1982 is coded 0.

```
MTB > plot c3 c1

 Sales   -
         -                                               *
         -
   2000+
         -                                      *    *
         -                                 *
         -
         -
   1500+
         -                         *          *
         -                 *            x
         -
         -
   1000+
         -              *
         -       *     *
         -
         ----+---------+---------+---------+---------+---------+--Year
          1982.0    1984.0    1986.0    1988.0    1990.0    1992.0

MTB > regr c3 1 c2

The regression equation is
Sales = 786 + 127 Code

Predictor      Coef    Stdev    t-ratio       p
Constant     786.45    53.66      14.66    0.000
Code        127.109    9.070      14.01    0.000
```

b. $Y' = 786 + 127t,$ found by MINITAB with 1982 coded as 0, 1983 as 1, and so on.

c. 1984: $Y' = 786 + 127(2) = \$1,040$
   1990: $Y' = 786 + 127(8) = \$1,802$

d. $127 million.

e. $2,691 million.

19. a. Using the MINITAB system the output is as follows. The year 1983 is coded as 0.

```
The regression equation is
Log-10 = 0.904 + 0.114 Code

Predictor        Coef        Stdev     t-ratio         p
Constant     0.903900     0.002316      390.35     0.000
Code         0.113669     0.000391      290.41     0.000
```

Log $Y' = 0.903900 + 0.113669t$ is the regression equation.

b. For 1985 the code is 3. Log $Y' = 0.903900 + 0.113669(3) = 1.244907$. Antilog is 17.575.
For 1990 the code is 7. Log $Y' = 0.903900 + 0.113669(8) = 1.813252$. Antilog is 65.051.

c. The yearly rate of increase is 29.9 percent, found by taking the antilog of 0.113669 and subtracting 1.

d. Log $Y' = 0.903900 + 0.113669(11) = 2.154259$. Antilog is 142.646. $ million.

21. a. The regression equation is (1980 is coded as 0)
Log $Y' = 0.00909 + 0.21978t$.

```
The regression equation is
Logten = 0.0091 + 0.220 Code

Predictor      Coef      Stdev   t-ratio      p
Constant    0.00909    0.07390     0.12    0.905
Code        0.21978    0.01384    15.88    0.000
```

b. $Y' = 0.00909 + 0.21978(13) = 2.86623$. The antilog is 734.903.

c. The antilog of 0.21978 is 1.659, so the number of households with VCRs increased about 65.9 percent per year.

23. a. July 87.5, August, 92.9, September, 99.3, October 109.1.

b.

| Month | Mean | Corrected |
|-------|------|-----------|
| July | 87.225 | 86.777 |
| Aug. | 92.025 | 91.552 |
| Sept. | 98.750 | 98.242 |
| Oct. | 105.100 | 104.500 |
| Nov. | 124.050 | 123.412 |
| Dec. | 143.075 | 142.340 |
| Jan. | 83.375 | 82.946 |
| Feb. | 74.375 | 73.993 |
| Mar. | 86.825 | 86.379 |
| Apr. | 120.325 | 119.707 |
| May | 99.025 | 98.516 |
| June | 92.025 | 91.552 |
| | 1206.200 | |

Correction $1200/1206.02 = .99486$

c. April, November, and December are periods of high sales. February is the lowest month.

25. a. The output from the CBS software is as follows.

(The first five periods are shown.)

```
Model:                              Seasonal Indices
Number of Periods:                  24
```

```
             Classical Seasonal Indices

Period   Quarter     Value     Trend      S-I

  1         1         142        -          -
            2         312        -          -
            3         488       288       1.6944
            4         208      289.2500   0.7191
  2         1         146       293       0.4983
```

```
         Seasonal Index by Quarter

               Average SI   Seasonal
    Quarter    Component     Index

       1        0.5014       0.5027
       2        1.0909       1.0936
       3        1.7709       1.7753
       4        0.6354       0.6370
```

b.  The production is largest in the third quarter. It is 77.5 percent above the average quarter. The second quarter is also above average. The first and fourth quarters are well below average, with the first quarter at about 50 percent of a typical quarter.

27. The CBS system was used to determine the seasonal indexes. (The first five periods are shown.)

```
Model:                              Seasonal Indices
Number of Periods:                  20
```

```
             Classical Seasonal Indices

Period   Quarter     Value     Trend      S-I

  1         1        4.4000      -          -
            2        6.1000      -          -
            3       11.7000    7.3125     1.6000
            4        7.2000    7.3375     0.9813
  2         1        4.1000    7.3250     0.5597
```

```
         Seasonal Index by Quarter

               Average SI   Seasonal
    Quarter    Component     Index

       1        0.5549       0.5577
       2        0.8254       0.8296
       3        1.5102       1.5178
       4        1.0973       1.1029
```

b.   The MINITAB system was used to determine the trend equation, where the first period is coded 1.

```
The regression equation is
Deseason = 7.67 + 0.0023 Code

Predictor        Coef        Stdev      t-ratio        p
Constant       7.6696       0.3196      24.00       0.000
Code          0.00227      0.02876       0.08       0.938
```

c.
| Period | Turnover | Index | Forecast |
|--------|----------|--------|----------|
| 20 | 7.7150 | 0.5577 | 4.3026 |
| 21 | 7.7270 | 0.8296 | 6.4020 |
| 22 | 7.7200 | 1.5178 | 11.7274 |
| 23 | 7.7218 | 1.1029 | 8.5163 |

29.  Using the Hall and Adelman package, the seasonal indexes are:

| Quarter | Index |
|---------|--------|
| I | 120.53 |
| II | 102.12 |
| III | 63.01 |
| IV | 114.57 |

The total number of visitors in 1992 was 928. A 10 percent increase would mean 1,021 visitors in 1993. Using the seasonal adjustment, the number of visitors for 1993 is estimated as follows: The first step is to divide the 1993 estimate by 4, to obtain the quarterly estimate; then the seasonal factor is applied.

| Quarter | Visitors | Index | Estimate 1993 |
|---------|----------|--------|---------------|
| I | 255.25 | 120.53 | 307.65 |
| II | 255.25 | 102.12 | 260.66 |
| III | 255.25 | 63.01 | 160.83 |
| IV | 255.25 | 114.57 | 292.44 |

# CHAPTER 20   AN INTRODUCTION TO DECISION MAKING UNDER UNCERTAINTY

1.

$EMV(A_1) = .30(\$50) + .50(\$70) + .20(\$100) = \$70$

$EMV(A_2) = .30(\$90) + .50(\$40) + .20(\$80) = \$63$

$EMV(A_3) = .30(\$70) + .50(\$60) + .20(\$90) = \$69$

Decision: Choose alternative 1.

3.
| | Opportunity loss | | |
|---|---|---|---|
| | $S_1$ | $S_2$ | $S_3$ |
| $A_1$ | $40 | $ 0 | $ 0 |
| $A_2$ | 0 | 30 | 20 |
| $A_3$ | 20 | 10 | 10 |

5.   Answers in $000.

$EOL(A_1) = .30(\$40) + .50(\$0) + .20(\$0) = \$12$

$EOL(A_2) = .30(\$0) + .50(\$30) + .20(\$20) = \$19$

$EOL(A_3) = .30(\$20) + .50(\$10) + .20(\$10) = \$13$

7.   Expected value under conditions of certainty is $82, found by .30($90) + .50($70) + .20($100).

$$EVPI = \$82 - \$70 = \$12$$

9.   Yes, it changes the decision. Choose alternative 2.

$EMV(A_1) = .50(\$50) + .20(\$70) + .30(\$100) = \$69$

$EMV(A_2) = .50(\$90) + .20(\$40) + .30(\$80) = \$77$

$EMV(A_3) = .50(\$70) + .20(\$60) + .30(\$90) = \$74$

11.   a.

$EMV(\text{neither}) = .30(\$0) + .50(\$0) + .20(\$0) = \$0$

$EMV(1) = .30(\$125) + .50(\$65) + .20(\$30)$
  $= \$76.00(000)$

$EMV(2) = .30(\$105) + .50(\$60) + .20(\$30)$
  $= \$67.50(000)$

$EMV(\text{both}) = .30(\$220) + .50(\$110) + .20(\$40)$
  $= \$129.00(000)$

b.   Choose both.

c.
| | Opportunity loss | | |
|---|---|---|---|
| | $S_1$ | $S_2$ | $S_3$ |
| Neither | $220 | $110 | $40 |
| 1 | 95 | 45 | 10 |
| 2 | 115 | 50 | 10 |
| Both | 0 | 0 | 0 |

d.

$EOL(\text{neither}) = .30(\$220) + .50(\$110) + .20(\$40) = \$129.00$

$EOL(1) = .30(\$95) + .50(\$45) + .20(\$10)$  $= \$ 53.00$

$EOL(2) = .30(\$115) + .50(\$50) + .20(\$10)$  $= \$ 61.50$

$EOL(\text{both}) = .30(\$0) + .50(\$0) + .20(\$0)$  $= 0$

e.   EVPI = $0, found by $129 − $129.

Certainty = .30($220) + .50($110) + .20($40)
  = $129

13. The payoff table is as follows ($ 000):

| Production | Recession, $S_1$ | No recession, $S_2$ |
|---|---|---|
| Production | −10.0 | 15.0 |
| Stock | −5.0 | 12.0 |
| CD | 6.0 | 6.0 |

a. Purchase a CD.
b. Increase production.
c.

$$EMV(Prod.) = .2(-10) + .8(15.0) = \$10.0$$
$$EMV(Stock) = .2(-5) + .8(12.0) = \$8.6$$
$$EMV(CD) = .2(6) + .8(6) = \$6.0$$

Expand production.

d. $EVPI = [.2(6) + .8(15)] - [10.0] = 13.2 - 10.0$
$= 3.2$

15. a.

| Act | Event | | | | |
| | 10 | 11 | 12 | 13 | 14 |
|---|---|---|---|---|---|
| 10 | $ 500 | $ 500 | $500 | $500 | $500 |
| 11 | 200 | 550 | 550 | 550 | 550 |
| 12 | −100 | 250 | 600 | 600 | 600 |
| 13 | −400 | −50 | 300 | 650 | 650 |
| 14 | −700 | −350 | 0 | 350 | 700 |

b.

| Act | Expected profit |
|---|---|
| 10 | $ 500.00 |
| 11 | 504.50 |
| 12 | 421.50 |
| 13 | 233.50 |
| 14 | −31.50 |

Order 11 mobile homes because expected profit of $504.50 is the highest.

c.

| Supply | Opportunity loss | | | | |
| | 10 | 11 | 12 | 13 | 14 |
|---|---|---|---|---|---|
| 10 | $ 0 | $ 50 | $100 | $150 | $200 |
| 11 | 300 | 0 | 50 | 100 | 150 |
| 12 | 600 | 300 | 0 | 50 | 100 |
| 13 | 900 | 600 | 300 | 0 | 50 |
| 14 | 1,200 | 900 | 600 | 300 | 0 |

d.

| | Act | | | | |
| | 10 | 11 | 12 | 13 | 14 |
|---|---|---|---|---|---|
| Expected opportunity loss | $95.50 | $91 | $174 | $362 | $627 |

Decision: Order 11 homes because the opportunity loss of $91 is the smallest.

e. $91, found by:

$595.50  Profit under certainty
−504.50  Profit under uncertainty
$ 91.00  Value of perfect information

17. a.

| Act | Event | | | | | |
| | 41 | 42 | 43 | 44 | 45 | 46 |
|---|---|---|---|---|---|---|
| 41 | $410 | $410 | $410 | $410 | $410 | $410 |
| 42 | 405 | 420 | 420 | 420 | 420 | 420 |
| 43 | 400 | 415 | 430 | 430 | 430 | 430 |
| 44 | 395 | 410 | 425 | 440 | 440 | 440 |
| 45 | 390 | 405 | 420 | 435 | 450 | 450 |
| 46 | 385 | 400 | 415 | 430 | 445 | 460 |

b.

| Act | Expected profit |
|---|---|
| 41 | $410.00 |
| 42 | 419.10 |
| 43 | 426.70 |
| 44 | 432.20 |
| 45 | 431.70 |
| 46 | 427.45 |

c. Order 44 because $432.20 is the largest expected profit.

d. Expected opportunity loss:

| 41 | 42 | 43 | 44 | 45 | 46 |
|---|---|---|---|---|---|
| $28.30 | $19.20 | $11.60 | $6.10 | $6.60 | $10.85 |

e. Order 44 because the opportunity loss of $6.10 is the smallest. Yes, it agrees.

f. $6.10, found by:

$438.30  Profit under certainty
−432.20  Profit under uncertainty
$ 6.10  Value of perfect information

The maximum we should pay for perfect information is $6.10.

# CHAPTER 21  STATISTICAL QUALITY CONTROL

1. Chance variation is random in nature and *not* controllable. Assignable variation is due to some flaw or problem in the process and should be investigated.

3. a. The $A_2$ factor is 0.729.
   b. The value for $D_3$ is 0, and for $D_4$ it is 2.282.

5. a.

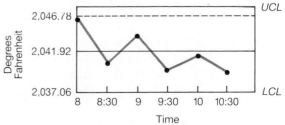

| Time | $\overline{X}$, Arithmetic means | $R$, range |
|------|------|------|
| 8:00 A.M. | 46 | 16 |
| 8:30 A.M. | 40.5 | 6 |
| 9:00 A.M. | 44 | 6 |
| 9:30 A.M. | 40 | 2 |
| 10:00 A.M. | 41.5 | 9 |
| 10:30 A.M. | 39.5 | 1 |
|  | 251.5 | 40 |

$$UCL = \overline{\overline{X}} + A_2\overline{R}$$
$$= 41.92 + 0.729(6.67)$$
$$= 46.78$$
$$LCL = \overline{\overline{X}} - A_2\overline{R}$$
$$= 41.92 - 0.729(6.67)$$
$$= 37.06$$

b.  Interpreting, the mean reading was 2,041.92 degrees Fahrenheit. If the oven continues operating as evidenced by the first six hourly readings, about 99.7 percent of the mean readings will lie between 2,037.06 degrees and 2,046.78 degrees.

7.  a.
$$\bar{p} = \frac{.48}{10} = .048$$

$$.048 \pm 3\sqrt{\frac{.048(1 - .048)}{50}} = .048 \pm .091$$

The limits are from 0 to .139.

b.  10/50 = .20, so this reading is out of control. The process should be adjusted.

9.  a.  $\bar{c} = \dfrac{24}{10} = 2.40$    $2.40 \pm 3\sqrt{2.40} = 2.40 \pm 4.65$

The limits are from 0 to 7.05.

b.  The unit that had 6 defects is not out of control because 6 < 7.05; that is, 6 falls below the UCL of 7.05.

11.

| Percent defective | Probability of accepting lot |
|------|------|
| 10 | .889 |
| 20 | .558 |
| 30 | .253 |
| 40 | .083 |

13.

$$P(X \le 1 \mid n = 10, p = .10) = .736$$
$$P(X \le 1 \mid n = 10, p = .20) = .376$$
$$P(X \le 1 \mid n = 10, p = .30) = .149$$
$$P(X \le 1 \mid n = 10, p = .40) = .046$$

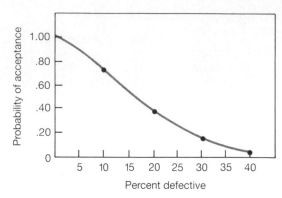

15.  a.  The limits for the mean are 9.86 ounces up to 10.14 ounces, found by:

$$10.00 \pm 0.577(0.25) = 10.00 \pm 0.14$$

The limits for the range are 0 to 0.53, found by

$$0.25(0) = 0 \quad\text{and}\quad 0.25(2.115) = 0.53$$

b.  The process is out of control for the mean but not for the range. The mean of 10.16 ounces is larger than the upper control limit of 10.14 ounces.

17.  a.  $\bar{p} = .465/15 = .031$

b.  
$$.031 \pm 3\sqrt{\frac{.031(1 - .031)}{200}} = .031 \pm .037$$

The limits are from 0 to .068, or 6.8 percent after 10.30 A.M.

c.  No. $\bar{p} = 10/200 = .05$, which is in control.

19.  For the mean chart: central line = 45.2; UCL = 54.3; LCL = 36.1. Control limits computed by $\overline{X} \pm A_2\overline{R} = 45.2 \pm .729(12.5)$. The factor $A_2$ is from Appendix L. For the range chart: central line = 12.5; UCL = 28.5; LCL = 0. Control limits computed by:

$$D_4\overline{R} = 2.282(12.5)$$
$$D_3\overline{R} = (0)(12.5)$$

Both factors are from Appendix L.

21.  a.  
$$\bar{p} = \frac{.80}{10} = .08$$

To find UCL and LCL:

$$.08 \pm 3\sqrt{\frac{(.08)(.92)}{50}}$$
$$.08 \pm 3(.038)$$
$$UCL = .1951$$
$$LCL = 0$$

b.

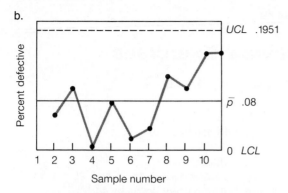

c.  The upper and lower control limits indicate that 99.73 percent of the percent defectives will be between 0 and 19.51, with a mean of 8 percent.

23.  $\bar{c} = 47/20 = 2.35$.
UCL and LCL $= 2.35 \pm 3\sqrt{2.35} = 0$ and 6.95.

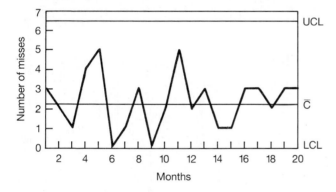

There is no trend upward.

$$P(x \le 3 \mid n = 20, p = .10) = .867$$
$$P(x \le 3 \mid n = 20, p = .20) = .411$$
$$P(x \le 3 \mid n = 20, p = .30) = .107$$

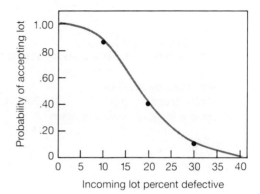

**Answers**

# Odd-Numbered Review Exercises

## A REVIEW OF CHAPTERS 1−4

1.  a. Sample.
    b. Ratio.
    c. $11.60, found by $58/5.
    d. $11.70. Half of the rates are above $11.70, half below it.
    e. 5.845, found by 23.38/(5 − 1)
    f. −.12409, found by 3($11.60 − $11.70)/2.4176. There is a slight negative skewness.

3.  a.

    | Number of rolls | Frequency |
    |---|---|
    | 3–5 | 2 |
    | 6–8 | 6 |
    | 9–11 | 8 |
    | 12–14 | 3 |
    | 15–17 | 1 |
    | | 20 |

    b.

    c. 9.25 rolls, found by 185/20 (using the raw data).
    d. 9.25.

    e. 10.
    f. 13, found by 16 − 3.
    g. 9.355.
    h. 3.059.
    i. 3.132 to 15.368, found by 9.25 ± 2(3.059).

5.  a. 8.82 percent, found by 44.1/5.
    b. 7.48 percent.
    c. Geometric mean, as it is more conservative. For the arithmetic mean, 19.5 is weighting the mean upward.

7.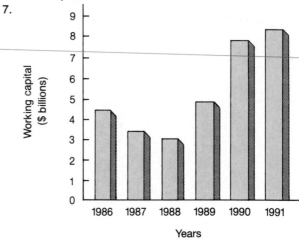

9.  Ordinal.
11. Less-than cumulative frequency polygon; 45; 35; 10; 5; 35.
13. 9.375, found by ($6/$64)(100).
15. Coefficient of variation.
17. 92 and 108, found by 100 ± 2(4).
19. Answers will vary.

## A REVIEW OF CHAPTERS 5−7

1.  Subjective.
3.  Event.
5.  Complement rule; 1 − P(X); .999.
7.  Discrete.
9.  Discrete.
11. Bell-shaped, symmetrical, asymptotic.

13. a. .10, found, by 20/200.
    b. .725, found by 145/200.
    c. .925, found by 1 − .075.
15. a. .1353, from Appendix C and a $\mu$ of 2.0.
    b. 346, found by .1353 × 400. Then 400 − 54 = 346.
    c. .3232, found by .1804 + .0902 + · · · + .0002.

# A REVIEW OF CHAPTERS 8–10

1. *b.*
3. *c.*
5. *d.*
7. *e.*
9. *a.*

11.
$$H_0: \mu = 36$$
$$H_1: \mu < 36$$

$H_0$ is rejected if the computed value of $z$ is less than $-1.645$.

$$z = \frac{35.5 - 36}{0.9/\sqrt{42}} = -3.60$$

The null hypothesis is rejected and the alternate accepted. The balls do not bounce up to a mean of 36 inches.

13. a. $n = .05(1 - .05)\left(\frac{1.96}{.02}\right)^2 = 456.19$

A sample of 457 is recommended.

b. The sample size could be reduced by increasing the level of confidence to 10 percent, for example.

The sample size could also be reduced by increasing the allowable error.

15. a. Let population 1 refer to Cartersville.
$$H_0: \mu_1 = \mu_2$$
$$H_1: \mu_1 \neq \mu_2$$

b. This is a two-tailed test, because no direction is specified.

c. $$z = \frac{\bar{X}_1 - \bar{X}_2}{\sqrt{\dfrac{s_1^2}{n_1} + \dfrac{s_2^2}{n_2}}}$$

d. $H_0$ is rejected if $z < -1.96$ or $z > 1.96$.

e.
$$z = \frac{\$10.92 - \$11.05}{\sqrt{\dfrac{(\$0.78)^2}{180} + \dfrac{(\$0.39)^2}{200}}} = \frac{\$-0.13}{0.0643467} = -2.02$$

$H_0$ is rejected because $-2.02$ falls in the area beyond $-1.96$. There is a difference in the mean wages.

# A REVIEW OF CHAPTERS 11 AND 12

1. *b.*
3. *a.*
5. *d.*
7. *d.* $H_1: \mu > \$80.$
9. *b,* because 1.90 lies beyond 1.725.
11. *e.* It is 5.57. $k - 1 = 3 - 1 = 2$ degrees of freedom in numerator; $N - k = 28 - 3 = 25$ degrees of freedom in denominator. Refer to Appendix G, .01 level.
13. $H_0: \mu = 20$. $H_1: \mu > 20$. Computed $t = 0.485$. Critical value of $t$ for $n - 1 = 9 - 1 = 8$ degrees of freedom is 1.860. Do not reject $H_0$. Calculations for $t$ and $s$ are:

$$t = \frac{21 - 20}{6.18/\sqrt{9}} = \frac{1}{2.06} = 0.485$$

$$s = \sqrt{\frac{306}{9 - 1}} = 6.18$$

$$\bar{X} = 189/9 = 21$$

15. a. $H_0: \mu_d = 0$ (no difference). $H_1: \mu_d > 0$ (differences are positive).

b.

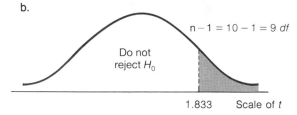

c. Computed $t = 0.21$, found by:

$$t = \frac{0.4}{6.11/\sqrt{10}}$$

and

$$s = \sqrt{\frac{388 - \dfrac{(0.4)^2}{10}}{10 - 1}} = 6.11$$

Do not reject $H_0$ because 0.21 is less than 1.833. Additive not effective.

17. a. (1) $H_0$: The treatment means are the same.
   $H_1$: The treatment means are not the same.
   (2) $H_0$: The block means are the same.
   $H_1$: The block means are not the same.

b. (1) 3.84 for treatments found by 4 in numerator, 8 in denominator, .05 level.

(2) 4.46 for blocks, found by 2 in numerator, 8 in denominator, .05 level.

c. (1) Reject $H_0$ for treatments because computed $F$ of $11.1 > 3.84$.
   (2) Do not reject $H_0$ for blocks because $3.05 < 4.46$.

$$F\text{ (Treatments)} = \frac{\text{MSTR}}{\text{MSE}} = \frac{41.43}{3.73} = 11.1$$

$$F\text{ (Blocks)} = \frac{\text{MSB}}{\text{MSE}} = \frac{11.4}{3.73} = 3.05$$

d. (1) There is a difference in the yields of the five fertilizer types.
   (2) There is no difference in the yields with respect to the type of soil. The fertilizers are equally effective.

# A REVIEW OF CHAPTERS 13–15

1. Coefficient of determination or coefficient of correlation.
3. $H_0: \rho = 0$, $H_1: \rho > 0$. Reject $H_0$ if $t > 1.671$ computed $t = 3.324$. Reject $H_0$. There is positive correlation.
5. In the stepwise method, independent variables are entered in the order in which they will increase $R^2$ the fastest.
7. $Y' = a + \beta_1 X_1 + \beta_2 X_2 + \beta_3 X_3 + \beta_4 X_4$
9. If $R = .86$, then $R^2 = (.86)^2 = .7376$. Nearly 74 percent of the variation in net profit is explained by the four independent variables.
11. a.

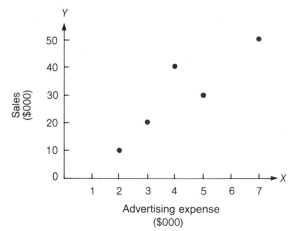

| Y | X | X² | XY | Y² |
|---|---|----|----|-----|
| 10 | 2 | 4 | 20 | 100 |
| 40 | 4 | 16 | 160 | 1,600 |
| 30 | 5 | 25 | 150 | 900 |
| 50 | 7 | 49 | 350 | 2,500 |
| 20 | 3 | 9 | 60 | 400 |
| 150 | 21 | 103 | 740 | 5,500 |

b. $r = \dfrac{5(740) - (21)(150)}{\sqrt{[5(103) - (21)^2][5(5,500) - (150)^2]}}$

$= \dfrac{550}{\sqrt{(74)(5,000)}}$

$= .904$

c. $R^2 = (.904)^2 = .82; \ 1 - R^2 = 1 - .82 = .18.$

d. $b = \dfrac{5(740) - (21)(150)}{5(103) - (21)^2} = \dfrac{550}{74} = 7.4324$

$a = \dfrac{150 - 7.4324(21)}{5} = -1.2161$

$Y' = -1.2161 + 7.4324\,X$

e. $Y' = -1.2161 + 7.4324(4.5) = 32.2297$

f. There is a strong positive association between sales and advertising expense. Further, an increase of $1,000 in advertising will result in an increase of $7,432 in sales.

13. a. .926, found by 1050.8/1134.6.
    b. 2.047, found by

$$\sqrt{\frac{83.8}{20}}$$

c. Using the global test, $F = 262.70/4.19 = 62.70$ critical value of $F$ at .05 significance level is 2.87. Reject $H_0$. Not all the regression coefficients are zero.

d. At the .05 significance level and 20 $df$, the critical value of $t$ is 2.086. $X_1$, $X_3$, and $X_4$ $t$-ratios are in the rejection region beyond 2.086. Therefore, these three variables are significant predictors. For $X_2$ the $t$ ratio is 1.29 and it is not a significant predictor and can be removed from the study.

# A REVIEW OF CHAPTERS 16 AND 17

1. Frequency observed, frequency expected.
3. Chi-square distribution.
5. Not rejected, because $11.248 < 12.592$. There are 6 degrees of freedom.
7. There is no difference between the observed set of frequencies and the expected frequencies.
9. At least nominal level.
11. To find out if two independent samples come from the same population.
13. To find out if three or more populations are equal.
15. The Kruskal-Wallis test.
17. Yes.

19. No. It is positively skewed.
21. Example:

$H_0$ : Median starting salary of accountants = \$27,000

$H_1$ : Median $\neq$ \$27,000

Use .05 level. Apply the sign test. This is a two-tailed test, so critical values are $+1.96$ and $-1.96$. Count the number of values above the median and below the median. Compute $z$. Reject $H_0$ if $z > 1.96$ or if $z < -1.96$. Otherwise, do not reject $H_0$. This assumes the sample is large.

# Index

## K–L

## M

## N

# T

# TABLE

## Special Symbols

| Symbol | Page | Meaning | Symbol | Page | Meaning |
|--------|------|---------|--------|------|---------|
| $A_2$ | 752 | Control chart factor for means | $\mu$ | 76 | Population mean |
| $a$ | 501 | $Y$-intercept | $Q_1$ | 131 | First quartile |
| A.D. | 114 | Average deviation | $Q_3$ | 131 | Third quartile |
| ANOVA | 424 | Analysis of variance | $Q$ | 660 | Quantity index |
| $b$ | 501 | Slope of the regression line | Q.D. | 133 | Quartile deviaiton |
| $\bar{c}$ | 764 | Mean number of defects per unit | $r^2$ | 473 | Coefficient of determination |
| $\chi^2$ | 577 | Chi-square statistic | $r_s$ | 478 | Rank-order correlation coefficient |
| $_nC_r$ | 195 | Combination of $n$ things taken $r$ at a time | $r$ | 470 | Sample correlation coefficient |
| C.V. | 137 | Coefficient of variation | $\rho$ | 477 | Population coefficient of correlation |
| CPI | 666 | Consumer price index | $\sigma^2$ | 117 | Population variance |
| $D_4$ | 755 | Control limit factor for the range | $\sigma_p$ | 316 | Standard error of the proportion |
| EMV | 725 | Expected monetary value | $\sigma$ | 119 | Population standard deviation |
| EOL | 728 | Expected opportunity loss | $\sigma_{\bar{x}}$ | 309 | Standard error of the mean |
| EVPI | 730 | Expected value of perfect information | $s^2$ | 120 | Sample variance |
| $f_e$ | 579 | Expected frequency | $s_d$ | 409 | Standard deviation of paired differences |
| $f_o$ | 577 | Observed frequency | $s_{y \cdot x}$ | 506 | Standard error of estimate |
| $F$ | 431 | $F$-Distribution | $s$ | 122 | Sample standard deviation |
| G.M. | 86 | Geometric mean | $sk$ | 139 | Coefficient of skewness |
| $H$ | 624 | Kruskal-Wallis test statistic | SS *total* | 434 | Sum of squares total |
| $k$ | 533 | Number of independent variables | SSB | 441 | Sum of squares blocks |
| MSE | 432 | Mean square error | SSE | 433 | Sum of squares error |
| MSTR | 438 | Mean square treatment | SSR | 518 | Sum of squares regression |
| $n$ | 75 | Number of items in the sample | SST | 432 | Sum of squares treatments |
| $N$ | 76 | Number of items in the population | $T_c^2$ | 433 | Treatment column total |
| $_nP_r$ | 192 | Permutation of $n$ things taken $r$ at a time | $t$ | 394 | Student's $t$-distribution |
| $\bar{p}_c$ | 376 | Weighted mean of sample proportions | $U$ | 618 | Mann-Whitney $U$ statistic |
| $\bar{p}$ | 307 | Proportion of success in a sample | $V$ | 662 | Value index |
| $p$ | 372 | Population proportion | $\bar{X}_c$ | 356 | Control limit for sample mean |
| $P$ | 655 | Price index | $\bar{X}_w$ | 79 | Weighted mean |
| $P(A)$ | 169 | Probability of an event happening | $\bar{X}$ | 75 | Sample mean |
| $P(B|A)\ P(A|B)$ | 180 | Probability of an even given that another event happened | $Y'$ | 501 | Predicted value of $Y$ |
|  |  |  | $z$ | 252 | Standard normal deviate |

# TABLE

## Areas under the Normal Curve

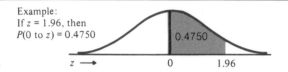

Example:
If $z = 1.96$, then
$P(0$ to $z) = 0.4750$

| Z | 0.00 | 0.01 | 0.02 | 0.03 | 0.04 | 0.05 | 0.06 | 0.07 | 0.08 | 0.09 |
|---|------|------|------|------|------|------|------|------|------|------|
| 0.0 | 0.0000 | 0.0040 | 0.0080 | 0.0120 | 0.0160 | 0.0199 | 0.0239 | 0.0279 | 0.0319 | 0.0359 |
| 0.1 | 0.0398 | 0.0438 | 0.0478 | 0.0517 | 0.0557 | 0.0596 | 0.0636 | 0.0675 | 0.0714 | 0.0753 |
| 0.2 | 0.0793 | 0.0832 | 0.0871 | 0.0910 | 0.0948 | 0.0987 | 0.1026 | 0.1064 | 0.1103 | 0.1141 |
| 0.3 | 0.1179 | 0.1217 | 0.1255 | 0.1293 | 0.1331 | 0.1368 | 0.1406 | 0.1443 | 0.1480 | 0.1517 |
| 0.4 | 0.1554 | 0.1591 | 0.1628 | 0.1664 | 0.1700 | 0.1736 | 0.1772 | 0.1808 | 0.1844 | 0.1879 |
| 0.5 | 0.1915 | 0.1950 | 0.1985 | 0.2019 | 0.2054 | 0.2088 | 0.2123 | 0.2157 | 0.2190 | 0.2224 |
| 0.6 | 0.2257 | 0.2291 | 0.2324 | 0.2357 | 0.2389 | 0.2422 | 0.2454 | 0.2486 | 0.2517 | 0.2549 |
| 0.7 | 0.2580 | 0.2611 | 0.2642 | 0.2673 | 0.2704 | 0.2734 | 0.2764 | 0.2794 | 0.2823 | 0.2852 |
| 0.8 | 0.2881 | 0.2910 | 0.2939 | 0.2967 | 0.2995 | 0.3023 | 0.3051 | 0.3078 | 0.3106 | 0.3133 |
| 0.9 | 0.3159 | 0.3186 | 0.3212 | 0.3238 | 0.3264 | 0.3289 | 0.3315 | 0.3340 | 0.3365 | 0.3389 |
| 1.0 | 0.3413 | 0.3438 | 0.3461 | 0.3485 | 0.3508 | 0.3531 | 0.3554 | 0.3577 | 0.3599 | 0.3621 |
| 1.1 | 0.3643 | 0.3665 | 0.3686 | 0.3708 | 0.3729 | 0.3749 | 0.3770 | 0.3790 | 0.3810 | 0.3830 |
| 1.2 | 0.3849 | 0.3869 | 0.3888 | 0.3907 | 0.3925 | 0.3944 | 0.3962 | 0.3980 | 0.3997 | 0.4015 |
| 1.3 | 0.4032 | 0.4049 | 0.4066 | 0.4082 | 0.4099 | 0.4115 | 0.4131 | 0.4147 | 0.4162 | 0.4177 |
| 1.4 | 0.4192 | 0.4207 | 0.4222 | 0.4236 | 0.4251 | 0.4265 | 0.4279 | 0.4292 | 0.4306 | 0.4319 |
| 1.5 | 0.4332 | 0.4345 | 0.4357 | 0.4370 | 0.4382 | 0.4394 | 0.4406 | 0.4418 | 0.4429 | 0.4441 |
| 1.6 | 0.4452 | 0.4463 | 0.4474 | 0.4484 | 0.4495 | 0.4505 | 0.4515 | 0.4525 | 0.4535 | 0.4545 |
| 1.7 | 0.4554 | 0.4564 | 0.4573 | 0.4582 | 0.4591 | 0.4599 | 0.4608 | 0.4616 | 0.4625 | 0.4633 |
| 1.8 | 0.4641 | 0.4649 | 0.4656 | 0.4664 | 0.4671 | 0.4678 | 0.4686 | 0.4693 | 0.4699 | 0.4706 |
| 1.9 | 0.4713 | 0.4719 | 0.4726 | 0.4732 | 0.4738 | 0.4744 | 0.4750 | 0.4756 | 0.4761 | 0.4767 |
| 2.0 | 0.4772 | 0.4778 | 0.4783 | 0.4788 | 0.4793 | 0.4798 | 0.4803 | 0.4808 | 0.4812 | 0.4817 |
| 2.1 | 0.4821 | 0.4826 | 0.4830 | 0.4834 | 0.4838 | 0.4842 | 0.4846 | 0.4850 | 0.4854 | 0.4857 |
| 2.2 | 0.4861 | 0.4864 | 0.4868 | 0.4871 | 0.4875 | 0.4878 | 0.4881 | 0.4884 | 0.4887 | 0.4890 |
| 2.3 | 0.4893 | 0.4896 | 0.4898 | 0.4901 | 0.4904 | 0.4906 | 0.4909 | 0.4911 | 0.4913 | 0.4916 |
| 2.4 | 0.4918 | 0.4920 | 0.4922 | 0.4925 | 0.4927 | 0.4929 | 0.4931 | 0.4932 | 0.4934 | 0.4936 |
| 2.5 | 0.4938 | 0.4940 | 0.4941 | 0.4943 | 0.4945 | 0.4946 | 0.4948 | 0.4949 | 0.4951 | 0.4952 |
| 2.6 | 0.4953 | 0.4955 | 0.4956 | 0.4957 | 0.4959 | 0.4960 | 0.4961 | 0.4962 | 0.4963 | 0.4964 |
| 2.7 | 0.4965 | 0.4966 | 0.4967 | 0.4968 | 0.4969 | 0.4970 | 0.4971 | 0.4972 | 0.4973 | 0.4974 |
| 2.8 | 0.4974 | 0.4975 | 0.4976 | 0.4977 | 0.4977 | 0.4978 | 0.4979 | 0.4979 | 0.4980 | 0.4981 |
| 2.9 | 0.4981 | 0.4982 | 0.4982 | 0.4983 | 0.4984 | 0.4984 | 0.4985 | 0.4985 | 0.4986 | 0.4986 |
| 3.0 | 0.4987 | 0.4987 | 0.4987 | 0.4988 | 0.4988 | 0.4989 | 0.4989 | 0.4989 | 0.4990 | 0.4990 |